SENSATION AND PERCEPTION

SENSATION AND PERCEPTION

An Integrated Approach

Fourth Edition

Harvey Richard Schiffman

Rutgers, The State University

JOHN WILEY & SONS, INC.

New York   Chichester   Brisbane   Toronto   Singapore

ACQUISITIONS EDITOR   Christopher Rogers
MARKETING MANAGER   Rebecca Herschler
SENIOR PRODUCTION EDITOR   Katharine Rubin
COPYEDITING SPECIALIST   Deborah Herbert
INTERIOR DESIGNER   David Levy
COVER DESIGNER   Michael Jung
MANUFACTURING MANAGER   Dorothy Sinclair
PHOTO EDITOR   Hilary Newman
ILLUSTRATION COORDINATOR   Rosa Bryant
PRODUCTION SERVICE   Spectrum Publisher Services, Inc.
COVER PHOTO   Gary Gay/The Image Bank

This book was set in 9/12 Garamond Light by TCSystems, Inc. and printed and bound by Donnelley Crawfordsville. The cover was printed by Phoenix Color, Inc.

Recognizing the importance of preserving what has been written, it is a
policy of John Wiley & Sons, Inc. to have books of enduring value published
in the United States printed on acid-free paper, and we exert our best
efforts to that end.

The paper in this book was manufactured by a mill whose forest management programs include
sustained yield harvesting of its timberlands. Sustained yield harvesting principles ensure that
the number of trees cut each year does not exceed the amount of new growth.

Library of Congress Cataloging in Publication Data:
Schiffman, Harvey Richard, 1934–
    Sensation and perception : an integrated approach / Harvey Richard
Schiffman. — 4th ed.
        p.   cm.
    Includes bibliographical references and index.
    ISBN 0–471–58620–X (cloth : alk. paper)
    1. Senses and sensation.   2. Perception.   I. Title.
BF233.S44   1995
152.1—dc20   95-21053
                                                         CIP

Printed in the United States of America

10 9 8 7 6 5 4 3 2 1

To Jan and Noah, again

PREFACE

Most individuals are curious about how they perceive the world that surrounds them but have surprisingly little understanding of the processes and mechanisms involved. How do the senses gather and secure information about the outside world? This critical question has been posed in many ways and in many contexts, and it has inspired a variety of answers. In *Sensation and Perception* I address this basic question by explaining how the physical world interacts with and stimulates the senses and, in turn, how the senses and the nervous system transform, integrate, and process the stimulation. I assume no specialized background on the part of the reader beyond a basic course in psychology and perhaps some biology.

The primary purpose of this fourth edition is to update coverage of the rapidly advancing field of sensation and perception. However, the goals of this revision extend considerably beyond keeping pace with the findings and conceptual advances that have emerged since the last edition. Any reader familiar with earlier editions will quickly observe that the fourth edition has a number of other significant changes as well. First, however, let's look at what is still true about the text.

WHAT HAS BEEN RETAINED?

As in previous editions of *Sensation and Perception,* a key objective of the fourth edition is to provide an integrated survey of sensation and perception within a biological behavioral context. To meet this goal, I have strived to represent a broad and balanced treatment of the theories, principles, and basic findings of the discipline. In addition, previous readers will recognize as the central theme of the text the emphasis on the adaptive, functional significance of the senses. Indeed, numerous instances of sensory and perceptual activities with obvious adaptive consequences will be found throughout the book. However, the text remains guardedly eclectic and does not concentrate on any particular view or theory.

Previous users will also note that all sensory systems are given their due. Although vision is emphasized, followed by hearing, no sense is treated as a "minor" sense. This is generally not true in other texts, where taste, smell, and the skin senses are often short-changed and the orienting sense and the perception of time are usually overlooked entirely. Here they are given full coverage with a separate chapter devoted to each.

WHAT HAS BEEN CHANGED?

The major change in the fourth edition is the substantial reorganization of the order in which the senses are presented. In earlier editions, the visual system was the culminating and final sensory system discussed. However, in this edition, after an introductory chapter and a chapter on methodology (psychophysics), I begin in Chapter 3 with a discussion of vision that continues through Chapter 11. There are several reasons for this change. Functionally, vision is the dominating, most essential sensory modality for a number of species, including the human. Accordingly, it has been studied in great detail and, arguably, more is known about it than any of the other senses. Probably for this reason most instructors prefer to present it as the first sensory-perceptual system in their course.

Moreover, confronting the very broad area of vision first, enables me to introduce and describe many general mechanisms and phenomena that are common to all the senses—to set the groundwork, in effect, for observing similarities among the senses.

There are other notable organizational changes. To accommodate additions to the vast detail on perceptual organization, Chapters 6 and 7, devoted to bottom-up and top-down processes, respectively, now replace the single chapter that was formerly devoted to this topic. The fourth edition retains two chapters on space perception, but they have been reorganized so that Chapter 9 principally covers monocular and binocular vision, and Chapter 10 deals with the constancies (lightness, size, and shape) and visual illusions. The material on perceptual development that was distributed over two chapters in earlier editions is now integrated and condensed into a single chapter (Chapter 11). The orienting sense (Chapter 15) now follows the auditory system (Chapters 12–14). This is a sensible link in that the major receptor organs for the orienting sense—the vestibular organs—are, in fact, part of the middle ear structures, and their sensory mechanisms possess the same essential mechanical properties observed with the auditory system. Two chapters that in previous editions dealt with the skin are now covered in a single chapter on the skin senses (Chapter 16). The coverage here of traditional topics has not changed, but the phenomena and theories, such as cutaneous communication and the spinal gate theory of pain, have been reevaluated and kept or deleted in light of their present status in the field. The previous edition contained a final, loosely organized chapter on cognitive topics and issues relevant to sensation and perception. It has been dropped and the material has either been omitted or incorporated in the chapters where it is most relevant. For example, the Stroop effect is now presented with the discussion of perceptual set (Chapter 7).

One of the broadest changes in the fourth edition is that virtually every chapter has been thoroughly evaluated for readability and upgraded with new information. Many sections are entirely new, and many discussions retained from earlier editions have been revised or rewritten. My overriding purpose has been to make the text clearer and more interesting to stu-

dents without sacrificing comprehensiveness about how the senses and perception function. To this end I added concrete, real-life examples of sensation and perception throughout the text.

WHAT IS NEW IN EACH CHAPTER?

Chapter 1 is completely new. It introduces the reader to the problems and issues of sensation and perception, placing them within a general historical and scientific framework. It outlines the major conceptual approaches to the field and presents some of the reasons why one should study these topics. Finally, Chapter 1 describes some of the basic facts, mechanisms, and concepts of neurophysiology relevant to sensory reception, including the cortical representation of the senses, in effect, surveying the general neural details of the sensory system that are assumed throughout the book.

Chapter 2, "Psychophysics," retains the traditional topics of psychophysics. However, the discussions of the threshold notions (absolute and difference), signal detection theory, Weber's fraction, and Fechner's law and Steven's law have been rewritten with numerous examples to illustrate the complex issue of how changes in the external environment quantitatively affect sensory experience. Unlike most texts in the field, psychophysics (especially the methods of threshold determination and signal detection theory) is not shunted to an appendix but is prominently discussed within the chapter. However, this topic can be easily amended or deleted without a loss of continuity.

Chapter 3, "The Visual System," introduces the visual system. It retains the treatment of the structural and functional processes of the eye found in previous editions, and includes a new discussion of neurophysiological factors mediating visual processes. Other topics include the pupillary phenomenon of "redeye," pathways of the eye to the brain, receptive fields for ganglion cells of the retina (X, Y, and W cells), receptive fields for the parvocellular and magnocellular divisions of the lateral geniculate nucleus, and the functional architecture of the visual cortex (orientation columns, hypercolumns, and cortical magnification of the cortex).

Chapter 4, "Fundamental Visual Functions and Phenomena," is a major reformulation of Chapter 12 of the third edition. However, it covers the same topics on basic visual function along with the inclusion of new sections on eye movements, reading, focal and ambient vision, and blindsight.

Chapter 5, "The Perception of Color," now includes color constancy, a detailed exposition of color matching, and new material on theories of color vision and defective color vision. A number of black-and-white illustrations and color plates are new to this chapter.

Chapter 6, "Basic Processes of Perceptual Organization," is updated and reorganized with new material on bottom-up processes, the preattentive and focused attention stages, textons, recognition-by-components, geons, the computational approach, and the connectionist model.

Chapter 7, "Higher Processes of Perceptual Organization," includes a new discussion of top-down processes. There are also new sections on figure-ground perception, Gestalt psychology, subjective contours, and perceptual set.

Chapter 8, "The Perception of Movement," retains its coverage of the traditional topics of the perception of movement. However, it has been reorganized with new material on motion detectors, corollary discharge and outflow signals, optic flow patterns, retinal expansion, and apparent movement.

Chapter 9, "Monocular and Binocular Vision," presents a new discussion of the physiological and psychological factors that mediate space perception. Moreover, the traditional approach to the subtopics of this chapter are supplemented by giving the reader firsthand experience with an autostereogram and by a new discussion of the physiological basis of binocular vision. In addition, several new figures have been added.

Chapter 10, "Constancy and Illusions," begins with a new treatment of lightness, size, and shape constancy, which is followed by the presentation of visual illusions that highlight the role played by constancy in creating illusory phenomena. In keeping with the theme of earlier editions, a major portion of this chapter is devoted to a discussion of various attempts to explain illusions. Some new illusory figures and some new explanations are presented.

Chapter 11, "Perceptual Development," still maintains a focus on the origins of perceptual abilities, but it has been reorganized to include a new discussion of various cortical and visual disorders (e.g., amblyopia) due to deprivation and biased stimulation during infancy.

Chapter 12, "The Auditory System," is now the first of three chapters devoted to hearing. It has been reorganized extensively from Chapter 4 of the third edition and includes new sections on phase and noise cancellation, impedance matching, and the acoustic reflex.

Chapter 13, "Psychoacoustics," has new figures. The discussion of equal-loudness contours has been rewritten.

Chapter 14, "Sound as Information," is an expanded exposition of the reception of meaningful sound. A new discussion of auditory localization includes material on echo delay-tuned neurons and a personal guidance system for the blind. The topic of speech perception has been rewritten and includes new material on the uniqueness of speech, the McGurk effect, and auditory scene analysis.

Chapter 15, "The Orienting Sense," has been extensively revised. There is a new discussion of postural stability and a section on postural sway. New also to this chapter is an explanation of motion sickness based on sensory conflict theory.

Chapter 16, "The Skin Senses," has increased coverage of relevant physiological mechanisms, specifically on receptive fields, Pacinian corpuscles, and rapidly adapting and slowly adapting fibers. The material on complex touch has been revised and clarified. The perception of thermal stimulation has been reorganized and rewritten to include a discussion of thermal conductivity. Many sections have been rewritten, and the material on the physiological and chemical mechanisms of pain has been reevaluated in the light of recent findings. In particular, the discussion on the spinal gate theory of pain has been revised, and the analgesic effect of the neurotransmitter chemical endorphin has been examined with respect to how it is affected by the administration of naloxone.

Chapters 17 and 18, "The Chemical Sense of Taste" and "The Chemical Sense of Smell," respectively, have been updated, reorganized, and rewritten. New material in Chapter 17 includes a discussion of taste abnormalities and disorders. In Chapter 18 smell disorders receive expanded treatment. The section on pheromones reevaluates the McClintock effect and now highlights various forms of pheromone-induced behavior. Finally, the section on the effects of the chemical capsaicin on the common chemical sense has been elaborated.

Although **Chapter 19,** "The Perception of Time," has been extensively reorganized and pared down, it essentially retains the main topics found in earlier editions. In particular, the discussions of Hoagland's hypothesis, Ornstein's information storage-size theory, and experiential space-time relativity have been abridged significantly. However, there is a new section on the effect of one's age on the passage of time.

PEDAGOGICAL FEATURES

The field of sensation and perception covers an enormously diverse set of topics. In an effort to maximize the flexibility of the book, each chapter has been written to be relatively self-contained and independent of other chapters. This enables instructors to tailor their courses by easily altering chapter sequence without an obvious loss in intellectual cohesion. Moreover, for those instructors who do not typically cover all the traditional subtopics of sensation and perception, individual sections, topics, and chapters can be deleted easily without affecting the continuity in the readings.

One of the strengths of the text is the ample use of illustrations. It is unlikely that any other text on sensation can match the number and the diversity of figures found in this edition.

The reader will find a preview at the beginning of each chapter that sets the stage for the topics to be discussed. The end of each chapter has a summary and a set of general survey questions that can be used for assignment, self-testing, or for discussion. These questions require the student to examine the critical topics and principles discussed in the chapter.

Because so many of the details of the subject matter of this book derive from other branches of science—anatomy, medicine, physics, chemistry, among others—the technical vocabulary of sensation and perception must reflect their terminology. I have intentionally restricted the number of technical terms, but readers will still confront an unfamiliar vocabulary. To ease the impact of this confrontation and to make the terms themselves interesting, in this edition I have added details on the origin and derivation of many of them. This also helps "de-mystify" the use of a term.

Key terms are printed in boldface when they first appear in the text to help the reader identify the important terms of the chapter. There is also a list of these key terms at the end of each chapter. In addition, a unified and updated glossary is included at the end of the book for readers' convenience in looking up terms that reappear from chapter to chapter.

This edition also highlights a series of interesting, easy-to-perform demonstrations that require little or no equipment. In most instances, they help clarify and illuminate specific sensory-perceptual concepts. In some cases, they also serve as focal points in class discussions and lectures. Moreover, by engaging the reader's attention and activity, the demonstrations make possible a firsthand experience with some of the phenomena described and thus provide direct evidence for the generalizations discussed within the text. In this sense, they help close the gap between the richness of our real-world sensory-perceptual experiences and their all too-often traditional treatment as abstract laboratory events.

HARVEY RICHARD SCHIFFMAN

ACKNOWLEDGMENTS

The preparation of this edition required an immense amount of support and help. I am grateful to the many individuals who contributed in various capacities to this project.

The technical content of the chapters was reviewed and criticized at various stages by a number of knowledgeable and expert psychologists, and I am indebted to them. Indeed, in many instances, sections of the revision were shaped and guided by the thoughtful and constructive suggestions of these individuals. Without any doubt, the revision has benefited considerably as a result of their contributions. The responsibility for any inaccuracies in fact or interpretation that remain is entirely mine. I hereby acknowledge my debt to:

Michael Babcock, *Montana State University*
Jan Berkhout, *The University of South Dakota*
Joseph S. Brown, *University of Nebraska at Omaha*
Gregory Burton, *Seton Hall University*
Richard Colker, *University of the District of Columbia*
Thaddeus M. Cowan, *Kansas State University*
Frank P. Gullotta, *Virginia Commonwealth University*
Frederick L. Kitterle, *The University of Toledo*
James M. Knight, *Humboldt State University*
Janice L. Nerger, *Colorado State University*
Zygmunt Pizlo, *Purdue University*
A. M. Prestrude, *Virginia Polytechnic Institute and State University*
Terry Rew-Gottfried, *Lawrence University*
Burton A. Weiss, *Drexel University*

I express my gratitude to many individuals at John Wiley for their effort in producing this edition. Special thanks are due to Helen Greenberg for her editing skill in paring down the manuscript while enhancing its clarity and to Deborah Herbert for supervising the copyediting. Katharine Rubin, the senior production editor, has my sincere gratitude for all of her help. After I submitted the completed manuscript Katy Rubin was usually the person I first called for any problem, and she was always helpful. Throughout, she supervised the production process with extreme patience, intelligence, expertise, and good humor. The enormous burden of finding appropriate photos and illustrations, and the task of preparing artwork was expertly handled by Hilary Newman and Rosa Bryant. Pam Kennedy, the production director, and Dawn Stanley, the art director for this edition, also have my thanks for their superb effort on this project.

A special acknowledgment is due to Karen Dubno, the psychology editor who convinced me to consider a major revision of the third edition. Karen was always enthusiastic and supportive, and in many ways helped me to formulate the goals of this revision. I am sorry that she is not still my editor. I miss her judgment. I would like her to know that this revision would probably not have happened without her early encouragement. I would also like to acknowledge the editorial assistance provided by Neil W. Sigda, who assisted Karen at the beginning of this project.

I owe a special debt of gratitude to Barbara Bredenko, the present editorial assistant for psychology. While she probably doesn't realize it, she served as a main source of stability on this project and continues as my primary resource for information at Wiley.

She helped me solve every problem I brought to her attention and she always returned my calls.

Finally, I acknowledge the vital contribution made by Kelly Ricci, production manager of Spectrum Publisher Services. She handled an enormous freight of details with poise and resourcefulness. Her professional commitment to this project was evident throughout the final production stage.

This is also my opportunity to acknowledge the special contributions made by a number of individuals at various stages of this revision. Several friends carefully read and commented on chapter sections, single chapters, or groups of chapters. For their assistance and valuable feedback I thank Noah Schiffman, Aileen Mroz, Harold Schiffman, and Lynsey Wollin. Special thanks are due Sue Greist-Bousquet. Many features in this revision are based on suggestions she made on earlier editions.

I also express my gratitude to the people who carried out various functions that either directly or indirectly contributed to the preparation of this edition. Jan Schiffman and Noah Schiffman devised and suggested a number of illustrations. Harold, Ellen, and Jennie Schiffman shared many ideas and never failed to find and correct flaws in my thinking. Marjorie F. W. Grigonis helped to take some of the original photographs. Ron Gandelman supplied me with several relevant literary references. Dr. James Hoyme helped me deal with several distracting preoccupations (for a while they were gone, but not forgotten). Diane Apadula assisted with the immense burden of correspondence and permissions and helped in many ways to assemble the final manuscript of this revision.

H. R. S.

CONTENTS

16 THE SKIN SENSES 413

17 THE CHEMICAL SENSE OF TASTE 449

chapter 1

AN INTRODUCTION TO SENSATION AND PERCEPTION

We are surrounded by a world of objects and events, and with apparently no conscious effort we sense their presence. Indeed, it seems so natural and almost effortless to be aware of the environment that, generally, we tend to take sensation and perception for granted. It is not unusual for the typical person to assume that the perception of the objects and events of the world is a given, offering no real problems to the psychologist other than perhaps very technical ones, such as trying to understand how a given sensory structure works. However, as Richard Gregory (1977) notes with vision:

> We are so familiar with seeing, that it takes a leap of imagination to realise that there are problems to be solved. But consider it. We are given tiny distorted upside-down images in the eyes, and we see separate solid objects in surrounding space. From the patterns of stimulation on the retina we perceive the world of objects, and this is nothing short of a miracle (p. 9).

While perhaps less than a miracle, it is quite a feat, especially when we consider that virtually everything we are aware of about the environment is based on a pattern of physical energies that directly affects our sensory receptors. For example, what we smell is based on a complex chemical reaction taking place in the inner reaches of the nasal cavity, what we see is the result of a changing pattern of radiant energies cast upon the back of the eyeball, and what we hear comes from a varying pattern of airborne vibrations conveyed to the receptors of the inner ear. Moreover, these environmental energy sources are in many ways impoverished and incomplete. In numerous instances–such as when we have barely a glimpse of the visual scene, when a sound is abrupt and faint, or when an object is only briefly felt by the fingertips, we are provided with only the weakest sensory clues as to the composition of our environment; yet, for the most part our perceptions are reasonably accurate.

How does this happen? It is obvious that all knowledge of the outside world depends on our senses and that there seems to be a very close link between the physical environment and our awareness of it. But how does all this information about the physical environment get into our heads? How do all the qualities and features of objects in our environment get constructed and seemingly recreated in our minds so that we "perceive" them as real coherent objects.

Consider another fundamental problem: Our awareness of physical reality —the objects and events that surround us—seems so tangible, so concrete and real, that we generally believe

figure **1.1** Two physically equal vertical lines. The "wings" added to the ends of the lines cause them to appear unequal in length. This is an example of the Müller-Lyer illusion, described in Chapter 10.

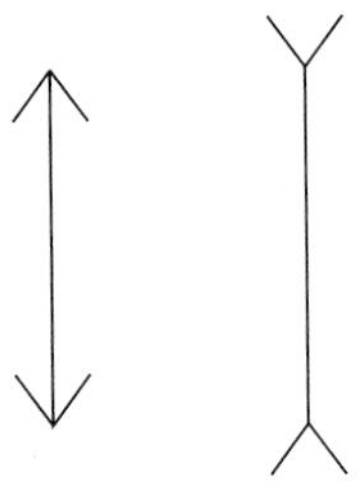

that the world must exist exactly as we perceive it or perhaps, at the very least, that our perceptions are just slightly off. But how close is the actual correspondence between the physical world and the inner subjective world created by our senses? Examine Figure 1.1. The two vertical lines appear unequal in length. However, despite the obvious evidence provided by our senses, the two lines are physically equal. We have, in fact, observed a well-known illusion of length called the Müller-Lyer *illusion. Thus, while our knowledge of the world depends on the senses, it is important to recognize that the world created by our senses does not always correspond exactly with physical reality. Indeed, certain sources of sensory information often subject us to errors and systematic distortions that misrepresent the world.*

How we become aware of our physical environment, and the relationship between the environment and our conscious experience, remains the central challenge to psychologists who study sensation and perception. An examination of the problems inherent in this challenge is one of the purposes of this book. This first chapter will orient us to these tasks.

This first chapter has several other purposes. It will introduce and describe the topics of sensation and perception and will examine the sorts of phenomena they deal with. It will give some of the history and background concerning sensation and perception and will locate the place of sensation and perception not only in psychology but, to an extent, in the history of intellectual and scientific thought. This chapter will then outline the main contemporary approaches to sensation and perception and the reasons one should study sensation and perception. Finally it will provide an introduction to the process by which physical signals from the environment are coded into neural activity; in particular, the chapter will describe the work of the receptor cells as a basic stage in initiating the sensory and perceptual response and will introduce the topics of sensory receptors and their task of converting environmental signals into neural activity.

SENSATION AND PERCEPTION

By tradition, certain distinctions are made between sensation and perception.

Sensation refers to the initial processes of detecting and encoding environmental energy. In other words, sensation is concerned with the first contact between the organism and its environment. Potential energy signals from the environment emit light, pressure, heat, chemicals, and so on, and our sense organs—our windows to the environment—receive this energy and transform it into a bioelectric neural code that is sent to the brain. This first step in sensing the world is performed by receptor cells (described later

in this chapter), which are special neural units that react to specific kinds of energy. Thus, specialized cells of the eye react to light energy and equally specialized cells of the tongue react to chemical molecules of compounds. Sensation involves the study of all of these biological events, but it concerns more than biological systems. A psychologist studying visual sensation would not only examine the physical structure of the eye and its reaction to light energy but would also attempt to establish how sensory experiences are related to both light stimulation from the environment and the functioning of the eye.

The *sensations* themselves refer to certain immediate, fundamental, and direct experiences, that is, the conscious awareness of qualities or attributes linked to the physical environment, such as "hard," "warm," "loud," "red," and so on, generally produced by simple, isolated physical stimuli.

Perception, on the other hand, generally refers to the result of psychological processes in which meaning, relationships, context, judgment, past experience, and memory play a role. According to this sensation–perception distinction, our eyes may initially register a fleeting series of colored images on the surface of a television screen (i.e., the work of sensation), but we see or perceive a representation of visual events with people and objects interacting spatially in a meaningful way. Similarly, our eardrums vibrate in a particular manner, producing some immediately recognizable tonal quality, such as loudness (sensation), but we hear or perceive a conversation or a melody. Thus, perception involves organizing, interpreting, and giving meaning to what the sense organs initially process. In other words, perception is the result of the organization and integration of sensations into an awareness of objects and environmental events.

Having made this distinction, we must note that it has a more historical than practical or functional significance. In many meaningful environmental encounters it is difficult, perhaps even impossible to make a clear distinction between sensation and perception. When we hear a tune, for example, are we initially aware of any isolated tonal qualities of the notes, such as their pitch and loudness, distinct from the melody? When we grasp a familiar object, such as a book or pencil, can we sense the pressure on our fingers and palm independent of how the object feels? The answer is no in both cases. In short, sensation and perception are unified, inseparable processes. Usually it is only in well-controlled laboratory conditions that one can initiate isolated sensations, which are distinct from meaning, context, past experience, and so on. Accordingly, although these terms will be part of our vocabulary, in this text we will generally avoid a clear sensation–perception distinction and maintain an integrated approach. That is, we will adopt the view that the outcome of environmental encounters generally provides useful information to the organism, some of which may be relatively basic and uncomplicated, such as the brightness of an object, and some of which may be more complex, such as what the object actually is.

THE HISTORICAL AND SCIENTIFIC ROOTS OF SENSATION AND PERCEPTION

Many of the problems examined by psychologists who study sensation and perception are not new. Indeed, concerns with issues and problems of sensation and perception can be traced to the very beginnings of human intellectual history. Philosophers since the ancient Greeks have inquired about how we know the world, that is, how we know what is out there. Aristotle (384–322 B.C.) was the first of the early Greek philosophers to advocate the careful observation and description of nature; for this reason, he is generally regarded as the first scientist. He believed that all knowledge of the external world is gained through experience provided by the senses. In addition, he established the long-held basic classification of the five senses into sight, hearing, taste, smell, and touch.

Empiricism and the Senses

Historically, the question of how we come to know the world remained a dominant issue, and the view that such knowledge is the result of experiences provided by the senses became a prominent philosophical school of thought of the seventeenth and eighteenth centuries called **empiricism.** Empiricism is the doctrine that the only source of true knowledge about the world is sensory experience, that is, what is seen, heard, tasted, smelled, or felt. In the early 1700s major empiricists such as Thomas Hobbes (1588–1679), John Locke (1632–1704), and George Berkeley (1685–1753) stressed the philosophical theme that *all* knowledge results from learning, associations, and experience given by the senses. Locke, in his view of empiricism, depicted the mind as initially empty, a *tabula rasa* or blank tablet, on which experiences provided by the senses are written. In short, according to Locke, the contents of our mind are the sum of our sensory experiences.

The philosopher George Berkeley (who was also the bishop of Cloyne, Ireland, and whose name has been memorialized by the university town in California), questioned the very existence of an external world, proposing the unusual (by contemporary standards) empiricistic view that the world exists *only* through perception. That is, the world of objects does not exist when it is not sensed. But wouldn't it follow, according to this notion, that a tree, for example, would cease to exist if no one was looking at it? (Another version of this query is the old philosophical conundrum: "If a tree falls in the forest but no one is around to hear it, does it make a sound?") Berkeley countered that God always perceives everything; hence, according to Berkeley, the apparent permanence of the world is a manifestation of the existence of God. A limerick by Ronald Knox (1888–1957) [cited by Bertrand Russell (1872–1970), 1945, p. 648], along with an anonymous reply, captures Berkeley's ideas concerning the permanence of the physical world in a rather whimsical manner:

There was a young man who said, "God
Must think it exceedingly odd
If he finds that this tree
Continues to be
When there's no one about in the Quad."

A reply by an anonymous donor is as follows:

Dear Sir:
Your astonishment's odd:
I am always about in the Quad,
And that's why the tree
Will continue to be,
Since observed by
*   Yours faithfully,*

*   God.*

The empiricist tradition persists and indeed pervades much contemporary analysis in perception, although in a greatly modified form. The contemporary view might focus on the role that experience (as opposed to unlearned or innate factors) plays in, for example, the attainment of space perception, speech perception, or taste preferences.

Of course, sensation and perception are areas of science and, accordingly, trace many of their most

basic problems as well as their exact, quantitative methodologies, to various fields of science. In fact, the topics and problems that concern psychologists who study sensation and perception are so interconnected with and draw so heavily from the biological, chemical, and physical sciences that we may consider them among the most derivative of all of psychology's subdisciplines. Historically, it is not easy to separate the problems of physiology and physics studied in the eighteenth century from those of sensation and perception. For example, until the beginning of the nineteenth century, the study of light and optics and the study of visual perception were intermixed, with light treated as subsidiary to visual perception. As Edwin Boring (1886–1968) observed in 1942 on this issue, "Light is a concept invented to explain vision, since it was perception that set the first problems for physics" (p. 97).

In many cases, the fundamental problems probed by the early physicists and physiologists concerned the nature of sensory experience. In vision, for example, the physicist Thomas Young (1773–1829), known especially for elaborating the wave theory of light, is also known for his basic work on color perception. The eminent physicist James Clerk Maxwell (1831–1879), the great Sir Isaac Newton (1642–1727), and perhaps perception's greatest scientific forebear, the physiologist Hermann von Helmholtz (1821–1894), also wrote extensively on color perception. In many respects their work set the foundation for much of our contemporary understanding of this complex topic (discussed in Chapter 5). Ernst Mach (1838–1916), famous for his classic work on mechanics (you may recognize his name applied to the *Mach number,* a unit of speed of an object expressed relative to the speed of sound), also studied sensation (writing a book in 1886 entitled *The Analysis of the Sensations*) and made numerous contributions to the study of visual contrast phenomena (one of which, called *Mach bands,* is described in Chapter 6).

Finally, before leaving the early scientists who helped establish and shape the field of sensation and perception, we must note the contribution of Wilhelm Wundt (1832–1920), the founder of experimental psychology. Wundt's formal training was in medicine and physiology, and his early work concentrated on the role of salt in urine formation. Of interest is the fact that one of Wundt's first colleagues in his early scientific endeavors was the chemist R. W. von Bunsen (1811–1899), who invented the gas burner that bears his name (Hothersall, 1984). In 1879 in Leipzig, Wundt began a critical series of laboratory studies on vision, hearing, attention, and reaction time (which he thought was a means of measuring the speed of thought) that placed the problems and issues of sensation and perception on a par with those of any science. Indeed, in many ways the problems of sensation and perception addressed by Wundt in the nineteenth century are variations of those we will encounter here.

Sensation and Perception as Interdisciplinary Sciences

We have seen that, historically, the problems of other sciences are closely bound up with those of sensation and perception. It follows that the study of sensation and perception requires knowledge from areas of science outside of psychology. For example, to study vision we must know something of the nature of light, how it is affected by its transmission through the various structures of the eye and the biochemical effects it has on the receptor cells of the eye. The same requirement applies to hearing: We must know something about the physics of sound propagation, understand how vibrations are transmitted within the inner ear, and how these vibrations are transformed into neural signals. In addition, basic knowledge of chemistry is a must to understand how we taste and smell. Similarly, we need knowledge of the physics of mechanical force and of heat transfer for touch, as well as the basics of gravitational and inertial force for an understanding of bodily orientation and position in space.

APPROACHES TO THE STUDY OF SENSATION AND PERCEPTION

A field as broad as sensation and perception uses a variety of approaches. In this section we outline some of the major approaches, but it is important to keep

in mind that they are presented as an introduction and will be discussed in greater detail in some of the following chapters.

Structuralism

When psychology was founded as an experimental science by Wilhelm Wundt in 1879, it was patterned after the prevailing sciences of the nineteenth century in an approach called **structuralism.** As the natural sciences focused on discovering the structure of basic elements of matter—atoms, molecules, cells—the view of psychology, especially in the hands of one of Wundt's most influential students, Edward Bradford Titchener (1867–1927), posed psychology's problem as discovering the *structure* of perception. That is, its goal was to uncover the simplest, most basic elements of conscious experience, namely, elementary sensations. According to Titchener, the task of psychology was to *reduce* perception to its constituent elements: its elementary sensations. A visual example is offered in Figure 1.2, which shows a structuralist's triangle.

According to the structuralist notion, each of the dot elements shown in Figure 1.2 produces a single, elementary sensation, and the total effect of these sensations creates the perception of a triangle. Of course, this is not what happens when we typically perceive aspects of the environment. Clearly the structuralist notion is mainly of historical significance, and its elemental assumptions are not taken seriously today. Structuralism did, however, provide an important impetus to another, quite different way of thinking about the role of elements comprising the environment.

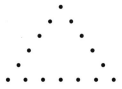

□ *figure 1.2* A structuralist triangle. According to a structuralist interpretation, each dot in the array of dots produces its own elementary sensation and the sum of these sensations creates the perception of a triangle.

Gestalt Psychology

A second school emerged, in part as a reaction to the structuralist approach. This approach, called **Gestalt psychology,** began around 1910 in Germany and argued against the prevailing structuralist notion that a perception is a combination of individual sensations that can be reduced to simple, individual elements. According to Gestalt psychologists, structural analysis ignored a significant factor of perception: the *relationship* between stimuli.

Examine Figure 1.3. What do you see? Certainly three dots. If you also see a triangle, you are experiencing a Gestalt perception. Instead of the mere sum of individual parts, you perceive a cohesive, integrated figure. The triangle that you perceive is a relational characteristic, a unique property not present in the individual elements or merely the sum of the elements. The elements of the figure are related to each other in such a way as to create a figure with properties and qualities that do not reside in its individual parts. As this example shows, the Gestalt approach stresses that we perceive the environment with respect to its inherent organizational properties, and we tend to perceive holistic, meaningful forms.

Without question, our awareness of the environment is filled with Gestalt-like perception. Consider a tune. Its meaningfulness is a function of the relationship between the notes. In fact, it is the *relationship* between the notes that defines the tune. The melody persists even if the notes are systematically altered (or transposed by an octave or key change), so long as the relationship between them does not change.

•

•   •

□ *figure 1.3* A Gestalt triangle. The perception of a triangle is the result of the *relation* of the three dots to each other rather than the sum of their individual sensory effects. The experience of a triangle from the dots highlights the relational, holistic nature of Gestalt perception.

While few contemporary psychologists would describe themselves as Gestalt psychologists, this does not mean that the Gestalt approach has been rejected or abandoned. Instead, the general Gestalt theme of holistic perception has been absorbed and integrated into the mainstream of sensation and perception studies, especially in areas that emphasize the organized nature of perception. We will have occasion to repeat this relational theme in later contexts; here, it is sufficient to cite the Gestalt credo: "*The whole is different from the sum of its parts.*"

Constructivist Approach

The **constructivist approach** emphasizes the active role played by the observer in the perceptual process. This approach presumes that perception is based on more than just the information in the stimulus input. It proposes that what we perceive at any moment is a *mental construction* based on our cognitive strategies, our collection of past experiences, biases, expectations, motives, attention, and so on. In short, the constructivist approach proposes that perceptions are constructed or even inferred by the observer based on an interpretation of the information provided by the environment. Central to this view is that some constructive process occurs within the observer, a process that mediates between the physical world of objects and events and its perception.

Look around you. You undoubtedly see objects arranged in a certain relation—some close by, some far away. But how do you know this? What tells you that a chair, for example, stands in front of a table? According to the constructivist approach, you are taking into account some prominent location cues provided by the scene. The chair perhaps overlaps or visually obscures part of the desk. According to the constructivist approach, your perception of the location of these objects derives, in part, from the recognition of this relationship. This somewhat active view presently flourishes in the work of researchers and theorists such as Irvin Rock (e.g., 1986), Julian Hochberg (e.g., 1981, 1988), and R. L. Gregory (1974, 1977).

ecological
Direct Perception

A very different approach was developed by James J. Gibson (1904–1979). Gibson proposed that inner mental processes play little or no role in perception. Central to his approach is that as an observer moves through the environment, he or she *directly* picks up the information needed for adaptive, effective perception. That is, the stimuli in the environment—the information provided in the visual image—contain all the necessary and sufficient information for the percep-

tion of the physical world directly; additional stages of processing or mediation are unnecessary. According to Gibson, one important source of spatial information is provided by changes in the texture of surfaces. Typically we see objects in the third dimension lying on surfaces extending outward from us in depth. These surfaces, which generally have a texture, are projected on the eye in an informative fashion: Elements of the texture always appear finer or denser as distance increases, and they appear coarser with decreasing distance (Figure 1.4). The graded change

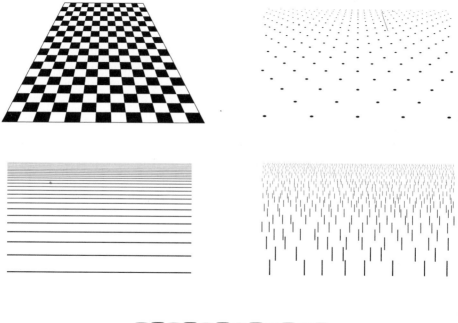

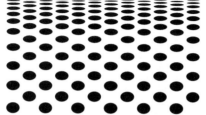

⬛ *figure 1.4* Spatial information from textured surfaces. The textured array of elements is arranged to depict a graded change in texture density, producing an impression of a continuous, receding plane. If you were to view the actual surfaces depicted above, the visual projections of the surface texture would appear coarse from the foreground and become finer and denser with distance. This graded change in surface texture with distance is called a *texture gradient*.

in the texture of a surface directly due to distance is called a **texture gradient.**

Another source of direct information concerning spatial perception is the manner in which images flow across the eyes as the objects or the observer shifts or moves within the environment: The pattern of changes in the images shifting across the eyes gives an immediate impression of the spatial layout of the environment relative to the observer, with no processing or analysis of depth or distance cues.

Compare this with the constructivist approach, in which perception is seen as the outcome of information processing. The contrast between the two is suggested in Figure 1.5, which shows disks differing in projected size. In viewing an actual scene of one depicted here, the disks appear similar in size but differ in projected sizes. According to the constructivist approach, this happens because the upper disk appears to be farther away and our perception of its size involves taking into account this apparent distance cue. That is, we compensate for the apparent distance by adjusting the apparent size. The approach of direct perception, in contrast, argues that no such compensation for apparent distance is needed because the scene itself provides sufficient information to perceive disk size directly, without incorporating distance information. Each disk covers about four texture units on the

apparent terrain. Thus in natural, real world viewing the constant texture covered by the disks directly indicates that they are the same size.

Gibson's direct approach, also referred to as the _ecological approach,_ further stresses the appealing point that perception is a natural process that has evolved to deal with the real world; hence, the study of perception should focus on the sorts of stimulation that the typical observer confronts while moving within the environment. It follows that the Gibson approach emphasizes naturalistic, real-world observations as opposed to artificial, strictly controlled laboratory investigations.

Computational Approach

The **computational approach** is attributed to David Marr (1945–1980), based on his monograph, _Vision,_ published posthumously in 1982. The computational concept involves a rigorous, mathematically oriented analysis of certain aspects of visual perception derived largely from the use of computer simulation and artificial intelligence. It accepts the basic idea of Gibson's direct perception: that all of the information needed for perception is provided in the environment. But the computational approach also proposes that the perception of characteristics such as shape and form

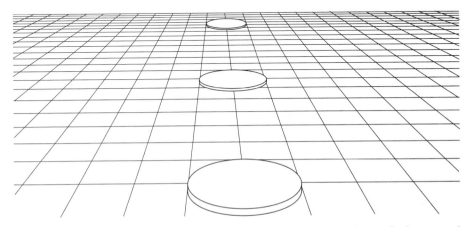

□ *figure 1.5* Equal-sized disks with distance and texture cues. Although projecting smaller images to the eye with increasing apparent distance, the disks seem about equal in size because each occupies the same amount of texture surface on its plane.

requires a form of problem solving or information processing of environmental stimuli by the observer—namely, the extraction, in a symbolic form, of certain features from the visual image of the environment such as its lines, edges, borders, contours, motion, and other discontinuities. According to the computational concept, this sort of information is "computed" from a form of mathematical analysis of changes in shading, lightness, and other subtle surface texture characteristics by an observer in much the same way that a computer program allows a machine to interpret selected sensory information to make decisions about features such as patterns and shapes.

The computational approach is a recent concept, and its influence is not as widespread as that of other approaches. This may be because many of the concepts and mechanisms invoked to explain perceptual phenomena are complicated, requiring detailed knowledge from disciplines other than psychology. However, it provides an innovative framework for studying sensation and perception, and it may provide a fruitful area of interaction between sensation and perception, on the one hand, and artificial intelligence and information processing, on the other.

Neurophysiological Approach

The neurophysiological approach argues that sensory and perceptual phenomena are best explained by known neural and physiological mechanisms serving sensory structures. This proposal invokes a form of *reductionism:* the idea that one can understand broad, apparently complex forms of behavior by studying their underlying biological processes (somewhat reminiscent of structuralism but here restricted to physiological mechanisms). Part of the argument in favor of this approach is that neural and physiological mechanisms pervade and underlie all aspects of behavior. More important, however, is that structures and processes of the sensory system analyze incoming sensory stimuli (which typically are degraded) to provide us with information about the environment. Indeed, as we shall learn throughout the text, there are analyzing mechanisms at the neural level that enable us to detect specific features and events in the environment. For example, nerve cells in various parts of the visual

system, as well as in the brain itself, are capable of responding selectively and precisely to specific features in the environment—shapes, orientation, length, color, and so on (e.g., Hubel & Wiesel, 1962, 1968). In fact, certain nerve cells in the brains of monkeys are activated only by complex combinations of stimulus features, such as the profile of a face or the outline of a hand held in a certain orientation (Desimone et al., 1984; Gross, Rocha-Miranda, & Bender, 1972). In short, certain neural mechanisms of the visual system extract coherent features from a relatively degraded visual image.

Another example is that our understanding of the neural complexity of the eye can account for our extraordinary acuity and color vision in bright light and our equally impressive sensitivity in dim light. As we shall observe when we discuss the visual system, different kinds of photoreceptors within the eye, along with their neural connections, promote these different visual functions.

Since our understanding of the sensory system draws extensively from neurophysiological mechanisms, this approach is somewhat reasonable. It plays the single most critical role in explaining phenomena at the sensory level. No experimental psychologist would question seriously the fact that discoveries in neurophysiology have provided some definitive answers to fundamental problems of sensation and perception. Clearly, neurophysiology has a permanent place in the study of sensation and perception (in fact, we will introduce or, hopefully, reintroduce some of its basic concepts in the last section of this chapter). However, neurophysiological mechanisms alone cannot explain the enormous complexity that exists between, for example, stimulating the eye and a conscious perceptual experience. The attempt to reduce *all* of sensation and perception to biological or neurophysiological mechanisms goes beyond the expectations of most experimental psychologists.

WHY STUDY SENSATION AND PERCEPTION?

Anyone confronting the vast, complex phenomena comprising sensation and perception might well ask, why study them? Of course, we would not have asked this question without having many good answers. First, as we have observed, the topics and major themes of sensation and perception are essential to the history of science in general and are central to experimental psychology in particular. Recall that basic philosophical questions on how we come to know the external world focused on the role of the senses. In fact, experimental psychology itself began with problems of sensation and perception.

Another reason we study sensation and perception is that they have many practical applications and apply to many everyday questions. For example, what sounds and colors are the most readily perceived danger signals? Is red really the best color to denote "danger?" Why should natural substances with unpleasant tastes, especially bitter ones, generally be avoided? What is the relation of "stereo" listening to auditory localization?

The study of sensation and perception allows educators and psychologists to identify and treat students with reading disabilities involving eye movements and acuity. Psychologists may link excessive noise or noise pollution to specific deficits in hearing. They may relate changes in sensation and perception to specific environmental events. Important practical applications, for example, pain management, may develop from research questions such as why the same painful stimulus varies so much, depending on the circumstances in which it occurs.

Yet another reason to study sensation and perception was proposed at the beginning of this chapter: Our perception of the physical world poses important scientific problems that must be examined. As Howard (1982) observes, "Many people do not realize that perception is a problem; they perceive that world so effortlessly and continuously that they take the mechanism for granted. Perception is the most neglected of all the major problems of scier   nd this may be because it is the most difficult   lem of them all" (p. 1). Let us examine two exa ples of perception as posing problems: *Necker's rhomboid* (Figure 1.6a) and the perception of subjective contours (Figure 1.6b).

Generally, we are not aware of the problem of perception unless we are confronted with unusual examples. As you view Figure 1.6a you are certainly

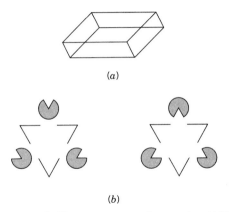

(a)

(b)

□ *figure 1.6* Two problems of perception. (a) Necker's rhomboid. (b) Subjective contours.

not aware of the reception of light energy, or the formation of an image in the back of the eye, or the propagation of information along neural paths to the brain, and you remain unaware of the processing that gives rise to its perception: all of this occurs without effort. However, we easily perceive a depiction of a three-dimensional figure. This immediate experience—the perception of a form of a three-dimensional figure from a two-dimensional surface—in itself is both profound and extraordinary. However, consider further that with continued viewing of the figure and with no change in light energy, or the image projected on the back of the eyeball, or additional neural information, the simple transparent figure reverses in depth: what was once a front surface becomes a surface in the back of the figure. A change in perception occurs without any change in the stimulus that gives rise to it. Although this example of a problem of perception is unusual, our normal perceptions are equally extraordinary events (based on a description by the Swiss naturalist L. A. Necker in 1832). We will return to the problem of viewing Necker's figure in Chapters 7 and 10.

The left side of Figure 1.6b is a design made up of angular elements and disks with "Pac Man-like" cutout sectors. However, when the disks are specially aligned (shown at right of Figure 1.6b), a white triangle appears to lie in front of the disks. You can verify that the white triangle is an illusory perception by covering the cutout disks. This phenomenon, called a **subjective contour,** will be discussed in Chapter 7.

Finally, we study sensation and perception because they are intrinsically interesting topics and help us answer basic questions concerning our daily existence: how we see, hear, taste, and so on. Clearly, we possess an impressive arsenal of sensory equipment, and its functioning provides an amazing amount of information on the physical world.

PHYSIOLOGICAL PERSPECTIVE: NEURONAL COMMUNICATION

In this final section, we outline some elementary neurophysiology because throughout the text there will be numerous discussions in which concepts and terms of the physiology of the nervous system will be mentioned or assumed. Our purpose here is not to present the function of the nervous system in detail, but rather to provide a selective, condensed, general introduction to neural activity in sensory systems.

The Neuron

The basic elements of the nervous system are **neurons** (or *nerve cells*), the main processors and transmitters of information used by the body. The human nervous system has an estimated 100 billion neurons (Thompson, 1985). Each neuron is a separate cell and serves as the basic unit of communication within the nervous system (Figure 1.7). There are different types of neurons, each specialized for a specific neural task. Some neurons serve as receptor cells of the sensory organs, reacting to specific forms of physical energy from the environment, such as light or pressure or chemicals. These neurons **transduce** or convert, the physical energy affecting them into nerve impulses (i.e., fire individual neurons), which are then sent to other neurons as part of the overall communication system of the nervous system. In other words **transduction** is the conversion of physical energy into a neural form of stimulation, accomplished by specialized neurons in the sense organs. *Sensory neurons* transmit information from sensory receptors to the brain, *motor neurons* conduct information from the

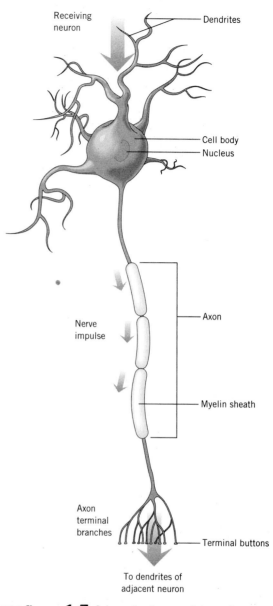

□ *figure 1.7* Schematic diagram of the main parts of a neuron. Typically, the nerve impulse travels from the dendrites and the cell body to the axon until it reaches the terminal buttons of the axon; here the nerve impulse synapses, or connects, with dendrites of another neuron, continuing the nerve impulse (as schematized in Figure 1.8).

brain to the muscles, and *interneurons* transmit information between neurons. All neurons, regardless of their function, consist of a separate cell with three distinct parts: (1) the *cell body,* or *soma,* which contains the nucleus of the cell that regulates the chemical activities of the neuron and receives and collects incoming messages; (2) radiating from the cell body are branching structures called **dendrites** (from the Greek, *dendron,* which means "tree"), which make contact and receive neural information from other neurons; and (3) the **axon,** long, thin fibers that carry information from the cell body to other neurons.

Typically, axons carry outgoing messages from the neuron, either relaying them to nearby neurons or directing a muscle or gland to take action. Some axons are only about 0.1 mm long; others may stretch up to 1 m or more within the human adult's nervous system. Typically, axons connect with and transmit impulses to the dendrites of other neurons. That is, the axon is the part of the neuron's communication system that transfers information, as neural impulses, outward, whereas the dendrites transfer information inward toward the neuron's cell body. Many neurons have axons that are covered with a fatty layer or sheath made up of a substance called **myelin.** Myelin is made of protective and nutritive cells (called *glial cells*) that cover the axon, forming the insulating myelin sheath around the axon. This myelin sheath helps to increase significantly the speed at which a nerve impulse travels along a neuron.

The end of the axon assumes a branching, tree-like shape, and each branch ends in a structure called a **terminal button.** At the terminal button, the axon connects with the dendrite of another neuron.

Neural Transmission

Underlying all sensory behavior—seeing, hearing, feeling, and so on—is the communication of information. Information in the form of neural signals is passed along neurons by a complex interaction of electrical and chemical changes. Neurons are filled with and surrounded by electrically charged atoms called *ions,* particularly sodium (Na^+) and potassium (K^+) ions (technically, positively charged ions, such as K^+ and Na^+, are called *cations*). For an inactive or unstimu-

lated neuron, differing concentrations of these electrically charged ions lie both inside and outside the neuron's membrane, with a higher concentration of negatively charged ions inside. The net effect of this unequal distribution of ions is that the fluid inside an inactive neuron is negative relative to the outside, which causes a tiny electrical charge to exist across its cell membrane. In general, in the human, the inside of the neuron has a charge of about −70 millivolts (mv) (a millivolt is 1/1000th of a volt) relative to the outside. This *inactive* state of a neuron is called a **resting potential** (or membrane potential).

However, when a neuron is excited by a stimulus or by the axon of another neuron, the resting potential is altered for a fraction of a second; the inside of the cell membrane becomes positively charged with respect to the outside. This brief alteration creates an electric charge that flows rapidly down the axon of the neuron, after which the resting potential is restored to its original state. This brief change in the electrical charge sets the first stage for the firing of a neuron and for sending messages (by way of the axon) within the nervous system. This occurs for all sensory events.

Action Potentials   Neurons do not necessarily fire and transmit impulses to adjacent neurons every time they generate an electric charge or every time they are stimulated. Every neuron has a minimum level of stimulation that must be reached in order for it to fire and transmit an impulse. This minimum level of stimulation necessary for a neuron to fire is called the *neural threshold* (other, more behavioral thresholds will be encountered in the next chapter). Thus, when several electrical charges within a neuron collect and exceed the neural threshold, the electrical state of the neuron changes rapidly—a change lasting 1 millisecond (msec or 1/1000th of a sec). This change is called an **action potential** (or a **spike potential** or just a *spike,* because at a given point the electric charge in a neuron rises rapidly to a peak and then declines equally rapidly).

Action potentials follow an **all-or-none principle.** That is, when the electrical charge reaches the neural threshold, an action potential occurs and an impulse is sent. If, on the other hand, the total electrical charge falls below the critical neural threshold level, no action potential results. In short, a neuron either fires an action potential or it doesn't; hence, its all-or-none characteristic. It should be pointed out that the force or intensity of the action potential remains constant regardless of stimulus intensity. That is, it always fires in the same way. However, as we readily recognize in dealing with the environment, the effects of a stimulus can range from very intense to barely detectable. So how can the all-or-none occurrence of action potentials represent the intensity of a physical stimulus? The answer lies in the *rate of firing* of action potentials: The stronger the stimulus, the more often the neuron will fire. So the difference between, for example, the sensory effects of a weak flashlight viewed from a great distance and a flashbulb going off in your face is a matter of the *rate* at which neurons fire action potentials, not their intensity.

Refractory Period   Action potentials are time limited. When an action potential has occurred, another one cannot be triggered for 1 msec. This brief duration of neural inactivity is called the **refractory period.** The refractory period thus limits the maximal frequency of neuron firing to 1000 action potentials per second or less. This fact has practical and theoretical consequences for neural excitation, especially in setting upper limits for the sensory system. Another way of saying this is that due to the refractory period the rate at which neural spikes can be sent along the nervous system cannot exceed 1000 spikes per second.

Speed of Neural Transmission   The neural impulse or action potential for mammals travels along a bare axon at about 2 to 3 m/sec. However, as we noted earlier, myelin covering axons, acting as an electrical insulation, greatly increase the speed of action potentials. In myelinated axons, the action potential can travel more than 100 m/sec (about 225 mph!). In the human, myelination of axons is incomplete until about age 12, which in part accounts for the fact that children cannot learn and react as fast or act as purposively as can adults. Their nervous systems cannot handle information with the speed and complexity necessary for certain tasks. Diseases such as multiple sclerosis destroy the myelin sheath. This re-

sults in a reduced rate of conduction of action potentials and eventual loss of sensory-motor coordination requiring nervous system integration.

Synaptic Connections   The billions of neurons in the nervous system cooperate with each other to coordinate all of the body's sensory and motor activities. How do they interact? In this section we examine how a signal or message travels from one neuron to another.

When an action potential is initiated, it creates an impulse that spreads along the neuron's membrane and travels down the axon until it reaches the terminal button (see Figure 1.7). There a chemical reaction occurs between the axon of one neuron (the presynaptic neuron) and the dendrite of another neuron (the receiving, or postsynaptic, neuron). This point of contact between neurons is a neural junction called a **synapse** (from the Greek word *synapsis,* meaning "clasp" or "connection"). Figure 1.8 provides a schematic view of a synapse and the *synaptic cleft* (or *synaptic space*), a microscopic gap between the terminal button of the presynaptic neuron and the cell membrane of the postsynaptic neuron. When the action potential reaches the end of the axon to the terminal button, minute amounts of neurotransmitter substances stored in tiny chambers or sacs of the terminal button, called *synaptic vesicles,* are released into the synaptic cleft. These neurotransmitters are special chemicals that momentarily bridge the synapse and stimulate the adjacent postsynaptic neuron.

Neurotransmitters   The neurotransmitter chemicals released at a synapse either excite or inhibit the postsynaptic neuron. When an action potential triggers an excitatory synapse, a neurotransmitter chemical is released that excites the neuron across the synaptic cleft. In contrast, when an action potential triggers an inhibitory synapse, a neurotransmitter is released that inhibits the adjacent neuron, making adjacent neurons less likely to transmit an action potential.

One important excitatory neurotransmitter is *acetylcholine (ACh),* which is markedly affected by drugs such as caffeine and cocaine. ACh is found in synapses of the brain, where it contributes to attention, arousal,

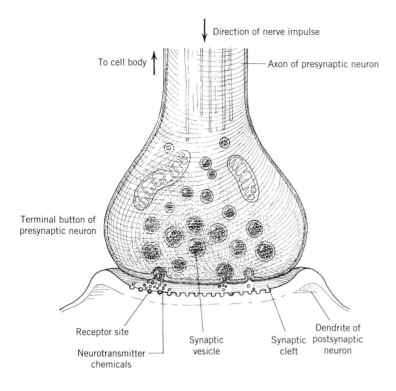

Direction of nerve impulse

To cell body ↑

Axon of presynaptic neuron

Terminal button of presynaptic neuron

Receptor site

Neurotransmitter chemicals

Synaptic vesicle

Synaptic cleft

Dendrite of postsynaptic neuron

▭ *figure* **1.8** Schematic diagram of neural transmission at a synapse. The nerve impulse sent along the axon causes the synaptic vesicles of the terminal button to release neurotransmitter chemicals. The chemicals then bridge the gap of the synaptic cleft between the axon of the presynaptic neuron and the dendrite of the receiving, or postsynaptic, neuron, thereby continuing the nerve impulse.

and memory and produces skeletal muscle activity by acting on motor nerves, to name only a few of its functions. An antagonist to ACh is *curare*, a potent paralyzing drug sometimes used by South American natives of the Amazon River Basin. Curare selectively blocks the action of ACh by essentially preventing it from reaching the synapses of neurons of nerves and muscles, resulting in total paralysis. *Norepinephrine (NE)* is another important excitatory neurotransmitter contributing to alertness and arousal; as is well known, cocaine and amphetamine prolong the action of NE, thereby promoting the highly stimulating psychological effects of these drugs.

A major inhibitory neurotransmitter is *GABA* (*gamma-amino butyric acid,* also called *glutamic acid*), which dampens the firing of neurons and thus aids in controlling the preciseness of muscle control. Without the inhibiting influence of GABA, nerve impulses become less precise and muscle activity becomes erratic, uncoordinated, and even convulsive. Another inhibitory neurotransmitter, quite relevant to any discussion of sensory processes, is *endorphin,*

which has been found to slow or block neural signals in the pain pathways. (We will return to a discussion of endorphins in a later chapter.) Similarly, common drugs such as barbiturates and alcohol act by suppressing the release of neurotransmitters.

Measuring the Action Potential Action potentials or spikes are often used as direct measures of sensory neural activity. Indeed, these neural-electrical signals (action potentials) are generated by individual neurons that make up the sensory code with which the nervous system communicates. Generally, these neural signals are measured and recorded utilizing sensitive, precise instruments that can pick up and amplify very weak electrical signals. One such instrument is the *microelectrode*—a tiny filament whose tip is tapered to a diameter of less than 1 micron (1/1000th of a millimeter or less than about 1/25,000th of an inch)—which ideally is inserted into a cell body of a single neuron or an axon. Electrical activity of the neuron is measured by a voltage meter and is displayed on an *oscilloscope* (consisting of a beam of electrons on a phosphor screen) that shows electrical change in the neuron over time, that is, it presents the pattern of action or spike potentials. Three such sample outputs are given in Figure 1.9, which displays microelectrode activity of the same neuron responding at different rates due to changes in the tactual (pressure) stimulation applied to a finger. These records of neural activity show that as the pressure applied to the finger increases, the rate of discharge of action potentials correspondingly increases (and the sensation changes).

The use of microelectrode recordings applied to the activity of single neurons enables us to understand fundamental processes of communication in the ner-

vous system. In general, it has led to important advances in sensory neurophysiology.

Sensory-Neural Transmission and Integration

A single neuron may be connected to thousands of other neurons by synaptic contacts. Since the human brain has perhaps 100 billion neurons, each with thousands of possible synaptic connections, the nervous system has at least 100,000 billion possible synaptic connections (i.e., 100 trillion!). Based on such magnitudes, Thompson (1985) has calculated the possibility that "the number of possible different combinations

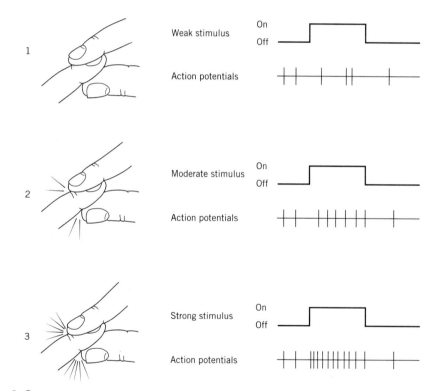

□ **figure 1.9** Three records of neuronal activity—action potentials—produced by three intensity levels of touch or pressure applied to a finger. In Record 1 the finger is lightly touched, the resultant sensation is a feeling of light touch, and the firing rate of action potentials is very low. In Record 2 the finger is squeezed with more force, the sensation is a feeling of pressure, and the action potentials fire at an increased rate. In Record 3 the pressure applied to the finger is still further increased, the sensation is of intense pressure (and perhaps pain), and the firing rate of action potentials is relatively high. Observe that the size (height) of action potentials for all records is constant, but the *rate* of firing (the number of action potentials over time) varies with the stimulus intensity applied. That is, the rate of firing correlates with intensity and sensation. (*Source:* Based on Dember, Jenkins, & Teyler, 1984.)

of synaptic connections among the neurons in a single human brain is larger than the total number of atomic particles that make up the known universe" (p. 3). The complexity of possible interconnections between neurons seems almost without limit and contributes to the immense possible diversity of the nervous system and its sensory capacities.

To be informative to the organism, the electrical signals in the neuron must be sent to the brain. This is done by the nerves, tracts, and nuclei of the nervous system. A **nerve** is a bundle of axons grouped to form a pathway to carry neural signals from one part of the nervous system to another. Just as there are sensory and motor neurons, there are also sensory and motor nerves. *Sensory nerves,* also called *afferent nerves* (from the Latin word *affere,* "to bring to"), carry sensory information to the brain and spinal cord and provide our sensory experience. *Motor nerves,* or *efferent nerves* (from the Latin word *effere,* "to bring forth"), send messages *from* the brain and spinal cord to effectors such as muscles.

Sensory information is carried by the nerves to the *central nervous system,* which consists of the spinal cord and the brain. Within the central nervous system, pathways are referred to as *tracts* (rather than nerves). In addition, there are many regions of the central nervous system where large groups of neurons converge to make synaptic connections called **nuclei.** Nuclei act as relay and switching stations to process, integrate, transform, and even perform simple analyses on sensory information. The **thalamus** of the brain (located in the forebrain, beneath the center of the cerebral hemispheres) is one such major nucleus. It is made up of numerous nuclei, each restricted to a specific sense. The signals picked up by the axons of the neurons travel to specific regions of the *cerebral cortex* of the brain. The cerebral cortex (from the Latin, *cortex,* meaning the "bark of a tree"), is a thin exterior covering of the cerebral hemispheres of the brain. It is only about 2 millimeters thick but it is very convoluted or furrowed, yielding an overall surface area of about 1.5 sq ft.

The regions of the brain specific to each sensory system are referred to as **primary cortical projection areas.** As shown in Figure 1.10, the primary projection, or receiving, area for hearing is in the temporal lobe (a **lobe** is an area of the cortex associated with a specific function) located on the side of the cortex; the primary projection area for touch (also called the **somatosensory cortex**) is in the **parietal lobe,** located at the top of the cortex; the primary projection area for sight (also called the **striate cortex**) is in the **occipital lobe,** located at the back of the cortex; and the region of the brain devoted to smell is the **olfactory bulb,** located beneath the temporal lobe.

It is in the brain that the sensory signals generated in the axons result in the psychological experience of perception. Each sensory nerve connects to a specific area of the brain that, when activated, determines a person's sensory experience. Thus, neural signals picked up from the ear and sent to the temporal lobe of the brain cause us to hear sounds; signals from the eyes transmitted to the occipital lobe of the brain cause us to see things; and so on. The sounds and sights result only when the sensory-neural signals reach the appropriate cortical projection areas of the brain.

Sensory Receptors

Up to this point, our discussion has centered on the activity of neurons in response to electrical stimulation. However, our main interest is in the function of the *sensory systems.* Although we focus primarily on the human senses, the text is organized around a broad, functional evolutionary theme: that the organism is adapted, both by sensory structure and by function, to interact successfully with its environment. For each species, the reception of specific features of its environment is vital to its adaptive success. Accordingly, we assume that evolutionary pressures and natural selection lead to the creation of adaptive sensory structures and functions that enable every species to receive specific features of the environment that are necessary for its survival. Thus, we will encounter many specialized forms of anatomy, physiology, and behavior with adaptive consequences.

All forms of life must interact with their surroundings to gain information and exchange energy. For a one-celled animal such as the amoeba, the simplest protozoan, there are no specialized receptors. Most of the amoeba's external surface is responsive to gravity,

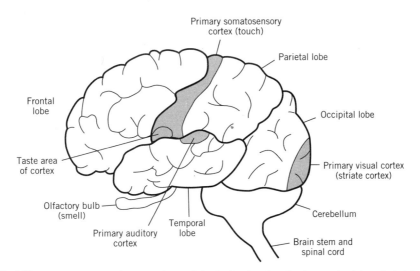

□ *figure **1.10*** Diagram of the left hemisphere of the brain showing the four major lobes (in bold outline) and the primary or cortical projection areas (shaded)—the specific brain regions—that mediate the various senses of hearing, touch, taste, and vision. The brain region for smell is the olfactory bulb, shown as an extension beneath the temporal lobe.

light, heat, and pressure or touch. However, most multicellular animals have evolved specialized receptor cells and units. All such receptor cells generate neural activity in response to stimulation.

Doctrine of Specific Nerve Energies

Aggregations of receptor units form sense organs with diverse structures and functions. Each sense organ is sensitive to energy changes in the environment of the organism. Thus, receptive parts of the eye receive and react neurally to light or radiant energy; taste buds react to chemical molecules in the mouth; the inner regions of the ear receive airborne pressure vibrations; and the skin surface responds to thermal and mechanical changes. However, mechanical energy, when applied as pressure, can produce effects on hearing and vision: You need merely press your finger against the side of a closed eye to get a visual sensation. This happens when receptors of the eye react to pressure stimulation, and it illustrates a fundamental principle of sensation: Regardless of how a receptor is stimulated, it produces only one kind of sensory experience. This is because the resultant sensation depends on the neural connection of the stimulated receptor to the brain, not on the form of physical energy that

initiates the process. This fact of neural specificity is generally attributed to Johannes Müller, who in 1826 proposed the **Doctrine of Specific Nerve Energies.** The doctrine states that the sensory quality experienced, such as a sound, touch, light, and so on, depends on which nerve is stimulated, not on *how* it is stimulated. In other words, according to Müller's doctrine, it is not the stimulus that determines the nature of the sensation but rather the specificity of the neurons, receptors, and nerves activated by the stimulus.

Finally, we must note in this context that because of the bioelectric nature of living tissue, electrical energy has the unique property of exciting all sensory units.

In general, specialized sense receptors have evolved to help a species survive by reacting specifically to particular forms of energy—energy that provides critical information about the species' habitat. Indeed, sense-receptor structures and mechanisms can be studied in terms of their function in behavior—the relationship of a species' sensory equipment to the behavioral requirements for survival in its habitat. For example, the bat possesses a highly developed, specialized acoustic anatomy, along with a remarkable range of sounds it can both emit and receive. These can be understood when the bat is viewed in an ecological context. Bats are most active at night and typically live in environments so dark that photoreceptors—light-sensitive mechanisms for its vision—are useless. Therefore, bats have evolved sensory structures and behavioral capacities for activity in a lightless habitat. Thus their peculiar auditory structures, as well as their extended range of sound emissions and receptions, can be examined in terms of the bat's remarkable ability to locate and catch prey on the wing, and to navigate and avoid obstacles in the complete absence of light.

Another such example is the extremely sensitive hands of the raccoon. Raccoons use their hands to forage for food, particularly in places where vision and smell are of limited value, such as in shallow water. Moreover, in captivity raccoons are often observed handling their food under water before eating it. Although this behavior has been labeled "washing," its function most likely is to soften the skin of the hands, increasing their sensitivity (Radinsky, 1976). Presumably the sensitivity of the raccoon's hands evolved in response to the need to compensate with touch for the reduced use of vision and smell. The area of the raccoon's brain that receives touch information from the hands is unusually enlarged compared to other cortical sensory areas (Welker & Campos, 1963).

Such unusual sensory adaptations are not restricted to lower mammals. The aye-aye is a nocturnal animal, somewhat resembling a squirrel, that lives in a relatively restricted region of coastal Madagascar. It is a species of lemur, a primate (in the same phylogenetic order as monkeys, apes, and humans) that has evolved a unique set of sensory structures and mechanisms to deal with its restricted, nocturnal habitat (Figure 1.11). Consider this description by Natalie Angier (1992):

> *Its hearing is so keen that it can tap on a tree trunk and detect the hollow regions within, indicating the presence of the beetle grubs it covets. The animal will then rip through the trunk with four chisel-shaped front teeth that, unlike those of other primates, will grow throughout life. And of course there is the aye-aye's extraordinary middle finger, a long thin digit that it can bend in every direction, even backward to touch its forearm. The finger is an all-purpose tool for delicately tapping the tree trunks, poking holes in eggs, pumping the liquid out of those eggs, and extracting milk from coconuts. (p. C-10)*

Sensory structures may also adapt to a *decrease* in the functional demands of the environment, as indicated by this unusual example:

> *The tunicate sea squirt in its larval form swims freely about, guided by its eyes and ears, finding food and avoiding predators. Reaching adulthood, it loses its tail and attaches itself to a rock.*

□ *figure **1.11*** The aye-aye of Madagascar, a species of primate whose sensory system is remarkably adapted to a nocturnal environment. (*Source:* Duane Hall/*The New York Times*)

For about two years, it sits on the rock, vegetating. Its eyes, its ears, and then its brain—all degenerate and become useless. (Alpern, Lawrence, & Wolsk, 1967, p. 1)

In general, however, the specialization of sensory structures increases the information that can be extracted from the environment. As the functional demands of a species increase, there is a need for greater sensitivity to energy and the capacity to make finer sensory discriminations. In the course of evolution, this is often provided by the development of more specialized sensory mechanisms.

SUMMARY

This chapter introduced the topics of sensation and perception, and revealed some of their fundamental problems and issues. Traditionally, sensations are considered basic, immediate, and isolated experiences directly linked to the physical environment; perceptions are the result of psychological processes such as meaning and past experience, which involve the organization and integration of sensations. However, in many environmental encounters, the distinction between sensation and perception is difficult.

Sensation and perception was further discussed in a scientific–historical context. This led to a discussion of various historical and contemporary approaches: structuralism, Gestalt psychology, the constructivist approach, J. J. Gibson's direct approach to perception, the computational approach, and the neurophysiological approach.

The final section introduced some basic notions of neural communication and nervous system functioning required for the study of sensation and perception. Some fundamental properties of the neuron and neural transmission were outlined, especially the role of the action potential. Functional aspects of neural transmission were described with respect to synaptic connections between neurons.

The relation between neurons, nerves, tracts, and nuclei was outlined, and their link between sensory receptors and specific regions of the brain—the primary cortical projection areas—was described.

Sensory reception was also discussed, and the specific connection between sensory receptors and environmental stimulation was stressed in the context of Müller's Doctrine of Specific Nerve Energies. The adaptive significance of sensory receptors was noted, and examples were presented.

KEY TERMS

Action Potential (or Spike Potential)

All-or-None Principle

Axons

Computational Approach

Constructivist Approach

Dendrites

Direct Approach (J. J. Gibson)

Direct Perception

Doctrine of Specific Nerve Energies (J. Müller)

Empiricism

Gestalt Psychology

Lobe

Myelin

Nerve

Neuron

Neurophysiological Approach

Nuclei

Occipital Lobe

Olfactory Bulb

Parietal Lobe

Perception

Primary Cortical Projection Areas

Refractory Period

Resting Potential

Sensation

Somatosensory Cortex

Striate Cortex

Structuralism (E. B. Titchener)

Subjective Contours

Synapse

Temporal Lobe

Terminal Button

Texture Gradient

Thalamus

Transduction

STUDY QUESTIONS

1. What are the traditional definitions of sensation and perception? Consider instances where the distinction between them may be inappropriate.

2. Describe some of the challenges and problems of perception. Analyze the relation between the physical environment and our perception of it.

3. What is the role of the philosophical school of empiricism in sensation and perception? Describe some of the contributions of physical scientists of the nineteenth century to the contemporary issues of sensation and perception, with examples.

4. Summarize the various approaches to sensation and perception. Compare the structuralist and Gestalt approaches regarding the relation between environmental stimuli and the organized nature of perception. Consider why the Gestalt approach has been integrated into the mainstream knowledge of sensation and perception.

5. Compare and contrast J. J. Gibson's direct approach with the constructivist approach. How does Gibson's approach deal with cognitive processes and past experience?

6. Describe why the neurophysiological approach is important. Cite examples in which an understanding of neural mechanisms can account for sensory and perceptual activities.

7. Why should one study sensation and perception? In your answer, consider some of the issues and problems concerning sensation and perception.

8. What are the main components of a neuron? Identify the axon and dendrite and indicate their roles in neural communication. Describe how neurons transmit information from sensory receptors to the brain.

9. Contrast the resting potential with the action potential and indicate what changes occur in a neuron during an action potential.

10. What is the all-or-none principle? How can the intensity of a physical stimulus be represented by the rate of firing of action potentials?

11. What is a synapse? How does synaptic activity enable communication between neurons? What role do neurotransmitters play at the synapse?

12. Identify the role of the thalamus in sensory processing. What are nerves, tracts, and nuclei?

13. What are the lobes of the cortex? What are the primary cortical projection areas? What is the relation between neural activity in the sensory receptor and the primary cortical projection areas?

14. What is J. Müller's Doctrine of Specific Nerve Energies, and what does it stress concerning the link between neural activity and sensory experience?

15. Give some examples of how specialized sensory receptors enable the processing of sensory information that is crucial to an animal's survival.

chapter 2

PSYCHOPHYSICS

*P*hysical energy from the environment, we have learned, is transduced, or converted into electrochemical messages that affect the nervous system and give rise to psychological experiences, that is, produce sensations and perceptions. This chapter further analyzes this process by introducing an essential tool for studying sensation and perception called **psychophysics.** This is the study of the quantitative relationship between environmental stimulation (the physical dimension) and sensory experience (the psychological dimension).

We will examine some of the basic issues and questions of psychophysics, such as those concerning the detection of very weak or **threshold** levels of stimulation. For example, what is the softest sound that can be heard? The softest touch that can be felt? The faintest odor that can be smelled? The dimmest light that can be seen? In general, the detection or threshold question is this: What is the minimum amount of physical energy for a particular sensory system that can just produce a sensation? There is also the related psychophysical question of the **difference threshold,** or the least difference between stimuli that can be detected: What is the smallest intensity difference between two stimuli that can just be detected? To answer such questions, we will outline the traditional **psychophysical methods.** We will also examine an alternative approach, called **Signal Detection**

Theory (SDT), which questions the very notion of a sensory threshold.

Finally, we examine ways to measure sensory experience and attempt to answer the general psychophysical question: If environmental stimulation is varied, what is the corresponding effect on sensory or perceptual experience? In other words, what is the relationship between changes in the physical dimension and resultant changes in the psychological or experiential dimension? As we can easily anticipate, this relationship is not a simple one. Consider the challenge involved in this task of psychophysics. While it is clear that features of the physical environment—such as sounds, lights, chemicals, and pressures—can be readily measured and quantified, it is also clear that the resulting psychological effects—sensations and perceptions—are private, unobservable experiences, which are not easily quantified. However, as we shall see, there are psychophysical methods and techniques that make it possible to express the relationship between the physical environment and its psychological effects.

Many of the general concerns of psychophysics are among the oldest in psychology. Historically, measuring sensory experience has often been tied to such central philosophical issues as the nature and meaning of conscious experience, as well as the continuing enigma of the relationship between the mind and the body

21

(generally referred to as the mind–body problem*). Although these concerns are not our focus
here, it is obvious that the topic of psychophysics
is critical to the study of sensation and perception, for in an important sense, what psychophysics attempts to do is to quantify and*
*relate changes in our inner mental experi-
ence—our sensations and perceptions—to
changes in external environmental stimulation. We begin by introducing the problem of
stimulus detection and the measurement of the
threshold.*

DETECTION AND THE ABSOLUTE THRESHOLD

In studying the relationship of certain features of environmental stimulation to sensory experience, an important experimental question arises: What is the minimal amount of stimulus required for detection? That
is, how intense must the stimulus be for an observer
to reliably distinguish its presence from its absence?
Clearly, no organism is responsive to *all* portions of
the possible range of physical energies. Instead, the
potential stimulus must be of sufficient minimal intensity (and duration) to cause the neural activation required to sense it.

The minimum stimulus necessary for detection
is generally known as the **absolute threshold** or
absolute limen (*limen* is Latin for threshold). Traditionally, these stimulus values define the approximate
lower limit of the organism's absolute sensitivity. If
the stimulus is too weak, not producing a reliable
response, its magnitude is said to be **subthreshold**
or **subliminal;** in contrast, above-threshold stimulus
values are termed **suprathreshold** or **supraliminal.**
Some threshold values, not to be taken too seriously
in their present form, are shown in Table 2.1. More
detailed and precise values for some senses will be
given in subsequent chapters. Obviously, the minimal
detectable stimulus varies with the sensory system
investigated, with testing conditions, and with individual differences between observers.

The concept of an absolute threshold assumes
that there is a precise stimulus point on the intensity
or energy dimension that, when reached, becomes
just perceptible and the observer responds, "Yes," he
or she detects the stimulus. It follows, then, that a
stimulus one unit weaker will not be detected. If this

were the case, then some form of the hypothetical
curve, such as that shown in Figure 2.1, would be
the result. That is, the observer would not detect the
stimulus until a certain energy level was reached (e.g.,
four units in the figure), at which point and beyond,
the stimulus would be detected 100% of the time. In
the detection of the threshold for tones, for example,
either a sound would be heard or complete silence
would result. However, this rarely happens. Rather,
empirical laboratory investigations typically yield
gradual empirical or *S-shaped* curves like that shown
in Figure 2.2.

Thus, we must conclude that no single absolute
value represents the minimum stimulus energy necessary for a detection response; that is, there is no fixed
point separating the energy levels that never yield a

□ *table 2.1* Some Approximate
Detection Threshold Values

Sense	Detection Threshold
Vision	A candle flame seen at 30 mi on a dark clear night.
Hearing	The tick of a watch under quiet conditions at 20 ft.
Taste	One teaspoon of sugar in 2 gal of water.
Smell	One drop of perfume diffused into the entire volume of a three-room apartment.
Touch	The wing of a bee falling on your back from a distance of 1 cm.

Source: Based on Galanter (1962).
Note: These threshold values are presented for illustrative purposes only, primarily to show the incredibly sensitive detection of
very weak environmental stimulation by humans. Some of these
values are based on extrapolations and assumptions that apply
only to ideal conditions, and it would be very difficult to verify or
replicate them. Consider, for example, the practical problem of
obtaining a watch that actually ticks.

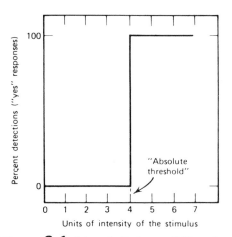

⌐ figure 2.1 A hypothetical curve linking stimulus intensity to absolute threshold. The vertical axis plots the proportion of trials on which the observer responds "Yes," he or she detects the stimulus. As shown, the threshold value is 4 units of stimulus intensity. Theoretically, below 4 units of intensity the stimulus is not detected, whereas for 4 units and above, the stimulus is detected 100% of the time.

detection response from those that always do. As one approximation of the threshold value, psychologists have adopted a statistical concept. By convention, the absolute threshold value is assumed to correspond to

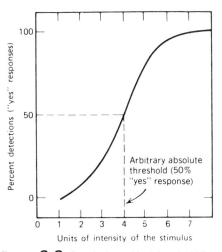

⌐ figure 2.2 A typical empirical threshold function. By convention the absolute threshold is defined as the intensity at which the stimulus is detected on 50% of the trials.

that stimulus magnitude eliciting a detection response on *half* of its test trials, that is, 50% of the time. This arbitrarily defined value is indicated by the dotted line in Figure 2.2.

Psychophysical Methods

The methods traditionally used to determine the threshold were devised by Gustav Theodor Fechner (1801–1887), a physicist and philosopher, who is generally regarded as the founder of psychophysics. Fechner was concerned with the relation between physical stimulation and mental experience. In order to study the relationship between the two, he devised a series of methods.

Method of Limits (Method of Minimal Change) One of the simplest methods is called the **method of limits** or the **method of minimal change.** For example, to determine the absolute threshold for the detection of light, we might start with a light sufficiently intense to be perceived by an observer and then systematically reduce its intensity in small, graded steps with a device such as a light dimmer until the observer reports that the light is no longer detectable. We then record that intensity level and then show the light at a still dimmer setting, but now gradually increasing its intensity level until the observer reports that it is just perceptible. After a number of *descending* and *ascending* series of trials, we compute an average based on the energy levels at which the stimulus just crosses the boundary between being undetectable and just becoming perceptible. That is, we compute a numerical estimate of the absolute threshold by taking the average of the stimulus intensities reached when the observer reaches a "limit" or makes a response shift for the ascending and descending series of stimuli. This average serves as the statistical measure of the threshold for that observer under the general experimental conditions of testing. See Table 2.2 for an example of the method of limits.

Although very useful, the method of limits is open to various sources of bias and error. One drawback of its simple form is that generally the change in stimulus intensity (increase or decrease) is orderly and regular;

◻ **table 2.2** Use of Method of Limits to Determine the Detection Threshold for a Visual Stimulus

Light Intensity (Arbitrary Units)	Observer's Response					
	Series					
	1	2	3	4	5	6
10	YES					
9	YES		YES			
8	YES	YES	YES		YES	
7	YES	NO	YES	YES	YES	YES
6	NO	NO	YES	NO	YES	NO
5		NO	NO	NO	NO	NO
4				NO		NO
3						NO
2						
1						
Limit value	6.5	7.5	5.5	6.5	5.5	6.5

Note: In the results of the three descending series of trials alternated with the three ascending series illustrated, the "YES" responses mean that on a given trial the stimulus is detected, and the "NO" responses mean that it is not detected. The horizontal bar in each series column represents the stimulus value of the limit in which a transition from detection to no detection, or vice versa, occurs. Typical of this method is some variation in the limit obtained for each series, which in this example ranges between 5.5 and 7.5. The threshold value is computed as the average of the limits obtained for each series, or (6.5 + 7.5 + 5.5 + 6.5 + 5.5 + 6.5)/6 = 6.333. That is, the threshold value for the detection of the light is 6.333 intensity units.

thus, it may be somewhat predictable by the observer. That is, the observer's expectation that each successive stimulus is increasing or decreasing may bias the response. Another similar source of bias is the error of *habituation,* the tendency to keep responding "Yes" in a descending series and "No" in an ascending series. In other words, observers make the same response in successive trials in a given series because they become "used to," or "habituate" to, a particular response, continuing to give it even after the threshold is reached. To counteract these and other related sources of bias and error, modifications of the method of limits are commonly used. In one form, called the *staircase* method (Cornsweet, 1962), the experimenter initially presents an intensity level below the assumed threshold value, yielding a "No" response, and increases it until the observer detects it, that is, reports "Yes." As soon as the report changes from "No" to "Yes," the direction of the magnitude of the stimulus is reversed. Now the experimenter decreases the stimulus values until the response changes again; that is, when the observer reports "No," the intensity increases again.

In a typical staircase method, the threshold is thus calculated as the average of all stimulus values at which the observer's response changes. Variations on this simple form of the staircase method are also employed.

Method of Constant Stimuli Another method of determining the absolute threshold is the **method of constant stimuli.** This method requires a series of forced-choice trials. A fixed number of stimuli of different intensities, extending over a relatively wide range, are singly presented many times in random order. On each presentation the observer must make a detection response—either "Yes" (detection) or "No" (no detection). For each stimulus intensity, the percentage of trials in which the stimulus value is detected is computed. The intensity of the stimulus value detected on 50% of the trials is generally used as the measure of the absolute threshold. While the method of constant stimuli is somewhat involved and laborious, it tends to yield the least variable and most accurate absolute threshold values.

Method of Adjustment (Method of Average Error) Finally, there is the **method of adjustment** (or **method of average error**). Here the intensity of the stimulus is under the *observer's control;* that is, the observer is required to adjust the intensity to a *just detectable* level. Once the observer adjusts the stimulus intensity until it is just detectable, the value of that intensity level defines the threshold. However, while this method is quick and direct, it is generally the least accurate. Its major drawback is that it yields somewhat variable threshold values, probably because observers vary significantly in the precision and care with which they do their adjusting in a typical detection task.

SIGNAL DETECTION THEORY (SDT)

In the absolute threshold in Figure 2.2, there is a *range* of weak intensity levels over which an observer sometimes responds that the stimulus is detected and sometimes that it is not detected. In other words, for some intensity levels the *same* stimulus may sometimes be detected and sometimes not. This difference in response to the same stimulus implies that the threshold value changes over time. This, of course, poses a serious challenge to the traditional all-or-none notion of a sensory threshold, namely, that there is a precise stimulus intensity value separating stimuli that are detectable from those that are not.

To appreciate this threshold problem, we should note that we are often unsure whether we have crossed the sensory threshold—that is, perceived a weak or marginal stimulus. Clearly, we confront many stimulus conditions that from a sensory point of view are ambiguous, yet generally we make decisions concerning them. Do we really hear the phone ring when mowing the lawn or that knock on the door when we are in the shower? Do we really see that faint star in the night sky?

As an example of such an ambiguous situation, suppose that you are alone in your room and anxiously awaiting the return of a friend. You are aware that his arrival will be signaled by his footsteps in the stairwell. So, from a psychophysical point of view, you are listening for a certain kind of sound—the sound of footsteps. Since the sounds will occur outside the room, they will be faint and will be heard against constant background noise—street noise. In a situation like this, you will probably sometimes hear the sound of the footsteps when they really occur, and at other times you will be certain that you hear them when no one is even close by. Of course, you try to form some sensory impression of the sound of footsteps. You will also attempt to distinguish among the various sounds you hear or think you hear. Indeed, sometimes when the sound of footsteps really occurs, you will not hear them, and sometimes you will swear you heard footsteps—perhaps because you really want to hear them—when the sounds are really only part of the background street noise.

It seems clear from this example that decisions concerning the presence of weak stimuli pose special problems for the traditional threshold notion. Are our decisions based exclusively on the effects of the stimuli or are there psychological biases within us that influence our decisions? This section presents an approach to situations in which psychological factors may predispose us toward making certain decisions—the sorts of factors that the traditional threshold notion does not take into account.

Sensitivity Versus Response Bias

Because the magnitude of the stimulus required for a threshold or detection response varies, especially under weak or marginal conditions of stimulation, factors in addition to the observer's detection abilities, or **sensitivity,** may play a role in the task of detecting weak stimuli (or **signals,** as they are called in this context). These factors may include the level of the observer's attention to the stimulus, the motivation for performing the detection task, the expectation that a stimulus is present, and other *nonsensory* factors—collectively referred to as **response bias**—that may affect the observer's decision as to whether a signal is present or absent. Hence, during a detection task, when the observer sometimes responds "Yes" and at other times "No" to a constant signal or stimulus intensity, we do not know for sure whether this is a result of some change in the observer's sensitivity or whether it is merely the effect of nonsensory factors such as fluctuations in the observer's attention or motivation. Indeed, observers may even sometimes say that they detect a stimulus when actually they are uncertain.

Detection and Noise

Why does the detection of a weak stimulus show such variability? What is the source of this variability? Consider what happens to the sensory system when any weak environmental signal occurs, such as a dim light or a faint sound. If it is sufficiently intense, at the neural level sensory receptors may register action potentials that can influence neural activity in the brain. This activity signals the observer's nervous system that a light or a sound has occurred. However, spontaneous neural activity occurs continuously in the sensory systems and the brain, even in the total absence of external stimulation. This spontaneous sensory-neural activity is due, in part, to random patterns of neural firing—like static heard on AM radio or "snow" seen on TV—and is considered a form of extraneous background **noise (N)** in the sensory system (thus *noise* in this context is in no way restricted to the auditory sense). In addition to spontaneous sensory-neural activity, neural noise may include the unpredictable, random effects of fatigue, and the observer's fluctuating level of attention, expectations, and anticipations.

Although noise is not part of the environmental stimulation (or signal), when it occurs in an ambiguous situation, it can significantly influence the detection of a weak signal. In fact, what an observer tries to do in a typical threshold detection experiment is to decide, on each presentation or trial, whether the sensory effects experienced—the sensations—are due to background noise (*N*) alone or to the signal heard against the background noises (i.e., the signal-plus-noise, or *SN*).

The distribution of the sensory effects of noise on the observer's sensory system is outlined in Figure 2.3. The familiar bell-shaped curve of Figure 2.3*a* shows that the level of sensory activity attributed to

noise alone in the sensory system varies considerably. The *x*-axis gives the level (low to moderate to high) of sensory activity, and the *y*-axis plots the frequency (rare to frequent) of different levels of sensory activity. Sometimes the noise level is minimal and sometimes it is extreme, but most frequently it is of moderate or average intensity, labeled $\bar{X}_n$. However, when an environmental event (e.g., a sound or light) stimulates a sensory receptor, it produces sensory activity (a *signal*) that is added to the effects of the background noise. Specifically, if a signal of *constant* intensity is added to all possible levels of the randomly varying background noise, the composite effect on sensory activity caused by the *SN* will appear as in the normal distribution, or bell-shape curve, of Figure 2.3*b*. As we noted with the effects of *N* alone, the level of sensory activity of *SN* also varies, sometimes high, sometimes low, but it hovers around an average value (labeled $\bar{X}_{stn}$) that is clearly higher than the average level of *N* alone (i.e., it is displaced to the right of $\bar{X}_n$ in Figure 2.3*a*). However, as Figure 2.3*c* shows, the sensory effects of *N* alone and *SN* overlap. That is, they produce some common effects on the sensory system so that, when attempting to determine whether a weak stimulus is present or not, the observer must decide if the particular level of activity in his or her sensory system is due to the effects of *N* alone—that is, to extraneous or irrelevant background activity— or to the effects of *SN*.

The Criterion In short, the observer's task in the typical signal detection experiment is to decide whether the sensation experienced on a given trial (based on the level of sensory activity) came from a signal (*SN*) or from noise alone (*N*). According to SDT, observers adopt some cutoff point, or internal **criterion** (usually symbolized by the Greek letter **β**), of overall sensory activity in deciding whether a signal is present. One such criterion level is indicated on the *x*-axis of Figure 2.4. According to the criterion, the observer will respond "Yes" when the level of sensory activity shown on the *x*-axis exceeds that point and "No" when the sensory effect is less. Note that in both instances the observer may be in error. The observer can respond that a signal was present when in fact the sensory effect came only from the *N* distribution,

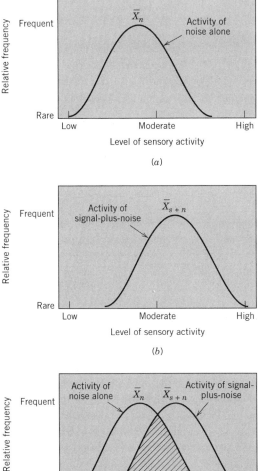

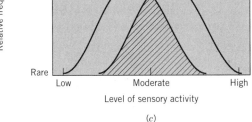

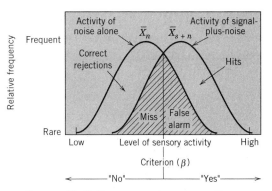

figure 2.4 Frequency of sensory effects produced by N and by SN and the observer's criterion value. The x-axis shows a hypothetical decision point or criterion value (β) at which the observer decides whether to report "Yes" or "No" regarding the presence of a signal on a given trial. Any number of criterion values could be adopted. In this hypothetical one, all signals whose effects lie below the criterion sensory level (i.e., to its left) take a "No" response; all signals whose effects lie above the criterion level (i.e., to its right) take a "Yes" response. Also shown for the hypothetical criterion are the regions of sensory activity for correct rejections and hits.

figure 2.3 (a) Frequency of varying levels of sensory activity produced by N alone on the sensory system. The frequencies vary from rare to frequent. As shown, the most frequently occurring level of sensory activity is a moderate one that hovers around a midpoint at $\bar{X}_n$. (b) Frequency of different levels of sensory activity produced by SN on the sensory system. Shown is the frequency of sensory effects when a stimulus or signal is added to all values of N given in (a). (c) Frequency of various levels of sensory activity produced by distributions of N and SN on the sensory system. The average sensory-neural effect of SN is greater than the average effect of N due to addition of the SN to the N effects. However,

that is, from noise alone (shown on the figure as a **false alarm**); likewise, the observer could respond that a signal was not present when actually one did occur (i.e., a **miss**). This follows because, as we noted in Figure 2.3c, the sensory effects of the SN and N distributions overlap, making it impossible for an observer to set a sensory criterion that permits a correct response on *every* presentation of the signal. In fact, the shape of the overlap of the SN and N distributions in Figures 2.3c and 2.4 shows the possibility that on some SN trials (in which the signal actually occurs), the sensory effects on the observer may be less than those resulting from noise alone.

Outcome Matrix As we noted in describing Figure 2.4, on a given signal detection trial the

the sensory effects of N alone and SN overlap and produce some sensory effects in common. That is, there is a range of sensory effects—shown in the shaded area—that could come from *either* the N or the SN distribution.

observer must decide whether the sensory activity is produced by the *SN* or the *N* effects, and the decision is determined by the criterion adopted at the moment. If the level of sensory activity is below the observer's criterion, he or she will respond "No"; if the level of sensory activity is above this criterion, he or she will respond "Yes." These responses result in one of four possible outcomes, as shown in Table 2.3. A **hit** results when the observer reports "Yes" and correctly detects the presence of a stimulus. As we noted, a false alarm occurs when the observer reports "Yes," that a stimulus is present when actually it is not, and a miss occurs when the observer reports "No," that a stimulus is not present when in fact it is. Finally, a **correct rejection** occurs when the observer correctly reports "No," a stimulus is not present, when in fact it is absent. Of course, as shown in Figure 2.4, false alarms and misses are errors due to the overlap of the sensory effects from the *SN* and *N* distributions and their relation to the criterion set by the observer for deciding whether a stimulus is present or not.

Criteria Effects: Expectation and Motivation

According to SDT, the ability to detect a weak stimulus varies from moment to moment because several relatively independent sources affect the observer's performance. One factor, of course, is that the level of noise itself in the sensory system varies. That is, the sensory effects from varying background noise, or from a constant signal plus varying background noise, from presentation to presentation, give rise to variations in the ability to detect a marginal stimulus. This point was illustrated in the bell-shaped curves of Figure 2.3. Another factor that affects the performance is the observer's *expectation* about the presence of a signal. This is actually a nonsensory response bias that affects the setting of the observer's criterion (β) level, and it may be created during the course of the experiment. If the signal occurs on almost every trial, then the observer may almost always expect a signal to be presented. As a result, the observer will adopt a relatively generous or liberal criterion (a shift of the criterion to the left in Figure 2.4). The result is a bias in the observer's performance shown as an increase in the tendency to respond "Yes" even when no signal is present. The result would be a high probability of hits, but due to the observer's expectation, the probability of false alarms will be higher than if no such expectation was created. In contrast, if the signal is rarely present, the observer may tend to respond "No" even when the signal is present (a shift of the criterion to the right in Figure 2.4). The result in this case is fewer false alarms but more misses. Table 2.4*a* presents some reported response proportions for the case when the signal is presented on 90% of the trials and not presented on 10% (trials in which no signal is presented are typically referred to as **catch trials** in signal detection research). Table 2.4*b* shows the response proportions for the case when the signal is presented on 10% of the trials and no signal is presented on 90%. The difference in the two tables for the same signal shows that the variation in the proportion of signal presentations markedly affects the expectations and perfor-

□ *table 2.3* Stimulus–Response Outcome Matrix for the Observer Responding Either "Yes" or "No" on Each Trial of a Signal Detection Experiment

		Response Alternatives	
STIMULUS ALTERNATIVES		*"Yes, signal is present."*	*"No, signal is absent."*
	SIGNAL + NOISE	Probability of a positive response when the signal is present Hit	Probability of a negative response when the signal is present Miss
	NOISE	Probability of a positive response when *no* signal is present False Alarm	Probability of a negative response when *no* signal is present Correct Rejection

▭ *table 2.4a* Response Proportions
for a Signal Presented on 90% of the
Trials and No Signal on 10%

		Response	
		Yes	No
S	Present	0.95	0.05
i			
g			
n			
a			
l	Absent	0.78	0.22

mance of the observer; consequently, he or she produces systematic changes in the proportion of hits and false alarms. That is, variations in the proportion of hits and false alarms are attributable to the observer's varying criterion (in this case, due to expectation) in reaction to the change in the proportion of catch trials. The differences in the response proportions of Tables 2.4*a* and 2.4*b* also indicate that changes occur in detection performance to a constant stimulus, with no corresponding change in stimulus intensity. In other words, the presumed detection threshold changes due to changes in the observer's *expectation* that a stimulus will occur, not to any change in the stimulus itself.

Another nonsensory response bias factor that affects the criterion (β) level is the *motivation* to detect a specific outcome, that is, the observer's concern with the consequences of the detection response. For instance, if the observer is highly motivated to detect the signal—trying to never miss it—he or she will likely lower the criterion or β level for reporting its

presence, increasing the number of "Yes" responses and hits (again, a shift of the criterion to the left in Figure 2.4). Increasing the number of "Yes" responses will also raise the number of false alarms. On the other hand, the use of a more restrictive, conservative criterion (i.e., moving the β level in Figure 2.4 to the right) increases the number of "No" responses; although this strategy may yield fewer false alarms, it also results in fewer hits.

An experimental task in which β is intentionally manipulated shows how an observer's motivation may affect the proportion of hits and false alarms. Suppose that you are an observer in the following signal detection experiment. You are instructed that on each trial you may or may not hear a very faint tone. Accordingly, after each trial you are to respond "Yes" or "No," depending on whether or not you heard a tone. Moreover, your response has certain monetary consequences. Consider three different outcome or payoff conditions:

1. For each hit, you win $1. Of course, you would tend to respond "Yes" on almost every trial, even when you are unsure if you heard a tone.
2. Similarly, for each hit you win $1, but you are penalized 50 cents for a false alarm. You will still tend to respond "Yes" when you are unsure, though somewhat less likely than in condition (1), where there was no penalty for a false alarm.
3. In contrast to the payoff conditions in (1) and (2), you receive 50 cents for each hit but are penalized $1 for a false alarm. You will tend to respond cautiously, answering "Yes" only when you are very sure.

▭ *table 2.4b* Response Proportions
for a Signal Presented on 10% of the
Trials and No Signal on 90%

		Response	
		Yes	No
S	Present	0.28	0.72
i			
g			
n			
a			
l	Absent	0.04	0.96

A summary of some observed response proportions of hits and false alarms appropriate to these three payoff conditions is given in Table 2.5.

What we have described is a change in the criterion or β and a variation in the proportion of hits and false alarms due to the payoff of the response. The same stimuli may elicit a "Yes" or a "No" response, depending on the consequences—the rewards and penalties—independent of the observer's sensitivity to the stimuli.

□ **table 2.5** Proportion of Hits and False Alarms for Three Payoff Conditions

	Response Proportion Made by Observer	
Payoff Condition	Hits	False Alarms
Observer gets:		
1. $1 for hit	.95	.95
2. $1 for hit and 50-cent penalty for false alarm	.85	.70
3. 50 cents for hit and $1 penalty for false alarm	.40	.10

Note: Varying the outcome or payoff produces variation in the proportion of hits and false alarms for the same stimuli.

Thus, even in a relatively simple psychophysical task like deciding whether a weak signal is present or not, the observer's performance is significantly affected by nonsensory factors, that is, response bias. This should make it clear that there is no simply observed, absolute threshold value. Rather, the observer adjusts the response criterion to both the intensity of the signal and to certain nonsensory variables, such as motivation on the task and the expectation of the signal's occurrence.

ROC Curves

SDT holds that we cannot extract an absolute threshold value. However, we can obtain a measure of an observer's *sensitivity* to the presentation of a stimulus and his or her decision criterion or β level at the same time. The separate effects of the observer's sensitivity in detecting the signal and the effects of a shifting criterion are derived by analyzing the relationship between the proportion of hits and the proportion of false alarms—a relationship, as we have noted, that shifts as the criterion is varied. Typically, the proportion of hits (saying "Yes" to *SN* activity) is plotted on the *y*-axis and the proportion of false alarms (saying "Yes" to *N* activity alone) is plotted on the *x*-axis. The resultant curves, called **receiver operating characteristic curves** or, more simply, **ROC curves** graphi-

cally display the relationship between the proportions of hits and false alarms for a constant stimulus intensity (see Figure 2.5 for an example of an ROC curve, whose derivation we describe below).

The term *ROC* refers to the idea that the curve measures and describes the operating or sensitivity characteristics of the receiver (i.e., the observer) in detecting signals. Consider how an ROC curve may describe an observer's sensitivity measure for a particular signal whose intensity is fixed, that is, where the intensity level is held constant. Table 2.6 illustrates how the probability of a signal affects the proportion of hits and false alarms for a hypothetical experiment in which the signal intensity is held constant (some of these signal proportions are taken from Tables 2.4*a* and 2.4*b*). Thus, if the signal is almost always present in the trials of a signal detection experiment (e.g., 90% of Table 2.6), the observer tends to increase the probability of saying "Yes." The result is an increase in the proportion of hits (.95 for this example), with a corresponding increase in the proportion of false alarms (.78). In contrast, when the signal is presented on only 10% of the trials (i.e., 90% catch trials), for the *same signal intensity,* the proportion of hits is .28 and the proportion of false alarms is .04. Clearly, when

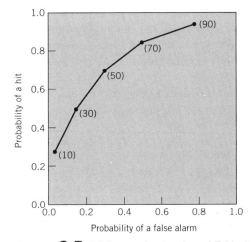

□ **figure 2.5** ROC curve for the data of Table 2.6. The probability of a hit (*y*-axis) is plotted against the probability of a false alarm (*x*-axis). Each point plotted represents the hits and false alarms for a different percentage of signal presentations (shown in parentheses). (Note that the curve is fitted by eye.)

▭ **table 2.6** Proportion of Hits and False Alarms for Different Percentages of Signal Presentations (Hypothetical Data)

Percentage of Trials Containing a Signal	Proportion of:	
	Hits	False Alarms
90	.95	.78
70	.85	.50
50	.70	.30
30	.50	.15
10	.28	.04

Note: These proportions are derived from presentation of a signal of constant intensity. Hence, the differences in the proportions of hits and false alarms reflect the effects of differences in criteria, or β, produced by varying the percentage of signals and catch trials (10% to 90%) over the course of many trials.

the signal is infrequent—actually present in only 10% of the trials—the observer tends to say "No." As a result, while the proportion of false alarms is quite small (.04) the proportion of hits is also relatively low (.28). Figure 2.5 is an ROC curve based on these values. Note, for example, that the top value is for the condition in which 90% of the trials had a signal. Referring to the table, we note that the hit rate plotted on the *y*-axis is .95 and the false alarm rate plotted on the *x*-axis is .78. When all the data points of Table 2.6 are plotted, an obvious trend emerges: The data points appear to lie on a symmetrical curve bowed to the left. If more trials were administered, using the same *stimulus intensity* but with probabilities of signals to catch trials different from those plotted here, their hit and false alarm proportions would no doubt differ from those in Table 2.6—reflecting the effect of a shifting criterion—but when plotted on Figure 2.5, they would lie somewhere *on* the curve. That is, a given ROC curve reflects the observer's detection performance for a single stimulus intensity. Thus, for a given ROC curve, the observer's sensitivity is constant for all points along the curve. The signal intensity and the observer's sensory ability do not change. What does change is the proportion of hits and false alarms due to variations in the observer's criterion or β level.

We have stressed that the points plotted in Figure 2.5 are for a signal of constant intensity. When the signal is more intense, it becomes more detectable

and a different ROC curve is generated. For a weaker, less detectable signal, still another ROC curve is derived (examples of different ROC curves are given in Figure 2.6). Thus an ROC curve illustrates how varying the observer's β level (in this case, by varying the expectation of a signal) affects the proportion of hits and false alarms for a fixed signal intensity. Each ROC curve graphically shows the effect of the observer's sensitivity to a constant signal intensity *plus* the effects of the observer's β level.

Sensitivity: d' As an aid to visualization, the general features of an ROC curve are given in Figure 2.7, showing how the curvature of the ROC curve represents the observer's sensitivity to the signal and his or her response bias or criterion effects. As we noted, when the signal is made more intense, it becomes more detectable and, as indicated earlier in Figure 2.6, the ROC curve is bowed higher to the left; when the signal is weaker, the ROC curve lies closer to the 45° diagonal (the diagonal line represents the

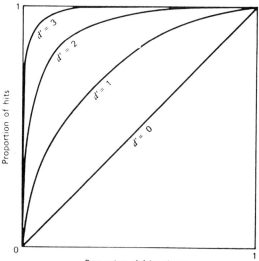

▭ **figure 2.6** ROC curves for three signals that are detectable to different degrees. The proportion of hits (*y*-axis) is plotted against the proportion of false alarms (*x*-axis). Each curve expresses a specific value of sensitivity to a specific signal intensity. (The *d'* value represents a numerical measure of the observer's sensitivity, described in the text.)

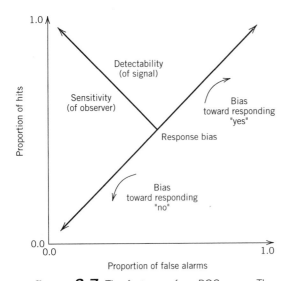

Proportion of hits

Detectability
(of signal)

Sensitivity
(of observer)

Bias
toward responding
"yes"

Response bias

Bias
toward responding
"no"

0.0

0.0   1.0

Proportion of false alarms

□ **figure 2.7** The features of an ROC curve. The 45° diagonal response bias line represents chance performance, where the hit rate equals the observer's false alarm rate.

observer's chance performance, i.e., where the hit and false alarm rates are equal). In short, the bow of the ROC curve to the left, i.e., away from the 45° line, is determined by the intensity of the signal and is independent of the observer's response bias. A measure of the bowedness or curvature of the ROC curve, called **d′**, can be calculated; it is a statistical measure of the observer's sensitivity to a given signal intensity. In practice, the value of $d′$ is estimated by the linear distance of a given ROC curve from the 45° diagonal chance line. Figure 2.6 gives ROC curves for values of $d′$ ranging from 0 to 3. Note that the higher the $d′$ value (and the more bowed the curve), the higher the hit rate and the lower the rate of false alarms. In short, the greater the $d′$ value, the more sensitive is the observer to the particular signal intensity. Thus the hit and false alarm rates are used to derive a $d′$ value that is a psychophysical measure of the observer's sensitivity to a particular signal intensity. In other words, the degree of bowing in the ROC curve can serve as a measure of the observer's sensitivity to a signal of constant intensity. Alternatively, it should be noted that increasing the signal intensity will also render the signal more detectable. Thus the upward

bow of an ROC curve is produced both by the observer's sensitivity and by an increase in signal intensity.

The procedure for computing $d′$ is beyond the scope of this book. However, it is important to understand that $d′$ serves as a measure of the observer's sensitivity to the signal's intensity independent of his or her β or response bias effects. This can be visualized by graphing the sensory effects from which the ROC curves of Figure 2.6 are derived. Observe that $d′$ represents the linear distance between the two sensory distributions introduced at the beginning of the discussion of SDT, namely, the N and SN distributions (see Figure 2.8). With increasing signal intensity, the SN distribution moves farther to the right of the N distribution. In contrast, if the intensity of the signal is very weak, the N and SN distributions lie very close together. For example, for $d′ = 1$, the distributions of N and SN lie relatively close together; the signal is moderately weak, and therefore it is somewhat difficult to detect (incidentally, the $d′$ value for the data of Table 2.6 plotted in Figure 2.5 is 1). In contrast, for $d′ = 3$, the signal is relatively intense and its effect on the sensory system is quite easy to detect from the effect of noise. Thus, with increasing signal intensity, the SN distribution is displaced farther from the N distribution, resulting in a larger value of $d′$. In short, a high $d′$ value means that the signal is intense (or that the observer is sensitive). Thus the $d′$ value provides a measure of sensitivity to the signal independent of such nonsensory factors as the observer's expectations and other decision-making strategies.

How is this information relevant? We began with the problem of determining the absolute limen or threshold, but to do so, we have gone through a psychophysical procedure that seems unusually complex and elaborate. First, what SDT points out about the detection of weak stimuli is that even simple, commonplace tasks, such as deciding whether a stimulus was present or not, is not nearly as precise as we might think. Moreover, SDT allows a researcher to do what the traditional approach to thresholds does not: to assess the role of nonsensory bias effects (β) on the observer's decision in a signal detection task. Clearly, as we have observed, the observer's decision depends on the experiences that he or she brings to the task, as well as expectations, motives, attentional

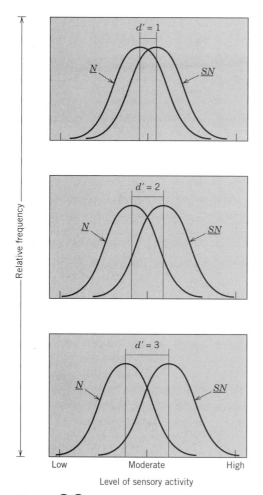

Given what we have discussed above, there appears to be no single, absolute minimal magnitude value of a stimulus—a threshold value—for its detection. However, this is not to say that the sensory threshold notion should be discarded. Rather, it is reasonable to assume that the general notion of a threshold encompasses and describes a *range* of values whose expression is influenced by a variety of nonsensory environmental and observer effects. In fact, a threshold, as a statistical average, is a very useful concept that has widespread application. In terms of energy values, it provides an important approximation of the range and limits of the sensory system. We conclude that it is necessary to interpret threshold statements cautiously; they serve as statistical approximations suggesting an average magnitude and/or a range of magnitudes rather than as a single energy value.

Before leaving the threshold notion and its problems, we must consider the controversial idea that a stimulus magnitude that lies below the level of apparent detection, that is, a subthreshold or *subliminal* stimulus, may have a measurable effect on the observer's behavior.

□ figure 2.8 A graphic representation of the distributions of N and SN for the three ROC curves of Figure 2.7. Here the value of d' is shown to vary with the sensory effects of the SN distribution relative to the effects of the N distribution. This is indicated by the distance between the average of the distributions of N and SN. Of course, for $d' = 0$ the distributions of N and SN fully overlap. The value of d', then, represents a measure of signal intensity and the observer's sensitivity to the signal, independent of response bias.

SUBLIMINAL PERCEPTION

As we have noted, there are marginal conditions of stimulation—for example, when stimuli are presented at very weak intensity levels or at extremely fast exposure times—in which the stimuli apparently do not yield a detection response. Nonetheless, these imperceptible stimuli may produce indirect but measurable effects on the individual's behavior. Here we address the role played by *subliminal* stimulation which, although apparently below the detection level, still exerts an observable influence on various response parameters.

This raises the obvious but controversial question: Can material, in some way, be detected at a level below conscious awareness? In other words, can stimulation of which the observer is *unaware* still exert a measurable influence on certain response outcomes?

Concern with **subliminal perception** has led to an extensive conceptual and empirical literature, but

factors, and probably other nonsensory psychological factors. Indeed, perhaps the most significant feature of SDT is that it allows us to isolate and evaluate the separate effects of the observer's sensory capacity apart from the observer's nonsensory response bias on his or her performance.

at the same time its validity has been a source of much controversy (e.g., Cheesman & Merikle, 1984; Dixon, 1971; Duncan, 1985; Erdelyi, 1974; Vokey & Read, 1985). The evidence offered in support of subliminal perception comes from a variety of experimental sources; here, several representative examples are presented.

Fowler et al. (1981) performed a study suggesting that the *meaning* of subliminal stimuli may be available to the observer even when the stimuli themselves are not detectable. In this experiment, words (such as "cook") were flashed on a screen so rapidly that observers were not aware of what was presented. This was followed by the presentation of two suprathreshold words (e.g., "bake" and "view"). Observers were instructed to make a forced-choice response, that is, to choose or even guess which word was most like the subliminally flashed word (e.g., "cook"). The result was that the observers' choices were significantly better than chance. For example, the observers were more likely to choose "bake" over "view" when it followed the undetected word "cook." These results suggest that semantic properties such as the meaning of material that is presented below a stimulus magnitude necessary for detection is received and processed by the observer.

Semantic Priming

Another demonstration of subliminal perception, similar to the above example, is given by a technique called **semantic priming.** Basically, this involves a condition in which two successive words are presented, and the meaning of the first word biases or "primes" the response to the second word. Thus, presenting the word "nurse" may serve as a prime for the target word "doctor"; accordingly, an observer's response (such as naming the word) to "doctor" when preceded by the priming word "nurse" is faster than when it is preceded by an unrelated word like "yard." In one experiment by Balota (1983), one group of observers was presented with word primes at a subliminal level (i.e., presented so briefly that observers did not report seeing the primes), whereas another group of observers received the word primes at a

suprathreshold level. For a given target word (e.g., "yard"), the primes were related (e.g., "inch"), unrelated (e.g., "frog"), or neutral ("xxxx"). The major result of the priming task was that observers responded more quickly to a given target word when it was preceded by a related prime (e.g., "inch–yard") than when it was preceded by an unrelated prime (e.g., "frog–yard"). The facilitative effect of semantic priming was observed in both the suprathreshold and subliminal priming condition. These results on subliminal semantic priming thus also provide evidence that material of which the viewer is not aware can influence ongoing perceptual judgment (see also Marcel, 1983; note, however, that there is some dispute concerning the status of subliminal semantic priming—see Bernstein et al., 1989).

It thus appears that weak—subliminal—stimuli can be picked up and registered by the sensory system and encoded at a level beneath conscious awareness. However, it is important to stress that there is no empirical support that subliminal sensory input and its accompanying neural encoding have a substantial impact on one's thoughts or beliefs, or that it can in any way modify or influence behavior (Vokey & Read, 1985). That is, the evidence for subliminal perception per se does not imply that humans can be "controlled" or persuaded by subliminal messages. Thus the suggestion made from time to time that advertisers can influence behavior has little scientific merit. This controversial issue does, however, draw attention to the distinction between simple response processes such as the detection and recognition of stimuli in the laboratory and more complex responses such as purchasing or preference behavior.

As a final point on subliminal perception, we present Dixon's (1971) provocative speculation concerning its origin and function.

It can be argued that this [subliminal perception] is no evolutionary accident. With the evolving of brains that provided the potential for conscious experience, there had to evolve control mechanisms whereby this new, limited-capacity, system could be used to maximal advantage. In theory, this control could be exercised in two ways, either by a drastic restriction on peripheral sensory inflow, or by a variable restriction on entry into consciousness. From an evolutionary point of view, the first of these two alternatives would obviously have low survival value. (p. 321)

THE DIFFERENCE THRESHOLD

The **difference threshold** (or **difference limen**) is the smallest difference between two stimuli that is required to detect them as different. In other words, it is a measure of the smallest detectable difference between two stimuli. Basically, it answers the psychophysical question: How different must two stimuli— say, two weights, two colors, two sounds, or two textures—be from each other in order to detect them as different stimuli?

In practice, the difference threshold, like the absolute threshold described at the beginning of this chapter, is a derived statistical measure: it is the difference in magnitude between two stimuli, usually a standard and a comparison stimulus, that is detected 50% of the time. For instance, if two tones of the same intensity or nearly the same intensity are presented, one immediately following the other, the listener will generally report that they are identical in loudness. However, as we gradually increase the intensity difference between the two tones, a difference in intensity will be reached at which a different judgment will be reported on 50% of the trials. The magnitude of this difference specifies the difference threshold. In other words, the difference threshold is the amount of change in a physical stimulus necessary to produce a **just noticeable difference (JND)** in sensation. As an example, if the magnitude of a physical stimulus—say, a sound—is 100 units, and the sound has to be increased to 110 units to produce a just noticeable change in the sound, the difference threshold of 10 units (i.e., 110 − 100) corresponds to one JND.

The difference threshold is a measure of the ability to discriminate two stimulus magnitudes from each other; as such, it is measured in physical units. By contrast, the JND refers to the resultant psychological unit; that is, it represents the unit of subjective experience or sensory magnitude.

Weber's Fraction

The investigation of the difference threshold is significant in the history of the measurement of sensation. In 1834, E. H. Weber, a German physiologist, investigated the ability of observers to perform discrimination tasks. He noted that discrimination is a matter of relative rather than absolute judgment. He observed that the amount of change—increase or decrease— in a stimulus necessary to detect it as different is proportional to the absolute magnitude of the stimulus. Weber found, for example, that while the addition of 1 candle to 60 lit ones resulted in the perception of a difference in brightness, 1 candle added to 120 did not. For a JND in the brightness of 120 candles, at least 2 candles were required. Extending this example, the difference threshold for the brightness of 300 candles requires 5 or more lit candles; for 600 candles, 10 additional ones are required; and so forth.

That the detection of a change in a stimulus is relative to the intensity of the stimulus makes intuitive sense. For instance, while a couple of drops of water will be easily detected when added to the contents of a small test tube, the same two drops will probably produce no sensory effect when added to a gallon of water.

We have described a fundamental principle of relative sensitivity referred to as **Weber's fraction** (or **Weber's ratio**), which is symbolized as follows:

$$\frac{\Delta I}{I} = k$$

where I is the magnitude of the stimulus intensity at which the threshold is obtained; ΔI (read as "delta" I) is the difference threshold value or the increment of intensity that, when added to the stimulus intensity I, produces a JND (i.e., the increment of change in sensation); and k is a constant that varies with the sensory system being measured. The equation states that the smallest detectable increment (ΔI) in the intensity continuum of a stimulus is a constant proportion (k) of the intensity of the original stimulus (I). Weber's fraction thus indicates the proportion by which a stimulus intensity must be changed in order to detect the change (i.e., produce a JND), and k is constant within a given stimulus dimension such as brightness, loudness, weight, and so on. Thus, in the example of the brightness of candles, the ΔI values for 60, 120, 300, and 600 lit candles would be 1, 2, 5, and 10, and the respective Weber fractions would be 1/60, 2/120, 5/300, and 10/600, which all reduce to $k = 1/60$. Thus, in general, k is solved by computing the proportion of a stimulus that must be changed in order to yield a JND.

Table 2.7 gives the representative Weber fractions for a variety of sensory dimensions. Observe that for these sensory dimensions, the Weber fractions vary from a high of 0.083 (8.3%) for salty taste to a low of 0.013 (1.3%) for electric shock. Using "heaviness" for a computational example, the Weber fraction is 0.02 or 2/100; this means that we must increase the weight of a stimulus by 0.02 or 2% to produce a JND. Thus 2 grams must be added to a 100-gram weight, 4 grams must be added to a 200-gram weight, and 20 grams must be added to a 1000-gram weight for a difference to be detected.

The size of the Weber fraction gives a measure of the overall sensitivity to differences in intensity along a particular sensory dimension. Thus, the smaller the fraction, the greater the sensitivity to stimulus differences. In other words, the smaller the fraction, the smaller the change in intensity necessary to

□ **table 2.7** Representative Weber Fractions for Different Sensory Dimensions

Dimension	Weber Value
Taste (salt)	0.083
Brightness	0.079
Loudness	0.048
Vibration (at fingertip)	0.036
Line length	0.029
Heaviness	0.020
Electric shock	0.013

Source: Based on Teghtsoonian (1971).
Note: Weber values are expressed in decimal form for ease in making computations. For example, "Heaviness," 0.020, expressed as a fraction, is 1/50 (or 2%). The smaller the Weber value, the smaller the change in the intensity of a stimulus necessary to produce a JND.

produce a JND. With respect to the values given in Table 2.7, we note that individuals are least sensitive to differences in taste and brightness—requiring an 8.3% and 7.9% change, respectively—whereas they are most sensitive to differences in electric shock and heaviness—requiring only a 1.3% and 2% change, respectively.

How accurate is Weber's fraction? In general, it is reasonably valid for a wide range of stimulus intensities, including most of our everyday experiences, but it tends to break down for very weak and very strong intensity levels along all sensory dimensions. We conclude that within a broad middle range of intensities, the Weber fraction provides a useful measure of discriminability. However, beyond practical considerations, Weber's fraction has played an important role in the measurement of sensation, and it stands as one of the broadest empirical generalizations in the history of experimental psychology.

FECHNER'S LAW

In 1860 Gustave Theodor Fechner published *The Elements of Psychophysics,* which had a profound effect on the measurement of sensation and perception. His basic premise was that mental experience—sensation—is quantitatively related to the physical stimulus. He attempted to derive an expression of the relation between the two, developing a numerical scale of sensation for a given sensory modality. Fechner's work led to an important equation relating the magnitude of sensation to the magnitude of the stimulus. More specifically, he proposed that the difference threshold (ΔI) that produces the JND could be used as a standard unit to measure the subjective magnitude of sensation (recall that the difference threshold refers to the incremental change in stimulus intensity that produces a JND). What Fechner attempted was a scale that related subjective experience—sensations, in units of JND—to changes in stimulus intensity, in units of ΔI. He began with the assumption that, for a given sensory system, all JNDs represent subjectively equal units of sensation. This means that the subjective impression of the difference between two stimuli separated by one JND is the same, regardless of the values of the two stimuli. Thus, if you take two stimuli at the low end of the intensity scale that are separated by one JND, then the sensation of the difference between them is the same as it is for two stimuli separated by one JND taken from the high end of the intensity scale. In essence, according to Fechner's assumption, every JND, regardless of its location on the intensity scale, is equal to every other JND.

Recall that according to Weber's constant fraction, a given JND corresponds to a constant proportional increase in the stimulus (i.e., $\Delta I/I$ is a constant, so as I increases, ΔI must increase correspondingly). This means that if the basic intensity is low, the increment of change necessary to produce a JND is correspondingly small; by contrast, if the initial intensity is high, the stimulus increment necessary for the JND is correspondingly large. In other words, at the low end of the intensity scale, two stimuli will be separated by one JND when they are physically close together, while at the high end of the intensity scale, two stimuli will be separated by one JND when they are widely separated physically. This relation between sensation and stimulation is illustrated in Figure 2.9. Under the assumption that all JNDs are psychologically equal, it follows that as the sensation scale (y-axis) increases in equal units, the stimulus intensity scale increases in progressively larger and larger units. As Figure 2.9 shows, larger and larger outputs in stimulus intensity are required to obtain corresponding effects in sensory

experience. In other words, as the number of sensation units (i.e., JNDs) grows arithmetically (y-axis), the stimulus intensity increases geometrically (x-axis). Geometric increases in the intensity scale and arithmetic increases in the sensory scale express a logarithmic relationship.

The arithmetic to geometric progression between sensation and intensity reduces mathematically to a logarithmic relation known as **Fechner's law.** That is, the magnitude of a sensation is a logarithmic function of the stimulus, or

$$S = k \log I$$

where S is the magnitude of the sensation, I is the logarithm of the physical intensity of the stimulus, and k is a constant that takes into account the specific Weber fraction for a given sensory dimension. This logarithmic relationship shows that sensation increases less rapidly than stimulus intensity; as stimulus intensity increases, a greater increase in intensity is necessary to produce the same sensory effect. In short, larger and larger steps in intensity are required to produce equal sensory effects.

How effective is Fechner's law in describing the relation between sensation and stimulus intensity? Like Weber's law, on which it is based, Fechner's law is reasonably accurate under many conditions, but it is limited, serving best as an approximation of the

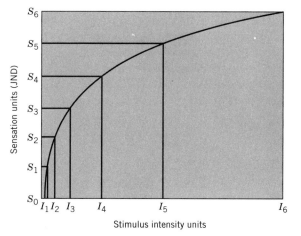

□ *figure 2.9* The relationship between the sensation continuum and the stimulus continuum according to Fechner's law. Notice that larger and larger differences between stimulus units (*I*) are required with increases in the stimulus continuum in order to maintain equal differences between sensation units (*S*) on the sensation continuum. That is, as the sensation increases in equal steps (arithmetically), the corresponding stimulus continuum increases in physically unequal but proportional steps (geometrically). A logarithmic function represents the relationship between an arithmetic and geometric series; hence, $S = k \log I$. (*Source:* Based on J. P. Guilford, *Psychometric methods.* New York, McGraw-Hill. 1954)

relationship of sensory magnitude to stimulus magnitude. In fact, the key assumption in Fechner's law that all JNDs are subjectively equal is questionable. For example, according to this assumption, a tone 20 JND units above the absolute threshold should sound twice as loud as one 10 JND units above the threshold (since one tone contains twice as many JND units as the other tone). In fact, however, the tone 20 JND units above the threshold sounds far more than twice as loud as one 10 JND units above the threshold. In short, all JNDs for a given sensory dimension do not produce equal sensory effects.

STEVENS' POWER LAW

Fechner devised a psychophysical scale of sensation based on the difference threshold and the constancy of Weber's fraction along a given sensory dimension. A different psychophysical scale, based on different assumptions, was devised principally by S. S. Stevens about 100 years after Fechner's work. Stevens proposed that the relation between sensory magnitude and stimulus magnitude is not logarithmic. Indeed, one of Stevens' papers disputing Fechner's logarithmic equation is pointedly titled, "To Honor Fechner and Repeal His Law" (Stevens, 1961a). Stevens contended that one could obtain a direct estimation of an observer's sensory experience using several methods in which observers directly translate estimates of their sensations into numbers. When using the most frequently employed method, called **magnitude estimation,** the observer is presented with a standard stimulus, called a **modulus,** such as a light or a tone of moderate intensity, and is instructed to assign a numerical value to it, say 10 or 100. Then the observer is presented, one at a time, with a series of randomly ordered stimuli that vary along a single dimension, say physical intensity. For each stimulus, the observer gives a number that expresses his or her judgment of the stimulus relative to the standard (modulus). In essence, the observer is estimating directly the magnitude of the sensory impression of each stimulus with a number. For an example, using tones and a modulus value of 100, if the observer is presented with a tone that sounds

twice as loud as the standard modulus, he or she will assign the number 200; a tone that the observer estimates to be half as loud as the modulus is assigned the number 50; a tone that sounds only one-fourth as loud as the standard modulus is rated 25; and so on. In short, the observer attempts to match the perceived intensity of each stimulus in the series with a number relative to the standard modulus number. When the task is completed, the physical intensities of the tones presented can be directly compared with the magnitude estimates made by the observers. The result is a scale of loudness.

Using such methods, Stevens and numerous other workers have found a mathematical relationship between the magnitude of the stimulus dimension and the magnitude of sensation called the **power law.** According to the power law, sensory or subjective magnitude grows in proportion to the physical intensity of the stimulus raised to a power. In other words, sensory magnitude is equal to physical intensity raised to a power. Stated as an equation,

$$S = kI^b$$

where S is sensation, k is a constant (a scale factor that takes into account the choice of units used in a given sensory dimension, e.g., inches, grams, amps), I is stimulus intensity, and b is the exponent to which the intensity is raised (this is a constant for a given sensory dimension).

Two points must be stressed: (1) the exponent of the equation—b—reflects the relation between sensory magnitude and stimulus magnitude, and (2) each sensory dimension—brightness, loudness, and so on—has its own exponent (b). Some of the sensory dimensions that conform to a power law relation, along with their exponents, are shown in Table 2.8. Thus, by using a power law formulation, it is possible to show that the sensory dimensions for various perceptual tasks differ from each other in the extent to which the sensory magnitude changes with stimulus intensity. For example, when the magnitude estimation method is used for the judged length of a line, the exponent of the calculated power equation is very close to 1.00 and the

▭ **table 2.8** Representative Exponents (b) of the Power Functions Relating Psychological Magnitude to Stimulus Magnitude

Continuum	Measured Exponent (b)	Stimulus Condition
Loudness	0.6	Both ears
Brightness	0.33	Small target in dark
Smell	0.55	Coffee
Taste	1.3	Sucrose
Taste	0.8	Saccharine
Taste	1.3	Salt
Temperature	1.0	Cold on arm
Temperature	1.6	Warmth on arm
Vibration	0.95	60 Hz on finger
Duration	1.1	White noise stimuli
Pressure on palm	1.1	Static force on skin
Heaviness	1.45	Lifted weights
Force of handgrip	1.7	Hand dynamometer
Electric shock	3.5	Current through fingers
Tactual roughness	1.5	Rubbing emery cloths
Tactual hardness	0.8	Squeezing rubber
Visual length	1.0	Projected line

Source: Based on Stevens (1961b, 1970, 1975).

equation reduces to $S = kI$. This means that apparent length grows in direct proportion to physical length. The relationship between sensation (or psychological magnitude) and stimulus magnitude can be plotted as a curve called a **power function.** This is depicted in Figure 2.10 as a straight 45° line power function. This relation between sensation and stimulation for line length means, for example, that a line 10 inches long looks twice as long as one 5 inches long, and that a 10-inch line looks half as long as a 20-inch line. For the sensation of brightness, as derived by the direct method of magnitude estimation, the exponent is about 0.33. When the relation between stimulus magnitude and sensory or psychological magnitude is plotted, as in Figure 2.10, the power function relationship is a curve that is concave downward. This means that brightness (the sensory dimension) increases much more slowly than light intensity—a *compression* of the sensory or response dimension. For example, to double the brightness sensation of a light, a considerable amount of light intensity—clearly in excess of the doubling of light intensity—must be expended.

▯ **DEMONSTRATION:**
Response Compression

It is reasonably easy to demonstrate that doubling light intensity does not double brightness by using a couple of lamps, each with a 60-watt bulb. In an otherwise dark room, turn on one lamp—producing a stimulus intensity based on 60 watts—and observe the brightness (without staring at the bulb). Then turn on the other lamp. This will *double* the physical light intensity of the room based on 120 watts; however, your sensory experience will clearly be nowhere near doubled. That is, the room will not seem nearly twice as bright when lit with two lamps, even though the light intensity has been doubled; there is a response compression. Actually, about an eightfold increase in light intensity is required to double brightness.

In contrast to brightness, the exponent for electric shock applied to the finger is about 3.5. As shown in

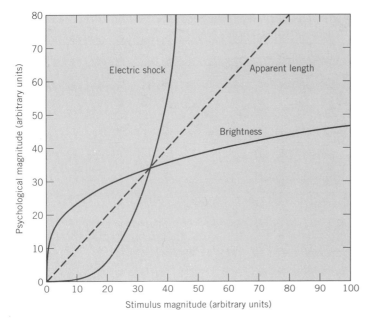

Psychological magnitude (arbitrary units) — vertical axis
Stimulus magnitude (arbitrary units) — horizontal axis

Electric shock

Apparent length

Brightness

□ *figure* **2.10** Power functions relating sensation (psychological magnitude) to stimulus intensity (stimulus magnitude). The shape of a power function is related to its exponent: A curve is concave upward when its exponent is greater than 1.0 and concave downward when its exponent is less than 1.0. Thus the sensory magnitudes of electric shock and brightness follow different growth curves because their power law exponents (*b*) are 3.5 and 0.33, respectively. The power function for apparent length is almost straight because its exponent is about 1.00. Here the scale units of the *x*- and *y*-axes have been chosen arbitrarily to show the relative form of the curves on a single graph. (*Source:* Reprinted from S. S. Stevens, "Psychophysics of sensory function," in W. A. Rosenblith (Ed.), *Sensory Communication,* 1961, by permission of the M.I.T. Press, Cambridge, Mass.)

Figure 2.10, its power function is represented by a curve that is concave upward. Clearly, even a small amount of electric current applied to the finger tip (which may, of course, also signal pain) results in a significant sensory effect—in this case, an expansion of the sensory dimension. Indeed, a doubling of the electric current flow through one's finger tip results in considerably more than a doubling of sensation (more like a 10-fold increase), that is, response expansion.

In general, the exponent of the power function determines its curvature and indicates how sensory magnitude grows with stimulus magnitude. An exponent close to 1.00 results in a straight-line curve. A power function with an exponent greater than 1.00 is represented by a curve that is concave upward, with a response expansion; if the exponent is less than 1.00, the curvature is concave downward, reflecting a response compression. However, a convenient property of power functions is that when stimulus intensity and sensory or psychological magnitude are plotted in log-log coordinates (i.e., logarithmic scales

on both *x*- and *y*-axes, generally achieved by using special graph paper that has both axes stretched out logarithmically), the power law equation describes a straight line whose *slope* (or measure of steepness) is the exponent, *b*. That is, when both sensory magnitude and stimulus magnitude are plotted on logarithmic scales, the curvature of the functions disappears and the slope of the resultant straight line becomes a direct measure of the exponent of the power equation. Accordingly, as shown in Figure 2.11, when the power function curves of Figure 2.10 are replotted in log-log coordinates, differences in curvature become differences in slope. In log-log coordinates the high exponent for the sensation of electric shock gives a steep slope, brightness gives a relatively flat slope, and the linear function for perceived length results in a 45° line with a slope of about 1.00.

Stevens' power law has proved to be very useful in psychophysics because almost any sensory dimension—within which observers can reliably assign a numerical value to their subjective impression or sensation—can be readily scaled. Indeed, there is increas-

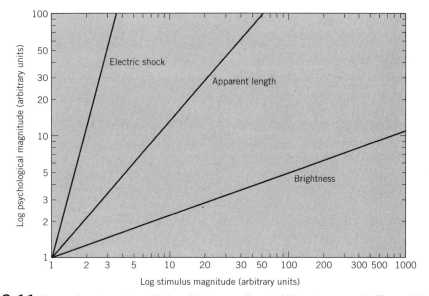

Log stimulus magnitude (arbitrary units)

□ *figure 2.11* Power functions plotted in logarithmic coordinates. When the curves in Figure 2.10 are replotted in log-log coordinates, they become straight lines. The slope of the line corresponds to the exponent of the power function governing the growth of the sensation (psychological magnitude). (*Source:* Reprinted from S. S. Stevens, "Psychophysics of sensory function," in W. A. Rosenblith (Ed.), *Sensory Communication,* 1961, by permission of the M.I.T. Press, Cambridge, Mass.)

ing general agreement that the power law provides a valid representation of the relationship between subjective experience (sensation) and physical intensity.

THE RELATIVITY OF PSYCHOPHYSICAL JUDGMENTS

A stimulus is rarely perceived in total isolation, except perhaps in certain laboratory conditions. It follows, then, that the perception of a stimulus may also be affected by relations that exist between the stimulus and its apparent context or background. For example, the horizontal center line in Figure 2.12*a* appears to be a bit shorter than the one in Figure 2.12*b*, but physically the two lines are equal. In fact, they are aligned in the figure, so their equality should be obvious, yet the center line in Figure 2.12*b* still appears longer. Clearly, the boxes flanking each center line strongly affect the apparent line lengths, giving rise to a perceptual distortion. This points out that we cannot neglect or discount the influence of *context—*

the effect of surrounding (or preceding or subsequent) stimuli on the perception of a stimulus (a comprehensive approach to this general psychophysical issue is found in Helson, 1964).

This finding merits a general principle in perception, namely, that the perception of a stimulus de-

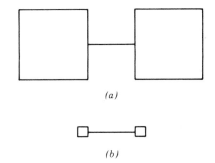

□ *figure 2.12* The effect of context on apparent length. The center lines at (*a*) and (*b*) are equal, but because of contextual stimuli—the different-sized flanking boxes—the line at (*b*) appears longer. (This is called the *Baldwin illusion.*)

pends not only on the immediate sensory information generated by the stimulus, such as its size, shape, orientation, color, and so on, but also on the context in which the stimulus appears. In other words, the perception of a target is affected by all of the background stimulation, including stimulation that precedes (and, in some cases, follows) the target.

Interestingly, this phenomenon is not restricted to humans. Flaherty and his colleagues (e.g., Flaherty, 1982; Flaherty & Grigson, 1988) demonstrated that certain forms of consummatory behavior in rats are also influenced by context and contrast effects. One striking form of this relativity phenomenon is called *successive negative contrast.* For example, one group of rats are exposed to a high reward level (e.g., a high concentration of a sweet solution) and then shifted to a lower level of reward (a low concentration of sweet solution). The performance of these animals, whose reward has been shifted downward, becomes poorer than that of a control group that has been exposed only to the lower level of reward. That is, the *contrast* between the two levels of reward for the shifted group exaggerates the reduced sweetness of the lower level of reward, thus reducing their performance. In effect, the initial exposure to the high-concentration sweet solution makes the low-concentration solution appear less sweet.

SUMMARY

This chapter outlined some of the main issues of *psychophysics,* which examines the relationship between physical stimulation and subjective experience. To this end, the concepts of absolute and difference threshold, including general techniques for their assessment, were described. The absolute threshold (or absolute limen) was defined as the minimum amount of energy required to detect a stimulus. However, the idea of an absolute threshold was questioned. Many factors make the notion of a single, immutable value for stimulus detection untenable.

The absolute threshold was also questioned by a discussion of Signal Detection Theory (SDT). SDT stresses that, when confronting marginal or very weak stimulus conditions, an observer's decision as to whether or not a stimulus (or signal) is present is affected by certain nonsensory response biases—such as the observer's attention, expectation, and motivation. It was also noted that SDT makes it possible to isolate and evaluate the effects of sensory capacity and response bias on the observer's performance.

The controversial concept of subliminal perception—the detection of stimuli whose magnitude lies below the level of conscious detection—was introduced. Several types of research were discussed in which stimulation imperceptible to the observer exerts measurable influence on his or her behavior. It was concluded that in certain conditions, subliminal stimulation may be received and registered by the observer and may influence the detection or recognition of subsequent stimuli.

The difference threshold was introduced as the amount of change in stimulus energy necessary to produce a detectable difference between two stimuli. This led to a discussion of Weber's fraction, which states that the amount of change in a stimulus necessary to detect it as different is proportional to the magnitude of the stimulus. We then described Fechner's extension of Weber's fraction. Fechner formulated a mathematical equation linking sensation to stimulation. Fechner's equation states that the magnitude of a sensation is proportional to the logarithm of the physical intensity of the stimulus. Although the general validity of both Weber's fraction and especially Fechner's equation has been questioned, their impact on measurement in psychology has been significant.

An alternative to Fechner's law concerning psychological scaling is Stevens' power law. This law holds that for many kinds of sensory and perceptual phenomena, the relation between sensation and stimulation can be expressed by an exponential function; that is, sensation grows in proportion to the physical intensity of the stimulus raised to a power. This formulation expresses the relationship between sensation and stimulation that has been applied effectively in many diverse domains of psychology.

Finally, we noted that judgments about a stimulus do not occur in isolation. Judgments in psychophysical tasks are relative, influenced by the role of context or the background of a stimulus. A general perceptual principle is that the perception of a stimulus depends not only on absolute, immediate factors but also on comparative relations between the stimulus and the context in which it appears. That is, the perception of a stimulus may be markedly influenced by what precedes it, what follows it, and what serves as its background.

KEY TERMS

Absolute Threshold (Absolute Limen)

Catch Trials

Correct Rejection

Criterion (β)

d'

Difference Threshold (Difference Limen)

False Alarm

Fechner's Law

Hit

Just Noticeable Difference (JND)

Magnitude Estimation

Method of Adjustment (Average Error)

Method of Constant Stimuli

Method of Limits (Minimal Change)

Miss

Modulus

Noise (N)

Power Function

Power Law

Psychophysical Methods

Psychophysics

Response Bias

Receiver Operating Characteristic (ROC) Curve

Semantic Priming

Sensitivity

Signal

Signal Detection Theory (SDT)

Subliminal Perception

Subthreshold (Subliminal)

Suprathreshold (Supraliminal)

Threshold

Weber's Fraction (or Ratio)

STUDY QUESTIONS

1. What is the role of psychophysics? What does the use of psychophysical techniques enable psychologists to determine about the state of subjective experience?

2. What is the absolute threshold? How can it be assessed? What are the main methods used to determine the absolute threshold?

3. What alternatives are there to the notion of an absolute threshold?

4. What is signal detection theory? How does it relate to the traditional notion of an absolute threshold?

5. How do signal detection techniques include the observer's decision criteria and various nonsensory factors in assessing an observer's sensitivity?

6. Enumerate factors that influence an observer's judgment about whether a stimulus is present or absent.

7. What is meant by the decision-making strategy of the observer in a typical signal detection task?

8. What does the value of d' represent? How is this illustrated by the ROC curve? What factors increase the probability of a hit or a false alarm?

9. What is subliminal perception, and how can it be demonstrated? How does research on semantic priming bear on subliminal perception? Why is subliminal perception a controversial research area?

10. What is the difference threshold, and how can it be demonstrated? What is the relation of the difference threshold to the observer's ability to discriminate between stimuli? How is the difference threshold affected by the magnitude of the stimulus intensity under observation?

11. Consider the relation of Weber's fraction to the notion of a JND.

12. What is Fechner's law or equation? What does it state concerning the relation of stimulation to sensation? How is it related to Weber's fraction?

13. How does Stevens' power law relate sensation to stimulation? How does Stevens' power law differ from Fechner's equation?

14. What is a power function? What are some methods used to scale sensation using Stevens' power law? What does the exponent of a power func-

tion represent concerning the relation of sensation to stimulation?

15. Why is the judgment of various aspects of a stimulus a relative matter? What factors in addition to the stimulus enter into its perception?

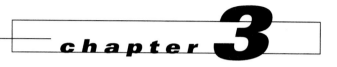

THE VISUAL SYSTEM

This first chapter on the sensory systems introduces the visual system. First, we describe the physical stimulus—light—and outline many of the anatomic features, structural mechanisms, and functional properties of the eye. Next, we describe how the eye and the visual system transform, process, and modify light energy from the environment into neural activity. Finally, we trace the pathways of this information to various areas of the visual system, including the brain.

There are good reasons for beginning with the visual system. It is probably the best-understood sensory system. In part, this is due to methodological and technical factors: The anatomy and related structures of the visual system are reasonably accessible and, for the most part, visual stimulation is well defined and can be subjected to precise controls. But probably a more important reason relates to the functional significance of vision. For many forms of life, vision is crucial for gaining knowledge about objects and events in the environment. This knowledge depends on information such as shape and texture, size and distance, brightness and lightness, color and movement.

Vision is probably the dominant sensory system for human beings. This can be demonstrated, in part, when vision is put in conflict with another sensory system. Rock and Victor (1964; see also Rock & Harris, 1967) examined

*the priority of vision over touch by making a square look like a rectangle; this was done by having subjects view the square through a special distorting lens that produced an optical compression of the height (Figure 3.1). When a subject both felt and saw the square through the distorting lens system, the square was perceived as a rectangle! That is, the stimulus was perceived on the basis of how it looked rather than how it felt. The phenomenon that an object "feels" as if it has the size or shape seen is called **visual capture** (e.g., Rock, 1986). In other words, in visual capture our perceptions conform to how things appear visually, even when there is conflicting (and accurate) information from another sensory system. Although the results of other studies may not make so compelling a case for the overriding influence of vision when there is a sensory distortion or conflict (e.g., Power, 1980; Heller, 1983, 1989), it is clear that, for humans, vision is critical for survival.*

For all of these reasons, vision has been studied in great detail, and more is known about it than about the other senses. Accordingly, we will have more to say about the visual sense than about any other sensory system. In addition, introducing vision first enables us to consider many general mechanisms and phenomena that are common to all the senses. We begin with a discussion of light and its relation to the visual system.

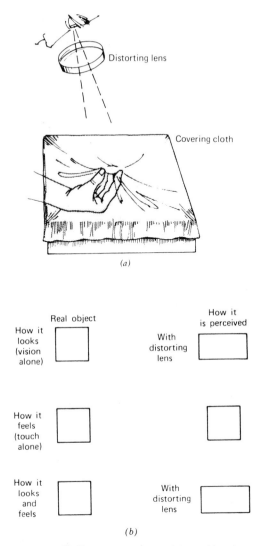

(a)

(b)

▭ **figure 3.1** Experiment in which a subject is presented with contradictory information from vision and from touch. The apparatus included a distorting lens, a cloth over the subjects' hands so that they would not deduce from the distorted appearance of their hands that they were looking through a distorting lens, and a square made of hard plastic. In the experiment depicted, the subject looked at the square and simultaneously grasped it. The lens optically showed a rectangle. The results for this and other conditions are schematized in (b).

THE PHYSICAL STIMULUS

The physical stimulus for the visual system is light. Light is a form of **radiant electromagnetic energy** that belongs to the same class of phenomena as X-rays, radar waves, and radio waves (Figure 3.2). The physical characteristics of light are compatible with two complementary properties: (1) it is a vibratory phenomenon—a continuous cycle of waves of energy pulsating, or oscillating, at a certain frequency that can be converted into units of wavelength (discussed in the next section), and (2) it behaves as if it is emitted as a stream of minute, discrete particles, or quanta, of energy. The quantum unit of radiant energy is called a **photon,** and the number of photon units emitted by a light source—the amount of radiant energy—specifies its **intensity.** Light, then, is generally described by both its wavelength and its intensity. These two physical characteristics are related to different psychological phenomena.

Wavelength

We have noted that light, as a form of radiant electromagnetic energy, travels in a continuous cycle of waves. This creates a regular pattern of peaks and troughs, or depressions, that can be described in units of wavelength. The **wavelength** of a light source refers to the physical distance of a single wave cycle measured from peak to peak, and it underlies a critical physical property that has a significant effect on sensation and perception. The corresponding subjective or psychological effect that different wavelengths of light have on the observer is the perception of different *colors* or *hues* (color perception is discussed in detail in Chapter 5).

Wavelengths of electromagnetic energy vary from trillionths of a meter to many kilometers in length. Very short and very long wavelengths of energy are not visible. As shown in Figure 3.2, very short wavelengths of energy include gamma waves, X-rays, and ultraviolet rays, whereas long wavelengths characterize electrical energy (AC circuits) and radio waves. However, the wavelengths of radiant energy of significance to the visual systems of most animal species occupy a relatively small region of the total electro-

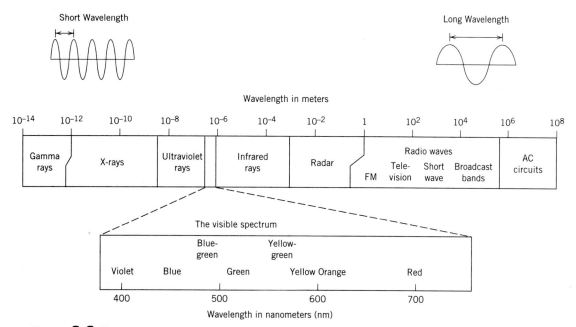

□ *figure 3.2* The electromagnetic spectrum. The visible portion of the spectrum is enlarged in the lower part of the figure. The spectrum is in units of wavelength, which refers to the distance between two adjacent peaks of a continuous waveform. This is suggested by the schematic drawings of short and long wavelengths above the spectrum.

magnetic energy spectrum. Insects, some birds, and perhaps certain rodents (Jacobs et al., 1991), may be sensitive to near-ultraviolet radiation; in addition, some snakes possess specialized sense organs for receiving infrared radiations. However, under normal conditions, for most vertebrates, radiations—light—extend from about 380 nm (**nm, nanometer,** billionth of a meter) to about 760 nm. This range constitutes only a narrow band, about one-seventieth of the total spectrum. Part of the reason for the reception to only a limited portion of the spectrum may be due to the filtering of light energy by a presumably intact ozone layer (15 miles above the Earth), so that 80% of the solar energy reaching the Earth lies between 300 and 1100 nm. In addition, as light enters water, it undergoes a number of physical changes, including absorption, scattering, and, even at moderate depths, extinction. By one account, the short ultraviolet waves are almost extinguished in a few millimeters of water and the infrared waves are eliminated in about a meter, thereby leaving the narrow band of the visible spectrum shown expanded in Figure 3.2 (Walls, 1963,

p. 373). Thus, sea-dwelling, or aquatic, creatures whose vision is adapted to the available light spectrum and those land-bound, or terrestrial, animals owing their origins to aquatic forms of life share a similar visible spectrum.

There are, however, some notable exceptions to this generalization. The emission of infrared radiation by warm-blooded animals has been exploited by some night-active, or nocturnal, cold-blooded animals. Snakes such as the pit viper and the rattlesnake hunt for small mammals and birds in the absence of visible light by utilizing specialized organs located alongside their eyes that are capable of forming an infrared or "heat" image of the immediate surroundings, especially of their warm-blooded prey.

Intensity

As we have noted, the physical intensity of light refers to the amount of radiant energy contained in the light source. The corresponding subjective or psychological effect that intensity has on the observer is called

brightness. Here we must stress the difference between intensity and brightness because it points out the important general distinction between physical stimulation and its corresponding psychological reactions. Although brightness typically varies with intensity, the term *brightness* is restricted to the sensory impression—the individual's subjective experience—resulting from the intensity of light. In other words, whereas *intensity* is a physical property of light, *brightness* is the impression produced by the intensity of light striking the visual system. This distinction was highlighted in the previous chapter, where we introduced Stevens' power law. We observed, for example, that varying the physical intensity of a light does not necessarily produce a proportional change in sensory experience, that is, in brightness. Thus, doubling light intensity does not produce a doubling in brightness. About an eightfold increase in physical intensity is required to double the corresponding sensory impression—to double brightness.

Measurement of the intensity of a light stimulus requires technical procedures and equipment, and the results are specified in a diverse, almost bewildering, array of units. Consider the different aspects of a lighted environment that must be measured: the amount of light coming from a light source (called *radiance*), the amount of light falling on or illuminating a surface, and the light reflected from a surface. Table 3.1 summarizes some of the often used measures of light.

Illuminance Two aspects of environmental light are important to this discussion. The first, **illuminance,** refers to the physical intensity of the light falling on or illuminating a surface, that is, the amount of *incident* light. A common English unit of illuminance is the *foot-candle* (ft-c). A metric unit of illuminance is the *meter-candle*.

Luminance Ordinarily, we do not look directly at a light source; most of the light that we see is reflected from surfaces. The intensity of the light reflected from an illuminated surface is called **luminance.** An English unit of luminance is the *foot-lambert* (ft-L). Other common units of luminance are the *millilambert* (mL) and candela per square meter

(cd/m^2). Table 3.2 shows luminance levels, expressed in millilamberts, for some typical sources of stimulation.

It is useful to summarize several of the features of light specification relevant to our discussion. Consider the characteristics of light necessary to read this page: The amount of light energy emanating from the bulb of your room or your desk lamp specifies radiant energy or *radiance;* the amount of light falling on this page is *illuminance;* the amount of light reflected from the page is *luminance;* and the psychological-sensory effect of the image on your visual system is *brightness.*

LIGHT RECEPTION

Radiant energy is informative only when it affects a visual system. In the initial stage of vision, radiant energy must be transduced, or transformed, into a neural form. That is, the physical energy acts on light-sensitive tissue to produce impulses that convey sensory information. The kind of tissue that is responsive to radiant energy is found in the simplest organisms. Some organisms, such as the single-celled amoeba, possess no specialized light receptors; rather, the entire body is light sensitive. However, most animals have a region on their body that is maximally sensitive to light. Of course, mere responsivity to light is quite different from actually forming a visual image. Indeed, many of the light-sensitive structures of lower forms of life act primarily to concentrate light on a light-sensitive pigment. That is, they serve as *light-gathering* rather than *image-forming* organs. It is in advanced stages of evolution that an image-forming eye developed. The structural transition in light-sensitive organs from simple light gatherer to image former is suggested in Figure 3.3.

According to Wald (1959), only three of the major phyla have developed image-forming eyes: the arthropods (animals with an external skeleton, e.g., insects and crabs; Figure 3.4), mollusks (e.g., squid and octopus), and vertebrates (animals with an internal skeleton). Many different optical devices for forming an image have evolved within these phyla. For example, the mollusk *Nautilus* (shown

▭ *table 3.1* Photometric Terms, Units, and Measures

Term	Unit	Measure
Illuminance (Light falling on a surface)	Foot-candle (ft-c)	The illumination received on a surface 1 foot square located 1 foot from a standard candle
	Meter-candle (m-c)	The illumination on a surface of 1 meter square located 1 meter from a standard candle. (1 m-c = 0.0929 ft-c or 1 ft-c = 10.76 m-c)
Luminance (Light reflected from a surface)	Foot-lambert (ft-L)	The total amount of light emitted in all directions from a perfectly reflecting and diffusing surface illuminated by 1 foot-candle
	Millilambert (mL)	1 mL = 0.929 ft-L, or 1 ft-L = 1.076 mL
	Candela per square meter (cd/m^2)	The amount of light given off by a perfectly diffuse reflecting surface illuminated by 1 meter-candle. (1 cd/m^2 = 0.3142 mL or 0.2919 ft-L)

Note: Riggs (1965) suggests that the unwieldy, confusing array of terms used in specifying lighting conditions arose because photometry, or the measurement of light, initially grew out of a number of specific technological needs of the lighting industry.

▭ *table 3.2* Luminance Values for Typical Visual Stimuli

	Scale of Luminance (millilamberts)	
	10^{10}	
Sun's surface at noon	10^9	Damaging
	10^8	
	10^7	
Tungsten filament	10^6	
	10^5	Color vision
White paper in sunlight	10^4	
	10^3	
	10^2	
Comfortable reading	10^*	
	1	
	10^{-1}	
White paper in moonlight	10^{-2}	
	10^{-3}	Colorless vision
White paper in starlight	10^{-4}	
	10^{-5}	
Absolute threshold	10^{-6}	

*10 mL equals approximately 9.3 ft-L or 32 cd/m^2.

Source: L. A. Riggs, in *Vision and Visual Perception*, edited by C. H. Graham, John Wiley, New York, 1965, p. 26. Reprinted by permission of the publisher.

in Figure 3.3) has a pinhole eye (generally, a small hole in an opaque surface forms an image on a surface behind it). The tiny arthropod *Copilia* has a lens and a single attached light receptor that moves back and forth, scanning the image in a way similar to that of a TV camera.

All image-forming eyes have advantages and limitations. The pinhole eye forms a target image that is in focus at all distances from which the target is viewed. However, it admits only a very small amount of light to its photosensitive tissue. The **compound eye** of arthropods (Figure 3.4) consists of a mosaic of tubular units called **ommatidia** (literally, "little eyes" in Greek) that are clustered tightly together and arranged so that the outer surface forms a hemisphere. Each ommatidium registers only the light directly in front of it; this produces a single image constructed from an enormous number of separate signals. In other words, the image is a pattern or mosaic of as many points of light as there are ommatidia. Thus, the image formed is a coarse one, somewhat analogous to the grainy image printed by a dot matrix printer. However, since the movements of objects in the immediate visual field

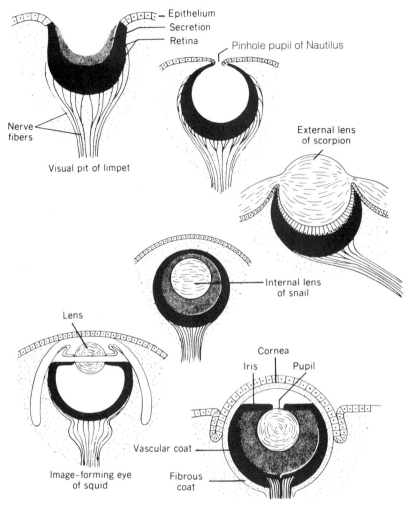

▭ figure 3.3 Examples of some light-receiving structures, including primitive eyes and the vertebrate eye. A trend in optical sophistication is suggested by the change from the light-gathering property of the pit of the limpet to the image-forming feature of the vertebrate eye. (*Source:* Gregory, 1973, p. 24. Reprinted by permission of the author.)

are recorded successively across ommatidia, the compound eye is especially effective for detecting the slightest movement of prey or enemy, as you have no doubt experienced when trying to catch a fly.

Each ommatidium is essentially a fixed-focus, image-forming device that refracts only a tiny spot of nearby light or shade; accordingly, the compound eye is particularly effective only for seeing targets that are

very close. In contrast, the vertebrate eye is quite effective for long-range viewing, but it cannot resolve images at the short distances at which the arthropod eye is so effective. However, no matter what design or variation on the basic image-forming eye a species has adopted, it is clear that, in general, the eye is adapted in different ways in different species to maximize the capture of information in the optic array. In

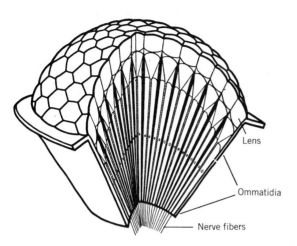

Lens

Ommatidia

Nerve fibers

☐ *figure 3.4* Three-dimensional cutaway view of the compound eye of an arthropod. Essentially, the compound eye is composed of a cluster of hundreds or thousands of narrow tubes called ommatidia, each with a lens at its outer surface and a central nerve fiber to transmit stimulation. The outer surface of the cluster is arranged so that it forms a hemisphere. Each ommatidium is separated and insulated from every other one, with each one registering only the light directly in front of it.

short, the eye of a given species is uniquely related to the demands of its environment and its way of life.

ANATOMY OF THE VERTEBRATE EYE

The vertebrate eye is built on a single basic plan: From fish to mammal, all vertebrate eyes possess a photosensitive layer called a **retina** and a **lens** whose optical properties cause it to focus an image on the retina. Figure 3.5 presents a cross-sectional slice of the human eye. We first describe its major structural components and then discuss several important functional mechanisms.

The eyeball, lying in a protective socket of the skull, is a globular structure just under 1 inch (about 20 mm) in diameter. The outer covering of the eyeball is a tough white, opaque coat about 1 mm in thickness called the *sclera* (seen as the white of the eye). The sclera at the front of the eye becomes the translucent membrane called the **cornea.** Light rays entering the cornea are refracted, or bent, by its surface. In fact, most of the refraction of light rays reaching the eye is performed by the cornea. A second layer of the eyeball, the **choroid,** is attached to the sclera. The choroid is about 0.2 mm thick. It consists largely of blood vessels and provides a major source of nutrition for the eye. In addition, the choroid is a heavily pigmented, dark structure; this enables the absorption

of most extraneous light entering the eye, thereby reducing reflections within the eyeball that might blur the image. However, some nocturnal animals possess a retinal layer, called the **tapetum,** that reflects back some of the light entering the eye. It is the reflection of light from the retina that accounts for the eerie glow, or "eyeshine," that appears occasionally from the eyes of many familiar nocturnal animals. When we drive past a cat or dog at night, the animal's eyes reflect back some of the light of the car's headlights rather than absorbing the light, as does the human choroid layer. The function of the tapetum is not clear. Walls (1963) suggests that the limited amount of light reflected on the environment from the tapetum and then *back* into the tapetum may enhance vision in nocturnal conditions.

Iris, Pupil, and Whytt's Reflex

In the front of the eye the choroid is modified to form the **iris.** The iris is a disklike, colored membrane, consisting of two smooth muscles, that lies between the cornea and the lens. One function of the iris is to regulate the amount of light entering the eye— a structural analogy to the diaphragm of a camera (Figure 3.6). When lighting conditions are poor, the iris opens (or *dilates*) to increase the size of the **pupil**—the round black opening surrounded by the iris (Figure 3.7). By contrast, in bright light the iris

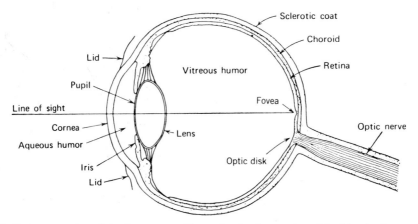

Sclerotic coat
Choroid
Retina
Lid
Vitreous humor
Pupil
Fovea
Line of sight
Cornea
Lens
Optic nerve
Aqueous humor
Optic disk
Iris
Lid

◻ *figure* **3.5** Cross section of the human eye. The main structures relevant to this chapter are indicated. The cornea and the lens focus the incoming light on the retina, the surface at the back of the eye. The retina contains light-sensitive receptors that convert light energy into a neural message that is sent to further stages in the visual system via optic nerve fibers. The region where optic nerve fibers leave the eye is the optic disk. The small pit in the retina, the fovea, is the region of sharpest vision. The remainder of the retina, the peripheral retina, functions best in low levels of light.

closes, *constricting,* or reducing, the size of the pupil. Pupil size is controlled by two opposing smooth muscles of the iris, the *sphincter* and the *dilator* (identified in Figure 3.8), which constrict and dilate the pupil, respectively.

In the human young adult, pupil size ranges from about 2 to 9 mm in diameter. This enables more than a 20-fold variation in area and in the amount of light admitted into the eye (since the area is proportional to the square of the diameter).

Generally, the pupil's reaction to the overall conditions of lighting is reflexive. Shining a bright light in the eye produces **Whytt's reflex** (a reflex identified by the physiologist, Robert Whytt in 1751): an immediate constriction of the pupil in response to bright light. In fact, Whytt's reflex has important diagnostic value concerning the function of the central nervous system:

◻ *figure* **3.6** Optical similarity of the diaphragm of a camera and the iris of the eye. Both adjust to the intensity of light.

The inability to demonstrate Whytt's reflex may indicate neural injury.

The human pupil is circular, but a variety of shapes exists in different species. Figure 3.9 shows the vertical slit pupil of a cat during dilation and constriction. Such a pupil allows an essentially nocturnal animal (e.g., the cat) to hunt in bright daylight or to bask in the comfort of the sun (e.g., the crocodile) (Duke-Elder, 1958).

Red-Eye An interesting effect on the human choroid is produced by the pupil's reaction to flashes of light. Although the human eye does not usually reflect eyeshine, there are times when we are aware of some of the incident light reflected back from the choroid. The most familiar instance of eyeshine in the human is the **red-eye** seen in pictures taken with a flash. Red-eye is produced in conditions of dim light where the pupil is probably at or near its maximum dilation, and typically where a flash is required to obtain a reasonably distinct photograph. Although the pupil's reaction to bright light is reasonably quick (between 250 and 500 msec—0.25 to 0.5 sec), it is still too slow to constrict effectively when the flash strikes it. Red-eye is the effect of a brief burst of bright light through a widely dilated pupil that is reflected back from the choroid.

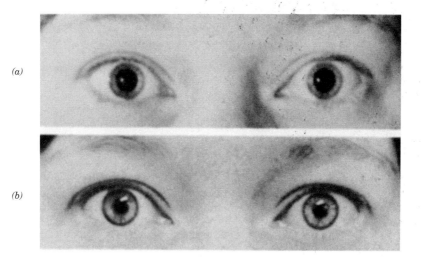

(a)

(b)

▭ **figure 3.7** The size of the pupil changes with the level of light. The photo for (a) was taken in dimmer light than the one for (b), although they appear about equally bright. Accordingly, the pupils shown in (a) are dilated, whereas those in (b) are constricted. (*Source:* From Buss, 1978, p. 139)

Sophisticated cameras incorporate a red-eye reduction process. Essentially, they send a preliminary burst of light to the pupil about 0.75 sec before the actual exposure of the film. This gives the pupil time to constrict, so the effect of the second exposure-linked flash on the choroid is minimized. The red-eye reduction process reduces the amount of light reaching the choroid, since it is the light of the flash reflected back from the choroid that produces the eerie red glow in a photograph. Thus, firing a small

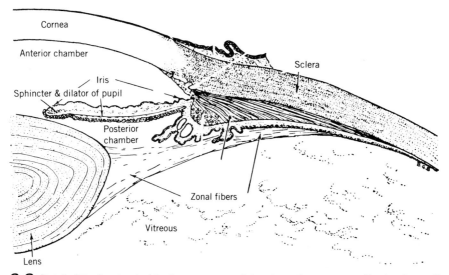

▭ **figure 3.8** Detail of the front part of the human eye, outlining the main structures affecting the pupillary response and the curvature of the lens. The sphincter and dilator structures of the iris, shown just to the right of the lens, control the size of the pupil. The ciliary muscle is attached by ligaments, the zonal fibers, to the lens and controls the curvature of the lens. These structures are shown just below the sclera.

but effective burst of light *before* the exposure causes the pupil to constrict, transmitting less light to the choroid of the retina. This does not totally eliminate red-eye, but constricting the pupil reduces its size.

This has been a relatively long discussion of an infrequent photographic distortion resulting from the use of indoor environments. But if you understand the phenomenon and the means of reducing it, you have gained an appreciation of the function of the choroid and the pupil's reaction to light.

Finally, we should note a secondary effect of the red-eye reduction process: The people photographed have artificially reduced pupils, which, in normal circumstances, may convey something about their attitude and interest. The relevance of this effect will be examined in a later section on the function of changes in pupil size.

The Lens

The transparent, flexible lens of the vertebrate eye divides it into two unequal chambers—a small one in front filled with watery fluid held under pressure, the *aqueous humor,* which helps to maintain the shape of the eye and provides the metabolic requirements of the cornea, and a larger chamber behind the lens filled with a jelly-like protein, the *vitreous humor.* These fluids, both transparent, help hold the lens in place and allow its housing to be flexible. However, whereas aqueous fluid is continuously renewed, vitreous fluid does not change. This causes the accumulation of microscopic amounts of optical waste matter such as shed cells. You may be aware of some of the debris in the vitreous fluid when you occasionally see "floaters," small specks that float about. Sometimes when gazing at a bright, uniform surface such as a lamp or even at a bright sky, old cells—floaters—cast shadows on the retina, which appear as dark spots flitting about in your field of view.

A set of muscles, the **ciliary muscles,** attached to the lens by ligaments (the *zonal fibers* of Figure 3.8), controls its curvature, which varies depending on the distance of the object focused. (We will discuss this mechanism shortly in a separate section.) From a comparative viewpoint, lens size bears an interesting relation to the normal lighting conditions of an ani-

mal's habitat. Because large lenses can collect more light than smaller ones, nocturnal animals have evolved larger lenses relative to the size of their eyeballs than have day-active animals.

The Retina

Light passes through the lens to the retina at the back of the eyeball. The retina, which covers nearly 200° of the inside of the eyeball, is composed of a coating of interconnected nerve cells and photoreceptors that absorb light energy and transduce, or convert, it into neural form. Two types of photoreceptors in the retina have been identified: **rods** and **cones,** named for their cylindrical and conic shapes, respectively (Figure 3.10). The outer surface of both rods and cones contains a light-absorbing pigment. There are between 120 and 130 million rods, each averaging about 0.002 mm in width. Rods are heavily concentrated in the peripheral region of the retina.

There are 6 to 8 million cones, each between 0.003 and 0.008 mm in width. In contrast to the location of rods, cones are primarily concentrated in a small pit or indentation less than 1 mm across called the **fovea** (Latin for "small pit"), shown in Figure 3.5. Although some cones are found outside the fovea mixed with rods, the fovea contains *only* cones. The central region of the retina that includes the fovea is marked by a yellow pigment, the *macula lutea* (Latin for "yellow spot"), over an area 2 to 3 mm in diameter.

The approximate distribution of rods and cones over the retina is illustrated in Figure 3.11. The gap in the curve corresponds to that part of the retina called the **optic disk,** where optic nerve fibers leave the eye en route to the brain (Figure 3.5). Since there are no photoreceptors here, there is no vision when light strikes this region of the retina, and it creates a perceptual **blind spot.**

□ **DEMONSTRATION:**
The Blind Spot

A demonstration confirming the blind spot is given in Figure 3.12. If you follow the simple directions, you will experience the unusual impression

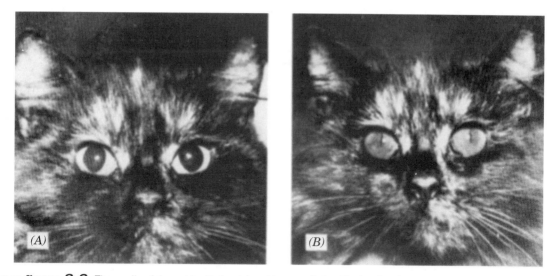

◻ *figure 3.9* The pupils of the cat in dilation (*a*) and in constriction (*b*) showing the extremely narrow vertical slits. (From S. Duke-Elder, *System of Opthalmology.* Volume 1, *The Eye in Evolution,* C. V. Mosby, St. Louis, 1958, p. 613. Reproduced by permission of the publisher.)

of a visible image suddenly "disappearing." Specifically, at some critical viewing distance, the image of the caged dog will project onto the optic disk and disappear completely. Also of interest is the observation that when the dog disappears, you do not see a blank area; instead, the region is "filled in" by the surrounding background cage bars (Brown & Thurmond, 1993; Ramachandran, 1992; this filling-in phenomenon is an instance of a general perceptual process described in Chapter 7).

As illustrated in Figure 3.10, there is an apparently illogical relation between the location of the photoreceptors and incoming light in that the receptors do not face the light. In most vertebrates, the photoreceptors are located in the back of the retina and nerve fibers connected to them are gathered together in front. This means that light must travel through the network of nerve fibers, blood vessels, and other supporting cells before it reaches the photoreceptors: the retina thus appears anatomically inside out. However, functionally this poses little problem, for the blood vessels are quite small and the nerve fibers and related cells are more or less transparent. Further-

more, as Figure 3.13 points out, the nerve cells of the fovea are arranged in a spoke-like fashion so that they do not interfere with the incoming light rays.

Neural Connections in the Retina Stimulation of rods and cones is transmitted through the retina by a chain of neural connections to the optic nerve, which, in turn, sends signals to the visual area of the brain. Several kinds of neural connections are illustrated in Figure 3.10. The figure shows that there are both vertical and horizontal connections between the photoreceptors and the optic nerve. Indeed, the retina appears as a network (the Latin word for "net" is *rete*) of interconnections. Consider first the chain of vertical connections that connect the photoreceptors to the optic nerve: Groups of rods (sometimes with cones) and cones (sometimes singly) are connected to *intermediate cells* called **bipolar cells** (literally, "having two ends"). Bipolar cells, in turn, connect to **ganglion cells,** whose axons are the optic nerve fibers.

In addition to the intermediate bipolar and ganglion cells, there are two layers of horizontal connections that link adjacent bipolar and ganglion cells to

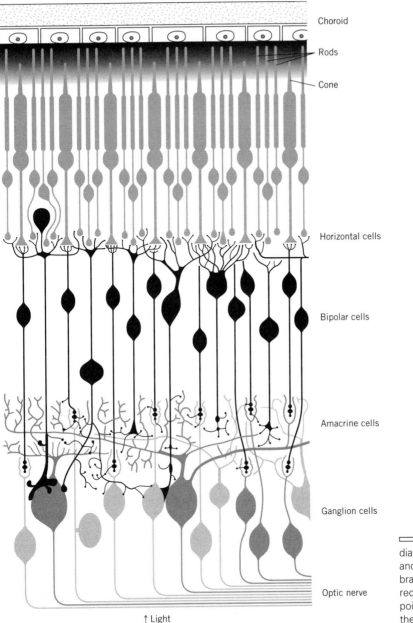

Choroid

Rods

Cone

Horizontal cells

Bipolar cells

Amacrine cells

Ganglion cells

Optic nerve

↑ Light

▭ *figure* **3.10** Schematic diagram of the neural structures and interconnections of the vertebrate retina. Notice that the photoreceptors do not face the light but point toward the choroid layer at the top.

each other. As shown in Figure 3.10, one group, appropriately labeled *horizontal cells,* has a neural network that extends across the retinal layer, lying between the photoreceptors and the bipolar cells. A second set of lateral connections, the *amacrine cells*

(meaning "cells without axons"), lies between the bipolar cells and the ganglion cells. One function of these lateral connections is to enable a form of interaction between neighboring cells so that the signals from the photoreceptors can be modified. For exam-

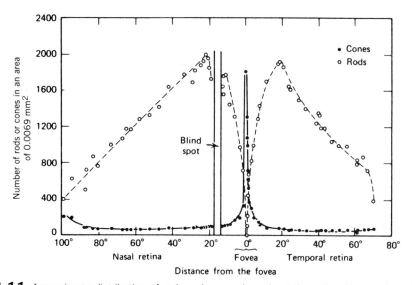

figure 3.11 Approximate distribution of rods and cones throughout the retina. The number of receptors per unit area from the fovea to the extreme periphery of the retina has been plotted. Cones are represented by solid circles and rods by open circles. At about 20° from the fovea, the density of rods approximately matches the density of cones at the fovea. The gap in the figure, labeled the "blind spot," corresponds to the place (the optic disk) on the retina where optic nerve fibers leave the eye. Since there are no photoreceptors in this area, there is no visual response when light strikes it. (*Source:* Chapanis, 1949, p. 7.)

ple, stimulating a number of neighboring photoreceptors has a different effect on any one of the receptors than when only a single photoreceptor is stimulated.

Acuity and Sensitivity

Several important functions can be attributed directly to the arrangement of the rods and cones in relation to the bipolar and ganglion cells. The total number of bipolar and ganglion cells present in the periphery of the retina is much less than the number of rods. It follows that each bipolar and ganglion cell receives the input from a large number of rods. In the extreme peripheral regions of the retina—away from the fovea—as many as several hundred rods may be connected to a single bipolar cell. Thus, the activity of a very large number of rods may be represented in a single intermediate cell. In contrast, in the cone-rich area of the retina, the fovea, the number of cones comes much closer to matching the number of intermediate cells. In fact, many cones in the fovea are each independently connected to a single bipolar and ganglion cell. Thus,

cones have fewer intermediate connections than do rods; hence, the most direct transmission between the retina and the optic nerve is with cones in the fovea.

Consider the functional significance of the neural connections of rods and cones to the intermediate cells. The fact that a number of rods share a ganglion cell means that there is *convergence* or *pooling* of receptor information from an appreciable part of the retina at a single ganglion cell. This convergence of stimulation increases the likelihood of the common ganglion cell's reaching the energy level necessary to fire (Figure 3.14). This "many-to-few" neural relation between rods and intermediate cells increases **sensitivity,** the capacity to perceive in *low* levels of illumination. In addition to pooling signals at a common ganglion cell, rods have another advantage: A single rod requires less light than a single cone in order to be activated. Thus, although individual signals may be weak, when they are pooled together at a common ganglion cell the cumulative effect may be strong enough to activate the ganglion cell. The convergence of the signals from a number of rods on a single

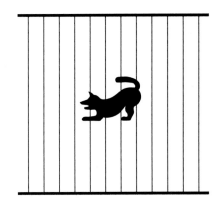

(a)

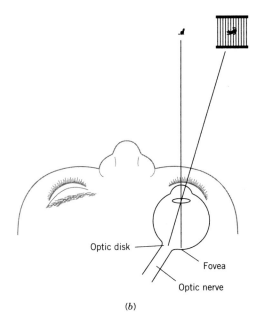

Optic disk

Fovea

Optic nerve

(b)

▭ **figure 3.12** Demonstration of the blind spot. (a) Close or cover your left eye and hold the page about 10 in. from your face. Focus your right eye on the cat at the left and, at the same time, slowly move the page back and forth from the eye. At some point, generally between 5 and 15 in. from the eye, the dog will "disappear," that is, the cage will appear empty. As shown in (b), the image of the dog is falling on the optic disk—the region of the retina where the nerve fibers group together and leave the eye. There are no photoreceptors at this region; hence, no visual response, or a blind spot occurs. (Part a revised from Smith, 1989.)

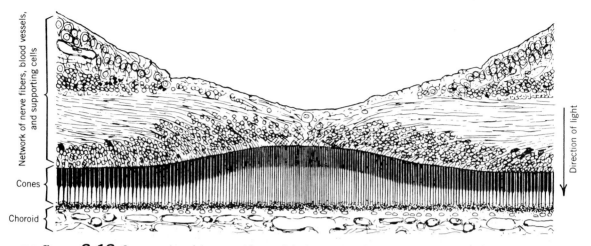

Network of nerve fibers, blood vessels, and supporting cells

Cones

Choroid

Direction of light

▭ *figure 3.13* Cross section of the central fovea of the human eye. Shown are the cones and the layer of neurons above the cones containing a network of blood vessels and nerve fibers. At the centermost region the cones are thin, long, and tightly grouped together. Note that the network of vessels and fibers above the cones is much thinner in the center region. This reduces interference and distortion of the incoming light rays and facilitates the passage of light rays to the cones. (From S. Polyak, *The Vertebrate Visual System*, University of Chicago Press, 1957, p. 276. Reprinted by permission of the publisher.)

intermediate ganglion cell helps explain why we see better in very dim light when we look at the target stimulus indirectly or out of the corner of our eye. What we are doing is positioning our eyes so that

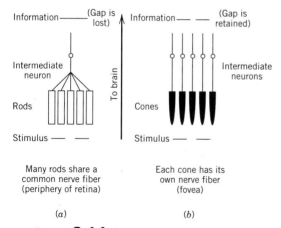

Information —— (Gap is lost)

Intermediate neuron

Rods

Stimulus —— ——

To brain

Information —— —— (Gap is retained)

Intermediate neurons

Cones

Stimulus —— ——

Many rods share a common nerve fiber (periphery of retina)

Each cone has its own nerve fiber (fovea)

(a)

(b)

▭ *figure 3.14* Schematic of neural connections of rods and cones to intermediate neurons. In (a) the stimulation from a number of rods converge on a single neuron. Thus sensitivity is high but acuity is low and information of the gap in the stimulus line is lost. In (b) there is no convergence of cone stimulation, and acuity is high.

what we wish to see falls on the rods, which are more sensitive than the cones. A familiar example of this is looking at a faint star at night; we are more successful when we do not fixate directly on the star. By doing this, we ensure that the image falls on the sensitive rods in the peripheral retina rather than on the presumably all-cone fovea.

Of course, the pooling of stimulus information from a number of rods at the ganglion cell level reduces the information given by any single rod. Hence **acuity,** the ability to see sharp details, is correspondingly coarse when rods alone are stimulated. In contrast to the neural connections of rods within the retina, foveal cones are more directly connected to ganglion cells; thus, cones at the fovea have a relatively independent or private line to the brain. The result is that cones are more capable of contributing independent information concerning the source of their stimulation—information required for resolving stimulus patterns and seeing fine details. It follows, then, that a foveal cone, with its relatively direct neural connection to the intermediate cells, is more capable of relaying information about its place of stimulation than is a rod. At the fovea there is a heavy concentration of cones, and hence a greater number of independently stimulated bipolar and ganglion cells, which results in a greater capacity for differentiating an image. The fovea, then, is the part of the retina that is specialized for clear, detailed vision. In fact, when we look directly at a target in order to see it sharply and in detail, we automatically position our eyes so that the image of the target falls directly on the fovea.

DEMONSTRATION:
Foveal Acuity

You can demonstrate the acuity of foveal vision quite easily by fixating, at a distance of about 5 inches, on the **"X"** centered on the following string of letters:

C T W J K R L N **X** E P V Z M B G U

You will see the **X,** of course, and only a few neighboring letters. What is seen clearly is due to foveal stimulation; more distant letters fall on the rods of the peripheral retina, and as you can readily determine, rods are not very useful for perceiving details.

It should be clear that increasing acuity reduces sensitivity. Thus, the relatively independent connections of cones promote greater acuity, and the convergence of rods onto intermediate ganglion cells provides greater sensitivity. The difference in the way the rods and cones are connected to the intermediate bipolar and ganglion cells explains why sensitivity develops as a trade-off to acuity. Figure 3.14 demonstrates this schematically. (We will discuss acuity in more detail in the next chapter.)

VARIATIONS IN EYE POSITION: MOBILITY AND PLACEMENT

In this section, we discuss two aspects of visual exploration: eye mobility, the ability to move the eyes independently of the head or body, and the placement of the eyes in the head (i.e., the direction of the eyes: frontal versus lateral).

Eye Mobility

Human eyes are set in sockets and are capable of rotating within the skull. The eyes are moved about by three pairs of muscles called *oculomotor muscles,* illustrated in Figure 3.15. Eye mobility allows us to maintain the image of moving objects on the retina— to track objects—by moving the eyes smoothly without turning the head or body. Without independent eye movements, the precision, speed, and overall efficiency with which we explore the environment would be greatly reduced.

Independent eye movements are not available to many kinds of animals. For example, the eyes of the nocturnal owl are so large relative to the size of the skull that they almost touch each other. No space is available in the eyeball socket for the muscles needed to move the eyes; as a consequence, the owl's eyes are fixed and immobile. The solution to the owl's need to explore the environment visually is to move its head. According to Walls (1963), the owl can revolve its head by 270° or more, in a sense trading eye muscles for neck muscles. A more drastic limitation in exploration occurs with certain crustacea (a class of arthropods having a hard outer shell or crust) whose eyes are rigid, immobile parts of the head. Visual exploration of these organisms usually involves movement of the entire body, significantly restricting the ability to track moving targets. (A separate section on eye movements is presented in the next chapter.)

Placement of the Eyes and the Visual Field

Vertebrates have either two laterally directed eyes at the sides of the head or two frontally directed eyes. Examples of eye placement for a prey animal (the rabbit) and a predator (the cat) are given in Figure 3.16a. As illustrated in Figure 3.16b, animals with laterally directed eyes generally have two separate or monocular fields of vision, a small region of the visual field that is seen in common by both eyes (called *binocular overlap*), and a relatively large total view.

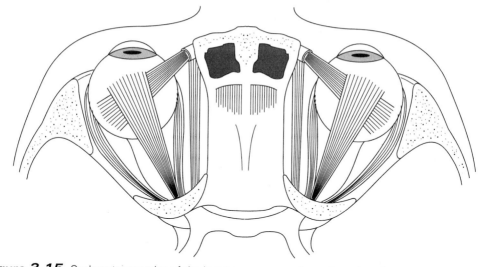

━ **figure 3.15** Oculomotor muscles of the human eye as seen from above in a dissected head. The eyeball is controlled by six muscles that move it and enable it to direct the gaze smoothly to any position. (Revised from G. L. Walls, *The vertebrate eye and its adaptive radiations,* New York, Hafner, 1963.)

Laterally directed eyes are an obvious anatomical adaptation for prey animals that must maintain continual vigilance against predators. Their survival depends on the early detection of predators, in whatever direction, and rapid escape from them. The panoramic vision of the rabbit, one of the most defenseless mammals, is an example. As shown in Figure 3.16*b*, its left and right eyes have separate monocular visual fields of about 170°, and both eyes share a small region of binocular overlap directly in front and in back.

In contrast, animals with frontally directed eyes, typical of predators such as the cat, have smaller monocular visual fields but relatively large areas of binocular overlap, as well as blind areas behind them. That is, there are relatively large areas of the visual field that register almost the same array of visual information on both eyes. As shown in Figure 3.16*b*, the cat has a binocular visual field of 120°. While this narrows the total visual field, a greater degree of binocular overlap offers significant advantages. It enhances the perception of depth and distance and provides an accurate means of locating objects in space. These factors are especially important to predatory animals and animals like primates (including the human; see Figure 3.16*c*), which require acute depth perception to perform

manipulatory skills with their hands, such as holding and grasping and, in the case of tree-dwellers, to enable leaping. Thus, there is a trade-off between frontal and lateral viewing, with the style adopted depending on the survival needs of the species.

ACCOMMODATION

As we noted at the beginning of the section on the structure of the vertebrate eye, as light rays enter the eyeball, they are initially refracted, or bent, by the cornea. They are further refracted by the lens by a dynamic automatic process called **accommodation.** Accommodation is the mechanism that changes the shape of the lens in order to bring an image into sharp focus on the retina. The flatter the lens, the less it refracts light rays; the more the lens bulges or thickens, the more it refracts or converges light rays. In other words, accommodation enables the lens to fine-tune and focus light rays that come from objects of varying distances.

To understand accommodation, we must recognize that the light rays entering the eye are refracted and converge at a point on the surface of the retina. However, light rays reaching the eye from nearby

Prey

Predator

(a)

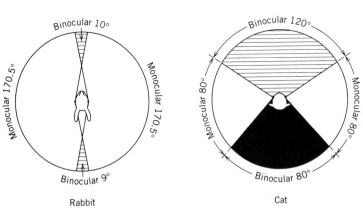

Binocular 10°

Monocular 170.5°

Monocular 170.5°

Binocular 9°

Rabbit

Binocular 120°

Monocular 80°

Monocular 80°

Binocular 80°

Cat

(b)

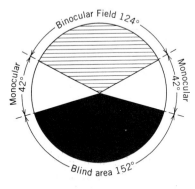

Binocular Field 124°

Monocular 42°

Monocular 42°

Blind area 152°

Primate

(c)

▭ **figure 3.16** Placement of the eyes and the fields of vision. (a) Laterally directed eyes of the rabbit, typical of prey animal, look off to the side. The frontally directed eyes of the cat, typical of predators, face forward. (b) The visual field of the rabbit: each eye has a separate monocular visual field of about 170°, with a small region of binocular overlap in front and in back, accounting for the rabbit's panoramic view of the environment. The visual field of the cat includes a relatively large area of binocular overlap—the area common to both eyes—along with independent monocular visual fields for each eye and a blind area. (c) The visual field of the frontally oriented primate. Frontal viewing reduces the total visual field but facilitates activities that require depth perception. (Based on Duke-Elder, 1958.)

stimuli are different from those coming from far targets; the light rays from a target located more than 20 feet away from the eye are essentially parallel to each other, and are easily refracted and brought to focus on the retina. In contrast, the light rays from a target that is relatively close to the eye are somewhat divergent from each other, and if not sufficiently refracted, they are brought to a focal point behind the retina. (The insufficiently refracted light rays would not actually pass through the retina, but they would produce an out-of-focus, blurred image on the retina.) However, this is generally avoided by accommodation: For focusing on nearby targets the lens changes its curvature—thickens—thus refracting or converging the light rays entering the lens and bringing them to a sharp focus on the retina. The change in the shape of the lens depending on the target's distance is outlined in Figure 3.17.

Accommodation is not found in all levels of vertebrates, and it may differ somewhat for different animals. In general, two different accommodative techniques are used by vertebrates to achieve a focused image—moving the lens in relation to the retina or changing the curvature of the lens. The former technique is similar to the focusing mechanisms employed in the camera. The camera lens moves forward for focusing on a nearby target and moves backward for focusing on a distant target. This accommodative technique involving movement of the lens is used by fish, for example.

The second technique of accommodation, used by mammals, is the mechanism described above: changing the curvature and shape of the lens. The change in lens shape is effected by relaxing or contracting the ciliary muscle, which is attached to ligaments that suspend the lens in place (these are the zonal fibers shown in Figure 3.8). When focusing on distant targets, the ciliary muscle is relaxed and the lens is relatively flat. When focusing on targets near the eye, the ciliary muscle contracts, causing the lens to bulge and assume a rounder, more spherical shape.

Accommodation has limits. As a target is gradually brought close to the eye, the ciliary muscle contracts and the lens bulges. However, a distance will be reached at which even the strongest contraction of the ciliary muscle will not produce a distinct image

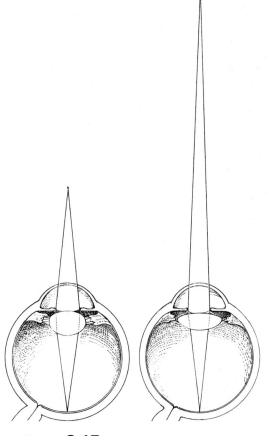

□ *figure* **3.17** Accommodation of the lens. The lens is relatively flat or thin for focusing the light rays of a distant target (shown at the right) and bulges to focus the divergent light rays of a near target.

of the target. This is because the resultant light rays of the very close target are so divergent that, even with full accommodation, the lens system cannot converge them sufficiently to bring them to a focus on the retina.

The closest distance at which a target can be seen clearly, with full accommodation, is called the **near point;** thus, a target held closer than the near point will be out of focus or blurred. If we are forced to maintain continued focus on objects that are close to the near point, say, 6 in. or less, the ciliary muscle soon fatigues and eye strain sets in. Generally, we must use optical devices for prolonged examination of objects located close to the eye.

For the human, accommodation changes during infancy. The newborn human infant, less than 1 month of age, can focus only on targets at one distance, whose median value is 19 cm (about 7.5 in.; Haynes, White, & Held, 1965). Images of targets nearer or farther away are proportionately blurred. However, during the second month of infancy the accommodative system begins to respond adaptively to changes in target distance and approximates adult performance at 9 weeks (Banks, 1980).

Refractive Errors

Presbyopia The ability of the human eye to accommodate deteriorates with age, resulting in a form of refractive error called **presbyopia** (literally, Greek for "old eyes"). With increasing age, the elasticity of the lens progressively diminishes, so that it becomes sclerotic or hardens, making it more difficult for the ciliary muscles to change the lens' curvature to accommodate or converge the divergent light rays from nearby objects. One result of presbyopia is that the refracting capacity of the lens decreases and, as Figure 3.18 illustrates, the near point increases during the aging process. Hence, older persons with uncorrected lenses must often hold reading material abnormally far from their faces in order to focus adequately. Fortunately, this condition is easily remedied by wearing reading glasses, essentially convex lenses that converge the divergent light rays of nearby targets on the retina (the familiar magnifying glass is an example of a convex lens).

Hyperopia When the ciliary muscle is relaxed, an *emmetropic,* or optically normal eye, forms an image of a distant target on the retina. This condition is shown in Figure 3.19a. As the target is brought closer to the eye, the light rays diverge. Hence, the lens must thicken or bulge in order to bend or refract the light rays so that they converge on the retina; otherwise, the rays of the image will be brought to a focus behind the retina, resulting in a blurred retinal image. In this case, the lack of proper convergence is called **hyperopia** or *farsightedness* (also referred to as **hypermetropia**). This condition is depicted in Figure 3.19b. Hyperopia occurs because the lens is too weak or the eyeball is too short for the refractive capacity of the lens. Though the eye can adequately focus the parallel light rays of a distant target, it cannot focus accurately on the divergent light rays of nearby targets. To correct for hyperopia, a *convex* lens that converges light rays must be worn to increase the refraction of the lens.

Myopia The condition of **myopia** or *nearsightedness* is shown in Figure 3.19c. Myopia is a highly prevalent refractive disorder of the lens, affecting approximately 25% of the adult population (Zadnik et al., 1994). Myopia is an inability to focus the light rays from distant targets. This may be due to a number of factors, but two forms are especially prevalent: (1) *axial myopia,* in which the eyeball is too long for the refractive capacity of the lens, and (2) *refractive myopia,* in which the cornea and the lens abnormally refract the incoming light rays. The problem with the myopic eye is that while it can effectively focus the divergent light rays of nearby targets on the retina, it cannot focus accurately the parallel light rays of distant targets on the retinal plane; these rays are brought to a focus in front of the retina. To correct for myopia, a *concave* lens is used. This causes the parallel light rays reaching the eye to diverge, compensating for the abnormal refractive capacity of the myopic eye and focusing the light rays on the retina.

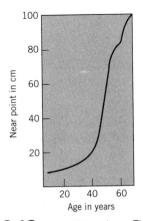

□ **figure 3.18** Near point and age. The near point, the closest distance at which a target can be seen clearly, increases with age.

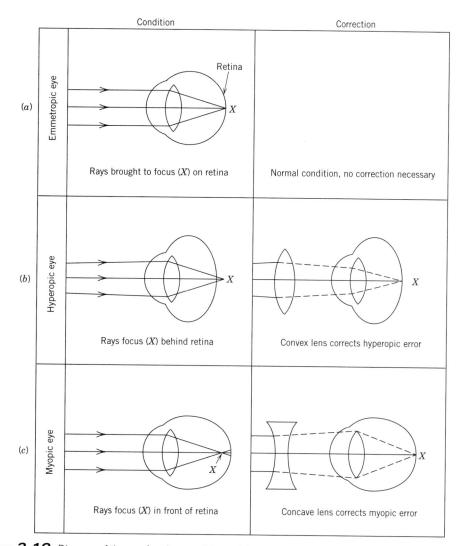

figure 3.19 Diagram of three refractive conditions of the eye and the kinds of lenses required to focus light rays on the retina. (*a*) The emmetropic (normal) lens focuses the light rays of far objects on the retina (noted at the **X** in the figure) and thus requires no correction. (*b*) The hyperopic (farsighted) lens cannot refract the divergent light rays *sufficiently* from nearby objects; hence, it focuses the light rays from near targets behind the plane of the retina. As shown at the right of (*b*), the use of a convex lens, which bends and converges the light rays, corrects this problem. (*c*) The myopic (nearsighted) lens overrefracts the parallel light rays from distant objects, bringing them to a focus in front of the retina. As shown at the right, the myopic lens is corrected by using a concave lens, which diverges the light rays from far objects.

Development of Myopia Many researchers contend that the origin of myopia has a genetic basis (e.g., Gwiazda, Thorn, & Bauer, 1993; Zadnik et al., 1994). Myopia is more prevalent among the children of myopic parents than among the children of nonmyopic parents. Moreover, even before the onset of myopia, children of myopic parents generally have longer than normal eyeballs, resembling the elongated eyeball typical of myopia (Zadnik et al., 1994).

However, there is evidence that myopia may also have an environmental basis. For example, Young (1970) has indicated that myopia may be partly due to a substantial amount of near viewing during childhood, the kind that requires continuous accommodation (e.g., as in learning to read). That is, a causal relationship may exist between excessive near vision and myopia (see Curtin, 1970; Wiesel & Raviola, 1986). This notion is sometimes referred to as the **near-work** or **use-abuse theory** (e.g., Angle & Wissman, 1980; Owens & Wolf-Kelly, 1987). Evidence for an experiential or environmental origin of myopia comes from research with animals. In one study almost 70% of a group of kittens deprived of distance vision (i.e., restricted to near vision) developed myopia, whereas about 90% of a comparison group that had ample experience with distance vision were hyperopic (Rose, Yinon, & Belkin, 1974). Similar evidence is found with birds. Chicks whose vision was restricted to the frontal field of view (by means of special occluders; see Figure 3.20) from hatching until 4 to 7 weeks became extremely myopic, whereas the vision of chicks restricted to a lateral visual field did not differ from the vision of normal animals (Schaeffel, Glasser, & Howland, 1988; Wallman et al., 1987). Similar myopic effects were observed with primates (Macaque monkeys); refractive errors were produced experimentally by restricting and degrading form vision from birth to 1 year (by suturing the eyes shut; Raviola & Wiesel, 1985; Wiesel & Raviola, 1986).

(a)   *(b)*

▭ **figure 3.20** Occluding devices used to restrict the visual fields (fitted upon hatching). (*a*) Restriction to frontal vision. (*b*) Restriction to lateral vision. It was assumed that animals restricted to frontal vision experienced more close viewing than animals restricted to lateral vision. (Photo courtesy of J. Wallman.)

While no clear statement has yet emerged as to the cause of myopia, research does demonstrate that specific visual exposure, especially restricted form vision, blurred vision, and excessive near viewing, as in long periods of reading, may contribute to refractive errors and perhaps alter the structure of the eye (Wallman et al., 1987; Wiesel & Raviola, 1986). Relatedly, there are some proposals, and evidence in humans, suggesting that specific controlled visual experience (i.e., by behavior modification) may reduce certain forms of myopia (Rosen, Schiffman, & Cohen, 1984; Rosen, Schiffman, & Myers, 1984). Based on our discussion, it seems reasonable to conclude that myopia has both a genetic and an environmental basis.

Lens Aberrations

Other kinds of refractive errors, not directly related to lens accommodation, may also affect the focus of light rays on the retina. Figure 3.21*a* illustrates a refractive error called **spherical aberration:** The light rays passing through the peripheral parts of a spherical lens are refracted more strongly and brought to a focus at a point closer to the lens than the rays passing through the central regions. Rather than meeting at a common focal point, the rays from the marginal and central portions of the lens meet at different points and are spread over an area, creating a "blur circle." Uncorrected, this condition results in a significantly blurred image. However, several mechanisms of the cornea and lens can compensate, in part, for spherical aberration. Furthermore, under moderately good lighting conditions, the pupil constricts to limit the rays of light to the central parts of the lens.

A second form of lens aberration, **chromatic aberration,** is shown in Figure 3.21*b*. Chromatic aberration is due to the fact that lenses made of a single material refract rays of short wavelengths (e.g., "blues") more strongly than those of long wavelengths (e.g., "reds"). Thus, light rays that appear violet or blue, for example, are brought to a focus at a point closer to the lens than are rays that appear red. Uncorrected, this condition would result in a blurry, colored image. However, this is rarely a problem, since many of the very short wavelengths (which appear blue and

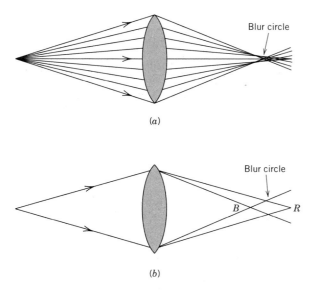

(a)

Blur circle

(b)

B R

Blur circle

▭ *figure* **3.21** (*a*) Schematic of spherical aberration. The light rays that pass through the edge of a spherical lens are brought to a shorter focus than those that pass through the center. Thus, instead of meeting at a common point, the light rays are spread over an area. The result is that the image formed of a point is a blur circle. (*b*) Schematic of chromatic aberration. When light of various wavelengths is refracted by a lens made of a single material, the light of shorter wavelengths is refracted more than that of longer wavelengths. For example, blue (B), which appears from short wavelengths of light, is brought to a shorter focus than long-wavelength red (R) light. The result is that the image formed of a white point is a chromatic blur circle.

for which chromatic error is greatest) are absorbed by the yellow pigment of the *macular lutea,* the region surrounding the fovea, which acts as a yellow screen (Riggs, 1965, p. 331).

Astigmatism

Ideally, the refractive surfaces of the cornea and the lens are spherical and symmetrical, with the vertical and horizontal curvatures equalized. When the corneal surface is not spherical and symmetrical, an error of refraction called **astigmatism** occurs. The effects of astigmatism are illustrated in Figures 3.22 and 3.23. Almost all eyes have some degree of astigmatism, since the cornea is usually not perfectly shaped. The astigmatic surface of the cornea produces different degrees of curvature for the vertical and horizontal orientations. In most instances of astigmatism, the surface of the cornea is flatter from side to side than it is vertically, resulting in blurring and distortion of parts of images, depending on their orientation; that is, vertical lines may appear sharp, whereas horizontal lines may appear blurred. Astigmatism is corrected with lenses that compensate for different degrees of curvature of the cornea.

PUPIL MOBILITY

The variable pupil, controlled by the iris, has several reflexive functions. As we noted earlier, it maintains an optimal intensity of light entering the eye. Too little light will not sufficiently excite the photoreceptors in the retina, and too much light will render them inefficient or perhaps injure them. When there is little light, the pupil opens wide—dilates. When there is much light, the pupil narrows—constricts. A constricted pupil also reduces the blurring effects of spherical aberra-

▭ *figure* **3.22** Astigmatism chart. To an astigmatic viewer, some sets of lines appear blurred relative to others.

figure 3.23 Astigmatism and Op art. A number of unusual perceptual effects are produced by viewing this reproduction of a painting. The most striking perception is of a pattern of pulsating squares. The clarity of different groups of oblique lines varies. This result is attributed to the common effects of astigmatism, which becomes more pronounced when the figure's prominent contours are vertical and horizontal rather than oblique. This is easily accomplished by tilting the figure 45°. (*Source:* Square of Three, by Reginald Neal; reproduction courtesy of the State Museum of New Jersey, Trenton, NJ.)

tion. As you may recall from the section on spherical aberration, light that strikes the periphery of the lens is brought to a focus at a different plane than light that strikes the center of the lens. Thus, in intense light, constriction of the pupil tends to keep out peripheral light

rays, restricting incoming light mainly to the central part of the lens, which provides the best focus. This, of course, increases acuity.

A small pupil also enhances acuity by keeping extraneous light from entering the eye and reaching the retina. We do this when squinting in the presence of glare, restricting the light that enters the eye. The same effect may be achieved by viewing a well-lighted area through a long tube, which yields a sharper image than can be obtained with the naked eye. Of course, the restriction of peripheral light cannot occur when lighting is poor and a maximum opening—full dilation—is required. Thus, acuity, or image resolution, is greatest when the available light is intense and the pupil is appropriately constricted.

Pupillometry

The amount of available light is not the only determiner of changes in pupil size. Heinrich in 1896 (see Bakan, 1967) and more recently Hess (e.g., 1965) have noted that the size of the pupil varies in response to strong emotional states and certain forms of ongoing mental activity and, in general, serves as a measure of arousal. The study of such psychological factors affecting the pupillary response is called **pupillometry** (Hess, 1975*a*; Janisse, 1977). Hess (1965; Hess & Polt, 1960, 1966) demonstrated that while a subject is viewing visual stimuli, pupil size may serve as an indication of the interest value of the stimuli. For example, the pupils of males dilated in reaction to viewing pictures of female pinups, and they constricted slightly to male pinups. In contrast, the pupils of female subjects constricted to the pictures of female pinups but dilated to male pinups (Hess & Polt, 1960; Metalis & Hess, 1982). Correlated attitude and emotional factors with pupillary reactions have also been observed for such diverse stimuli as foods (Hess & Polt, 1966), political figures (Barlow, 1969), and pictures of unusual skin disorders (Metalis & Hess, 1982).

Mental activity also appears to produce changes in pupil size. In one study, Hess and Polt (1964) had subjects solve a graded series of verbally presented multiplication problems. Typically, the size of the pupils of each subject gradually increased, beginning with the presentation of the problem and reached a maximum dilation immediately before the verbal answer was given. In addition, the more difficult the problem, the greater the increase in pupil size. Along similar lines, Schluroff (1982) found that the degree of pupil dilation correlated positively with the gram-

matical complexity of auditorily presented sentences (for related findings, see Ahern & Beatty, 1979; Beatty & Wagoner, 1978). While research on pupillometry has been somewhat controversial, the evidence generally suggests that pupil size reflects mental effort.

Finally, in this context, we should note Hess' (1975*a,b*) proposal that pupil size plays a major role in certain forms of nonverbal communication. For example, in social interactions, large (dilated) pupils tend to be associated with and communicate positive attributes such as friendliness and attractiveness.

EYEBLINKS

Eyeblinks, under normal conditions of vision, occur every few seconds, typically about 15 per minute. During the duration of the blink, which may range between about 100 and 400 msec, virtually all visual information to the eye is interrupted. However, despite this break in the flow of light stimuli, perception is relatively unaffected: Generally, the effect of the blink is scarcely noticed. This is all the more surprising in that if, say, room lighting were interrupted for even a briefer interval than produced by a typical eyeblink, the visual environment would appear dark.

Why is the perceptual effect of an eyeblink so small compared with the actual change it produces on the retina? One explanation is based on the finding that a neural mechanism in the brain generates a cancellation or inhibitory signal that accompanies the eyeblink. This inhibitory signal acts as a visual suppressor and decreases the sensitivity for visual stimuli during the duration of the blink (Riggs, Volkmann, & Moore, 1981). Thus, a neural inhibitory mechanism accompanying the eyeblink diminishes its effects, contributing to the stability and continuity of vision.

Although we may scarcely notice the effects of our own eyeblinks, we may at times be aware of the blinks of other individuals, especially in certain situations. People tend to blink more frequently when they are startled, excited, or anxious and under stress, as well as when they are tired. By contrast, the eyeblink rate is reduced when performing visually demanding tasks. When reading, for example, the typical blink rate of 15 per minute drops to less than 5 per minute. However, reduced eyeblink rates do not occur randomly. Stern and Strock (1987) note that blinks occur during times when the acquisition of visual information is minimal. Thus eyeblinks during reading are most likely to occur as the reader shifts from one line or page of text to another, as well as at the end of sentences and paragraphs—when a blink would be least likely to disrupt the reader's attention or the intake of information. In general, blinks occur at places in reading text where the acquisition of new information is lowest, and blinks are somewhat inhibited when stimuli requiring attention and information processing are presented (Fogarty & Stern, 1989; Orchard & Stern, 1991).

EYE AND BRAIN

In this section, we present an overview of the neural pathway between the retina and the visual projection area of the brain. Then we describe some complex neural processing that occurs at several levels of the visual system, including the ganglion cells of the retina, major relay centers of the visual system, and finally, the visual area of the brain.

Visual Pathway of Eye to Brain

A schematic diagram of the human visual system, linking the visual fields of the eyes to the brain, is shown in Figure 3.24. The optic nerves leave the eye and converge at an X-shaped region called the **optic chiasma** (or **chiasm,** after *chi,* the Greek letter for *x*). At the chiasma, fibers of the optic nerve from the inner or *nasal* half of each retina cross, whereas those from the outside or *temporal* half of each retina stay on the same side. In short, the optic chiasma is the location where only the inner optic nerve fibers of each eye cross over to the opposite side en route to the brain.

Consider the relation of the visual fields to the retina and to the occipital lobe of the brain. As shown in Figure 3.24, light from the right visual field stimulates the left half of each retina (i.e., the temporal and nasal halves of the left and right eyes, respectively), and light from the left visual field stimulates the right half of each retina (the temporal and nasal halves of the right and left eyes, respectively). Following the pathway in Figure 3.24, we also note that each eye sends projections to both the right and left occipital lobes. Thus, the optic nerve fibers from the left half of each retina are sent to the left occipital lobe. Correspondingly, optic fibers from the right half of each retina are sent to the right occipital lobe. Functionally, this ensures that information from the same side of each eye reaches the same brain hemisphere. With respect to the relation of the visual field to the brain, this means that the right visual field is represented on the left side of the brain and the left visual field projects on the right side of the brain. Thus, one-half of the total visual field is projected on each occipital lobe.

The partial crossing of optic fibers at the chiasma holds true only for mammals. According to Walls (1963), for most vertebrates below mammals (e.g., fish, amphibia, and birds), all the optic nerve fibers from each eye cross over at the chiasma to form *optic tracts* on the opposite side. Thus, each eye is connected only to the opposite half of the brain. For mammals, the relative amount of uncrossed fibers is related to the extent to which the eyes face frontally. Thus, with reference to the placement of the eyes in the head (see Figure 3.16), very few of the optic fibers of the rabbit remain uncrossed relative to those of the cat. Walls (1963) states that about 12–16% of the fibers remain uncrossed in the horse, 20% in the rat and oppossum, 25% in the dog, and one-third in the cat, reaching a maximum of one-half in higher primates, including humans.

The Superior Colliculus After crossing at the optic chiasma, the majority of axons of the ganglion cells project to two relay centers located in the brain (Figure 3.25). About one-fifth of the axons of the ganglion cells project and connect, or synapse, with cells in a region at the top of the midbrain called the **superior colliculus.** In evolutionary terms, the superior colliculus is an old visual processing center, and in many lower species of animals, such as fish, amphibia, and birds, it serves as the major processing center for all visual input. However, for most higher animals, the superior colliculus plays a somewhat specific role in coordinating certain eye movements, in

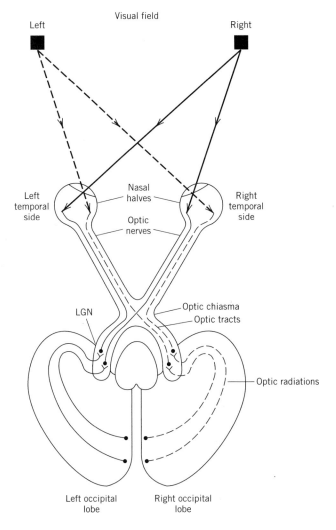

Visual field
Left   Right

Left
temporal
side

Nasal
halves

Right
temporal
side

Optic
nerves

LGN

Optic chiasma
Optic tracts

Optic radiations

Left occipital
lobe

Right occipital
lobe

▭ *figure 3.24* Schematic of the human visual system showing projection of the visual field through the system. Fibers originating in the inner, or nasal, halves of the retinas intercross at the optic chiasma, and fibers originating in the outer, or temporal, halves of the retinas do not. In addition, the right half of the visual field projects (shown by the continuous line) on the left half of each retina (and to the left occipital lobe of the brain). The left half of the visual field projects (shown by the dashed line) on the right half of each retina (and to the right occipital lobe). Thus, each half of the visual field is projected on the opposite side of each eye and onto the opposite occipital lobe of the brain.

visual and postural reflexes, and in spatial localization. An example of a reflex mediated by the superior colliculus is orienting to and blinking in response to an object that suddenly appears in the visual field. This is a very useful reaction for many species of animals: When cells of the superior colliculus are stimulated by sudden movement of an object, the signals quickly result in an eye movement that projects the image of the object on the fovea, so that the animal can see it more clearly. The superior colliculus also receives sensory input from the ears (and other senses), and it has cells that are organized to integrate input on

the location and direction of auditory and visual movement. These cells respond exclusively to visual and auditory signals that originate simultaneously from a common spatial region. In other words, these spatially linked cells fire *only* when the place where you see an object is also the place where you hear it. This is an obvious aid in locating and following moving objects. However, the superior colliculus is not capable of a detailed analysis of specific spatial features. It contributes to object location rather than object recognition and identification. The latter task is performed by the visual cortex (where, in a region called

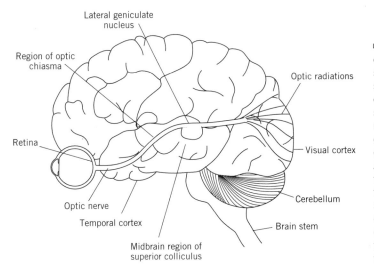

Lateral geniculate nucleus

Region of optic chiasma

Retina

Optic nerve

Temporal cortex

Midbrain region of superior colliculus

Optic radiations

Visual cortex

Cerebellum

Brain stem

◻ **figure 3.25** Relative positions of major structures of the human visual system. Shown is a side view, with visual structures presented relative to each other. Highlighted are the three major sites where processing and synaptic connections take place: the retina, the lateral geniculate nucleus (LGN), and the visual cortex of the occipital lobe of the brain. Also shown are the general location of the superior colliculus of the midbrain, the temporal cortex, and some collateral structures, such as the region of the optic chiasma and brain stem. (Note: Only half of the visual system is shown and with the exception of the eyeball, the structures shown actually lie within the brain.)

the *extrastriate cortex* or *secondary visual cortex,* fibers from the superior colliculus project).

The Lateral Geniculate Nucleus After crossing at the optic chiasma, the majority of axons of the ganglion cells from each eye synapse with cells in each **lateral geniculate nucleus (LGN),** a small cluster of neurons in the **thalamus,** that serves as the major sensory relay center (in Figure 3.24, note that there are a pair of lateral geniculate nuclei, each residing in a separate hemisphere). The LGN resembles a slightly curved or bent structure (its name derives from the Latin word *geniculate,* meaning "kneelike"). Ganglion cell axons from the retina synapse with cells in the LGN in an orderly and systematic manner. In fact, cells from neighboring regions of the retina connect with neighboring regions of the LGN, creating a precise representation or topographical "map" of the retina in the LGN. A map-like representation of the retina is called a **retinotopic map** (*topos* is the Greek word for "place"); a number of such maps are found in the brain.

The Visual Cortex As Figures 3.24 and 3.25 show, when the axons leave the LGN, they fan out in a group of fibers called *optic radiations.* These optic radiations synapse with a specific cluster of neurons of the occipital lobe of the cerebral cortex, which

lies at the back of the brain. A number of names have been attached to this region of the visual system. Because of its striped patterns, or striations, it is often referred to as the *striated cortex.* Alternatively, because it is the region where the fibers from the LGN terminate, it is also referred to as the *primary visual cortex* (identified in Chapter 1, Figure 1.10). Finally, with reference to specific labeling systems applied to the anatomy of the brain, it is also referred to as *Brodmann's Area 17* or *visual area I* (or *V 1).*

To sum up, visual stimulation originating in the environment and projected onto the retina is processed and transmitted to three prominent levels of the visual system: *Ganglion cells* of the retina send the majority of their axons to the *LGN* of the thalamus, whose axons, in turn, reach the *primary visual cortex* of the occipital lobe (recall that a small proportion of ganglion cells also project to the superior colliculus). In the next section, we see that the cells within each of these levels react in specific ways to environmental stimulation projected onto the retina.

RECEPTIVE FIELDS

There are many complex interconnections between the photoreceptors of the retina and the cortical cells of the visual area of the brain. The relationship between the retina and various regions of the visual system can be studied directly by recording the electrical responses of single nerve cells to light patterns. A tiny, fine-tipped filament or wire called a *microelectrode* is surgically inserted into various parts of the visual system of an experimental animal; ideally, this is in a single ganglion cell or a cell in the LGN, or in the visual area of the cortex. Then an assortment of stimuli varying along certain dimensions, such as size, movement, intensity, orientation, pattern, and so on, are projected singly on various parts of the animal's retina until one of them produces a measurable change in electrical activity (i.e., produces action potentials or spikes) in the cell or neuron under examination (Figure 3.26). As a result, an area of the visual field or of the retina called a **receptive field** is mapped out. Presenting a stimulus of sufficient intensity or quality to the receptive field alters the firing activity of a sensory cell. In short, the receptive field for a given receptor cell is the region of the visual field, or the corresponding region of the retina, that, when appropriately stimulated, excites or inhibits the cell's firing pattern. Using this technique, the receptive fields for various locations of the visual system have been mapped. It allows us to determine the specific sorts of environmental stimulation that excite cells in various processing regions of the visual system. We now examine the receptive fields of some of these regions.

Receptive Fields for Ganglion Cells: Center-Surround Organization

Typically, ganglion cells fire at fairly steady rates in the absence of any light stimulation (20 to 30 times per second). In one pioneering investigation, a microelectrode was inserted in a ganglion cell of a cat (Kuffler, 1953). When a tiny spot of light was then projected into the cat's eye and was moved over various regions of the retina, the steady state was observed to vary. Specifically, the ganglion cell's rate of discharge was maximally altered by shining a small spot of light on its receptive field—a circular retinal area about 1 to 2 mm in area. This indicates that the receptive field of the ganglion cell is small and approximately circular.

It is important to note, as Figure 3.27 illustrates, that light alters the ganglion cell's discharge rate in different ways, depending on the part of the receptive field stimulated. In one type of ganglion cell, the receptive field consists of a small circular "ON" area, in which the impulse rate of the cell increases at the onset of the light. Light stimulation to a surrounding peripheral annular (or outer ring) "OFF" zone inhibits the ganglion cell's neural activity, and the cell shows a burst of impulses when the light stimulus is removed. These ganglion cells thus have opposing or antagonistic, concentric receptive fields called **center-surround receptive fields.**

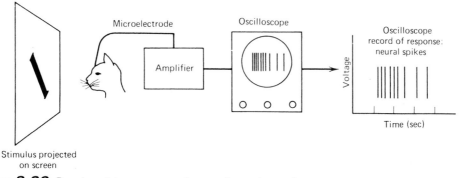

□ *figure 3.26* Experimental arrangement for mapping and recording receptive fields. An electrode is inserted into a cell at some point in the visual system of the experimental animal. Various light stimuli are projected on a screen in front of the animal's eyes. The eyes are generally paralyzed so that particular locations on the screen project to particular locations on the animal's retina. The impulse activity of an individual cell in response to the stimuli (shown in the oscilloscope record) indicates the characteristics of that cell's receptive field.

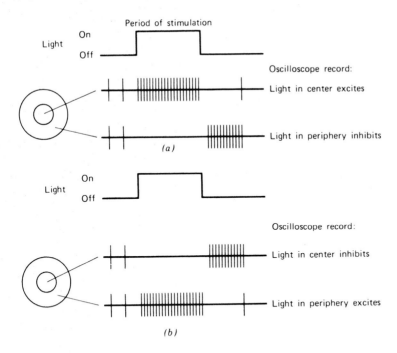

(a) Oscilloscope record shows strong firing by an ON-center ganglion cell when a circular spot of light strikes the field's center. If the spot hits the annular OFF-surround area, the firing is suppressed until the light goes off. This cell thus has a center-surround receptive field. (b) Oscilloscope record for a ganglion cell with an OFF-center and an excitatory ON-surround. If the light strikes the field's center, the discharge rate is suppressed, but there is a strong discharge when the light is terminated.

Another type of ganglion cell, also with a concentric center-surround, antagonistic organization, has a reversed form of receptive field consisting of an inhibitory OFF-center and an excitatory ON-surround. If the annular ON-surround region is illuminated, the cell's firing rate increases; if the OFF-center region is illuminated, the firing rate is suppressed. However, when the illumination of the OFF-center is terminated, there is a vigorous rebound discharge.

Light striking only an ON region produces a strong excitatory response. The more ON area thus stimulated, the more vigorous the response. However, ON and OFF regions are mutually antagonistic: If one spot of light is shone on an ON area and a second spot on its adjacent OFF area, opposite effects are produced; the two effects tend to neutralize each other, resulting in very weak ON or OFF responses. Thus, lighting up the whole retina diffusely or uniformly, thereby simultaneously affecting receptors throughout the retina, does not affect a single ganglion cell as much as does a small spot of light precisely covering its excitatory receptive field. In summary, the antagonistic arrangement of concentric center-surround receptive fields of retinal ganglion cells requires that they compare and react to differences in the illumination levels of physically adjacent areas of the retina. Thus, center-surround receptive fields are most effective for detecting contrasting regions rather than for overall illumination (Schiller, 1992).

X, Y, and W Cells

In addition to the general receptive field characteristics described above, there are three different kinds of ganglion cells, referred to simply as **X, Y,** and **W cells.** Their major differences lie in their number, the rapidity with which they react to neural signals, the size of their receptive fields, and their location. The most common of these ganglion cells, X cells, have a slow conduction speed and react in a steady, sustained fashion when stimulated. The X cells also have small center-surround receptive fields and respond accordingly to precise, fine details of stationary stimuli. Consistent with their processing of small details, X cells are neurally linked to the fovea (the retinal region responsible for acuity). The X cells are also involved in processing color information.

In contrast, Y cells have a fast conduction speed and respond abruptly with transient reactions—showing a brief burst of activity on stimulation and quickly becoming inactive. Compared to X cells, Y cells have large center-surround receptive fields and accordingly contribute very little to acuity. This follows from the observation that cells with large receptive fields are relatively incapable of responding to small, precise differences in stimulation; hence, they are less able to contribute to the fine discriminations characteristic of acuity tasks. This is consistent with the observation that Y cells are concentrated in the peripheral retina, with no connections to the fovea. Instead, the abrupt response of Y cells, with brief, transient bursts of activity, suggests that their main property is responding to movement. Thus, X cells seem specialized for a fine analysis of stationary patterns, and Y cells seem specialized for detecting movement. Table 3.3 summarizes the differences in the X and Y ganglion cells.

Both X and Y cells have center-surround receptive fields (though their sizes differ). However, the receptive field distribution for W cells is more variable. While some W cells possess center-surround receptive fields, many of them respond only to uniformly distributed stimulation that moves in a specific way. Generally speaking, W cells have a greater, more variable range of receptive fields, some being very complex and unique—unlike the center-surround receptive fields shared by X and Y cells. In addition, W cells are the most sluggish and slowest-conducting of the three types of retinal ganglion cells.

What are we to make of these distinctions between ganglion cells of the retina? The preceding discussion makes an important statement about the functional complexity of the retina, especially the ganglion cells: The retina does not merely transduce light energy and transmit neural signals. Rather, the varied properties and activities of the different ganglion cells show that complex processing of the stimulus input is performed within the retina. Moreover, the receptive field organization of retinal ganglion cells is also prominent in the LGN. In fact, axons of all three types of ganglion cells form the optic nerve and project to the LGN. However, it is assumed that some Y cells and the majority of W cells bypass the LGN and project to the superior colliculus.

Receptive Fields for the LGN

The majority of ganglion cells of the retina cross at the optic chiasma and transmit their signals via optic tracts to cells of the LGN in the thalamus. The distinction between X and Y cells is also maintained in the LGN. Thus, the receptive fields for cells of the LGN closely resemble those of the ganglion cells of the retina. For one thing, cells of the LGN have an ON-center and an OFF-surround, or the reverse. Also, like their retinal ganglion counterparts, LGN cells differ from each other both in their anatomy and functionally, in the kind of information they process and transmit.

These functional and anatomical differences are maintained by two distinct divisions within the LGN (Hubel & Livingstone, 1987; Livingstone & Hubel, 1987, 1988). A small cell division in the LGN called the **parvocellular division** receives signals from retinal ganglion X cells with small receptive fields, and a large cell division called the **magnocellular division** receives signals from the Y ganglion cells with relatively large receptive fields (the names for the LGN divisions are derived from the Latin words *magnus,* meaning "large," and *parvus,* meaning "small").

The Parvocellular Division In addition to reacting to the presence or absence of light shone

□ **table 3.3** Properties of X and Y Ganglion Cells

Property	X cells	Y cells
Size of receptive field	Small	Large
Speed of response	Slow, sustained	Fast, transient
Retinal location	Fovea	Peripheral retina
Probable function	Fine-detail vision	Movement

within the center (or the surround) of its receptive fields, the parvocellular division is sensitive to differences in the wavelength of light; that is, cells of this division react differentially to the hue, or color, of the light. For example, a strong response may be elicited for color-sensitive cells if the center of their receptive fields is illuminated by light of a particular color (e.g., green) and inhibited when it is illuminated with the "opposite" color (e.g., red).

The receptive fields of cells of the parvocellular division are much smaller than those of the magnocellular division. Thus, they are more capable of distinguishing between small visual features and making a fine-grained analysis of the spatial details of stationary stimuli than are cells of the magnocellular division. Evidence that the parvocellular division conveys both color and fine detail vision comes from findings that specific damage to cells of the parvocellular division of primates causes loss of color vision and the capacity to resolve fine details (Merigan & Eskin, 1986). Cells of the parvocellular division also respond relatively slowly with a sustained, relatively prolonged response.

The parvocellular division is highly developed only in primates, one of the very few groups of mammals that possess both highly efficient color and fine-detail acuity vision. Based on this observation, Livingstone and Hubel (1988) speculate that in mammals the parvocellular division probably evolved after the magnocellular division.

The Magnocellular Division The more basic magnocellular division is found in all mammals. Functionally it is involved with depth and movement and, along with the parvocellular division, aids form and shape perception (Livingstone & Hubel, 1988). The receptive fields of cells of the magnocellular division are relatively large—as much as two or three times as large as the receptive fields of the parvocellular division—and thus are relatively inefficient in detecting fine details.

Cells of the magnocellular division are more sensitive than cells of the parvocellular division to low-contrast stimuli; that is, they are able to detect smaller contrasts between light and dark areas. Whereas the parvocellular division may be better at detecting high-contrast stimuli, say a black stimulus against a white background, the magnocellular division is more effective in detecting a gray stimulus against another slightly darker gray background. In other words, the magnocellular division is more effective in detecting faint images than the parvocellular division. This characteristic enhances the perception of spatial relationships between surfaces and objects and their background, which, in turn, contributes to depth perception.

Cells at the magnocellular level also respond faster and more transiently—showing a brisk response to stimulus onset and quickly terminate—than cells at the parvocellular level. Like their Y cell inputs from the retinal ganglion cells, the speed of response of cells of the magnocellular division are particularly well suited for detecting movement (Livingstone & Hubel, 1988).

In summary, cells of the parvocellular division are color sensitive, have small receptive fields (hence are able to distinguish between fine visual details), give a slow, relatively prolonged response, and are relatively unresponsive to low contrasts. Cells of the magnocellular division are insensitive to color, have large receptive fields and low resolution of small visual features, respond quickly in a transient manner, and are relatively sensitive to low-contrast stimuli. The major differences between the two divisions imply that they may be responsible for very different aspects of vision. Neuroscientists often refer to the magnocellular and parvocellular divisions, respectively, as the *where* and the *what* divisions. We may conclude that the parvocellular division contributes to the perception of color and acuity, whereas the magnocellular division deals with movement and depth. Table 3.4 summarizes these differences in the two divisions of the visual system.

Receptive Fields for the Visual Cortex

The receptive fields for cells of the LGN of the thalamus are similar to those of the retinal ganglion cells, that is, such cells have an ON-center and OFF-surround or the reverse. However, as receptive fields are plotted for cells lying closer to the visual cortex,

□ **table 3.4** Properties of the Parvocellular and Magnocellular Divisions

Property	Parvocellular	Magnocellular
Responds to:		
Color	Yes	No
Fine details	Yes	No
Size of receptive field	Small	Large
Sensitivity to low contrast	Low	High
Sensitivity to high contrast	High	Low
Speed of response	Slow, sustained	Fast, transient
Retinal input	X cells	Y cells
Probable functions	Color vision, Acuity	Movement, depth perception

the optic array necessary for excitation becomes more precise. Indeed, paralleling the increases in anatomical complexity on ascending from the retinal to the cortical cells, there appears to be an increase in stimulus complexity needed for cells to respond. The research of David Hubel and Torsten Wiesel (Nobel laureates for physiology in 1981) on the functioning of the mammalian visual brain has illuminated our knowledge on this topic (e.g., Hubel, 1982; Hubel & Wiesel, 1959, 1962, 1979). Much of their seminal research consists of exploring and plotting the receptive fields of the primary visual cortex (i.e., the striate cortex, or Brodmann's Area 17) that receives the primary connections from the LGN.

Hubel and Weisel found that instead of circular receptive fields with concentric ON and OFF regions, as in ganglion cells of the retina and cells of the LGN, the receptive fields of neurons of the visual cortex have linear properties; that is, the most effective stimuli are lines, bars, and various rectangular segments with definite edges. Cortical neurons vary in a number of ways. Some possess extremely small receptive fields and some possess relatively large receptive fields, especially those linked to peripheral regions of the retina (Hubel & Wiesel, 1962). However, there are more specific differences in the receptive fields of cells of the cortex that we must describe.

Simple Cells Some cells have comparatively simple receptive fields; a vigorous response will occur from a small, elongated straight-line segment, such as that formed by a narrow slit or bar of light (e.g., a dark bar against a light background or the reverse) or an edge. The receptive fields of these cortical cells also require the stimulus to be in a particular location and in a certain orientation (Figure 3.28). If the angle of the bar is altered as little as 15°, the cell's response decreases. Hubel and Wiesel labeled the cells that respond to such simple but selective environmental features **simple cells.**

Complex Cells Another class of cells identified by Hubel and Wiesel are labeled **complex cells.** Like simple cells, complex cells are *orientation specific,* that is, they react maximally to stimuli that are in a particular orientation. However, the receptive fields of complex cells are usually larger than those

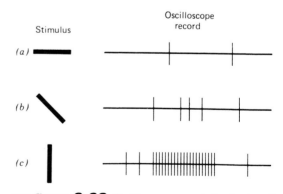

□ **figure 3.28** Oscilloscope record of a simple cell whose maximal response is to a vertically oriented bar of light. The horizontal bar (a) produces no response; the oblique bar (b) produces a weak response; the vertical bar (c) produces a strong response.

of simple cells. Moreover, compared to simple cells, the properly oriented stimulus may occur anywhere within a relatively large region of the visual field. That is, the exact location of the stimulus feature within the visual field is not critical. Another distinguishing characteristic of a complex cell is that it responds to *movement* of its particular feature within its receptive field area. But, as shown in Figure 3.29, it responds most strongly to movement of the stimulus feature in a specific direction. Thus, for example, a line moved down is responded to vigorously, but not when it is moved up (or to the right or left).

Hypercomplex Cells Hubel and Wiesel also identified a third class of cortical cells that they labeled **hypercomplex cells.** These are similar to complex cells, with receptive fields that are optimally responsive to movement and to specifically oriented stimuli, including corners and edges. For example, one group of hypercomplex cells may respond vigorously to two bars of light set at right angles to each other, suggesting that these cells react selectively to angles and corners. However, the most distinguishing characteristic of a hypercomplex cell is that it responds best to stimuli of a *particular length*. This is illustrated

in Figure 3.30. This feature suggests that hypercomplex cells respond to changes in boundaries. Thus, a hypercomplex cortical cell has a receptive field that will produce maximal cortical activity if the light stimulus is properly oriented, moves in a certain direction across the retina, and is of limited length. Deviations from these requirements may yield weak responses or none at all in the cortical cell whose activity is being recorded.

Overall there appears to be a complex transformation of neural information at various levels in the visual system; cells become more selective and generate greater visual abstraction as stimulation ascends to higher centers. Thus, photoreceptors at the retina react merely when light strikes them; ganglion cells and LGN cells fire vigorously only if the centers (or the contrasting surrounds) of their receptive fields are illuminated; simple cells of the cortex fire to linear segments viewed at specific orientations; complex cells require specific sorts of movement; and hypercomplex cells require stimuli falling within their receptive fields to be of a particular size. Kandel (1985) summarizes this neural hierarchy in the visual system as follows:

> *At the lowest level of the system, the level of the retinal ganglion and lateral geniculate cells, neurons respond primarily to brightness contrast. As we move up the hierarchy to the simple and complex cells of the cortex, cells begin to respond to line segments and boundaries. The hypercomplex cells respond to changes in boundaries. Thus, as we progress up the system the stimulus requirements necessary to activate a cell become more precise. . . . At each level, each cell sees more than do the cells at the lower level, and higher cells have a greater capacity for abstraction. (p. 381)*

Orientation Columns and Hypercolumns Another receptive field property of simple, complex, and hypercomplex cells within the visual cortex applies specifically to the *orientation* of stimuli projected to the visual system; this property describes a very interesting aspect of the physical organization—the *functional architecture*—of the visual cortex. A useful way to introduce this feature is to describe

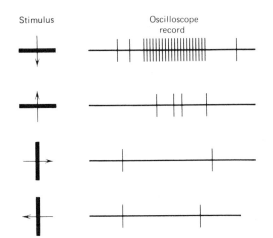

□ **figure 3.29** Oscilloscope record of a complex cell sensitive to the direction of motion. This cell responds strongly only to downward stimulus motion. It responds weakly to upward motion and does not respond at all to sideways motion.

Stimulus   Oscilloscope record

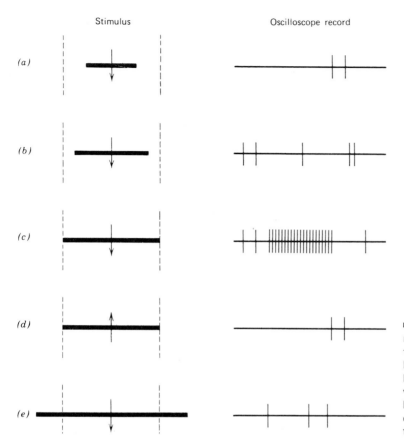

figure **3.30** Oscilloscope record of a hypercomplex cell sensitive to direction and length of stimulus. Only a stimulus of a certain length and moving downward (c) yields a strong response. (The length of the receptive field is indicated by the distance bounded by the dashed vertical lines.)

the procedures used to produce it (Hubel & Wiesel, 1974). A microelectrode is inserted straight down into the cortex in a direction perpendicular to the surface (Figure 3.31). As the microelectrode penetrates through the cortical layers (a distance of about 2 mm), the receptive fields of the vertical stack of tens of thousands of simple, complex, and hypercomplex cells encountered all show the same preferred orientation. In other words, the receptive fields of all the cells aligned within a given column react best to a single stimulus orientation. This vertical arrangement of cells that show the same orientation preference is appropriately labeled **orientation columns.**

By systematically moving and reinserting the microelectrode over parts of the surface of the cortex, Hubel and Wiesel revealed the existence of series of orientation columns. In the process, they observed an interesting phenomenon: The receptive fields for the

cells of adjacent columns showed a gradual but progressive shift in orientation preference (Figure 3.32). Starting from, say, a horizontal bar oriented at 0°, the receptive fields of cells for the immediately adjacent column (about 0.05 mm away) showed a preference for a stimulus oriented at about 10°; in turn, the orientation preference for the next column was for a stimulus oriented at 20°, and so on, until the preferred orientation was to a 90° vertical stimulus, then gradually shifting back to a horizontal stimulus, thereby completing a cycle of orientations (i.e., rotating 180°). This progression through a complete set of orientations is analogous to the positions assumed by the sweep of the second hand of a watch: Beginning horizontally at 9:00 o'clock, gradually advancing to vertical at 12:00 o'clock, and then back to horizontal at 3:00 o'clock. In Hubel and Wiesel's observation, the completion of a full cycle of all orientations spanned

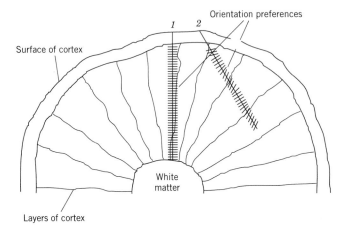

□ **figure 3.31** Vertical columns of the visual cortex. If a microelectrode is inserted perpendicular to the surface of the cortex, the receptive fields of all cells through which it passes assume the same orientation. This is shown for the microelectrode at position *1*. The vertical stack of cells that have the same orientation preference is the orientation column. The microelectrode at position *2* penetrates the cortex at a somewhat oblique angle, crossing over a number of different columns and stimulating cells with a mixture of orientation preferences. (Based on Hubel & Wiesel, 1962.)

about 18 to 20 columns and extended over a distance of about 1 mm. Thus, they revealed the existence of a series or cluster of adjacent columns whose cells possessed receptive fields that systematically represented all possible orientations.

Orientation columns are also organized with regard to which eye is stimulated. Although cells in the cortex receive information from both eyes, they are more receptive and usually show a greater response to stimulation by either the left or the right eye. Cortical cells show a greater response to stimulation of one eye or the other, a tendency called *ocular dominance*. In fact, Hubel and Wiesel (1977) observed that the surface of the cortex is made up of an alternating

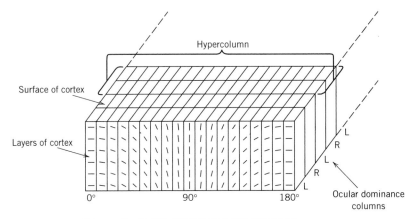

Columns of cells with different orientation preferences

□ **figure 3.32** Schematic diagram of orientation columns and hypercolumns in a cross section of the visual cortex. The receptive fields of all cells in a column have the same orientation preference. However, the receptive fields of cells within adjacent columns have different orientation preferences. As illustrated, the orientation preferences change in a gradual but systematic fashion. Each orientation column is about 0.05 mm in width and changes by about 10° in orientation preference. Accordingly, a distance of approximately 1 mm includes all possible orientations.

Ocular dominance is shown at the right of the figure. Columns of cells dominated by the left eye alternate with columns dominated by the right eye. A cluster or module of about 18 to 20 adjacent orientation columns (required to complete a full cycle of stimulus orientation preferences), which includes columns for the left and the right eye (i.e., ocular dominance columns), is called a *hypercolumn*.

series of ocular dominance columns (indicated in Figure 3.32), with each column favoring the stimulation received from either the left or the right eye. Thus, the cortex is organized into ocular dominance columns as well as orientation columns. As shown in Figure 3.32, a cluster (or *module,* as it is sometimes called) of adjacent columns that includes all possible orientations, as well as columns for the left and right eyes (i.e., ocular dominance columns), is called a **hypercolumn.**

Cortical Magnification There are tens of thousands of hypercolumns and they occur throughout the visual cortex, each serving a small region of the retina. That is, each hypercolumn reacts to a particular location on the retina. However, while the hypercolumns are approximately uniform in size, they are not equally linked to all areas of the retina. Instead, the retinal area near the fovea is allotted much more cortical space, and hence more hypercolumns, than an area of similar size of the peripheral retina. This unequal but functionally relevant allocation of cortical representation of the area of the fovea relative to the peripheral retina is called **cortical magnification.** This arrangement makes sense given that the foveal receptors are very dense, whereas the peripheral receptors are much more diffuse. Moreover, while cortical magnification means that a large area of the cortex is devoted to a small area of the retina, it also means that more cortical space is allotted to the specific parts of the retina that are responsible for perceiving fine detail and acute vision (i.e., the fovea). This is also an example of an important organizing principle of the nervous system: The amount of neural tissue of a feature-analyzing structure or region (e.g., the LGN or the cortex) devoted to a receptor surface (the fovea, in this case) is proportional to the functional importance of that surface rather than to its size or area (Kandel, Schwartz, & Jessell, 1995).

Cortical Cells and Feature Detection

We have observed that information processing occurs in a number of regions within the visual system. It occurs within the ganglion level of the retina and within the LGN. In addition, cells of the primary visual cortex fire in response to fairly specific features of the stimulus, in particular to stimulus orientation, movement, and size. The reaction of cells to specific features is even more pronounced in certain areas of the cortex that lie outside the primary visual cortex of the occipital lobe. One area of the brain that appears to contribute to specific, complex feature detection is located in the **temporal lobe** (which corresponds roughly to the region of the brain that lies right behind the temples of the skull). A particularly interesting area of the temporal lobe for feature detection is located in its lower portion, the *inferotemporal cortex.* Gross, Rocha-Miranda, and Bender (1972) identified a small group of cortical cells in the inferotemporal cortex of the Macaque monkey whose receptive fields were specifically sensitive to size, shape, orientation, direction of movement, and color characteristics. Moreover, there were some rather unusual, even startling, response characteristics. Gross et al. found one cell in this cortical region whose activity was triggered by the outline shape of a monkey's hand. Interestingly, an outline of the fingers pointing down elicited very little response compared with the outline of the fingers pointing upward or laterally; these latter orientations, of course, are the ones in which the monkey would ordinarily see its own hand. In addition, some cells of the monkey's inferotemporal cortex have been identified that markedly alter their activity pattern and respond more vigorously to the profiles of monkey faces than to other stimuli (Desimone et al., 1984; see also Desimone, 1991). As Figure 3.33 illustrates, such cells responded strongly to the monkey profiles and very weakly to rear or front views or to stimuli such as a bottle brush. Additionally, altering or removing some of the elements of the profiles significantly reduced cell response.

Striking response specificity has also been observed in another region of the temporal lobe called the *superior temporal cortex.* Bruce, Desimone, and Gross (1981) found some cells in this region of the monkey's brain that responded most vigorously to drawings of a monkey's full face. Removing the eyes or showing a cartoon-like caricature significantly reduced cell response. Another region of the temporal

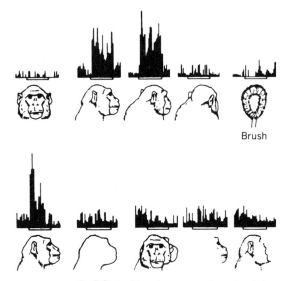

Brush

━━ *figure* **3.33** Activity of neurons of monkey inferotemporal cortex to profiles. Shown are some of the stimulus figures presented and a graphic rendering of the activity
pattern of certain neurons of the monkeys' cortex. The
graphs above each figure give the number of action potentials or spikes discharged by the neurons (vertical axis)
over time (horizontal axis). The time during which each
stimulus was presented is represented by the line under
each graph. (From R. Desimone et al., *Journal of Neuroscience,*
4, 1984, p. 2159. Reprinted by permission of the Society for Neuroscience.)

lobe of the monkey is responsible for the identification
of particular faces (Young & Yamane, 1992).

Feature Detection in Lower Animals

It should be recognized that feature-specific cells are
not restricted to primates. Kendrick and Baldwin
(1987) observed cells in the temporal cortex of a
horned breed of sheep (while the sheep were conscious) that responded preferentially to life-sized projections of various faces, ranging from those of other
sheep to those of other animals, including human
faces. They reported that cells specifically responsive
to facial stimuli could be linked to factors relevant to
social interactions among sheep. For example, they
found groups of cells selectively responsive to the
presence and size of the horns on sheep faces, "possibly allowing for a rapid estimation of the perceived

animal's sex or position in the dominance hierarchy"
(p. 450).

The cortical organization outlined in the preceding sections is not typical of the visual systems of many
lower species. Animals possessing a comparatively
primitive visual cortex (e.g., the rabbit and ground
squirrel) or lacking it completely (e.g., the pigeon and
frog) usually have highly integrative mechanisms in
the retina (Michael, 1969).

Lettvin and his colleagues (1959) published a classic neurophysiological analysis of the frog's vision
that identifies several distinct kinds of pattern or form
detectors in the retina of the frog. By recording the
neural activity of single fibers in the frog's optic nerve
in response to different visual stimuli, several distinct
types of fibers were identified, each type concerned
with a different sort of pattern or visual event. Some
fibers reacted to sharp edges and borders, movement
of edges, and general dimming or darkening of illumination. Most interesting were the "bug perceivers,"
so called by the authors because these were nerve
fibers that responded best to small, dark objects intermittently moving across the visual field. In the authors' words:

> *Such a fiber responds best when a dark object,*
> *smaller than a receptive field, enters that field,*
> *stops, and moves about intermittently thereafter.*
> *The response is not affected if the lighting changes*
> *or if the background (say a picture of grass and*
> *flowers) is moving, and is not there if only the*
> *background, moving or still, is in the field. Could*
> *one better describe a system for detecting an acces-*
> *sible bug? (p. 1951).*

The functional value of bug perceivers to the frog,
primarily an insect eater, is obvious. Thus the frog,
possessing a primitive brain, has a highly complex
retina that enables much of the processing, organizing,
and interpretation of visual stimuli to occur within the
eye itself. It appears that whether visual information
is processed at the retina or in the brain depends on
the evolutionary development of the species.

Are There Feature Detectors? Gi-

ven the preceding discussion, especially for primate

vision, it is reasonable to question the role that cortical cells play in global perception. Is our perception of specific objects—for example, biologically relevant objects like faces and hands—due directly and exclusively to the firing of certain cells in the brain? In short, are there specific and unique cortical cells for detecting specific features? Probably the answer is no. For one thing, the vast majority of cortical cells are not sufficiently precise or finely tuned enough for specific objects; in fact, to some degree, most cells respond to any complex stimulus. The notion of specific feature detector cells is also questioned on statistical grounds: Even given the enormous number of cortical cells, there are just too many details, features, and objects in the visual environment to assign a specific cortical cell to each one. Moreover, each distinct perception would have to be backed up by a collection of identical cells; otherwise, the death of a single cell (which occurs frequently) could mean the loss of a particular perception, that is, the loss of the ability to recognize a specific object or feature.

A reasonable alternative to the idea of individual cortical cells as feature detectors is based on the fact that cortical cells do not act in isolation. They interact and participate with each other in a broad network of cortical activity. Probably a single cortical cell participates in many perceptual tasks, and the perception of an object such as a face results from the activity of a constellation of cortical cells. In other words, the representation of an object or a specific complex feature is probably the result of a pattern of activity across a network of interacting cells, cells linked by a tendency to react to similar stimulus features and properties—not the activation of a single feature detector cell.

Additionally, we may consider the role played in feature detection by the various retinotopic maps that exist within the cortex. As noted in an earlier discussion, the retina projects on the LGN: That is, the LGN contains an orderly representation, or topographic map, of the retina. Preservation of the topography of the retina is also found in the cellular organization of the visual cortex. In fact, there are retinotopic maps in a number of cortical regions creating multiple representations of the retina and the visual field in the cortex. For example, a number of regions of both the occipital lobe and the temporal lobe each have separate representations of the visual world mapped onto them. Why are there multiple retinotopic maps? Each cortical area performs different processing tasks, each requiring specific information of a stimulus that falls within the visual field. Some regions may be specialized for analyzing color, some for movement, orientation, or depth, and so on. This specialization and segregation of function is not unfamiliar, considering the distinctions between the X, Y, and W cells at the ganglion level, and between the parvocellular and magnocellular division in the LGN. Accordingly, each retinotopic map isolates and extracts some necessary and specific property or feature of the array in the visual field. This functional segregation implies that impairment of any of these cortical maps (or specific visual pathways leading to them) could cause subtle disruptions in normal visual abilities, depending on the map or pathway affected. In examining this possibility, Livingstone and her colleagues (1991) studied the relation of defects in the magnocellular division of the LGN to *dyslexia* (a disorder of unknown origin involving selective impairment in perceptual skills, such as reading, despite normal intelligence and sensory function). These researchers found that dyslexics, who perform poorly in tests requiring rapid visual processing of low-contrast stimuli, also have abnormalities in cells of the magnocellular division of the LGN (fast-acting cells relatively responsive to low-contrast stimuli). This suggests that dyslexia is linked, at least in part, to defective functioning of a specific set of brain cells. This relationship also supports the broader notion that the discrimination of specific environmental signals—perhaps perceptions in general—is represented by the activity of specialized neural units segregated in specific regions of the visual system.

Our purpose in this chapter was to introduce basic visual structures, functions, and phenomena; to survey the neurophysiological bases of visual processing; and to examine the flow of information throughout the visual system. The primary neural units and pathways involved in the exchange of neural information are presented in Figure 3.34. In the next chapter, we extend our discussion of vision to specific visual functions and properties, drawing on some of the physio-

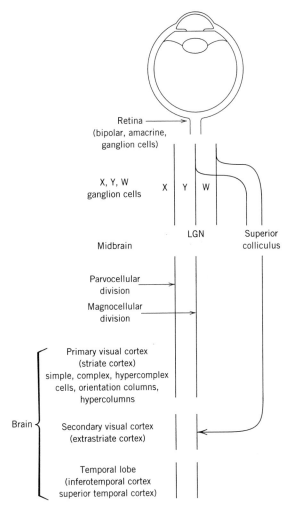

Retina
(bipolar, amacrine,
ganglion cells)

X, Y, W
ganglion cells   X | Y | W

                        LGN   Superior
Midbrain   colliculus

Parvocellular
   division
Magnocellular
   division

Primary visual cortex
   (striate cortex)
simple, complex, hypercomplex
cells, orientation columns,
        hypercolumns

Brain   Secondary visual cortex
               (extrastriate cortex)

         Temporal lobe
   (inferotemporal cortex
   superior temporal cortex)

□ *figure* **3.34** Schematic summarizing some of the structures, connections, major pathways, and neural routes that lie between the retina and the brain. Some of the structures and their connections comprise functional processing units or systems of the visual system. The *geniculostriate visual system*—involved in object identification and recognition—consists of the central retina (including the fovea), the LGN, and the primary visual cortex. The *retinotectal visual system*—involved in locating objects—consists of the central and peripheral retina, the superior colliculus, and the secondary visual cortex. The functional significance of both of these processing systems for identification and localization is described in the next chapter.

logical principles described in this chapter. In general, this chapter and the next also lay the groundwork for the remainder of the book. Many of the properties and characteristics of the eye and the visual system illustrate general principles governing the translation of sensory information that pertain to all the senses.

SUMMARY

This chapter introduced the subject of vision. We began with a discussion of the nature of the visual stimulus—light, noting that the corresponding psychologi-

cal effects that the physical dimensions of the wavelength and intensity of light have on the observer are color (or hue) and brightness, respectively. The specification and measurement of light intensity was examined with respect to the radiant energy falling on the surface—incident light, or illuminance—and the intensity of the light reaching the eye from a surface—reflected light, or luminance.

The basic anatomical structures and functions of the eye were elaborated. The major parts outlined were the cornea, the iris and pupil, the lens, and their supporting structures. This was followed by a description of the retina, its neural connections and photoreceptors—the rods and cones. The functional significance of the neural connections of rods and cones for sensitivity and acuity, respectively, was also examined.

Some evolutionary trends in the placement of the eyes and the size of the visual field were described. A tendency was noted for prey animals to possess laterally directed eyes, resulting in a larger total visual field, and for predatory animals or animals with strong manipulative skill such as primates, to possess frontally directed eyes.

The dynamic processes of the lens, especially accommodation, were described. Some problems of lens refraction were specified: presbyopia, hypermetropia, myopia, spherical and chromatic aberration, and astigmatism. It was concluded that specific forms of visual exposure, especially excessive near viewing in young individuals, may contribute significantly to myopia. Psychological factors in eyeblinks and changes in pupil size were also considered.

Next, we examined the structural and functional mechanisms in the neural pathways between the retina and the primary visual projection area of the brain. Neural structures that serve as processing and transmission centers for the visual signals from the retina to the primary visual cortex were described. We then considered the superior colliculus and the relation between ganglion cells of the retina to the LGN of the thalamus.

The notion of receptive fields for various locations in the visual system was discussed. Briefly, a receptive field for a given receptor cell or neuron is the region of the retina or visual field that, when appropriately stimulated, excites or inhibits the cell's firing pattern. Many different kinds of receptive fields and cells were identified. Receptive fields and their functions were described for ganglion cells of the retina, called X, Y, and W cells. Receptive fields and their functions were also described for the LGN; these consist of small and large receptive cell divisions called the parvocellular and magnocellular divisions, respectively. Finally, receptive fields for the visual cortex were discussed, including simple cells, complex cells, and hypercomplex cells. The structural and functional organization of the receptive fields of the visual cortex were considered, in particular, orientation columns, hyperco-

lumns, and cortical magnification. The chapter ended with a discussion on the role of cortical cells in feature detection.

KEY TERMS

Accommodation

Acuity

Astigmatism

Bipolar Cells

Blind Spot

Brightness

Center-Surround Receptive Fields

Choroid

Chromatic Aberration

Ciliary Muscles

Color

Complex Cells

Compound Eye

Cones

Cornea

Cortical Magnification

Fovea

Ganglion Cells

Hue

Hypercolumns

Hypercomplex Cells

Hyperopia (or Hypermetropia)

Illuminance

Intensity

Iris

Lateral Geniculate Nucleus (LGN)

Lens

Luminance

Macula lutea

Magnocellular Division (of the LGN)

Myopia

Nanometer (nm)

Near Point

Near-Work (Use-Abuse) Theory

Ommatidia

Optic Chiasma (or Chiasm)

Optic Disk

Orientation Columns

Parvocellular Division (of the LGN)

Photon

Presbyopia

Pupil

Pupillometry

Radiant Electromagnetic Energy

Receptive Field

Red-Eye

Refractive Errors

Retina

Retinotopic Map

Rods

Sclera

Sensitivity

Simple Cells

Spherical Aberration

Superior Colliculus

Tapetum

Temporal Lobe

Thalamus

Visual Capture

W Cells

Wavelength

Whytt's Reflex

X Cells

Y Cells

STUDY QUESTIONS

1. Discuss the importance of vision for gaining spatial information. Indicate the kinds of information that are received by the visual system.

2. Distinguish between intensity and brightness and between illuminance and luminance.

3. What structural components are common to various kinds of image-forming eyes? Consider in what way the eye is like a camera.

4. Describe the functioning of each major component of the anterior of the eye, including the cornea, iris (or pupil), and lens. Explain how the change in pupil size is due to changes in light conditions.

5. Identify the retina and its major photoreceptor elements (rods and cones), describing the functional purposes of the rods and cones. Distinguish between rods and cones with respect to their location relative to the fovea and their relative distribution in the retina. Define visual sensitivity and acuity and explain how the different neural connections of the rods and cones may account for sensitivity and acuity, respectively.

6. What is the functional significance of frontal and lateral placement of the eyes in the head for different species? Indicate the benefit of each for meeting the survival needs of a given species.

7. Outline the mechanism of accommodation, and indicate how it is measured. Discuss its limits and describe the accommodative or refractive errors of presbyopia, hypermetropia, and myopia. Consider the origin of myopia. Outline evidence supporting the notion that myopia may be caused, in part, by experiential factors.

8. Describe lens aberrations and astigmatism. What limiting or distortion effects do these conditions have on the refractive capacity of the lens to form a true or useful image?

9. Outline the sorts of lighting conditions and cognitive processing tasks that affect pupil mobility. What stimulus features appear to cause pupil constriction and dilation?

10. Why don't we momentarily "see" darkness every time we blink? What is the relationship between eyeblinks and attention and information processing?

11. Outline the major connections between the eye and brain, indicating the interaction of neural tracts at the optic chiasma, relay stages at the LGN, and optical projections to the occipital lobe of the brain.

12. Explain how the right visual field is represented on the left side of the brain and how the left visual field is represented on the right side of the brain. Indicate these connections by tracing the visual field projections to the retina and the retinal projections to the occipital lobe.

13. What are receptive fields for vision? Identify and describe the different kinds of receptive fields for the retina and the LGN. What are X, Y, and W ganglion cells? Identify and compare the parvocellular and magnocellular divisions of the LGN.

14. Identify and describe the different kinds of cortical cells defined by receptive field excitation (i.e., simple, complex, and hypercomplex cells).

What are orientation columns and hypercolumns of the visual cortex?

15. Discuss the various sorts of stimuli that are effective for stimulating the receptive fields of cells of the visual cortex. Examine the possibility that there are specific cortical cells for detecting specific features. Consider the role played by various parts of the temporal lobe in feature detection.

chapter 4

FUNDAMENTAL VISUAL FUNCTIONS AND PHENOMENA

The previous chapter emphasized the visual stimulus and the means by which the visual system translates light into neural information. In the present chapter we continue this discussion, with greater emphasis on some of the basic functional properties and processes that make the visual system more efficient. To do so, we elaborate on the distinction made between vision performed by rods and by cones, and we describe the different activities most effectively performed by each. In particular, we describe the forms of stimulation that significantly affect the efficiency of rod and cone vision, stressing the perceptual and physiological events that occur in dim and bright environments. This brings us to the factors affecting thresholds for vision, such as the size of the retinal area stimulated, as well as the effect of the intensity, duration, wavelength, and movement of light on stimulus detection. We then discuss visual acuity, indicating how it is measured and identifying some of the main factors that enhance or degrade it. This is followed by a section on the main categories of eye movements, including their role in general visual exploration and in visually guided cognitive tasks such as reading. Finally, we end this chapter with a proposal: There are two kinds of visual systems, each with its own set of neural connections linking the retina to the brain—the primary focal one, for identifying objects, and a secondary ambient one, for localizing objects. This discussion includes a brief discussion of "blindsight," the unusual notion that some individuals, totally blind with respect to the primary system, are still able to use the localization system.

SCOTOPIC AND PHOTOPIC VISION

In the preceding chapter, we distinguished between rods and cones with respect to anatomy, location, relative distribution, and neural connections. Some of these distinctions are reflected in their functional properties. Vision performed with cones is termed **photopic** vision (from the Greek stem *phot,* meaning "light," and *optos,* meaning "to see"), whereas vision accomplished with rods is called **scotopic** vision (from the Greek *skotos,* meaning "darkness"). The properties of rods and cones are summarized in Table 4.1. Several of these properties have been introduced; some will be described in the sections to follow.

The rods and cones in the retinas of many species show adaptive trends. In nocturnal animals, the retina consists primarily of rods, best suited for night vision; that is, the retina has high light *sensitivity* rather than acuity. In contrast, in day-active animals, the retina is

□ *table 4.1* Properties of Photopic (Cone) and Scotopic (Rod) Vision of Humans

	Photopic	Scotopic
Receptor	Cones (ca. 7 million)	Rods (ca. 125 million)
Retinal location	Concentration in fovea	Peripheral retina
Functional luminance level	Daylight	Night light
Peak wavelength	550 nm	500 nm
Color vision	Yes	No
Dark adaptation	Rapid (ca. 5 min)	Slow (ca. 30 min)
Spatial resolution	High acuity, low sensitivity	Low acuity, high sensitivity

either almost totally dominated by cones (e.g., most species of birds) and possesses high *acuity,* or has both rods and cones (e.g., primates), with both sensitivity and acuity.

In general, cone-mediated vision is poor in a dimly lit environment and scotopic vision dominates. Thus, when gazing at a faint star at night, we are more successful with indirect vision, that is, when we do not fixate directly on the star. By doing this, we ensure that the image falls on the sensitive rods in the peripheral regions of the retina rather than on the cone-concentrated fovea.

ADAPTATION

One fundamental difference between rods and cones is in their response to general lighting conditions. When moving abruptly from a well-lit to a poorly lit or dark environment, we initially experience temporary blindness. However, gradually some of the visual features in the dim surroundings become visible, and we are able to see some details; that is, our sensitivity gradually increases. The process of adjusting to a dimly illuminated environment is called **dark adaptation.** We experience it almost every time we enter a dimly lit auditorium or movie theater.

Just as exposure to the dark increases the sensitivity of the retina, exposure to the light decreases it in a process called **light adaptation.** Exposure of the dark-adapted eye to light results at first in a rapid elevation of the threshold (i.e., a loss in sensitivity) that continues briefly, but at a slower and slower rate, and then levels off in several minutes. The behavioral effects of light adaptation may be strong. When the

dark-adapted retina is suddenly confronted with intense light, as when entering bright daylight from a dark auditorium, the immediate sensation may be quite unpleasant, even painful.

In the sections to follow, we will describe some of the phenomena related to both dark and light adaptation of the visual system and to changes in the conditions of lighting. However, as it has been studied in greater detail, our focus will be on dark adaptation.

Measuring Dark Adaptation

One means of measuring dark adaptation is as follows: The subject is first exposed to a highly illuminated surface (in essence, to a controlled form of light adaptation) for a short period of time. This reduces the subject's sensitivity and provides a well-defined starting level from which the time course of dark adaptation can be traced. The subject is then exposed to a dark environment, and at various intervals, the absolute threshold for a light stimulus is measured. The light stimulus is of a specific wavelength, duration, and energy level and strikes a precise area on the retina. The result is a curve relating the minimum energy required to reach threshold to the amount of time in the dark. Figure 4.1 presents a typical dark adaptation curve. The figure shows the decrease in the threshold (or increase in sensitivity, plotted on the *y*-axis) with continued exposure to the darkened environment (shown on the *x*-axis).

The dark adaptation curve of Figure 4.1 is composed of two segments, reflecting the two different rates of adaptive change taking place. The upper branch is for cones and the lower one is for rods. During the early stages of adaptation, there is an initial

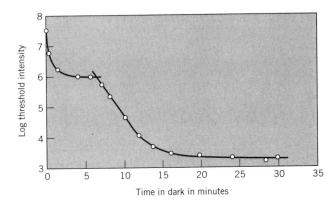

□ **figure 4.1** Change in the visual threshold during dark adaptation. The top branch of the curve is for cones, the bottom one for the rods. (After Hecht & Shlaer, 1938.)

rapid fall in threshold that quickly reaches a stable plateau; this reflects the increase in sensitivity for cones. The total gain in the sensitivity of cones is much less extensive than that of the rods, and it is completed in about 5 to 10 minutes of dark exposure. The lower segment of the curve of Figure 4.1 represents the dark adaptation of rods. The increase in sensitivity over time for rods requires 20 to 30 minutes of continual exposure to the dark. Thus, after about a half hour of dark adaptation, the sensitivity of the eye is many times greater than it was at the onset of the dark adaptation process.

DEMONSTRATION:
Light and Dark Adaptation

However, even though the gain in sensitivity due to dark adaptation is typically gradual and takes time to complete, it can be terminated by a brief exposure to bright light. Consider this demonstration, which not only points out the fragile nature of dark adaptation but also contrasts the experience of dark adaptation with that of light adaptation. Remain in a relatively dark room for about 20 to 30 minutes or until the eyes are fully dark adapted. Your sensitivity will then be high, and you will be able to see clearly any available light. Now tightly cover one eye so that nothing is seen by it and turn on a bright light for a second or two, looking at it

(and thus light-adapting it) only with your uncovered eye. Immediately turn off the light and compare the vision in the two eyes, opening one, then the other. The eye that was covered during the light exposure still retains its sensitivity, whereas the uncovered eye that has been light adapted is essentially blind. Thus, what has taken about a half hour to complete (i.e., dark adaptation) has been wiped out in a moment of light adaptation.

We are ordinarily unaware of the course of dark adaptation because the normal transition from daylight to night occurs so gradually. A speculation on the typical time course of dark adaptation is offered by Buss (1973):

At first glance the half hour required to adapt fully to the dark of night would appear to be maladaptive. A visually deficient animal would surely fall prey to other animals under these conditions, but . . . rapid changes from light to dark occur mainly in man's technological advanced civilization. In nature a rapid change from light to dark would occur only when an animal entered a cave, and most animals tend to avoid caves. The natural transition from light to dark requires approximately 20 minutes—the period of twilight between the sun's setting and darkness of night—and this period matches the time it takes for dark adaptation to be completed. (pp. 196–197)

The Photochemical Basis of Dark Adaptation

Adaptation to the dark involves a complex chemical change within the rods. The rods of most vertebrates contain a light-absorbing pigment called **rhodopsin;** stimulation of this pigment marks the first stage in response to light energy. A form of rhodopsin was originally discovered in the rods of the frog by Franz Boll of the University of Rome in 1876. It was a brilliant red pigment, and accordingly called *rhodopsin* (from the Greek *rhodon,* meaning "rose," and *opsis,* for "sight" or "vision"; Le Grand, 1968; Wald, 1950).

Rhodopsin is an unstable chemical readily altered by light energy; when exposed to light, it is broken down, or *bleached* (so called because the apparent color of the pigment changes in stages from red to colorless; technically, the molecular change in rhodopsin on light exposure is termed *isomerization*). In contrast, rhodopsin regenerates in darkness.

Although there are important neural changes relevant to dark adaptation, rhodopsin regeneration is the basic photochemical process underlying dark adaptation for rods. The multistate cycle of bleaching and the synthesis of rhodopsin as a function of the light environment of the eye are diagrammed in Figure 4.2. Rhodopsin is bleached by light to form *retinal,* a yellow plant pigment found in all photoreceptors, and *opsin,* a colorless protein. With continued bleaching, retinal is converted to a form of vitamin A (also called

retinol). In the regenerative portion of the cycle, when the eye is kept in the dark, vitamin A joins with opsin to reconstitute rhodopsin. Thus, an equilibrium is established between the decomposition of rhodopsin by light and its subsequent regeneration, or synthesis, from its constituent elements in the dark.

Night Blindness Since vitamin A is integral to the restoration of rhodopsin, a serious deficiency of it will markedly alter dark adaptation. In fact, a critical lack of vitamin A in the diet may produce a pathological difficulty in seeing at night or in dim illumination called **night blindness** (or **nyctalopia** or sometimes called *hemeralopia*). There is evidence of extensive retinal damage due to continued vitamin A deficiency. Dowling and Wald (1960) deprived rats (which have mainly rod retinas) of vitamin A. After 8 weeks the rats' sensitivity decreased radically; they required up to 1000 times more light to produce a neural response from the retina. With continued vitamin A depletion the poor cell nutrition became irreversible, the rods degenerated, and the rats became permanently blind (see also Dowling, 1966).

The Neural Basis of Dark Adaptation Factors other than changes in rhodopsin concentration may be involved in adaptation (Schnapf & Baylor, 1987; Wang et al., 1994). In fact, visual sensitivity may vary somewhat without correspondingly large changes in the concentration of rhodopsin. Moreover, the cycle of rhodopsin bleaching and regeneration occurs more slowly than does the change in threshold and sensitivity (Baker, 1953). Along with the photochemical processes just outlined, there are neural processes that may contribute to some of the threshold and sensitivity changes in adaptation. For example, according to MacLeod, Chen, and Crognale (1989), the rise in the visual threshold and the adjustment in sensitivity produced by the bleaching of rhodopsin do not take place within the rods themselves; instead, they contend, adaptation occurs at a later neural site (perhaps at the bipolar level), where signals from many rods are pooled (recall from Chapter 3 that the pooling of signals is a dominant neural characteristic of rods). According to this view, each rod that is illumi-

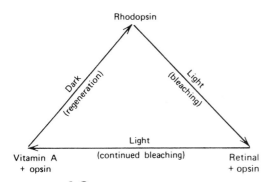

◻ *figure* **4.2** Simplified diagram of the photochemical cycle underlying dark adaptation. Rhodopsin also undergoes several intermediate chemical stages of decomposition before its molecule splits into retinal and opsin.

nated and bleached sends a signal to a neural "adaptation pool," which then regulates the sensitivity of a large group of rods, suggesting that adaptation does not occur in a single stage. However, these neural processes are not well understood. We conclude that adaptation is likely mediated by both photochemical and neural processes (see Pugh, 1988).

To summarize, there are several important functional differences between rods and cones. Cones dark adapt more swiftly than do rods but are ultimately far less sensitive; although relatively slow to dark adapt, rods enable greater sensitivity in dim lighting conditions than do cones. There is an additional important functional difference between rods and cones. This difference is linked not only to the overall conditions of illumination and adaptation but also to the *wavelength* of the illumination.

Spectral Sensitivity and the Purkinje Shift

Another functional distinction between photopic and scotopic vision is that rods and cones are not equally sensitive to the entire visible spectrum. Different wavelengths of light differ markedly in their effect on the photoreceptors of the eye. This is illustrated by Figure 4.3, where threshold values are plotted against wavelengths to obtain **spectral threshold curves.** This is a complex functional relationship because threshold level—the amount of radiant energy necessary for light of a particular wavelength to be detected—depends on the adaptive state of the eye and the kinds of receptors that are stimulated. The threshold values for photopic vision, shown in the upper curve, result when the eye is light adapted to moderately high intensities, such as in daylight. It is quite elevated relative to the threshold values for the scotopic vision of the dark-adapted eye, shown in the lower curve. Reading from the figure, the wavelength with the lowest threshold for photopic vision is in the region of 550 nm (appearing as a yellow-green color), whereas for scotopic vision the lowest threshold is in the region of 500 nm.

Recall that threshold and sensitivity are inversely related. Thus, the difference in sensitivity between photopic and scotopic vision for wavelength can be

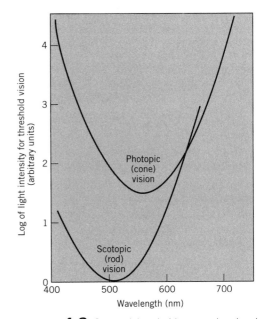

□ *figure 4.3* Spectral threshold curves showing the relative amounts of light energy required to reach threshold as a function of wavelength. The rods require less radiant energy than the cones for threshold visibility at all wavelengths except the very long ones (about 650 nm and above), where photopic cone vision has a slightly lower threshold (i.e., it is slightly more sensitive; see Figure 4.4). The vertical distance between the two curves represents the colorless photochromatic interval. (Based on Wald, 1945; revised from Chapanis, 1949, p. 12.)

plotted as the reciprocal of threshold values. This is given in Figure 4.4, which yields **spectral sensitivity curves.** As illustrated, the peak sensitivity for rods (centered at about 500 nm) is for shorter wavelengths than the peak sensitivity for cones (centered at about 550 nm). This difference in the sensitivity of rods and cones to different wavelengths of light means that as vision shifts from photopic to scotopic during dark adaptation, it becomes more sensitive to short wavelengths of light. In perceptual terms, certain wavelengths of light will appear brighter than others, depending on whether photopic or scotopic vision is used.

Only when light levels are sufficient to activate photopic vision does the perception of colors or hues occur. When visual stimulation reaches only scotopic levels, stimulating only rods, weak lights are visible

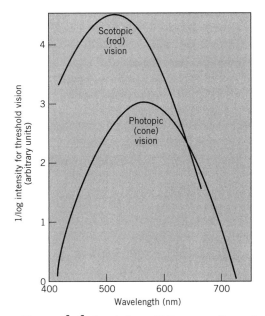

figure 4.4 Spectral sensitivity curves. The reciprocal of the threshold values of Figure 4.3 is plotted on the *y*-axis to illustrate the sensitivity of scotopic and photopic vision across wavelength. As shown, scotopic rod vision is more sensitive than photopic cone vision for all wavelengths up to about 650 nm. Beyond that level, photopic vision is more sensitive.

but colorless; that is, all wavelengths are seen as a series of grays. This is illustrated in Figure 4.3. The colorless interval in radiant energy for a given wavelength—the interval between seeing only a light and seeing a color—is given as the vertical distance between the scotopic and photopic threshold curves. This is called the **photochromatic interval.** The photochromatic, or colorless, interval is largest at the short-wavelength end and smallest at the long-wavelength end of the spectrum, where rods and cones are both insensitive. In fact, as illustrated in Figure 4.4, at the long-wavelength end (ca. 650 nm and beyond), the cones are slightly more sensitive than the rods (Cornsweet, 1970; Wald, 1945). This means that if dim lights, whose wavelengths are 650 nm or more, are intense enough to be seen at all, they are also seen as colored (i.e., as red). That is, the intensity of a light around 650 nm that can just stimulate the rods is also sufficiently intense to stimulate the cones (which mediate colors). In fact, because

of the insensitivity of rods to long wavelengths of light, stimulation with light beyond about 650 nm will probably not excite rods at all.

The Purkinje Shift These facts help to explain why, when light intensity is decreased so that vision changes from photopic to scotopic levels, the relative brightness of different colors may change. For example, two equally light surfaces in the photopic conditions of daylight, one red and one green, will differ in brightness when viewed under the scotopic conditions of dim lighting; the formerly red surface appears to be darker than the green one. The shift from photopic to scotopic sensitivity is called the **Purkinje shift,** named for Johannes (Jan) Evangelista von Purkinje, the Czech physiologist who described it in 1825.

In fact, the shift is based on Purkinje's own real-world observation. According to Le Grand (1968), Purkinje noticed that signposts painted in blue and red looked somewhat different at different times of the day. Although the two colors appeared equally bright during the day, at dawn the blue appeared brighter than the red. What was occurring was a change in the brightness of certain wavelengths coincident with the shift from photopic to scotopic vision. It follows that in reduced illumination, utilizing scotopic rod vision, the visual system is more sensitive to shorter wavelengths (see Figure 4.4); hence, the light composed of shorter wavelengths appears to be relatively brighter than when it is observed in high illumination. Thus, using photopic vision during the approach of twilight, the long wavelength "reds" initially appear relatively bright compared to the short wavelength "greens", but as twilight progresses and scotopic vision takes over, the reddish colors appear darker. Since scotopic vision is colorless, within a certain illumination interval daylight greens change to moonlight grays and daylight reds change to moonlight blacks. It is then, as the English dramatist, John Heywood, wrote in 1546, "When all candles be out, all cats be gray."

Red Light and Dark Adaptation The wavelength of the preadapting test light used in dark adaptation has a practical consequence. If the light just prior to adaptation consists of only a single long wavelength (650 nm or more, appearing red), dark adaptation proceeds much more rapidly after the pre-adapting light is turned off than if other wavelengths are used. This is because the photoreceptors are relatively insensitive to the long-wavelength end of the spectrum; hence, they show little light adaptation effect.

There is an interesting practical application. If one must go rapidly from a well-lit to a dimly-lit environment, dark adaptation may be begun in the light by wearing red lenses or goggles (which transmit only long-wavelength light) prior to entering the darkened environment. In fact, preadaptation with long-wavelength ("red") light is nearly as effective a preparation for night vision as being in darkness.

The red goggles serve several functions: Like any light filter, they reduce the amount of light reaching the eyes, so that the eyes are light adapted to a lower intensity level. More important, red goggles let in only long-wavelength red light, to which the rods are especially insensitive. Although the cones are also insensitive to long-wavelength red light, with sufficient intensity they will still function while the more insensitive rods are undergoing dark adaptation. In other words, the available red light only stimulates the cones. Thus, it is only the cones that must subsequently undergo dark adaptation when the goggles are removed in the dark, and, as indicated in the top branch of Figure 4.1, dark adaptation proceeds most rapidly for cone-mediated photopic vision.

LIMITS OF BASIC VISUAL FUNCTION

The Absolute Threshold

Under optimal conditions of testing, the least amount of light necessary to produce a visual sensation—the absolute threshold—is a remarkably small amount. The definitive, classic experiment on threshold determination was performed by Hecht, Shlaer, and Pirenne (1941, 1942). They derived some striking threshold measures under conditions conducive to assessing maximum sensitivity—such as testing the most sensitive part of the dark-adapted retina with the wavelength of light to which it is most sensitive.

They found that the absolute threshold was in the range of 5 to 14 quanta (in luminance terms, the absolute threshold was of the order of 0.000001 mL!). They also estimated that under optimal conditions a single quantum of radiant energy may be sufficient to activate a single rod. Although these values are derived ones and pertain only to the maximal sensitivity that is theoretically possible, they do stress the remarkable sensitivity of the human eye as a light detector.

The limiting capacity of threshold vision appears to be linked to the physical nature of light, suggesting that if the eye were much more sensitive, under certain conditions the discreteness of photon emission might be perceptible and light would then not be perceived as continuous or steady.

Factors Affecting the Absolute Threshold

Aside from stimulus intensity, many other variables affect the absolute threshold of vision: the size of the stimulated area, the duration and wavelength of the light stimulus, and the region of the retina on which the stimulus falls.

Size of the Retina Stimulated: Ricco's Law For relatively small visual areas in the central part of the retina, the likelihood of stimulus detection or a threshold response can be increased by increasing either the stimulus intensity or the size of the retinal area stimulated. There is a trade-off between the size of the area stimulated and the intensity of the stimulus. Thus, within certain limits, all stimuli possessing the same product of area and intensity are equally detectable. This relationship, known as **Ricco's law,** is stated mathematically as follows:

$$A \times I = C$$

where the product of area (A) and intensity (I) produces a constant threshold value (C). In general, Ricco's law states that a constant threshold value is maintained by increasing the area stimulated while decreasing stimulus intensity, or the reverse: If we increase the intensity of a stimulus, we can decrease its size, or vice versa, and still be able to detect it.

This makes intuitive sense, since the same products of area and intensity contain identical amounts of total light energy.

However, for peripheral areas of the retina, covering substantial regions, there is no gain in stimulation from increasing the size of the stimulated area; here the threshold depends on intensity alone. That is, $I = C$. It appears that no single law extends over the full range of the retinal area.

Duration of the Stimulus: Bloch's Law

Within limits, a form of stimulus summation over time also occurs. For relatively brief periods (about 100 msec or less), stimulus intensity and time have a reciprocal relationship for a constant threshold value. That is, a less intense light acting for a relatively long time, and a more intense light acting for a relatively short time, may produce the same effect. Thus, in certain conditions, stimuli with the same product of time and intensity are equally detectable. This is known as **Bloch's law** (or sometimes as **Bunsen-Roscoe law**). With I and C as defined above and T as the stimulus duration, $T \times I = C$. The relationship between intensity and time described by Bloch's law holds best for stimulation of peripheral retinal regions (where the neural convergence of rods is dominant). The effective duration involved may be as long as 100 msec; thereafter, however, the threshold is determined by the intensity of the stimulus alone. Obviously, the reciprocal relationship between time and intensity cannot hold over an indefinite range. That would imply that we could detect a light stimulus of almost infinitesimal intensity, provided it was exposed long enough.

The relationship between time and intensity (for relatively short periods) allows us to take reasonably comparable photographs under varying light conditions. When the light is poor, the exposure time is lengthened in order to collect enough light to expose the film properly. When the light level is high, such as in bright daylight or with a flash, the exposure time may be significantly shortened. What is important to recognize is that the same amount of light energy is necessary to expose the film properly in each condition of light. It just takes less time for the required

amount to be collected in bright light than it does in poor light.

Retinal Location and Wavelength

Two additional points noted earlier must be restated in this context. As the spectral threshold curves (Figure 4.3) show, the absolute threshold depends on the photoreceptors stimulated. Photopic vision, mediated by the cone-concentrated fovea, has a much higher threshold (i.e., is less sensitive) than the scotopic vision of the peripheral retina, containing rods. In general, the eye is most sensitive when light strikes the retinal area where the density of rods is maximal.

The absolute threshold is not equally affected by radiant energy from all portions of the spectrum: It is affected by the wavelength of the light (again, see Figure 4.3).

Perceiving Continuity from Intermittent Light: The CFF

Under certain conditions, a flickering or flashing light may be perceived as continuous. Many common light sources (e.g., fluorescent lights, television screens, motion pictures) appear to give off a steady, constant illumination when, in fact, they emit light that is continuously interrupted. Fluorescent light, for example, flashes about 120 times each second, which means that the bulb is also offset—hence, totally dark—120 times every second. Yet none of this interrupted light is perceived; rather, when a light is flashed at a certain rate, it is perceived as fused, or continuous. That the interrupted light goes undetected is due, in part, to the fact that, once initiated, a visual image persists for a brief period after the physical stimulus is terminated.

The minimum flash or flicker rate of a light source that results in a perceptual shift from apparent flicker to apparent steady, continuous light is known as the **critical flicker frequency (CFF).** (CFF is sometimes applied to the functionally equivalent phenomenon, the **critical fusion frequency**.) In other words, the CFF marks the border between seeing flicker and seeing fusion.

Generally, the more intense the fluctuating stimulus, the higher the frequency rate required to eliminate flicker: The brighter an intermittent light source appears, the easier it is to detect its flicker. Relatedly, weak flashes show greater persistence and fuse at comparatively slow rates. The ability to detect flicker also increases with the size of the flickering display and with the region of the retina that it stimulates. We can often detect the flicker of a sizable light source better when it strikes the peripheral retina rather than the fovea. You have probably verified this for yourself when you noticed, from the "corner of your eye" (i.e., from the edge of your visual field), the annoying flicker when a fluorescent light was defective. When you looked directly at the light, no flicker was apparent.

As we noted, the more intense the stimulus, the greater the frequency required for the threshold of apparent fusion to be reached. However, beyond a certain frequency, fusion occurs regardless of intensity. In addition to the variables of intensity, stimulus size, and retinal location, the CFF is affected by the wavelength of the intermittent light.

ACUITY

In the previous chapter, we discussed briefly some of the anatomical bases of visual acuity. Here we deal primarily with its measurement. Visual acuity, in a broad sense, refers to the ability to resolve fine details and to distinguish different parts of the visual field from each other (Figure 4.5). Actually, there are five types of acuity, each involving a different task—detection, localization, resolution, recognition, and dynamic acuity.

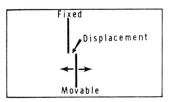

□ *figure* **4.6** Vernier acuity measurement with a movable line. The acuity task is to detect the displacement.

Detection acuity refers to detection of a target stimulus in the visual field. Often a small object of a specified size must be detected against a darker background.

Vernier or **localization** acuity is the ability to detect whether two lines, laid end to end, are continuous or whether one line is offset or displaced relative to the other (Figure 4.6). The amount of displacement can be varied, and the level at which the viewer cannot perceive the misalignment of the two lines sets the level of acuity. Whenever we must line up or match two points or lines, such as unlocking a combination lock or aligning a dial on a scale in precision equipment, we are using localization or vernier acuity.

Resolution acuity is the ability to perceive a separation between discrete elements of a pattern (Figure 4.7). Thus, one might determine whether a pattern of line gratings can be seen as distinct and lying in a certain orientation (e.g., vertical versus horizontal; Figure 4.7*c*). As the lines become thinner and closer together, the discrete lines or orientation of the grating pattern gradually seem to disappear. The *Landholt rings* shown in Figure 4.8 are also used to assess

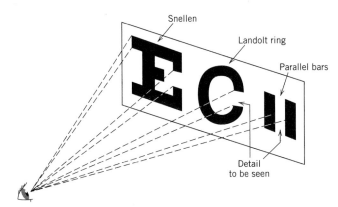

□ *figure* **4.5** Details of targets used in the measurement of visual acuity. The Snellen letters measure recognition acuity; the other two targets assess resolution acuity. The viewer must report the position of the break in the Landolt ring and the orientation of the parallel bars.

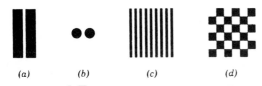

(a)   (b)   (c)   (d)

▭ *figure **4.7*** Targets for resolution acuity. The task requires detection of the separation or gap between elements of the pattern. (*a*) Parallel bars, (*b*) double-dot target, (*c*) acuity grating, (*d*) checkerboard. Most commonly used is a grating pattern (*c*) in which the widths of the dark and bright lines are made equal. A series of gratings ranging from coarse to fine is presented, and visual acuity is specified in terms of the angular width of the line of the finest grating that can be resolved.

resolution acuity. (There is a more definitive measure of acuity involving grating patterns called *contrast sensitivity*. However, because its description requires assumptions about the visual system that have not yet been introduced, we defer its discussion until Chapter 6.)

Recognition acuity is perhaps the most familiar form of acuity. It usually requires the viewer to name the target stimuli. The *Snellen letters* of the familiar eye chart are used to measure recognition acuity (Figure 4.9). We will return to recognition acuity and the Snellen eye chart in a later section.

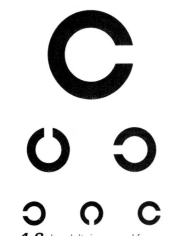

▭ *figure **4.8*** Landolt rings used for assessing resolution acuity. The thickness of the ring is one-fifth the outer diameter. The gap width is also one-fifth the outer diameter.

▭ *figure **4.9*** Snellen letters used for measuring recognition acuity. The letters are composed of lines with a thickness that is one-fifth the height or width of the whole letter. The Snellen eye chart was devised by the Dutch ophthalmologist Herman Snellen in 1862.

Dynamic acuity is the detection and location of areas in moving targets. It is critical in activities such as driving. Table 4.2 summarizes the five types of acuity.

Visual Angle

As we have observed, there are many types of acuity and the degree of acuity differs for each type. For example, detection acuity is higher than recognition acuity. However, before comparing the various acuities further, we will introduce a single measure for specifying acuity that applies to all types. First, we must note that the visibility of a target varies with both

▭ *table **4.2*** Acuities and Acuity Tasks

Acuity	Task
Detection	Detecting the presence of target
Vernier, localization	Detecting displacement, misalignment
Resolution	Detecting a separation or gap
Recognition	Identifying an item (e.g., a letter)
Dynamic acuity	Detecting and locating a moving target

its size and its distance from the observer. So, what we need is a single measure that takes into account both the target's physical size and its distance. Such a measure, called the **visual angle,** is the size of the retinal image formed by the target. This point, and the fact that visual angle takes into account the target's size *and* its distance from the observer, is illustrated in Figure 4.10*a*.

Visual angle is given in degrees (°), minutes ('), and seconds (") of arc. In angular measure, 1° (degree) = 60' (minutes), 1' = 60" (seconds), and 1" = 1/3600°. Figure 4.10*b* offers a relatively simple computation of visual angle (involving a bit of trigonometry), taking into account the size and observer distance of several targets.

For those who wish to avoid using trigonometry, an approximate unit of visual angle is based literally on a general "rule of thumb." Robert O'Shea (1991) has calculated that the visual angle of the width of the average thumb (for both males and females) held at arm's length is about 2°. Using your thumb this way as a measuring device, you can easily approximate

the visual angles of much larger but more distant objects, such as the moon (which is 0.5° or 30'). Relatedly, observe from Figure 4.10 that targets 1, 2, and 3 all have the same visual angle of *β*. In other words, if targets of very different physical size are appropriately adjusted in terms of their distance from the observer, they will all have the same visual angle.

One advantage of using the visual angle, then, is that it avoids having to specify both the target's size and its distance from the observer. In addition, since it is given by a single value, it enables a comparison of different acuities. For example, in terms of visual angle, the five types of acuity introduced earlier have approximately the following optimal values for human vision: detection acuity—0.5 sec of arc (Olzak & Thomas, 1986); vernier or localization acuity—2 sec of arc (Matin, 1986); for both resolution and recognition—30 sec of arc. Dynamic visual acuity is poorer than the static acuities. According to Schiff (1980), for stimuli moving at a rate of 60° per sec, dynamic acuity is about 1 to 2 min of arc. Visual angle values associated with some typical objects and ocular structures are given in Table 4.3.

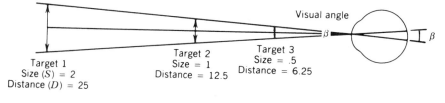

(a)

□ *figure 4.10* (a) The visual angle. The angle, *β*, is the visual angle of a target of size, *S*, that lies at a distance, *D*. from the retina along the line of regard. Note that other targets (e.g., Targets 2 and 3) of different sizes, lying at different distances, have the same visual angle, *β*. (b) Computation of the visual angle. Given the values of *S* and *D* for Target 1, it is possible to compute the visual angle of a target using the equation

$$\tan\frac{\beta}{2} = \frac{S}{2D}$$

where tan *β*/2 represents the trigonometric function for half of the visual angle. *S* represents the size of the target, and *D* represents the distance of the target from the retina. The target distance is 25 units, and along the line of regard the target size is 2 units; hence, tangent *β*/2 is $\frac{2}{2 \times 25}$ or 1/25 or 0.04; that is, one-half of the target height divided by the distance of the target from the eye, or 1 divided by 25. The angle whose tangent is 0.04 is 2°18'. But this is only one-half of the target angle *β*; hence, the full visual angle that the target image occupies on the retina is twice this value, or 4°36'. In many situations where the visual angle is relatively small, say 10° or less, the formula tan *β* = *S/D* is applicable.

⊐ *table 4.3* Visual Angle Associated with Some Typical Objects and Ocular Structures

Alphanumeric character on a CRT screen at 50 cm	17′
Diameter of the sun and moon	30′
Lowercase pica-type letter at a reading distance of 40 cm (about 16 in.)	13′
Quarter at arm's length	2°
Quarter at 90 yards (about 82 m)	1′
Quarter at 3 mi. (about 5 km)	1″
Diameter of the fovea	1°
Diameter of the foveal receptor	30″
Position of the inner edge of a blind spot	12° from fovea
Size of the blind spot	7.5° (vertical), 5° (horizontal)

Source: Based on T. N. Cornsweet, *Visual perception* (New York: Academic Press, 1970), and G. Westheimer, The eye as an optical instrument, in K. R. Boff, L. Kaufman, & J. P. Thomas (Eds.), *Handbook of perception and human performance:* Vol. 1. *Sensory processes and perception* (New York: Wiley, 1986).

Recognition Acuity and the Eye Chart

Because of its widespread use, we have more to say about recognition acuity. The most common form of acuity assessed in clinical practice is recognition acuity, and it is usually measured by means of the familiar eye chart. Typically, the chart contains lines of Snellen letters that vary in size. The viewer reads the line with the smallest letters that can be read with accuracy. When this type of acuity is assessed, it is specified relative to the performance of a normal or typical viewer. That is, the resultant value is expressed as a ratio of the distance at which a line of letters can just be correctly seen to the farthest distance at which the hypothetical average person with normal vision can just read the same line. Accordingly, a ratio of 20/20 indicates that the viewer correctly sees at 20 feet letters that the average person can just read at 20 feet (20/20 = 1 min of arc). A ratio of 20/15 means that the viewer just sees at 20 feet what the average person can just see at 15 feet—obviously better than average acuity. On the other hand, a ratio of 20/30 means that the viewer can just read at 20 feet letters that are large enough for the average person to read at 30 feet—poorer than average acuity.

We noted that many nocturnal animals have greater sensitivity in dim lighting than the human. In contrast, many day-active animals, especially birds,

possess an extraordinary degree of visual acuity. It has been estimated that the resolution acuity of the eagle may be 3.6 times human visual acuity (Reymond, 1985; Shlaer, 1972). The vision of the falcon is estimated to be 2.6 times more acute than that of the human (Fox, Lehmkuhle, & Westendorf, 1976). In environmental terms, these findings suggest that the falcon can just detect a target of 1 mm at 18 meters!

Hyperacuity

Some of the acuity values given above are quite spectacular (e.g., 2 sec for vernier acuity). Since we have just stressed the functional significance of photoreceptor cones in acuity, it seems reasonable to conclude that the limiting factor in high-performance acuity tasks—assessing the minimum detectable detail—is an anatomical one based on the size of the individual retinal receptors, the cones. Thus, to detect whether one line is displaced relative to another, as illustrated by the example of vernier acuity shown in Figure 4.6, at least one unstimulated receptor must lie between the receptors stimulated by the two vertical lines. In other words, to detect the spatial displacement or gap between the two vertical lines, some sort of "neural gap" must be registered on the fovea. Therefore, a detectable detail cannot be finer than the width or diameter of a cone; otherwise, there would be no differential effect in stimulation on the fovea. However, the reported vernier acuity value of 2 sec of arc is less than one-tenth of the width of a single foveal cone (which is about 20″ of arc). This means that a single photoreceptor cone is actually much larger than the detail detected or, as Howard (1982) puts it, "the spatial resolving power or pattern acuity of the eye may be very much better than the 'grain' of the retinal mosaic" (p. 36).

The extraordinary acuity for details of less than 10 sec of arc has been termed **hyperacuity** (Westheimer, 1976); however, our understanding of how this happens is fairly limited. Still, it is a fact that humans can detect details finer than a fraction of the diameter of an individual photoreceptor. This suggests that some sort of complex neural pooling and integration of spatial information over several receptors serving very small areas of the fovea must be involved in certain hyperacuity tasks (Poggio, Fahle, & Edelman, 1992; Wilson, 1986).

Acuity and Retinal Location

Sensitivity, we have noted, is highest where the density of rods is greatest. Relatedly, acuity is best when the image falls on the fovea, where the cones are most densely packed, and worsens as the image stimulates areas peripheral to the fovea. The variation in visual acuity generated by stimulating different regions of the human retina is shown in Figure 4.11. That acuity is dependent on the distribution of cones becomes obvious when we compare Figure 4.11 with a plot of the distribution of rods and cones in the retina (see Figure 3.11). Acuity falls off rapidly as the image of a visual target moves from the fovea to the periphery of the retina.

DEMONSTRATION:
Acuity and Retinal Position

Study the chart shown in Figure 4.12 on page 102, devised by S. M. Anstis (1974). It provides a pictorial impression of the variation in acuity as a function of increasing target distance from the fovea. According to Anstis's analysis, when the center of the chart is fixated, all the letters should be equally legible at any viewing distance. This is because any increase in viewing distance makes the retinal image of each letter smaller, but at the same time it projects each letter closer toward the fovea, where acuity is higher. In brief, all letters appear equally legible since the size of the target letters decreases at the same rate as visual acuity increases.

Acuity also depends on the level of illumination; it is highest under photopic conditions. The contrast between the target and its background is another important consideration, as is the amount of time spent viewing the target; generally, the more time spent looking at a target, the more visible it is (e.g., McKee & Westheimer, 1978). Furthermore, the viewer's eye movements, the size of the pupil, the wavelength of the target stimulus and its background, the age and experience of the viewer, and other psychological factors may have an important effect on the level of acuity (Olzak & Thomas, 1986). One of these factors, eye movements, is so important, not only to acuity but also for a general understanding of the visual system, that it warrants a separate discussion.

EYE MOVEMENTS

As we observed in Chapter 3, the eyes are moved about almost effortlessly by the action of the oculomotor muscles (see Figure 3.15). We note here that eye movements are biologically adapted to orienting and searching for targets that lie in different directions and at different distances. They not only enable the observer to position the eyes to fixate and focus on a target, so that its image falls on the fovea, they also allow the observer to continuously change and redirect the gaze. In other words, the eyes are capable of fixating on a target, as well as continuously moving, so that the images of moving stimuli will continue to fall directly on the small central region of clearest, most acute vision—the fovea.

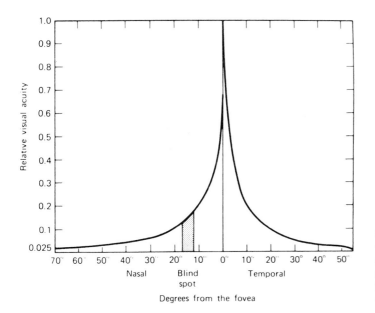

□ *figure **4.11*** Visual acuity at different retinal positions. These results were obtained from a grating target. All values are expressed as proportions of foveal acuity. (From Chapanis, 1949, p. 27; after Wertheim, 1894.)

Many different types of eye movements have been identified.

Saccades

The most common form of eye movement is called the **saccade** (from the French verb, *saccader*, meaning "to jerk" or "flick"), a rapid and abrupt jump (of about 50 msec duration) made by the eye as it moves from one fixation to another. Saccades may be small (less than 3 min of visual angle) or large (20° of angle). Saccades are *ballistic-type* movements, in that they are guided and have a predetermined destination; that is, the direction and distance of their excursions are planned by the nervous system prior to their execution. Zingale and Kowler (1987) have reported that, like many voluntary motor tasks involving the limbs and fingers, saccadic eye movements are preset or planned as patterned sequences prior to their execution.

Because vision is impaired during eye movements, it is not surprising that these movements are extremely rapid. Indeed, the muscles responsible for saccadic eye movements are among the fastest in the body. Typically, there are 1 to 3 saccades per second,

but they occur so rapidly that they occupy only about 10% of the total viewing time. Saccades are generally voluntary, for they can be made with the eyes closed or in total darkness, and they can be aimed or suppressed. However, they also have a reflexive nature. A suddenly appearing, flickering, or moving stimulus seen out of the corner of the eye can result in a saccade that moves the gaze directly on the stimulus. This is of adaptive significance "for in the primitive world, a slight movement glimpsed from the corner of the eye . . . might be the first warning of an attack" (Llewellyn–Thomas, 1969, p. 406).

Saccades are used primarily to search and explore the visual field and to place images of selected visual details on the fovea, where visual acuity is maximal; accordingly, they are especially functional in such tasks as reading and the examination of stationary scenes. As Figure 4.13 shows, the pattern of eye movements may be partially determined by the kind of information to be extracted from a scene.

Saccades and Reading Saccadic eye movements are functional acts that contribute to the process of reading. It is well known that the pattern of eye movements during reading does not consist of

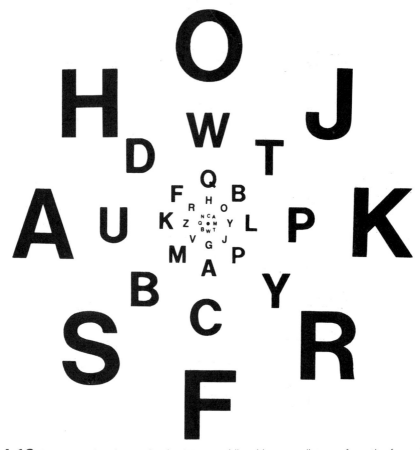

□ **figure 4.12** Demonstration that acuity decreases rapidly with target distance from the fovea. The chart was specially designed so that, with proper fixation, all letters appear equally legible. (From S. M. Anstis, A chart demonstrating variations in acuity with retinal position. *Vision Research, 14,* 1974, p. 591. Reprinted by permission of the author and Pergamon Press.)

smoothly executed tracking movements of successive rows of letter and words. Instead, as Figure 4.14 shows, during reading the eyes execute a series of saccades interspersed with pauses, or *fixations,* and some refixations or regressive eye movements (called *regressions*). It is during fixation that reading occurs, since functional vision is essentially blocked during saccadic movements. The length and frequency of saccades in reading are affected by the reader's ability to resolve individual letters and by how well the letters form coherent, easily recognizable perceptual units (e.g., Kowler & Anton, 1987; Nazir,

Heller, & Sussmann, 1992). In general, the skilled reader makes fewer but longer saccades, fewer and briefer fixations, and fewer regressions than the poorer one.

This may be because the skilled reader is making efficient use of some obvious visual features provided by text to organize and guide the pattern of saccades while reading. Thus, the skilled reader may use information from peripheral vision to guide the line of sight during reading (Carr, 1986; Schiffman, 1972). Clearly, it would be more efficient for the reader to use peripheral vision to search for and fixate on salient,

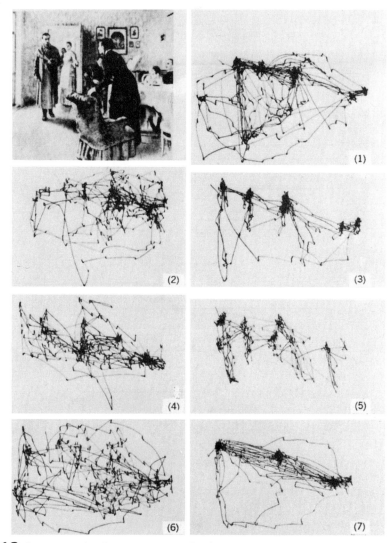

□ **figure 4.13** Seven records of eye movements by the same subject made to the same picture but viewed under different instructions. Each line segment represents a saccade. Each record lasted for 3 min. The subject examined the picture with both eyes. (1) Free examination of the picture. Before the subsequent recording sessions, the subject was asked to (2) estimate the material circumstances of the family in the picture, (3) give the ages of the people, (4) surmise what the family had been doing before the arrival of the "unexpected visitor," (5) remember the clothes worn by the people, (6) remember the position of the people and objects in the room, (7) estimate how long the unexpected visitor had been away from the family. (From A. L. Yarbus, *Eye Movement and Vision,* Plenum Press, New York, 1967, p. 174. Reprinted with permission of Plenum Press.)

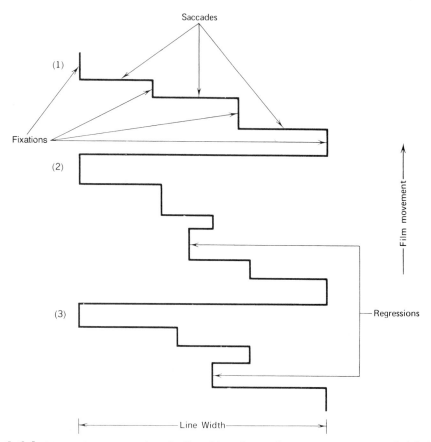

□ *figure 4.14* Schematic representation of a film of lateral saccadic eye movements recorded during reading of three lines of text. Note that since the film moves up, the recording progresses down. The extent of saccadic movements is given by the length of the horizontal line segments; the duration of the fixations is registered by the vertical segments. For the first line of text (1), the record shows three saccades and four fixations. The records for lines 2 and 3 show regressions (i.e., returns to previously passed text).

nonredundant, important words than to pause on common words or on the spaces between each word (Balota & Raynor, 1983; Zola, 1984). In fact, when viewing stationary visual displays, readers tend to fixate on high-content areas; for reading in particular, the optimal location for a fixation is on the word (Epelboim, Booth, & Steinman, 1994; McConkie et al., 1989; Nazir et al., 1992).

In addition, since the spaces between words appear to define the shapes of words visually, it seems reasonable to assume that such spaces are critical to the pattern of eye movements and efficient reading.

If this is true, then eliminating the spaces should affect the programming of saccades, with a correspondingly adverse effect on reading. Indeed, this seems to happen when initially reading unspaced text.

DEMONSTRATION:
Reading Without Interword Spaces

Begin to read the unusually dense paragraph of Figure 4.15. As you do so, it should seem difficult,

Pursuitmovementsarealmostcompletely
automaticandgenerallyrequireaphysically
movingstimulus.Incontrasttosaccades,
pursuitmovementsaresmoothlyexecuted
andarecomparativelyslow.Generally,they
areusedtotrackanobjectmovingina
stationaryenvironment;hencetarget
velocityratherthantargetlocationisthe
appropriatestimulus.Inthiscase,the
velocityofthepursuitmovementofthe
eyematchesthevelocityofthemoving
stimulus.Thisservestomoreorlesscast
andpreservethestationaryimageofthe
targetontheretina.Movingtheeyein
accordancewiththemovementofa
stimulusmayalsoenhancetheperception
oftheformofastimulus.Youwillsoonread
thismaterialagainbecauseitisrepeatedin
thenextsection,butwithspacesbetween
thewords.

▭ *figure **4.15*** Text in which interword spaces are eliminated. (Based on a demonstration by Epelboim et al., 1994.)

requiring almost letter-by-letter fixation. However, as you continue to read (ensuring that the text is observed in good lighting and is highly visible), it should become surprisingly easy. In fact, based on an extensive study on this issue, Epelboim, Booth, and Steinman (1994) report that the only major effect on the pattern of eye movements of reading dense, unspaced text is that it requires smaller saccades and slightly longer fixations on individual words than are needed for reading spaced text.

The findings discussed in the Demonstration do not deny a role to peripheral vision in efficient reading, nor do they imply that word spaces are trivial in facilitating word recognition in a typical reading task; what they do suggest, however, is that *words,* rather than *word spaces* are the perceptual unit guiding the line of sight across the text. Thus, word spaces may serve a secondary perceptual role by facilitating word visi-

bility and recognition. In fact, Epelboim, Booth, and Steinman (1994) remark that word spaces were introduced in the late eighth century to make it possible to read under poor lighting conditions and to compensate for presbyopia; this underscores the idea that the main function of word spaces is to increase visibility rather than to direct saccades.

Pursuit Movements

Pursuit movements are almost completely automatic and generally require a physically moving stimulus. In contrast to saccades, pursuit movements are smoothly executed and comparatively slow. Generally, they are used to *track* an object moving in a stationary environment; hence, target velocity rather than target location is the appropriate stimulus. In this case, the velocity of the pursuit movement of the eye matches the velocity of the moving stimulus. This serves to more or less cast and preserve a stationary image of the target on the retina. Moving the eye in accordance with the movement of a stimulus may also enhance the perception of the form of a stimulus. This is because it is easier for the visual system to perceive the form of an image if it is stationary on the retina rather than moving.

Saccades and pursuit movements are only two parts of a general planning mechanism that involves controlled movements of the head and certain body muscles in directing the eyes to a target (Mack et al., 1985). In addition, specialized eye movements (vestibulo-ocular eye movements, described in the next section) are initiated to stabilize eye position when there is any movement of the head or body in space. In this case, bodily movement is compensated for by eye movements.

Vestibulo-Ocular Eye Movements

Moving about in space is a common activity, yet in spite of the resulting change in position of the head and body, we continually perceive a stable environment. The reason is this: Whenever the head or body moves in space, a pattern of reflexive **vestibulo-ocular eye movements** (also called the *vestibulo-ocular reflex* or *VOR*) are initiated to stabilize the position of the eyes relative to the environment. (In fact, the eye movements are driven by stimuli that arise in the *vestibular system* of the inner ear, a sensory system involved with bodily movement, discussed in detail in Chapter 15). This role of vestibulo-ocular eye movements is demonstrated whenever you move your head or body while fixating visually on an object. In fact, while moving about, precise eye movements are generated that compensate for head or body movements so that you can maintain fixation on particular regions of the environment.

DEMONSTRATION:
Vestibulo-Ocular Eye Movement

Have someone hold his eyes fixated on your nose while turning his head from side to side. If you look at his eyes as he moves his head, you will observe a pattern of eye movements made in direct response to his head movements (Figure 4.16). As his head turns to the right, his eyes rotate smoothly to the left (Figure 4.16a); and as his head turns to the left, his eyes rotate to the right (Figure 4.16b). What is happening is that signals concerning head movements are analyzed and linked by the brain to the eye muscles, causing compensatory eye movements. In short, automatic, smooth, rapid, and exact eye movements compensate precisely for head

movements, enabling the retinal image of a target to be stabilized on the fovea.

Vergence Movements

The most recently evolved type of eye movements—called **vergence movements**—are those that involve the coordinated movements of both eyes. Vergence movements move the eyes in opposite directions in the horizontal plane, toward or away from each other, so that both eyes can focus on the same target. Such movements are found in animals like primates with frontal vision, for which the visual fields from both eyes overlap. A lack of proper vergence movements may result in *diplopia,* or "double vision."

Miniature Eye Movements

There are also a number of reflexive, so-called **miniature eye movements** that may be identified and measured during maintained fixation. When a person maintains deliberate fixation on a target, a pattern of extremely small, involuntary, tremor-like eye movements is observable with proper recording techniques. Although in continual movement during fixation, the eye does not wander very far from its average focal position. It is recognized that if the involuntary miniature eye movements were entirely eliminated, the image on the retina would fade and disappear. However,

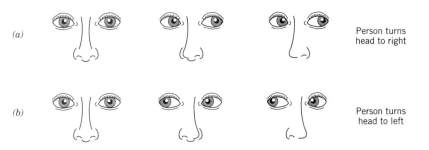

□ *figure 4.16* Schematic of vestibulo-ocular eye movements made to compensate for side-to-side head movements while maintaining fixation. (*a*) As the head turns to the right, the eyes move to the left. (*b*) As the head turns to the left, the eyes move to the right.

attempts to implicate miniature eye movements as necessary for perceptual capacities such as acuity and form perception have been seriously questioned (Steinman, 1986).

Mixed-Mode Eye Movements

Although we have identified and distinguished between several different types of eye movements, it should be stressed that most natural activities involving visual interaction with the environment employ a combination of the various eye movements—a category of eye movements that Hallett (1986) labels **mixed-mode eye movements.** For example, tracking a moving object in depth involves saccades, smooth pursuit, and vergence movements.

Our capacity to track moving objects visually is remarkable. Edward Llewellyn–Thomas (1981) describes, in somewhat dramatic, hyperbolic fashion, a specific but representative task of dynamic visual acuity—tracking a pitched baseball.

> *It's astounding that any of us can hit one at all. A ball is travelling a hundred miles an hour. A visual sample is taken from a bad angle in a single fixation from which the batter has to compute and extrapolate the ball's trajectory while initiating the voluntary muscle movements to guide a round club along a convoluted curve so it impacts the ball hard at a unique point in time and space! Impossible—all those differential equations to solve, and curves to plot in milliseconds! (p. 318)*

In the interest of accuracy, we must note that the batter cannot really follow the path of a fastball pitch (i.e., between 60 and 100 mph). Bahill and LaRitz (1984) studied the batter's ability to do this and found that their subjects (college students, college baseball players, and even a professional baseball player) could not follow the total flight of the ball. In short, they were unable to follow the batting axiom "Keep your eye on the ball." Bahill and LaRitz found that a typical batter tracks the pitched ball until it is about 9 ft (of the total 60 ft, 6 in. distance) in front of the plate, at which point the image of the ball falls off the

fovea. Moreover as the authors point out, how would it help the batter to see the ball hit the bat? Because of the human's relatively slow reaction time, the information gained from the last part of the ball's flight could not be used to alter the swing of the bat. In fact, given the ball's velocity, any useful change in batting would have to be made well before the ball nears the plate. This aside, however, eye movements are extremely useful in general visual exploration.

How does the visual system integrate rapidly changing images with controlled muscle movements? The mechanism is far from clear. However, it appears that a saccadic eye movement immediately after the ball is pitched may help some batters anticipate the ball's trajectory. The batter does not actually see the ball as it approaches the plate. The saccade aims the eyes where the batter anticipates the ball will be at the moment it crosses the plate.

According to Bahill and LaRitz, such predictive saccades explain only part of the accuracy shown by some batters in hitting fast pitches. In fact, they note that their most accurate subject, a professional baseball player, used more pursuit movements than anticipatory saccades when batting. Generally, what distinguished the professional player was the efficiency of his eye movements. Indeed, accurate visual tracking, of which viewing a pitched ball is only an unusual example, may involve development of efficient eye movements—the topic to which we now turn.

Development of Efficient Eye Movements

Finally, we consider the role of experience in the development of efficient eye movements. As we have noted, eye movements are essential motor activities for processing the visual scene. Efficient eye movements involve skilled muscle movements that appear to improve with practice. Kowler and Martins (1982) observed that the eye movements of preschool children 4 and 5 years of age differed from those of adults in a number of ways that affect efficient vision. For example, the children could not easily maintain steady fixation. When instructed to fixate on a small, bright, stationary target in an otherwise darkened room, their line of sight was extremely unstable: Their eyes darted about, scanning an area 100 times larger than would a typical adult in the same condition. In addition, when tracking a moving target, the children had difficulty controlling the timing of their saccades, and, unlike adults, they could not anticipate any change in the direction of the target's movement, even when the change was predictable; in fact, Kowler and Martins reported that about 200 msec elapsed before the children changed the direction of their eye movements.

Clearly, preschool children do not perform simple oculomotor tasks with the same efficiency as adults. Some of the difference in performance between the two groups may be attributed to the immature and incomplete oculomotor development of the children. It is also possible that, as with the acquisition of skilled motor habits in general, preschool children have not yet learned efficient oculomotor control and, accordingly, have not acquired the specific motor skills necessary to perform effectively. It is reasonable to assume that developing efficient eye movements is a skill acquired gradually, with practice and experience extending well beyond the preschool years.

One function of controlled eye movements is to enable scanning and fixation on targets. This greatly improves visually guided behaviors such as locating and identifying objects and events. However, as we note in the next and last section of this chapter, object identification and localization appear to require far more than the information provided by eye movements.

OBJECT IDENTIFICATION AND LOCALIZATION: FOCAL AND AMBIENT SYSTEMS

Two anatomically distinct neural pathways or systems are proposed for processing spatial information, each with its own functional properties. The primary **focal system** concerns the *identification* and *recognition* of objects. In humans it is mediated by the *geniculostriate visual system,* which includes the central retina (including the fovea), the LGN, and the primary visual or striate cortex. (While we have much more to say

about object identification in later chapters, our purpose here is to draw on and integrate some of the structures and functions introduced in this chapter and in Chapter 3; see Figure 3.34).

The other, secondary system, termed the **ambient system,** is involved in *locating* objects. It is mediated by the *retinotectal visual system,* which consists of both central and peripheral regions of the retina, the superior colliculus, and the secondary visual or extrastriate cortex.

The superior colliculus is important to localization. This is shown by the observation that surgical removal of the visual cortex of hamsters did not produce total blindness (Schneider, 1969). It did eliminate the ability to discriminate between patterns, but as long as the superior colliculus was unaffected, some residual visual capacity, such as localizing objects, was left intact. In comparison, when the superior colliculus was destroyed and the visual cortex was left intact, the hamsters could not localize objects but were capable of pattern discrimination. Further support for the importance of the superior colliculus comes from similar findings with monkeys (Humphrey, 1974; Trevarthen, 1968) and, to an extent, with humans. According to this idea, the cortically driven focal system helps the animal identify *what kind* of object is present, whereas the ambient system, mediated by the superior colliculus, indicates *where* the object is located.

Blindsight

Evidence in support of the focal and ambient systems in the human comes from observations that a similar residual localization capacity persists in blind individuals who appear capable of localizing and orienting to objects without seeing them. The ability of some blind individuals to look at, point to, and, in a general way, be aware of attributes of objects that they cannot see, has been labeled **blindsight** (Weiskrantz, 1977, 1992). One explanation for blindsight is based on the residual functioning of the ambient system when the focal system is useless. That is, although some blind individuals cannot identify objects due to damage or injury of the central pathway and visual cortex, an alternative secondary pathway (the ambient system) allows them to make accurate orientation responses,

⎯ **Color plate 1** Variation in saturation. The saturated patch at the right
changes from a rich, vivid blue to successively paler shades of blue as saturation
decreases. The completely desaturated patch at the left appears to lack any hue
characteristic.

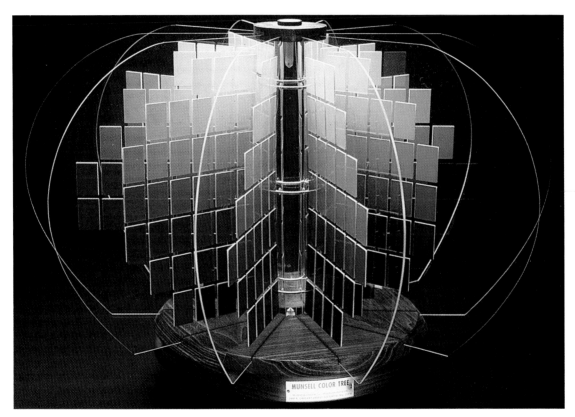

⎯ **Color plate 2** A color version of the schematic color spindle shown in Figure 5.2. All three
Psychological dimensions are shown. Hue is represented around the perimeter or circumference,
brightness is represented along the vertical axis, and saturation is represented along the radius, from
the center to the perimeter. *(Courtesy Kollmorgen Corporation.)*

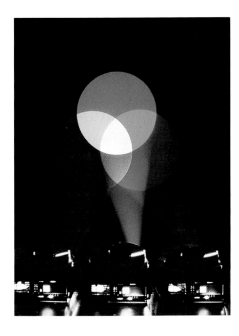

Color plate 3 Additive color mixtures. Additive colors involve the mixing of lights. Thus the partially superimposed projections of red, green, and blue lights result in additive color mixtures. For example, red and green lights combine to yield yellow, etc., The excitations from all lights sent to the visual system (shown at the center) yields white. *(Courtesy Spear et al.)*

A

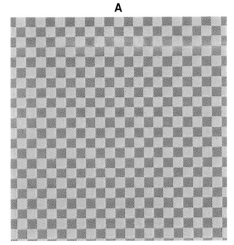

B

Color plate 4 Additive color mixture. The chromatic surface of square (A) is composed of a mosaic of red and green squares, each taken from the two stripes shown below square (A). The chromatic surface of square (B) has a homogeneous yellow-orange appearance. In fact, squares (A) and (B) reflect very different sets of wavelengths and appear very different from each other. However, when the two squares are viewed from a distance of 10–12 ft *(and lighted by an incandescent light)*, the two surfaces appear almost identical. What has occurred is that, when viewed from a distance, the small red and green squares of (A) cannot be resolved individually and their combined *(i.e., additive)* effect on the visual system creates a chromatic match with square (B).

⊂⊃ **Color plate 5** A photographed enlargement of a small area of a color television screen. Observe that only spots of blue, green and red are used. Various color sensations are produced by varying the intensity of the spots. When viewed from the typical viewing distance, the illuminated colors apparently fuse (i.e., as an additive color mixture) to produce the wide range of colors seen in television viewing. Thus, for example, illuminating only the green and red spots produces a yellow sensation and when all three spots are equally illuminated white is perceived. *(Photograph courtesy of James Bolish.)*

⊂⊃ **Color plate 6** Subtractive color mixture. Mixing paints and pigments involves mutual absorption or subtraction of certain wavelengths of the component colors in the mixture, leaving the reflection of only the wavelengths that the pigments reflect in common. For example, mixing yellow and blue paints, as shown, yields green: blue absorbs yellow and reflects blue and *green*, whereas yellow absorbs blue and reflects yellow and some *green*. Accordingly, when they are mixed, the mutual absorption or sub-traction of blue and yellow wavelengths leaves green. In contrast, when blue and yellow *lights* are mixed, as an additive color mixture they are complementary to each other, therefore canceling each other's effect and yielding gray. In subtractive color mixtures the colors seen are the sensory effects produced by the pigments *after* they have been mixed together.

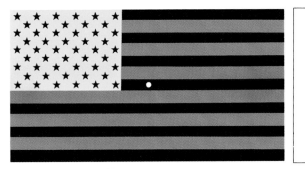

Color plate 7 Complementary or chromatic negative afterimages. Stare at the white dot at the middle of the flag for about 30 sec. and then shift the gaze to the dot in the middle of the rectangle. Colors complementary to the green, yellow, and black—the American flag in its normal colors—will appear as afterimages.

Color plate 8 Complementary afterimage and successive contrast. Stare at the fixation cross of the blue patch for 30 sec., then transfer the gaze to the cross of the yellow surface. A supersaturated yellow patch will appear.

Color plate 9
Desaturation with continued exposure. Cover the right half of the rectangle with a piece of gray paper and stare at the fixation cross for 60 sec. Then remove the gray sheet while continuing to stare at the fixation mark. The left side will appear less saturated than the previously covered right side.

Color plate 10 Simultaneous contrast. Stare at the cross for 20 sec. "Shimmering" effects may be seen at the border of the patch and its background because the two colors are complementaries.

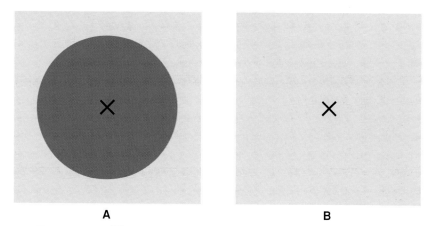

A **B**

Color plate 11 Color aftereffect. Stare at the fixation **x** in (A) for about 30 sec. and then transfer your fixation to the **x** in (B). You will see a yellow color.

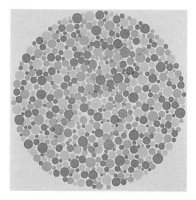
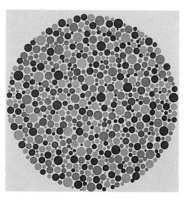

Color plate 12 (A) Individuals with normal color vision—trichromats—see the number 3, whereas red-green-deficient dichromats see no number, only a random pattern of dots. (B) Individuals with normal color vision see the number 42, dichromatic deuteranopes see only the digit 4, and protanopes see only the digit 2. *(Courtesy of Graham-Field Surgical Company.)*

A

B

C

D

▭ *Color plate **13*** Approximate appearance of chromatic scene to individuals with normal color vision and to dichromats.
(A) Approximate appearance of chromatic scene to normal observer.
(B) Approximate appearance to a protanope.
(C) Approximate appearance to a deuteranope.
(D) Approximate appearance to a tritanope.
(*Burnham, Hanes, & Bartleson, Color. John Wiley & Sons, 1963.*)

A		B		C	
BLUE	YELLOW			YELLOW	RED
GREEN	RED			GREEN	GREEN
RED	BLUE			BLUE	YELLOW
YELLOW	GREEN			RED	GREEN
RED	RED			YELLOW	BLUE
YELLOW	YELLOW			RED	RED
GREEN	BLUE			GREEN	YELLOW
BLUE	GREEN			BLUE	RED
RED	YELLOW			YELLOW	BLUE
GREEN	BLUE			BLUE	RED
YELLOW	YELLOW			GREEN	BLUE
GREEN	GREEN			BLUE	GREEN
BLUE	RED			GREEN	RED
RED	BLUE			YELLOW	YELLOW

A   **B**   **C**

Color plate **14** The Stroop effect. The times required to read list of color names in (A) or to name the color of each patch in (B) are significantly less than the time needed to name the colors of the list of color words in (C).

🞄 *Color plate 15* "The Girl with a Red Hat" by Jan Vermeer (1632–1675). Depth and luminance quality is enhanced in the painting by the use of shading and diffused highlights. *(The painting, c. 1665, was done on a wood panel. National Gallery of Art.)*

🞄 *Color plate 16* A reproduction of "Self-portrait as a Young Man" by Rembrandt van Rijn (1606–1669). When viewed directly, Rembrandt's self-portrait is an outstanding illustration of depth and distance in a picture. However, if viewed through a tube, reducing the cues of the picture's flatness, the depth effect is rendered more striking, approaching a real-world perception. *(The picture was painted in oil on wood when Rembrandt was about 23 years old and represents the first of about 60 self-portraits painted by Rembrandt during his lifetime. The series itself is a dramatic study of the progression of physical age, rendered pictorially. Mauritshuis, The Hague.)*

such as pointing to or directing their eye movements to a target. Interestingly, while doing so, they claim that they do not actually see the target and are merely guessing (Weiskrantz, 1992). It is assumed that some alternative visual pathway, probably involving the superior colliculus, enables certain blind individuals to localize objects they do not see. However, even though numerous studies support the idea of separate visual systems for identification and localization, the precise anatomical structures (such as the superior colliculus) remain problematic and controversial (e.g., Baringa, 1992; Cowey & Stoerig, 1991; Fendrich, Wessinger, & Gazzaniga, 1992; Mishkin et al., 1983).

The notion of two functionally distinct visual systems may have important practical consequences. Leibowitz and his colleagues (Leibowitz et al., 1982; Leibowitz & Owens, 1977) point out that during night driving in dim light, a relatively dangerous activity, the focal and ambient systems are both needed. The focal system is needed for identifying objects and obstacles and judging distances, and the ambient system is needed for localization information in orienting the car to the road. However, in dim light, the centrally driven focal system is impaired, involving loss of acuity (especially dynamic acuity) and loss of contrast perception, that is, a reduced ability to discern an object from its background. But since the ambient system is relatively intact, the night driver appears to suffer little overall loss of steering ability and may thus be unaware of the reduced function of the focal system. This situation is potentially dangerous. Since visual impairment is only partial, the driver is unaware of the loss of focal function and its source of acuity information, and may thus fail to take adequate precautions.

SUMMARY

This chapter focused on the phenomena and functioning of the visual system. The distinctions between rods and cones introduced in the preceding chapter were stressed throughout. Vision accomplished with rods is called scotopic vision, and cone-mediated vision is called photopic vision.

A major functional difference between photopic and scotopic vision in response to general lighting conditions was stressed, with photopic vision used at higher lighting levels and scotopic vision at low levels. We described dark adaptation, the functional and photochemical adjustment to dim light. The photochemical change involved can be traced to the change in the photopigment of rods called rhodopsin: It is bleached and broken down by light and regenerates in the dark. Next, we described sensitivity differences in photopic and scotopic vision as a function of the wavelength of stimulating light. This led to an examination of related phenomena such as the Purkinje shift, the change in the brightness of certain wavelengths due to a shift from photopic to scotopic vision.

Absolute thresholds for light were examined, and several factors were identified. For the absolute threshold, stimulus intensity is inversely related to the size or area of the retina stimulated (Ricco's law); for the absolute threshold, stimulus intensity is inversely related to the duration of the stimulus (Bloch's law). The absolute threshold for light is also affected by the region of the retina stimulated (i.e., rods or cones) and the wavelength of the light. This was followed by a discussion of threshold factors involved in perceiving continuous or steady light from physically intermittent light. In particular, the role of the flicker rate (CFF) of intermittent light was described.

Visual acuity was discussed, and five types were identified: detection, vernier (or localization), resolution, recognition, and dynamic acuity. The measurement of visual acuity in terms of units of visual angle was outlined. This section ended with a brief discussion of hyperacuity.

The next section dealt with eye movements, and several types were discussed. These included saccades (and their relevance to reading), pursuit, vestibulo-ocular, vergence, miniature, and mixed-mode eye movements. Finally, in this section, the development of efficient eye movements was examined. We noted that the eye movements of preschool children are less efficient than those of adults. This may be due to the immature oculomotor development and unskilled oculomotor habits of children.

The last section of the chapter dealt with the possibility of two anatomically and functionally distinct neural pathways or systems for processing spatial information. The focal system deals with the identification and recognition of objects and the ambient system with locating objects. Some support for the idea of two functionally distinct neural systems is provided by blindsight, the ability of some blind individuals to be aware of certain attributes of objects (such as their general location) while being unable to see them.

KEY TERMS

Ambient System

Blindsight

Bloch's Law (Bunsen-Roscoe Law)

Critical Flicker Frequency (CFF)

Critical Fusion Frequency

Dark Adaptation

Detection Acuity

Dynamic Acuity

Focal System

Hyperacuity

Light Adaptation

Localization (Vernier) Acuity

Miniature Eye Movements

Mixed-Mode Eye Movements

Night Blindness (Nyctalopia)

Photochromatic Interval

Photopic

Purkinje Shift

Pursuit Movements

Recognition Acuity

Resolution Acuity

Rhodopsin

Ricco's Law

Saccade

Scotopic

Spectral Sensitivity Curves

Spectral Threshold Curves

Vergence Movements

Visual Angle

Vestibulo-Ocular Eye Movements

STUDY QUESTIONS

1. Compare the functional properties of scotopic and photopic vision, emphasizing the visual activities of each. Compare the vision of nocturnal and day-active animals based on their use of photopic and scotopic vision.

2. Explain dark adaptation. How is it demonstrated? What do the two segments of a typical dark adaptation curve illustrate about photopic and scotopic vision?

3. Outline the photochemical basis of dark adaptation, indicating the changing state of rhodopsin relative to light exposure.

4. Identify and explain the Purkinje shift with respect to spectral threshold curves. What does the Purkinje shift indicate about perception in bright and dim light? What are the differences and similarities of photopic and scotopic vision in long-wavelength (i.e., 650 nm or ''red'') light?

5. What are the minimal radiant energy requirements of the visual system to produce a sensation?

6. Identify the main influences on the absolute threshold for vision. Consider the role of stimulus intensity, area, duration, the region of the retina stimulated, and the wavelength of the stimulus applied. Examine these factors with respect to the Purkinje shift.

7. Describe the CFF. What effect does stimulus intensity and stimulus localization have on the CFF?

8. Identify and distinguish between the various kinds of acuities, and consider the ways in which they are measured. What is the visual angle, and why is it useful in describing acuity? What is hyperacuity?

9. What are some of the factors that affect visual acuity? Consider the effect on acuity of stimulus intensity and the area of the retina stimulated.

10. Identify the major forms of eye movements and indicate the role of each in efficiency of the visual system. In particular, consider the use of

saccadic eye movements in exploring the visual field and in reading.

11. Examine the role of experience in the development of efficient eye movements. How do the eye movements of preschool children differ from those of adults?

12. Define the focal and ambient systems and describe their functional difference. What evidence supports a role for the superior colliculus in the ambient system? What is blindsight, and how do the focal and ambient systems contribute to it?

COLOR VISION

This chapter deals with the perception of color. Few topics in sensation and perception have had as persistent and controversial a history as this one. Artists, philosophers, poets, and physicists, as well as physiologists and psychologists, have enhanced our knowledge of color perception. Interest in this subject is not difficult to understand. Color is a pervasive characteristic of the environment that not only specifies a fundamental attribute or quality of surfaces and objects but also, in the case of humans, often creates profound aesthetic and emotional effects, influenced by associations and preferences. To most individuals, much of the visual environment seems dominated by its colors. Colors attract and often overwhelm our attention, highlight the world, appeal to our aesthetic sense, and, most important, provide information: They enhance the contrast between surfaces, facilitating the visual detection and discrimination of objects, and they often provide a clear recognition cue to many objects, thus giving a sense of stability to the world around us.

Our goal in this chapter is to understand how color perception arises from reflected light. We consider how the visual system converts the components of radiant energy into color experience. To do this, we introduce and describe the
nature of color. We then describe and discuss the perceptual effects of color mixtures and the fleeting effects of afterimages *with illustrations and demonstrations, and we discuss some of the long-term effects of colors on our perception. We examine* color constancy, *the tendency to perceive colors as unchanging in spite of changes in light. The major explanations of color vision will be outlined, along with the main forms of defective color vision. Finally, we describe and explain the unusual effects of* subjective colors, *that is, perceiving color from black-and-white stimuli.*

Not all animals have color perception. Although color vision occurs widely throughout the animal world, there are no clear overall phylogenetic trends. While the color vision of most primates is highly developed—matched only by that of birds—few other species of mammals possess a well-developed color sense. Among lower mammals, some degree of color perception has been observed in certain species of squirrels (Crescitelli & Pollack, 1965; Michels & Schumaker, 1968), cats (Brown et al., 1973; Loop & Bruce, 1978), and prairie dogs (Jacobs & Pulliam, 1973). In contrast to most mammals, many birds, fish, amphibia, reptiles, and arthropods have highly developed color vision (Ingle, 1985).

THE FUNCTION OF COLOR VISION

The evolution of color vision probably had a strong biological advantage. Creatures with color vision see another dimension of the environment beyond the edges, boundaries, and borders based on intensity differences alone. Color provides an additional source of contrast between objects that greatly increases their visibility and generally provides a sense of solidity to the visual environment. Compare, if possible, the images displayed on a black-and-white TV screen with the same images displayed on a color screen. There is a significant gain in the visual information on the color screen. Many surface characteristics such as textures and patterns, as well as objects themselves, would go undetected in a world devoid of color. In this sense, color vision is part of a general adaptive capacity to perceive the composition of surfaces and objects in the environment. As Walls (1963) comments: "To the first animals which developed a system of color vision, it meant the life-saving difference between being sometimes able to discriminate enemies and prey against their backgrounds, and being *usually* able to do so" (p. 463). Wright (1967) proposes that, along with using it for object identification, "primitive man must have used colour . . . to tell him about his crops, to help him judge the fertility of the soil, [and] to make his weather forecast from the colour of the sunset" (p. 21).

Animals often employ color vision or body coloration to their advantage, enhancing their survival capability. Color clearly plays a dominant role in the mating behavior of birds, in which the plumage serves to lure mates. However, distinctive coloration may have also evolved in response to predation pressures rather than sexual attraction. Many prey animals take advantage of their predators' color vision by possessing some concealment coloration or bodily camouflage, generally limited to nature's colors—greens and browns. Their special coloring enables them to avoid their predators by hiding their presence. In contrast, some birds use "flash coloration," the abrupt exposure of brightly colored plumage, to startle or confuse an attacking predator, enabling them to escape (Baker & Parker, 1979). Consider this very different survival function of the brilliant, exotic bright orange and black plumage of the hooded *pitohui*, a small bird native to New Guinea. Its feathers and skin harbor a highly concentrated neurotoxin so potent that it instantly repels any animal that so much as licks one of its feathers (Dumbacher, et al., 1992). Therefore, rather than a sexual adornment, the flashy plumage of the *pitohui* serves as a conspicuous warning to its potential predators that it is extremely poisonous and should be avoided. The *pitohui* also emits a strong sour odor, suggesting that its chemical defense is signaled to potential predators by olfactory (smell) as well as visual cues.

THE NATURE OF COLOR

Perceiving color depends primarily on the wavelength of the light stimulating the visual system. In humans, the light that produces a color experience falls within the highly restricted visibility range of the electromagnetic spectrum—between about 380 and 760 nm. Therefore, when we refer to a "blue" or a "red" light, we really mean the light of short or long wavelengths, respectively, whose effects on the visual system produce the sensations of blue or red.

Color sensations are totally subjective effects produced by reflected light from certain wavelengths of the visible spectrum on the nervous system. In other words, the colors depend on the way the visual system interprets the different wavelengths of light that are reflected from objects and strike the eye. Light rays, paints, filters, and so on have no color. They merely use radiant energy in a selective manner, producing or transmitting some wavelengths, reflecting some, and absorbing others. In short, color is a product of the visual system, not an inherent property of the visible spectrum.

This important distinction between the physical dimension specified by the wavelengths and the psychological phenomenon of color vision is summarized well by Wright (in an essay entitled "The Rays Are Not Coloured," 1963, 1967): "Our sensations of colour are within us and colour cannot exist unless there is an observer to perceive them. Colour does not exist even in the chain of events between the retinal receptors and the visual cortex, but only when the information is finally interpreted in the consciousness of the observer" (p. 20).

Objects thus appear colored because they reflect specific wavelengths of light to our visual system. When "white" light from the sun or an overhead source illuminates a surface or object, some of the wavelengths are absorbed by light-sensitive pigments within the surface and others are reflected. In fact, the color we do perceive from a surface or object is based on the wavelengths of light it reflects. For example, to humans, wavelengths of around 580 nm appear yellow. So does a lemon when it is illuminated by white light. In fact, the peel of a lemon appears yellow because it *absorbs* most of the wavelengths striking it except for a small band of wavelengths around 580 nm; that is, the lemon reflects predominantly the yellow-appearing wavelengths around 580 nm. Similarly, wavelengths of about 500 nm appear green to most individuals. For example, the skin of a pepper looks green because it absorbs most wavelengths and reflects those in the region of 500 nm. In contrast to both examples, black shoes appear black because they absorb almost all the light that illuminates them, and this page appears white because it reflects most of the light falling on it more or less uniformly.

The Dimensions of Color

With these distinctions in mind, we should note that color sensations are related in consistent and measurable ways to the physical features of light. To describe this relationship, we must first identify the stimulus dimensions for color vision. As noted above, the dominant physical characteristic of the color of a light is its wavelength. This was observed in one of the earliest comprehensive treatments of color vision, by Sir Isaac Newton (in his treatise "Optiks," 1704/1952). In the seventeenth century, he demonstrated that when a pinpoint beam of white light (containing all of the visible wavelengths) is passed through a prism, it is refracted, or bent, and split into a number of rays of light of different wavelengths, forming the colored spectrum (Figure 5.1). The amount of refraction is determined by the wavelength, with short wavelengths refracted most and long wavelengths least. In fact, the colored spectrum is seen as a rainbow of colors, extending from violet and blue (short wavelengths) to yellow and red (long wavelengths). Newton's prism demonstration decomposed white light into its *spectral* components—visible radiations of different wavelengths—that *appear* as colors.

Hue The main, and obvious, physical component of a color is the wavelength of the reflected

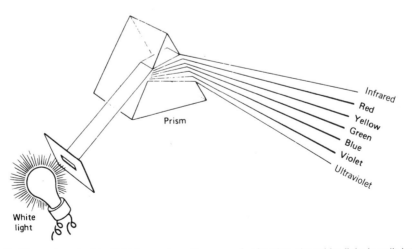

□ *figure 5.1* Dispersion of white light by a prism. Because of refraction, the white light is split into rays of light of different wavelengths, apparent as different colors.

⮐ *table* **5.1** Relation Between Physical and Psychological Dimensions of Color

Physical Dimension	Psychological Dimension
Wavelength	Hue
Intensity	Brightness
Spectral purity	Saturation

light that produces it. However, the color sensation is actually determined by three physical attributes of light: *wavelength, intensity,* and *spectral purity.* Each of these attributes is linked to a specific psychological quality of the color sensation: *hue, brightness,* and *saturation,* respectively (Table 5.1).

Hue corresponds to the common meaning of color. If a color has a recognizable spectral hue, we perceive it as, say, blue, green, yellow, or red. Hue generally varies with changes in wavelength (Table 5.2). (For convenience and simplicity, we will generally use the terms *hue* and *color* interchangeably. We will also use color names to refer to spectral stimuli

⮐ *table* **5.2** Typical Hue Names Associated with Spectral Energy Bands

Approximate Wavelength Region (in nm)	Associated Hue
380–470	Reddish blue
470–475	Blue
475–480	Greenish blue
480–485	Blue-green
485–495	Bluish green
495–535	Green
535–555	Yellowish green
555–565	Green-yellow
565–575	Greenish yellow
575–580	Yellow
580–585	Reddish yellow
585–595	Yellow-red
595–770	Yellowish red*

Source: *Color: A guide to basic facts and concepts,* by R. W. Burnham, R. M. Hanes, and C. J. Bartleson, John Wiley, New York, 1963, p. 56. Reprinted by permission of the publisher.

* A pure red with no tinge of yellow requires some blue (400 nm). Accordingly, a unique red is "extraspectral" in that no single wavelength produces it.

having specific sensory effects. However, keep in mind that when we refer to a "red" light, for example, we are really talking about those long wavelengths of light that elicit the sensation of red.)

Recognizing the close relationship between the wavelength of light and color sensation enables us to understand why the sky usually appears blue. This is due to a special sort of light reflection that occurs in an atmosphere like the sky, which contains molecules of gases, water vapor, and dust. When sunlight passes through the earth's atmosphere, molecules of various gases *scatter* the light. But they selectively scatter the short, blue-appearing wavelengths of light more than the long wavelengths. Hence the sky takes on a blue appearance. Relatedly, when there is a lot of dust and moisture in the atmosphere, these larger particles scatter the longer wavelengths, causing the blue sky to appear paler. Similarly, fog and clouds appear white because they contain water particles, which are even larger. These particles act as diffuse reflectors of light, reflecting all visible wavelengths about equally. In contrast, beginning at about 10 mi above the earth's surface, there are no particles of any kind to scatter the sunlight and the sky appears black (Mueller & Rudolph, 1966; Riggs, 1965).

Brightness A given color is also specified by its **brightness,** which varies with physical intensity. As we noted earlier, brightness is related to the intensity of the light. Generally, the more intense the light, the brighter it appears; decreasing intensity produces a darker appearance. However, for a given intensity, some hues, such as yellow, appear brighter than hues produced by shorter wavelengths, such as blue. In addition, the perceived hue of a stimulus will change slightly depending on the stimulus intensity. If the intensity of relatively long-wavelength lights that appear as yellow-greens and yellow-reds is increased, these lights will not only appear brighter but will also take on a more yellow hue. Similarly, short-wavelength lights that are seen as blue-greens and violets begin to appear bluer when their intensity is increased. This change in hue with changes in intensity is called the **Bezold-Brücke shift.**

Saturation Saturation is the psychological attribute that refers to the relative *amount* of a hue of a surface or object. Saturation is related to the physical dimension of **spectral purity.** A light of only a single wavelength—called *monochromatic*—is a *pure* light and appears very saturated. However, the addition of other wavelengths, or of white or gray light, to monochromatic light reduces its purity and desaturates its appearance. If made sufficiently impure, the light seems to lose all its hue and appears gray. In other words, reducing the purity of a light makes the hue of the original light appear washed out. For example, reducing the purity of a monochromatic long-wavelength red light by adding white or gray to it will desaturate it and change its appearance to a pinkish hue. In fact, we may consider pink to be a desaturated red. The gradual decrease in the saturation of a blue hue is illustrated in Color Plate 1. When the purity of a pure, deep blue is gradually decreased, it appears washed out, becoming perhaps a sky blue, a baby blue, and then a powder blue. Finally, when completely desaturated, lacking any hue, it appears as a neutral gray.

Color Spindle The relationship between the three psychological dimensions of hue, saturation, and brightness is simplified and represented visually in the **color spindle** or solid shown in Figure 5.2 and Color Plate 2. Brightness is shown along the vertical axis, extending from white at the top to black at the base. The vertical line through the middle of the spindle represents various shades of gray. Saturation is shown laterally and varies from the center out to the periphery, with the most saturated colors located on the rim of the central circle and at the midpoint of the vertical distance between white and black. The conical shape of the spindle reflects the fact that saturation is maximal only at moderate or intermediate brightness levels. In other words, saturation depends secondarily on brightness. The farther from the middle of the brightness axis, either lighter or darker, the less is the saturation of a hue; the addition of either white or black desaturates a hue. This also means that no very bright or very dark color is highly saturated. At the extremes of the color spindle—toward white or black—lights appear colorless.

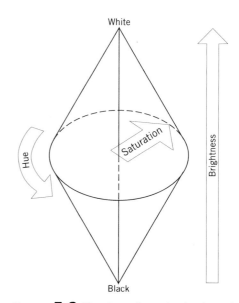

◻ ***figure 5.2*** The three-dimensional color spindle. The spindle is constructed so as to locate every possible color sensation somewhere within the three-dimensional color space.

COLOR MIXTURE

Generally, pure colors generated by a single wavelength—monochromatic colors—occur rarely, and then only under precise laboratory conditions. Most often the light that reaches the eye is composed of a mixture of wavelengths. It is important to recall here a point made earlier in this chapter: The colors we see are based on the responses of the visual system to different wavelengths of light. The wavelengths themselves are unaffected by the mixture. With this in mind, we turn to a discussion of two kinds of color mixtures: *additive* and *subtractive*. Since additive color mixtures are much more relevant to the understanding of color perception, we have much more to say about them.

Additive Color Mixture

Additive color mixtures result when lights of various wavelengths are combined. This means that we are *adding* the effects—the visual excitations—of different wavelengths in the visual system. Thus, when we observe an additive mixture of 530-nm green and 650-nm red, we experience their combined effects— the effects of a middle-wavelength green light *plus* the effects of a long-wavelength red light on the visual system. Several rules or principles governing the mixing of various wavelengths of light have been worked out, and we will highlight some of them by describing two schemes: one based on a color appearance system using a *color circle* and a more precise scheme based on *color matching*. Both are useful, but each stresses different points concerning the phenomena of color mixture.

Color Circle, Complementary Colors, and Metamers
Some of the essential phenomena of additive color mixture are summarized in the **color circle** of Figure 5.3. The color circle corresponds to the central circle of the color spindle of Figure 5.2. The color circle is the midpoint slice of the spindle. Lights of various spectral wavelengths and their corresponding color sensations are arranged along the circle's circumference, and degrees of satu-

ration are represented along its radius; the saturation of a color decreases with the distance from the circumference to the center of the circle.

In creating the color circle, the colors were specially arranged to highlight certain essential phenomena. Every color has its **complementary color** that lies diametrically opposite it on the color circle. When mixed together in the proper proportions, the color and its complement produces a mixture that appears gray. Complementary colors cancel each other's effects on the visual system. The following are common pairs of complementary colors: blue and yellow, red and blue-green, green and purple. (Note that purple lies within the gap of the color circle—an "extraspectral" region representing colors or hues that cannot be specified by a single wavelength but must be produced by mixtures of spectral lights.)

Mixtures of noncomplementary colors result in sensations that lie intermediate on the color circle between the colors mixed. Thus, if the colors are mixed in equal amounts, a new color lies on the color circle halfway between the two component colors. An example of this is given at *A* of Figure 5.3. Here

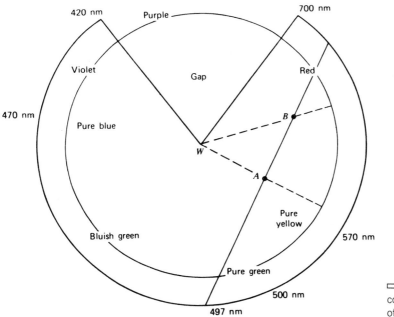

□ *figure 5.3* The color circle corresponding to the central circle of the color spindle of Figure 5.2.

equal proportions of red and green produce a yellow color sensation. That is, the color sensation produced by the mixture of red and green light matches the sensation produced by a yellow light. Pairs of colors like these, which appear to be the same color but come from different wavelengths, are called **metamers.** That is, metamers are pairs of lights of physically different wavelengths that have the same effect on the visual system and hence appear identical in color. In our example, the mixture of red and green appears identical to yellow; thus, they are *metamers* or *metameric pairs,* and the color match between the pair of colors is called a *metameric match*. Metamers illustrate an important point about mixing colored lights: Once the lights are combined, the visual system cannot distinguish the individual components.

If the colors are mixed in unequal amounts, we can approximate the resultant color on the color circle by drawing a line connecting the two component colors and placing a point on the line representing the proportion in which they are mixed. The location of the point designates the color and its saturation. As *B* of Figure 5.3 shows, when more red than green is mixed, the resultant color of the mixture lies closer to the component that makes the greater contribution, namely, red.

The saturation of the mixture is less than the saturation of one or both of the component colors. As an approximate rule, the farther away the constituent colors lie from each other, the less is the saturation of the resultant color. This is depicted graphically by the examples of *A* and *B* in Figure 5.3: Any mixture falls closer to the center (the desaturated region) of the color circle than do the components that comprise it.

Color Matching The color circle, while providing a good qualitative summary of many of the basic phenomena of color mixture, is limited. A more precise way of expressing and designating color mixture uses a system of color matching that relies on a *trichromatic* notion of color vision. The trichromatic notion is based on the fact that any color can be produced by combining various amounts of three specially chosen colored lights. The colors of these lights are called **primary colors** because they appear psychologically unique, not easily reducible to compo-

nent colors. Although generally lights that appear blue, green, and red are chosen as the three primaries, many different sets of primaries are possible as long as no primary can be matched by a mixture of the other two or can cancel out another's effect (i.e., no primary is complementary to another primary). In short, with certain limitations, primary colors can be combined in various proportions to match all spectral colors, including white (with the possible exception of the so-called metallic colors: silver, gold, and copper). Color Plate 3 illustrates some of the colors that result from the mixture of three primaries. Note that when the three primary colors are mixed together in equal amounts—shown at the intersection of the primaries—they produce the sensation of white light.

By using the following procedure, it is possible to match any color. Spectral light of a given wavelength is shown on a *test field,* and the viewer adjusts the proportion of the three primaries that are mixed on an adjacent *comparison field* until a match is made (Figure 5.4). This method of color matching is a form of metameric matching. The match is purely a subjective psychological effect: Although the two fields create equal effects on the visual system and thus appear identical in color, the wavelength compositions of each may differ greatly from each other. As we noted earlier, once the spectral lights are mixed in the comparison field, the visual system cannot distinguish the individual components. We cannot recognize or ana-

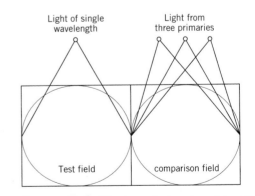

▭ figure 5.4 Stimulus display for the color-matching task. The test field consists of a surface illuminated by a single wavelength. The viewer adjusts the amount of the three primaries in the comparison field until it matches the color in the test field.

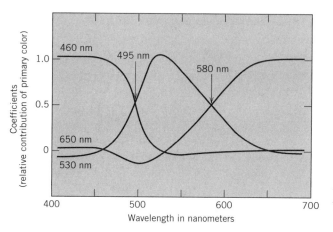

□ *figure* **5.5** Color-mixture curves. Plotted are the relative amounts of each primary needed to match any part of the visual spectrum. (The colors of some short and very long wavelengths cannot be matched without first modifying them. A negative value indicates that in order to match these colors, one of the primary colors was first added to it; this was necessary to reduce its saturation to a point where it could be matched by a mixture of the two remaining primaries. In this example of matching a 495-nm bluish-green, it was necessary to first add some 650-nm red before it could be matched by the blue and green lights.) (After Wright, 1928.)

lyze a color mixture into its spectral components by merely viewing it.

When this procedure is applied throughout the spectrum, a set of curves like those shown in Figure 5.5, called **color-mixture curves,** results. Though many sets of tristimuli (i.e., lights composed of three different wavelengths) are possible, the primaries used in Figure 5.5 are a 460-nm blue, a 530-nm green, and a 650-nm red. Based on a tristimulus specification of any color (C), a general color equation can be stated:

$$(C) = xR + yG + zB$$

where x, y, and z are the coefficients or proportions of the three fixed wavelengths (plotted on the y-axis of Figure 5.5) whose contributions vary depending on the color to be matched. Thus, for example, under proper conditions, the mixture of equal amounts of red (650 nm) and green (530 nm) (and no 460-nm blue) perfectly match a yellow (roughly at 580 nm). In fact, as we noted, if they are properly matched, it is not possible to tell which is which. A 580-nm yellow light has the same effect on the visual system as does the mixture of 530-nm green and 650-nm red light.

In addition to the color circle and color matching technique there are various procedures for showing the additive nature of mixing lights. This is done by projecting beams of light from three projectors onto a screen, with each projector equipped with a different colored filter. This is how the color mixtures illustrated

in Color Plate 3 were made: Colors apparent at the intersections of the beams illustrate the effect of the additive mixture of lights. Thus, for example, where only the red and green beams overlap, the light appears yellow; and in the center, where the three beams overlap (so that the visual system receives the reflected light from all three primaries), the light appears white.

Another simple means of observing an additive color mixture is to use a color wheel on which disks of colored paper are assembled (Figure 5.6). The colored disks can be overlapped and adjusted so that different-sized angular sectors of each color are exposed, thereby varying the proportions of the component colors. When the wheel is rotated rapidly, the component colors stimulate the visual system but they cannot

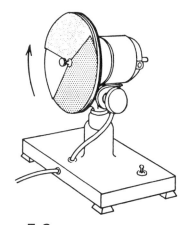

□ *figure* **5.6** A color wheel.

be individually resolved; instead, a completely fused and uniform color is seen based on the additive mixture of the constituent colors.

Artists have also used an additive method of color mixture directly on the canvas. In the technique called *pointillism* or *divisionism,* used by the French Impressionist painters (e.g., Seurat and Signac), the paints were not mixed; instead, the artist placed tiny, discrete dots of colored paint close together on the canvas. When viewed from a certain distance, the discrete dots are not visible as such, but apparently fuse to produce an additive color mixture. An example of this sort of color mixture is given in Color Plate 4.

Perhaps the most common example of additive color mixture is color television. Generally, the screen of a color television set is composed of a mosaic of closely packed spots of only three colors, usually red, green, and blue, whose intensity can be individually varied (see Color Plate 5). Thus, when the screen displays various colors, it does so by individually varying the intensity of the spots. Because the spots are very small, they cannot be seen separately at the usual viewing distance: Hence, they appear fused, or blended together, and their combined effect—an additive color mixture—results in the sensation of a distinct color.

DEMONSTRATION:
Additive Color Mixture

It may not be obvious in casual viewing, but an apparent patch of "yellow" seen on a color television screen is composed of small red and green spots. To demonstrate this for yourself, place a magnifying glass against a "yellow" patch on the television screen. The discrete spots that now appear are clearly not yellow. The same procedure applied to a "white" area on the screen will reveal that the white sensation is in fact created by equally illuminated blue, green, and red spots. Both of these examples are consistent with what we have said about additive color mixture.

Subtractive Color Mixture

The phenomena illustrated by the color circle and color matching technique apply to the mixture of colored lights but not to the mixing of pigments, paints, or dyes. Mixtures of lights and mixtures of pigments are physically quite different. In the former case, involving additive color mixtures, lights are combined—colored lights *add* their dominant wavelengths to the mixture. This is an *additive* process in that when light strikes the eye, the effects of the individual wavelengths of the light are added together in the nervous system.

In contrast, we can understand the idea of **subtractive color mixture** by recalling a point made earlier in this chapter: The color of a surface depends on the wavelengths it absorbs and reflects. Thus, when light strikes colored paint, for example, pigments in the paint selectively absorb or *subtract* some wavelengths striking them and reflect the remaining wavelengths that give the paint its unique color. A blue surface appears blue because the surface pigment absorbs or subtracts all but the wavelengths of light that appear as blue. Hence, when white light falls on the surface, its blue wavelengths are largely reflected to the eyes of the viewer, and the other wavelengths are largely absorbed. Similarly, mixing two paints involves a mutual absorption or subtraction process, canceling the reflectance of all wavelengths but those that the pigments in the two paints reflect in common (Color Plate 6).

A practical distinction can be made between additive and subtractive color mixtures with respect to where the light mixture occurs. With additive color mixtures, the lights are mixed together in the eyes, that is, excitations from the component lights are added together in the visual system. In contrast, with subtractive color mixtures, the component colors are first mixed together on a palette or in a paint can, where the subtraction of colors by light absorption occurs, and only the remaining light reaches the eye.

As another example of the difference between additive and subtractive color mixtures, consider the familiar pair of complementaries, blue and yellow (Figure 5.7). As lights (Figure 5.7*a*), the additive mix-

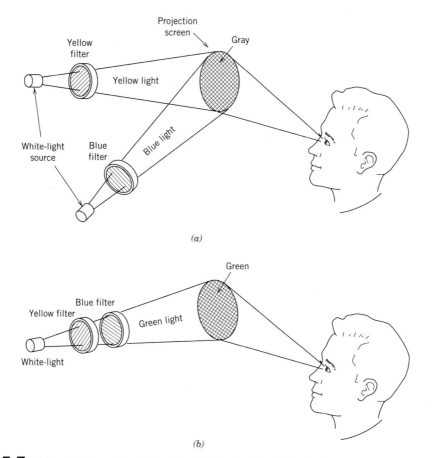

□ *figure* **5.7** (*a*) An additive mixture. When blue light and yellow light, which are complementary to each other, are projected onto the surface of a projection screen and then reflected to the eyes the mixture appears gray. (*b*) A subtractive mixture of yellow and blue produces green. (Note that the filters placed in series, here, produce the same effect as does the mixing of pigments.)

ture yields gray—the combined effect of the two lights on the visual system—whereas as a *subtractive color mixture* of pigments (Figure 5.7*b*), their combined absorption produces the reflection of wavelengths that appear predominantly green. Specifically, the yellow pigment of the first filter absorbs (i.e., subtracts) mainly short wavelengths (e.g., blue, violet) and transmits medium and long ones. These strike the blue pigment of the second filter, which absorbs primarily long wavelengths (i.e., yellow, orange, and red) and transmits medium and short ones. Thus, the long wavelengths are removed by the blue filter and the

short wavelengths by the yellow filter; this leaves the residual middle band of wavelengths that are transmitted by both pigments and that, when reflected from the screen onto the viewer's eyes, appear green. That is, all other wavelengths but those that appear green are absorbed in the combination.

In practice, it is difficult to predict accurately the resultant color from a mixture of pigments—certainly much more difficult than is the case for additive color mixtures. This is because, with subtractive mixtures, we must know the precise wavelengths absorbed by each of the component pigments. However, the absorption properties of the typical pigment are strongly dependent on its complex physical and chemical composition and generally are not readily determined by inspection alone.

In the next section, we describe some color phenomena, called *afterimages,* that relate to some of the principles of color mixture.

AFTERIMAGES

Effects of a visual stimulus may persist after its physical termination in a form called **afterimages.** The usual means of demonstrating afterimages is to have a viewer stare at a stimulus patch for about 30 to 60 sec, after which the gaze is transferred to a different surface. There are two kinds of afterimages. One, much less frequent and more fleeting, is called a *positive afterimage,* in that the afterimage maintains the same black–white brightness relations and colors as the original stimulus. Positive afterimages most often occur after brief, intense stimulation of the dark-adapted eye (e.g., the effects of a flashbulb). The more frequent *negative afterimage* refers to the persistence of the image in a reversed state. That is, the black and white and colored effects are reversed, as in a photographic negative.

▯ **DEMONSTRATION:**
An Achromatic Example of a Negative Afterimage

Figure 5.8 presents an achromatic example of a negative afterimage. Stare at the dot in the white profile for about 30 sec and then shift your gaze to the dot in the white square. You should see a negative afterimage in the white square, that is, a dark profile instead of a white one.

Successive and Simultaneous Contrast

Continued exposure to a specific color—**color adaptation**—may reduce one's sensitivity to the color. Some unusual effects may be produced by selective

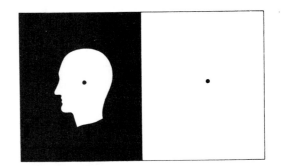

▱ *figure 5.8* Demonstration of an achromatic negative afterimage.

color adaptation. If a colored stimulus is stared at and the gaze is then directed to a neutral white or gray surface, a negative afterimage results that is the complementary color of the initial stimulus. This phenomenon, called **successive color contrast,** is an example of a **complementary afterimage.** Color Plate 7 demonstrates a complementary afterimage of a familiar object.

How long a complementary afterimages lasts depends on the intensity and length of exposure to the adapting color. Such afterimages last long enough (about 30 sec or more) to be "projected" onto other colored surfaces. The complementary afterimage then combines with the new colored surface to yield a single fused color sensation. By using a color's complementary afterimage, striking, unnatural color effects may be produced. For example, if a blue patch is fixated on for a minute, after which the gaze is transferred to a yellow surface, the surface will appear excessively saturated, or "supersaturated" (Color Plate 8). Here the complementary afterimage of the blue patch (yellow) has been projected onto a yellow surface. This is illustrated in Color Plates 8 and 9.

▯ **DEMONSTRATION:**
Adaptation and Complementary Afterimages

If the instructions for Color Plates 8 and 9 are correctly followed, it will be clear that continual exposure of a particular region of the fovea by a particular color produces a loss in sensitivity to that color. Interestingly, as Color Plate 9 demonstrates, the loss occurs with no clear or immediate perception of a change in saturation. Thus, during fixation of the blue patch, the region of the retina that is stimulated becomes *adapted*, fatigued, or less sensitive to that particular color, and it appears relatively desaturated.

This is functionally equivalent to making the same retinal area more sensitive to its complementary, yellow. That is, prolonged exposure of a region of the retina to blue increases the sensitivity of that region to yellow. Thus, when continued inspection of the blue patch fatigues the receptors normally mediating a blue sensation, a yellow afterimage results. If the gaze then shifts to a yellow surface (as shown in Color Plate 8), the additive mixture of the yellow afterimage and the yellow surface makes the yellow surface appear more saturated than is normal.

Similar effects are seen with **simultaneous contrast** (sometimes termed *spatial induction of the complementary*). After continued fixation of a colored stimulus patch that appears against a neutral or gray background, the edge of the background bordering the patch appears to be tinged with its complementary. In part, this is because, with continued inspection, the color patch loses saturation (coinciding with the induction of its complementary). Since the eyes move slightly, even during fixation, the retinal image of the patch is not perfectly stationary, and the decreased saturation or slight appearance of the patch's complementary appears at its edges. If the color's complement is substituted for the neutral background, the usual complementary tinge of the patch sums with the chromatic background to produce a simultaneous supersaturation at the edges of the patch (see Color Plate 10).

MEMORY COLOR

An additional factor that may influence the perception of an object's color is its familiarity and color associations. This is especially true when stimuli whose colors are to be matched have characteristic and distinctive shapes that are closely associated with objects that typically occur in a single color. An example would be perceiving the color of a gray stimulus shaped like a banana as slightly yellow or a leaf as slightly green. The effects of familiarity and past experience on apparent color are due to what Ewald Hering (1920) termed **memory color.**

A classic study by Duncker (1939) illustrates memory color. Cutouts of a leaf and a donkey made from the same green felt material were successively shown bathed by hidden red illumination that was the complementary of the color of the green cutouts; thus, each stimulus cutout reflected the same gray. According to the notion of memory color, past experience with objects associated with these shapes influences their apparent color. Therefore, the cutout of the leaf, typically green, should appear greener than the cutout of the characteristically gray donkey. Matches of the apparent color of each stimulus made on an adjustable red-green color wheel indicated that the amount of green required to match the color of the cutout of the leaf was about twice as much as that needed to match the color of the cutout of the donkey. That is, although both stimuli reflected the same gray light, the cutout of the leaf, presumably owing to the influence of memory color, appeared to be somewhat greener than the cutout of the donkey. The obvious conclusion is that previous color and form associations—*memory color*—do have a strong effect on perceived color. This experiment, in a number of variations, has been repeated and its essential findings confirmed (e.g., Delk & Fillenbaum, 1965; Epstein, 1967).

A variation of memory color using afterimages was reported by White and Montgomery (1976). In their demonstration, observers formed afterimages of either a flag-like pattern (i.e., an American flag printed in its complementary colors, consisting of black stars, an orange field, and blue-green stripes, like Color Plate 7) or a simple blue-green striped pattern (identical to the stripes in the flag pattern). Observers then adjusted a color display to match the afterimage colors. The observers generally perceived the complementary afterimages of the stripes in the flag pattern as more red than they did the afterimages of the same stripes in the simple striped pattern. These results indicate that memory color plays a role in afterimages: Afterimages that represent familiar objects are affected by the colors in which the objects normally appear.

COLOR CONSTANCY

As we have noted, the wavelength reflected from the surface of an object is the major determinant of its color. However, in natural viewing, the light reflected from a surface depends not only on the wavelengths it reflects but also on the light illuminating the surface. If the spectral components—the wavelengths—illuminating an object change, so will the wavelengths of the reflected light. You don't have to perform a formal demonstration to convince yourself of this. The yellowish tint of the familiar tungsten light bulb (dominated by long wavelengths) differs markedly from the bluish tint of fluorescent bulbs (dominated by short wavelengths), and both differ from the natural light of the sun (which contains about an equal distribution of all visible wavelengths). It would seem, then, that the perceived color of an object illuminated in turn by these light sources should also change. Nevertheless, within limits, we see objects and surfaces as retaining the same color in spite of changes in the spectral composition of the illuminating light. In other words, while the light reflected from an object's surface actually changes when the spectrum of light illuminating it changes, we do not generally notice much, if any, of a change in its color. The tendency for an object's color to remain *constant,* in spite of wavelength changes in the light illuminating it, is called **color constancy.** Color constancy is so common that we are usually unaware of it. However, it is easily verified by using some of the colors mentioned in this chapter. A green surface appears about the same green whether it is illuminated by fluorescent light or by a tungsten bulb; thus, color constancy prevails. Yet, if you view the same green surface through an "artificial pupil" (a small hole punched in a piece of opaque cardboard)—blocking out everything except the green color surface—its color will differ somewhat, depending on how it is illuminated. It will appear bluish-green when illuminated by the fluorescent light

and yellowish-green when seen under the tungsten bulb; under these restrictive viewing conditions, color constancy is eliminated.

Factors Influencing Color Constancy

A complete explanation of color constancy remains elusive, but two factors seem to play a role.

Effects of Background The previous example of restrictive viewing points out that the visual system seems capable of taking into account and compensating for spectral changes in illumination that affect the *entire* visual scene equally. Thus, for color constancy to occur, the spectral changes in illumination that result from, say, going from natural outdoor sunlight to artificial indoor fluorescent or tungsten light must fall over the entire visual scene. This makes sense since, in natural viewing, adjacent objects and surfaces are seen together. Natural variations in overhead illumination typically fall on the entire visual scene, not just on a small region seen in isolation. A change in overhead illumination that affects only a single object or a small, isolated area is an unnatural occurrence.

Color Adaptation Another factor that may contribute to color constancy is *color adaptation,* based on the visual system's adaptation to the dominant wavelengths lighting up a scene. If a scene is illuminated by a tungsten light bulb, the visual system soon becomes less sensitive to the dominant long wavelengths of tungsten light. A white sheet of paper illuminated by a tungsten light source would appear very yellow if the visual system did not adapt to the general conditions of illumination. In other words, the visual system adapts to the yellowish wavelengths of tungsten, and they thus appear less yellowish. Adaptation also occurs with the dominant wavelengths of fluorescent lighting, decreasing the eye's sensitivity to short, bluish wavelengths. In other words, due to color adaptation, the visual system compensates for any dominant long or short wavelengths produced by artificial light. This relative insensitivity to dominant wavelengths illuminating a scene reduces or cancels their effect on the perception of colors—producing a sensory correction—and this results in color constancy.

Function of Color Constancy

Color constancy (along with other constancies described later in this text) strongly influences our perception of a stable environment. Imagine the problem of recognizing objects if every change in illumination changed the perception of their color. It would be necessary, for example, to assign different color names to the same objects just because of changes in the dominant wavelengths of their illumination. Under such conditions, we would be forced to ignore, or discount, or somehow "neutralize" the sensory effects of the colors of objects rather than utilize them.

Although color constancy allows us to correct for the dominant wavelengths of artificial light, it probably evolved to compensate for the variations in natural conditions of lighting. That is, it probably adjusts for the relatively small changes in illumination that occur between the rising and setting sun (depending on atmospheric conditions)—from the red of dawn, to the intense yellow-orange of noon, to the bluish or sometimes deep reddish glow of twilight.

Color constancy has limits. On occasion, we are very much aware of a change in the color of an object when lighting conditions vary. We are dismayed to see, for example, that a piece of fabric that appeared to be a certain blue when seen under fluorescent light is a very different blue in sunlight. For this reason, the color-conscious shopper often observes samples of colored fabrics in various lighting conditions before making a purchase.

THEORIES OF COLOR PERCEPTION

Numerous theories have tried to account for the many phenomena of color perception. Two main theories (more accurately, levels of explanation) have emerged as most consistent with contemporary research. Our discussion will be confined largely to them.

Trichromatic Receptor Theory (Young–Helmholtz Theory)

The phenomena of color mixture suggest certain structural, functional, and neural mechanisms of the retina. Because lights of three distinct wavelengths are enough to produce the complete visible spectrum, it is possible that there are three corresponding types of receptors in the human retina, each with different spectral sensitivities.

Thomas Young, an English scientist (who deciphered the Rosetta stone), in 1802 proposed such a trichromatic receptor theory. It was revived in 1866 by Herman von Helmholtz, who extended Young's initial theory by postulating the existence of three types of receptors with maximal sensitivity to the wavelengths corresponding to blue, green, and red colors. Each type of receptor, he proposed, is most sensitive to a specific band of wavelengths that appear either blue, green, or red; however, the responses of each type are graded, or relative, with each showing some activity to the wavelengths of other colors as well. That is, the sensitivities of the different receptor types somewhat overlap each other.

Thus in its simplest form, the **trichromatic receptor theory** (sometimes called the **Young–Helmholtz theory**) maintains that only three types of receptors are required to produce all the colors resulting from the distribution of spectral lights. Accordingly, all color sensations are produced by the appropriate proportional contribution of a three-receptor or trichromatic system.

[We pause here to acknowledge a matter concerning the history of the trichromatic receptor theory. Although this theory is generally attributed to Young and Helmholtz, equally important contributions were made earlier by other scientists. Wasserman (1978) notes that the work of Isaac Newton and the work of the physicist James Clerk Maxwell were especially significant.]

S, M, and L Cones There is strong physiological evidence for the existence of a three-receptor system at the level of the retina. Three distinct groups of cones exist, each maximally responsive to a different wavelength. Actually, three classes of *photopigments* are segregated in three kinds of cones. Marks, Dobelle, and MacNichol (1964) directed a fine beam of light on isolated cone photoreceptors of the retinas of monkeys and humans and measured the absorption of light by the pigment of a single cone for different spectral wavelengths. The more a given wavelength was absorbed by the pigment of a cone, the more sensitive that cone was to light of that wavelength. The results, shown in Figure 5.9, indicate that for cones, peaks of absorption fall into three major groups, with maximum absorption of one cone type to short wavelengths at about 445 nm (labeled "S"), another to medium wavelengths with its peak at about 535 nm ("M"), and a third to long wavelengths with a peak at 570 nm ("L"). [Several later studies substantiated the existence of three light-sensitive pigments, each found in a different cone type; the peak wavelength absorptions of these pigments are similar to the absorption peaks of the pigments cited above and described in Figure 5.9 (e.g., see Brown & Wald, 1964; Merbs & Nathans, 1992; Schnapf, Kraft, & Baylor, 1987).]

Note, however, the overlap in the absorption curves of Figure 5.9; this indicates that each cone pigment absorbs a relatively broad range of wavelengths. The cone pigments that maximally absorb medium and long wavelengths are sensitive across most of the visible spectrum, whereas the cone pig-

ment sensitive to short wavelengths responds to less than half of the spectrum. As a result, many wavelengths of light stimulate more than one type of cone. In other words, different wavelengths of light activate each type of cone to different extents. For example, as shown in Figure 5.9, a 450-nm light shone on the retina creates a strong absorption effect by the short-wavelength cones and has little effect on the medium- and long-wavelength cones (and appears blue), whereas a 560-nm light affects only the cones with peak absorption of the medium and long wavelengths (and appears greenish-yellow). Although not shown in the figure, if a spot of white light is projected on the retina, all three types of cones are stimulated equally, creating a white sensation. Relating all color sensations to the activity of only three independent cone types suggests that the visual system employs the trichromatic principle of color television introduced in the section on additive color mixture, but in reverse: Instead of displaying the colors, it analyzes them.

Further support for the existence of specific cone pigments has come from the research of Rushton (1962; Baker & Rushton, 1965), using different measuring techniques. He reported the existence of a photosensitive pigment for green called **chlorolabe** (from the Greek, meaning "green catcher"); a pigment for red, **erythrolabe** ("red catcher"); and the possible existence of a third pigment for blue, **cyanolabe** ("blue catcher"). Although we conclude that there are three different types of cones, with a single distinct pigment residing in each type, they are not equal in

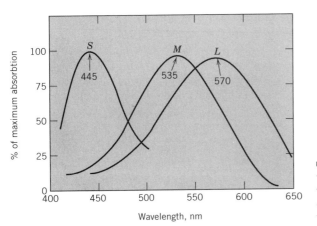

□ *figure* **5.9** Absorption curves. Note that all three cone types absorb light over a wide range of wavelengths and that their absorption curves overlap each other; thus, many wavelengths of light may activate more than one type of cone.

number. The blue-pigment cones, sensitive to short wavelengths, are quite sparse relative to the cones sensitive to medium and long wavelengths. Furthermore, there seem to be twice as many cones with a pigment sensitive to long wavelengths as there are cones with a pigment sensitive to medium wavelengths (Cicerone & Nerger, 1989; Nerger & Cicerone, 1992).

Thus, three types of cone pigments are specialized to absorb portions of light over a limited range of wavelengths, each with a peak absorption at a particular region of the spectrum. Because of their peak sensitivities to short, medium, and long wavelengths, these three cone pigments are often referred to as **S cones,** **M cones,** and **L cones,** respectively.

These and numerous other studies, along with many of the facts of color mixture, support the trichromatic theory of color vision, at least at the level of the retina. The trichromatic theory is also consistent with the phenomena of complementary afterimages. If we assume that there is, roughly speaking, an S (blue), an M (green), and an L (red) cone, then if you stare at a blue patch for a short time as suggested by the demonstration of Color Plate 11, the pigment in the S cones (blue) becomes selectively adapted or fatigued. When the foveal gaze is transferred to a chromatically neutral white or gray surface, only the two unadapted cone pigments are active—the M (green) and the L (red) cones—creating the yellow-appearing complementary afterimage; the additive mixture of L cone (red) and M cone (green) activity on the visual system produces a yellow sensation (which is the complementary of blue). Relatedly, staring at a yellow surface selectively adapts the cones that produce a yellowish sensation—namely, the L (red) and M (green) cones—so that the blue-appearing negative afterimage is due to the activity of the remaining unadapted S cones (blue).

The trichromatic receptor theory also allows us to understand the phenomenon introduced in the section on color mixture: that a yellow sensation produced by monochromatic 580-nm light is identical to the yellow sensation produced by the additive mixture of green medium-wavelength and red long-wavelength light (e.g., as on a TV screen). Although they are quite different in physical stimuli, both lights are absorbed by the pigments of the M and L cones to exactly the same extent. They produce the *same effect* on the visual system. In this sense, neither one is more or less "yellow" than the other. Both lights have the same absorption effects on the receptive cone pigments. Finally, the trichromatic receptor theory is consistent with the finding that when all pigments are stimulated equally, we see white.

Opponent-Process Theory

A second major theory of theory of color vision, the **opponent-process theory,** is traced to Ewald Hering, a German physiologist (1920). Like the Young–Helmholtz trichomatic receptor theory, it proposes three independent mechanisms, each assumed to be composed of a pair of *opponent* color processes of neural systems: a blue-yellow, a green-red, and a white-black opponent process. Each receptor is capable of two kinds of sensory responses that are antagonistic to each other. That is, a receptor can respond in only one of two possible ways. It follows that either red *or* green and yellow *or* blue is experienced, but not yellow *and* blue or red *and* green.

As with the trichromatic notion, observations on complementary afterimages conform to the opponent-process theory. If the stimulation of one member of a receptor pair is prolonged (and presumably fatigued) and the gaze is then shifted to an achromatic or colorless surface, a complementary afterimage will appear (as illustrated by Color Plates 7 and 11). If both members of a receptor pair are equally stimulated, they cancel each other out (as with mixtures of complementary colors such as blue and yellow), resulting in a gray or colorless sensation.

A more recent approach to the idea of opponent processes mediating color vision has been taken by Hurvich and Jameson (e.g., 1955, 1957, 1974). In keeping with the trichromatic notion, they have proposed that there are three types of retinal photoreceptors (or cones), each sensitive to a different region of the visible spectrum. But they have elaborated on Hering's original notion by proposing that these receptor types are linked to three pairs of neural opponent processes that lie at further levels of the visual system. In keeping with Hering's idea, they postulate a *blue-yellow* process, a *green-red* process, and an achromatic *white-black* process (whose function is to transmit light intensity rather than hue). Within each pair of neural processes, one physiological response characteristic is antagonistic to the other (i.e., blue is antagonistic to yellow and green is antagonistic to red). For example, the red-green opponent process is organized so that it reacts in opposite ways to red and green lights.

Therefore, according to Hurvich and Jameson, three different kinds of receptors process wavelength information at the retinal level of the cones, and these feed into three opponent processes at a neural level beyond the receptors. Essentially, Hurvich and Jameson propose that color coding is a *two-stage process:* Antagonistic or opponent properties result from stimulation of receptors with trichomatic properties.

Measuring the Opponent Process

Based on an opponent-process notion, it is possible to measure the color sensation for any given wavelength of light. Because the two members of an opponent process are mutually antagonistic, they cancel each other's color sensation (as do complementary colors). Therefore, the magnitude of a given color response can be measured by the amount of the opponent member needed to cancel the color sensation. This is called the **null** or **hue cancellation method.** For example, the strength of a blue sensory response is determined by the amount of yellow light that must be added to *cancel* or *neutralize* the blue sensation. Similarly, the strength of the yellow sensory response is determined by the amount of blue light that must be added to cancel the yellow sensation. The same is true of the green and red sensations. The null method, serving as a direct measure of opponent-process activity, allows us to assess color sensation at all wavelengths across the visible spectrum.

Physiological Basis of Opponent Processes

A good deal of neurophysiological evidence shows that opponent processes operate beyond the cone level of the retina. Recall from Chapter 3 that the X cells at the retinal ganglion level, which mediate acuity, also process color information. In addition, color-sensitive cells are part of the parvocellular division linking the LGN with the cortex. Neural activity recorded from the ganglion level of the retina and the LGN reveals that some cells increase their rates of firing (above a spontaneous or baseline level) for foveal stimulation by some wavelengths and decrease them for others. In short, they show color-opponent properties.

Consider some evidence for opponent-color processing with various species of animals. Wagner, MacNichol, and Wolbarsht (1960; see also Daw, 1967; Svaetichin, 1956) found that the ganglion cells of the goldfish gave ON-OFF responses to stimulation by white light. However, when lights of a single wavelength were presented, an excitatory, or ON, response to a band of wavelengths for a given cell turned into an inhibitory, or OFF, response to other wavelengths. That is, for a given cell, the ON-OFF response differed for different wavelengths.

DeValois, Abramov, and Jacobs (1966; DeValois & Jacobs, 1984) inserted microelectrodes into single cells in the LGN of the Macaque monkey (which has essentially the same color vision as the human) and recorded the neural activity in response to different wavelengths. Some cells directly increased or decreased their rates of firing in response to any wavelength. However, there were opponent-type cells whose overall response rates varied with wavelength; they were excited by some wavelengths and inhibited by others, and they generally showed differing firing rates to different wavelengths. Figure 5.10 shows one such cell. If the cell is stimulated with long-wavelength red light (633 nm), it fires vigorously at the onset and throughout the duration of the light, whereas it is relatively inhibited at the offset of the light. In contrast, short and moderate wavelengths of light that appear blue or green inhibit the cell during presentation of the light, followed by vigorous activity at offset. This type of cell, showing excitation to red light and inhibition to green light, is labeled an $+R - G$ *opponent cell*. The opponency of the cell in responding to red and green is essentially the process proposed by Hering. Subsequent research has revealed many different types of cells with antagonistic or opponent properties. They are excited by wavelengths at one end of the spectrum and inhibited by wavelengths at the other end, and thus encode color information in terms of excitation and inhibition.

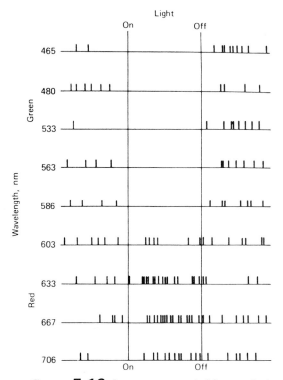

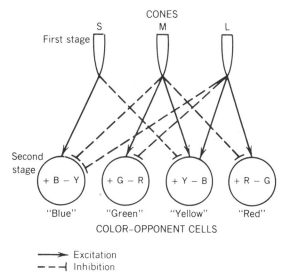

□ figure 5.10 Responses recorded from a single microelectrode inserted in a cell of the LGN of a monkey. [The firing before the stimulation (light onset) is due to the spontaneous firing of the cell.] (After DeValois et al., 1966.)

□ figure 5.11 Schematic depiction of two-stage color theory. Three classes of cones with peak sensitivities at short (S), medium (M), and long (L) wavelengths feed into color-opponent cells of the second stage. For example, a +B −Y opponent cell is excited by S cones and inhibited by both M and L cones (recall that activity of M and L cones produces a yellow sensation). In contrast, the +Y −B cell is excited by M and L cones and inhibited by S cones. Similar logic applies to activation of the +G −R and +R −G cells.

The discovery of color-opponent cells has been incorporated in a two-stage theory in which the color information processed by three types of receptors, as in the trichromatic receptor theory, feeds into color-opponent cells at further levels in the visual system. This two-stage color theory is depicted in Figure 5.11.

We conclude that both the trichromatic receptor and opponent-process mechanisms mediate color perception. The trichromatic mechanism applies to color coding at the level of the retinal receptors (the cones), whereas opponent processes operate on specific cells further along in the visual system. We will now describe opponent process activity that occurs within neurons in the visual cortex.

Color Coding in the Brain: Blobs

Color-opponent neurons have been identified in the visual cortex, but their organization is more compli-

cated than that of opponent cells at the retinal ganglion level or in the LGN. Livingstone and Hubel (1984; Hubel & Livingstone, 1983; Livingstone, 1987) have reported a somewhat regular mosaic or dot-like pattern of dark regions (each about 0.2 mm in diameter), distributed in layers over the primary visual or striate cortex, that they call *blobs.*

Blobs are composed of neurons that are not tuned to orientation, shape, or movement but react exclusively to color. Moreover, the activity of color-coded cortical neurons from these regions differs substantially from that of the opponent color cells discussed so far. We have been dealing with a simple opponent process in which a cell is excited by one color and inhibited by another. However, many color opponent cells of the cortex possess concentric, **double-opponent receptive fields** (Michael, 1978*a*, 1978*b*). Double-opponent cells have an antagonistic center-surround organization, with each component having a dual effect; that is, both the center and the surround are color opponent. Thus, the center increases its activity to one color and decreases it to the complementary color; in contrast, its surround has exactly the opposite pattern. Figure 5.12 shows the organization of a double-opponent cortical cell in which the center of its receptive field shows excitation to red and inhibition to green, whereas its surround shows inhibition to red and increased activity to green.

Figures 5.12b and 5.12c suggest how a linear arrangement of the receptive fields of double-opponent color-coded neurons of the cortex may be organized to react to chromatic bars and rectangles. Shown are the cells of one opponent-color system (e.g., +R −G center) that have antagonistic flanking regions with a reverse double-opponent arrangement (+G −R surround). The neural activity of the concentric cells feeds into a simple cortical cell. Figure 5.12c shows the response to chromatic bars of light. Clearly, of the stimulus possibilities examined, the greatest neural response to the stimulus occurs when a red bar covers the central region and is flanked by two green bars (see row 5 of Figure 5.12c). The red bar stimulates the +R −G centers, whereas the adjacent green bars stimulate the +G −R surrounds. In short, the excitation from the red in the center is combined with the excitation of the green in the surround, causing each cell to fire at its maximum. It seems reasonable to propose that the organization of double-opponent process cells plays some role in simultaneous contrast, such as shown in Color Plate 10. The activity of cells possessing double-opponent receptive fields is consistent with the exaggerated brightness that is apparent when fixation is on the border region of the two adjacent complementary colors (i.e., a red center and a green surround).

Much is yet to be worked out, but it is reasonable to conclude that the characteristics of a color stimulus are processed and neurally transmitted along the visual system by means of opponent-type color coding cells. Thus, there is clear evidence for an initial trichromatic receptor stage of photosensitivity, followed by opponent processing beginning at the ganglion level of the retina (X cells), extending to the LGN (parvocellular division) and to the cortex itself (blobs). In short, three-color information is processed by the cones and encoded into two-color ON-OFF neural signals by opponent processes for transmission to higher visual centers.

DEFECTIVE COLOR VISION

Although the vast majority of humans possess normal color vision, a small proportion have some color defect. Color-deficient individuals require different amounts of primary colors to match spectral colors than do individuals with normal color vision.

Except for acquired forms of color defects based on pathology (discussed below), defective color vision is inherited. Nathans and his colleagues (Nathans, Thomas, & Hogness, 1986; see also Botstein, 1986; Hunt et al., 1995) have identified the genetic coding of the three retinal cone pigments that mediate color vision. Each cone contains a single pigment, and each pigment has its own gene. Moreover, the green and red genes are nearly identical and are localized on the X chromosome, which is critical in determining gender. Accordingly, red and green defective color vision is usually a genetically transmitted, sex-linked recessive characteristic and, as such, occurs primarily in males; about 9% of the male population and less than 0.5% of the female population have some genetically transmitted color vision defect.

Color deficiencies may be divided into three major classes. The main forms are termed *anomalous trichromatism, dichromatism,* and *monochromatism.* Table 5.3 summarizes the main forms of color deficiencies and their prevalence in the population.

Anomalous Trichromatism

Normal color vision is trichromatic; that is, individuals with normal color vision require three primary colors to match the colors of the spectrum. By contrast, individuals with **anomalous trichromatism** require different amounts of the three primary colors to match the spectrum than do individuals with normal color vision. The major forms of anomalous trichromatism are **protoanomaly** and **deuteranomaly.** The protoanomalous individual appears to have a deficiency in the L cone pigment and, accordingly, shows re-

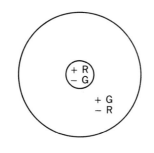

(a)

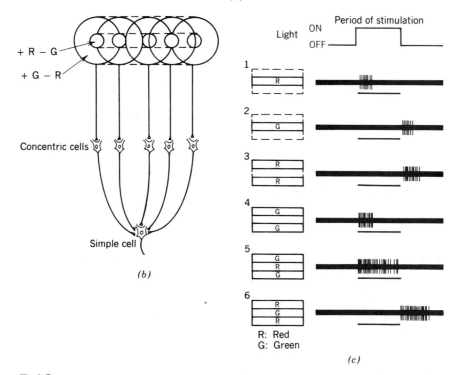

R: Red
G: Green

(c)

▭ *figure 5.12* Double-opponent color-coded cortical cells with concentric receptive fields. (*a*) Receptive field of a double-opponent color-coded cortical cell. The center is +R −G, and the surround is +G −R. (*b*) Linear arrangement of double-opponent receptive fields that are organized to respond to bars and rectangles of one opponent color system. (*c*) Neural record of activity of simple cortical cell to bars of lights (red: 620 nm; green: 500 nm): (1) A red bar covering the central strip produced an ON response. (2) A green bar covering the central strip produced an OFF response. (3) Two red bars covering the antagonistic surround elicited an OFF response. (4) Two green bars covering the surround evoked an ON response. (5) A red bar covering the central strip and flanked by two green ones evoked a strong ON response that extended for the duration of the stimulation. (6) A green bar covering the central strip and flanked by two red ones elicited a vigorous OFF response. (Based on Michael, 1978*b*; modified from Gouras, 1981.)

▭ *table 5.3* Color Vision Defects

	Incidence	
Classification	(% Males)	(% Females)
Anomalous trichromats		
Protoanomaly (L cone pigment deficiency)	1.3	0.02
Deuteranomaly (M cone pigment deficiency)	5.0	0.35
Dichromatism		
Protanopia (L cone pigment absent)	1.3	0.02
Deuteranopia (M cone pigment absent)	1.2	0.01
Tritanopia (S cone pigment absent)	0.001	0.003
Monochromatism (all cone pigments absent)	0.00001 for males and females	

Source: Based, in part, on Gouras (1991).

duced sensitivity to the reddish colors produced by long-wavelength light. The deuteranomalous individual is deficient in the M cone pigment and is correspondingly less sensitive to the greenish colors resulting from moderate-wavelength light.

Anomalous trichromatism can be assessed by a color mixture task. Recall that yellow can be matched by an additive mixture of red and green. This fact is taken into account by a special device used to assess such defects, appropriately called an **anomaloscope.** This is a special kind of color mixer that measures the proportions of monochromatic red that must be mixed with monochromatic green to match a monochromatic yellow. Anomalous trichomats require more red or green in the mixture than do normals: The protoanomalous individual requires more red, and the deuteranomalous person needs more green.

Dichromatism

Individuals with **dichromatism** match the spectrum with the appropriate combination of only two colors rather than the three required by color-normal viewers. Dichromats may be divided into those with *deuteranopia* and *protanopia,* which refer to green and red color deficiencies, respectively. **Deuteranopes** lack the M cone pigment and **protanopes** lack the L cone pigment. Consistent with this deficiency, persons who have deuteranopia are insensitive to the medium wavelengths in the green region, whereas those with protanopia are insensitive to the long wavelengths;

that is, much higher than normal intensities of red light are required to be seen by protanopes (Color Plates 12 and 13).

However, for both deuteranopes and protanopes, the short-wavelength region of the spectrum appears blue and the long-wavelength region appears yellow. Moreover, both deuteranopes and protanopes confuse red and green; when made sufficiently intense, they appear as desaturated yellow (Graham & Hsia, 1954, 1958; Hsia & Graham, 1965).

Although it is not possible to know how the colors that a dichromat sees compare with those seen by a normal person, some evidence has been obtained from an unusual clinical study. Graham and Hsia (1958) reported the case of a unilaterally color-blind subject, a woman who was a deuteranope in her left eye but normal in her right eye. By using color-matching procedures in which different hues were shown to each eye independently, it was possible to measure the color vision in the defective left eye. The procedure was as follows: For each color presented to her defective left eye, the woman adjusted the color using her normal right eye so that it appeared as the same hue. The results of this color-matching procedure are shown in Figure 5.13. To her defective eye, the colors spanning the entire spectral range from green to red (502 to 700 nm) appeared identical to a single hue of yellow (about 570 nm), as seen by her normal right eye, and all the colors from green to violet looked blue (about 470 nm). The green region (which occurred at about 502 nm) was seen as a neutral gray by the defective eye.

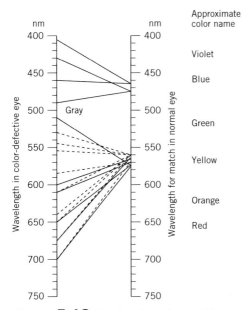

□ *figure 5.13* Results of a color-matching experiment with a unilateral color-defective individual. The wavelengths seen by the color-defective eye (left scale) are matched by the indicated wavelengths in the normal eye (right scale). Approximate color names for various wavelengths used in the matching task are indicated by the right column. (From Graham & Hsia, 1958.)

A rare third form of dichromatism, called **tritanopia,** is caused by a lack of S cone pigment. Tritanopes have a deficiency in seeing blue and yellow; they see only reds and greens, and confuse yellows, grays, and blues. In addition, tritanopes see only neutral gray in the neighborhood of 570 nm (which appears yellow to individuals with normal color vision); longer wavelengths appear reddish, and shorter wavelengths appear greenish (see Color Plate 13).

Monochromatism

Finally, a very small group of individuals suffers from **monochromatism.** Monochromats need only one primary color to match all wavelengths of the spectrum. This group can be truly termed "color-blind." Essentially, they have no color response and usually a reduction in other visual functions as well. They probably have an abnormality in the number and kinds of cones in their retinas. Although monochromatism is also considered to be inherited, its prevalence is about the same for males and females.

The Structural Basis of Defective Color Vision

Color defects have important theoretical implications for color vision. As we noted, specific color defects are consistent with the trichromatic notion that there are three classes of cones, each with a distinct pigment, and for the color-defective individual, one or more of the cones' photopigment types is missing or absent. Accordingly, the anatomical distinction between deuteranopes, protanopes, and tritanopes is that each has a set of cones with a relative lack of the M, L, or S cone pigment, respectively. No cones are absent, nor are the other functions of cones impeded—which squares with the fact that the acuity of most color-deficient persons, except the monochromat, is normal. However, they do possess an abnormal distribution of cone photopigments or an abnormal set of cones that are less sensitive than normal cones to certain spectral lights (Frome, Piantanida, & Kelly, 1982).

Thus, consistent with the trichromatic notion at the receptor level, specific color defects arise from the relative lack of particular cone pigments. In addition, consistent with the postreceptor opponent-process notion, individuals who are defective in seeing red are also defective in seeing green; likewise, those who cannot see blue normally also have a problem in seeing yellow.

Many color-defective individuals, especially when their defect is moderate, do not realize their lack of color vision until it is called to their attention. In part, this is because light waves that strike the eye are rarely monochromatic (i.e., composed of only a single wavelength); as a result, the cones of the color-defective individual may be sensitive to some of the reflected wavelengths. As we observed earlier with subtractive color mixtures, blue and yellow paint each reflects some green light, so a tritanope, while seeing neither blue or yellow, may sense the residual green wavelengths. Similarly, many green surfaces reflect some blue and many red surfaces reflect some yellow.

Therefore, some familiar color-specific signals, such as red warning lights and red and green traffic lights, may still be perceived on the basis of their reflected wavelengths by some dichromats due to the reflection of some yellow from the red light and some blue from the green light.

Although dichromats have trouble discriminating between the lights of certain wavelengths, this does not mean that the lights themselves are invisible. Dichromats can still discriminate between lights on the basis of intensity differences. Therefore, aside from the subtle yellow and blue tints that may be picked up from the red and green traffic lights, respectively, the red-green-deficient dichromat may use a difference in the *brightness* in one or the other signal to decide whether to stop or go. For this reason, traffic lights almost everywhere have the red on top.

Finally, aside from defects that are genetic in origin, there are *acquired color deficiencies* attributable to pathological changes in the eye, the optic nerve, or the brain itself, caused by degenerative disease (e.g., diabetes, glaucoma) and injury. An example of an acquired color defect due to brain injury is given in the next section.

Cortical Color Blindness

As we noted earlier, regions of the visual cortex have specialized neurons for color coding. Accordingly, localized damage to such regions from injury, strokes, multiple sclerosis, or tumors may seriously impair color perception. While this is rare, several clinical cases of total **cortical color blindness** (or, technically, cerebral **achromatopsia**) have been described and merit a brief discussion. The most unusual case (summarized by Sacks & Wasserman, 1987; see also Sacks, 1995) is that of a 65-year-old successful abstract painter with normal vision, who suffered a concussion (and apparent damage to the visual association area of the cortex) as a direct result of an automobile accident. Immediately after the accident, the patient discovered his total lack of color vision. Reds and greens appeared black, and yellows and blues appeared almost white; moreover there was excessive contrast between visible objects and surfaces and a lack of brightness gradation that is typical of normal vision. Curiously, other aspects of vision were either unaffected or, as in the case of acuity, seemed heightened, due perhaps to the augmented contrast.

Not only was the patient totally unable to see colors, but colored surfaces had an unnatural and unpleasant appearance. For example, he saw people's flesh, including his own, as an abhorrent gray; "flesh-colored" appeared "rat-colored" after his accident. Perhaps because he was an artist, the patient's loss of color vision also caused a profound sense of personal loss, at times bordering on extreme depression and despondency.

The results of this clinical study underscore the personal significance that color has for the individual. Also, at a physiological level, they help support the notion that regions of the cortex contain specialized and distinct color-analyzing mechanisms. Moreover, the study makes clear that the nervous system uses separate parallel channels to transmit and process achromatic and chromatic information about the visual environment (see also Livingstone, 1987). Certainly the observation that green and red appeared to the patient as black, whereas blue and yellow were seen as white, is suggestive of the opponent processes mentioned earlier in describing color vision (see Pearlman, Birch, & Meadows, 1979, for another example of this rare anomaly).

SUBJECTIVE COLORS

We end this chapter with a brief discussion on the production of chromatic sensations from colorless stimulation. We have noted repeatedly that color sensations result principally from the different wavelength compositions of light. However, it is possible to produce some color sensations, called **subjective colors,** from only black and white stimuli. One configuration used to demonstrate subjective colors, called **Benham's top,** is shown in Figure 5.14. By rotating the disk clockwise at a rate of 5 to 10 revolutions per second, very desaturated blues, greens, yellows, and reds may appear. When the direction of rotation is reversed, the order of the appearance of the colors also reverses. Clearly, neither wavelength variation of the physical stimulus nor differential

☐ *figure 5.14* Benham's top. When rotated, the figure produces various temporal sequences of black and white. However, subjective colors—desaturated blues, greens, yellows, and reds—may appear.

bleaching of the cone pigments plays a role in the resultant color sensations. It is plausible that the patterns of black and white alternations bypass the contribution of the retina. That is, the step normally performed at the retina is eliminated, and patterns of excitation are set up beyond the retinal level. This implies that the intermittent stimulation created by rotation of the Benham disk produces a sequence of neural events that mimics the different temporal patterns of neural activity that normally result from viewing colored stimuli (Wade, 1977, 1978).

In a related study, Festinger, Allyn, and White (1971) demonstrated subjective colors with a stationary pattern of flickering lights. The sequence of light changes created by the flicker resulted in reliable color sensations.

DEMONSTRATION:
Subjective Colors from an Achromatic Pattern

Figure 5.15 gives a simple demonstration of subjective colors from a black-and-white stationary pattern. Examine the central region of the diagonal pattern of lines shown in the figure for about 15 sec. A faint, shimmering stream of pale colors will

appear, often zigzagging or moving perpendicular to the diagonal black lines. During inspection of the pattern, small voluntary and involuntary eye movements occur. These eye movements constantly displace the image of the diagonal lines over the retinal receptors, producing a pattern of receptor activity that typically occurs from viewing colored stimuli (e.g., Piggins, Kingham, & Holmes, 1972; Young, 1977).

SUMMARY

In this chapter, we discussed the general nature and phenomena of color. To highlight the subjective nature of color vision, a color sensation was analyzed and described based on three psychological attributes—hue, brightness, and saturation. These sensory components were related to the physical dimensions of wavelength, intensity, and purity.

The major facts and bases of color mixtures (additive and subtractive) and color matching were presented. Additive color mixtures were shown to involve many color phenomena, such as adaptation, color aftereffects and afterimages (especially negative afterimages), and successive and simultaneous contrast.

The discussion of memory color highlighted the role of past experience with objects having a characteristic color on color experience. This was followed by a discussion of color constancy—the tendency of an object's color to remain unchanged despite changes in the wavelengths of light illuminating the object.

Two major theoretical notions of color perception were outlined: the Young–Helmholtz trichromatic receptor theory and the opponent-process theory. Evidence of each was summarized, with the conclusion that aspects of both theories are consistent with contemporary research findings. In support of the trichromatic theory, it was noted that there are three types of foveal cones (S, M, and L), each with a different photopigment that is maximally sensitive to a different part of the visible spectrum. Evidence of an opponent process in mediating color experience was described

□ **figure 5.15** Subjective colors from an achromatic pattern.

based on the neural activity of nerve fibers that lie beyond the retinal level.

We then considered blobs—regions of the visual cortex containing certain neurons whose activity is restricted to color stimuli. It was noted that many color-coded cortical neurons from blobs have double-opponent receptive fields: That is, they have an antagonistic center-surround organization, each component (center and surround) of which has a dual effect on stimulation by color.

This was followed by a presentation of defective color vision. A number of forms, both genetic (anomalous trichromatism, dichromatism, and monochromatism) and acquired (e.g., achromatopsia), were outlined.

In the last section, the perception of subjective colors was summarized. Subjective colors indicate that color sensations can occur without wavelength variation.

KEY TERMS

Achromatopsia (Cortical Color Blindness)

Additive Color Mixture

Afterimages

Anomaloscope

Anomalous Trichromatism

Benham's top

Bezold-Brücke Shift

Blobs

Brightness

Chlorolabe

Color Adaptation

Color Circle

Color Constancy

Color Mixture Curves

Color Spindle

Complementary Afterimage

Complementary Colors

Cyanolabe

Deuteranomaly

Deuteranopia

Dichromatism

Double-Opponent Receptive Fields

Erythrolabe

Hue

L Cones

M Cones

Memory Color

Metamers

Monochromatism

Null (Hue Cancellation) Method

Opponent-Process Theory

Primary Colors

Protoanomaly

Protanopia

S Cones

Saturation

Simultaneous Contrast

Spectral Purity

Subjective Colors

Subtractive Color Mixture

Successive Color Contrast

Trichromatic Receptor Theory
(Young–Helmholtz Theory)

Tritanopia

STUDY QUESTIONS

1. Describe some of the functions of color vision. Discuss the notion that color is a subjective experience. Distinguish between the physical dimensions of color and the psychological phenomenon of color vision.

2. Indicate how the color spindle and color circle represent and summarize the psychological dimensions of hue, saturation, and brightness. Outline some of the features illustrated by the color circle.

3. Describe trichromatic matching and indicate how three primary colors can be combined to match most color experiences.

4. What are complementary colors? How are they related to the color spindle or circle? How can they be demonstrated? What are metamers?

5. Distinguish between additive and subtractive color mixtures. Indicate what additive effects are demonstrated by metamers and colors that are complementary to each other. Describe how the color circle summarizes some of the effects of additive color mixtures.

6. Explain why the colors seen on color television and the artist's technique of pointillism are based on an additive color mixture. Explain why mixtures of blue and yellow paints produce a green color, whereas a mixture of blue and yellow light appears as an achromatic gray.

7. What is a negative afterimage? Explain successive and simultaneous contrast using negative afterimages.

8. What do negative afterimages indicate about the efficiency of cones after continual chromatic exposure? What role do involuntary eye movements play in producing simultaneous contrast?

9. What is memory color? Outline the contributions of past experiences and associations to the apparent colors of familiar objects.

10. Define color constancy and describe the factors that affect it. Explain the functional advantages it gives the individual viewing colored surfaces when environmental lighting conditions change.

11. Outline the Young–Helmholtz (trichromatic receptor) theory, indicating supporting evidence based on cone activity.

12. Describe the opponent-process theory, drawing on the neural response activity of regions beyond the retina.

13. Describe blobs and indicate how they enable an opponent-process type of color coding. Define the concentric double-opponent receptive field that is characteristic of blobs.

14. Describe how the trichromatic and opponent-process theories account for the phenomena of chromatic afterimages, such as successive and simultaneous contrast.

15. Summarize how the trichromatic and opponent-process theories may be integrated and may both be consistent with the phenomena of color perception.

16. State the main color vision defects. In particular, distinguish between the two forms of dichromatism, protanopia and deuteranopia, and indicate their possible causes.

17. Consider the implications of the clinical study of cortical color blindness for the opponent-process theory.

18. What are subjective colors, and how can they be demonstrated? Note the contribution of sequences of colorless, intermittent stimulation in producing subjective colors. Consider how small, transient, involuntary eye movements may produce the neural activity that normally occurs when viewing colored stimuli.

chapter 6

BASIC PROPERTIES OF PERCEPTUAL ORGANIZATION

In discussing vision up to this point, we have described the nature of the stimulus and have considered how light enters the visual system and is initially processed. However, perception involves more than reception and processing of light signals. After all, the image reflected on the retina is little more than an array of discrete light signals of varying intensities and wavelengths— an image far too impoverished and degraded to provide the rich visual characteristics we perceive. Yet, in spite of the discrete nature of the retinal signals, we perceive integrated units. The visual world, as we perceive it, is organized into distinctive objects and surfaces with cohesive forms and shapes. Clearly, perception then is not merely an inherent direct feature of signals reflected on the visual system. It is a constructive achievement resulting from the unify-

ing processes and organization of the visual system.

In this chapter and the next, we show how the information given in the distribution of light on our retinas is transformed into the world of meaningful objects. To this end, we trace the development of perceptual organization, beginning with fundamental physiological mechanisms and processes at the retinal level that enhance the perception of boundaries and edges. We also consider various approaches to percep- tual organization, particularly stressing the role of bottom-up processing, whereby simple features are organized to allow the perception of complex forms. Finally, we outline the computational-type approaches, in which vision is defined as the product of a series of information-processing routines performed on the information in the retinal image.

CONTOUR AND CONTRAST PERCEPTION

Contours dominate our perceptions. They are fundamental to perceiving an object's shape; in fact, they define an object's edges and borders and hence enable its visual perception. Generally, we see contours when there is some contrast in the light between adjacent areas. Contrast enables the visual system to distinguish

contours due to neural interactions of receptor elements. As we know, an enormous number of interconnections exist among neighboring receptor cells within the eye and related structures; some of these contribute directly to the perception of sharp visual contours.

Our understanding of neural interactions in relation to the perception of contours comes from studies of the visual system of the horseshoe crab (more a spider than a crab), **Limulus,** which has existed for millions of years in the same form as a kind of living fossil. The eye of the *Limulus* provides a simple model for analyzing higher visual systems. It is a compound eye consisting of about 1000 facets, or ommatidia (introduced in Chapter 3; see Figure 3.4). Each ommatidium is attached to its own intermediate neural cell and optic nerve, and each one directly registers the light striking it. In addition, ommatidia are independent of each other, so excitation of one ommatidium does not spread to adjacent ommatidia. However, at a further neural stage, adjacent ommatidia are linked to each other by a network of neural connections that extend sideways, or laterally, called the *lateral plexus* (see Figure 6.1), so that there is an interaction in their mutual activity when neighboring ommatidia are simultaneously stimulated. The nature of this lateral interaction is described next.

Lateral Inhibition

In **lateral inhibition,** neighboring ommatidia mutually suppress each other. In other words, the presence of light on one ommatidium decreases the activity of nearby receptors to light. Thus, when two neighboring ommatidia are simultaneously illuminated, each discharges fewer impulses than when only a single ommatidium receives the same amount of light by itself. The nature of lateral inhibition is illustrated in Figure 6.1. The upper record at (*a*) shows the neural record for a single ommatidium (A) when it is illuminated with various levels of light. The bottom records at (*b*) show the neural record for the same ommatidium (A) when nearby ommatidia (at B) are simultaneously illuminated at different intensities. Although the illumination at A has not changed, the simultaneous illumination of nearby ommatidia (B) inhibits the neural activity of A. What this illustrates is that neural activity of a photoreceptor is affected not only by its illumination but also by the stimulation of nearby photoreceptors. The greater the illumination of nearby receptors, the stronger the inhibitory effect. Although not shown in Figure 6.1, the more widely separated the ommatidia from each other, the smaller the mutual inhibitory effect. Thus, the more a receptor is stimulated and

the closer it is to another receptor, the greater the mutual inhibition.

How does lateral inhibition apply to human vision? Recall that there are several levels of lateral connections in the retina (see Figure 3.10). In fact, in certain ways the lateral connections at the ganglion level function very similarly to the inhibitory interactions observed with the eye of *Limulus.* Ganglion cells of the retina do not generally fire in isolation. The complex interconnections at the ganglion level of the retina ensure that at any moment many cells are firing and a great deal of lateral interaction is occurring. In short, cells within the human retina affect each others' activity through lateral inhibition, and as we shall see, it enhances the perception of edges and borders.

Mach Bands Lateral inhibition is important where there are abrupt changes in the illumination of adjacent ommatidia, such as where there is a sharp boundary between a dimly and a brightly lit area reflected on the eye—at borders and edges of light patterns. For example, when looking at a "step pattern" consisting of a series of uniform rectangles graded from black to white, as in Figure 6.2*a,* each vertical rectangle appears to be slightly lighter on the left than on the right, producing a scalloping effect (illustrated in Figures 6.2*b* and *c*). In fact, however, each rectangle of Figure 6.2*a* is uniform in intensity from edge to edge. This is evident when the figure is covered, so that only a single rectangle is visible. These illusory regions of heightened and reduced brightnesses are called **Mach bands** (named after their discoverer, the nineteenth-century Austrian physicist-physiologist, Ernst Mach; see Figure 6.3 for an illustration of a white Mach band). Mach bands are an example of a process that occurs at the regions of greatest change in luminance: The physical contrast that already exists at the border is accentuated still further.

An explanation of Mach bands due to lateral inhibition at the retinal ganglion cells is presented in Figure 6.4. The subjectively enhanced regions—the Mach bands—result from the luminance from adjacent regions interacting with each other. On the bright side, cell D is illuminated by the same amount of light as cell E, but since it is adjacent to a dimly illuminated

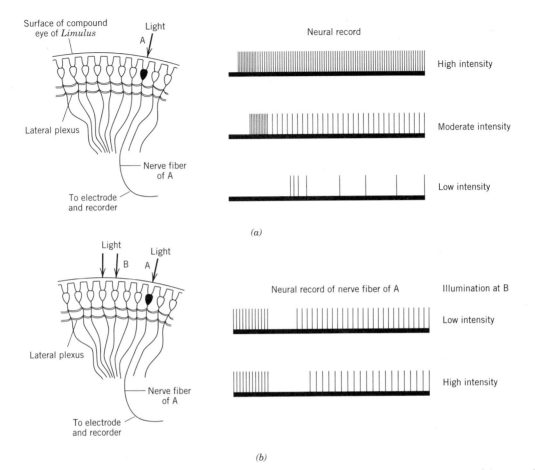

figure 6.1 (a) Neural activity of an ommatidium of Limulus. The top record gives the response of **A** to steady, high-intensity light. The middle record shows the response to light of moderate intensity and the lower record the response to light of low intensity. (b) Lateral inhibition of the nerve fiber of the steadily illuminated ommatidium **A**, produced when neighboring ommatidia at **B** are simultaneously illuminated. This is shown in the neural record of **A** as a decrease in the rate of discharge of nerve impulses. The upper record shows the effects on **A** of moderate-intensity illumination of **B**. The lower record shows the effect on **A** of high-intensity illumination of **B**. (Based on Ratliff, 1972.)

cell at C, it receives less inhibition than does E (i.e., it is inhibited from only one side); therefore, cell D shows greater neural activity than cell E, and the region stimulated by cell D appears lighter than any adjacent region. Consider next the neural activity of cell C, located at the edge of the dark side: It is receiving the same low level of stimulation as cell B. However, whereas cell C is weakly inhibited on one side by neighboring cell B, it is strongly inhibited on the other side by cell D, which is highly illuminated. Thus,

while B and C are equally illuminated, C, which is located right at the light–dark border, is more strongly inhibited than cell B. This means that its neural activity is reduced, causing the region stimulated by cell C to appear dimmer than any other region. The result of the inhibitory interaction between neighboring receptors is that the border or edge in a visual pattern is highly emphasized: The dark edge appears extra dark, and the light edge appears extra light.

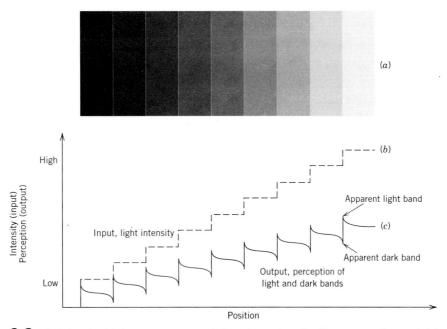

□ *figure 6.2* Mach bands. (*a*) A step pattern consisting of a series of uniform rectangles graded from black to white. (*b*) The physical intensity of the step pattern is plotted showing a simple series of ascending steps. (*c*) For each rectangle shown in (*a*), the left edge (adjacent to its darker neighbor) appears lighter than the remaining area of the rectangle, whereas the right edge (adjacent to the lighter neighbor) appears darker (note that the printing process may degrade the apparent light and dark edges). For illustrative purposes, the intensity (input) and perception (output) curves are displaced vertically and plotted on the same figure.

Lateral inhibition results from the lights from different regions interacting with each other. Perceptually, it exaggerates the difference in the neural firing rates of receptors stimulated by regions located at the light–dark boundary. One function of lateral inhibition is clear: It enhances the perception of contours and edges. Since the perception of contours and edges is integral to the perception of shape, enhancement of contour perception is a necessary step in form perception. Lateral inhibition also facilitates the perception of visual discontinuities or changes, which, as we will see in a later section, is necessary for the stable perception of form.

First, however, we will examine two contrast effects in which adjacent light and dark regions interact spatially to either reduce (the *Hermann grid*) or enhance (*lightness contrast*) the perception of lightness.

Hermann Grid

Examine the **Hermann grid** pattern of Figure 6.5. Although the luminance of the white stripes is uniform throughout, faint gray spots are apparent at the intersections where four black corners occur. Like Mach bands, this results from the luminance of different regions interacting with each other. It is believed that the gray spots result from activity at the retinal ganglion level of cells with an antagonistic center-surround receptive field organization (Jung & Spillman, 1970). As shown in the right insert of Figure 6.5, a receptor or unit (whose presumed receptive field has an excitatory center and an inhibitory surround) that is activated by an intersection of the white stripes has more of its inhibitory surround illuminated than a unit stimulated by a region located away from the intersection. Therefore, there is more inhibition of units stimulated by the center of the intersection, and

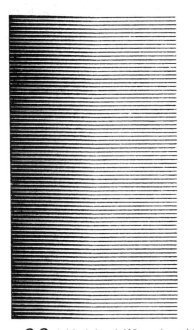

□ *figure 6.3* A Mach band. When viewed from a short distance, a vertical white Mach band is observed at about the center of this pattern of horizontal lines. This illusory band is due to the contrast created by the arrangement of lines.

the region appears dimmer. In short, the lightness of the intersection is weakened relative to the lightness of the neighboring regions, hence the perception of gray spots.

Inspection of the Hermann grid also shows that the gray spots do not appear at the points of fixation (i.e., when the images of the intersections fall on the fovea), but only at those intersections that fall on the peripheral retina. In part, this is because the receptive fields for the fovea are much smaller than those for the periphery (Frisby, 1980; Jung & Spillman, 1970). Thus, when you look *directly* at an intersection of Figure 6.5, you are stimulating the receptive fields of cells whose centers and surrounds are so small that they *both* fall within the region. This is schematized in Figure 6.6*a*, which shows a region of the grid that stimulates the small receptive fields of cells of the fovea. These fields all receive the same illumination within the excitatory center and the inhibitory surround; hence, all cells around the region of fixation

yield the same response, regardless whether they are stimulated by the intersection or not. As a result, the intersection does not appear dimmer than any adjacent region, and no gray spots are apparent. This implies that if the intersections of the grid were made sufficiently small, gray spots would be seen at *every* intersection, regardless of fixation. This is, in fact, what happens in Figure 6.6*b*. Here the white lines are made sufficiently thin so that the small center-surround receptive fields of the fovea do not fit completely within the lines and the inhibitory conditions for producing gray spots at the intersections prevail.

Lightness Contrast

Another form of spatial interaction, in which contrasting regions are adjacent, produces **lightness contrast** effects. Here the lightness of a smaller enclosed area can be modified by the intensity of the large background region on which it lies. Figure 6.7 illustrates the effects of lightness contrast. The inner four gray squares are identical in the intensity of light they reflect, yet their perceived lightness differs. The inner square on the far right (seen against a dark background) appears to be lighter than a physically identical one on the far left (against a light background). This shows that the lightness of a region depends on the intensity of its background. (The term *lightness*, as used here, refers to a surface quality whose perception is relatively unaffected by variations in the intensity of the light reflected by a surface. As we noted in Chapters 3, 4, and 5, *brightness* refers to the subjective-perceptual effect that varies with light intensity; that is, generally, changes in intensity produce changes in brightness. Note here that contrast effects promote lightness effects rather than brightness effects.)

The Ganzfeld: Perception in a Homogeneous Field

Stimulation from the environment usually contains changes or discontinuities of luminance and surface textures. However, when a completely textureless field of uniform brightness—an entirely homogeneous field called a **Ganzfeld**—is viewed, we per-

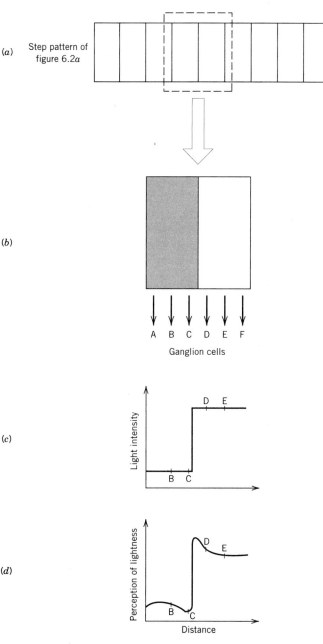

(a) Step pattern of figure 6.2a

(b)

(c)

(d)

Light intensity

D E

B C

Ganglion cells

A B C D E F

Perception of lightness

D

E

B

C

Distance

□ *figure* **6.4** Schematic of lateral inhibition and Mach bands. (a) Outline of the pattern of light changes in Figure 6.2a. (b) Enlargement of two contrasting rectangles, a dark one adjacent to a light one. When reflected on the cells of the retina, the abrupt change in light intensity between the rectangle occurs between cells C and D. Recall from Figure 6.1b that the stronger the illumination, the stronger the inhibitory effect. Assume then that the lighter of the two rectangles, shown at the right, results in two units of inhibition to each adjacent ganglion cell, while the darker rectangle results in only one unit of inhibition to the cells that it illuminates. It follows that cell E receives four units of inhibition (two units from D and two units from F), whereas cell D, located right at the border of the dark and light rectangles, receives only three units of inhibition (one from C, the darker rectangle, and two from E). Therefore, cell D, stimulated at the dark-light border, is *less* inhibited than cell E. This means that it will signal the presence of more light and thus accounts for the border's lighter appearance.

Consider the neural activity of cell C, located at the edge of the dark side: it is receiving the same low level of stimulation as B. However, whereas C is weakly inhibited by its neighbor cell B (1 unit), it is strongly inhibited on the other side by the higher illuminated cell D (2 units). Specifically, cell B receives 2 units of inhibition (one unit each from cells A and C), whereas cell C receives 3 units of inhibition (one unit from cell B and 2 units from cell D). Thus although cells B and C are equally illuminated, cell C, located at the light-dark border, is more strongly inhibited than is cell B. Specifically, this means that the neural activity of cell C is reduced, hence the region stimulated by cell C appears dimmer than any other region within the physically uniform rectangle.

The effects of the different levels of inhibition on cells C and D, producing Mach bands is given in figures (c) and (d). (c) Plot of the physical intensity distribution of the two adjacent rectangles of (b). (d) Plot of the dark and light perceptual effects.

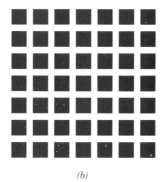

◻ *figure* **6.5** The Hermann grid.

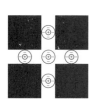

(a)

(b)

◻ *figure* **6.6** Schematic of receptive field stimulation with foveal stimulation. [It may be necessary to move the small grid at (b) closer to or farther from the usual fixation distance to ensure that the foveal cells are properly stimulated.]

◻ *figure* **6.7** Lightness contrast effects.

ceive an unstructured, ambiguous, and disoriented environment.

There are several ways of producing a Ganzfeld—for example, having subjects look into a translucent globe (Gibson & Waddell, 1952) or wear ping-pong ball halves over their eyes (Hochberg, Triebel, & Seaman, 1951). Under such conditions, viewers experience a uniform, undifferentiated space extending for an indefinite distance. A "diffuse fog" is one representative characterization (Cohen, 1957, p. 406). Such uniformity, although quite unnatural, occurs from a very simple level of stimulation and produces a very simple perceptual experience. When the Ganzfeld surface is illuminated with colored light, observers generally report that the color quality disappears within minutes (Hochberg et al., 1951; Cohen, 1958). A very primitive level of form perception appears in the Ganzfeld with the introduction of a simple luminance change such as a shadow or a gradient of intensity. With further stimulus changes, using definite contours, segregation of parts of the Ganzfeld into a figure and a background occurs, and forms, figures, and surfaces may become perceptible. Not surprisingly, the greater the stimulus change, the greater is the perception of form qualities.

Stabilized Image

The Ganzfeld experience indicates that the visual system cannot function effectively with completely uniform stimulation. Normally this is not a problem. As we noted in Chapter 4, the eye is constantly in motion. Even when the eye is fixated on a stationary target, small involuntary eye movements persist. Accordingly, the target image on the retina is kept in constant motion. However, it is possible to control or cancel the effects of eye movements on the retinal image. Several methods for stabilizing the retinal image exist, but the general findings are similar, so we need consider only the following procedure. A contact lens on which is mounted a tiny, self-contained optical projector is fitted directly over the cornea (Figure 6.8). This device is set so that a focused image falls on the retina. Because the contact lens and projector move with the eye, the image projected onto the retina will not shift over the retina with movement of the eyeball.

As a result, the effects of eye movements are eliminated. When a **stabilized image** is produced in this way or by other methods, the image soon fades and disappears, leaving an unstructured gray field. However, it can be quickly restored by the introduction of stimulus changes such as flickering of the image, changing its intensity level, and movement of the image after its disappearance.

DEMONSTRATION:
Stimulus Change and
Contour Perception

The significance of stimulus change on the perception of contour is illustrated by the demonstration of Figure 6.9. The two disks reflect the same amount of light; however, disk *1* has a blurry, indistinct contour and disk *2* has a sharp, well-defined contour. Staring steadily with one eye at the center fixation of disk *1* soon causes it to fade and disappear. However, it will reappear if you blink or shift fixation to the **X** at the right. In contrast, even prolonged fixation of disk *2* will not produce its disappearance.

This phenomenon is explained by the principle introduced in earlier discussions of stimulus change and adaptation: All sensory channels require a certain level of stimulus change to maintain perception. When fixation is maintained on disk *2*, patterns of very slight and abrupt, involuntary eye movements occur. The result is that the eye movements produce strong intensity changes on the retina. In short, because of the involuntary eye movements, the retinal region receiving the sharp contour stimulation is constantly changing, and such changes help keep the disk continually visible. However, consider the effect of eye movements when disk *1* is fixated. Due to its blurry contour, involuntary eye movements produce only a negligible change in intensity on the retina; that is, with fixation, the changes in stimulation due to the involuntary eye movements are not sufficient to maintain perception. In this condition, no region of the retina undergoes even moderate changes in intensity. It follows that visibility of the

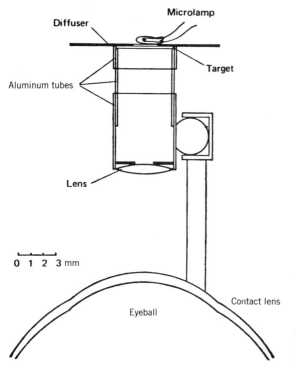

▭ *figure 6.8* Stabilized-image device. The entire optical device weighs only 0.25 gram. (From Pritchard, Heron, & Hebb, 1960, p. 69.)

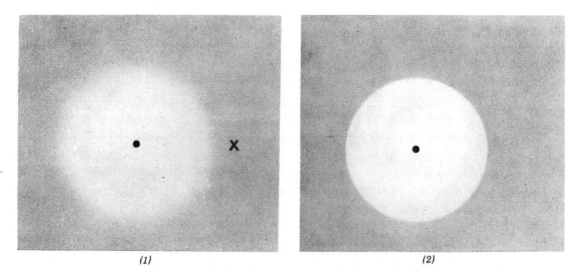

▭ *figure 6.9* Stabilized-image effect. (*Source:* Based on Cornsweet, 1969, 409.)

blurred disk can be restored only after a significant change in illumination, such as from a large eye movement (e.g., shifting the gaze to the **X**) or opening and closing the eyes.

Stabilizing projections on the retina or rendering eye movements ineffective in promoting stimulus change, as in Figure 6.9, yield results similar to that produced by the Ganzfeld. In each case, eye movements are rendered incapable of changing the pattern of stimulation. In general, these phenomena demonstrate that variation and inhomogeneity of visual stimulation are necessary for the formation and maintenance of a visual image.

SPATIAL FREQUENCY ANALYSIS

We have stressed that the ability to perceive visual details is strongly affected by contrast phenomena; there is a heightened perception of lightness due to the contrast of adjacent light and dark areas. In fact, if we critically inspect the visual scene at any moment (without regard to color), we recognize that, at a certain level of analysis, it is actually composed of patterns of alternating light and dark regions. It is possible to reduce any complex visual scene to a mosaic of light and dark regions. In doing this, two components of the visual display are especially relevant: the *number* or *frequency* of contrasting areas and the degree of *contrast* between adjacent areas. As artificial as this analysis may seem, these two components of a visual pattern are descriptive enough to represent a complex scene, and they have been applied to describe the basic units used by the visual system to encode the visual environment. (However, as we shall see later, psychologists have identified many other components of the physical stimulus that also serve this purpose.)

Spatial Frequencies

We can analyze and transform the composition of a visual display, consisting of contrasting light and dark areas, into its **spatial frequencies**—that is, the number of variations in luminance over a given space. In more graphic terms, spatial frequencies are the *number of cycles* of alternating dark and light bars or stripes over a given region of the visual field. The more bars or stripes per unit area of a pattern, the higher its spatial frequency. Technically, spatial frequency is the number of cycles of luminance changes per degree of visual angle (*cycles/degree*). This links the unit of spatial frequency to a specific retinal image size—the *visual angle* (see Chapter 4), and thus avoids the need to specify the size of the individual contrasting areas and the distance from which they are viewed.

Grating Patterns and Contrast The patterns of adjacent light and dark bars or stripes are referred to as *grating patterns*. They are useful because they serve as the building blocks in constructing a complex visual scene. Examples of typical grating patterns are given in Figure 6.10*a, b* and *c*. The associated intensity distributions of light, referred to as *luminance profiles,* are plotted below each pattern. Note that the stripes of the gratings of Figures 6.10*a* and 6.10*b* do not have sharp edges; instead, there is a gradual transition from bright to dark areas. It follows that the luminance profiles of the grating patterns show a series of gradual peaks and troughs, tracing a sine wave function; for this reason, such patterns are called *sinusoidal* or *sine-wave gratings*. It is also possible to produce patterns whose luminance profile contains sharp edges rather than curves. Figure 6.10*c* presents such a pattern, called a *square wave grating*. A square wave corresponds to a series of regularly repeating, very dark and very light bands that have crisp, sharp edges.

The distribution of intensity given by the luminance profile of a grating pattern indicates the degree of contrast across the pattern. Note that the grating patterns of Figures 6.10 all have the same number of cycles, or spatial frequencies, but differ in the distribution of intensity, or contrast. In general terms, *contrast* here refers to the difference in luminance between the light and dark areas. The greater the difference, the greater is the contrast.

Fourier Analysis How is a complex visual scene related to sinusoidal grating patterns? First, recall that the visual scene is composed of a complex

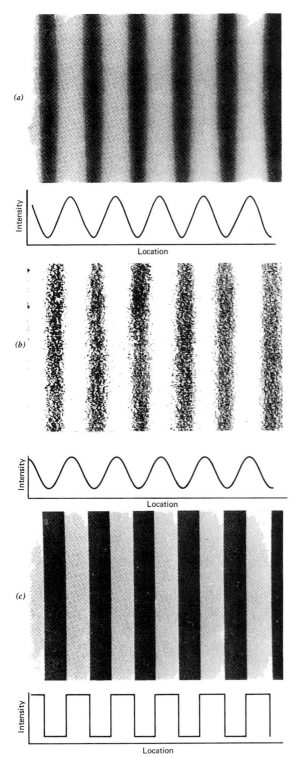

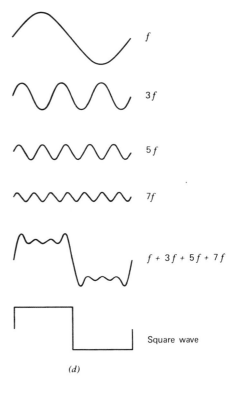

▭ **figure 6.10** Grating patterns (below each is its luminance profile or intensity distribution). (*a*) Sinusoidal grating pattern. (*b*) Sinusoidal grating pattern with same frequency as (*a*) but lower in contrast. (*c*) Square wave grating pattern. (*d*) The Fourier synthesis of a square wave. The addition of Fourier components results in an approximation of a square wave (*f* refers to the frequency of the original sine wave, which depicts one cycle.)

pattern of various light intensities distributed across space, that is, it is the sum of a series of simple sinusoidal components. Using a special mathematical technique called **Fourier analysis,** we can take the complex spatial distribution of light comprising the scene and transform it into its simple component sine waves (called *Fourier components*). The technique is based on *Fourier's theorem,* a mathematical principle devised in the early nineteenth century by the French physicist–mathematician Jean Baptiste Fourier. Briefly, Fourier's theorem states that it is possible to analyze any complex, repeating pattern into a series of simple sine waves. Conversely, the component sine waves can be summed to produce the complex pattern. This recombination process is called a *Fourier synthesis.* An example of a Fourier synthesis is given in Figure 6.10*d,* which shows how the sine waves, labeled *f, 3f, 5f,* and *7f* can be combined to make a pattern whose intensity distribution or luminance profile approximates a square wave (*f + 3f + 5f + 7f*). Observe that the resemblance of this distribution to the square wave distribution of Figure 6.10*c* increases as higher odd frequencies (e.g., *9f, 11f, 13f*) are properly added.

Spatial Frequency Detectors

Let us assume that the visual system does perform a spatial frequency analysis on a complex visual image. A typical visual scene, decomposed and analyzed as we suggest here, would likely contain regions of high and low spatial frequency components and high and low contrasts; those areas containing fine, detailed parts of the visual scene would be made up of high spatial frequencies (with many luminance changes), whereas the coarser, larger, less detailed parts would be made up of low spatial frequencies (with fewer luminance changes). As we will soon learn, there is evidence of specialized cells or channels in the visual system—**spatial frequency detectors**—tuned to particular variations in luminance; that is, certain neural units in the visual system are maximally sensitive to specific spatial frequencies. Thus, our perception of a complex visual scene results from the visual system's analysis and synthesis of the spatial frequencies making up the scene. In short, the brain reconstructs a visual image of a scene by integrating the information from the various spatial frequency channels stimulated by the components of the scene.

Contrast Sensitivity Function

As we noted above, a pattern may be characterized by its spatial frequency (i.e., the number of intensity or luminance variations) and its contrast (difference in intensity between pattern elements). There is a relation between spatial frequency and contrast in which certain spatial frequencies are seen more clearly than others, depending on the contrast between the elements comprising the spatial frequency pattern. That is, less contrast is required to distinguish some spatial frequencies than others, indicating that the visual system is more sensitive to certain spatial frequencies than to others. This is apparent when spatial frequency patterns of luminance variations are viewed, such as the one in Figure 6.11*a.* The display consists of a varying sinusoidal grating pattern whose frequency increases from left to right and whose contrast increases from top to bottom. Thus the farther down on the pattern necessary to just distinguish the particular spatial frequencies, the greater is the degree of contrast required (i.e., the higher the threshold) and the less is the sensitivity of the visual system to those spatial frequencies. Similarly, the less contrast required to make certain spatial frequencies visible, the greater is the sensitivity to those frequencies.

We can examine the functional relation of threshold levels of contrast to spatial frequency that describes the visual system's sensitivity for the range of spatial frequencies to which it responds. The relation between spatial frequency and threshold levels of contrast is called the **contrast sensitivity function.** The variation of contrast sensitivity with spatial frequency in Figure 6.11*a* is illustrated in the contrast sensitivity function of Figure 6.11*b.* Generally for patterns having low spatial frequencies (i.e., comprised of broad grating elements), the contrast threshold is high (left ordinate) and the sensitivity is low (right ordinate); that is, high contrast is required to detect the pattern. As spatial frequency increases (e.g., moving from left to

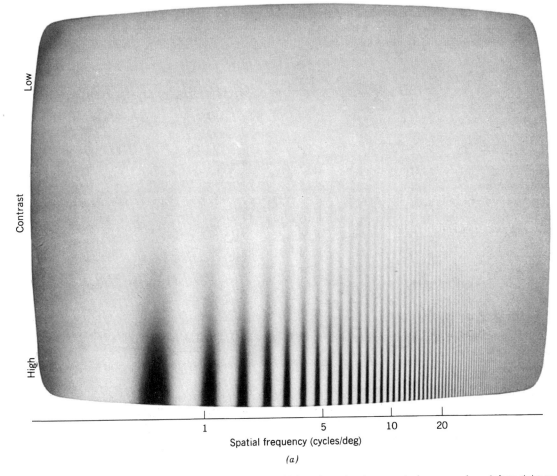

Low

Contrast

High

1   5   10   20

Spatial frequency (cycles/deg)

(a)

□ *figure* **6.11** (a) Stimulus pattern containing sinusoidal gratings that increase in frequency from left to right and in contrast from top to bottom. For most viewers, the spatial frequencies in the middle appear most distinctly. Because of the printing process, this rendering degrades or eliminates some of the original detail of the pattern and serves only as an approximation. (*Source:* Courtesy of F. W. Campbell.)

right in Figure 6.11*a*), less contrast is required for visibility and the contrast threshold decreases (and sensitivity increases). However, for patterns having *very* high spatial frequencies (approximated on the far right in Figure 6.11*a*), the contrast threshold increases and sensitivity falls again.

Figure 6.11*b* is a plot of the physical contrast necessary to detect a grating pattern relative to the pattern's intensity changes or spatial frequency. It shows that intensity changes are most effective in making a grating pattern visible when they occur at intermediate

spatial frequencies (with a peak at about 3 cycles/degree). When the intensity changes occur too frequently (i.e., very high spatial frequencies) or too infrequently (i.e., very low frequencies), sensitivity to the changes is reduced. In short, the visual system is less sensitive to very low and very high spatial frequencies than it is to intermediate ones.

One particular interest in spatial frequencies is based on the notion, introduced earlier, that a visual scene may be represented by a complex set of patterns specifiable in units of spatial frequencies. Thus, at a

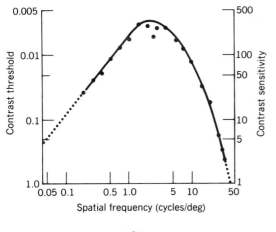

(b)

▭ *figure 6.11* (*Continued*). (*b*) Contrast sensitivity function. The curve relates threshold contrast and sensitivity to the range of spatial frequencies to which the visual system responds. The left ordinate specifies the contrast threshold values necessary to just distinguish each frequency. Sensitivity plotted on the right ordinate, is the reciprocal of the threshold value. The moderate spatial frequencies are visible with less contrast than either the low or high spatial frequencies. Hence of the range of frequencies examined, sensitivity is greatest for moderate spatial frequencies (i.e., around 3 cycles/deg.) (Based on Howard, 1982.)

certain level, the visual system may be performing a Fourier analysis on the spatial frequency content of the complex visual stimuli, that is, analyzing and determining the Fourier components of the pattern. If this is the case, then the visual system may have a distinct signal or response for the individual sinusoidal components (i.e., Fourier components) of a complex pattern. In other words, there may be discrete, independent neurons or channels in the visual system, each tuned to a different but limited range of spatial frequencies to which it maximally responds. One means of demonstrating independent *spatial frequency channels* involves the use of selective adaptation.

Selective Adaptation

The existence of channels in the visual system specific to spatial frequencies can be demonstrated by using Figure 6.12.

DEMONSTRATION:
Spatial Frequency Channels in Human Vision

Study Figure 6.12. The top grating pattern at (*a*) is of a relatively low frequency, whereas the bottom grating pattern is of a high frequency. The spatial frequencies of the two grating patterns on the right at (*b*) are identical and are intermediate in spatial frequency to those at (*a*). Cover the patterns at (*b*) and focus on the two patterns at (*a*) for at least 60 sec, but with the gaze wandering back and forth along the horizontal fixation bar that separates the two patterns. After this period of adaptation, transfer the gaze to the fixation point between the two patterns of the right at (*b*). They will no longer appear identical in spatial frequency: The grating of a higher spatial frequency than the corresponding adapting grating will appear higher (top grating at *b*), and the grating with a lower spatial frequency than the appropriate adapting grating will appear lower in spatial frequency (bottom grating at *b*). What has occurred is an effect of the technique of **selective adaptation**: The fatiguing of channels (or neurons) that respond to low spatial frequencies, in the region of the upper grating of (*a*), causes the medium-frequency grating of the upper right at (*b*) to shift toward higher frequencies; similarly, adaptation of the channels that respond to high spatial frequencies, in the region of the bottom grating at (*a*), causes the medium-frequency grating on the bottom right at (*b*) to appear lower in frequency than that of the adapting grating. In other words if the visual system becomes adapted (and less sensitive) to a grating of a given spatial frequency, the apparent spatial frequencies of gratings with similar frequencies are shifted in just the way that one would predict from the existence of distinct and independent channels for spatial frequencies, namely, in a direction away from the spatial frequency of the adapting grating.

In general, if an observer steadily views a grating pattern with a particular spatial frequency, the recep-

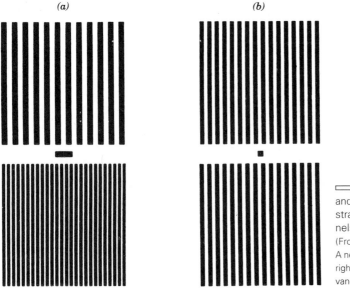

(a)   *(b)*

□ *figure* **6.12** Inspection patterns (*a*) and test grating patterns (*b*) used to demonstrate the existence of spatial frequency channels in human vision. See text for explanation. (From C. Blakemore and P. Sutton, "Size adaptation: A new aftereffect," *Science, 166,* 1969, p. 245. Copyright © 1969 by the American Association for the Advancement of Science.)

tors or channels that respond to that frequency will selectively fatigue, reducing or weakening their sensitivity to that frequency while leaving the sensitivity to other frequencies relatively unaffected. The loss in sensitivity to a particular spatial frequency (or band of spatial frequencies) due to selective exposure of that frequency implies that there are different channels for detecting different spatial frequencies.

The analyses of spatial frequencies and selective adaptation are not restricted to simple sinusoidal-type grating patterns. Figure 6.13 emphasizes this point with an additional demonstration using spatial adaptation.

DEMONSTRATION:
Adaptation of Spatial Frequencies

Study Figure 6.13. Cover the pattern at (*b*) and gaze at the central horizontal bar at (*a*) for about 60 sec, moving your eyes back and forth along the bar. Then rapidly switch your gaze to the central spot at (*b*). For a brief time, the material in the lower pattern of (*b*) will appear coarser (i.e., lower in frequency) and the upper material will appear denser (higher

in frequency). Try this with both the text and the dot patterns.

Most visual displays can be described and analyzed in spatial frequency terms. A spatial frequency analysis applied to complex forms, described next, further indicates the potential role played by Fourier analysis in image processing.

Image-Processing: Block Portraits

An example of a spatial frequency analysis on form perception is given in Figure 6.14*a.* The photograph— a **block portrait**—of a U.S. president is the product of a picture that has undergone a special form of computer processing; the original picture was divided into a pattern of small rectangles or blocks, with each block printed with the average dark-light intensity of the original block portion of the picture. That is, each block has been made uniform in luminance throughout its area, or *block-averaged* (also called *quantized* or *digitized* images; Harmon, 1973; Harmon & Julesz, 1973). The original picture is thus reduced to a collection of adjacent homogeneous light and dark blocks.

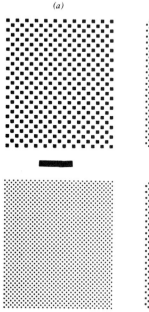

(a) *(b)*

he second editor
estseller introduc
odern psycholog
udy of mental m
ms...concentrate
test research in n
tention and perc
demonstrates, w
rpts from curren
re, how recent de
ents in cognitive

odern psychology...the
udy of mental mechan—
ns...concentrates on the
est research in memory,
ention and perception.
demonstrates, with ex —
rpts from current litera-
re, how recent develop—
ents in cognitive
ychology explain human in
havior, everyday learning
oblems to stress perfor-
ance, skills memory,
ention. Ideal for courses
Memory, Information
cessing, Verbal Learning
d Cognitive Psychology

chapter as introduces the student to
influences aspects of the senses and
and emotion perception in an integral
students manner. Covers the main
The seconacts cf psychophysics,
bestseller ructures and unctions
modern pshe orientations sense, au
study of mon, touch, taste, smell a
isms...conision. Extensively illustr
latest resead; inclnt cognitive theo
attention apper diding the place of
It demonstrates courses ness in moderi
cerpts from n on or emotional and
ture, how recent ational concepts
ments in cognitive ology of cognition
psychology explanation processing,
behavior, everyday of competing
problems to stresses, and a novel
mance, skills, men concept of arousal
attention. Ideal for the role of the aut
in Memory, Information nervous syste

odern psychology...the
udy of mental mechan—
ns...concentrates on the
est research in memory,
ention and perception.
demonstrates, with ex —
rpts from current litera-
re, how recent develop—
ents in cognitive
ychology explain human in
havior, everyday learning
oblems to stress perfor-
ance, skills memory,
ention. Ideal for courses
Memory, Information
cessing, Verbal Learning
d Cognitive Psychology

(a) *(b)*

◻ ***figure 6.13*** Spatial frequency aftereffect for two examples of nongrating patterns (text and dots).

This removes much of the sharpness and detail of the original picture because high spatial frequencies have been removed by the averaging process applied to each block. At the same time, as an artifact of the block-averaging procedure, a form of high-frequency noise has been introduced by the creation of sharp edges between the blocks. This noise also serves to camouflage many of the informative low-frequency components remaining from the original picture.

As a result, when viewed directly and up close, the block portrait does not show an easily recognizable person. However, recognition is greatly improved by blurred viewing (e.g., by viewing it at a distance or by squinting). The obvious explanation is that the blurring selectively filters out and reduces much of the noise created by constructing a block portrait; as a result, many of the remaining low frequencies may be revealed. That is, blurring of the image of the portrait reduces the perception of the artificial sharp edges of the blocks produced by block averaging (Figure 6.14*b*). Once the extraneous high-frequency details are removed, the low-frequency information becomes visible and helps enable recognition.

Spatial Frequency and Acuity

Analyzing visual performance in terms of contrast sensitivity provides a more informative measure of visual acuity than, say, the resolution acuity described in Chapter 4, which assesses acuity only at a single high spatial frequency and contrast level. For example, an individual may have average sensitivity at one end of the spatial frequency spectrum and below-average sensitivity at the other end. Owsley, Sekuler, and Siemsen (1983; see also Crassini, Brown, & Bowman, 1988) found that contrast sensitivity for high spatial frequencies deteriorates rapidly with age, while sensitivity for low spatial frequencies remains relatively unchanged. This finding would not ordinarily be picked up by, say, the familiar Snellen eye chart test, described in Chapter 4. In addition, human infants are poorer than adults at distinguishing most spatial frequencies (Dobson & Teller, 1978; Gwiazda, Brill, & Held, 1979; Norcia & Tyler, 1985).

Relatedly, Ginsburg (1981, 1986) reported evidence that the vision of individuals whose profession demands high visual acuity, such as aviators, may be

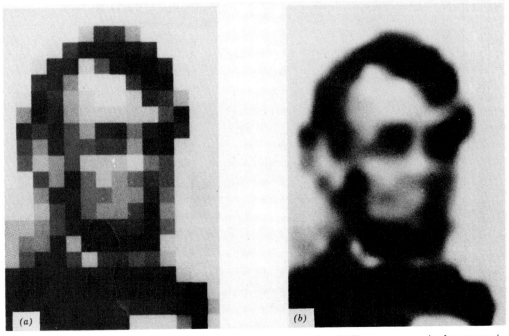

figure 6.14 (a) A block portrait produced by computer processing. (b) The same portrait after removal of the high-frequency noise. (*Source:* Courtesy of Leon D. Harmon.)

normal in terms of traditional acuity measures but, based on their contrast sensitivity functions, may show significant individual differences. In fact, Ginsburg (1981) found that some pilots showed higher contrast sensitivity to low spatial frequencies than did pilots who had greater visual acuity scores on the Snellen test (which is restricted to high frequencies). This heightened selective sensitivity may translate into an increased visibility of objects located at great distances or viewed in degraded conditions such as in fog. Ginsburg (1986; Ginsburg et al., 1984) proposes that about 10–15% of the population has good acuity, as measured by Snellen testing, but low contrast sensitivity to low and moderate spatial frequencies.

The Role of Spatial Frequency Analysis in Vision

What direct role does spatial frequency analysis play in vision? Clearly it provides a simple, elegant means of describing and summarizing a specifiable dimension of the physical stimulus. It is also useful for de-scribing the systematic manner in which the visual system analyzes, collates, and integrates the activity of an enormous number of receptors and links them in a coherent way with a specifiable feature of the physical stimulus. As we have observed, the description of the visual stimulus in terms of its spatial frequencies is useful in assessing acuity and is far more informative than the traditional Snellen eye chart. At the very least, spatial frequency analyses specifies a quantitative, descriptive means that the visual system could encode complex visual information for further processing.

PERCEPTUAL PROCESSING

This introduction to perceptual organization and form perception has stressed structural physiological mechanisms and certain biological details concerning how environmental stimulation enters and is initially processed in the visual system. However, perception is much more than the transmission of neural impulses by the sensory system to specific regions of the brain.

Perception also involves some sort of internal aware-ness and representation of the stimulation; for this to occur, we must first make sense of the sensory input. In other words, perception is a process of drawing meaning from the stimulation that reaches our sensory receptors. It is thus reasonable, at this point, to ap-proach perception as a problem-solving task in which the sensory input is analyzed, processed, and interpre-ted to create a meaningful representation of the visual world. In the next section, we will examine perception as if it were the end product of a sequence of mental operations performed by an observer on the stimulus input. In doing this, we will make several distinctions in information processing.

Bottom-Up and Top-Down Processes

There are two basic approaches to perceptual analysis and processing: bottom-up and top-down. **Bottom-up processes** (also called **data-driven processes),** begin with simple, basic elements—the discrete sen-sory features provided by the sensory receptors. Such features may be luminance differences, spatial fre-quencies, or element orientations. The visual system functions in a bottom-up fashion when its basic ele-ments are combined to form identifiable patterns and shapes: The information flows from a basic, "bottom" level up toward higher, more integrative levels.

In contrast, in **top-down processes** (also called **conceptually driven processes**), higher, global, ab-stract levels of analysis affect the operation of lower processes: Top-down processes emphasize the ob-server's prior knowledge, experience, meaning, and interpretation, as well as expectations in shaping per-ception. Both are active processes, however, and many perceptual events require them to interact. In the remainder of this chapter, we will outline some approaches that apply primarily to bottom-up pro-cesses, examining the basic processing stages and the primitive units and elements extracted from the vi-sual image.

Preattentive and Focused Attention Stages

There is growing agreement that perception of the features of an object results from two major processing stages that differ from each other in the amount of directed attention and effort required (e.g., Julesz, 1986; Treisman's 1986 version of this two-stage pro-cess is called *Feature Integration Theory).* The initial or **preattentive stage** immediately extracts and pro-cesses the sensory information received by the recep-tors, allowing perception of very simple, conspicuous features that may serve as the basic elements of per-ception. The preattentive stage perceives these ele-ments automatically, rapidly, and without conscious effort or scrutiny. The preattentive stage also involves *parallel processing,* in which all elements in a visual display are processed simultaneously. Figure 6.15 shows a preattentive visual task that requires no con-scious effort by the observer. It depicts a display of +'s at various orientations embedded in an array of L's (and some T's). Even with the most cursory glance, the two arrays are immediately and effortlessly per-ceived as distinct from each other.

In contrast, the **focused attention stage** is not instantaneous, but requires effort and conscious scru-tiny by the observer. Thus, perceiving the T-shaped area (upper left part of Figure 6.15) requires a time-consuming *serial search*—an element-by-element ex-amination of much of the display. In contrast to the rapidly performed parallel processing of the preatten-tive stage, the focused attention task requires scrutiny and conscious attention. As we shall see (mostly in the following chapter), the focused attention stage enables the observer to perceptually group the distinct basic elements uncovered by the preattentive stage into complex unitary objects.

Elements of the Preattentive Stage: Textons
Why are the +'s so easily detected in Figure 6.15? According to Bela Julesz (e.g., 1984, 1986, 1988), textural discriminations are rendered most readily when there are differences in certain primitive textural features of a display that he labels **textons.** Textons are specific, distinguishable characteristics or features of the elements that comprise a texture. Julesz identifies such basic features as elongated shapes (e.g., rectangles, ellipses, and line segments), their widths, lengths, end connections, angular orienta-tions, and their intersections. According to Julesz, the

◻ **figure 6.15** Preattention and focused attention. The immediate and effortless (preattentive) texture discrimination is shown between areas composed of +'s and L's. In contrast, texture discrimination of an area composed of T's, embedded in the texture of L's (upper left quadrant) requires an element by element (focused attention) scrutiny of the display. (Figure courtesy of Bela Julesz.)

greater the differences between textons in an array, the more readily the discrimination. Thus the textural regions of Figure 6.15 composed of +'s are rapidly, effortlessly, and hence preattentively distinguished from the L's and T's; this is because, although all elements of the figure have in common the textural features, or textons, of horizontal and vertical line segments, the + elements have the additional texton of an intersection. In contrast, textural regions composed of L's and T's are constructed from the same number of equally informative textons of horizontal and vertical line segments; hence, discriminating one from the other requires closer scrutiny. Specifically, it depends on detecting the unique spatial relation of the line segment textons from each other. This involves a serially executed, element-by-element analysis: clearly a task requiring focused attention. We now examine a bottom-up proposal concerning the way objects are recognized.

Object Identification: Recognition by Components

Julesz's notion of textons offers a basic unit useful in understanding texture perception. However, are there also primitive features that set the stage for the recognition and identification of objects? A theory proposed by Irving Biederman (1987*a*, 1990), called **recognition by components,** proposes that object recognition begins with the processing of a set of primitive features. Biederman's main assumption is that the perception of any three-dimensional object can be reduced to, or decomposed into, an arrangement of a set of geometric modules or components. According to Biederman (1990), there are about 24 such basic three-dimensional geometric forms called **geons** (for "geometrical ions"), which can be combined and arranged to create the shape of almost any object. Moreover, according to Biederman, geons can be easily distinguished from each other from almost any angle, and they resist various types of visual distortions.

Thus, geons are proposed as the perceptual building blocks of all volumetric or three-dimensional objects. A sample of geons and some objects created by them is given in Figure 6.16.

According to the recognition by components approach, we recognize an object and its three-dimensional shape by uncovering its primitive geons and their relations to each other. Thus, if we perceive a cylindrical geon with a tubular arc geon over its top, it appears as a pail, whereas if the arc appears on the side, the object is seen as a cup (Figure 6.16). If geons do, in fact, represent the primitive, distinctive three-dimensional features that characterize an object, then the more geons an object has, the more readily we recognize it. Thus, complex objects such as airplanes and elephants, composed of many geons, are more easily recognized than simple objects such as cups and lamps, composed of only a few geons. In one experiment reported by Biederman (1987*a*), when line drawings of

objects (e.g., an airplane, a telephone, a flashlight) were individually flashed (for 0.1 sec) at observers, the greater the number of geons presented for a given object, the more rapid and accurate was its recognition. Moreover, Biederman (1987*b*) found that an object could be accurately identified when only a few of its geons were present, stressing the basic defining character of geons for object recognition. For example, a line drawing of an airplane or a penguin (Figure 6.17) was correctly recognized when less than half of their geons were given. Biederman (1990) reports that, generally, three geons are sufficient to recognize an object.

The units involved in spatial frequency analyses, as well as Julesz's textons and Biederman's geons, are proposed as primitive elements integral to bottom-up processing. In the next section, we will continue to examine bottom-up mechanisms, but at a different level of analysis. Actually, we will be concerned more with a general *approach* to perceptual analysis than

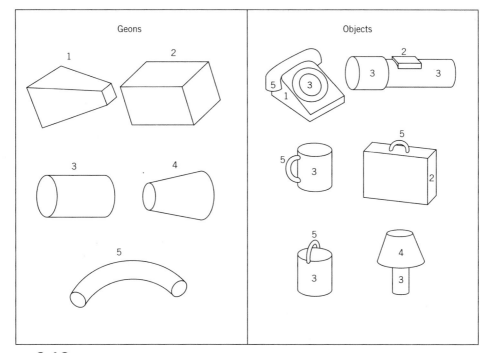

☐ *figure 6.16* Left: five geons. Right: objects formed from these geons. The numbers on the objects at the right indicate which geons are present. Only two or three geons are necessary to uniquely specify an object. Also, the arrangement of the geons is important to object recognition. Thus, the cup and pail are both composed of the same two geons but are distinguished by the different arrangement of the arc geon (5). (Figure courtesy of Irving Biederman.)

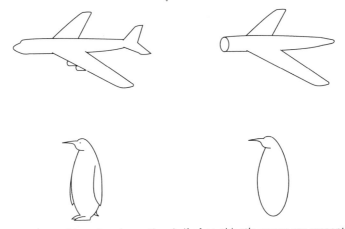

□ **figure 6.17** Object recognition when fewer than half of an object's geons are presented. Left: The complete line drawings of the airplane and penguin require nine geons. Right: These objects are recognized when only three of their geons are present.

with the specific elements of analysis. Our next topic of perceptual processing is called a *computational approach* because it assumes that perception (or vision) is a constructive process involving a series of processing routines or mathematical computations that are performed directly on information contained in the image projected on the retina.

The Computational Approach

The **computational approach** is generally considered to be the influential legacy of David Marr (1945–1980), who died at the age of 35, just before the completion of his major work on the topic. Central to the computational approach is that meaningful perception, such as object recognition, involves solving a kind of an *information processing* problem posed to the visual system. At the beginning of his major work on the computational approach (*Vision,* 1982, p. 3), Marr asks us and tells us: "What does it mean to see? The plain man's answer . . . would be, to know what is where by looking. In other words, vision is the *process* of discovering from images what is present in the world, and where it is. Vision is therefore, first and foremost, an information-processing task."

Marr states that the visual system analyzes the retinal image to extract information in ways similar to the analyses performed by computers in solving

problems. In fact, according to the computational approach, the way a computer (or a related machine designed especially for "seeing") might analyze an image provides a general basis for understanding how perception occurs (an approach shared by the closely related areas called *artificial intelligence* and *machine vision*). It first breaks down a global task—such as recognizing an object—into a sequence of manageable processing tasks, each uncovering information and providing data for the next task, until the solution is reached—the object is recognized. (Note: The proposed analyses performed on the retinal image by the various processing stages are highly technical ones, described in mathematical terms that go well beyond the scope of this text. Accordingly, we can only describe the computational approach in very general terms. Furthermore, we highlight Marr's work only to give some idea of this approach; computational approaches to vision extend in numerous directions and are finding applications in many areas of human visual performance [e.g., Barrow & Tenenbaum, 1986; Ullman, 1991].)

According to Marr's theory, the image on the retina provides the input—the stimulation to be analyzed for information. The information processing task involves a precise set of computational analyses, each extracting some critical information from the retinal image. Marr identified three levels of sequential analysis on information in the retinal image: the *primal sketch,* the *2 1/2-D sketch,* and the *3-D model representation.*

The Primal Sketch   The starting point for perception is the retinal image. This image contains various intensities created by the way light is reflected by the physical structures being viewed and the way the light is focused by the observer's eye (Figure 6.18). The goal of this early visual processing stage is to create a description and representation of these physical structures: in particular, their textures, shapes, orientations, and distances from the viewer. The first step is to create the **primal sketch,** which locates discontinuities—sharp changes—in light intensity and regions where intensity values are changing rapidly (such as those shown in Figure 6.18). This is an important step because the changes in intensity often convey critical information about edges, contours, and boundaries, which contribute to knowledge about the shape and orientation of objects. The primal sketch consists of primary information extracted from the retinal image concerning edges and boundaries, their location, and so on.

The 2 1/2-D Sketch   The next level of information processing is performed on the primal

sketch to determine the orientation and depth relationships of structures in the visual environment *relative to the observer.* In other words, it extracts information concerning the layout of these structures from a particular viewpoint. Marr labeled this viewer-oriented representation the **2 1/2-D sketch.** In a sense, the 2 1/2-D sketch marks the point at which a rough picture of the world is beginning to emerge, but one that is structured with reference only to the observer.

The 3-D Model Representation   In the final processing stage of vision, the 2 1/2-D sketch is transformed into the **3-D model representation.** With this representation, the observer has attained a general model of the visual world that is largely independent of any particular viewing position and orientation. At this stage of information processing, the observer recognizes a particular object.

The computational approach is quite different from typical bottom-up approaches to perceptual processing. It describes perceptual activities, such as object recognition, as the product of several levels of processing and computations, each describing some aspect of the information in the retinal image. In short, the workings of the visual system are expressed as a set of computations performed on the retinal image. Thus, as we noted above, it is more like describing a sequence of

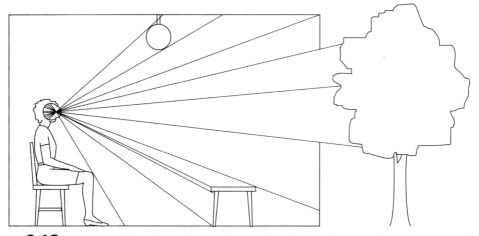

▭ *figure* **6.18** The array of light reflected from objects and surfaces in the visual field onto the eye. The light is structured by the environment. This creates patterns of various intensities on the retina that contain information about the shape, orientation, and location of objects and surfaces. (Based on Gibson, 1979.)

computations performed by a computer program in processing and analyzing certain physical properties of the visual world than more typical descriptions of how the visual system and brain processes sensory input. Largely for this reason, the computational approach has an unusually strong affinity with fields such as artificial intelligence and computer science; many of the refinements and achievements of this relatively new approach come from these allied fields.

The Connectionist Model

Marr's computational approach treats perception as a series of computational processes applied to the retinal input, which gradually extracts a description of the visual scene. In this section, we will briefly outline another computer-oriented approach to perception, called the **connectionist model** (or *parallel distributed processes* [*PDP*]; attributed largely to the early work of Rosenblatt, 1962, and, more recently, to Rumelhart & McClelland, 1986). The connectionist model builds on the idea that the sensory system possesses a large but finite set of functional neural units, with the pattern or network of activity across many such units representing specific features. According to the connectionist model, subsets of these units—*networks of neural connections*—can represent the features of a complex stimulus. One appealing aspect of the connectionist model is that it takes a biologically plausible approach to the recognition problem (Bienenstock & Doursat, 1991). That is, it attempts to link an image, for instance, directly to a specific pattern of activity across neural units. Thus, according to the connectionist approach, a given perceptual event—for example, the recognition of an alphabet letter—is expressable in terms of a particular activity pattern across a specific subset of units.

Consider the very simple network of connections for letter recognition given in Figure 6.19. The top of the network contains the letters, and the functional neural units for its specific linear features are given at the bottom of the network: These features are verticals, horizontals, and left and right diagonal segments. As indicated, connections between features and letters may be excitatory or inhibitory (the connections are also assigned a numerical value indicating the degree of excitation or inhibition). An excitatory connection

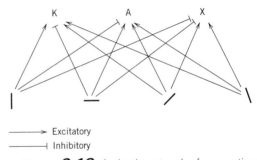

> Excitatory
> Inhibitory

□ *figure* **6.19** A simple network of connections. (Based on Johnston & McClelland, 1980.)

shows that the feature is part of the letter; an inhibitory connection shows that the feature is not part of the letter. Thus, in this very simple network, the letter is described by the features it contains as well as by the features it lacks. To see how this network can be used to distinguish between similar letters, consider what occurs when the letter **K** is presented. It will activate the vertical and the two diagonal features, and it will inhibit the horizontal feature. The letters **A** and **X** will also excite the two diagonal features, but the **K** is distinguished from them because the **A** activates the horizontal feature and inhibits the vertical feature, while the **X** inhibits both the vertical and horizontal features. In short, a particular network of activity represents a specific letter.

To summarize, perceptual recognition, according to the connectionist model, involves the simultaneous activity of simple feature-specific units interacting in a complex network to represent a complex stimulus. However, we have presented no more than a sketch of the connectionist model. Like the computational approach, its conceptual and technical details are beyond the scope of this book. But as the connectionist model appears to be influential, we must understand both its general nature and its basic premise: that complex sensory events may be represented by a network of interactions between simple functional neural units. As Gordon (1989) puts it, "The one major insight which designers of PDP [i.e., the connectionist model] have led us to is that systems using simple components can do very complicated things, provided these components are allowed to compete and interact" (p. 220).

Our goal in this chapter was to introduce fundamental processes and mechanisms that contribute to visual perception. Some of these, such as lateral inhibition, are a result of basic physiological processes; other, higher-level activities, involving bottom-up processing, extract information by isolating primitive units such as textons and geons. In the next chapter, we will continue our discussion of perceptual organization and shape perception with a consideration of figure-ground perception and top-down processes.

SUMMARY

In this chapter, we began a general discussion of form perception and perceptual organization. First, we described some fundamental visual processes and mechanisms involved in perceiving contours and contrast; it was noted that lateral inhibition, a form of neural inhibition at the retinal level, increases the perception of luminance discontinuities, contrast, and contours. The role of lateral inhibition in producing contrast effects in Mach bands and Hermann grids, was described.

The importance of stimulus change was examined. Discontinuities, necessary for form perception, were illustrated by the Ganzfeld and stabilized imagery.

Next, we discussed spatial frequency analysis, which concerns analyzing a visual display in terms of its physically contrasting areas—its spatial frequencies (the number of luminance changes in a given space), and its luminance profiles (the degree of contrast of the luminance changes). This required a discussion of Fourier analysis and synthesis and of contrast sensitivity functions. In particular, Fourier analysis and synthesis was then applied to spatial frequencies. It is possible that a complex spatial scene can be represented in units of its spatial frequencies and contrast. It is also possible that the visual system may be performing a Fourier analysis on the spatial frequencies of the visual input. Related phenomena and research, such as selective adaptation to spatial frequencies and block portraits, were discussed. The influence of spatial frequencies on acuity was also outlined.

Perceptual processing was introduced in terms of bottom-up and top-down perceptual processes. The remainder of the chapter dealt with several bottom-up notions, including the preattentive stages (basic, automatic) and the focused attention stages (intensional, scrutinized) as basic initial stages in processing

visual information. The textural elements processed by the preattentive stage—textons—were illustrated.

Another form of bottom-up processing considered critical for the recognition and identification of objects is recognition by components. This involves a set of 24 primitive three-dimensional features called geons, combined and arranged by the visual system for the perception of almost any object.

Finally, the computational and connectionist approaches to perception were outlined. Both are derived from a computer-oriented analysis of information extraction from the retinal image.

The computational approach assumes that perception is a constructive, information-processing task. Accordingly, the retinal image processes information in stages, with each stage involving a set of mathematical computations. As a result, each stage extracts a different level of information about the visual display. Three significant interconnected stages were identified: the primal sketch, the 2 1/2-D sketch, and the 3-D model representation.

The connectionist model assumes that perception results from the activity of a network of feature-specific neural units. It attempts to link an image directly to a specific network of activity across simple feature-specific neural units. Like the computational approach, the connectionist model was only briefly outlined.

The next chapter extends our discussion of form perception and perceptual organization to conditions involving top-down processing.

KEY TERMS

Block Portrait

Bottom-Up Processes (Data-Driven)

Computational Approach

Connectionist Model

Contrast Sensitivity Function

Focused Attention Stage

Fourier Analysis

Ganzfeld

Geons

Hermann Grid

Lateral Inhibition

Lightness Contrast

Limulus

Mach Bands

Preattentive Stage

Primal Sketch

Recognition by Components

Selective Adaptation

Spatial Frequencies

Spatial Frequency Detectors

Stabilized Image

Textons

3-D Model Representation

Top-Down Processes (Conceptually Driven)

2 1/2-D Sketch

STUDY QUESTIONS

1. What is lateral inhibition? Discuss how it enhances the perception of contrast and the detection of contours in human vision based on the activity of the *Limulus* eye. Show how the inhibition of receptor cells varies with the distribution of light across the retina.

2. What is a Mach band? Relate the perception of Mach bands to lateral inhibition of retinal ganglion cells.

3. Explain the perception of gray spots in the Hermann grid. Show the role of antagonistic center-surround receptive fields in producing inhibitory regions. Also, show the effect of grid size in producing gray spots.

4. What is lightness contrast? Show how the background of a region affects the perception of its lightness.

5. Identify the ocular mechanisms and phenomena that stress the necessity of stimulus change for the perception of form.

6. Describe spatial frequencies and luminance profiles applied to a visual display. What is a spatial frequency analysis and synthesis? Present evidence showing that the visual system performs a spatial frequency analysis on the visual scene projected on the retina.

7. What does a spatial frequency analysis indicate about variation in the sensitivity of the visual system with luminance changes and contrast? How does a Fourier analysis enable us to analyze a complex spatial pattern into components of simple spatial patterns?

8. Describe the computation of a contrast sensitivity function. How is human contrast sensitivity related to spatial frequency?

9. Indicate how selective adaptation supports the notion of independent channels in the visual system for detecting different spatial frequencies.

10. What does the perception of block portraits tell us about the spatial frequency analysis of complex images?

11. In what ways does a spatial frequency analysis add to the traditional measures of visual acuity?

12. Distinguish between bottom-up and top-down processing.

13. Examine the role of preattentive and focused attention stages in perceiving a complex visual display. What are textons? In which processing stage would their detection be critical?

14. Describe the role of recognition by components in object identification. Identify geons and indicate their relevance to recognizing three-dimensional objects.

15. Briefly describe the computational approach. Discuss its relationship to sequential computer information processing. Describe the three levels of analysis performed on the retinal image, as proposed by the computational approach.

16. Describe the connectionist model and indicate how networks of neural units may be involved in recognizing images.

chapter 7

HIGHER PROCESSES OF PERCEPTUAL ORGANIZATION

In this chapter, we continue our discussion of perceptual organization and shape perception, drawing largely on top-down processes. Accordingly, we will describe those forms of organization in which the stimulus is initially interpreted in terms of global, abstract features *drawn from the observer's past experience and expectations, as well as the context of the stimulus. We begin by describing an important aspect of perceptual organization called* figure— ground *perception.*

FIGURE-GROUND PERCEPTION

The observation that the book before you appears as a distinct, complete object, physically separate from the desk or table on which it lies, is, in certain ways, a remarkable achievement. As Rock and Palmer (1990) observe, in many respects the arrays of light "coming from different parts of the same object have no more affinity for one another than those coming from two different objects" (p. 85). Nevertheless, when we view the world, objects are immediately separated perceptually from their backgrounds. What is it about the relationship between objects and their backgrounds that enables them to be immediately and effortlessly seen as distinct from each other? Part of the answer is based on the fact that there are often physical differences between objects and their backgrounds, and as we observed in Chapter 6, we tend perceptually to highlight physical differences in the visual field. However, apart from this, we tend to divide up the visual field perceptually—to see it as composed of distinct, self-integrated regions. In other words, a fundamental

step in seeing a world organized into physically separate objects and surfaces is that certain parts of the visual display stand out from other parts. As the Danish psychologist Edgar Rubin pointed out in 1915, the part that appears as a distinct, sharply defined shape is known as the **figure,** and the remainder is called the **ground.** In the simplest case, where the total visual field consists of only two different portions, one portion is most likely to be seen as the figure (and usually appears closer to the observer), and the remaining part appears as the ground (Figure 7.1).

Functionally, in figure–ground perception we tend to see parts of a visual scene as composed of solid, well-defined objects standing out from their background. What determines which part will be seen as figure and which part as ground? According to Rubin, there is a fundamental principle involved in figure–ground organization: "If one of the two homogeneous, different-colored fields is larger than and encloses the other, there is a great likelihood that the small, surrounded field will be seen as figure" (Rubin, 1915/1958, p. 202). However, it is possible that *any*

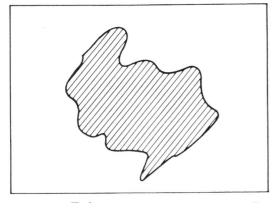

▭ *figure* **7.1** A simple figure–ground relation. The enclosed striped area appears as the figure, lying on a white background.

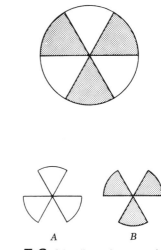

▭ *figure* **7.3** Stimuli used to examine the role of angle sector on figure–ground perception. (Based on Oyama, 1960.)

well-marked part of the visual field may appear as the figure, leaving the remainder as the ground. An unusual illustration of figure–ground organization appears in Figure 7.2.

A quantitative approach to the tendency to see a figure as a function of its relation to the total stimulus was developed by Oyama (1960). He presented the stimulus pattern shown in Figure 7.3 and instructed subjects to indicate whether the white *A* or gray *B* crosses appeared as figure. When the angle of the sectors was varied, for either the *A* or *B* crosses, the result was that the thinner the cross, the more likely it was to be seen as figure, regardless of whether it was gray or white.

Ambiguous Figure–Ground Relationships

The above example points to an interesting variation of figure–ground differentiation: the presence of two distinct, homogeneous regions, neither enclosed by the other. In addition, both parts share a common contour, so that there is no tendency for either part to be seen as figure. Some examples of such configurations are shown in Figure 7.4*a–d*. In viewing ambiguous figures like these, one part is initially perceived as the figure, followed by a reversal. Figure 7.4*a* shows a radially marked cross alternating with a concentrically marked cross. If the concentric cross is seen as figure, the radial lines form the ground. However, when the radial cross is seen as figure, the concentric lines, as part of the ground, do not appear to be interrupted. Thus, one has the impression that the concentric circles continue behind the figure.

After viewing some ambiguous figure–ground configurations for a brief period, the figure and ground can be reversed by a shift in attention: If you change

▭ *figure* **7.2** A central square is typically perceived, yet a design composed of diagonal lines at right angles may be seen as an alternative figure–ground organization (see Lawson et al. 1977, for an empirical analysis).

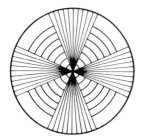

(a)

(b)

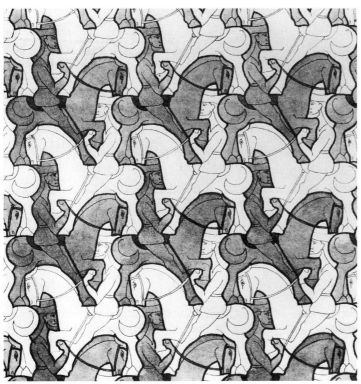

(c)

(d)

□ **figure 7.4** (a) Figure–ground reversal. (Based on Rubin, 1915/1958.) (b) Ambiguous figure–ground patterns. Either a series of black, irregular shapes against a white background or white words on a black ground may be seen. The perception of white words may be difficult initially because the black shapes have a strong tendency to be seen as figure. (From Davis, Schiffman, & Greist–Bousquet, 1990.) (c) Reversible figure–ground pattern of procession of horsemen. (*Source:* Based on a woodcut of M. C. Escher, Beeldrect, Amsterdam/VAGA, New York, 1982, Collection Haags Gemeentemuseum.) (d) A reversible figure–ground pattern. The perceptions of either pairs of goblets or pairs of silhouetted faces in profile alternate with each other. (Courtesy of Suzanne Greist–Bousquet.)

the focus of attention, you change the region seen as figure. Moreover, as indicated by Figure 7.4*b*, the organization seen as the figure can also be facilitated by cognitive factors, such as recognizing that the white space surrounding the black shapes spells words (Hint: The words spell a baseball batter's goal; based on Davis, Schiffman, & Greist-Bousquet, 1990). We should realize, however, that ordinarily we have no difficulty resolving figure and ground. Ambiguous displays such as those in Figure 7.4 rarely occur in the real world—and certainly not as natural objects.

Perceptual Differences Between Figure and Ground

Rubin (1915/1958) identified the main differences between figure and ground as follows:

1. The figure has the quality of a "thing," and the contour appears at the edge of the figure's shape. In contrast, the ground has the quality of a "substance" and appears relatively formless.
2. The figure appears closer to the viewer and in front of the ground, whereas the ground appears less clearly localized, extending continuously behind the figure. In fact, Wong and Weisstein (1982) found an advantage when seeing a target stimulus on the part of the visual field seen as figure rather than when the same part of the visual field is seen as ground. Thus, when a subject viewed a target

that was flashed on what was seen as the figure of an ambiguous figure–ground pattern (a version of the goblet profiles of Figure 7.4*d*), the subject was at least three times as accurate in discriminating the orientation of the target as when the same region was seen as ground (see also Brown & Weisstein, 1988).
3. In relation to the ground, the figure appears more impressive, dominant, and better remembered. Also, the figure suggests more associations of meaningful shapes than does the ground. As Figure 7.4*d* shows, the configurations appearing either as profiles or as goblets are easily assigned meaning, whereas the ground in either case is seen as shapeless.

Figure–Ground and Lightness

In addition to the perceived differences in figure and ground identified by Rubin, there are striking figure–ground effects on the perception of an area's lightness. As Figure 7.5 shows, a region perceived as figure appears lighter than when the same region is perceived as ground. In other words, a region of the visual field with a constant luminance underoges a greater contrast effect when it is perceived as figure than when it is perceived as ground.

Wolff Effect Generally, figures show greater contrast effects than grounds. A demonstration of this,

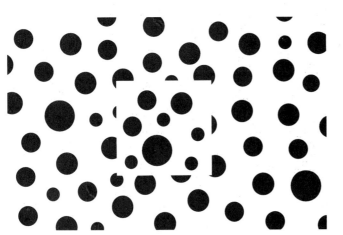

figure 7.5 Lightness of figure relative to ground. The central square, seen as figure, appears lighter than its background. In fact, the entire surface is covered with black disks on a homogeneous white surface. The contours creating the perception of the central square are called *subjective contours* and are the subject of discussion later in this chapter. (Kanizsa, 1979, p. 177. Reprinted with permission.)

reconstructed by Kanizsa (1979) and by Rock (1986)—labeled the **Wolff effect** (Wolff, 1935)—is given in Figure 7.6. The light and dark gray areas of (*a*) and *b*) are physically identical, but the enclosed light gray circles at (*a*), seen as *figure,* appear lighter than the identical gray region at (*b*), seen as *ground.* Similarly, the dark gray circles in (*b*), seen as figure, appear darker than the same dark gray seen as ground in (*a*). Note that the total areas of light and dark regions in (*a*) and (*b*) are equal. This indicates that a region seen as figure is affected more by its contrast with its ground than a region seen as ground is affected by its contrast with the figure.

Koffka Rings A demonstration, different from those above since it apparently opposes contrast effects, concerns the classic **Koffka rings,** shown in Figure 7.7*a*. (As a point of historical interest, this phenomenon is generally attributed to Koffka, 1935; however, Osgood, 1953, notes that much earlier, a form of it was used in lecture demonstrations by Wundt.) Figure 7.7*a* contains all the elements for a contrast effect. The neutral gray ring is half against a black ground and half against a white ground, yet there is little or no lightness contrast. The portion of the ring on the left in (*a*) does not appear lighter than the portion on the right, although this effect would be predicted based on the effects of contrast discussed, in the previous chapter (see Figure 6.7). Instead, the ring appears a homogeneous neutral gray throughout.

Figure 7.7*a* may illustrate the dominant effect of the unity or total organization of a figure on percep-tion; the coherence of a unified configuration over-rides contrast effects. Thus, being perceived as a single integrated unit, the entire ring is perceived as uniform gray. However, contrast effects immediately appear if vertical contours are introduced that separate the ring into two parts, as shown in Figure 7.7*b,* or when the two halves of the rings are shifted vertically with respect to each other, as shown in Figure 7.7*c.* Thus, when the ring is divided, it becomes two half rings, each seen against a different background, and the contrast effects occur appropriately to each half ring with its background. Moreover, as Figures 7.7*d* and 7.7*e* show, the imposed contour restricts apparent lightness to entire portions of the divided rings, even when part of a ring extends into an opposing back-ground. That is, within limits, the contour prevents the lightness effect in one part of the ring from affect-ing the lightness in the other part, even when the parts of the ring, as defined by the contours, are seen against contrasting areas.

Figure–Ground and Perceptual Organization

Figure–ground differentiation is one of the simplest steps in form perception. Evidence for a fundamental organizing tendency resulting in figure–ground sepa-ration comes from reports by von Senden (1960) on adult patients who had surgery for lifelong congenital cataracts (a disorder clouding the lenses at birth, so that only areas of light and dark can be detected). When given first sight at maturity, patients showed figure–ground differentiation before they were able to discriminate and recognize different figures. The perception of figure–ground in the patients' first expo-sures in using their new vision strongly hints that it is unlearned and independent of experience. That figure–ground is a basic, fundamental step in percep-tual organization is further demonstrated by the fact that many lower animals, including some species of insects (e.g., Srinivasan, 1992), can distinguish figure from ground even with minimal visual experience.

Of related interest is that figure–ground differenti-ation occurs tactually as well as visually. When a raised-line version of a reversible drawing such as that depicted in Figure 7.8 was examined tactually by blind

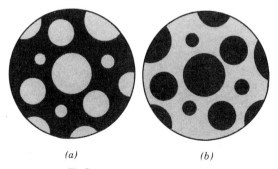

(a)   *(b)*

▭ *figure* **7.6** The Wolff effect showing differential lightness contrast effects of figure and ground. (After Rock, 1986; Kanizsa, 1979.)

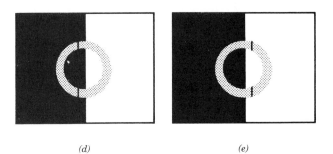

(a)   (b)   (c)

(d)   (e)

□ **figure 7.7** The Koffka rings.

children, they experienced figural effects similar to those encountered when sighted viewers examine the figure visually (Kennedy, 1983; Kennedy & Domander, 1984). That is, on the basis of feeling the centrally located raised contour, the blind children interpreted, say, a profile as looking to the right as

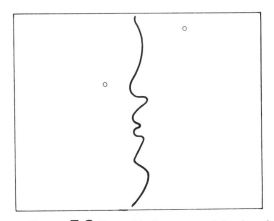

□ **figure 7.8** Reversible figure–ground drawing of profiles formed by the same contour.

figure, immediately followed by the perception of a different profile as figure, this one looking to the left. However, in perceiving the second profile (i.e., looking left), they did not understand that they were using the same contour that they had felt only a moment before (a profile looking right). In short, without their awareness, the same contour was used in the perception of two different profile figures. This not only indicates that the reversal of figure–ground can occur tactually, but it also suggests that, "like the sighted, blind people have pictorial impressions that can modify their perception of unchanging forms. They seem to have something akin to a sighted person's perception of pictured foreground and background" (Kennedy, 1984, p. 23).

THE GESTALT APPROACH

Why do some elements of the visual field form the unified figure and others become ground? As we have seen, this is the result of an organizing tendency based on certain features of the stimulus. The factors determining the formation of figure-like shapes were studied by a group of German psychologists (in particular, Max Wertheimer, Kurt Koffka, and Wolfgang Köhler) at the beginning of the twentieth century. The area of psychology they founded is called **Gestalt psychology** (*Gestalt* is the German word for "form," "shape," or "whole configuration").

Gestalt Psychology versus Structuralism

In Chapter 1, we noted that the Gestalt psychologists studied patterns of stimuli and observed that some stimuli appeared to be spontaneously grouped together, with figure-like qualities. This approach questioned the prevailing analytical view in psychology called **structuralism.** The structuralist view was influenced strongly by a form of *elementism* that dominated the physical and biological sciences in the latter nineteenth century. In chemistry, for example, significant advances were made as compounds were analyzed into molecules and atoms. Taking its cue from these striking achievements, the emerging scientific psychology stressed the *structural* character of the mind and its perceptions. Thus, the psychology of structuralism assumed a kind of "mental chemistry," and, by employing a form of mental analysis called **analytical introspection** (involving a highly disciplined technique of self-observation), the structuralists attempted to determine the fundamental, irreducible units—the elementary sensations or "mental molecules"—of perception. It followed that the structuralists assumed that perceptions are composed of a sum of basic, elemental units—raw sensations.

In marked contrast, the Gestalt psychologists believed that a perception cannot be decomposed into its components. Rather, they proposed that the basic units of perception are themselves the perceptions—the "Gestalts" (or *Gestalten*) *are* the fundamental units. They argued that to attempt to break down and reduce a perception to presumed elementary sensory units would be to lose sight of the perception. Consider as a Gestalt (as we did in Chapter 1) the perception of a tune. It is possible to hear a tune played in

one key; yet when it is played again, in another key, but with none of the original notes replayed, it is still recognized as the same tune. Clearly, something besides the reception of a sequence of notes is involved when we recognize a tune. Thus, we readily recognize that a tune cannot be meaningfully decomposed into its individual notes. In fact, we probably cannot learn very much about a tune by examining its notes in isolation. What is important in our example, then, is not the musical notes per se, but the relationship between them. In other words, it is the perceived relationship between the notes that gives rise to a unique tonal configuration—to a Gestalt-like perception. In short, the perception of the whole dominates the perception of its parts. Indeed, the basic

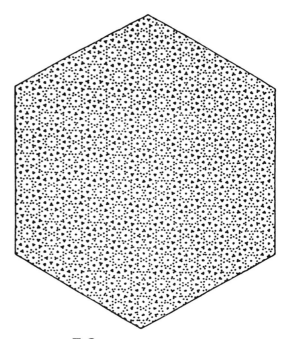

□ *figure 7.9* An example of a Gestalt-like perceptual organization. There is a tendency to organize the elements of this pattern into different perceptual patterns, usually ones involving circular shapes. Different groupings and arrangements of the elements emerge spontaneously and seem to compete and alternate with each other. (After J. L. Marroquin, *Human visual perception of structure.* Master's thesis, 1976, MIT. Printed with permission of the Massachusetts Institute of Technology.)

□ **figure 7.10** Due to the principle of proximity, the enclosed circles are seen as arranged in pairs.

Gestalt theme is embodied in the often applied summary phrase: *The whole is different from the sum of its parts.*

Gestalt psychology emphasizes the unique role of the overall structure and the relationship between components in producing perceptual organization. A compelling visual demonstration of the role of the relationship between discrete elements in perceptual organization is given in Figure 7.9. This figure reveals an overwhelming tendency to group specifically arranged elements to form unique patterns. As Marr (1982) observed, "The pattern apparently seethes with activity as the rival organizations seem to compete with one another" (p. 50). We will now discuss the Gestalt principles underlying this grouping tendency.

Gestalt Grouping Principles

One of the most significant and enduring contributions of Gestalt psychology is the identification of the figural properties that enable us to perceive forms. According to the Gestalt psychologists, there appears to be a fundamental, largely unlearned organizing tendency to perceive global, coherent characteristics

of the visual environment on the basis of the arrangement, location, and interaction of its constituents. A set of **Gestalt grouping principles,** supported by numerous elegant and convincing illustrations, has been described by Max Wertheimer (1923; based on a 1958 translation by Michael Wertheimer). In the following section, we present an abridged summary of these principles.

Proximity (Nearness) According to the principle of **proximity** or **nearness,** elements may be grouped according to their perceived closeness. In other words, elements that appear close together tend to be grouped together (Figure 7.10). The perceived proximity that creates grouping effects may be either spatial or temporal.

Similarity With the proximity of elements equated, elements that are similar physically tend to be grouped together. Figure 7.11 shows grouping on the basis of **similarity.**

Good Continuation Elements that appear to follow in the same direction, such as along a straight line or a simple curve, are readily perceived as forming a group. Figure 7.12 presents an example of **good continuation.** All such elements appear to follow in a uniform direction, allowing the continuation of an

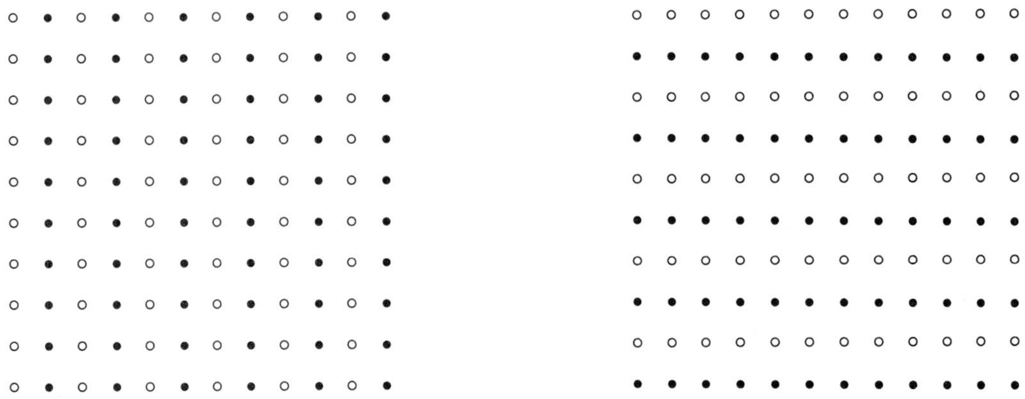

(a)

(b)

□ **figure 7.11** Because of the principle of similarity, the series of open and closed circles are seen as organized in columns in (a) and as rows in (b).

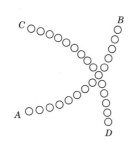

figure 7.12 Due to the principle of good continuation, two intersecting but distinct curves are perceived: an upward (segment *A–B*) and a downward curve (segment *C–D*). Although it is possible to see segments *A–D* and *C–B*, due to grouping based on good continuation they are unlikely perceptions.

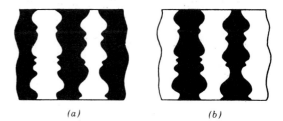

(a)   (b)

figure 7.13 The contours of the vertical shapes are identical, but in (*a*) one sees the white columns and in (*b*) the black ones. In both cases, perceptual organization follows the symmetrical pattern. (After Zusne, 1970.)

aspect of a figure (in this case, a curve) whose movement or direction has been established. (An unusual example of good continuation coupled with other organizing relations is shown later in Figure 7.17.)

Common Fate According to the principle of **common fate,** elements that move in the same direction are perceptually grouped together. This is grouping on the basis of similarity, but applied to *moving* elements. Thus, if a number of elements are seen in motion, those that apppear to be moving in parallel paths tend to be grouped together to form a coherent pattern. For example, a group of runners or a flock of birds when seen moving in the same direction appear as units. Similarly, the familiar "wave" created by the arm movements of fans at a sporting event illustrates the principle of common fate.

Symmetry In **symmetry,** priority in grouping is given to the more natural, balanced, and symmetrical figure over the asymmetrical ones (Figure 7.13).

Closure In **closure,** grouping occurs in a way that favors perception of the more enclosed or complete figure (Figure 7.14). Within limits, physically incomplete figures tend to be perceived as wholes. This is especially the case when stimuli are presented very briefly.

Like all the Gestalt grouping principles, good continuation and closure enhance the perception of a

stable environment. Consider the following typical and somewhat unusual examples. The drawing in Figure 7.15 can be perceived as three discrete shapes, yet the most likely perception is that of two bars, one in front of the other, the partially covered bar appearing continuous. Figure 7.16 sketches a Gestalt-like grouping of elements—the Big Dipper in the night sky—based largely on good continuation and closure.

Another example of the effect of good continuation and closure on grouping is given in Figure 7.17. In (*a*) an apparently random scattering of irregular fragments shows no tendency to group into any meaningful pattern. However, in (*b*) the same shapes, left intact but apparently covered by a "school of fish," produce a striking reorganization of the fragments: An irregular arrangement of five heart shapes is perceived. That is, one sees a group of hearts covered by a school of fish. Note, however, that, as with Figure 7.15, other spatial–figural relationships, including past experience with related shapes, are involved in promoting a meaningful grouping in this figure (see Brown and Koch, 1993, for an analysis of some of the variables in such fragmented pictures).

Measures of Grouping Effects

Clearly, observers are sensitive to the structure of Gestalt patterns. In one experiment on the characteristics that affect perceptual organization, Beck (1966, 1982) showed that perceptual separation or grouping of two-line figures may be influenced by the orientation of the lines comprising the figure. When subjects were

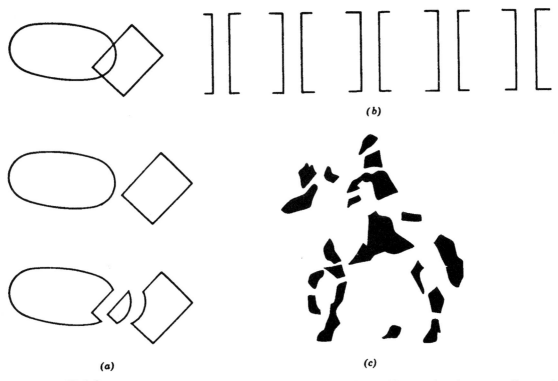

(b)

(a)

(c)

□ *figure* **7.14** (a) Due to the operation of closure, one sees two distinct and intersecting shapes, an ellipse and a rectangle, rather than three discrete, enclosed areas. (b) One tends to see rectangles: the principle of closure predominates. (c) One tends to perceive a completed figure, although only fragmentary stimuli are present.

instructed to divide the pattern shown in Figure 7.18 into two parts, the division was based primarily on the *orientation* of the figures; that is, figures with lines oriented in the same direction were grouped together. In this example, the physical similarity of figures was not important in perceptual grouping.

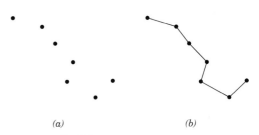

(a)   (b)

□ *figure* **7.16** The Big Dipper. The perceptions of early astronomers were likely affected by the Gestalt grouping tendencies of good continuation and closure when a particular constellation of seven stars suggested a familiar shape. The approximate physical relation of the stars to each other is given at (a). At (b) the stars are connected to reveal the famous Big Dipper. In fact, the stars comprising the Big Dipper are unrelated to each other. They complete a clearly recognizable figure by accident because of the line of sight from which they are viewed from Earth. (Jastrow & Thompson, 1974.)

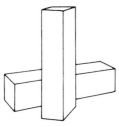

□ *figure* **7.15** At least three discrete shapes may be perceived in the line drawing. Good continuation and closure tend to favor the perception of two bars, one lying in front of the other.

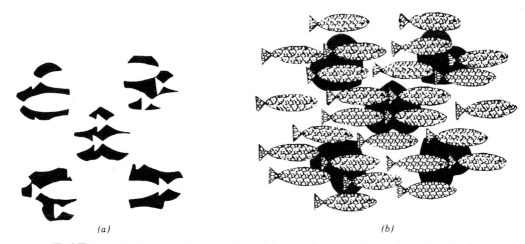

(a)   *(b)*

▭ *figure 7.17* Organization by good continuation and closure. (Courtesy of Jan and Sue. Based on Bregman, 1981.)

In a different grouping experiment, Girgus and her colleagues (Coren & Girgus, 1980; Enns & Girgus, 1985) demonstrated that Gestalt factors that promote perceptual grouping and enhance perceptual organization have direct and measurable consequences. They had subjects estimate the apparent distance between elements embedded in patterns that illustrated the Gestalt grouping principles of proximity, similarity, closure, and good continuation (Figure 7.19). The subjects appeared sensitive to the structural relations in the Gestalt patterns and reflected this in a spatial distortion of their distance judgments. Thus subjects judged the distance between elements that were apparently embedded in the same perceptual pattern as smaller—that is, the elements appeared closer together—than they judged the same physical distance between elements that appeared in perceptual groups

unrelated to each other in a Gestalt sense. In other words, elements subject to various grouping tendencies appeared to lie closer to each other than elements at identical distances from each other but not linked together in any Gestalt relation. (However, as Enns and Girgus, 1985, note, the magnitude of these distances distortions decreases with age.)

Law of Prägnanz

Many of the Gestalt principles stated earlier, along with several corollaries, have been codified under the general label of the **law of Prägnanz,** or the law of the *good figure,* which refers to the tendency to perceive the simplest and most stable figure of all possible alternatives. However, as used by the Gestaltists, the descriptive term "good," although possessing some

(a)   *(b)*   *(c)*

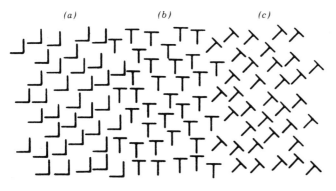

▭ *figure 7.18* Stimulus pattern used by Beck. The elements of (*a*) and (*b*) appear to form a group distinct from the elements of (*c*), although the elements of (*b*) have greater physical similarity to those of (*c*) than to those of (*a*). (From J. Beck, "Effect of orientation and of shape similarity on perceptual grouping," *Perception & Psychophysics, 1,* 1966, p. 300. Reprinted by permission of Psychonomic Society, Inc.)

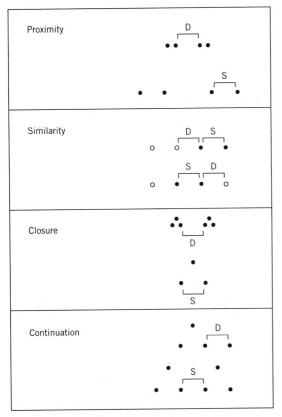

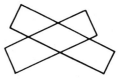

□ figure 7.19 The effects of Gestalt grouping principles on the apparent distance between pattern elements. Subjects judged the linear distance between the extent markers, shown above selected dot pairs, by choosing from a graded series of horizontal distances (note that the extent markers did not appear on the patterns shown to subjects). The distance between the elements that appeared to be part of the same Gestalt pattern or group (labeled "S") was distorted, that is, judged less than the physically identical distance between elements appearing in different perceptual groups (labeled "D"). Thus, elements linked by Gestalt grouping principles appear closer together than elements that do not. (Based on Coren & Girgus, 1980; Enns & Girgus, 1985.)

intuitive appeal, demands further elaboration. One attempt to develop a quantitative index of the structural properties of figural goodness was made by Hochberg and McAlister (1953). They suggested that figural goodness is inversely proportional to the amount of information necessary to specify a figure. That is, the less information needed to define a given

organization compared to other alternatives, the more likely is the perception of that organization and the greater is its figural goodness. In short, the good figure in the Gestalt sense is the simpler, more stable one.

The general Gestalt law of Prägnanz incorporates the effects of the Gestalt grouping principles. Organizing the visual pattern on the basis of Gestalt principles leads to efficient, simpler perceptions. For example, a closed figure can be more easily defined than an open one—not requiring specification of the gap's size and location—and a symmetrical figure can be succinctly described by indicating half of its features because the remaining half is its mirror image. Look at Figure 7.20. It is generally described as two overlapping rectangles. Alternatively, however, it can be interpreted as five irregular shapes. In this case, more angles, lines, and points of intersection are required to specify the general pattern. Hence, according to the analysis of Hochberg and McAlister, this is the least likely perception. In contrast, because less information is necessary to specify the pattern as two rectangles, this is the figure most likely seen, and it possesses greater figural goodness than its alternatives. (Note that Figures 7.14 and 7.15 also illustrate the law of Prägnanz.)

In general, well-organized, good figures in the Gestalt sense are remembered better than disorganized ones (Howe & Brandau, 1983; Howe & Jung, 1986). Perhaps this is because they are easier to encode and, accordingly, make fewer demands on cognitive resources (Hatfield & Epstein, 1985). Mermelstein, Banks, and Prinzmetal (1979) have shown that when a visual configuration such as a picture of a face is organized and remembered as a good or unitary Gestalt figure, later detection of its component parts is facilitated (see also Purcell & Stewart, 1988).

□ figure 7.20 Less information is required to specify this figure as two overlapping rectangles (8 line segments and 8 angles) than the alternative construction of five irregular shapes (16 lines segments and 16 angles).

Much evidence supports the notion that wholes are perceived better than their parts. In one investigation, Schendel and Shaw (1976) compared the perception of whole letters to that of specific letter fragments (i.e., the interior linear segments comprising the letters). For example, when subjects had to decide whether a flashed fragment was a short horizontal line (——) or a negatively sloped diagonal (\) line, their performance was superior when the target fragments were part of the letters H or N (which contain the critical linear segments that just distinguish H from N) than when the fragments were presented in isolation. That is, the subjects' responses were more rapid and accurate when they were required to process entire letters rather than the fragments alone (for a similar facilitative relation of words to letters, see Johnston & McClelland, 1973, 1974). There are also reports that target identification is easier when the target is part of a configuration that appears to be a three-dimensional drawing (Enns & Prinzmetal, 1984) or when the target appears to be part of some basic configuration compared to when the target is presented in isolation (Lanze, Maguire, & Weisstein, 1985).

The next section deals with perceptual phenomena—called *subjective contours*—that seem to derive from Gestalt closure-like tendencies. However, while they seem to exemplify the holistic, global, and spontaneous nature of the Gestalt approach to perception, other factors of also seem to play a role.

SUBJECTIVE CONTOURS

A process resembling a closure-type process may occur across a blank portion of the visual field, producing the appearance of edges or outlines called **subjective contours** (also referred to as *illusory contours* or *apparent contours;* in some cases, not only contours, but also an overall figure seems to emerge). Although these contours are illusory, they can be measured and quantified (Banton & Levi, 1992). Several examples of subjective contours are given in Figure 7.21.

Many explanations has been proposed to account for subjective contours, but none has been complete or fully accepted. For example, it has been proposed that a subjective contour is the edge of an apparent

plane in depth (Coren, 1972); thus, the contour serves to simplify a complex two-dimensional array of elements into an easily coded three-dimensional array of meaningful elements. However, as Rock (1986) points out, the depth effect generally arises *after* the perception of a figure with subjective contours.

It has been argued that subjective contours derive from differences in the lightnesses of adjacent regions due to lightness contrast effects (e.g., Frisby, 1980; Jory & Day, 1979; Petry & Meyer, 1987). That is, the subjective contour is the perceived edge of a region that appears lighter than its background due to significant luminance differences. However, clear subjective contours appear even when the conditions for producing contrast effects are minimal (e.g., Figure 7.22; see Kennedy, 1988).

A Gestalt–cognitive explanation for the lightness difference between the apparent shape formed by the subjective contour and the background has been proposed by Bradley and Dumais (1975; Bradley & Petry, 1977; Dumais & Bradley, 1976). It is based on an effect of figure–ground organization noted earlier; the figure generally appears lighter or more intense than the background of equal reflectance. Thus, for example, since the central areas in Figures 7.5 and 7.21*a* appear as figures (i.e., circles, triangles, rectangles), it follows that they will be perceived as lighter than their backgrounds. Thus, the lightness effect is secondary to the perception of a figure. A provocative example of this cognitive approach to subjective contours is demonstrated by Figure 7.23, which shows a variation, with subjective contours, of a Necker cube (a variation of this was described in Chapter 1). The initial and most prominent perception is of a three-dimensional cube-like form in which each corner of the cube appears to lie in front of a black disk, and "bars" connecting the corners of the cube appear between the disks. Although the entire cube is seen, those portions apparent between the disks are illusory. In an alternative perceptual organization for this figure, subjective contours are *not* apparent. The perceptual alternative is aided by assuming that the eight disks are eight holes on an interposing white surface. Thus, a cube appears to lie against a dark background behind the white surface, so that each corner of the cube is visible through one of the holes, while the

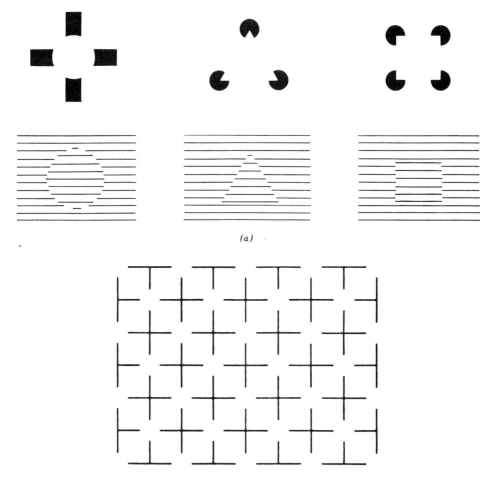

(a)

(b)

▭ *figure 7.21* (a) Subjective contours produce apparent shapes (i.e., circles, triangles, and rectangles). (b) Diagonal contours connected by circles are apparent at the missing intersections of the grid lines. (Based on Ehrenstein, 1941.)

remainder of the cube is covered by the interposing white surface. With this "cube-in-back" perceptual organization, the subjective contours previously seen extending between the disks do not appear.

Apparent Overlap

Clearly, the formation of subjective contours is probably due to several observer and stimulus variables. However, one primary feature in the formation of subjective contours for shapes is the perception of a central figure. What faciliates this perception is that the contour-inducing elements—the "cut-out" gaps, wedges, and line endings—that enclose and surround the edges and corners of the "figure" appear interrupted and incomplete; the shapes of the elements suggest that some form or surface—the edges of the figure—is partially covering or *overlapping* them in a consistent manner. In fact, the more this overlapping feature—that is, **apparent overlap** by a central surface or figure—appears within the configuration, the more immediate and compelling is the formation of

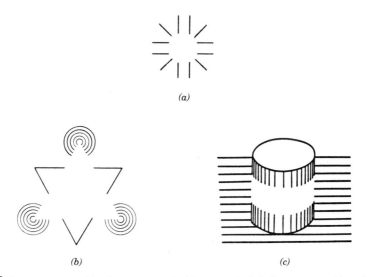

(a)

(b)   (c)

figure 7.22 Low-contrast subjective contours. In (a) a central circle is apparent, although only radiating lines are used. In (b) a triangle is apparent between the gaps of the three elements composed of concentric circles. In (c) the central portion of a cylinder, seen with a depth-like quality, is created by a series of linear segments. (Note that the bottom row of Figure 7.21 (a), as well as Figure 7.21 (b), also demonstrates subjective contour formation from low-contrast linear elements.)

the subjective contours (Figure 7.24). On the other hand, when the contour-inducing elements are themselves identifiable as complete and coherent figures, subjective contour formation is weak or does not occur. In this case, the apparently *un*interrupted shape of the contour-inducing elements is inconsistent with the perception of a central overlapping figure. Both

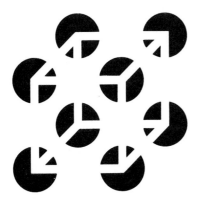

figure 7.23 A subjective Necker cube from which two perceptual alternatives are possible. (Based on Bradley, Dumais, & Petry, 1976.)

of these alternatives are illustrated in Figure 7.25. The central figures at (*a*) (appearing as a rectangle and a triangle) appear to overlap or cover part of each corner-inducing element. The shapes of the apparently fragmented elements help define the shape of the central figure and the nature of its subjective contours. However, at (*b*), the corner elements are complete, self-contained figural shapes that are not consistent with any overlap by a central shape: They do not appear to be covered or overlapped by part of any figure; accordingly, neither figure nor subjective contours emerge. In general, subjective contours are significantly linked to the shape of the edge-inducing elements (e.g., Kennedy, 1988).

The context (i.e., the overlapped elements) in which the stimulus appears causes the perception of a specific shape. This suggests strongly that subjective contours are a product of *top-down processing*: Apparent overlap generates the perception of edges in the figure, and the edges generate the apparent contours. In short, the global organization leads to the perception of a specific shape. Relatedly, Rock (1986) refers to the resultant lightness effect producing the subjec-

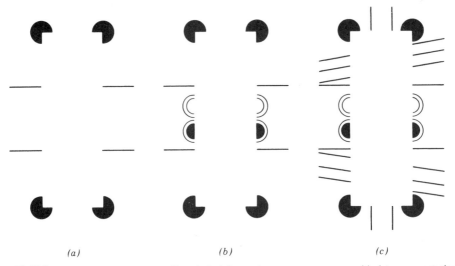

▭ *figure* **7.24** The subjective contour effect is heightened as more cues are added to suggest that a central figure overlaps the background. Although moderate subjective contours may be observable in (*a*), when additional cues are added that enhance the perception of an overlapping rectangle, as in (*b*) and (*c*), the contours appear stronger.

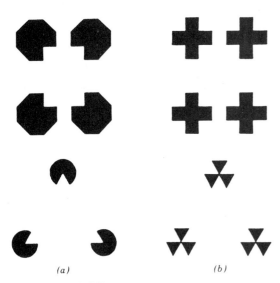

▭ *figure* **7.25** In (*a*) central figures are seen with subjective contours. The figures appear to overlay or cover part of the fragments at the corners or vertices. In (*b*) the elements at the corners and vertices are figural, self-contained units that do not contribute to the perception of a central shape.

tive contours as a **cognitive invention** that serves to make sense of the perception of a figure. Clearly, apparent overlap and some form of cognitive invention aid meaningful perception of the unusual configurations in Figure 7.26*a* where contours define shapes that appear to pass through planes formed by line segments.

However, apparent overlap may not be the only cognitive factor allowing us to perceive subjective contours and illusory figures. Many other cognitive variables have been proposed: for example, familiarity with specific shapes (Wallach & Slaughter, 1988) and selective attention (Gurnsey, Humphrey, & Kapitan, 1992; for general reviews, see Parks, 1984; Petry & Myer, 1987; Purghé & Coren, 1992). Moreover, as Figure 7.26*b* illustrates, subjective contours and the perception of a familiar shape may appear even when there is no apparent overlap (Purghé, 1993).

In addition, there is growing evidence that some cortical cells react to certain types of subjective contours; for example, neural activity in the cortex of alert monkeys is associated with subjective contours (Heydt & Peterhans, 1989*a*, 1989*b*; Heydt, Peterhans, & Baumgartner, 1984; see also Grossberg & Min-

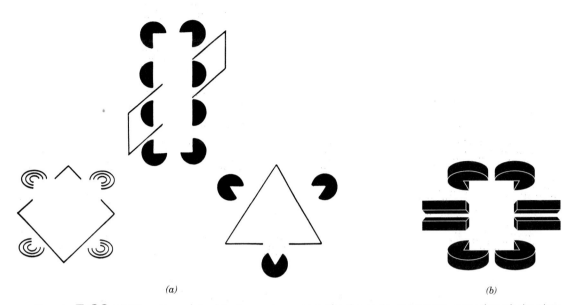

(b)

▭ *figure **7.26*** (a) When lines and subjective contours intersect, the contours appear to pass through the plane formed by the lines. (Based on Kanizsa, 1979.) (b) Subjective contours without apparent overlap. A central rectangle is seen, but its "corners" or "sides" do not appear to overlap any of the surrounding contour-inducing figures. (From Purghé, 1993, p. 810.)

golla, 1987; Winckelgren, 1992). There are also indications that cats, as well as humans and monkeys, see subjective contours (Bravo, Blake, & Morrison, 1988). This brings into question an explanation of subjective contours based on cognitive factors alone. Many issues remain to be clarified before the nature of subjective contours is well understood.

TEMPORAL FACTORS IN SHAPE PERCEPTION

Perception requires time, so it is not surprising that the time relations between stimuli affect their visibility. We will discuss two different phenomena in which time factors work in different ways to affect perception: *masking* and *aftereffects*.

Masking

Whenever stimul occur close together in time or space, they may interfere with, or *mask*, each other's perception. In **visual masking,** the perception of a target

stimulus is obscured by presenting a masking stimulus at or close to the same time. The resulting impairment in the perception of the target stimulus by a masking stimulus presented before it and close in time is called **forward masking.** The condition when the masking stimulus immediately follows the target stimulus is called **backward masking.** In backward masking, the masking stimulus appears after the target and interferes with its perception.

Consider, for example, a circular target disk and a masking ring just circumscribing it (Figure 7.27) presented briefly and in sequence. When the pause between the target and mask, called the **interstimulus interval (ISI),** is 200 msec or less in duration, the target may not be perceived, or it may appear dimmer or less structured than if it were presented without the mask.

We have no fully acceptable explanation of masking. However, it may result, at least in part, from some form of **visual persistence,** a sluggishness in neural activity following stimulation, so that the impression of a stimulus may be present even *after* its physical

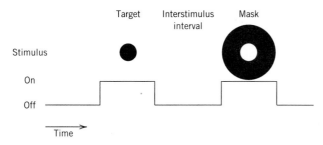

□ **figure 7.27** An arrangement for demonstrating masking. Presentation of the masking stimulus 200 msec or less after the presentation of the target impairs perception of the target. This arrangement illustrates backward masking since the mask follows the target. Masking could also be produced by having the mask coincide with or precede the target (i.e., forward masking).

offset (e.g., Long & Wurst, 1984). Thus, brief stimulus events that do not physically overlap in space or time may be perceived as occurring simultaneously or may somehow impair each other's perception.

Masking and Facilitative Interaction With visual masking, the interaction of successive but *different* visual stimuli (i.e., target and mask), may result in impaired perception. This is based on the notion that some of the information in a briefly flashed stimulus momentarily lingers after its physical termination (i.e., visual persistence) and interferes with the perception of the stimulus that immediately precedes or follows it. Thus, it is possible that a similar integrative mechanism will *facilitate* perception if the two successive stimuli are identical. In other words, if the two *different* stimuli—the target and the masking stimulus—when presented in sequence, interact to reduce recognition, then we can assume that if two stimuli are *identical,* their effect on the visual system will summate to produce a **facilitative interaction** effect.

A study by Eriksen and Collins (1967) illustrates this. They presented very briefly (6 msec) the dot pattern in Figure 7.28*a* followed by the dot pattern in Figure 7.28*b,* with a brief ISI (25 to 100 msec) between presentations. Each pattern by itself appears to be meaningless. However, when they are properly aligned and exposed simultaneously, the resulting perception is of the nonsense syllable "VOH" in Figure 7.28*c*. Eriksen and Collins found that with sequential presentation of the stimuli, identification of the nonsense syllable increased as the pause time between presentation of the two dot patterns decreased. The sensory effects of each stimulus presentation were

apparently summed or integrated visually to reveal the nonsense word.

Ordinarily, we are not passive observers of masking stimuli flashed at us. However, there is a common condition in which masking effects appear to be important in preserving the appearance of a stable, clear, and continuous visual world: that of *saccadic eye movements.*

Masking and Saccadic Omission As we noted in Chapter 4, vision is interrupted several times each second by rapid saccadic eye movements. During these movements, the visual scene literally sweeps across the retina, which should produce a brief period of retinal blurring. However, no blurred vision is generated by the saccades, nor are we even aware of the saccadic eye movements themselves. In fact, even when we gaze at a mirror while moving our eyes, we do not see any movement. In contrast, if we look at another person's eyes performing the same task, their eye movements are readily perceived. The lack of awareness of any blur during saccadic eye movements is generally referred to as **saccadic omission.**

Why are we not aware of our eye movements, and why do we not experience blurred vision during the movements? The reason may be based on visual masking. That is, the stimuli we perceive immediately before and after the saccadic eye movements may mask the blur created by the saccade. To assess this possibility, Campbell and Wurtz (1978; see also Cornfield, Frosdick, & Campbell, 1978) had subjects make saccadic eye movements, but in a condition in which masking could *not* occur. The subject sat in a darkened

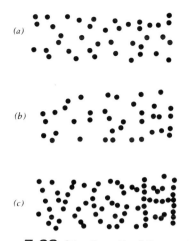

▭ *figure 7.28* Stimuli used by Eriksen and Collins. When the upper two dot patterns, (a) and (b), are superimposed or when the interval separating their sequential presentation is 100 msec or less, the likely perceptual result is the stimulus pattern in (c), in which the nonsense syllable "VOH" can be read. To minimize the possibility of guessing the nonsense syllable from the dots on only one dot pattern, camouflaging dots were distributed over each pattern. (From C. W. Eriksen and J. F. Collins, "Some temporal characteristics of visual pattern recognition," *Journal of Experimental Psychology, 74,* 1967, p. 477. Reprinted by permission of the American Psychological Association.)

room with only two small red fixation lights and was instructed to make a saccade by moving the eyes from one light to the other. When this was done, a signal triggered a light flash that illuminated the room, but only during the duration of the saccade (50–70 msec). In other words, illumination of the room occurred *only* during the saccade, eliminating the possibility of masking before and after the saccade. As a result, when the light was flashed during the saccade, the room, although visible, appeared blurred. However, when the duration of the light was extended for an additional 40 msec to illuminate the room—not only during the execution of the saccade but also during the fixation period preceding or following the saccade, or both—the subjects reported that the room and its furnishings appeared to be clear (unblurred). This indicates that the normal visual image formed during the visual fixation preceding or following a saccade masks the perception of the blurred image created during the saccade.

Aftereffects

We now turn to the general topic of **aftereffects.** Perhaps the most common and pervasive aftereffect results from inadvertently viewing the very brief but intense light of a flash bulb. Colored aftereffects were described in Chapter 5; if you stare at a colored shape for 30 sec and then shift the gaze to a neutral colorless surface, the shape is still perceived, but in its opponent or complementary color. In other cases, prolonged inspection of a stimulus not only causes stimulus persistance but also creates a measurable distortion in the perception of other figures (recall the demonstration of Figures 6.12 and 6.13). Several classes of aftereffects have been distinguished, in particular *figural, shape,* and *contingent* aftereffects.

Figural Aftereffects A classic example of **figural aftereffects** is the demonstration by Köhler and Wallach (1944) that the contours of shapes appear displaced from their original location. The typical arrangement is shown in Figure 7.29. If the x in Figure 7.29*a* is fixated for 40 sec and then the gaze is transferred to the x in Figure 7.29*b*, the distance between the two left squares in (*b*) will appear greater than that between the two right squares; in fact, the distances are equal. Although this distortion is due to the prior inspection of Figure 7.29*a*, there is no fully acceptable explanation for it. Köhler and Wallach explained the apparent displacement as due to the effects of *satiation.* That is, when a figure has been exposed for a period of time to a given region of the retina, its receptors, as well as the receptors for those areas immediately adjacent to that retinal site, become fatigued, resistant to stimulation, or satiated. This causes new figures projected near the satiated retinal areas to appear displaced from it. According to the satiation notion, then, the distortion—the shift in apparent location—of the squares in Figure 7.29*b* is due to their proximity to the retinal regions to which the inspection figures had been previously exposed and thus fatigued. Figure 7.29*c* is a schematic of the relation, indicating the appearance of components (*a*) and (*b*) of Figure 7.29 if they were combined. Thus, according to satiation, the two left squares appear pushed apart and the two right squares appear pushed

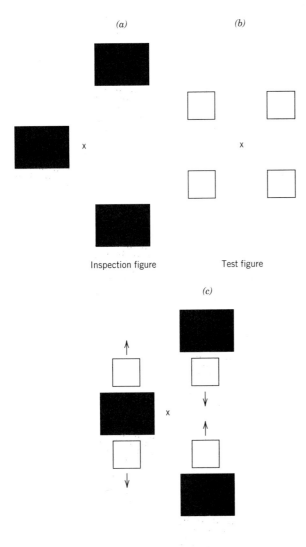

(a)   *(b)*

x   x

Inspection figure   Test figure

(c)

x

□ *figure 7.29* Inspection or inducing figure (*a*) and test figure (*b*) used to demonstrate figural aftereffects. The arrows in (*c*) indicate the direction of apparent displacement. (After Köhler & Wallach, 1944.)

together—displaced from the retinal region that was satiated.

at (*b*). This causes the vertical grating patterns at (*b*) to appear tilted in the direction opposite to the grating patterns at (*a*).

□
DEMONSTRATION:
Tilt Aftereffects

Figure 7.30 demonstrates a related figural aftereffect called the *tilt aftereffect*. As instructed by the caption, gaze at the central horizontal bar between the two tilted grating patterns at (*a*). After about 30–40 sec, transfer your gaze to the fixation circle

Shape Aftereffects   A second form of aftereffect called **shape** (or *curvature*) **aftereffects** refers to changes in the apparent shape of figures due to exposure. An experiment by J. J. Gibson in 1933 with simple lines—outlined in Figure 7.31—illustrates this. Subjects wore special distorting prism glasses that displaced the incoming light rays so that straight

(a)   (b)

figure 7.30 The tilt aftereffect. Cover the vertical gratings of (b) and gaze at the tilted gratings of (a) for 30–40 sec, with your gaze wandering back and forth along the central horizontal bar. Then rapidly transfer your gaze to the fixation circle of (b) that lies between the two vertical gratings. The vertical bars of (b) will briefly appear tilted in directions opposite to those of the gratings in (a).

vertical lines appeared as curved (see the second row of Figure 7.31). During exposure, the subjects reported that the apparent curvature gradually diminished. That is, the straight line "curved" by the prism glasses began to appear more straight. Moreover, when the prism glasses were removed, an *aftereffect* of wearing them was recorded: Straight lines appeared curved in the opposite direction of the apparent curvature produced by the glasses (see the bottom row of Figure 7.31). Gibson and Radner (1937) found that after a period of continuous visual inspection of tilted or curved lines, the same aftereffect occurred: Vertical straight lines appeared tilted or curved in the direction opposite to that of the initial inspection.

DEMONSTRATION:
Shape Aftereffects

A similar shape aftereffect is illustrated in Figure 7.32. As indicated in the caption, gaze at the center dot between the two curves at (a) for 30 sec; then shift your gaze to the fixation dot between the two vertical lines at (b). The lines at (b) appear bowed in the direction opposite to the curves at (a).

The shape aftereffect is not restricted to vision. In his original study, Gibson reported that if a blindfolded subject feels along a curved edge for a while, a straight edge feels curved in the opposite direction.

Contingent Aftereffects In the previous examples, prolonged exposure produces displacement or shape distortion in subsequent perception. In addition, there are aftereffects that are linked to *combinations* of stimulus properties, such as color with orientation or color with shape. Typically one of the features is color, and the resultant color aftereffect is contingent on, or linked to, the presentation of the other stimulus feature. Perhaps the first direct report of **contingent aftereffects** linked to a combination of stimulus properties is that of McCollough (1965). She presented a grating pattern consisting of vertical black and orange stripes for a few seconds, followed by an identical grating pattern of horizontal black and blue-green stripes (Figure 7.33); these two patterns

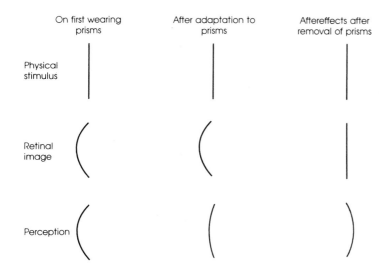

On first wearing   After adaptation to   Aftereffects after
prisms   prisms   removal of prisms

Physical
stimulus

Retinal
image

Perception

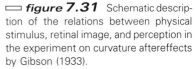 **figure 7.31** Schematic description of the relations between physical stimulus, retinal image, and perception in the experiment on curvature aftereffects by Gibson (1933).

were alternated for a total presentation time of about 4 min. She then presented test patterns consisting of a vertically and a horizontally oriented black-and-white grating pattern (shown at the right of Figure 7.33). The observer reported a faint blue-green aftereffect on the vertically oriented black-and-white test pattern and a faint orange aftereffect on the horizontally oriented test pattern. The two colors that McCollough used were complementary; orange is opponent to blue-green. Recall from Chapter 5 that when the visual system is continuously stimulated by a specific hue (i.e., wavelength), it becomes less sensitive to it and, as an aftereffect, produces the sensation of its opponent or complementary color. In short, fatiguing orange produces blue-green, and vice versa. What is

(a)   (b)

□ **figure 7.32** Shape aftereffects. Stare at the central dot in (a) for 30 sec, then transfer your gaze to the central dot in (b). The physically vertical lines in (b) will appear to be bowed in the opposite direction to those of (a).

interesting in this case is that the specific color aftereffect is linked to the *orientation* of the pattern's contours. In other words, exposure to colored stimuli in a particular orientation fatigues the units linked to that particular combination of color and orientation.

In Chapter 3, we noted that some neurons in the brain respond best to lines and edges in certain orientations. Since aftereffects are color sensitive *and* specific to the orientation of the pattern's contours, there may be neural analyzers in the human visual system that are selectively tuned to both color *and* orientation.

Contingent aftereffects that are movement specific have also been found. Hepler (1968) reported that after subjects alternately viewed green stripes (across a black background) moving up and red stripes against a similar ground moving down, they saw a pink aftereffect when white stripes moved up and a green aftereffect when white stripes moved down. That is, the paired-stimulus attributes of color and movement produced color aftereffects that were movement contingent. Many other studies have shown related variations on the theme of adaptation producing color- and movement-contingent aftereffects (e.g., Favreau, Emerson, & Corballis, 1972). In fact, color-contingent aftereffects have been demonstrated in combinations of almost every stimulus subject to adaptation and fatigue effects, including spatial frequency components (e.g., Zhou & May, 1993). Wy-

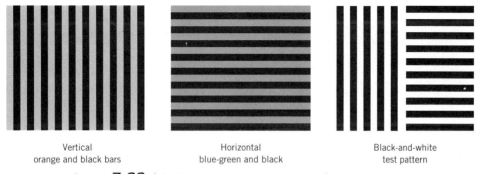

Vertical
orange and black bars

Horizontal
blue-green and black

Black-and-white
test pattern

◻ *figure 7.33* Stimuli used to demonstrate the McCollough (1965) effect.

att (1974) has even demonstrated contingent aftereffects for a combination of three stimulus properties: color, orientation, and spatial frequency. Contingent aftereffects suggest that the visual system is differentially sensitive to (and thus adapted by) *combinations* of specific stimulus features. However, the precise nature of the channels remains to be clarified.

FIGURAL ORIENTATION AND FORM PERCEPTION

Many factors are involved in the recognition of a stimulus figure. Two additional factors are the apparent orientation and context of the figure. *Orientation* here refers to the location of the top, bottom, and sides of a figure as perceived by the observer. If these are altered in certain ways, perception changes. The unfamiliar shapes in Figure 7.34a, look different from those in Figure 7.34b; the shapes in each row are geometrically equal but are shown in different orientations. Clearly, to the naïve observer, each shape appears quite different.

In addition, for figures with a recognizable shape, it is not the orientation of the shape on the retina that is crucial to its perception, but rather how the shape appears to be oriented with respect to gravity and to the viewer's visual frame of reference—what Rock (1973) labels **environmental orientation.** Generally a figure will not appear different in shape if its orientation is changed only in its retinal coordinates. Thus, once seen as upright, with an assigned top, the ambig-

uous shape in Figure 7.35a viewed with the head titled 90° to the right side continues to be perceived as a bearded profile; similarly, viewing Figure 7.35b with the head titled 90° to the left still results in the perception of an outline map of the United States. However, in each case, the image of the shape on the retina is oriented for the reverse perception. Thus, the environmentally upright rather than the retinally upright version of the figure is the one recognized.

Another effect of orientation and context is given in Figure 7.36, where the two small inner figures at

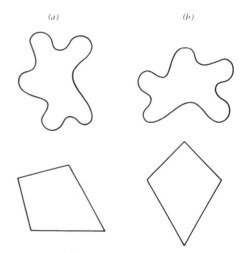

◻ *figure 7.34* The shapes in (a) appear different from those in (b). However, the shapes within each row are geometrically equivalent, except that they have been rotated to the right. The upper left shape has been rotated 90° and the bottom left shape 45°. (Modified from Rock, 1974.)

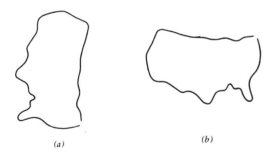

(a)   *(b)*

▭ *figure 7.35* This ambiguous figure above can be perceived as a different shape depending on its orientation. (Modified from Rock, 1973.)

the top and bottom have the same retinal orientation but different apparent orientation relative to their surrounding rectangles, that is, they differ in environmental orientation. Due to their different environmental orientations, the inner figures appear very different from each other. The top figure, surrounded by an apparently slanted rectangle, is seen as a correspond-

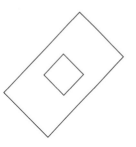

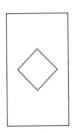

▭ *figure 7.36* Environmental orientation and context. (Based on Kaufman, 1979.)

ingly tilted square, whereas the bottom figure (which is retinally identical) appears as a diamond.

Shapes are perceived on the basis of their environmental orientation rather than their retinal orientation because the perceptual system tends to compensate automatically for head or body tilt. Perception based on environmental orientation is clearly adaptive in perceiving a stable environment. It makes far more sense for a biological system to compensate for its own physical displacements with regard to the environment than to perceive the environment as tilted with every tilt of the body. The latter would result in visual chaos.

There are, however, interesting exceptions to the general rule that retinal orientation does not markedly affect perception. In particular, the perception of complex figures—usually seen in only one orientation and composed of several meaningfully related parts in a Gestalt sense—may be affected by a change in retinal orientation. Thus, printed or written words seen upside down or inverted photographs of faces are not easily recognized. As Figure 7.37 shows, we readily perceive an inverted face, but distorted details of its individual parts are unnoticed until the photograph is seen upright.

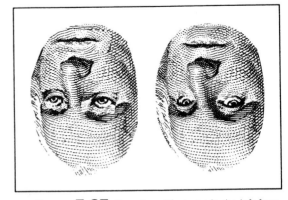

▭ *figure 7.37* The altered features in the left face do not seem to contribute to an extreme distortion in its expression until the face is viewed upright. The face on the right is the original photograph which was altered by inverting only the eyes and mouth. (*Source:* Based on Thompson, 1980.)

PERCEPTUAL SET

As we noted at the beginning of Chapter 6, perception involves more than the reception of stimuli at the retina. The optical array reflected from the environment—patterns of discrete stimuli composed of lines, dots, and luminance changes—cannot account by itself for the meaningful, structured visual world we experience. Perception of the environment is also due to certain dispositions and intentions within the perceiver. There are psychological processes, more specific and modifiable than the Gestalt principles described earlier, that play a role in organizing the incoming stimuli. Perception is directed by past experience and memories, expectation, suggestion, and the surrounding context, resulting in a readiness, or bias, to organize visual input in a certain way. In other words, due to various influences, the observer is primed, or *set,* to perceive the visual environment in a particular way. William Shakespeare hinted at the role of suggestion in organizing and assigning meaning to familiar but apparently amorphous configurations—cloud formations—in *Hamlet*. We see it in this piece of dialogue in which Hamlet mockingly questions Polonius:

HAMLET: Do you see yonder cloud that's almost in shape of a camel?

POLONIUS: By the mass, and 'tis like a camel, indeed.

HAMLET: Methinks it is like a weasel.

POLONIUS: It is backed like a weasel.

HAMLET: Or like a whale?

POLONIUS: Very like a whale.

Perceptual set, then, refers to a form of perceptual priming to perceive the world derived from past experience and environmental context. In general, perceptual set uses *top-down processing*. That is, assumptions and past experience are used to create general organizational strategies that are applied to the entire configuration; these strategies, in turn, determine the perception of the elements and their details. In short, the initial "big picture" determines the perception of its elements.

An interesting example of perceptual set involving a top-down process is given in Figure 7.38. An array of seven white irregular shapes on a black ground is shown. However, what is almost immediately perceived is a familiar face in semiprofile. This perception is not merely the result of detecting its contours. The shapes at the right in Figure 7.38 isolate the prominant contours, and they alone are insufficient to perceive the profile. Integral to perceiving the face in profile is the assumption of partial illumination and apparent shading of the entire figure. The "shading" apparent in the stimulus predisposes the viewer to organize the shapes into a global configuration that coincides with past experience, namely, a face. (It may occur to the reader that the "profile" apparent in Figure 7.38 also seems to be a product of Gestalt organization, involving figure–ground separation, good continuation, and closure.)

The influence of perceptual set in guiding perception is demonstrated by Figure 7.39. Depending on whether (*a*) or (*b*) is seen prior to (*c*), the viewer sees

◻ *figure **7.38*** Set and top-down processing. The figure on the left is easily seen as a familiar face in profile. However, its contours alone, presented at the right, are insufficient for recognition. What is required is an assumption of illumination and the resultant apparent shading attached to the entire figure. (Figure courtesy of Patrick Cavanaugh.)

(a)

(b)

(c)

▭ *figure 7.39* Whether a young woman or an old woman is seen in (c) can be due to the viewer's set. If (a) is seen first, the drawing in (c) is seen as a young woman; if (b) is seen first, (c) appears as an old woman. (Adapted from Boring, 1930.)

(c) as a drawing of either a young or an old woman. In this case, perception results from a set caused by the prior inspection of either (a) or (b). Another example is given by the classic duck-rabbit figure shown in Figure 7.40.

Perceptual set is not restricted to figures depicting familiar objects. Long, Toppino, and Mondin (1992) presented the ambiguous, reversible Necker cube-like figure composed of a series of overlapping squares shown in Figure 7.41c). By itself, this figure was seen

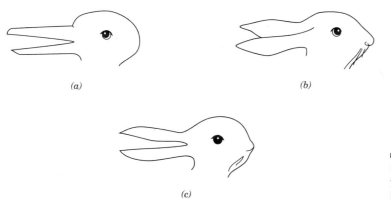

(a)

(b)

(c)

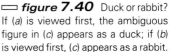

figure 7.40 Duck or rabbit? If (a) is viewed first, the ambiguous figure in (c) appears as a duck; if (b) is viewed first, (c) appears as a rabbit.

as a series of squares receding up *or* down. However, perception became restricted when Figure 7.41*c* was very briefly preceded by Figure 7.41*a* or Figure 7.41*b*. In other words, the observer's perception of (c) was primed or set by prior exposure. When presentation of (c) was preceded by a brief exposure (less than 100 msec) of (a), it was seen as a series of overlapping squares receding down, from left to right. In contrast, if (b) was briefly presented first, (c) was seen as a series of overlapping squares receding up, from right to left. In general, then, the stimulus first presented establishes the context that determines the perception of an ambiguous figure. [It should be stressed, how-

ever, that the *duration* of the preexposure Necker cube-like figure is important in inducing set effects. Long et al. report that if the preexposure duration of (a) or (b) of Figure 7.41 exceeds 100 msec, set effects are eliminated and the opposite alternative to set effects are perceived: Fatigue or adaptation rather than set effects are reported. We will return to this point in Chapter 10.]

Perceptual set facilitates meaningful perception under suboptimal conditions, such as when an object is shaded, overlapped, or obscured by background stimuli. This role of set is important, since environmental stimuli are usually indistinct or incomplete. Fre-

(a)

(b)

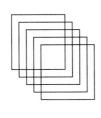

(c)

figure 7.41 Set-inducing stimuli used by Long, Toppino, and Mondin (1992). (Courtesy of G. Long.)

□ *figure* **7.42** Concealed figure. Examine the apparently unstructured configuration. Among its details is a familiar shape. The solution is given in Figure 7.46 on page 192. (From K. M. Dallenbach, A puzzle-picture with a new principle of concealment, *American Journal of Psychology, 64,* 1951, p. 432. Reprinted with permission of University of Illinois Press.)

quently, an expectation, based on prior experience, of what "should be there" enables meaningful interpretation and perception of what "is there." Figure 7.42 shows how set contributes to meaningful perception of seemingly formless stimuli.

Perceptual Set, Reading, and the Stroop Effect

Because reading is such a well-learned and practiced activity, it can be used to demonstrate set. Read the two lines of Figure 7.43. Most individuals read the top line as the numerals from 11 to 14 and the bottom

11 12 13 14

A B C D

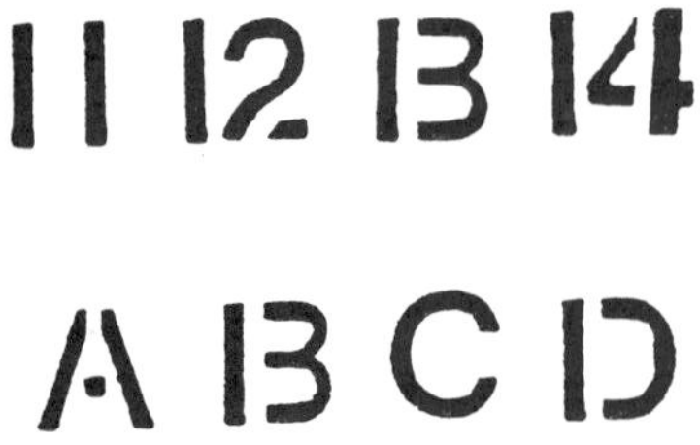

□ *figure* **7.43** The top line appears to be composed exclusively of numerals, whereas the bottom line is made up of letters. However, one ambiguous symbol is common to both lines.

line as the first four letters of the alphabet. Note, however, that the numeral read as 13 and the letter read as B are identical. We tend to "read" an ambiguous stimulus in accordance with an expectation determined by the context.

In fact, whenever we are confronted with textual stimuli such as words, the tendency to read them is overwhelming. This tendency to read seems to be so habitual, well practiced, and overlearned that it occurs automatically and can even interfere with other activities. This is demonstrated with the **Stroop effect.** This effect (1935, 1938), named for the psychologist J. Ridley Stroop, consists of a disruption and delay in naming the colors of words printed in colored ink when the letters of the words spell the names of incongruous or nonmatching colors. In the typical procedure, a subject is presented with a list of names of colors, each printed in an ink that is a different color from the one spelled by the word: for example, the word RED printed in blue ink (Color Plate 14). The subject must go through the list as rapidly as possible, naming *only* the color of the ink of each word. In other words, the Stroop task requires that the subject *ignore* the color words and respond only to the colors of the inks in which they are printed. However, during this task, there is a powerful set, or tendency, to read the word: Subjects may even feel the effects of suppressing the set to read, and show signs of strain and increased effort. As a result, the loudness of the voice may increase, vocalization itself my falter, and occasionally the printed word rather than its color is mistakenly reported.

The color-naming task of the Stroop test is difficult because we cannot ignore or suppress the reading response: the presence of text triggers the incorrect but automatic perceptual set to read. This competes with the correct response of color naming creating response conflict and interference.

Perceptual Set and Scene Perception

The types of set introduced above generally deal with unusual or simple stimuli presented in isolation. To what extent do factors of set such as *expectation* (involving top-down processing) apply to the more complex stimuli encountered in the real world? Typically, the spatial view that confronts an observer is a visual "scene" of the environment, composed of an array of objects against a background. Clearly, **scene perception** differs from the perception of an individual object or a display of isolated objects. Objects in a scene have spatial and contextual relationships to one another and to the background that contribute to an overall cohesive and meaningful perception.

Biederman (1981) has studied extensively the role played by the normal relationships among objects, and between objects and their environment, in the perception of an organized, well-formed, rational scene. For example, certain objects characteristically occur in specific positions in a scene and not in others. To use one of Biederman's examples, fire hydrants typically appear on the sidewalk, not on mailboxes or counters. Moreover, many objects have familiar, expected sizes; accordingly, in real-world scenes, the relative sizes of objects are meaningfully incorporated. Thus, in a typical kitchen scene, a cup will not be bigger than the stove.

In one experiment in which several of these relationships were studied, Biederman, Mezzanotte, and Rabinowitz (1982) had observers decide whether a specified target object was located at a particular location in a scene. Immediately before each trial, the observer was given the name of the target, for example, a "fire hydrant." A fixation point was presented, followed by a brief (150-msec) presentation of the scene, which in turn was followed by a cue marking some position in the scene presented. The observer had to report whether the target had appeared in the location marked by the cue. However, sometimes the target object was in its normal position, and sometimes it violated one or more natural scene relations. Figure 7.44*a* shows a normal scene in which the target is the fire hydrant. In contrast, the location of the hydrant in Figures 7.44*b* and 7.44*c* is inappropriate and violates the natural relations among objects. Observers viewing scenes where the target object was incongruously located made many more errors in detecting the object than when the target object was in a natural, appropriate location. In short, the observers' expectation of where fire hydrants belong influenced their ability to detect the hydrants.

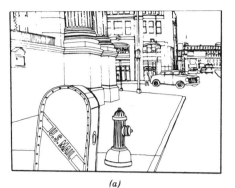

(a)

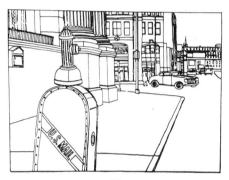

(b)

(c)

□ **figure 7.44** Scenes used by Biederman et al. (1982). (From I. Biederman, R. J. Mezzanotte, and J. C. Rabinowitz. *Cognitive psychology, 14,* 1982, p. 153. Reprinted by permission of the author and Academic Press.)

Clearly, a scene containing objects that share a coherent relationship to each other and to their background creates strong expectancies that can facilitate the detection of a single object, even when the viewer is allowed only a single glance of less than a fifth of a second of the scene.

Bottom-up or Top-Down Processing?

In Chapter 6, we introduced and stressed the notion of bottom-up processing, in which recognition begins with the extraction of basic sensory information registered on the receptors (e.g., luminance differences, contours, orientations). This information is then processed by the visual system until the stimulus is perceived. In contrast, many of the topics discussed in this chapter emphasized top-down processing, in which context, past experience and general knowledge, perceptual set, expectations, and the like guide organized perception.

Perception involves *both* bottom-up and top-down processes: Our typical perceptions are influenced not only by sequential extraction and analysis of the basic details of stimuli, but also by set-inducing context and expectations. For example, a very brief glance into the kitchen reveals the vague figure shown in Figure 7.45. Given the context—a kitchen—you will probably see it as a loaf of bread. However, the same stimulus, briefly glimpsed at down a country road, is likely to be seen as a mailbox. In short, the context—using top-down processing—provides the appropriate perception (Palmer, 1975). Consider also a glance into a large pot cooking on the stove, with no expectation of what it contains. In order to learn what is cooking, we need to extract a series of features. We might begin by extracting shapes (long, thin,

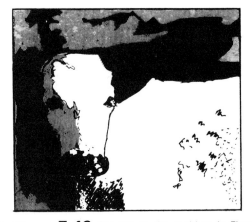

□ *figure 7.46* Solution to the problem in Figure 7.42. The head of a cow facing forward at the left is outlined from the detail of Figure 7.42. Once you see the cow's head, it is easy to see it in Figure 7.42. (From J. Hochberg, Visual perception, in *Stevens' Handbook of Experimental Psychology,* 2nd ed., Volume 1, John Wiley, New York, 1988, p. 258. Reprinted by permission of the publisher.)

strand-like), color (pale), and other characteristics until we recognize it as some form of pasta. In short, here we use bottom-up processing. Perception, then, typically derives from both top-down and bottom-up processes.

SUMMARY

In this chapter, we continued the discussion of perceptual organization begun in Chapter 6, but with a stress on top-down processes. We began with the perceptual relationship between objects or figures and their general backgrounds called figure–ground perception. Several figure–ground phenomena and relationships were described, including the special effect of the figure on the perception of lightness. This was also illustrated by the Wolff effect and Koffka rings.

This led to the discussion of Gestalt psychology, which stresses the use of unlearned organizing tendencies to perceive relations between visual stimuli. Gestalt grouping principles were outlined: proximity, similarity, good continuation, common fate, closure, and the law of Prägnanz. Some contemporary research yielding measures of grouping effects was briefly presented.

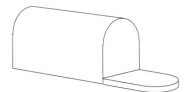

□ *figure 7.45* Context and top-down processing.

Subjective contours—illusory contours and shapes due to the special arrangement of fragmentary background stimuli—were then discussed. An explanation was offered based on the idea that the apparent contour derives from the perception of a shape apparently overlapping aspects of the background. While the notion of apparent overlap is useful for explaining many types of apparent contours, it is not a complete explanation.

Some time-related effects between stimuli on form perception were described next: visual masking and aftereffects. Various forms of masking, as well as their disruptive and facilitative effects on perception, were outlined, including the related notion of figural persistence and the role of masking on saccadic eye movements. Three main types of aftereffects were identified and discussed: figural, shape, and contingent. In general, aftereffects result from selective adaptation or fatigue of channels or units in the visual system specific to stimulus features such as color, orientation, shape, direction, and movement.

The role of physical and apparent orientation on perception was outlined next. We stressed environmental orientation—how an object appears to be oriented visually with respect to the observer.

In the final section, perceptual set was introduced and its priming role in perceptual organization was discussed. We tend to organize sensory input based on anticipations, expectations, and past experience. Several illustrations of perceptual set were presented, including the Stroop effect and scene perception.

KEY TERMS

Aftereffects

Analytical Introspection

Apparent Overlap

Backward Masking

Closure

Cognitive Invention

Common Fate

Contingent Aftereffects

Environmental Orientation

Facilitative Interaction

Figural Aftereffect

Figure–Ground

Forward Masking

Gestalt Psychology

Gestalt Grouping principles

Good Continuation

Interstimulus Interval (ISI)

Koffka Rings

Law of Prägnanz

Perceptual Set

Proximity (Nearness)

Saccadic Omission

Scene Perception

Shape Aftereffects

Similarity

Stroop Effect

Structuralism

Subjective Contours

Symmetry

Top-Down Processes

Visual Masking

Visual Persistence

Wolff Effect

STUDY QUESTIONS

1. What is figure-ground differentiation, and what fundamental principle does it illustrate about organized perception of the visual field?

2. What are some of the stimulus features that affect figure-ground differentiation? What factors determine whether a given region will be perceived as figure or ground?

3. What are the perceptual differences between figure and ground? Analyze the tendency of the figure to appear lighter than the ground, drawing on the Wolff figure and by the Koffka rings.

4. Discuss the ways in which figure-ground differentiation aids perceptual organization and object identification. Describe the importance of the contour to figure-ground differentiation.

5. What is Gestalt psychology? How does it treat the notion of fundamental units of perception? What does it propose concerning the relational character of stimuli for perceptual organization?

6. Distinguish between Gestalt psychology and structuralism. How does each deal with the notion of elementary sensations?

7. Identify the main Gestalt organizing principles, and present examples of proximity, similarity, good continuation, and closure.

8. Indicate how grouping effects may be measured.

9. What are subjective contours? What stimulus factors are critical in their formation? To what extent is an apparent partial overlap of the background by the subjective contour necessary for their formation?

10. How does Rock's notion of a cognitive invention explain the emergence of subjective contours?

11. What is a good figure in the Gestalt sense? How can its characteristics be assessed? What are the general features of good figures? To what extent are parts embedded in wholes better recognized than when they appear in isolation?

12. Describe masking, indicating its main forms (backward and forward). Indicate what variables affect masking.

13. What does masking indicate about the interaction effect of processing simultaneously and successively presented stimuli? Consider the question of why we don't experience blurred vision from the changing visual fixations created by saccadic eye movements.

14. Describe facilitative interaction due to the integration of successive visual stimulation. What does facilitative interaction indicate about the integration of stimuli over time and space by the visual system?

15. Indicate how aftereffects can be demonstrated. Describe the main forms, indicating figural, tilt, shape, and contingent aftereffects. To what extent do aftereffects support the existence of selective neural channels for specific stimulus features?

16. To what extent does the perceptual system compensate for head tilt on the position of the upright? How does the perception of an object's shape differ when it is tilted 90° to the right of a stationary observer, from when the object is kept stationary but the observer shifts his or her head 90° to the right? In examining this question consider Rock's notion of environmental orientation.

17. What is perceptual set? What does set stress about the role of expectation and anticipation on perceptual processing? Discuss the contribution of past experience on perceptual set.

18. Identify the Stroop effect and scene perception. In what ways are they instances of the operation of perceptual set?

19. What topics in this chapter can be readily described as top-down processes? Indicate why they are top-down processes.

THE PERCEPTION OF MOVEMENT

*O*ur *discussion of visual perception has been confined to static or immobile stimuli by a stationary viewer. However, we also perceive* movement *in the environment. Most organisms are relatively mobile and move about in an environment containing a variety of moving objects—objects to be pursued or potentially dangerous objects to be avoided. Clearly, the perception of movement has important biological utility. To move about effectively, animals must be able to detect the location, the direction, and often even the rate of movement of objects. Perhaps for all species information about movement is essential for survival.*

Gregory (1977) speculates that movement perception may have evolutionary priority over shape perception:

> *Something of the evolutionary development of the eye, from movement to shape perception, can be seen embalmed in the human retina. The edge of the retina is sensitive only to movement. This may be seen by getting someone to wave an object around the side of the visual field, where only the edge of the retina is stimulated. It will be found that movement is seen but it is impossible to identify the object. When the movement stops, the object becomes invisible. This is as close as we can come to experiencing primitive perception. The very extreme edge of the retina is even more primitive: when stimulated by movement we experience nothing, but a reflex is initiated which rotates the eye to bring the moving object into central vision, so that the highly developed foveal region with its associated central neural network is brought into play for identifying the object. The edge of the retina is thus an early-warning device, used to rotate the eyes to aim the sophisticated object-recognition part of the system on to objects likely to be friend or foe or food rather than neutral. (p. 93)*

MOTION DETECTORS

The ability to perceive movement is basic; it is observed in the young of many species and in primitive animals. There is also evidence of specific neural units for the detection of movement in many species (Cremieux, Orban, & Duysens, 1984; Frost & Nakayama, 1983). In Chapter 3, we observed that the Y cells found at the retinal ganglion level may react specifically to moving stimuli (Yang & Masland, 1992). We described the role played by the magnocellular division of the LGN in processing stimulus movement. At the level of the visual cortex (occipital lobe), we find strong evidence for specialized cells for stimulus movement. As we noted in the discussion of receptive fields for cortical cells in Chapter 3, there are cells that react

,ot only to movement but to movement in a specific direction. Furthermore, there is evidence that a region of the medial temporal (MT) lobe of the cortex receives input from motion-sensitive cells of the visual cortex (e.g., Movshon & Newsome, 1992). Whereas these motion-sensitive cells possess relatively precise, small receptive fields and thus react to local movement, many MT cells respond to movement over larger regions of the visual field. It may be that MT cells integrate various sorts of movement, acting as generalized motion detectors (Albright, 1992; Logethetis & Schall, 1989; Saltzman & Newsome, 1994).

The following clinical study highlights the specific role played by the cortex in human perception of movement. Zihl, von Cramon, and Mai (1983) reported the case of a patient who suffered from cortical lesions. Although she retained other visual functions such as visual acuity, binocular vision, and form and color perception, she lost the ability to perceive most movement in all three dimensions. Clinical assessments showed that while she had some movement perception along the vertical and horizontal axes, her perception was restricted to a small region of the inner visual field. In addition, she was totally unable to see motion in depth. "She had difficulty, for example, in pouring tea or coffee into a cup because the fluid appeared to be frozen, like a glacier. In addition she could not stop pouring at the right time since she was unable to perceive the movement in the cup (or a pot) when the fluid rose" (p. 315). She also complained of difficulty following a conversation because she could not see the movements of the face, especially the speaker's mouth. In a room where more than two other people were moving about, she felt extremely uncomfortable and usually left immediately because "people were suddenly here or there, but I have not seen them moving" (p. 315). The patient experienced this problem to a greater extent in crowded places and where there was considerable movement, like the outdoors, which she avoided as much as possible. Thus, she could not cross the street because of her inability to estimate the speed of the cars, although she could easily identify the car. "When I'm looking at the car first, it seems far away. But then, when I want to cross the road, suddenly the car is very near"

(p. 315). Eventually, however, she learned to judge the distance of moving vehicles by their increase in loudness as they approached. It is of interest that her lack of movement perception was specific and limited to the visual modality. She was able to perceive motion given by tactual means (e.g., a stimulus moving over her skin surface) and by auditory cues (a moving sound source) with ease.

MOVEMENT SYSTEMS OF THE EYE

The most general way of perceiving movement is by the stimulation of a succession of neighboring retinal elements by an image. However, retinal displacement does not include all forms of movement perception. The movement of a stimulus may be perceived when its image is held relatively stationary on the retina, such as when the eyes follow or track a moving object. Here eye movements match the target's movement, resulting in a more or less motionless retinal image.

Gregory (1977) has identified and proposed two interdependent movement systems: the **image–retina movement system** and the **eye–head movement system** (Figure 8.1).

Image–Retina Movement System

For the image–retina system, effective stimulation for the perception of movement is successive stimulation of adjacent retinal receptors. Generally, when the eye if held relatively still, as during fixation, a series of images produced by a moving stimulus shifts across the retina. The movement thus registered is due to the sequential activity of the retinal receptors in the path of the image of the stimulus. This movement detection system is well suited to the mosaic of ommatidia found in the compound eye of the arthropod (described in Chapter 3; see Figure 3.4). A neural model of a movement detector coincident with the image–retina movement system is suggested in Figure 8.2 (Schouten, 1967).

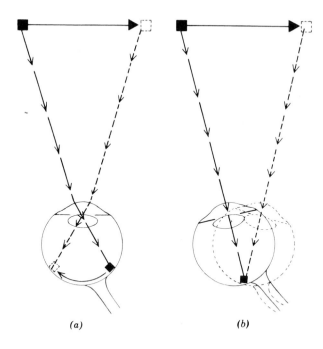

(a)   **(b)**

□ *figure 8.1* Movement systems of the eye. (*a*) Image–retina movement system. The succession of images of a moving target stimulus across the retina provides information of movement to a stationary eye. (*b*) Eye–head movement system. A moving-target stimulus is tracked by a moving eye so that the image remains stationary on the retina, yet movement of the target stimulus is still perceived. Images that move across the retina are perceived as stationary background stimuli, and images that remain stationary on the retina while the eye moves are perceived as moving. (Adapted from Gregory, 1973.)

Eye–Head Movement System

When we follow a moving target with our eyes, the image of the target remains more or less fixed on the same retinal region. In this case, eye movement

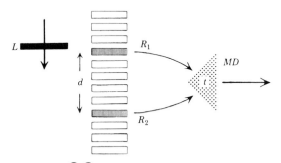

□ *figure 8.2* Neural model of a movement detector. Two retinal receptors, R_1 and R_2, spaced d apart, feed into the movement detector, *MD*. The movement detector reacts if the light, *L*, strikes receptor R_1 first and then, after or within a given period of time, *t*, strikes receptor R_2. (From J. F. Schouten, Subjective stroboscopy and a model of visual movement detectors, in W. Wathen-Dunn (Ed.), *Modes for the Perception of Visual Form*, M.I.T. Press, Cambridge, Massachusetts, 1967. By permission of the M.I.T. Press.)

compensates for target movement, yet we still perceive the target's movement. If the moving target is tracked against a stationary textured background, the target's background moves across the retina. However, the perception of movement results even when there is no background stimulation. A moving dot of light in an otherwise darkened room provides enough information for movement perception, yet as the eye follows the dot, no background imagery shifts across the retina. This means that with no stimulation of the image–retina system, a *self-initiated* neural signal—called an **efferent signal**—that produces rotation of the eyes in their sockets provides information for the perception of movement. That is, a neural mechanism takes account of command signals that move the eyes and relates them to the image on the retina. These neural command signals to the eye muscles, a direct response to object movement, occur only when the eyes are *voluntarily* moved. The nature of these self-initiated efferent signals is discussed next.

Corollary Discharge and Outflow Signals We frequently scan a stationary visual en-

vironment and perceive it as stationary. This raises a basic question: Why doesn't the visual environment appear to move as our eyes move? Clearly, when we intentionally move our eyes, a continuous flow of images streams across our retina; this stimulates the image–retina system, and we should perceive movement. Yet, we do not. The reason seems to be that when the eyes are voluntarily moved, the efferent motor command signals sent from the brain to the eye muscles somehow neutralize or cancel the perception of the flow of images that these self-induced eye movement generate. More specifically, it has been proposed that when the brain sends an efferent signal, or outgoing message, to the eye muscles to move, a related or **corollary discharge signal** (also called an *outflow signal*) of this message is also sent to a hypothetical **comparator** center of the nervous system (Figure 8.3). Thus, when the eyes voluntarily move, the resultant **afferent signal** or incoming message conveying information on changes in retinal image position (i.e., information for the image–retina system) is compared with the corollary discharge signal sent to the comparator (Matin, 1986). The outcome is *cancellation* of the stimulus to the image–retina movement system, and the visual scene appears stable in spite of the changes in the retinal iamge. We are thus able to differentiate between movements in the retinal image produced only by voluntary eye movements and movements in the retinal image produced

by the actual physical movements of objects. In short, when we scan intentionally, the perception of a stationary environment in spite of a changing retinal image is due to self-induced, *intentional* efferent motor commands to execute the eye movements.

When we track a moving object, what is *not* perceptually canceled out by corollary discharge signals is the image of the object that remains fixed on the retina. This is what we see as motion. In other words, when the eyes voluntarily move in tracking an object, the visual field of the target's stationary background appears stable and only physically moving stimuli appear to move.

From this analysis of the eye–head system, it follows that when eye movements are *not* voluntary—and corollary discharge signals are absent—the changing retinal images cannot be canceled and movement of the environment will be perceived. This is verified by the demonstration (attributed to Herman von Helmholtz) that when eyeball movement is initiated *passively*, thereby stimulating *only* the image–retina system, the total visual environment is erroneously seen as in movement.

DEMONSTRATION:
Passively Moving the Eyeball

You can verify this easily. If you close one eye and gently move a finger against the bottom lid of the open eye, moving the eye sideways or up, the visual scene appears to move in the direction opposite to the eye movement. In fact, pushing on your eyeball causes your eye to move, and this, in turn, causes the image of the scene to move on the retina. However, since the movement is *passive* (i.e., made by your finger rather than by a self-induced command from your brain to your eye muscles), it is a signal only for the image–retina system; correspondingly thus, there is no corollary discharge to cancel the moving scene. Hence, a moving scene is perceived. In other words, the visual scene appears to move because the the eye is passively moved, and impulses voluntarily directing eye movements and their accompanying corollary dis-

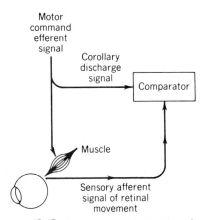

□ **figure 8.3** Schematic of the function of corollary discharge signals.

charge signals are lacking (Bridgeman & Delgardo, 1984).

Further evidence on the role of corollary discharge signals in movement perception comes from Ernst Mach, who performed a demonstration opposite to that of Helmholtz (Gregory, 1973). That is, rather than passively moving the eyeballs, Mach immobilized his eyes with putty. When he then attempted to move his eyes, the visual scene appeared to move in the same direction as the attempted movement. In this condition, eye movement command signals and corollary discharge signals are generated but, due to the experimental immobilization of the eyes, they are *not* accompanied by any movement of the retinal image. In other words, the visual field is displaced in the direction of the intended but unexecuted eye movement. (More recent studies of experimental eye immobilization to examine the role of voluntary eye movements can be found in Stevens et al., 1976 and Matin et al., 1982.)

In summary, passive movements of the eyeball produce image–retina signals *without* corresponding corollary discharge signals, and the visual field appears to move. In contrast, voluntary eye movements create corollary discharge signals that cancel the image–retina movement signals, and the visual field appears stationary. Table 8.1 summarizes some of the outcomes of environmental (object) and retinal movement we have been describing, with and without voluntary eye movements (and corollary discharge signals). In (1) the image–retina system alone is active: An object moves across the visual field and the retinal image changes, but the eyes are stationary. There is

no corollary discharge to cancel the retinal changes, and movement is perceived. This may happen when you are fixating on a stationary target and another object moves across your field of view. In (2) the eye–head system is active: The eyes move across a stationary scene, causing the retinal image to change. However, since the eye movements are voluntary, the resultant corollary discharge signals cancel the retinal changes at the comparator, and movement is not perceived. This may happen when you are merely scanning the visual scene. In (3), the eye–head system is also active: An object moves against a stationary background and the eyes correspondingly move, tracking the object, whose image remains fixed on the retina. The result is that since the eyes voluntarily move, the corollary discharge signals cancel the changes in the retinal image produced by the background, which thus appear stationary; however, since they do not cancel the stationary retinal image of the moving object being tracked, it is perceived as moving. This typically occurs when your eyes track a moving object.

Finally, it should be noted that, in general, the visual world does not appear to move very much as we move our heads or bodies independent of eye movements. This indicates that the central nervous system also takes into account an interplay of visual and orientational information, so that we perceive a stable visual environment. For example, the intentional motor command signals we make when we walk or run or jump are integrated with and cancel the resultant images moving across the retina. Thus, as a result of voluntarily moving about, we perceive a relatively stationary visual environment. The functional advantage of this is obvious.

▭ *table **8.1*** Outcomes of Object Movement, Retinal Image Changes, and Voluntary Eye Movements on the Perception of Movement

Movement System	Typical Activity	Activity of Object (or Environment)	Retinal Image	Voluntary Eye Movements and Corollary Discharge	Perception
1. Image–retina	Fixation	Moves	Changes	No	Movement
2. Eye–head	Scanning	Stationary	Changes	Yes	No Movement
3. Eye–head	Tracking	Moves	Stationary	Yes	Movement

THE PATTERN OF OPTICAL STIMULATION FOR MOVEMENT PERCEPTION

In the visual world things move about, and they move in different ways, in different directions, at different velocities, and with different accelerations. In addition, as an observer moves, the location from which the world is viewed continuously changes. All these dynamic events produce corresponding changes in the light array imaged on the retina. Thus, the perception of movement is affected by the complex pattern of changing stimulation in the retinal projection. Several variables, indexed by these changes, are especially informative in perceiving movement and are identified here.

Optic Flow Patterns

As an individual moves through the visual world, the image on the retina changes with movement. In other words, the optic array of most surfaces (e.g., floors, walls, ceilings, roads, fields) continuously changes with the viewer's movement. This pattern of changes created by the viewer's movement is called an **optic flow pattern.** As outlined in Figure 8.4, when the

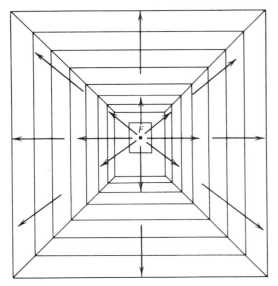

□ **figure 8.4** Optic flow pattern.

observer moves toward the frontal surface while focusing on point (*F*), contours appear to flow radially away (i.e., to fan out) from the focal point, flowing farther and farther to the edge of the visual field. The vectors in the figure suggest the changing optic patterns of the array. Since the optic flow pattern is generated by the movement of the observer, it should be reliable for gauging the *direction* of movement (Warren & Hannon, 1988, 1990; Warren, Morris, & Kalish, 1988). (It is the manipulation of optic flow patterns that produces the striking movement effects in most video games.)

Retinal Expansion and Rate of Movement

Information in the pattern of retinal changes also helps us to gauge the relative *rate* of the observer's movement. With movement toward a stationary surface, the size of the retinal image of the surface expands; the resulting source of information on movement is called **retinal expansion**. As the observer moves toward a surface, the rate of retinal expansion (i.e., of the retinal image of the surface) reflects the rate of the observer's approach. If the retinal image of the surface expands rapidly as the observer approaches, it can be a potent indicator of impending *collision* with the surface. Similarly, consider the condition where surfaces or objects appear to move toward a stationary observer. Movement of an object in the frontal (near-far) plane may be perceived when the approach of the object is signaled by its retinal expansion. That is, the increase in the object's image on the retina of the stationary observer is perceived as movement toward the observer, and the rate of increase indicates the velocity of the object. (This is called *looming* and is discussed in detail in Chapter 11.)

Changes in the image size of an object may also signal the infrequent, and hence unlikely, size change in a stationary object. Thus, an expanding retinal image of an object could mean that the object is stationary with respect to the observer, but is enlarging or growing, *or* that it is actually moving closer at a uniform rate. Considering the basis of perceiving size changes in an object as signals of the object's movement, rather than as cues of its expansion, Regan, Beverley, and Cynader (1979) propose that

> as long as an object's shape remains constant the visual system (possibly by means of some neural biasing system) responds as though changing size were caused by motion in depth. This might be described as a "best guess" solution. For an animal (including the human one) there would be little survival advantage conferred by a visual system that submitted for leisurely intellectual judgment the question of whether a predator was approaching rapidly or swelling rapidly! (p. 142)

Thresholds for Movement

How effective are we in detecting movement? At one extreme, objects can move across a visual field so swiftly that we can, at best, see only a blur. At the other extreme, there are objects and events whose rates of movement are so slow that we cannot detect any movement. We notice no movement in the hour hand of a clock and probably have some trouble seeing the minute hand move as well. Threshold values for the perception of movement—the minimum velocity that can be detected—vary with many physical and psychophysiological factors other than the actual velocity of an object. The movement threshold varies with such factors as target size, target distance, target background (e.g., homogeneous versus textured), luminance level, the region of the retina stimulated, and the adaptive state of the eye. For example, threshold values for movement are lowest for well-illuminated stimuli moving across a stationary background whose image falls on the fovea. Consider the following specific threshold conditions: When the fovea is stimulated, the movement of a well-illuminated target 0.8 cm² seen at a viewing distance of 2 m is just detected when it moves at about 0.2 cm/sec (Brown, 1931; see Spigel, 1965). In comparison, when the velocity of a moving target at 2 m from the viewer exceeds about 150 cm/sec, the target appears as a blur rather than as a moving stimulus. Specific values aside, there is both a lower threshold—a minimum velocity, below which motion is not perceived (Bonnett, 1982)—and an upper threshold—a maximum veloc-

ity value, above which motion is not perceived (Burr & Ross, 1982; see Mack, 1986, for an analysis and summary of threshold measures for motion). In other words, objects that move too slowly *or* too quickly are not perceived as moving.

BIOLOGICAL MOTION

Thus far we have dealt with the perception of movement per se, but one kind of environmental movement must be highlighted: the perception of movements made by moving humans. We quickly recognize whether a person is walking or running, skipping or dancing, and so on. Moreover, we can detect slight deviations from the general norms of these motions. For example, we easily note a slight limp in one's walk and the slower gait of the aged, and we may even recognize (and mimic) a person on the basis of characteristic posture, style of walk, and pattern of gestures. The complex pattern of movements determining the perception of these Gestalt-like acts of motion are constructed from combinations of pendulum-type motions that are specific for each type of activity. These complex patterns of motion have been studied extensively and labeled **biological motion** by Johansson (1973, 1975).

Johansson has devised an elegant method for directly studying visual information for perceiving pure biological motion without any interference by the shape of the moving form. In one experiment, an actor's movement was recorded on videotape. However, the movement was done in complete darkness, and only points or dots of light placed at 10 main body joints were visible. This eliminated any traces of the visual field background or the actor's body contours (Figure 8.5). When viewing the moving dot configuration shown in Figure 8.5*b*, the spontaneous perception of activity resulted even after the actor had taken only one or two steps. Indeed, the effect of the patterns of movement made by the joints was so compelling that subjects could not combine the moving dots to establish alternative impressions of movement and could not see the dots merely as a series of unrelated points of light in motion. When the motion ceased, the light configurations did not

(a)   (b)

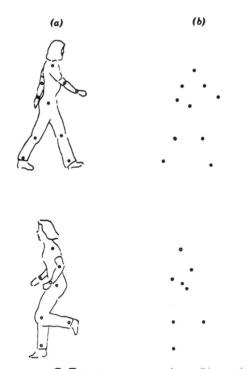

□ *figure 8.5* Outline contours of a walking and a running subject (*a*) and the corresponding dot configurations (*b*). After the first one or two steps, subjects viewing the dots of light perceive a walking (top dot configuration) or a running (bottom configuration) person. (From G. Johansson, Visual perception of biological motion and a model for its analysis, *Perception & Psychophysics, 14,* 1973, p. 202. Reprinted by permission of the Psychonomic Society, Inc.)

appear to represent a human form. This showed that it was the *pattern of movement* that determined the perception of the particular kind of motion.

Further studies of gait perception using point–light kinetic or moving displays as stimuli have established that it is possible to recognize one's own walk, as well as those of friends (Cutting & Kozlowski, 1977). Moreover, male and female walkers have distinctive and identifiable patterns of movement (Cutting & Proffitt, 1981; Cutting, Proffitt, & Kozlowski, 1978). Point–light sequences were identified as male when the perception of shoulder movement was greater than that of hip movement, and as female for the reverse pattern (Barclay, Cutting, & Kozlowski, 1978; Cutting, 1978; Runeson & Frykholm, 1983).

The pickup of biological motion is immediate, apparently requiring no complex processing by the observer. For example, short segments containing instances of biological motion flashed for only 100 msec are sufficient for viewers to identify aspects of familiar movements (Johansson, von Hofsten, & Jansson, 1980).

The perception of biological motion, even when defined by patterns of moving points of light on a television screen, is not restricted to adult humans. Fox and McDaniel (1982) found that human infants not only discriminate between simulations of biological and nonbiological forms of motion, but also show a distinct preference for the former. The finding that biological motion is perceived with little experience and at very brief durations suggests that the stimuli signaling biological motion are easily organized and may provide a basic source of information. This conclusion is further supported by the finding that the cat perceives biological motion when the "motion" is created by changing sequences of points of light (Blake, 1993).

In summary, general body movements, even when represented by lights set at body joints, are sufficiently informative to evoke strong and identifiable impressions of complex human movement. Moreover, it is possible to identify gender and even a familiar person from a dynamic point–light display.

DISTORTIONS IN THE PERCEPTION OF MOVEMENT

Many dynamic events have in common a distortion of movement, promoted by either a reinterpretation or a misperception of the physical movement occurring in the visual field.

Motion-Produced Depth: Kinetic Depth Effect

If a pattern of two-dimensional shadows, such as those created by rotation of a wire cube form, is cast on a translucent screen, as shown in Figure 8.6, the impression is of a rotating rigid object in three dimensions. This has been termed the **kinetic depth effect** by

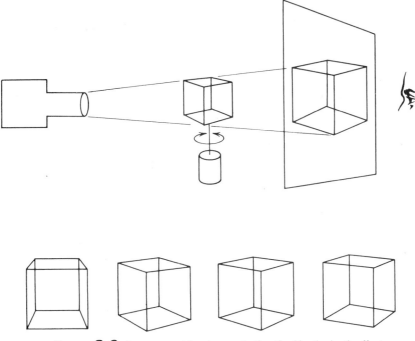

▭ *figure* **8.6** Arrangement for demonstrating the kinetic depth effect.

Wallach and O'Connell (1953). When the figure is stationary, the shadow of the wire cube form appears flat, in two dimensions. However, when set in rotation around its vertical axis, the changing shadow pattern is perceived as coming from a solid rotating cube, even though all the movement is imaged on a flat plane. Here a sequence of visual images is projected on the retina that corresponds to the continuous imagery normally resulting from the rotation of an actual three-dimensional object. As a result, the visual system interprets the changes in the pattern of shadows as those of a rotating three-dimensional object rather than as a succession of changing flat patterns.

Viewing a totally unfamiliar object, such as a randomly bent wire, also provides the same effect. As a stationary stimulus it would appear as a flat curve, and its shape would not be detectable; however, when rotated using the arrangement of Figure 8.6, its shape in three dimensions would be immediately perceived. Thus the kinetic depth effect demonstrates an extremely important point: The perception of an object's

motion may contribute to the perception of the object's *form.*

Anorthoscopic Perception

The framework in which the movement is seen strongly influences the character of the perceived movement. Parks (1965) demonstrated that when a picture of a figure is moved horizontally behind an opaque cover with a stationary slit that is smaller than the figure, a viewer observing the pattern of stimulation at the slit will perceive the figure as a whole in the general vicinity of the slit (see Figures 8.7 and 8.8). This unusual effect, attributed to Zöllner in 1862, is called **anorthoscopic perception** (see Rock, 1986, for a brief history). Interestingly, with an anorthoscopic display, the entire figure can be recognized, even though only a narrow strip of it is visible at any instant. This suggests that, over time, the visual system can integrate or assemble a set of successive parts that fall on the same retinal region into a single unitary

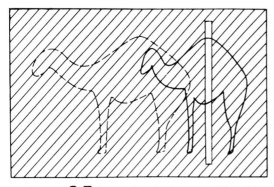

⊂⊃ *figure 8.7* A sample stimulus and outline of the arrangement for the demonstration of Park's effect. (From T. E. Parks, Post-retinal visual storage, *American Journal of Psychology, 78,* 1965, p. 148. Reprinted with permission of the publisher, University of Illinois Press.)

form. Along with the shape of the slit, the figure's perceived shape depends on the speed at which the figure travels behind the slit. At relatively slow speeds, the figure appears slightly elongated; at relatively high speeds, it appears compressed or condensed (Anstis & Atkinson, 1967; Haber & Nathanson, 1968). In addition, the figure appears displaced on the direction of its movement.

Induced Movement

What an observer perceives to be in motion is not always what is actually in motion. The perception of movement is strongly influenced by the spatial context in which the moving stimuli are seen. If two lighted figures of different sizes are seen against a dark field and only the larger figure is in physical motion, generally only the smaller one appears to move. The larger moving stimulus is said to *induce* the movement of the smaller one. If a stationary luminous dot is enclosed by a luminous rectangle in the dark and the rectangle is slowly moved to the right, the enclosed dot appears to move to the left. That is, the apparent movement of the dot is induced by the physical displacement of the rectangle. This is outlined in Figure 8.9. In a more familiar example, sometimes the moon appears to race behind apparently stationary clouds, yet clearly it is the clouds that are moving and covering the sta-

tionary moon. Thus **induced movement** is a visual illusion in which there is physical movement, but it is attributed to the wrong part of the stimulus array. In general, the smaller and more enclosed stimulus appears to move relative to the larger and enclosing stimulus. Perhaps this is because we know that it is usually small objects in our environment that move, whereas large objects are stable.

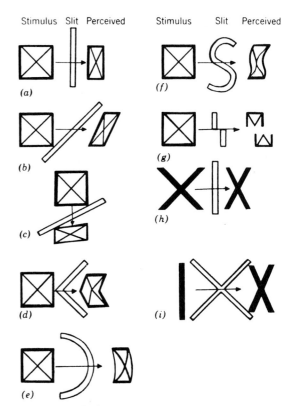

⊂⊃ *figure 8.8* Examples of the distorted perception of figures moving behind a stationary slit. (*a*) The perceived figure appears displaced and compressed in the direction of its movement. (*b–g*) Slits that are tilted, curved or multiple make moving figures appear tilted, curved or multiple, respectively. (*h, i*) The shape of the figure and the slit can be interchanged. An "X"-shape figure seen through a vertical-line slit appears the same as a vertical-line figure seen through an "X"-shape slit. (From S. M. Anstis and J. Atkinson, Distortions in moving figures viewed through a stationary slit, *American Journal of Psychology, 80,* 1967, p. 573. Reprinted with permission of the publisher, University of Illinois Press.)

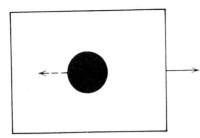

◻ *figure 8.9* Induced movement. A luminous stationary dot enclosed by a luminous rectangle is seen in the dark. If the rectangle is physically displaced to the right (solid arrow), the enclosed dot appears to move to the left (dashed arrow). The apparent movement of the stationary dot is induced by the physical displacement of the rectangle.

Induced movement is not restricted to apparent linear paths. Duncker (1929), in his classic treatise on induced movement, reported that movement of a patterned stationary disk can be induced by the rotation of a surrounding concentric patterned annulus (see Figure 8.10 for a demonstration of a related effect. See Anstis and Reinhardt-Rutland, 1976, and Day, 1981).

Pulfrich Effect

An interesting perceptual distortion of physical movement, known as the **Pulfrich pendulum effect**, may occur when the two eyes are stimulated by different intensities of light. This effect is schematized in Figure 8.11. The pendulum bob is swung back and forth in a straight path in a plane perpendicular to the viewer's line of sight. However, when both eyes are open, but one eye is covered with a dark glass or light filter (e.g., one lens of a pair of sunglasses), the pendulum bob appears to swing in an elliptical path arching toward and away from the viewer. According to Gregory (1973) and others (Brauner & Lit, 1976; Enright, 1970), this distortion is due largely to the fact that the reaction time of the visual system varies with stimulus intensity. The filter reduces the amount of light reaching one eye, which in turn results in a slight but neurally significant delay in the signals from that eye reaching the brain. That is, at any instant the apparent position of the pendulum bob coded by the filtered eye lags slightly behind the position of the pendulum bob coded by the unfiltered eye. The fact that for the filtered eye the pendulum bob is seen slightly later in space means that at any given moment the pendulum bob appears at slightly different locations for each eye. The disparity between the information arriving at the brain from both retinas is reconciled by an apparent displacement of the pendulum bob in an elliptical path in depth.

Ironically, this phenomenon was explained in 1922 by the German physicist Carl Pulfrich, who was blind in one eye and thus was never able to experience the distortion effect. (A detailed account of the procedures, and presumed processes, involved in the Pulfrich pendulum effect may be found in Emerson and Pesta, 1992; Fineman, 1981; and Walker, 1978.)

APPARENT MOVEMENT

Apparent movement refers to the perception of movement when there is no actual physical movement of an object in space. In other words, it is the *illusion* of movement from stationary stimuli. However, apparent movement is more than a rare perceptual curiosity observed in the laboratory; in fact, apparent movement is a familiar event. Every time we see a movie or watch television, we experience it. In this section, we will discuss several conditions that give rise to apparent movement, beginning with one of the simplest forms: *stroboscopic movement*.

Stroboscopic Movement

One of the earliest studied and most convincing examples of apparent movement occurs when two stationary lights, set a short distance apart, are alternately flashed at a certain rate (Figure 8.12). As light *A* flashes on and off, light *B* flashes off and on; that is, one light is onset as the other offsets. The character of the apparent movement depends on the time interval, or ISI, between the two flashing lights. Generally, some form of apparent movement is seen when the ISI of the two flashing lights is set between 30 and 200 msec.

□ *figure* **8.10** A rotary-induced movement effect. Focus on the center cogwheel from about 12 in. When the page is oscillated back and forth at a rate of about once per second, the outside wheels will appear to move in one direction and the center cogwheel in the opposite direction. (Based on Le Grand, 1967.)

If the ISI is very long (more than 200 msec), only succession is perceived—two lights alternately flashing. If the ISI is too brief (less than 30 msec), the perception of apparent movement changes to one of simultaneity—two lights, *A* and *B*, are perceived flashing, each at its own location. If, however, the ISI is about 60 msec, optimal movement is perceived: the perception of a single light moving across the intervening space between lights *A* and *B*. (When the ISI is about 100 msec, an unusual type of apparent movement called *phi movement* is perceived. In phi movement, observers sense movement from the displaced flashing lights, but they do not actually see an object move from one light to the other.)

This form of apparent movement, created by manipulating the timing between flashes of the lights, is termed **stroboscopic movement** or **beta (β) movement.** You have probably seen this form of apparent movement from a series of lights on billboards and railroad crossings, as well as from the flashing neon signs directing you to diners, parking lots, and motels.

The nature of stroboscopic movement is determined by the interval between flashes of lights (ISI), the intensity of the lights, and the spatial distance between them. The complex interactions of these three variables were worked out by Korte in 1915 and are appropriately labeled *Korte's laws* (see Boring, 1942, p. 598). For example, as the physical distance between the flashing lights is increased, either their intensity or their ISI must be increased to maintain the perception of stroboscopic movement.

Motion Pictures

As shown in Figure 8.13, apparent movement from sequential stationary stimuli is not limited to simple lights or dots. The principles involved are the basis of one of the most familiar and compelling examples of apparent movement—**motion pictures**. In motion pictures, a series of still frames of slightly different photographs are projected on a screen in rapid succession. Each frame is a view of a slightly different spatial

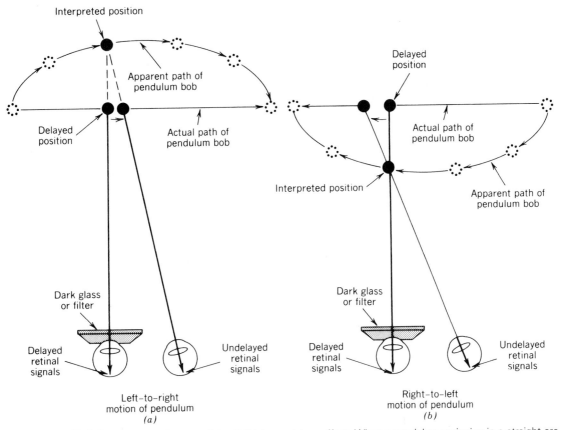

□ *figure* **8.11** Schematic diagram of the Pulfrich pendulum effect. When a pendulum swinging in a straight arc in a plane perpendicular to the line of sight is viewed with a filter over one eye, it appears to swing in an elliptical path. This is due to the signals being delayed from the eye covered by the filter. The perceptual effect is that there is an apparent displacement of the pendulum bob *away* from the viewer when it moves from left to right, that is, from the filtered to the unfiltered side of the visual field (a), and a displacement *toward* the viewer when the pendulum bob moves in the opposite direction (b).

In both (a) and (b) the apparent paths created by the series of interpreted positions of the pendulum bob conform to the set of visual signals that would reach each eye if the pendulum bob actually moved away from and toward the viewer, that is, moved in depth.

position of a moving object. When this succession of static frames is projected at the proper rate (usually at least 24 frames per second), movement is perceived. As with stroboscopic movement, the quality of the movement varies with the rate of projection. If the rate is too slow, a succession of flickers (or at even slower rates, frames of discrete photographs) are seen; if the rate is too fast, a blur of images is seen. (Wead and Lellis, 1981, offer a concise history and technology of motion pictures, as well as an analysis of its percep-

tion; see also Hochberg, 1986, for an extensive and provocative analysis of this topic.)

As noted earlier (e.g., in visual masking; see Chapter 7), once begun, a visual response persists for a brief period even after the physical stimulus ends. In the case of motion pictures, when the frames of photographs are shown at the proper rate, the image of each frame apparently fuses with the image of the preceding and following frames, producing the perception of steady movement. Thus, the visual sys-

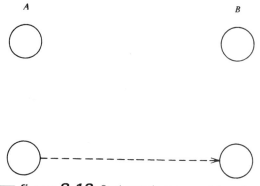

=== **figure 8.12** Stroboscopic movement from two alternately flashing stationary lights, A and B. Depending on the intensity of the light flashes, the physical distance separating them, and the time interval between light flashes, the illusion of one light moving from A to B—schematized in the bottom figure with the dashed line—can be created with two lights flashing sequentially.

tem can integrate a series of successive, discrete images, producing an apparently continuous visual environment or event.

However, while *persistence* of the visual response is important in producing the perception of smooth, continuous movement from a succession of discrete images—especially enabling the darkness between images to go unnoticed—another significant factor is also involved. The smooth integration of the frames is aided by a close correspondence between the features of each frame and the context they share. The greater their relationship and the more structurally similar the adjoining frames are to each other—the greater their "phenomenal identity"—the more easily the visual system combines the sequential information, allowing us to perceive fluid movement from physically discrete stimuli.

=== **figure 8.13** Apparent movement with two successive stationary stimuli. When the vertical line (a) is succeeded by the horizontal line (b) after an interval of about 60 msec, the vertical line will appear to rotate 90° clockwise, as shown by (c).

When we view a segment of a movie—for example, of a person running—and the changes in the separate units (e.g., arms, legs, body) are *consistent* from frame to frame, the units of the frame retain their apparent cohesiveness and structural integrity. That is, the visual system interprets these consistent changes as *movement*. By contrast, a succession of dissimilar, seemingly incompatible frames may challenge the visual system; while there may be fleeting experiences of one form becoming another, the perception of smooth apparent movement is reduced. The conditions for producing this effect would probably occur only in a perception laboratory.

Wagon Wheel Effect In practice, the light projected from each frame to the screen by most professional motion picture projectors is interrupted several times before advancing to the next frame. This is necessary because, at only 24 frames per second, we would still see flicker. To avoid this, each frame is usually shown three times. This is done with a shutter arrangement, with each frame projected on the screen as three flashes, resulting in a frequency of 72 flashes per second. Old home movies run at 16 frames per second (48 flashes or projections per second), but because they are usually shown at a lower intensity level, they fuse more readily and there is less of a tendency to see flicker. The image produced on the television screen results from a similar fusion principle, although it is technically different.

In this context, we offer an explanation of the *wagon wheel effect,* by which the spokes of the wheels of vehicles obviously moving forward, as shown in motion pictures, sometimes appear to move backward. Christman (1979) and Fineman (1981) note that there is no illusion of movement (other than the apparent movement induced by the succession of frames themselves) but rather that there is a mismatch between the number of wheel revolutions per second and the number of frames photographed per second. If the camera takes 24 frames per second and the wheel is rotating at 23 revolutions per second (or some multiple thereof), each successive frame of film will capture the wheel slightly *before* it completes a full revolution. When the film is shown, the wheel will appear to be moving backward at the rate of 1 revolution per second. If the wheel actually rotates at 24 revolutions per second—the same rate at which the film is projected (i.e., 24 frames per second)—it will appear stationary. Finally, if the camera takes 24 frames per second but the wheel turns at 25 revolutions per second (or some multiple thereof), when projected, the wheel will appear to move forward at the rate of 1 revolution per second.

In summary, the perception of motion pictures from a series of discrete, intermittent images results from the persistence of vision and the recognition of related features and consistent changes from frame to frame. However, we do not yet have a full explanation. As Wead and Lellis (1981) conclude, "Science has not explained the cause of the illusion [motion pictures]. We know that under the right conditions we tend to perceive discrete objects as continuous units, but no one yet knows why this trickery occurs" (p. 41).

Autokinetic Movement

An experience of movement may occur when fixating on a stationary point of light in a completely dark room. In this condition, a spatial background is lacking, and there is no fixed visual framework to which the point of light may be referred. The result is that a single stationary point of light appears to drift about, an effect termed **autokinetic movement.** Typically, the point of light appears to make small excursions, but often with considerable movement. There are wide individual differences in the extent and direction of autokinetic movement, which is strongly affected by social influences (Sherif, 1936).

Several explanations for autokinetic movement, based primarily on the role of eye movements, have been proposed (Mack, 1986; Post & Leibowitz, 1985). One appealing explanation offered by Gregory (1973) is based on the varying efficiency of the eye muscles in maintaining fixation on the stationary point of light. During continued fixation, slight tremors of the eyes cause fluctuations in fixation. Moreover, during prolonged fixation, the eye muscles fatigue. To compensate for the lack of maintained fixation as well as for fatigue, the eye muscles require *abnormal command signals* to hold the gaze on the point of light. These abnormal signals are the same sort of signals that

normally move the eyes when tracking moving stimuli. Thus, according to Gregory, it is not the eyes moving, but the correcting signals applied to *prevent* them from moving, that "cause" the spot of light to wander in the dark.

Movement Aftereffects

Just after an extended period of gazing at the moving landscape, a passenger on a stopped train sees the now stationary landscape moving forward so realistically that the train may be perceived as slowly moving backward. This is an example of a **movement aftereffect (MAE)**, in which perceived movement may persist after the moving stimulus ends. Similarly, if you stare at part of a waterfall for a while and then look at a stationary scene, the scene will appear to move up. This is an instance of a specific MAE called the *waterfall illusion* (described by Addams, 1834, and by Bowditch and Hall, 1882; see Fineman, 1981, for details). An early device used to create the MAE is shown in Figure 8.14. A somewhat different MAE, due in part, to the pattern of involuntary eye movements during fixation, is shown in the geometric patterns of Figure 8.15.

Neural Basis of MAEs A general explanation for MAEs is based on the notion of *aftereffects* and *selective adaptation* described in various contexts in Chapters 5, 6, and 7. That is, MAEs are caused by the selective adaptation of motion-sensitive detectors that are specific to the viewer's perceived movement of the objects. Applied to the waterfall illusion, for example, this means that after gazing exclusively at *downward*-moving stimuli for a while, the detectors sensitive to downward movement become fatigued or adapted and thus less sensitive. So, when the viewer suddenly shifts his or her gaze and looks at a stationary scene, activity of the "downward" movement detectors is reduced, resulting in the impression of the scene moving up.

Where in the visual system are the detectors for MAEs located? Some idea can be obtained by varying the conditions under which they occur. Thus, if they lie at the level of the retina, then if only one eye receives the adapting moving stimuli, testing with the

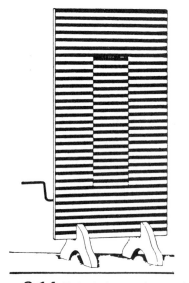

□ **figure 8.14** Early device used to produce the waterfall illusion. A crank moves a striped band, seen through the central aperture, down (or up). When movement of the band ceases, the subject sees a reverse movement if he or she looks at the background or at another surface. (Generally attributed to Bowditch and Hall, 1882, although Boring, 1942, speculates that a version of this device may be traced to William James.)

other, unstimulated eye should reveal *no* MAE. That is, if MAEs are retinal in origin, there should be no transfer of the adaptation effects between the eyes. However, when this experiment was performed, MAEs were found to be present, indicating that they are likely central or cortical in origin (Mitchell, Readon, & Muir, 1975; Mitchell & Ware, 1975).

THE PREDICTION OF MOTION PATHS

This final section is more concerned with *predicting* how objects move than it is with perception of their movement. However, this topic warrants a brief discussion because some of the factors that explain why people assume objects move in certain ways derive from some general phenomena of movement perception.

As we have stressed, most individuals constantly observe and interact with dynamic events in the environment, particularly those involving objects in motion. It is reasonable to assume that, based on this extensive experience, they would come to understand some of the basic principles and laws of physics, and recognize that objects in motion move in predictable ways. However, certain misconceptions and erroneous beliefs persist about the motion of objects in seemingly simple conditions. McCloskey, Carramazza, and Green (1980; see also Kaiser, Proffitt, & McCloskey, 1985) have assessed the ability of individuals to make accurate predictions about the path of objects in motion based on the responses to simple physical problems, such as the first two presented in Figure 8.16. When asked to indicate the **motion path** that a moving object would follow on emerging from the tube, a surprising number of subjects (all college students, of whom almost 70% had at least a high school physics course) revealed some naïveté. Their answer was that when a moving object is passed through a curved tube, it will continue in a curved path even when no external force is applied. Moreover, the increase in errors from Problem 1 to Problem 2 suggests that many subjects thought that the longer the moving object is in the curved tube, the more curved its motion will be when it emerges. The correct answer to both problems follows directly from the *law of inertia,* or Newton's first law of motion: *There is no change in the motion of a body unless a resultant force acts on it. If the body is at rest, it will continue at rest. If it is in motion, it will continue in motion at a constant speed in a straight line unless there is an externally applied force.*

Based on postexperimental interviews with the subjects, it appears that their incorrect prediction was not a matter of a visual distortion or a perceptual bias; instead, it was due to the nature of their naïve notions about motion. Their general misconception was based on the belief that an object forced to travel in a curved path in a tube acquires a "momentum" or impetus that causes it to continue in curvilinear motion for a while even after it emerges from the tube and is uninfluenced by the original force; thus, only after the impetus gradually disappears does the object's

◻ *figure 8.15* An example of a geometric pattern that produces afterimages in which motion can be perceived. If the center of the pattern is fixated for approximately 20 sec and then the afterimage is projected on a plain white surface, rotary motion is usually perceived. (From D. M. MacKay, Ways of looking at perception, in W. Wather-Dunn (Ed.), *Models for the perception of visual form,* M.I.T. Press, Cambridge, Massachusetts, 1967. By permission of the M.I.T. Press.)

trajectory become linear. McCloskey (1983*a*) traces these naïve notions of motion—clearly at odds with classical physics—to the pre-Newtonian *impetus* theory of motion prevalent during the Middle Ages. This theory claimed that an object set in motion acquires a force, or impetus, that maintains the motion; the impetus gradually disappears, causing deceleration and the eventual end of the object's motion.

Further evidence that naïve notions about physical mechanics, rather than incorrect perceptual processes, is based on the finding that subjects do *recognize* the correct trajectory of objects when they are observed in motion, as in Problems 1 and 2 of Figure 8.16 (Kaiser, Proffitt, & Anderson, 1985). When shown simulated sequences on a video screen of balls rolling through curved tubes and following a variety of straight and curved paths on exit, almost all subjects selected the correct path. That is, when viewing a depiction of the ongoing event, subjects perceived the correct straight path as the most natural path, not the wrong trajectory that was often predicted in stationary representations.

However, there are also wrong predictions about falling objects that may be based on perceptual pro-

Problem 1   Problem 2

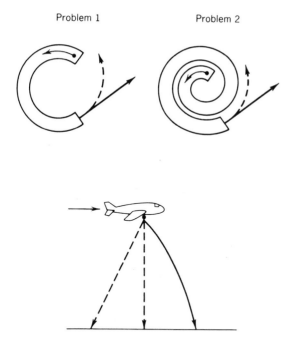

Problem 3

□ *figure 8.16* Motion problems with correct solutions (solid lines) and common incorrect responses (dashed lines). (Based on McCloskey, 1983a; Kaiser, Proffitt, and McCloskey, 1985; McCloskey, Caramazza, Green, 1980).

cessing. Problem 3 of Figure 8.16 shows an aircraft traveling at a constant altitude and velocity that drops an object; the task is to show the object's trajectory from the moment it is dropped to the moment of its impact with the ground. The correct, as well as two common incorrect trajectories are given in the figure. The correct answer is that the object will continue to move forward while falling in a parabolic arc. McCloskey (1983a, 1983b) and his colleagues (Kaiser et al., 1985; McCloskey, Washburn, & Felch, 1983) suggest that the common misconceptions are due to a visual illusion based on extensive experience that objects dropped from a moving carrier often appear to fall straight down. When a person drops something while walking or running, he or she acts as a frame of reference against which the falling object is viewed. (This is closely linked to the earlier discussions of *induced* movement and refers to a phenomenon related to the

effect in Figure 8.9.) That is, the perception of the object's falling motion is viewed against a moving frame of reference—the moving person. Accordingly, the object's motion *relative* to the moving background may be mistakenly perceived as motion relative to a stationary environment and thus may be misinterpreted as the object's absolute motion. In short, an object dropped from a moving carrier falls straight down *relative to its carrier,* so it may be perceived as falling in a straight vertical path. Generally, misconceptions about the trajectories of carried objects develop after repeatedly perceiving the motion against a moving reference frame (see also Kaiser et al., 1985).

SUMMARY

In this chapter, we have described the perception of various forms of real and apparent movement. For the perception of real movement, two main interdependent movement systems were identified: the image–retina system and the eye–head movement system. In addition, the contribution made by outflow or corollary discharge signals during voluntary eye movements to the eye–head system was noted.

Several types of optical stimulation for movement perception were described. Also described was the unique perception of human biological activity and the kinds of information obtained from biological motion.

Distortions in the perception of physical movement were discussed: kinetic depth effect, anorthoscopic perception, induced movement, and the Pulfrich pendulum effect.

Apparent movement—the perception of movement in the absence of physical movement—was examined. We focused especially on stroboscopic movement. The relation of stroboscopic motion to motion pictures was noted, and an explanation of the latter was offered in terms of visual persistence and recognition of the consistency and correspondence of elements from frame to frame. In this context, an explanation was given of the unusual phenomenon of the wagon wheel effect. Another form of apparent movement, the autokinetic effect, involving perception in an ambiguous spatial context, was introduced. The aftereffects of perceiving certain kinds of motion were briefly considered.

The final section was devoted to prediction of the paths of motion that are followed by physically moving objects. It was concluded that certain forms of motion paths are incorrectly predicted because of misconceptions about physical movement. Other forms of motion paths are wrongly predicted due to a bias in perceptual processing—a visual illusion likely based on induced movement.

KEY TERMS

Afferent Signal

Anorthoscopic Perception

Apparent Movement

Autokinetic Movement

Biological Motion

Comparator

Corollary Discharge Signal (Outflow Signal)

Efferent Signal

Eye–Head Movement System

Image–Retina Movement System

Induced Movement

Kinetic Depth Effect

Motion Paths

Motion Pictures

Movement Aftereffect (MAE)

Optic Flow Pattern

Pulfrich Pendulum Effect

Retinal Expansion

Stroboscopic (β) Movement

STUDY QUESTIONS

1. Discuss the significance of movement perception for an animal's survival. Examine the kinds of environmental information received by viewing objects and events in motion.

2. Compare the image–retina system with the eye–head movement system. Indicate the conditions in which each plays a dominant role.

3. Explain why the visual environment appears stationary when the eyes are voluntarily moved. Explain why passive movements of the eyeball cause apparent movement of the visual environment. Consider the role of corollary discharge and outflow signals in your answer.

4. Identify the main patterns of changes in the retinal projection as an object or an observer moves through the visual environment. Examine optic flow patterns in your discussion.

5. What is biological motion? What kinds of information does it convey? What stimulus factors are most informative?

6. Identify the kinetic depth effect. Consider how the perception of an object's motion may contribute to the perception of its shape.

7. What is anorthoscopic perception? What effect does the shape of the aperture have on the perception of the shape of the stimulus moving behind it?

8. Explain induced movement and describe how it can be demonstrated. What are some of the factors between an object and its background that may promote induced movement?

9. Explain the Pulfrich pendulum effect, taking into account delay of the retinal signals. Indicate how the effect simulates a pattern of visual signals that correspond to environmental depth.

10. What are apparent movement and stroboscopic movement? How does apparent movement differ from induced movement? What factors are crucial in producing apparent movement?

11. Explain the perception of motion pictures as an elaboration of stroboscopic motion. What factors explain the apparent integration and fusion of the separate frames of motion pictures film?

12. Explain why the spoked wheels of vehicles that are apparently moving forward sometimes appear to move backward when they are seen in movies and on television.

13. Distinguish autokinetic movement from induced movement. Explain autokinetic movement with

respect to prolonged eye fixations and eye muscle fatigue.

14. How can movement aftereffects be demonstrated? What are some common examples?

15. What are some misconceptions about the predicted paths of objects set in motion based on the shapes of the structures that emit them? To what extent do they fail to take into account the law of inertia? What kinds of errors are made concerning the predicted trajectories made by falling objects from moving vehicles? How may the effects of induced movement contribute to these errors?

chapter 9

MONOCULAR AND BINOCULAR VISION

*T*his chapter and the following one discuss the primary function of vision: the perception of space. The visual system has evolved the ability to register the spatial arrangement of objects and surfaces. Every glimpse of the visual scene underscores this point. Objects are generally seen as solid forms, spatially arranged and lying at some depth or distance in the terrain. However, the perception of space in depth and distance presents a problem: How can visual space normally be experienced as three-dimensional, yet the retina and the corresponding retinal images are essentially two-dimensional surfaces? Part of the answer lies in the nature of the stimulation at the retina. For example, one sees differences in the brightness of different surfaces; objects take up different amounts of visual angle and are seen with varying degrees of clarity; some objects appear to partially cover other objects. Clearly, the optic array projected on the retina conveys information or "cues" that enable us to perceive a three-dimensional space.

Our primary function in this chapter is to describe and discuss these cues, along with relevant processes and mechanisms of the visual system that enable us to perceive depth and distance. Additionally, because perception of object size is so closely related to the perception of objects' depth and distance, we will discuss the factors that affect apparent size.

MONOCULAR CUES FOR SPATIAL PERCEPTION

A number of spatial cues require only a single eye for their reception and are labeled **monocular cues**. Graphics artists employ *static* monocular cues (i.e., where the viewer and the scene are stationary), called **pictorial cues**, to represent depth pictorially, that is, to produce the impression of three-dimensional space on a two-dimensional surface, such as in pictures, photographs, and movies.

Interposition

Interposition refers to the appearance of one object partially concealing or overlapping another. If one object is partially covered by another, the fully exposed one is perceived as nearer. Examples of interposition are shown in Figure 9.1. When the images are of familiar objects, interposition is more effective in showing relative distance. As a static pictorial cue it is quite effective, but it provides only *relative* depth information—whether one object is nearer or farther

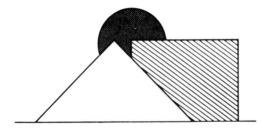

(a)

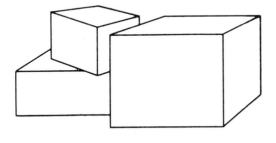

(b)

 figure 9.1 *(a)* The circle appears to lie behind the rectangle, which appears to lie behind the triangle. *(b)* Interposition contributes to the perception of the relative positions of line drawings of three-dimensional shapes.

than another from the viewer—not absolute depth, or distance information.

Aerial Perspective or Clearness

When viewing the terrain outdoors, objects far away are generally seen less clearly than objects close by. This effect is called **aerial perspective** (or *clearness*) and is due to the effect of very small particles in the atmosphere on light. Light rays traveling through suspended particles of dust, water vapor, and other atmospheric constituents are scattered, decreasing the clarity of the details and the lightness of the images of objects reflected to the eye. Since light reflected from distant objects passes through more of the atmosphere than light from nearby objects, the more distant objects appear hazy, dim, and even blurry in contrast to the appearance of nearby objects. Thus, relatively large structures such as buildings appear closer when

viewed on a clear day than on a hazy one. Aerial perspective may play a role in spatial perception, particularly when one is viewing over extensive distances. Aerial perspective is shown later in Figure 9.13.

Shading and Lighting

Generally, the surface of an object nearest the light source is the brightest. As the surface recedes from the light, it appears less bright and more darkly shadowed. The pattern of **shading** and **lighting** also contributes to the perception of apparent depth on a discontinuous surface. Observe the bumps and irregular indentations of Figure 9.2; then turn the page around. A convexity–concavity change has taken place. We are accustomed to the source of light coming from above (e.g., sunlight, ceiling lighting). Thus, when the picture is inverted, the bumps and indentations reverse because we continue to presume an overhead light source. In fact, Berbaum and his colleagues (Berbaum, Bever, & Chung, 1983, 1984; Berbaum, Tharp, & Mroczek, 1983) have shown that areas of highlights and shading in a two-dimensional picture provide a potent source of depth information. Moreover, the impression of depth increases as the contrast between highlights and shadows increases.

The successful use of shading in a painting to suggest depth is shown in Color Plate 15, a reproduction of one of Vermeer's works. Vermeer's art is known for its creative use of shading and lighting to produce compelling depth and luminance qualities on a flat surface.

Children as young as 3 years of age assume an overhead source of lighting and can discriminate concavities from convexities (i.e., pits from bumps) on the basis of shading (Benson & Yonas, 1973; Yonas, Kuskowski, & Sternfels, 1979). Moreover, chickens, like humans, react to stimuli as if they are lighted by an overhead source (Hershberger, 1970), suggesting that the use of shading as a spatial cue is phylogenetically primitive.

Shading and Shape The appropriate use of changes in surface shading may also provide cues to the *shape* of objects (Berbaum et al., 1984; Kleffner & Ramachandran, 1992). Generally, illumination from a

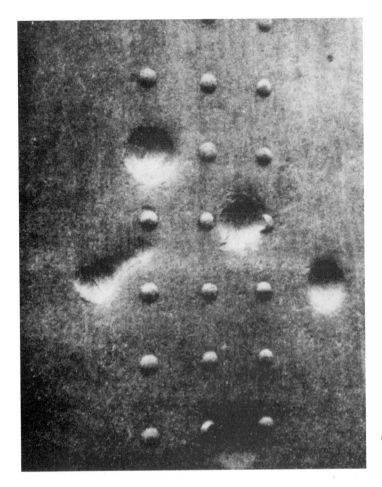

☐ *figure* **9.2** Light and shade used as depth cues. When the figure is inverted, bumps and pits reverse.

single light source will fall on a three-dimensional object in a consistent pattern. Since those surfaces closest to the light source receive the most illumination, the shape of the object has an effect on the pattern of light and dark areas produced: Surfaces that face the light source appear lighter, while opposing surfaces are darker or shaded (Figure 9.3). In addition, the distribution of lightness and darkness across an object aids in the perception of its surface characteristics. Thus the perception of a curved surface may result from a gradual transition from light to dark, whereas an abrupt, sudden change from light to dark may be perceived as a change in planes such as a sharp edge or corner. Clearly, shading is a basic source of spatial information. Perhaps, as Kleffner and Rama-chandran (1992) speculate, there are neural elements

specialized for extracting shape information from shading.

Elevation

Generally speaking, the horizon is higher in the vertical dimension of the visual field than is the foreground. Accordingly, objects appearing higher in the visual field (as long as they also appear to lie *below* the horizon) are generally perceived as being located farther from the viewer than are objects appearing lower in the visual field. **Elevation** (sometimes called **height in the visual field**) may play a role in the perception of both relative and absolute distance (Wallach & O'Leary, 1982). Elevation also serves as a spatial cue when viewing two-dimensional pictures

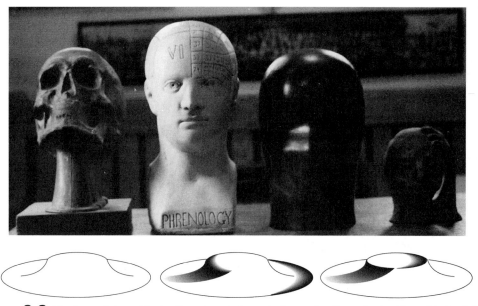

□ **figure 9.3** Shading and shape. The top figure is a photograph of some familiar and unfamiliar solid objects in which shading aids shape perception. The bottom figure consists of three drawings illustrating that variation in shading significantly affects the perception of an object's shape. The same outline is used in all drawings. Adding shading depicts a bump or hill in the central drawing; however, as the drawing on the right shows, the same outline with different shading gives the appearance of a depression or crater. (Top figure courtesy of Harvey Schiffman; bottom figure based on Wyburn, Pickford, & Hirst, 1964.)

that attempt to depict a depth relationship (Berbaum, Tharp, & Mroczek, 1983).

Linear Perspective

The perception of depth on a flat surface can be aided by the use of **linear perspective** (often referred to as *perspective*). This involves systematically decreasing the size of more distant elements and the space separating them (Figure 9.4). The image of a three-dimensional object is so transformed as it is projected on the retina. A typical example is railroad tracks, as shown in Figure 9.5. The parallel tracks appear to converge at a point in the distance called the *vanishing point*. Another illustration of perspective using converging lines is given in Figure 9.6. Observe that the edges that appear farther away are smaller than those that appear closer. Artistic examples of the bizarre use of linear perspective are given in Figure 9.7.

The history of linear perspective as a graphic technique is controversial. However, it is generally agreed

that this technique was discovered early in the fifteenth century by the Italian architect and sculptor Brunelleschi (Janson, 1962; Lynes, 1980) and soon afterward was formalized by Alberti (Fineman, 1981; Kubovy, 1986).

Texture Gradients

A form of microstructure, generally seen as a grain or texture, is characteristic of most surfaces. This is obvious in many natural surfaces such as fields of grass, foliage, and trees, as well as in artificial surfaces such as roads, floors, and fabrics. As described by James J. Gibson (1950), the texture of these surfaces possesses a continuous density change, or *gradient*, that structures the light in the optic array in a way that is consistent with the arrangement of objects and surfaces. Specifically, when we look at any textured surface, the elements comprising the texture become denser as distance increases. As with linear perspec-

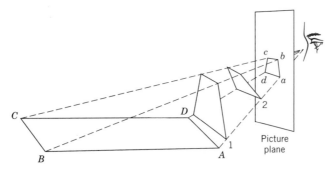

▭ *figure* **9.4** The image of the rectangle is shown in perspective on the picture plane. The two-dimensional projection of the rectangle *ABCD* is shown as trapezoid *abcd* on the picture plane. Clearly, the distances separating the more distant elements of the rectangle (segment *BC*) are decreased in their projection on the picture plane (*bc*). Note also that since the stimulus pattern for the eye is in two dimensions (as depicted on the picture plane), an infinite number of arrangements in three dimensions (shapes 1, 2, etc.) will produce the same pattern at the eye. (Modified from Hochberg, 1964.)

tive, the size of the elements and the distance separating the elements decrease with distance.

Textural information also provides graded cues to depth and distance in flat surfaces such as photographs (e.g., Gibson & Bridgeman, 1987). This is illustrated in Figure 9.8, which gives two examples of textural gradations called **texture gradients**. The gradient, or gradual change in the size, shape, and spacing of elements comprising the pattern of the texture, provides information on distance. In Figure 9.9a, the longitudinal surface *XY* projects a retinal image, *xy*; the latter possesses a gradient of texture from coarse to dense, the coarser elements closer to *x*, the denser elements closer to *y*. The gradient of texture transmitted in *xy* provides information that one is viewing a receding surface. Note that with respect to the eye, the change in texture reflected from the surface *XY* is at a constant rate. The frontal surface *YZ*, which is perpendicular to the line of sight, projects a different image: there is no gradient since all the elements are equidistant from the eye. Thus, the pattern *YZ*, (which projects a retinal image *yz* in Figure 9.9*a*) is perceived as a wall, forming a 90° angle with the floor of pattern *XY*, as shown in Figure 9.9*b*.

As Figure 9.10 makes clear, textural changes are such a powerful source of information that even simple line drawings provide a strong spatial sense. The figure provides examples that curves and edges, as well as the shape and inclination of a surface, are

detected from discontinuities in the texture and from texture changes that are not at a constant rate.

Texture gradients, along with interposition and linear perspective, may be useful in determining perceived size. Neisser (1968) has noted that the increase in texture density on the retina, corresponding to an increase in the distance from the observer, provides a "scale" for object sizes. In the ideal case when all texture units are identical, figures of the same real size but different retinal sizes, owing to their different distances from the observer, will cover or overlap the same number of texture units (Figure 9.11). In other words, the relation between the retinal texture size and the object's retinal image is constant, in spite of changes in distance.

Relative Size

The cue to distance called **relative size** applies when two similar or identical shapes of different sizes are viewed simultaneously or in close succession; in such cases the larger stimulus generally appears closer to the viewer (e.g., Hochberg, 1964). Relative size is a cue to distance, as illustrated in Figure 9.12. This cue to distance does not require previous experience with the objects; rather, in certain situations, images of the same shapes but of different sizes are sufficient stimuli for a depth relationship.

▭ **figure 9.5** Perhaps the most common and most striking instance of linear perspective is the apparent convergence in the distance of parallel railroad tracks. The actual space between the tracks is constant, but the corresponding retinal images and, accordingly, the size of the apparent separation of the tracks decrease with the distance of the tracks.

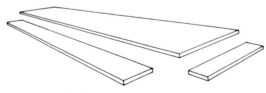

▭ **figure 9.6** Planks drawn in perspective. Parts of apparently rectangular planks that are diminished in size appear farther away.

Familiar Size

When we view familiar objects, there are not only visual cues to depth and distance but also nonvisual cues to the objects' spatial characteristics, such as their size and shape, attained as a result of past experience. Although not, strictly speaking, a visual cue to depth or distance, **familiar size** may contribute significantly to spatial perception. In other words, we know the sizes of many objects in our immediate surrounding and can give reasonably accurate size estimations of them from memory. However, to what extent we use this size information is not known.

Several studies suggest that the role of familiar size in determining the apparent size of objects depends

□ *figure* **9.7** An artist's bizarre use of perspective. The sixteenth-century portrait shown in (*1*) was drawn in distorted perspective. When viewed obliquely through a notch in the frame, the distortion is corrected, as seen in (*2*). This also can be accomplished by holding the edge of the page to your eye and looking at the picture in (*1*). (Edward VI, by William Scrots. Reprinted by permission of The National Portrait Gallery, London.)

largely on the conditions under which the objects are observed. In judging the sizes of familiar objects under typical conditions of viewing, in which visual cues are prominent, familiar size is probably *not* used (Fillenbaum, Schiffman, & Butcher, 1965). By contrast, when objects are observed under poor viewing conditions, such as when lighting and distance cues are degraded or absent, knowledge of the objects' size—that is, *familiar size*—may be important in size judgments (Schiffman, 1967). In other words, size informa-

□ **figure 9.8** Examples of gradients of textures. These gradients produce an impression of depth or distance on a flat surface.

tion based on past experience with similar objects is used when visual cues to distance are lacking or significantly reduced.

Furthermore, under certain conditions, the known size of a familiar object affects the perception of the object's *location*. In one experiment, Epstein (1963, 1967) presented realistic representations of three coins (photographs of a dime, quarter, and half-dollar), which, of course, differed in familiar size. However, unknown to the observers, the photographs were al-

tered in size so that the pictures of the coins appeared identical in physical size. Specifically, the photograph of the dime was enlarged to the size of the quarter, and that of the half-dollar was reduced to the size of the quarter. The coins were then viewed under conditions of reduced visual cues (restricting viewing to one eye, dim lighting, etc.). When the coins were presented at the *same* distance (thus projecting the same retinal size), the dime was judged closer than the quarter, which, in turn, was judged closer than

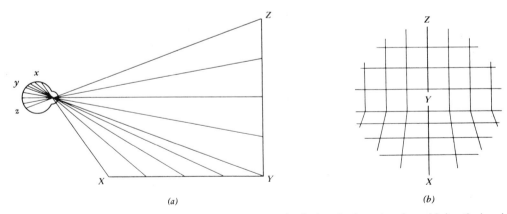

(a)   (b)

□ **figure 9.9** Two views of the optical projection of a longitudinal and a frontal surface. (*a*) A retinal projection from coarse to dense, *xy*, is produced by the longitudinal surface *XY*. A frontal surface, *YZ*, projects a uniform texture to the retina at *yz*. (*b*) Another view of the optical projections of the surfaces *XY* and *YZ*. The longitudinal projection from the surface *XY* is perceived as a "floor"; the frontal projection from the uniform texture of surface *YZ* is seen as a "wall." (Based on Gibson, 1950.)

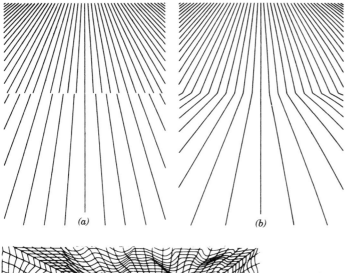

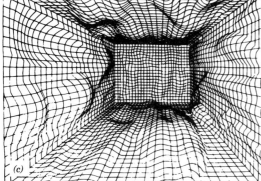

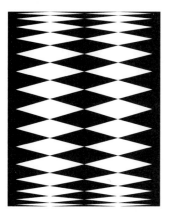

□ *figure* **9.10** Examples of apparent depth given by texture gradients with discontinuities and examples of texture changes that are not a constant rate. Discontinuities in texture: an edge is seen in (*a*), a corner in (*b*). In (*c*), the discontinuities in the surfaces increase the apparent depth of a "mesh" or "wire" room. In (*d*), a somewhat delicate variation in texture helps determine the shape of the rounded surface of a drum. (*Source:* (*c*), courtesy of the Carpenter Center for the Visual Arts, Harvard University, Cambridge, Mass.)

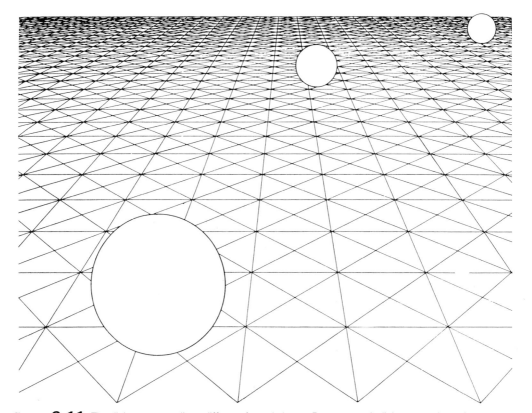

the half-dollar. In other words, observers judged the dime, which was made larger than normal, to be closer, whereas, the half-dollar, which was smaller than normal, was judged to be farther away. Therefore, in spite of the fact that all coins projected the

▭ *figure* **9.12** Relative size. Images of the same shapes but of different sizes may furnish a depth cue. In this figure the larger squares give the appearance of lying closer to the viewer than do the smaller ones.

same retinal size, their different familiar sizes (created by photographically altering the sizes of the coins) determined their apparent distance. This means that when cues to distance are scarce, the familiar size of objects may influence the observer's judgment of their distance (see also Fitzpatrick, Pasnak, & Tyler, 1982; Gogel & DaSilva, 1987).

Pictorial Perception

The cues of linear perspective, texture gradients, and relative size express a common principle: the size of an object's image on the retina is proportional to the distance between the observer and the object. That is, these static monocular cues directly take into account the fact that the size of the retinal image decreases with increasing distance. This principle enables the representation of depth and distance on a flat, two-dimensional surface. In fact, the use of all the static monocular cues that we have described (e.g., interposition, shading and lighting, linear perspective) within a photograph or picture enables **pictorial perception**—the impression of depth from a two-dimensional surface (Figure 9.13).

The picture shown in Figure 9.14 also illustrates pictorial perception, but it contains a bizarre mixture of spatial cues. Although some spatial cues are used appropriately, other conflicting cues create impossible spatial relationships.

FRONTISPIECE TO KERBY.

▭ *figure* **9.14** An artist's intentional misuse of some static depth cues is illustrated in this 1754 engraving by William Hogarth, entitled "False Perspective." The print was used originally as an illustration for the frontispiece or the title page of a book, and its accompanying description on the role of perspective is worth repeating: "Whosoever maketh a print without the knowledge of perspective will be liable to such absurdities as are shown on the frontispiece."

Clearly other cues besides perspective are misapplied in Hogarth's print, notably interposition and relative size. (Reproduced by permission of the Bettmann Archives.)

▭ *figure* **9.13** Pictorial perception and aerial perception. Various static monocular cues are prominent in an aerial photograph. Due to aerial perspective, the nearby details, depicted in the foreground, appear clearer and sharper than do details in the receding background. (Courtesy of Margaret Burke-White Estate, *Life Magazine,* Copyright © by Time, Inc.)

Another factor that affects pictorial perception is the amount of detail depicted. In viewing real-world scenes, less detail is perceived as elements recede in the distance. Thus, pictorial perception may also be promoted by varying the *detail* of elements that appear to lie on a flat surface. Leonardo da Vinci termed the gradient of detail in a picture the "perspective of disappearance" and observed that objects in a picture "ought to be less finished as they are remote" (Bloomer, 1976, p. 83). Thus, since greater detail is characteristic of nearness, an artist can manipulate apparent distance on the flat picture plane by varying the degree of detail.

Note that Vermeer's painting in Color Plate 15 also exploits this principle in enhancing the depth effect.

Pictorial perception can be increased by reducing *flatness cues,* that is, by reducing the information indicating that the image is actually of a flat surface. For example, looking at a two-dimensional picture through a rolled-up paper tube not only eliminates the frame effect of the picture but also reduces the cue that the picture is a flat surface. This considerably enhances the depth effect (Schlosberg, 1941). Thus, viewing Color Plate 16 through a paper tube makes the depth effects of the Rembrandt more striking. In general, *any* manipulation that reduces the perception of the static, flat quality of the picture plane will enhance the detection of its depth information.

Finally, we note that pictorial perception appears early in the human. In fact, pictorial perception from a television image has been demonstrated with humans as young as 14 months of age (Meltzoff, 1988). In one experiment, babies watched a black-and-white television screen on which they saw a man solve a toy puzzle. These babies were then able to solve the same puzzle, indicating that they could pick up and absorb information depicted in two-dimensional imagery. In short, babies, with limited spatial experience, can relate two-dimensional pictorial representations to their own actions on real objects in three-dimensional space.

The pictorial cues described above are static, monocular cues that give the impression of depth on a two-dimensional surface. In addition, there are several important monocular sources of dynamic, or kinetic, information that also contribute to the perception of depth. However, unlike static cues, these monocular cues cannot be represented in two-dimensional images. They are called *motion parallax, motion perspective,* and *accommodation.*

Motion Parallax

When the observer or objects move, a source of monocular information on the depth and distance of objects relative to each other is produced called **motion parallax** (from *parallaxis,* Greek for "change"). Specifically, motion parallax refers to differences in the displacement of the images of objects that lie at different distances relative to each other when the head moves. Therefore, when the observer fixates on some point in the visual scene and the head moves (even very slightly), objects in the visual field that lie closer than the point of fixation appear to move faster than do distantly located objects. In short, near objects seem to move rapidly and far objects appear to move slowly.

In addition, the apparent direction of movement differs for near and far objects: objects closer than the fixation point appear to move in a direction opposite to the observer's head movement, whereas farther objects appear to move in the same direction as the head movement. Thus, both the relative velocity and the direction of the perceived movement depend on the location of the observer's fixation point, and together they provide a continuous source of information on the relative position of objects in the field of view.

Figure 9.15*a* schematically depicts the relative velocity changes in the retinal images of a near object (a square) and a far object (circle) as the eye moves from right (1) to left (2). At position 1 the eye is fixated on a central X. The square lies in front of the X, and the circle lies beyond the fixation point. However, when the eye moves slightly to the left, from position 1 to position 2 (arrow), the images of the near square and the far circle move by different amounts across

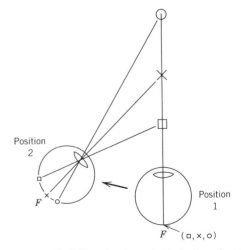

□ *figure* **9.15a** A schematic illustration of motion parallax. (Figure courtesy of Janice L. Nerger.)

the retina. Specifically, with fixation maintained on X, when the eye moves to the left—to position 2—the image of the near square travels a slightly greater distance across the retinal surface than does the image of the far circle. As shown in position 2, the distance between the images of the fixation X and the square on the retina is greater than the distance between the images of the X and the circle. Thus, with just a small movement in the position of the eye, the image of a nearby object moves a greater distance over the retina, and therefore moves more rapidly across the viewer's field of view than does the image of a far object. Note also that due to movement of the eye, the images of the near and far objects move *opposite* to each other relative to the fixation point. Adjusting for the reversal in the retinal images due to the optical property of the lens, the observer sees the near object moving in the opposite direction to the eyes, whereas the far object appears to move in the same direction as the eyes.

Although motion parallax seems to be a complex cue, it is actually a common source of information about the relative distances of objects in space under conditions where the observer and/or the environment move. Thus, it also occurs when the head is relatively stationary and the environment seems to flow by, such as when we ride in a car. Motion parallax in one set of dynamic conditions is illustrated in Figure 9.15*b*. This diagram shows how the terrain appears to move as an observer gazes out of a vehicle moving

to the left. While the observer maintains fixation at point *F*, the nearer objects seem to move to the right, in a direction *opposite* to the observer's motion, whereas objects located beyond the fixation point appear to move to the left in the *same* direction as the observer. In addition, objects located at different distances move at different velocities. The perceived velocity of an object diminishes the closer it lies to *F* (as indicated by the length of the arrows).

DEMONSTRATION:
Motion Parallax

Motion parallax can be simply demonstrated as follows: close one eye and hold up two objects, such as your fingers, in the direct line of sight, one about 25 cm (10 in.) in front of the other. If you move your head from side to side while maintaining fixation on the far finger, the image of the near finger will appear to move in the direction opposite to the movement of your head. If you fixate on the near finger, the far finger will appear to move in the same direction as the movement of your head.

Motion parallax, the relative apparent movement of objects in the field of view, provides an important source of depth and distance information and is partic-

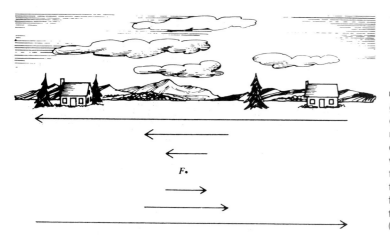

□ *figure* **9.15b** Schematic diagram of motion parallax. If an object located at *F* is fixated while the observer moves to the left, the images of the nearer objects appear to move to the right, whereas farther objects seem to move to the left. The length of the arrows indicates that the apparent velocity of objects in the field of view increases in direct relation to their distance from the fixation point. (Based on Gibson, 1950.)

ularly effective for such spatial tasks as perceiving an object standing out from its background. As we shall observe in a later section (on the visual cliff), motion parallax is also a potent cue employed by many different species of animals (including insects; e.g., Srinivasan, 1992) for avoiding depth.

Motion Perspective

Another source of depth and distance information provided by movement is the optic flow patterns described in the preceding chapter (see Figure 8.4). Recall that the optic flow patterns created by movement toward or parallel to surfaces provide information about velocity and the direction of movement. They also convey information about the relative *distance* of objects from the moving observer. J. J. Gibson labeled the source of information on distance of objects in the optic flow pattern **motion perspective**. When movement is toward a surface, for example, the location of objects relative to oneself can be gauged based on the continuous change in the perspective or position from which the objects are viewed (e.g., Clocksin, 1980; McCleod & Ross, 1983). It is a familiar experience that as you move through the terrain, objects that are close appear to flow by more rapidly than distant objects, producing a pattern of streaming of the retinal image and thus a strong cue for relative distance.

Accommodation

We described accommodation in Chapter 3 as a mechanism for focusing the lens to form a sharp retinal image. Because accommodating responses differ in focusing on near and far objects, it is possible that oculomotor adjusting signals from the ciliary muscles (i.e., the degree of muscle contraction) furnish information of a target's spatial location. In other words, because the adjustment of the lens is correlated with the distance of objects observed, **accommodation** may provide depth and distance information. However, accommodation is probably a limited source of spatial information. For the human, it is useful only for distances up to about 2 meters; for targets located

beyond this point, accommodation does not furnish accurate information about distance.

BINOCULAR CUES

Monocular cues provide a lot of spatial information, and on the basis of monocular vision many visually guided skilled tasks can be performed. However, some sources of information require the activity of both eyes. We introduced some of the structural and functional aspects of binocular vision in earlier chapters. We now turn to the kinds of spatial information provided by perception with two eyes: the **binocular cues.**

Convergence

Convergence refers to the tendency of the eyes to turn toward each other in a coordinated action to fixate on targets located nearby (Figure 9.16). Targets located far away from the viewer, on the other hand, are fixated with the lines of sight of the eyes parallel to each other. Because the degree of convergence is controlled by muscles attached to the eyeballs, different states of muscular tension for viewing near and far objects may furnish a cue to depth or distance. However, like accommodation, convergent eye movements as a source of depth or distance information are useful only for nearby objects.

Binocular Disparity

We noted in Chapter 3 that for some animals, particularly predators and primates, the two frontally directed eyes receive two slightly different images of the same three-dimensional scene. This is outlined in Figure 9.17, which depicts the different views of the same visual scene seen by the left and right eyes. In the human, this is due to the fact that the eyes are set about 2 to 3 in. apart. The slightly different views can be easily observed by sighting on a nearby object with each eye individually. Depending on the location of the fixation point, the visual field seen by one eye is somewhat different from the visual field seen by the

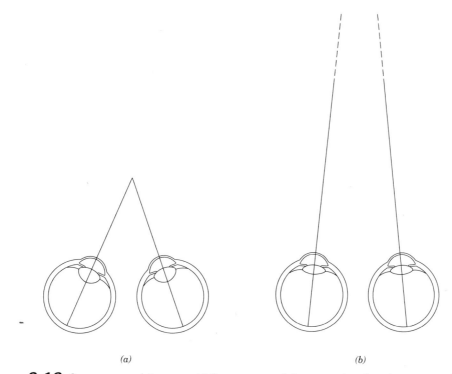

(a)

(b)

□ **figure 9.16** Convergence of the eyes. (a) Convergence of the eyes when focusing on a nearby target; the eyes pivot inward toward each other. (b) Relative position of the eyes when focusing on a distant target; the lines of sight of the left and right eyes are essentially parallel. Accommodation of the eyes also differs in the two viewing conditions. At (a) the lens bulges for nearby viewing; at (b) the lens is relatively flat.

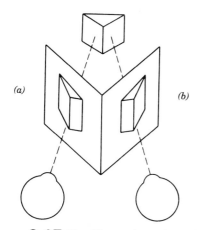

(a)

(b)

□ **figure 9.17** The different views of a wedge seen by the two eyes. (a) The image of the three-dimensional wedge seen by the left eye. (b) The image seen by the right eye.

other (Figure 9.18). This difference in the two retinal images is called **binocular disparity** (or sometimes **binocular parallax**). Figure 9.19 shows how disparity is created in a simple viewing condition in which two lines are located at different distances from the observer.

The visual system's ability to use binocular disparity information to detect the difference in depth between two objects is impressive. According to Yellot (1981), a depth difference between two objects that corresponds to 1 micrometer (0.001 mm) in retinal disparity can be detected. That is, a difference of only 1 micrometer in the position of the images of objects reflected on the left and right retinas is detectable. This means that the visual system can reliably detect disparities substantially smaller than the diameter of most retinal photoreceptors.

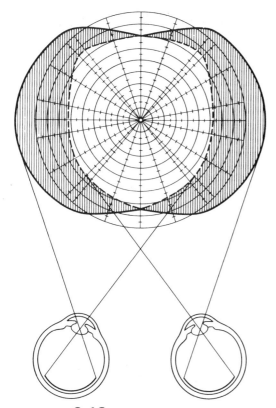

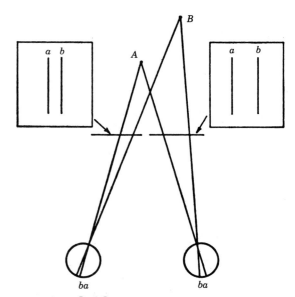

□ *figure* **9.19** The perception of relative distance of two objects with binocular disparity information. The perception of the relative distance between two lines is due to the slight disparity in separation of the retinal images projected on the left and right eyes (i.e., the distance between *b* and *a*), as indicated by the projections in the two boxes. The distance between retinal images of the two lines is larger in the right eye. That is, the distance *ba* in the right eye is larger than the distance *ba* in the left eye. The difference in these distances specifies the degree of binocular disparity. In general, the farther away one object is from another, the greater the disparity.

□ *figure* **9.18** The approximate visual fields of each eye (gray hatched areas) and the binocular visual field (central white area). Note that the area seen by one eye does not fully coincide with the area seen by the other. The white central area seen by both eyes is the binocular visual field.

□
DEMONSTRATION:
Depth Based on Binocular Disparity

Consider this practical illustration of the keen depth judgment made possible with binocular disparity. If you hold two vertically oriented objects such as pencils, one in each hand, at arm's length, you can detect whether one of them is as little as 1 millimeter (about 0.04 in.) closer to you than the other. The contribution of binocular disparity is evident if you close one eye as you do this. You will immediately observe that the remaining monocular cues are insufficient to detect the difference in depth between the two pencils. A more practical and familiar illustration of binocular disparity is that of trying to thread a needle with one eye closed. Try it, and you will be immediately aware of the importance of binocular disparity.

Corresponding Retinal Points and the Horopter

Disparity may be further analyzed for information of depth and distance. When a relatively small target is fixated, it forms images on the foveas of both eyes.

However, the fixated target will appear single, since the two eyes are converged to project the target image on identical or corresponding parts of both eyes. That is, if the left retina and its target image were superimposed on the right retina and its target image, so that the foveas were made to coincide, the two target images would also coincide. Such retinal locations that are identical in both eyes are called **corresponding retinal points.**

Other targets that are not fixated on, but are located at about the same distance as the fixation target, will also project onto identical or corresponding retinal points on both retinas, and will be fused and seen as single. In fact, for a given degree of fixation and convergence, there is a set of spatial points that project onto corresponding retinal points. A target located at any one of these points is seen singly and is perceived as being the same distance from the observer as the fixation target.

If we map out all the spatial locations where targets lie at about the same fixation or convergence distance, and that project onto corresponding retinal points, we will trace out a surface called the **horopter** (Figure 9.20). The horopter is an imaginary curved surface that passes through the fixation point, and all points lying on its surface project images that fall on corresponding retinal points of the two eyes and appear single. However, targets *not* lying on the horopter for a particular fixation distance produce *diplopia,* or double images, because they stimulate disparate or **noncorresponding retinal points.** That is, targets located nearer or farther than the fixated target project images in *different* positions on each retina, giving rise to disparity and double images.

An important exception to this generalization involves noncorresponding retinal points projected from a spatial region that lies within a narrow horizontal band surrounding the horopter. This region, shown in Figure 9.20, is called **Panum's fusion area (PFA)** (named for the Danish physiologist who first noted its importance). Spatial points that stimulate noncorresponding retinal points but lie within PFA are also fused into single images. That is, PFA is a small zone surrounding a given horopter that projects mildly disparate images that also appear fused. In fact, spatial

stimuli lying within the PFA are seen as single objects that appear at slightly different distances from the observer than the fixation distance.

Thus, for a given fixation distance, there is a spatial region of fused, single images flanked by areas of double images. Whatever the distance of the target we fixate on, other targets at the same distance project onto corresponding retinal points on the two eyes and appear single; targets at different distances (and lying outside the PFA) project onto noncorresponding retinal points and appear double. There is a different horoptor for every point of fixation: only objects located at the *same* convergence and fixation distance are fused and seen as single. In other words, for each fixation distance there is a separate and distinct set of corresponding retinal points, and a different horopter (along with its appropriate PFA), on which objects appear single.

The perception of double images produced by stimulating noncorresponding retinal points is given in the following demonstration.

□ **DEMONSTRATION:**
Double Images and Binocular Disparity

Hold a near and a far object as indicated in Figure 9.21. If you fixate on the near object, you will produce a single image of the near object and double images of the far, nonfixated object. The image of the near object falls on corresponding retinal points of the fovea (*F*) of both eyes, whereas the images of the nonfixated, far object fall on noncorresponding retinal points of each retina. The solid lines represent the light reflected from the near and far objects. The two close-up dashed lines show the apparent paths of the projected images from the far, nonfixated object, indicating that it projects two separate images and appears double.

This demonstration summarizes some of the points just made. When fixation is on the near object,

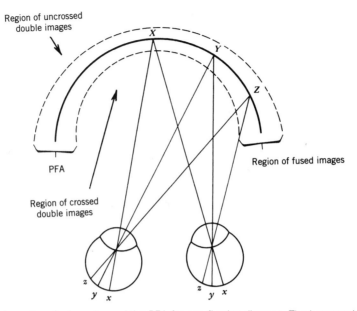

□ figure 9.20 A version of a horopter and the PFA for one fixation distance. The horopter is an imaginary plane mapping the locations of all objects whose image fall on corresponding retinal points and appear single. Thus images of the points, *X, Y,* and *Z* fall on corresponding retinal points in the two retinas and are seen as single points. While not falling on corresponding retinal points, the images of spatial points lying within PFA will also be fused and seen as single. Spatial points not lying on the horopter (and falling outside of the PFA) will appear as double images. Objects located more distant than the region of fixation (i.e., farther than the horopter and PFA) produce double images with uncrossed disparity, whereas objects located closer than the horopter and PFA produce double images with crossed disparity. The horopter (and the associated PFA) vary with fixation distance and ocular convergence, so that different fixations produce different horopters and fusion areas.

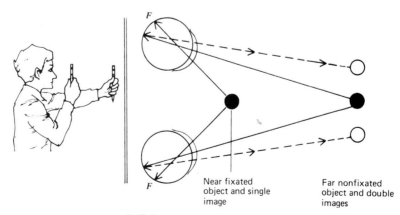

□ figure 9.21 Double images and binocular disparity.

the image falls on the foveas of both eyes. However, images of the far, nonfixated object fall on noncorresponding retinal points, and two different images of the far object are observed. Although not depicted in this figure, when fixation is on the far object, the image of the near, nonfixated object will appear double (and the two images will appear crossed with respect to each other). In fact, the pattern of double images is different, depending on whether the double images appear to lie in front or in back of the fixated target. Objects farther than the point of fixation are seen in *uncrossed disparity,* whereas objects closer than the fixated target appear in *crossed disparity.* Thus, the pattern of double images may serve as a cue to relative distance (though perhaps one of which we are not generally very conscious).

To review, as long as fixation is maintained on some point on a given horopter, all objects located anywhere on the plane produce images on corresponding retinal areas and hence appear single. Objects that lie closer or farther than the horopter (actually, objects that lie outside of the PTA for a given horopter) fall on noncorresponding retinal points; thus, they are not fused and are seen as double images. Objects that lie closer than the horopter are seen in crossed disparity, and objects that lie farther than the horopter are seen in uncrossed disparity. Although the pattern of double images is linked to the distance of objects relative to the horopter, in general, double images of nonfixated objects are usually suppressed and go unnoticed except under special conditions (see Figure 9.22 for the following demonstration).

DEMONSTRATION:
Binocular Disparity

Binocular disparity may be used to create amusing effects. Bring the index fingers about 12 in. in front of your face at eye level so that your fingers are pointing at each other but are separated by about 1 in. (*1*) Focus straight ahead, past the fingers, on a wall or distant surface, shown in Figure 9.22 by the fixation X. A phantom floating finger joint or sausage-like shape will appear between the fingers

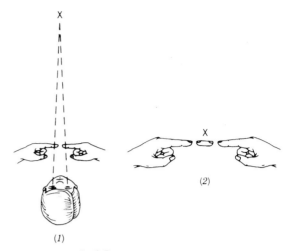

□ *figure* **9.22** Binocular disparity and phantom images.

(*2*). With a little practice, you will be able to focus on the "sausage," and by moving your fingers up and down slightly, you may experience some unusual effects. In addition, as you slowly move toward the surface on which you focus, the size of the sausage will shrink.

The sausage is actually the result of the fused images of the tips of each finger as seen by the left and right eyes. This can be easily verified by alternately blinking. Monocular imagery prevails, and the sausage disappears. However, when both eyes are opened, the two monocular images are fused and the sausage soon reappears. (This demonstration was described by Sharp, 1928.)

Binocular Disparity and Stereopsis

The disparity of the images projected on each eye gives rise to the unique appearance of depth with solidity called **stereopsis** (from the Greek, *stereos,* for "solid," and *opsis,* for "vision," hence "solid sight"). One of the most impressive examples of stereopsis is the entertaining depth effect experienced when viewing slides in the familiar stereo viewer (such as a View–Master). The original stereo viewer, called a **stereoscope** was an optical instrument devised in 1838 by the English physicist Charles Wheatstone, who reasoned that it should be possible to produce a synthetic impression of depth by casting on each eye similar but slightly disparate pictures called **stereograms** (also called *stereo pairs* or *stereo half-fields*). A Victorian-style stereoscope popular in the middle and late 1800s is presented in Figure 9.23*a;* some examples of stereograms are presented in Figures 9.23*b* and 9.23*c.*

Stereograms then are pairs of pictures representing those views of objects and scenes that are observed by the separate eyes. When the slightly disparate pictures are properly paired and shown in a stereoscope, the scene appears in stereoscopic depth; that is, a vivid and compelling experience of a single three-dimensional scene is seen.

The common View–Master stereo viewer performs the same function as the stereoscope in that it gives the viewer two different pictures of the same scene taken with a stereo camera—a camera that has two lenses separated from each other by about the same distance as the two eyes. The two pictures thus taken are slightly different, corresponding to the views seen by the left and right eyes. When these pictures are processed and each one is presented by means of a stereo viewer to the appropriate eye (ensuring that the left eye sees only the picture taken by the left lens and the right eye sees only the picture taken with the right lens), the images fuse and the striking effect of stereopsis occurs.

Within limits, the greater the disparity of the two pictures shown in a stereoscope or stereo viewer, the greater the impression of solidity or three-dimensional depth. This suggests a general point concerning the relation between the degree of stereopsis and object distance when binocularly viewing the real world. Typically, viewing nearby objects requires greater convergence of the two eyes and produces greater disparity; hence, the closer the object is to the observer, the greater the stereoscopic depth effect. For example, gazing at your palm when it is held close to your face creates disparate images and gives a very strong effect of three-dimensionality. When binocularly viewed close up, the roundness and solidarity of the fingers and the crevices and ridges of the palm stand out in vivid depth. (Indeed, abruptly close one eye and the strong three-dimensional effect is lost!).

In contrast, for very far objects, the images received by each eye are almost identical, with little or no binocular disparity; consequently, as objects increase in distance from the viewer, binocular disparity decreases, and objects appear increasingly flat.

Anaglyphs There is an alternative way of experiencing stereopsis that is probably more familiar (and convenient) than using a stereoscope or stereo viewer. Effective stereopsis may be experienced by viewing an **anaglyph** of a stereogram (*anaglyph* derives from the Greek word for "carving in relief"). An anaglyph is a special version of stereogram produced by printing the stereo pairs on top of each other in different inks (usually red and green) to produce a composite picture. When the anaglyph is normally viewed, the two colors printed on top of each other create a blurry image. However, when viewed through special color-tinted glasses (with different colors, either red or green, over the left and right eyes), each eye sorts out its appropriate single image (the eye with the red tint in front sees only the green image, and the eye with the green tint in front sees only the red image), and the anaglyph is seen in stereoscopic depth. Most "3-D" movies use the anaglyph process; hence, you must wear the red and green color-tinted glasses in order to see them stereoscopically.

Binocular Rivalry As we noted earlier in the discussion of the horopter, fusion of the images projected on the left and right eyes occurs only when the two images are reasonably similar. When they are very different, an unusual phenomenon called **binocular rivalry** results. When binocular rivalry occurs, several outcomes are possible. The very different images projected to the right and left eyes may fuse to provide a somewhat fragile and fleeting composite image, or one image may be dominant over the other. That is, at one moment the stimuli from one eye may be dominant, with a corresponding suppression of the stimuli from the other eye; moreover, dominance may fluctuate from eye to eye (e.g., see Engel, 1958).

The perceptual effects that result from presenting each eye with different imagery can have practical consequences. Because the visual system is sensitive to very slight binocular disparity information, stereo-

Pairs of stereo pictures
or stereograms, shown
below in *b* and *c*, are
inserted in the holder so
as to face the eyepiece

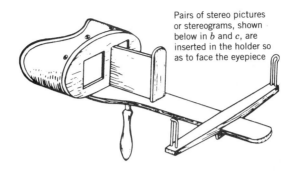

(*a*)

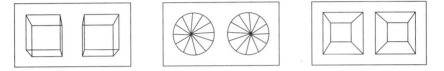

(*b*)

(*c*)

□ *figure* **9.23** (*a*) A typical hand-held stereoscope presenting different images to each eye. This type of stereoscope was designed by Oliver Wendall Holmes, Sr. (the father of the renowned Supreme Court justice). (*b*) Three simple line-drawn stereograms. The elements of the pairs of figures are arranged so that when they are viewed in a stereoscope and fused, a single object is seen in depth. The figures in each stereogram depict the views that would be seen by the left and right eyes when actually viewing such linear scenes.

(*c*) An early photographic stereogram. When viewed in a stereoscope, the left and right images are projected on the left and right eyes, respectively. When fused, a single image containing a "Poem in Trees" is seen in stereoscopic depth. Although the two pictures seem identical, close inspection reveals slight differences. The stereogram is actually composed of two slightly different views of the same scene that was made by photographing each view from about the position of each eye. Thus, the picture on the left is the image seen by the left eye, and the picture on the right is the image seen by the right eye. The slight differences between the two images result in binocular disparity, and when they are shown to each eye separately in a stereoscope, the scene appears in depth. (Courtesy of Harvey Schiffman.)

scopic viewing allows us to detect minute differences between similar images. For example, stereoscopic viewing can help detect counterfeit currency. If each eye sees a genuine bill, there is no disparity in the two images, and a single fused image of the bill will appear on a flat plane. However, if one eye views a counterfeit bill (even a very good one) and the other sees a genuine one, the disparity in the two images will immediately expose slight differences; some areas will appear to stand out from others. Similarly, ballistic experts view enlarged photographs of different bullets stereoscopically to discover if they have been fired from the same weapon (Bloomer, 1976). If the markings are identical (i.e., if no disparity exists)—which would be the case if both bullets were fired by the same gun—then a single fused image is seen.

Cyclopean Perception

Bela Julesz (1964, 1965, 1971, 1978) devised an unusual and innovative form of stereo viewing employing a unique kind of stereogram. He termed it **cyclopean perception** because the special stereo image projected on each eye appears meaningless by itself to the visual system. A meaningful perception of objects in depth appears only *after* the two images are combined in some central visual area. In his words:

> The mythical cyclops looked out on the world through a single eye in the middle of his forehead. We too, in a sense, perceive the world with a single eye in the middle of the head. But our cyclopean eye sits not on the forehead, but rather some distance behind it in the areas of the brain that are devoted to visual perception. (1971, p. xi)

The stereograms that Julesz used to demonstrate cyclopean perception are unusual. Julesz had a computer program print out two nearly identical displays of random-dot patterns (generally referred to as **random-dot stereograms**). A pair of such patterns is shown in Figure 9.24a. The two patterns possess identical random-dot textures, except for a small central area that is also identical in both patterns but is displaced laterally in opposite directions on each pattern. Although it is impossible to see any depth or

shape by looking at either half of the pair of random-dot patterns, when the two patterns are stereoscopically fused, a small central square corresponding to the horizontally shifted area is vividly seen in its own depth plane, floating above the surrounding texture (Figure 9.24b). As indicated in Figure 9.25, the regions that are shifted differ for the left and right squares of the random-dot stereogram. In the left square the shift is to the right, and in the right square the shift is to the left. This provides the disparate views that would project onto the left and right eyes if the small central square was actually lying on a separate plane in front of the random background texture. As a result, there is binocular disparity between elements of texture for this small central region, and, when stereoscopically viewed, it is perceived as lying on a plane above the random background texture. If the disparity relationship between the left and right squares is reversed, the small shifted region appears to lie on a surface behind the random texture.

According to Julesz (1964, 1971), stereopsis from these random-dot stereograms is produced by the process of searching for and evaluating disparities. In fact, it appears that binocular disparity alone is sufficient for achieving stereopsis, since there is nothing in the pattern of the random-dot stereograms, such as pictorial depth cues or familiar shapes, to suggest that one region is displaced relative to another.

Local versus Global Stereopsis

Random-dot stereograms present a unique problem of ambiguity. When viewing simple stereograms such as those illustrated in Figures 9.23b and 9.23c, there is no ambiguity as to which of the line segments in the left and right retinal projections correspond to each other. Such stereograms provide ample, monocularly recognizable stimuli in each of the pictures projected on the left and right eyes that can be matched, point for point, by the visual system to create the stereoscopic effect. This unambiguous depth localization is termed **local stereopsis.** In contrast, random-dot stereograms provide no recognizable structures; nothing in the two features of a random-dot stereogram informs the visual system that there are groups of common elements that could be paired up to provide

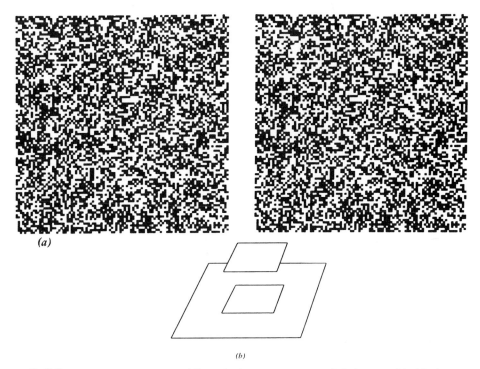

□ *figure 9.24* Random-dot stereogram. When the images are monocularly inspected in (*a*), they appear to be composed of uniformly random elements with no depth characteristics, but when stereoscopically fused a center square is seen floating above the background in vivid depth (as depicted in *b*). Similarly, when an anaglyph of this stereogram is viewed with appropriately tinted glasses, a center square is seen above the surround. (From B. Julesz, *Foundations of Cyclopean Perception*, 1971, p. 21. Reprinted by permission of the author and publisher.)

1	0	1	0	1	0	0	1	0	1
1	0	0	1	0	1	0	1	0	0
0	0	1	1	0	1	1	0	1	0
0	1	0	Y	A	A	B	B	0	1
1	1	1	X	B	A	B	A	0	1
0	0	1	X	A	A	B	A	1	0
1	1	1	Y	B	B	A	B	0	1
1	0	0	1	1	0	1	1	0	1
1	1	0	0	1	1	0	1	1	1
0	1	0	0	0	1	1	1	1	0

1	0	1	0	1	0	0	1	0	1
1	0	0	1	0	1	0	1	0	0
0	0	1	1	0	1	1	0	1	0
0	1	0	A	A	B	B	X	0	1
1	1	1	B	A	B	A	Y	0	1
0	0	1	A	A	B	A	Y	1	0
1	1	1	B	B	A	B	X	0	1
1	0	0	1	1	0	1	1	0	1
1	1	0	0	1	1	0	1	1	1
0	1	0	0	0	1	1	1	1	0

□ *figure 9.25* A schematic diagram indicating the process by which the random-dot stereogram of Figure 9.24 was generated. The left and right images are identical random-dot textures except for certain areas that are shifted in opposite directions relative to each other in the horizontal direction as though they were solid sheets. The shifted areas, indicated by A and B cells, cover certain areas of the background, indicated by 1 and 0 cells; owing to the shift, areas become uncovered (X and Y cells) which are filled in by additional random elements. (From B. Julesz, *Foundations of Cyclopean Perception*, 1971, p. 21. Reprinted by permission of the author and publisher.)

stereopsis. Thus, random-dot stereograms are *ambiguous* with regard to which elements in the left and right retinal projections correspond to each other. Any element projected on one eye could conceivably be matched to any other neighboring element projected on the other eye. Instead, however, the visual system matches up the patterns of disparity in the two eyes. Here a *global* process is required to search for the many disparities necessary to perceive a three-dimensional surface. Since there must be an overall or global matching of disparate elements common to both halves of the random-dot stereogram, rather than a point for point or local matching, the presumed process yielding stereoscopic perception from random-dot stereograms is termed **global stereopsis.**

Autostereograms Because of technical limitations, we cannot demonstrate global stereopsis here with random-dot stereograms (unless the reader takes the trouble to fuse the stereo pairs of Figure 9.24*a* by viewing them through a stereoscope). However, with some effort it is possible, using free viewing alone, to experience global stereopsis by viewing an **autostereogram.** An autostereogram is a special form of stereogram developed by Christopher Tyler (Pugliese, 1991; Tyler & Clarke, 1990; see also Stork & Rocca, 1989) that contains complete information for both eyes on a single printed image and, like a random-dot stereogram, reveals no recognizable monocular cues. Figure 9.26 presents an autostereogram. The instructions for obtaining stereopsis in the figure are presented in the following demonstration. (Incidentally, these same instructions for free-viewing may be used to fuse the images of the two line stereograms of Figure 9.23*b*.)

DEMONSTRATION:
Viewing an Autostereogram

When Figure 9.26*a* is properly viewed, an image of a familiar object will be seen on a plane lying in front of the background texture. The viewer's task is to cross the eyes and focus on the two fixation dots so that they appear as three dots. This means

that the eyes must converge on a point that lies in front of the figure plane. Several techniques for doing this follow. It might be helpful to have someone else read these instructions to you while you attempt to get the stereo image.

As illustrated in Figure 9.26*b*, hold a pencil about 6 in. in front of the figure, with its point aimed about halfway between the two dots. As you fixate on the pencil point, you should also be able to see the two dots at the top of the figure. While focusing on the pencil point, slowly move the pencil back and forth until you see the two dots appear as three dots in a line (you are now crossing your eyes to the correct extent). Maintain this focus for a few moments until the images of the pencil point and fused "center" dot appear sharp; then slowly move your fixation to the center dot and remove the pencil. If your eyes tend to flip back to the plane of the page, keep trying until the three-dot configuration can be stably maintained. For some observers, an image of an object in stereoscopic depth may pop out immediately; others may have to maintain the fixation for several minutes.

If this doesn't work after repeated attempts, try these alternative methods. As above, hold the pencil in front of the figure, with its point aimed about halfway between the two fixation dots. However, focus your eyes on the plane of the figure rather than on the pencil. Since you are focusing on the figure, you should see crossed double images of the pencil. Slowly move the pencil so that the two pencil images appear somewhat aligned with the two fixation dots at the top of the figure. Then, slowly focus on the pencil point. The two blurred images of the pencil should converge into a single image that points at a center dot. Continue focusing on the pencil point until the center dot appears sharp. This may take some time, but when it happens you will see a central figure emerge in depth from the background.

A third method, but one that will produce the hidden object at a depth plane *below* the textured surface (because the eyes will converge on a point that lies below the figure plane), is as follows: As you look at the top of the figure, try to focus your gaze at a point past the dots, such as on the floor

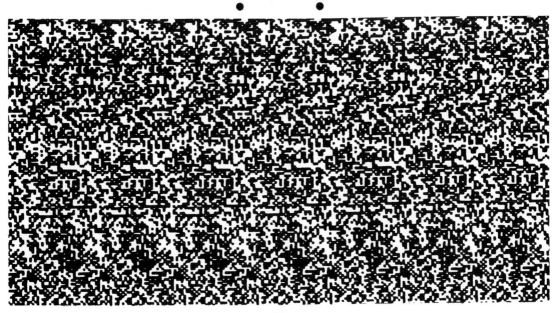

(a)

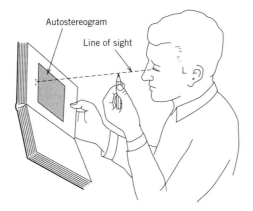

(b)

▭ **figure 9.26** An autostereogram (a) and illustration for viewing it (b). (Autostereogram courtesy of Christopher Tyler.)

or wall, until the two dots appear as three. Hold your gaze steadily on the three dots for a few moments and, without changing your focus, slowly move your eyes down until you see the figure in depth. Hint (although it won't hasten the process): the figure that can be seen in depth is also depicted in Figure 7.17 of Chapter 7.

The autostereogram poses an unfamiliar, difficult task for the visual system because you have to focus your eyes at a distance that is different from the location of the figure plane; but unless you are a monocular or a *stereoblind* individual (see the next section), with practice you should be able to see the stereo image.

The depth effect is difficult for many individuals to experience the first time. For some, it may take several minutes of oculomotor effort, but with patience and practice, it should be achieved by most viewers. Interestingly, as Pugliese (1991) points out, you might have inadvertently induced the same stereoscopic effect when gazing at a repetitively tiled floor or wallpaper pattern, and had the disconcerting sensation of seeing the tiles floating off the floor or the patterns floating in front of the wall on an imaginary plane in front of you.

One of the most significant findings of cyclopean research with random-dot stereograms is that stereopsis may occur in the total absence of monocular depth cues and even recognizable or familiar contours or shapes. When random-dot stereograms are viewed monocularly, they appear to be completely random arrays of textures, with no hint of recognizable forms or shapes. Thus, stereopsis may not only precede the perception of shape, but it may occur in the absence of shape recognition. In other words, the perception of contours and shapes is not a prerequisite for achieving stereopsis. As Gulick and Lawson (1976) have stated cyclopean perception indicates that "instead of contours giving rise to depth, it is rather depth that gives rise to contours" (p. 272).

Stereopsis using random-dot stereograms is not limited to the adult human. It emerges in the human at between 3 ½ to 6 months of age (Fox et al., 1980; Petrig et al., 1981). Moreover, this form of stereopsis occurs in other species. Falcons (Fox, Lehmkuhl, & Bush, 1977), cats (Fox & Blake, 1970), and monkeys (Bough, 1970) appear capable of perceiving depth with random-dot stereograms.

Cyclopean stimulation occurs in a unique set of laboratory conditions in which the monocular and binocular forms of information are separated. Most spatial events are viewed without such restriction. Typically, space perception is accomplished in an environment containing a number of cues, and effective space perception depends on their integration.

However, the attainment of stereopsis does confer some special advantage to the spatial perception of the environment. It not only enables us to extract information about the relative depth of objects and surfaces, but it also contributes to the *unitary* percep-

tion of those features that lie at a similar depth; that is, grouping together features that lie at a similar depth from the viewer promotes object recognition. In line with this, Frisby (1980) speculates that

perhaps the initial evolutionary advantage of having two eyes was as a solution to the problem of decoding camouflage. Perhaps two-eyed vision really came into its own when it provided a means of grouping together stripe features belonging to the tiger (or other predator, or desirable but hidden prey), and separating them from stripe features produced by the branches, twigs and leaves of the tree in which he was hiding, ready to pounce. This speculation is certainly in keeping with the discovery of random-dot stereograms, because they show just how superb a camouflage-breaking system stereopsis is: only after their binocular fusion can any object whatsoever be seen . . . perhaps with the special kind of depth perception which is stereopsis in its armoury, the visual system is very much better able to break up a scene into its constituent regions, and thereby to get on with the job of seeing what is present. (p. 155)

Physiological Basis of Binocular Disparity

The physiological basis of stereopsis is supported by evidence of binocular disparity-selective cells in various mammalian species, including the human. That is, there are cells that show little response to monocular stimulation, responding instead to a range of binocular disparity stimulation. These cells—referred to as *disparity detectors*—are activated when neighboring clusters of stimuli of similar disparities reach each retina (e.g., Ferster, 1981; Heydt et al., 1978; Hubel & Wiesel, 1970; Ohzawa, DeAngelis, & Freeman, 1990; Poggio, 1995; Poggio & Poggio, 1984). This means that binocular stimulation selectively stimulates various pools of disparity detector cells, which are tuned to different disparities. Some cells are narrowly tuned and react to stimuli with little or no binocular disparity, essentially excited by stimuli lying on or close to the fixation distance only (i.e., stimuli falling within the PFA of the horopter; see Figure 9.20). Other cells respond selectively only to stimuli lying in front of or beyond the fixation distance.

For example, Poggio and Fischer (1977) conditioned a monkey to fixate on a point located at a specific distance. They then presented it with targets positioned either in front or in back of the fixation point. As the monkey maintained fixation on the point, the experimenters recorded the activity of various single cells in its cortex. They found some cells that fired only to targets in front of the fixation point (which were inhibited by targets located behind the fixation) and other cells that fired only to targets beyond the fixation point (and inhibited by targets in front of the fixation). This suggests that the primate visual cortex has binocularly driven cells that are specifically responsive to targets whose distance is related to the point of fixation.

These findings suggest that there are at least three classes of binocular depth processing cells: cells specifically tuned to the fixation plane and the PFA; cells excited by stimuli lying in front of the fixation plane and inhibited by stimuli lying behind it; and cells excited by stimuli lying behind the fixation and inhibited by stimuli lying in front of it (see also Poggio, 1995).

There are some psychophysical findings in the human supporting the existence of disparity-detector cells that have a specific distance relation to the point of fixation (Richards, 1970, 1971; Richards & Regan, 1973; see also Blake & Cormack, 1979; Cormack, Stevenson, & Schor, 1993). Individuals with **stereoblindness** are unable to localize the depth of an object by means of stereoscopic or binocular disparity cues alone (although they can perceive depth using other cues). Some individuals are partially stereoblind: they cannot use stereoscopic cues to localize an object that lies either beyond or in front of the fixation plane. These observations are consistent with the existence of three sets of disparity detectors: one for objects lying on the fixation plane (having zero disparity) and within the PFA; another class for objects lying beyond the fixation plane; and a third for objects lying in front of it. Thus, given the physiological findings described above, the stereoblind (or partially stereoblind) individual may lack any or all sets of disparity detectors.

THE INTERACTION OF CUES TO SPACE

We have discussed several monocular and binocular cues for depth and distance that are normally well represented in environmental stimulation. However, there are several questions about their use and origin. Which cues are the most important? How effective is monocular depth perception? Is the perception of space gradually acquired through environmental encounters or is it a given—a perceptual feat that results directly from stimulation of the retina, one requiring no processing by the observer? We will consider these issues in the last sections of this chapter, but they will also figure in the next two chapters. First, we will outline two approaches, introduced in Chapter 1, concerning the nature and source of visual information available to the observer for perceiving depth and distance.

Constructivist Approach to Spatial Cues

According to the **constructivist approach,** the observer plays an active role in combining, evaluating, and interpreting the spatial information provided by the various spatial cues. That is, the observer must process the information provided by various spatial cues in order to "construct" the perception. It follows that the construction is aided by the observer's experience and knowledge of the spatial environment. Consider the cue of *interposition,* introduced at the beginning of this chapter: if one object partially overlaps or covers another object, we perceive, almost immediately, that the partially obscured object is farther away than the object that covers it. But how do we know this? That is, how do we recognize partial overlap as a source of information on the relative location of objects? According to the constructivist approach, the association between object interposition and distance perception is acquired through experience with objects covering each other. Similarly, what is there about the converging lines of railroad tracks that creates the perception of apparent distance (i.e., linear perspective)? Again, environmental interactions are key. We could make a similar case for many of the other cues discussed above, but the general point of the constructivist approach is this: experience with the various depth and distance cues enables us to make inferences about the spatial layout of the environment. We "construct" the visual environment based on our interpretation of the many spatial relationships between elements that appear in visual space (e.g., Hochberg, 1988; Rock, 1986).

Gibson's Direct Approach

Few psychologists in the last several decades have developed as influential an approach to the perception of space as has James J. Gibson (1950, 1966, 1979). Perhaps most unique and controversial in Gibson's approach is his notion of **direct perception,** which holds that, in most natural settings, enough information about the spatial layout of the environment is picked up *directly,* rather than as a result of processing and analyzing various depth and distance cues. That is, Gibson starts with the view that the information for depth and distance is contained fully within the optic array projected on the eyes and, by itself, provides reliable information about the visual world. According to this view, then, the optic array provides enough information to account fully for the perception of the visual world; no interpretation or evaluation of spatial cues is needed. The information contained within the optic array is picked up rather than processed.

Gibson also stresses the role played by systematic changes in the optic array that result from dynamic interactions as the observer moves through the natural environment. In spite of a moving observer, a changing environment, and a changing retinal image, certain sources of dynamic information remain constant; such information Gibson labels **invariants.** As an example, consider *optic flow patterns* (described in Chapter 8) and *motion perspective* (described earlier in this chapter). As an observer moves, contours sweep across the retina—with elements from all sides successively passing out of the bounded visual field as new elements enter—but the *pattern* of the optic flow does not change. The *flow* of the array remains constant as the observer moves. Texture gradients also offer invariant information: texture elements always appear

finer or denser as distance increases, and they appear coarser with decreasing distance. A similar case concerns the information for *motion parallax.* The apparent velocity differences of different regions of the visual field resulting from movement of the observer directly reveal relative distance information.

Most scientists who study vision find much to agree and disagree with in Gibson's approach. Clearly, the spatial variables stressed by Gibson, such as texture gradients and the optic flow pattern streaming past the moving observer, do provide potent sources of invariant information about depth and distance. However, his notion that space perception is, in most cases, directly registered in the optic array, with no inferential or cognitive processing or past experience, may be too exclusionary and restrictive for many visual scientists (e.g., see Bruce & Green, 1990; Hochberg, 1981; Ullman, 1980). As we noted earlier in this chapter, many spatial cues draw on experience and require some sort of processing. Indeed, as we have observed in earlier discussions, most researchers believe that perception is a product of various monocular and binocular depth cues, as well as invariant information. Thus, it seems reasonable to assume that, at least in part, we do not see the world directly; instead, we draw on many sources of spatial cues to construct it.

However, the impact of Gibson's approach is immense. It has contributed, both in its inspiration and in its identification and emphasis, to our knowledge of the rich, potent sources of dynamic information available to the observer in real-world scenes, namely, the invariant information in the optic array.

The Visual Cliff

When we confront a natural environment with depth and distance, several sources of information are usually available, and they almost always provide consistent spatial information. It is reasonable to assume that the more cues available, the more spatial information is conveyed to the observer and the more accurate the perception of depth and distance. However, is one cue more critical than another? In fact, is effective depth possible with monocular vision? An important step in answering these and other basic questions concerning the depth perception of a number of animal species was taken by Eleanor Gibson and Richard Walk (1961), making use of an apparatus they devised called the **visual cliff.** One version of the visual cliff is illustrated in Figure 9.27, which shows a centrally located start platform that divides the floor of the apparatus into two sides, each side providing different kinds of stimulation. The "shallow" side lies directly over a patterned surface; on the "deep" side, the same patterned surface is placed some distance below. Actually, a sheet of glass extends over both the deep and shallow sides for safety and to equate sources of thermal, smell, and sound reflection cues for both sides. Therefore, with lighting equalized for both sides, only intentional visual information is allowed. In the usual situation, an animal is placed on the start platform separating the shallow from the deep side. From this position, the animal can see the shallow or "safe" side and the deep or "dangerous" side, an edge with a dropoff beyond it similar to what the animal would see if it were actually looking over the edge of a cliff and facing a sharp drop.

A basic assumption in testing animals on the visual cliff is that animals tend to avoid a fall; hence, they will descend to the shallow side. Since depth perception is an adaptive ability that preserves the species, it is reasonable to expect that most animals have it. Furthermore, this ability should be effective by the time the animal moves about on its own. The existence of this ability is demonstrated by a descent preference for the shallow side; and in fact, this is the overwhelming finding in tests using the visual cliff. Based on research with a wide range of animals, including amphibia, birds, many species of small and some large mammals, primates, and human infants, a strong tendency to avoid the deep side has been found.

Moreover, by systematically varying the sources of information on the deep and shallow sides, Gibson and Walk were able to isolate the depth features that influence the depth perception of the animals. When all possible cues were independently varied and equated for both sides (relative size, texture gradients), animals still descended to the shallow side. In fact, regardless of the visual restrictions, so long as they could move about or move their heads, animals avoided the deep side. The one cue that could not be equated for the shallow and deep sides, and which

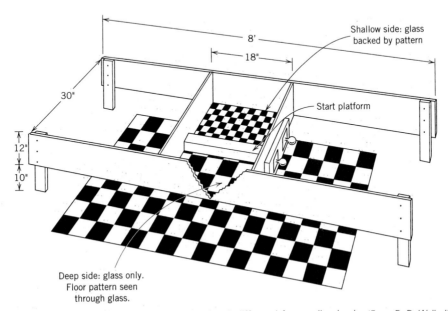

□ **figure 9.27** A schematic of a model of the visual cliff used for small animals. (From R. D. Walk, "The study of visual depth and distance perception in animals," in D. S. Lehrman, R. A. Hinde, and E. Shaw (Eds.). *Advances in the study of behavior,* Academic Press, 1965, p. 103. Reprinted by permission of the author and the publisher.)

appeared to dominate effective descent behavior, was *motion parallax*. That is, the relative rate at which elements moved over the retina as the animal scanned the two sides of the visual cliff apparatus provided the necessary information for perceiving the different depths.

The effectiveness of monocular vision for depth perception was also tested. The descents of monocular animals tested on the visual cliff, when compared with those of binocular animals, clearly indicate that one eye is adequate. That is, avoidance of the deep side is as effective with monocular viewing as it is with binocular viewing. As an interesting aside, the usefulness of monocular viewing for perceiving depth has often been demonstrated by individuals who, using only one eye, have been skillful in navigating within very complicated spatial contexts, such as professional sports and even in aviation. One of the more celebrated and dramatic examples of effective one-eye vision is that of Wiley Post, a pioneer of early flight, who made the first solo flight around the world in 1933. Not only was Post one-eyed, but he flew at a time when pilots flew "by the seat of their pants." That is, their main source of spatial information consisted of what they saw and felt; very little flight information was derived from cockpit instruments. The conclusion for us is that, given some experience, we can get by pretty well with only one eye. However, because of the loss of the keeness of vision provided by binocular disparity (as well as the obvious loss of half of our visual field), we must conclude that we get around much better with two eyes.

SUMMARY

In this chapter, we identified and described the stimulus indicators and visual processes that help us to perceive three-dimensional space. These stimulus features were described in terms of monocular and binocular cues, depending on whether or not the joint function of both eyes is necessary. Static monocular cues include interposition, aerial perspective, shading and lighting, elevation, linear perspective, texture gradients, relative size, and familiar size. It was noted that static monocular cues enable us to perceive depth on a

flat surface—pictorial perception. Three nonpictorial, dynamic monocular cues to depth were also described: motion parallax, motion perspective, and accommodation.

Binocular cues, which require the integration of input from the two eyes, were discussed next. These cues are convergence and binocular disparity. Related to the discussion of binocular cues, we examined corresponding retinal points, the horopter, and Panum's fusion area (PFA), and described how these contribute to stereopsis—the perception of depth with solidity. This led to a discussion of an unusual form of stereopsis called cyclopean perception, which uses random-dot stereograms. In this context, we also dealt with local and global stereopsis and presented an example of an autostereogram. We stressed an important contribution made by cyclopean perception and random-dot stereograms: not only does stereopsis precede shape perception, but it can occur in the absence of shape perception. Shape perception is not necessary for stereopsis.

The physiological basis of binocular disparity and the notion that some cells serve as disparity detectors were outlined. The evidence concerning the existence of different classes of disparity detectors appears consistent with the phenomenon of stereoblindness.

In the final section of this chapter, we discussed the interaction of spatial cues, focusing on two approaches to space perception: the constructivist approach and J. J. Gibson's direct approach. The constructivist approach contends that depth perception is based on experience and knowledge of the spatial environment, as well as processing and evaluating the available spatial cues. The direct approach, in contrast, holds that in most natural settings enough information about the depth and distance of objects and surfaces is contained in the optic array; moreover, this information is picked up directly by the observer, with no processing, evaluation, or reliance on experience. According to this view, the information from cues such as texture density and motion parallax reveals depth and distance information directly, with no mediation or evaluation required.

Finally, the visual cliff apparatus and some of the research findings from its use were discussed. It was concluded that the dynamic monocular cue of motion parallax provides enough information to mediate depth perception.

KEY TERMS

Accommodation

Aerial Perspective (Clearness)

Anaglyph

Autostereogram

Binocular Cues

Binocular Disparity (Binocular Parallax)

Binocular Rivalry

Constructivist Approach

Convergence

Corresponding Retinal Points

Cyclopean Perception

Direct Perception

Elevation (Height in the Visual Field)

Familiar Size

Horopter

Interposition

Invariants

Linear Perspective

Local and Global Stereopsis

Monocular Cues

Motion Parallax

Motion Perspective

Noncorresponding Retinal Points

Panum's Fusion Area (PFA)

Pictorial Cues

Pictorial Perception

Random-Dot Stereogram

Relative Size

Shading and Lighting

Stereoblindness

Stereograms

Stereopsis

Stereoscope

Texture Gradients

Visual Cliff

STUDY QUESTIONS

1. Identify the monocular cues that contribute to the perception of a three-dimensional environment. Indicate the static monocular pictorial cues and distinguish them from dynamic monocular cues that require movement. In particular, describe linear perspective and motion parallax, and indicate how they are utilized.

2. Explain why the scattering of the short wavelengths of light, involved in aerial perspective, causes the sky to appear blue.

3. Distinguish between the monocular cues of relative size and familiar size. Which one is based on experience? In what viewing conditions would familiar size be especially useful?

4. What is pictorial perception? What cues contribute to it?

5. Distinguish between motion parallax and motion perspective. Outline the process of motion parallax and describe its importance as a monocular cue to depth and distance. What feature do motion parallax, motion perspective, and accommodation have in common? In what ways are they dynamic cues?

6. Identify the binocular cues to depth and distance. What information, in addition to that conveyed by monocular cues, do binocular cues provide for spatial perception?

7. Describe binocular disparity, taking into account the horopter and the PFA. In what ways does binocular disparity provide information on the relative distance of objects to each other?

8. What are corresponding and noncorresponding retinal points? Describe how noncorresponding retinal points enable both binocular fusion (within the PFA) and double images.

9. What is stereopsis? Analyze this process, indicating how it can be simulated by viewing stereograms through a stereoscope.

10. What is cyclopean perception? How is it demonstrated, and how does it differ from typical

stereo viewing? Distinguish between local and global stereopsis.

11. What does cyclopean perception indicate about the necessity of monocular static cues, convergence, and the familiarity of objects for attaining stereopsis? To what extent is the monocular perception of contours a prerequisite for stereopsis?

12. Examine stereopsis in terms of the information it gives the observer. Indicate in what ways and to what extent species with specific spatial needs profit by it.

13. How necessary is binocular vision for efficient spatial perception? What spatial tasks does it enable? Consider the possibility of performing precise spatial tasks based on monocular information alone.

14. Distinguish between the constructivist approach and Gibson's direct approach to the perception of space. What are invariants in the direct approach? What role does each theory assign to past experience and cognitive processing of cues for the perception of space?

15. Describe the perceptual capacities that can be demonstrated and assessed on the visual cliff. Summarize the findings concerning the critical cues for depth perception on the visual cliff.

chapter 10

CONSTANCY AND ILLUSIONS

Observers generally move about and see objects from very different distances and angles under many lighting conditions. These moment-to-moment changes cause great variations in the stimulation reaching the retinas. However, in spite of these retinal changes, the perceptual world remains remarkably stable or constant. *We continue to perceive accurately the color, lightness, size, and shape of objects despite much stimulus variation. We refer to this ability as* perceptual constancy, *and we significantly extend our discussion of space perception by discussing it in this chapter.*

*Much of this chapter will also focus on those conditions that create systematic distortions in spatial perception—*visual illusions. *We will ex-*

amine the role of perceptual constancy, as well as spatial cues to depth and distance, in creating certain illusions. We will outline some of the attempts to explain illusions, and we will point out how empirically based attempts to come to terms with them may help us understand some of the processes of real-world space perception. There are a vast number of visual illusions, and many are included in this chapter. However, we will focus on only a representative group that is clearly relevant to the perception of space and that has been the subject of relatively recent or classic research. In several cases, we present provisional explanations embodying principles of perception; in almost all cases, there is no fully acceptable explanation.

PERCEPTUAL CONSTANCY

As we have just noted, the pattern of light reaching an observer undergoes continual, substantial variation as the spatial orientation of the object relative to the observer changes. This can occur by spatial displacement of the object, as well as by movements of the observer. Accompanying the spatial changes are changes in the distribution of the light striking the observer's retinas. These may result in variations in the object's projected size, shape, and luminance. However, in spite of these changes in stimulation, the

enduring qualities of the object are usually perceived. Indeed, the world we perceive, by and large, is a stable one. This stability of perception in the presence of variation in physical stimulation is termed **perceptual constancy.**

Perceptual constancy is one of the most impressive achievements of the visual system. It also challenges our understanding of space perception. Importantly, it is automatic and ever-present; indeed, it is so prevalent that we are generally unaware of its operation and effects. The page before you appears white whether it is illuminated by moonlight or by a high-intensity desk lamp. Its size does not appear to shrink or expand much as you move away or approach it. Yet the laws of geometry dictate precise size changes in the image corresponding to the distance of the page from your retina. The shape of this page looks rectangular regardless of the angle at which it is viewed, yet the shape of its retinal image is almost always trapezoidal. Clearly, as these examples indicate, perception is based on more than the absolute amount of reflected light or the shape and size of the retinal image. Our ability to perceive the enduring characteristics of the environment—perceptual constancy—depends on more than receiving isolated physical features of stimulation. The observer must somehow evaluate and interpret the stimulus input, taking into account the full circumstances in which the input occurs.

The fact that perception is linked to the *invariant* physical properties of objects—for example, actual size and shape—rather than the enormously changing light patterns reaching the visual system is very important: We perceive and deal with a world of reasonably stable objects with relatively permanent physical properties. Clearly, without perceptual constancy, the moment-to-moment variations in stimulation would appear as just that—a series of chaotic visual sensations.

Lightness Constancy

Although the terms are sometimes used interchangeably, the distinction made in previous chapters between lightness and brightness must be restated here (Jacobsen & Gilchrist, 1988). Technically, *lightness* refers to the surface quality—the degree of gray of an object or surface, ranging from black to white—that is independent of illumination. The *brightness* of a surface refers to the perceptual effects of the intensity of the light reflected by a surface, or *luminance*. Thus, for example, the lightness of a sheet of white paper will not change when viewed in intense or dim light (i.e., with luminance changes, it will continue to appear white), whereas its brightness will vary. In short,

brightness changes with illumination, whereas lightness generally does not.

Lightness constancy (sometimes called *whiteness constancy*) refers to the fact that the lightness of an object remains relatively constant even though its illumination changes. Thus, for example, we perceive a patch of snow in dark shadow as white and a chunk of coal in sunlight as black, yet the light reflected from the coal may be far more intense than that from the snow. Somehow we are taking into account information on the light reflected from these surfaces, as well as information about the general conditions of illumination.

The notion of perceiving a reflected light as constant, despite physical changes in the luminance reaching our eyes, should be familiar. Recall our discussion of *color constancy* from Chapter 5: Perception of the hue of objects and surfaces remains relatively constant in spite of changes in the wavelengths illuminating them. As we noted then, we appear to compensate, taking into account the overall illumination of a scene, so that whether illuminated by sunlight, tungsten, or fluorescent light, an object's color appears constant. A similar compensatory mechanism occurs with lightness constancy. In fact, lightness constancy is sometimes considered to be an instance of color constancy.

Albedo In trying to explain lightness constancy, we must consider a constant surface property called **albedo** or *reflectance*. The albedo is the proportion of incoming, or incident, light that is reflected (i.e., the proportion of reflected/incident light) from an object or surface. Albedo is a surface property that is independent of the degree of illumination. That is, the *proportion* of light reflected from an object or surface remains constant regardless of the degree of illumination. For example, a sheet of white bond paper (similar to this page) may have an albedo of, say, 0.80; this means it reflects approximately 80% of the light it receives. Therefore, whether the page is intensely or dimly illuminated, it will still reflect a constant proportion—80%—of the light that strikes it.

In addition, if, under ordinary conditions, part of the sheet of paper is placed under dim illumination (perhaps because of a shadow), so that all parts of the sheet are not illuminated equally, the entire sheet is still perceived as more or less uniform in lightness. This stability in lightness occurs because the entire surface of the sheet reflects a constant proportion of the light received, even though the amount of incident light may differ for different parts of the sheet's surface.

Relational Properties of Lightness Constancy

To use albedo effectively, we must know the overall conditions of lighting. In natural scenes, there are many cues to the source as well as the intensity of the illumination. Generally we are aware of the obvious sources, such as sunlight and artificial overhead or desk lighting. Also, since more than one object is usually visible, the amount of illumination falling on one object will also fall on nearby objects. This means that if the lighting on an object of our focus suddenly changes—for whatever reason—it also changes for nearby objects as well. Somehow the visual system takes into account the constant change in overall illumination and compensates for it accordingly, preserving lightness constancy. For example, as you look at this page placed on a desk or propped up against your lap, and the intensity of the overhead light is reduced by a constant amount, the appearance of the book, as well as all the surrounding objects and surfaces, will be dimmed. In short, with a change in overall illumination, most objects in the field of view are equally affected, but because of their individual albedos, they will continue to reflect the same *constant* proportion of the incident light that they did before the illumination change.

The effect on the perception of nearby objects is familiar to us. In discussing contrast phenomena in Chapter 6, we observed how a surface's background can affect its appearance. Applied in this context, within limits, lightness is strongly influenced by the lighting of the surrounding region. In a classic demonstration, Hans Wallach (e.g., 1948, 1963) illustrated this relation as follows: he projected a disk of light on a screen in a dark room and surrounded the disk with a ring of light. He found that the lightness of the

disk could be shifted from light to dark simply by varying the luminance of the surrounding ring of light from low to high.

In his most celebrated study on the relational basis of lightness constancy, Wallach found that if the intensities of both the ring and disk are changed by the *same* proportion, the lightness of the disks remains constant. The arrangement for demonstrating this is illustrated in Figure 10.1. Wallach projected two disks of light, each surrounded by a ring, in a dark room. When an observer adjusted the intensity of the test disk (at *b*) to match the lightness of the standard disk (at *a*), rather than setting it at a level for a physically equal match (i.e., 180 millilamberts or mL), the adjustment was to 90 mL. That is, the intensity *ratio* of ring to disk of (*a*)—360/180 or 2 : 1—was maintained at

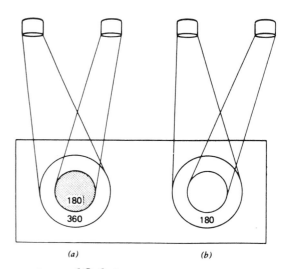

(a)

(a)   (b)

▭ **figure 10.1** Sample arrangement for demonstrating lightness constancy as a function of the relative illumination of an area to its background. Each disk and its surrounding ring of light in (*a*) and (*b*) is projected on a screen in an otherwise darkened room by a pair of projectors. The intensities of the disks and rings are separately controlled. In (*a*), the ratio of ring intensity to disk intensity is set at 2 : 1 (360 mL : 180 mL). In order for the disk at (*b*), with the intensity level of its ring set at 180 mL, to appear as light as the disk in (*a*), a setting of 90 mL is required. So long as the ratios of the intensities between the disks and their backgrounds remain constant, the two disks appear equally light in spite of the changes in overall illumination. (Based on Wallach, 1963.)

(b)—180/90 or 2:1—to produce an equal-lightness match. It is as if the overall level of illumination of (a) is halved at (b) and the observer adjusts to this lower level for an equality match. This clearly shows that perceived lightness is determined not by the absolute amount of light intensity but by the *ratios* of light intensities of adjacent regions.

This fixed proportional change is what occurs in natural settings when the overall illumination changes. As we noted earlier, objects normally do not appear isolated in the visual field. Therefore, when illumination changes, all objects and surfaces in the field of view are equally affected. Figure 10.2 outlines the effect of dramatically changing the illumination of a

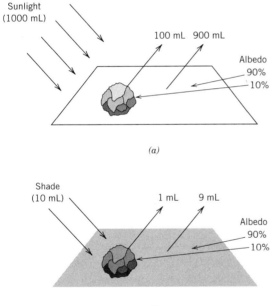

(a)

(b)

□ *figure 10.2* A chunk of coal and a piece of white paper in two conditions of illumination. The objects of the scene in (b) are uniformly illuminated by 1/100th of the amount of incident light in (a). However, since the objects reflect a constant proportion of the incident light (indicated by the albedos or reflectances), the intensity ratios of the chunk of coal to the sheet of paper in the scenes at (a) and in (b) are constant (1:9). Accordingly, the objects appear equally light in both scenes. (Modified from Hochberg, 1964.)

chunk of coal lying on a white sheet of paper. Although the illumination is very different in the two situations, the two objects—coal and paper—each reflect a constant proportion of the incident light (i.e., albedos of 0.1 and 0.9, or reflections of 10% and 90%, respectively). Thus, the *ratio* of the light intensities reflected from the chunk of coal to the paper remains constant at 1:9 under both levels of illumination. In general, as long as the light illuminating an object or surface also falls equally on regions surrounding it, the luminance ratios of the light of the object or surface to adjacent regions will remain constant in spite of changes in overall illumination. As a result, the lightness of an object seen against the background does not appear to change with changes in its illumination since *all* adjacent objects are equally affected.

It follows, then, that constancy should be poor in conditions where the sources of incident lighting and background illumination are obscured or lacking. In fact, if illumination is restricted to the object alone (e.g., by a hidden light source and a special means of projection, so that no light falls on the background), the perceived lightness of the object will depend entirely on its illumination, and lightness constancy is absent. Clearly, the visual system responds to the luminance relations of objects and surfaces in the field of view. Therefore, we conclude that one of the important factors of lightness constancy is that changes in the illumination of objects and surfaces are perceived relative to each other.

Lightness constancy is not perfect, especially when background cues are lacking. An isolated piece of white bond paper may appear somewhat gray when viewed in very dim illumination and white when bathed by intense light, showing a breakdown in lightness constancy. However, our own knowledge may override the absence of a background effect. In fact, it may contribute to lightness constancy in such situations. For example, knowing that an object is a sheet of white paper or a chunk of coal may have a strong effect on the perception of its lightness, even when viewed in conditions that reduce lightness constancy, such as in total isolation.

Size Constancy

We begin our discussion of size constancy with a demonstration.

▯ DEMONSTRATION:
Size Constancy

Consider this simple demonstration. Prop this book up and observe its size (it's about 9 1/2 in. high). Then slowly walk away from it while you continue to observe its size. Do this at about 5 ft, then at 10 ft, and finally at 15 ft. The apparent size of the book remains unchanged. Moreover, as you reverse the process and gradually approach the book, its size will still appear constant. With this seemingly trivial demonstration, you have verified some important points about the constancy of perceived size. Moving away from the book and then approaching it creates significant changes in the size of its retinal image; specifically, as the distance between your eyes and the book increases, the size of the retinal image decreases, and vice versa. The geometric relation between retinal image and object distance is outlined in Figure 10.3. Generally, however, the size of an object's image on the retina may change considerably with variation in the object's distance from the viewer, but the size changes go relatively unnoticed with normal viewing. You demonstrated

this for yourself by walking away from and back to the book, and you do so every time the distance of objects from you physically changes: Within limits, *objects don't appear to shrink and expand as their distance varies.* Thus, as implied in Figure 10.3, a person standing 15 ft away appears about as large as when he or she stands 30 ft away, even though the first image projected on the retina is twice the size of the second.

To sum up, the perceived size of an object in normal viewing conditions does not depend solely on the size of its image on the retina. Indeed, over a wide range of distances, perceived size is somewhat independent of retinal size. The tendency of objects to appear constant in size as their distance (and retinal images) changes is due to **size constancy.** Size constancy is the tendency of objects to remain relatively constant in size despite changes in the size of the retinal image cast by them as they are viewed from different distances. Although many factors affect size constancy, the most important are apparent distance cues and background stimuli. As Figure 10.4 shows, when used properly, distance information in a scene enables size constancy in a two-dimensional picture. That is, size constancy compensates for apparent distance.

Size constancy seems to occur automatically. However, the distance information required to trigger

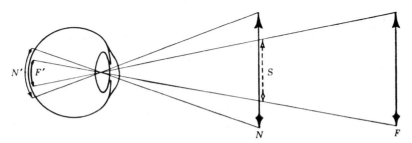

□ *figure 10.3* A schematic diagram showing the relative size of two retinal images, *N'* and *F'*, from the same-sized objects, *N* and *F*, but located at different distances. Object *F* is twice as far from the eye as object *N*; hence, its image on the retina is half as large. This is in accordance with the fact that the size of the retinal image is inversely proportional to the distance of the object from the eye. The smaller retinal image cast by object *F* could also be produced by the smaller object, *S* (smaller by one-half), located at the position of object *N*.

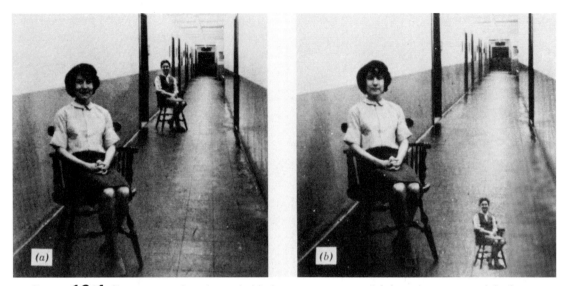

□ **figure 10.4** Size constancy in a picture. In (a), the near woman was 9 ft from the camera and the far woman 27 ft. The relative distances, and thus the relative retinal heights, are in the ratio 1 : 3. Size constancy is not complete; the distant woman appears somewhat smaller, but clearly not in the ratio 1 : 3, which is correct for the two women in the photograph. Compare this with (b). The far woman of (a) was cut out of the picture, brought forward next to the other woman, and pasted there with the apparent distance from the viewer equal for the two. The size ratio 1 : 3 is now apparent. The right-hand woman looks considerably smaller in (b) than she did in (a), although physically unchanged in size on the page. This is an *example* of size constancy in a picture with perspective and elevation cues for distance. [Note that the size constancy of (a) is diminished when the picture is inverted.] *Source:* (From E. G. Boring, "Size constance in a picture," *American Journal of Psychology, 77,* 1964, 497. Reprinted with permission of University of Illinois Press.)

size constancy is continuously taken into account as we interact spatially with the environment. Moreover, the spatial cues that trigger size constancy may be subtle.

DEMONSTRATION:
The Role of Distance Cues for Size Constancy

A variation of the pencil demonstration given in Figure 9.21 illustrates the points made above. Hold up two identical pencils, with their erasers upright, side by side, about 2 in. apart and about 10 in. from your face. Observe that the eraser tops appear the same size. Then keep one pencil at 10 in. and move the other one levelly to about 20 in. from your face while maintaining the same 2-in. separation be-

tween the two pencils. Note that although one pencil is now twice as far from your face as the other, both erasers continue to appear the same size. This is due to size constancy. Now close one eye and move the near pencil laterally until the image of its eraser appears next to the image of the far eraser. At this point, note that the two erasers appear quite different in size; the eraser of the near pencil is larger than the eraser of the pencil held at 20 in. Viewing in this fashion, you have experienced the effect of a reduction in the distance cues ordinarily used in dealing with the visual environment: when cues are reduced, size constancy is weakened. (The breakdown of size constancy is not due to monocular viewing per se. In fact, closing one eye not only enables you to align the images of the two erasers retinally, it reduces some of the background distance cues, and it eliminates the distracting double images created by viewing nearby objects with binocular vision. As we will observe in a classic experiment described in the next section, size constancy for more distant objects is quite good with monocular viewing. In general, that experiment reveals a clear causal link between distance cues and size constancy.)

The Holway–Boring Experiment

The classic **Holway–Boring experiment** (1941) on size constancy examines several of its influences. In the experiment, the observer was stationed at the intersection of two long, darkened corridors, as illustrated in Figure 10.5. An adjustable, lighted comparison disk was placed 10 ft (about 3 m) from the observer in one corridor; standard disks were placed one at a time at a number of distances varying from 10 to 120 ft (about 3 to 36 m) in the other corridor. The sizes of the standard disks were graduated so as to cast the same-sized retinal image (a visual angle of 1°) at every distance from the viewer's eye. In other words, the physical sizes of the disks were increased in proportion to their distance from the observer so as to always project the same-sized retinal image.

The viewer's task was to adjust the comparison disk so that it would look the same size as the standard disk. There were four experimental conditions: condition 1 provided normal binocular observation; condition 2 allowed monocular viewing only; condition 3 allowed monocular viewing through a small hole, called an *artificial pupil,* which removed some of the sources of information normally used in distance perception, such as binocular cues and head movements; and condition 4 provided an even further reduction of distance cues by surrounding each standard disk with black cloth, creating a tunnel of black cloth,

virtually eliminating the distance cues originally provided by the floor, walls, and ceiling.

The amount of constancy exhibited in each condition is shown in Figure 10.6. The top dashed line shows what the judgments would ideally be for perfect constancy: the adjusted size of the comparison disk would be exactly the same size as the standard disks that increased in size with distance. The bottom dashed line indicates the complete lack of constancy: the adjusted size of the comparison disk would be set to the size of the standard disk at 10 ft (namely, a visual angle of 1°), regardless of the distance at which the standard disk was viewed—in short, a *retinal* match.

With binocular and monocular viewing (conditions 1 and 2), the achievement of size constancy was excellent, indicating that it makes little difference whether one eye or both eyes are used. Both sets of adjustments conform closely to what would be predicted if size constancy were perfect.

Artificial restrictions on observation, as in condition 3, in which viewing was through a small hole, caused a big drop in constancy. Condition 4 produced an almost total loss of distance cues and a greater decrease in constancy. Judgments in these two conditions, intentionally less influenced by distance cues, were based mainly on the size of the image projected on the retina. In other words, with few or no distance cues available, perception is based on the size of the visual angle projected on the retina. Hence, when the observer could see only the disks surrounded by darkness, their sizes were judged to be about the same at all distances. *Constancy almost disappeared with a complete lack of distance cues.* Clearly, then, distance cues and a visual framework are critical for size constancy.

□ *figure* **10.5** Schematic diagram of experimental arrangement used by Holway and Boring for testing size constancy. The comparison stimulus was located 10 ft from the observer. The standard stimuli, located at various positions from 10 to 120 ft, always projected a visual angle of 1°. (After Holway and Boring, 1941.)

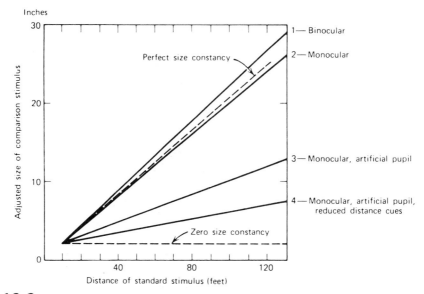

□ *figure* **10.6** Size constancy as function of distance cues. A standard disk was displayed at various distances from the observer, shown on the *x*-axis. The physical size of the standard disk was increased as its distance was increased to maintain a constant size retinal *image* (a visual angle of 1°). The observer adjusted a comparison disk to match the size of each of the standard disks, shown on the *y*-axis. The results were that size constancy was high for conditions 1 and 2, which allowed distance cues provided by binocular and monocular vision, respectively. In condition 3, which significantly reduced distance cues, size constancy was correspondingly reduced; and when all distance cues were eliminated, as in condition 4, size constancy was almost totally lacking. In condition 4, the perception of the disks was based almost entirely on the size of the retinal image. Thus, the degree of size constancy varied with the amount of visual information. (After Holway & Boring, 1941.)

□ **DEMONSTRATION:**
Reducing Size Constancy

A simple demonstration suggested by Dember, Jenkins, and Teyler (1984) allows you to simulate some aspects of the Holway–Boring experiment and, to an extent, to experience firsthand the strong influence of distance cues on perceiving an environment composed of objects with a constant size. First, find a visual environment where several people are seated, some near you, some far away (a classroom or library setting is fine). Then examine the apparent sizes of the heads of the people. Consistent with size constancy, all the heads, regardless of distance, will appear about the same size. Now close one eye, hold the thumb and forefinger of one hand close to your opened eye, and visually isolate or "bracket" the head belonging to one of the persons nearby (Figure 10.7); then do the same for the head of a distant person, keeping your hand at the same distance from your eye in both cases. You will observe that the head of the distant person shrinks considerably. The reason for this change in perceived head size is that, by bracketing the image of the head, you are seeing it with distance cues somewhat blocked out—similar to condition 3 of the Holway–Boring experiment. It follows that with a reduction in distance cues, perception depends on retinal size. This means that size constancy is weakened, and objects that ordinarily remain constant in size (e.g., people's heads) appear to vary.

Emmert's Law It should now be clear that the perceived size of an object is based on its retinal image size *and* its apparent distance. The relationship between these two factors is a powerful one that is

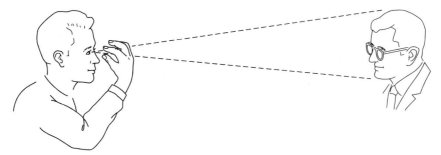

□ *figure* **10.7** Viewing conditions for reducing size constancy.

expressed in many spatial situations. Under certain conditions, the perceived size of an object, when it is viewed as an *afterimage* (an image that persists after the original stimulus ends; see Chapter 5), is determined by the distance of the surface on which the image is projected (Figure 10.8). The perceived size of the afterimage is directly proportional to the distance of the projection surface from the eye, a relationship known as **Emmert's law** (named after E. Emmert, who discovered it in 1881). This relationship—that the more distant an afterimage appears, the larger it appears—can be stated as a general equation:

$$Ps = k(RIs \times Pd)$$

where *Ps* is the perceived size of the afterimage, *k* is a constant, *RIs* is the size of the retinal image, and *Pd* is the perceived distance of the afterimage. For example, if the retinal image (*RIs*) is constant in size (as in Figure 10.8), increasing the distance of the sur-

face on which the afterimage is projected (*Pd*) will increase the perceived size of the afterimage (*Ps*).

□ **DEMONSTRATION:**
Emmert's Law

Emmert's law can be easily demonstrated. Stare at a small black shape on a white background, or the shape given in Figure 5.8 of Chapter 5, for about 30 to 40 seconds to overstimulate and fatigue a specific area of the retina, producing an afterimage. Then hold a sheet of white paper about 12 in. in front of you, focus at a spot on its center, and observe the size of the afterimage. Next, move the sheet of paper to arm's length and focus in the same manner. The afterimage will now appear about twice as large (since the projection surface—the sheet of paper—is now about twice as far). If you can still maintain

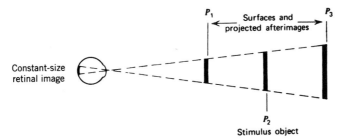

□ *figure* **10.8** Outline of Emmert's law. A simple stimulus object shown at surface P_2 is fixated on for about 30 to 40 seconds to form an afterimage. Immediately afterward, the fixation falls on a surface located nearer (P_1) or farther (P_3). The afterimage will thus appear to be projected on the fixated surface, and its perceived size will be directly proportional to the distance of the fixated surface from the eye. Note that regardless of the distance of the fixated surface from the eye, the retinal image remains constant in size.

the afterimage (you can aid this by blinking), focus on a more distant surface such as a blank far wall: the afterimage will appear even larger (but in direct proportion to its greater distance).

Thus, according to Emmert's law, the afterimage appears to grow larger as the surface on which it projects increases in distance. This is because the area on the retina responsible for the afterimage is constant in size. Remember that the afterimage is produced by fatiguing a constant area on the retina. It follows, then, as the distance of the projection surface is increased, the size of an object necessary to reflect a constant retinal size must be proportionally increased. In other words, the size of the area covered by the afterimage varies directly with its distance. Although Emmert's law specifically applies to afterimages, it is actually a special case of the general relationship between retinal image size and apparent distance that applies directly to conditions promoting size constancy: namely, that with the size of the retinal image held constant, perceived size varies with perceived distance.

Limits of Size Constancy Size constancy has limits. It appears to be less effective when we view over great expanses, even though distance cues of the environment may be available. You may experience the breakdown of size constancy when looking down from a tall building or peering over the edge of a steep cliff. In these viewing conditions, people, trees, cars, and so on assume a toy-like quality. Instead of compensating for distance and interpreting the small retinal images as reflected from normal-sized objects, but located far away—that is, triggering size constancy—you perceive the images as coming from small objects. In other words, when viewing from considerable height, the apparent size of objects is based mainly on retinal size. This may be due largely to the unfamiliarity of the extreme viewing conditions, especially when looking down or up. At any rate, there appears to be no adaptive benefit for the human of a mechanism to compensate for the very small retinal images induced by viewing objects from far

above or below—that is, for a size constancy mechanism for unusual, infrequent situations.

Shape Constancy

We have seen that an object viewed under very different conditions of illumination may appear equally light and that an object viewed from different distances with different projected sizes may appear the same size. In addition, an object may appear to possess the same *shape* even when the angle of view changes radically. This last property is called **shape constancy.** A typical window frame or a door appears to be more or less rectangular no matter at what angle it is viewed. Yet geometrically it casts a rectangular image *only* when it is viewed from a certain position directly in front of the viewer (Figure 10.9).

Shape constancy is typically assessed when a subject judges the shape of an object such as a circular plate or disk tilted or slanted at an angle. It has been found that the estimated shape (see Figure 10.10) obtained by having subjects draw the shape of a tilted disk or match it against a series of ellipses is more circular than the elliptical shape projected on the observers' retinas (Thouless, 1931).

Shape constancy maintains the perceptual integrity of the object's shape. As in size constancy, the degree of shape constancy varies with the availability of spatial information on orientation, such as the tilt of the object or the slant of the surface on which the object rests (Sedgwick, 1986). In general, shape constancy varies with cues to the distance and displacement of all spatial aspects of the object. It follows that when there is no visual information on the object's position relative to the viewer, shape constancy is impaired or breaks down completely.

Shape Constancy and Apparent Depth When we view certain configurations, the processes underlying shape constancy may be automatic and may not be voluntarily suppressed (Shepard, 1981). As we saw in Figure 10.9, when we look at certain two-dimensional drawings, we tend to interpret them as two-dimensional drawings of three-dimensional objects. Thus doors, cubes, and even unfamiliar shapes appear rectilinear, regardless of their

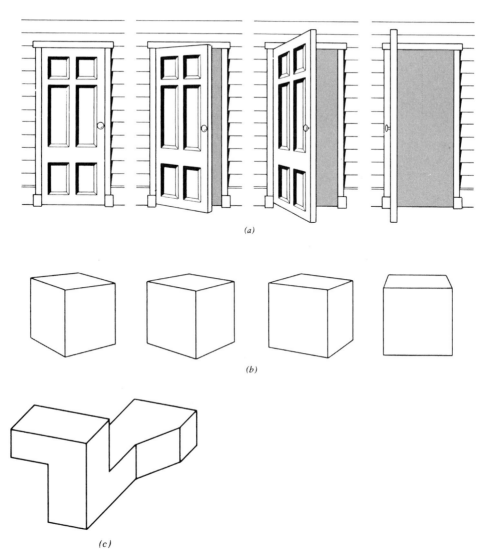

□ *figure 10.9* Shape constancy. (*a*) Various projected images from an opening door are quite different, yet a rectangular door is perceived. (*b*) Similarly, various projections of trapezoids and parallelograms yield the perception of the faces of a cube as seen from different perspectives. (*c*) A drawing of an unfamiliar object that appears to be a composite of many right angles and rectangular shapes. However, as depicted, the figure does not contain any right angles. (Devised by Noah in 1988.)

actual retinal projections as trapezoids, parallelograms, and other unusual shapes. In fact, it is difficult to see these configurations as comprised of trapezoids and parallelograms, all lying on the same flat plane. Our difficulty in seeing certain two-dimensional drawings as merely flat linear shapes, independent of any

three-dimensional interpretation, is illustrated in the perception of the shapes in Figure 10.11a and 10.11b. In Figure 10.11a two identical shaded parallelograms are presented, one with its long axis vertically oriented and the other with its long axis horizontally oriented. Most observers perceive only a small effect of appar-

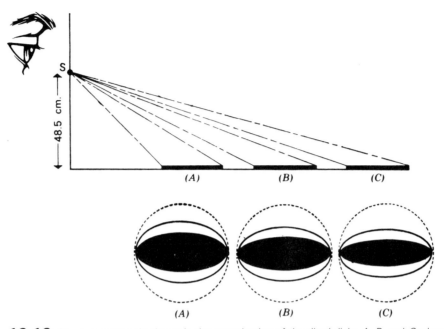

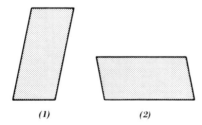

□ **figure 10.10** Shape constancy is shown in the reproduction of the tilted disks *A, B,* and *C* whose projected shapes are indicated by the black figures. The broken line shows the physical shape, and the continuous line gives the reproduced shape. The reproduced shape indicates that the perceived shape is more circular than the projected shape. (From Thouless, 1931.)

ent depth; accordingly, only a small difference in apparent size is noted between the two. However, as shown in Figure 10.11*b,* when these parallelograms appear as the top surfaces of two-dimensional drawings that strongly suggest three-dimensional rectang-

□ **figure 10.11a** The shaded parallelogram with its long axis vertically oriented (*1*) is identical to the shaded parallelogram with its long axis horizontally oriented (*2*). For most observers only a slight variation in size may be perceived and the physical identity of the figures is clear. However, a striking change in their appearance occurs when they are each seen as parts of more complex figures, as shown in Figure 10.11*b.*

ular shapes in depth, a startling change in their appearance occurs. This tendency toward three-dimensionality and depth biases the observer to perceive the parallelogram with the long vertical axis (*1*) as representing a foreshortened rectangle sloping back in depth. In this context, it looks much longer and more narrow than the rectangle portrayed by the physically identical parallelogram in (*2*).

Finally, we must emphasize that the effects of constancy result from the interplay of many factors. An obvious one, which likely plays some role in all the constancies, is familiarity of the objects in the visual field. As we noted with lightness constancy, experience and familiarity may stabilize our perception of the visual input in spite of continual variations and apparent distortions of objects and surrounding stimuli. However, constancy equally affects unfamiliar stimuli. Moreover, constancy appears very early in human perceptual development (e.g., Cook & Birch, 1984; Day & McKenzie, 1981), and it is found in animals far below the human (e.g., Ingle, 1985). In other

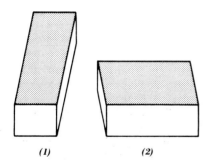

□ *figure* **10.11b** The parallelograms of Figure 10.11a, as surfaces of apparent rectangular shapes. When embedded in representations of three-dimensional shapes in depth, the two shaded identical parallelograms appear quite different from each other in size and shape. (Based on Shepard, 1981.)

words, constancy occurs where learning and familiarity are unlikely to play much of a role.

Perceptual constancy enables the perceptual world to correspond closely to the physical world. In this sense, perceptual constancy is a clear instance of an adaptive, biologically relevant mechanism. Ironically, however, there are conditions in which constancy seems to reduce the integrity and accuracy of our perception, leading us to distorted or erroneous perceptions—*illusory perceptions.* In the sections that follow, we will examine how this happens.

VISUAL ILLUSIONS

Numerous visual events carry potential perceptual ambiguity, and under certain conditions they may provide a distorted, illusory view of the physical environment. It would be an oversimplification, however, to dismiss these illusory events as mere curiosities, errors of perception, or occasional exceptions to perceptual constancy. Rather, they are the consistent effects of ongoing perceptual processes and mechanisms used in perceiving space. Thus, the study of illusions may give clues to the more general mechanisms and principles of space perception. Accordingly, in the remainder of this chapter, we will discuss some representative visual illusions, presenting some of the attempts to explain them and, where possible, attempt to relate them to general mechanisms of space perception.

TRANSACTIONALISM AND THE AMES ILLUSIONS

We begin by introducing a provocative approach to spatial perception that is highlighted by a related set of illusions. They were devised by Adelbert Ames Jr., (1946), and have particular relevance to constancy and the cues to depth and distance. They were an outgrowth of his examination of **aniseikonia** (literally, "unequal images") at the Dartmouth Eye Clinic. Aniseikonia is an optical anomaly in which the image in one eye is larger than the image in the other, resulting in a significant disparity between the images in each eye. This effect can be simulated with a special lens worn over one eye (Figure 10.12). However, although optically there is a marked difference in the size of the two images—with confusing depth cues—persons with aniseikonia often see relatively normally. Objects and surfaces such as floors and walls appear to be rectilinear, although the images on the retina are sufficiently different to produce severe distortions.

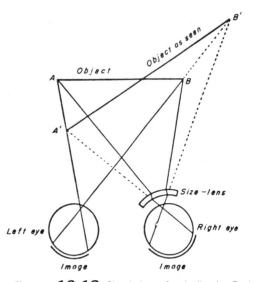

□ *figure* **10.12** Simulation of aniseikonia. Both eyes gaze on object AB. However, a size-distorting lens worn over the right eye reflects an image different in size from the one reflected on the left eye. As indicated by the dashed projection lines, the image of the object (A'B') reflected on the right eye is considerably larger than the image on the left eye, creating incorrect and confusing depth cues. (Based on Woodworth & Schlosberg, 1954.)

The seeming contradiction between the accurate perception and the distorted optical stimulation led Ames and his colleagues (see Kilpatrick, 1961) to theorize that spatial *experience* in dealing with specific objects and surfaces plays a dominant role in normal perception. This theory, called **Transactionalism,** proposes that visual perception is based largely on experiences in dealing with the visual environment.

Fundamental to Transactional theory is the fact that almost any image projected onto the retina can be produced by an unlimited number of objects (Figure 10.13). However, what is actually perceived is usually limited. According to the Transactionalists, this limitation is due to the experience acquired during the individual's active interactions, or *transactions,* with the environment. Thus, the perceptual alternatives associated with any retinal image become focused and restricted in a way that conforms to the experience

gained from interacting with the world of real objects. In other words, according to the Transactionalists, we *assume* (and therefore perceive) the world to be organized in a manner that derives from and coincides with our past experience with it.

The Ames Illusions

The Ames illusions are particularly effective in illustrating the role of experience in perception. When observed—generally under restricted and contrived conditions (i.e., without binocular and motion cues)—they highlight the assumptions about spatial relations acquired during environmental interactions. The illusions are most striking when the individual is forced to violate one set of assumptions about the spatial environment to preserve another. Although there are numerous Ames demonstrations, we will consider the two most famous ones.

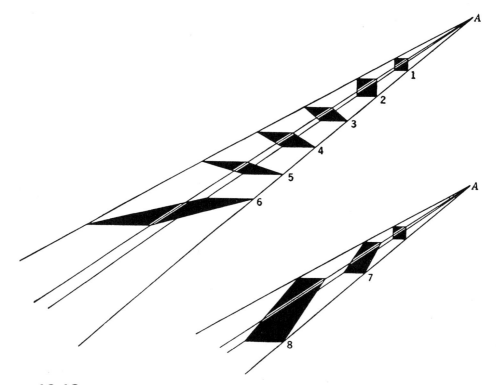

□ *figure 10.13* An infinite number of surfaces, differently oriented with regard to the line of sight, may project the same visual angle at *A* as does the square at 1 and therefore may be perceived as a square when accompanying cues to space are lacking. (From S. H. Bartley, in *Handbook of Experimental Psychology*, edited by S. S. Stevens, John Wiley, New York, 1951, p. 924. Reprinted by permission of the publisher.)

The Trapezoidal Window The dramatic perceptual effects of the rotating trapezoid must be observed to be fully appreciated. The physical device consists of a trapezoidal surface with panes and shadows painted on both sides so as to appear convincingly as a partially turned rectangular window (Figure 10.14); the object is, in fact, a **trapezoidal window.** When observed frontally, it appears to be rectangular, but turned at an angle (so long as there are not enough depth and distance cues to indicate that it is not actually slanted or turned). The window is mounted on a rod connected to a motor that can rotate at a slow constant speed (about 3–6 rpm) about its vertical axis. When it is observed with one eye from about 3 m (about 10 ft) or with both eyes at 6 m or more, the trapezoidal window seems to rotate through 180°, and then seems to stop momentarily and reverse direction. That is, it is perceived not as a rotating trapezoid but as an *oscillating* rectangular window reversing its direction once every 180°.

In terms of the available stimulus information, there are two mutually exclusive perceptual alternatives: an oscillating rectangle *or* a rotating trapezoid. However, based on the viewer's assumptions created by past experience, this ambiguous stimulus figure is usually perceived as a normal rectangular window turned slightly. Therefore, if it is seen as a rectangular window, its movement must be perceived as an oscillation because the continuous array of images could occur only from a rectangular surface that oscillates.

The perception of the true motion of the surface—rotation—is inconsistent with the assumption that the figure is a rectangular window. In normal rotation of a rectangular surface, the retinal projection of only the farther edge reduces in size. However, in a rotating trapezoidal window, one of its sides remains *always* longer than the other. Hence, the longer side continuously appears closer to the viewer, even when it is physically farther away. This sort of image could occur only from a moving rectangular surface when it oscillates. Hence, it follows that the projection of the apparently nearer long side appears to oscillate.

To assess the effect of past experience and assumptions about the environment on the illusory effect of the rotating trapezoidal window, Allport and Pettigrew (1957) performed a cross-cultural test of the illusion. The rotating trapezoid illusion was presented to subjects from cultures that differed in their experiences with rectangular environments. Some subjects came from cultures with almost no windows and surfaces with right angles and straight lines, whereas other subjects came from typical urban environments. When the rotating trapezoid was presented under optimal conditions for producing the illusion, all subjects showed the illusion (i.e., perceived oscillation rather than actual rotation) despite their cultural differences. However, under conditions that were marginal for perceiving the illusion (i.e., close up with binocular vision), the subjects with less experience with rectangles were less susceptible to the illusion. (Attempts have been made to explain the rotating trapezoid illusion without assuming that past experience leads one to perceive rectangular shapes; see e.g., Braunstein, 1976.)

Axis of rotation

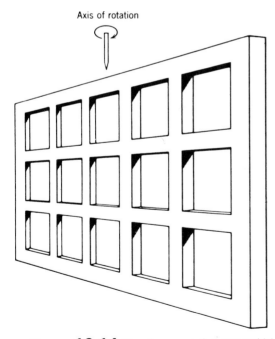

▭ *figure* **10.14** The Ames rotating trapezoidal window. A rendering of the frontal view (perpendicular to the line of sight) of the rotating trapezoid. It was designed to appear as a rectangular window slanted to the left (as it does here).

The Distorted Room Figure 10.15*a* suggests a view of a specially built room. The room is

(a)

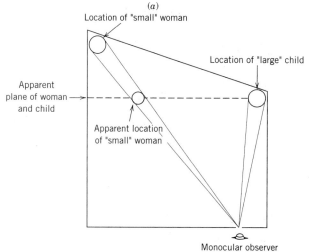

(b)

▭ *figure* **10.15** The distorted room illusion. The woman on the left in (a) appears distorted relative to the child on the right. Actually, the woman is much taller than the child. The illusion is created by the design of the room, as indicated by its floor plan in (b). The room is constructed so as to make the woman and child appear equidistant from the viewer. Actually, however, the woman is standing about twice as far away from the viewer as is the child. (*Source: a* from Barron Wolman/Woodfin Camp & Associates.)

usually seen through a small peephole that allows only a monocular view, eliminating many depth and distance cues. Under these conditions, most observers see two individuals, one unusually smaller than the other, standing at the back wall of an ordinary room.

It is an illusory perception—called the *distorted room illusion*—since the actual sizes of the individuals are the reverse of what they appear to be, whereas the room is quite unusual. In fact, the "small" woman is really located farther away from the viewer than the "large" child. She does not appear so, according to the Transactionalists, due to the compelling influence of assumptions about the environment formed by past experience. They contend that due to extensive experience with rectangular rooms, the viewer assumes that the two people are standing against the usual background of a rectangular room. However, the floor, ceiling, some walls, and the far windows of the room are actually trapezoidal surfaces. As the outline structure in Figure 10.15*b* shows, the room is carefully constructed so as to create the apparent size distortion. In particular, the left corner of the room is about twice as far from the viewer as the right corner. The more distant aspects of the room are correspondingly increased in size so that, when seen in perspective, the near and far parts appear to be at the same distance from the observer. As with the rotating trapezoid, there are two perceptual alternatives in the distorted room illusion: two persons of normal size relative to each other, at different locations from the observer and standing against a trapezoidal surface; or two persons, unusually different in size, standing against a rectangular background. The typical perception is of a rectangular room with the sizes of the occupants distorted. In other words, perceptually, the assumption of a stable rectangular environment overrides the physical conditions. This follows since rooms are almost always rectangular, whereas objects within them do differ in size.

The rotating trapezoid and the distorted room are only two of a series of unusual demonstrations by Ames and his colleagues in support of Transactionalism. However, all point to the same conclusion: under the proper physical conditions, past experience is critical in determining space perception.

ILLUSIONS OF DEPTH, DISTANCE, AND CONSTANCY

The Transactionalist approach exemplified by the Ames illusions illustrates the role of learning and past experience in spatial perception. However, they do so by manipulating false depth and distance cues that deceive the viewer's impression of the shape and location of objects and surfaces. We now continue our examination of the role played by spatial factors such as depth, distance, and constancy factors, focusing on four primary illusions: the moon, Müller-Lyer, Ponzo, and Poggendorff illusions. Although they are very different from each other in detail, they share an explanation based, in part, on the pickup and processing of distance cues and the use of size constancy.

THE MOON ILLUSION

In the **moon illusion,** the moon appears larger (by as much as 1.5 times) when it is viewed at the horizon rather than at the zenith, although the projected images in both cases are identical. In fact, the moon (as well as the sun) occupies a far smaller fraction of the visible sky than most individuals assume. The visual angle projected on the retina by the moon is almost exactly 0.5° (Tolansky, 1964). An object as small as 0.25 in. (about 6 mm) across, held 30 in. (76 cm) from the eye, projects a visual angle of about 0.5°, yet when it is held in the correct position, it is large enough to blot out the image of the moon. Interest in the moon illusion has been extensive, and many explanations have been offered (see Hershenson, 1989, for a collection of such explanations). Several prominent attempts to explain it follow.

Angle-of-Regard Hypothesis

Boring (1943; Holway & Boring, 1940; Taylor & Boring, 1942) and, more recently, Suzuki (1991) proposed that the apparent size of the moon is affected by the angle of the eyes relative to the head. That is, according to the **angle-of-regard hypothesis,** the moon illusion is produced by changes in the position of the eyes in the head accompanying changes in the angle of elevation of the moon. In one task, Holway and Boring (1940) had subjects match the moon, as they saw it, with one of a series of disks of light projected on a nearby screen. Viewing the horizon moon with eyes level, most subjects selected a disk considerably larger than the disk chosen when their eyes were raised 30° to match the zenith moon. Similarly, when a subject lying on a flat table viewed the zenith moon from a supine position, with no raising or lowering of the eyes, or when a subject viewing from a supine position hung his or her head over the edge of a table to view the horizon moon with the eyes elevated, the illusion was reversed: the horizon moon appeared smaller than the zenith moon. This latter effect can also be obtained by doubling over and looking at the horizon moon between one's legs.

Boring concluded that the moon illusion depends on raising or lowering the eyes with respect to the head. Mere movements of the neck, head, and body are not causal factors. However, there is no convincing psychological process to explain Boring's evidence that visual space is altered with vertical eye movements. As he stated in 1943:

> *There is no satisfactory . . . theory for explaining this phenomenon. It is not due to physical causes outside the visual mechanism. . . . There remains only the suggestion that the effort of raising or lowering the eyes shrinks the perceived size of the moon. . . . Since we do not know why muscular effort in the visual mechanism should affect visually perceived size . . . we are forced to leave the problem there without ultimate solution. (pp. 59–60)*

Apparent Distance Hypothesis

An explanation of the moon illusion based on perceptual factors can be traced to Ptolemy (ca. 150 A.D.), the second-century astronomer and geometrician. He proposed that an object seen through filled space, such as the moon viewed across terrain at the horizon, is perceived as being farther away than an object located physically at the same distance but seen through empty space, as in the case of the moon at its zenith. The projected images of the moon in both cases are identical in size, but the horizon moon *appears farther away.* It also appears larger, following from the linear relationship between apparent size and apparent distance that we introduced in our discussion of the factors that promote size constancy. Thus, if two objects project the same-sized retinal image but appear at different distances from the viewer, the object that appears farther from the viewer will typically be perceived as larger (Figure 10.16). This relationship is called the **apparent distance hypothesis** (also called the **size-distance invariance hypothesis**). Applied here, the moon appears farther away at the horizon and hence appears larger. You

may recognize this as an expression of *size constancy:* that is, size constancy is triggered by the presence of depth and distance cues that cause the horizon moon to appear larger.

Kaufman and Rock (1962a, 1962b; Rock & Kaufman, 1962) examined the apparent distance hypothesis extensively. They questioned the angle-of-regard hypothesis and, in particular, the method used to determine the moon's apparent size. They argued that because the real moon is so far away from the observer, it appears as a large object but one of indeterminate size. To judge the size of a stimulus of indeterminate size with nearby comparison disks having a visibly specific size is to ask the viewer to compare things that are essentially different. Instead, Kaufman and Rock had subjects compare and match against each other two artificial "moons" seen against the sky. This, of course, is fundamentally the same sort of comparison as in the original illusion, though in the original case the two real moons are separated by both space and time. Kaufman and Rock used a projection device that permitted an observer to view an adjustable disk of light (artificial moon) on the sky. Using a pair of these devices, the observer was able to compare a standard disk set at one position (e.g., the horizon) with a variable disk set at another position (e.g., the zenith). The size of the variable disk chosen by the observer to match the size of the standard provided a measure of the magnitude of the illusion.

The result was that, regardless of eye elevation, the horizon moon was perceived as being much larger than the zenith moon. From a series of studies, these researchers concluded that the horizon moon appears farther away than the zenith moon and that this impression of the horizon moon's greater distance is produced by the terrain viewed as a plane extended outward from the observer.

As we noted earlier in regard to size constancy, if two objects have the same projected size but appear to lie at different distances from the viewer, the one that seems farther away will look larger. Therefore, it follows from the apparent distance notion of Kaufman and Rock that the apparently farther moon should appear larger. In other words, due to size constancy, perceived size is a function of perceived distance; with retinal size constant, the greater the apparent distance, the larger the perceived size.

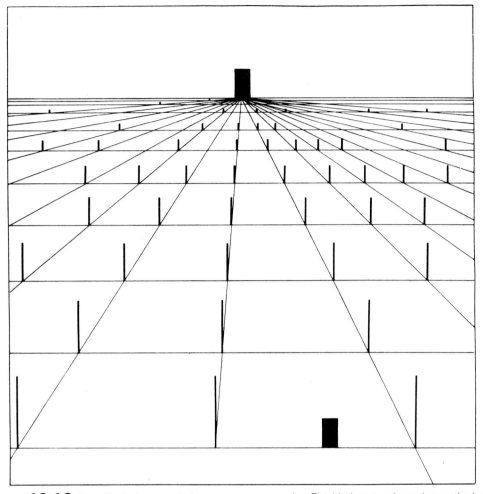

◻ *figure 10.16* The effect of apparent distance on apparent size. The black rectangle resting on the horizon is drawn so as to appear farther away, hence larger than the one in the foreground, although they are identical in size. (From I. Rock and L. Kaufman, "The moon illusion. II." *Science, 136,* 1962, p. 1029. Copyright © 1962 by the American Association for the Advancement of Science.)

Criticism of Apparent Distance Hypotheses: The Distance Paradox

While appealing, the apparent distance notion cannot account for all instances of the moon illusion. For example, Suzuki (1991) compared the judgments of light stimuli projected on the horizon with those projected on the zenith of a dome screen of a completely darkened planetarium. This environment provided few if any distance cues, yet a reliable moon illusion effect was obtained. However, more critical to the apparent distance theory is the frequent observation that the horizon moon not only appears larger than the zenith moon, it also appears *closer* than it! This appearance is referred to as the **distance paradox** or sometimes as the *further-larger-nearer* phenomenon. This poses a serious problem for the apparent distance notion, which holds that the horizon moon appears larger because distance cues associated with the terrain make it look farther away than the zenith moon, since the horizon moon often seems closer than the zenith moon. Kaufman and Rock (1989; see also Coren & Aks, 1990) explain the distance paradox of the horizon moon as due to a *serial* or *sequence* effect that is required in processing distance and size information in order to make size and distance judgments, respectively. That is, judgments of the size of the moon and its distance from the observer are *not* made simultaneously or based on the same set of visual cues. According to the apparent distance notion and size constancy, the horizon moon is perceived to be located farther away, and therefore appears larger than the zenith moon. This is the result of an immediate, unintentional or *unconscious inference* about the relation between apparent distance and apparent size typical of size constancy. However, when a distance judgment about the horizon moon is made, it is the result of a deliberate, *conscious decision* based on its apparent size. Since the horizon moon appears larger than the zenith moon, it must also be closer.

Coren and Aks (1990) explain the distance paradox—that the horizon moon appears larger *and* closer than the zenith moon—as follows:

> *This result is, of course, quite consistent and non-paradoxical if we accept the idea that we are dealing with a serial system, where first the registered depth cue triggers size constancy and results in distortion of the size of the moon. The perceptually enlarged horizon moon is then processed to evaluate apparent distance. It appears closer because it is larger. The two judgments are made on different data bases. . . . Thus one illusory percept (the size illusion) serves as the source of a secondary illusion (the apparent-distance difference) in the moon illusion. (p. 377)*

Relative Size Hypothesis

Although the apparent distance hypothesis is the most influential account of the moon illusion, numerous other explanations, largely cognitive, abound. Restle (1970) proposed an explanation that does not depend on processing apparent distance information. The basic assumption of his *relative size hypothesis* is that the perceived size of an object depends not only on its retinal size but also on the size of its immediate

visual surround. The smaller its boundary or frame of reference, the larger its apparent size. Accordingly, if the moon is judged relative to its immediate surround, the horizon moon appears to be larger because it is compared with a small space (1° to the horizon). At the zenith the moon appears smaller because it is located in a large expanse of empty visual space (90° to the horizon). In this case, the moon illusion is considered an example of the relativity of perceived size; the same object may appear large in one context and small in another. Some role, perhaps subordinate to a version of the apparent distance hypothesis, is quite possibly played by relative size (see also Baird, 1982).

There are many other explanations for the moon illusion that we cannot describe here (see, e.g., Hershenson, 1989, and McCready, 1986). However, explanations aside, it should not be surprising that there is a constant error in perceiving the moon. After all, in judging the size of the moon, we are actually attempting to appraise the size of a celestial object over 2000 miles in diameter viewed at a distance of about 250,000 miles!

THE MÜLLER-LYER ILLUSION

The illusion shown in Figure 10.17, known as the *Müller-Lyer illusion* since it was devised by Franz Müller-Lyer in 1889, is probably the most familiar and extensively studied geometric illusion.

Perspective-Constancy Theory

Although there are many theories to account for this distortion, we will deal first with extensions of a **perspective-constancy theory,** which holds that certain stimulus features, like the arrowheads of the Müller-Lyer figure, are indicators of apparent distance. The perspective-constancy theory has been elaborated by Gregory (1963, 1966, 1968) and Day (1972) to account for many size illusions. In the case of the Müller-Lyer figure, they contend that perspective features furnished by the arrowheads of the figure, however subtle, provide false distance cues. As a result, size constancy is inappropriately induced to compen-

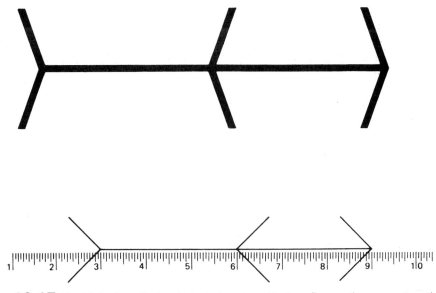

□ *figure* **10.17** The Müller-Lyer illusion. In both the top and bottom figures, the segment on the left appears longer than the one on the right, although the left and right segments are the same length. The bottom figure indicates that the illusion persists in spite of the presence of a disconfirming measure.

sate for the apparent distance of the line segments. The result is a consistent error in the perceived length of the lines.

An example illustrating this is given in Figure 10.18. Drawings of corners and edges in perspective are shown with corresponding outline drawings of Müller-Lyer figures. According to a perspective-constancy explanation, the Müller-Lyer figures, as well as the outline drawings, are two-dimensional projections of three-dimensional shapes in depth; hence, due to the operation of a size-constancy mechanism, parts of the illustration that appear farther away are perceived as larger. In other words, size constancy compensates for the apparent distance of objects—a compensatory correction that normally occurs for a diminishing retinal image size when distance is increased—but here it is *inappropriately* invoked.

Criticisms of the Perspective-Constancy Theory

While the perspective-constancy theory offers an appealing explanation of the Müller-Lyer illusion, it has not gone unchallenged. Figure 10.19 presents several variations of the Müller-

Lyer illusion. However, while all of the forms generate compelling illusory effects, several of them are inconsistent with the central requirement of the perspective-constancy explanation of the Müller-Lyer illusion: namely, that, due to linear perspective cues, some of the line segments or regions of the figure appear to be farther away from the viewer than others. Indeed, observe that examples (*c*) and (*d*) of Figure 10.19 seem to violate this requirement. Clearly, these variations of the Müller-Lyer illusion produce significant distortion effects, yet neither (*c*) nor (*d*) contains perspective or any other obvious source of apparent depth or distance information.

Further criticism of the perspective-constancy theory comes from the finding that blind and normally sighted, blindfolded persons examining solid forms of illusory figures by touch—and presumably lacking the apparent depth cues of a two-dimensional visual display—are also susceptible to the Müller-Lyer illusion (Lucca, Dellantonio, & Riggio, 1986; Patterson & Deffenbacher, 1972). Moreover, reliable illusory effects also occur with visual inspection of three-dimensional versions of the figure (DeLucia & Hoch-

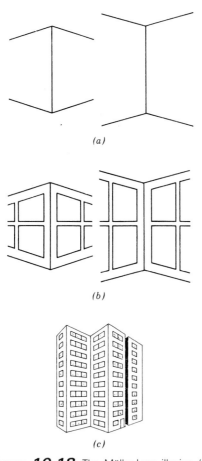

(a)

(b)

(c)

□ *figure* **10.18** The Müller-Lyer illusion (a) and perspective drawings of structures whose outlines match the illusion (b). The left drawing in (b) is characteristic of an outside corner of a building—the corner closer to the viewer. The right drawing in (b) suggests the inside corner of a building—the corner farther away from the viewer. Perspective causes an apparent enlargement of the vertical projection of the farthest corner to compensate for its apparently greater distance from the viewer. How this perspective-constancy notion accounts for the Müller-Lyer illusion may be more readily seen in (c), which depicts a building in perspective. Since when actually viewing such a building we see all its vertical extents as about the same height, we are obviously compensating for apparent distance: the apparent length of the farthest inside corner is enlarged and the nearer outside corner is reduced in apparent length.

berg, 1991; see also Nijhawan, 1991); accordingly, such stimuli do not project any apparent distance information and hence should not inappropriately invoke a size constancy mechanism. It seems, then, that the processes creating the Müller-Lyer illusion are not restricted to conditions providing perspective-distance cues and inappropriately promoting size constancy on a two-dimensional surface.

Finally, general applicability of a perspective-constancy notion is weakened by evidence that the Müller-Lyer illusion occurs with lower animals: it has been reported for the pigeon (Mallott & Mallott, 1970), the ringdove (Warden & Baar, 1929), the fish (cited in Gregory, 1966), and the fly (Geiger & Poggio, 1975). Understandably, it is not clear whether these animals are capable of interpreting the arrowheads or wings as perspective cues for depth or distance.

It should not necessarily be assumed from the above that apparent spatial cues and constancy are not causal factors. More likely, there is no single factor or phenomenon that determines the Müller-Lyer illusion. It seems reasonable to assume that the illusion results from the composite activity of several length-distorting mechanisms and that various factors, to different degrees, may affect or contribute to the Müller-Lyer illusion. For example, stimulus variables as diverse as the figure's color (Pollack & Jaeger, 1991) and the viewer's focus of attention (e.g., Pressey & Pressey, 1992) have been reported to affect the magnitude of the Müller-Lyer illusion. Finally, we should note evidence suggesting that the standard Müller-Lyer illusion is actually a composite of two distinct processes, one acting on the wings-inward version (causing an underestimation) and one affecting the wings-outward figure (producing overestimation) (Greist-Bousquet & Schiffman, 1981*a,* 1981*c*).

THE PONZO ILLUSION

An example of the **Ponzo illusion,** devised by Mario Ponzo in 1913, is given in Figure 10.20. Although the two horizontal lines are identical in length, the line

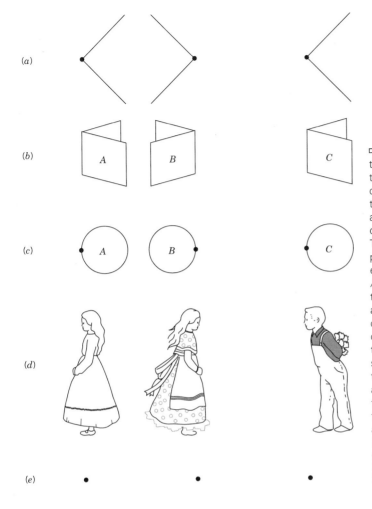

▭ *figure* **10.19** Müller-Lyer variations. (*a*) The distance between the dots on
the arrowheads facing each other on the left
does not appear equal to the distance between the dots on the arrowheads facing
away from each other on the right. (*b*) A three-
dimensional version of (*a*) is suggested here.
The distance between the corners of two apparently upright folded sheets of paper facing
each other, shown as the segment between
A and *B*, appears unequal to the corners of
the folds facing away from each other, shown
as the segment between *B* and *C*. (*c*) The
distance between the dots on the outer border of circles *A* and *B* does not appear equal
to the distance between the dots on the right
side of *B* and the left side of *C*. (*d*) The distance between the eyes of the girl on the left
and in the middle does not appear equal to
the distance between the eyes of the boy on
the right and the girl in the middle. (*e*) The
actual distances described in (*a*), (*b*), (*c*), and
(*d*) are physically equal, as indicated by the
equated line segments. (Part *b* is based on an
illustration from DeLucia & Hochberg, 1991; *d* is
based on a demonstration by Edward Gorey, 1979.)

closer to the point of convergence of the two bounding lines appears to be longer.

The Ponzo Illusion and Perspective

The Ponzo illusion is so closely linked to an explanation based on perspective (or a perspective-constancy
notion) that it is often referred to as the *Ponzo perspective figure*. The perspective feature in the figure is
obviously produced by the converging lines ordinarily
associated with distance: that is, the two oblique lines
appear to converge toward the horizon or a vanishing
point. Therefore, the perspective cue falsely suggests

depth or distance, with the result that the top horizontal line appears farther away. This provokes a size
constancy correction and, accordingly, it is perceived
as longer.

In examining the factors influencing this phenomenon, Leibowitz and his colleagues (1969) had subjects view, both monocularly and binocularly, the actual scene illustrated in Figure 10.21*b* from the point at
which the photograph was taken. In a second phase,
students were tested with the four two-dimensional
pictorial stimuli shown in Figure 10.21. The upper line
in the actual scene and in each subfigure of Figure
10.21 was held constant while a series of lower lines
were individually and randomly presented for an

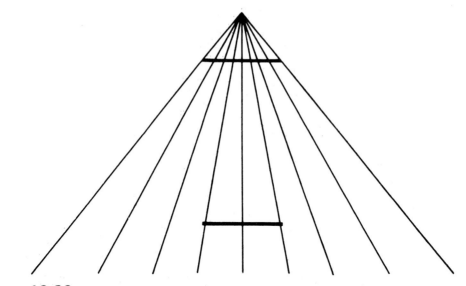

□ **figure 10.20** A version of the Ponzo illusion. The two horizontal lines are equal. (Devised by M. Ponzo in 1913.)

equality match with the upper line. The results for all viewing conditions are given in Figure 10.22. The findings generally indicate that the magnitude of the Ponzo illusion depends on the presence of a context of cues to depth: the greater the context—the more the photographs simulate the real scene—the greater the magnitude of the illusion. Figure 10.22 indicates that the upper of two lines, when shown alone (*d*), is slightly overestimated. This is likely due to the cue of elevation. The addition of converging lines (*a*) produces an illusion value of approximately 10% (percentage overestimation of the upper line). When the two horizontal lines are shown against texture cues (*c*), a 20% illusory effect results; the addition of perspective cues such as railroad tracks (*b*) results in about a 30% illusion. However, the greatest illusion resulted from the actual scene. This study is important in showing that the more the two-dimensional photograph approximates a representation of a three-dimensional scene—the more spatial cues to depth are available—the greater the magnitude of the illusion.

Leibowitz et al. also examined the role of experience on the magnitude of the Ponzo illusion depicted

in Figure 10.21 by comparing the judgments described earlier (made by Pennsylvania college students) with those made by students native to Guam who presumably had less experience with perspective cues, owing to the relatively flat terrain of Guam. The illusory effects were significantly higher for the Pennsylvania students than for the Guam students. The results thus suggest that the magnitude of the illusion depends upon previous experience with topographical features (as represented in Figures 10.21*b* and 10.21*c*). Other related findings (Leibowitz & Pick, 1972) indicate that experience with pictorial depth (as in two-dimensional printed material and media sources such as photographs, movies, and television) similarly affects the magnitude of the Ponzo illusion.

The Ponzo Illusion and Framing Effects

Although a perspective-constancy explanation of the Ponzo illusion appears reasonable and a constancy mechanism likely plays a dominant role, it is probably not the complete explanation. For example, when the interior lines are changed from their normal horizontal

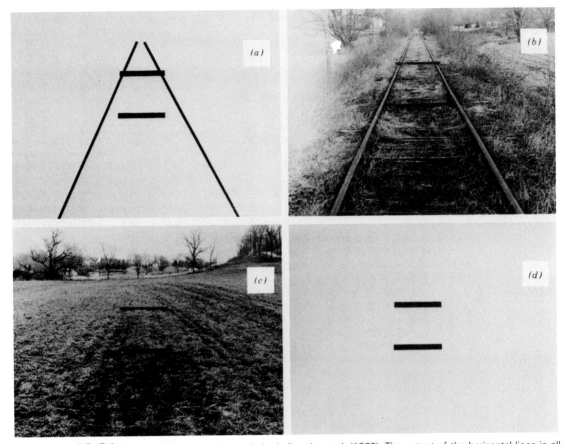

□ figure 10.21 The stimuli used in the study by Leibowitz et al. (1969). The extent of the horizontal lines in all figures is the same. (*Source:* From Leibowitz, H. W., Brislin, R., Perlmutter, L., & Hennessy, R. Ponzo perspective illusion as a manifestation of space perception. *Science, 166,* 1969, p. 1175. Copyright © by the American Association for the Advancement of Science. Reprinted by permission of the authors and publisher.)

orientation to a vertical orientation, the illusion is eliminated (Gillam, 1980; Schiffman & Thompson, 1978). Moreover, there is evidence to suggest that a factor in addition to implied distance and constancy may help produce the Ponzo illusion. An alternative approach to explaining the illusion is based on difference in the degree of enclosure, or *framing,* of the two horizontal lines—that is, the gap between the two horizontal lines and the surrounding converging lines (e.g., Fisher, 1973; Jordan & Randall, 1987; the framing notion is reminiscent of Restle's *relative size hypothesis* applied to the moon illusion). According to this notion, the difference in the separation, or gap, of the

two horizontal lines from the framing converging lines may determine, or at least contribute to, the magnitude of the distortion. In other words, the *closer* a line segment is to its enclosing border or frame, the longer it appears. In fact, the apparently longer horizontal line of Figure 10.20, located near the vertex of the surrounding oblique lines, does lie closer to the borders than the line located near the diverging region. Several variations in the **framing effects** of horizontal lines devoid of obvious perspective cues are presented in Figure 10.23. Accordingly, an effect based on the proximity of adjacent stimuli in framing the two horizontal lines, apart from any apparent

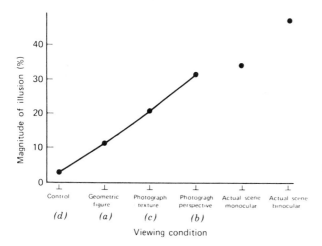

 figure 10.22 The magnitude of the Ponzo illusion for the various conditions of the experiment by Leibowitz et al. (1969). The magnitude of the illusion represents the percentage overestimation of the upper member of the pairs of horizontal lines shown in the preceding figure. (After Leibowitz et al., 1969.)

distance cues, may help contribute to the Ponzo illusion.

The pigeon appears subject to the framing effect of the Ponzo illusion (Fujita, Blough, & Blough, 1991, 1993). Using a variation of the Ponzo figure, pigeons reinforced for responding to "long" line lengths showed greater activity in response to line segments located close to their surrounding frames (i.e., near the vertex) than they did to segments farther away from their frames; this occurred regardless of whether the framing oblique lines converged upward or downward (i.e., vertex upward or downward). In contrast, the upright figure (i.e., where the vertex is at the top) usually produces a greater illusory effect in humans. Moreover, unlike the result of human observation of the Ponzo illusion, the addition of perspective cues did not enhance the illusion for pigeons. However, we do not really know whether the pigeon and the human employ any similar perceptual processes in viewing the Ponzo illusion.

THE POGGENDORFF ILLUSION

The **Poggendorff illusion,** presented in Figure 10.24a, was actually derived from another illusory figure. In 1860, J. C. Poggendorff, the editor of a journal of physics and chemistry, received a monograph from F. Zöllner, an astronomer, that described an illusion he accidentally noticed in a sample design pattern printed on cloth (Luckiesh, 1922). His illusion, the *Zöllner illusion,* presented in Figure 10.24b, shows that parallel lines intersected by a pattern of short diagonal lines appear to diverge. On his part, Poggendorff noticed and described another effect of the apparent misalignment of the diagonal lines in

 **figure 10.23** Variations of the Ponzo illusion involving a framing effect. The horizontal lines of each pair of figures are identical but vary in the extent to which they are framed by elements. Although the elements framing the horizontal lines do not create any obvious perspective features, a small but reliable illusory effect still results.

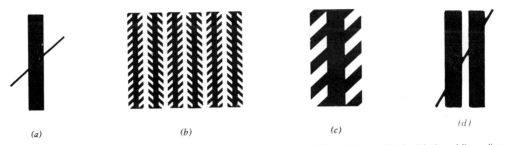

(a) (b) (c) (d)

▭ *figure* **10.24** The standard Poggendorff illusion (*a*) and the Zöllner illusion (*b*). In (*a*) the oblique lines are collinear, although they appear to be misaligned. In (*b*) the parallel lines appear to converge and diverge. An enlargement of a portion of (*b*) is shown in (*c*). Note in (*c*) that the oblique line segments forming the Zöllner illusion also appear misaligned. A variation of the Poggendorff illusion in (*d*) shows that when interrupted by two vertical rectangles, the segments of the continuous diagonal line appear to be even more offset than the version in (*a*).

Zöllner's figure (Figure 10.24*c*); as a result, the Poggendorff illusion bears the name of the observant journal editor (Coren & Girgus, 1978*a*).

Unlike the visual illusions described earlier, the Poggendorff illusion is usually considered an illusion of direction or misalignment rather than a distortion of size or distance. The two interrupted diagonal or oblique lines in Figure 10.24*a* are actually *collinear* (i.e., aligned on a straight line); yet, to most observers, an imaginary extension of the left line segment appears to be misaligned with or offset by the right line segment.

Generally speaking, the Poggendorff effect is a perceptual misalignment that results when diagonally tracking across a space that appears to be covered by an object or surface. It is not limited to simple line drawings. Indeed, the Poggendorff effect occurs in real-life settings such as reading graphs (Poulton, 1985), viewing actual scenes (Lucas & Fisher, 1969), and viewing photographs.

The Poggendorff Illusion and Perspective Constancy

Although there are many explanations of the Poggendorff illusion, we begin with a version of the familiar perspective-constancy notion described earlier, which assumes that apparent depth or distance is depicted in the illusory figure (Gillam, 1971, 1980). As applied to the Poggendorff figure, the oblique lines are perceived as the outlines of apparently receding

horizontal surfaces that lie on different planes (Figure 10.25), whereas the central rectangle is perceived as lying on a single plane in front of the viewer. Figure 10.25 shows that using perspective cues and depicting the oblique lines as lying on different depth planes disrupts the perceived alignment of the oblique lines.

It follows from the perspective-constancy notion that if the rectangle of the figure is changed to depict a surface that appears to recede into the distance in the same apparent orientation as the oblique lines, the illusory misalignment effect should greatly weaken. As illustrated in Figure 10.26, with such a display, this is exactly what happens (Gillam, 1971). The oblique lines appear essentially aligned or collinear.

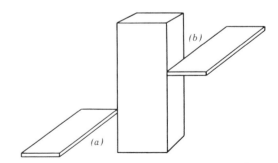

▭ *figure* **10.25** An elaboration of the Poggendorff figure that illustrates the perspective-constancy explanation of the illusory misalignment. In this case the obliques of the figure (*a* and *b*) are processed as belonging to different horizontal planes rather than as a single continuous receding plane. (Based on Rock, 1975.)

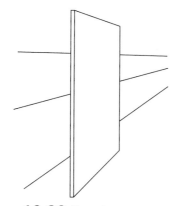

□ *figure* **10.26** The misalignment effect is significantly reduced when perspective cues depict all elements of the Poggendorff illusion lying on a single receding plane. (Devised by Noah.)

However, as with other illusions, perspective-constancy alone does not completely explain the full range of Poggendorff variations. For example, Figure 10.27 shows persistence of the misalignment for variations of the Poggendorff illusion that contain no apparent perspective features. Moreover, a perspective-constancy notion cannot account for the observation in Figure 10.28 that when the standard Poggendorff figure is tilted so that the interrupted oblique lines are set vertically at 90° or horizontally at 180°, the illusory misalignment effect weakens or disappears (see Masini et al., 1992; Spivey-Knowlton & Bridgeman, 1993). Indeed, merely tilting the figure should not greatly change any presumed perspective features of the standard figure. At the very least, this indicates that factors other than apparent perspective must also be involved in the apparent misalignment of the Poggendorff figure (see Greene & Fiser, 1994; Greene & Verloop, 1994).

Several well-known illusions to be described next do not rely obviously on apparent depth features and the misapplication of size constancy. Perhaps the simplest of these, at least in the number of components necessary to produce the effect, is the horizontal-vertical illusion.

THE HORIZONTAL-VERTICAL ILLUSION

A version of the **horizontal–vertical illusion**, introduced by Wundt in 1858, is presented in Figure 10.29*a*. The two intersecting lines are equal in length, although the vertical line appears to be much longer. Typically, when adjusting the horizontal line to match in length the vertical one, the horizontal line is extended over 30% longer than the vertical one (Figure

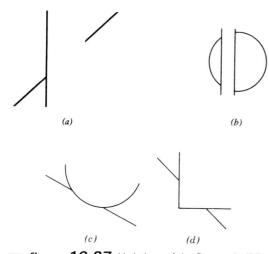

(a)   (b)

(c)   (d)

□ *figure* **10.27** Variations of the Poggendorff figure that also produce misalignment effects. In (*a*) the oblique line segments would form a continuous line, but appear to be offset. In (*b*) the circle appears to be segments of two circles with different diameters when intercepted by the parallel lines. Misalignment effects also occur in (*c*) and (*d*). (See Greene, 1988.)

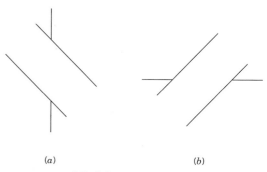

(a)   (b)

□ *figure* **10.28** A tilted Poggendorff illusion. When the standard figure is tilted so that the oblique lines are (*a*) aligned vertically at 90°, or (*b*) horizontally at 180°, the misalignment effect is slight.

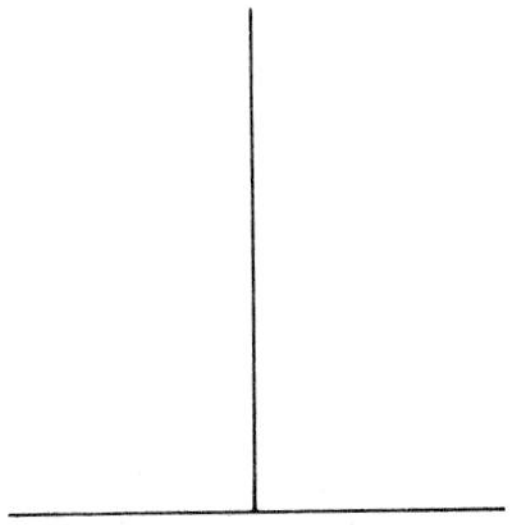

figure than when it is presented singly. That is, the horizontal–vertical illusion involves both an apparent lengthe ing of the vertical line *and* an apparent shortening of the horizontal line.

CONTRAST ILLUSIONS

Contrast illusions consist of distortion effects in which surrounding or contextual stimuli exert an opposing or *contrasting* effect on the perception of an embedded stimulus. Contrast illusions are of particular interest since they stress the contribution of the visual context in the perception of area, length, shape, and orientation.

The illusion introduced at the end of Chapter 2 (called the *Baldwin illusion;* see Figure 2.12) and the *Ebbinghaus illusion,* depicted in Figure 10.30, are prime examples of consistent distortions effects produced by contrast. The two inner circles in Figure 10.30, at *A* and *B*, are physically equal. However, the area of the surrounded circle in *A* appears enlarged due to the presence of the smaller contextual circles, whereas the identical center circle at *B* appears smaller due to the presence of the larger contextual circles. The *Jastrow illusion* in Figure 10.31 also illustrates the effect of contrast on size perception. The bottom curved area at *B* appears longer than the one at *A,* yet they are identical. Figure 10.32 presents the *tilt contrast illusion,* in which enclosed vertical lines appear tilted by the contrasting tilt of background lines.

□ *figure* **10.29a** The horizontal–vertical illusion. The vertical and horizontal lines are the same length.

10.29*b*; however, according to Prinzmetal and Gettleman, 1993, the magnitude of the illusion is somewhat less than this value when it is viewed monocularly).

The perceptually distorted relationship between vertical and horizontal length is not confined to simple line drawings. Chapanis and Mankin (1967) demonstrated an overestimation of perceived vertical extent with such everyday objects as buildings, parking meters, and large trees, all viewed in a natural setting. In fact, generally speaking, vertical lines usually appear longer than physically equal horizontal ones, an observation, no doubt used in architecture, interior design, and fashion.

While there is no fully accepted explanation of the horizontal–vertical illusion, it is worth noting that the horizontal and vertical segments each contribute to the overall magnitude of the illusion. Masin and Vidotto (1983) found that the vertical line in the illusory figure appears longer than the same vertical line presented in isolation; similarly, the horizontal line appears shorter when it is embedded in the illusory

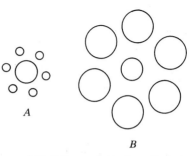

A

B

□ *figure* **10.30** The Ebbinghaus illusion and contrast effects. The center circle in *A* appears enlarged due to the smaller surrounding circles. The identical circle in the center of *B* appears diminished due to the larger surrounding circles. (Described by Ebbinghaus in 1902.)

□ *figure* **10.29b** Apparently equal vertical and horizontal lines. To most observers the horizontal and vertical lines appear equal; however, the horizontal line is over 30% longer than the vertical line.

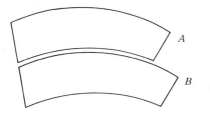

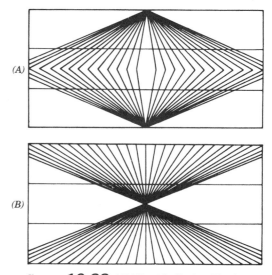

□ **figure 10.31** An illusion attributed to J. Jastrow in 1891. Although the two figures are identical, *B* appears longer than *A*. The shorter side of *A* is apparently contrasted against the longer side of *B;* thus, *A* appears shorter and *B* appears longer.

Contrast effects, involving distortion of shape, are obvious in the *Wundt* and *Hering illusions* of Figure 10.33. The two sets of horizontal lines are straight and parallel, yet they appear to bow inward in the Wundt illusion and outward in the Hering illusion. Similar distortion effects due to the contrast between adjacent areas appear in the *Fraser illusion* of Figure 10.34. Obvious contrast effects between adjacent black and white rectangles disrupt the perception of physically parallel rectangles in the *Münsterberg illusion* and its variants, shown in Figure 10.35. The effect is so

□ **figure 10.33** (*A*) Wundt's illusion. The horizontal parallel lines appear to bend toward the middle. (Proposed by W. Wundt in 1896.) (*B*) Hering's illusion. The horizontal parallel lines appear to bow apart in the middle. (Proposed by E. Hering in 1861.)

compelling that you may have to hold a straight edge alongside a line of horizontal elements to verify that they are indeed lines of parallel rectangles.

AMBIGUOUS, REVERSIBLE, AND MULTISTABLE FIGURES

Many figural organizations (similar to those of figure–ground, described in Chapter 7) have inherent depth characteristics that may be ambiguously perceived in terms of their main spatial orientation. After a brief inspection of any of the drawings shown in Figure 10.36, there is a spontaneous reversal in its spatial orientation. With continued inspection the reversal may occur periodically. The reversal occurs because there is not enough stimulus information in a given figure to assign to it a completely stable and unitary orientation in depth. Attneave (1971) refers to the figures characterized by ambiguous and equivocal depth information as **multistable figures.** These figures are also referred to as **reversible figures.** For example, in the standard Necker cube (Figure 10.36*a*) two simple three-dimensional organizations of a cube

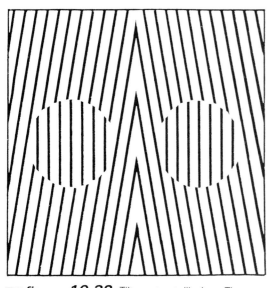

□ **figure 10.32** Tilt contrast illusion. The surrounded circular areas contain vertical lines, yet their apparent orientation is displaced in the direction opposite to the lines in the surrounding fields.

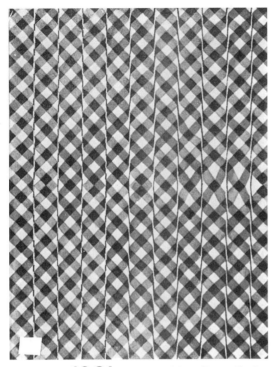

□ *figure* **10.34** Twisted cord or Fraser illusion. The straight lines seen against a checkerboard-like pattern appear curved. This illusion is called the twisted cord illusion because the effect can be obtained by viewing a twisted cord against a checkered background. (Devised by J. Fraser, 1908.)

in depth are about equally possible: the cube can be seen as projecting upward *or* downward in depth, but not both ways at the same time.

Multistable Figures and Adaptation

In general, when the available depth information is ambiguous enough to favor two or more different depth interpretations equally (or nearly equally), alternative perceptions may be induced by the same figure.

In fact, after continued viewing of multistable figures such as the Necker cube, there is an increase in spontaneous reversals. An explanation of this is based on a presumed *selective-adaptation* and fatigue-recovery mechanism. This account assumes that different visual channels mediate each perceived variation of the reversible figure (Long, Toppino, & Kostenbauder, 1983; Long, Toppino & Mondin, 1992; Toppino & Long, 1987; von Grünau, Wiggins, & Reed, 1984). Moreover, these channels involve mutually antagonistic processes enabling only one variation in orientation to be seen at a time (similar in nature to the presumed specific channels producing aftereffects of shape, color, tilt, and movement, discussed in earlier chapters). When one orientation of the multistable figure is perceived for a period of time, the perception of that orientation is selectively adapted and gradually fatigues; it is then supplanted by the alternative orientation. Over time, this second alternative also fatigues

□ *figure* **10.35** The Münsterberg illusion. The edges of each row of the checkerboard pattern appear nonparallel. (Proposed by H. Münsterberg in 1897.)

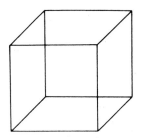

⚊ *figure* **10.36a** The Necker cube. After a brief period of inspection the cube spontaneously reverses in depth. (Based on a rhomboid figure devised by L. A. Necker in 1832.)

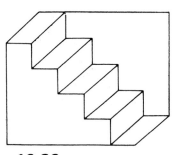

⚊ *figure* **10.36c** Schröder's staircase. The figure reverses from a staircase to an overhanging cornice. (Devised by H. Schröder in 1858.)

and is replaced by the original orientation, which meanwhile has "recovered" from fatigue. However, this recovery is incomplete, so that fatigue and reversal occur again, but more rapidly. With extended viewing, this process continues, but more and more rapidly, until spontaneous reversals occur at a constant rate. Thus the fluctuations in the perceived orientation of figures with ambiguous spatial characteristics result from a cyclical process of fatigue and recovery. (Recall, however, from Chapter 7, Figure 7.41, that spatially ambiguous, reversible figures like the Necker cube are subject to perceptual bias or *set* effects rather than adaptation-fatigue effects. According to Long, Toppino, and Mondin (1992), whether set *or* adaptation-induced spontaneous reversals occur from inspecting a Necker cube depends on the *length* of the inspection. As described in Chapter 7, for very short inspection periods—less than 100 msec—set effects

occur. For longer inspection times, as in the present section, adaptation-fatigue effects occur and spontaneous reversals are perceived.)

In contrast to the cycle of spontaneous reversals, when depth cues favoring a particular orientation are added to an ambiguous figure like the Necker cube, the perception appropriate to that orientation dominates. As illustrated in Figure 10.37, we tend to use perception appropriate to the spatially favored orientation, with a marked decrease in spontaneous reversals.

MULTIPLE DETERMINANTS OF ILLUSIONS

No theory posing a unitary mechanism or process explains the major spatial illusions satisfactorily or completely. It may well be that there is no one process or mechanism that accounts for any given illusion. It thus seems reasonable to consider the notion that individual illusions may be produced by several different sources, some coming from the structure of the

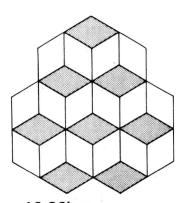

⚊ *figure* **10.36b** The figure reverses so that either six or seven cubes are perceived.

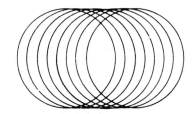

⚊ *figure* **10.36d** Either end of the series of rings may be seen as the near or far end of a tube.

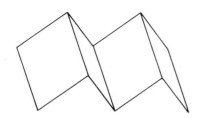

□ **figure 10.36e** Mach illusion. With continued inspection the two-dimensional drawing of a folded sheet of paper will reverse in its orientation. (Devised by E. Mach in 1866.)

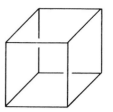

□ **figure 10.37** Altered Necker cube. When the overlapping (or interposition) of line segments is made distinct, spatial ambiguity is reduced and the Necker cube is significantly less likely to reverse its apparent orientation.

eye and from neural interactions within the retina, and some coming from higher-level cognitive factors involving judgment and past experience. Along these lines, Coren and Girgus (1978a, 1978b) propose that there are two independent, primary levels of distortion mechanisms, each of which may help create illusory perceptions; we label them here as *optical-retinal* (or structural) *components* and *cognitive components*.

Optical-Retinal Components

Optical-retinal components derive directly from anatomical or physiological (i.e., structural) mechanisms of the visual system. Structural factors include distortions created by the image-forming mechanisms of the eye such as the cornea and lens. A structural component is illustrated by the *subjective curvature*

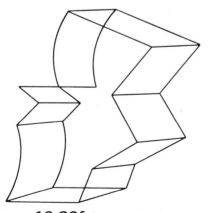

□ **figure 10.36f** An example of an ambiguous figure constructed without familiar shapes, right angles, or circles. (Devised by Noah in 1979.)

of Figure 10.38. Subjective curvature of straight lines occurs principally in indirect, peripheral vision since the image is projected on a curved retinal surface. Perhaps because we seldom rely on peripheral vision alone for form or shape judgments, we are not usually aware of subjective curvature; however, when shapes are isolated, as in Figure 10.38, they provide compelling examples of visual distortions.

Another optical-retinal effect that may contribute to the perception of visual illusions, especially those that contain converging lines, angles, and contrasting regions, is due to the smearing or blurring of the retinal image owing to the imperfections of the lens and cornea in projecting images on the retina. In general, when contours intersect or lie close together on the retina, there may be enough retinal blur and inhibitory interactions to distort apparent orientation (e.g., Greene, 1993), apparent location (e.g., Badcock & Westheimer, 1985; Westheimer, 1990), and contrast (e.g., Pollack & Jaeger, 1994; Greene & Verloop, 1994).

Furthermore, Ginsburg (1986) suggests that similar contour distortions may occur due to channels in the visual system that are differentially tuned to different spatial frequencies. According to this notion, certain spatial frequency components of a visual image may be more readily extracted than others by specialized filters in the visual system. If the visual system filters information in this way for a particular display, pattern detail may be lost for those elements that contain spatial frequencies to which the visual system is relatively insensitive. This could introduce distortions much like the errors produced by visual illusions.

Structural factors of the eye, the retina, and relevant neural connections may help to form visual illu-

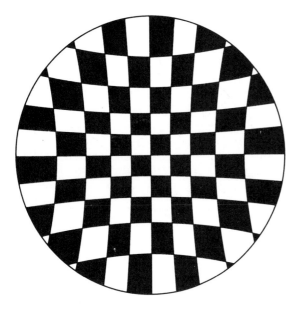

▭ *figure* **10.38** Subjective curvature. With one eye closed fixate on the center of the curved checkerboard design from about the distance specified by the vertical line segment on the right. The perception is of an ordinary checkerboard pattern comprised of black and white squares, approximately equal in size and arranged in straight lines. The curvatures of the lines used in the construction of this pattern were chosen to compensate for the subjective curvature of the lines that is seen in peripheral vision. (Based on a demonstration by Helmholtz in 1866.)

sions, especially where figures contain angles, intersecting lines, and contrasting areas (and, accordingly, especially applicable to such illusions such as those depicted in Figures 10.32 to 10.35). However, optical-retinal effects in general are limited in scope, and they cannot be extended to the full range of illusory figures. It appears that a significant portion of illusory effects may be due to cognitive components.

Cognitive Components

Cognitive components that contribute to illusions include past experience, learning, and attention. Obvious examples are those factors presumably involving a perspective-constancy mechanism in such illusions as the moon, Ponzo, and Müller-Lyer illusions. Generally, apparent sources of depth and distance information trigger a compensatory size constancy mechanism. For example, this notion suggests that viewers are especially sensitive to the converging lines in the Ponzo illusion because they have a lot of experience with converging lines representing distance.

Accordingly, in such distance-dependent figures, there is no appeal to structural factors of the eye. In fact, for many of the illusions described earlier, there

is evidence that their main determinant must lie beyond the level of the optical processes of the eye. Schiller and Wiener (1962) presented many illusions, such as the Ponzo, Poggendorff, Zöllner, horizontal-vertical, and Ebbinghaus illusions, *stereoscopically,* in which different parts of a given illusory figure were flashed to each eye. For example, with the Ponzo illusion, the two horizontal lines were flashed to one eye and the surrounding converging lines to the other. The results showed that the distortions effects were almost the same as those obtained with normal viewing of the figures. Using similar procedures, Weiss, Hewitt, and Mentzer (1979) reported evidence supporting the central basis of the Poggendorff illusion. They also found that the Jastrow and Hering illusions have a central rather than a retinal origin. Julesz (1971) also verified the central basis of several illusory figures, including the Müller-Lyer illusion, using the random-dot stereogram format described in the preceding chapter. These findings indicate that the distortion effects of these illusions are not induced by optical-retinal components but occur somewhat centrally in the visual system, beyond the retinal level; that is, they are located at least beyond the level in the visual system where the inputs from the two eyes first come together.

The viewer's *attention* is a prime cognitive component that may be involved in visual illusions. For example, in viewing Figure 10.39, you may find your own attention directed inward or outward by the arrows to create an apparent distortion in the perception of the circles. Even without direct manipulation of the viewer's attention, a reduced illusion is observed when the wings of the Müller-Lyer figure (see Figure 10.17) are colored differently from the central segment (Sadza & de Weert, 1984). This may be due to indirect manipulation of attention, making the wings less likely to enter into the comparison.

In addition to attention, *exposure* and *learning* seem to be other cognitive factors involved in visual illusions. It is well known that many visual illusions decline in magnitude with prolonged inspection. Feedback (or knowledge of the illusion) has been identified as playing a critical role in this decrement effect (Watson, Greist-Bousquet, & Schiffman, 1991). However, it should be noted that even if the magnitude of many visual illusions decreases with continued inspection, the illusion does not decrease to zero. For example, no matter how long or often one inspects the Müller-Lyer figure shown in Figure 10.17, the illusion does not disappear.

Multiple-Illusion Figures

The notion that visual illusions result from many contributing factors is consistent with the observation that some visual illusions probably have several more basic illusory effects embedded within them. For example,

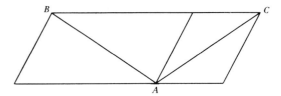

□ **figure 10.40** The Sander parallelogram. Diagonal line segment *AB* appears longer than segment *AC* although they are both the same length. Note that components of the wings-inward Müller-Lyer figure are embedded in the parallelogram. (Devised by F. Sander in 1926.)

the observant reader may notice that the Sandor parallelogram shown in Figure 10.40 contains Müller-Lyer components.

If we can dissect certain visual illusions into more basic illusory effects, we can also combine predictable illusory effects to produce more dramatic visual illusions. For example, the unusual spatial distortion apparent in Figure 10.41 is the result of combining the Müller-Lyer illusion and the Ponzo illusion, which is still further enhanced by the addition of perspective cues.

In summary, most visual illusions probably involve many causes. The illusory perception may owe some distortion effects to the structure of the eye, to neural-retinal interactions, and to cognitive processes. Accordingly, the search for one mechanism seems less

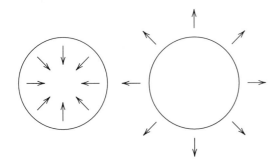

□ **figure 10.39** The two circles are equal, but attention to the arrows makes the one on the left appear to contract and the one on the right appear to expand.

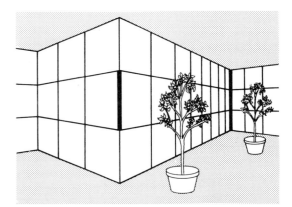

□ **figure 10.41** A multiple illusion figure that contains the Müller-Lyer illusion, the Ponzo illusion, and further enhancement due to additional perspective cues. The heavy vertical line at the right appears longer than the one at the left; however, both are identical.

reasonable than the general assumption that visual illusions may result either from several levels of visual processing mechanisms or from a combination of several illusory effects.

IMPOSSIBLE FIGURES

We end our discussion of illusions with the curious set of figures that, by their name and definition, do not physically exist; yet, at the same time, they challenge our understanding of space perception because, at first glance, they appear to represent real, coherent objects. Indeed, so-called **impossible figures,** such as those shown in Figure 10.42, can be disturbing as well as confusing to observers who attempt to see them as depicting stable, three-dimensional objects. This is because such displays contain inconsistent and contradictory sets of depth information that cannot be suppressed individually. As illustrated in Figure 10.43, when the impossible triangle of Figure 17.42*b* is viewed as a collection of individual linear segments and angles, they appear to represent parts of a simple three-dimensional object in depth; that is, when seen in isolation, the segments are "locally interpretable" (Simon, 1967). However, when seen globally as unitary objects, the depth characteristics of the individual features appear to conflict with each other and the

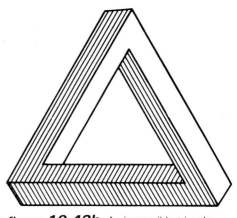

□ *figure* **10.42b** An impossible triangle.

figures appear spatially impossible. Thus, the depth interpretation assigned to each part individually cannot be extended to the figure as a whole.

Some of the remarkable graphic drawings of the Dutch artist Maurits C. Escher (1971; see especially M. L. Teuber, 1974), utilizing contradictory depth cues, are fascinating examples of impossible three-dimensional scenes. As you attempt to follow the direction of water flow in Figure 10.44 you will readily

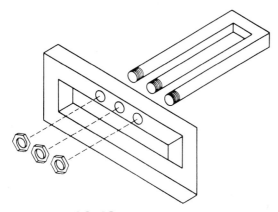

□ *figure* **10.42a** An "impossible" construction. The three-pronged figure is called a *trident.* (From *North American Aviation's Skywriter,* February 18, 1966, Braun & Co., Inc.)

□ *figure* **10.42c** A variation of the impossible triangle is portrayed on a Swedish postage stamp. Note also that a change in figure–ground organization enables the perception of a centrally located "star."

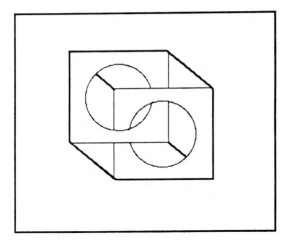

□ figure 10.42d An impossible Necker cube. (Devised by Jan in 1989.)

recognize the challenge of trying to sensibly perceive an impossible scene.

A final statement concerning spatial illusions is in order. We have stressed in earlier chapters—as well as at the beginning of this chapter with perceptual constancy—that the primate visual system evolved to extract useful, accurate spatial information from natural scenes. Our treatment of illusions in no way violates this; we have merely exaggerated their presence in order to understand them. Indeed, in spite of the vast array of visual illusions that have been documented (only a few of which were discussed in this chapter), it remains a remarkable measure of the evolutionary success of our visual system that it is so rarely deceived into making incorrect and distorted spatial perceptions.

SUMMARY

This chapter extended the discussion of space perception begun in Chapter 9, focusing on perceptual constancy and visual illusions. In particular, we discussed the various forms of perceptual constancy, the tendency to perceive the visual world as composed of objects that remain stable, or constant, in their lightness, size, and shape, despite changes in the stimulation that they project to the visual system.

Lightness constancy is the tendency of the lightness of an object to remain constant despite fluctuations in the light illuminating it. Lightness constancy was explained, in part, by taking into account the

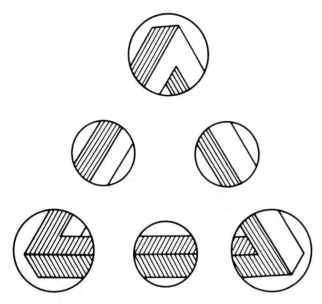

□ figure 10.43 When isolated parts of the impossible triangle (Figure 10.42b) are seen, they appear as simple drawings of angles and line lengths in depth. However, when the figure is viewed as a whole, apparently depicting a three-dimensional object, the depth interpretations assigned to the isolated features are in conflict with each other. (After Lindsay & Norman, 1977.)

☐ **figure 10.44** Impossible scene drawn by M. C. Escher (1971). According to Escher the figure incorporates the triangle of Figure 10.42b. (*Source:* Beeldrect, Amsterdam/VAGA, New York, 1982, Collection Haags Gemeentemuseum.)

constant properties of the light reflected from objects and surfaces, such as albedo and the luminance relation of objects relative to their surroundings.

Size constancy is the tendency of objects to remain constant in size despite variations in the size of their retinal images as their distance from the viewer changes. Size constancy was examined in terms of the presence of cues to depth and distance. When such spatial cues are reduced or absent, size constancy is correspondingly reduced or lacking.

Shape constancy is the tendency to perceive the shape of an object as constant even when it is viewed from very different angles. As in size constancy, the shape of an object appears stable to the extent that relevant spatial information concerning such factors as slant and orientation is available.

The remainder of the chapter dealt with visual illusions, drawing on the role of spatial cues, especially size constancy. We began by discussing Transactionalism, which holds that the perception of the visual environment is based largely on experience in dealing with the visual environment. We also examined two of the related Ames illusions—the trapezoidal window and the distorted room—that highlight the role of past experience in visual perception.

Next, we described several illusions, each apparently based on depth and distance cues and the misapplication of size constancy: the moon illusion, the Müller-Lyer illusion, the Ponzo illusion, and the Poggendorff illusion. In attempting to explain these illusions, several notions of spatial perception were introduced: for the moon illusion, in particular, we described the apparent distance and relative size hypotheses and the distance paradox. All four illusions were generally explained with regard to the perspective-constancy notion, which is based on the assumption that parts of the illusory figures contain linear perspective cues. It follows that perspective suggests apparent distance on a two-dimensional surface, which, in turn, erroneously triggers a size constancy mechanism. Accordingly, due to the compensatory nature of a size-constancy mechanism, those parts of the illusory figures that seem distant appear correspondingly larger. However, while we found the per-spective-constancy notion useful, it was not considered fully acceptable or complete.

The remainder of the section on illusions described the horizontal-vertical illusion and some contrast illusions. Contrast illusions result from distortion effects in which background stimuli exert opposing effects on the perception of an embedded figure. Among the contrast illusions examined were the Ebbinghaus illusion, the Jastrow illusion, the tilt contrast illusion, the Wundt and Hering illusions, the Fraser illusion, and the Münsterberg illusion.

Figures projecting ambiguous or contradictory depth information were next discussed. We concluded that the perceptual ambiguity in so-called ambiguous, reversible, and multistable figures (e.g., the Necker cube) is due to the fact that their inherent depth indicators equally favor two or more perceptual organizations.

In general, it was assumed that many visual illusions have several determinants. This notion stresses that visual illusions may be the result of several different sources, and two primary classes were proposed: optical-retinal components and cognitive components. Optical-retinal components are anatomical and physiological properties of the eye and visual system that promote illusory effects. The resultant effects include subjective curvature, retinal blur, and differential filtering of certain spatial frequencies. Cognitive components include the perspective-constancy mechanism, attention, experience, and learning. It was noted that some classic visual illusion figures may contain several more basic illusory effects.

The last section of this chapter briefly dealt with so-called impossible figures, which are created by merging incompatible depth cues within the same figure. When these depth features are viewed in isolation, they are easily interpretable, but when they are viewed together so as to appear as a unitary rendering of a three-dimensional object in depth, the total configuration seems spatially impossible.

KEY TERMS

Albedo

Ames Illusions

Angle-of-Regard Hypothesis

Aniseikonia

Apparent Distance Hypothesis (Size-Distance
   Invariance Hypothesis)

Cognitive Components

Contrast Illusions

Distance Paradox

Distorted Room Illusion

Emmert's Law

Framing Effects (Ponzo Illusion)

Holway–Boring Experiment

Horizontal–Vertical Illusion

Impossible Figures

Lightness Constancy

Moon Illusion

Müller-Lyer Illusion

Multistable Figures (Reversible Figures)

Optical-Retinal Components

Perceptual Constancy

Perspective-Constancy Theory

Poggendorff Illusion

Ponzo Illusion

Shape Constancy

Size Constancy

Subjective Curvature

Transactionalism

Trapezoidal Window

STUDY QUESTIONS

1. Describe the general notion of perceptual constancy and indicate its importance as an adaptive mechanism.

2. Explain lightness constancy, using the related notions of albedo and the relationship of the reflected light of an object to the light reflected by the background.

3. Outline the Holway–Boring experiment and summarize its significance and importance in explaining size constancy. Describe Emmert's law and indicate in what ways it demonstrates size constancy processes.

4. Discuss shape constancy and indicate how it can be demonstrated, drawing on familiar shapes such as circles, ellipses, squares, and trapezoids. Examine the contribution made by spatial cues to depth and distance, as well as slant and orientation, in promoting shape constancy.

5. Describe Transactionalism and the Transactional view of space perception. Explain the Ames illusions (the trapezoidal window and the distorted room) on the basis of perceptual assumptions about the spatial world developed through learning and experience. To what extent do size and shape constancy enter into the illusory effects produced by the trapezoidal window and the distorted room?

6. Examine the importance of two-dimensional pictorial cues in promoting visual illusions.

7. Indicate how a correction for apparent distance may promote illusions. Which of the prominent illusions described appear most prone to the effects of pictorial cues?

8. How is the moon illusion demonstrated? What role do apparent distance cues play in producing the illusion? How may a constancy mechanism help to produce the illusion?

9. Outline additional theories proposed to explain the moon illusion and explain the distance paradox.

10. How can the inappropriate elicitation of a perspective-constancy mechanism explain the Müller-Lyer illusion?

11. In what ways does the perspective-constancy notion apply to the Ponzo illusion?

12. Outline and evaluate the explanations of the Poggendorff illusion. In particular, describe how structural aspects of the Müller-Lyer figure are embedded within the Poggendorff figure.

13. Consider how the horizontal-vertical illusion may be due to the combined perceptual effect of a lengthened vertical segment and a shortened horizontal segment.

14. Examine the general proposition that many illusions have multiple determinants. Identify possible structural and cognitive distortion components that may contribute to illusions.

15. Consider to what extent optical–retinal factors play a role in promoting illusions. Examine the effects of cognitive components such as attention and learning in observing the illusions.

16. Explain the perceptual effect of reversible or multistable figures. Explain the effects of reversible figures on the basis of adaptation, fatigue, and recovery.

17. What are "impossible" figures, and how can they be "explained?"

18. Discuss the contribution made to a general understanding of spatial perception by an analysis of visual illusions.

PERCEPTUAL DEVELOPMENT

In the last eight chapters, we have seen that our visual system provides us with a remarkable arsenal of perceptual abilities. In this chapter, we discuss the factors that determine and affect the attainment and development of these perceptual abilities. Although we have already encountered many developmental issues in various contexts, in this chapter they are the primary focus.

Central to any treatment of perceptual development is the problem of the origin of perceptual abilities: Is the ability to perceive spatial features of the world a totally acquired *capacity, completely dependent on experience and learning, or is it based wholly on* innate, genetic *factors predetermined by the biology of the sensory systems? This issue—often referred to as* **nativism versus empiricism** *(or sometimes the* innate–learned *or* nature–nurture *issue)—can be traced to the writings of seventeenth- and eighteenth-century philosophers and nineteenth-century scientists. Historically, the* nativist *approach, proposed by Descartes, Kant, and others asserts that perceptual abilities are inborn. More recently, the Gestalt school has also supported a modified nativist position, claiming that much organization of the perceptual world is governed by tendencies and mechanisms that are unlearned. On the other hand, the* empiricists, *including Hobbes, Locke, Berkeley, and Helmholtz (introduced in Chapter 1), and, more recently, the Transactionalists maintained that perception occurs through a learning process—from interactions and experience with the environment.*

Although the empiricism–nativism issue has had a strong influence on psychology, both as a philosophical and as an empirical disagreement, it has been impossible to resolve. Most contemporary psychologists hold that some forms of perceptual abilities and mechanisms are available soon enough after birth so as to reject a strictly empirical interpretation of the origin of perceptual abilities. Similarly, most psychologists also agree that experience plays a necessary, useful role in perception (e.g., that experience modifies or stabilizes certain genetically endowed sensory mechanisms). As a contemporary controversy, then, the origin of perceptual abilities is largely one of emphasis rather than exclusion. Accordingly, the view taken here is that mutually exclusive alternatives such as nativism versus empiricism are unnecessary. As we will readily observe in this chapter, it is possible to study and identify the factors that control and affect the development of perceptual abilities without appealing to the innate–learned issue.

Although much of what we will describe can apply to all the senses, the topics discussed will generally focus on the development of visual processes. Specifically, in this chapter we will examine several related questions that are central to perceptual development. What are the basic perceptual abilities of the newborn? When and how do they develop? And what factors govern their emergence, their functioning, and their maintenance?

DEVELOPMENT OF THE SENSORY SYSTEM

The sensory system of the newborn human is surprisingly well developed. In fact, identifiable eye movements and blink–startle responses begin prior to birth, soon after 24 weeks of fetal life (Birnholz, 1981; Birnholz & Benacerraf, 1983). The cornea and lens are capable of focusing an image on the retina, which is also quite functional. At higher levels of the visual system, structures including the pathways between the lateral geniculate nucleus (LGN) and the cortex, as well as parts of the cortex, are undergoing rapid development, so that a reasonable level of maturity in anatomy occurs by about 6 to 8 weeks of prenatal age (Banks & Salapatek, 1983). In addition, studies of kittens and monkeys indicate that many of the functions observed for the cortical cells of the adult of the species are also present in the cells of the infant. For example, like the receptive field activity of cortical cells of adult animals, the cells of the newborn show significant activity when bars of light, set at particular orientations, are shone onto a specific region of the retina.

The development of the visual system is sensitive to environmental influences. During an animal's infancy, the development of sensory structures (such as the rods and cones) and perceptual processes (such as monocular and binocular vision) is susceptible to change and may even be irreversibly affected by restrictive or abnormal experience (Harwerth et al., 1986). This applies as well to cortical neurons and neural connections. Changes in the performance of components of the sensory nervous system due to visual deprivation or select visual experience suggest that the development and maintenance of normal visual function may be due to an interplay of genetic factors and experience.

We will first consider some of the evidence that select forms of visual deprivation and biased stimulation may affect the organization of the visual cortex.

Cortical Effects of Visual Deprivation

Some of the pioneering research of Hubel and Wiesel (1963) point to the complex interactions of inborn factors and experience in attaining and maintaining certain perceptual abilities. For example, the innate mechanism underlying the perception of visual movement requires appropriate stimulation to continue proper functioning. In kittens reared without patterned light for 2 months, the cortical cells that normally react to visual movement showed little activity. Absence of the neural response due to extended light deprivation means that visual experience is necessary to maintain a largely inborn ability. Generally speaking, in animals completely deprived of visual stimulation by extended rearing in the dark from birth, the cells of the visual cortex become unresponsive to stimulation of any kind. Light deprivation of the newborn animal, especially when extensive, has serious consequences in adulthood.

Monocular Deprivation Many neurons of the mammalian visual cortex respond to stimulation from either eye. However, this changes when light experience is limited to one eye. Restricting vision to one eye is called **monocular deprivation.** The neurophysiological effects of depriving one eye of vision are more subtle than total light deprivation. Consider the condition in which a kitten is monocularly deprived from birth, so that it views the world through only one eye; when it is tested later, the vast majority of its cortical cells will fire *only* when the normal, undeprived eye is stimulated. A drastic loss of binocularly driven neurons has resulted from the monocular deprivation (LeVay, Wiesel, & Hubel, 1980; Wiesel & Hubel, 1963). The loss of binocular cells has a significant consequence for the perceptual world of the animal. Thus monkeys who have lost a majority of their binocular cells due to experimental restrictions lose much of their ability to use binocular disparity to perceive depth (Crawford et al., 1984).

Critical Periods The physiological effects of monocular deprivation appear to depend on *when* deprivation begins. If it begins at about 3 weeks to 3 or 4 months of age (in the cat), it has a sizable effect; however, if it is delayed 4 months of age or more, then even after extended periods of monocular deprivation, there is little or no effect on cortical activity. This suggests that there is a **critical period:**

a particular developmental period when the visual deprivation has a major effect on the establishment of normal binocular neural organization. Once the critical period is past, visual deprivation has little permanent developmental effect. The cat's critical period lasts for about 3 to 4 months; the human's critical period for certain visual abilities may extend up to 4 or 5 years.

The deprivation period does not have to be very long to significantly restrict cortical activity. As long as deprivation occurs during the critical period, for some species such as the cat, periods as short as 1 day may strongly affect the responses of cortical cells (Freeman, Mallach, & Hartley, 1981; Olson & Freeman, 1975). We now turn to the effects on the developing visual system of allowing only very selective stimulation.

Cortical Effects of Biased and Selective Visual Stimulation

If depriving one or both eyes of *all* visual experience has a drastic effect on the development of cortical neurons, what is the effect of restricting visual experience to *specific forms* of stimuli? This question was addressed, in part, by an experiment that restricted kittens to a visual world comprised of specific forms of stimulation containing lines of only a single orientation. Hirsch and Spinelli (1970) reared kittens from birth until 10 to 12 weeks of age with special masks that completely controlled their vision; one eye was exposed only to three black horizontal lines on a white field and the other eye to three black vertical lines, also on a white field (see also Muir & Mitchell, 1973). After the exposure period, the researchers recorded from cells in the kittens' visual cortex and assessed the stimulus orientations that caused the greatest response from each cell. In marked contrast to normal kittens whose cortical cells respond to all orientations, including diagonal ones, there was a drastic alteration in the neural responses of the experimental animals. Neurons in the visual cortex were either horizontally or vertically oriented and showed little activity to oblique or diagonally oriented stimuli. Moreover, the cortical

neurons excited by horizontally oriented stimuli were activated *only* by the eye initially exposed to the horizontal lines; conversely, neurons fired by vertical stimuli were activated *only* by the eye exposed to the vertical lines. As the authors' conclude: "The change in the distribution of orientations of cortical unit(s) . . . that we found when kittens were raised with both eyes viewing different patterns demonstrates that functional neural connections can be selectively and predictably modified by environmental stimulation" (p. 871).

This result—that selective deprivation alters cortical organization—was confirmed by Blakemore and Cooper (1970) using a different rearing situation. Beginning at 2 weeks of age, two kittens were placed in a restrictive drum or cylinder lined with horizontal or vertical stripes on the side and mirrors above and below to give the impression of a continuous stimulus pattern (Figure 11.1). They were kept in the cylinder for about 5 hours a day, with the remainder of the time spent in darkness. After approximately 5 months, their vision was tested with stripes of various orientations. The kittens appeared blind to stripes oriented differently from those expe-

□ *figure 11.1* The vertically striped cylinder environment used by Blakemore and Cooper (1970).

rienced during the rearing conditions. They responded only to the contour orientation to which they had been exposed as kittens: the kitten reared with the horizontal stripes reacted only to horizontal stimulation, and those reared with vertical stripes responded only to vertical stimulation. When a black rod, for example, was held horizontally, only the cat reared with black horizontal lines attempted to play with it; the vertically reared cat ignored it. When the rod was suddenly changed to a vertical orientation, their roles were reversed: the vertically reared cat played with the rod, while the other kitten ignored it.

The cats' cortical cell activity showed the same orientational selectivity as the cats' behavior. Cortical units of the kitten reared with horizontal stripes reacted only to horizontal stripes; cortical units of the kitten reared with vertical stripes responded only to vertical stripes. It was as if stimulating the visual system with only a single orientation during rearing—horizontal *or* vertical—was a form of **environmental surgery:** it systematically eliminated the eye's ability to respond to any orientation other than the one to which it had been exposed during rearing. Selective visual deprivation changed the visual system with no physical intervention.

The dramatic effects on cortical neuron organization created by restriction to vertical or horizontal experience led to many other investigations in which animals' vision were restricted to various sorts of stimulus features. In general, evidence indicates that early, selective visual experience modifies cortical cell development; the cells react best to the stimulus features to which they were exposed.

Consider the following unusual experiment showing that early, specific visual experience modifies receptive field development. Kittens were reared in a planetarium-like environment, essentially a dome with spots of light on it so that their visual environment was restricted to point sources of light, with no straight-line contours (Pettigrew & Freeman, 1973). When the kittens were later tested, their cortical neurons were found to be highly sensitive to spots of light but did not respond to straight lines, again reflecting the stimulus effects during rearing.

Effects of Biased Stimulation for the Human

These findings raise an obvious question: can the organization of neurons in the human be modified by early abnormal visual stimulation (e.g., Freeman, Mitchell, & Millodot, 1972; Freeman & Thibos, 1973)? We cannot submit the human infant to the forms of selective deprivation just described. However, based on an analysis of the perceptual effects of certain ocular defects that produce early abnormal experience—analogous in many ways to the experimental restrictions imposed on cats—the answer seems to be a qualified "yes." Some supporting evidence follows.

Meridional Amblyopia Certain forms of adult ocular *astigmatism,* appear to result from an early, uncorrected distortion of the cornea. Astigmatism, as noted in Chapter 3, is an optical defect in which the corneal surface is not a perfect sphere. As a result, astigmatic individuals see lines in one orientation (usually horizontal *or* vertical) more clearly than lines in the other orientation. Some older children and adults who are astigmatic have permanently reduced acuity for the contours of a specific orientation, a condition called **meridional amblyopia** (sometimes called *astigmatic amblyopia* or *ametropic amblyopia;* there are many forms of *amblyopia,* a name that derives from the Greek words for "dull vision").

Why is it that the astigmatism (or low vision for a certain orientation) in older children and adults with meridional amblyopia *cannot* be corrected optically? It is generally accepted that this form of acuity loss has a neural basis: the blurring induced by astigmatism during an early critical period in the development of the visual system has altered the neural connections and permanently modified the brain (e.g., Freeman et al., 1972). Specifically, the neural effect of the early astigmatism appears in adulthood as a scarcity of cortical neurons that can respond to the astigmatic orientation. This means that even if the distortion or optical error is corrected by compensating lenses, so that a sharp image of all orientations occurs, the orientation originally blurred by the early astigmatism is still impaired. The adult visual system cannot correct or compensate optically for the deficient cortical neurons because the problem lies in the brain, *not* in the optics of the eye (e.g., Annis & Frost, 1973; Mitchell, 1980). The argument that early astigmatism may permanently modify the brain is well summarized by Freeman et al. (1972):

> *Suppose that the retinal image of a developing visual system suffers from astigmatism that causes extensive blur along the horizontal, but not the vertical, axis. The visual cortex could adapt to the discordant input from the retina by "tuning" itself to the features clearly imaged along the vertical axis. A logical effect of the cortical adaptation would be an [unequal] development of the neural connections involved in resolution. And as a consequence, the resolution capacity for horizontally imaged details would be reduced. (p. 1385)*

Some evidence with children supports a causal link between early astigmatism and meridional amblyopia. Jane Gwiazda and her colleagues (Gwiazda et al., 1986; 1989) found a strong correlation between astigmatism in infancy and meridional amblyopia in childhood (average age, 8 to 9 years). Accordingly, they propose that the blur of early astigmatism (i.e., in the critical period ranging from age 6 months to 2 years) may be a factor in the onset of later amblyopia.

Stimulus Deprivation Amblyopia

Lack of early visual experience during the critical period may play a role in one of the most common forms of amblyopia, stimulus deprivation amblyopia (Hubel, 1988). In **stimulus deprivation amblyopia** (also called *amblyopia ex anopsia* or *disuse amblyopia*), there is a sizable permanent reduction in the acuity of one eye. This form of amblyopia has been observed in individuals who, as babies or young children, had very reduced or restricted use of one eye following an injury or surgery, strongly suggesting that it results from visual deprivation during the critical period. Like the monocularly deprived kitten described earlier, the stimulus-deprived amblyopic individual may lack normal function in the cortical cells linked to the visually deprived eye. Evidence from animal studies supports this idea. Eggers and Blakemore (1978) induced amblyopia in kittens by having them wear a distorting, high-power lens in front of one eye during rearing. When they were tested after about 2 to 4 months, their cortical neurons were found to be far more dominated by the normal eye than by the originally defocused eye. This experimentally induced amblyopia created a deficiency in cortical neuronal development (see also Thomas, Mohindra, & Held, 1979).

Strabismus

Stereoblindness, introduced in Chapter 9, is closely associated with certain visual disorders of early childhood. The most common childhood disorder impeding the development of stereopsis is called **strabismus,** derived from the Greek, "to squint", an inability to coordinate the movement of the two eyes (technically, strabismus is also a form of amblyopia, sometimes called *strabismic amblyopia*). The defect is actually in the ability to coordinate the eye muscles that ordinarily fixate the two eyes on a single target. The two eyes may be misaligned inward or outward, causing the individual to be either *esotropic* ("cross-eyed") or *exotropic* ("wall-eyed"), respectively. In either case, the eyes point in different directions and thus have different images. Strabismic individuals cannot fixate on a single object with both eyes. This causes the brain to receive conflicting images from the eyes, leading to double images, or *diplopia*. Generally, however, double vision rarely persists in children. Instead, the child alternates fixations between the two eyes, looking first with one eye and then with the other. Soon, however, the child's visual system comes to favor one eye and totally suppresses the vision in the other eye. This eventually causes functional deterioration in the suppressed eye. Over time, in many respects, strabismic individuals perceive the world as though they have only monocular vision. In this sense, early strabismus has induced a form of stimulus deprivation amblyopia (see Shors, Wright, & Greene, 1992). Any of these effects of strabismus—diplopia (double images), fixation alternation, or suppression—eliminates the possibility of extracting binocular disparity information, and stereopsis generally does not develop.

The cause of strabismus is unknown. If it is not corrected surgically before school age (about 4–5 years), there will be a critical lack of binocular experience and permanent stereoblindness will result. In other words, the basis of this perceptual deficit is the loss of binocularly driven cortical cells (i.e., cells that respond best when both eyes view the same stimulus) resulting from early uncorrected strabismus (Crawford et al., 1986; Mitchell, 1978; Mitchell & Ware, 1974).

Supporting evidence indicates that there is a critical period for the attainment and development of binocularly driven cells in the brain. This critical period begins early during the first year, peaks at 2 years, and declines gradually after 4 years (Banks, Aslin, & Letson, 1975; Hohmann & Creutzfeldt, 1975). Therefore, delaying the treatment of strabismus—which correspondingly reduces binocular experience during the critical period—causes an appreciable loss of these cells. Thus, even if the strabismus is eventually repaired surgically in late childhood or in adulthood and the eyes are aligned with each other, the binocular cells lost because of strabismus during the critical period are unrecoverable, and the stereoblindness remains (Hubel, 1988).

Restored Sight with Humans

The effects of light deprivation and biased stimulation stress the role of innate factors and sensitivity to environmental influences in the development of perception. But experimental manipulations such as restricted and biased stimulation are not possible with humans. However, in many clinical observations, otherwise normal individuals, functionally blind from birth because of congenital visual defects such as *cataracts* of the lens (a condition that eliminates pattern vision, allowing only clouded patches of light, described later), have had their vision surgically restored (Gregory & Wallace, 1963; Gregory, 1974; Sacks, 1993, 1995; Senden, 1960).

Since 1728, when the first scientific citation on the effects of **restored sight** was made, many successful operations have been reported (see Pastore, 1971, for a history of restored vision). Generally, newly sighted

persons do not "see" much at first. They perceive colored unitary shapes against a background—that is, they perceive color and figure–ground organization—and they can fixate, scan, and follow moving figures. Although they may differentiate between objects, there is difficulty at first in identifying and recognizing an object as a member of a class of objects (Hebb, 1949; London, 1960; Senden, 1960).

Some sense of restored vision is given in a clinical report by Gregory and Wallace (1963; Gregory, 1974, 1977). The patient, S.B., was a 52-year-old male, blind since the age of 10 months, who had a successful corneal transplant. When the surgical bandages were removed, he did not suddenly see a world of objects but only one of blurs. Yet within days he did attain some functional vision; he could walk the hospital corridors without using touch; he was able to tell the time from a large wall clock; and presumably, based on his use of Braille, he could read uppercase letters. He made rapid progress in general visual abilities, and within months he could recognize the faces of friends and could name familiar objects with ease. However, he found it very difficult to perceive depth and distance. As Gregory (1977) writes, "We found that his perception of distance was peculiar. . . . He thought he would just be able to touch the ground below his window with his hands; but in fact the distance down was at least ten times his height" (p. 195). He also had difficulties with *pictorial perception,* such as in making sense out of pictures in a magazine. Generally, S.B. appeared to lack *perceptual constancy* (Gregory, 1974). Interestingly, he was relatively unsusceptible to certain geometric illusions with apparent depth features. For example, he did not "reverse" ambiguous reversible figures such as the Necker cube and Schröder's staircase (illustrated in Chapter 10), nor did he experience the usual effect for the Poggendorff illusion. Moreover he was only minimally affected by a variation of the Ponzo illusion, and while he did show an illusory effect when viewing the Müller-Lyer figure, his errors were much smaller than that of the typical subject. Of course, not all these illusions involve the scaling of apparent space, but it is interesting that figures typically seen in depth, such as the Necker cube, not only did not reverse to S.B. but, in fact, were not seen in depth by him. According to Gregory

(1974), S.B.'s spatial skills were so arrested that he was never able to even grasp the concept of depth.

A more recent clinical observation by the neurologist Oliver Sacks (1993, 1995) on the restored sight of a 50-year-old man confirms these points. Although he could recognize and identify many objects, most relevant to us here is his patient's poor distance perception, together with an apparently total lack of perceptual constancy and pictorial perception, closely paralleling the findings of Gregory and Wallace (1963) with patient S.B. In fact, Sacks reports that his patient could not even understand the representation of meaningful objects in two-dimensional pictures; nor could he make sense of the moving pictures on a TV screen. He perceived it to be little more than a display of streaks of light, colors, and motions.

Two visual events that posed special problems to Sacks' patient—obviously related to his poor spatial skills—were shadows and steps. Sacks (1993) describes his patient's difficulties as follows: "sometimes he would get confused by his own shadow—the whole concept of shadows, of objects blocking light, was puzzling to him—and [he] would come to a stop, or trip, or try to step over it. Steps, in particular, posed a special hazard, because all he could see was a confusion, a flat surface, of parallel and crisscrossing lines; he could not see them (although he knew them) as solid objects going up or coming down in three-dimensional space" (p. 63).

Based on the observations of Gregory and Wallace and of Sacks concerning their patients' poor spatial abilities and lack of constancy, it is tempting to propose that perceptual constancy and perhaps space perception in general, require learning or, at the least, exposure to spatial events early in life.

What meaning can we assign to these case studies? Since effective figural identification and recognition occurred only after a period of experience and training, these studies have been interpreted to mean that these abilities are acquired rather than innate, and it has been incorporated into an empiricistic theory of perception (Hebb, 1949). However, we cannot directly compare the behavior of the visually naïve but otherwise sophisticated adult with that of the completely naïve infant. The blind adult with knowledge gained from the other senses is very different from

the inexperienced infant. In addition, as we noted earlier, there may be some neural recognition in the adult due to early stimulus deprivation of the optical system, so that the lack of certain perceptual abilities (e.g., size constancy) cannot be attributed to experience alone. Thus, while the effects of vision restoration are of obvious interest and may suggest the role of learning a newly acquired sense, they may not offer any straightforward conclusions (Wertheimer, 1951).

PERCEPTION OF THE NEWBORN HUMAN

The classical empiricist position holds that the newborn human sees merely an undifferentiated blur—that its visual world is, in the words of the eminent nineteenth-century psychologist William James (1890), "one great blooming, buzzing confusion" (p. 488). However, as we shall see, there is considerable evidence against this assertion. Accordingly, our purpose in this section is to expand and, elaborate our examination of human infant perception, outlining some of the capacities and mechanisms that function with minimal visual experience.

Dramatic proof that the very newborn human is capable of reacting perceptually to the environment is found in a study in which an infant was tested for spatial localization 3 minutes after birth (Wertheimer, 1961). As the infant lay on her back, a toy "cricket" was clicked next to either her right or her left ear. The perceptual response was whether her eyes moved to the right, to the left, or at all. On most of the trials on which eye movement occurred, her eyes moved in the direction of the click. When the experiment was over, the subject was only 10 minutes old! This study tells us that, without any experience, some spatial features of stimulation—directionally specific auditory signals—are capable of guiding behavior in the newborn human: the very newborn human is innately capable of a basic form of auditory localization. It also suggests that there is innate coordination between auditory space and visual space. We will return to this relationship later, in a discussion of older infants. First, we will examine the ability of infants to deal with more basic tasks, such as efficiently scanning and fixating on specific regions of the visual environment.

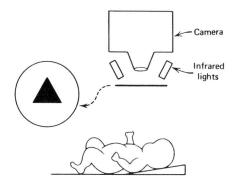

□ **figure 11.2a** Arrangement for measuring ocular fixations of the infant. The camera records the location of the infant's pupils that are marked by infrared lights. (From W. Kessen, in *Early Behavior*, edited by H. W. Stevenson, E. H. Hess, and H. L. Rheingold, John Wiley, New York, 1967, p. 153. Reprinted by permission of the publisher.)

Eye Fixations and Scanning

An important aspect of the infant's perceptual world concerns the features of a visual display that attract its attention. For example, do infants look at certain parts of a figure more than others? Do they fixate and scan individual parts of the figure or do they fixate on the whole figure? A series of studies by Salapatek and Kessen (1966; Kessen, 1967) concentrated on the relation between particular features of a figure and eye fixations made by the infant. As shown in Figure 11.2a, they exposed a black equilateral triangle on a white field to a group of 1-month-old infants and examined their scanning and fixation activity by recording the movements of the infants' eyes. The infants showed concentrated fixations on the outer contours, particularly the vertices (corners) of the triangle.

The sample record for one infant, given in Figure 11.2b, shows that 1-month-old infants tend to fixate on a single vertex, with little scanning of the sides of the triangle. This general tendency of infants to fixate on a limited portion of a figure was also found with various geometric figures (Salapatek, 1969; Salapatek & Kessen, 1973).

Is there any special functional significance of the infant's tendency to scan select parts of figures, especially vertices? Perhaps, as Haith (1978, 1980) suggests, this happens because more stimulus changes, and hence more information, lies at corners and vertices (and edges in general) than at most other regions. In other words, by scanning the distinctive, defining areas of a figure, the infant also scans the most informative areas.

Developmental Changes in Scanning and Fixation Scanning is subject to marked developmental changes. Infants during the first month of life fixate on a single element. In contrast, a broader scanning pattern is shown by older infants. In particular, the fixations of 1-month-old infants are confined to the extremities and external contours of a stimulus pattern or figure, with little fixation on internal elements (as in the infants' scanning pattern on the vertices of a triangle, noted in Figure 11.2b), whereas the scanning of the 2-month-old infant is broader and more extensive. For example, Maurer and Salapatek (1976) reported that the 2-month-old infant is more likely than the 1-month-old to scan the internal elements of a display, such as the features of a face (see also Milewski, 1976). In contrast

Subject 7 Day 1 Position 1   Subject 7 Day 1 Position 2

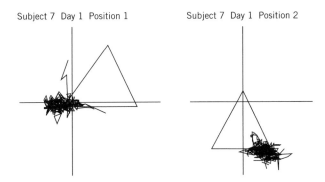

□ **figure 11.2b** Sample records of ocular fixations for a subject in the experimental group. The triangle represents the outline of the solid, black, equilateral triangle presented to the experimental subjects. (From W. Kessen, in *Early Behavior*, edited by H. W. Stevenson, E. H. Hess, and H. L. Rheingold, John Wiley, New York, 1967, p. 174. Reprinted by permission of the publisher.)

to both ages, 4-month-old infants scan *both* internal and external elements.

The progressive broadening in scanning activity with age is likely linked to other developmental changes in the infant's rapidly maturing nervous system. Salapatak (1975) speculates that at about 2 months there is enough cortical maturation so that the infant can employ memory (e.g., Davis & Rovee-Collier, 1983; Rovee-Collier, 1993; Rovee-Collier & Hayne, 1987). This suggests that memory contributes to more exploratory and integrative scanning activity.

Subsidiary visual capacities that also appear early in development probably contribute directly to scanning activity. Maurer and Lewis (1979) report that 3-month-old infants can discriminate between grossly different figures located as far out as 30° toward the periphery. That is, the 3-month-old infant can process stimuli perceived with peripheral vision.

Therefore, it is reasonable to propose that, as various visual and cognitive capabilities develop, infants' perception progresses from the focus on parts to the perception of wholes (Aslin & Salapatek, 1975). The broader scanning pattern with increasing age suggests that the infant comes to integrate individually fixated elements and features, perceiving forms as a whole. We can conclude, then, that the human newborn will select and focus on a few features of a visual pattern and then progress to more informative, integrative scanning, enabling the perception of global forms. In the next section, we continue to examine the stimulus features that attract the attention of the infant, but with particular relevance to the infant's emerging perception of form.

Form and Pattern Perception

Experiments indicate that human infants can perceive forms to varying degrees. R. L. Fantz's (1961, 1963, 1966) pioneer studies concentrated on those stimulus features that are discriminable from each other by human infants. Fantz used the **preferential looking method,** which is based on the observation that infants are highly attentive to selective features in their environment, preferring to look at certain kinds of features and stimuli more than others. It follows that if the infant consistently looks longer at one stimulus

or stimulus feature than at another, the infant is discriminating visually between the two.

One version of the apparatus used by Fantz for assessing preferential looking is shown in Figure 11.3. Typically, the infant is placed on its back in a small hammock crib inside a test or "looking chamber," so that it must look up toward two panels containing pairs of contrasting stimuli. The experimenter, looking through a small hole in the roof of the chamber, watches the infant's eyes and records their movements to determine which of the two panels the infant looks at more often and for a longer duration. By systematically varying the stimuli, the preferential looking method makes it possible to learn a great deal about early infant perception. Different looking preferences not only provide evidence of the discriminative capacities of the infant, but they also suggest what sorts of stimuli attract the attention of the newborn.

In one experiment, infants 1 to 15 weeks of age were shown several pairs of test patterns (Fantz, 1961). The paired patterns, and results for the pairs yielding significant preference differences, are shown in Figure 11.4. In terms of looking time, the more complex pairs drew the most attention. Furthermore, the relative attraction of the members of a pair depended on whether a clear pattern difference was present. Thus, there were strong preferential looking differences between the stripes and bull's eye and between the checkerboard and square, but not between the other pairs (i.e., a cross versus a circle and two identical triangles). Although not shown in the figure, infants prefer a black-and-white patterned surface over a plain patch even when the patch is brighter and in color. Since these preferences were shown at all ages tested, the role of learning appears to be minimal.

The Perception of Faces Facial patterns receive special attention from infants. When the preferential looking method was used with various patterned stimuli, including a sketch of a face, as well as plain unpatterned colored stimuli, patterned stimuli appeared more attractive (Fantz, 1961, 1963, 1966). In one experiment, preference for patterned and unpatterned stimuli was assessed with very young infants (10 hours to 5 days old) and older infants (2 to 6 months old). Three stimuli had a distinguishing pat-

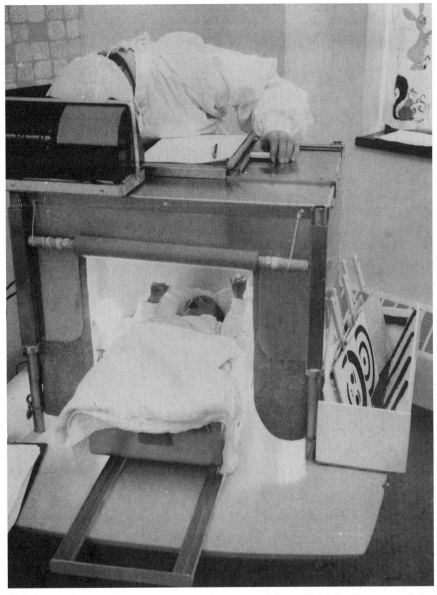

□ figure 11.3 Chamber for measuring visual preferences in infants. The infant lies on a crib in the chamber, looking up at stimuli placed in panels at the ceiling. The experimenter peers through a peephole and records the attention given each object. (*Source:* From Fantz, R. L. Pattern vision in newborn infants. *Science,* 1963, 140, 296–297. Copyright © 1963 by the American Association for the Advancement of Science.)

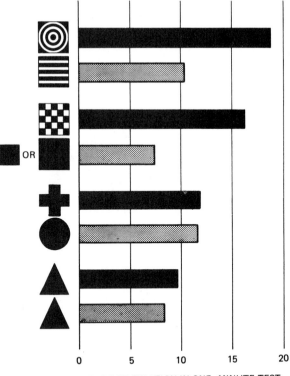

AVERAGE SECONDS OF FIXATION IN ONE–MINUTE TEST

tern: a schematic face, a bull's eye, and a patch of newsprint. Three stimuli consisted of plain patches of color: red, yellow, and white. The response measure, given in Figure 11.5, was the duration of the first fixation on each stimulus. It is clear from the figure that patterned stimuli were preferred over unpatterned colored patches; in particular, infants in both age groups preferred the schematic face.

The preference for facial patterns was further examined with three patterns in the size and shape of a head (Fantz, 1961, 1965*b*). One pattern had a schematic face, the second pattern had the same features but in scrambled form, and the third pattern had the same amounts of black and white areas as the other stimuli, but condensed into two solid sections (Figure 11.6). The three stimuli were paired in all possible combinations and shown to infants ranging in age from 4 days to 6 months. The schematic face was preferred over the other two patterns by almost all

infants. Fantz's results suggest that face-like patterns have a potent distinguishing property.

Because face-like patterns may have adaptive significance, it is tempting to suggest that representations of the human face are innately recognized. But before drawing this conclusion, consider the stimulus complexity of a face, even a schematic one. It contains figure–ground differences, contours, boundaries, edges, brightness contrasts, shadings, symmetry, and so on, each of which may be a compelling, attention-demanding feature of a stimulus independent of any specific structural or organizational (i.e., facial) relation. Moreover, attention to face-like patterns over abstract forms has not been shown consistently for all infants (Kagan, 1970).

Although infants appear to prefer face-like patterns, precisely what features of the pattern are critical is not clear. However, the visual fixation records of infants looking at real adult faces provide some age-

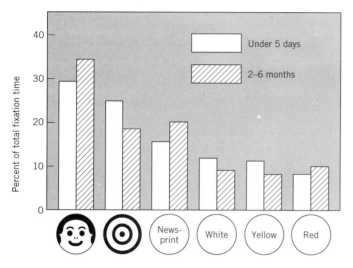

☐ *figure* **11.5** Visual preferences of newborn and older infants for black-and-white patterned disks over plain and colored disks. (From Fantz, 1966.)

dependent hints and trends. Haith, Bergman, and Moore (1977) recorded the eye fixations of 3- to 5-week-old, 7-week-old, and 9- to 11-week-old infants as the infants scanned an adult face. They found that between 5 and 7 weeks of age there is a dramatic increase in face fixations, especially on the eyes of the adult face. Recall from the section on scanning that, at about 2 months, infants begin to explore the interior components of a pattern, such as a face. Interestingly, when the adult was speaking, fixations on the eye area intensified in the two older groups. This suggests that the physical attributes of the face (such as lip and chin movement and lip–tooth contrast) are not sufficiently attractive by themselves to direct fixations away from the eye area. Perhaps, as the authors propose, the eyes become attractive to 7-week-old infants partly because they convey socially

relevant information and thus become important for social interaction.

In any case, with increasing age, infants not only can recognize a person's face but, by 4 to 6 months, may be able to recognize a familiar face even when it is seen in a different pose or viewed from a different position (Fagen, 1976). Infants of this age can also discriminate between a happy and an angry facial expression (Walker-Andrews, 1989); they can perceive a difference between male and female faces (Leinbach & Fagot, 1993; Walker-Andrews et al., 1991) and they prefer to look at attractive rather than unattractive adult and infant faces (as rated by male and female undergraduates), regardless of gender (Langlois et al., 1991; Samuels et al., 1994).

Color Perception

Very young infants possess color vision to some degree, but it is not fully developed at birth. Using a variation of the preferential looking method, Adams, Maurer, and Davis (1986) observed that infants 1 to 5 days of age can discriminate between wavelengths that typically appear red, yellow, and green, but they are not sensitive to wavelengths that ordinarily appear blue. Thus, the color vision of very young infants appears to be similar to that of individuals with *tritanopia*, a form of dichromatic color defect (described

☐ *figure* **11.6** Variations of facial patterns used by Fantz. Shown are a schematic face, a scrambled face, and a pattern containing the same amount of black and white as the faces but in only two sections.

in Chapter 5; see also Varner et al., 1985). This color-weak condition continues until about 2 to 3 months of age, at which time infants may show color discriminability approximating that of a normal adult.

Although the infant is able to discriminate between different wavelengths, we cannot conclude that it sees the same colors or hues as the adult. Do infants, like adults, see short wavelengths (about 480 nm) as blue and medium wavelengths (about 510 nm) as green? The answer with older infants appears to be "yes."

Habituation Technique To demonstrate this, Bornstein, Kessen, and Weiskopf (1976) used a basic **habituation** technique. Habituation in this case means that an infant shows less attention to (i.e., looks less at or *habituates* to) a stimulus that is repeatedly presented. Consequently when given the opportunity, the infant will choose to look at a different stimulus. The following increase in looking time to a new or changed stimulus is termed *dishabituation* or recovery from habituation.

Four-month-old infants were habituated to a blue 480-nm stimulus by a series of repeated presentations. Their looking behavior (i.e., the *amount* of looking time) was then assessed by the preferential looking method. Two physically different stimuli were presented; one color stimulus came from the same color category as the habituation stimulus (450 nm, also seen as blue by the adult human) and the other from a different color category, but equally close in wavelength to the habituation stimulus (510 nm, perceived by the human adult as green). Thus, the blue habituation stimulus (480 nm) was the same physical distance from a stimulus that to typical trichromatic adults appears blue (450 nm) as it was from a stimulus that to adults appears green (510 nm), namely, 30 nm. In this color example, infants consistently looked more at the 510-nm green stimulus (taken from a different color category, at least for adults) than they did at the 450-nm blue stimulus (chosen from the same color category); that is, they *dishabituated* to the 510-nm stimulus but not to the 450-nm stimulus. This indicates that 450- and 480-nm spectral wavelengths (both perceived as blue to adults) also appear similar to infants, and both of these wavelengths appear different from

the 510-nm green stimulus. Similar results were reported when the color boundaries of green, yellow, and red were subjected to the same habituation and preferential looking techniques. These findings indicate that 4-month-old-infants possess color vision and that the four primary color categories seen by trichromatic adults—blue, green, yellow, and red—are matched by infants. In short, the color categories of infants and adults are similarly organized.

Visual Acuity

Visual acuity is one of the most basic measures of pattern vision development in the human infant. It is a dynamic ability, displaying progressive developmental changes. Several electrophysiological and behavioral (or preference) techniques are used to assess acuity, each yielding somewhat different values (see Dobson & Teller, 1978). We will focus on the method using preferential looking.

Preferential Looking and Acuity
The typical *preferential looking* method for assessing infant acuity involves a modification of the forced-choice preferential looking procedure of Fantz, described earlier. This procedure uses grating patterns specified in terms of their spatial frequency (cycles per degree of visual angle, or c/deg; spatial frequency was discussed in Chapter 6). Infants are placed before a display screen on which the experimenter flashes a grating pattern on one side and a uniform gray field of equal size and luminance on the other side (Figure 11.7). The experimenter then records which side the infant fixates on. A consistent preference indicates that the grating is discriminable to the infant. Typically, gratings are presented in order of increasing spatial frequency: when coarse patterns, of low spatial frequency (i.e., comprised of wide gratings), are paired with the uniform gray field, the grating is initially fixated; however, as the spatial frequency pattern increases (and the gratings become finer), preference for the pattern decreases. The acuity threshold is reached when infants fail to show a consistent or significant looking preference for either the uniform gray field or the grating pattern, that is, when the infant's preference for the grating pattern drops to

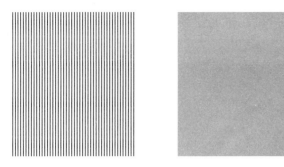

▭ *figure* **11.7** An example of stimuli used to assess visual acuity with infants using the preferential looking method.

about 50%. Thus, the highest spatial frequency preferentially fixated by the infant marks the acuity threshold value.

This procedure shows that visual acuity is poor at birth but develops rapidly in the first 6 months of life. It is poor at birth mainly because of the immaturity of the visual cortex and the retina—especially the fovea (Abramov et al., 1982; Banks & Bennett, 1988; Wilson, 1988; Youdelis & Hendrickson, 1986). At birth the density of cones in the fovea is less than a third of that of the adult fovea, but it rapidly increases within the first 6 months of life. The rise in visual acuity during this period of infancy thus depends primarily on the overall maturation of the visual system.

Specified in Snellen notation (described in Chapter 4) and spatial frequency, acuity in the newborn varies from 20/1200 (about 0.5 c/deg) to 20/600 (1 c/deg); it is 20/200 (about 3 c/deg) at 4 months of age, 20/100 (6 c/deg) at 6 months, and 20/50 (about 12 c/deg) at 1 year (Dobson & Teller, 1978; Gwiazda, Brill, & Held, 1979). By comparison, that normal adult acuity is 20/20, or 30 c/deg.

Oblique Effect The acuity measures described are based on grating patterns that were horizontally or vertically oriented. When the patterns are obliquely oriented, acuity measures are much lower. Moreover, when oblique grating patterns are paired with horizontal or vertical gratings matched in spatial frequency, there is a marked preference for the vertical and horizontal grating patterns over the oblique ones. This reduced acuity for oblique grating patterns is termed the **oblique effect.** Figure 11.8 provides a self-demonstration of the oblique effect.

DEMONSTRATION:
The Oblique Effect

While you view Figure 11.8 from a comfortable reading distance, look across each row and count how many patterns have gratings that are detectable. If you are subject to the oblique effect, you will be able to see further along the row of vertical and horizontal grating patterns (90° and 180°) than along either of the two rows of oblique grating patterns (45° and 135°). Due to your own astigmatism, you may see the horizontal grating pattern more clearly than the vertical one, or vice versa.

The oblique effect is found in many species (Appelle, 1972), including the monkey (Bauer et al., 1979), as well as in most human infants, children, and adults; moreover, it is present throughout life and even appears to increase with age (Mayer, 1977). It emerges between 6 weeks and 3 months of age (Braddick, Wattam-Bell, & Atkinson, 1986; Gwiazda et al., 1978; Leehey et al., 1975; Sokol, Moskowitz, & Hansen, 1987).

Interestingly, the oblique effect has also been attributed to experience with an urban environment (e.g., Annis & Frost, 1973; Mitchell, 1980), when vertical and horizontal contours predominate over oblique ones. However, considering the infant's generally supine physical position and the visual environment it provides, it is unlikely that the typical infant's retina is exposed to more vertical and horizontal contours than oblique ones. Moreover, the findings of an

□ *figure 11.8* Self-demonstration of the oblique effect. While the page is at a normal reading distance, look across each row and count how many grating patterns are detectable. (Note that the gratings in each column are identical and are merely shown at different angular orientations). (Based on a demonstration by Donald E. Mitchell, 1988; figure courtesy of Dr. Mitchell.)

oblique effect in early human infancy (Leehey et al., 1975) and in a wide range of lower species (Appelle, 1972) cast doubt on a primary explanation based on environmental biasing. It seems likely, then, that the oblique effect has an innate, genetic origin.

Space Perception

This section focuses on the development of space perception. Although our major concern is with human perception, a large body of research on the space perception of lower animals bears directly on general issues of perceptual development and warrants our attention here. We begin by examining the origins of

one of the most crucial visual abilities: *depth perception*.

Depth Perception

Animal Studies Many studies on the development of depth perception involve animals reared from birth in a light-restricted environment. Such studies assume that if an animal reared without light experience shows efficient depth perception when it first emerges into the light, this ability is likely unlearned.

Research using the visual cliff apparatus (described in Chapter 9) on many species of animals with no light experience indicates that they can discriminate depth on their first experience in a lighted environment. Thus, for many animals, depth perception appears to require no training (e.g., Carr & McGuigan, 1965; Walk, Trychin, & Karmel, 1965). In fact, infant rats demonstrated depth perception immediately after their eyes opened for the first time (Bauer, 1973; Lore & Sawatski, 1969). Similar findings have been reported for hamsters (Schiffman, 1971), goats (Walk & Gibson, 1961), monkeys (Rosenblum & Cross, 1963), and chicks (Shinkman, 1963). The fact that the chick moves about, pecks accurately, and demonstrates depth perception almost immediately after hatching indicates its innate origin for this animal. In general, for most animals, visual depth perception appears to be innate (Walk, 1978).

Human Studies Is depth perception innate in the human infant? There is no precise answer based on infant visual cliff studies. In general, early experience in the human infant cannot be rigorously controlled. For obvious reasons, light restriction experiments cannot be performed. Moreover, the typical infant must be at least 6 months of age (and thus somewhat visually experienced) before it can crawl and move about and thus even be tested on the visual cliff apparatus. However, from numerous other studies, especially those involving reaching for and avoiding objects, we know that infants possess visual depth perception well before they can crawl—probably soon after birth (e.g., Bower, 1974; Campos et al., 1978; Fox et al., 1980; Walk, 1978). Interestingly, depth perception appears to develop even before the onset of a fear of heights. In one study reported by Bertenthal and Campos (1989), locomotor (i.e., capable of crawling) and prelocomotor infants about 7 months old were placed directly on the glass over the deep side of a visual cliff. Fear of height was assessed based on acceleration in heart rate. Only the infants with locomotor experience showed the accelerated heart rate indicative of fear of height. It appears that *fear* of height appears to come about shortly afterward, probably as a direct result of crawling experience (e.g., Campos et al., 1978; Bertenthal & Campos, 1989).

Object Avoidance: Looming An object hurled at a person in the direct field of view, appearing as if it will collide, produces an automatic avoidance reaction. The complex spatial information that specifies an *imminent collision* with a moving object is called **looming** (Schiff, 1965). This information occurs from an accelerated magnification—a continuous increase in the retinal size—of an approaching shape or silhouette of an object. The rapid expansion of the retinal image of the object causes it to *loom* up as it approaches the viewer.

One apparatus used to study looming with human infants, shown in Figure 11.9, consists of a point source of light from a shadow-casting device that projects the silhouette of an object onto a projection screen. By the appropriate movement of the object between the light and screen, the projected shadow can be made to undergo continuous expansion or contraction. Expansion or magnification of the shadow results in the impression of an object approaching at a uniform speed, that is, it specifies *looming*. Contraction or minification yields the impression of an object receding into the distance, which Schiff (1980) calls *zooming*. Notice that in looming and zooming nothing actually needs to approach the ob-

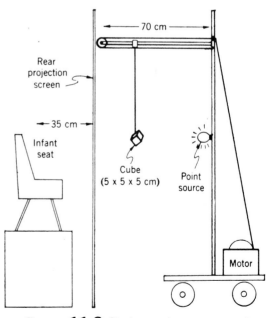

□ figure 11.9 Shadow-casting apparatus. (From W. Ball and E. Tronick, "Infant responses to impending collision: Optical and real, "*Science, 171,* 1971, p. 819. Copyright © 1971 by the American Association for the Advancement of Science.)

server; the physical information only simulates something approaching or receding.

Animal Studies This apparatus has been used in studies with a variety of animals, including crabs, frogs, turtles, chicks, kittens, and infant and adult monkeys. Crabs responded to a looming pattern by running, flinching, or flattening out. Frogs reacted most often by jumping away from a looming image. Chicks responded with various avoidance behaviors: flinching, "back pedaling," crouching or squatting, and hopping. Although the reaction of kittens was less consistent and conclusive, they also showed an avoidance reaction to image magnification simulating looming (Schiff, 1965). Turtles reacted to a looming pattern by withdrawing their heads into their shells (Hayes & Saiff, 1967). Both adult and infant monkeys rapidly withdrew, leaping to the rear of their cage (Schiff, Caviness, & Gibson, 1962). Alarm cries often accompanied the retreat of the younger animals. By contrast, for most animals, a receding form—zooming—produced exploratory rather than avoidance or alarm reactions.

Human Studies Human infants react similarly to a looming pattern simulating collision. For example, in a study by Ball and Tronick (1971) with 24 human infants ranging in age from 2 to 11 weeks, the responses to a looming silhouette of a cube on a direct collision course were various forms of avoidance activities (e.g., blinking, moving the head back and away from the screen, bringing the arms toward the face, stiffening the body, and fear vocalizations). These responses did not occur for expanding images of an object approaching the infant on a *miss* path (in these cases, the infants showed tracking rather than avoidance responses) or for zooming silhouettes. These results were observed in all infants, regardless of age, and duplicated the results obtained when real objects rather than silhouettes were used. Similar results have been reported with 6- to 20-day-old infants. The avoidance responses observed to a looming stimulus consisted of the eyes opening wide, backward movement of the head, and movement of both hands between the object and the face (Bower, Broughton, & Moore, 1971; Dunkeld & Bower, 1980; Nanez, 1988).

An avoidance reaction to a rapidly approaching object is clearly adaptive: *avoidance prevents collision.* That the perception of imminent collision and its avoidance occurs at a very early age, and in a wide range of animal species, indicates that it is probably unlearned. Moreover, responses to looming probably have a biological basis. This is consistent with the suggestion made in Chapter 8 in regard to *retinal expansion:* the visual system may contain neural subunits or channels for picking up and processing rapid size changes in the retinal image—the sorts of retinal changes that signal looming (e.g., Regan, Beverley, & Cynader, 1979; Regan, Kaufman, & Lincoln, 1986).

Spatial Cues and Pictorial Perception As we observed in Chapter 9, the perception of space is mediated by information from monocular and binocular spatial cues. However, all of the spatial cues available to the adult may not be functional in the infant. Moreover, the availability of some cues depends on the age of the infant. For example, 7-month-old infants can perceive depth using *interposition* (i.e., the monocular cue whereby one object or surface appears to cover another), whereas 5-month-olds cannot (Granrud & Yonas, 1984).

Static monocular cues such as interposition, shading and lighting, linear perspective, texture gradients, and so on that enable *pictorial perception*—the impression of depth on a two-dimensional surface—become functional between the ages of 5 and 7 months (e.g., Granrud & Yonas, 1984; Granrud, Yonas, & Opland, 1985; Yonas, Granrud, Arterberry, & Hanson, 1986). The use of binocular disparity for stereoscopic vision develops by about 3 1/2 to 4 months of age (Fox et al., 1980; Held, Birch, & Gwiazda, 1980; Petrig et al., 1981).

Size and Shape Constancy Two important integrative abilities derived from spatial cues are *size* and *shape constancy.* Recall from Chapter 10 that the perception of an object's size and shape does not change very much even when the size and shape of the projected retinal image change. The size and shape of an object remain constant even when we view it from different distances and angles. Do infants perceive a stable spatial visual environment? Evidence indicates that constancy develops as the infant learns to use cues to depth and slant; this ability is reasonably well developed by 6 months of age. Hence, size and shape constancy are functional at least by 6 months of age, and possibly even sooner (e.g., Caron, Caron, & Carlson, 1979; McKenzie, Tootell, & Day, 1980).

Auditory-Visual Events   We introduced the section on perception in the human newborn by showing that an infant almost immediately after birth could make an appropriate spatial response to an auditory signal. The ability to link auditory and visual stimulation appropriately develops further with age, enabling more complicated activities. For example, infants 1–2 months of age showed distress on hearing their mothers' voices while the voices were displaced in space (Aronson & Rosenbloom, 1971). In the experiment, the mother was located in a room with a window that directly faced the infant. The infant viewed its mother, but by the use of a stereo amplifier system heard her voice emanate from 90° to the right or left. In other words, the infant's mother appeared directly in front, but her voice was heard coming from the right or left. The result—that the infants recognized and reacted emotionally to this spatial discrepancy—indicates that infants perceive the *relationship* between normally correlated auditory and visual stimulation.

Changes in Sights and Sounds   Perception of many spatial events with sound-emitting objects involves *changes* in sounds synchronized with *changes* in apparent distance. Thus, when we see an object such as an automobile move toward or away from us, there is a corresponding change in the engine sounds we hear. For the adult, variation in the sound is closely linked to variation in the image, creating the perception of a single, unified spatial event. Do infants perceive the same relationship between the sight and sound of a moving object? This question was studied by Walker-Andrews and Lennon (1985; Walker-Andrews, 1989, 1994). Five-month-old infants were presented with two films side by side, one of an automobile approaching *and* another of an automobile driving away; simultaneously, the infants heard a single sound track that either increased *or* decreased in

sound intensity but was appropriate to only one of the films (i.e., appropriately, the sound track increased in loudness for the film showing an automobile approaching and became softer for the film of an automobile driving away). The infants' looking behavior (i.e., fixation time) was significantly greater for the appropriately sound-matched film. That is, infants preferred to view the film that was spatially synchronized with the sound, verifying that infants as young as 5 months of age can detect the relation between the sight and sound of a moving object (see also Lewkowicz, 1992).

Facial and Auditory Expressions of Emotions   Infants also appear capable of matching facial expressions with vocal expressions of emotions. Arlene Walker-Andrews (1986) studied this ability in 7-month-old infants using differences in looking behavior similar to those of the preceding experiment. Infants watched a pair of films, projected side by side, of an angry *and* a happy speaker while they heard a recording of either an angry *or* a happy voice. (Note that the lower third of the face of each film was covered so that infants could not simply match the voice to lip movements on the film). The infants increased their fixations to a particular facial expression when it was matched by the appropriate vocalization. Infants who heard the happy voice tended to watch the happy face, whereas infants who heard the angry voice tended to watch the angry face. Interestingly, no particular emotional expression was preferred; that is, infants did not look longer at the happy or the angry face, independent of the sound manipulation (see also Walker-Andrews & Lennon, 1991).

Voice Recognition in Infancy   The ability of an infant to recognize its mother's voice develops very early. There is evidence that the newborn infant less than 3 days of age will suck on a nonnutritive nipple in a specific manner to produce its mother's voice in preference to the voice of another female adult (DeCasper & Fifer, 1980). The preference for the mother's voice in infants with very limited maternal experience suggests that a very brief period shortly after birth is sufficient for initiating recognition of her voice. Moreover, in addition to preferring their own mother's voice, newborn infants showed a preference for a specific *Dr. Seuss* passage that was read aloud by the mother during her third trimester of pregnancy (DeCasper & Spence, 1986; see also Gandelman, 1992, pp. 36–40).

Before moving on to a different set of topics involving the development of *perceptual–motor abilities,* we should take stock of the extensive perceptual abilities available in infancy. Reflecting on the capacities we have discussed, it is clear that during the first year—probably by 6 or 7 months of age—the infant has acquired the basic perceptual abilities. Perceptual development is, of course, an ongoing process. The interplay of physiology, maturation, and experience continues to increase the competence of the perceptual abilities acquired during the first year of life.

DEVELOPMENT OF PERCEPTUAL–MOTOR COORDINATION

In some of the research discussed in the preceding sections, aspects of perceptual development were assessed by observing limb or body-part movement. An animal was seen to ward off a looming object or to move toward a shallow rather than a deep surface (depth perception). The acquisition of such visually guided behavior clearly involves the development of a link between the organism's perception and its self-initiated movement, that is, the development of **perceptual–motor coordination.**

Perceptual–Motor Coordination

Normal visually guided behavior—even very simple activities such as reaching out your hand and turning this page—involves a precise and intentional muscular or motor movement in response to optical stimulation. An enormous number of almost effortlessly executed daily activities involve perceptual–motor coordination. Important questions for us here are these: How does the ability to execute smooth motor movements in response to the visual environment develop? Do we have to learn to coordinate our move-

ments with our perception? In other words, what is the functional relationship between intentional, self-initiated movement and normal perceptual development?

Active versus Passive Experience: Carousel Experiment   The acquisition of accurate perceptual-motor coordination seems to depend on *experience* with active bodily movements under visual guidance. That is, the organism must *actively* interact with the spatial environment to develop perceptual–motor development. This conclusion is based on **carousel experiments** performed by Richard Held and his colleagues in studying the development of visually guided spatial behavior.

Held and Hein (1963) raised kittens in the dark until they developed enough motor maturity to move about (at about 8 to 12 weeks of age). At testing, the kittens were paired off and given 3 hours of daily light exposure in the "carousel" apparatus shown in Figure 11.10. The pair members were assigned to an *active* (A) and a *passive* (P) movement condition. Kitten A was placed in a neck harness and body clamp that allowed it to move in a circular path within a cylinder whose inside surface was painted in vertical stripes; kitten P was restricted to a gondola whose movements varied directly with those of kitten A. The experiment was devised to provide identical optical and motion stimulation to each member of a pair. By means of the apparatus, the self-produced locomotor activity of kitten A controlled the activity of its mate, kitten P. In brief, the apparatus provided equivalent visual and motion stimulation to each member of a pair, but the motion was active and self-produced for kitten A and passively imposed for kitten P. Note also that kitten P was not immobilized. It was free to move its head and could also move its paws along the floor of the gondola. However, the movements of kitten P, unlike those of kitten A, were not systematically and functionally associated with changes in the visual input.

The behavioral tests for assessing the effect of active versus passive movement experience included (1) a test for *visual placing* (the automatic, visually mediated extension, or reaching out, of the paw as if to prevent collision when the animal is moved toward

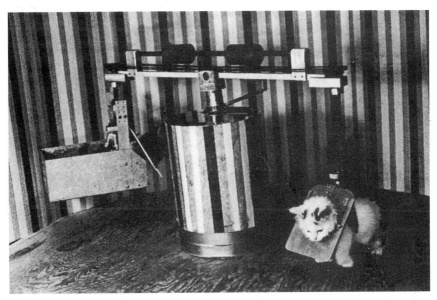

◁▷ *figure 11.10* Carousel apparatus used to control visual and movement information for kittens. The passive kitten (P) on the left sits in an elevated gondola, while the active (A) kitten on the right wears a harness that controls the movement of the carousel. Thus, as the active kitten moves in a circular path, it also moves the gondola and the passive kitten. The result is that both kittens receive identical visual experience from the circular environment, but only the active kitten receives visual feedback from its own movement. (*Source:* From Kimble, Garmezy, and Zigler, 1980, 94.)

a surface—similar to looming); (2) blinking to an approaching object; and (3) depth perception on the visual cliff apparatus. Differences between active and passive kittens occurred on all tests. Onset of the visual placing and blinking responses was significantly delayed for the passive kittens. Tests on the visual cliff showed that the active kittens performed like normally reared animals, whereas the passive kittens showed little evidence of depth discrimination. That is, the active kittens did not descend to the deep side, whereas the passive kittens descended to both the shallow and deep sides on a chance basis.

It appears that mere passive experience in the carousel interfered with the normal maturational process by which these responses develop. (However, these perceptual-motor deficiencies of the passive kittens were readily remedied; after 48 hours of free movement in an illuminated room, the passive kittens performed normally on the tests.)

The major point raised by this study is that if movement and perception are not properly inte-

grated, but instead develop independently, deficiencies in perceptual–motor development result. Thus, *changes* in visual stimulation simultaneous with active, self-produced movement are essential for the normal development of perceptual–motor coordination and visually guided spatial activity. In other words, the development of perceptual–motor coordination requires more than exposure to changing visual stimulation; it also requires that the organism actively promote the changes using self-produced movement.

Parallel results on visually guided reaching with monkeys (Bauer & Held, 1975; Held & Bauer, 1967) confirm the observations with kittens. Extensions of this research to the human infant also stress the importance of self-produced movement for the development of perceptual–motor coordination, particularly exploratory activities such as reaching and grasping (White 1969; White, Castle, & Held, 1964; Zelazo, Zelazo, & Kolb, 1972). It is clear that for a wide range of mammals, including the human infant, the sight of its own actively moving body parts is necessary to develop visually coordinated movements of those parts.

PERCEPTUAL ADAPTATION TO DISTORTED VISUAL STIMULATION

Closely related to perceptual–motor development is the modifiability of perception when visual stimulation is distorted. Here we focus on the consistent rearrangement or alteration in the usual relationship between the external environment and an organism's normal optical stimulation. A familiar example concerns the novice wearer of prescription eyeglasses. The first day or two may be marked by visual distortion and perhaps by minor motor disturbances such as inaccurately reaching or placing or, in general, poorly executed visually guided motor activities. However, these problems soon disappear. Indeed, to the person wearing the glasses, it seems that the total visual system effortlessly adjusts, or *adapts,* to the initial distortion, and the world as viewed through the glasses appears normal (in fact, there should be an overall gain—the glasses should increase the viewer's acuity). This general process of readjustment is referred to as **adaptation,** and it appears to involve a form of learning or relearning.

There are several reasons for studying the modifiability of the perceptual system. For one thing, it is important to examine how the perception of consistently rearranged or distorted directional information can continue to guide spatial responses. Moreover, studying the adaptability of the perceptual–motor system to consistent spatial displacement may help us understand the development and perhaps the origin of spatial perception. That is, the conditions that mediate adaptation may provide clues to the variables that affect and control perceptual–motor development. The point we are making here is that there may be factors common to adaptation in the adult and the development of perceptual–motor coordination in the newborn. Thus, it is possible that the way the mature organism adapts to consistent spatial distortions basically re-creates the way in which perception normally develops in infancy.

Although this comparison is appealing, it must be qualified because the perceptual abilities of the adult are far more rich and complex than those of the infant. Many compensatory mechanisms and preestablished relationships normally available to the adult may be used for adaptation. This suggests that by analyzing adaptation to optical distortions in the mature organism, we may not be studying an original developmental process. More likely, we may be studying an instance of the mature adult's well-established capacity to deal with consistent changes in visual stimulation. However, with these reservations in mind, there is still much to learn from studying perceptual modifications in the adult. In fact, findings on how the visual system adapts to consistent distortions in stimulation can provide some broad insights, or at least hints, concerning the overall malleability of the visual system.

Adaptation to Prism-Induced Distortion

Studies on adaptation to distorted stimulation generally require that viewers wear optical devices producing controlled transformations or rearrangements of visual stimulation; after these devices are worn for a while, the effects on the viewer's perceptual–motor performance of specific activities are measured. The optical distortions include those achieved by lens systems that induce inversion, reversal, lateral displacement, and curvature of the contours of the visual input.

One optical device used to produce consistent distortion is the wedge prism, illustrated in Figure 11.11. It is a wedge-shaped lens that bends light so that the objects viewed through it appear to be shifted laterally in the direction of the apex. Howard (1982) has suggested a simple demonstration, using a wedge prism and a target-pointing task, in which the effects of lateral displacement can be easily experienced. As shown in Figure 11.12, several numbers are marked on the edge of a card placed horizontally under the viewer's chin. With one eye closed, the viewer looks through the prism and is directed to extend the arm and point a finger toward a number on the edge of the card. The viewer then brings the arm down, after which the aiming movement is repeated several times to each of the numbers on the edge of the card in

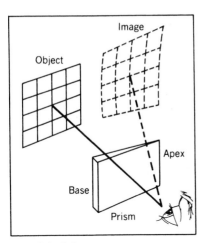

□ *figure* **11.11** A wedge prism and its optical properties. The prism produces a lateral displacement of the visual field. As a result of the varying thickness of the prism and the angle of incidence of the light rays, the visual field appears displaced and expanded on the apex (or pointed) side and relatively compressed on the base side. In addition, vertical contours appear curved, particularly toward the apex side. Finally, up–down head movements performed while viewing through the prism induce an apparent seesaw motion of the visual field, whereas lateral head movements cause an alternative expansion and compression of the visual field. (After Welch, 1986.)

random order. The error in pointing is obvious in the first several trials, but soon the viewer's aim becomes accurate; that is, the viewer *adapts* to the displaced image. After adaptation is achieved and the prism is

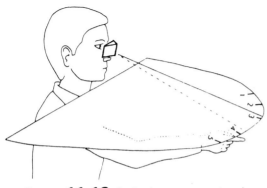

□ *figure* **11.12** A simple arrangement, using a wedge prism, for demonstrating adaptation of pointing to displaced vision. (After Howard, 1982, p. 493.)

removed, the first few aims of the finger at a given number will be off target in the opposite direction of the error first made when the prism was in place.

Adaptation to Optical Inversion and Reversal

Although lateral displacement of the visual scene due to prism wearing is initially an unusual experience, it is mild compared to the kinds of displacement induced in the classic **Stratton experiment** and **Kohler experiment.**

Stratton Experiment   In a classic experiment in 1896, George Stratton wore a specially designed optical system that produced an up–down inversion and a left–right reversal of the visual image. The subject, who in this case was Stratton himself, saw all objects reversed and upside down, as if the physical scene were rotated 180°. From a reading of his reports, there seems to have been marked disruption and disorientation of perceptual-motor coordination initially, but after several days he reported fleeting impressions of his visual world as normally oriented with a waning tendency to correct intentionally for his movements. With still longer experience with the displacing optical system, a greater degree of normalcy was reported (Stratton, 1897*a,* 1897*b*). In general, there was a strong suggestion that he was making some sort of adaptation to his new visual world, although it is not clear from his account whether he began to "see" the world right side up or whether he only learned to adjust his behavior to a world that appeared reversed and upside down. The conclusion that some adjustment was made, despite the maintenance of a retinally distorted image, is strengthened by the fact that removal of the system produced an *aftereffect*: the world briefly appeared slightly distorted. Generally, these reports have been substantiated (Ewert, 1930; Snyder & Pronko, 1952).

Kohler Experiment   Ivo Kohler (1962, 1964) reported an extensive investigation on adaptation to various forms of optical rearrangement. For example, after wearing spectacles that produced a reversal of left and right (i.e., mirror reversal) continually for 15 days, one subject reported the following: "It seems that everything in vision is the way it really is; the house, for instance, which I see through the right window, really appears to be on the right; and the parts of the car look just as they would feel if I were to touch them" (p. 154). Kohler writes that on the eighteenth day "very paradoxical impressions resulted. Approaching pedestrians were seen on the correct side, but their right shoulders were seen on the subject's right side. Inscriptions on buildings, or advertisements, were still seen in mirror writing, but the objects containing them were seen in the correct location. Vehicles . . . carried license numbers in mirror writing. A strange world indeed!" (p. 155). After 37 days, the subject

> *achieved almost completely correct impressions, even where letters and numbers were involved. In reading, for example, the first words to rectify themselves were the common ones, whereas those that had to be looked at attentively remained reversed. . . . After much practice, "mirror reading" became so well established and previous memories so secondary that even print looked all right, as long as attention was not too critical.* (p. 160)

It appears that individuals eventually adjust and adapt to optically reversed input. This is reasonable in light of the fact that a reversing optical system does provide a consistent and essentially intact source of information about the environment, although in an altered form. In fact, Kohler found that adaptation to spatial reversal was eventually sufficient to allow complicated perceptual-motor activities such as skiing and bicycling.

Of course, we cannot conclude that a real change in visual perception occurs after wearing the devices over time; that is, it is not clear whether visual space appears normally oriented over time when wearing devices that optically alter the retinal image.

Active Movement and Adaptation

Adaptation to optical rearrangement poses an important question: What conditions and variables are necessary to produce the adaptation? That is, how must the viewer interact with the distorted optical input in order to achieve adaptation? Earlier, we observed that the development of normal perceptual–motor coordination requires active movements by kittens. It also appears that adaptation depends on stimulation resulting from self-produced, *active movements*. A series of experiments, using considerably less drastic optical changes than those employed by Stratton and Kohler, clarify the nature of this source of stimulation for achieving adaptation.

Held and his colleagues (Held & Gottlieb, 1958; Held & Hein, 1958; Held & Schlank, 1959) performed experiments with human adults that compared the effectiveness of active, self-produced movements with that of passive movements to a displaced visual input. In one experiment, viewers watched their hand through a wedge prism, which, as illustrated in Figure 11.11, produced an apparently lateral displacement of the image. An *active* group watched their hand movements through the prism while they intentionally moved it from side to side. In contrast, a *passive* group watched their hand movements through the prism while it was moved by the experimenter. Immediately after several minutes of wedge prism viewing, members of both groups were required to perform a simple task consisting of making a mark at the corners of a square.

Only the group allowed active movement showed a compensating shift in the marking task and adapted to the displaced image produced by the prism-viewing experience. That is, only members of the active group were accurate in marking the corners of a target whose image was laterally displaced. Thus, even though all members of both the active and passive groups received the same displaced visual input concerning body-part movement, when the movements were passively imposed—with no sensory feedback from self-produced movement—the visual input was insufficient to produce adaptation.

Adaptation and Negative Aftereffects Adaptation to the distortion produced by prism viewing may also induce a related aftereffect. After adaptation occurred for the active group and the wedge prisms were removed, for a short time the visual environment appeared to be shifted laterally in the direction *opposite* to the optical displacement induced by the prism. In other words, prism viewing by the active group incurred a temporary but measurable *negative aftereffect* (discussed in several other contexts, notably in Chapters 5 and 7). The negative aftereffects may be thought of as a continuation of the adaptation effects, but now imposed on normal viewing conditions. However, this postexposure error or negative aftereffect due to prism viewing is transient and gradually declines (Welch et al., 1993).

The role of active movements for adaptation and postexposure negative aftereffects has also been documented for movements of the entire body (e.g., Hay, 1981; Held & Bossom, 1961). In one experiment, subjects wore wedge prisms that displaced the retinal image 11° to the left. An active group walked unaided for an hour along an outdoor path. In contrast, each subject in a passive group sat in a wheelchair and was moved along the same path for the same period. The logic of the experiment was as follows: if prism adaptation is successful, the subject should, over time, perceive the leftward-displaced retinal location as being straight ahead. Thus, when the prisms are removed after adaptation and the subject is directed to point straight ahead, he or she should now point to 11° to the *right* side (i.e., showing a negative aftereffect). The results coincide with the previous studies on adaptation of hand movement: adaptation and a postexposure negative aftereffect occurred only in the active group.

Adaptation and Perceptual-Motor Correlation
A critical aspect of active movement in these and many related studies is that the optical displacement must be *systematically* and *consistently* related to the organism's motor or movement activity: motor output and sensory input must be *correlated*. In other words, the causal link between actual movement and visual feedback—no matter how perturbed or distorted—must be stable (Welch, 1986). In contrast, adaptation is not possible when signals from the motor system are wholly independent of visual feedback. If the sensory feedback from the environment is inconsistent with what one actively does to the environment—referred to as **decorrelated feedback**—adaptation is not possible. Generally, the conditions that

produce decorrelated feedback are signs of environmental instability—for example, when muscle movements do not produce corresponding bodily movement (e.g., the astronaut in free flight on zero-gravity maneuvers), in certain neurological disorders where afferent or efferent transmission is blocked or distorted, or where all bodily movements are produced entirely by external forces. Fortunately, under normal conditions, these events are rare.

There are many questions about the role of active movements in adaptation. For example, what is changed when adaptation to optical distortions occurs? Is the site of the adaptation visual or positional? Is it cognitive or sensory? Harris (1965, 1980) suggests that the position sense is modified. For instance, when wearing image-reversing lenses, wearers feel their arms and legs to be where the lenses show them to be. That is, the felt position of the body becomes congruent with the visual input.

What makes active movement effective in achieving perceptual–motor adaptation? Perhaps, in part, it is due to the greater total stimulation of the active compared to the passive viewer. Maybe the passive viewer is less motivated to engage in visual exploration and, hence, samples less of the stimulation available to the active viewer.

Another factor that may contribute to adaptation is that the active movements made to optical displacement provide more direct information on the discrepancy between what is seen and what is felt than passive movements (Lackner, 1977). In other words, feedback from active movement provides direct, immediate information on the extent and direction of placement errors, which in turn may provide a basis for correction or for learning a new relation. Thus, according to this view, what appears to be crucial for adaptation is visual feedback cues on the mismatch between actual movement and its consequence.

Active movement provides a source of corrective feedback, indicating the direction and extent of the error induced by viewing an optically distorted display, and it plays a critical role in perceptual–motor learning and performance (Keele, 1986). It follows that the more information the viewer has concerning the nature of the error, the greater the perceptual–motor adaptation to optical distortions.

Comparative Studies of Adaptation

Adaptation to optical displacement is not limited to humans. Foley (1940) reported that monkeys adjusted some of their movements after wearing an inverting lens for 8 days. Bossom and Hamilton (1963) found that monkeys adapted to lateral displacement after 2 days. Cats (Howard & Templeton, 1966) and chickens also adapted to optically displaced vision. Rossi (1968, 1969) reported that chicks, wearing laterally displacing prisms from the day of hatching, adapted after 8 days of displacement.

Adaptation to optically displaced vision, however, has limitations. Of interest to this discussion are studies with amphibia in which drastic spatial rearrangement was introduced by surgical modification of the visual system. In one of a series of studies performed by Roger Sperry (1951), the eyeballs of a frog were rotated through 180° and healed in this new position; optically, this produced both up–down inversion and front–back reversal. When tested for object localization, the frog reacted in the same manner as did humans after first wearing inverting lenses. As illustrated in Figure 11.13, when an object (a fly) moved in one direction, the frog responded by moving in the diametrically opposite direction. However, unlike subsequent adaptation by mammals and birds to systematic optical displacements, the frog's inappropriate and obviously maladaptive responses (inappropriate to the physical environment, not to the visual image) persisted, uncorrected by experience.

The phylogenetic differences in adaptation indicate that not all species can benefit from systematic perceptual–motor feedback. Taub (1968) proposed that adaptation to optically rearranged stimulation involves a unique form of learning that alters the appearance of visual space (see also Bedford, 1989). If a form of learning is central to adaptation, then the phylogenetic differences in adaptation to optical displacement may in fact reflect phylogenetic differences in the ability to learn the necessary components for adaptation. While a firm conclusion is not possible, we conclude that mammals (and birds) possess the learning capacities required for adaptation to a systematic optical rearrangement, whereas amphibia and perhaps lower animals do not.

VISION AND AGING

Most of the perceptual processes and abilities described in this chapter that develop progressively appear to stabilize early in life. However, in adulthood, some visual capacities tend to decrease with aging, especially during the middle to later years. Some of this reduced efficiency may be due to the natural effects of aging or to diseases that become more prevalent with age.

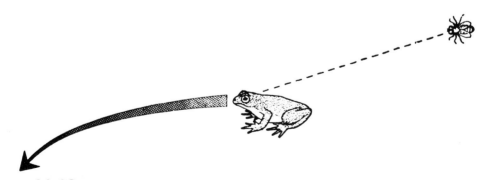

□ *figure 11.13* Error in spatial localization of an object following rotation of the eyeball of a frog. With the eye rotated 180°, the frog strikes at a point in the visual field diametrically opposite the place where an object (a fly) is actually located. This inappropriate reaction is not corrected with repeated experience. (Revised from Sperry, 1951.)

The Eye and Aging

Age-related impairment in vision may be due to changes in the efficiency of some of the structures of the eye, namely, the cornea, pupil, lens, and ocular muscles. Generally, these changes first appear between 35 and 45 years of age. As we noted in Chapter 3 in discussing *presbyopia,* with age the lens hardens and loses its flexibility. Part of the reason is that the lens is composed of epithelial cells like those found in hair, nails, and skin that continue to grow throughout life. However, unlike the skin or nails, the lens cannot shed its excess cells; with age, it becomes densely packed and less flexible. The major effect of loss of flexibility in the lens is a reduction in its ability to *accommodate.* That is, the lens loses its capacity to change its shape to focus on nearby objects. With age the lens also becomes more yellow, which acts as a light filter, reducing the amount of light reaching the retina; moreover, since yellow absorbs wavelengths from the blue-green end of the spectrum, there is a reduction in the sensitivity to surfaces that reflect short wavelengths.

Cataracts   The lens is the site of still another age-related condition called **cataracts.** Cataracts are a form of opacity, or clouding, of the normally transparent lens that impairs its ability to transmit light to the retina. In advanced cases, cataracts may even make the normally black pupil appear yellowish or white. The dominant visual effect of cataracts is a significant blurring of vision. There are many types of cataracts, and they can occur at any age (they may even be present at birth); however, the most common type, called *senile cataracts,* usually develops gradually over many years and frequently occurs in the aged population. It is estimated that well over half of the population over the age of 65 possess senile cataracts in one or both eyes. Although the exact cause of cataracts is not known, excessive exposure to the ultraviolet radiation of the sun increases the risk (Taylor et al., 1988). Fortunately, in the vast majority of cases, cataracts can be effectively treated with surgery.

Senile Miosis   The effective size of the pupil also decreases with age. In dim lighting, maximum dilation becomes limited (e.g., Mayer et al., 1988). In fact, in old adults, the largest possible pupil opening may be less than half that of young adults. This greatly reduces the amount of light reaching the retina. Reduced dilation of the pupil due to age is called **senile miosis.**

In addition, the pupil's response to changes in illumination—for both dilation and constriction—becomes sluggish with age. Accordingly, the reaction time for the pupil to react to both bright and dim light increases with age.

The Retina and Aging

Along with the age-related effects on the anterior structures of the eye is the likelihood of damage to the photoreceptors at the retina. Retinal damage is due largely to an overall reduction in circulation and blood supply. However, increasing age also increases the possibility of disease. Such effects become particularly noticeable between 55 and 65 years of age.

Macular Degeneration   A particularly serious retinal disease that afflicts the elderly is age-related **macular degeneration.** This disease causes deterioration of the *macula* region of the retina (the center area of the retina, which includes the fovea) where vision is acute, generally sparing peripheral vision. The result is distortion, blurring, and dimming of central vision, greatly reducing the individual's ability to perform close visual tasks. The disease builds slowly, progressing until visual acuity is severely affected, declining to between 20/50 and 20/100 or less. Within this range, acuity is sufficiently reduced so that visual tasks such as reading are possible only with high-powered magnification.

Glaucoma   **Glaucoma** is one of the most prevalent visual diseases and a leading cause of blindness in middle and late adulthood. It is estimated that 2 out of every 100 persons over the age of 35 will have their vision threatened by this disease. Glaucoma results from the buildup of abnormal fluid pressure within the eyeball (called *intraocular pressure*), which, if untreated, may cause irreparable damage to the optic nerve. Major effects of glaucoma include severe reduction in the size of the visual field (usually with blind spots and loss of peripheral vision) and in acuity. Although the nerve damage produced by glaucoma is not reversible, it is important to detect it in its early stages (typically by measuring the intraocular pressure in the eyeball as part of an eye examination). Proper medication can reduce the abnormal pressure, preventing further nerve damage and preserving the existing vision.

Diabetic Retinopathy Another retinal disease is **diabetic retinopathy,** which afflicts a high proportion of older individuals with diabetes mellitus (a disorder that impairs the body's ability to use and store sugar). In diabetic retinopathy, tiny blood vessels and capillaries in the retina rupture and hemorrhage; this results in pockets of swelling and light-distorting deposits that reduce or even block the transmission of light. The perceptual effects of diabetic retinopathy are a gradual blurring and distortion of images on the retina and a significantly reduced ability to perform close work such as reading. According to the American Academy of Ophthalmology, the risk of developing diabetic retinopathy increases with the duration of diabetes. Early detection is important since, if left untreated, it can result in severe loss of sight and even blindness.

Visual Acuity and Aging

Visual function is degraded in general and visual acuity in particular is reduced with age (e.g., Kline & Schieber, 1981; Pollack, 1978). By about the seventh decade of life, the cumulative effects of an inflexible, yellowing lens, a diminished pupil, and a lifetime of eye use render poor acuity a common occurrence (although generally offset by corrective glasses). This is not surprising when we consider the estimate made by Sekuler and Blake (1987) that "by age 60 our eyes have been exposed to more light energy than would be unleashed by a nuclear blast" (p. 51).

Evidence also points to an age-related decrease in the efficiency of specific aspects of spatial vision. Using grating patterns (and controlling for visual acuity and ocular pathology), it has been observed that sensitivity to grating patterns of high spatial frequencies decreases with age, while sensitivity to patterns of low spatial frequencies (composed of wide gratings) remains relatively unaffected throughout adulthood (e.g., Crasini, Brown, & Bowman, 1988; Owsley, Sekuler, & Siemsen, 1983). Moreover, there is evidence that sensitivity to moving grating targets also decreases with age (Owsley et al., 1983; Sekuler, Hutman, & Owsley, 1980).

These sensory–perceptual reductions that accompany age may have serious implications for certain visually dependent abilities of the aging human. Many routine, but critical, activities that require the detection of fine details and the perception of dynamic events, such as driving, and perhaps even postural stabilization, may be adversely affected by the reduced sensitivity to high spatial frequencies and moving targets. One obvious practical implication concerns traffic safety, in particular observing road signs from a moving vehicle: Evans and Ginsburg (1982) state that young observers can discriminate a road sign at a distance 24% greater than can older individuals.

SUMMARY

In this chapter, we discussed the emergence and development of visual perception. The development of the sensory system and of perceptual abilities was examined in terms of environmental (learning) factors and biological (innate) factors. Drawing largely on animal studies of deprivation (e.g., monocular deprivation) or distortion of early visual experience, we noted that cortical physiology and visual abilities may be significantly modified by environmental stimulation. Specifically, restriction and biased stimulation during a critical developmental period in infancy may modify and disrupt the organization of cortical neurons, receptive fields, and functional neural connections in the visual system. The role of restricted, biased, and abnormal early stimulation (e.g., astigmatism) on human ocular defects (e.g., amblyopia, strabismus, stereoblindness) and cortical physiology was also examined.

Understanding of perceptual development in the human was examined in terms of two clinical studies on restored vision; both studies concerned individuals blind for most of their lives who, as adults, had their sight surgically restored. Tentative conclusions about the role of experience in the development of normal space perception and constancy were outlined.

The human infant can respond in many meaningful ways to its environment. Analysis of perception in the newborn human included eye fixation and scanning, form and pattern perception, and the perception of faces. Regarding the development of color, we presented evidence indicating that, by 4 months of age, infants possess color vision and perceive the adult hue categories of blue, green, yellow, and red.

In discussing the development of visual acuity, we concluded that while the visual acuity of the newborn is poor, it increases rapidly during the first year of life. This section also described the origins of the oblique effect (i.e., greater acuity for patterns and line segments with horizontal and vertical orientations than for stimuli with diagonal ones); it was concluded that the oblique effect is probably not learned.

A discussion of the development of space perception covered depth perception, looming (the pickup of and avoidance reaction to imminent collision with an approaching object), pictorial perception, and constancy. It was concluded that by about 6 or 7 months of life, the human infant has acquired basic perceptual and spatial abilities. This section also outlined development of the perception of auditory–visual events, facial and auditory expressions of emotions, and voice recognition.

The next section focused on how species acquire perceptual–motor coordination and develop accurate visually guided behavior. Studies were reviewed, such as the carousel experiment using biased sensory input, which involved rearing animals without experience of visual stimulation integrated with and related to self-produced movement. It was concluded that without such active experience, perceptual–motor coordination and precise visually guided activity do not develop properly.

Next, adaptation and negative aftereffects to systematically distorted optical stimulation (e.g., optical inversion, reversal, lateral displacement created by distorting lens and prisms) were discussed. It was noted that experience with active movements is important in adaptation. A summary of the early work of Stratton and Kohler underscored this point. Comparative studies of adaptation to systematic optical rearrangements suggest that a unique form of learning may play a role. Mammals and birds appear to be capable of this form of learning for adaptation; amphibia are not.

The final section focused on the effect of aging on vision. Several age-related changes and disorders of the lens and iris (pupil) that reduce visual function were described. Among these are cataracts of the lens and senile miosis of the iris. Further, it was noted that with advancing age, certain disorders and diseases of the visual system, particularly in the retina, are more likely to develop. In this context, we briefly described macula degeneration, glaucoma, and diabetic retinopathy. It was noted that the effects of age particularly influence visual acuity. For example, the vision of older humans is much less sensitive to targets with fine-grained, high spatial frequencies and to moving targets than is the vision of young adults.

KEY TERMS

Adaptation

Carousel Experiments

Cataracts

Critical Period

Decorrelated Feedback

Diabetic Retinopathy

Environmental Surgery

Glaucoma

Habituation

Kohler Experiment

Looming

Macular Degeneration

Meridional Amblyopia

Monocular Deprivation

Nativism versus Empiricism

Oblique Effect

Perceptual–Motor Coordination

Preferential Looking Method

Restored Sight

Senile Miosis

Stimulus Deprivation Amblyopia

Strabismus

Stratton Experiment

STUDY QUESTIONS

1. What is the nativism–empiricism issue as applied to the study of the development of sensation and perception? Are there any generalizations about the role of learning versus innate factors that would lead to a resolution of this issue? Consider whether it is a useful issue.

2. Summarize the effects of sensory deprivation on the development of the visual system. Examine the extent to which biased or selective visual stimulation modifies the visual system and its cortical organization. Include the effects of monocular deprivation and the notion of critical periods in the development of receptive fields.

3. What is meant by environmental surgery? Outline several experiments in which it is used to demonstrate the role of early experience in the development of the optical system.

4. What is amblyopia? Describe the possible role of early astigmatism in the development of meridional amblyopia. How does strabismus affect the development of stereoblindness?

5. Summarize the clinical studies on restored sight with humans. What are the implications for understanding the acquisition and development of perception?

6. Outline the section on eye fixations and scanning and indicate relevant developmental changes. What tendencies do human infants show with respect to visual scanning and eye fixations? What stimulus aspects are most appealing or most likely to be fixated?

7. What is the preferential looking method, and what perceptual abilities does it assess?

8. Examine the infant's preference for looking at faces. Indicate developmental changes in face fixations. What general trends exist in the development of preferences for and recognition of human-like faces?

9. Outline the evidence indicating that the human infant has color vision and perceives adult-like hues. Describe the use of habituation in examining early color vision and summarize age-dependent changes.

10. What visual acuity abilities does the infant possess? Describe how acuity changes within the first year of life. What is the oblique effect, and what causes it?

11. Summarize the research on depth perception in the infant. How is the development of fear of height related to the perception of depth? What role does locomotion experience play in the development of fear of height?

12. What is looming, and how is it demonstrated? In general, how is looming related to species and age? What is the functional significance of looming?

13. Examine the ability of the human infant to process and integrate temporally and spatially related visual and auditory events. Consider the infant's ability to relate facial expressions of emotion to appropriate vocal expressions.

14. Summarize studies on the importance of sensory feedback from self-initiated, active movements in the development of perceptual–motor coordination and visually guided behavior. Summarize the carousel and related experiments.

15. What conditions are necessary for adaptation to rearrangements and distortions of optical stimulation? Discuss the importance of systematic and consistent rearrangements of the stimulation.

16. Examine the possibility that the perception of an inverted visual field created by wearing lenses will eventually appear upright and normal. To what extent is this possibility related to the acquisition and development of visually guided behavior in the infant?

17. Indicate how the use of a wedge prism demonstrates adaptation. Relatedly, discuss why removing the prism following adaptation briefly produces a negative aftereffect, that is, distortion in the direction opposite to the optical displacement experienced when the prism was first used.

18. Discuss the importance of self-produced, active movements in adapting to prism distortion. To

what extent is adaptation to optical displacement restricted to certain species? What role does learning play in adaptation to consistent optical displacement?

19. What kinds of information are provided by active and passive movements for promoting adaptation?

20. Outline the general effects of aging on vision. How are the lens and pupil affected by the aging process? How does aging affect the function of visual processes? Describe age-related effects on acuity, taking into account the disorders of cataracts, presbyopia, senile miosis, macular degeneration, and glaucoma.

THE AUDITORY SYSTEM

With this chapter, we begin a discussion of hearing and the auditory system that will span three chapters. Next to sight, hearing is the most extensively studied sensory–perceptual system, and in many respects it enables environmental interactions that approach those of vision. The sense of hearing provides a unique source of information on what is occurring in our immediate surroundings. It is one of the primary sentinels of our senses: always vigilant, always on the alert for sounds. And indeed, we live in a sound-filled environment. Pay attention for a moment to the sounds that surround you and try to reflect on the variety that enter your awareness. Some sounds are mere noise—hums and whirls and clangs and squeals—for the most part, uninformative, incidental sounds deriving from our loud machine technology. But some of the sounds inform you about the nature of the immediate environment. In particular, such sounds enable us to localize objects: without hesitation, we seem to be aware immediately of the
location of many sound-emitting sources relative to ourselves.

For many animals hearing is also vital to communication, and the use of sounds pervades the social structure of many species. By vocalization and hearing, many birds and mammals signal to each other critical information about recognition and warning. The evolution of the human's extraordinary vocal apparatus and large, complex brain has enabled a unique form of vocal communication using language. We will have much to say about these and other functions of hearing in the chapters to follow, especially in Chapter 14.

The major purpose of this chapter is to identify and describe the characteristics of the auditory stimulus, as well as the physiological events and processes of the auditory system that result in the perception of sounds. To do this, we will also outline certain disorders of the auditory system. We begin by discussing the physical stimulation for hearing—sounds.

THE PHYSICAL STIMULUS

The sounds we hear are created from a form of mechanical energy. They are actually patterns of successive pressure disturbances occurring in a medium, which may be gaseous, liquid, or solid. Ordinarily the sounds we hear are transmitted in the air. For example,
as shown in Figure 12.1, when a tuning fork is struck, it produces sounds by vibrating—actually, moving back and forth—creating a succession of *compressions* alternating with decompressions (called *rarefactions*) of the air molecules surrounding the tines of the fork. Probably a more familiar example of a vibrating body that generates sound is the loudspeaker of

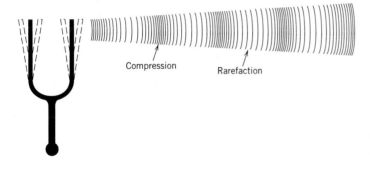

a stereo or a radio. The active speaker cone pushes against the air, causing compression of the air molecules, and then retracts, causing a partial vacuum or rarefaction of the air molecules. In fact, the speaker cone moves back and forth hundreds or even thousands of times a second, creating a pattern of pressure changes (i.e., compressions alternating with rarefactions) that travels outward from the speaker cone. The pattern of air pressure changes, depicted as a series of peaks and troughs, is called a **sound wave.** As we will see in later sections, the nature of the sounds we experience is directly related to the physical characteristics of the sound wave.

The simplest kind of sound wave is one that causes successive pressure changes over time in the form of a single repeating *sine wave.* A graphic plot of the compressions and rarefactions of a simple sound wave passing by a given point in space is shown in Figure 12.2. A complete change in pressure, from compression to rarefaction and back to compression, defines a *cycle.*

Though sound waves move progressively from place to place within the medium, the medium itself does not necessarily vibrate or move. That is, the air molecules do not travel with the wave, but rather pass along a wave of motion through the air. A visual

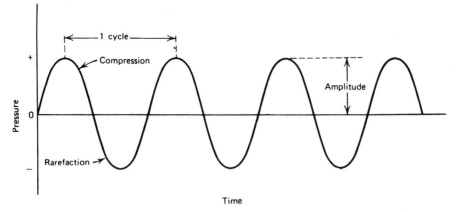

□ *figure* **12.2** Graphic sinusoidal representation of pressure variation—successive compressions and rarefactions—produced by a simple sound wave. The graph describes the pressure changes (*y*-axis) passing by a given point at a fixed distance from the sound source as a function of time (*x*-axis). The figure also shows the time taken for one complete cycle (i.e., a complete cycle of pressure changes) to move past a particular point in space. This is indicated by the interval measured from wave peak to wave peak. The *frequency* of the sound wave is equal to the number of cycles completed in a second. The *amplitude* of the sound, shown as the height of the wave, indicates the degree of compression (or rarefaction) of the sound wave.

analogy to sound wave transmission occurs when the calm surface of a pond is disturbed by throwing a pebble into it. The entry of the pebble causes a pattern of disturbances, seen as radiating circles of ripples, that move progressively from place to place in the water without carrying the water with them.

It should be clear that sounds require a medium through which the pressure variations can be transmitted. That is, sound cannot exist in a vacuum where there is nothing to compress. Moreover, the physical characteristics of the medium affect the velocity (v) of sound transmission: sound travels much faster in solids than in liquids or gases. For example, the rate of sound transmission in air is about 1100 ft/sec (335 m/sec), about four times faster in water, and another four times faster in steel or glass. In general, sound travels faster in denser media. Sound velocity is also affected by the temperature of the medium; in air, for example, it increases about 2 ft (61 cm) per second for every degree Centigrade rise in temperature.

The principal *physical* properties of sound waves may be characterized by their frequency, amplitude or intensity, and complexity. We will discuss each one separately and indicate its corresponding *psychological* effects (*pitch, loudness,* and *timbre,* respectively).

Frequency

Sound waves are conventionally described by the *number of pressure changes* (i.e., compression to rarefaction and back to compression) completed in a second, that is, how rapidly the cycle of pressure changes occurs. The measure is referred to as **frequency** (*f*), where the unit of frequency—the number of pressure changes per second—is denoted by the term **Hertz (Hz),** named for the nineteenth-century German physicist Heinrich Hertz. Thus, for example, in the case of 1000-Hz sound, there would be 1000 cycles, or pressure changes, in 1 second. Figure 12.2 depicts the frequency of a sound wave as the number of its pressure changes, or cycles, passing a given point in a second. It is generally accepted that the range of hearing in the young human adult is 20

to 20,000 Hz; sounds with frequencies below 20 Hz and above 20,000 Hz are inaudible.

Frequency and Wavelength Sound waves can also be described with respect to the length of a single wave. As we will observe in Chapter 14, specifying a sound in terms of wavelength can be useful in understanding aspects of sound localization. As shown in Figure 12.3, the **wavelength** of a sound wave is the linear distance between two successive compressions (abbreviated by the Greek letter *lambda,* λ). Wavelength and frequency are inversely related (actually, $\lambda = v/f$). Thus, in air, with velocity constant at 1100 ft/sec (335 m/sec), a 1100-Hz sound

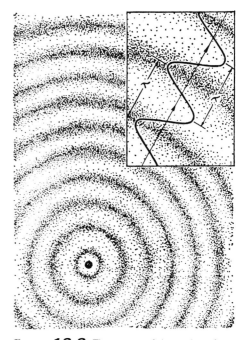

◻ *figure 12.3* The center of the series of concentric circles represents a sound-emitting source. The molecules of air around the sound source are distributed as shown. Some molecules are grouped closely and some loosely, representing compression and rarefaction, respectively. A graph of this variation in pressure, shown in the enlarged insert at the upper right, appears as a sine wave. (From D. R. Griffin, *Echoes of Bats and Men,* Anchor Books/ Doubleday, Garden City, N. Y., 1959, p. 39. Reprinted by permission of the author.)

has a wavelength of 1 ft (30.48 cm); a 550-Hz sound has a wavelength of 2 ft, and a 2,200-Hz sound has a wavelength of 0.5 ft. A higher frequency means that more pressure changes occur in a given unit of time and closer to each other in space, producing a shorter wavelength. Thus, a low-frequency sound has a long wavelength, whereas a high-frequency sound has a short wavelength. Figure 12.4 illustrates the relationship between wavelength and frequency. You can see from this graph that a sound of 1100 Hz has a wavelength of 1 ft.

Pitch *Frequency* refers to a *physical* property of the sound wave—the number of pressure changes per second. In contrast, the auditory sensation—the *psychological* attribute of frequency—is called **pitch,** which refers to how high or low a sound is experienced by a listener. This may range from very low bass sounds to extremely high treble sounds. Some

familiar musical sound sources specified in terms of their frequencies are presented in Figure 12.5.

Amplitude

Sound waves also vary in **amplitude,** the *amount* of change in pressure—that is, the extent of displacement (compression or rarefaction) of the molecules from a position of rest (see Figure 12.2). When air pressure is low, the amplitude of the sound wave is low and a weak sound results. When air pressure is high, the amplitude of the sound wave is high and an intense sound results. (We will use the terms *amplitude* and *intensity* interchangeably.)

In physical terms, the amplitude, or intensity, of a sound depends on the pressure or force applied to a sound-emitting source. The fundamental measure of pressure is *force per unit area*. Although sound pressure can be expressed in many different units, by

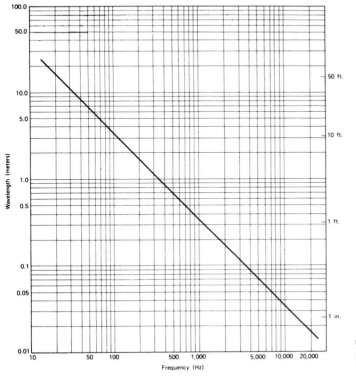

▭ *figure* **12.4** Wavelength as a function of frequency (measured in air at 15° C).

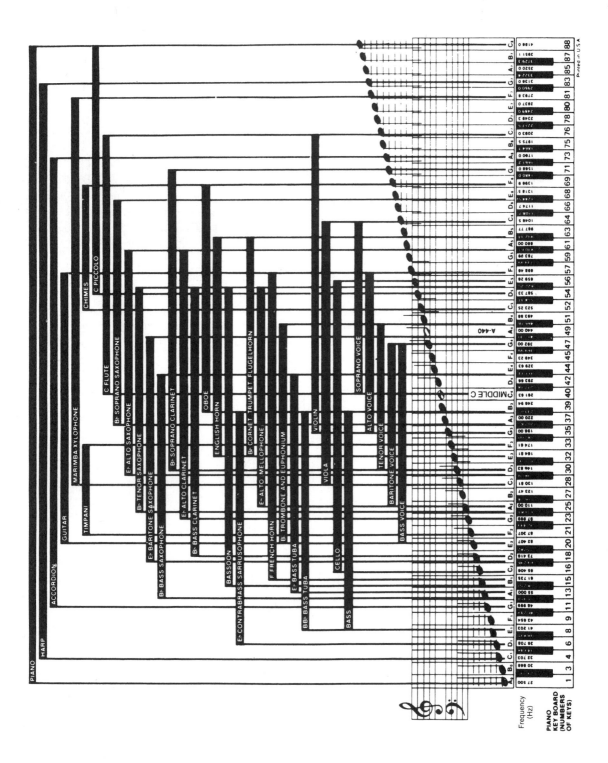

convention in *acoustics* (the area of physical science concerned with sound), pressure is measured in *dynes per square centimeter* (*dynes/cm²*). (Sometimes sound pressure is stated in the equivalent unit, the *microbar,* abbreviated as μbar. More recently employed units of pressure variation are *Newtons per square meter,* N/m^2, and *microPascal,* μPa.)

The Decibel (dB)   The ear is sensitive to an enormously wide range of pressure amplitudes. The range in sensitivity from the strongest to the weakest sound that the human can hear is on the order of billions to 1. Because of this immense range, it is convenient to use a logarithmic scale of pressures called the **decibel (dB)** scale, named in honor of Alexander Graham Bell. The advantage of using the logarithmic decibel scale for amplitude is that it compresses the tremendous range of possible values so that the entire auditory amplitude scale is contained within a manageable range of values from 0 to approximately 160.

The decibel formula is

$$N_{dB} = 20 \log P^e/P^r$$

where N_{dB} is the number of decibels, P^e is the sound pressure to be expressed in decibels, and P^r is a standard reference pressure, 0.0002 dynes/cm². The sound pressure to be converted to decibels (P^e) is specified relative to a particular reference pressure. This reference pressure was chosen because it is close to the average threshold of human hearing (for a 1000-Hz tone).

Decibels are not absolute, fixed units like inches, grams, or Watts. When we specify a sound in decibels, we mean that it is a certain number of times greater or less than some other pressure—the reference pressure, P^r. The decibel scale, using the presumed threshold reference pressure of 0.0002 dynes/cm², is conventionally termed *sound pressure level* (*SPL*). The designation SPL is usually given since, for practical reasons, other reference pressures are sometimes used for calculating decibels.

Table 12.1 presents the number of decibels calculated from the formula given above for a range of pressures (P^e) produced by some familiar sound sources. For illustrative purposes, the pressure values were selected to differ from each other by a factor of 10 (e.g., 200 dynes/cm² is 10 times the pressure of 20 dynes/cm², which is 10 times greater than 2.0, and so on). Table 12.1 shows that the relationship between changes in pressure and decibels is logarithmic rather than linear. The resultant decibel values show that each *10-fold increase* in sound pressure (P^e) results in the addition of *20 db*. For example, the difference between a 60-dB and an 80-dB sound means that the pressure amplitude of the 80-dB sound is 10 times greater than that of the 60-dB sound. Observe also that a whisper is 20 dB higher than the 0-dB reference level. This also corresponds to a 10-fold increase in sound pressure. In comparison, the sound amplitude of a normal conversation is 60 dB higher than the reference level, which corresponds to an increase in pressure that is 1000 times the reference value.

The nonlinear relationship between changes in pressure amplitude and decibels suggests caution in interpreting decibel values. As noted, every time pressure is increased by a factor of 10, we add 20 dB. In addition, a *doubling* of sound pressure amplitude increases the decibel level by 6 dB (likewise, halving the pressure amplitude decreases the decibel scale by 6 dB). This means that if we have a sound with a pressure amplitude of 20 dB SPL and we double its pressure, this does *not* double the decibel level to 40. Rather, the amplitude changes from 20 to 26 dB. Similarly, if we have a sound with a pressure amplitude of 40 dB SPL and reduce its amplitude by half, its dB level will change from 40 to 34 dB SPL.

Loudness   The corresponding auditory sensation, or psychological attribute, of pressure amplitude is **loudness.** Thus, high-amplitude sound waves

---

□ *figure* **12.5** Tonal frequencies of a keyboard, the human voice, and various orchestral instruments. (Courtesy of Conn Ltd., Oakbrook, Ill.)

□ **table 12.1** Relation Between Sound Pressures and Decibels (SPL) for Some Familiar Sounds

Pressures, P^e (dynes/cm^2)	dB	Source
2000	140	Jet aircraft at takeoff; may cause pain and injury
200	120	Loud thunder, amplified rock music
20	100	Heavy automobile traffic, subway noise, pneumatic drill
2.0	80	Factory noise, hair dryer, vacuum cleaner
0.2	60	Normal conversation
0.02	40	Quiet office or residential setting
0.002	20	Whisper, leaves rustling
0.0002	0	Threshold of hearing

express large pressure changes and create the experience of loud sounds, whereas low-amplitude waves reflect small pressure changes and are heard as soft or faint sounds. Note that although the sound wave's amplitude is the major determinant of the sound's loudness, it is not the only factor; variations in its frequency, for example, can affect the experience of loudness. In addition, amplitude and loudness are not linearly related. As we noted above, a 26-dB sound is double the intensity of a 20-dB sound, but it is not double in loudness. Both of these points will be elaborated on in the next chapter.

Complexity

The sounds that occur in nature rarely have the simple sinusoidal form shown in Figure 12.2. A sound described by a perfect sine curve representing a constant frequency and amplitude is usually achieved in the laboratory. Most sound-producing sources emit sounds that do not vibrate at a single frequency; for this reason, their waveform is characterized by **complexity.** Thus, sounds produced by, say, the human voice, by animals, by traffic, by musical instruments, and the like are produced by the interaction of many different waves of varying frequencies. That is, such sounds possess extremely complex cycles of pressure variations—cycles of compression and rarefaction. Some examples of complex waveforms are shown in Figure 12.6.

The complex waveforms produced by musical instruments reveal an important characteristic of vibrating sources. In general, a complex sound-emitting source vibrates simultaneously at a number of frequencies. The lowest frequency, called the **fundamental frequency** (or *first harmonic*) determines the *pitch* of a complex sound. If a violin or guitar string is plucked, it vibrates as a whole, alternately compressing and rarefying the surrounding air molecules. However, in addition to the full length of vibration (the fundamental frequency), there are simultaneous vibrations of shorter lengths that are precise divisions of the string's length. This is illustrated in Figure 12.7. These additional vibrations, whose frequencies are multiples of the fundamental frequency, are called **harmonics** (or *overtones*). In other words, the *fundamental frequency* is the *lowest* frequency in a complex waveform; all the higher frequencies that are multiples of the fundamental are the *harmonics* of the fundamental. We will shortly return to the role played by the fundamental frequency and its harmonics in the quality of hearing.

Fourier Analysis and Complexity

Although a complex sound cannot be represented by a single sine wave, it can be expressed by a *series* of sine waves. Recall our discussion of Fourier analysis in Chapter 6. There we described how a complex visual scene can be analyzed into a series of simple sine waves. The same analysis applies to complex sound waves. Briefly, Fourier's theorem states that any complex periodic waveform can be expressed as the sum of a series of simple sine waves, each with

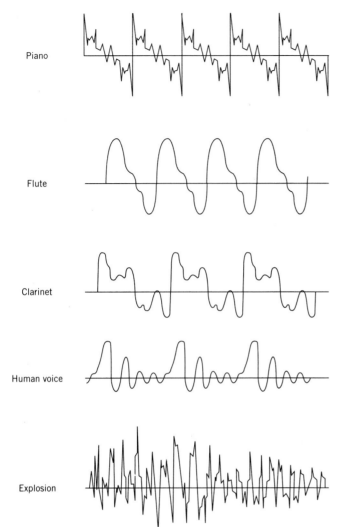

Piano

Flute

Clarinet

Human voice

Explosion

□ *figure* **12.6** Typical sound waves for various sounds. The sound waves for the human voice are for repetitions of the vowel sound of *a,* as in "father." (Sound wave of the human voice from Kinsler & Frey, 1962.)

its own frequency and amplitude. The breakdown of a complex waveform into its components is called **Fourier analysis.** The construction of a complex waveform from a series of sine waves is called **Fourier synthesis.**

As an example of how a complex wave is constructed, examine Figure 12.8. A complete cycle of the complex wave is shown at the lower right (roughly a "square wave" produced by some sirens). Fourier analysis of this tone reveals that five components, seen in the left column, make it up. In the right column

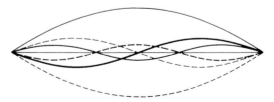

□ *figure* **12.7** The figure shows the complex way in which a plucked string vibrates. In addition to the full-length vibration, which produces the string's fundamental tone, there are simultaneous vibrations of shorter lengths (harmonics) that are precise divisions of the string's length—in this example, one-half and one-third.

Component   Composite

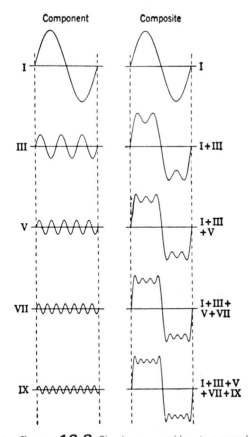

□ *figure 12.8* Simple waves add up to a complex wave. The relative frequency of each component corresponds to the numbers I, III, V, VII, and IX, to the left of each line. If enough additional odd harmonics were added, the "square wave," a rectangular form that is already apparent in the form at the lower right corner of the figure, would be even more closely approximated. (From E. G. Boring, H. S. Langfeld, and H. P. Weld, *Foundations of Psychology*, John Wiley, New York, 1948, p. 316. Reprinted by permission of the publisher.)

are the composite waveforms as each component is added in succession. Mathematically, Fourier analysis begins with the *fundamental frequency*—the lowest frequency within the series of sounds of the complex wave. To the fundamental frequency are added sine waves of higher frequencies that are multiples of the fundamental.

Note that the fundamental frequency of a complex tone determines its pitch. If a listener is instructed to adjust the frequency of a simple sine wave so that its pitch matches that of a complex tone, the frequency of the simple wave will be set close to the fundamental frequency of the complex tone. In other words, the pitch of a complex tone is about the same as the pitch of its fundamental frequency (Moore, 1994).

Ohm's Acoustical Law The auditory system can perform a crude Fourier analysis on a complex wave, decomposing it into its separate components and sending information about which frequencies are present to higher auditory centers. This phenomenon, known as **Ohm's acoustical law** (named after the nineteenth-century German physicist Georg Ohm, better known for his law on electricity), means that when we are exposed to a complex sound such as a musical chord, created by striking several notes together, we can recognize the contribution made by each note separately. In other words, Ohm's law refers to the fact that, within limits, we can hear the individual frequency components of a complex sound.

Timbre The characteristic sensory experience corresponding to a sound's complexity is called **timbre** (pronounced "tam'ber"; derived from an old French word meaning "a small bell"). Timbre refers to a sound's distinctive tonal quality produced by the number and intensity of the harmonics (or overtones) it produces. A complex sound emitted from a musical instrument, for example, is composed of a fundamental frequency combined with a number of harmonic frequencies (always multiples of the fundamental frequency) present in varying amounts. Different instruments emit and emphasize different harmonics and, accordingly, vary in timbre. It is on the basis of timbre that we are able to distinguish between the sounds of musical instruments even when they play the same note and have the same pitch quality. Their different timbre quality is due to the variation in their harmonic contributions.

In summary, the fundamental frequency mainly determines the *pitch* of a complex sound, whereas the harmonics determine its *timbre*. Generally speaking, instruments that produce many harmonics, like the guitar and certain piano notes, give fuller, richer tones than instruments that emit very few harmonics, such as the flute, which gives a relatively pure, clear tone.

Phase

A complete sound pressure wave, or cycle, extends from a position of rest to compression to rest to rarefaction and to rest again (see Figure 12.2). A complete cycle is specified as extending for 360°. The beginning is taken as 0°, the first compression peak as 90°, rest as 180°, rarefaction peak as 270°, and rest again as 360°. **Phase** refers to that part of the cycle the sound wave has reached at a given point in time.

Two sounds of the same frequency, simultaneously sounded, will move alike at every instant and their waveforms will be "in phase." However, if two sounds are produced of the same frequency but displaced slightly in time, their waveforms will differ in the time at which the waves rest or reach compression. For example, the same tone emitted from two separate speakers may differ in phase if the tones must travel different distances to reach a listener's ear. Alternatively, a tone from a single speaker may have to travel different distances to reach each of the two ears of a listener, causing a difference in arrival time (and, therefore, phase) at the two ears. These sounds will be "out of phase", and the phase difference is expressed in degrees.

Some examples of phase differences are given in Figure 12.9. If one sine wave is in compression one-quarter of a cycle sooner than another, the waves are 90° out of phase (Figure 12.9, wave *B*). If one wave occurs one-half of a cycle sooner than the other, they are 180° out of phase (Figure 12.9, wave *C*). In this case, if both waves have the same frequency and amplitude, they exert opposite effects on the air pressure, canceling each other's effects, and no sound would be heard. With respect to Figure 12.9, wave *C*, which appears as a mirror image of wave *A*, is said to have the "reverse" phase of wave *A*.

Phase and "Noise Cancellation"
The fact that sound pressure waves 180° out of phase cancel each other's effects has a significant practical consequence. The cancellation, or neutralization, of

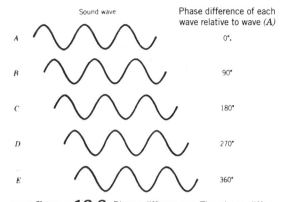

□ figure 12.9 Phase differences. The phase difference between two waves is produced by differences in the time at which the waves reach compression. In this example, the phase differences are calculated relative to wave *A*. For example, wave *B* reaches its peak compression 90° after wave *A*, wave *C* reaches compression 180° after wave *A*, and so on. (From W. A. van Bergeijk, J. R. Pierce, and E. E. David, Jr., *Waves and the Ear,* Anchor/Doubleday, Garden City, N. Y., 1960, p. 85. Reprinted by permission of Doubleday & Company, Inc.)

sound pressure by actively generating an exact pressure wave, but in its reverse phase, can be used to reduce noise (Alper, 1991). This **noise cancellation** is particularly applicable to predictable, continuous, or repetitive complex noises such as the unpleasant, distracting, and, at times, potentially harmful drones, hums, whines, roars, and throbs produced by large air conditioning units, industrial machinery, and aircraft engines. The procedure, in outline, is that in a matter of microseconds a microphone samples the offensive, unwanted noise and a computer analyzes it, essentially performing a Fourier analysis, which reveals its underlying harmonics and periodic elements. Almost immediately, an identical complex sound pressure waveform is computer generated, with the same frequency and amplitude characteristics as the unwanted noise but in its reverse form, that is, 180° out of phase. When the two sets of complex wave patterns are sounded together, the result is "anti-noise," or silence. This leaves desired sounds that are not predictable and repetitive, such as speech, unaffected while eliminating the offending sounds. In a real sense this technique of noise cancellation "makes twice as much noise," but none of it is heard.

Resonance

Most solid objects vibrate at a specific frequency when struck or driven with the necessary force. For example, strike the rim of a crystal glass with a spoon and it will vibrate at a specific frequency. The frequency at which the object vibrates is called its *natural* or *resonant* frequency, and it is a function of the mass and stiffness, or tension, of the object. Many different driving forces, including sound pressures, can cause an object to vibrate sympathetically, or *resonate*. Causing an object to vibrate when the frequency of a sound-emitting source matches the natural or resonant frequency of the object is called **resonance.**

Generally, the ease of resonant vibration or frequency enhancement depends on how closely the driving or imposed frequency matches the object's resonant frequency. An emitted sound having the same frequency as the resonant frequency of an object will be most likely to set the object into sympathetic vibration. You have probably experienced resonance when a glass vibrates after you turn up the volume of your stereo. Some of the sounds coming from the speakers have the same resonant frequency as the glass, inducing vibrations in the glass. Resonance will become important when we discuss sound waves entering the ear, since the outer ear and ear canal resonate to particular frequencies, and thus favor and amplify specific sounds entering them.

ANATOMY AND MECHANISMS OF THE EAR

We will now analyze the mechanisms of the ear that enable the complex pressure variations just described to produce the perception of sound. Specifically, our concern is with the receptor organs and mechanisms that transduce sound energy into nerve impulses and with how these organs function. Though there are numerous structures in nature for picking up acoustic energy, we will focus primarily on the human ear

(Figure 12.10). As shown in Figure 12.11, this auditory system can be grossly divided into three major structural components: the outer ear, the middle ear, and the inner ear.

The Outer Ear

The outer ear of most mammals consists of an earflap called the *pinna* (or the *auricle*), the *external auditory canal,* and the *eardrum* (or *tympanic membrane*).

The Pinna   The **pinna** (Latin for "feather"), a fleshy, wrinkled flap that lies on the side of the head, has several functions. It protects the sensitive, delicate inner structures, preventing foreign bodies from entering the ear passage, and it collects and funnels air vibrations into the external auditory canal. The shell-like folds of the pinna also amplify high-frequency sounds of around 4000 Hz (Gulick, Gescheider, & Frisina, 1989). In addition, the pinna plays a role in localizing sounds; it is especially helpful in differentiating between front and back sound sources (e.g., Batteau, 1968; Freedman & Fisher, 1968). It may also be useful in localizing sounds in the vertical plane (Butler & Humanski, 1992; we will return to its role in sound localization in Chapter 14).

Although the human normally does not have functional control over the muscle system that controls the pinnas, many mammals do; it is common to observe lower mammals orient their mobile pinnas in the direction of a sound source, obviously enhancing the pinnas' localization. Pinnas are not found in all mammals. Sea-dwelling mammals such as the porpoise and whale do not possess pinnas, perhaps because water-borne sound waves would pass directly through them. Moreover, the protuberance created by earflaps would reduce the streamlining of the outer body surface and decrease mobility. This may also be the reason why lower vertebrates such as fish, amphibia, reptiles, and birds lack pinnas. In fact, some birds have a covering of feathers over their ear passage that may even hinder their hearing; this covering is required to reduce wind noise during flight (Marler & Hamilton, 1966).

The External Auditory Canal   The **external auditory canal** is a cylindrical cavity about

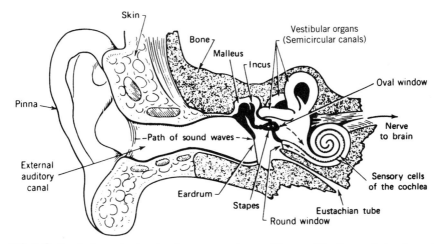

■ **figure 12.10** Semischematic showing the gross anatomy of the ear. Vibrations entering the external auditory canal affect the eardrum. Vibrations of the eardrum are transmitted through the middle ear by the chain of bones or ossicles—malleus (hammer), incus (anvil), and stapes (stirrup). The footplate of the stapes carries the vibration to the fluid of the cochlea. The vestibular organs, lying directly above the cochlea, are a set of sensory structures concerned with balance, bodily position, and the detection of gravity.

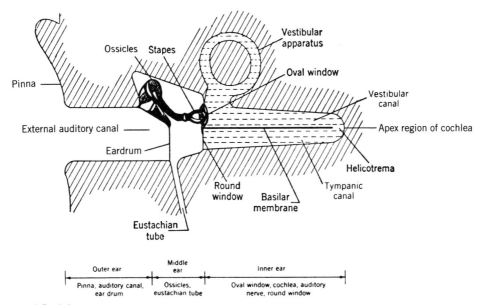

■ **figure 12.11** Schematic of the ear. The cochlea is uncoiled in this drawing (as Figure 12.12 illustrates). When the footplate of the stapes moves inward, the fluid inside the cochlea flows in the direction of the helicotrema and makes the round window membrane bulge outward. (From G. von Békésy and W. A. Rosenblith, "The mechanical properties of the ear," in S. S. Stevens (Ed.), *Handbook of Experimental Psychology*, John Wiley, New York, 1951, p. 1076. Reprinted by permission of the publisher.)

2.5 to 3 cm long (about 1 to 1¼ in.) and 7 mm (about 0.3 in.) in diameter, open on the outside and bounded on the inside. It functions primarily to conduct vibrations to the eardrum, but it also protects against foreign bodies and it controls the temperature and humidity in the vicinity of the eardrum. The auditory canal acts like a horn, especially for sound frequencies of around 3000 Hz, reinforcing, amplifying, and prolonging the sound pressure by induced vibrations, or resonance. For sounds at the canal's resonant frequency of 3000 Hz, the sensitivity of the ear can be increased by as much as 8 to 10 dB (Békésy & Rosenblith, 1951; Gulick et al., 1989). Of interest is the fact that in the human, the resonant frequency of the external auditory canal (3000 Hz) corresponds closely to the frequency range to which the auditory system is most sensitive.

The Eardrum   The **eardrum** (or *tympanic membrane*), a thin, translucent membrane, is stretched across the inner end of the auditory canal and seals off the cavity of the middle ear. The eardrum vibrates in response to the pressure waves of sound, and it is at the eardrum that pressure variations are transformed into mechanical motion. The displacements of the eardrum by pressure waves required to produce hearing at threshold levels are minute. For the detection of some sound frequencies near 3000 Hz, the displacements of the eardrum's vibrations are smaller than the diameter of a hydrogen atom (Békésy & Rosenblith, 1951).

The Middle Ear

As shown in Figures 12.10 and 12.11, the eardrum closes off the air-filled cavity of the middle ear. The middle ear transmits the vibratory motions of the eardrum by a mechanical linkage to the inner ear. Attached to the eardrum is the **malleus** (or *hammer*), the first of a chain of three small bones (the smallest bones in the human) called **ossicles** (known by both their Latin and English names) that link the middle ear to the inner ear. The malleus connects to the **incus** (or *anvil*), which, in turn, connects to the **stapes** (or *stirrup*, the smallest of the bones), whose footplate finally connects to the membrane of the **oval window,** which, as Figure 12.11 shows, is the entrance

to the inner ear. The ossicles, which have a total length of about 18 mm, are firmly connected by ligaments and transmit the vibrations acting on the eardrum by a lever system—with the motion of the footplate of the stapes acting as a piston—to the oval window.

Functions of the Middle Ear: Impedance Matching   The outer and middle ear cavities are air-filled, whereas the inner ear is filled with a watery liquid. This difference has an important effect on the transmission of sounds to the inner ear. Air is an easily compressible medium, whereas water, which is dense, is much more resistant to movement. This means that more force is required to transmit sound waves in water than in air. The difference between the resistance, or impedance, of air and water is illustrated by the ease with which you can move your cupped hand through air compared to the resistance experienced when you move it through water. The resistance to the transmission of sound waves is called *impedance,* and the difference between the resistance of sound pressure transmitted from the middle ear to the inner ear is referred to as an **impedance mismatch.** Thus, the change in the sound wave medium from the airborne vibrations of the middle ear cavity to the fluid-filled inner ear chambers of the cochlea creates an impedance mismatch, posing a special mechanical problem for sound conduction. Unless they are transformed, airborne vibrations will be poorly transmitted to the dense, watery fluid of the inner ear, and the auditory system will lose much of its sensitivity.

In fact, the major function of the middle ear is to reduce impedance mismatch and ensure the efficient transfer of sound vibrations from the air to the fluid of the inner ear. The middle ear performs two important mechanical transformations to increase the efficiency of sound transmission to the inner ear. The transfer of vibrations from the eardrum to the stapes and oval window is enhanced to a small but important extent by the ossicles, which serve as a lever. Although not obvious from their depictions in Figures 12.10 and 12.11, the ossicles are hinged in a way that creates a mechanical advantage to the action of the stapes, increasing the force of vibrations at the stapes and oval window by a factor of about 1.3.

More significantly, however, the transformation of vibrations derives principally from the difference in the effective areas of the eardrum and the footplate of the stapes. The eardrum (with an average area of about 70 mm²) is much larger than the area of the footplate of the stapes (about 3 mm²) connecting with the oval window. Concentrating the vibrations of the relatively large eardrum on the much smaller stapes significantly increases the pressure (specifically, it increases the pressure per unit area). In other words, if the same force is applied to both a large and a small area, the force applied to the small area will result in a greater pressure change (in the same way, hitting your desk with a hammer may merely dent it, but if the same force is applied to the much smaller area of a nail point, it will pierce the surface). In fact, the difference in area between the two structures increases pressure on the footplate of the stapes and oval window roughly 20 to 25 times as great as the pressure on the eardrum; this effectively compensates for the impedance mismatch caused by the increased resistance of the fluid of the inner ear. For this reason, the middle ear is often referred to as an *impedance-matching device* (Moore, 1989).

The middle ear thus acts as a mechanical transformer, essentially providing the change necessary for air pressure to move the dense fluid of the inner ear. Persons with impaired ossicles, and thus middle ear dysfunction, may have significant hearing loss. By contrast, most marine life, which does not ordinarily deal with airborne sounds, has no need for the mechanical transformation provided by a middle ear mechanism. Accordingly, many species of fish have no outer or middle ear structures (e.g., Fay, 1970). In fact, the bony ossicles of the middle ear in amphibia and reptiles evolved from the jawbones of fish and were further elaborated in mammals. Thus, from an evolutionary viewpoint, as animals moved from the sea, to amphibian existence to land, a sensitive middle ear mechanism evolved that matched the high resistance of the fluid-filled inner ear with airborne stimulation.

Acoustic Reflex Besides acting as an impedance-matching device to mechanically transform the auditory signal, the middle ear has a protective function. Two sets of small muscles are attached to the ossicles: the *tensor tympani* is attached to the malleus near the eardrum, and the *stapedius muscle* is attached to the stapes. When exposed to intense sounds that could possibly damage the delicate inner ear structures (particularly for frequencies below 1000 Hz), the muscles contract reflexively and reduce the transmission of vibrations through the middle ear. The combined action of these muscles to reduce the efficiency of the middle ear to intense sounds is called the **acoustic reflex.**

In general, the acoustic reflex parallels the constriction of the pupil of the eye when it is exposed to potentially harmful, intense light (recall Whytt's reflex, discussed in Chapter 3). Moreover, like the pupil's relatively sluggish response to brief, sudden-onset, intense light (e.g., flashbulbs), the acoustic reflex is not instantaneous. The reaction time of the acoustic reflex is too slow to protect against abrupt, transient, brief sounds such as gunshots, firecrackers, or even hammer blows. However, it is useful in reducing the transmission of gradual-onset, intense, low-frequency sounds. Interestingly, the acoustic reflex is activated just before vocalization, so it is especially useful in reducing self-generated, intense sounds of moderate frequency such as shouts.

The Eustachian Tube As we noted, in addition to making incoming sound waves more effective, the middle ear protects the delicate inner ear from intense sounds by the acoustic reflex. However, another structural factor also plays a protective role. Although the middle ear chamber is sealed off from outside atmospheric pressure changes, it connects with the back of the mouth cavity through the **Eustachian tube.** This connection allows pressure from the outside to be equalized with air pressure in the middle ear. Thus, when the mouth is open, air pressure on both sides of the eardrum is equalized.

The effects of a small difference in pressure are experienced when we have a head cold. The Eustachian tube becomes clogged, so that the pressure in the middle ear cannot adjust adequately to the outside air. The result of this small inequality in pressure is a temporary reduction in hearing. Extreme pressure differences on both sides of the eardrum may produce abnormal and even painful displacements of the ear-drum. When we are confronted with extremely loud sounds or abrupt air pressure changes, such as when altitude changes, the sudden pressure changes may burst or rupture the eardrum.

Bone Conduction Normally sound travels from the outer ear to the middle ear, and then to the sensitive inner ear. However, an alternative route of sound transmission to the inner ear is **bone conduction.** This involves direct transmission between a vibrating sound source and the inner ear, bypassing the eardrum, ossicles, and other middle-ear structures. In bone conduction, the sounds produce vibrations in the bones of the skull that stimulate the inner ear directly. However, bone conduction is much less efficient than normal middle-ear sound conduction.

Bone-conducted sound occurs more frequently than you might think. You have, for example, experienced the vibrations transmitted by bone conduction when you chewed on hard food such as a carrot or a stale pretzel. Similarly, the loud sound of the dentist's drill when it is in contact with your tooth is transmitted largely by bone conduction: vibrations from the drill travel from your tooth to your skull and to the inner ear structures.

☐ **DEMONSTRATION:**
Bone Conduction

It is quite easy to experience the effects of bone conduction: close off your external auditory canal with ear plugs, or even by gently inserting the fingertips, and hum or speak. The sounds you hear are bone-conducted sounds that have reached the inner ear without access to any outer or middle-ear structures. The vibrations of the air created by your oral cavity are transmitted to your cheeks, from there to the lower jaw, and then to the sensitive structures of the inner ear.

The transmission of sounds by bone conduction explains why the playback of your tape-recorded voice sounds less familiar to you than to your friends. Actually, it is not the voice that you usually hear when speaking. Normally, when speaking, you not only hear the air-conducted sounds that others hear, you also hear the sounds transmitted by bone conduction; however, when listening to your recorded voice on playback, you hear only what was recorded—air-conducted sound.

The Inner Ear

Next in the relay of pressure variations is movement in the *inner ear,* specifically the movement of the stapes on the watery fluid of the inner ear. The inner ear is a small, tubular structure about 25 to 35 mm (about 1 to 1 1/2 in.) in length, resembling a snail shell: for this reason, it is called the **cochlea** (Latin for "snail"). The cochlea is coiled on itself about three turns. Figure 12.12 is a schematic of the cochlea, uncoiled to show its main components. The cochlea contains three chambers, or canals. Along most of its length it is divided by its central canal, the **cochlear duct,** into two canals. The upper canal, the **vestibular canal,** starts at the oval window and connects with the lower canal, the **tympanic canal;** the upper and lower canals connect at the tip, or apex, of the cochlea by way of a small opening called the *helicotrema.* A membrane-covered opening called the **round window** is found at the base of the tympanic canal (see Figures 12.10 and 12.11). The membrane of the round window expands to accommodate fluid displaced by the stapes against the oval window. The vestibular and tympanic canals are fluid-filled. The cochlear duct is also fluid-filled, but it is independent of the other two canals.

The cochlear duct is bounded by two membranes. It is divided from the vestibular canal by **Reissner's membrane,** and it is separated from the tympanic canal by the **basilar membrane.** The basilar membrane is a tough, flexible membrane that moves or displaces itself in direct response to the frequency of the incoming sound. Whereas the cochlea narrows toward the apex, as shown in Figure 12.13, the basilar membrane becomes progressively wider. At the base, near the stapes, it measures less than 0.10 mm in width; near the apex or helicotrema end, it broadens

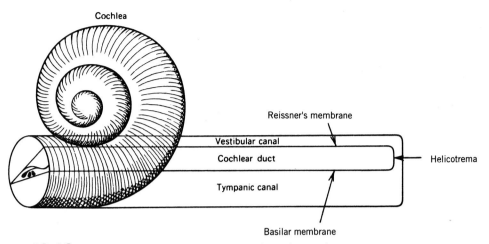

□ figure 12.12 Schematic of the cochlea uncoiled to show the canals.

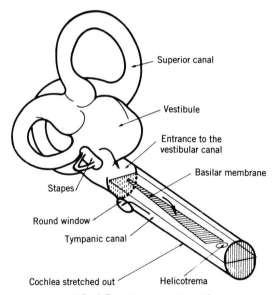

□ figure 12.13 Schematic of the inner ear with the cochlea uncoiled. The basilar membrane increases in width as it extends toward the helicotrema. The superior canal and the vestibule are structures of the vestibular organs, mentioned in Figure 12.10. (From G. von Békésy, "Experimental models of the cochlea with and without nerve supply," in G. L. Rasmussen and W. F. Windle (Eds.), *Neural Mechanisms of the Auditory and Vestibular Systems,* Charles C. Thomas, Springfield, Ill., 1960; also see G. von Békésy, *Sensory Inhibition,* Princeton University Press, Princeton, N. J., 1967, p. 137. Reprinted by permission of the publisher.)

to about 0.5 mm. In addition, the basilar membrane at the base of the cochlea is about 100 times stiffer than it is at the apex. As we shall soon see, the activity of the basilar membrane is especially important in understanding the physiological analysis of sound because the receptors for hearing—the *hair cells*—rest on it.

Organ of Corti The central cochlear duct contains the specialized sensory structures, nerves, and supporting tissues for transducing vibrations to nerve impulses. Collectively these form a receptor structure called the **organ of Corti** (named for its discover, Alfonso Corti), which rests on and extends along the length of the basilar membrane. The structures that form the organ of Corti are illustrated in the cross section of the cochlea shown in Figure 12.14. It contains columns of specialized *hair cells* arranged in two sets, divided by an arch (tunnel of Corti), called the **inner hair cells,** which number about 3500, and the **outer hair cells,** which number about 20,000. In turn, each hair cell has up to 100 tiny bristles or filaments called *stereocilia* or usually just *cilia*. The inner set has a single column of hair cells, whereas the outer set has three columns. An estimated 50,000 auditory nerve fibers connect with the inner and outer hair cells. However, the distribution of nerve fibers is neither equal nor proportional to the number of inner

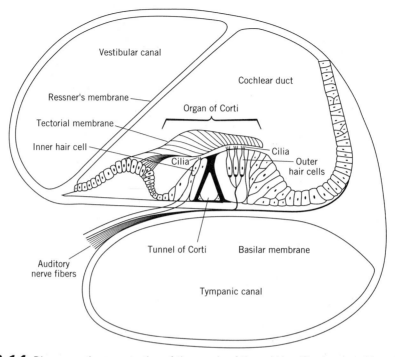

□ *figure 12.14* Diagrammatic cross section of the canals of the cochlea. The inner cochlear duct is separated from the vestibular canal by Reissner's membrane and from the tympanic canal by the basilar membrane. The cochlear duct contains the organ of Corti, which consists of the tectorial membrane, the inner and outer hair cells, and their attached cilia and auditory nerve fibers.

and outer hair cells; about 90–95% of the nerve fibers make contact with the relatively sparse inner hair cells, and the remaining 5–10% of nerve fibers link with the more numerous outer hair cells.

Given these significant structural-neural differences between the inner and outer hair cells, it is likely that they transmit different types of auditory information. It has been suggested, for example, that, based on their greater representation in the distribution of auditory nerves, the inner hair cells encode frequency information, whereas the corresponding outer hair cells amplify the movement of the basilar membrane to sharpen the frequency response of the inner hair cells (e.g., Dallos, 1992; Pickles, 1988; Scharf & Buus, 1986). Evidence also suggests that the outer hair cells register low-amplitude, weak sounds and are essential for sound detection close to the

absolute threshold (Prosen, Moody, Stebbins, & Hawkins, 1981).

Regardless of their function, what is clear is that these sensory hair cells are the ultimate transducers of mechanical vibrations into nerve impulses. As shown in Figure 12.14, the longer filaments, or cilia, of the outer hair cells attach to an overhanging **tectorial membrane.** The tectorial membrane is attached at only one end and partially extends lengthwise across the cochlear duct. Movement of the stapes against the oval window creates vibrations within the cochlea that cause motion of the basilar membrane. In turn, the movement of the basilar membrane bends the cilia of the hair cells against the tectorial membrane. This stimulation of the cilia triggers an electrical change in the hair cells, which initiates the first stage in the neural conduction process; here mechanical energy, in a vibratory form, is transformed into nerve impulses.

The Auditory Nerve

Nerve fibers from the hair cells of the organ of Corti orginate along the full length of the basilar membrane and make up the auditory nerve. The separate fibers are bundled together in such a way that fibers from neighboring regions on the basilar membrane tend to remain together as they ascend to the auditory receiving area of the brain. This arrangement has functional significance. The front or apex of the basilar membrane near the helicotrema is particularly concerned with encoding low-frequency sound waves into neural responses, while successively higher frequencies stimulate hair cells on the basilar membrane that lie progressively closer to the base, near the stapes (Figure 12.15). In other words, the basilar membrane performs a *frequency analysis*. This orderly spatial arrangement of neural elements corresponding to the separation of different frequencies is known as a **tonotopic organization.** Functionally, a tonotopic organization is a systematic way to keep information about similar frequencies represented in adjacent neural areas. Thus, a particular region of the auditory cortex responds selectively to particular frequencies.

In fact, specificity in response to frequency appears to exist at all levels of the auditory system. We will return to the tonotopic organization of the basilar membrane later.

Recordings of the Auditory Nerve

Measures of the electrical activity of the individual fibers of the auditory nerve in response to various sounds indicate that a form of specificity exists for the fibers comprising the auditory nerve. Although many fibers react to various sound characteristics, there is a dominant class of fibers, sometimes referred to as **tuned fibers,** that are frequency selective. That is, they are most sensitive to sounds over a very narrow range of frequencies. As outlined in the **frequency tuning curves** of Figure 12.16, each tuned fiber has a **best** or **characteristic frequency** to which it is most sensitive—a frequency where the intensity necessary for the fiber to reach its absolute threshold is at a minimum. It follows that with changes from the best frequency in either direction, the sensitivity of the fiber decreases and its absolute threshold rises. From such measurements, we know that the auditory nerve has fibers that are selectively and sharply tuned to frequencies extending over the entire range of audibility.

We now examine how the action of the inner ear reacts to and processes different frequencies.

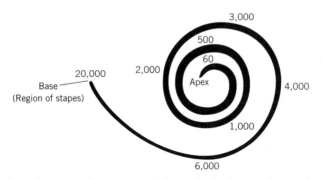

▭ *figure 12.15* Schematic map of frequency analysis on the basilar membrane, showing that the location on the basilar membrane that is maximally stimulated depends on the frequency of the sound. The locations and values indicated are only estimates. However, the important point of the figure is that sounds of different frequencies produce maximal effects at different places along the basilar membrane. Specifically, the apex end of the cochlea, where the basilar membrane is broad, reacts best to low-frequency sounds, whereas the basal end, where the basilar membrane is narrow, reacts best to high-frequency sounds.

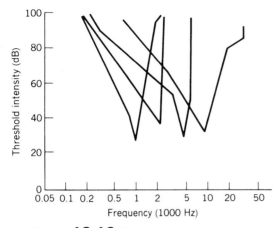

□ *figure 12.16* Frequency tuning curves for four different auditory nerve fibers. The response of a given fiber varies with stimulus frequency. Each curve is generated by determining the lowest intensity of a tone of a specific frequency necessary to produce a detectable or threshold response. The frequency of the tone to which the absolute threshold of a given fiber is at a minimum is called its characteristic or best frequency. Thus, for example, the second fiber yields a threshold response when stimulated by its best stimulus of about 2000 Hz, that is, 2(1000Hz), at about 38 dB. Observe that for a given nerve fiber its threshold increases with a change in frequency from its best stimulus in either direction.

Note that the frequency axis is plotted on a logarithmic scale. (Based on data of Katsuki, 1961; Katsuki, Watanabe, & Suga, 1959.)

FUNCTIONING OF THE INNER EAR

The chain of vibration transmission that produces hearing normally proceeds from the eardrum to the ossicles of the middle ear, to the oval window, and then to the cochlea. However, it is the movement of the cochlear duct that activates and affects, to varying degrees, the hair cells and associated nerve fibers. Thus, to understand how auditory messages are produced, we must focus primarily on how the basilar membrane and the organ of Corti respond to incoming sound waves.

There are two main theories (actually, mechanisms) to account for the way the sensory structures of the ear encode sound frequencies, allowing us to perceive pitch. Although there are several variations, they are conventionally referred to as the *place* and the *frequency* or *frequency-matching theory.*

The Place Theory

The **place theory** assumes that the organ of Corti is organized in strictly tonotopic fashion; that is, that there is an orderly spatial representation of stimulus frequency on the basilar membrane, as suggested by Figure 12.15. Accordingly, different frequencies of vibrations in the cochlear fluid displace different regions of the basilar membrane. These different regions of deflection, in turn, stimulate different hair cells and their corresponding auditory nerve fibers. Specifically, hair cells near the base of the basilar membrane are more affected by high-frequency tones, and hair cells near the apex, or helicotrema, are more responsive to low-frequency tones. Moreover, as we have noted, the nerve fibers from the basilar membrane to the auditory cortex are organized tonotopically, that is, in accordance with the part of the basilar membrane they innervate. The place theory thus describes a spatial code for frequency: It maintains that different frequencies excite different regions of the basilar membrane (and related hair cells and auditory nerve fibers) and produce different pitch sensations.

An early version of a place theory was proposed by Hermann von Helmholtz in 1863 based on assumed resonance properties of the cochlea. However, the major contemporary proponent of a place theory is Georg von Békésy, the Nobel laureate for his work on the mechanisms of the ear (in 1961 for medicine and physiology). Békésy has traced and documented the operation of the inner ear and has reported a number of research findings that support a place theory of hearing.

Traveling Wave Motion in the Cochlea Békésy's contribution to our understanding of the mechanics of the ear concerns the *hydrodynamics* (i.e., transmission of motion in a fluid medium) of the inner ear and the unique effect of sound frequency on the movement of the basilar membrane.

When the action of the stapes causes the oval window to vibrate, the vibrations are transmitted to the basilar membrane, on which the auditory recep-

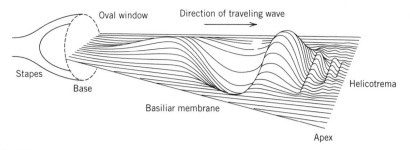

Oval window

Direction of traveling wave

Stapes

Base

Basiliar membrane

Helicotrema

Apex

◻ *figure* **12.17** Schematic of a traveling wave deforming the basilar membrane from the base to the apex.

tors—the hair cells—rest. The resulting *pattern* of vibration along the basilar membrane reflects a unique kind of wave motion called a **traveling wave.** In general, a traveling wave is analogous to a moving wave on the surface of water. To clarify the notion of a traveling wave, imagine a length of rope fastened at one end to a stationary structure, such as a door or wall, and the free end held in your hand. As you flick your wrist, the movement of the rope creates what appears to be a wave that travels along the rope away from the hand. The place along the rope where the peak of the wave occurs depends on how rapidly you flick the rope.

Likewise, the movement of the cochlear fluid by the action of the stapes on the oval window causes traveling waves to move down the basilar membrane from the base (near the oval window and stapes) to the apex (near the helicotrema). Figure 12.17 is a schematic of such a wave. The wave reaches a peak amplitude then rapidly falls. A traveling wave, then, is a unique moving waveform whose point of maximal displacement traces out a specific set of locations. The shape described by the set of these locations along the basilar membrane is called the **envelope of the traveling wave** (Figure 12.18). The point along the basilar membrane where the displacement is maximal depends on the frequency of the sound. The maximum point of displacement, and hence the envelope traced by a traveling wave, differs for each frequency. The traveling wave for high-frequency sounds causes only a small portion of the basilar membrane near the stapes region to move significantly, with very little activity in the remainder of the membrane; in contrast, the traveling wave created by low frequencies causes

almost the entire basilar membrane to move. In short, the vibration pattern created by the action of the stapes converts different sound frequencies into activity at different locations along the basilar membrane. The formation of a traveling wave is critical in the analysis of sound by the auditory system, since the *pattern* of movement of the basilar membrane depends on the *frequency* of the sound.

Ingenious experiments by Békésy support the notion of the transport of vibrations by traveling waves. The sensory effect of much of the physical activity in the cochlear duct has been duplicated by mechanical models designed by Békésy (1955) that accurately reproduce many of the elastic properties and couplings among the components of the inner ear. In addition to using these mechanical models, Békésy observed the activity of the cochlea directly. He observed wave motion on the basilar membrane in fresh and preserved specimens of human and animal cochleas. In some investigations, he placed particles of

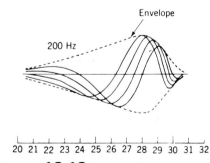

Envelope

200 Hz

20 21 22 23 24 25 26 27 28 29 30 31 32

◻ *figure* **12.18** Envelope formed by a 200-Hz tone. The shape of the envelope is described by the set of momentary locations traced out by the traveling wave along the basilar membrane. (From Békésy, 1953.)

fine metals or carbon in the cochlea and observed their movements during stimulation under magnification. He also cut windows into the human cochlea at various locations and noted the traveling wave vibration pattern of the basilar membrane for selected frequencies. The results of one of these investigations are presented in Figure 12.19. The movement patterns closely corresponded to those obtained with the mechanical models. In short, *the location of maximal displacement of the basilar membrane varies progressively with changes in the frequency of stimulation at the oval window.*

In summary, according to Békésy's observations, movement of the stapes against the oval window creates fluid displacement and a traveling wave that begins at the base of the basilar membrane and travels to the apex of the basilar membrane. En route, the wave stimulates the cochlear duct and mechanically displaces its neighboring components, particularly the cilia of the hair cells. As seen in Figure 12.20, high-frequency vibrations create traveling waves whose points of maximal displacement are near the stapes and then quickly dissipate, whereas low-frequency vibrations produce traveling waves with somewhat flattened displacements near the apex of the cochlea. In fact, for very low frequency tones, almost the entire basilar membrane moves as a single unit, although maximum vibration occurs at the apex. In short, the place theory describes a spatial code for frequency.

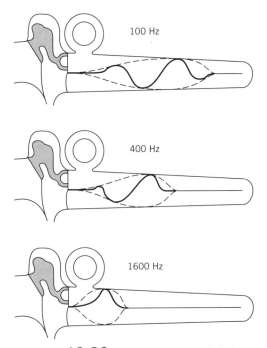

□ **figure 12.20** Traveling waves and their envelopes for three different frequencies in schematic depictions of the cochlea. Observe that the traveling wave of low frequencies (e.g., 100 Hz) extends far along the length of the cochlea, but the amplitude of its displacement is relatively flat. Note also that with increases in frequency, the peak of maximal displacement of the traveling wave within each envelope moves progressively toward the base (stapes region). In fact, as exemplified by the bottom figure (1600 Hz), the displacement within the cochlea created by high frequencies is confined to the base region. The frequency specification and configuration of all waveforms are approximate. (Based on Yost & Nielsen, 1977.)

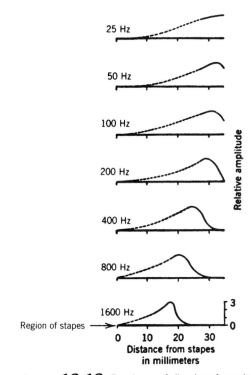

□ **figure 12.19** Envelopes of vibrations for various frequencies over the basilar membrane in a human cadaver. As the frequency of the stimulus increases, the amplitude of maximum displacement moves progressively toward the stapes. The actual data observed are indicated by the continuous line; the broken line is an extrapolation. (From Békésy, 1949.)

Two related points should be stressed here. (1) The location of the peak of the traveling wave is determined by the *frequency* of the originating sound. High-frequency sounds create traveling waveforms that peak close to the stapes region (Figure 12.20), whereas low-frequency sounds produce broader waveforms with a relatively flat response region whose maximum is near the apex. (2) The peak of the traveling wave is the *place* where the basilar membrane is most deflected. This means that the hair cells and their cilia lying on this part of the basilar membrane are correspondingly displaced most by the traveling wave. In other words, the frequency of vibration and the corresponding traveling wave cause the basilar membrane to deflect maximally at one location, thereby maximally stimulating a particular group of hair cells. Thus, the differential action of the basilar membrane is the basis of a frequency analysis.

In addition to accounting for frequency reception, the place theory has been used to explain how a sound's pressure intensity, or amplitude (hence loudness), is registered on the basilar membrane. It assumes that the more intense a sound, the greater the proportion of the basilar membrane called into action (e.g., Glaser & Haven, 1972). Thus, for a given frequency, the intensity of a sound determines the amplitude or height of the peak of the resulting traveling wave. Increases in the amplitude of the basilar membrane's movement cause greater stimulation of the hair cells and cilia, an increase in nerve fiber activity— overall, a larger neural response—and a resulting increase in the perception of loudness.

In summary, frequency analysis and the perception of pitch, according to the place theory, depend on differential activity along the basilar membrane and on the innervation of specific hair cells. The encoding of intensity or amplitude and the resulting sensation of loudness are explained on the basis of the number of nerve impulses generated by basilar membrane displacement.

The Frequency-Matching Theory

The major alternative to the Békésy place theory is called the **frequency-matching theory** (also referred to as the **frequency** or **telephone theory;** Wever & Bray, 1930). It holds that the basilar membrane vibrates as a single unit, reproducing the frequency of vibrations of the sound. This causes neurons in the auditory system to fire at the same frequency as that of the sound. Frequency thus is transmitted directly by the vibrations of the cochlear elements to the auditory nerve, much as the telephone or microphone diaphragm directly transduces sounds. The pitch heard, according to the frequency-matching notion, is determined by the frequency of impulses traveling up the auditory nerve, which, in turn, is correlated with the frequency of the sound wave. The brain, then, serves as the analyzing instrument for pitch perception.

Evidence supports a frequency-matching notion for coding moderately low frequencies; that is, the firing pattern of nerve fibers is closely synchronized with the frequency of the stimulating sound (Rose et al., 1967). As an example, in response to a 250-Hz tone, a fiber might fire every 4 msec, or 250 times per second. Its neural discharge would thus be **phase locked** or **time locked** to the 250-Hz tone; that is, the successive discharges of the fiber would be regular and locked in time to the frequency of the tone. Accordingly, information about the tone's frequency can be encoded and transmitted by the pattern of the fiber's activity over time.

Evidence of a frequency-matching mechanism comes from studies on frequency detection and discrimination in fish. Fish have hair cells and auditory nerves but lack all of the peripheral frequency analyzers required by a place mechanism, such as a cochlea or basilar membrane. However, based solely on a frequency-matching mechanism, goldfish and catfish have been shown to be sensitive to sounds within a frequencies range of 100 to about 4000 Hz, with peak sensitivity between 600 and 700 Hz (Weiss, 1966; Weiss, Strother, & Hartig, 1969). Similarly, based on a frequency mechanism alone, goldfish have shown the ability to discriminate between frequencies up to about 1000 Hz (Fay, 1970).

The Volley Principle A major criticism of the frequency-matching theory is that a single nerve fiber cannot respond directly more than 1000 times per second—hence, it cannot transmit frequencies above 1000 Hz—so it certainly cannot transmit all the frequencies within the audible range. The frequency-matching theory has been modified by Wever and Bray (1937) under the assumption that every nerve fiber does not fire at the same moment; rather, total neural activity is distributed over a series of auditory nerve fibers (Figure 12.21). Thus, fibers are believed to cooperate, so that squads, or *volleys,* of fibers fire at different times; the overall effect is that the neural pattern of firing corresponds directly to the frequency of the stimulus. In other words, groups of fibers that have a staggered discharge rate together yield impulses synchronized with the frequency of the stimulus. This explanation is called the **volley principle** (Wever, 1949). Some sort of volleying has been reported from the responses of single neurons (e.g., for frequencies up to 1050 Hz; Galambos & Davis, 1943).

The volley principle also accounts for variations in sound intensity (and hence in the sensation of loudness), independent of frequency. Increases in intensity create increased firings in each volley. In other words, as a sound's intensity increases, more auditory nerve fibers enter the volleys. The total effect of increasing intensity is to produce more impulses per volley without changing frequency.

Cooperation of Place and Frequency-Matching Mechanisms

Modern hearing theory generally draws from both the place and frequency-matching theories. Pitch may thus be mediated by two independent mechanisms, each operating for a limited range of frequencies. High frequencies are efficiently encoded by a place mechanism. As evidence, the location of basilar membrane displacement is quite specific and narrowly tuned for high frequencies. That is, high-frequency sounds produce traveling waves that peak at specific places along the basilar membrane. The specific region of basilar membrane displacement, in turn, activates different groups of hair cells and auditory nerves.

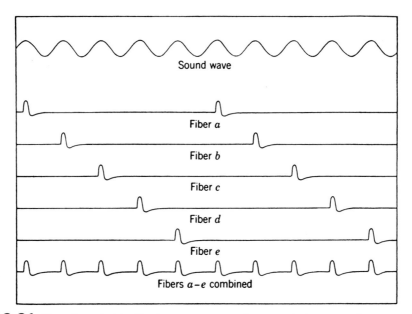

◻ *figure 12.21* The volley principle. The top curve represents a sound whose waveform appears at a rate too rapid for a single fiber to follow. However, its total activity can be staggered and distributed over a set of fibers. Shown below the sound wave is such a set of auditory nerve fibers (labeled *a, b, c, d,* and *e*) that fire at different times, but in such a way that each fiber responds to different peaks of the sound wave. The bottom curve describes the effect of combining the discharges of all the fibers (*a* to *e* combined): the total response reproduces precisely the full frequency of the stimulating sound waveform.

However, recall that low frequencies (i.e., below 1000 Hz) create a rather broad or flat pattern of vibratory activity on the basilar membrane (see Figures 12.19 and 12.20). This means that the displacement pattern is much less specific and localizable than the peak displacement of high frequencies. Low frequencies thus pose a problem for a place mechanism since, as we noted, the place mechanism encodes frequency information according to the precise place along the basilar membrane that is maximally deflected by the vibration pattern. However, a frequency-matching mechanism can handle low frequencies efficiently. That is, for frequencies below 1000 Hz, the entire basilar membrane can vibrate in synchrony with the frequency of pressure changes registered in the cochlea.

It is reasonable to conclude that both the place and frequency-matching mechanisms are used to encode frequency information. E. G. Wever (1949), a major proponent of the frequency-matching theory, has written: "the low-tone region is that in which frequency (i.e., frequency-matching) holds sway, the high-tone region that for place representation, and the middle-tone region one where both frequency and place work side by side" (p. 190). Békésy (1963) has likewise commented that only the frequency-matching mechanism is active below 50 Hz, the place mechanism alone above 3000 Hz, and both appear to play a role between 50 and 3000 Hz. (Interestingly, as we will observe in Chapter 14, the frequency range in which both mechanisms may operate includes the majority of sounds that are critical to the human.)

Evidence supports this functional cooperation. Simmons et al. (1965) implanted electrodes in different parts of the auditory nerve of a subject's deaf ear and found that different pitch effects were produced when differently located electrodes were stimulated; that is, in support of a place mechanism, pitch effects were produced that correlated with the *place* of stimulation (see also Townshend et al., 1987). However, Simmons et al. also found evidence of a frequency-matching mechanism: variations in stimulus frequency from about 20 to 300 Hz, regardless of electrode location, produced changes in the pitch of the resulting sound (see also Rose et al., 1967).

AUDITORY PATHOLOGY

Auditory pathology ranges from various hearing impairments that produce systematic distortions in hearing sounds to a complete failure of the auditory mechanism to respond to any sounds. In this section we consider a few of the major forms of pathology of the auditory system.

Tinnitus

Tinnitus is a condition in which a tone or noise is continuously heard in one or both ears in the absence of an outside stimulus. The most obvious sign is a persistent humming or ringing in the ears, usually of a high pitch. It has a variety of causes and may also occur in the absence of any known pathology. Tinnitus itself is not considered a disease; rather, it is a symptom of an underlying disorder. It is an important symptom of several ear disorders; it accompanies certain infections and high fevers; and frequently it follows cochlea damage caused by mechanical injury, exposure to high-intensity sounds, or certain drugs. It is estimated that as much as 1% of the population suffer from debilitating or occasionally annoying tinnitus.

One treatment of tinnitus consists of alleviating the disturbing noise by introducing another sound that serves as a masking noise. The masker is introduced by a device worn like a hearing aid or portable stereo. For some individuals, the masker covers up and reduces but does not eliminate, the tinnitus.

Presbyacusis

Hearing loss attributed to the effects of aging is known as **presbyacusis** (from the Greek *presbys* for "old" and *akousis* for "hearing"). Advancing age is by far the most common cause of inner ear hearing deficiencies and, either directly or indirectly, it is probably the leading cause of all hearing loss. Many effects due directly to age may play a role: various forms of middle-ear impairment, loss of elasticity of the basilar membrane, restriction of vascular flow to auditory structures, and gradual degeneration and loss of sensorineural elements in the central nervous system, particularly the cochlea.

Age-related hearing loss is selective and specific: Sensitivity to high-frequency sound decreases progressively throughout life. Although the upper limit for frequency reception may be as high as 23,000 Hz in children, it gradually decreases. In one rather depressing citation, individuals in their forties regularly lost 80 Hz from their upper limit of hearing every 6 months (Békésy, 1957). Loss of sensitivity to high-frequency sound supports Békésy's place notion: the nerve degeneration characteristic of presbyacusis occurs mainly at the basal end of the cochlea—where, according to the place notion, high-frequency sounds are mediated (e.g., Johnsson & Hawkins, 1972).

Although presbyacusis is probably due to deterioration in neural and other supporting structures directly related to the aging process, indirect effects likely also play a role—that is, the cumulative influence of infections, occasional abnormal noise exposure, and the collection of usual and unusual acoustic events that occur throughout life.

Finally, in this context, we should note an effect of gradual age-related hearing loss that could play a role in psychopathology. Clinical and audiometric assessments of elderly mental patients reveal that hearing loss and deafness are especially prevalent among those diagnosed as paranoid (e.g., Zimbardo, Anderson, & Kabat, 1981). One process by which significant hearing loss and deafness in the aged may contribute to paranoia is based on the gradual onset of the hearing impairment. Because hearing loss is gradual, a person may be totally unaware that his or her hearing is affected. Thus a person, not recognizing a hearing loss, continually confronts situations such as not hearing what others are apparently saying. Nearby individuals, speaking at a normal conversational level, may be interpreted as whispering. In turn, their denial that they are whispering may be judged by the elderly, hearing-impaired person as a lie, since it is clearly different from what is apparent: individuals in animated conversation, but at an inaudible level. Uncorrected, this interpretation and resultant interaction can lead to frustration and hostility; over time, social relationships deteriorate and eventually the person becomes isolated, eliminating the social feedback required to correct or modify false beliefs.

Hearing Loss

Deafness refers to hearing threshold levels for speech reception above 92 dB (Davis & Silverman, 1978). At these levels, normal auditory communication is almost impossible. In contrast, *hearing loss* refers to a measurable loss of sensitivity that does not prevent auditory communication. Generally, we will restrict our discussion to hearing loss.

Conduction and Sensorineural Hearing Loss

There are two main types of hearing loss: *conduction* and *sensorineural*. **Conduction hearing loss** results from deficiencies in the conduction mechanism of the auditory system, particularly involving the structure and function of the external auditory canal, the eardrum, or the ossicles. **Sensorineural hearing loss** occurs from deficiencies in or damage to the auditory nerve, to structures of the organ of Corti, or other closely linked neural connection in the cochlea.

The Audiometer

An important instrument for studying hearing loss is the **audiometer.** It usually consists of a tone generator that provides pure tones at many different frequencies and allows for intensity to be set at levels at which the tone is just audible. At each test frequency, the intensity necessary for the tone to be barely audible is measured and is compared with previously established standards. The resulting graph from the manipulations, an **audiogram,** shows any departure from normal sensitivity, that is, hearing loss, in decibels for the different test frequencies.

Typical audiograms are given in Figure 12.22. The curve for a person with normal hearing (shown by Curve *A*) remains relatively close to zero in hearing loss in all frequencies. The other curves are typical for persons with hearing deficiencies. Curve *B* shows the hearing loss for a person with sensorineural hearing loss. In this form of auditory pathology, hearing loss is usually pronounced for the high frequencies and much less for the lower frequencies. Curve *C* shows the hearing loss for a person with conduction

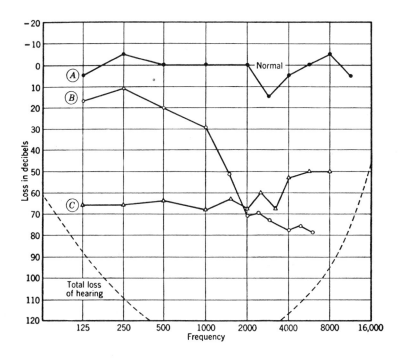

hearing loss. The curve shows that the severe hearing loss is approximately the same at all frequencies.

Békésy Tracking Procedure: Tonal Gaps

Another form of audiogram or audiometric function, shown in Figure 12.23, is based on a different procedure called the **Békésy tracking procedure.** In this procedure, the subject generates the absolute threshold level for tones of various frequencies. (In fact, it is an adaptation of the psychophysical *method of adjustment* introduced in Chapter 2.) The subject presses a button when he or she hears a tone and releases the button when the tone just becomes inaudible. However, pressing the button decreases the intensity of the tone, whereas releasing it increases the intensity.

The procedure is as follows. A tone of a specified frequency is presented at a subthreshold intensity level and is gradually increased until it just becomes audible. The subject then presses the button, which gradually reduces the tone's intensity until it fades away and is no longer audible. At this point the subject releases the button, whereupon the tone's intensity

increases gradually until it again becomes audible; and again the subject presses the button. In other words, the subject alternates pressing and releasing the button until the tone hovers around a just audible or threshold level. In addition, the frequency of the

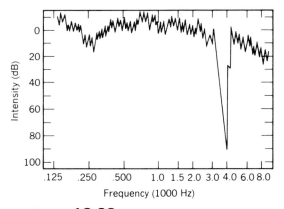

□ **figure 12.23** Audiometric function generated by the Békésy tracking procedure. The curve shows threshold intensity as a function of frequency. The curve reveals a tonal gap—an insensitivity to a band of tonal frequencies—at about 4000 Hz.

tone is automatically and gradually advanced so that, as the subject responds, a continuous record of the subject's threshold for various frequencies is generated.

The audiometric function is plotted by a pen moving along a chart that tracks the subject's threshold responses as a function of frequency. Thus, as the frequency of the tone is gradually changed, the pen runs up and down across the chart, reversing direction each time the button is pressed or released; this accounts for the rather zigzag curve seen in Figure 12.23. The Békésy tracking procedure is useful clinically, as it can reveal **tonal gaps**—narrow ranges of frequencies that are inaudible to the subject and of which the subject may be totally unaware.

Causes of Hearing Loss and Deafness

Hearing loss and deafness are due to a wide range of conditions, including chronic infection (particularly viral) of the middle and inner ears, vascular disorders, acoustic trauma, prolonged exposure to intense noise, and the use of certain antibiotics in high dosages, such as streptomycin, neomycin, and kanamycin. In fact, the pathological effects on the auditory system of some antibiotics are so fast-acting, strong, and predictable that they have been used in studies on the effects of selective destruction of the hair cells of the organ of Corti (e.g., Cazals et al., 1980; Prosen et al., 1981). The ability of certain antibiotics to destroy the hair cells was first discovered when treating tuberculosis with streptomycin (Rosenzweig & Leiman, 1982).

In addition to antibiotics, other drugs and chemicals, such as aspirin (salicylate), quinine, certain diuretics, carbon monoxide, lead, mercury, and tobacco, may contribute to hearing loss on a temporary or permanent basis (e.g., McFadden & Plattsmier, 1983; Stypulkowski, 1990; Zelman, 1973). In this discussion, we must also include the effects of aging on hearing deficiency (see the earlier section on presbyacusis).

Sound-Induced Hearing Loss One result of abnormal exposure to intense sounds or noise (i.e., unwanted sound) that warrants special mention is called **sound-** or **noise-induced hearing loss.**

Exposure to excessive, prolonged acoustic stimulation—"noise pollution"—can produce severe hearing losses that may be temporary or permanent. It has been estimated that more than 16 million Americans have some permanent hearing loss from exposure to intense sound. For example, it has been known for decades that hearing loss is an occupational hazard when the work environment involves exposure to intense noise for long periods of time. In one early study, workers exposed to noise levels of close to 100 dB for 8 hours a day, 5 days a week, had absolute thresholds 35 dB higher than the thresholds of an unexposed group (Taylor et al., 1965). In other words, the extensive exposure to intense noise reduced their hearing, so that sounds had to be far more intense than normal in order to be heard. Relatedly, structural changes caused by exposure to intense noise can be seen in the guinea pig cochlea: exposure to sounds of 140 dB for only 30 seconds produces gross distortions of the outer hair cells and tears them off the basilar membrane (*Lancet,* 1975, p. 215).

Recreational activities may also contribute to hearing loss, including listening to high-intensity amplified music (e.g., Hanson & Fearn, 1975). In fact, many individuals report some hearing loss (and tinnitus)—often lasting for hours—after listening to a highly amplified concert. The familiar personal stereo (e.g., the Walkman) at high intensity levels may also produce hearing loss. A rule of thumb is that if individuals other than the user can hear the sound (coming from the user's ear phones while being worn), then it is probably set at far too intense a level.

Weiss and Brandspiegel (1990) found that certain sports events also create excessive, potentially damaging sound levels. They measured the noise generated at six enclosed sports areas during typical basketball games, both professional and collegiate. Of course, we need no data to convince us that these are noisy events: shouting, cheering, stamping, clapping, and so on, along with occasional intense bursts of organ or band music, create continual, intense background noise. Weiss and Brandspiegel found that spectators at such sports events are not merely exposed to a noisy environment. They found that, with few exceptions, the sound levels often generated during a typical game far exceeded the safety levels set for human hearing.

In light of this discussion, a cautionary note is in order. We live in a noisy environment, and the potential for hearing loss due to excessive noise exposure is ever present. However, once progressive hearing loss begins, it may occur so gradually that we may scarcely detect it. Ironically, an insidious result of gradual hearing loss due to exposure to intense sound is that sounds must then be made more intense in order to be heard, which, in turn, further damages the auditory process. Although we cannot eliminate, or even avoid, many noisy situations, we should be aware of and vigilant to the potential damage posed by intense noise.

COMPARATIVE AUDITORY STRUCTURES

As we have observed, the human ear is an immensely complicated and efficient organ. Yet many of its basic processes and mechanisms are shared by lower forms of vertebrate life. Accordingly, we may gain some insight into its functioning by examining the hearing and auditory structures of other species.

The auditory structures of a turtle, a bird, and a mammal are sketched in Figure 12.24. The various upper ring-like structures are the *vestibular organs,*

concerned with registering gravity and balance, to be discussed in detail in Chapter 15. Here, however, it is relevant to note that the basilar membrane lengthens with the evolution of birds and mammals. Generally, the basilar membrane is shortest in amphibia and reptiles, somewhat longer in birds, and longest in mammals (Manley, 1971).

The length of the basilar membrane is obviously linked to certain aspects of auditory reception. One suggestion about the significance of these phylogenetic differences is given by Masterton and Diamond (1973): "Because sounds of different frequencies result in stimulation at different places along the basilar membrane, this lengthening of the receptor organ almost certainly means that there existed a strong and persistent pressure on the ancestors of mammals for a wider range and finer discrimination of frequency" (p. 411).

Structures other than those of the inner ear are important to the audible range of hearing. Masterton, Heffner, and Ravizza (1968) have pointed out that high-frequency hearing (above 32,000 Hz) is unique to mammals and is due to the evolution, in mammals only, of the middle-ear ossicles.

Of interest here is the relationship of hearing range to gross bodily dimensions. Békésy (1960) surmised that the overall *physical size* of the animal bears some relationship to the minimum frequency that is detect-

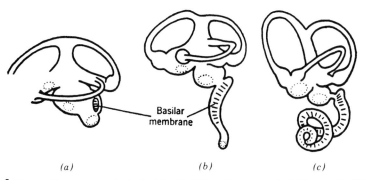

Basilar membrane

(a)   *(b)*   *(c)*

▭ *figure* **12.24** The auditory organs of a turtle (*a*), a bird (*b*), and a mammal (*c*). The length of the basilar membrane increases dramatically from the turtle to the mammal. The parallel dashes within the basilar membrane represent the auditory nerve endings. The top ring-like structures and the dotted ellipses are the vestibular organs, which react to gravity and register bodily position and balance. [From G. von Békésy, "Frequency in the cochlea of various animals," in E. G. Wever (Trans. and Ed.), *Experiments in Hearing,* McGraw-Hill, New York, 1960; and G. von Békésy and W. A. Rosenblith, "The mechanical properties of the ear," in S. S. Stevens (Ed.), *Handbook of Experimental Psychology,* John Wiley, New York, 1951, p. 1102. Reprinted by permission of the publisher.]

able. Specifically, he suggested that the lower-frequency limit is shifted downward with increases in animal size. This is related to the general enlargement of the ear. When sound is transmitted along the ear's main surfaces, the sound absorption is less for low-frequency tones than for high ones. Accordingly, when auditory passages are relatively large, there is an advantage to the reception of low-frequency tones: they last longer and thus travel farther.

Moreover, according to Békésy and Rosenblith (1951), favoring low-frequency tones offers an ecological advantage to large animals: "The wisdom of nature is evident in all this, because it is certainly important for large animals to hear over great distances. If the sound is propagated along the ground, the absorption will in general affect low-frequency sounds less than high-frequency sounds. Hence the usefulness of favoring the low frequencies" (p. 1104).

It has also been suggested that mammals with a small *interaural distance* (i.e., the functional distance between the two ears) have been subjected to more selective pressure to hear high frequencies than mammals with more widely set ears; that is, the ability to hear high-frequency sounds is inversely related to the distance between the two ears. As we will see in Chapter 14, because of the shorter wavelengths involved, high-frequency hearing for small mammals is especially important for sound localization. Generally, mammals with large heads and wide-set ears have a more restricted high-frequency limit than those with small heads and small interaural distances. Thus, while the average mammalian high-frequency hearing limit is of the order of 55 kHz (k = kilo, or thousand), the upper limit for mammals with large physical dimensions such as the elephant is relatively small, about 10 kHz (Heffner & Heffner, 1980).

An additional observation concerning the audible frequency range for mammals bears examination. Heffner and Heffner (1983a, 1983b) have analyzed evidence on the frequency range of audibility for various mammalian species and have observed an overall trend. Generally, there is a trade-off between high- and low-frequency hearing: across mammalian species, low-frequency hearing improves as the ability to hear high frequencies declines. In short, mammals that have relatively good high-frequency hearing have

□ **table 12.2** Range of Audible Sound Frequencies (Hz) for Various Mammalian Species

	Low-Frequency Limit	High-Frequency Limit
Elephant	17	10,000
Human	20	20,000
Cattle	23	35,000
Horse	55	33,500
Dog	60	45,000
Monkey	110	45,000
Rat	650	60,000
Mouse	1000	90,000
Bat	3000	120,000

Source: Approximated from Heffner and Heffner (1983a, 1983b).

somewhat restricted low-frequency hearing, and vice versa. Table 12.2 gives some approximate values illustrating this trend.

SUMMARY

In this chapter, we introduced the auditory system and some basic phenomena of hearing. We began by describing the physical characteristics of the sound stimulus and their corresponding psychological effects on the auditory system. We discussed the main physical properties of the waveform of sounds, noting that they are characterized by variation in frequency (given in terms of the number of pressure changes per second, or Hz), amplitude or intensity (specified in decibels, or dB units), and complexity. Frequency is related to the psychological experience of pitch; amplitude, or intensity, to loudness; and complexity to timbre. In discussing complexity, we discussed the notion of harmonics, the fundamental frequency, and Ohm's acoustical law. In addition, we outlined how the auditory system performs a Fourier analysis on the auditory stimulus. We also described the phase of a sound—that part of the pressure wave (which varies from peak, or compression to trough, or rarefaction) reached at a given point in time. In discussing phase, we noted the possibility of cancelling noise by simultaneously presenting an identical set of noise stimuli, but exactly 180° out of phase. Finally, in the section on the auditory stimulus, we introduced the notion of resonance, the tendency of an object to vibrate sympathetically when the frequency of a sound-emitting source matches the natural or resonant frequency of the object.

The next section concerned the anatomy and mechanisms of the ear. Three main divisions were identified (the outer, middle, and inner ear), and the physiological events and processes of the auditory system that promote sound perception were outlined.

The main function of the middle ear is to deal with impedance mismatch, the difference in the resistance of sound pressure transmitted from the airborne media of the middle ear to the fluid-filled media of the inner ear. We also noted the protective function of the middle ear, stressing the acoustic reflex—a reflex of two small muscles in the middle ear to reduce the transmission of very intense sounds to the inner ear. Relatedly, we noted that the Eustachian tube equalizes air pressure on both sides of the eardrum—between the outer and middle ears. We also noted that sound vibrations may bypass the outer and middle ears completely, reach the inner ear by bone conduction—in which sounds vibrate the bones of the skull, which, in turn, stimulate the inner ear directly.

The main anatomical structures and their functioning of the inner ear were outlined, with particular attention on the organ of Corti. The organ of Corti rests on and extends the length of the basilar membrane. It contains columns of inner and outer hair cells that transform the mechanical vibrations of sound into neural activity.

The auditory nerve was discussed next, and its organizational and spatial relation to basilar membrane displacement was stressed. We pointed out that there is an orderly spatial arrangement of neural elements along the basilar membrane corresponding to specific frequencies. These neural elements systematically connect with separate fibers of the auditory nerve and ascend to the auditory receiving area of the brain, where they are spatially arranged to correspond directly to their basilar membrane origin—an arrangement called tonotopic organization. Many auditory nerve fibers are frequency selective, supporting the notion of a tonotopic organization of the auditory nerve in the auditory brain.

In the context of inner ear function, we considered two main theories (actually, mechanisms) of pitch perception: Békésy's place theory and frequency-matching theory (and the volley principle). The place theory assumes that stimulus frequencies are represented systematically on the basilar membrane: Specifically, neural elements near the base of the basilar membrane (near the stapes) are more affected by high-frequency tones and elements located near the apex of the basilar membrane are more responsive to low-frequency tones. In short, according to place theory, different frequencies excite different regions of the basilar membrane and produce different pitch sensations. Much evidence was summarized in support of a place notion of pitch perception, including traveling wave activity within the cochlea and the relation between the pitch experienced and the differential displacement of the basilar membrane.

The frequency-matching notion holds that the basilar membrane, along with the auditory nerve and its neurons, vibrates as a single unit, reproducing the frequency of pressure changes in a sound. Accordingly, the pitch experienced is directly correlated with the frequency of impulses traveling up the auditory nerve, which, in turn, is correlated with the frequency of the sound waves reaching the eardrum.

It is likely that both notions play a role in hearing. The perception of low-frequency sounds may be determined by a frequency-matching mechanism, whereas high-frequency sounds may be handled by the place mechanism.

The next section dealt with general auditory pathology, hearing loss, and deafness. Several common pathologies of the auditory were outlined: tinnitus, presbyacusis, conduction and sensorineural hearing loss, and sound-induced hearing loss. The possible cause and measurement of hearing loss were analyzed, with a brief discussion of the audiometer and the Békésy tracking procedure. We noted that the latter can uncover tonal gaps—narrow ranges of frequencies which are inaudible and of which the individual may be totally unaware.

Finally, we briefly discussed comparative auditory structures. We noted that the basilar membrane lengthened with increases in phylogenetic development. Some general trends were observed. For mammalian species, the ability to hear high frequencies appears to be inversely related to the distance between the two ears: the smaller this distance, the higher the frequency range perceived. It was also noted that for mammals, high-frequency hearing occurs at a sacrifice in the ability to hear low frequencies, and vice versa.

KEY TERMS

Acoustic Reflex

Amplitude

Audiogram

Audiometer

Basilar Membrane

Békésy Tracking Procedure

Best (Characteristic) Frequency

Bone Conduction

Cochlea

Cochlear Duct

Complexity

Conduction Hearing Loss

Decibel (dB)

Eardrum

Envelope of the Traveling Wave

Eustachian Tube

External Auditory Canal

Fourier Analysis

Fourier Synthesis

Frequency

Frequency-Matching Theory (Frequency Theory, Telephone Theory)

Frequency Tuning Curves

Fundamental Frequency

Harmonics

Hertz (Hz)

Impedance Mismatch

Incus

Inner Hair Cells

Loudness

Malleus

Noise Cancellation

Ohm's Acoustical Law

Organ of Corti

Ossicles

Outer Hair Cells

Oval Window

Phase

Phase-Locked (Time-Locked)

Pinna

Pitch

Place Theory

Presbyacusis

Reissner's Membrane

Resonance

Round Window

Sensorineural Hearing Loss

Sound- (Noise-) Induced Hearing Loss

Soundwave

Stapes

Tectorial Membrane

Timbre

Tinnitus

Tonal Gap

Tonotopic Organization

Traveling Wave

Tuned Fibers

Tympanic Canal

Vestibular Canal

Volley Principle

Wavelength

STUDY QUESTIONS

1. Describe the physical and psychological dimensions of a sound. Consider a sound's frequency, amplitude or intensity, and complexity, and link

these physical dimensions to the appropriate subjective dimensions of pitch, loudness, and timbre.

2. What is the decibel? Discuss the relationship between increases in sound pressure and increases in decibel values. What is the advantage of using a decibel scale?

3. Explain the complexity–timbre relationship of a sound, including harmonics, the fundamental frequency, Fourier analysis, and Ohm's acoustical law.

4. What is the phase of a sound pressure wave? How is it specified? Consider how an unwanted noise may be cancelled by the synthesis of its reverse waveform 180° out of phase.

5. Describe resonance. What factors cause an object to resonate, or vibrate, sympathetically?

6. Distinguish between the major anatomical components of the outer, middle, and inner ear. Trace the route of a sound from the external environment to the transducers in the inner ear.

7. Outline the function of the middle ear. Discuss impedance mismatch and the acoustic reflex, and highlight the role of the Eustachian tube.

8. What is bone conduction? How does it enable sounds to be transmitted to the cochlea of the inner ear, bypassing the action of the outer and middle ear components?

9. Outline the main components of the inner ear and indicate their function in sound reception. Focus on the structures of the organ of Corti, including the basilar membrane and the specialized inner and outer hairs that lie on it.

10. What kinds of frequency specificity exist within the auditory nerve? How does the observation that nerve fibers may be selectively and sharply tuned to frequency apply to pitch perception? Be sure to discuss frequency tuning curves.

11. Compare and contrast the place and frequency-matching theories of pitch perception. Indicate their major differences and discuss how they complement each other. What is the status of the theories of pitch perception? Outline evidence in support of the place and frequency-matching notions, noting the modification introduced by the volley principle.

12. What is a traveling wave? How does it support a place notion of pitch perception?

13. Indicate how the place and frequency-matching notions register intensity and account for loudness perception.

14. Outline the major disorders of the auditory system. Distinguish between disorders due to illness and disease, those due to abnormal noise exposure, and those due to aging. Distinguish between conduction and sensorineural hearing loss.

15. What is an audiometer? In what ways is the Békésy tracking procedure an absolute threshold detection technique? How does it reveal tonal gaps?

16. Examine some of the differences in the range of audibility related to a species' anatomy. What anatomical characteristics favor the reception of high- and low-frequency sounds?

chapter **13**

PSYCHOACOUSTICS

In the previous chapter, we introduced the physical stimulus for sound and described the physiological mechanisms that enable hearing. In this chapter, our primary focus is on the sensory or psychological effects produced by simple sounds. Much of our discussion concerns how the perceptual, or sensory, dimensions of hearing are related to the acoustic events that produce them. As we noted in the previous chapter, *the primary physical dimensions of a simple sound are its intensity (or pressure amplitude) and frequency, which are functionally related to the psychological dimensions of loudness and pitch, respectively. We will now examine some of the quantitative relationships between these dimensions, beginning with the sensitivity of the auditory system to sound intensity.*

INTENSITY

The sensitivity of the vertebrate auditory system to sound is extraordinary. The human threshold to sound has been measured by finding the lowest intensity that just produces a detection response, or sensation of hearing. At frequencies of about 3000 Hz, the human threshold for sound approaches the reception of the sounds made by the random movement of air molecules! Considering this degree of sensitivity along with the fact that the ear is also capable of hearing sounds millions of times as intense indicates what a remarkable physiological mechanism the ear is just in terms of its performance range.

To obtain precise threshold measurements, listeners are often tested in specially constructed environments that totally lack sound-reflecting objects. One such environment is called an *anechoic chamber* (i.e., free of echoes) in which all walls, ceilings, and floors

are covered by a highly absorbent material to eliminate interfering sound reflection. Figure 13.1 plots the threshold values in decibels for the range of pure sound frequencies that are audible to the human measured in such an acoustically controlled environment. The figure makes it clear that the sensitivity of the human auditory system depends on the frequency of the sound. That is, each frequency has its own threshold value. In general, maximal sensitivity (and the lowest threshold value) is for those frequencies in the region of 3000 Hz. This means that with intensity held constant, a sound of 3000 Hz sounds louder than sounds of other frequencies. This bias for frequencies around 3000 Hz corresponds to the natural resonance of the external auditory canal noted in the previous chapter. In functional terms, the benefit to the human of this particular frequency-related sensitivity may lie in the alarming and piercing quality of a cry that occurs in the 3000-Hz range. Perhaps, as Milne and Milne

350

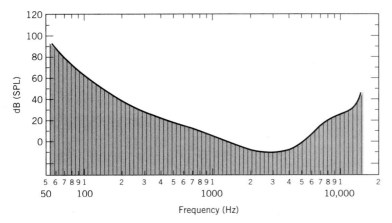

figure 13.1 Auditory threshold as a function of frequency. The values were generated by an observer facing the sound source and listening with both ears. Note that sounds with dB and Hz values that fall in the shaded region below the curve are below threshold and hence are inaudible. (Based on Sivian & White, 1933.)

(1967) speculate, we have a "channel open—as though reserved for emergencies—for any high-pitched scream" (p. 43).

Intensity Discrimination

An important aspect of intensity reception is the degree to which the stimulus intensity of a sound must be changed (either increased or decreased) in order to just perceive a difference. This value is referred to as the *difference threshold* (often noted as ΔI; see Chapter 2). The difference threshold depends on several factors, including the duration, intensity, and kinds of sounds (e.g., whether pure or complex sounds or noise bursts) on which the measurement is made. Generally speaking, the minimum change in the intensity of a sound (i.e., ΔI) that produces a perceptual difference is about 1 to 2 dB (perhaps less at high intensity levels; Gulick et al., 1989; Scharf & Buus, 1986). As we will see in the next chapter, intensity discrimination is helpful in localizing sounds.

Loudness

Recall that loudness refers to the psychological dimension of audition—an aspect of sensory experience that, as we have noted, is generally determined by the physical intensity, or pressure amplitude of the sound. However, the relationship between loudness and intensity is imperfect and complex; loudness does not correspond to physical intensity alone.

Based on the results of Stevens' magnitude estimation technique (described in Chapter 2), the relationship between loudness and physical intensity is that increases in intensity produce lower proportional increases in loudness. In other words, loudness grows more slowly than intensity. This imperfect relationship is further elaborated by the *sone scale*.

The Sone Scale It has been useful to adopt a standard unit of loudness. Stevens and Davis (1938) proposed the term **sone:** 1 sone is defined as the loudness of a 1000-Hz tone at 40-dB SPL intensity level. Both the sone unit and its referents have been universally adopted as the standard of loudness. A function relating intensity level to the sone scale is given in Figure 13.2. If you examine the figure carefully, you will observe that loudness (specified in sones on the *y*-axis) doubles when the sound intensity level of a sound (given in decibel units on the *x*-axis) increases by 10 dB. For example, a 70-dB tone (which has a loudness level of about 8 sones) is twice as loud as a 60-dB tone (which has a loudness of about 4 sones).

Another relation that should be noted in this context is that increasing a sound by 10 dB corresponds to about a tripling of its intensity. Relating this fact to changes in loudness means that a twofold increase in loudness is produced by a threefold (or 10-dB) in-

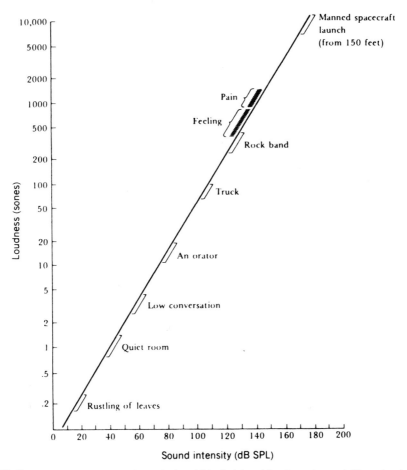

⌐ **figure 13.2** Relationship between intensity level (decibels) and loudness (sones). Note that in this function a 10-dB increase in the intensity scale increases loudness by a factor of 2. Loudness and intensity are scaled logarithmically. (From Lindsay & Norman, 1977, p. 161. Reprinted by permission of the publisher.)

crease in intensity. Thus, reading directly from Figure 13.2, a 50-dB SPL tone with a loudness of about 2 sones sounds twice as loud (and is three times as intense) as a 40-dB tone with a loudness of about 1 sone. In summary, adding 10 dB to a sound triples its intensity and doubles its loudness.

Loudness and Frequency

Specifying only the decibel level of a sound will not fully describe its loudness. As we noted in Figure 13.1, loudness is not only a matter of physical intensity; it also depends on the frequency of the sound. The

dependence of loudness on frequency is apparent when two tones with different frequencies are adjusted in intensity so that they appear matched in loudness; when their respective intensities are compared, they may be found to differ considerably. That is, even though the two tones may appear equal in loudness, due to their frequency difference they may be very different from each other in intensity.

Equal-Loudness Contours Using psychophysical methods, we can specify the different frequencies and intensities of sounds that are perceived as *equally loud*. For example, a subject listens to two tones that differ in both frequency and intensity. One tone has a fixed frequency (usually set at 1000 Hz) and intensity and is called the *standard tone*. A second, *comparison tone* is presented at a different frequency and intensity. The subject's task is to listen alternatively to the standard and comparison tones and adjust the intensity of the comparison tone so that it matches the loudness of the standard tone. In other words, the subject sets the intensity level of the comparison tone until it sounds just as loud as the standard tone. When this is done on many different comparison tones, a curve of the results can be plotted that describes the intensity at which tones of various frequencies appear just as loud as the standard tone. Appropriately, such curves are referred to as **equal-loudness contours** (or *isophonic contours,* or sometimes *Fletcher–Munson curves,* named after their originators). Each equal-loudness contour of Figure 13.3

shows the result of such a procedure for a different sound intensity standard.

The curves are labeled in **phons,** which serve as a measure of the loudness of all tones that lie on a given curve. All tones lying on the same equal-loudness contour sound equally loud and are assigned the same value of phons. The phon value for a given curve is actually the number of decibels of a standard 1000-Hz tone that sounds equal in loudness to all tones lying on the curve. In other words, the number of phons of a given tone (regardless of its frequency) is numerically equal to the number of decibels of a 1000-Hz tone that sounds as loud as the tone. For example, consider the curve labeled "30" in Figure 13.3. Any sound whose frequency *and* intensity lie on this curve appears just as loud as any other sound on the curve, although the frequency and intensity of the two sounds will differ. It follows that a 60-Hz tone

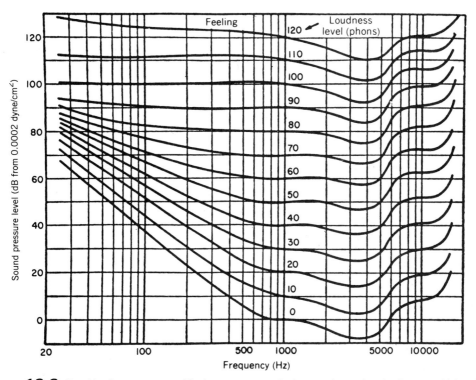

□ *figure* **13.3** Equal-loudness contours. The bottom curve—0 phons—shows the absolute sensitivity of the ear as a function of frequency. Presumably tones below this curve are not audible. (Revised from H. Fletcher and W. A. Munson, "Loudness, its definition, measurement, and calculation," *Journal of the Acoustical Society of America,* 5, 1933, pp. 82–108. Reprinted by permission of the American Institute of Physics.)

at a 65-dB intensity level and a 300-Hz tone at a 40-dB intensity level both sound as loud as a 1000-Hz tone at a 30-dB intensity level (or, by definition, 30 phons), and a 6000-Hz tone at about a 35-dB intensity level. Thus, the 60-, 300-, and 6000-Hz tones at 65, 40, and 35 dB, respectively, all have a loudness level of 30 phons, and any sound whose frequency and intensity also fall on this curve (i.e., 30 phons) has a loudness level of 30 phons. (It is important not to confuse the *phon* with the *sone* unit described in the preceding section. The phon is used only as a convenient way of expressing the loudness level of any tone with respect to the intensity of a 1000-Hz reference tone that sounds equal in loudness).

The curves presented in Figure 13.3 relate perceived loudness to intensity and frequency and point out a number of important facts about the perception of loudness, particularly to what extent loudness is affected by frequency. First of all, most of the curves are not flat, indicating that the loudness of a given tone is affected by its frequency. Indeed, tones of the same intensity but different in frequency do not sound equally loud. The effect of frequency on loudness is greatest at moderate and low levels of intensity (about 60 phons or less); at high intensity levels (above 60 phons), frequency is not important in the perception of loudness, and the equal-loudness contours are relatively flat. In other words, if tones are sufficiently intense, they tend to sound equally loud, regardless of frequency. At relatively moderate and low intensity levels, frequencies lower than about 1000 Hz and higher than 4000 Hz sound softer than do intermediate frequencies at the same intensity. The bow shape of the curves indicates that such frequencies require higher levels of intensity in order to sound as loud as frequencies between about 1000 and 4000 Hz. The dip in the curves also indicates the extent to which low and high frequencies must be boosted in intensity in order to maintain a constant loudness level.

This relationship appears not only in laboratory conditions with pure sound waves but also in ordinary listening experiences. For example, when music is heard from a loudspeaker at low intensity, it may seem to lack bass. This is because, at a low intensity level, our hearing is less sensitive to the low-frequency tones heard as bass tones. Because of this effect, many stereo amplifiers possess a compensatory adjustment circuit for listening at low intensity levels called a *loudness compensatator* (usually a button or switch labeled "loudness"), which overemphasizes the low frequencies (and sometimes the very high frequencies as well). In other words, the loudness circuit compensates by adding extra bass. It is necessary because in turning the "volume" (which is actually a misnomer) of the amplifier down, the relative loudness of various frequencies is changed as shown in Figure 13.3.

FREQUENCY

Although the perception of sound involves the interaction of intensity and frequency, many aspects of frequency reception can be analyzed separately. For normal or typical hearing, the limits of hearing for frequency fall between 20 and 20,000 Hz. Below 20 Hz only a feeling of vibration or "fluttering" sound is perceived; above 20,000 Hz, only a "tickling" is experienced. As we observed in Figures 13.1 and 13.3, the threshold of hearing varies with both sound intensity and frequency, and at the extremes of frequency, sounds must be intense in order to be audible.

Frequency Discrimination

The discrimination (or difference threshold) question raised for intensity can also be asked for frequency, namely, how much of a change in frequency (Δf) must occur in order to be detected by the observer? Some findings indicate that, for moderate intensities, the human can detect a frequency change of about 3 Hz for frequencies up to about 1000 Hz (Harris, 1952). However, for frequencies between about 1000 and 10,000, discriminability is a constant, small fraction of the frequency to be discriminated. The Weber fraction (see Chapter 2) for this frequency interval over a wide range of intensities remains constant (specifically, $\Delta f/f$ approximates 0.004). For example, at about 10,000 Hz, a 40-Hz change is required for a change to be perceived (i.e., $0.004 \times 10,000 \text{ Hz} = 40 \text{ Hz}$).

One important variable that affects the determination of the minimal discriminable change (or difference threshold) in frequency is the intensity level of the sounds measured. The Δf for frequency increases as stimulus intensity decreases. In other words, as a sound grows softer, it becomes more difficult to detect it as different from other sounds close to it in frequency.

Pitch

As we noted in Chapter 12, *pitch* is the subjective dimension of hearing; it refers to how high or low a sound appears. Pitch is determined mainly, but not exclusively, by the frequency of the sound. Typically, high-pitched sounds are heard from high-frequency tones and low-pitch sounds result from low-frequency tones. However, the relationship between pitch and frequency is not a simple linear one.

The Mel Scale   The relationship between pitch and frequency was determined by using an arbitrary unit called the **mel** with a special psychophysical scaling procedure called the *method of fractionation* (Stevens & Volkmann, 1940). By definition, the experience or sensation of pitch created by a 1000-Hz tone at 40 dB was assigned a value of 1000 mels. The fractionation method using the 1000 Hz standard is basically as follows. An observer is presented alternately with two tones, both at a constant intensity level, but only one tone is maintained at a fixed frequency. The other tone is varied in frequency by the observer until its pitch is experienced as, say, one-half of the pitch of the fixed tone. Since by definition 1000 mels is assigned to the pitch of a 1000-Hz tone, the frequency of a tone that sounds half as high in pitch as the 1000-mel tone would be assigned 500 mels. In like manner, the frequency of a tone that appears twice as high in pitch as the 1000-Hz tone is assigned a value of 2000 mels, and the frequency of a tone three times as high in pitch is given a value of 3000 mels. Extending this procedure to other frequencies and extrapolating the results produces the frequency–pitch scale of Figure 13.4, which depicts the number of mels associated with different frequencies. Observe from the figure that the only instance where the number of frequencies equals the number of mels is for a 1000 Hz tone (by definition).

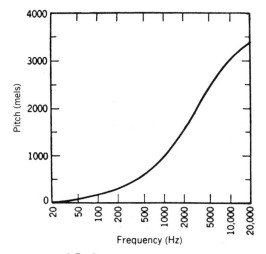

◻ *figure 13.4* The frequency–pitch function. Pitch in mels is plotted against frequency (in Hz). The curve shows how the perceived pitch of a tone varies with its frequency. Observe that pitch increases more rapidly than frequency for tones below 1000 Hz but less rapidly for tones above 1000 Hz. (Frequency is plotted on a logarithmic scale. After Stevens & Volkmann, 1940.)

The mel scale indicates that pitch is not directly related to frequency. In general, pitch increases more rapidly than frequency for tones below 1000 Hz and less rapidly for tones above 1000 Hz. That is, for frequencies above 1000 Hz, a greater change in frequency is needed to produce a change in pitch. As Figure 13.4 shows, tones of 500, 2000, and 3000 mels (that produce pitch sensations that are half, twice, and three times as high as the pitch of the 1000-Hz standard) correspond to frequencies of about 400, 3000, and 10,000 Hz, respectively. (Although the mel scale is useful in tracing the imperfect relationship between frequency and pitch for relatively simple sounds, it does not apply equally well to certain musical relations.)

Pitch and Intensity

Intensity has a measurable effect on the pitch of relatively pure tones. In a classic study, Stevens (1935), using a single trained observer, determined the effect of intensity on the pitch of tones for 11 frequencies ranging from 150 to 12,000 Hz. Two tones of slightly different frequencies were presented in succession to the observer, who adjusted the intensity of one tone until both tones were perceived as equal in pitch. In short, the observer was able to compensate for frequency differences by varying the intensity. In general, as the frequency of a tone (for tones of 3000 Hz or more) was increased, its pitch was kept constant by *decreasing* its intensity; in contrast, as the frequency of a tone (500 Hz or lower) was increased, its pitch was kept constant by *increasing* its intensity. Stated differently, the dependency of pitch on intensity is as follows: when intensity is increased, the pitch of high tones increases and the pitch of low tones decreases. For frequencies in the middle range (1000–2000 Hz), the effect of intensity on pitch is minimal (see also Gulick, 1971).

Before leaving our separate discussions of loudness and pitch, it is prudent to underscore the distinction between the physical and psychological dimensions of sound. That is, it is important not to confuse the physical properties of a sound—its intensity (or amplitude) and frequency (and complexity)—with its psychological properties of loudness and pitch (and timbre): they refer to quite different dimensions of sound. Moreover, although important relationships exist between intensity and loudness, and between frequency and pitch, as we observed, the relationship between them is not straightforward; for example, doubling intensity does not double loudness, nor does doubling frequency double pitch. Furthermore, as we observed with equal-loudness contours, varying the frequency of a sound not only affects its pitch but may also affect its loudness. Table 13.1 summarizes the physical and psychological dimensions of sound and their units of measure.

▭ *table 13.1* Physical and Sensory Dimensions of Sound and Their Units

Physical Dimension	Unit	Sensory Dimension	Unit
Intensity, amplitude	Decibel (dB)	Loudness	Sone, phon
Frequency	Hertz (Hz)	Pitch	Mel
Complexity		Timbre	

HEARING AND SOUND DURATION

Since hearing is largely a matter of stimulus reception over time, we would expect time to influence the perception of sound. Indeed, recognizable tonal quality require some minimal duration of the sound. For example, if a tone of an audible frequency and intensity is presented for only a few milliseconds, it will lose its tonal character and will either be inaudible or be heard as a click. According to Gulick et al. (1989), the length of time a given frequency must last in order to produce the perception of a stable and recognizable pitch is about 250 msec. In general, we are better able to recognize tones and to discriminate between tones of different frequencies when their duration is lengthened.

Loudness is also affected by the duration of the sound. As the duration of a sound becomes progressively briefer than 200 msec, intensity must be increased to maintain a constant level of loudness. In other words, sounds lasting for less than 200 msec are heard as softer than longer sounds of equal intensity. Thus, although the sound heard depends primarily on its frequency and intensity, both its pitch and its loudness are secondarily affected by the duration of the exposure. Within limits, loudness and pitch recognition increases as the duration of a brief burst of sound is lengthened.

EFFECTS OF MULTIPLE TONAL STIMULATION

Beats

When simultaneously listening to two tones of similar intensity but slightly different in frequency, one may perceive **beats**—perhaps best described as a perception of a single throbbing tone with a single pitch midway between the two tones but periodically varying in loudness: in short, an alternate waxing and waning in loudness.

The frequency with which the loudness fluctuates in beating is precisely the difference between the frequencies of the two sounds that are combined. The reason beats occur is purely physical: there is a contin-

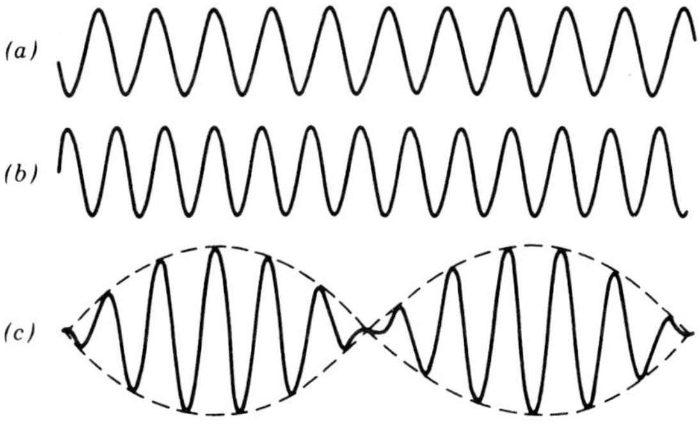

(a)
(b)
(c)

□ figure 13.5 Beats. Shown are the sound waves, *a* and *b*, of two tones, where *b* is slightly higher in frequency than *a*. When the tones are sounded together, the waves interact to form a complex tone that varies in intensity at a rate equal to the frequency difference of the two tones. The variation in intensity, called the beat frequency, is shown by the dotted enclosing segments in *c*. (From M. Mayer, *Sensory Perception Laboratory Manual*, Wiley, New York, 1982, p. 91. Reprinted by permission of the publisher.)

uous change in the relative phase of two simultaneously applied tones, so that the tones alternately reinforce and cancel each other. As illustrated in Figure 13.5, this produces a complex tone that varies in intensity at a rate equal to the frequency difference of the two tones. Thus, for example, when two tones that differ by 2 Hz are simultaneously produced, the sound waves generated by each will be in compression, or "in phase," at the same time two times each second and will be exactly out of phase at the same time two times each second; that is, the tones will systematically vary between reinforcing and canceling each other two times a second. The ear hears this phase alternation as periodic variations in loudness, that is, as *beats*. Indeed, one tone is said to be "beating" against the other.

As the difference between tones increases, beats become faster and soon lose their individuality. With sufficient increases in the frequency difference (at about 30 Hz), the resultant sound begins to assume a "roughness."

Masking

The perception of a sound depends not only on its own frequency and intensity but also on other sounds present at the same time. Generally, when two tones close in frequency are sounded but one has greater intensity, the more intense tone will reduce or eliminate the perception of the softer tone. It is familiar to experience one sound "drowning out" another one. As you have no doubt experienced, typical classroom sounds created by movement, coughing, whispering, rustling of papers, and the like may all make the in-

structor's voice difficult to hear. This phenomenon is called **masking.** Technically, masking is defined as the rise in the threshold of one tone (*test tone*) due to the presence of a second (*masker*) tone.

The classic study of masking was done by Wegel and Lane (1924); Zwicker and Scharf (1965) have also provided the findings summarized in Figure 13.6. The figure shows the masking effects of a narrow band of frequencies centered at a 1200-Hz band of noise (the masker, indicated by the arrow on the *x*-axis) sounded

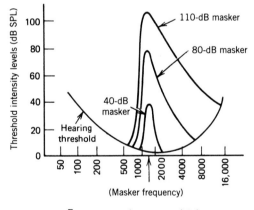

Frequency of test tone (Hz)

□ figure 13.6 Masking. Shown are thresholds for tones in the presence of a narrow band of frequencies (masker) centered at 1200 Hz and at three intensity levels. The intensity of the masker is given on each curve in decibels. The magnitude of masking is shown by the height of the threshold curves. The higher the curve, the greater the masking effect. For maskers greater than 40 dB, tones higher in frequency than the masker are clearly affected, whereas those lower in frequency show a negligible effect. (Based on Zwicker & Scharf, 1965.)

at three sample intensity levels on tones of various frequencies. Each curve represents the degree of masking: it is measured as the rise in the intensity level from threshold necessary for test tones (whose frequencies are distributed along the *x*-axis) to be heard in the presence of the 1200-Hz masker. As the figure shows, a masking tone raises the threshold of hearing by an amount that varies with intensity and frequency. More specifically, tones close in frequency to the masker are more strongly masked than those far away in frequency. That is, the masker must lie near the frequency of the test tone for masking to result. By examining the collective results for the three sample intensity levels of the masking tone, we can see that more masking results when the masker is made more intense.

Also apparent from the figure is the asymmetry of the 80- and 110-dB curves with respect to the frequency range of the masking effects. This indicates that the effect of masking is greater on test tones whose frequencies are above the masker frequency than for those below it. That is, lower frequencies mask higher-frequency sounds much more effectively than the reverse. The effects of the masker on frequencies below it are very slight even for the 110-dB masker. Observe also in the figure that this general trend in the asymmetry of masking effects applies only at masker levels above about 40 dB SPL. Indeed, the effect of the 40-dB masker appears somewhat symmetrical.

Masking and Basilar Membrane Activity: The Line-Busy Hypothesis

Much masking may be explained in a very simplified way by analyzing the interaction and interference of displacement patterns on the basilar membrane. This explanation is sometimes referred to as the **line-busy hypothesis** (e.g., Scharf & Buus, 1986). The line-busy hypothesis assumes that to mask the test tone, the masker excites the same restricted group of auditory nerve fibers, preventing them from responding to the test tone. In short, masking occurs when the neural elements that normally respond to a given tone are kept too "busy" by the masker to respond adequately.

Support for the line-busy hypothesis comes from the displacement pattern on the basilar membrane. Recall that there is a spatial representation of frequency on the basilar membrane (see Figures 12.15 and 12.20 in Chapter 12). Note further from Figure 12.20 that there is an asymmetry in the spread of displacement along the basilar membrane: low-frequency tones produce a relatively broad displacement pattern extending over much of the membrane, whereas high-frequency tones produce patterns that are sharper, more restricted in area, and have peaks lying close to the stapes and oval window.

Figure 13.7 outlines the effect of basilar membrane displacement in producing masking effects. As Figure 13.7*a* shows, when the masker is higher in frequency and more intense than the test tone, its pattern of displacement extends only partway along the basilar membrane (recall that the waveforms of higher frequencies peak closer to the stapes, which would be shown as closer to the left in Figure 13.7). Since the lower-frequency test tone produces displacement in a separate, nonoverlapping region, the interference by the masker is relatively slight and the test tone is detectable.

In contrast, when the masker has a lower frequency than the weaker test tone, as shown in Figure 13.7*b*, the masker's displacement pattern tends to engulf or cover that of the test tone, and the detectability of the test tone is reduced or eliminated. However, the test tone can be detected if its intensity is sufficiently increased so that its displacement pattern on the basilar membrane is distinct from that produced by the masker; this is shown in Figure 13.7*c*.

Masking is not restricted to the simultaneous presentation of the masker and the test tone. Interference effects can also occur when the masker precedes (forward masking) or follows (backward masking) the test tone. For example, in backward masking, a test tone, followed after a brief interval, say 50 msec, by a more intense masker tone, may make the prior sounded test tone inaudible.

In addition, a sound delivered to one ear may mask a weaker sound sent to the other—an effect called *interaural masking*. The site of the source of

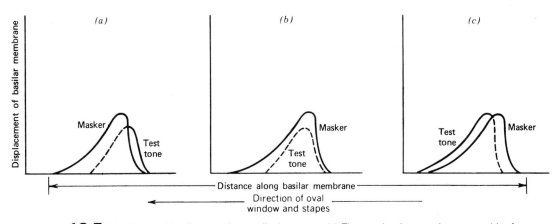

□ **figure 13.7** Masking and basilar membrane displacement. (a) The masker is more intense and its frequency is higher than the test tone. The lower-frequency test tone produces displacement in a nonoverlapping portion of the basilar membrane, away from the stapes and oval window (recall that higher frequencies cause maximal displacement of the basilar membrane closer to the region of the stapes and oval window, i.e., to the left in each figure). Thus, interference by the masker is not complete, and the test tone is detectable. (b) The masker has a lower frequency and is more intense than the test tone. Here the interference effect of the masker's basilar membrane displacement pattern on the test tone is strong, so that the test tone is not distinguishable from that of the masker. (c) This masker also has a lower frequency than the test tone, but the intensity of the test tone is increased enough to be detected as a separate tone.

interference for interaural masking is believed to be centrally located within the auditory nervous system.

Auditory Fatigue and Auditory Adaptation

Ordinarily, normal threshold sensitivity to a premasking level is restored very soon after the masking tone ends. However, even then, the effects of masking are not necessarily eliminated.

Auditory Fatigue and Threshold Shifts

When very intense masking has been applied for long periods, an elevated threshold may extend for hours or even days, producing a temporary form of hearing loss called *auditory fatigue*. **Auditory fatigue** is thus a temporary loss of sensitivity to sounds immediately *following* exposure to intense sounds. As with the effects of masking, there is an upward shift in the threshold for sounds (or a reduction in their perceived loudness). However, masking is a temporary loss in sensitivity *during* (or shortly before or after) exposure to another tone. Not unexpectedly,

the length and severity of auditory fatigue depend on the duration and intensity of the inducing sound. The measure of auditory fatigue—the elevation in threshold—is called a **temporary threshold shift (TTS).** Threshold values, measured for many different frequencies immediately after exposure to the tone, are compared with preexposure measures of threshold sensitivity. The shift in threshold at different frequencies is taken as the measure of hearing loss induced by auditory fatigue.

The audiogram of Figure 13.8 shows the amount of hearing loss due to auditory fatigue induced by prior exposure to *white noise* (a form of noise containing a mixture of a wide range of audible frequencies of various intensities). The horizontal zero line represents the preexposure sensitivity of the ear. The curves specify temporary hearing loss for various rest periods after exposure to the noise. The figure shows clearly that temporary hearing loss due to exposure to intense noise is greater for high frequencies (between about 2500 and 6000 Hz), and that as the rest period increases, hearing sensitivity approaches preexposure sensitivity.

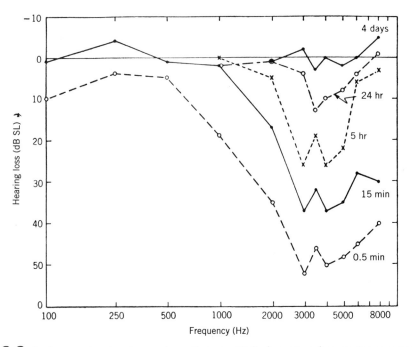

figure 13.8 Audiogram showing changes in auditory sensitivity for various frequencies as a result of exposure to intense white noise (115 dB) for 20 minutes. The individual curves specify the temporary shift in sensitivity (hearing loss) measured at different times (or after different rest periods) following exposure to the intense noise. The figure shows that hearing sensitivity returns to its original level (plotted as the horizontal zero line) as the duration of the rest period increases. The temporary hearing loss due to intense noise exposure is greatest for frequencies between about 2500 and 6000 Hz. (From Postman & Egan, 1949.)

There is also a type of induced threshold shift that is permanent, called a **permanent threshold shift (PTS).** A PTS is a change in sensitivity due to noise exposure in which the threshold *never* returns to its preexposure level. Although a PTS can be produced by a single loud noise such as an explosion, or by repeated exposure to loud music, it usually results from years of exposure to intense, chronic noise of the sort observed in certain industrial environments (recall the section on *sound-induced hearing loss* in Chapter 12).

Auditory Adaptation A related reaction to the threshold shift observed with auditory fatigue, called **auditory adaptation,** occurs when a sound is presented continuously and its perceived loudness decreases over time. That is, the loudness of a *continuous* tone appears to diminish over time. Usually the

reduction in loudness goes unnoticed by the listener. The practical relevance of auditory adaptation is that the ability to hear steady sounds declines over time; after a while, continuous sounds that are well above threshold appear softer and some sounds close to threshold levels may become inaudible. Moore (1989) reports that continuous 3-minute exposure to a sound of 80 dB may bring a loss in sensitivity to that sound of about 20 dB. In other words, after 3 minutes of continuously hearing an 80-dB sound, it will appear to be only as loud as if it were 60 dB.

If continuous exposure to a steady sound reduces the sensitivity to loudness, then it seems reasonable to assume that continuous exposure to a relatively silent acoustic environment will increase the sensitivity to low-level sounds. The increase in sensitivity due to the relative *lack* of sound is analogous to the dark adaptation process described for vision (Chapter 4), in which sensitivity to dim light increases significantly after a period of light deprivation. Thus, it is suggested that the cumulative effect of all the persistent noise and sounds heard during the day's activity probably reduces the ear's sensitivity to sound at night. It also suggests that after a night's sleep, there should be a corresponding recovery of sensitivity due to the reduced sound experience that generally accompanies sleep. This would explain why the wakeup call of a radio alarm seems so much louder in the morning—following the relative silence of a night's sleep—than it did when you set it the night before. Of course, it is equally possible that the morning wakeup sound appears so jarring (and loud) for reasons that have little to do with recovery from the previous day's acoustic exposure (such as just not wanting to get up).

SUBJECTIVE TONAL ATTRIBUTES

Volume and Density

The literature on psychoacoustics contains references to qualities of pure tones that cannot be accounted for by pitch and loudness alone. One of these subjective characteristics is termed **volume,** which refers to the apparent size, expansiveness, or voluminousness of a tone. It is based on the assumption that certain sounds, independently matched in pitch and loudness, appear to occupy more space than others. (The term *volume,* as used here, is different from the misnamed "volume" control found on radios, receivers, and amplifiers.) When observers are required to order tones along a *large–small dimension,* considerable agreement occurs in that tones of high frequency sound smaller or less "voluminous" than tones of low frequency.

Another tonal quality also has been reported called **density.** Density refers to the apparent compactness or tightness of a sound, with greater density for tones of high frequency. Density appears to be reciprocally related to volume—the higher the density, the lower the volume, and vice versa—except that both increase with increases in intensity: with sufficient increases in intensity, a low-frequency tone can be matched in density with a high-frequency tone (Guirao & Stevens, 1964).

Consonance and Dissonance

For most observers, when two tones are sounded together, the resultant combination sounds either pleasant or unpleasant. Those combinations that sound pleasant—that tend to fuse or blend well together—are characterized as **consonant.** Those combinations that sound discordant or harsh are termed **dissonant.** Although it is likely true that nonauditory attributes such as custom, culture, and related learning factors have a role in the consonance–dissonance attribute of combined tones, other auditory processes are also involved.

In deciding whether two sounds are heard as consonant or dissonant, an important acoustic consideration is their frequency difference. One explanation is that dissonance occurs when the upper harmonics of the two fundamentals are close in frequency, producing a roughness in the sound (the basis for this was described in the section on beats; see Terhardt, 1977), whereas consonance occurs when the harmonics of the two fundamentals differ sufficiently in frequency to be heard as distinct sounds, or when they coincide and reinforce each other.

Musical instruments produce complex tones containing many higher harmonic frequencies, increasing the likelihood of roughness. It follows that two tones produced by musical instruments are more likely to be dissonant than two tones represented by simple sine waves.

Laboratory versus Natural Sounds

We have presented many important facts about psychoacoustics. However, we must note that most of the vast body of research on sound, although extremely useful and informative, has been performed in laboratories using precisely controlled tones—usually relatively long-lasting pure tones—quite unlike those that ordinarily occur in nature. Perhaps the greatest departure of these laboratory tones from natural ones lies in their purity and duration. Clearly, long-duration pure tones occur infrequently in nature. As Masterton and Diamond (1973, p. 419) state: "most natural sounds and almost all natural sounds that warn an animal of a potentially dangerous intruder are very brief sounds . . . made up not of enduring pure tones or even their simple combinations, but instead, of sounds such as snaps, pops, crackles, thumps, and thuds" (p. 419).

SUMMARY

In this chapter, we described some of the quantitative and qualitative relationships between the physical dimensions of simple sounds and their subjective psychological dimensions. We observed that the frequency of pressure changes, in Hertz (Hz), mainly determines pitch, whereas the physical dimension of intensity or pressure amplitude, given in decibels (dB), directly affects loudness.

We discussed the measurement of intensity at threshold levels within the range of frequencies audible to the human. It was concluded that the lowest threshold value, and hence maximal sensitivity, is for frequencies in the region of 3000 Hz. The difference threshold was also discussed and it was noted that, generally, the minimum change in the intensity of a sound that produces a perceptual difference is about 1 to 2 dB.

The quantitative relation between intensity and loudness is that loudness grows more slowly than intensity. The sone scale of loudness was described in this context. Using this scale, it was noted that the loudness of a sound doubles when its intensity is tripled (or increased by 10 dB).

The effect of frequency on loudness was analyzed by equal-loudness contours. It was noted that, within limits, a sound's frequency affects its loudness; specifically, for moderately low intensity levels, the human is more sensitive to sound frequencies between about 1000 and 4000 Hz than to other frequencies within the audible range. In terms of loudness, this means that, with intensity held constant, sounds in the neighborhood of 3000 Hz appear louder than sounds of other frequencies.

Frequency and frequency discrimination were discussed next. We noted that the difference threshold for frequencies up to about 1000 Hz is about 3 Hz, whereas for frequencies between 1000 and 10,000 Hz, the Weber fraction remains constant at about 0.004.

We also noted that the intensity level of sounds affects the difference threshold: the lower the intensity level, the higher the difference threshold. In short, the softer the sound, the more difficult it is to detect it as different from other sounds close in frequency.

Pitch was examined with respect to the mel scale, which shows that pitch is not linearly related to frequency. It was noted that pitch generally increases more rapidly than frequency for tones below 1000 Hz and less rapidly for tones above this level. It was also observed that the pitch of a sound depends secondarily on its intensity: generally, when intensity is increased, the pitch of high tones increases and the pitch of low tones decreases.

Next, several phenomena and stimulus variables that influence the perception of sound were examined. After discussing the effects of tone duration, we noted that it is easier to recognize tones and to discriminate between tones of different frequencies when the duration of the tones is lengthened. It was also noted that auditory beats are produced when two tones of different frequencies are simultaneously sounded. Beating occurs because the waveforms of the two tones alternately reinforce and cancel each other. The beat frequency of the complex tone that is produced is equal to the frequency difference of the two tones.

Masking was outlined next. In masking, the presence of one sound interferes with and reduces the perception of another sound. Several general points were made: the more intense a masking tone, the greater is the masking effect; a given masking tone interferes more with the perception of tones close in frequency than with tones far apart in frequency; and for intense masking tones, the masking effect is far greater on tones whose frequencies lie above the masking tone than for those that lie below it. Finally, we analyzed masking based on competing basilar membrane displacements created by the tones. The explanation of masking on the basis of interference on the basilar membrane is called the line-busy hypothesis.

Next, auditory fatigue and adaptation were described. Auditory fatigue is a temporary loss in sensitivity, or an elevated threshold, to sounds immediately following exposure to intense sounds. The elevation in threshold caused by auditory fatigue is called a temporary threshold shift (TTS). It was further noted that exposure to intense sound can also cause a permanent threshold shift (PTS). Auditory adaptation is a reduction in sensitivity to a steady sound after continuous exposure to it. In practical terms, this means that the loudness of a physically constant sound declines over time.

In the final section, we described briefly four subjective tonal attributes: volume, density, consonance, and dissonance.

KEY TERMS

Auditory Adaptation

Auditory Fatigue

Beats

Consonance

Density

Dissonance

Equal-Loudness Contours

Line-Busy Hypothesis

Masking

Mel

Permanent Threshold Shift (PTS)

Phons

Sone

Temporary Threshold Shift (TTS)

Volume

STUDY QUESTIONS

1. What effect does variation in frequency have on the detection or absolute threshold values for intensity? What is the maximal sensitivity range for human audibility with respect to variations in intensity?

2. Describe the quantitative relation of loudness to the physical intensity of sound. Discuss the extent to which the loudness of a sound is affected by its intensity level, making use of the sone scale.

3. What are equal-loudness contours and phon units? What do they indicate concerning the effect of frequency on loudness? With intensity held constant, what range of frequencies are heard louder than others?

4. Discuss the general relationship between frequency and pitch using the mel scale of pitch. How is pitch affected by intensity?

5. Summarize intensity and frequency discrimination. What are the difference thresholds for intensity and for frequency?

6. In what general ways is the pitch and loudness of a sound affected by its duration?

7. What are beats? Outline how the phase and frequency difference between two tones produce beats.

8. Describe auditory masking and outline the conditions that produce masking. What are the general relations between a masking sound and the sounds that it masks? Describe why a high intensity masking tone interferes with or masks tones higher than it is more than it interferes or masks tones lower than it is. Explain masking phenomena by an analysis of interference effects on the basilar membrane, drawing on the notion of the line-busy hypothesis.

9. Outline the basis of auditory fatigue and auditory adaptation and indicate their effect on thresholds. Distinguish between auditory masking, auditory fatigue, and auditory adaptation.

10. Describe the subjective tonal characteristics of volume and density. How do sound frequency and intensity affect each? What is consonance and dissonance? What factors determine whether a combination of tones are heard as consonant or dissonant? Examine the role of frequency in producing consonance and dissonance.

SOUND AS INFORMATION

In this chapter, we discuss the reception of sound as meaningful information. Sounds in nature may provide enough information to enable us to perceive spatial features, such as location and identification. Moreover, the vocalization and reception of sounds is an important form of communication for a wide variety of animal species. In the human, the pickup of meaningful sounds supports two unique skills: it enables us to perceive music and it also allows speech—a vocal-auditory behavior that extends well beyond the sound communication of non-human species.

Accordingly, we will stress here the functional effects of sound reception, emphasizing auditory space perception, and the localization of sound-emitting events, the perception of music, and sound communication between animals, particularly the perception of speech in the human. We begin by describing the neural connection between the ear and the brain.

THE AUDITORY PATHWAY AND CENTRAL STRUCTURES

In the previous two chapters, we described the auditory system as if it consisted of a single unit—the ear. However, one ear is only half of the listening apparatus. As we noted with the two eyes, the possession of two ears is not merely a duplication of structure; the ears do not function independently of each other, but rather interact both neurally and behaviorally. Understanding this interaction is key to an understanding of some of the functional results of hearing, which is the primary focus of this chapter. Accordingly, in this section we pick up on some of the physiological aspects of audition that we began to consider in Chapter 12. However, the neural structures, mechanisms, and relationships described here are especially relevant to sound localization and communication.

The general scheme of neural connections between the ear and brain is sketched in Figure 14.1. After leaving the inner ear, the fibers of the auditory nerve make a series of synaptic connections at various relay stations along the auditory nerve's pathway to the brain. The first relay point of the auditory nerve from the inner ear is the *cochlear nucleus,* which lies at the base of the back of the brain. The output of the cochlear nucleus involves multiple paths. Each cochlear nucleus sends some of its auditory nerve fibers to the *olivary nucleus* on the same (or *ipsilateral*) side of the brain, but the majority of the fibers of the cochlear nucleus cross over to the opposite (or *contralateral*) olivary nucleus. Thus, the majority of nerve fibers from one ear (about 60%) cross over to the opposite side of the brain. In fact, this largely contralateral connection of neural elements from one side of the body to the opposite side, or hemisphere,

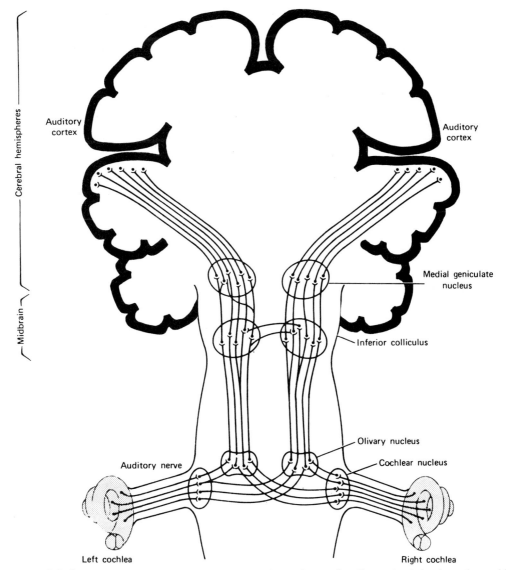

◻ *figure* **14.1** Semischematic diagram of the conduction pathway of auditory stimulation from the cochlea of each ear to the cerebral cortex.

of the brain is characteristic of most of the neural systems of the body. Since the olivary nucleus receives input from both ears, it can compare aspects of *binaural,* or two-ear, stimulation. As we will see, binaural interactions in the auditory system analyze differences in the neural message from each ear—an important source of sound localization information.

Each olivary nucleus, having input from each ear, sends its binaural neural message to the *inferior colliculus*. There a further crossing of fibers takes place, so that each inferior colliculus receives auditory signals from each ear. This further ensures that neural signals from both ears are represented on both sides of the brain. Neural signals from each inferior colliculus are then passed on to the *medial geniculate nucleus,* an important sensory structure of the thalamus. From there, fibers project to the **auditory cortex,** found in a region of the temporal lobe, which lies in each cerebral hemisphere. Thus, the auditory message originating at the organ of Corti of each ear passes through a sequence of five synaptic or relay levels before terminating within the auditory cortex of each hemisphere.

Because neural signals cross at the olivary nucleus and inferior colliculus, most cortical neurons within the auditory cortex receive signals from both ears. Moreover, there is an orderly, systematic relationship between the spatial locations of neurons within the brain and the frequencies of sounds to which these neurons are sensitive. In fact, there is a spatial map of frequency represented in the auditory cortex: neurons sensitive to similar frequencies are located near one another. In short, cortical neurons (as well as the neurons making up much of the auditory pathways) are *tonotopically* organized.

We now turn to the functional relevance of some of the structural relations of the auditory pathway. First, we will outline the basic neural transmission between the ear and the brain. Then we will discuss how neural organization contributes to sound localization in space.

Cerebral Dominance and Hearing

As we have noted, the auditory cortex is primarily dominated by the fibers that cross; neural conduction of auditory signals is faster, and the signals themselves are more intense for the crossed pathways than for the uncrossed pathways. This means that each ear is better represented on the opposite cerebral hemisphere of the brain, so that a sound produced on one side of the body results in greater cortical activity on the opposite hemisphere of the brain (Rosenzweig, 1961).

Another lateral difference in the auditory pathways is that the left and right hemispheres of the brain predominate in different functions (e.g., Springer & Deutsch, 1993; Witelson, 1985). Specifically, the auditory cortex of the two hemispheres differs in the way certain characteristics of sound are perceived and

probably in the way information is processed. This general functional specialization in sound processing is referred to as **cerebral dominance** (or *brain asymmetry.*) Many studies have found that the auditory cortex of the left hemisphere governs the perception of speech and language-related stimulation, whereas the auditory cortex of the right hemisphere predominates in the processing and perception of certain nonverbal sounds. These differences have been uncovered by studies using brain-imaging procedures, such as position emission tomography (PET) scan (which pinpoints areas of ongoing brain activity; see, e.g., Zatorre et al., 1992). Many behavioral studies also support hemispheric differences, as well as revealing many related phenomena. Accordingly, the next section will focus on a special behavioral procedure: dichotic listening.

Dichotic Listening The functional difference between the left and right auditory cortices has been observed with an auditory technique called **dichotic listening** (different or competing stimulation delivered to each ear is called *dichotic*). An observer wearing an independently driven earphone over each ear is simultaneously presented with two independent messages—a different message to each ear. In one early study using the dichotic listening technique, pairs of different digits were delivered simultaneously to each ear. When the subjects reported what they heard, significantly more of the digits that had entered the right ear (and cross over, to be registered in the auditory cortex of the left hemisphere) were correctly reported than were digits delivered to the left ear (Kimura, 1961). This finding—that the right ear and left hemisphere dominate in processing linguistic material—has been replicated and extended (see reviews by Bradshaw & Nettelton, 1983; Springer & Deutsch, 1985, 1993).

Moreover, even when speech-like sounds such as those produced by the reverse playback of recorded speech are presented to the left and right ears, the sounds arriving at the right ear are more accurately identified than those arriving at the left (Kimura & Folb, 1968). On the other hand, for musical stimulation (solo instrumental passages), a reversal in ear dominance occurs: melodies delivered to the left ear are better recalled than similar musical stimuli sent to the right ear (Johnson & Kozma, 1977; Kimura, 1964, 1967). This is also the case for chords and notes from musical instruments (Sidtis & Bryden, 1978) and pure tones (Spreen, Spellacy, & Reid, 1970). Moreover, reaction times to musical sounds are faster when delivered to the left ear (Kallman & Corballis, 1975).

For nonmusical sounds, left-ear dominance is also observed with environmental noise [e.g., a phone ring, dog bark, and clock tick (Curry, 1967; Knox & Kimura, 1970)]. Furthermore, left-ear superiority is reported for nonverbal vocalization (e.g., a cry, sigh, and laugh; see Carmon & Nachson, 1973). It appears that for verbal stimuli, the right ear is dominant, that is, has a better path to the speech-processing area of the left cerebral hemisphere; in contrast, for nonverbal stimuli, the left ear (and right cerebral hemisphere) is more important. It should also be noted that these hemispheric differences occur early in development: MacKain et al. (1983) have reported that the left hemisphere plays a dominant role in language processing in infancy.

Interestingly, Corina, Vaid, and Bellugi (1992) found that deaf individuals too show a left hemispheric specialization in processing linguistic material when language is manually expressed or gestured (i.e., by signing) rather than spoken; that is, deaf individuals are much more likely to transmit linguistic material with their right hand than their left (the right hand is controlled mainly by the left hemisphere). In contrast, when deaf individuals perform skilled nonlinguistic motor movements or make conventional symbolic gestures (e.g., waving good-bye), no right-hand or left hemispheric bias is observed.

However, we should not necessarily conclude that something inherent in the nature of verbal stimuli per se accounts for left-hemisphere dominance. There is evidence that the kind or level of analytic processing characteristic of verbal or language-related stimuli is crucial. For example, Bever and Chiarello (1974; Kellar & Bever, 1980) have reported that musically experienced listeners recognize simple melodies better when sent to the right ear (hence dominant processing by the left hemisphere) than when sent to the left ear, whereas the reverse is the case for naïve listeners. They propose that experienced musicians use different listening strategies for music: they analyze the melodic information in a way similar to that required for speech perception. Thus the musically experienced "have learned to perceive a melody as an articulated set of relations among components, rather than as a whole," whereas musically naïve listeners "focus on the overall melodic contour"; that is, they "treat melodies as unanalyzed wholes" (p. 538).

A specific case history bearing on this hemispheric structural–functional issue is that of the French composer Maurice Ravel, who at the age of 56, at the peak of his career, suffered severe damage to his left hemisphere (Alajouanine, 1948). Afterward, he was able to recognize and appreciate music much like a naïve listener, but most of his sophisticated analytical skills with music were lost, and he was never able to deal with music as a highly trained musician: he could no longer read or compose in musical notation, play the piano, or even sing in tune.

AUDITORY SPACE PERCEPTION

The ability to localize sounds in space is important for humans and animals. It helps locate and avoid sound-emitting objects and events, and it guides the direction of visual attention. The auditory system is extraordinarily accurate in localizing sounds in space. To do this precisely, both the *direction* and the *distance* of sound-emitting objects and events must be perceived. This information is provided by *monaural* (one-ear) and *binaural* (two-ear) cues.

Monaural Cues

Sound that can be picked up by only one ear—**monaural cues**—may be useful for evaluating an object's relative *distance* (although some coarse sound *localization* is possible with monaural hearing; see Oldfield & Parker, 1986, Slattery & Middlebrooks, 1994). In judging the distance of a sound source, an important cue is the intensity, or loudness of the sound wave reaching the ear. The louder the sound, the closer the object appears to be. If two sounds are heard, the louder one is ordinarily perceived as closer. If the loudness of a single sound gradually changes, so does the perception of its location. The sound is perceived to approach if it grows louder and to recede if it grows softer. A familiar example is the change in the loudness of a siren's wail as a cue to the changing distance of a fast-moving emergency vehicle.

Doppler Shift Another cue to the changing distance of a moving object is the shift in the frequency (and pitch) of a sound source moving in relation to a stationary listener. This is called the **Doppler shift,** named after its discoverer, a nineteenth-century Austrian physicist, Christian Doppler. The basis of the shift is as follows: as a sound-emitting object moves, each of its successive sound waves is emitted slightly farther ahead in its path. However, the waves, though moving in all directions at a constant speed, do not share a common center (as would be the case with a stationary sound source). Instead, the sound waves tend to bunch up in front of the moving sound source; this reduces the distance between successive waves and creates an increase in sound frequency. The perceptual result is that as the frequency of the sound waves that pass a given point increases, the *pitch* heard at that point increases. After the object passes, a reversal in pitch occurs; that is, the distance between waves is stretched, frequency decreases, and to the listener, the pitch lowers.

Binaural Cues

Although relative distance information is available monaurally, the ability to perceive the *direction* of a sound, especially a very brief one, is seriously affected when using only one ear. To a stationary monaural listener, the sound could be perceived as lying at any number of locations. However, it should be noted that if the sound is repetitive or long-lasting, the monaural listener can localize it using head movements: By moving the head toward and away from a stationary sound source (such as by rotating the head slightly), the listener receives a pattern of loudness changes that helps specify the location of the sound. Specifically, as the single functional ear moves toward the sound source, it appears louder; as the ear moves away, the sound appears softer.

However, most effective and reliable localization depends on stimulation of the two ears—on **binaural cues.** In this case, the auditory system uses the physical differences in stimulation that arise because the two ears are separated in space. In short, it compares the sounds from a single source reaching the two ears.

Time Differences The information in binaural stimulation provides several cues for sound localization. One cue, called **interaural time difference,** is the slight time differences produced when a sound, especially one with a sharp onset such as a click, reaches one ear before it reaches the other. As shown in Figure 14.2, any sound from source *B* is equidistant from both ears and thus produces equal effects on the two ears (called *diotic* stimulation). In contrast, a sound arriving from a lateral location, such as source *A*, travels farther to reach the right ear than

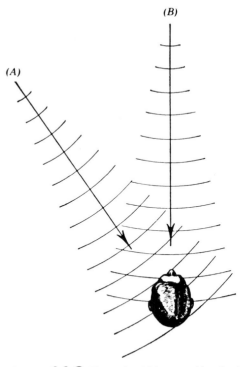

□ *figure 14.2* Binaural cues for sound localization. Sound waves coming from source *B* in the median plane affect both ears equally. A sound from source *A* reaches the left ear before the right ear, and it is more intense because the right ear is slightly "shadowed" by the head.

the left. It follows that the sound waves from *A* will arrive later at the right ear than at the left. In general, a sound source closer to one ear than to the other sends sound waves that reach the nearer ear sooner than the farther one. The difference may be slight, but usually it is sufficient to locate the sound source (Wallach, Newman, & Rosenzweig, 1949). In fact, sounds whose time of arrival differs by as little as 0.0001 second or less (with no intensity differences) are sufficient to serve as cues for localizing sound in space. This seems to be the result of a neural mechanism because such an interval is too short to allow the individual sounds to be heard as separate stimuli (Rosenzweig, 1961).

A series of experiments by Rosenzweig (1951, 1954, 1961; see also Yin, Kuwada, & Sujaku, 1984) supports the notion that sound localization using interaural time differences has a neural basis. Using anesthetized cats, Rosenzweig reported that small interaural time differences produce reliable differential responses in the auditory cortex. Independent auditory signals were produced by separate earphones, one on each ear. The neural effect of the signals were recorded by tiny electrodes inserted in the auditory cortex. Although responses occurred on both sides of the auditory cortex, when only the right ear was stimulated, the responses at the left side were stronger. When both ears were stimulated, but with a small time interval between stimuli (clicks), the resultant cortical response resembled the responses to the single stimulus. For example, when a click delivered to one ear preceded the click sent to the other ear, by say 0.0002 second, the amplitude of the cortical response from the initially stimulated ear was slightly larger than that from the other ear. As previously described, this is based on the fact that each ear is better represented on the opposite side of the brain: thus, for example, a sound delivered to the left ear before the right one produces more neural activity in the right hemisphere of the brain (and, in fact, partially inhibits the response from the right ear). The neural response pattern therefore reflects the time difference in stimulation.

Finally, some findings suggest that the location of a sound is based on the temporal firing pattern of a specific population of neurons in the auditory cortex.

Middlebrooks et al., (1994) recorded the neural activity of several "localization-coding" neurons in the auditory cortex of anesthetized cats while they moved a sound source to different locations in a 360° arc around their heads. They observed that the firing pattern of the individual neurons depended on the location of the sound. In other words, certain cortical neurons appear to encode sounds from different spatial directions by a specific temporal firing pattern.

While the results are not conclusive, they do stress the role of time on the neural level of auditory localization. Indeed, since sounds occur over time as well as space, it makes sense that the auditory system would have developed a way of using a temporal code for localization.

The Precedence Effect   In normal listening conditions, the sound from a stationary source reaches the ears by many different paths (Figure 14.3). Some sound waves reach the ears directly, but many others arrive only after being reflected from the surfaces of objects in the immediate environment. In spite of the many reflections (or echoes) created by single sounds, typically only a *single sound* is heard whose location is based largely on the *first* sound received. In fact, we do not even hear the echoes unless the reflecting surface is so far away that the echoes take a long amount of time to reach our ears (about 35 msec or more). This hearing of only a single sound whose location is determined primarily by the arrival of the first sound is called the **precedence effect.**

DEMONSTRATION:
The Precedence Effect

The precedence effect can be partly demonstrated by employing two speakers of a home stereo system set to monaural, or "mono," so that the speakers will deliver identical acoustic stimuli (stereophonic listening is described in a following section). If you are seated equidistant from the two speakers, you will hear the sound originating from both speakers simultaneously. However, if you move to the left or right, only one of the speakers

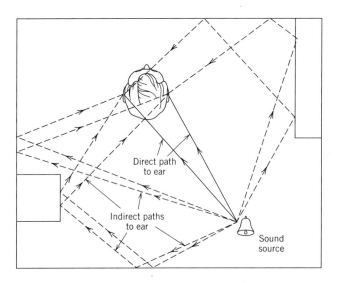

Direct path
to ear

Indirect paths
to ear

Sound
source

□ **figure 14.3** Schematic of some paths of sounds created by a single sound source.

will appear to be sounding. That is, the nearer speaker will appear to be the only active sound source. The sound reaching the ears from the farther speaker may be delayed only a few milliseconds relative to the sound of the nearer speaker. However, this slight time difference is enough to suppress the sound of the farther speaker, at least with respect to its apparent location. In fact, you may even need to verify that the other speaker is still on. The sound from the farther speaker, though apparently inaudible, does affect the quality of the sound coming from the nearer speaker. In fact, when the farther speaker is turned off, the sound from the nearer, audible speaker will seem weaker and less expansive.

This demonstration of the precedence effect stresses that the auditory system weighs the first sounds more heavily and tends to suppress later-arriving sounds, so that generally only one sound originating from a particular direction is perceived (Pickles, 1988; Wallach et al., 1949). Without the precedence effect, hearing everyday sounds in an acoustic environment with reflections and echoes would be very confusing. In an environment, with prominent reflections and echoes, the waveforms of the first sounds contain the most accurate information on their location. The waveforms of later sounds generally give a false impression since they originate from objects that have reflected the first waveforms (Green, 1976).

Phase Differences Under certain conditions, especially for low frequencies, sound localization may be aided by detecting a difference in phase between the sounds reaching the two ears. Sounds of low frequency have wavelengths longer than the diameter of the head; such sounds are diffracted around the head and may produce phase differences. That is, the waveform of the sound reaching one ear may be in a different part of its compression–rarefaction cycle than the waveform of the sound arriving at the other ear. However, above about 1000 Hz, phase differences, at least for pure tones, are not important for sound localization (Oster, 1973).

Intensity Differences Another binaural cue, called **interaural intensity difference,** results from the intensity difference between the sounds reaching each ear. A sound that lies at different distances from each ear not only strikes the nearer ear first, but it also delivers a slightly more intense sound to that ear. This is primarily because the head becomes an acoustic obstacle that blocks or interferes with the sound's propagation to the more distant ear. As Figure 14.2 shows, the head casts a sound "shadow" and the ear opposite to the sound source lies in this shadow. Hence, sound waves that must pass around the head are disrupted and reach the farther ear with less intensity than the nearer one.

To cast a sound shadow, objects must be large in proportion to the wavelengths of the sound. This means that the long wavelengths of low-frequency sounds tend to bend around the head, casting no shadow. It follows that the influence of sound shadows on interaural intensity differences increases as frequency increases (i.e., as wavelength decreases). Kinsler and Frey (1962) point out that the difference in the intensities reaching the two ears from distant sound sources, with frequencies below about 1000 Hz, is neglible. In these cases, the location of the sounds is based almost completely on interaural time differences. This means that sound localization, at least for pure tones, involves a dual system: interaural time differences are best for localizing low-frequency sounds, and interaural intensity differences are most effective for localizing high-frequency sounds. However, high-frequency *complex* sounds, which contain various harmonics, may also be localized on the basis of interaural time differences.

In the typical listening situation, complex sounds of both high and low frequencies usually occur simultaneously. Therefore, sources of both intensity and time differences are accessible, and likely play a role in successful spatial localization (Hafter et al., 1990).

Interaural Intensity Differences and Deaf Feigning When a tone is presented to both ears simultaneously but made more intense to one ear, the listener hears the tone as coming only from the direction of the more intensely stimulated ear. By analogy to the precedence effect, the tone appears to stimulate only the ear receiving the more intense signal. However, the weaker signal, although not audible, contributes to the loudness of the more intense tone in that if the weaker tone is abruptly terminated, the loudness of the more intense tone decreases.

DEMONSTRATION:
Interaural Intensity Difference and Localization

The localization effect based on the interaural intensity difference can be easily experienced using earphones with a home stereo system set to "mono." While wearing the earphones, manipulate the "balance" control (which modulates the intensity of the sound reaching the left and right ears individually) until the sound appears to come from only one earphone. By listening to each earphone individually, you will find that sound is actually coming from the other, less intense earphone. You just don't hear it when the other ear is more intensely stimulated!

Using this demonstration, we can better understand the following historical anecdote on auditory localization. According to Rosenzweig (1961), shortly after 1900 the German physician Stenger devised a clinical test to expose individuals feigning deafness in one ear. The test, which is still used, is based on some of the points made in the text and in the above demonstration. For example, a person who pretends to be deaf in the left ear will report hearing a tone if it is presented to the right ear through an earphone. What happens if the same tone is now presented to the right ear and *simultaneously, but more intensely* to the left ear? According to the demonstration and the text, the listener with normal hearing will hear the sound as coming *only* from the left. Of course, a person truly deaf in the left ear will hear *only* the less intense tone sent to the right ear. In contrast, the malingerer (who has normal hearing) will be revealed by stating that he or she does *not hear any* sound, even though sound of audible intensity is being delivered to the admittedly normal right ear! According to Rosenzweig, "The effectiveness of this test makes it clear that the listener hears only a single localized sound and does not compare separate sensations arising at the two ears" (p. 132).

Stereophonic Listening As we have noted, in typical binaural hearing, each ear receives a slightly different sound; this difference is created primarily by the time and intensity differences produced by sound-emitting objects located at different distances from each ear. Accordingly, to record an acoustic event that accurately reproduces active *binaural listening,* a separate microphone must be placed very close to the auditory canal of each ear. The sounds thus recorded preserve all the binaural differences ordinarily heard (including the effects produced by the pinnas, described below). When the two independent recordings are played back over stereo earphones, they sound strikingly like the original acoustic event.

The unique auditory experience of **stereophonic listening** produced from stereophonic recordings requires a playback system of two loudspeakers or earphones so that slightly different auditory messages can be delivered to each ear. However, the message sent to each ear to create the stereo effect is more a product of sound signals mixed by an engineer in a recording studio than an achievement of the true binaural differences in each message. Actually, modern stereophonic recording uses the sounds picked up by several microphones. In practice, recording engineers selectively combine the input from the microphones into two distinct channels, one for each ear, to obtain the proper spatial effect in playback. Moreover, stereo stimulation is created almost entirely by intensity rather than time differences in the two channels (Moore, 1989).

As we should understand at this point, if sounds come from only a single channel or if one channel is made more intense than the other, the sounds will be heard as located in the direction of that channel. Obviously, if the sounds are equally intense in both channels, they will be heard as located equidistant between the two channels.

Head Movements Interaural time and intensity differences reaching the ears of binaural listeners enable them to locate horizontal sound-emitting sources. However, the vertical location of sounds (i.e., above or below the observer) poses a problem, since the same time and intensity differences in stimulation may reach the ears from sounds located above as those from below the listener. Furthermore, if a sound source is located in the *median plane* (the imaginary vertical plane that passes through the middle of the head from front to back), its correct direction cannot be determined by a stationary observer. As shown in Figure 14.4, confusion in locating sounds here results because no matter where the sounds originate on the median plane, they are always the same distance from each ear, thereby producing the same interaural time and intensity differences (identical to condition *B* in Figure 14.2).

These localization problems can be solved by allowing free movement of the head: When the head moves, time and intensity changes in sound reception occur. It follows, then, that if the head turns to the left of the midline, a sound directly behind is heard sooner and louder by the left ear than by the right ear. Similarly, by moving the head up and down, vertical sound sources can be located. Generally speaking, any bodily movement creating differences in the stimulation reaching the two ears that are directly linked to the position of the sound source may help us to perceive its location.

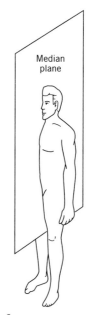

□ *figure 14.4* The median plane of a listener.

The Pinna and Localization

The complex surface created by the folds and corrugations of the **pinna** (i.e., the fleshy external ear flap in most mammals, introduced in Chapter 12) modifies and reflects sounds of different frequencies (especially high frequencies) by different amounts before they enter the external auditory canal. Along with head movements, consistent changes in the distribution of sound waves produced by the pinna may thus provide cues to sound localization (e.g., see Batteau, 1967, and Butler, 1987, for monaural localization; and Butler & Humanski, 1992, and Oldfield & Parker, 1986, for binaural localization).

In action, the wrinkles and convolutions of the pinna serve as small reflecting surfaces that create different echo patterns for complex sound sources lying at different directions from the listener; thus, in some situations, sounds originating in front of or above the listener may be heard as different from those located behind or below the listener. In one investigation, when the pinna's sound-reflecting ability was rendered ineffective by filling the pinna cavities with molded rubber plugs, localization accuracy was greatly reduced (Gardner & Gardner, 1973).

DEMONSTRATION:
The Effect of the Pinna on Sound Perception

You can experience firsthand the different patterns of sounds created by the pinna by the following simple demonstration. While listening to someone speaking, grasp the outer part of each pinna with the thumb and forefinger, pulling them forward. This catches more sound waves, increasing the echoes created by the pinnas. The speaker's voice will sound deeper or fuller and a bit louder. Now, grasping the pinnas as above, pull them back so that they are more or less flat against the sides of your head. This reduces their ability to catch sound waves and decreases echoes; in this case, the speaker's voice sounds thinner and somewhat higher in pitch.

Localization without a Pinna   Most of this discussion is related to animals with pinnas and symmetrical ears. However, nocturnal barn owls, like birds in general, do not have pinnas. Instead, they have a skin flap—essentially a fold of skin—that covers each auditory canal. In addition, the ears in barn owls are not symmetrical; their left ear is higher than the right, which is helpful in determining the vertical location of acoustic targets. Thus, to the barn owl, a sound in its median plane reaches one ear first, whereas in most other vertebrates, both ears receive the sound at the same instant. We can reasonably conclude that the asymmetry of the barn owl's ears is a special adaptation: the barn owl stalks its prey (generally small rodents and insects) on the wing at night, and must locate it mainly by faint, brief, transient sounds.

The barn owl's auditory cortex is also uniquely adapted for enhancing auditory localization. It has specialized neurons that react to sounds only when they originate from certain spatial regions, thus creating a neural map of auditory space (Knudsen & Brainard, 1991; Knudsen & Konishi, 1978).

Echolocation

The natural habitats of many mammals, including bats, porpoises, whales, and perhaps some small nocturnal rodents, require activity in places where vision is severely reduced or eliminated. For example, bats—the only mammals that can fly—are active at night and in the dark; similarly, marine mammals such as porpoises and whales may dwell in murky waters and at depths of little light. To navigate effectively in such environments, these animals have developed the ability to evaluate the echoes of their own sounds from objects in their surroundings. By using these echoes, they gain accurate and almost immediate information about the range or distance and direction (and likely the velocity, trajectory, size, shape, and identity) of objects at a distance in the absence of sight. The use of self-produced echoes to gain such biologically relevant information is termed **echolocation.**

Much of the research on echolocation has been done with bats, whose principal sensory modality is audition. An estimated 600 living species of bats pursue prey guided by echolocation (Simmons, Fenton, & O'Farrell, 1979). The bat avoids obstacles—which may be as thin as a human hair and only 0.1 in. long—when flying in the dark, and it can locate and capture prey with near-perfect accuracy while it and its prey fly at relatively high speeds. Bats perform these feats by producing and receiving the echoes of extremely brief *ultrasonic* cries, chirps, or *pulses* (i.e., sounds above the frequency limit of human hearing) whose frequencies exceed 100 kHz (Figure 14.5).

The emission and reception of *ultrasonic* sounds are necessary for bats to identify and track prey and avoid obstacles. This is due to several factors in sound transmission: high-frequency sounds are reflected less diffusely than low-frequency sounds. More important, the reflection of sound depends on the length of the sound wave striking an object relative to the size of the object. In other words, to be reflected and thus return useful information, the sound must have a wavelength smaller than the object; otherwise, the sound wave will bend around the object. For the bat, small insects are the favored prey, so the use of high-frequency sounds (i.e., sounds with short wavelengths) is critical. This point underscores the value of the bat's extended upper limit of hearing.

Echolocation involves evaluation of the returning echo. Some bats home in on their targets by emitting very brief chirps or pulses that rapidly change in frequency. This type of sound emission, called *frequency modulated* (*FM*), is a very sophisticated range-measuring mechanism. When a pulse is used whose frequency changes with time, echoes returning from targets located at different distances return at different times and thus are heard at different frequencies (the actual frequencies emitted, as well as the pattern of emissions over time, differ for different species of bats). In the case of a single returning echo with a varying frequency, if it reaches one ear before the other, it is heard at a different frequency in each ear.

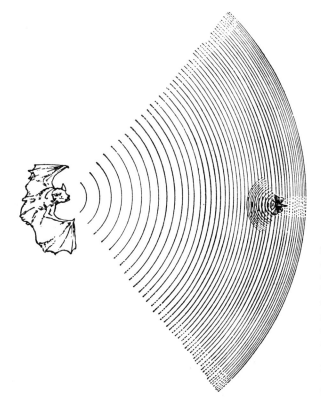

□ *figure 14.5* A flying bat and a representation of its emitted ultrasonic pulse. The curved lines represent individual sound waves in a single pulse. The frequency and wavelength of a bat's sound may vary during each pulse. The figure, which according to its author is drawn to scale, illustrates the small amount of sound reflected by one insect. In some species of bats, such as the familiar brown bat, common in the Northeast, the effective echolocation range may reach 20 ft. (From D. R. Griffin, *Echoes of Bats and Man*, Anchor Books/Doubleday, Garden City, N. Y., 1959, p. 86. Reprinted by permission of the author.)

The bat's anatomy, like its auditory system, is linked to auditory localization. In fact, the mechanisms supporting its echolocation ability—some of which appear to humans as frightening deformities (the ears and especially the snout)—take up much of the bat's small frame. Structural peculiarities of the bat's auditory and vocal anatomy specifically facilitate the reception of high frequencies. For example, the region of the cochlea concerned with high-frequency reception—nearest the middle ear—is unusually large in bats. Furthermore, the bat's vocal structures are especially well engineered for producing intense ultrasonic pulses (Griffin, 1958, 1959). Bats are also able to receive unusually weak echo signals.

Although different species of bats have varying echolocating mechanisms, the general mechanism uses a series of short ultrasonic chirps or pulses and their comparison with the returning echoes. This may involve the evaluation of time, intensity, and frequency differences between the emitted pulse burst and its echo. In many respects, this mechanism is similar to the technical instruments used for sound navigation in water (i.e., **so**und **n**avigation **a**nd **r**anging, hence the term **sonar**).

Echo Delay-Tuned Neurons

There is also evidence of a neural basis for echolocation in the bat. Dear, Simmons, and Fritz (1993) propose that the auditory-processing part of the bat's brain is comprised of neurons specially tuned to process the *time interval* (or delay time) that elapses between the emission of a pulse by the bat and the return of its echo after the pulse strikes an object. They call these special neurons **echo delay-tuned neurons.** This means that different populations of such time-sensitive neurons in the bat's brain are tuned to respond to echoes arriving at specific time intervals following pulse emissions, that is, they respond to different delay times. Thus, echoes with a short delay time (i.e., reflected from nearby obstacles) affect a different set of neurons than echoes with a long delay time (reflected from more distant obstacles). Groups of echo delay-tuned neurons simultaneously stimulated at any given moment thus provide the bat with an "acoustic image" of its immediate spatial environment.

Obstacle Perception by the Blind

Many blind individuals appear able to detect and thus avoid colliding with nearby obstacles. They are usually unable to explain this unusual and often baffling ability. As a result, several theories of nonvisual localization in the human have been developed. An early, once prominent theory held that the touch and temperature senses developed sufficiently in certain blind individuals to enable them to feel air currents as they are affected by nearby obstacles. Since the location of this ability was attributed to the face, the term "facial vision" was applied. In contrast, auditory cues in the form of echoes from objects are another explanation for obstacle perception by the blind. A series of experiments performed in the 1940s to evaluate these two explanations will now be described.

Human Echolocation

Using normally sighted blindfolded and blind subjects, Supra, Cotzin, and Dallenbach (1944) tested the effectiveness of auditory cues for obstacle perception. The subject was instructed to walk down a hallway, indicate when he thought he was approaching a wall, and walk up as close as possible to it without striking it. When sound cues were reduced—such as by having subjects walk in their stocking feet over thick carpeting or by stopping up their ears—obstacle avoidance was poor or eliminated. This result occurred in most cases, even though potential information from air currents to the head, arms, and hands was readily available. This indicated that touch is not sufficient to perceive obstacles at a distance. Moreover, when subjects wore earphones creating a background masking noise that eliminated the perception of echoes, obstacle avoidance was poor.

Thus, sound alone appears to be the critical source of information for obstacle avoidance. This conclusion is further supported by an unusual experiment in which all sensory channels except the auditory one were eliminated. Subjects were placed in a sound-proof room and were told to judge the *experimenter's* approach to an obstacle using the sounds of the experimenter's footsteps. These sounds were picked up by a microphone worn by the experimenter at ear height and transmitted to the subject's earphones through an amplifying system. All subjects tested were able to perceive the experimenter's approach to the obstacle. This ability was only slightly less than when they themselves walked toward the obstacle. All of these experiments show that the blind can perceive obstacles on the basis of reflected sound information.

The use of self-produced echoes by blind humans to obtain spatial information is not limited to the laboratory. The tapping cane of a blind person helps provide distance information derived directly from the touch of the cane against surfaces; however, the sounds of the taps themselves also generate echoes that reflect off nearby surfaces and may possibly provide the cane's user with some useful information about other surfaces and obstacles.

A striking nonlaboratory demonstration of the use of reflected sound for deriving location information was provided by a nationally ranked intercollegiate equestrienne who has been blind since birth. Her ability to navigate the corners and winding turns on the course during competition is based on the reflected echoes produced by the sounds of her ride. As she describes it, "I can hear my horse's hooves echo off the rails when they hit the ground" (Knouse, 1988, p. 8).

Several questions arise about human echolocation: How accurate are sound cues for spatial perception? What additional spatial discriminations are possible using sound reflections? A definitive set of studies was performed by Kellog (1962), who compared the performance of the blind with that of blindfolded, normally sighted control subjects on several spatial localization tasks. Of particular interest is that subjects were allowed to make any sound they wanted to produce echoes to aid them in localization. Although the subjects sometimes used tongue clicking, finger snapping, hissing, or whistling, coupled with head bobbing, the preferred source of self-produced sound was the human voice used repeatedly—that is, saying the same word over and over.

Kellogg found that blind subjects were able to derive distance and size information on the basis of self-produced sounds, whereas blindfolded, normally sighted subjects performed at about chance level. Blind subjects also were able to discriminate between surfaces of different texture, such as metal, glass,

wood, denim, and velvet, whereas blindfolded, normally sighted subjects could not. The conclusion is that experience using echoes from self-emitted sounds not only enables the blind individual to avoid obstacles but also provides enough information to make fine discriminations between objects.

The critical factors in reflected sounds for localization of obstacles are changes in the pitch of echoes (Cotzin & Dallenbach, 1950). Rice (1967) found that self-produced sounds of moderately high frequency are most effective in object localization. This is probably because the higher the frequency, the shorter the wavelength (see Chapter 12), and shorter wavelengths provide more accurate reflections. As we have noted, wavelength size limits object localization: an object must be at least as large as the wavelength of the sound striking it to reflect an effective echo. In other words, to reflect a useful echo, the wavelength of the sound striking an object should be smaller than the object.

Visual Experience and Nonvisual Spatial Navigation
The age at which the individual is blinded may play a role in spatial localization and environmental orientation. There is some evidence that individuals with visual experience before losing their sight are more effective on certain spatial tasks involving object localization and orientation than those who are congenitally blind or were blinded very early in life (Hollins & Kelley, 1988; Veraart & Wanet-Defalque, 1987). One proposal is that some early visual experience enables the blind individual to gain a better grasp of the notion of spatial relationships and to develop mental pictures of the environment. According to this view, prior visual experience makes it easier to use nonvisual *external* reference cues in developing an accurate spatial framework.

However, the precise role of prior visual experience in the spatial competence and orientation of the blind remains problematic. In fact, Loomis et al. (1993) observed that some congenitally blind individuals outperformed some normally sighted, blindfolded individuals on certain spatial tasks, such as traveling a complex route and retracing it in the reverse direction. While it seems reasonable to assume that prior visual experience offers some advantage to the blind in localization and orientation, we do not know which aspects of the ability to navigate without vision are aided.

Before leaving this topic, we will briefly note recent work on a *personal guidance system* devised as a nonvisual navigational aid.

Personal Guidance System Loomis, Golledge, and their colleagues (Golledge et al., 1991; Golledge, Loomis, & Klatsky, 1994; Loomis et al., 1994) have developed a multicomponent navigational system to help the blind, mobile individual to move about. They call it a **personal guidance system.** This system uses sound to inform the individual about his or her current position and orientation. Briefly, it works as follows: a computerized relay device picks up visual signals about the position of objects near the individual, translates them into directionally accurate sound signals, and relays the signals via binaural earphones to the listener. In one version, the blind individual actually hears the obstacles identify themselves with recognizable sounds or even words. Moreover, these binaural auditory signals from an object contain the same time and intensity differences that would ordinarily come from a sound-emitting object at a specific location relative to the person. In other words, each ear receives sounds from a given object, with the same timing and intensity that would occur if the object were actually making a sound. As a result, objects appear as sounds lying at their correct location within the auditory space of the blind navigator, allowing the individual to create a "spatial map" from an "auditory map."

While it is still in development and many technical problems remain, a personal guidance system will allow the blind to maneuver on the basis of auditory rather than visual cues. The system "will allow users to travel without assistance over unfamiliar territory and will instill in them feelings of independence and confidence that are lacking in all but the most adventurous of blind travelers" (Loomis et al., 1994, p. 2).

PERCEPTION OF MUSIC

We have discussed a wide range of psychoacoustic principles, processes, and facts that generally concern the reception of simple laboratory sounds. However, the human can also experience the succession of sounds that vary in frequency, intensity, complexity, and duration in a unique way—as *music.*

Music, we must stress, is a special and complex kind of acoustic information. To characterize musical tones solely on the basis of their physical attributes and properties would not help very much in explaining them as music. First of all, we perceive music as much more than a series of discrete sounds; instead, the sounds are psychologically integrated and heard as well-formed, organized, and coherent patterns that we recognize as musical phrases or melodies. In fact, a melodic pattern may be so compelling, so evocative, that often, after hearing it only once, we can recognize it or even reproduce it from memory.

What distinguishes music from a mere collection of sounds that vary in physical dimension? The answer appears to lie in the organized nature of the stimulation—the relation among the individual tones, or their *context.* For our purposes, music can be characterized as a succession of tones *in relation to each other* as a coherent, rhythmic pattern, a *melody.* In other words, music is an organized experience derived from the context in which the tones appear.

Dimensions of Music

A complete understanding of the perception of music requires a discussion of many technical details that go well beyond the scope of this chapter. We can, however, draw on our earlier discussions of psychoacoustics, outlining the relation between some of the basic psychological phenomena of music and the physical characteristics of musical tones or notes that contribute to their perception as music.

Octaves The fifth century B.C. Greek mathematician and philosopher Pythagoras (472–497 B.C.) discovered the simple numerical relationship of musical sounds from which Western musical scales derive; he observed that the pitch of sound from a stringed instrument depends on the length of the string that produces it. He also observed that when one string is exactly twice the length of another equally taut string, it will produce a sound that is half as high in frequency as the shorter string. Any two such tones, whose frequencies have a 2 : 1 ratio, are separated by an *octave*. In other words, an **octave** is the interval between any two tones, one of which is exactly twice the frequency of the other. Thus, to move a tone an octave higher, you simply double its frequency. For example, a tone whose frequency is 880 Hz (i.e., A_5, in musical notation described below) is one octave higher than a tone whose frequency is 440 Hz (A_4).

Musical Notation In Western musical notation, a tone is represented by a letter that specifies its position within a given octave, along with a number that indicates the particular octave in which it occurs. Thus, the letters used for tones *within* a given octave are C, D, E, F, G, A, B, and back to C again. In addition, the letters are assigned a number—for example, C_3, D_4, E_5—that specifies the particular octave in which the tones lie.

Tones such as C_3, C_4, and C_5 stand in an *octave relation* to each other and have a strong psychological similarity. Thus, in the example above, even though the 880-Hz tone (A_5) sounds higher in pitch, it sounds very similar to the 440-Hz tone (A_4). In fact, tones that are exactly one octave apart seem more similar to each other than do sounds separated by less than an octave. As an example, the two tones whose frequencies are 261.63 and 523.25 Hz (i.e., C_4 and C_5), separated by an octave, sound much closer to each other than do the two tones corresponding to 261.63 and 392 Hz (i.e., C_4 and G_4), which are separated by considerably less than an octave.

Octave Equivalence, Tone Height, and Tone Chroma The relation of every tone to every other tone within a given octave is constant across changes of octave. For example, whereas E_4 sounds similar to but lower in pitch than E_5, the relation of E_4 to D_4 and F_4 is the same as the relation of E_5 to D_5 and F_5. The perceptual similarity of tones that stand in an octave relation (e.g., E_4 to E_5; D_4 to D_5) is called **octave equivalence** and underscores the point that, in a musical context, a tone must be analyzed by more than just a single dimension of pitch. This can be illustrated by an unusual configuration, similar

to an old-time barber pole, shown in Figure 14.6, that deforms the scale of pitch into the spiral shape of a helix (this configuration is based on a scheme proposed by M. W. Drobisch in 1846; cited in Ruckmick, 1929). The vertical dimension, termed **tone height,** specifies overall pitch level (i.e., the sense of high and low pitch) and varies with stimulus frequency. The circular plane, called **tone chroma,** represents the relative position of a tone within a given octave. A complete turn, or rotation, of the helix in the horizontal plane accommodates a single octave. Within each turn of the helix, tones standing in an octave relation to each other (e.g., G_2, G_3, G_4) are vertically aligned and appear to lie close to each other on the vertical axis.

In addition to octave similarity, other relations between musical tones are important for perception. For example, when one tone is 1.5 times the frequency of another (i.e., a 3 : 2 ratio called a *perfect fifth*) or

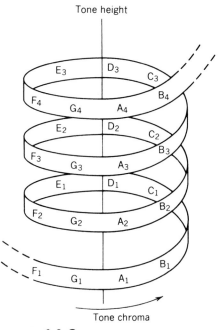

□ *figure* **14.6** Bidimensional representation of pitch: *tone height* represents overall pitch, which depends upon stimulus frequency; *tone chroma* represents the position of a tone within a given octave.

in a 4:3 ratio, the two tones are more pleasing, or consonant, when sounded together than are tones separated by other frequencies (with the exception of the 2:1 ratio of the octave interval; Krumhansl & Kessler, 1982).

Absolute or Perfect Pitch and Tone Deafness

Some individuals can identify and even reproduce isolated musical notes with no apparent musical reference or standard. This ability is called **absolute** or **perfect pitch.** It is rare, even among professional musicians, possessed by less than 1% of the population (Moore, 1989). Although individuals with absolute pitch can readily identify a musical note, they may misidentify the octave in which the tone is located (probably because of octave equivalence). Whereas prolonged training appears to enhance pitch recognition, perfect pitch appears to be genetically derived. Moreover, it has a neural basis in the left hemisphere (Schlaug et al., 1995). However, it requires proper exposure and training during early development to be realized fully (Miyazaki, 1988).

An anecdote about absolute pitch concerns the musical prodigy Wolfgang Amadeus Mozart (Stevens & Warshofsky, 1965). At the age of 7, Mozart could tell that his violin was tuned "half a quarter of a tone" sharper than his friend's violin, which he had last played days earlier!

In some ways, the opposite of absolute pitch may be the deficiency in expressing music sounds called *tone deafness*. The term itself is clearly a misnomer since almost all such individuals are as capable of discriminating between the pitch of two tones as normal individuals. According to Moore (1989), individuals who are considered tone deaf may merely find it more difficult than the average person to reproduce or sing passages of musical notes that fall outside of the range they normally use in speech. Moreover, these individuals improve with practice and musical training in general, indicating that the primary basis of tone deafness is limited experience in dealing with musical material.

Perception of Pitch Sequences: Melodies

Gestalt Organizing Principles Although music consists of an ordered sequence of tones occurring over time, we do not ordinarily hear the individual tones. Instead, sequences of tones appear to combine to form distinct auditory groups. In fact, melodies seem to be perceived on the basis of certain global properties of a sequence of tones, along with organizing tendencies of the listener—structurally analogous to the Gestalt grouping processes for form and pattern perception in vision, described in Chapter 7 (Deliege, 1987; Deutsch, 1982; Sloboda, 1985). Only some of the basic principles governing these tendencies in musical audition can be noted here, but they well illustrate the Gestalt-like organization imposed by the listener in perceiving music.

Proximity In the Gestalt principle of *proximity,* elements close to each other in space or time tend to be organized or grouped together. Applied to music, notes in a sequence that follow each other rapidly and thus appear close to each other in time (i.e., close in terms of note onset) tend to be perceived or grouped together as part of the same musical unit (Monahan, Kendall, & Carterette, 1987).

Similarity The Gestalt principle of *similarity* also applies to the apparently organized nature of music. Tones similar to each other in pitch are perceived as belonging together, that is, as forming a common perceptual group.

Common Fate When adjacent tones in a sequence combine to form changes in the pitch pattern, such as rising and falling together, or form changes in the intensity pattern such as starting and stopping together, they are perceived as a group or as part of the same sequence. In other words, if two or more components in a complex musical sound passage undergo the same kinds of change at the same time, they are grouped and perceived as part of a common unit. This is an example based on the Gestalt principle of *common fate,* which, in the visual modality, means that similar elements that move together in the same direction are perceived as part of the same perceptual unit.

Closure Psychologically related sounds such as music (as well as conversation) coming from a constant source are frequently interrupted and briefly obscured or masked by other sounds. However, even when intense interfering sounds occur, the listener typically hears the music as continuous. For example, when we listen to music on the car radio while driving, motor and traffic noise repeatedly interferes with the music signal, yet we are relatively unaware of any gaps in the music. Recall from Chapter 7 that this tendency to perceptually "fill in" and perceive physically incomplete sequences as continuous is called *closure.*

Figure–Ground Organization Finally, *figure–ground* organization may occur in the perception of music. We tend to perceive the part of the musical passage that dominates as the melody (the figure) and the accompaniment to the melody as the ground. Moreover, generally only one melody stands out as figural at any given time. Thus, a musical sequence causes the listener to group the more prominent tones together to be heard as the figure, distinct from the background of the overall sequence.

The Constancy of Melodies When played in different keys or on different instruments, or even when sung by different voices, melodies retain some invariant characteristics and continue to sound the same or very similar. Indeed, melodies appear to retain their perceptual identities even when they are systematically altered, such as when sequences of tones are *transposed* to different pitch ranges (e.g., moving all the tones up or down an octave), provided that the relationship between the successive tones and pitches comprising the melody remains unchanged. In other words, when listening to music, one attends more to pitch *relations* than to absolute pitch sounds. This underscores the point that the perception of melodies is not based on the sequential reception of a series of specific notes alone, but rather is due to the perception of constant, global, relational properties

of the sequence. In this sense, the perception of music exhibits a form of *constancy* that has much in common with the constancy phenomena observed in the visual system.

Among the important global properties and relations in the perception of melody are the spacing between discrete notes and the sequence of pitch changes—the rises and falls—between successive notes. In fact, it is this unique pattern of frequency peaks and troughs—a sort of *musical contour*—that characterizes a melody (Deutsch, 1986; Dowling, 1978).

Temporal Organization The perception of music is also strongly influenced by the rate at which the individual tones are presented, by their duration, and by other time-dependent variations between musical tones in a given sequence. Indeed, most musical passages have internal temporal properties, such as a *rhythm,* that may markedly affect how the listener hears groups of tones as forming a perceptual unit. In fact, sequences of tones can be readily grouped perceptually by manipulating their rate of presentation or by using *temporal proximity.* As we noted earlier with the Gestalt principle of proximity, musical notes that occur close together are perceived as part of the same perceptual unit; thus, temporally accenting a sequence of notes, such as by imposing a gap between groups of notes, can markedly affect the perceptual organization of the sequence and even influence the perception of a segment's melody (Jones, 1987). That is, introducing intervals between groups of notes can spontaneously alter the rhythmic structure and thus influence the hearing of discrete musical units distinct from other units in the sequence. This, in turn, can affect the perception of the overall contour and melody. In general, rhythmic organization appears to conform to an auditory equivalent of the Gestalt organizing principles of grouping (Monahan et al., 1987; Povel & Essens, 1985).

Chromesthesia and Music

In **synesthesia,** stimulation of one sensory modality almost simultaneously evokes an experience in a different sensory domain (Marks, 1975, 1978). **Chromes-**

thesia (also termed *chromaesthesia,* or *color hearing*) is a specific form of synesthesia in which sounds not only register an auditory sensation but produce vivid color sensations as well. This interplay of sensory experience occurs especially with musical sounds. Although there is considerable variation among individuals, the tone–color relationship does show certain general uniformities and trends. For example, Langfeld (1914) reported the synesthetic responses of a musician-composer when she was 23 and 30 years of age, observing that treble notes resulted in relatively stable sensations of lighter colors and bass notes induced darker colors. Moreover, the results spanning a 7-year period, were quite similar. Remarkedly, the subject could sense or "see" the color at the mere mention of the musical note.

Conditioned Color Associations

More recently, Cutietta and Haggerty (1987) investigated the colors associated with auditory sensations (which they label *color association* rather than true chromesthesia) to determine whether or not the effect is due to some form of experiential conditioning. Because of the large subject population used, their procedure is of interest: they examined the color associations of 1256 subjects ranging in age from 3 to 78 years. Subjects were instructed to listen to three tape-recorded musical passages. The musical examples were selected because each had a unique overall musical quality. They were (1) a "majestic and vigorous" passage (Gustav Holt's *Suite No. 1 in E flat major,* third movement, "March"), (2) a "plodding and laboring" passage (Moussorgsky's, *Pictures at an Exhibition,* fourth movement, "Bydlo"), and (3) a "lively, dance-like piece," played by a trio of woodwinds, (Handel's *Music for the Royal Fireworks,* "Bourrée," measures 11–26).

While listening to each music passage, subjects were instructed to indicate the colors of which the music "reminded them or made them think, or that they associated with the music." While there was significant variation, there was also overall consistency in color responses. The "majestic" example (1) was associated with the color red, the "plodding" example (2) evoked blue, and the "lively" example (3) was linked to yellow. Consistency of color associations to

the music passages was noted in children at about age 9; this consistency was observed into early adulthood. However, for subjects in their 40s and 50s, greater variability was found. While the finding is clear that across many age groups there are consistent color–music associations, the origin and basis of the link is elusive.

Function of Music Perception

Finally, we consider the status of music perception in terms of general auditory system function. Without doubt, music provides intensely experienced aesthetic pleasure. The amalgam of complex but ordered patterns, intertwined with emotion, tension, change, uncertainty, and even surprise, common to most aesthetic experience, is probably basic to its intrinsic appeal. Indeed, music has been characterized as "designed uncertainty" (L. B. Myers, cited in Smith, 1987). Clearly, by almost any criterion, music is a highly evolved art form and a prominent part of human culture. However, in a biological context, consider the proposal by the physicist J. G. Roederer (1973) that, in the course of evolution, music perception developed *incidentally* as a result of the complex demands placed on the auditory system to serve, first, as a distance and location detector and, later, as a communication system.

PERCEPTION OF SPEECH

The auditory system in the human is vital in vocal communication—the perception of *speech.* As with music, speech perception is based on the interplay of an enormous number of complex psychological factors. Here we can only briefly outline the processes and phenomena involved.

Consider how remarkable the perception of speech is. It requires us to make very fine discriminations between sounds. For example, a spoken word consists of a short pattern of sounds lasting less than a second. Moreover, the perception of speech persists even when the sounds comprising words change greatly. In fact, words retain their identity and are perceived accurately under many distorting conditions: for example, varying accents, dialects and voice qualities; masking background noises and sound omissions; and distortions produced by electrical means such as telephones or other mass communications systems. Even when most physical characteristics of speech sounds have been changed to some degree, the sounds may still be intelligible. That meaningful speech occurs under these conditions points out a striking perceptual achievement.

Range of Speech Sounds

The frequency range of actual speech sounds is limited by the anatomy of the vocal apparatus rather than by the potential of the ear to hear. Human speech is produced by the mechanics of the vocal cords and the vocal tract, which includes cavities of the mouth, throat, and nose. The air in the cavities is set into vibration by movement of the vocal cords producing sound waves. The potential for varying frequency is determined by a number of factors. Different frequencies may be produced by the combined action of the vocal tract and the positioning of the tongue, lips, cheeks, and jaw.

The resonant frequency of the oral cavity is governed by the physical length of the tract and the mass of the vocal cords. For the average man this frequency is close to 500 Hz; for women, 727 Hz; and for children, 850 Hz (Bergeijk, Pierce, & David, 1960). The highest useful frequencies for speech production lie close to 6500 Hz. Thus, speech sounds occupy about one-third of the total range of frequencies presumably audible to humans.

Much speech energy occurs at low frequencies, less than 1000 Hz (especially for vowels, where the human is less sensitive). However, the frequencies defining the majority of consonants, which are critical for speech perception, are in the range of 1000 to 5000 Hz (where the human is most sensitive). The range of produced intensities is likewise narrow. Between the softest sounds (whispers) and the loudest sounds (shouts) that may naturally occur from the human voice is a range of about 70 dB. The energy levels at both of these extremes are far from the limits of human audibility.

Phonemes   To comprehend our fine discrimination between words, we must focus on the individual sounds of a language. A major unit of the speech is the **phoneme,** the smallest unit of the speech sounds of a language that enables one utterance to be distinguished from another (Table 14.1). Phonemes by themselves are meaningless and in isolation may not even be pronounceable (such as *ng* in "sing"), but with other phonemes they form syllables and words. For example, the word "pet" is composed of three phonemes, /p,/ /e/, and /t/. By changing only one of these phonemes at a time, numerous other words can be created (e.g., "pit, pat, pot, put, pen, let"), each differing from the original word, "pet," by just a single phoneme.

Vowels and Consonants   Another way of classifying speech sounds is based on how the vocal apparatus is used in producing the vowels and consonants that comprise phonemes. *Vowels* are produced by the vocal cords, the resonance of the throat cavities, and the open mouth. In fact, you will readily notice the change in the shape of the mouth as you say the vowels *a, e, i, o,* and *u* out loud. *Consonants* are produced by constriction of the passage through the throat and mouth, aided greatly by movement of the tongue and lips. Vowels are longer in duration and louder than consonants, although the loudness of consonants varies greatly. The energy in vowel sounds is almost entirely in the frequency range below 3000 Hz, whereas the energy in a *ch* or *s* consonant sound, for example, lies above 3000 Hz.

The Spectogram   The ease with which we perceive speech hides an immensely complicated mechanism. Most speech sounds represent a complex, changing pattern of intensities and frequencies over time. A record that indicates the changes in this pattern of utterances over time is called a **spectogram.** A spectogram gives a graphic picture of the energy produced by speech (or any complex set of sounds). A characteristic spectogram is shown in Figure 14.7. Three components of speech sounds are displayed: time is plotted on the *x*-axis, frequency is plotted on the *y*-axis, and the concentration of dark areas, called

▭ **table 14.1** The Phonemes of General American English[a,b]

Vowels	Consonants	
ee as in heat	t as in tee	s as in see
I as in hit	p as in pea	sh as in shell
e as in head	k as in key	h as in he
ae as in had	b as in bee	v as in view
ah as in father	d as in dawn	th as in then
aw as in call	g as in go	z as in zoo
U as in put	m as in me	zh as in garage
oo as in cool	n as in no	l as in law
△ as in ton	ng as in sing	r as in red
uh as in the	f as in fee	y as in you
er as in bird	θ as in thin	w as in we
oi as in toil	ch as in church	g as in gin
au as in shout		
ei as in take		
ou as in tone		
ai as in might		

[a] General American is the dialect of English spoken in midwestern and western areas of the United States. Certain phonemes of other regional dialects (e.g., southern) can be different. The phonemes of General American English include about 16 vowels and 24 consonants, as shown above.

[b] Some phonemes are represented by the letters of the Roman alphabet and others by special characters.

Source: Based on Denes and Pinson (1973).

formants, represents the intensity of various frequencies over time.

Note that there are time intervals where little or no energy is shown on the spectogram. However, these "silent" intervals do not necessarily correspond to the gaps between words when speaking. In fact, we don't actually pause between each word when speaking fluently, so there are no silent intervals between successive words. In general, there is very little connection between the breaks in the speech record as shown on a typical spectogram and the gaps between words. (We will return to the relevance of this point later in the chapter.)

However, although not directly linked to the perception of distinct words, a brief period of silence between adjacent syllables can provide an important cue for the perceptual grouping of sounds in fluent speech. For example, as Moore (1989) points out, the introduction of a silent interval helps the listener distinguish between such phrases as "light house-keeper" and "lighthouse keeper."

Speech Perception with Sound Distortion

Understanding speech perception involves much more than an analysis of sound reception. In fact, a complex cognitive integrative mechanism is required to perceive speech. Moreover, we continue to perceive intelligible speech even when the flow of speech is reduced or distorted. In this section, we highlight this point by describing several experiments and procedures in which aspects of speech were severely distorted, degraded, or eliminated to determine their effect on the intelligibility of speech.

Frequency Cutoff One form of speech degradation involves filtering out whole ranges of frequencies from speech. This procedure is known as **frequency cutoff.** In a classic study by French and Steinberg (1947), subjects heard a series of recorded words from which whole bands of frequencies either above or below 1900 Hz were completely removed.

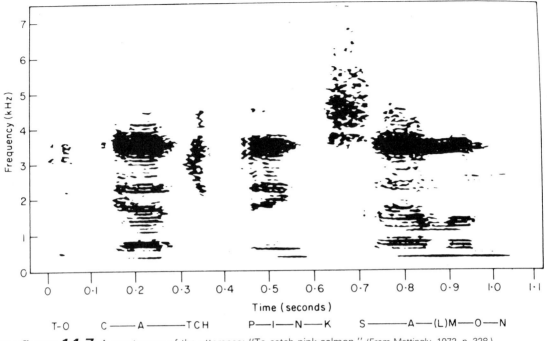

□ *figure 14.7* A spectogram of the utterance: "To catch pink salmon." (From Mattingly, 1972, p. 328.)

When frequencies above 1900 Hz were filtered out, about 70% of the words were still intelligible. The same result was obtained with the elimination of all sounds below 1900 Hz. This means that as much of the total intelligibility is carried by frequencies below 1900 Hz as is carried by frequencies above 1900 Hz. Hence, the critical stimulus information for speech perception is not confined to any frequency range.

Frequency cutoff illustrates a trade-off in information retained and removed: eliminating the high frequencies affects the perception of consonants more than vowels, whereas filtering out the low frequencies affects vowels more than consonants. Thus, neither all the high-frequency nor all the low-frequency speech components are necessary. Only a surprisingly narrow band of frequencies is enough for reasonable intelligibility.

Missing Sounds and Context In typical interactions involving sound, small segments of speech are commonly eliminated and replaced with an assortment of brief extraneous sounds, such as traffic noise, footsteps, door bells, door slams, general conversational sounds, coughs, and so on. However, most of the time, the absence of speech sounds goes unnoticed, and the sounds are apparently restored by the listener. This makes a very important point: the perception of continuous speech does not depend solely on the fixed acoustic stimulation that occurs at any given moment. It also depends on *anticipations* and *expectations* of what the stimulation should be based on the cognitive framework created by preceding and following speech sounds. In other words, extra information for perceiving speech is provided by the linguistic **context** in which sounds are heard.

The importance of context for speech perception is obvious in the following example of a phenomenon called the **phonemic restoration effect** (Bashford, Riener, & Warren, 1992; Warren, 1970; Warren & Warren, 1970). Listeners heard sentences like the following:

"It was found that the (   )eel was on the orange." A missing speech sound (a phoneme), represented by the blank space, was replaced by an apparently extraneous sound—a loud cough. That is, the sound of a cough was inserted just before the "eel" sound. On hearing this (and other similar sentences), listeners reported that, rather than hearing the cough before the "eel" sound, they heard the sound of a phoneme appropriate to the *context* of the sentence; that is, they perceptually restored the phoneme "p" and heard the word "peel." This means that the perception of the missing phoneme of the word fragment "(   )eel" was determined by the context provided by the last word in the sentence. Other words used to complete the sentence and alter the context were "axle" and "shoe." Each restored a different speech sound for the preceding word fragment and apparently replaced the sound of the cough; listeners heard the words "wheel," and "heel," respectively. Thus, phonemic restoration conforms to the context provided. Note again that the perception of the missing sound was aided by words that occurred *after* the cough. This indicates that the listener stores incomplete information until the necessary context is established. Interestingly, although the missing sound and its location were "heard" clearly, the perception of where the cough occurred was poor. In contrast, when a silent gap rather than a cough replaced the missing phoneme, listeners easily recognized the location of the gap.

The role of context may also *reduce* inaccuracies or "slips of the ear" in the perception of fluent conversational speech. This occurs especially when the acoustic input is ambiguous or the same utterance has readily accessible alternative perceptions (Garrett, 1982). That is, the same acoustic input, received phonetically in the same manner, may be perceived quite differently, depending on the context in which the input occurs. Thus, in the childhood chant "I scream, you scream, we all scream for ice cream," one hears the words "I scream" and "ice cream," appropriate to their respective context. Compare the term "euthanasia" with the almost phonetically identical phrase "youth in Asia."

An often cited and amusing inaccuracy in speech perception, presumably owing to the *lack* of context, was described by *The New York Times* columnist William Safire (1979) about a woman who, on first hearing some lyrics of the well-known Beatles' song "Lucy in the Sky with Diamonds," perceived "the girl with kaleidoscope eyes" as "the girl with colitis goes by." In this example, the context (or the *lack* of the proper context) contributed to the way in which sounds were segmented into separate words.

More recently, Safire (1994) recounted an example (originally reported by the writer Sylvia Wright), concerning the contextually misunderstood title of the church hymn "Gladly the Cross I'd Bear." Instead of using the hymn's title correctly, children happily sang in church about a big animal named "Gladly" with a vision problem (strabismus). That is, they sang, "Gladly, the cross-eyed bear." Consider also this more timely misperception of a musical composition owing to the lack of proper context (or perhaps based on a self-imposed contemporary context): on a test of music composers and the names of their compositions, one elementary school child answered that George Gershwin wrote "Rap City in Blue" (Root, 1994; see Pinker, 1994, for a collection of such contextually induced misperceptions).

Finally, perception of isolated words and even smaller units of speech, such as vowels, is influenced by their context. For example, Pollack and Pickett (1964) recorded the conversations of subjects as they were waiting to be tested in an experiment. Afterward the subjects were given recordings of isolated words and short phrases taken from their own fluent conversation. Subjects given only an isolated word were far less accurate in recognizing them than when several adjacent words were presented—that is, in context. The role of context also applies to the perception of word fragments. Rakerd (1984) reported that vowels heard in the presence of neighboring consonants—a relation termed *consonantal context*—are perceived quite differently (i.e., more linguistically) than when they are presented in isolation.

It is clear, then, that context is vital in the processing and perception of speech signals, especially in establishing word boundaries and in cases of speech ambiguity.

Speech Blanking A result similar to the perceptual filling-in effect of context occurs when sections of speech are eliminated by periodically turning the speech on and off or by systematically blanking out sections of speech flow by turning a masking noise on and off. This form of speech disruption is called **speech blanking.**

The general trend for various proportions of speech blanking as derived by Miller (1947), is given by Figure 14.8. According to this figure, when conversation was blanked out for 50% of the time (at a rate of nine blinks per second), speech intelligibility was altered, but only about 15% of the words were lost. Thus, a reasonable degree of speech intelligibility may be retained even though the auditory system hears the speech only half of the time.

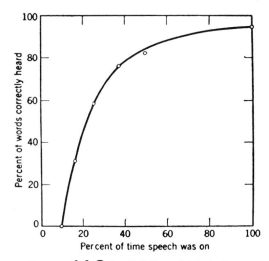

□ *figure* **14.8** Intelligibility of blanked speech. Speech was turned on and off nine times per second. Quite short bursts of speech are enough to give good intelligibility. (After Miller, 1947.)

□ *DEMONSTRATION:*
Speech Blanking

It is possible to approximate the effect of speech blanking. While listening to a radio news broadcast, rapidly adjust the volume or loudness control back and forth so that silence alternates with audible speech. You will find that although the perception of speech flow is greatly disrupted, a surprising number of words can be recognized. Of course, the overall intelligibility of the broadcast depends on how fast you turn the loudness control back and forth and thus how long you pause for silence or speech.

In general, speech perception is remarkably resistant to degradation. Speech remains reasonably intelligible even with background noise and even when chunks of linguistic elements are eliminated—including phonemes and whole frequency bands—conditions that are clearly far from ideal. That speech perception persists in spite of great variability in the sounds reaching the listener—including acoustic effects due to differences in the speakers' age, gender, dialect, and even emotional state—indicates that the information carried in speech is highly redundant. Hence, distorting or eliminating some of the speech

cues still provides enough information to convey a message from the remaining cues. As Moore (1989) observes, "This is of great practical advantage. If speech perception depended on a near-perfect transmission of sound from speaker to listener, then speech communication in most real situations would become extremely difficult. Nature has designed the speech communication process so that it can operate under a great variety of adverse conditions" (p. 281).

GENERAL ISSUES IN SPEECH PERCEPTION

It should now be clear that the ability to perceive speech is extraordinary. When confronted with the sequence of continuous sounds comprising speech we recognize, almost immediately and without effort, a specific cognitive message. Moreover, we perceive intelligible speech even when the speech sounds are drastically altered or distorted and the elements of speech are incomplete. In the following sections, we will discuss several general issues that supply hints on how the continuous output of vocalized sounds is heard as speech.

Perception of Words

We are now able to confront a basic question in the understanding of speech perception: how do we perceive the sequence of sounds in the spoken message as composed of individual words when the physical signals alone provide few cues to divide the verbal message properly into discrete words? We perceive boundaries between words, but they are only apparent: there are no physical breaks or other markers corresponding to the separations perceived. Moreover, as we noted earlier, the perceived boundaries between words have no corresponding gaps in the spectogram—that is, they are not physically represented by intervals of silence in the speech flow reaching the ears. Instead, the phonetic segments comprising speech physically merge into each other and reach the listener as a continuous stream of acoustic stimulation.

A stranger to a language immediately confronts the problem of perceptually segmenting individual words. A truly foreign language is heard merely as a rapid, continuous stream of utterances. The naïve listener does not even know what sets of sounds refer to discrete words or even where one word ends and another begins based only on their sounds. In fact, as Jusczyk (1986) observes, "Given the continuous nature of the signal, perhaps it is not surprising that nonnative listeners have difficulty in pinpointing word boundaries and that they complain that English is spoken too rapidly by a native speaker. Rather, the real surprise is that native speakers *do* hear this continuous signal as a series of discrete word-size units" (p. 27-3).

One critical factor in perceiving discrete words from the stream of sounds of conversational speech is the *familiarity* of the sounds to the listener. Certainly knowledge of the language, especially familiarity with its sounds, helps us perceive breaks between words where none exist. That is, word boundaries are heard, at least in part, because we are familiar with certain sounds as forming words. Indeed, the more familiar the listener is with the speech sounds of the language, the more readily the sounds are perceived as distinct words. Relatedly, familiarity with the speaker's voice helps us perceive his or her spoken words. Nygaard, Sommers, and Pisoni (1994) found that the recognition of words heard against a noise background was significantly higher when the listener was familiar with the speaker's voice than when the listener heard the same words uttered by an unfamiliar voice (see also Palmeri, Goldinger, & Pisoni, 1993). Thus, it seems that experience with the speaker's speech pattern increases the intelligibility of words produced by that speaker. Finally, as we described earlier with the *phonemic restoration effect,* hearing sounds in the context of other sounds aids us in perceiving word boundaries.

Uniqueness of Speech

Is speech special? Does the auditory system recognize and treat speech as a special form of stimulation—different from other sounds in the environment—requiring its own processing mechanisms? Or is speech simply a form of complex sound stimulation perceived by the same mechanisms used to analyze other complex sound stimuli? Neither view has been completely adopted by researchers and theorists. There are strong arguments for and against both of them, and the unique status of speech remains problematic.

In this section, we will examine the possibility that speech perception differs greatly from the perception of nonspeech sounds and that special mechanisms have evolved to recognize and analyze speech sounds. We will also consider the notion that speech perception is the output of a neurally distinct processing system specialized for extracting linguistic elements from the sounds that transmit them. We begin with a brief introduction to the motor theory of speech.

Motor Theory of Speech The motor theory derives largely from the observation that there is a very close link between the perception of speech sounds and the way they are produced by the vocal tract. In other words, "the sounds of speech are somehow perceived by reference to the ways we generate them" (Liberman et al., 1967*a,* p. 70; Liberman & Studdert-Kennedy, 1978). It is called a **motor theory** because listeners are assumed to use the motor–articulatory gestures ordinarily involved in speaking. In effect, the motor theory assumes that *speech production* is basic to speech recognition: listeners somehow engage their own speech-motor systems in perceiving the speech of others. Speech is obviously special, according to the motor theory, since it holds that speech perception is linked to speech production by a specialized speech–motor system.

Categorical Perception The notion that speech differs from other forms of sound stimuli has also been advanced, in part, by **categorical perception.** Categorical perception is said to occur when the ability to discriminate among members of the *same* category is substantially inferior to the ability to discriminate between members of different categories (e.g., Jusczyk, 1986). As applied to speech sounds, categorical perception means that two different linguistic sounds, such as the consonants /p/ and /b/ (or /d/ and /t/), should be easier to discriminate than different forms of /p/ or of /b/.

Phonetic consonants such as /p/ and /b/ are produced by slightly different vocal activities. Both sounds are produced by closing the lips, then opening them and releasing air, and by vocal cord vibration (called *voicing*). However, in producing /b/, the vocal cords begin vibrating almost simultaneously with the release of air, whereas for /p/ there is a short gap between air release and vocal cord vibration; specifically, in articulating /p/, the vocal cords vibrate about 50 to 60 msec after the release of air. The time between air release and vocal cord vibration, or voicing, is referred to as the **voice-onset time (VOT).** Of particular relevance here is that listeners use VOT as a cue in determining whether a /b/ or a /p/ has been uttered.

In a basic and illustrative demonstration of consonant discrimination (using synthesized or computer-generated speech sounds), the VOT is systematically varied in small increments, and the listener's task at each step is to indicate whether, for instance, a /b/ or a /p/ is heard. In our example of distinguishing between the phonemes /b/ and /p/, listeners will initially hear /b/ (since we begin with air release and voicing occurring simultaneously). The perception of the /b/ phoneme will persist in spite of small, incremental changes in VOT until the VOT reaches a certain point—the phonetic boundary—whereupon the pho-

neme /b/ sound will suddenly change to the phoneme /p/ sound. The **phonetic boundary,** then, is the particular VOT that changes the perceived phoneme. Thus, even though the VOT may change considerably on either side of the phonetic boundary, it does not result in continuous perceptual changes; instead, the listener hears only two categories of sounds: either /b/ or /p/, depending on which side of the phonetic boundary the VOT lies.

To those who believe that speech sounds are special, categorical perception indicates a special speech processor that is activated when variations in the VOT of phonetic sounds such as /b/ reach a critical point—at the phonetic boundary. In effect, the particular VOT engages a special speech mechanism that produces a perceptual change in the phoneme perceived.

Categorical perception also supports the motor theory, illustrating a close relationship between the perception of certain speech sounds and the way they are produced. In short, according to categorical perception, speech perception is tied to speech articulation. That we perceive sounds discontinuously—for example, /b/ *or* /p/—is paralleled by the way we produce these sounds. In natural speech, considerable variation in VOT may occur, yet we continue to hear the same consonant, /b/. Then, at the phonetic boundary, where the speaker produces a specific VOT, perception abruptly changes and we hear /p/. Thus, a particular change in articulation produces a corresponding change in perception.

However, categorical perception is not restricted to speech sounds. Similar categorization effects have been demonstrated for the perception of nonspeech sounds such as "buzz" noises (Miller et al., 1976). Perhaps more challenging to the notion that categorical perception involves a special speech-processing mechanism is the fact that it occurs in nonhuman species, which are denied the use of a spoken language (e.g., the monkey: Kuhl & Padden, 1983; Morse & Snowden, 1975; the chinchilla: Kuhl & Miller, 1975; the Japanese quail: Kluender, Diehl, & Killeen, 1987; and the dog: Adams & Molfese, 1987).

Neural Mechanisms of Speech Perception There are also physiological approaches to the idea that speech is different from other forms of sounds. These contend that special neural units and mechanisms are used in decoding speech from sound. Several forms of this notion are described in the next section.

Linguistic Feature Detectors Does the human brain contain specialized neurons—neural speech detectors—uniquely responsive to human speech sounds? The search for such neurons is based on the assumption that there are specific **linguistic feature detectors** in the brain. These are presumed to be fine-tuned to respond exclusively to specific characteristics and features of the speech signal (e.g., VOT). One means of demonstrating their existence is to use a **selective adaptation procedure** that fatigues or adapts a presumed specific linguistic feature by a controlled form of stimulus overexposure. If there is a specific detector for a given feature of speech—produced by, say, the phoneme /t/—then it follows that after repeatedly hearing this feature, the linguistic detector will fatigue and the listener will be less likely to hear that particular speech sound.

In an experiment using selective adaptation, Eimas and Corbit (1973) prepared a series of computer-generated, artificial speech sounds, including two pairs of consonants, /t/, /d/ and /b/, /p/. They also computer-synthesized a series of *intermediate* speech sounds for the two pairs of sounds—/t/–/d/ and /b/–/p/—that were sufficiently ambiguous so that *either* /t/ or /d/ (or /b/ or /p/) could be heard from the corresponding synthesized speech signal. In other words, along with the pairs of distinctive, unambiguous consonants of /t/, /d/ and /b/, /p/, artificial speech sounds were synthesized that were heard at the *linguistic boundary* between the two distinct consonant categories. For example, the ambiguous /t/–/d/ sound was as likely to be heard as /t/ as it was as /d/.

Eimas and Corbit had subjects repeatedly hear the sound of the unambiguous consonant, /d/, for 2 min. This served to selectively adapt a presumed detector that responds to the linguistic features of the /d/ consonant (you may recall this as similar to the procedure for demonstrating negative afterimages described in Chapter 5). When the adaptation phase was followed by an appropriate ambiguous consonant (/t/–/d/,

originally heard as either /t/ *or* /d/), the subject was less likely to hear the unambiguous consonant that was repeatedly exposed; that is, the subject tended to hear /t/ rather than /d/. The same procedure yielded similar results when applied to the /b/, /p/ consonant pair. In summary, repeated presentation of a linguistic stimulus selectively fatigues a presumed detector that is sensitive to one of the distinctive features of that stimulus, reducing its activity.

The notion that specific feature detectors are the primary mechanism for speech perception has been questioned on several grounds. The most serious problem is that selective adaptation effects are not confined to speech sounds but occur readily for various nonspeech sounds (e.g., Sawusch & Jusczyk, 1981). This means that there is nothing inherent in the *linguistic* or phonetic character of the acoustic input that produces selective adaptation. Indeed, adaptation may be selectively fatiguing detectors that respond to the *frequencies* of the adapting stimulus rather than its specific linguistic or speech feature. In other words, while specific neural feature detectors seem to exist, they are probably responsible for processing sounds in general, not speech sounds in particular. While we do not reject a role for feature detectors in the perception of speech (Samuel, 1986, 1989), other speech processing mechanisms are probably also involved. In the next section, we examine an alternative to linguistic feature detectors: a *speech mode*.

Speech Mode of Perception Like all sounds that reach the auditory system, speech sounds consist of stimuli that vary physically (e.g., intensity, frequency, complexity, duration). Since speech sounds are complex symbols, they must undergo some form of special processing to uncover their message. Indeed, to perceive speech, the listener must not only extract information about the presence or location of the sounds, but must also uncover the meaning—the *semantic message*—encoded in the sounds. It follows from this viewpoint, then, that speech perception is distinct from other forms of auditory perception and thus requires its own special processing mechanism.

With this in mind, a broad biologically based theory has been proposed. According to this theory, the human nervous system has a special processing **speech mode**—a *phonetic* or *speech module*—exclusively for extracting sounds identified as speech.

Perhaps the most convincing evidence of a special speech mode emerges from research indicating that the same acoustic signals are processed and perceived quite differently, depending on whether the listener treats them as speech or as nonspeech information. That is, listeners appear to use different strategies and criteria for evaluating sounds perceived as speech than for those they perceive as nonspeech (Best, Morrongiello, & Robson, 1981; Reméz et al., 1981).

In addition to studies demonstrating that the same speech sounds may be perceived on different occasions as speech or as nonspeech, there are special circumstances in which the same physical stimulus can simultaneously evoke a nonspeech (or psychoacoustic) mode *and* a phonetic or speech mode. This effect of hearing sound signals simultaneously as speech and as nonspeech is called **duplex perception.** It is proposed that duplex perception reflects mutually distinct psychoacoustic and linguistic ways of perceiving the same stimulus.

In one demonstration of this phenomenon reported by Whalen and Liberman (1987), complex computer-generated sounds were synthesized that were heard as /da/ and /ga/ at relatively low intensity levels, but when presented at higher intensities, duplex perception occurred. That is, with an increase in the intensity level of the same acoustic input, subjects heard not only the /da/ and /ga/ sounds but also simultaneously heard a nonspeech whistling sound. According to the researchers, the speech processing mode takes priority over the nonspeech mode, and only when the signals are made sufficiently intense does the nonspeech mode enter: "the duplex phenomenon supports the hypothesis that the phonetic mode takes precedence in processing the input signals, using them for its special linguistic purposes until, having appropriated its share, it passes on the remainder to be perceived by the nonspeech system as auditory whistles. Such precedence reflects the profound biological significance of speech" (p. 171).

Speech acquisition occurs gradually beginning in infancy. Although infants first process speech in terms of its physical or psychoacoustic properties, they seem predisposed to discriminate between sounds corresponding to different phonemes and to learn the particular phonemes that are important for communication (e.g., Friederici & Wessels, 1993; Kuhl, 1983; MacKain et al., 1983).

At some point during language acquisition, infants begin to take into account the phonological (language-sound) structure and other general rules of the language and begin to process the same input differently. In effect, the infant's classification of speech sounds shifts from their physical basis to their linguistic relevance. It follows, then, that speech develops as a result of acquiring language skills and attempting to attach linguistic meaning to the acoustic input.

Speech Areas of the Brain Another line of physiological evidence suggesting that speech is special is based on the fact that localized regions of the brain are specialized for dealing with speech. At the beginning of this chapter, we discussed the functional difference between the left and right hemispheres of the brain in processing language and nonlinguistic stimulation, noting that speech is more readily decoded in the left hemisphere than in the right. Indeed, there are well-defined regions within the left hemisphere for various language-related activities. The two main cortical areas for processing linguistic stimulation are indicated in Figure 14.9. The lower part of the frontal lobe contains **Broca's area,** named for the French surgeon, Paul Broca, who observed in 1861 that this particular region controls speech expression or *production*. The region in the left temporal lobe that controls speech *comprehension* is called **Wernicke's area** (after the German neurologist-psychiatrist Carl Wernicke). Injury to either of these cortical regions can produce speech defects known as *aphasias*. In particular, damage to Broca's area severely reduces the ability to speak (called *Broca's* or *motor aphasia*), and damage to Wernicke's area markedly affects the understanding of speech (and is called *Wernicke's* or *sensory aphasia*). Relevant to our discussion is that neither form of aphasia necessarily disrupts other nonspeech abilities, such as auditory acuity or sound localization.

Given the parsimony of the nervous system, it seems reasonable to assume that if specific regions of

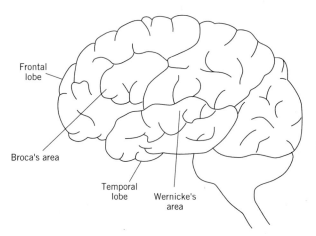

Frontal
lobe

Broca's area

Temporal
lobe

Wernicke's
area

□ *figure **14.9*** Schematic view of the left side of the human brain. Indicated are Broca's area and Wernicke's area, which are important for producing and perceiving speech, respectively. In addition, there is a bundle of nerve fibers (not shown), called the *arcuate fasciculus,* that connects the two speech areas.

the brain have evolved for speech production and comprehension, then the elements of speech must comprise a special, biologically relevant form of stimulation. At the least, the fact that distinct regions of the left hemisphere are dedicated to specific speech functions is consistent with the notion of a special speech processing system.

Audiovisual Integration: The Mc-Gurk Effect Finally, speech may be special in the sense that the speaker provides the listener not only with acoustic speech signals but also, in typical verbal interactions, with accompanying movements of the face and lips. In other words, when we listen to a speaker, we also often see the speaker's face forming the speech sounds. Can these visual cues influence our perception of speech? To any extent, is our perception of speech influenced by seeing the speaker's face?

The most impressive evidence that the speaker's visual cues influence speech perception—that is, audiovisual integration—comes from the McGurk effect. In the **McGurk effect,** auditory and visual information on speech interact with each other and affect what is heard. In short, the visual display of speech influences what the listener hears.

In the original investigation, McGurk and Mac-Donald (1976; see also Dodd, 1977) created a condition in which auditory signals of a spoken syllable were in direct conflict with the visual signals linked

to form the syllable. In one example, they prepared a videotape recording of a woman repeatedly forming the syllables, /ga-ga/ while the synchronized sound track gave a different sound, /ba-ba/. When observers closed their eyes and only the /ba-ba/ sound was available, they identified it accurately. Moreover, when they saw the lip movement of the speaker with the sound off, they were reasonably accurate in naming the syllables mouthed by the speaker, /ga-ga/ (verifying that, when necessary, we can lipread, and we probably do it more than we realize). However when the conflicting sources were presented together, observers heard syllables that were not present in either the audio or video portion of the signal. For example, when observers saw the woman forming the syllables /ga-ga/ while simultaneously presented with the acoustic signal /ba-ba/, they heard a different syllable—/da-da/! Interestingly, most observers were not aware of the disparity between the auditory and visual cues.

The seemingly automatic audiovisual integration appears to apply in a general manner. Green et al. (1991) showed that the influence of visual input on sound perception persists even when there is an obvious disparity between the sex of the speaker and the dubbed sound of the voice. If observers see the tape of a man mouthing /ga/, but it is synchronized with the sound of a woman saying /ba/, they recognize the conflict in the two signals, although they still perceive the illusory phoneme, /da/. In other words, the visual source continues to influence the perception of the sound.

Visible displays of vocal *effort* can also influence the perceived loudness of sounds. Rosenblum and Fowler (1991) presented subjects with audiovisual displays of a man producing syllable sounds, but the visible displays of effort with which the syllables were apparently spoken were mismatched with the intensity of the sound emitted. For example, subjects saw the individual appear to speak a syllable with great effort (indicative of a loud sound), but the corresponding dubbed sound was a softly spoken syllable. Even though subjects were instructed to base their loudness judgments only on the sound they heard, the sight of someone speaking a syllable with intense effort greatly increased the perceived loudness of the syllable. In fact, the greater the visible display of vocal effort, the louder the sounds were judged to be.

Audiovisual integration demonstrated by the McGurk effect suggests that, under the right circumstances, speech perception depends on more than the auditory signals. However, does the integration of activities such as lip movements with speech sounds alone support the claim that speech is different? Probably not. For one thing, audiovisual integration also occurs for nonspeech sounds for humans and animals (Heffner & Heffner, 1992; Saldaña & Rosenblum, 1993). Sound localization in general is subject to visual influences; that is, to an extent, what you see helps determine where you see it. Moreover, lip movements and other visual cues to speech are not crucial for attaining high levels of speech intelligibility. The accuracy of the blind to speech and personal experience with radio listening make this point clearly. However, audiovisual integration does indicate that, when available, a visual component to speech provides a complementary source of information that is integrated with the speech sound. This can be very useful in making speech less ambiguous in many noisy social circumstances. In particular, in situations containing several speech messages, the intelligibility of the one we attend to is increased greatly by observing the speaker's lips.

In summary, speech perception derives from a variety of cues, some available in the speech wave itself, others imposed by tendencies within the listener. However, the question asked at the beginning of this section—"Is speech special?"—still awaits an answer. While we cannot conclude with certainty that speech is a special form of auditory stimulation that requires a special mechanism or mode, it is an inviting notion and a distinct possibility.

A general statement is in order before leaving the topic of speech perception. At the very least, our brief discussion underscores the enormity of the task of arriving at a useful and reasonably complete explanation of speech perception. Perhaps as with other complex human activities and capacities, more than one method or strategy is involved in speech perception. In any event, it should be clear that an understanding of speech perception goes well beyond the physical dimensions of the speech waveform and sound reception in the ear.

AUDITORY SCENE ANALYSIS

Many of the activities described in this chapter, such as localizing sounds and hearing music and speech, have been described as if the auditory system deals primarily with unitary events. Thus, we hear a sound and immediately localize it; we hear a group of tones and recognize a melody; we hear a series of phonemes and perceive intelligible speech. However, in most natural situations, we are exposed to a vastly complex acoustic environment—an *auditory scene*—in which many different sound sources and acoustic events occur at the same time. Thus, at any given moment, sources of music, speech, and an array of background noise may surround us and blend into a complex sound stream. However, in spite of this acoustic complexity, we usually hear distinct, separate auditory events. That is, we do not typically hear the cacophonous jumble of sounds reaching our ears; instead, we recognize the various auditory sources as individual events. In short, we perceptually *analyze* the complex auditory scene into its constituent elements.

To appreciate this ability, consider the familiar situation where several conversations are going on at the same time; many of the word sounds from these conversations reach us at the same moment, yet we can easily follow the speech of a single individual.

How is it possible to pick out and focus on a particular acoustic message from the complex mixture of acoustic energy that our auditory system receives? In other words, how does the auditory system analyze and decide which parts of the sensory stimulation come from the same acoustic event? Albert Bregman (e.g., 1981, 1990; Rogers & Bregman, 1993), who has studied this problem, refers to the ability to perceive the complex acoustic scene in terms of its separate sources as an **auditory scene analysis.** According to Bregman, auditory scene analysis is accomplished by an acoustic analogue of the Gestalt organizational or grouping principles for visual forms (introduced in Chapter 7 and reintroduced earlier in this chapter in the section on music).

Auditory Streams

What are the acoustic properties that promote perceptual grouping in hearing? According to auditory scene analysis, we tend to hear **auditory streams**—groups of sounds that appear to come from a common source because they possess homogeneous features or share some perceptual characteristics. Thus, groups of sounds that, over time, are similar—for example, in pitch, loudness, and timbre—tend to be organized and perceived as distinct and separate acoustic events, and they appear to emanate from a single source. For example, when we confront several different conversations, each may have its own acoustic signature in terms of pitch and loudness, and accordingly, we hear them as distinct from each other. To some extent, this happens because each may come from a specific location, creating its own pattern of pitch and loudness.

The recognition of individual differences in the speech patterns of different speakers may also influence the perceptual segregation of distinct, separate acoustic events. Indeed, there is often sufficient variation in the voice characteristics (e.g., accent, phrasing, intonations) of speakers to distinguish one voice from another and thus for each voice to be represented by a distinct auditory stream (e.g., Nygaard et al., 1994). In general listening conditions, there is usually some grouping feature that enables each conversation to become a perceptually independent event. In short,

the auditory system separates perceptually similar acoustic events into their own auditory stream.

Stream Segregation Imagine what happens when two simple, familiar tunes, "Daisy" and "Greensleeves," are played together as follows: not only are both tunes played in the same approximate pitch range, but the individual notes of each tune are alternated in sequence (see Dowling, 1973; Dowling & Harwood, 1986). Thus, the first note of "Daisy" is followed by the first note of "Greensleeves," which is followed by the second note of "Daisy," and so on. The perceptual effect of hearing this mixture would be a more or less jumbled sound message, with neither tune recognizable. However, if we gradually change the frequency components of each tune, so that, say, all the notes of "Daisy" are heard slightly higher in pitch than the notes of "Greensleeves" (without changing the *tone chroma,* or tonal relationship, of the notes within a given tune to each other), the two tunes will emerge as two distinguishable streams. That is, the tendency to perceptually group together notes of similar pitches will segregate the series of alternating tones into high and low streams—into perceptually distinct auditory events. This splitting of the composite acoustic signal into separate auditory streams is called **stream segregation** (see Bregman, 1990). Generally speaking, the readiness of an alternating sequence of tones to form two distinct auditory streams increases with the pitch separation between the high and low tones.

We also depend on the focus of attention, as well as experience and learned factors, to help us interpret, analyze, and segregate the complex auditory scene. The physician listening to the patient's heartbeat or lung activity through a stethoscope has detailed knowledge concerning the patterns of sounds that demand attention, and on that basis can separate critical signals from extraneous ones. Finally, auditory scene analysis is aided by conditions that favor auditory localization. The more cues provided that enable the listener to distinguish one sound source from another, the greater is the scene analysis. Anecdotal evidence suggests that monaural listeners are poorer in perceiving auditory streams and segregating acoustic events than binaural listeners (N. Schiffman, 1994). In other words, the ability to localize sounds is a general aid in analyzing the auditory scene.

ANIMAL COMMUNICATION

Although it is generally agreed that only humans have linguistic behavior, the sounds produced by many animals, ranging from insects to primates, including fish, amphibia, and birds, may be used for a form of intraspecies information exchange. Communicative behavior patterns are highly characteristic for the species, both in their production and in the sorts of information they convey. Insects such as the cicada, katydid, and cricket (especially the male), for example, use signals to convey information on courting and other mating-related activities and for maintaining contact with each other. Birds use sound signals—calls or songs—for such diverse activities as territorial defense, nesting, parental recognition, and the establishment and maintenance of pair bonds. For example, the extensive song repertoire and mimicry of the northern mockingbird appear to be used for attracting mates. Indeed, unmated males sing significantly more than mated males; moreover, they are more active than the mated, flying from perch to perch so as to deliver their song from a number of different locations and hence increase the likelihood of attracting a mate (Breitwisch & Whitesides, 1987; Lewin, 1987).

Mammals also use vocalization extensively for within-species communication. By howling, wolves communicate their identity, their location, and perhaps something of their emotional state (Theberge, 1971). Communication on the basis of emitted sounds also applies to their more recent relatives, dogs.

Dog Sounds

Stanley Coren (1994), an experimental psychologist as well as a dog breeder and trainer, has analyzed dog sounds. He believes that many have particular meanings and are used to communicate specific events. He has observed that low-pitched sounds usually indicate threats, anger, and the possibility of aggression. Generally, sustained, low-pitched sounds signal behavior that is about to happen, such as the growl that precedes an attack. Higher-pitched, briefer sounds, such as yelps, can mean fear or pain; however, the same high-pitched sounds, emitted at a slow rate, may signal pleasure or playfulness. The rate of sounds may also convey specific meanings. Repetitive, rapid sounds indicate excitement and urgency; prolonged whining is a demand for attention.

Primate Sounds

Primates also emit and exchange signals in an informative way. Perhaps the most closely studied group has been the rhesus monkey. Rowell (1962) described distinct cries produced by the rhesus that express some aspects of the animal's condition in certain situations. For example, a long, fairly loud roar is made by a very confident rhesus monkey when threatening another of inferior rank. In contrast, a short, very high-pitched squeak is made by a defeated animal at the end of a fight.

Evidence also exists that species of monkeys make acoustically distinct and different alarm calls to at least three different classes of predators: leopards, eagles, and pythons (Seyforth, Cheney, & Marler, 1980). Field recordings made in Kenya yielded the following: leopard alarms were "short tonal calls, typically produced in a series of both exhalation and inhalation," eagle alarm calls were "low-pitched, staccato grunts," and the python alarm calls were "high-pitched 'chutters'." Moreover, these calls appear to contribute to a form of communication. When recordings of the alarms were played back in the absence of actual predators, adult monkeys displayed apparently adaptive activity specific to the hunting behavior of the predator represented by the recording. Thus, when the monkeys were on the ground, the leopard alarm was likely to cause them to climb up into trees (apparently rendering them safest from the ambush attack typical of leopards). Eagle alarm calls caused the monkeys to look up or run to cover. Python alarm calls caused the monkeys to look down at the ground around them. "Such responses suggested that each alarm call effectively represented, or signified, a different class of external danger" (p. 802).

It is interesting to consider the evolution of language in terms of animal communication. The principal factor in language development is believed to be the unusual intellect that is uniquely human; that is, language is a unique reflection of human intellect, and accordingly, it is afforded only to the human (see Lenneberg, 1967). Furthermore, it has been argued that the human vocal tract evolved from something like that of a chimpanzee (e.g., Lieberman & Crelin, 1971; Lieberman, Crelin, & Klatt, 1972). Thus, the attainment of human spoken language must be viewed as the product of a long evolutionary process that involved changes in anatomical structure through mutation, successive variation, and natural selection, which culminated in vocal communication—speech.

SUMMARY

In this chapter, we focused mainly on the functional and informative aspects of sound and hearing, stressing object localization and the perception of music and speech. We began by describing the auditory pathway and cerebral dominance. It was noted that the neural message originating in the left ear is predominantly registered in the auditory region of the right hemisphere of the brain; likewise, the message from the right ear principally affects the left hemisphere. Some of the functional hemispheric differences revealed by using dichotic listening were discussed.

The next section concerned the spatial perception of sounds—their distance and location—on the basis of monaural and especially binaural hearing. Generally, monaural hearing uses the intensity of a sound source, enabling the evaluation of a sound's relative distance. A change in pitch, owing to the Doppler shift, may also signal the relative distance of a moving sound source. However, for precise sound localization, binaural cues are required. The binaural cues of interaural time and intensity differences received from a sound were described, and these were linked to several factors relevant to sound localization, such as the precedence effect, stereophonic listening, the role of head movements and the pinna, and echolocation by animals and humans. The bat's remarkable localization abilities using echolocation were discussed. Hu-

man echolocation focused on the ability of mobile, blind individuals to avoid obstacles. Briefly considered were the role of early experience in the blind individual's nonvisual spatial abilities and research on a personal guidance system as a navigational aid for the blind.

The perception of music was next considered, drawing especially on the notion that music is a psychological experience based on how the listener perceives notes in relation to each other in a specific context. Phenomena relevant to the perception of music were outlined, including elementary musical notation, absolute pitch, and the octave relationship. Drawing on the notion of octave equivalence, we analyzed pitch based on a bidimensional scale, using tone height and tone chroma. We observed that the perception of melodies is based on recognizing certain relational and invariant global features of a musical passage; specifically, perception is based on tendencies of the listener drawn from many of the Gestalt organizing principles, such as proximity, similarity, common fate, closure, and figure–ground perception. A final section described chromesthesia and conditioned color associations, with a brief speculation on the function of music.

Next, the role of the auditory system in speech communication was outlined. Certain physical characteristics of sounds were identified and analyzed in terms of their contribution to production and perception as the basic elements of speech. Included was a discussion of the role of the phoneme and the spectogram in speech perception. We noted that speech perception is robust: reasonably intelligible speech can be perceived in spite of significant distortion and corruption, including the elimination of frequencies, specific sounds, phonemes, and so on.

Several general issues critical to speech perception were discussed. For example, how does the listener separate aspects of the verbal message so that distinct words emerge from a continuous stream of sound? It was noted that word familiarity and linguistic context aid the perception of separate words.

Next, we considered whether speech is a unique acoustic stimulus, requiring a special set of analyzing and processing mechanisms. Several theories and concepts that appear to support this notion were outlined. We began with the motor theory of speech, which assumes that speech perception is based on knowledge of the motor gestures involved in speech production. The notion that speech is special was also supported by categorical perception, the finding that it is easier to discriminate between two phonemes that differ in voice-onset time (VOT), such as /b/ and /p/, than it is to discriminate between two forms of the same phoneme that may have the same difference in VOT, such as pairs of /b/'s or /p/'s. In other words, listeners can discriminate between two similar sounds only if they fall on different sides of a phonemic boundary.

Several neurally based notions that speech is a fundamentally different form of sound were also discussed. Linguistic feature detectors assume that there are specialized neural detectors tuned to react exclusively to specific features of human speech sounds. The speech mode of perception holds that speech perception results from a special processing mode—a speech module—in which sounds that are recognized as speech undergo a unique form of processing and analysis. This led to a description of duplex perception, in which the same physical sound stimuli can simultaneously evoke a nonspeech and a speech mode. The presumed specialness of speech was further supported by the physiological evidence that speech function—both production and recognition—is mediated by specific regions of the brain (Broca's and Wernicke's areas). Finally, in this section we considered how visual factors, such as viewing the speaker's face and lip activity during speech production, aids the perception of speech. We found that auditory and visual cues to speech interact with each other and affect what is heard—the McGurk effect. We concluded that the issue whether speech is a special form of auditory stimulation requiring a special speech processing system remains unresolved.

The tendency to hear distinct and independent auditory sources—auditory streams—from the complex acoustic environment was discussed. This tendency, called auditory scene analysis, is due to an auditory analogue of the Gestalt organizational grouping principles. Features from the complex acoustic scene that promote grouping and form auditory streams were identified.

Lastly, we briefly discussed nonlinguistic aural communication in animals, describing typical sounds produced by dogs and primates that may have particular meanings and communicate specific events.

KEY TERMS

Absolute (Perfect) Pitch

Auditory Cortex

Auditory Scene Analysis

Auditory Streams

Binaural Cues

Broca's Area

Categorical Perception

Cerebral Dominance

Chromesthesia

Context

Dichotic Listening

Doppler Shift

Duplex Perception

Echo Delay-Tuned Neurons

Echolocation

Formants

Frequency Cutoff

Interaural Intensity Difference

Interaural Time Difference

Linguistic Feature Detectors

McGurk Effect

Monaural Cues

Motor Theory

Octave

Octave Equivalence

Personal Guidance System

Phonemes

Phonemic Restoration Effect

Phonetic Boundary

Pinna

Precedence Effect

Selective Adaptation Procedure

Sonar

Spectogram

Speech Blanking

Speech Mode

Stereophonic Listening

Stream Segregation

Synesthesia

Tone Chroma

Tone Height

Voice-Onset Time (VOT)

Wernicke's Area

STUDY QUESTIONS

1. Trace the neural connections of the auditory system from the ear to the brain and describe how they contribute to sound localization.

2. What evidence indicates that the two cerebral hemispheres of the brain are functionally different? Describe the role of dichotic listening in revealing such differences. What are some of the functional differences?

3. Enumerate the monaural and binaural cues for auditory perception. Describe how interaural time and interaural intensity differences contribute to auditory localization. Discuss the precedence effect for auditory localization. How do head movements resolve localization ambiguity, such as when sounds occur in the listener's median plane?

4. Drawing from basic principles on auditory localization, outline a procedure revealing whether someone who claims to be deaf in one ear is faking. Consider the implications of the procedure for auditory localization and stereophonic listening.

5. How does the pinna contribute to auditory localization?

6. What is echolocation, and how is it used by different species? What evidence suggests that humans may be capable of echolocation?

7. Describe the role of sounds and their echoes in the spatial perception of the blind. What aspects of sounds are most informative for localization? How may early visual experience aid the blind in nonvisual spatial localization?

8. How are musical sounds different from nonmusical sounds? What tonal properties and acoustic dimensions enable a succession of sounds to be heard as musical sounds?

9. Identify the notation used to describe musical sounds. Indicate the significance of the octave relationship to the perception of music. Consider why pitch is analyzed in terms of both tone chroma and tone height for musical sounds.

10. What is unique about a melody? Why do melodies remain essentially unchanged in spite of changes in the pitch range of the tones comprising them? What global features and Gestalt organizing principles enter into the perception of a melody?

11. What is chromesthesia? How can it be demonstrated?

12. Outline the human vocal apparatus and its operation in producing speech. What are the physical ranges of speech sounds? What are the fundamental units of speech? Identify the roles of phonemes, vowels, and consonants in speech perception.

13. What is a spectogram? What does it indicate about the link between the flow of acoustic energy and speech perception? Discuss the difficulty in describing speech only on the basis of its physical dimensions.

14. Discuss speech perception when there are acoustic distortions in the speech message. Describe speech perception when selected frequencies are eliminated (i.e., frequency cutoff), when speech sounds are missing, and when speech blanking occurs.

15. Examine the linguistic context in which sounds are heard for speech perception. Describe the phonemic restoration effect.

16. Discuss how discrete words are perceived. Examine the relation between the perception of a series of words and the sequence of sounds in the physical speech flow. How does familiarity

with the sounds of a language contribute to the perception of words?

17. Examine the proposal that speech is a special form of complex acoustic stimulation different from general forms of environmental sounds. Present evidence that both supports and refutes this proposal.

18. What is the motor theory of speech perception? What does it imply about the notion that speech is a special form of stimulation? Examine categorical perception in terms of the specialness of speech stimulation.

19. What are linguistic feature detectors? How does selective adaptation support the notion of linguistic feature detectors? What problems are there for linguistic speech detectors in explaining speech perception?

20. Describe the speech mode of perception, taking duplex perception into account. Discuss how the speech mode may develop.

21. Identify the areas of brain that appear to play a direct role in speech perception.

22. What is the McGurk effect? What does it imply about the contribution of visual information to speech perception?

23. What is auditory scene analysis? Describe auditory streams. What factors help us perceive auditory streams? What enhances stream segregation?

24. Discuss the proposal that animals other than the human produce and perceive sounds for communication. What behaviors and environmental events are especially relevant to animal communication?

chapter 15

THE ORIENTING SENSE

Animals at all levels of evolution that move about must remain oriented to their surroundings: to do so, they have evolved special mechanisms that detect the position and motion of the body in space. Unlike the sensations of sights, sounds, touches, tastes, and smells, the sensations of orientation and movement seem intangible and generally go unnoticed. There are, of course, certain situations in which we do become aware of bodily movement. As we will see, there are unusual conditions of movement and orientation that, as a by-product, yield prominent sensations—dizziness, nausea—that can over-whelm our consciousness. However, even then, the responses induced by abnormal vestibular stimulation occur automatically, without conscious control.

Nevertheless, even though we never become consciously aware of orientation information, it is essential. Orientation is critical for most motor activities involving changes in bodily position, such as maintaining balance and posture, reflexively adjusting eye position when the head is moving, and coordinating overall bodily movement with the environment.

RECEPTORS FOR ORIENTATION

The organs and receptors for detecting orientational information (as well as for hearing in vertebrates) are thought to have evolved from primitive sensory organs located in the fluid-filled depressions in the skin of sea-dwelling animals. These depressions were lined with sensory hair cells, or cilia, receptive to mechanical stimulation: that is, they were sensitive to movements and vibrations of the fluid filling the depression. During evolution, these depressions and their sensory cells and receptors became specialized and account for the bony cavities of the inner ears of mammals (sometimes called the *labyrinth*).

Probably for all animals, *gravity* is the basic plane of reference. Organs and receptors sensitive to gravita-tional force are very old in the evolutionary scale. They are found in every animal phylum, and their general mode of functioning is similar. In all receptors, excitation depends on mechanical changes. Accordingly, they are called **mechanoreceptors.**

In their simplest form, in invertebrates (animals without a backbone), gravity detectors are known as **statocysts** (from the Greek words *statos* for "stationary" and *kystis* for "sac"), and they are perhaps the earliest specialized sense organs to develop in the entire animal kingdom. Although the physical mechanisms of statocysts among animal groups are diverse, their general sensory structure operates on the same basic principle. The statocyst is a fluid-filled cavity lined with a membrane of receptive tissue containing cilia. Small, freely moving particles called **statoliths** (from the Greek *lith,* for "stone") lie within the stato-cyst (Figure 15.1). The statoliths are heavier than the fluid of the statocyst cavity and are relatively free to move. Due to inertial force and gravity, linear bodily movements displace the statoliths relative to the membrane of receptor tissue lined with the ciliated hair cells (Figure 15.2). The statoliths thus react to gravity or linear (straight-line) movement—up–down, forward–backward, left–right—and exert pressure on specific sensory hair cell receptors.

The same general anatomical structures and principles apply to vertebrates. The gravity detectors are called **otocysts** (from the Greek *oto,* for "ear") in vertebrates; the freely moving particles that lie within the otocyst cavity are called **otoliths** (literally, "stones of the ear") and react similarly to gravity or linear movement.

The general principle of processing gravity, linear movement, and inertial force by the use of a statocyst is well illustrated by a crustacean such as a crayfish. The crayfish regularly molts (sheds) the lining of its statocyst along with the rest of its external covering.

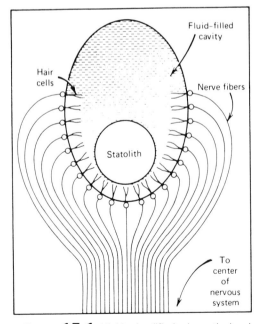

□ *figure 15.1* Highly simplified schematic drawing of a statocyst cavity, statolith, receptive hair cells, and a set of nerve fibers.

The statoliths, which for the crayfish are grains of sand, are also shed while molting. After molting is complete, the crayfish places new grains of sand in the new statocyst with its claws. Like all statoliths, the grains of sand react to inertial forces and thus stimulate the sensory cells as the crayfish moves about.

However, if a crayfish is placed in the unusual laboratory condition where the only potential replacement statoliths available are iron filings, it will also place them in its statocyst. If a magnet is now moved about the head of the crayfish, the replacement statoliths will be attracted and the crayfish will alter its bodily orientation according to the location of the iron filings (this classic experiment was performed by Kreidl in 1893; see Howard, 1982).

MAMMALIAN ORIENTING SYSTEM

The organs for detecting orientational information in mammals are a closely linked set of functional receptive structures called the *saccule,* the *utricle,* and the *semicircular canals.*

Saccule and Utricle

The advanced development of the otocyst mechanism is seen in a set of mammalian structures that are collectively labeled the **vestibular organs** (Figures 15.3 and 15.4): the saccule (from the Latin, *sacculus,* for "little sac"), the utricle (from the Latin, *utriculus,* for "little bag"), and the *semicircular canals* (described in the next section).

The saccule and utricle are fluid-filled, membranous sacs that act as otocysts. The sensory receptor surface of both the saccule and utricle is called the *macula.* As shown in Figure 15.5, the macula is composed of sensory hair cells embedded in the inner surface of the saccule and utricle. According to Howard (1986), there are about 33,000 hair cells in the utricle and about 19,000 in the saccule, the number decreasing with age (Johnsson & Hawkins, 1972). The ciliated hair cells of the macula surface innervate nerve fibers that extend to various regions of the brain, notably the *cerebellum,* a balance center that mediates

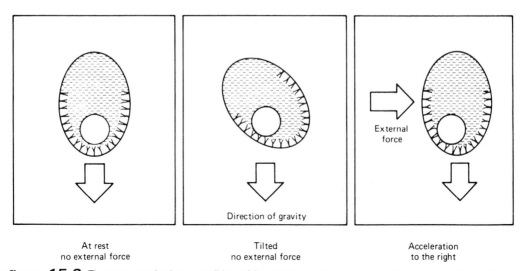

At rest
no external force

Tilted
no external force

Acceleration
to the right

⬄ *figure* **15.2** The statocyst in three conditions. Movement causes the statolith to stimulate different hair cells and, accordingly, register changes in position and linear acceleration.

many of the reflexes involved in coordinated movement.

The otoliths in the saccule and utricle sacs are loosely attached to a gelatinous mass that lies along the surface of the macula. The otoliths are dense calcium carbonate crystals (almost three times as dense as water, according to Parker, 1980). In operation, the hair cells are bent by the otoliths in accordance with the extent and direction of linear displacement and bodily position with respect to gravity. Presumably

when the body is speeding up or slowing down in a straight-line motion (i.e., with linear acceleration or *changes* in the rate of motion), or when the head is tilted, the inertia of the otoliths' particles bends the hair cells, with a resulting discharge by the attached

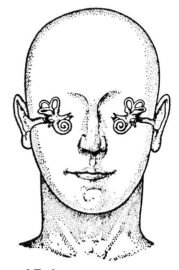

⬄ *figure* **15.4** Schematic of the vestibular organs in the head. For purposes of illustration, the size of the structures is exaggerated and their location is laterally displaced. (Based on Krech & Crutchfield, 1958.)

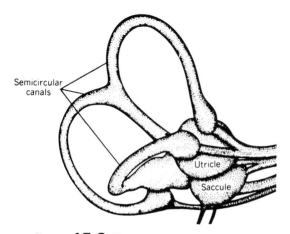

⬄ *figure* **15.3** The human vestibular organs. (Based on Mueller, 1965.)

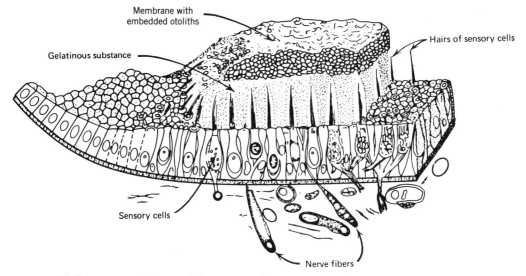

Membrane with
embedded otoliths

Hairs of sensory cells

Gelatinous substance

Sensory cells

Nerve fibers

□ **figure 15.5** Structure of the macula in cross section.

nerve fibers. The saccule is so positioned that its stato-liths register vertical (up–down) movement of the body, whereas the utricle senses horizontal linear movement; however, both react to gravity.

Semicircular Canals

The functioning of the saccule and utricle overlaps with that of a second dynamic vestibular organ whose primary function is to register the direction and extent of circular movement, or *rotary acceleration*. Most vertebrates, from fish up, have developed specialized structures to detect rotary acceleration called **semicircular canals.** Semicircular canals are fluid-filled enclosures that lie approximately at right angles to each other, and each canal relates to a major plane of the body (Figure 15.6). Together the canals form a three-coordinate system to which rotary motion of the body can be referred. In other words, since the three semicircular canals lie in different planes, they detect angular acceleration of the head in any direction in three-dimensional space.

Each canal widens at its base into a somewhat spherical, fluid-filled chamber called an *ampulla,* which contains the vestibular receptors (Figure 15.7). Each ampulla contains a tongue-shaped sensory struc-

ture called the *cupula.* The cupula is composed of crests of hair tufts from the vestibular nerve and is encased in a gelatinous mass (Figure 15.8). The cupula has a fixed base called the *crista,* which houses the sensory hair cells and fibers of the vestibular nerve. However, it swings freely into the ampullar cavity and can be bent by pressure of the fluid in the canal. This movement at the crista for a given canal stimulates the hair cells, which transmit impulses on the nature of the movement to the brain.

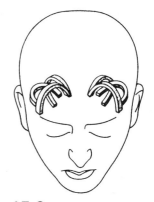

□ **figure 15.6** Highly schematic drawing of the semicircular canals. They are approximately at right angles to each other. (Based on Mueller, 1965.)

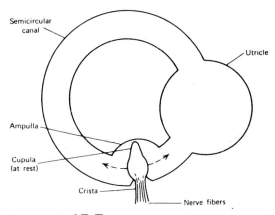

□ **figure 15.7** Schematic of a semicircular canal with ampulla, cupula, and crista. The dashed arrows indicate the potential deflection of the cupula by displacement of the endolymph fluid produced by appropriate rotation of the head.

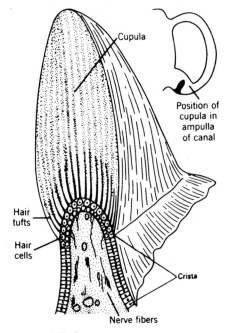

□ **figure 15.8** Cross section of the cupula, showing the ridge of hair tufts and cells fixed at the base (crista). The small insert shows the position of the ampulla of the semicircular canal.

Figure 15.9 shows the activity of the cupula and crista of a single canal during rotary acceleration, such as when the head is turned, or rotated, on a given axis. The fluid of the canal circulates and becomes displaced in accordance with the head turn, creating pressure. This pressure causes a bending of the cupula that is proportional to the force of the head turn. The rotary acceleration thus causes specific deflection of the cupula (and stimulation of the hair cell receptors in each canal) and is analyzable into its spatial components. When the rotation stops or its rate stabilizes, the deflection is canceled and the cupula returns to its normal position. In contrast, linear acceleration and gravitational force have little effect on the cupula.

Vestibular Stimulation

The orienting system evolved as an adaptation to the conditions that normally confront animals, such as active movements and perhaps brief passive movements. It is not surprising, then, that the system is not well suited to cope with spatial conditions that rarely

□ **figure 15.9** Schematic of activity of the cupula and crista during rotary head movement. When the head starts turning, the fluid of the ampulla at first lags behind, bending the cupula and the hair tufts of the crista in the direction opposite to the head movement. As the movement of the head continues, the ampullar fluid and the cupula move at the same rate as the rotary movement of the head, and the hair tufts of the crista become erect (which also occurs when there is no head movement). As long as the head is moving in a constant direction and at a constant speed, the cupula and the hair tufts of the crista remain erect. However, when the head movement stops, the inertial force of the ampullar fluid carries the cupula forward and the hair tufts are bent in the forward direction. Thus, starts and stops move the fluid of the semicircular canals, bend the cupula, deform the hair tufts, and stimulate the hair cells of the crista, whereas constant motion, as shown in the central figure, produces no deflection and transmits no neural impulses. (Based on Krech and Crutchfield, 1958.)

or never occur. For example, the vestibular system does not register sustained passive movements at a constant rate. If the velocity is kept stable, as n high-speed vehicular transport (e.g., trains, planes, or elevators), motion is not detectable. This follows from the fact that with constant passive motion the fluids, otoliths, and receptors soon move at the same speed, gravitational and inertial forces are overcome, and there is no relative movement between the components of the vestibular mechanism: hence, there is no stimulation.

The kinds of motion to which the vestibular receptors respond are acceleration or deceleration—*changes in the rate of motion.* In other words, the vestibular organs are suited to detect starts and stops and changes in motion, *not* constant velocities.

Although head movements are adequate stimuli for the vestibular organs, the receptors can be stimulated experimentally by electrical, mechanical, chemical, or even thermal stimuli. For example, since vestibular organs are kept thermally constant, they may be stimulated by irrigation of the external auditory canal with water that is either warmer or colder than the canal wall (generally, cold water is used). This produces a heat exchange that is readily transmitted to the vestibular organs, particularly to the fluid of the semicircular canal. The heating or cooling of the fluid causes it to expand or contract, respectively; this, in turn, causes upward or downward movement of the fluid, which then deflects the cupula (Wendt, 1951). This form of cupula displacement produces a brief feeling of bodily motion, which may even induce reflexive eye movements and a change in the posture of the head even though the visual scene remains unchanged.

Vestibular Nystagmus and Vestibulo-Ocular Eye Movements

Stimulation of the vestibular receptors is transmitted to the lower centers of the brain (e.g., the cerebellum), from which connections are made with motor fibers to the neck, trunk, limb, and ocular muscles. Of particular concern here is the relation of bodily position to patterns of eye movements. When an individual is rotated about his or her body axis, the resulting stimulation of the semicircular canals creates rhythmic, reflexive eye movements. During the acceleration, the eyes move slowly opposite to the movement of the rotation and then rapidly back; during deceleration, the direction of eye movements reverses. These rhythmic, reflexive eye movements in response to stimulation of the semicircular canals from rotary movement are termed **vestibular nystagmus.** Vestibular nystagmus appears to be a fundamental response to rotation, occurring in all vertebrates with mobile eyes; it is also quite prominent in the newborn human (Howard, 1986).

Vestibular stimulation also causes eye movements that help us perceive a constant, stable visual environment. As we move in space, our heads bob and weave continuously. To adjust for changes in the visual imagery due to this continual head movement, our eyes change their position accordingly. Recall from Chapter 4 (see Figure 4.16) that *vestibulo-ocular eye movements* help stabilize vision by coordinating eye and head positions. This is done by a complex reflex system that smoothly, effortlessly, and automatically compensates for each head movement by an equal and opposite movement of the eyes. Thus, for example, if you lock your gaze on an object in the environment while turning your head to the right, your eyes automatically move to the left; the result is that the visual image of the fixated object remains stabilized on the retina.

Visually Induced Illusions of Movement

Self-Vection Sometimes observers report that they are moving when in fact they are stationary and the visual field is in motion. Perhaps the most common such experience, **self-vection,** occurs when an observer, looking out of the window of a stationary train that restricts viewing to a nearby moving train, erroneously perceives that his or her train is in motion. The illusion is especially strong when the nearby train is viewed out of the corner of the eye. In this situation, there is ambiguous visual stimulation concerning movement but no vestibular stimulation concerning movement. In other words, lacking any vestibular information and using vision alone, *either* train can be perceived as moving. However, there seems to be a basic tendency to perceive a stable, constant visual environment, so that the observer usually perceives the visual field as stationary and erroneously senses that his or her own train is moving. Moreover, to a stationary passenger in this ambiguous situation, the *entire* visual scene as observed from the window (which is limited to the image of the nearby train) appears to move. This global visual scene in motion simulates what we typically see while moving through a stationary environment. In other words, we normally see the *total* scene move only when we are actually moving relative to a stationary environment. Hence, in an ambiguous situation, when vision tells us that the environment is moving, we reasonably (but in error) attribute the movement to ourselves.

Postural Sway Experiments involving conditions similar to those that produce self-vection illustrate the compelling role of vision in the illusion of bodily movement and the control of posture. Lee and his colleagues (Lee & Aronson, 1974; Lishman & Lee, 1973) observed that when a stationary observer is enclosed in an illuminated box room whose walls and ceiling can swing back and forth, the observer begins to sway in synchrony with the swinging room. As shown in Figure 15.10, **postural sway** is imposed by the movement of the visual surroundings, and it occurs in the direction in which the room is moved. This makes sense because the swinging room duplicates the optical stimulation that normally results when the body actually swings back and forth. Thus, in the experiment, when the walls and ceiling of the swinging room moved toward the stationary observer, they produced the visual stimulation that would occur if the observer was actually swaying forward in a stationary room; accordingly, to correct or compensate for the apparent forward movement, the observer leaned backward. Correspondingly, when the swinging room moved away from the stationary observer, it duplicated the visual stimulus that the observer was swaying backward, so the observer leaned forward.

Note that postural adjustment, or sway, occurs only in response to a changing visual scene with no corresponding vestibular stimulation. Postural sway applies to infants as well as adults, although it is more pronounced in infants, often resulting in a loss of balance or even a fall in the direction in which the swinging room is moved (see Butterworth & Hicks, 1977).

As we have seen, visually induced sensations of motion often appear equivalent to those produced by actual bodily motion. This suggests that movement of the visual scene alone has the same or a similar effect on the individual's nervous system as does stimulation of the vestibular organs. In fact, there is evidence of cortical cells in lower animals that react both to direct stimulation of the vestibular organs *and* to motion of the visual environment (Daunton & Thomsen, 1979; Dichgans & Brandt, 1978).

DEMONSTRATION:
The Role of Vision on Maintaining Balance

The above observations underscore the importance of vision in bodily orientation. The critical role of vision in maintaining postural stability and balance can be easily demonstrated. Stand on one foot, raising the knee of the other foot to about waist level. With your eyes open, you will likely have little difficulty balancing on one foot. However, when you try this with your eyes closed, maintaining balance becomes difficult. This shows the importance of visual surroundings in enabling us to adjust our muscles continuously and smoothly to maintain our balance.

Vestibular Habituation

The vestibular system is subject to **adaptation** and **habituation:** If acceleration or rotation is sustained, the feeling of motion will gradually decrease and eventually may totally subside. Technically, the long-term decrease in vestibular effects with prolonged exposure is termed vestibular *habituation;* by contrast, *adaptation* effects are rapidly induced and dissipated.

Movement of room →

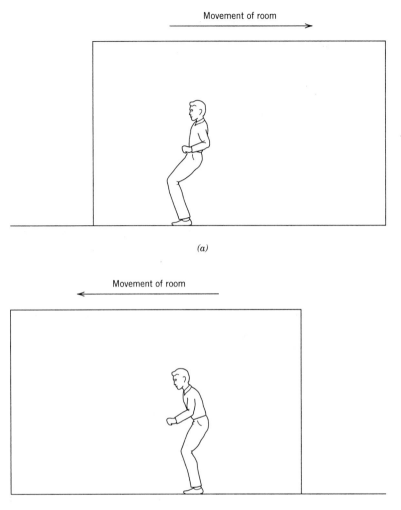

(a)

← Movement of room

(b)

☐ **figure 15.10** Effect of the visual scene on postural sway. When the walls and ceiling surrounding a stationary observer begin to move, the observer begins to sway in synchrony. As shown in (a), when the room moves toward the stationary observer, the visual scene projected is the one that would normally accompany forward movement; as a compensatory postural adjustment the observer sways backward. Correspondingly, as shown in (b), when the room moves away from the stationary observer, it creates a visual scene that would result if the observer actually moved backward; in compensation for the apparent movement of the room, the observer sways forward.

Nystagmus (reflexive eye movements) may habituate with long exposure to the abnormal vestibular stimulation that occurs with continual motion, such as in sailors, aviators, acrobats, and dancers. Other results of rotation, such as vertigo (the sensation of whirling accompanied by involuntary swaying), dizziness, and nausea, also habituate for these individuals. For example, experienced figure skaters were reported to be able to walk straight ahead after being rotated in a chair: the usual tendency of naïve skaters to veer off had been completely habituated (McCabe, in Marler & Hamilton, 1966).

Several techniques can either reduce or even override certain vestibular phenomena while the body remains in motion. Ballet dancers, for example, are known to reduce nystagmus while spinning by "spotting": fixating their gaze on some distant point, generally in the audience. Typically, the dancer keeps the head pointing to the audience as long as possible and then flicks the head around faster than the body until it again faces the same way and can regain fixation. While the body of the dancer is continually moving, the vestibular organs are stimulated *only* during the head movement that serves to regain fixation on the distant point. Thus, spotting reduces vestibular stimulation while providing a somewhat stable visual environment.

Deficiencies of the Vestibular Mechanism

A cat or rabbit suspended upside down by its paws and then released, whether in a light or dark environment, will usually right itself during the fall (in less than a second) and land on its feet (Figure 15.11). This is known as the **air-righting reflex** (Howard, 1986; Warkentin & Carmichael, 1939). This feat of bodily orientation in midair, physically extremely complex, is controlled by the vestibular organs. An animal lacking proper vestibular functioning does not show this adaptive reaction to falling and lands in a heap (e.g., Watt, 1976).

In the human, the loss of vestibular function is accompanied by a general disorientation that eventually subsides. Initially the individual cannot stand upright steadily with the eyes closed and may suffer from vertigo. However, with the use of vision the individual eventually compensates for the loss. In congenitally deaf individuals, whose vestibular organs may be totally degenerate (due to the close anatomical and physiological relationship of the vestibular organs to the auditory ones), equilibrium and postural adjustment are effective. However, when the use of vision is reduced or visual cues are ambiguous, general bodily orientation is sharply reduced. Boring (1942, p. 542) writes that some deaf people do not go very deep underwater when swimming because what is up and down get confused and there is danger of drowning.

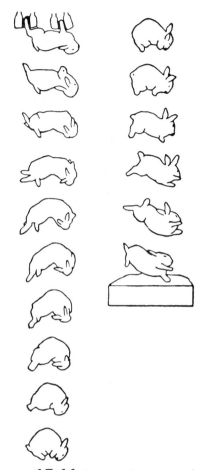

▭ figure 15.11 Tracings of successive frames of a motion picture (64 frames per second) of a 20-day-old rabbit dropped while upside down. (From G. R. Wendt, "Vestibular functions," in S. S. Stevens, (Ed.), *Handbook of Experimental Psychology*, Chap. 31, John Wiley, New York, 1951; and J. Warkentin and L. A. Carmichael, "A study of the development of the air-righting reflex in cats and rabbits," *Journal of Genetic Psychology, 55,* 1939, pp. 67–80. Reprinted by permission of the Helen Dwight Reid Educational Foundation. Published by Heldref Publications, 4000 Albemarle St., N. W., Washington, D. C. 20016, Copyright © 1939.)

This underscores the point that the sense of orientation—the nonvisual awareness of which way is up and which way is down—is derived from vestibular detectors.

Individuals both deaf and blind face a more serious problem in maintaining equilibrium. Of a group of 10 deaf-blind subjects, 9 were unable to maintain balance for more than a second or two when standing on one foot (Worshel & Dallenbach, 1948). Furthermore, the same nine subjects showed no vestibular nystagmus, nausea, dizziness, or vertigo after 30 sec of rotation. It is likely that these subjects had absolutely no vestibular function. It follows that individuals who suffer total loss of vestibular function are not susceptible to motion sickness (Reason & Brand, 1975).

Ménière's Disease   There is an incurable condition that affects both vestibular function and hearing. It is held to be due to an overproduction and elevated pressure of the enclosed fluid of the labyrinth (i.e., the inner ear and the vestibular organs). The patient afflicted with **Ménière's disease** experiences episodes of sudden, violent vestibular activity causing turbulent nystagmic eye movements, extreme vertigo, severe nausea, and often distortions in hearing; high-pitched sounds especially may sound tinny, hollow, or fuzzy.

Ménière's disease is often progressive; in later stages, hearing and vestibular function may be permanently lost. While there is no cure, surgery can sometimes drain off excess fluid, relieving pressure on the inner ear and reducing the debilitating symptoms. There is also a drastic procedure to alleviate the symptoms that essentially severs the vestibular nerve to the brain.

Relatedly, it is possible that unusual physical activity may cause some damage to the vestibular organs. Weintraub (1994) reports that for some enthusiasts, regular high-impact aerobic activity (at least 3 to 4 days a week) can injure the otoliths and distort the signals from the vestibular organs. The cause of the damage appears to be the intense, repetitive jarring produced by the aerobic activity. Among the most common effects of the vestibular damage are vertigo with accompanying orientation and balance problems.

MOTION SICKNESS

When we enter a vehicle or device that transports us passively, we may experience the effects of unusual or abnormal vestibular stimulation. In certain controlled conditions, this experience can be positive. For many individuals, driving, sailing, skiing, and flying are appealing. Moreover, some people enjoy activities that severely challenge their vestibular and visual systems. This is amply verified by the popularity of amusement park rides—from the mild rotation of the merry-go-round to the extremely complex motions induced by the roller coaster and even more exotic rides.

However, some of these same motions may induce an extremely unpleasant experience. Perhaps the most immediate, distressing, and debilitating feature of abnormal vestibular stimulation is **motion sickness.** This widespread sensation occurs in a number of species as well as the human (though usually not in the infant), including monkeys, sheep, horses, and some birds and fish, but apparently not in rabbits or guinea pigs (Treisman, 1977). In the human it is disabling and extremely unpleasant, causing dizziness, pallor, nausea, vertigo, hyperventilation, "cold sweating," and general malaise, often accompanied by vomiting.

Motion sickness often occurs when motion information signaled by vision is mismatched with that signaled by the vestibular sense. In addition, the potentially sickness-inducing motion seems to involve acceleration (or deceleration). Thus, motion sickness does not generally result from being transported at a steady speed.

Some forms of motion are more likely to produce motion sickness than others. Motion sickness can be produced by repeated vertical motion of moderate frequency—for example, the pattern of motion affecting a passive, seated passenger in turbulent air on an aircraft or on a heaving ship in rough water. In fact, the word "nausea" derives from the Greek word *nautia,* for "seasickness."

Active versus Passive Movement

An important factor in motion sickness is whether the individual is *actively* or *passively* moved. Generally, motion sickness does not result from active, self-produced movement. Thus, a series of short, self-imposed, rapidly repeated movements, as in walking, jogging, and running, are not effective. Similarly, motion sickness is less frequent and severe when the individual is passively moved but can exert some control over the movement. For example, the driver of a car, while still transported passively, is less likely than a passenger to become sick. Perhaps this is because the driver—clearly the more active member—plays a principal role in inducing the movement. Thus, the driver can anticipate the movement and make compensatory motor adjustments to maintain proper orientation and match the visual to the vestibular input.

Other common passively experienced events, even with no actual bodily movement, may also cause motion sickness: visual disorientation, visual illusions of movement, unpleasant odors, uncomfortable warmth, drugs (e.g., alcohol, narcotics), inner ear infections, prolonged exposure to loud sounds, and certain emotional factors, such as anxiety, may contribute.

Cause of Motion Sickness: Sensory Conflict Theory

The vestibular and visual systems are consistent and closely correlated spatial reference systems. Ordinarily, the sensory inputs for both systems function together and are continuously coordinated with each other in maintaining body equilibrium and general orientation. However, a series of irregular or unpredictable, passive movements can disrupt this relationship and produce a sensory conflict. According to the **sensory conflict theory,** the disparity between visual and vestibular information on spatial orientation causes motion sickness. For example, a ship's cabin in choppy waters is a stable visual environment, but the vestibular organs register the body in continual movement. It is the inability of the nervous system to resolve this sensory conflict that induces the compelling and disturbing effects of motion sickness.

Treisman (1977) proposes an interesting explanation of why the sensory conflict may induce vomiting. It is based on the fact that the visual–vestibular sensory conflict resulting from irregular passive movements simulates the same effects that occur when natural poisons are ingested. In fact, poisons that affect the central nervous system are likely to alter the visual input and disrupt motor coordination in the same way that unusual passive movement does. That is, the

ingestion of a poison also disrupts the closely linked visual and vestibular inputs.

It follows, then, that vomiting in response to repeated sensory conflict is beneficial and even adaptive if the sensory conflict is due to a poison. Clearly, it would serve as an early warning system for detecting the central effects of the poison and, further, provides a means of eliminating it from the body—by *vomiting*. In fact, dogs that have had their vestibular organs removed do not vomit after ingesting poisons (Money & Cheung, 1983).

Thus, according to Treisman, it is the avoidance of food poisoning that provides the biological incentive for motion sickness. Viewed this way, motion sickness (especially vomiting) is a biologically adaptive response to an *inappropriate stimulus* (i.e., motion rather than poison). In other words, motion sickness is a response to *any* of the conditions that generate repeated challenges to the closely correlated vestibular and visual reference systems.

Reducing Motion Sickness

One obvious way to reduce motion sickness is to minimize body movements, especially head movements when the body moves. If independent head movements are allowed, especially during body rotation, complex forces act on the vestibular system, increasing the possibility and severity of motion sickness. For some individuals, motion sickness may be relieved or reduced if the information provided by the visual sense is made somewhat consistent with the vestibular stimulation. In the cabin of a continuously heaving ship, the individual could gaze out at the rough water and anticipate the movements of the ship (and one's body); alternatively, the individual could use the horizon as a constant reference signaling that he or she is indeed rocking up and down. But for most individuals who are especially prone to motion sickness, even with these precautions, the abnormal, passively imposed motion signals are often too upsetting for anything but a moderate reduction in the distress experienced.

Fortunately, most individuals eventually habituate to the stimuli that cause motion sickness. Some of these conditions are habituated to quickly; others require a few hours or longer. For example, the motion-induced distress of astronauts in orbit is eliminated only after about 5 days of flight (Lackner & Grabiel, 1986). Moreover, there are numerous so-called motion sickness drugs that, when taken beforehand, reduce, inhibit, and even prevent some of the symptoms of motion sickness (e.g., Graybiel & Lackner, 1987). Most of the drugs (e.g., Dramamine, Bonine, meclizine, promethazine, and scopolomine, which can even be administered gradually by a skin patch worn behind the ear) depress the central nervous system by decreasing the activity of certain neurotransmitters.

Finally, we must consider the wider biological implications of motion sickness and make an obvious point: although motion sickness is a wretched and debilitating experience, it is also a self-inflicted one. Motion sickness is just one of the biological results of using modern technology to improve passive human travel. In contrast, the human vestibular system, along with those of most forms of earth-bound life, is limited to serving a totally self-propelled animal: that is, it is basically suited to animals that actively move about in a three-dimensional world, subject to normal earth gravity—not animals that are passively transported.

OTHER MECHANISMS FOR ORIENTATION

In the human, bodily orientation is produced by a complex interaction between visual and vestibular stimulation (e.g., Nemire & Cohen, 1993; Witkin, 1959). However, as we have seen, visual input usually dominates vestibular input. It follows that injury to the vestibular organs of the human (and of primates in general) is less serious than it is for most lower animals, especially nocturnal ones, whose vision is relatively ineffective in bodily orientation.

On the other hand, some lower animals have orientation mechanisms that are not available to the human. For example, modified mechanoreceptors found in many species of fish are specialized to detect electric fields. In addition, fish possess a specialized structure that is highly susceptible to low-frequency vibrations or pressure changes in the surrounding water. It appears as a line running along the side of the fish's body from head to tail called the *lateral line*. A small, fluid-filled tube that runs under the skin beneath the lateral line contains bundles of sensory cells that respond to faint vibratory stimuli. The lateral line provides information on orientation and localization (e.g., Weiss, 1969; Weiss & Martini, 1970) and is especially useful in detecting the location of prey (Montgomery & MacDonald, 1987).

Magnetic Sense

In various species, there is evidence of a **magnetic sense** for certain forms of orientation. Honeybees appear to orient to the earth's magnetic fields (i.e., magnetic force fields that flow around the earth from the South Pole to the North Pole) aided by magnetic material located in the front of their abdomen (Gould, Kirschvink, & Diffeyes, 1978). Similarly, Lohmann and Lohmann (1994) have reported that turtles have magnetic mineral particles in their brains that enable them to use the earth's magnetic field as a navigational aid.

There is also evidence that the pigeon's legendary homing ability may be aided by magnetic field information (Kirschvink, Jones, & MacFadden, 1985; Walcott, Gould, & Kirschvink, 1979). When the pickup of information about the earth's magnetic field is disrupted, such as by attaching small magnets to their heads, pigeons usually fail to orient properly; this is especially the case when other visual navigational cues are unavailable (such as on cloudy days). However, some studies with pigeons have failed to demonstrate a magnetic sense, so this issue remains unresolved (e.g., Griffin, 1987).

The goal orientation behavior of blindfolded humans over long distances raises the possibility of a *human magnetic sense* (Baker, 1980; Baker, Mather, & Kennaugh, 1983; see Barinaga, 1992). In one experiment (Baker, 1980), 31 blindfolded subjects were driven in a complex, roundabout way 16 km from a home site; 15 of them wore bar magnets fastened at the backs of their heads. When they were tested for orientation (i.e., to indicate the direction of the home site), the estimations made by subjects who wore magnets were found to be much less accurate than those of the subjects who did not. In fact, the direction estimates of the group that did not wear magnets were significantly clustered toward the home site. The results, while far from conclusive, lend some support to the possibility of a magnetic sense for goal orientation in the blindfolded human. However, as with the research on pigeons, further confirmation of a magnetic sense for humans (and other mammals) is lacking. (See Gould & Able, 1981, and Adler & Pelke, 1985, for failures to replicate this finding with humans. See Madden & Phillips, 1987, for negative findings with small mammals.) It appears that if a magnetic sense does indeed exist, it is extremely weak.

SUMMARY

This chapter covered the orienting system, the sensory system that enables the organism to orient physically to its environment. In mammals, the sensory organs that do this are the saccule, the utricle, and the semicircular canals, collectively labeled the vestibular organs. The saccule and utricle register gravity and linear acceleration (or deceleration), and the semicircular canals register the direction and extent of rotary acceleration. The effective stimulation for the vestibular system is acceleration or deceleration—changes in the rate of motion. The vestibular organs do not register constant or uniform velocities.

Several conditions due to vestibular activity were presented. Vestibular nystagmus is the reflexive movements of the eye caused by vestibular stimulation. Two visually induced illusions of movement were described: self-vection and postural sway. It was noted that the vestibular system habituates and adapts to continual, uniform vestibular stimulation.

Some deficiencies of the vestibular system were discussed. We considered the air-righting reflex in some small mammals, Ménière's disease in the human, and the possibility that high-impact aerobics can injure the vestibular organs.

Next, we discussed the effect of passive movements and the sensory conflict between vestibular and visual input concerning bodily orientation in causing motion sickness. The nature of motion sickness was

considered, and some guidelines were offered on how to reduce it.

In the final section, we described several alternatives to the vestibular system for orientation. It was noted that fish have receptors sensitive to electric fields, as well as a specialized structure sensitive to low-frequency vibrations called the lateral line. We briefly discussed the possibility that a number of animal species, including the human, have a magnetic sense.

KEY TERMS

Adaptation

Air-Righting Reflex

Habituation

Magnetic Sense

Mechanoreceptor

Ménière's Disease

Motion Sickness

Otocyst

Otolith

Postural Sway

Saccule

Self-Vection

Semicircular Canals

Sensory Conflict Theory

Statocyst

Statolith

Utricle

Vestibular Nystagmus

Vestibular Organs

STUDY QUESTIONS

1. Identify the receptors and structures for registering gravity and body orientation in space. Explain how they function.

2. Describe the mechanism used by mammals to register the direction and extent of rotary acceleration. What general principle do the saccule and utricle share with the semicircular canals?

3. The vestibular system is best suited to detect what kinds of environmental movement? It is least suited to register what sorts of movement?

4. Describe vestibular nystagmus and vestibulo-ocular eye movements. What kinds of motion cause these reflexive eye movements?

5. What are self-vection and postural sway? Explain the role of visual stimulation in producing these reactions. Compare the roles of visual stimulation and vestibular stimulation in maintaining postural stability and balance.

6. Consider the habituation and adaptation of the vestibular system to sustained motion. What are some techniques used by persons such as dancers to overcome the side effects of sustained motion?

7. Identify and describe some of the deficiencies of the vestibular function. What effect does vestibular deficiency have on the air-righting reflex? How do individuals who lack or have defective vestibular function react to motion?

8. What is motion sickness, and what are its effects? What role does the vestibular system play in causing motion sickness?

9. What sorts of motion are most likely to promote motion sickness? Consider the role of head movements.

10. Explain why active movement is less likely to promote motion sickness than passive motion.

11. Describe the sensory conflict theory of motion sickness.

12. In what ways is motion sickness a result of advances in technology? Describe how motion sickness can be considered a self-inflicted disorder.

13. Explain the effects of motion sickness as an adaptive response to the ingestion of a poison.

14. Are there alternatives to the vestibular system for gaining information on body orientation? Which mechanism is used by fish? What is the status of a magnetic sense for spatial orientation?

chapter 16

THE SKIN SENSES

*T*his chapter is devoted to perceptions received by the skin or the cutaneous sense (from the Latin, cutis, for "skin"). The skin responds to physical events next to the organism; accordingly, it gives information about the nature of surfaces and objects that directly contact it. Thus, we perceive objects and surfaces by touching and being touched, we feel warmth and coldness, and we experience pain. However, cutaneous sensitivity is not restricted to these broad sensory events. We also feel complex "blended" sensations such as oiliness, stickiness, wetness, tickle, roughness, smoothness, itch, vibration, and so on. Moreover, by feeling objects, such as when we handle or grasp them, we can also recognize their three-dimensional shape. In this case, we not only use touch or pressure information from the skin, we also incorporate stress and strain information—kinesthetic *information*—from the muscles, tendons, and joints of the fingers and hands. Kinesthetic and cutaneous information are sometimes collectively labeled the "bodily" sense or somesthesis.

Generally, cutaneous information is registered by direct mechanical stimulation of the body's surface or by thermal stimulation from a radiant source. In the human this stimulation comes mainly from the skin, particularly certain appendages such as the hands and fingers. However, cutaneous information is picked up not only directly by the skin but also indirectly by other surface structures such as hairs and nails. In lower animals, pressure stimulation may also come from claws, hooves, horns, vibrissae (whiskers), and antennae—intermediate structures that separate an organism from its environment.

The skin sense differs from other senses in that its receptors are not restricted to a specialized, well-defined, localized sensory structure, like the retina for vision or the cochlea for hearing. Instead, its sensory surface covers nearly the entire body, and it serves many purposes—especially protective ones—besides mediating cutaneous sensations. However, this in no way lessens its critical value as a sensory organ. Consider how the sensory world would be reduced if we suddenly lost the ability to feel anything. Aside from the immediate loss of pressure, thermal, and pain sensations, we would lose the ability to move about. Without feedback from touch, even the most ordinary skilled movements of the limbs would be unlikely; consider the difficulty in walking after your foot has "fallen asleep." Or consider the effect on the touch-sensitive face when the lips, mouth, or tongue have been anesthetized by novocaine. The affected parts of the face become totally nonfunctional, and eating and even speaking may be difficult or even impossible.

In this chapter, we will first describe the receptors and structures of the skin and indicate their connection to the brain. Then we will discuss the mechanisms and phenomena specific to touch or pressure, followed by the perception of temperature and, lastly, pain. One emphasis, evident throughout the chapter, is on the unusual array of functional, adaptive information about the environment provided by the skin.

FUNCTIONS OF THE SKIN: PROTECTION AND SENSATION

The human skin, viewed both as a sensory organ and as a protective organ, is remarkable. The skin is by far the largest organ, covering the entire body. The adult human of average weight and body build has about 3000 in.^{2} (about 1.8 m^2) of skin area (this is about 1000 times the area of the retinal surface); on average, the skin weighs about 9 lb (4 to 5 kg). The vastness of the skin as a sensory organ is suggested by Figure 16.1. In contrast to the magnitude of its area, the skin is quite thin, although it is much thinner in some areas than in others: in facial regions it may be as thin as 0.5 mm, whereas on the sole of the foot it may be 4.0 mm or more.

The skin is also the most versatile sensory organ of the body, serving as a flexible, continuously renewable shield against many foreign agents and mechanical injury. It holds in vital body fluids. It wards off the harmful light waves (ultraviolet and infrared radiation) of the sun and, by means of its pigmentation, protects against the loss of light-sensitive elements. When appropriate, it regulates and stabilizes body temperature (in birds and mammals), either cooling the body or limiting heat loss. It also helps to regulate the pressure and direction of blood flow.

Finally, as a sensory organ, the skin has specialized

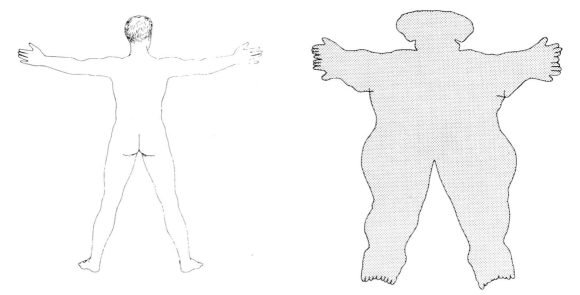

□ *figure* **16.1** Total surface area of the skin (right). It seems surprisingly large in contrast to the outline of the human figure (left). It was calculated by adding the areas of a series of cylinders constructed from an average of leg, arm, and torso circumferences. (From W. Montagna, "The skin," *Scientific American,* 1965, pp. 58–59. Copyright 1965 by Scientific American, Inc. All rights reserved.)

nerve endings embedded in it that can be stimulated in a variety of ways to mediate different sensations. These nerve endings inform the organism of what is next to the body, including thermal information and especially unpleasant, potentially harmful stimuli.

Externally, the skin is a highly irregular covering with a variety of surface qualities and extensions—hairs, ridges, grooves and creases, valleys and pores, colorations and thicknesses—in different areas. However, an internal view indicates that the skin is not a single structural unit but is composed of layers. These layers, along with sensory nerve endings, are identified and illustrated in cross section in Figure 16.2. The *epidermis,* or outer part of the skin, is composed of two to four layers, depending on the area of the body it covers. The *dermis,* or inner part of the skin, has two layers and contains the nerve endings of the cutaneous receptors.

Cutaneous Sensitivity

The sensory effect of skin stimulation is termed **cutaneous sensitivity.** Three primary cutaneous qualities have been identified: *pressure* or *touch* (also referred to as *contact, tactual,* or *tactile stimulation*), *temperature* (cold or warm), and *pain.*

Regional Distribution of Cutaneous Sensitivity

One of the first things to be noted about the skin is that its surface is not uniformly sensitive to cutaneous stimulation. If we drew a grid of millimeter squares on part of the skin of a blindfolded observer and systematically explored the squares of that grid in turn with a heated rod and a cold rod, a stiff, fine hair filament, and a needle point, our observer would probably report the cutaneous sensations of warmth, cold, pressure, and pain, respectively.

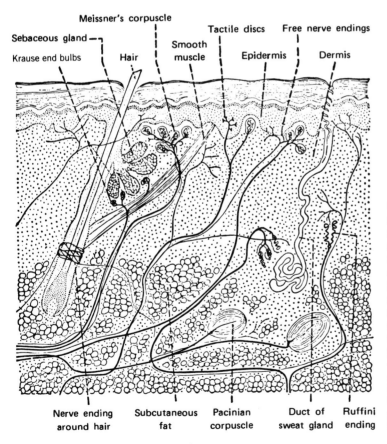

□ *figure 16.2* Composite diagram of the skin in cross section. The chief layers—epidermis, dermis, and subcutaneous tissue—are shown, as are also a hair follicle, the smooth muscle that erects the hair, and several kinds of nerve endings. The epidermis contains tactile discs and free nerve endings; in the dermis are Meissner corpuscles, Krause end bulbs, and Ruffini endings. The subcutaneous tissue is chiefly fatty and vascular but contains Pacinian corpuscles, the largest of the specialized nerve endings. (From E. Gardner, *Fundamentals of Neurology,* W. B. Saunders, Philadelphia, 1947. Reprinted by permission of the author and publisher.)

A plot of the regional distribution of sensitive "spots" would form a map of cutaneous sensitivity. However, in mapping all the spots for which temperature, pain, and pressure are represented, we find that regions of the skin are not uniformly sensitive to all cutaneous stimuli. Some areas may be sensitive to very slight pressure, whereas others are insensitive to even intense pressure. Some areas may be sensitive to warm and relatively insensitive to cold stimuli or the reverse. Moreover, while most regions of the skin are sensitive to pain, different regions may be much more sensitive than others.

It has been proposed that different sensory qualities are mediated by different receptors embedded in the skin (e.g., Uttal, 1973, pp. 131–136). This would mean that, for example, regions that are sensitive to warm—"warm spots"—but not to cold are innervated by distinct "warm" fibers. However, as we shall see in the next section, the evidence for this is not conclusive.

Cutaneous Receptors   Some of the proposed nerve endings for cutaneous receptors are identified and shown in cross section in Figure 16.2. About 95% of the skin surface of human female and male bodies is covered with hairs (most of which are not easily visible); the presumed major nerve endings for hairy skin regions are called *basket cells* (because they resemble a woven basket wrapped around the bottom of the hair shaft embedded within the inner skin layer). The hairless remainder of the skin, called *glabrous* skin, is thicker, and is found on the smooth surfaces of the soles and toes of the feet, the palms and fingers of the hand, and certain facial regions, including the lips and mouth. The primary sensory receptors for the sparse glabrous skin are specialized structures called *encapsulated end organs,* which come in a wide variety of forms. The major nerve endings embedded in glabrous skin are the deeply placed **Pacinian corpuscles** which have an onion-like appearance (other presumed cutaneous receptors are *Meissner's corpuscles* and *tactile disks* for touch or pressure, *Ruffini endings* for warmth, and *Krause end bulbs* for cold). Additionally, both hairy and hairless (glabrous) skin regions contain receptors called **free nerve endings** that lack specialized receptor cells and are unattached to any specific skin region. Free nerve endings are found almost everywhere within the skin surface and are by far the most common skin receptors (as we shall note later in the chapter, free nerve endings are the primary receptors for pain, although they are also sensitive to temperature and pressure).

However, in spite of the wide variety of skin receptors, we cannot conclude that there is a simple relationship between a particular cutaneous sensitivity and a particular skin receptor type. The major types of receptors—basket cells, Pacinian corpuscles, and free nerve endings—all yield some sort of pressure or touch sensation when stimulated. In fact, a given cutaneous pressure sensation may be produced by many different specialized skin receptors rather than by a single one. Indeed, there is no conclusive evidence that stimulation of a particular type of skin receptors alone produces a specific cutaneous sensation. An unusual example of the lack of specificity concerns the cornea of the eye: it contains *only* free nerve endings, yet it is very sensitive to pressure, temperature, and pain. In summary, then, highly specialized, anatomically distinct receptors are not excited exclusively by a particular type of stimulus, nor do they elicit only one cutaneous sensation when stimulated. Instead, all skin receptors seem to respond somewhat to several types of sensory stimulation.

THE SKIN AND THE BRAIN

The ultimate destination of the neural message sent by cutaneous receptors is a region of each hemisphere of the brain called the **somatosensory cortex** (Figure 16.3). In this section, we will describe how cutaneous information is transmitted to this area.

Cutaneous Representation in the Brain: The Homunculus

Stimulation of the skin provides an extraordinary amount of cutaneous information; this is due largely to the way the skin is *topographically* projected and arranged in the somatosensory cortex: nerve fibers from each part of the skin surface are spatially represented in the somatosensory cortex. Generally, neigh-

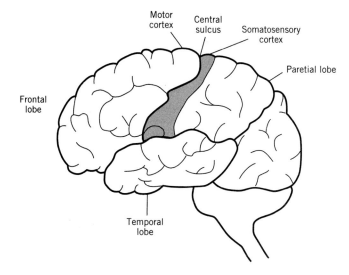

Motor cortex
Central sulcus
Somatosensory cortex
Parietal lobe
Frontal lobe
Temporal lobe

▭ *figure* **16.3** Outline of the human brain. The shaded area is the region of the somatosensory cortex in the parietal lobe that receives and processes cutaneous stimulation. Also indicated at the left of the somatosensory cortex is the region of the motor cortex, which controls voluntary body movements. The somatosensory cortex is divided from the motor cortex by a long fissure or crevice called the *central sulcus.*

boring areas of the skin are represented in neighboring regions of the somatosensory cortex. Some areas of the skin, such as the fingers, lips, and tongue, are more densely supplied with nerve fibers, which makes them more easily excited. Thus, they are represented by larger areas of the somatosensory cortex and hence are more sensitive to processing fine details than other areas of the skin, such as the shoulder and calf. This relationship is suggested by the distortion obvious in the sensory **homunculus** (literally, "a little man"). The homunculus, sketched in Figures 16.4*a* and 16.4*b*, is a topographic representation of the brain areas devoted to various parts of the body. The construction of the sensory homunculus derives largely from the cutaneous responses of surgical patients whose somatosensory cortex was exposed and electrically stimulated when their skulls were opened for tumor removal (Penfield & Rasmussen, 1950). In general, the more cortical tissue devoted to an area of the skin, the more sensitive that area is to processing stimulus features such as location and textural details (Of course, depending on their different anatomies and varying reliance on different sensory mechanisms than the human, in other species the sensory "homunculi"—not, strictly speaking, *homun*culi—may be markedly different than the one described here; e.g., see Thompson, 1993, pp. 252–254).

The exaggeration in cortical area illustrated by the sensory homunculus applies not only to the height-

ened sensitivity of specific skin regions but also to the area of the cortex involved in the motor control of these regions. Thus, skin areas that involve the muscles controlling very fine movements—such as the fingers and lips—are represented by more area of the somatosensory cortex and of the neighboring motor cortex (identified in Figure 16.3) than are skin areas that involve muscles controlling coarse movements—such as the calf and thigh. As we know, we have much finer control in moving our fingers than in moving our toes. Correspondingly, a larger area of the somatosensory and motor cortices is devoted to controlling the fingers than the toes. In general, the finer the muscle control of a given bodily region, the greater its representation in the somatosensory cortex and the closely allied motor cortex.

Lemniscal and Spinothalamic Pathways

The relationship between the skin and neural pathways to the somatosensory cortex is linked to two major neural systems—the *lemniscal* and *spinothalamic* pathways or systems—and each transmits different classes of information. Nerve fibers that make up the **lemniscal pathway** are large in diameter and fast conducting; they transmit precise positional information about touch and movement stimulation. Cuta-

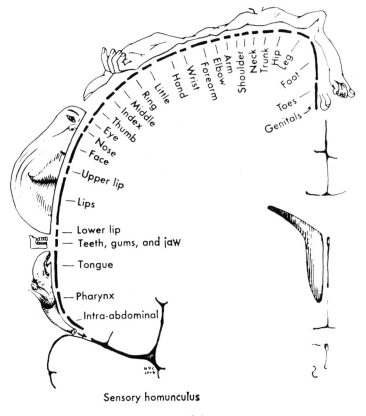

Little
Ring
Middle
Index
Thumb
Eye
Nose
Face
Hand
Wrist
Forearm
Elbow
Arm
Shoulder
Neck
Trunk
Hip
Leg
Foot
Toes
Genitals

—Upper lip

— Lips

— Lower lip
— Teeth, gums, and jaw

— Tongue

— Pharynx

—Intra-abdominal

Sensory homunculus

(a)

(b)

neous input carried by the lemniscal system for the left side of the body terminates in the somatosensory cortex of the right hemisphere of the brain, and cutaneous input for the right side of the body terminates in the somatosensory cortex of the left hemisphere.

In contrast, the fibers of the **spinothalamic pathway** are small in diameter, slow conducting, and carry cutaneous input concerning nonlocalized touch, temperature, and pain to both sides of the brain. A good example of a poorly localized, slowly conducted sensation carried by the spinothalamic pathway is the sensation of bladder fullness (Bridgeman, 1988).

Receptive Fields

In addition to representation of particular skin regions in the somatosensory cortex, its neural activity is also linked to stimulation of specific skin regions. For each neuron of the somatosensory cortex, there is a precise region of the skin that, if appropriately stimulated, alters the neuron's firing rate. The skin region linked to a particular neuron is called the neuron's *receptive field*. (Recall from Chapter 3 that the same receptive field relationship between the retina and the visual brain was described for the visual system.) In other words, the **receptive field** is a specific area on the skin that, when properly stimulated, either excites or increases (or inhibits or decreases) the firing of a specific neuron of the somatosensory cortex.

Variation in the *size* and *density* of the receptive fields reflects differences in the functioning of the lemniscal and spinothalamic pathways. The receptive fields for neurons of the lemniscal pathway are more numerous and smaller, with sharply defined, distinct borders (i.e., each represents a small, precise area of skin surface), whereas receptive fields of neurons of the spinothalamic pathway are fewer, each covering relatively large, less distinct regions of the skin (Figure

16.5). The more numerous and dense receptive field organization of the lemniscal system is clearly an aid to tactual acuity and the ability to resolve fine spatial detail. Having numerous receptive fields that each represent only a small area of the skin, and having them densely packed, enables finer tactual discriminations to be made when they are stimulated. The somatosensory neurons for areas of the skin that are most sensitive to pressure and touch, and accordingly have the greatest cortical representation—the tongue, lips, and fingertips—have the smallest receptive fields and the largest number of receptive fields per unit area of skin.

In addition to neurons that fire to simple pressure stimulation, there are more complex cortical neurons that fire only to relatively specialized stimulus *changes* in the skin. For example, there are neurons that do not react well to mere touch or pressure but do respond vigorously to *movement* of a textured surface in a specific *direction* on the skin (e.g., Costanzo & Gardner, 1980; Darian-Smith et al., 1982). Still other cells respond best to an edge moved across the skin in a particular direction. Clearly, complex cells help the skin to explore, pick up, and process information— for example, to identify and differentiate between textured surfaces and to recognize the contours of objects.

As we note in the next section, complex cells that react to brief *changes* in tactual stimulation are innervated by nerve fibers that *adapt* rapidly to constant stimulation.

Slowly and Rapidly Adapting Fibers

The *nerve fibers* that innervate and link the receptors of the skin with the neurons of the brain can be distinguished by their rate of adaptation. Two such fiber types have been identified based on their different responses to the manner in which stimulation is ap-

---

□ *figure* **16.4** Two versions of the sensory homunculus. In (*a*) various human body regions are projected on a cross section of the somatosensory cortex. The length of each line segment represents the proportion of the somatosensory cortex devoted to the body part identified by the label. The caricatures of the body parts are drawn in about the same proportion as the line segments. In (*b*) the completed homunculus depicts the body surface, with each part drawn in proportion to the size of its representation in the somatosensory cortex. Clearly, regions of the face and hands claim disproportionate amounts of the somatosensory cortex. [(*a*) based on McClintic, 1978; (*b*) modified from Rosenzweig & Leiman, 1982.]

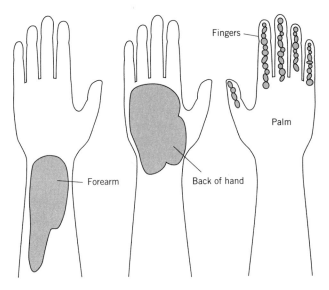

Fingers

Palm

Forearm

Back of hand

□ *figure* **16.5** Highly schematic receptive fields on the hand and arm. The receptive field is indicated by the spots and areas of shading on the limb. Very sensitive regions involved with manipulation, such as the fingers, have very small receptive fields; less sensitive regions where less important mechanical events occur, such as the back of the hand and forearm, have large receptive fields.

plied to the skin region linked to the fibers (Johansson & Vallbo, 1979; Bolanowski et al., 1988). One class of fibers responds best when pressure is applied to and maintained on the skin surface. This class is called **slowly adapting (SA) fibers.** That is, maintained pressure on the skin gives rise to a steady pattern of discharge. Another class of fibers responds only when pressure begins (and perhaps when it is terminated). These fibers are called **rapidly adapting (RA) fibers** (e.g., Gardner & Palmer, 1990). RA fibers adapt rapidly and are unresponsive to sustained pressure. Both classes of fibers feed into the lemniscal and spinothalamic tracts, so that four different fiber types can be distinguished: fibers with small receptive fields that adapt either rapidly (1) or slowly (2) and fibers with large receptive fields that also adapt rapidly (3) or slowly (4). Each of these four types may transmit a distinct neural message to the brain, since each relates to a particular kind of cutaneous stimulation. Thus, along with spatial characteristics of the cutaneous stimulus (provided by the receptive field), the adaptation property of the cutaneous stimulus is also encoded. This means that differences in both spatial and temporal response properties enable each class of fibers to transmit something different about the source of stimulation in their receptive fields.

We have introduced only a small part of the neural complexities linking the skin with the brain. Tactual perception also involves neural integration and association within the cortex that includes the input from other senses. Typically, touch stimulation interacts with bodily position and visual information to make us aware of our immediate environment.

TOUCH AND PRESSURE

Although we will use the terms *touch* and *pressure* interchangeably, there are a number of distinctions within cutaneous sensitivity. One major distinction is that between *passive touch* (in which the observer does not control the reception of stimulation, such as when objects are placed against the person's skin) and *active touch* (in which the observer actively controls stimulus pickup, such as by picking objects up; e.g., Gibson, 1962, 1966). Many of the psychophysical findings discussed in the following sections concern simple forms of stimulation imposed on a passive observer to determine cutaneous thresholds and related basic phenomena; that is, they concern the effects of passive touch. In later sections, involving more complex forms of touch stimulation, we will deal with the conditions of active touch.

Touch Stimulation and Reception

Stimulus for Touch Although the term *touch* commonly refers to any cutaneous sensation, it is more precisely applied to mechanical encounters that produce a deflection of the skin, such as an indentation or a change in the shape of the skin. Generally, uniformly applied pressure or very gradual, continuous changes in pressure are not sufficiently deforming; hence, they do not stimulate the cutaneous sense.

DEMONSTRATION:
The Effect of Stimulus Change on Touch Perception

You can easily verify the importance of stimulus change in perceiving texture. With your eyes closed, have someone place a piece of highly textured fabric such as corduroy, suede, terry cloth, or heavy knit against your fingertip and hold it there without moving. Although you will be aware that something is touching your fingertip, you probably will not be able to identify the material. However, if the fabric is moved back and forth over the surface of your fingertip (or, better yet, if you move your finger over the fabric), its texture will be readily recognized. This simple example demonstrates that the skin is not very effective with uniformly applied pressure, but it reacts well to touch stimulation that changes over time and space (e.g., see Hollins, Faldowski, Rao, & Young, 1993).

Receptors for Touch Although the outer surface of the skin as a whole responds to the pressure or touch of the environment, the guiding and exploratory parts of the body—the fingers, the hands, parts of the mouth, and the tip of the tongue—are most sensitive to touch. Less sensitive areas, like the legs, arms and trunk, are regions where less important mechanical events occur.

Mechanical disturbances received by the skin are registered by specialized receptors called *mechanoreceptors*. In turn, nerve fibers from these receptors transmit neural impulses to the brain by way of nerve pathways in the spinal cord. As described before, in the brain cutaneous information is processed in special cortical regions of the *somatosensory cortex*—regions that are topographically linked to the surface of the skin.

Pacinian Corpuscle We noted earlier that there are several different nerve ending receptors for mediating touch stimulation; however, the pressure receptor that is best understood because of its size, accessibility, and extreme sensitivity to touch is the encapsulated **Pacinian corpuscle** (shown in Figures 16.2 and 16.6). It is located relatively deep in the skin (as well as in tissue of the joints, muscle tendons, and ligaments) and it is the largest cutaneous receptor—even visible in laboratory preparations—typically about 0.5 mm wide and 1.0 mm long, although it can achieve a size of 1 by 4 mm (Sherrick & Cholewiak, 1986).

Each Pacinian corpuscle consists of 50 or more concentric, onion-like layers of tissue and fluid surrounding its sensory nerve. Because of its many layers, the Pacinian corpuscle does not respond to sustained pressure: only the initial stimulus impact causes the sensory nerve to fire. In other words, due to its structure, the Pacinian corpuscle responds best to the onset (or offset) of brief touch stimulation, such as rapid pressure changes or vibrations—the sort of stimulation produced when the finger is moved over the surface of a textured object. That it responds only when a stimulus changes, and not to continuous pressure, indicates that the Pacinian corpuscle is innervated by RA fibers. Pacinian corpuscles also have large receptive fields, but since they are so densely packed in certain skin regions and so sensitive to pressure (requiring movement of only about 0.0001 in. for excitation), they are effective in signaling the location and certain textural characteristics of a brief stimulus.

Having described some of the sensory structures available for processing different sorts of information provided by touch, we will now discuss some of the abilities it provides.

Thresholds for Touch

Absolute Threshold The skin surface is very sensitive to light pressure. Under ideal laboratory conditions, skin displacement of less than 0.001 mm

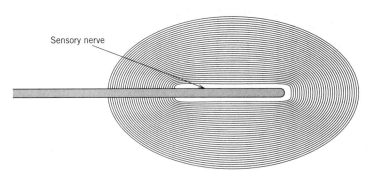

Sensory nerve

□ **figure 16.6** Schematic of a cross section of a Pacinian corpuscle.

(0.00004 in.) creates a sensation of pressure (Verillo, 1975). However, the sensitivity to touch stimulation varies not only with the intensity of the stimulus applied but also from one region of the body to another. Thus, for example, we recognize that it takes more pressure to feel something on the thigh or the sole of the foot than on the fingertips or face.

To assess absolute threshold levels of touch or pressure, Weinstein (1968) stimulated various bodily sites of observers using fine nylon filaments (whose force could be precisely calibrated in milligrams). The results for the right and left sides of the body, shown in Figure 16.7, indicate that the face is the most pressure-sensitive part of the body; parts of the trunk are next, closely followed by the fingers and arms (see also Stevens, 1990).

Point Localization for Touch We can easily identify the location of the skin that is touched. An itch on the back is accurately scratched; a light tap on the arm or shoulder is readily identified. The ability to localize touch sensations on the stimulated region of the skin is called **point localization.** Like the absolute threshold, it varies with the region of the body stimulated.

Since a major sensory function of the skin is to inform the organism of what is next to it, it is not surprising that in general, stimulation of the more mobile and exploratory skin regions of the body, with finer muscular control for manipulation (e.g., the hands and mouth) results in more accurate point localization (see Figure 16.8). For example, stimulation of the fingertip or the lip is extremely well localized; the error in pinpointing it is only about 2 mm. In contrast,

stimulation of the upper arm, thigh, or back produces a localization error of more than 1 cm. Relating this to our discussion of receptive fields and the cortical representation of various skin regions, we can conclude that localization accuracy is directly linked to the amount of cortical representation of the skin receptors in that body region.

Two-Point Threshold Another important measure of the localizing ability of the skin is the two-point threshold. The **two-point threshold** refers to the smallest separation of two separate but adjacent points of stimulation on the skin that just produces two distinct impressions of touch (Figure 16.9). That is, if the two stimuli were placed any closer together, they would produce a single touch sensation. As with the ability to localize a single stimulus, more mobile skin regions (e.g., the hands and parts of the face) are more sensitive and have lower two-point thresholds. For example, the two-point threshold for the mobile thumb is about 4 mm (i.e., the two contact points on the thumb have to be 4 mm apart in order to be felt as two separate touches), whereas for the relatively immobile calf the two-point threshold is about 48 mm—about a 12-fold increase!

Aristotle's Illusion

A unique tactual experience attributed to the Greek philosopher Aristotle (e.g., Benedetti, 1985)—**Aristotle's illusion**—bears on some of the phenomena just described, especially tactual localization. According to Benedetti, Aristotle noted that if two adjacent

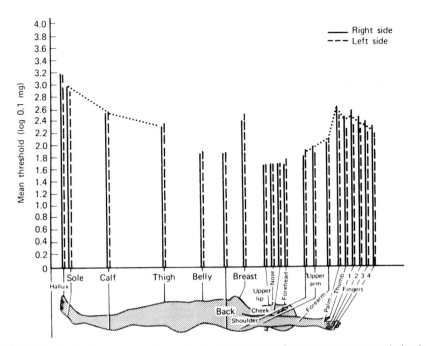

▭ **figure 16.7** Thresholds for pressure. The ordinate represents the force necessary to reach the threshold level. The figure is for females, but corresponding thresholds for males are similar. (From S. Weinstein, "Intensive and extensive aspects of tactile sensitivity as a function of body part, sex, and laterality," in D. R. Kenshalo (Ed.), *The Skin Senses*, Charles C. Thomas, Springfield, Ill., 1968, p. 201. Reprinted by permission of the author and publisher.)

fingers are crossed (most easily accomplished with the index and middle finger), creating a V by the fingertips, and if the V of the two crossed fingers is stimulated by a small object such as a bead, a sensation of touching *two* beads will result. A version of this is illustrated in Figure 16.10.

▯ **DEMONSTRATION:**
Aristotle's Illusion

Follow the instructions given in Figure 16.10. Cross the fingers, as shown in Figure 16.10*b*. When a single pencil is shifted back and forth against both fingers, you will feel two touch sensations.

According to Benedetti's extensive analysis (1985, 1986*a*, 1986*b*, 1988, 1991), the unusual experience of sensing two stimuli from a single stimulus when the fingers are crossed (Figure 16.10*b*) follows from the fact that the skin areas of the two fingers that are simultaneously stimulated (i.e., their outsides) are the ones that ordinarily require the application of two stimuli. In other words, it is not usually possible for a single object to stimulate the outsides of two different fingers; stimulating the outsides of two uncrossed fingers would typically occur only with two tactual stimuli (as indicated in Figure 16.10*d*). Thus, stimulating the two crossed fingers with one object duplicates the pattern of stimulation that typically requires two stimuli: one stimulus in contact with the outside of one finger and another stimulus touching the outside of the other finger. Moreover, since stimulation of the outsides of the fingers signals to the observer that two stimuli have been applied, the spatial information obtained by stimulation with the fingers crossed is processed and produces the same experience that would occur if the fingers were uncrossed.

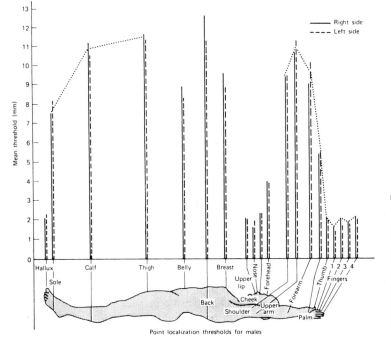

□ *figure* **16.8** Point localization thresholds. The ordinate represents the distance between the body point stimulated and the subject's perception of where stimulation occurred. (From S. Weinstein, "Intensive and extensive aspects of tactile sensitivity as a function of body part, sex, and laterality," in D. R. Kenshalo (Ed.), *The Skin Senses*, Charles C. Thomas, Springfield, Ill., 1968, p. 204. Reprinted by permission of the author and publisher.)

Coren, Porac, and Ward (1984) suggest a neural organization that coincides with this description. They propose that when an object stimulates the insides of two adjacent fingers (i.e., Figure 16.10*a*), the touch information is sent to two related or overlapping areas of the somatosensory cortex, resulting in a single touch sensation. In fact, as indicated in Figure 16.10*c*, the cutaneous experience created by two concurrently applied stimuli to adjacent skin regions is of a single touch. However, when the fingers are crossed and a stimulus contacts the outsides of the two fingers (Figure 16.10*b*), the information is sent to two separate, unrelated areas of the sensory cortex, producing a *double touch* sensation.

Adaptation to Touch

Continued steady pressure or touching may result in a decrease or even a complete elimination of sensation: touch sensations undergo *adaptation*. Adaptation to pressure is a common experience. For example, even after a short time, we do not usually feel the pressure

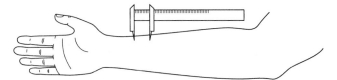

□ *figure* **16.9** Determination of the two-point threshold. This caliper-ruler device has two very fine contact points whose separation can be varied. The caliper-ruler is applied to various regions of the body, and the smallest separation of the contact points that gives rise to two discrete touch sensations is the measure of the two-point threshold for that skin region.

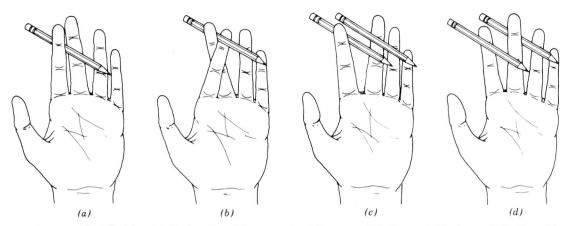

(a)   (b)   (c)   (d)

▭ *figure* **16.10** Aristotle's illusion: Perceiving two stimuli from one. This demonstration is most effective with the eyes closed. (a) Stimulate the two fingers as shown. A slight shifting of a pen or pencil is adequate to demonstrate the sensation of a single touch. (b) When the fingers are crossed and the same stimulus is applied, two sensations of touch result. Compare these sensations with the following ones. (c) Stimulation of the insides of uncrossed adjacent fingers by two simultaneously applied stimuli produces a single touch experience. (d) Stimulation of the outsides of uncrossed fingers produces two sensations of touch. The conditions of touch in (b) essentially duplicate stimulation of the outside areas of the uncrossed fingers in (d), but the latter requires the simultaneous application of two stimuli, as indicated.

[Note that although conditions (b) and (d) are similar with respect to stimulation of the outsides of both fingers, there are cutaneous and kinesthetic (kinesthesis is described later in the chapter) stimulation differences: when the fingers are crossed, it is difficult to stimulate exactly the same cutaneous areas of both fingers that are stimulated when they are uncrossed. In addition, when the fingers are crossed, they are in different relative positions to each other, producing kinesthetic stimulation that is lacking when they are uncrossed.]

of our watch band on the wrist or the clothes against the body. The time course of adaptation varies with several factors, particularly the intensity of the stimulus and the size and region of the skin contacted. When a weight is resting on the skin, the time required for the sensation to disappear completely is directly proportional to the intensity of the stimulus and inversely proportional to the size of the area contacted (Geldard, 1972). The heavier the pressure applied to the skin, the longer it takes for the sensation to disappear, but the larger the skin area covered by the pressure, the less the time required for the sensation to disappear. Once adaptation occurs, however, the touch sensation can be quickly restored by a brief movement or an abrupt change in the stimulation to the adapted skin area. Continuous change in stimulation is what normally occurs when the individual *actively* touches surfaces and objects. Some forms of complex information picked up from active, self-produced touching are discussed next.

COMPLEX TOUCH

Braille System

We have noted that the fingers are sensitive to point localization and two-point discrimination. It is not surprising, then, that some sort of complex communication can occur from active touching. One example is the well-known **Braille system** devised by Louis Braille in the nineteenth century. The Braille alphabet is actually a reading system composed of dots embossed on a surface that can be "read" by the skin, usually the tips of the fingers. As shown in Figures 16.11 and 16.12, various combinations of dots are used to represent letters and words. By moving the finger over the raised surfaces, the experienced adult Braille reader can reach 100 words per minute (Foulke & Berlá, 1978; Kennedy, 1984).

Because Braille is displayed in a manner similar to print symbols, it retains many of the advantages of the print code: for example, the Braille reader can

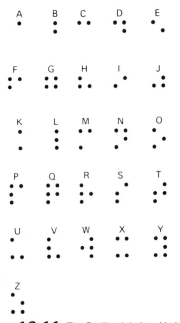

◻ figure 16.11 The Braille alphabet. Various combinations of from one to six embossed dots are used to represent letters and short words. Each dot stands 1 mm above the surface and dot separations are 2.3 mm. (From Kenshalo, 1978.)

vary the reading rate and can reread ambiguous material. Since Braille symbols are displayed spatially, the reader can also read paragraph indentation and centered headings. Moreover, the same basic cognitive methods may be involved in processing printed visual text and Braille tactual text. Krueger (1982b; Krueger & Ward, 1983) found that Braille letters (like print letters)

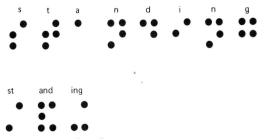

◻ figure 16.12 The word "standing" written in Braille symbols (top) and written in a contracted form (bottom) in which frequently recurring letter groups are assigned specific patterns. (After Foulke & Berlá, 1978.)

are detected more rapidly and accurately when embedded in words than in nonwords (see also Heller, 1980).

Tadoma Method

Cutaneous stimulation can also be used to communicate speech, as demonstrated by some individuals who are both blind and deaf, using the **Tadoma method** of speech reception (Reed, Doherty, Braida, & Durlach, 1982). In the Tadoma method the listener touches specific parts of the speaker's lips, face, and neck so that the hand receives some of the complex movement patterns produced by the speaker (see Figure 16.13). If the rate of speech is moderated

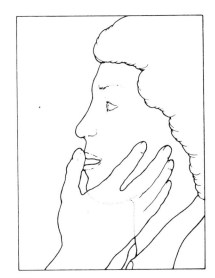

◻ figure 16.13 Representation of hand placement using the Tadoma method of speech perception. The deaf-blind "listener's" hand is placed on the speaker's face and neck. The thumb is placed vertically with its tip over the speaker's upper lip, the little finger is placed over the jaw with its tip against the jaw (i.e., the temporal-mandibular joint), and the remaining fingers fan out over the speaker's cheek. As the speaker talks, the listener can directly pick up information that is closely tied to articulation, that is, stimulation from lip and jaw movements, laryngeal vibrations, and oral air flow. (From J. M. Loomis and S. J. Lederman, "Tactual perception," in *Handbook of Perception and Human Performance*, Volume II, Wiley, New York, 1986, pp. 31–19. Reprinted by permission of the publisher.)

and if the listener is experienced, the Tadoma method permits a reasonable level of speech comprehension.

The hand, held against the vocal apparatus of the speaker in using the Tadoma system, is receiving an informative pattern of pressure changes or *vibrations*. However, the technique is not confined to receiving stimulation directly from the vocal apparatus. Krueger (1982*a*, p. 13) cites the case of a deaf girl who "could understand what a normal girl was saying in a dark room if she laid her hand on the breast of the speaking girl. Another deaf person could 'listen' to and understand vibrations transmitted from the speaker by means of a billiard cue stick or a bowed piece of paper." By placing a hand on an audio speaker, deaf individuals can use this technique of vibration transmission to "listen" to music. Remarkably, there is a deaf Scottish musician "who can feel the trembling of the separate instruments of an orchestra, can modulate her voice's timbre with real beauty, can even understand words through vibrations" (Solomon, 1994, p. 44).

Seeing with the Skin: Tactual–Visual Substitution System

Another possible means of skin communication is to use the skin surface as a direct channel for pictorial material. A group of researchers (White et al., 1970; Collins, 1971) have developed a **tactual–visual substitution system** to convert a visual image into a direct cutaneous display. The apparatus for this is shown in Figure 16.14. It consists of a tripod-mounted television camera—the "eye"of the system—that is connected to a 20×20 matrix of 400 vibrators mounted on the back of a stationary dental chair (Figure 16.15). The video image is electronically transformed so that a vibrator is active when its location is within an illuminated region of the camera field. The subject seated in the chair with his or her back against the vibrators is appropriately stimulated when the camera picks up an image. Thus, when a subject moves the television camera across a scene, patterns of light intensity in the visual field are reproduced in successions of tactual impressions on the skin surface of the back.

The results from presentation of this coarse tactual image are remarkable. Subjects, both blind and blindfolded, normally sighted, were able to perceive some simple displays very soon after they had been introduced to the system. Simple geometric shapes—a circle, a triangle, and a square—were accurately identified when subjects were allowed to scan the figures by moving the television camera and were corrected immediately after a wrong response. With enough experience, a collection of 25 complex items (e.g., a coffee cup, telephone, stuffed animal) were identifiable.

Furthermore, experienced subjects were able to identify the objects and describe their arrangements on a table when the objects were viewed by the camera from slightly above (an angle of 20° off the horizontal). Some objects at the rear were partially occluded by those in front, suggesting that some of the depth and distance information of the visual scene is provided in the corresponding tactual image. One such cue for the location of an object in depth was its vertical position on the cutaneous display: the farther back its location on the table top, the higher up on the display. A second cue for tactually perceiving depth is based on the familiar inverse relationship between the projected size of the image and the physical distance of an object. The change in image size normally projected on the eye as the object's distance is varied also occurred on the skin surface in this arrangement. One of the subjects was a blind psychologist who has taught this relationship (i.e., an inverse relation between the projected size of an object on the retinal surface and its physical distance from an observer) to his classes for years, but obviously he had never directly perceived it. His experience of the increase in the size of a tactual image as an object was brought closer and closer to the camera and a decrease in image size as object distance from the camera was increased produced in him a perceptual realization about the relation between projected size and physical distance—"a genuine 'aha' experience."

Some variables are critical in gaining skill with the tactual–visual substitution system. It is crucial that the television camera not be kept in a fixed position and that the subject *actively* control the movement of the camera. It appears that enabling subjects to explore

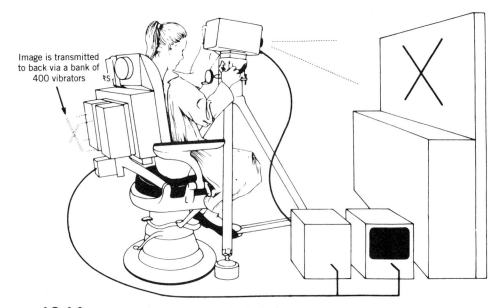

Image is transmitted
to back via a bank of
400 vibrators

□ *figure* **16.14** Schematic of the tactual–visual substitution system. (From B. W. White, F. A. Saunders, L. Scadden, P. Bach-y-Rita, and C. C. Collins, "Seeing with the skin," *Perception & Psychophysics, 7,* 1970, p. 23. Reprinted by permission of Psychonomic Society, Inc.)

□ *figure* **16.15** The vibrator array mounted in the back of the chair. (From B. W. White, F. A. Saunders, L. Scadden, P. Bach-y-Rita, and C. C. Collins, "Seeing with the skin," *Perception & Psychophysics, 7,* 1970, p. 26. Reprinted by permission of Psychonomic Society, Inc.)

figures by sweeping the camera over the display results in the successive changes in vibrator activity that are necessary for meaningful tactual images to be perceived.

The tactual–visual substitution system has been further developed to increase both its portability and the amount of tactual information received. To this end, various versions of tactual displays have been employed, modified for use with different regions of the skin, such as the abdomen and forehead (e.g., Cholewiak & Sherrick, 1981) and fingertips and palm (Craig & Johnson, cited in Amato, 1992; Lambert & Lederman, 1989; Shimizu, 1986; Shimizu, Saida, & Shimura, 1993). A tactual display enabling shape and pattern recognition by the fingers and palms of blind individuals is shown in Figure 16.16.

In this context, it is possible that the blind, using touch, can understand many visual spatial concepts. By running their hands over "pictorially correct" raised surfaces, they can readily perceive representations of depth and distance, relative size, and certain figural relationships (e.g., figure–ground or foreground–background) (Heller, 1991; Kennedy, 1983; Kennedy &

□ *figure* **16.16** A tactual display for use with the finger and palm. The display is composed of a matrix of almost 4000 blunt pins, whose heights can be adjusted to produce a particular stimulus pattern. The pins are spaced 2 mm apart, creating a total display area of 120 × 120 mm. The example pattern shown above is obviously of a palm. (Courtesy of Prof. Y. Shimizu; from Shimizu, Saida, & Shimura, 1993, p. 45.)

Campbell, 1985; Kennedy, Gabias, & Nicholls, 1991). In fact, certain complex and spatially detailed artworks, including representational sculpture and bas relief murals, are especially designed for tactual perception by the blind (e.g., Good, 1988; Kennedy, 1993).

In the next section, we describe how the integration of skin stimulation with information about body part movement and location provides further detail about the local environment.

KINESTHESIS

The hand is a remarkable device for exploring environmental space, such as the shapes of objects. As we have noted, moving the fingers over various surfaces enables us to discover various textural qualities. However, when the hand is used to examine an object, involving grasping and manipulation, information from the skin's pressure receptors is coordinated and combined with another kind of information called *kinesthesis.*

Kinesthesis (or *kinesthesia,* from the Greek *kineo,* "to move") refers to the perception of body part position and movement—the posture, location, and movement in space of the limbs and other mobile parts of the jointed skeleton (e.g., fingers, wrist, limbs, head, trunk, vertebrate column; this positional information is sometimes referred to as *proprioception*). At least two sources of mechanical stimulation may contribute to the kinesthetic sense: those from the joints and those from the muscles and tendons. The mechanoreceptors for joint information are a form of Pacinian corpuscles, which lie in the muscles, tendons, and mobile joints of the skeletal system, and Ruffini cylinders. These receptors are stimulated by contact between the parts of the joint surfaces that occurs with changes in the angles at which the bones are held. In a sense, these mechanoreceptors are subcutaneous pressure receptors.

Another source of information that contributes to kinesthesis results from innervation of muscles and tendons. Muscles, and the tendons that connect them to the bone, are well supplied with nerve endings (*Golgi tendon organs,* as well as Pacinian corpuscles) and sensory nerves that respond to changes in tension when the muscle fiber is stretched or contracted. Stimulation of the appropriate receptors produces patterns of excitation that lead to the perception of stretch and strain, as when weight is supported. That is, a feeling of strain becomes part of the total kinesthetic information when there is resistance to limb movement. In addition, the receptors from muscles and tendons may contribute to the control of postural reflex actions, automatically adjusting tension to the needs of the limb.

Although kinesthetic stimulation does not generally result in a clear or conscious sensation such as hearing a sound or seeing an image, the kinesthetic system continually provides important information. Without difficulty we know the position, posture, and direction of movement of our limbs in space. We scratch an itch we cannot see; we walk safely down a flight of stairs without gazing directly at our feet; and, in general, we accurately touch any part of our bodies in the dark. Laboratory studies have shown that a person is capable of pointing accurately with the limbs without using vision (e.g., L. A. Cohen, 1958; Wood, 1969). When an individual is instructed to point with a hand-held rod to the gravitational vertical or horizontal, the average error is only a few degrees (Gibson, 1966; Rymer & D'Almeida, 1980). The ability of the receptors at the joints to supply information about angles and distances is seen when a person accurately uses the distance between the two palms to mark off length, regardless of whether the eyes are opened or closed. The main sensory receptors for this particular action reside in the shoulder joints and associated muscles. Similarly, the gap spanned by the index finger and its opposable thumb is accurately used to mark off width or short distances (see Figure 16.17). Here the receptors are in the knuckle and wrist joints. The accuracy of these abilities has been amply demonstrated in the laboratory (e.g., Jones, Hunter, & Irwin, 1992; Teghtsoonian & Teghtsoonian, 1970; Wertheimer, 1954). No doubt it is this activity that is meant when we say we can measure an object or compare two objects on the basis of "touch."

Tickling and Self-Produced Stimulation

Do we experience the same tactual sensation when we intentionally touch a region of our own skin as when someone else touches the same region in precisely the same way? That is, are both self-produced and externally applied touches perceived the same way? We often touch our own skin in various ways and even, on occasion, stroke the soles of our feet or touch our rib cage and armpits. From a sensory point of view, these activities are not particularly eventful. However, if *someone else* strokes the soles of our feet

⊏ figure 16.17 Kinesthetic information from the knuckle and wrist joint used to indicate linear extent. The size of the gap made by the thumb and index finger can serve as a measure of thickness and small distance.

or our rib cage or armpits—even if they do so exactly as we do it to ourselves—for most individuals it produces the sensation of being *tickled*. Depending on the social and perceptual circumstances, a tickle may range from a mildly pleasant, even exciting, sensation to an extremely unpleasant, aversive one. While we cannot here describe the neural and psychological basis of tickling, it is due in part to the unpredictable and random nature of light tactual stimulation applied to very sensitive skin regions. We can, however, examine the question of why we don't seem to be able to tickle ourselves.

The answer appears to be the ability of the nervous system to compare and differentiate between the stimulation produced when we touch our own skin from when someone else does it. When we intentionally touch our own skin, we first send a motor command (efferent) signal to the appropriate muscles to touch the skin in a specific manner and at a specific location; a corresponding afferent (incoming) touch sensation is received by the brain. An identical afferent signal is also received when someone else touches us in the same place and in precisely the same way. However, when the touch sensation is *self-produced,* it is matched by and compared with the outgoing efferent motor command signal sent from the brain to touch that region of the skin. Thus, for example, when we stroke the soles of our feet, the outgoing efferent command signals sent to the muscles and tendons of the fingers are compared with the resulting afferent sensations from the soles. The fact that the touch is self-produced *eliminates* the unpredictable nature typical of a tickle. In contrast, when someone else strokes our soles (producing the same afferent signals), there are no corresponding command signals for a comparison with the touch sensations. Accordingly, the same incoming, afferent tactual signals are perceived as tickles. (The reader may recall a related discussion in Chapter 8 on *outflow signals* to explain how self-produced eye movements neutralize or cancel the flow of images produced by these same eye movements.) In other words, when it is self-produced, a touch eliminates the unpredictable characteristic of a tickle while still eliciting a touch sensation.

Weiskrantz, Elliott, and Darlington (1971) examined the neutralizing role of self-produced stimulation in tickling by using a special device that enabled the tickling stroke to be controlled and moved over the sole of the bare foot of a subject in three ways: by the experimenter alone, by the subject alone, or by the experimenter with the subject's hand on the device so that the arm passively followed the movement of the tickling stimulus. In general, the strokes administered by the experimenter were most ticklish, self-administered stroking was least ticklish, and the condition featuring passive movement of the subject's arm was intermediate between the two. These results show that self-produced stroking is much less effective in producing a tickling sensation than stroking by someone else, and that the degree of self-produced stroking determines the degree of tickling experienced.

HAPTIC SYSTEM

The combined input from the skin and kinesthesis provides the basis of a perceptual channel called the **haptic system** (from the Greek term *hapsis,* "to grasp" or "hold"). The haptic system is responsible for the perception of geometric properties—shapes, dimensions, and proportions of objects that are handled. Moreover, by various manipulations, the haptic system not only extracts geometric properties but also gives information on the weight and consistency of objects (Figure 16.18). According to James J. Gibson (1966), an early proponent of the importance of this channel for normal tactual exploration, the haptic system puts organisms literally "in touch" with the environment. (Credit for recognizing the role of the haptic system must also be given to David Katz; see Krueger, 1982*a;* Katz, 1989). Consider some of the many functions of haptic perception:

> *the sensing of fabrics by the hand; the sensing of food texture by the mouth; the sensing of vibrations in machinery that signify normal or abnormal operation; the identification of solid objects and their spatial arrangement; the sensing of imperfections and dirt on the surfaces of objects; the examination of internal organs of the body by palpation; the examination of unseen portions of the teeth using dental probes; and the sensing of weight, center of gravity, and the moment of iner-*

> *tia of hefted objects. . . . For humans . . . it contributes much to social and sexual communication, to individual development, and to the aesthetic appreciation of both art and daily life. (Loomis & Lederman, 1986, pp. 31–26)*

Haptic perception normally results from a broad range of contacts between the environment and the body. Indeed, most self-produced, perceptual–motor encounters produce combined kinesthetic and skin stimulation. For example, when we identify an object by handling it, we also obtain information about its shape from the position of our fingers (i.e., from kinesthesis) and from skin contact (from cutaneous stimulation; Klatzky et al., 1993). Distinct receptors act in conjunction to produce what is clearly a *unitary* experience. Furthermore, the nerve pathways for the cutaneous sense and kinesthesis are functionally linked: they are both projected to the same area of the somatosensory cortex, and for experimental convenience they have usually been investigated together. In brief, kinesthetic and cutaneous inputs combine to act as a single functional perceptual system.

It is not passive cutaneous and kinesthetic stimulation that provides and registers the necessary information for haptic perception but *active touch:* concurrent cutaneous and kinesthetic stimulation that results from purposive, self-produced exploration. The gathering of such stimulation is what we refer to when we say we "touch," "feel," "grasp," or "hold" something with our fingers or hands. A common example of such a haptic ability is *tactual stereognosis.*

Tactual Stereognosis

Tactual stereognosis refers to the familiar and quite accurate ability to perceive three-dimensional shapes by palpation or by exploring with the hands. In one investigation, Klatzky, Lederman, and Metzger (1985) studied the ability of 20 subjects to identify common objects on the basis of touch alone. Blindfolded subjects handled 100 common objects, each easily identifiable by name—for example, a toothbrush, onion, paper clip, screwdriver, and fork. The results were impressive: out of 2000 responses, approximately 96%

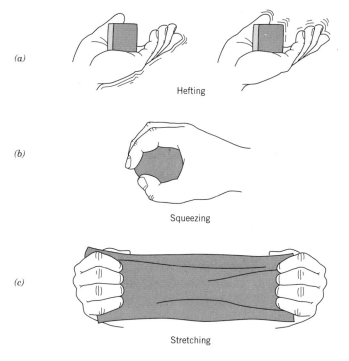

(a)

Hefting

(b)

Squeezing

(c)

Stretching

▭ *figure **16.18*** Examples of haptic perception. (*a*) To determine the weight of an object, we heft it; that is, we move the hand up and down to produce a pattern of stimulation from the skin, joints, and muscles. To gauge the consistency (i.e., the soft–firm, elastic–rigid dimension) of an object, we squeeze it (*b*) or stretch it (*c*). Squeezing an object reveals how soft or hard it is, whereas pulling at it with both hands establishes how elastic it is.

were correct and 94% of the correct responses occurred within 5 sec of handling by the subject!

Active touch need not be restricted to the hands and fingers. As we noted earlier with the tactual–visual substitution system, the surface of the back (not itself very touch sensitive) may be quite informative if stimulation is *actively* obtained rather than imposed. Indeed, various parts of the body surface may be quite informative if stimulation is properly obtained. In fact, a prosthesis called a *sensate hand prosthesis* for artificial hands enables the wearer to obtain a sense of touch from its fingers. Contact sensors built into the fingertips of the artificial hand generate recognizable signals in the form of high-frequency vibrations. The thumb and index finger each transmit vibrations at a distinctive frequency, and the other three fingers generate a third frequency. On contact of the fingers, the vibrations are transmitted to the base of the artificial hand that adjoins the bony stump of the natural limb, and the wearer feels the vibrations in the arm. According to the inventor, a plastic surgeon (V. C. Giampapa, 1989), wearers quickly learn to distinguish the three signals from the different fingers and can

derive some tactual information on the objects and surfaces in direct contact with the fingers.

Roughness Enhancement

Sensitivity of the skin to actively self-imposed pressure or touch stimulation is increased by using a simple surface aid. An individual may detect the surface deflections and undulations of an object more accurately when moving a thin, intermediate sheet of paper across the surface than when the bare fingers are used (Gordon & Cooper, 1975). This method of feeling, referred to as **roughness enhancement** (see Loomis & Lederman, 1986), has long been employed by craftsmen and in auto body shops to examine the smoothness of the finish on repaired or reworked surfaces. According to Lederman (1978), as the bare fingers are moved over certain textured surfaces, lateral (or shear) forces are applied to the skin of the fingertips; such forces mask some of the critical skin deformation stimuli for roughness that are produced, in part, by normal (or downward) force. When an individual moves the intermediate sheet of paper across the surface, the paper reduces the shear force, which also reduces the interfering masking. As a result, the individual is more sensitive to the roughness of a surface when it is felt through the sheet of paper moving with the fingers than when it is experienced with the bare fingers.

□ **DEMONSTRATION:**
Roughness Enhancement

Roughness enhancement can be easily demonstrated. Rub your fingers over the glazed surface of an apparently smooth piece of ceramic pottery. [An alternative surface is an auto body. Note that the choice of surface used is important. As Green (1981) points out, roughness enhancement will not occur with all textured surfaces.] Then place a piece of very thin paper (such as "onion skin" or the kind of paper attached to a carbon) and rub the paper over the same surface with your finger. When the ceramic surface is rubbed with the paper over it, it will feel slightly rougher than when the surface is felt by only the skin of the fingertip.

Finally in this section on detecting surface qualities, it is worth noting that we can also make accurate judgments on the *hardness* of a surface using self-imposed touch. Even with reflected sound cues (as echoes) excluded, briefly tapping a surface with the fingernail is often enough to determine whether the surface is made of wood, metal, or plastic (Geldard, 1972).

TEMPERATURE

As we noted at the beginning of this chapter, the skin helps to regulate the body's thermal environment by both retaining and dissipating heat. When body temperature rises appreciably, heat from the internal organs is transported into a fine network of small, dilated blood vessels just below the skin surface and is dissipated. At the same time, the pores of the skin open, carrying perspiration, which on contact with air evaporates and cools the skin surface. Conversely, when body temperature markedly drops, the flow of heat to the skin surface falls off, the pores constrict (hence "goose bumps"), and the individual may shiver, generating heat from the muscles. The result is a slowing of heat loss.

The skin also responds to temperature by providing *thermal sensations*. These sensations are registered by cutaneous stimulation from the temperature of the surface that is in direct contact with the skin. Thermal sensations also contribute to the body's temperature-regulating system. Clearly, most animals cannot live at the extremes of temperature; thus, to survive, they must be aware of the rate at which their bodies are gaining and losing heat. When heat loss is too great (and the body feels cold), the organism must reduce it, such as by seeking shelter or insulation or a direct source of heat like sunlight or a fire. Similarly, if the heat gain is too great (and the body feels hot), the organism seeks a cooler environment such as shade or perhaps brief immersion in water. Accordingly, we may treat a sensory system for the perception of thermal information as an adaptation to help avoid temperature extremes, thereby contributing to thermal equilibrium.

Temperature Receptors and Thermal Spots

No single, specialized receptor type is *the* thermal receptor; however, it is generally accepted that a form of **free nerve endings** (which are also the main receptors for pain) mediate thermal sensations. Moreover, warmth and coolness are detected by different groups of temperature receptors that lie at different depths within the skin: receptors for cold lie relatively close to the skin surface, while receptors for warm are located at deeper levels (Carlson, 1991). In addition, the nerve fibers innervating the receptors for both warm and cold increase their firing rate when appropriately stimulated: warm fibers fire rapidly to warm temperatures (e.g., 45°C [113°F] or more) and decrease their firing rate as temperature drops. In contrast, cold fibers fire rapidly to cold stimulation and reduce firing as the temperature rises. In fact, warm and cold fibers each respond to an overlapping range of temperatures. That is, either cold or warm fibers may fire to temperatures between about 30° to 45°C.

Sensitivity to temperature is irregularly distributed in thermal "spots" (about 1 mm in diameter) over the skin surface. Exploration of the skin surface with warm or cold stimuli reveals that some skin spots are especially sensitive to warm stimulation, whereas other, more numerous spots are more sensitive to cold stimulation. However, as shown in Figure 16.19, the sensitivity of a given thermal spot may vary markedly over time. Part of this variability may be due to temperature shifts within the skin itself, that is, to normal heat exchanges on the skin surface. Skin tissue is continually warming or cooling owing to heat radiation, conduction, and convection from moisture evaporation and dilation or constriction of the blood vessels of the subcutaneous tissue. All or any of these factors may account for the fact that, in contrast to point localization for touch or pressure, localization for warmth is poor (Green, 1977).

In general, however, the body surface remains in a relatively stable thermal equilibrium with its environment. Over the clothed areas of the body and the face, skin temperature is close to 35°C (95°F); on the hands and arms, at about 33°C (91°F); and, of course, under the tongue at 37°C (about 98.6°F). Where blood flow is sluggish, as in the ear lobe, the temperature may be significantly lower (20°C or 68°F).

Thermal Conductivity

However, neither the temperature of the skin by itself nor the temperature of a surface or medium in contact with the skin is an accurate predictor of thermal experience. "Warm" and "cold" are comparative terms describing the temperature of the skin *relative* to the temperature of things in the environment that contact

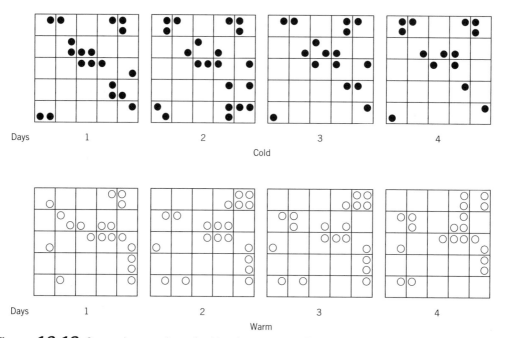

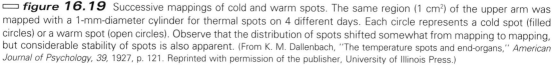

figure 16.19 Successive mappings of cold and warm spots. The same region (1 cm²) of the upper arm was mapped with a 1-mm-diameter cylinder for thermal spots on 4 different days. Each circle represents a cold spot (filled circles) or a warm spot (open circles). Observe that the distribution of spots shifted somewhat from mapping to mapping, but considerable stability of spots is also apparent. (From K. M. Dallenbach, "The temperature spots and end-organs," *American Journal of Psychology, 39,* 1927, p. 121. Reprinted with permission of the publisher, University of Illinois Press.)

the skin. Things that are warmer than the skin feel warm to the touch because heat energy is flowing to the skin surface (by conduction or radiation); things that are cooler than the skin feel cool because heat energy is moving away from the skin surface.

This relates to the observation that at a constant room temperature, many surfaces feel warm or cool to the touch. The reason is that thermal sensations are due partly to the *rate* at which heat is conducted to or from the skin, and some surfaces are better thermal conductors than others. The rate at which an object or surface conducts heat from or to the region of the skin in contact with the surface is called **thermal conductivity.** Thus, for example, touching a metal surface made of copper or aluminum (or, perhaps more familiarly, standing barefoot on bathroom floor tiles) usually feels cool because such surfaces have high thermal conductivity; in contrast, most fibrous materials, such as cloth fabrics and many wood surfaces, feel thermally neutral or perhaps slightly warm because they have low thermal conductivity.

Clearly, thermal conductivity plays an important part in a given thermal experience. Another critical factor that affects thermal sensations is *thermal adaptation.*

Thermal Adaptation

Thermal sensations from the skin undergo adaptation. Initial exposure to a moderately cold or warm environment, as in immersion in a swimming pool or bath, may initially result in a cool or hot experience, but eventually the thermal sensation will diminish and the water will feel only slightly cold or warm, depending on the prior thermal conditions. Prolonged warm or cold stimulation is likely to reduce the thermal sensitivity (i.e., raise the threshold values) for warmth and coldness, respectively. Moreover, both warm and cold sensitivities are simultaneously affected by warm or cold stimulation. Adaptation to a warm stimulus also lowers the threshold (i.e., increases the sensitivity) for cold. Similarly, prolonged cold stimulation reduces the threshold for warmth, so that lower than normal temperatures are sufficient to produce a sensation of warmth.

Physiological Zero A unique aspect of complete adaptation to thermal stimulation is that the thermal quality of the adapting stimulus—warm or cold—is not experienced: it becomes neutral. The adapting temperature that fails to produce a thermal sensation is called **physiological zero.** In other words, physiological zero is the skin temperature at which no thermal sensations are elicited. There is a narrow range of temperatures around the actual adapting temperature, or physiological zero, to which a response of neither warm nor cold occurs. That is, there is a *neutral zone* of complete thermal adaptation or thermal indifference. The size of the neutral zone varies with several factors, but it is usually about 2°–4°C on either side of physiological zero. Thus, a change in temperature that extends beyond this neutral zone is required to produce a thermal experience, and the resulting thermal quality varies with the direction of the temperature change. Normally, physiological zero corresponds to the skin temperature at 33°C (91°F). In other words, temperatures applied to the skin that are close to 33°C feel neither warm nor cold.

However, the skin temperature for producing physiological zero can vary markedly from this value. A demonstration attributed to the British philosopher John Locke in 1690 makes this point. As outlined in Figure 16.20, the right hand is immersed in a 40°C (104°F) basin of water and the left hand in a 20°C (68°F) basin. At first, the right and left hands will feel warm and cold, respectively. However, if both hands are kept in their respective thermal environments for several minutes, they will adapt, so that neither hand will feel any thermal sensation. If, after adaptation, both hands are placed in one 33°C (91°F) basin of water, the water will feel cool to the right hand that was originally in the warm (40°C) water and warm to the left hand that had adapted to the cold (20°C) water. Clearly, physiological zero has shifted for each hand as a result of thermal adaptation.

This relationship of the adapted skin temperature to the temperature of a new thermal environment also demonstrates that the skin does not provide completely accurate temperature information: as indicated by the demonstration of Figure 16.20, the same physical temperature can feel cool to one hand and warm to the other. Thus, thermal sensation is based on the *relation*

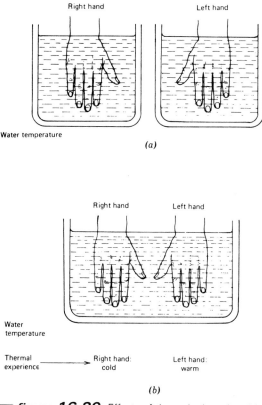

Right hand   Left hand

Water temperature

(a)

Right hand   Left hand

Water temperature

Thermal   ⟶   Right hand: Left hand:
experience   cold   warm

(b)

□ *figure* **16.20** Effects of thermal adaptation. (*a*) Each hand is placed in a separate basin of water and is thermally adapted to a different temperature. (*b*) When both hands are then placed in the 33°C water, the right hand previously adapted to warm water feels cold, and the left hand previously adapted to cold water feels warm. These effects of adaptation show that the skin is not a good indicator of physical temperature.

of the temperature of the skin surface to the temperature of its surroundings rather than on absolute physical temperature. This explanation also applies to the familiar experience of briefly feeling cold after coming out of a heated swimming pool or a hot bath or shower during the summer. What has occurred is that the skin has adapted to the water temperature of the pool, bath, or shower. Thus, even though the air of the poolside or bathroom is quite warm, relative to the temperature of the previously exposed water the air feels cool (evaporation of water from the skin surface may also cause a cooling effect, regardless of the immediate ther-

mal environment). Accordingly, the *temperature differential,* like that affecting the right hand in Figure 16.20*b*, promotes a brief cooling sensation.

In general, the more extreme the temperature, the longer the time required for adaptation. However, complete thermal adaptation occurs only within a restricted range of temperatures. Extremes of temperature do not completely adapt. Immersion of the hands, for example, in very cold or very hot water will produce persistent cold and hot sensations. The range of temperatures within which adaptation occurs is generally 16°–42°C (61°–108°F). However, these limits vary with the bodily region thermally stimulated. In one study using the skin of the forearm, only a very narrow range of temperatures—between 29°C (84°F) and 37°C (99°F)—was subject to adaptation (Kenshalo & Scott, 1966). It was found that temperatures between these rather moderate extremes reached physiological zero rapidly. However, temperatures below or above these values did not undergo complete adaptation but continued to elicit the feeling of coldness or warmth, respectively.

Paradoxical and Synthetic Thermal Sensations

Under certain stimulus conditions, cold skin spots—small skin regions whose stimulation elicits only a cold sensation—will produce a cold sensation when stimulated with a very warm stimulus (45°–50°C or 113°–122°F). This condition is referred to as **paradoxical cold** (discovered by von Frey in 1895). It is paradoxical in that a hot stimulus produces a cold sensation. The neural explanation of this effect relies on the fact that some nerve fibers innervating cold spots respond vigorously not only to cold temperatures but also to high temperatures. No matter how they are stimulated, cold spots elicit *only* a cold sensation.

Relatedly, it is possible to experience *heat* when appropriately stimulated with a warm stimulus. If a stimulus of about 45°C is applied to a small region of the skin that is sensitive to both warmth and coldness, the experience of heat occurs. Warm spots are appropriately activated by the warm stimulus; however, simultaneously, the same warm stimulus paradoxically activates cold spots. Apparently the warm and cold sensations elicited by the same warm thermal stimulus fuse and produce an overall sensation of intense heat (Geldard, 1972; Sherrick & Cholewiak, 1986).

We can simulate or synthesize the heat experience by simultaneously applying warm and cold stimulation to neighboring warm and cold spots on the skin. One approach uses the "heat grill" shown in Figure 16.21. Each set of tubes represents markedly different thermal ranges (the cold coil at, say, 20°C or 68°F and the warm coil at 40°C or 104°F). Touching the heat grill with a region of the arm containing both warm and cold spots produces a sensation of intense heat, that is, it feels about in the 50°–60°C (122°–140°F range). In fact, for some individuals it feels so hot that the limb is quickly withdrawn from the grill as if to avoid a burn, even though the grill is not hot. (This demonstration, like that of paradoxical cold, is not successful with all individuals—which underscores the subjective and somewhat elusive nature of the thermal cutaneous sense and its sensations; see, e.g., Geldard, 1972; Sherrick & Cholewiak, 1986).

Distinct temperature sensations may also be induced by thermally neutral chemicals applied directly to the skin. The cooling effect of menthol on mucous membranes is probably the most familiar example. Synthetic compounds called *icilins* produce sensations of cold by selectively stimulating peripheral skin receptors (Wei & Seid, 1983). Other familiar chemicals such as ether, alcohol, acetone, and gasoline also produce cool sensations when they are applied to the skin surface and then allowed to evaporate. On the other hand, there are chemicals that produce sensations of warmth; some examples are carbon dioxide (when its evaporation is prevented), methyl salicylate (found in ointments such as Ben-Gay), and capsaicin (the main pungent component of hot pepper). They produce a very mild irritation that brings blood to the skin surface, and an intense feeling of warmth results.

PAIN

It is obvious that when the temperature of the skin surface moves toward the extremes—freezing and boiling—thermal experience merges with pain. This is an adaptive association because intense thermal stimulation can produce tissue damage. The painful stimuli immediately cause the organism to respond, protecting it against harmful and perhaps even lethal thermal extremes. We can thus propose that the perception of pain serves an important biological role: it serves as a warning of potential biological harm.

Function of Pain Perception

Although tissue damage is neither necessary nor sufficient to produce pain, most pain-producing stimuli are potentially damaging: intense thermal, sound, light, chemical, and electrical stimulation, under certain conditions, can result in serious bodily harm. Thus, from an evolutionary point of view, pain offers an important biological advantage for survival. Failure to perceive pain can be extremely maladaptive. Reports of self-inflicted injury due to pathological pain

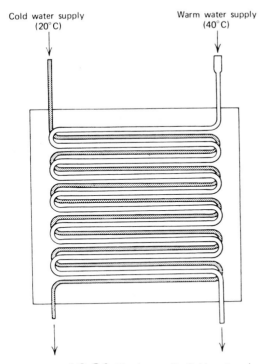

Cold water supply (20°C) Warm water supply (40°C)

□ *figure* **16.21** The heat grill. Cold water circulates through one coil, and warm water circulates through the other coil. If a skin area is placed firmly against the grill, the experience of heat results, although neither of the coils is hot.

insensitivity include serious injuries of the skin, flesh, and bones; burns from hot surfaces and liquids; and even chewing off the tip of the tongue (e.g., Cohen, Kipnes, Kunkle, & Kubzansky, 1955).

In one clinical study of pain-insensitive children, it was noted that they have pushed their eyeballs out of their sockets, pulled their teeth out, and had their fingernails pulled off with almost no discomfort; males were indifferent to testicular compression (Jewesbury, 1951). Among the most well-documented and dramatic instances of chronic insensitivity to pain, and one that illustrates the need for pain mechanisms and perception, is the clinical case reported by Baxter and Olszewski (1960).

The patient, the daughter of a physician, was a young Canadian student at McGill University in Montreal who appeared normal in all ways except that she had never experienced pain. Her apparent insensitivity to pain was noted at an early age. She bit her tongue on so many occasions that it was permanently deformed. Early childhood injuries involving numerous cuts, bruises, burns, frostbites, and abscesses (and their incisions) were experienced without any pain. In addition she denied having any pain from headache, toothache, earache, or stomach ache. By the age of 8 she had been hospitalized on three occasions for orthopedic problems, which were to continue into her adult years. By this age she was aware of her unusual insensitivity to typically painful, tissue-damaging incidents and learned to take precautions to ensure that she had not sustained any unnoticed but serious lacerations.

At the age of 22 she underwent extensive neurological examinations and appeared insensitive to the administration of any noxious stimuli. For example, she experienced no pain to prolonged ice baths (0°C or 32°F for 8 min) or to immersion in hot water (50°C or 122°F for 5 to 8 min); in fact, attempts to establish a pain threshold for heat ended when the patient failed to experience any pain despite thermal stimuli sufficient to cause skin blistering. Of interest is that she also failed to show typical physiological reactions to pain, such as changes in pulse rate, blood pressure, and respiration. However, she did exhibit the expected variations in these measures when subjected to stressful psychological tests that did not use physically noxious stimuli.

Despite her pain insensitivity, she could experience and localize touch, and could distinguish between warm and cold objects anywhere on the body surface, even when the difference between two temperatures was small. Her neurological examination did not reveal any evidence of organic neurological disease. However, her lifelong orthopedic problems became more severe. At age 23 she began to limp and exhibited pathological changes in her hip joint and spine, which were soon followed by numbness and marked muscle weakness in her lower extremities. Several orthopedic operations, including spinal decompression and fusion, were performed but without success. According to Melzack's (1973, p. 16) analysis, the pathological changes were "due to the lack of protection to joints usually given by pain sensations. She apparently failed to shift her weight when standing, to turn over in her sleep, or to avoid certain postures, which normally prevent inflammation of joints."

The patient died at the age of 29 due to intractable massive infections of her hip. During her last month she finally complained of pain in the region of her left hip. According to Baxter and Olszewski (1960, p. 392), "Her lack of pain appreciation was so great that she suffered extensive skin and bone trauma which contributed in a direct fashion to her death."

Qualities of Pain

It is possible to distinguish pain from most other sensory experiences and even to distinguish between classes of pain. Brief skin pain may be characterized as sharp or bright. It is well localized and causes an immediate reaction. It is experienced as being quite different from dull pain originating from deep within the body (the chest and abdomen), which may produce other bodily reactions (e.g., sweating, palpitations) and, in general, is poorly localized (Békésy, 1971).

In the present discussion, we stress the skin as a primary receptive surface for pain. Obviously, however, the locus for pain is not so confined. Pain can result from stimulation of almost any body region, internal as well as on the surface.

At times pain originating from internal organs may appear to occur from another region of the body, usually the surface of the skin. This is called *referred pain*. For example, the intense pain arising from the heart associated with angina pectoris appears to come from the chest wall and from a skin region lying on the inner surface of the upper arm (Lenz et al., 1994). The pain sensations from the oxygen-deprived heart muscles during a heart attack are also mislocalized—often felt in the left shoulder or running down the left arm.

Under certain circumstances, *double pain* may be experienced. That is, two kinds of pain, sharp and dull, occurring from the same stimulation, may be distinguished. The sharp pain is rapidly aroused and is gradually followed by a more persistent dull pain. The sharp and dull pain sensations are independently mediated by fibers of the lemniscal and spinothalamic pathways, respectively. Other pain sensations are pricking pain, produced by a very brief skin surface contact, and burning pain, where the pain-producing stimulus is of greater duration. The list of pains can be further extended to include irritations. For example, an *itch,* produced clinically by mechanical and chemical means, is considered a low-grade pain.

The vast array of pain qualities is suggested by the following catalogue by Dallenbach (1939):

> *achy, beating, biting, boring, bright, burning, clear, cutting, dark, digging, dragging, drawing, dull, fluttering, gnawing, hard, heavy, itchy, nipping, palpitating, penetrating, piercing, pinching, pressing, pricking, quick, quivering, radiating, raking, savage, sharp, smarting, squeezing, stabbing, sticking, stinging, tearing, thrilling, throbbing, thrusting, tugging, twiching, ugly, vicious.* (p. 614)

Pain Stimulus and Pain Thresholds

When the skin is mechanically stimulated, pain is produced by the lengthwise stretching of the skin (Bishop, 1949; Geldard, 1972). This is supported by the observation that injury to the skin such as cutting will be painful if, in the process, the skin is stretched. If cutting is done on skin that is rendered immobile, little or no pain is felt.

Because of marked individual differences in pain experience, general statements about the psychophysics of pain are difficult to make. Another problem is that pain can be elicited by very different stimuli that may not produce the same pain quality. Also, the same stimulus at different intensities can produce very different painful experiences. Furthermore, if tissue damage occurs, side effects, such as inflammation and swelling, further complicate evaluation of the pain experience.

Pain thresholds may be affected not only by the amount of painful stimulation but also by how that stimulation is distributed. Messing and Campbell (1971) demonstrated with rats that when electric shock (presumably painful) was divided over two distinct and widely separated areas (neck *and* tail), the avoidance response was less than when the same electric shock was applied to a single region (neck *or* tail): "Rats preferred shock in two (anatomical) locations to an equal amount in one location" (p. 225).

Relatedly, pain can often be masked or dulled by simultaneously introducing another nonpainful but intense cutaneous sensation. Competing, nonpainful stimulation may displace and thus diminish the pain sensation. This explains why rubbing the skin around an injury often reduces its pain. Similarly, scratching an itch temporarily reduces its low-grade pain. Pain may also be reduced by introducing a second pain, thereby creating a "counterirritation." Thus, tightly squeezing a finger undergoing splinter removal often reduces the pain of the irritated wound.

There are also gender-related effects and differences in pain sensitivity and thresholds. Goolkasian (1980) reported that women with normal menstrual periods had heightened sensitivity to pain during ovulation. In contrast, for women in whom ovulation was inhibited (by the use of oral contraceptives), there was no change in pain sensitivity across the menstrual phase. There is also evidence of gender differences in reaction to pain. Using electrocutaneous shock, Jones and Gwynn (1984) reported that women typically rated the same shock as more painful than men. Rollman and Harris (1987), also employing electric shock, observed that women had significantly lower pain thresholds.

While there appears to be a gender difference in response to electrocutaneous shock, Lautenbacher and Strian (1991) found no pain threshold difference between men and women when a heat stimulus was used. Generally speaking, there is not enough convincing evidence to conclude that pain thresholds for men and women differ reliably from each other.

Subjective Factors in Pain Experience

Pain is a subjective experience; as such, it involves more than the use of a noxious stimulus. Psychological factors such as expectation and attitude, attention and suggestion, motivation, emotional states and cognitive processes, and the meanings attached to the source of the pain may greatly affect the intensity and quality of the pain experienced. Indeed, the observation of a uniform sensation threshold that depends only on and is directly proportional to the pain stimuli applied is usually restricted to the laboratory. In the real world, psychological factors can radically modify the pain experience. A stimulus that is extremely painful in one situation may not be in another. Thus, an injury sustained in battle or sports may not be as painful as when it occurs in a less emotional situation. Moreover, the same injury may produce different effects in different persons.

From time to time, various sociocultural and ethnic effects have also been proposed to affect pain thresholds directly (e.g., Hardy, Wolff, & Goodell, 1952) and pain tolerance levels (Sternbach & Tursky, 1965). Melzack (1973) describes several culturally based initiation rites and rituals (of India and of the North American Plains Indians) that involve suspending and swinging celebrants by skewers and hooks inserted into their chest and backs as part of a religious ceremony. Rather than showing the effects of pain, the celebrants appear to be in a state of exaltation and ecstasy. That the range of pain tolerance may be linked to culture is further supported by some clinical observations following major surgery. H. Keim (1981), an orthopedic surgeon, reported that he performed spinal grafts or fusions (in which bone fragments are

chipped from regions of the pelvic bone and placed over vertebrae) on Canadian Indians on one day, and on the next day they walked about as if without any pain. Such stoic behavior was rarely observed in members of other cultural groups.

Overall, we may conclude that psychological factors can exert potent effects on pain experience and account for a high degree of variability in perceived and reported pain. It is worth noting that pain is not a single sensation produced by a single or specific stimulus. It may include a range of different, unpleasant experiences produced by a large set of potentially noxious events that are linked to one's personal history.

Pain Adaptation

Most people who have suffered prolonged, unrelenting pain—toothache, headache, burn, nerve trauma—agree that the pain seems to last indefinitely; that is, it does not seem to adapt. Moreover, from an evolutionary point of view, it could be argued that pain should not adapt, for that would reduce its survival value. However, adaptation to pain is not necessarily maladaptive. The profound biological benefit of pain, especially cutaneous pain, is seen in its *initial* effect. Because of the very urgent, almost primitive nature of pain, it usually demands immediate attention and elicits an immediate response. Thus, so long as the initial pain is perceived and quickly reacted to (generally by withdrawal), no further biological advantage is conferred by prolonging it. Moreover, a long period of unadapted pain may even be harmful. In fact, it is reasonable that after its initial impact, pain should adapt because continued attention to it could detract from or interfere with survival activities, especially those that help avoid or eliminate the source of the pain (and accompanying potential tissue injury). In short, pain should be reduced when the organism must engage in activities vital to its survival.

Furthermore, in cases where cutaneous pain does not adapt, it is not always clear if the stimulus and receptor conditions in the region of the injury are held constant (which is necessary for adaptation). Most painful conditions occur with continual variations at the site of injury. Thus, skin pain may not *appear* to adapt, either because neighboring but different regions are continually being stimulated or because the stimulation of a single region is varying.

Evidence strongly suggests that, within limits, cutaneous pain does adapt. Depending on the stimulus conditions, the skin adapts to the pain of thermal extremes. Complete pain adaptation, for example, occurs within 5 min when the hand is immersed in 0°C water. The pain due to temperatures up to about 47°C (117°F) may also be adapted to, although the pain from even higher temperatures, in the range of tissue damage, appears to be nonadapting (Hardy, Stolwijk, & Hoffman, 1968; Kenshalo, 1971). In general, the rate of adaptation to pain varies with the amount of skin involved: the smaller the skin area, the sooner the pain adaptation induced by both warm and cold stimulation.

When pain is induced mechanically, such as by the insertion of a needle, adaptation occurs because of a *lack* of effective stimulation. For example, the pain produced by inserting a needle soon adapts, but it recurs when the needle is withdrawn. The tissue movement is the painful stimulation; thus, when the needle is held steady within the skin, it causes no stimulation, hence no pain sensation.

In the next section, we consider the receptor for pain and then discuss how cutaneous pain is transmitted to the brain. In the final sections of this chapter, we will examine physiological and chemical mechanisms that appear to reduce or inhibit the transmission and experience of pain.

The Nociceptor

It is generally accepted that pain is a unique perceptual experience resulting from the excitation of a specialized receptor—a **nociceptor** (from the Latin, *nocere,* "to injure"; a receptor whose stimulation produces injury to the body and whose sensations are unpleasant)—that can be triggered by a wide range of stimuli. This is supported by the fact that, using mapping techniques, there are regions or spots of the skin that, when stimulated, yield only pain. Of interest is that pain spots are more numerous than pressure and thermal spots, and their distribution appears to be diffuse. Further evidence for pain as a separate sense comes

from measurements taken when the skin is made insensitive by the use of morphine. Morphine renders the skin insensitive to pain but has little effect on the other cutaneous sensations. In the dramatic case of congenital pain insensitivity noted earlier, the woman was able to perceive pressure and to make thermal discriminations (Baxter & Olszewski, 1960). Also, the thresholds for pain and touch have been shown to differ greatly (Gibson, 1968).

The identification of a special receptor for pain has been a problem for the nociceptor notion. However, based, in part, on the observation that *free nerve endings* are distributed throughout the skin, as well as in much of the internal anatomy, muscles, tendons, joints, and connective tissue of the viscera, they are believed to be the nociceptor.

Spinal Gate Control Theory

The notion of a specific nociceptor for pain (free nerve endings) is well accepted, but it cannot account for all of the circumstances in which psychological factors affect the quality and amount of pain felt. If stimulation of free nerve endings alone is responsible for pain, then we should always experience pain when they are stimulated by noxious stimuli, and the degree of pain should vary closely with the degree of stimulation. However, as we noted earlier (and probably personally experienced by the reader from time to time), pain can vary greatly, depending on psychological factors such as emotional state, expectation, attention, attitude, and even the social context in which the painful stimulus is applied. In short, both cognitive-psychological factors and nociceptors are involved in the experience of pain.

One attempt to incorporate many of the psychological factors associated with pain perception with the effects of nociceptor stimulation is the **spinal gate control theory** (Melzack & Walls, 1965). The theory proposes that a neurological gate control system within the spinal cord modulates, or "gates," the amount of painful neural activity transmitted from the peripheral receptors and fibers of the skin to the brain via the spinal cord (depicted in simplified form, indicating the operation of the *spinal gate,* in Figure 16.22). It is assumed that the gate control system re-

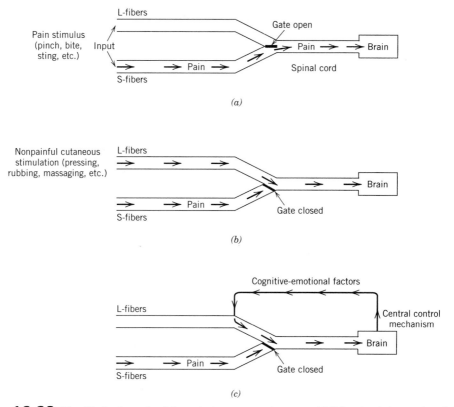

figure 16.22 Simplified schematic of the spinal gate control system. (*a*) Pain stimulation excites S-fibers; this opens the spinal gate, and pain signals are sent by way of the spinal cord to the brain. (*b*) Pain stimulation excites S-fibers. However, some forms of nonpainful cutaneous stimulation also excite L-fibers, which override S-fiber activity. This closes the spinal gate and reduces pain. (*c*) Pain stimulation excites S-fibers. However, the central control mechanism in the brain is activated by cognitive-emotional factors such as stress and excitement. This sends neural signals down, closing the spinal gate and reducing pain.

ceives neural inputs from three sources: (1) large-diameter fibers linked to cutaneous receptors, (2) small-diameter fibers also linked to skin receptors, and (3) a *central control mechanism* that transmits neuronal activity from the brain. The large-diameter fibers (*L-fibers*) are *rapidly conducting* fibers that convey sharp, quickly adapting pain, as well as other sensory events (e.g., low-frequency vibration, massage, gentle rubbing). The small-diameter fibers (*S-fibers*) are *slowly conducting* fibers that transmit dull, aching or burning pain. (Recall from an earlier discussion that fast-conducting, large-diameter fibers are part of the *lemniscal* system and slow-conducting,

small-diameter fibers are from the *spinothalamic* system.) We will first consider the role of the L- and S-fibers on pain transmission.

L- and S-fibers exert different effects on the spinal gate that, in turn, create opposite effects on pain transmission. While both transmit certain forms of pain, stimulation of the rapidly conducting L-fibers also *closes* the spinal gate, which *reduces* pain transmission. In contrast, stimulation of the S-fibers holds the gate in a relatively *open* position and *increases* pain transmission. This means that pain can be relieved by either reducing S-fiber activity or increasing L-fiber activity. Thus, at levels of high stimulation that accompany injury, bursts of S-fiber activity open the gate, and pain results. If, however, gentle stimulation, such as rubbing or massage, is applied to a region of the skin near the site of a painful wound, the transmission will contain rapidly conducted L-fiber impulses that arrive sooner than the pain signals from the slower S-fiber signals. This partially closes the gate and reduces pain. Accordingly, it is the competitive activity of fast L-fibers and slow S-fibers in the spinal cord that determines how much pain is experienced. In short, the spinal gate notion explains pain as the result of an increase in the activity of S-fibers and/or a decrease in the activity of L-fibers.

As we indicated above, inhibitory neural input to the gate control mechanism is also transmitted from a cortical *central control mechanism,* producing a cognitive-emotional effect on the pain experience. The central control is the neural mechanism whereby psychological factors such as excitement or emotions, attention, attitude, and social circumstances influence sensory input through the spinal gate system. The central control thus inhibits the influence on pain sensation by sending neural messages down from the brain via neural pathways to stimulate the rapid L-fibers and close the spinal gate. This accounts for the many instances in which ongoing mental activity—intense emotions, stress, great excitement—seem to block or reduce pain even when tissue injury is substantial. This inhibitory response to pain under stressful conditions has been labeled *stress-induced analgesia.*

The spinal gate control theory is not universally accepted, in part, because there is little direct physiological evidence of it and because some of its details are incorrect (e.g., Besson & Chaouch, 1987). Still, it is a convenient neural scheme that accounts for many different observations on pain, as well as the central idea that pain has a strong perceptual-psychological basis along with a biological cause. Moreover, many of its clinical implications have proven empirically useful in treating pain. In particular, the notion that stimulation of L-fibers closes the spinal gate and reduces pain has been applied to the management of chronic pain. In fact, the spinal gate control theory explains the early finding by Livingston (1948) that *causalgia* (a severe, prolonged buring pain produced

by lesions to peripheral nerves) could be controlled by therapy such as bathing the injured region in gently moving water followed by massage—both of which appear to stimulate L-fiber activity. Later, Wall and Sweet (1967) applied low-intensity electrical pulses—experienced as tingling—to patients with chronic cutaneous pain. These stimulated mainly L-fibers and presumably closed the spinal gate. After a 2-min application of this electrical stimulation, four of eight patients with chronic peripheral nerve diseases experienced significant relief of their pain. Chronic pain is also relieved by a device that transmits a form of low-voltage electrical stimulation called *transcutaneous electrical nerve stimulation (TENS).* Although by itself TENS produces only a tingling sensation, for some individuals it does appear to provide long-term clinical pain relief during and after stimulation, presumably by stimulating L-fibers.

The gate control notion also accounts for *phantom limb pain*—apparently vivid, intense pain in an amputated limb. Although phantom limb pain usually decreases and eventually disappears, there are cases where the pain intensifies over time (Katz & Melzack, 1990; Melzack, 1992). It is difficult to account for such pain because the peripheral pain receptors are removed along with the limbs. However, Melzack (1970) has noted that when a limb is amputated, about half of the cut nerve fibers that still remain in the stump die. The rest regenerate and grow into stump tissue, and these fibers are usually S-fibers. Thus, the full range of fiber sizes is missing in the stump. Pertinent to our present discussion is that the lack of L-fibers produces a corresponding lack of inhibitory effect in the sensory pathway from the spinal cord to the brain. In short, lacking L-fibers, the presumed spinal gate is kept open, resulting in chronic phantom pain. (Note that other explanations of the source of phantom limb pain exist, e.g., Ramachandran, 1993.)

Acupuncture

Striking and sometimes profound anesthetic effects are produced by the traditional Asian therapy for the treatment of disease and control of pain, **acupuncture** (from the Latin, *acus,* for "needle" and *pungere,* "to sting"). Here we are not concerned with the merits of acupuncture for the treatment of disease but rather with its application to pain. In most cases, electrified needles, set in movement (twirled) and often heated, are inserted at various bodily locations. The potential needle sites are charted precisely and vary with the pain site. Although Western medicine has been cautious in accepting acupuncture as valid, most of the reports so far have been positive (e.g., Gwei-Djen & Needham, 1979). Precisely how acupuncture works to eliminate pain is still debated. However, the gate control theory provides a reasonable explanation. The sensory input appears to be a critical factor. Perhaps electrifying, twirling, and heating the needles produce a stream of nonpainful sensations that stimulate the L-fibers of the sensory nerves, which close the gate in the spinal cord. Accordingly, the needles, by selectively and continuously stimulating the L-fibers, block pain impulses that travel along the S-fibers. This, of course, does not explain the full range of anesthetic effects produced by acupuncture, such as inserting needles in the arm to allow painless dental extractions.

Endorphins and Enkephalins

Acupuncture may also induce the neural secretion of an endogenous pain suppressor, an opiate-like chemical (opiates are a class of chemical compounds derived from the opium poppy plant). Indeed, endogenous chemicals called **enkephalins** (from the Greek, *kephalé,* meaning "head") and **endorphins** (from "endogenous morphine") have been isolated. These chemicals appear to be neurotransmitters for events relating to pain and perhaps other bodily processes (Marx, 1979; Wasacz, 1981). Although endorphin is used as a general term to describe both normally occurring opiate-like substances, endorphins are found in high concentrations in the pituitary, whereas enkephalins are found broadly and unevenly distributed in the brain, spinal cord, and intestines (e.g., Akil et al., 1978; Lewis et al., 1981).

Endorphins appear to have specific binding sites or receptors (Pasternak, Childers, & Snyder, 1980), which in some cases are the same as the binding sites of the opiates (e.g., morphine and heroin). It is reasonable to speculate that specific binding or receptor sites did not evolve in the human solely to receive external chemical stimuli such as the opiates: These receptor sites must have developed for substances produced within the body (Wasacz, 1981). It is of interest that one form of brain endogenous opiate, β-endorphin, shows an even higher affinity for the body's opiate receptor sites than does morphine; it also has stronger analgesic properties than does morphine (Kelly, 1984). As with exogenous opiates, chronic administration of β-endorphin produces tolerance (i.e., progressive weakening of its analgesic effects), and its abrupt withdrawal initiates all the distressing effects of morphine addiction.

Endorphins and Naloxone The pain-reducing role of endorphins has been firmly established based on its interaction with a potent opiate-antagonist substance called **naloxone.** Because of its strong inhibitory effect on opiates, naloxone is often given to individuals who have overdosed on opiate-derived narcotics such as morphine and heroin. Naloxone counters or reverses the pain-relieving activity of opiates by binding with pain receptors so that they cannot be excited by opiates.

Just as it does for opiates, naloxone reduces the pain-suppressing effect of endorphins. For example, rats repeatedly given unavoidable electric shock secrete larger amounts of endorphin and later appear less sensitive to pain (i.e., show elevated pain thresholds) than rats that do not experience the inescapable shock (e.g., Lewis, Cannon, & Liebeskind, 1980). However, the injection of naloxone reverses the pain insensitivity. Thus, in situations where endorphins are secreted and pain is reduced, the injection of naloxone lowers the pain threshold to preendorphin levels (Fanselow, 1979; Maier, Drugan, & Grau, 1982). This indicates that the pain-reducing effect of the unavoidable shock is mediated by the release of endorphins.

Naloxone also reverses the pain-suppressing effect of acupuncture but not the effects of hypnosis, suggesting that only acupuncture involves the release of endorphins (Goldstein & Hilgard, 1975; Spiegel & Albert, 1983). The analgesic effect of endorphins is also consistent with the spinal gate control notion. The spinal cord is highly enriched with both opiate receptors (Yaksh, 1978) and endorphin-containing neurons (Neale et al., 1978; Snyder, 1977). Accordingly, endorphins secreted by the brain and spinal cord may selectively stimulate L-fibers, which then close the presumed spinal gate and suppress the transmission of pain.

Endorphins and Stress Certain forms of severe stress may help activate an endogenous analgesia system—stress-induced analgesia—suggesting that endorphins may serve a biologically significant role in pain management and control (e.g., Terman et al., 1984). However, as we emphasized earlier, pain provides an immense biological advantage: it normally demands immediate attention, and it may initiate adaptive action necessary for survival. Accordingly a system that suppresses pain should be used only in emergencies where the normal reaction to pain could disrupt coping strategies and prove dangerous. That is, there may be conditions where the suppression or reduction of pain is useful for survival (e.g., Willer, Dehen, & Cambier, 1981).

Laboratory studies of animals confronting stresslike conditions support this notion. For example, endorphin system activity has been observed in pregnant rats (Gintzler, 1980) and with food deprivation (Gambert, Garthwaite, Pontzer, & Hagen, 1980; Mandenoff, Fumeron, Apfelbaum, & Margules, 1982; McGivern & Berntson, 1980). It has been reported that the pain produced by exposure to inescapable foot shock, administered to rats intermittently for 30 min, caused significant analgesic effects (Lewis, Cannon, & Liebeskind, 1980). It has also been reported that after repeated exposure to physical attack, defeated mice secrete endorphins and show effects of pain suppression (Miczek, Thompson, & Shuster, 1982). Associated with these analgesic effects are displays of submissive behavior and the typical posture of defeat in mice, characterized by an upright position, limp forepaws, upwardly angled head, and retracted ears. However, it should be noted that although severe stress appears to trigger pain suppression through endorphin activity, the exact mechanisms have not been identified.

We do not understand all of the physiological and psychological mechanisms involved in pain. Clearly, pain is produced by a huge variety of physical contacts, especially intense mechanical ones that stimulate the nociceptors (free nerve endings) over the skin. However, pain mediation can also be examined at a biochemical level. While this topic extends well beyond the scope of this chapter, it is important for a full understanding the mechanisms that produce pain.

When tissue is damaged, the injured cells release a variety of potent pain-inducing chemicals—including *histamine, bradykinin,* and *prostaglandin*—that activate nociceptors and decrease the pain threshold. Moreover, a complex interaction between some of the chemical agents heightens the pain by sensitizing the nociceptors. Thus, when bradykinin is released by injured cells, it enhances the synthesis and release of prostaglandin, which, in turn, increases the sensitivity of the nociceptor free nerve endings to histamine. The pain-reducing effect of common analgesics such as aspirin is based on the fact that, in part, they interfere with prostaglandin synthesis.

SUMMARY

This chapter has focused on the skin or cutaneous sense and its sensitivity to touch (or pressure), temperature, and pain. It was noted that cutaneous sensations are registered by mechanical or thermal stimulation of the skin. However, the skin is not uniformly sensitive to cutaneous stimulation: some regions are more sensitive than others.

The receptors and nerve endings that appear to mediate cutaneous sensations were identified: mainly the basket cells, encapsulated end organs, Pacinian corpuscles, and free nerve endings; however, there is no precise relationship between cutaneous sensation and receptor type. We concluded that a given cutaneous sensation may be produced by different specialized receptors in the skin: many different receptors show some reaction to a variety of stimuli.

Cutaneous representation of the skin in the region of the brain responsible for skin sensations (the somatosensory cortex) was discussed. It was noted that the skin is topographically projected onto the somatosensory cortex. We concluded that the skin areas that are most sensitive to stimulation—such as the fingers and certain facial regions—are more densely supplied with nerve fibers and are thus represented by larger areas of the somatosensory cortex. The functional link between the topographic representation of the brain and the skin region was illustrated by the sensory homunculus.

The link between the skin and neural pathways to the somatosensory cortex was next described: nerve fibers of the lemniscal pathway are large in diameter, conduct rapidly, and transmit precise positional information about touch, movement, and sharp pain. The nerve fibers of the spinothalamic pathway are small in diameter, conduct slowly, and transmit information on nonlocalized touch, temperature, and pain. It was observed that the receptive fields of neurons of the somatosensory cortex is a specific area of the skin that, when stimulated, alter the firing rate of the neurons. The receptive fields of neurons in the lemniscal pathway are more numerous, smaller, and more densely distributed than those of the spinothalamic pathway. This enables finer tactual discriminations by neurons of the lemniscal pathway.

Another neural distinction was made between nerve fibers of the cutaneous sense. One class of fibers responds best when pressure is applied and maintained on the skin surface. These are called slowly adapting (SA) fibers. Another class of fibers responds only when pressure begins and ends. These fibers are called rapidly adapting (RA) fibers.

The next section focused on touch or pressure. In describing the stimulus for touch, we distinguished between active and passive touch. We also noted that the stimulus for touch is an indentation or change in the shape of the skin: uniform or very gradual continuous changes in pressure are not effective stimuli for touch. The mechanoreceptor for touch was introduced, with a brief discussion of the largest touch receptor, the Pacinian corpuscle.

Several thresholds for touch were presented: the absolute, point localization, and two-point thresholds. It was noted that regions of the face and fingers are the most touch-sensitive parts of the body. For point localization—localizing the point on the skin touched—the more mobile the skin region stimulated (e.g., the hands and parts of the face), the more acute the point localization. This also applies to the two-point threshold, the smallest separation between two

adjacent points of stimulation on the skin that just produces two distinct impressions of touch. In the context of touch thresholds, Aristotle's illusion was introduced. In this illusion, two distinct sensations may arise from a single stimulus if it is simultaneously applied to two regions of the fingers that are not ordinarily stimulated together (such as when two adjacent fingers are crossed, and the V created by the fingertips is stimulated with a single object). Finally in this context, adaptation to touch was discussed and some of the variables that affect it were identified.

The next section dealt with three systems in which touch stimulation enables the pickup of complex information about the environment: the Braille system of tactual reading, the Tadoma method of speech reception for the deaf-blind, and the tactual–visual substitution system. In the last system, a visual image converted into a complex pattern of touch is applied to the skin surface. This allows the individual to perceive a meaningful sensation directly related to the visual image.

Kinesthesis was described as the reception of information about the posture, location, and movement in space of the limbs and other mobile parts of the jointed skeleton. The receptors for kinesthesis are located at the joints, muscles, and tendons. Due to the interaction of cutaneous and kinesthetic stimulation, we are unable to tickle ourselves when stroking certain regions of our own bodies. In contrast, when someone else touches the same regions, only cutaneous stimulation is available and a tickling results.

The last section on touch focused on combined input from the skin and kinesthesis in the haptic system. This system helps us perceive geometric properties of objects (e.g., shape, weight, consistency, size) by handling them. This led to a discussion of roughness enhancement and tactual stereognosis; the latter is the ability to perceive three-dimensional shapes by handling and palpation.

Next, the perception of temperature was discussed. It was noted that thermal experience depends on the relation between the temperature of the skin surface and that of its surroundings. Thermal receptors and thermal spots on the skin surface were briefly discussed. We noted that sensitivity to temperature is irregularly distributed over the skin surface. This led to a discussion of thermal conductivity: the rate at which a surface draws heat from or to the skin. Within limits, if the thermal environment is held constant, the sensation of either warmth or coldness decreases until adaptation—the complete absence of thermal sensation—results. The temperature range of stimuli required for adaptation is called physiological zero. The last section on temperature sensation covered paradoxical and synthetic thermal sensations.

The final section of this chapter dealt with the perception of pain. Its informative role, as well as its benefit for survival, was stressed. The qualities of pain and the variety of stimuli that induce pain were outlined, and the conditions that modify pain, such as adaptation, gender, and various psychological-emotional factors, were discussed.

It was noted that pain results from stimulation of a specialized receptor—a nociceptor—that can be triggered by a wide range of stimuli. The nociceptor nerve endings are assumed to be free nerve endings.

The spinal gate control theory of pain was outlined. It proposes that pain results from the action of a neurological gate control system in the spinal cord that reduces, or "gates out," the neural activity transmitted from the skin to the brain by way of the spinal cord. Large-diameter, fast-conducting fibers (L-fibers) in the sensory nerves running from the skin to the central nervous system close a "gate" in the pain-signaling system of the spinal cord, reducing the pain received; small-diameter, slow-conducting fibers (S-fibers) open the spinal gate and increase the pain signals reaching the brain. The theory also proposes a central control mechanism that transmits neural activity from the brain to the gate control system; this mechanism allows cognitive-emotional effects to close the gate, reducing pain experience. Evidence and clinical observations that support or weaken the spinal gate control theory were outlined.

Finally, we discussed conditions that affect pain experience: the presumed analgesic effects of acupuncture and endorphins, which are endogenous, opiate-like chemicals. Their possible link to the spinal gate control theory was noted.

KEY TERMS

Acupuncture
Aristotle's Illusion
Braille System
Cutaneous Sensitivity
Endorphins
Enkephalins
Free Nerve Endings
Haptic System
Homunculus
Kinesthesis
Lemniscal Pathway
Naloxone
Nociceptor
Pacinian Corpuscles
Paradoxical Cold
Physiological Zero
Point Localization
Rapidly Adapting (RA) Fibers
Receptive Field
Roughness Enhancement
Slowly Adapting (SA) Fibers
Somatosensory Cortex
Spinal Gate Control Theory
Spinothalamic Pathway
Tactual Stereognosis
Tactual–Visual Substitution System
Tadoma Method
Thermal Conductivity
Two-Point Threshold

STUDY QUESTIONS

1. Discuss the function of the skin. Distinguish between its protective and sensory functions.

2. Identify the cutaneous sensations and describe how cutaneous receptors are distributed over the skin surface.

3. Identify the nerve endings and receptors controlling cutaneous sensations. Describe the main factors linking a specific sensation to a specific receptor.

4. What is the homunculus, and what does it indicate about the relation between the skin surface and the somatosensory cortex?

5. Compare the lemniscal neural pathway with the spinothalamic pathway, indicating the different kinds of stimulation each transmits. Discuss the two pathways with reference to the receptive fields of the skin. Indicate how the size and density of receptive fields influence tactual sensitivity.

6. Distinguish between slowly adapting (SA) and rapidly adapting (RA) fibers that link the skin to the nervous system. Indicate the different sorts of stimulation that they encode and transmit to the brain.

7. Describe the effective stimulus for touch sensation. What is the difference between active and passive touch? Identify and describe the function of the Pacinian corpuscle for touch.

8. Describe the different kinds of thresholds for touch. Indicate the general relationship between skin region location and touch sensitivity.

9. Describe and explain Aristotle's illusion. Identify the stimulus factors that affect adaptation to touch.

10. Describe how complex touch changes on the skin convey spatial information and enable communication. Consider the Braille system, the Tadoma method, and the tactual–visual substitution system. Could complex touch stimulation provide spatial information to the blind individual? Elaborate on this.

11. Identify and examine the role of kinesthesis in gaining information about body position.

12. Explain why you can't seem to tickle youself.

13. What is the haptic system, and how does the combined use of kinesthesis and cutaneous stimulation enable tactual stereognosis?

14. Describe the function of a sensory-perceptual system that provides sensations of warm and cold.

15. What are the receptors for thermal sensations? What are thermal spots? Examine the relationship between skin temperature and thermal experience. Consider whether the physical temperature of the skin is effective in producing thermal sensations.

16. What is thermal conductivity, and what is its role in producing thermal sensations? Examine thermal adaptation and physiological zero. What are the ranges and limits of thermal adaptation?

17. What is paradoxical cold? Explain the sensation of heat with respect to the combined sensations of warm and cold. Include the heat grill in your discussion.

18. Discuss the adaptive role of pain and indicate its function. Examine the effect on general health if pain sensations are totally and permanently eliminated.

19. Discuss the general stimulus conditions that induce pain sensations. Describe the qualities of pain.

20. What variables affect pain thresholds? What threshold effects can be attributed to gender and to subjective-psychological factors such as expectation, attention, suggestion, and culture?

21. Examine adaptation to pain. Is this adaptation maladaptive?

22. What is the primary receptor for pain? Discuss the nociceptor and identify the nerve ending that appears to serve as the nociceptor for the skin.

23. Outline the spinal gate control theory of pain, indicating evidence and clinical observations that support it. How does this theory explain stress-induced analgesia and phantom limb pain?

24. Describe acupuncture and assess its role in pain control. What are endorphins? What environmental conditions promote the activity of an endorphin system?

25. Examine the relation of acupuncture and endorphins to the spinal gate control theory. How can naloxone assess the role of endorphins in pain experience? What effect does histamine, bradykinin, and prostaglandin have on pain experience?

chapter 17

THE CHEMICAL SENSE OF TASTE

*Our focus in this chapter and the following one will be on the chemical senses: taste (**gustation;** from the Latin gustare, "to taste") and smell (olfaction). Both taste and smell depend on receptors that are normally stimulated by chemical substances. Accordingly, these receptors are termed **chemoreceptors.** Aside from the fact that taste and smell are both activated by chemical stimuli, they are functionally related. The interdependence of smell and taste in food ingestion is common. If our ability to smell is reduced or eliminated by blockage of the air passages of the nostrils (such as with a bad cold), different foods may taste similar. For example, a raw potato tastes surprisingly similar to an apple. Relatedly, individuals lacking a sense of smell cannot distinguish between different meats on the basis of their taste alone (Moncrieff, 1951).*

DEMONSTRATION:
The Effect of Odor on Taste

Many taste qualities assigned to food are actually due to their odors. You can verify this easily with differently flavored jelly beans. Without looking at their colors, chew them one at a time while holding your nostrils closed. You will most likely find that they all taste like the same sugary paste. However, if you suddenly release your nostrils while chewing one of them, the flavor of a distinct jelly bean will emerge. Similarly, without the ability to smell them, the characteristic sensations from many appealing substances such as chocolate and vanilla are lost (Freedman, 1993). In other words, these sensations are much more affected by smell than by taste. This suggests a diet aid for certain individuals: reducing the odor of foods, rendering them somewhat tasteless, may decrease their appeal and perhaps their consumption.

THE DIVERSITY AND ORIGINS OF CHEMORECEPTION

It is neither necessary nor even possible to make a clear distinction between taste and smell in all animals. There is evidence that many forms of marine life can detect nearby chemical substances. Fish possess a pit resembling a nose lined with chemoreceptors, as well as taste receptors scattered over the surface of the body and mouth. In water the ability to detect chemical substances is not easily separated into smell and taste, since both give information about chemical substances in a surrounding medium. Perhaps when amphibians emerged from the sea, a general chemore-

449

ceptive system separated into two anatomically distinct but functionally united mechanisms to take into account the chemical information occurring in two different environments.

However, since receptors for taste (taste buds) occur in almost all vertebrates, a taste system developed early in the evolution of vertebrate phylogeny. According to Glass (1967), taste preceded smell. Smell developed as a means of extracting chemical information from air—"taste at a distance"—typically occurring as a by-product of breathing and sniffing. It is an active process enabling the detection of events at a distance by means of their odors. In fact, the close relationship between breathing and smelling suggests that a channel of information is continually open and explains the strong alertness of many organisms to odors. In contrast, the capacity to detect information from liquids became limited to the mouth and tongue; the mouth, being somewhat internalized, retained a liquid base of saliva and moist mucosa. In addition to its receptors for perceiving chemical solutions, the mouth is able to perceive cutaneous, haptic information such as the relative location, bulk, texture, and temperature of substances.

The Functions of Chemoreception

Chemical signals mediate a constant flow of information and thus can be powerful, immediate guides for biological and behavioral action. Accordingly, chemoreception in the human is the result of a long evolutionary pressure to react to a dynamic and highly informative chemical environment. Because seeking and ingesting food are vital to survival, it is reasonable that chemoreception evolved to serve a primary nutritional function. As suggested by J. J. Gibson (1966) and others, functionally, taste and smell together may be considered a food-seeking and sampling system, consisting of numerous dietary activities—seeking, testing, and selecting or rejecting the food or drink. Of course, smell precedes taste in this process. As Moncrieff (1951) puts it, "Smell is the distance receptor for food and taste gives the food the final check, approving it, or disapproving, such disapproval being the forerunner of disgust" (p. 58). However, for certain environmental events, taste and smell may be inde-

pendently employed. Smell may be used to pick up nonnutritive information such as the presence of a predator or prey or for sexual activities, whereas taste helps us to regulate the intake of nutrients and to avoid tainted and toxic substances (Palmerino et al., 1980). That is, taste enables an organism to sample substances prior to ingestion. For example, taste alone is responsible for certain dietary preferences, as in the case of the salt-deprived rat, which, when confronted with a series of foods, chooses the salty one (Richter, 1942).

TASTE PRIMARIES AND THE CHEMICAL STIMULUS

Taste Primaries

On the basis of human experience, four basic or **primary tastes** have been distinguished: *sweet, sour, salty,* and *bitter.* Other tastes have also been suggested as possible primaries. For example, Lawless (1987) notes the possibility of a primary *metallic* taste and an *umami* taste, the latter considered a basic taste in Japanese psychophysics (see also S. S. Schiffman, 1988; Scott & Plata-Salaman, 1991, p. 351). **Umami** is translated loosely as "delicious taste" or "savoriness" and refers to the taste sensations elicited by MSG (*monosodium glutamate,* an amino acid substance we will discuss later in the section on taste modifiers). Generally, however, most discussions and the vast research literature on human taste continue to recognize the existence of only four primaries (e.g., Bartoshuk, 1988; Erickson, 1984; Levinson, 1995).

That there are only four primary tastes should not, however, lead to the conclusion that the range of taste sensations is greatly limited. Recall from Chapter 5 that an immense range of color sensations results from the activity of only three kinds of cone photoreceptors. Indeed, as we shall see in a later section on taste interactions, a wide variety of complex tastes can be derived from the four primaries.

Origins of Taste Primaries

There has been a good deal of speculation about the significance of these primary tastes to the human. According to Moncrieff (1951), saltiness and sourness are more basic owing to the evolutionary development of taste from sea life: "As we are descended from sea-inhabiting invertebrates we should expect the salt taste to be the most primitive, followed by the acid [sour] taste, which would function chiefly as a warning. These two tastes are more concerned with environment and safety than with food. Later, when bitter and sweet tastes made their appearance they were concerned with nutrition" (p. 131). Salt is obviously basic to sea life; sourness may indicate foul water, corrosion, or bacterial decomposition. Sweet tastes, so appealing to many species, usually occur in substances with nutritional value. Bitter tastes may signal noxious or toxic substances.

The appeal of salt warrants a special discussion. It is clear that salt serves an adaptive function, playing a unique role in the regulation of bodily fluid. Many chemical reactions require salt. Some processes, such as those involved in the mechanics of the heart, even require a precise concentration of salt in blood plasma. Through perspiration and the regulatory activity of the kidneys, small amounts of salt are gradually lost. If the salt loss is not replaced and becomes excessive, the salt in the blood may fall to a critical level. The body reacts to this imbalance by excreting water in an attempt to raise the concentration of salt in the blood to its functional level. Thus, with a continued inadequate salt level, the body cannot retain water and dehydration sets in; as a result, blood volume plummets, the heart can no longer effectively pump blood, and heart failure occurs.

Clearly, the ingestion of enough salt is necessary for survival. As we recognize in our own lives, an acute, critical loss of sodium stimulates a craving for salty foods (e.g., Beauchamp, 1987). Indeed, salt has been held in high esteem for centuries. It was the custom to allot Roman soldiers a fixed stipend as part of their pay called *salarium argentum* ("salt money") with which to purchase rations of salt. The modern term for a regular payment or wage—*salary*—derives from this custom.

In contrast to what we said earlier, an interesting speculation is that salt did not evolve to ensure an adequate salt diet (with the possible exception of herbivorous animals, such as sheep and deer, who do appear to have a specific "salt hunger"). Instead, the sensitivity to salt evolved primarily as a *warning* against the ingestion of intolerably high concentrations of salt, that is, as a guard against *hypersalinity* (Denton, 1982; Dethier, 1977). In this light, the sensitivity to salt may be viewed as part of a monitoring and regulatory system to detect the presence of excess salts. Indeed, it would be especially critical for animals living near maritime shores to detect excessive salt in their dietary water.

However, in spite of a presumed mechanism for regulating salt intake, the human shows a powerful, perhaps even an unhealthy preference for salt. According to Logue (1991), adult humans need only 1 to 3 grams daily. However, in the United States, they consume 6 to 8 grams or more, far exceeding any nutritional requirements (Beauchamp, 1987; Denton, 1986). The potential health hazard is worth stressing since an overconsumption of salt may be an important factor in hypertension in many individuals.

Chemical Stimulus for Taste

What are the chemical stimuli that give rise to the primary taste sensations? First of all, *all* potential taste stimuli must be dissolved or soluble substances. Normally, to be tasted, a potentially *sapid,* or tastable, substance must go into solution on coming in contact with saliva, which limits tastable chemicals to water-soluble molecules. Accordingly, oily substances are generally poor stimuli for taste.

The chemical characteristics of a substance are the critical determinants of its taste. In general, a sour taste results primarily from acid compounds. In fact, it is speculated that the sour taste may have evolved as a warning taste against substances undergoing bacterial decomposition, most of which become acidic. However, not all acids taste sour (e.g., amino acids and sulfonic acids are sweet), and chemical substances other than acids may also taste sour. Salts generally taste salty, but not always (e.g., cesium chloride is bitter). Bitter tastes occur from alkaloids such as strychnine, quinine, nicotine, and cocaine, but other chemicals also taste bitter (e.g., potassium iodine and magnesium sulfate taste bitter). Sweet tastes, generally resulting from nutrients, are associated with organic substances composed of carbon, hydrogen, and oxygen, such as carbohydrates and amino acids. However, at low concentrations, the nonnutritional synthetic saccharin also tastes sweet (as do chloroform, lead acetate—known as "sugar of lead"—and beryllium salts; in fact, beryllium was originally called *glucinum,* Latin for "sweet element"). In addition, two proteins found in some tropical fruits contain no carbohydrates yet taste intensely sweet (Cagan, 1973).

Specifying the adequate stimulus for a primary taste is even more complex because, for some substances, taste quality changes with concentration. Thus, the taste of sodium saccharin shifts from predominantly sweet to bitter with increased concentration. A similar concentration-dependent effect occurs with some inorganic salts. For example, lithium chloride tastes sweet at low concentrations, and changes to sour and salty as the concentration increases (Dzendolet & Meiselman, 1967).

There are too many exceptions to allow us to account for all tastes on the basis of chemical composition. In fact, there are no definitive rules relating taste experience to the chemical composition of substances. It is even possible to produce a taste experience by injecting a chemical directly into the bloodstream. For example, when injected, saccharin produces the taste experience of sweetness. Taste sensations produced by electrical stimulation are also possible. When the tongue is electrically stimulated by a steady direct current, a sour taste results. The taste experienced depends on the frequency and intensity of the current. Moreover, alternating and direct current may produce different tastes (Pfaffmann, 1959).

ANATOMY AND PHYSIOLOGY OF TASTE

Taste Receptors

The basic receptor structures for taste, called **taste buds** (Figure 17.1), are specialized receptor organs located in tiny pits and grooves of the mouth, throat, pharynx, inside of the cheeks, soft palate (the upper part of the mouth, just above the back of the tongue), and particularly along the dorsal surface or back of the tongue. The human possesses between 9000 and

10,000 taste buds. They are generally found in clusters lying within small but visible elevations on the tongue, called **papillae** (Latin for "nipples"). Several different types of papillae, distinguished by shape and location, have been identified: *fungiform, foliate, circumvallate,* and *filiform* (Figure 17.2). The filiform papillae, primarily located in the center of the tongue, are the only ones that contain no taste buds.

The 50 to 150 cells comprising each taste bud terminate in figure-like projections called *microvilli* (*villus* is Latin for "hair tuft"; Figure 17.1a), which extend into taste pores and are in direct contact with chemical solutions applied to the surface of the tongue. Taste cells have a short life (several days) and are renewed constantly. Indeed, the taste cell is one of the most rapidly aging cells in the body. As the taste cell ages, it moves from the edge of a taste bud toward the center. This suggests that different cell types within a taste bud actually represent different stages in the development, degeneration, and migration of the taste cell. It is proposed that the sensitivity of a taste cell varies with its age. Accordingly, as the organism ages, taste cell replacement slows and the sense of taste diminishes. According to one observation, the taste qualities of sweetness and saltiness show the greatest decrease with age, and bitter and sour tastes are heightened (S. S. Schiffman, 1974*b*). However, the sense of smell declines much more rapidly than the sense of taste. "Hence, foods which are bitter but have a pleasant odor (e.g., green pepper, many other vegetables, chocolate) are experienced as just plain bitter by an aged person because the pleasant odor no longer contributes to the flavor" (S. S. Schiffman, 1975).

Taste Pathways to the Brain

Taste receptors have a multiple nerve supply: the *chorda tympani* branch of the facial nerve serves the front part of the tongue, the *glossopharyngeal nerve* serves the back of the tongue, and the *vagus nerve* serves the deeper recesses of the throat, pharynx, and larynx. The precise neural pathways taken by the taste nerve fibers to the brain are not well established. However, it is known that the nerve fibers travel from the mouth to the thalamus and from there to several

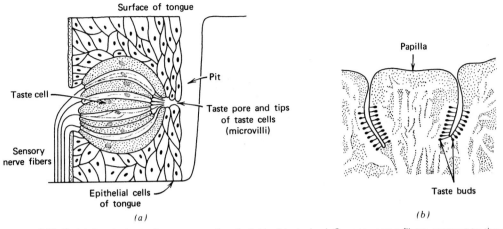

Surface of tongue

Taste cell

Sensory
nerve fibers

Pit

Taste pore and tips
of taste cells
(microvilli)

Epithelial cells
of tongue

(a)

Papilla

Taste buds

(b)

▭ **figure 17.1** (a) Semischematic structure of an individual taste bud. Sensory nerve fibers connect to the taste cells. The tips of the taste cells project microvilli into the taste pore. (b) Clusters of taste buds form papillae.

cortical regions, mainly to the base of the *somatosensory cortex* of the parietal lobe—a cortical region where cutaneous information from the face and mouth is projected (see Figure 1.10 Chapter 1).

Neural Recoding of Taste Receptors

We understand the physiology of taste largely from studying the electrophysiological activity of the taste system. For example, when a microelectrode is inserted into a single taste cell and a taste solution is flowed over the tongue, a measurable change in frequency discharge occurs. Applying various chemical substances to the cell reveals that, in general, a single cell responds to more than one taste solution. Some cells respond to many stimuli, others to relatively few. Also evident is that different cells show different sensitivities to the same stimuli.

Single nerve fiber recordings from the cat's chorda tympani show the same lack of specificity. These recordings show that most fibers respond to more than a single primary taste stimulus. Sensitivity to all four basic qualities has also been demonstrated in single taste buds of human fungiform papillae (Arvidson & Friberg, 1980). Recordings of the neural activity of single cells, taste buds, and nerve fiber stimulation in several species show little evidence of specificity for coding taste stimuli.

Cross-Fiber Patterning

This lack of neural specificity makes it hard to understand taste experiences. Pfaffmann (1959, 1964) proposed an **afferent code** for taste. He argued that taste is based on activity across a population of fibers. Individual fibers may fire to more than one taste stimulus, but they do not all have the same pattern of firing. That each fiber has its own sensitivity profile suggests that taste quality, rather than being coded by a single fiber or set of specific fibers, depends on the *pattern* developed across a great number of fibers. Since there is no neural specificity, a reasonable speculation is that at least part of the coding of taste occurs at more central levels—in the pathways to the brain or in the brain itself.

A critical question about neural activity is what relation these discharge patterns have to the different taste qualities, that is, to the actual tastes experienced? Erickson (1963) developed an interesting behavioral test to investigate **cross-fiber patterning.** He recorded the firings of many chorda tympani fibers in response to different salts. Figure 17.3 shows the neural activity of 13 taste fibers when stimulated by three different salt solutions: sodium chloride (NaCl), potassium chloride (KCl), and ammonium chloride (NH₄Cl). Stimulation with ammonium chloride and potassium chloride produces similar cross-fiber patterns in rates of firing. The neural firing pattern of

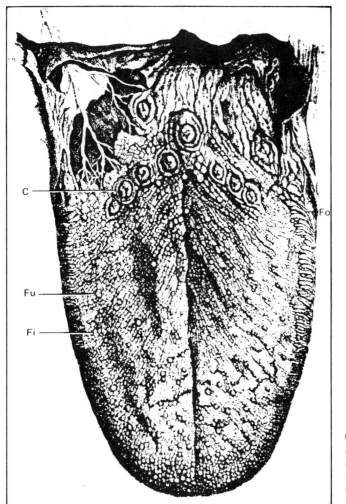

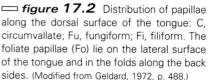

figure 17.2 Distribution of papillae along the dorsal surface of the tongue: C, circumvallate; Fu, fungiform; Fi, filiform. The foliate papillae (Fo) lie on the lateral surface of the tongue and in the folds along the back sides. (Modified from Geldard, 1972, p. 488.)

sodium chloride is different. To decide whether these neural similarities and differences relate to actual taste sensations, a behavioral test based on taste generalization was used. The question asked was: do ammonium and potassium chlorides taste similar to each other, and does the taste of sodium chloride differ from both? Rats were trained to avoid one of the salts by shocking them when they ingested a solution of it. When they avoided this test solution, they were tested with the other solutions. This was done for all three salts. One group was shocked for drinking ammonium chloride,

one for potassium chloride, and one for sodium chloride. When tested with the two salts for which they were *not* shocked, the rats showed a significant avoidance response to the salt most similar in neural response pattern to the salt for which they were shocked. Thus, rats that had been trained initially to avoid ammonium chloride avoided the potassium chloride significantly more than they avoided the sodium chloride. Likewise, rats that had learned to avoid potassium chloride avoided the ammonium chloride much more than they did the sodium chloride. Finally,

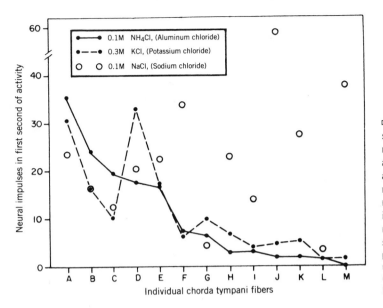

figure 17.3 The neural response of 13 chorda tympani fibers of a rat's tongue to three salts. The fibers are arranged in order of responsiveness to ammonium chloride. It is clear from the neural cross-fiber patterning in firing rates that the potassium chloride pattern is similar to that of the ammonium chloride, and both patterns differ from the sodium chloride pattern. (Reprinted with permission from R. P. Erickson, "Sensory neural patterns and gustation," in Y. Zotterman (Ed.), *Olfaction and Taste*, Pergamon Press, New York, 1963.)

rats trained to avoid sodium chloride showed little avoidance of either ammonium chloride or potassium chloride.

> *Therefore, in addition to concluding that there are many fiber types in gustation, one may conclude that the neural message for gustatory quality is a pattern made up of the amount of neural activity across many neural elements. (Erickson, 1963, p. 213)*

Thus, according to Erickson's analysis, different firing patterns across taste fibers account for different sensations.

The Best Stimulus and Labeled Lines

As we noted above, most taste fibers are broadly tuned and display many sensitivities when stimulated by the four primary taste qualities. However, when a large population of single taste fibers are examined, many fibers show some bias for a particular taste quality. Usually one class of stimuli will be most effective in eliciting the strongest discharge from a given taste fiber and can be designated as the **best stimulus**

of that fiber. Thus, taste receptor specificity can be described on the basis of a given taste fiber's reaction to different taste stimuli.

Therefore, although individual taste fibers may not respond to only one taste quality, they do seem to be biased, or "tuned," to certain stimuli. In other words, the fibers fire most readily and actively to their *best stimulus* and less actively to other taste stimuli. Recordings of the neural activity of single-taste nerve fibers' response of the hamster (Frank, 1973, 1977), the monkey (Pfaffmann, 1974; Pfaffman et al., 1976), and the rat (Nowlis et al., 1980; Scott & Chang, 1984) support this notion.

Evidence exists for four major clusters of fibers with selective sensitivity for each of the primary taste qualities (Pfaffmann, 1978; Smith, 1984). Moreover, each of these main clusters provides the basis of a **labeled line** (i.e., specifying, or labeling, nerve fibers based on the taste quality of their best stimulus). Thus although fibers may display many sensitivities—even responding to all taste stimuli to some degree—a given fiber may also show maximal sensitivity to its best stimulus. According to this analysis, taste fibers can be labeled on the basis of their maximal sensitivities. For example, when a sucrose-best cluster of nerve fibers is activated, the sensation is of sweetness.

The basis of a labeled line, as well as cross-fiber patterning, is illustrated in Figure 17.4. The line graphs show the response activity profiles of five salt and five sweet hamster chorda tympani fibers to the four primary taste qualities. Each curve represents the neural activity of an individual nerve fiber to each of the four primary taste stimuli. Although each taste fiber responds to more than one taste quality, it responds *best* to only one primary taste substance, and the common profile of a cluster of such fibers codes a particular taste quality.

The coding of taste appears to draw from both the cross-fiber patterning of neural activity and the preferential sensitivity of clusters of nerve fibers—the best stimulus and the labeled line approach. Accordingly, these two approaches may not be mutually exclusive. Labeled-line clusters could differentiate *be-tween* the four primary taste qualities, whereas cross-fiber patterning could signal differences *within* a primary taste cluster [e.g., as between salts such as sodium chloride (NaCl) and potassium chloride (KCl), as illustrated in Figure 17.3].

Taste Abnormalities and Disease

Certain diseases, injuries, nutritional deficiencies, and drugs can adversely affect taste thresholds and alter taste experiences. Among the more commonly identified impairments and malfunctions of taste are **ageusia** (or *ageustia* from *geustos,* Greek for "tasting"), the absence of taste (a rare disorder); **hypogeusia,** dulled or diminished taste; **hypergeusia,** increased sensitivity to taste; and **phantogeusia,** the perception of specific tastes—sweet, sour, salty, metallic or other-

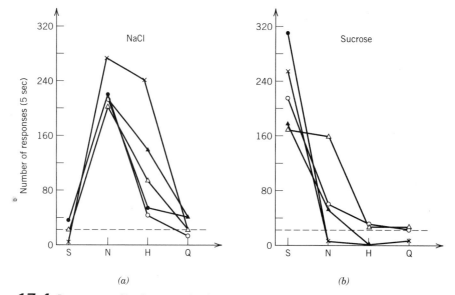

(a)   *(b)*

▭ **figure 17.4** Response profiles for a sample of chorda tympani fibers of the hamster. Each line graph in (*a*) and (*b*) plots the activity of a single nerve fiber to each of the four basic taste substances. The horizontal axis plots four basic taste substances administered to the fibers: S for sucrose (sweet), N for NaCl (salty), H for HCl (sour), and Q for quinine (bitter). The vertical axis shows the number of nerve impulses given by each nerve fiber to each taste substance in the first 5 sec of response. The dashed horizontal line represents an arbitrary response threshold.

Part (*a*) illustrates the profiles of five taste fibers that responded most strongly to NaCl ("salt-best" labeled line), and part (*b*) plots the profiles of five taste fibers that responded most strongly to sucrose ("sweet-best" labeled line). Fibers in the same taste category (i.e. salt-best or sweet-best) show somewhat similar response profiles across the basic taste substances. Thus, for example, the five salt-best fibers shown at (*a*) respond maximally to salt (N), marginally to HCl (H), and very weakly (close to the dotted threshold line) or not at all to sucrose (S) and quinine (Q). Accordingly, the labeled lines of these five fibers would be "sweet." (Based on Frank, 1973.)

wise unpleasant tastes—without the presence of any oral stimulus. Phantogeusic tastes can be quite unusual: Robert Henkin (1993), a specialist on disorders of the chemosensory system, described a phantogeustic taste disorder with the tongue-twisting label *torquegeusic phantogeusia* (i.e., a phantom "twisted taste") in a woman runner who experienced a strong metallic taste only while running or hard jogging. Actually, the phantom taste appeared somewhat reliably only after about 30 min of running. Although the cause could not be determined, the taste was not apparently due to physical exertion alone, since it never appeared when she otherwise exercised at a comparable intensity level and duration (e.g., when playing tennis or bicycling).

Perhaps the most common taste disorder is **dysgeusia,** a distortion of taste sensations (such as when an unpleasant taste results from a normally pleasant-tasting substance). According to Lawless (1987), the more common dysgeusic complaints are those of persistent metallic, burning, and sour tastes that are inappropriate to substances in the mouth; paradoxically, in these instances the responses to the four primary tastes may remain normal.

Among the proposed causes of taste abnormalities are certain diseases, viruses, endocrine disorders, poor oral hygiene and gum disease, nutritional deficiencies, and drug effects. Diseases that can produce taste malfunctions include Bell's palsy, multiple sclerosis, diabetes, chronic kidney disease, hepatitis, and cirrhosis of the liver. Some patients with liver disease also report specific food aversions and food cravings related to the illness (Deems et al., 1991).

Nutritional deficiencies of vitamins B_{12}, A, niacin, and the minerals zinc, copper, and nickel have been associated with taste impairments. Drugs that can disrupt normal taste function include anesthetics, antihistamines, antibiotics, and diuretics. Other possible causes of taste dysfunctions are general malnutrition, head trauma, radiation therapy of the head region (as in the treatment of cancer), and the general effects of aging. (For detailed surveys and evaluations of the causes of taste disorders, see Getchell et al., 1991; S. S. Schiffman, 1983, 1993; S. S. Schiffman, E. Gatlin, 1993).

TASTE THRESHOLDS

We now turn to the problem of assessing the human's sensitivity to taste and the general issue of absolute taste thresholds. It is an especially difficult problem because so many stimulus conditions affect taste sensitivity. Perhaps most basic is the chemical state of the mouth. Saliva has a complex chemical composition that dissolves food. It contains constituents of chlorides, phosphates, sulfates, and carbonates, as well as organic components of proteins, digestive enzymes, and carbon dioxide. Saliva also contains a weak solution of salt that adapts the tongue to salt. In fact, when the tongue is continually rinsed with distilled water, rendering the taste receptors relatively saliva-free, the threshold for salt is significantly decreased (McBurney & Pfaffman, 1963; O'Mahoney & Wingate, 1974).

Other variables that affect taste thresholds are the chemical nature of the stimulus and its concentration. Not surprisingly, thresholds may vary greatly from one substance to another. Thresholds are also strongly influenced by prior dietary conditions, the temperature of the chemical stimulus, the location and size of the area of application, the age of the taster, and various procedural variables of testing (e.g., Lawless, 1987; O'Mahoney et al., 1976). Several of these variables are examined in the next several sections.

Taste Thresholds and Temperature

Depending on the substance and taste quality examined, hot or cold temperatures, or both, affect taste sensitivity. Some of the effects of temperature on taste thresholds, reported by McBurney, Collings, and Glanz (1973), are summarized in Figure 17.5.

Observe that thresholds for all sample substances, each representing a different taste quality, are lowest for temperatures between 22°C and 32°C (about 72°F to 90°F). This coincides with the conclusion of Lawless (1987) that maximal sensitivity to most compounds occurs in the range between room and body temperature. All curves are somewhat U-shaped, but the degree of temperature dependence for maximal sensitivity differs somewhat by substance. Salted foods taste more salty when they are heated or cooled to the 22°C to 32°C range. Similarly, a hot

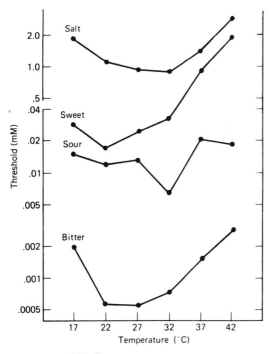

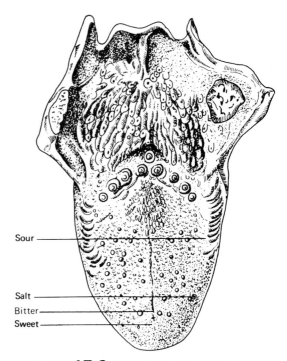

figure 17.5 Threshold values for the four taste qualities, each represented by a different sample compound, taken at six temperatures. (Salt: NaCl; sweet: Dulcin; sour: HCl; bitter: QSO_4. Note that the threshold concentrations are given in units of millimolars mM.) (Based on McBurney et al., 1973.)

figure 17.6 Approximate location on the tongue of regions of greatest taste sensitivity for the four primary taste qualities. For the bitter taste, the soft palate (the fleshy region above the back of the mouth, not shown) is the most sensitive region.

sweetened beverage tastes sweeter as the temperature of the liquid cools to about 22°C. In general, of course, the cook's caveat applies: food seasoning should be adjusted to the temperature at which the food will be served.

Taste Thresholds and Tongue Regions

Taste thresholds are greatly influenced by the region of the tongue stimulated. While all four primary tastes can be detected over most of the tongue, not all tongue regions are equally sensitive to all of them. Figures 17.6 and 17.7 show how sensitivity differs for regions of the tongue and the soft palate. For the sweet taste, the threshold is lowest at the front; for sour, the rear sides are the most sensitive; for salt, the front and sides are the most sensitive; and for bitter, the front and especially the soft palate are the most sensitive regions (Collings, 1974). Note the similarity in thresholds across the tongue locations for the two bitter substances studied; this suggests that they are coded by a common mechanism.

Taste Thresholds and Genetics

Taste thresholds for some chemical solutions also vary considerably from taster to taster. Two such chemicals are vanillin and the intensely bitter substance phenylthiocarbamide (**PTC,** or its synthetic equivalent, known as *PROP*). The variability of threshold values for PTC is interesting because its threshold distribution is bimodal. In other words, sensitivity to it is distributed over two widely separated groups: it is quite bitter to one group (called *tasters*) but is barely detect-

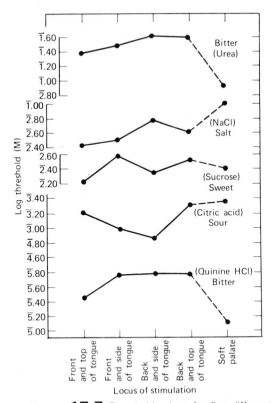

figure 17.7 Threshold values for five different taste stimuli applied to four tongue locations and the soft palate. Note the similar response patterns across locations for the two bitter substances, quinine and urea. (The ordinate, in log molar concentrations, is modified so that all taste qualities can be plotted on a single figure.) (Based on V. B. Collings, "Human taste response as a function of locus of stimulation on the tongue and soft palate," *Perception & Psychophysics, 16,* 1974, p. 170. Reprinted by permission of the Psychonomic Society, Inc.)

able or tasteless to the remaining group (*nontasters*), with very few individuals between these two extremes.

The ability to taste PTC (and PTC-like substances such as PROP) depends on the inheritance of a single pair of genes. Tasters have one or both dominant genes, and nontasters have a pair of recessive genes (Bartoshuk, 1988). About a third of the Caucasian and Asian populations are nontasters of PTC (who generally have otherwise normal taste capacities), whereas natives of Africa and South America are almost all tasters (McBurney, 1978). This "taste blindness" for

PTC may also extend to other compounds: Lawless (1987) notes that PTC nontasters may also be less sensitive to the bitterness of caffeine and relatively high concentrations of saccharin.

The threshold values for saccharin also provide another example of a genetically based bimodal distribution for a chemical substance. Bartoshuk (1979) reported that some individuals experience certain concentrations of saccharin as bitter, whereas others do not.

Taste Thresholds and Age

Taste thresholds are also affected by the normal process of aging. For example, on the average, taste thresholds for amino acids (S. S. Schiffman et al., 1979), sweeteners (S. S. Schiffman, 1983), and salt (Grzegorczyk et al., 1979) are two to two-and-a-half times higher in the elderly than in the young. Also, taste sensations at above-threshold levels are affected by aging (Murphy & Gilmore, 1989). However, an age-related threshold increase (and a general decline in taste functioning) does not apply to all individuals; in some older individuals, the taste function is essentially unimpaired (Weiffenbach, 1991).

It should be clear from our brief discussion of the variables affecting thresholds that their measurement is difficult and often unreliable. However, some absolute threshold determinations for the human have been made and are shown in Table 17.1. According to an analysis of threshold measures by Lawless (1987), a trend exists in terms of the primary tastes: bitter substances tend to yield low absolute threshold values, with sour (acids) next and salts and carbohydrate sweeteners a bit higher. However, exceptions such as the low threshold for saccharin relative to natural sweet substances and the high threshold for the bitter substance, urea, weaken any general guidelines for taste sensitivities.

ADAPTATION

Prolonged exposure of the tongue to a constant solution results in a decrease in or complete lack of sensitivity to the solution. This decrement in taste sensitiv-

Substance	Median Threshold (molar concentration)[a]
Caffeine	0.0007
Nicotine	0.000019
Quinine sulfate	0.000008
Citric acid	0.0023
Acetic acid	0.0018
Hydrochloric acid	0.0009
Sodium iodide	0.028
Sodium chloride	0.01
Sodium fluoride	0.005
Glucose	0.08
Sucrose	0.01
Sodium saccharin	0.000023

[a] Molar concentration represents the number of grams of solute divided by its molecular weight per liter of total solution.
Source: C. Pfaffmann, "The sense of taste," in J. Field, H. W. Magoun, and V. E. Hall (Eds.), *Handbook of physiology*, Vol. I (Washington, D.C.: American Physiological Society, 1959), Tables 2 (p. 514), 4 (p. 517), 6 (p. 519), and 8 (p. 521).

ity, which we observed in the other senses, is due to **adaptation.** Complete taste adaptation is primarily a laboratory condition since, in the normal course of tasting, tongue and chewing movements result in continual stimulus change. The shifting of chemical substances over different regions of the tongue, stimulating different receptors at different times, prevents the constant stimulation necessary for complete taste adaptation. Adaptation phenomena for taste, however, are shown clearly with isolated papillae.

The adaptation rate—the time required for the disappearance of the taste sensation—depends mainly on the concentration of the adapting solution. The higher the concentration, the more time required for adaptation. Of course, adaptation also depends on the chemical nature of the solution producing it.

Adaptation involves not only the loss of taste sensation but also an increase in the threshold level. During adaptation the absolute threshold increases until it is higher than the concentration of the adapting solution. Thus, at this point, adaptation is complete and no taste experience occurs. When the adapting solution is removed, reversing the adaptation process, the threshold falls back to its original value.

Adaptation-Produced Potentiation

Taste adaptation is a dynamic process, since various taste interactions and taste shifts are induced by the adapting process. For example, adaptation to certain chemicals not only changes the taste of other compounds that are sampled immediately afterward but can also impart a particular taste to water (e.g., Bartoshuk, 1968).

These special adaptation effects have been termed **adaptation-produced potentiation.** McBurney and Shick (1971) have shown that the four primary tastes can be induced by adaptation to certain chemicals. The effect of adaptation to bitter substances (e.g., caffeine) can elicit, or *potentiate,* a sweet taste from water; adaptation to sweet substances (sucrose, fructose, and saccharin) results in a sour and bitter taste from water; adaptation to salts potentiates sour, sweet, and some bitter water tastes; and a sour adapting solution (e.g., citric acid) can produce a sweet water taste.

Of the four basic tastes, the potentiation of a salt taste from water is most difficult to obtain. This may be because, as we noted earlier, saliva contains a substantial concentration of salt, so that the mouth is always somewhat adapted to a salty taste. Of 27 chemical compounds tested by McBurney and Schick (1971), only adaptation to urea (a sour-bitter-tasting substance found in urine) produced a reliable salty taste from water.

In addition, the taste quality induced by water after adaptation to a specific chemical solution sums .with the taste of another solution having the same quality to enhance the sensation of that taste. For example, adaptation to a normally bitter solution (e.g., quinine hydrochloride) produces a sweet water taste. When the adaptation to bitter is followed by a weak sucrose solution rather than water, the sucrose tastes sweeter than normal (McBurney, 1969). Similarly, when the tongue is sweet-adapted (producing a sour water taste), the taste intensity of a sour solution is increased.

DEMONSTRATION:
Adaptation-Produced Potentiation

You can easily demonstrate these potentiation effects using some of the substances described above (in fact, you have probably experienced them often while eating different-tasting foods in a single meal). For example, swish a mouthful of cool, strong black caffeinated coffee over your tongue for about 30 to 40 sec. Spit it out and then take a mouthful of plain water. It will taste slightly sweet (understandably, given the adapting solution identified above, you may not wish to attempt potentiating a salt taste).

Cross-Adaptation

There is evidence that different sapid substances that produce the same basic taste quality (e.g., sucrose and saccharin) can *cross-adapt* each other. In **cross-adaptation,** adaptation to one taste reduces the sensitivity of similar tastes. For example, adaptation to the salt taste of sodium chloride reduces the sensitivity to other salts while not affecting other basic taste qualities (Smith & McBurney, 1969). There is also strong evidence for cross-adaptation for sour. However, cross-adaptation to the sweet and bitter tastes are more complex. There is evidence of cross-adaptation between certain bitter substances but not between others (McBurney, 1978; McBurney et al., 1972). Similarly, some sweet compounds cross-adapt, while others do not.

The generalization of adaptation *within* a taste quality by different substances suggests that there may be a common neural-receptor mechanism for encoding the stimuli that elicit that quality. Thus, there may be separate receptor mechanisms that each encode and mediate the salt and sour tastes, but perhaps more than one type of neural-receptor mechanism for coding the sweet and bitter tastes (Bartoshuk, 1988). In other words, there may be no common or single chemical structure for substances that mediate sweet and bitter tastes. This is reasonable, since substances that are nutritional (and usually taste sweet) and substances that are toxic (and taste bitter) derive from an enormous range of very different sources in nature.

TASTE INTERACTIONS

So far, our discussion has focused primarily on the unitary taste qualities produced by a single chemical substance, or on those qualities due to taste adaptation effects caused by chemicals preceding or following a substance. However, typically tastes are due to stimulation involving interactions between various substances. Numerous complex interactions among the primary taste qualities prevent us from predicting the precise product of taste mixtures. Combining two chemical solutions whose components each appeal to a different taste is a complex psychophysiological event: the solutions do not function independently of each other, but, depending on the chemical substances, may show either facilitative or inhibitory effects in combination. Condiments work on this principle, selectively inhibiting and augmenting taste qualities.

A basic rule concerning taste mixtures is that no taste quality occurs from a mixture that is not originally present in the individual constituents of that mixture. Thus, a mixture of NaCl (salt) and quinine (bitter) will yield salty and bitter taste sensations, but not sweet or sour ones.

There is also evidence that different taste qualities may mutually suppress each other. However, if the two sapid substances of the taste mixture are sufficiently strong, they cannot mutually suppress each other to produce a *tasteless* mixture. In addition, when the components retain their distinct taste quality in the mixture, they are often judged to be less intense than when they are tasted in unmixed, isolated solutions. For example, a solution containing 0.3 M sucrose (sweet) and 0.0001 M quinine (bitter) is judged as less sweet than a solution containing *only* 0.3 M sucrose (no quinine) and less bitter than a solution containing *only* 0.0001 M quinine (no sucrose) (Lawless, 1986).

Taste Modifiers

Additional interactions affecting taste occur with some drugs and chemical compounds that have different effects on the four basic tastes. That is, there are substances that suppress some taste qualities and enhance others. One such substance that affects the palatability of food is **monosodium glutamate (MSG),** a relatively odorless component of glutamic acid that has been used in Asian cooking for nearly 2000 years and is commercially available under several trade names (e.g., Ać cent). Its precise action is unclear, but it appears to impart its own taste, which somehow accentuates the taste of food, hence serving as a taste stimulant. By itself, MSG seems to have a salty component, and at high concentrations it may accentuate sweet and salty tastes in food (Mosel & Kantrowitz, 1952). As we noted earlier, MSG has a special status, serving not only as a taste modifier but also as a culturally based primary taste quality, that is, as an umami or savory taste.

Organic acids from the leaves of the Indian plant *Gymnema sylvestre,* have been shown to suppress sweetness without affecting the response to salty, acid, or bitter substances. For example, sugar loses its taste and feels like sand after one chews the plant leaves.

Another chemical that differentially affects taste experience is *Synsepalum dulcificum* or *Richardella dulcifica,* most commonly called *miraculin,* a fruit plant indigenous to tropical West Africa. The plant produces olive-shaped berries 1 to 2 cm long—so-called miracle fruit—that turn red when ripe. The striking effect of the fruit is that, while tasteless itself, exposure of the tongue to the thin layer of fruit pulp for at least 3 min causes any sour substance to taste sweet; this effect can last for several hours. Miraculin somehow converts a sour taste into a sweet one without impairing the bitter, salt, or sweet response (Henning et al., 1969).

MSG, *Gymnema sylvestre,* and miraculin produce their effects by selectively affecting other tastes: sweet and sour tastes are modified by *Gymnema sylvestre* and miraculin, respectively. In contrast, for some individuals, exposure of the tongue to an artichoke (*Cynara scolymus*) can make water taste sweet (Bartoshuk et al., 1972). This effect appears to have a genetic

basis. For sensitive individuals, exposure of the tongue to the extract from one-fourth of an artichoke heart makes water taste as sweet as a solution of 2 teaspoons of sucrose in 6 oz of water, and the effect may last for more than 4 min. As has been written, the artichoke is a vegetable "of which there is more after it has been eaten."

One of the most common taste modifiers is *sodium lauryl sulfate,* a chemical component of toothpaste that can affect the taste of orange juice. According to S. S. Schiffman (1983), exposure of the tongue to sodium lauryl sulfate does not affect the usual sour taste of the citric acid in orange juice, but it increases the bitter taste of the juice and reduces the sweetness of the juice's sugar. This modifying effect of sodium lauryl sulfate explains the mildly unpleasant taste of orange juice that is occasionally experienced when drinking it right after brushing the teeth.

Sugar Substitutes

Finally, because of their wide use, a brief discussion of sugar substitutes is warranted.

Saccharin The most familiar sugar substitute is the nonnutritive *saccharin.* It was discovered in the late nineteenth century as a derivative of toluene (a solvent derived from coal tar). Saccharin is colorless, odorless, water-soluble, and totally noncaloric. Since it remains stable within a wide temperature range, it has been extensively used as a sweetener in cooking (however, high concentrations of saccharin taste bitter rather than sweet). Although some believe that its chronic use may pose a health risk to humans (based on evidence of bladder tumors in rats fed extremely high concentrations of saccharin), it remains readily available in most countries.

Aspartame Aspartame is a recently discovered (1965) low-calorie sweetener produced by a combination of two amino acids (aspartic acid and phenylalanine, which some individuals cannot metabolize). It is readily available (in those familiar blue packets) under the brand name NutraSweet. Unlike saccharin, aspartame degrades at high temperatures, so it is not useful in cooking. However, it is a good low-calorie sweetener in acid-containing beverages (used in many diet sodas). Interestingly, aspartame is digested by the body in the same way as other amino acids. In fact, gram for gram, it is equivalent in calories to sucrose (table sugar), but it is about 200 times sweeter. Hence, because only a very small amount is needed to sweeten many foods, aspartame has become known as a low-calorie sweetener (e.g., Mazur, 1977).

TASTE PREFERENCES AND TASTE WORLDS

Most of our discussion has focused on the taste qualities pertinent to human experience. However, taste experience among lower animals is somewhat different. Clearly, under many conditions, taste stimuli are motivating and can cause an organism to approach or avoid them. Although for the human sweet and salty solutions are positive, approach-type stimuli and bitter substances are negative, avoidance-type stimuli, this is not the case for all species. All animals do not react similarly to a given chemical solution. Generally, the chicken and the cat are indifferent to the sweet stimuli that are readily accepted by most species (Kare & Ficken, 1963; Zotterman, 1961). Sodium chloride preference is also species-specific. Whereas the rat, cat, rabbit, and sheep show strong salt appetites (Denton, 1982), the hamster shows aversion (Carpenter, 1956; Wong & Jones, 1978).

There appears to be no clear line of evolutionary development for taste receptors. Species differ in the type, location, and number of taste buds. Table 17.2

□ table 17.2 Average Number of Taste Buds in Various Animals

Snake	0
Chicken	24
Duck	200
Kitten	473
Bat	800
Human	9,000
Pig and goat	15,000
Rabbit	17,000
Catfish	175,000

lists the average number of taste buds found in certain animals. However, there is no obvious relationship between the number of taste buds and the taste experiences of the animals. Animals with many taste receptors do not necessarily taste more, nor are they more sensitive than those with fewer receptors.

The literature on food preferences of animals is complex, often equivocal, and sometimes contradictory. However, the taste preferences of a species have many nutritional and metabolic determinants, and may also reflect a given species' solution and adaptation to environmental challenges. We can conclude that there are different taste worlds for each species, and that the taste system of a particular species is adapted to the species' unique metabolic requirements.

Taste Preferences and Selective Deprivation

Compensatory taste appetites or cravings often arise from a state of nutritional or physiological need. A dramatic intake of NaCl (table salt) follows removal of the adrenal gland (which produces a marked salt deficiency), or the controlled dietary restriction of NaCl in the laboratory rat (e.g., Nachman, 1962; Richter, 1939, 1942). In fact, salt-deprived rats eat more of all salt concentrations, including weak solutions at a concentration level below that normally ingested (Pfaffmann, 1963; Wolf, 1969). A compensatory salt preference has also been shown by salt-deprived ruminants (e.g., sheep and goats; Bell, 1963) and humans. Human subjects depleted of salt through a combination of dietary restriction and diuretic use (drugs that increase the volume of urine) ate increased amounts of salt (Beauchamp et al., 1990).

Similarly, thiamine-deficient rats show a strong preference for compensatory diets containing thiamine as opposed to their experimental thiamine-deficient diet (Rodgers & Rozin, 1966; Zahorik & Maier, 1969). In addition to salt and thiamine, specific appetites have been observed in response to nutritional and metabolic imbalances of calcium, potassium, and sugar (S. S. Schiffman, 1983).

Perhaps most disturbing to many weight-conscious individuals is the occasional craving (usually in the late afternoon and evening) for foods high in fat. Fat, of course, is a necessary nutrient; however, our hunger for it far outweighs the amount needed by the body. Certainly our craving for fat—perhaps a biological legacy from our fat-scarce ancestry— has not kept up with the fat-abundant reality of the modern world.

In general, a deficit induced by food deprivation may amplify the role of taste in the control of food intake (Jacobs, 1967). It is inviting to consider that there are taste mechanisms in the human that may correct nutritional deficiencies by initiating substance-specific cravings and appetites.

Origins of Taste Preferences

For many animals, sweet and perhaps salty solutions are appealing and bitter ones are aversive. This suggests a functional relationship between taste preference, nutrients, and poisons. Moreover, for many animals, certain preferences appear early enough to suggest that they have a biological basis.

Supporting this is the fact that a functional taste mechanism appears early in development; moreover, taste receptors are exposed to natural stimuli in the amniotic fluid and oral secretions of the fetus and in the milk consumed by the suckling newborn (Mistretta, 1991). Thus, while the taste system for most species of mammals changes rapidly in the first few weeks after birth, we may assume that the sense of taste is operative at birth.

The sense of taste, at least for sweet, seems to be functional at birth in the rat (Jacobs, 1964), the pig (Houpt & Houpt, 1977), the sheep (Hill, 1987), and probably the human. For example, human infants 1 to 3 days of age can discriminate a sucrose solution from plain water and show a distinct preference for the sweet solution (Desor et al., 1973; see also Beauchamp & Moran, 1982). Newborn human infants also show an unlearned aversion to bitter and sour substances (Crook, 1978). Interestingly, the newborn infant appears indifferent to salt solutions until about 4 months of age, at which time a reliable salt preference appears (Beauchamp et al., 1986, 1990, 1991).

Culture and Taste Preferences

The cultural basis of taste preferences in the human infant was assessed by Jerome (1977), who compared cultures that feed dietary sugars soon after birth with those cultures whose infants thrive with a relatively sugar-free diet. Groups with a nonsugar tradition of infant feeding show the usual strong preference for sweet dietary items after they are introduced, suggesting that a sweet preference is unlearned.

However, it seems clear that there are both genetic and environmental influences in human taste preferences. The palatability of certain foods seems partially determined by education and custom. Specific seasonings, spices, and condiments have an ethnic origin and their use is culturally linked. That is, we cultivate or acquire a "taste" for certain foods. Who would risk sampling "the coagulated secretion of the modified skin-glands of a cow after it had undergone bacterial decomposition?" (Matthews & Knight, 1963, p. 205). Those who do have merely sampled cheese.

Some cultures and ethnic groups savor food considered inedible by others. While brains, insects, octopus tentacles, snails, and cattle blood may not be appealing to many North Americans, some of their favorite foods, such as peanut butter, corn on the cob, and root beer, are considered unpalatable in many regions of the world, including much of Europe, Africa, and Asia.

Clearly, the appeal of some bitter solutions, such as alcoholic beverages, coffee, and tea, is acquired through experience. It may be that the foods given us at certain critical times in our formative years determine, in part, many of the foods we prefer as adults. However, no matter what determines particular taste preferences, they vary considerably from individual to individual; and, as summarized in the Latin maxim *De gustibus non est disputandum* (which loosely translates as "you can't argue with taste").

Conditioned Taste Aversion

In addition to food preferences, when individuals are exposed—even once—to a substance under certain intensely unpleasant conditions a powerful aversion to that substance may be created. Garcia and his colleagues (Garcia et al., 1974; Gustavson & Garcia, 1974; Nicolaus et al., 1983) observed that when rats drink a solution of sugar and water containing a poison that makes them sick, they later reject or avoid the sugar solution. That is, a taste, paired with sickness conditions a taste aversion—a highly adaptive reaction called **conditioned taste aversion.**

The ability of animals to form conditioned associations between taste cues and later sickness provides an explanation for "bait shyness," sometimes observed with animals whose population growth must be controlled through poisons. Thus, for example, wild rats that ingest a nonlethal dose (but sufficient to produce illness) of a food treated with poison will avoid food laced with that particular poison in the future. To avoid bait shyness, poisons with novel tastes must constantly be employed.

Conditioned taste aversions have serious consequences in the human. Cancer patients undergoing radiation therapy and chemotherapy (which also induce nausea and sickness) frequently acquire taste aversions and reduced preferences for foods eaten close to the time of therapy (Bernstein, 1978, 1991; Bernstein & Webster, 1980). Thus, they may experience serious weight loss and even become malnourished. Accordingly, it is advisable that they not eat for several hours before or after treatment; certainly favorite foods should not be eaten immediately before or after therapy since aversions to any substance may develop, even for highly favored foods (S. S. Schiffman, 1983).

In the final section of this chapter, we will consider the sensory characteristics that may heighten the appeal of a food—its flavor.

Taste Preferences and Flavor

The hedonic (pleasant–unpleasant) character of taste stimuli for the human is affected by more than a unitary "taste" response. The overall appeal of a substance is due to a combination of sensory effects termed **flavor.** Flavor may include such factors as a substance's concentration, aroma, texture, temperature, color, and even the sound it makes when it is chewed on or bitten (Edmister & Vickers, 1985; Vickers, 1987); it may even include some irritability of the oral and nasal cavities (such as with carbonated beverages and spices). All these factors, as well as the dietary history and the hunger state of the taster, in combination, influence the hedonic judgment of the taste of a substance. S. S. Schiffman (1986) has called attention to the texture of food in affecting its flavor. Consider the following inventory of possible food textures:

> *hardness (soft, firm), brittleness (crumbly, crunchy, crisp, brittle), chewiness (tender, chewy, tough), gumminess, viscosity (thin, thick), adhesiveness (sticky, tacky, gooey), and fatty (oily, greasy), . . . airy, chalky, fibrous, flaky, fluffy, grainy, granular, gritty, lumpy, powdery, pulpy, sandy, stringy, creamy, doughy, elastic, heavy, juicy, light, mushy, rubbery, slimy, slippery, smooth, spongy, soggy, and springy. (p. 44P)*

We have assumed that an important purpose of the taste system is to regulate the ingestion of nutrients and the rejection of toxins. Although this may be acceptable for animals in the wild, the biological advantage of the taste system for the human must be tempered. A pertinent caveat has been expressed by Glass (1967):

> *Man himself, the most domesticated of mammals, seems to stand at a fresh crossroad in the evolution of the regulation of eating. Satiety is no longer a sufficient guard against overeating, and hunger is no longer a sufficient bulwark against dietary insufficiencies. Man has provided himself with too many foods unknown in the natural environment, too many natural goods appealing to his appetite but unbalanced or deleterious when consumed in great quantity. Even milk and milk products, as adult foods, come under grave suspicion. Man is too adaptable in diet, in spite of his cultural conservatism in matters of food and appetite, to pick and choose safely on the basis of flavor and appetite as guides to nutrition. (p. vi)*

SUMMARY

This chapter and the next one are concerned with chemoreception through the senses of taste and smell. Taste and smell together may function as a food-seeking and sampling system. In this chapter, the main focus is on the sense of taste.

The human possesses four primary tastes: salt, sour, sweet, and bitter. The precise chemical properties of the stimuli that create these tastes are not known.

The receptors for taste—taste cells, buds, papillae, and taste nerve fibers—are activated by soluble substances that go into solution on contact with saliva. Neural recording of the activity of individual taste cells reveals that they are relatively nonspecific: a single taste cell may respond to a broad range of stimuli. This lack of specificity also applies to the taste nerve fibers.

The lack of specificity of taste nerve fibers has led to the proposal of an afferent code for taste quality. As described by Pfaffmann, taste is based on activity across a population of fibers. This corresponds to the observation that individual taste fibers fire to more than one taste stimulus, but they do not show the same pattern of firing. Each fiber has its own firing profile, suggesting that taste quality, rather than being coded by a single fiber or set of fibers, is due to the firing pattern developed across a number of fibers. Some evidence for this notion was summarized.

An alternative notion is that taste fibers show some selectivity, responding most readily to one class of chemical stimuli associated with a primary taste. Neural recordings of single nerve fibers indicate that usually one class of chemicals elicits the most activity from a fiber. That particular class of stimuli is called the taste nerve fiber's best stimulus. There is also evidence of four major groups of fibers that are sensitive to each of the primary taste qualities. The nerve fibers of each group are specified, or labeled, on the basis of the taste quality of the stimulus that produces their maximal response. This labeling processing is called a labeled line.

Thresholds for taste were discussed next. We noted that these thresholds vary with the taste quality

investigated and are influenced by many factors, such as the chemical concentration, the tongue location and area of application, the prior chemical state of the tongue or mouth, the temperature of the solution, and the age and genetic background of the taster. For most sapid substances, the thresholds are lowest for temperatures between 22°C and 32°C (about 72°F and 90°F). Also, not all tongue regions respond equally to all chemical stimuli. Sensitivity to bitter solutions is greater at the front of the tongue and the soft palate, sweet at the front, sour along the rear sides, and salt over much of the tongue surface but best toward the front and sides. However, differential sensitivity in location has not led to corresponding specificity of taste buds or papillae (groups of taste buds).

We noted next that taste experience undergoes adaptation (becomes relatively insensitive) when the tongue is subject to prolonged exposure to a constant solution. Many factors affect adaptation, especially the concentration of the adapting solution. Moreover, the adaptation of one taste quality affects the taste of certain chemical solutions that are sampled right after the adapting solution. Adaptation can also impart a particular taste to water—an effect called adaptation-produced potentiation. For example, adaptation to caffeine (bitter) appears to potentiate a sweet taste from water. The thresholds for some substances vary considerably among individuals. In particular, sensitivity to PTC and certain concentrations of saccharin may have a genetic basis.

Several taste dysfunctions were identified. We noted that they have various causes, including, but not limited to, certain disease states, nutritional deficiencies, drugs, head trauma, and the general effects of aging.

The effects of taste modifiers such as MSG, gymnemic acid (a sweet suppressant), and the so-called miracle fruit (a sweet enhancer) were discussed. Also noted were several chemicals that appear to affect taste experience selectively. In addition, we stated that for some individuals, exposure of the tongue to the extract from an artichoke heart makes water taste sweet.

Taste preferences and their origin were discussed. It was noted that different species have different taste preferences, which are likely adapted to their nutritional and metabolic requirements.

Although specific appetites can be initiated in response to nutritional deficiencies, the taste preference for sweet substances in many different species appears to have a biological basis. The possibility of a conditioned taste aversion was also noted; that is, a taste paired with sickness conditions a strong taste aversion.

Clearly, in the human, the acceptability and palatability of certain foods are due largely to education and custom, as well as to a food's flavor—a combination of sensory effects, including concentration, aroma, temperature, and texture.

KEY TERMS

Adaptation

Adaptation-Produced Potentiation

Afferent Code

Ageusia

Best Stimulus

Chemoreceptors

Conditioned Taste Aversion

Cross-Adaptation

Cross-Fiber Patterning

Dysgeusia

Flavor

Hypergeusia

Hypogeusia

Labeled Line

Monosodium Glutamate (MSG)

Papillae

Phantogeusia

PTC

Taste Buds

Umami

STUDY QUESTIONS

1. Compare the chemical senses of taste and smell. What are the main differences in the necessary stimuli for each? To what extent do they overlap

functionally and serve a complementary role in nutrition?

2. Identify the basic tastes and indicate how they are related to the chemical composition of stimuli that typically elicit them. Consider the functional relevance of the ability to taste bitter, sweet, and salty substances.

3. What effect does the concentration of a substance have on taste quality?

4. Outline the main components of the taste system. Indicate what is unique about the life span of taste cells.

5. What does the neural activity of taste receptors to each of the four basic tastes indicate about the specificity of taste receptors?

6. How can cross-fiber patterning account for taste quality? Alternatively, examine the notion of a best stimulus and a labeled line for coding taste quality. Consider a compromise that can encompass both cross-fiber patterning and specificity of the labeled line to explain the coding of taste quality.

7. Identify the different kinds of taste abnormalities. What disorders, diseases, and deficiencies produce taste abnormalities?

8. Identify the main factors that have a significant effect on taste thresholds. What is the effect of temperature on taste thresholds? What effect does the part of the tongue stimulated have on the thresholds of the basic tastes? How does age influence taste thresholds?

9. Describe the effects of prolonged exposure to a specific taste on taste experience. Examine how the subsequent decrease in taste sensitivity—adaptation—affects other similar-tasting substances. Consider the effect that taste adaptation may have on the taste of water.

10. Describe the interactive effects on taste sensation when different tastes are combined. Explain how different taste qualities can enhance and suppress each other when combined.

11. How do taste modifiers affect taste? List some of the major taste modifiers.

12. Discuss the notion that different species have different primary tastes and taste preferences. Examine the basis of taste preferences and con-

sider the extent to which they may be biologically or culturally determined.

13. Discuss the possibility that deprivation of a nutrient may promote a compensatory taste appetite.

14. What is a conditioned taste aversion? What does it imply about temporary changes in taste preferences?

15. What is flavor? How does it differ from taste?

chapter 18

THE CHEMICAL SENSE OF SMELL

In this chapter we continue our discussion of chemosensory reception, but our main focus is on the sense of smell. At the end of the chapter, we will also describe a chemosensory receptor system that is neither taste nor smell but that senses and reacts to chemical irritants.

Functionally, the sense of smell or **olfaction** *(from the Latin,* olfactare, *"to smell") helps us receive information from distant as well as nearby chemical events. A familiar example is the dog's remarkable ability to track both air and ground scents. In many lower animals, the* sense of smell may be necessary for efficient interaction with the environment. One of the most distinctive aspects of the olfactory system in lower animals is the strong effect that odors have on behavior. This is especially true for nocturnal animals or those that dwell in poorly lit environments, since much of their activity depends on a source of nonvisual information. Animals possessing a keen sense of smell are called macrosmatic *(from the Greek,* osme *for "smell"); animals lacking a keen sense are* microsmatic, *and animals* totally *lacking a sense of smell are called* anosmic.

FUNCTION OF THE SENSE OF SMELL

For many animals, smell plays an important role in such diverse behaviors as territory marking, socialization, feeding, timing of the reproductive cycle, sexual selection and mating, and nursing the newborn. Some predators hunt their prey and some prey avoid their predators based on their sense of smell. There are some striking cases in which animals use the emission and pickup of odors for mating and survival. For example, the female gypsy moth emits a scent that, with proper wind conditions, can attract the male moth from miles away. The inky secretion discharged by a frightened octopus or squid serves not only to decrease an attacker's sight but also to dull the olfactory sensitivity of pursuing predator fish (Milne & Milne, 1967).

Olfaction is not equally important to all species. The pickup of chemical signals appears to be more important to land- and sea-dwelling species than to birds and tree-dwelling animals. But it may even be absent in some animals, such as the porpoise and perhaps the whale, which as lung-breathing marine mammals cannot use their noses underwater to receive odors (Altman, 1966). As we observed earlier (Chapter 14), in these animals the sense of hearing, especially for sound localization, has evolved to a degree that may compensate for their poor sense of smell.

The sense of smell for the human is much less important than it is for many other animals: certainly it is not necessary for survival. As Charles Darwin observed in 1871:

> The sense of smell is of the highest importance to the greater number of mammals—to . . . the ruminants, in warning them of danger; to . . . the carnivora, in finding their prey . . . . But the sense of smell is of extremely slight service, if any . . . [to man] . . . He inherits the power in an enfeebled and so far rudimentary condition, from some early progenitor, to whom it was highly serviceable, and by whom it was continually used. (pp. 405–406)

However, in combination with taste, smell provides important functions: it aids in food selection (e.g., detection of spoiled food and maintenance of a clean environment); in the case of certain odors, smell may provide some pleasant aesthetic sensations (e.g., the scent of food and of flowers). The following represents only a sample of the distinctive scents and odors—both natural and the technological products of our society—that one may encounter in an ordinary day: the scents from breath and perspiration, the smells of the toilet (both bodily wastes and of cleaners and cosmetics), the complex aromas of food and of the kitchen, the smells of auto exhausts, trains and buses, the smell of smoke, and the odors of plants. Certainly some are unpleasant, even foul—more stench than scent—but they are all intimately attached to our daily encounters and, for the most part, inform us by enabling us to perceive their sources in our environment.

The playwright Patrick Süskind, in describing the olfactory environment of eighteenth-century France in his 1986 novel *Perfume*, draws our attention to odorant quality in a particularly compelling, colorful, and somewhat disturbing fashion:

> . . . there reigned in the cities a stench barely conceivable to us modern men and women. The streets stank of manure, the courtyards of urine, the stairwells stank of moldering wood and rat droppings, the kitchens of spoiled cabbage and mutton fat; the unaired parlors stank of stale dust, the bedrooms of greasy sheets, damp featherbeds, and the pungently sweet aroma of chamber pots.

> The stench of sulfur rose from the chimneys, the stench of caustic lyes from the tanneries, and from the slaughterhouses came the stench of congealed blood. People stank of sweat and unwashed clothes; from their mouths came the stench of rotting teeth, from their bellies that of onions, and from their bodies, if they were no longer very young, came the stench of rancid cheese and sour milk and tumorous disease. The rivers stank, the marketplaces stank, the churches stank, it stank beneath the bridges and in the palaces. The peasant stank as did the priest, the apprentice as did his master's wife, the whole of the aristocracy stank, even the king himself stank, stank like a rank lion, and the queen like an old goat, summer and winter. For in the eighteenth century there was nothing to hinder bacteria busy at decomposition, and so there was no human activity, either constructive or destructive, no manifestation of germinating or decaying life that was not accompanied by stench. (pp. 3–4)

ODOR QUALITY

The Chemical Stimulus for Smell

The potential stimulus for the sense of smell must be a *volatile*, or readily vaporizable, substance. Accordingly, solids and liquids must pass into a gaseous state. Volatility, however, is necessary but not sufficient for stimulation of the smell system since many substances—water, for example—are volatile yet odorless. Potentially odorous substances must also be water and lipid (fatty) soluble in order to penetrate the watery film and lipid layer that covers the olfactory receptors.

In general, the normal chemical stimuli for olfaction are organic rather than inorganic substances. In fact, under usual circumstances, none of the elements occurring free in nature is odorous (in its atomic state). Odorants are usually mixtures of chemical compounds, often immensely complex: environmental odors emitted by vegetative life (fruits and flowers), decaying organic matter (vegetation, flesh and feces), and scent-producing glands of animals. In brief, the natural odors occur as signals for the recognition and location of nutrients, toxins, predators, and mates.

But, as we shall soon see, overall, the relationship between chemical properties and odor quality is far from clear. It seems most reasonable to conclude that many different properties of odor-producing molecules play a role in determining their odor quality.

Classification of Odor Quality

Unlike taste qualities, the primary qualities of smell are not known. In fact, there may not be a single set of primary odors. Many classifications of odors have been made on the basis of introspection and subjective experience, but a general problem is isolating a set of primary odors whose mixtures yield the 10,000 or more possible complex odors. One attempt to establish a classification of odors is based on a geometrical construction—*Henning's smell prism*—illustrated in Figure 18.1. The triangular prism is supposed to be hollow, with six *primary* odors—fragrant, putrid, ethereal (fruity), burned, resinous, and spicy—occupying the corners. Henning proposed that all odors lying along the edges between any two corners resembled only the primaries located on those corners, whereas intermediate odors that are blends of several primaries were located on the surface of the prism.

Other classifications have used fewer or greater numbers of basic odors. But all schemes have been challenged and are of questionable value: a major difficulty for classifications with few primary categories is that many odors may not be easily assignable to any of the primaries. On the other hand, classifications with many categories may be too broad and vague for assigning odors to a particular primary, thus defeating the purpose of identifying primary odor qualities. Moreover, using preassigned semantic descripters or labels such as "fragrant," "putrid," and "spicy" limits the ability to evaluate and categorize one's odor experience. In other words, the fact that odor judgment must conform to the available categories restricts one's description of a given odor to those categories.

A relatively recent scheme involving a sevenfold classification attempted to establish a direct link between certain chemical properties of substances and their perceived odors. Based on a group of terms most frequently used to describe the odors of most organic compounds, the seven odors, shown in Table 18.1, were proposed as probable primaries (Amoore, 1965). In addition, it was observed that many of the molecules of compounds that shared a similar primary odor had similar geometric properties; that is, these molecules all had about the same shape and diameter. For example, the molecules of compounds that had a

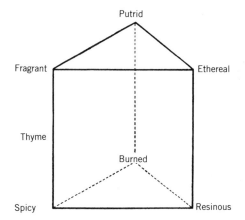

figure 18.1 Henning's smell prism. The corners of the prism were assumed to represent the six primary odor qualities of fragrant, putrid, ethereal (fruity), spicy, burned, and resinous. The edges and surfaces were assumed to represent odor qualities that consist of combinations of the primary qualities. Thus, for example, the odor of the seasoning thyme would lie on the edge of the prism midway between fragrant and spicy.

table 18.1 Primary Odors with Chemical and Familiar Examples

Primary Odor	Chemical Example	Familiar Example
Camphoraceous	Hexachloroethane, camphor	Moth repellent
Musky	Butylbenzene	Musk, civetone
Floral	Ethyl carbinol	Rose, lavender
Minty	Menthol	Peppermint
Ethereal	Diethyl ether	Cleaning fluid
Pungent	Formic acid	Vinegar, roasted coffee
Putrid	Butyl mercaptan, Hydrogen sulfide	Rotten egg

Source: J. E. Amoore, Current status of the steric theory of odor. *Annals of the New York Academy of Sciences, 116,* 1965, 457–476.

"camphoraceous" odor were roughly spherical and had the same approximate diameter. The theory was called the **stereochemical** (or *steric*) **theory** and was often referred to as a functional *lock-and-key theory:* the "key" is the molecule of the odorant chemical with specific geometric properties, and the "lock" is a presumed receptor site on the surface of the olfactory membrane that accommodates or "fits" only molecules with the specific geometric properties of the key. Accordingly, keys are specific to locks and both are specific to odors.

This was an appealing notion, especially since it attempted to relate perceived odor quality to specific chemical properties. However, it has been challenged on a number of grounds and is not widely accepted (e.g., Cain, 1978). This is due largely to a lack of evidence of distinct, specific receptor sites (i.e., "locks"), as well as some disconfirmatory evidence. For example, S. S. Schiffman (1974*a*) has reported that the compounds of certain odorants whose molecules have the same geometric properties may have very differently perceived odors. In short, it is not possible to reliably predict a compound's odor on the basis of its geometric properties alone. Thus, although some connection seems to exist between molecular shape and odor quality, other chemical properties are likely involved in determining odor quality. At present, there are no adequate odor classification schemes to describe or summarize the subtlety and enormity of odor experiences (see Doty, 1991; Dravnieks, 1982). However, an analysis of *specific anosmias* may provide some clues concerning basic odorant classes.

Specific Anosmias and Odor Qualities

Specific anosmias (sometimes referred to as "smell blindnesses") are olfactory disorders in which individuals are unable to smell one or a very limited specific class of odors (e.g., Amoore, 1991). These same individuals, however, may have normal sensitivity for all other odors. The fact that some individuals are unable to smell a specific range of odors suggests that they may have a deficiency or abnormality in a specific receptor type or mechanism tuned to coding that particular range of odor qualities. In fact, there is evidence suggesting that specific anosmias may be due to a genetic deficiency in the production of essen-

tial proteins necessary for the reception of a specific class of odorants (Buck, 1992; Buck & Axel, 1991). Several dozen specific anosmias have been identified, suggesting that the number of primary odor qualities (or the number of receptor proteins necessary to encode odor quality) may be quite high, certainly exceeding the number of primary qualities given by Henning's smell prism or the stereochemical theory (Amoore, 1991).

Finally, we must consider the possibility that, unlike the sense of taste, there are no real odor primaries. Perhaps instead there are many specific receptors whose complex interactions enable us to recognize the seemingly overwhelming number of discriminable odors.

ANATOMY AND PHYSIOLOGY OF THE OLFACTORY SYSTEM

The physiology of the olfactory process is elusive, particularly due to the inaccessibility of the receptors (Figures 18.2 and 18.3). The entire odor-sensitive tissue region, called the **olfactory epithelium** (literally a "smell surface membrane"), or **olfactory mucosa,** occupies a total area of about 1 in.^{2} It is located on both sides of the nasal cavity, which is divided by the nasal septum. The septum separates the two nostrils up into the area of the olfactory epithelium. It may serve as an aid in locating an odor, much like the auditory localization provided by the two ears.

Olfactory Receptors

The olfactory receptors, called **olfactory cells,** are located in the mucous membrane high in each side of the nasal cavity (see the upper left inset of Figure 18.3). They are relatively long, narrow, column-shaped cells surrounded by pigmented supporting cells. There are an estimated 10 million olfactory cells in the human (Wenzel, 1973) and perhaps more than 20 times as many in the dog, which likely accounts for the dog's phenomenal ability to track scents. On one end of the olfactory receptors cells, hair-like projections of the **olfactory cilia** project down into the fluid covering the mucous membrane of the olfactory

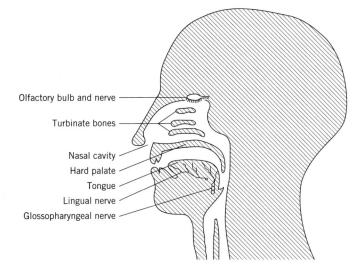

Olfactory bulb and nerve

Turbinate bones

Nasal cavity
Hard palate
Tongue
Lingual nerve
Glossopharyngeal nerve

▭ *figure* **18.2** The nasal passages. (From F. A. Geldard, *The Human Senses,* John Wiley, New York, 1972, p. 444. Reprinted by permission of the publisher.)

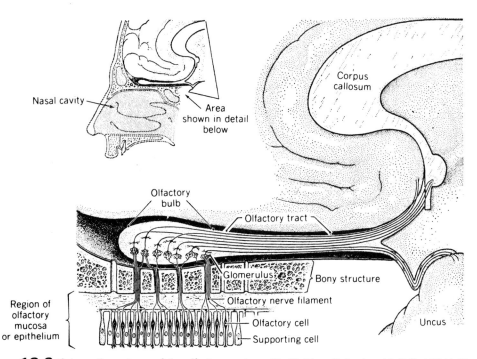

Nasal cavity

Area shown in detail below

Corpus callosum

Olfactory bulb

Olfactory tract

Glomerulus

Bony structure

Olfactory nerve filament

Olfactory cell

Supporting cell

Uncus

Region of olfactory mucosa or epithelium

▭ *figure* **18.3** Schematic anatomy of the olfactory system. (Modified from D. Krech and R. S. Crutchfield, *Elements of Psychology,* Alfred A. Knopf, New York, 1958, p. 184. Reprinted by permission of the authors.)

epithelium or mucosa (shown in Figure 18.4). It is generally thought that the cilia and their immediate connections, the *dendritic knobs* (shown in Figure 18.4), as well as the mucosa, are the receptor sites for odorants and are the structures involved in the initial stage of the transduction process (Getchell & Getchell, 1987). It is also thought that the mucosa contains molecules of a special protein (*olfactory binding protein*) that attaches, or binds, to odorant molecules so that they can be transported from the mucosa to the olfactory receptor cells (Dodd & Castellucci, 1991). In short, olfactory binding proteins in the mucosa may trap odorant molecules entering the nasal area and concentrate them on the olfactory receptors.

Extending from the olfactory receptor cells are nerve filaments comprising *olfactory nerve fibers,* which connect to the **olfactory bulb** of the brain at a relay or synaptic region called the **glomerulus** (from the Latin, *glomus,* meaning a "rounded mass" or "ball"; actually, there is a large cluster of such synaptic regions called *glomeruli)*; connections are then made from various glomeruli within the olfactory bulb to other parts of the brain by *olfactory tracts.* The olfactory receptor cells thus serve for both reception and conduction. As receptors, they transduce the chemical stimuli of odors into neural impulses; as conductors, they transmit these impulses to the olfactory brain by way of olfactory nerve fibers. Geldard (1972) pointed out that this dual function of cells is common in the relatively primitive nervous systems of lower vertebrates, reflecting the antiquity of the olfactory system in evolution.

Neural activity converges from the cilia to the olfactory bulb. At the mucosa, the activity of many cilia (6 to 12) serves a single olfactory receptor cell; many of the nerve fibers of olfactory cells converge on a single neuron in the olfactory bulb. The neurons, in turn, feed into olfactory tracts and proceed directly to the higher cortical regions (the limbic system, thalamus, and frontal cortex, described in the next section). At the olfactory bulb, there is an estimated 1000-to-1 reduction in the nerve fibers to each of the olfactory tracts conveying sensory information to the brain. In other words, the neural activity of as many as 1000 olfactory cells and their nerve fibers contributes to the activity of each neuron in the olfactory bulb. This general funneling of neural response (and summing of olfactory information) makes the olfactory system extremely sensitive. As a result of this pooling of neural activity, many very weak neural signals carried by many olfactory nerve fibers converge and are summed within the olfactory bulb to increase the reaction to minute concentrations of odorants. (In Chapter 3, we noted that a similar convergence of receptor activity for the rod photoreceptors contributes to visual sensitivity.)

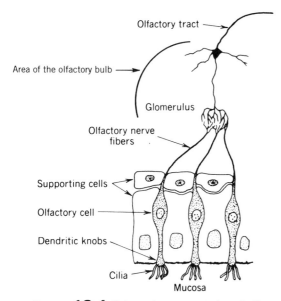

□ *figure* **18.4** Schematic representation of olfactory structures, detailing anatomy at the region of the epithelium. Shown are the dendritic knobs and the olfactory cilia embedded in the mucosa; collectively, these are the assumed structures for the initial transduction stage.

Olfactory Pathways to the Brain

The olfactory bulb sends tracts to several regions of the brain: one set goes to the thalamus, which projects to a region of the frontal cortex (Dodd & Castellucci, 1991; Scott, 1984); in addition, some tracts extend to parts of the *limbic system* (which is closely involved with our experience of emotion and memories, a topic we will discuss later in this chapter). Interestingly, it was once thought that what is now called the limbic system was part of the olfactory system. In fact, an old name for the brain region that includes the limbic system, the *rhinencephalon* (Greek for "smell brain"), is still used.

Active Sniffing and Odor Sensitivity

When air is inhaled, accompanying gaseous chemical stimuli are carried to the olfactory epithelium by small whirling currents. (Odor stimulation may also occur during exhalation, especially while eating.) The inhaled stream of air and odorant chemicals is warmed and filtered as it is deflected by three *turbinate bones* in the upper part of the nose (Figure 18.2). On reaching the upper regions of the nasal cavity, the chemical stimuli are dissolved in the olfactory epithelium by its fluid covering. This stimulates the cilia of the olfactory cells and adjacent structures and provokes the olfactory cells into neural activity.

It would seem intuitively sensible that the more vigorous the inhalation—as in active sniffing—the more the olfactory epithelium is bathed by the odorant and the greater is the stimulation. However, it appears that just sniffing normally is sufficient to produce the optimal amount of odorous chemicals for the olfactory system. As Laing (1983) noted, "it is very difficult to improve on the efficiency of sniffing techniques of individuals . . . a single natural sniff provides as much information about the presence and intensity of an odour as do seven or more sniffs" (p. 90).

Plasticity of Olfactory Receptor Cells

The olfactory system and its receptor cells, in particular, display a remarkable flexibility in dealing with a range of normal structural changes in neural processes. Like taste cells, olfactory receptor cells continually degenerate and regenerate; the life span of an olfactory receptor neuron is 4 to 8 weeks. Moreover, even after receptor cell damage and destruction due to injury and chemical irritation, the cells are usually renewed. Perhaps the continual cell replacement is an adaptive mechanism to cope with the cell loss resulting from the continual airflow and exposure to inhaled foreign substances. In fact, olfactory cells are probably the only sensory neurons in the adult mammal that can be replaced by new nerve cells (Costanzo & Graziadei, 1987). Interestingly, despite continuous receptor cell turnover, the capacity and functioning of the olfactory system is generally uninterrupted.

OLFACTORY CODING

The coding of olfactory stimuli—both odorant intensity (or strength) and quality (the particular odor sensed)—begins with the mucosa of the olfactory epithelium. Here the odorant compounds, represented as complex electrical and chemical signals, diffuse through the mucous layer to bind with chemically receptive membranes of the olfactory receptor cells.

Odor Intensity

The intensity of an odorant depends on the concentration of the odorant molecules reaching the receptor cells in the olfactory epithelium. It is assumed that electrical changes in the olfactory nerves at the surface of the olfactory epithelium serve as a measure of olfactory receptor cell activity. These responses increase in proportion to the concentration and duration of the odorant stimulus. For intense olfactory stimuli the electrical response rises rapidly, peaks higher, and decays relatively slowly in contrast to weak stimuli. Strong odors thus elicit more intense neural impulses than do weak odors (Gesteland, 1978; Kauer, 1987). You have verified this for yourself when nasal congestion from a cold has reduced the concentration of airborne odor molecules reaching the receptors, weakening the perceived intensity of odors.

Odor Quality

Odor quality is more difficult to understand than odor intensity. For one thing, odor quality cannot be easily characterized on the basis of specific neural activity. In fact, distinctive odorants do not activate specific receptor cells. Evidence for this comes from the activity of the frog's olfactory mechanism. For example, Gesteland and his colleagues (Gesteland et al., 1963,

1965) recorded the neural activity from the receptor cells of the frog's olfactory epithelium and observed that the odor response properties of single receptor cells are not specific. Instead, each cell is broadly tuned, responding to a wide variety of odorants. The same is true of olfactory nerves that connect the receptor cells with the glomeruli of the olfactory bulb. Like olfactory cells, most olfactory nerve fibers respond to a wide range of odorants, some of which may be very different from each other.

Patterns of Neural Activity: Response Profiles Although olfactory receptor neurons (and their nerve fibers) do not fire to specific odor compounds, there is some evidence of selective *patterns* of neural activity to distinctive odorants (Gesteland et al., 1963). When tested with 25 different odorants, each receptor was found to respond to several odorants, and the magnitude of the response varied from odorant to odorant. Thus, there do appear to be coherent, reliable differences in receptor cell sensitivity to various odorants that may enable us to discriminate odorant quality.

Accordingly, it has been proposed that odor quality is coded by a *spatial pattern* of neural activity across the olfactory bulb. That is, odor quality is mediated by a pattern of impulses across many receptor cells that vary in sensitivity. With this in mind, Kauer (1987) proposed a neural coding process that directly relates the broad tuning of receptor cells to the perception of olfactory quality. According to his analysis, there are groups or subunits of receptor cells, each having a wide range of sensitivities to various odorants but overlapping each other in their neural activity. Hence, stimulation with one odorant may activate a given subunit of receptor cells, yielding a particular pattern of neural activity, or *response profile,* for that group of receptor cells; stimulation by a different odorant activates another subunit of receptor cells, some of which may also respond to the first odorant. In other words, the same receptor cells may help code different odorants. Thus, there are no specialized olfactory cells for, say, coding the scent of a rose that are distinct from cells for coding the scent of lilacs or of coffee. What is specialized, or at least constant for coding odor quality at the receptor level, is the relation

of odor compounds to the response profiles of groups of receptor cells. Thus, odor quality depends on the *pattern of neural activity* across groups of olfactory cells that reach the glomeruli of the olfactory bulb. In short, different odorants produce characteristic, reliable patterns of neural activity within the olfactory bulb. A schematic example of the pattern of activity among subunits of receptor cells that can code particular odorants is given in Figure 18.5.

Many questions concerning the coding of odor quality remain unanswered. An appealing and empirically sound possibility is that there are a large number of olfactory receptors—perhaps hundreds—but probably far fewer than the number of discriminable odors. Accordingly, a firing pattern scheme like the one shown in Figure 18.5 may apply, but to a relatively large number of receptors, enabling coding of the thousands of odors that the human is capable of recognizing.

OLFACTORY DISORDERS

There are two main types of olfactory impairment: transport olfactory loss and sensorineural olfactory loss. *Transport olfactory loss* results from conditions that prevent an odorant from reaching the olfactory epithelium. This may be the result of obstruction of the nasal pathways owing to various forms of rhinitis (inflammation of the mucous membranes of the nasal cavity). *Sensorineural olfactory loss* results from conditions that directly affect the olfactory system. These include damage to the olfactory epithelium, tearing of olfactory nerve fibers, and injury to the olfactory cells by major head trauma, certain viral and bacterial infections (e.g., influenza, hepatitis), bronchial asthma, tumors that exert pressure on the olfactory bulb or tract, and burns to the olfactory receptors from the inhalation of certain toxic chemicals (e.g., ammonia, cocaine, lead, zinc sulfate, and other caustic agents) (Doty et al., 1991; S. S. Schiffman, 1983; Snow et al., 1991); impairment in odor detection and recognition may also be diagnostic of Alzheimer's disease (S. S. Schiffman & Gatlin, 1993).

The sense of smell also decreases with age; in fact, it is considerably more vulnerable to aging effects

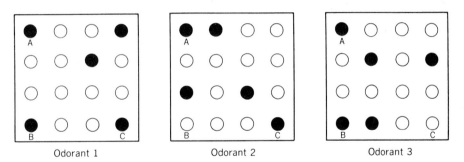

Odorant 1   Odorant 2   Odorant 3

▭ *figure **18.5*** A schematic description of the firing pattern of a sample of 16 receptor cells for three different odorants. Each circle represents an olfactory receptor cell, and black circles represent those receptor cells that fire in response to a particular odorant. Observe that receptor cell A is activated by all three odorants, receptor cell B is activated by odorant 1 and 3, and receptor cell C is activated by odorant 1 and 2. Thus, while individual receptor cells may be activated by several different odorants, each odorant activates a different group or *pattern* of receptor cells. Accordingly, a specific pattern of activated receptor cells signals or codes a specific odorant. (Based on Spear et al., 1988.)

than the sense of taste. According to Doty et al. (1991), over three-fourths of individuals over the age of 80 have some form of major olfactory impairment.

As with disorders of taste, there are numerous olfactory disorders. The most prominent effect of olfactory dysfunction, affecting about 2 million Americans, is the inability to smell, or *anosmia* (Costanzo & Zasler, 1991). The anosmia may be total, so that the individual cannot detect *any* odor quality, or (as previously described) partial, in that the individual is insensitive to only one or a limited number of odorants (i.e., specific anosmias). *Hyposmia* refers to decreased sensitivity to all or to a limited number of odorants. In contrast, *hyperosmia* refers to an increased sensitivity to all or to a limited number of odorants. *Dysosmia* (also called *parosmia)* refers to distortions of odor quality, as, for example, when an unpleasant odor is experienced in the presence of a normally pleasant odorant. *Phantosmia* refers to the perception of an odor (either pleasant or unpleasant), although no actual odorant is inhaled. Not surprisingly, since they are olfactory hallucinations, phantosmias are common among individuals with mental illness or brain damage.

While olfactory system impairment in the human is not life-threatening, it can be harmful. Odors alert us to poisonous gases, fires (through smoke), and spoiled foods. The individual with little or no sense of smell is deprived of an early warning of airborne dangers and must be especially alert. Olfactory dys-

function may also impair the quality of one's life. Effects can range from changes in appetite and diet, which can affect body weight and digestion, to a reduced feeling of well-being and may even provoke severe depression.

The Odor of Disease

It has long been known that for various diseases there are distinctive odors—often malodors—due largely to metabolic products or bacterial decomposition. These associations were once used by physicians as a source of diagnostic information. For example, historically, distinctive odors have been attributed to a critical deficiency of vitamin C or scurvy (putrid), yellow fever (butcher shop odor), typhoid fever (fresh baked brown bread), arsenic poisoning (garlic), liver failure (a mousy ammonia odor), and a sweet, fruity odor has been associated with diabetic coma (S. S. Schiffman, 1983). Some sense of the odors associated with diseased states recorded in eighteenth- and nineteenth-century France is strikingly captured by the medical historian Alain Corbin (1986):

What characterized the smell of the atmosphere of the hospital was the complex nature of the putrid odors. Patients' quickened respiration and foul-smelling sweat, their purulent sputum, the variety of pus that flowed from wounds, the contents of buckets and commodes, the pungency of medica-

tion, the effluvia of plasters, all amalgamated into stench that the practitioner tried to analyze as fast as possible in order to avert the risk of an epidemic. The sex, age, occupation, and temperment of the patients modified this overall fetidity, from which the effluvia of the dominant disease emerged. The worst was really "hospital fever," the odor of corpses that preceded and foreshadowed death; it rose from gangrenous limbs and from the sweat-impregnated beds reserved for the dying. (p. 51)

ODOR THRESHOLDS

Absolute thresholds have been determined for many odorants, indicating that extremely low concentrations are sufficient for detection. It has been estimated that olfaction is the more sensitive of the two chemical senses—perhaps 10,000 times as sensitive as taste, according to Moncrieff (1951). A striking example of olfactory sensitivity is given by the human's sensitivity to *mercaptan,* a foul-smelling compound often added to odorless gas to warn of its presence. A concentration of 1 molecule of mercaptan per 50 trillion molecules of air is detectable (Geldard, 1972). Another striking example is given by *skatol,* which has an objectionable fecal odor. Moncrieff (1951) describes the threshold concentration of skatol in very practical terms: 1 mg will produce an unpleasant odor in a hall 500 m long by 100 m wide and 50 m high. A final unusual example of the extraordinary power of olfactory stimuli and human sensitivity to odorants is drawn from the procedure used by Gibbons (1986) and Gilbert and Wysocki (1987; Wysocki et al., 1991) for a smell survey published by the National Geographic Society. They employed six "scratch-and-sniff" panels (each about 44 by 31 mm or $1\frac{3}{4}$ by $1\frac{1}{4}$ in.); less than 27 g (less than 1 oz) was needed for each odorant to microencapsulate it on nearly 11 million copies of the survey!

Because the amounts of odorous vapor required for the minimal detectable stimulus—that is, the *threshold concentration*—are so small, complicated methods of threshold measurement must be employed. Perhaps the most elaborate method of assessing olfactory sensitivity is the *olfactorium,* a glass double chamber in which the odor environment is completely controlled. For example, before the odorant is administered, all residual body odor is removed from the subject by intensive scrubbing and bathing. Thus, the vapor of the chamber consists only of the odorous chemicals administered, along with a known quantity of air at a controlled temperature and humidity (both of which can influence volatility and hence affect detection).

Threshold concentrations for some representative odorants are given in Table 18.2. However, threshold values are markedly affected by the methods used to introduce the odorant to the olfactory receptors and can vary greatly. Nevertheless, the extreme values of odorants such as mercaptan and musk (which should, at best, be taken only as approximations) make it clear that the human is remarkably sensitive to minute amounts of certain odorants. As Mozell (1971) points out, the olfactory system can detect fewer molecules than can most laboratory methods used for the same purpose.

In this context, we should again note the correlation between the number of olfactory receptors and detection thresholds. The average dog possesses at least 20 times the number of olfactory cells of the human. Not surprisingly, such animals, with more re-

□ *table* **18.2** Some Representative Odor Thresholds

Substance	Odor	Threshold Concentration[a,b]
Methyl salicylate	Wintergreen	0.100
Amyl acetate	Banana oil	0.039
Butyric acid	Perspiration	0.009
Hydrogen sulfide	Rotten eggs	0.00018
Coumarin	Vanilla-like	0.00002
Citral	Lemon	0.000003
Ethyl mercaptan	Decayed cabbage	0.00000066
Musk xylene	Musky	0.000000075

[a] Milligrams per liter of air.

[b] Note that absolute threshold determination is subject to large variations due to methodological differences; accordingly, other threshold values for the same substance can vary considerably from those given here. Still, the sample values in this table underscore the exquisite sensitivity of the human's olfactory system.

Source: Based on Murphy (1987); Wenger et al. (1956).

ceptor cells and more cilia per receptor, have a much keener sense of smell than the human.

Odor Thresholds and Gender

Thresholds for certain odorants may be affected by the interaction of gender and hormonal variation in the individual. It has been reported that the absolute threshold for **Exaltolide,** a musk-like synthetic odorant used as a fixative in perfume, varies in the human female according to the stage of the menstrual cycle. In a series of studies (Le Magnen, cited in Vierling & Rock, 1967; Good et al., 1976), it was noted that most sexually mature women perceived the odor of a sample of Exaltolide as intense, whereas most immature females and males, as well as mature males, either barely perceived it or were insensitive to it. Examination of the perception of the males revealed that of those studied, half were anosmic to Exaltolide; for the remaining men, the threshold was 1000 times greater than that of sexually mature women. Subsequent research on the absolute threshold of Exaltolide indicated that peaks in olfactory sensitivity occur at two points in the female reproductive cycle (Vierling & Rock, 1967). These peak times in sensitivity are approximately when estrogen secretion levels also peak, suggesting that the presence of estrogen influences the sensitivity to Exaltolide (Doty et al., 1981). This is supported by the findings that women deprived of normal estrogen by removal of their ovaries had higher thresholds than did normal females, but that restoration of the threshold to the normal range followed the administration of a form of estrogen. Of some further support is that a partially anosmic woman with abnormally low levels of estrogen became increasingly sensitive to the odor of Exaltolide while undergoing estrogen therapy (Good et al., 1976). It appears, then, that one's hormonal status may exert an effect on one's olfactory threshold (see Doty et al., 1981; Mair et al., 1978). We will return to the significance of the sensitivity to Exaltolide in a later section.

Females outperform males in identifying other odors (e.g., Doty, 1991; Doty et al., 1984). This olfactory superiority for females was also noted between prepubertal girls and boys, questioning the notion that sex differences in olfactory perception are always due exclusively to concurrent levels of circulating sex hormones.

Odor Threshold and Age

We noted earlier that the sense of smell declines much more rapidly with age than does the sense of taste. Some of the decreased sensitivities (increased thresholds) with age are striking: Kimbrell and Furtchgott (1968) reported approximately a 10-fold increase in threshold from the fourth to the seventh decade for certain odorants. Similarly, S. S. Schiffman, Moss, and Erickson (1976), using the odors of selected foods, reported that thresholds for elderly subjects (about 81 years old) were 11 times as high as those for young subjects (about 22 years old).

Performance on tasks requiring the identification, recognition, and short-term memory for odors also declines dramatically with age (Engen et al., 1991; Weiffenbach, 1991). Doty et al. (1984) studied odor recognition ability in almost 2000 subjects, ranging in age from 5 to 99 years, and observed clear age-dependent effects: the average ability to identify odors was greatest for those between 20 and 40 years and declined markedly thereafter up to the seventh decade. It was also observed that many of the elderly have major olfactory dysfunctions. Moreover, aside from serious olfactory impairments, almost 25% of the persons tested between the ages of 65 and 68, and nearly 50% of the persons tested over the age of 80, were anosmic (see also Doty et al., 1991; Murphy, 1987). At all ages, nonsmokers outperformed smokers.

ADAPTATION

Continued exposure to an odorant results in an increase in the threshold to that odorant—that is, **olfactory adaptation.** Depending on the odorant and its concentration, with sufficiently long exposure, odor experience tends to disappear.

Olfactory adaptation is a common experience. Owing to adaptation, we are usually unaware of our own potentially objectionable body odors (such as "morning breath" or perspiration, although we may be painfully aware of the odors of others). We are also unaware of the scent of perfume or cologne on our skin soon after it is applied, although other individuals readily smell the odor. Similarly, the cooking odors we initially experience when first entering a kitchen almost disappear after a few minutes. The odors are more or less constant, but they go relatively unnoticed because our olfactory system has adapted to them.

□ *DEMONSTRATION:*
Odor Adaptation

You can easily verify this in the kitchen. After you have adapted to the food odors of the kitchen and are barely aware of their presence, put your head out the window and take several deep breaths of fresh air. Then, when your olfactory system returns to the kitchen, the cooking odors suddenly reappear.

Although it can be useful to reduce the sensitivity to certain unpleasant and offensive odors, adaptation may also be dangerous. Miners once used canaries to detect lethal methane gas to which their own receptors had adapted before the presence of the gas was noted.

Self-Adaptation and Cross-Adaptation

Olfactory adaptation is selective. It is greatest when the adapting and test odors are identical—a situation called **self-adaptation.** Simply put, continued exposure to a specific odorant lessens your sensitivity (i.e., raises your threshold) when the same odorant is administered again. Adaptation to one odorant may also affect the threshold of another, related odor stimulus—an effect called **cross-adaptation.** Reduced sensitivity due to cross-adaptation varies with the similarity of the two odors. Thus, sensitivity to the scent of an orange will be lower (i.e., the threshold will be elevated) when immediately preceded by the smell

of a lemon than when preceded by a very different scent, say of moth balls or burning rubber.

In contrast to adaptation effects, the relative absence of odorants (as with exposure to pure air) can result in increased olfactory sensitivity. The average threshold drop due to prior exposure to pure air may be as much as 25%. However, like the effect of saliva on taste, our odor world is continually filled, so that usually we are at least partially odor-adapted.

Odor Mixtures

When two different odorants that do not react chemically are administered at the same time, several results are possible. The odorants may continue to be identified, depending on their initial distinctiveness. However, the more similar the components, the greater is the tendency for the odorants to blend and yield a third unitary odor. Another possibility is *masking*, which typically appears when the concentration of one odor sufficiently surpasses that of the other—an effect often wrongly called *deodorization*. True deodorization occurs only when the offensive odorous molecules are removed. This can be produced by treating the contaminated air with adsorbants such as activated charcoal. Of course, it is possible to eliminate the perception of odor quality by chemically producing anosmia. Thus, in weak solution, formalin (formaldehyde) vaporizes to cause temporary anosmia (Leukel, 1972). Odor quality can also be prevented from entering the airborne environment, which is what some of the chemicals in most underarm deodorants do. They inhibit perspiration and the growth of odorous bacteria.

ODOR PREFERENCES

As we noted, not all animals require or possess the same level of olfactory sensitivity, nor do they share the same spectrum of odor detectability. Because olfaction generally serves a biological function, it follows that, depending on the species, the odors best perceived are those that are biologically important.

Odor preference should also follow the functional, adaptive trend of odor reception, namely, that "Like or dislike of an odor, especially of food, is partly determined by the requirements of the body. What will be good for the body will usually be liked" (Moncrieff, 1966, p. 208). Thus, the odor of carrion, so repulsive to many animals, is attractive to the scavenger.

Moncrieff's (1966) investigation of the relationship of odor preferences to many human personality and constitutional variables has resulted in several generalizations. Using 132 different odorants, some natural and others synthetic, Moncrieff found that the ones best liked were those from flowers and fruits and from substances derived from natural products. A second finding of interest here is that odor preference is affected by concentration. Many chemicals yield pleasant odors when they are diluted. Often the perception of a given odorant will vary from pleasant to unpleasant as its concentration is increased.

Own-Odor Preference

In this context, there is some evidence for own-odor preference. In one study (McBurney et al., 1977), odor stimuli were produced by having male donors wear cotton undershirts continuously for 48 hours. When required to rate the pleasantness of the body odors from a large group of worn unidentified undershirts, subject donors typically rated their own odors (shirts) as more pleasant than did other raters; this occurred even though only about 25% of the subject donors correctly identified their own shirt based on its odor.

Preference for our own odors suggests that *familiarity* may be important in odor preference. This makes sense in that most biologically significant odors seem to be familiar ones. We are usually cautious, and perhaps even anxious, when confronting strange, unfamiliar, and especially unidentifiable odors (Engen, 1991).

It should also be recognized that—whether familiar or not—*unpleasant* odors create an immediate, almost indelible, effect. The pathologist-essayist Frank Gonzalez-Crussi (1989) points this out rather disturbingly:

> *You know the stubborn quality of a disagreeable smell. It assails you when you least expect it. One day, you stroll casually outdoors, and there it is: the repugnant companion of a revolting object.*

> *It hovers invisible over a dead and decomposed animal, a piece of carrion, or a heap of excrement. You turn away from the repelling sight, but it is no use: The smell has taken hold of you and does not leave. Or it diffuses relentlessly, from unseen origins. For it . . . has a presence of its own, and such power as can persecute you, and harass you, like a maddening obsession. (p. 79)*

IDENTIFICATION AND MEMORY OF ODORS

The human can identify the sources of a vast number of familiar odors. Some identifiable sources come from the human body, and the ability to identify some of them occurs early in life. An infant as young as 6 weeks of age can identify the scent of its mother (Russell, 1976).

There is evidence that sex identification is possible based only on the olfactory information in perspiration. Russell (1976) found that subjects could identify the gender of the wearers of undershirts worn by males and females for 24 hours who neither bathed nor used any deodorant or perfume. Wallace (1977) also observed that subjects could discriminate males from females with over 80% accuracy by smelling the person's hand. The males and females, whose hands served as the odorant-carrying surface, wore odor-free sterile gloves for 15 min prior to testing to promote perspiration. Consistent with an earlier discussion, females outperformed males on this task. Aside from the odor of perspiration, Doty et al. (1982) found that subjects were moderately successful in judging a person's gender only on the basis of his or her breath. Again, females were more accurate than males.

When the complex odors from familiar inanimate objects and materials are used in training procedures, identification by adults is quite good. In an investigation by Desor and Beauchamp (1974), the distinct odors of 64 common sources were used (e.g., coffee, popcorn, human urine, molasses). With some laboratory training in identifying odors, subjects approached near-perfect identification. The fact that training enhances odor identification points out the importance of learning (Rabin, 1988; Schab, 1991). Cain (1979) concluded that successful odorant identification depends on the familiarity of the odorant, the establishment of a long-standing association between an odor and its name, and help in recalling the odorant's name—that is, hints to individuals when they are in a "tip-of-the-nose" state (in which the individual realizes that the odor is familiar but is unable to identify or name its source; see Lawless, 1978; Lawless & Engen, 1977; Lyman & McDaniel, 1990).

Odor Memories versus Visual Memories

One of the striking aspects of odor memory is that although the initial identification and recognition of laboratory odors is not nearly as high as for visual stimuli, the memory for odors studied in the laboratory and **episodic odors** (i.e., odors associated with real-life experiences) are both long-lasting (Figure 18.6). In fact, although there is only moderate recognition for laboratory odors compared to pictures, the memory of such odors shows little loss over time. Engen and Ross

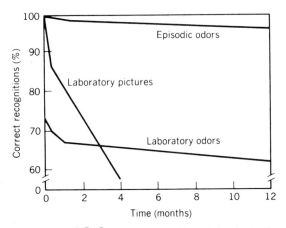

figure 18.6 Correct recognition of visual stimuli and laboratory and episodic odors (odors from real-life experiences) as a function of time. The memory for episodic odors remains stable and close to its initial high level over time. However, the memory for pictorial materials, while initially as high as the memory for episodic odors, falls off quite rapidly with time. Laboratory odors, while not well recognized after a short time, like episodic odors show little loss over time. (Based on Engen, 1987; Engen & Ross, 1973; Shepard, 1967.)

(1973) reported that when their subjects were given a set of 20 laboratory odors of familiar household products, they recognized about 70% when tested immediately after exposure. However, when tested again, 1, 7, 30, and 90 days later, almost 70% of the original odors were still correctly recognized. Moreover, when about 20% of the original subjects were tested 1 year later, their average recognition score was almost 65%. Coupled with comparable experiments with visual material (Shepard, 1967), this suggests that odor memory is much less influenced by the passage of time than visual memory.

Engen and Ross (1973) proposed that visual stimuli such as pictures are easily identified after a brief inspection because they contain many clear attributes (e.g., shape, color, size) that can be used in a memory-encoding process; in contrast, odors produce one-dimensional, all-or-none experiences. Thus, for recognition, the all-or-none coding of odors may influence the initial learning process and cause some immediate errors; however, the unitary character of odors also makes them resistant to later interference and confusion, enhancing their recognition. As Engen et al. (1991) suggest, "Odor perception is better characterized as *a system designed not to forget* rather than one designed to remember" (p. 318). This is especially true for lower animals in which certain odors play a survival role: thus, such critical odors and their relevance should be quickly learned and recognized and not easily forgotten.

Odors as Memory Cues

Odors can become associated with events and can serve as potent memory cues. What seems unique is that such associations may be learned after only a single exposure or event (and then only incidental to the event itself), yet even over a relatively long period, a particular odor can quickly call up the memory of the event (Schab, 1991).

Laboratory evidence supports this claim. For example, the presence of odors while examining visual stimuli (e.g., photographs) can aid their memory; in other words, a visual stimulus linked to a particular odor is more readily recognized in the presence of that odor (Cann & Ross, 1989). The association of odors and memories can also aid nonvisual cognitive tasks. Schab (1990) presented two groups of subjects with a list of 40 common adjectives (e.g., "large," "beautiful") with instructions to generate and list the antonyms of each adjective. While performing the word task, both groups of subjects were also exposed to the smell of chocolate. The next day, the two groups were directed to free-recall as many as possible of the antonyms they had listed in the first session. One group of subjects performed the recall task while exposed again to the chocolate odor originally present; the other group recalled their antonyms with no accompanying odor. The result was that the group exposed to the chocolate odor during the word task *and again* during the recall session recalled significantly more antonyms than did the group whose recall session was done without the chocolate odor. In other words, an odor present during both learning *and* testing aids memory, indicating that an ambient odor can be useful for retrieval. Incidently, the enhanced memory effect was not due to the appeal of chocolate odor alone; the same results occurred when the odor of mothballs was used instead.

The odor–memory relationship may be useful when studying for tests in courses or topics within a single time span (such as during finals). For example, a student studying for exams in several different courses might use a different odor for each course (of course, the student faces the formidable burden of re-creating the appropriate odor during each exam!).

Using odor as a retrieval cue can be viewed as a unique instance of *state-dependent learning* (e.g., Eich, 1980; Godden & Baddeley, 1975)—the tendency to recall material better if one is in the same physiological of psychological state as when the material was learned. According to this analysis, then, *any* sensory cue—visual, auditory, and so on—that is present during learning and available during the recall task could serve as a memory cue, influencing the state of the individual, and accordingly, could aid performance. However, it is possible that odors are more salient memory cues than other sensory stimuli. Thus, an odor is not only capable of cueing a memory, it may also evoke an *emotion,* suggesting a neural link be-

tween odors, memory, and emotions. We explore this possibility in the next section.

Odors and Emotions

Almost everyone has found that certain odors can create emotional arousal. This is largely because the olfactory bulb has a direct neural link with the *limbic system* of the brain, which is a center for emotional experience (as well as for memory). Thus, presumed experiences such as the "smell of fear" may not be farfetched. Even Ebenezer Scrooge, the notorious dour and unsentimental character of Charles Dickens' classic *A Christmas Carol,* was subject to the emotional arousal of odors: "He was conscious of a thousand odors floating in the air, each one connected with a thousand thoughts, and hopes, and joys, and cares long, long forgotten" (p. 29).

It doesn't take much stimulation for an odor to elicit an emotional response. Kirk-Smith et al. (1983) reported that if an unfamiliar neutral odor, even at a very low intensity level, is associated with a stressful emotional event or situation, then later the odor can elicit appropriate mood and attitudinal changes. Also, in this context, the link between odors and events can occur without the person's awareness (e.g., Kirk-Smith et al., 1983; Van Toller et al., 1983). Relatedly, Rubin et al. (1984) noted that odors evoke more vivid emotional memories than other types of cues (e.g., names or photographs). Such findings suggest that the apparent long-term status of many odor memories stems from their strong, emotionally significant associations. That is, memories of some odors persist in part because they have more definite, significant emotional referents, independent of any special attribute of the odor per se.

However, regardless of the source that provokes their enduring nature, we must conclude that odors, along with emotions, occupy a special place in memory; their capacity for pervading, even overwhelming, our conscious experience is without doubt. Reflecting on our general sensory loss with time, Gonzalez-Crussi (1989) hauntingly observes: "When the features of a loved face will have blurred; when pitch and inflection of cherished voice will no longer beckon distinctly; what a vivid pleasure, then, to open a flask and inhale the fundamental, irreducible reality of an odor. Oh, for the odor of the absent one!" (p. 92).

PSYCHOBIOLOGICAL FUNCTIONS OF OLFACTION: PHEROMONES

It is clear that the olfactory system receives biologically useful information; however, its importance varies among species. For many arthropods and mammalians, olfaction is important for survival. It enables the perception of the sources of odors—food, sex object, predator—and it conveys information for certain forms of behavior, such as orientation, sexual activity, territory and trail marking, aggression, and species recognition. In certain species, olfaction thus enables a form of chemical communication. One way this occurs involves the use of chemical communicants or signals called **pheromones** (from the Greek, *pherein,* "to carry," and *horman,* "to excite"). Pheromones are chemical substances secreted and exchanged among members of the same species. Unlike hormones, which are secreted in the bloodstream and regulate an organism's internal environment, pheromones are excreted by specialized glands of the skin or in the urine or saliva. These substances influence the behavior or physiology of receptive animals of the same species as the donor.

Releasers and Primers

The influence of pheromones, especially in reproduction, takes either of two forms, *releasers* and *primers*. **Releaser pheromones** produce an immediate and direct effect. A releaser, for example, attracts the male dog to a female dog in heat. In fact, a releaser compound has been identified in the vaginal secretions of female dogs in estrus (the brief period in the reproduction cycle when an animal is fertile and sexually receptive to mating). When small amounts of the releaser pheromone were applied to the genitals of unreceptive or spayed females, nearby males become sexually aroused and initiated mating behavior (Goodwin et al., 1979). The use of olfactory sex re-

leaser pheromones has also been identified for many insects, and synthetic variants are sometimes used for insect control (Linn et al., 1987; Silverstein, 1981). Releaser pheromones are also used for grouping in insects. For example, worker honeybees, on finding a source of food, release a scent that attracts other bees. This species also uses chemical signals for colony recognition.

Primer pheromones act by producing a long-lasting receptive state or physiological change (usually hormonal), such as that affecting the estrus cycle in the female. Several studies have identified chemical excretions of the mouse that influence hormonal activity, the estrus cycle, and hence the reproductive physiology and behavior of other mice (e.g., McClintock, 1984). In addition, it has been reported that removal of the olfactory bulb not only abolishes the estrus cycle but eliminates maternal behavior in lactating (nursing) mice (Gandelman et al., 1971). In a related study, olfactory bulb removal eliminated mating behavior in the male hamster (Murphy & Schneider, 1969).

It appears that the ability to smell is a prerequisite for reproductive behavior in many mammalian species. Some of the pheromonal effects are quite stylized. For example, Michael and Keverne (1968) mention that the releaser pheromones excreted by the boar immobilize the sow in estrus, so that the sow stands rigid while mating. The releaser pheromones promoting this activity have been identified; they are secreted by the boar's salivary glands (Patterson, 1968). When sexually excited, the boar salivates profusely, thereby providing what is termed the "swine sex odor" (Berry et al., 1971). The reception by an estrus sow of the pheromone present in the boar's saliva is essential for the characteristic immobilized mating stance (see also Amoore et al., 1977).

Territoriality and Trail Marking
Some mammals use pheromones to identify and mark their territorial boundaries by leaving chemical trails. The dog's vigorous ground sniffing and urination (which lays down the pheromone) is a common example. Many other means of territory marking exist. For example, reindeer have scent glands behind their hind toes that allow them to leave "cheesy" scent trails for

herd members (Gibbons, 1986). Rabbits have scent glands near their chin and anus, and elephants have glands located at their temple that are used to mark territorial boundaries.

You have probably seen ants apparently following a single trail from the ant colony hole to a food source and then back to the colony. In fact, many ant species leave a pheromonal chemical trail to guide other colony members to sources of food. According to Galluscio (1990), some worker ants returning from a food source not only leave a chemical trail for other ants to follow, but communicate the amount of the food by tapping colony members with their delicate antennae; the intensity and duration of the tapping also seem to determine the number of ants recruited to follow the chemical trail. Some ant species induce fellow colony workers to collect the food by releasing a special recruitment pheromone from a gland on their abdomen (Hölldobler & Wilson, 1990). The amount of the food source also determines the intensity of the chemical trail laid down by the ants; thus, as the food source is gradually depleted, the returning ants stop leaving a pheromonal trail.

Alarm Pheromones There are also classes of pheromones that appear to signal the presence of danger—*alarm pheromones*. In a study by Valenta and Rigby (1968), rats were trained to make a continuous simple response (bar press). When an air sample taken from the vicinity of another group of rats who were undergoing a stressful exposure (electric shock) was introduced into the test chamber of the trained rats, their bar press responses were interrupted. No such effect occurred when air from unstressed rats was introduced. The indication is that rats who were shocked excreted a detectable chemical—the alarm pheromone—that disrupted the learned behavior of the trained rats (see also Fanselow, 1985).

Primate Pheromones The role of pheromones in primates is not clear, but it has been noted that among certain lower primates, pheromones are used for territorial marking and sexual behavior. In higher primates, there is some evidence that sexual activity is partially mediated by a pheromone. In one study, experimentally anosmic male rhesus monkeys showed no interest in sexually receptive females until normal olfactory function was restored (Michael & Keverne, 1968). In addition, males with normal olfaction were more sexually responsive to females given estrogen than to females without this hormone. Although these findings suggest that a hormonal-dependent vaginal pheromone may affect primate sexual behavior, there is also evidence that the detection by the male primate of pheromones from the female is not *necessary* for copulatory behavior (Goldfoot et al., 1978).

Although pheromones may not play as dominant a role as visual or certain behavioral cues, and may not even be essential for primate breeding, they may confer an advantage in certain environments by identifying sexually receptive females, thereby increasing the likelihood of fertile matings (see Rogel, 1978).

The Vomeronasal System

Before leaving the topic of chemocommunication in nonhuman species, we should note that olfaction is probably not the only sensory system used to detect communicative odors from the environment. A system called the **vomeronasal system** appears to be specialized to deal with large, relatively nonvolatile (non-airborne) molecules that generally require physical contact (such as licking) for their reception. The vomeronasal organ is generally organized in parallel with the olfactory organ and in most animals lies above the hard palate of the mouth. The vomeronasal chemicals appear to mediate such activities as aggression, hormonal changes, female ovulation cycles, and certain aspects of courtship and reproduction (see Wysocki & Meredith, 1987).

Human Pheromones

The existence of pheromones in the human is far from certain, but there are suggestions and speculations. As we briefly noted earlier, some evidence exists that olfactory stimuli may enable accurate sexual identification. In the report by Russell (1976) previously cited, the gender of wearers of odor stimuli (i.e., worn undershirts) was correctly identified by a significant majority of subjects; in addition, the odors of the male donors were characterized as "musky," whereas those of the female donors were "sweet."

Some indirect hints emerge from applied chemical technology. Perfumers use certain mammalian sex pheromones such as civetone (produced by the anal glandular pouch of the male and female civet, a nocturnal felid, i.e., belonging to the cat family, found in Africa and Asia) and musk (from the anal scent glands of the male musk deer), substances used mainly as fixatives and extenders. Both pheromones are normally used by their donors for territory markings and as sex attractants.

Apart from their practical function of extending the more valued components of commercial perfumes, the odors of sex pheromones of lower mammals appear to have some attraction for the human. We noted earlier that Exaltolide, which is similar in odor and chemical structure to a mammalian sex attractant called muscone (Good et al., 1976), evokes a threshold response in the human female that varies according to her reproductive cycle. In addition its musk-like odor is pleasant and attractive to females ("sweet" and "like perfume" were the most frequent comments in one study; Vierling & Rock, 1967). Of some relevance to our discussion is that a compound found in human urine also has a sharp, musk-like odor, and the adult male secretes about twice as much as the adult female (Vierling & Rock, 1967). The conjecture here is that Exaltolide mimics a sexually relevant human pheromone. In addition, a female vaginal secretion of volatile fatty acids, similar to those possessing sex-attractant properties in other primate species, has been suggested as a possible human pheromone (Michael et al., 1974).

Clearly, the human possesses the glandular and other mechanisms to transmit chemical signals for chemocommunication. The human is amply supplied with apocrine glands that secrete odorants through sweat; moreover, the chemical composition of both secretions and excretions varies with emotional and perhaps mental state. For example, it has been reported that schizophrenics emit a peculiar and characteristic acidic odor in their sweat, and this substance has been identified (Smith et al., 1969).

Pheromones and Menstrual Synchrony: The McClintock Effect McClintock (1971) has reported a study on women (all dormitory residents of a women's college) indicating that the menstrual cycles of close friends and roommates fall into synchrony. This phenomenon is often referred to as the **McClintock effect.** The critical factor producing menstrual synchrony, according to McClintock, is that the individuals interact and remain physically close to each other. Further studies of menstrual synchrony also show that a critical factor in synchrony is the degree of association between the women (Graham & McGrew, 1980; Quadagno et al., 1981). In contrast, menstrual synchrony was not affected by the amount or nature of social interaction with males. One explanation for these findings is that the mechanism underlying menstrual synchrony (the McClintock effect) is pheromonal. There is evidence that a secretion from the axillary (armpit) gland is the chemical that mediates menstrual synchrony through olfaction. Generally, Russell et al. (1980) and Preti et al. (1986) found that when women had their upper lips swabbed three times per week with perspiration extract from the axillary glands of donor women, the women who received the extract began to menstruate in synchrony with the donor women between about their third and fifth menstrual cycles.

Another factor that may influence aspects of menstruation (i.e., length and timing) in humans is male axillary secretions. As in the previous study, Cutler et al. (1986) observed the effect of such secretions on females between the ages of 19 and 30 years who had somewhat irregular menstrual cycles (i.e., less than 26 or more than 32 days). After about 14 weeks of having their upper lips regularly swabbed with perspiration extract from the axillary glands of heterosexually active male donors, there was a reduction in the proportion of abnormal length cycles. Thus, there is some evidence to assume that for the human, a chemical signal from the male that would normally be transferred only during intimate physical contact exerts some regulatory control on the reproductive physiology of the female.

What adaptive advantage could menstrual synchronization confer on primates? According to Smith (1989), females with regular menstrual cycles seem to have a higher fertility rate than those with irregular cycles. Therefore, chemical signals that assist reproduction by regularizing the timing of ovulation through menstrual synchrony could improve the chances of successful mating and conception.

However, whether or not normal volatile genital secretions for both the human male and female act as sex attractants is far from clear. In fact, the evidence that women in close proximity over time influence each other's menstrual cycle through the exchange of chemical signals has been questioned on methodological grounds (e.g., Wilson, 1992). If, however, in the final analysis, naturally occurring bodily odorants do turn out to play some role in human physiology and/or sexual arousal, it would call into question the wide popularity and use of personal deodorants in a culture that seems to emphasize sexual attraction in so many other ways.

Although the notion of a human pheromone is appealing, the supporting evidence is speculative and, at best, circumstantial. Moreover, in the course of evolution, the human's spectacular ability to verbalize motivational and emotional states has reduced the need to communicate by smell. By the same token, however, the vast research literature on chemical communication systems and pheromones, at least for species below the primates, testifies to the important influence of olfaction on behavior.

THE COMMON CHEMICAL SENSE

Taste and smell are not the only sensory systems receptive to environmental chemicals. There is a system called the **common chemical sense** (or **trigeminal chemoreception)** that is stimulated by the action of chemical irritants (e.g., ammonia, pepper, mustard) on mucosal surfaces (i.e., surfaces found in the nose, mouth, eye, respiratory tract, anus, and genital regions).

The major neural structure mediating the common chemical sense for the head region is the **trigeminal nerve** (the fifth cranial nerve). Fibers of the trigeminal nerve form *free nerve endings* that provide sensory innervation to much of the mucous membrane of the head, including the nasal, oral and corneal regions of

the eyes. The free nerve endings thus relay information about certain irritating (or pain-inducing) chemical stimuli to the trigeminal nerve, which terminates in the trigeminal nuclei of the brain stem (Silver & Finger, 1991).

The common chemical sense serves as an irritant detector, or **chemonociceptor** (Silver, 1987; Silver & Maruniak, 1981). Thus, as a form of pain receptor, it protects the organism from potentially harmful chemicals. In fact, stimulation of its receptors by chemical irritants triggers a wide range of physiological reflexes that tend to eliminate the noxious stimuli from the eyes, nose, and mouth, thereby protecting the organism from further exposure. Indeed, stimulation of the common chemical sense, especially mucous membrane structures in the nasal cavity, produces some of the strongest reflexes in the body, often accompanied by intense stimulus rejection and withdrawal reactions such as coughing and sneezing, tearing, reduced respiration, and even spasm of the respiratory system. [Of course, reflexively and abruptly expelling air—sneezing—is not confined to inhaling chemical irritants. There is a genetically linked mechanism that causes some individuals to sneeze intensely when stimulated by bright light, such as when merely glancing at the sun. As the writer Diane Ackerman (1990) (herself a sufferer) notes, the effect is called *ACHOO* (an acronym for its intentionally formidable name) *autosomal dominant compelling helio-opthalmic outburst.*]

Stimulation of trigeminal receptors of the mouth with chemical irritants also produces profound rejection responses: increased salivation and nasal secretions, tearing, perspiration of the head and neck regions, and general vasodilation (flushing of the face and upper trunk and reddening of the conjunctiva—the membranous covering of the eyeball). The profuse perspiration (called "gustatory sweating") and salivary flow that accompany stimulation of oral trigeminal receptors increase with the intensity of the chemoirritant.

Reception via the common chemical sense is qualitatively different from taste and smell. For example, Doty et al. (1978; see also Mason & Silver, 1983) have reported that anosmic individuals can detect certain noxious chemicals in vapor form: in other words, they are able to detect these chemicals on the basis of their irritating properties rather than their odors.

Stimuli for the Common Chemical Sense

Generally speaking, to evoke the common chemical sense, the chemical concentration should be relatively high (i.e., higher than the olfactory threshold for a given chemical; Prah & Benignus, 1984), and it should be lipid (fat) soluble in order to reach chemoreceptive trigeminal nerve endings (Silver, 1987). The effective stimuli for trigeminal stimulation of the nasal cavity include pungent spices and vegetables such as onions, substances that irritate the eyes and produce tearing (lacrimatories), substances that provoke sneezing (sternutatories), tobacco smoke and ammonia (suffi-cants), and skin irritants (Silver, 1987).

Trigeminal chemoreceptors in the mouth react es-pecially to pungent spices such as chili and black pepper, ginger, mustard, cloves, and horseradish and to chemicals such as menthol (which, of course, pro-duces the sensation of coolness). Because of its ex-traordinary effect on the common chemical sense, the pungent chili pepper (and its active ingredient, capsaicin) has been studied in some detail and war-rants special discussion.

Capsaicin One of the most widely re-searched and effective chemoirritants for the common chemical sense is the active ingredient in chili peppers called **capsaicin** (named after *Capsicum*, a genus of the pepper plant). In fact, according to Silver and Finger (1991), much of the evidence that the receptors of the trigeminal nerve are receptors for chemically induced pain—that is, chemonociceptors—comes from studies using capsaicin. Capsaicin irritates recep-tors innervated by the trigeminal nerve and causes an extreme burning sensation. Ingesting even tiny amounts of chili pepper will dramatically verify this. According to Lawless (1987), the irritating heat effect in the mouth due to capsaicin can be detected by humans in solutions of one to two parts per million. However, over time, repeated ingestion of capsaicin renders individuals insensitive to the chemically in-duced pain and raises the threshold to chemical irrita-

tion. It is likely that chronic use of capsaicin desensi-tizes, damages, or even destroys chemonociceptors. This explains why individuals who repeatedly eat chili pepper seem to be able to tolerate considerably more of it than occasional users (Lawless, 1987; Lawless et al., 1985). A practical warning to the naïve user: if you have bitten into a chili pepper and wish to reduce some of the excruciating heat, don't count on water: while it won't hurt, it won't help. Some relief may be obtained by cold alcoholic or dairy beverages such as milk or yogurt. Some advocates also suggest eating starchy foods such as rice or bread.

The irritating quality due to the chemical potency of capsaicin is not confined to the common chemical sense in the mouth or nose (or to stimulation of fibers of the trigeminal nerve). Capsaicin applied to the skin surface elicits a burning, stinging sensation, with wide-spread local vasodilation. However, as with receptors of the trigeminal nerve, repeated application of capsa-icin to the skin surface eliminates both the irritating sensation and the vasodilation; moreover, repeated use of capsaicin also reduces the sensitivity of the skin to other forms of painful stimulation (Lynn, 1990). In fact, its general analgesic function is used in the popu-lar muscle ointment, "Heet," which is composed largely of capsaicin.

The Appeal of Irritating Chemical Stimuli

Finally, we may consider an interesting aspect of both nasal and oral trigeminal chemoreception. In humans, certain substances that are initially irritating, aversive, and abruptly rejected are eventually preferred. Famil-iar examples include pepper, mustard, horseradish, curry, ginger, vinegar, tobacco, and carbonated bever-ages. The observation that infants, children, and taste-naïve adults typically find the irritating properties of these substances aversive on first exposure, and reject and avoid them, suggests strongly that they are in-nately unappealing. However, in adulthood, many individuals acquire a preference for at least some of these aversive substances.

It has been suggested that chemical irritants of the common chemical sense interact with taste sensations, particularly bitter and sour tastes (Lawless, 1987). Perhaps in the human, the irritating factor serves to increase the palatability of the diet. It may interact with both taste and smell by adding a crispness or slight pungency to the overall sensory quality of food. By contrast, attempts to reverse the rejection and promote a preference for irritating chemical stimuli in animals other than the human, despite intensive and varied training procedures, have been unsuccessful (Rozin et al., 1979).

SUMMARY

This chapter covered the sense of smell, or olfaction. We noted that although the sense of smell is not necessary for human survival, it does provide critical, biologically relevant information for many species.

The necessary stimulus for smell is a volatile substance that is also water and lipid soluble. Generally, the natural chemical stimuli for the olfactory system are organic substances that are mixtures of chemical compounds.

The classification of odor qualities, along with specific anosmias, was discussed. It was concluded that, unlike the sense of taste, there are no basic categories of odors.

The anatomy and physiology of the olfactory system were outlined, and the relevance of the olfactory epithelium and the olfactory bulb for processing odors was discussed. We noted that the olfactory cells are used for both reception and conduction. We also noted that the dendritic knobs and the cilia of the olfactory cells are the structures involved in the initial stage of transduction. With respect to olfaction and the brain, it was pointed out that the olfactory bulb sends some neural tracts to the thalamus, which then projects to a region of the frontal cortex; some neural tracts also project to the limbic system.

The neural coding of olfactory stimulation was next presented. In regard to odor intensity, it was observed that neural activity increases with increases in the concentration of a given odor. For odor quality, it was noted that different odors do not activate specialized receptor cells. It was proposed that different odors produce different spatial and temporal patterns of neural activity across many olfactory receptors that

differ in sensitivity. This means that the same olfactory receptor may be activated by very different odors. A scheme for coding different odors, drawing on the neural activity of a set of olfactory receptors, was outlined.

Disorders of the olfactory system were next discussed. The two main classes are transport and sensorineural dysfunction. Several impairments of olfaction were discussed, including anosmia, hyposmia, hyperosmia, dysosmia (parosmia), and phantosmia. Some possible causes of olfactory impairment were given, such as injury, disease, and age. The odors of some disease states were briefly discussed.

Odor thresholds were considered, emphasizing that extremely low concentrations are sufficient for detection. The effect of sex and age on odor thresholds was described. It was noted that the odor threshold of the human female is lower than that of the male, particularly for certain odorant substances related to musk (e.g., Exaltolide); in addition, the female is superior to the male in odor identification. Odor thresholds increase greatly with age; in addition to being less sensitive to odors, older individuals develop strong olfactory impairments such as anosmia.

We discussed the notion that olfaction is a dynamic sense, subject to effects due to the interaction of odors, such as adaptation (as well as self- and cross-adaptation).

Some of the findings on odor preference were summarized, and some generalizations emerged: odor preference is partly determined by the odors that are biologically relevant to a given species. In addition, odors of flowers and fruits, especially in moderate or dilute concentrations, are preferred. There is also evidence of an own-odor preference.

The recognition and memory of odors was highlighted. It was noted that humans can identify their own clothing on the basis of perspiration. They can also identify the gender of individuals based only on the odor of the clothing they have worn. The memory for odors is high; in certain ways, it is superior to the memory for visual stimuli. Moreover, under the right circumstances, odors associated with events and objects are effective memory cues.

The relation between odors and emotion was discussed, with particular reference to memory. It was concluded that the strong memory for some odors is due largely to their emotional associations and their occurrence in emotional contexts.

Olfactory chemical communication by way of pheromones was described. Pheromones are chemical substances secreted and exchanged among members of the same species to produce behavioral or physiological reactions in receptive animals. Pheromonal communication has been shown for many species, including primates, but the evidence for a possible human pheromone is not compelling. However, some data suggest that secretions from the axillary gland of human females and males influence the human female menstrual cycle.

Finally, the common chemical sense was discussed. It is a chemosensory system, distinct from taste and smell, that is stimulated by the action of chemical irritants on mucosal surfaces (especially in the mouth and nose), and it is mediated by the trigeminal nerve. It has been proposed that the common chemical sense acts as an irritant detector, or chemonociceptor, to protect the individual from potentially harmful chemicals. However, the pungency of mild irritants, especially in the oral cavity, such as produced by mustard and the like, appears to increase the palatability of food for the human.

KEY TERMS

Anosmia

Capsaicin

Chemonociceptor

Common Chemical Sense (Trigeminal Chemoreception)

Cross-Adaptation

Episodic Odors

Exaltolide

Glomerulus

McClintock Effect

Olfaction

Olfactory Adaptation

Olfactory Bulb

Olfactory Cells

Olfactory Cilia

Olfactory Epithelium (Mucosa)

Pheromones

Primer Pheromones

Releaser Pheromones

Self-Adaptation

Specific Anosmias

Stereochemical Theory

Trigeminal Nerve

Vomeronasal System

STUDY QUESTIONS

1. Discuss the functional relevance of the olfactory system to various species.

2. What are the stimulus requirements for the olfactory system, and what are the natural sources of odorants?

3. Discuss the classification of odor quality. Examine Henning's smell prism, the stereochemical theory, and specific anosmias.

4. Outline the major components of the olfactory epithelium and indicate the probable reception sites for odorants.

5. What sorts of disease affect the olfactory system? Consider how disease affects one's body odor. What role could body odor serve in medical diagnoses?

6. Outline olfactory coding for both intensity and quality. Indicate how odor quality may be coded by a specific pattern of activity for groups of receptor cells. Consider how the activity of the same receptor cell may enter into the coding of more than one odorant.

7. Discuss olfactory thresholds, drawing on the sensitivity to specific substances, such as mercaptan and Exaltolide. Consider the role of gender in olfactory sensitivity and threshold values.

8. Discuss self- and cross-adaptation. Examine the possibility of eliminating unwanted odors by adding various odorants.

9. What factors determine or exert a significant effect on odor preferences?

10. Discuss the human's ability to recognize odors. What characteristics of an odorant are important to its recognition? What aspects of human odors enable gender recognition?

11. Explain the observation that the memory for odors, compared to visual stimuli, shows little loss over time. Consider the difference between visual and olfactory stimuli in explaining the memory difference. Describe the role of emotions in the memory for odors.

12. Describe pheromones and indicate what functions they perform. Describe the kinds of information pheromones transmit.

13. What is the vomeronasal system, and what role does it play in chemocommunication?

14. Outline evidence that suggests the possibility of a human pheromone. Indicate the effects that pheromonal-type chemicals may have on cyclic human physiology.

15. What is the common chemical sense, and how does it differ from the taste and smell systems?

16. What anatomical regions served by the trigeminal nerve are most prone to stimulation by the common chemical sense? What are some characteristic stimuli for the common chemical sense?

17. What is the function of the common chemical sense, and what are some typical reactions to the application of chemical irritants? How does the common chemical sense interact with the senses of smell and taste? Explain how stimuli of the common chemical sense may become appealing to the human.

THE PERCEPTION OF TIME

*I*n this brief final chapter, we deal with a unique perception resulting from the duration of events: the perception of the passage of time.

The nature of time pervades many areas of intellectual thought, particularly literature, philosophy, physics, and biology. It is no wonder, then, that the subjective perception of the duration of time is of special interest in psychology. It should be stressed that our interest here is not with the physical notion of time but rather with its perception—the duration of which one is aware. Indeed, the general notion of time concerns issues that go far beyond the limits of this text. Consider the religious philosopher St. Augustine's evasive reply to the enigmatic question "What is time?": "If no one asks me, I know what it is. If I wish to explain what it is to him who asks me, I do not know" (see Trefil, 1991). However, he wrote more confidently, though still arbitrarily, about the origin of time, saying essentially that time comes from the future—which does not exist yet; it moves into the present—which has no duration; and it goes into the past—which no longer exists (cited with credit to Anthony Scariano, 1991).

The perception of the passage of time has been termed **protensity** to distinguish it from physical duration (Woodrow, 1951). Time perception is an oddity in that its variables are more cognitive than physical or neural: clearly, there are no obvious sensory receptors or organs medi-ating it, nor are there any direct, observable sensations emanating from specific time-relevant stimuli. Indeed, "duration" does not have the thing-like quality of most physical stimuli. As Fraisse (1984) observes, "Duration has no existence in and of itself but is the intrinsic characteristic of that which endures" (p. 2).

These points, stressing the elusive nature of time experience, are cleverly elaborated by Hans Castorp, Thomas Mann's protagonist in The Magic Mountain:

> . . . what is time? Can you answer me that? Space we perceive with our organs, with our senses of sight and touch. Good. But which is our organ of time . . . how can we possibly measure anything about which we actually know nothing, not even a single one of its properties? We say of time that it passes. Very good, let it pass. But to be able to measure it . . . to be susceptible of being measured, time must flow evenly, but who ever said it did that? As far as our consciousness is concerned it doesn't, we only assume that it does, for the sake of convenience; our units of measurements are purely arbitrary, sheer conventions. (1927, p. 66)

As we shall see, there is good reason to assume, along with Fraisse and Mann, that time is not an immediately given property but is perceived indirectly: in other words, "time is a concept, somewhat like the value of pieces of money, that attaches to perception only through a judgmental process" (Woodrow, 1951, p. 1235).

Two main explanations will be examined— the biological *basis and the* cognitive *basis of* time perception. *These two explanations are neither mutually exclusive nor exhaustive.*

THE BIOLOGICAL BASIS OF TIME PERCEPTION

The cyclical nature of many bodily processes is well known. A clear example in the human is body temperature variation. There is about a 1.8°F difference in human temperature between the minimum at night and the maximum in the afternoon. Indeed, for most animals, many recurrent bodily changes and activities—such as temperature variations and the patterns of feeding and drinking—in some way reflect the daily cycle of day and night. Activity patterns that regularly recur on a daily basis are termed **circadian rhythms** (from the Latin, *circa,* "about," and *diem,* "day," because the cycles approximate 24 hours).

The body's circadian rhythms appear to be regulated mainly by exposure of the retina to light; retinal signals then travel through a special tract in the optic nerve to a clump of brain cells of the hypothalamus called the *suprachiasmatic nucleus.* From here the neural signals proceed to the *pineal gland,* a tiny structure located beneath the brain at the top of the brain stem. The pineal gland reacts directly to the presence and absence of light: it produces a hormone called *melatonin,* whose secretion is inhibited by light and stimulated by darkness (for this reason, it is sometimes referred to as the "Dracula" hormone; Lewy et al., 1980). Melatonin synchronizes the activity of certain organs and glands that regulate daily biological cycles. Interestingly, there is some evidence that the visual subsystem that mediates the light-induced suppression of melatonin secretion by the pineal gland remains functionally intact even in blind individuals (Czeisler et al., 1995).

The tendency of certain periodic changes in the natural environment to affect bodily rhythms and induce a behavioral reaction may provide a biological advantage. For example, the roosting behavior of birds when the sun sets is adaptive since birds are essentially sightless, and hence defenseless in dim lighting. In other words, the almost total physical inactivity characteristic of roosting serves as an evasive reaction to potential predators. Similarly, the hibernation of many mammals is an adaptive response to the drop in temperature of winter—when food is scarce and energy demands are immense.

Given the ample evidence of biobehavioral cyclical activity, it is reasonable to seek in the nervous system a **biological clock** for perceiving time (Hoagland, 1933, 1935; Holubář, 1969; Triesman, 1963). The concept of an internal time sense assumes that there is a continuous and automatic biological rhythm, not easily or directly influenced by external stimulation, with which the organism compares the duration of stimuli or events. Periodic events with measurable frequencies are found in the electrical activity of the brain, the pulse and heartbeat, respiration, metabolic and endocrine function, thermal regulation, and general activity cycles (although many of these would not be good reference rhythms because they are so markedly and easily affected by external stimulation, and hence can vary widely). The effects of some of these internal activities and processes on time perception have been studied. In particular, the effect of temperature and metabolic processes on the passage of time has led to a biologically based explanation of time perception.

Hoagland's Hypothesis: The Biological Clock

An attempt to develop a theory based on an internal biological clock was made by Hoagland (1933, 1935). He reportedly began his work when his wife became ill and developed a high fever. After she made a significant misjudgment of time, he explored the possibility that her fever had affected her sense of time. Hoagland then had her estimate the passage of time by counting to 60 at what she felt was a rate of one count per second. Relating this measure of her subjective minute to her oral temperature, he found the relationship between body temperature and time perception shown in Figure 19.1. Specifically, he found that a subjective or judged minute was shorter at higher temperatures than at lower ones. For example, reading directly from Figure 19.1, when body temperature was at 98°F, the passage of about 52 sec was judged equal to a minute, whereas when body temperature was at 101°F, an interval of only about 40 sec was judged equal to a minute. It should be clear that in both instances (i.e., judging the passage of 52 or 40 sec as equal to a minute), Hoagland's wife was *overestimating* the duration of time; however, as Figure 19.1 indicates, the overestimation increased with body temperature. Hoagland reasoned from this that an increase in body temperature speeds up bodily processes and causes overestimation of the passage of time. It follows, according to **Hoagland's hypothesis,** that there is a biological clock in the brain that regulates the body's rate of metabolism, which, in turn, affects perception of the passage of time.

Many studies have supported Hoagland's hypothesis that an internal biological clock accelerates when body temperature is raised. Thor (1962), Kleber et al. (1963), and Pfaff (1968) found that subjects overestimated the passage of time when their body temperature was raised.

It follows that time perception when body temperature is reduced should have the opposite effect: it should slow down bodily processes (and the presumed internal biological clock) and thus result in an *underestimation* of the passage of time. Baddeley (1966) tested this with scuba divers in cold water (4°C or 39°F) off the coast of Wales in March. Before and after the temperature of the subjects was lowered by a scuba dive, they estimated time by counting (to themselves) to 60 at what they felt was a rate of 1 per second (as did Hoagland's wife). The results pertinent to our discussion are shown in Table 19.1. Clearly, the subjects were colder after their dive and, in agreement with Hoagland's hypothesis, counted more slowly and thus underestimated time. [Note, however, that some studies found no consistent relationship between time perception and body temperature, making a firm conclusion impossible (e.g., Bell, 1965; Bell & Provins, 1963; Lockhart, 1967; see also the analysis of Wilsoncroft & Griffiths, 1985.)]

Our discussion suggests that variations in body temperature may influence the timing of a presumed internal biological clock by speeding up or slowing down bodily processes. In the next section, we examine the effects on time perception of another factor that influences the rate of bodily activity: drugs.

Drugs

There is compelling evidence that certain drugs influence the experience of time. Frankenhauser (1959) and Goldstone et al. (1958) found that amphetamines

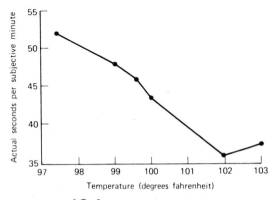

◻ figure 19.1 The relationship between body temperature and the estimated number of seconds in a timed minute. As temperature increases, fewer seconds are required for a subjective minute. (Based on data in Hoagland, 1933.)

◻ table 19.1 Mean Body Temperature and Time Judgment in Cold Water

	Oral Temp. (°F)	Time Judged as 1 min (sec)
Before diving	97.39	64.48
After diving	95.03	70.44[a]
Difference	2.36	−5.96

Source: Based on Baddeley (1966).

[a] Note that after diving the subjects required 70.44 sec to count to 60; that is, they judged the passage of 70.44 sec to be equal to a minute. Thus, the lowered temperature produced an underestimation of time.

lengthen time experience. Frankenhauser reported the same effect with caffeine; by contrast, pentobarbital, a sedative, had no such effect. Shortening of time experience has been observed with nitrous oxide (Steinberg, 1955) and other anesthetic gases (Adam et al., 1971). A general rule, according to Fraisse (1963), is that drugs that *accelerate* vital functions lead to an *overestimation* of time and those that slow them down have the reverse effect.

Among the most striking effects on time perception are those that occur with the administration of so-called psychedelic drugs (marijuana, mescaline, psilocybin, LSD, etc.). Generally, these drugs dramatically lengthen the perceived duration of time (e.g., Conrad et al., 1972; R. Fisher, 1967; Weil et al., 1968). However, whether the psychedelics produce their effect directly, by influencing an endogenous biological clock, or indirectly, by altering various bodily processes, is not clear. Moreover, most of these drugs are assumed to increase awareness and alertness, which could also influence temporal experience. We will consider the implications of this point shortly.

COGNITIVE THEORIES OF TIME PERCEPTION

A very different perspective of time experience is that it is the outcome of cognitive activity. Specifically, experience of the passage of time is assumed to be based on the nature and extent of the cognitive processing performed during a given interval of time. Several such cognitive theories of temporal experience have been proposed (e.g., Block, 1990; Gilliland et al., 1946; Kristofferson, 1967; Michon, 1966; Thomas & Weaver, 1975), but by far the most influential and most widely studied one is that proposed by Robert Ornstein (1969).

Ornstein's Theory: Information-Storage Size

Ornstein adopts an information-storage size or memory approach to time perception, assuming that perceived time duration is based on memory. The basic premise of his theory is that the amount of information

picked up consciously and stored in memory determines the perceived length of time. Relating his central theme to a *computer metaphor*, Ornstein comments:

> *If information is input to a computer and instructions are given to store that information in a certain way, we can check the size of the array or the number of spaces or number of words necessary to store the input information. A more complex input would require a larger storage space than a simpler. An input composed of many varied items would similarly require more space than more homogeneous input. . . . In the storage of a given interval, either increasing the number of stored events or the complexity of those events will increase the size of storage, and as storage size increases the experience of duration lengthens. (p. 41)*

Time perception, examined this way, can be easily analyzed. According to **Ornstein's information-storage size theory,** stimulus factors such as the number and complexity of events occurring during a span of time, along with the efficiency of coding and storage of the events, affect the amount of information that must be processed; thus, they strongly affect the experience of the passage of time. For example, increasing the number and complexity of the events in a given period of time demands increased information processing, and should thus lengthen the perceived duration of that time. In the next section, we examine the influence of several of these variables on time perception.

Number of Events Ornstein (1969) reported that duration experience is linked directly to the *number* of events in a given span of time. In one experiment, subjects were exposed to constant intervals of time (9 min, 20 sec), but the intervals varied in the number of stimuli they contained. Intervals were composed of sounds that occurred at the rate of either 40, 80, or 120 times per minute. As expected, increasing the number of stimuli (or the number of stimulus changes) within a constant period of time lengthened the perception of its duration. Specifically, the 120-sounds-per-minute interval was judged longer than the 80-sounds-per-minute interval, and both were judged longer than the 40-sounds-per-minute interval. These results also have been confirmed in the visual (Mescavage et al., 1971; Mo, 1971; H. R. Schiffman & Bobko, 1977) and tactual modalities (Buffardi, 1971). That is, durations with more elements were judged longer than durations with fewer elements. (This was also found in children as young as 6 years of age: Arlin, 1989.)

Kowal (1987) reported an interesting finding based on estimates of the duration of melodies. She found that sequences of musical notes that were judged to be more familiar, predictable, and organized were estimated as longer than their reverse melodic counterparts (i.e., the same melodies played backward). While these results appear inconsistent with Ornstein's information-storage size notion, Kowal also found that the familiar sequences were perceived to have far more notes than the unfamiliar sequences. Hence, Kowal's findings are consistent with the information-storage size notion that time perception varies positively with the number of events or elements *perceived* within an interval. Relatedly, Poynter and Homa (1983) and Block (1989) reported a positive relationship between duration estimations and the number of stimulus *changes* that occur within an interval of time.

Filled versus Unfilled Intervals Also consistent with this general relationship between numerosity and time perception is the well-documented observation that "filled" time intervals—containing stimuli such as sounds and lights—are typically judged longer than "empty" intervals—consisting only of a period of time between two bounding signals (e.g., Gomez & Robertson, 1979; Long & Beaton, 1980; Thomas & Brown, 1974; Thomas & Weaver, 1975).

However, in an offhand way, this situation also helps explain the lengthened time experience of the "empty" interval when one is anxiously waiting for something to happen—for example, the receipt of an important letter, a person's arrival, or the results of a test. The lengthening of time experience in such cases is attributed to the cognitive-emotional effects of anticipation or expectation. Expectancy leads to increased vigilance by the individual, so that there is more

"awareness of temporal input" and consequently a lengthening of perceived duration (Block et al., 1980; Cahoon & Edmonds, 1980; Ornstein, 1969; Zakay, 1993). This situation, in which the individual is waiting for an event to occur, is well summarized by the maxim "A watched pot never boils." (We will return to this phenomenon in a later section.)

In summary, then, an empty interval of time contains less information to process than a filled interval; hence, in comparison, it may be experienced as briefer. However, passively experiencing an empty interval of time can also increase awareness of the passage of time and correspondingly lengthen time experience. It thus appears that, depending on the nature of the situation and the task, an empty interval may be experienced as either longer *or* shorter than a filled interval of equal duration (see Boltz, 1991; Grondin & Rousseau, 1991; Grondin, 1993; Rammsayer & Lima, 1991).

Stimulus Complexity Ornstein (1969) and others (e.g., H. R. Schiffman & Bobko, 1974) have examined the effect of varying the *complexity* of the stimuli during an interval on the perception of time. Generally, time seems to increase as the complexity of the stimuli increases. This was the case when the stimuli presented to subjects during the interval were various visual shapes (whose complexity was based in the number of interior angles), as well as when the stimuli consisted of sounds of varying complexity. A similar effect on time experience was observed when subjects listened to melodies that varied in complexity: complex melodies were judged longer than simple ones (Yeager, 1969).

Organization and Memory According to the information-storage size notion, perceived duration is also affected by how information presented within an interval is organized (i.e., coded and stored in memory) and by the amount of stimulus information retained. It follows that the more information retained from a given interval, the longer its apparent duration. Relevant to this, Ornstein (1969) found that unpleasant stimuli are more poorly retained than neutral ones, and unpleasant events are judged to be shorter. It is common experience that pleasant or interesting events are likely to be regarded later on as longer than they actually were. The reason may be that these events are better retained than uneventful, ordinary events; hence, compared to ordinary events, they seem longer.

Mulligan and Schiffman (1979), in a direct approach to the role of organization and memory in altering apparent duration, reported evidence in support of this aspect of Ornstein's information-storage size theory. In one experiment they presented the ambiguous line drawing of Figure 19.2 for a fixed interval, telling the subjects to study and remember the figure. The time interval was judged shorter if it was preceded or followed by a simplifying cue—a descriptive verbal label or caption—than if no cue was provided. In other words, the clarifying cue reduced the ambiguity of the figure and thus made it easier to recall. These results support the assumption that the cue, even when presented *after* the figure, makes it easier to store the figure in memory: thus, intervals containing stimuli that are well organized in memory—requiring less information storage—are judged shorter than intervals in which the same stimuli are less organized.

An interesting implication of the role of memory on perceived duration comes from a variation of the *Zeigarnik effect*— in which finished tasks are recalled less well than unfinished ones. Most students have probably verified this in a casual way after taking a timed examination composed of brief, varied items such multiple-choice or fill-in questions. The items

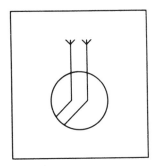

□ *figure* **19.2** Ambiguous line drawing used by Mulligan and Schiffman (1979). The cue for reducing the figure's ambiguity is "an early bird who caught a very strong worm."

most likely remembered after the test are usually the ones that were uncompleted or whose answers students were unsure of (i.e., "cognitively incomplete"). Thus, since the memory for uncompleted tasks is better than for completed tasks, the duration of uncompleted tasks should also be perceived as longer. In support of this, N. Schiffman and Greist-Bousquet (1992) found that subjects who were prevented from completing a series of simple tasks perceived them to be longer than did subjects who were allowed to finish (see also Fortin et al., 1993).

Before turning from Ornstein's information-storage approach to time perception, we should note that his approach is not the first to deal with temporal experience as principally a cognitive phenomenon (e.g., see Gilliland et al., 1946; Kristofferson, 1967; Michon, 1966), nor is it the only cognitive view of time perception, as evidenced in the next section.

Cognitive-Attentional Theory

An alternative to Ornstein's storage model of time perception holds that the *focus of attention* directly affects temporal experience. According to this **cognitive–attentional theory,** attention is divided between two processors: (1) a nontemporal **information processor** and (2) a **cognitive timer** that processes and encodes temporal information (see Thomas & Weaver, 1975; Underwood, 1975; Zakay, 1993). Thus, in a typical temporal task, observers divide their attention between the information-processing demands of the task and the processing of time information specific to the time span to be evaluated. It follows that the relative amount of attention given to these two processes directly determines the nature of the time experience: the perception of time *increases* with heightened temporal awareness and *shortens* with attention to nontemporal information processing. Based on this notion, temporal experience is directly related to the amount of *attention* focused on the passage of time. As Fraisse (1984) observes: "The more one pays attention to time, the longer it seems. . . . Reciprocally, duration seems short when the task is difficult and/or interesting" (p. 31).

This idea lends itself to a number of laboratory and common situations. Thus, the perception of an empty time interval noted earlier (with few or no sensory events or stimuli) may seem longer than a filled interval with attention-demanding stimuli (see Hogan, 1978). According to this notion, with a stimulus-filled interval of time, more attention is directed to meeting the cognitive demands of the task and less is allotted to the cognitive timer, minimizing temporal awareness. As a result, time seems to pass quickly. This is also supported by evidence that making the task more difficult seems to shorten the time (Brown, 1985; Hogan, 1978; Zakay & Fallach, 1984; Zakay et al., 1983).

With absorbing activities requiring effort (e.g., problem solving, test taking), there is an increase in information processing and a resultant decrease in temporal awareness; therefore, time seems to pass rapidly. In contrast, when waiting in line, performing repetitive, boring tasks, or experiencing the "watched pot" phenomenon (introduced earlier and explained in an alternative way by Ornstein's emphasis on the "awareness of input"), there is less information processing and more attention to the cognitive timer: the result is a greater temporal awareness—"time seems to weigh more heavily"—and temporal experience accordingly lengthens. In short, the more attention you pay to the passage of time, the longer it seems to be.

This analysis may also apply to the familiar experience summarized by the statement "time flies when you're having fun." In such cases, attention is focused more on the activities in which one is engaged—that is, nontemporal information processing—than on the cognitive timer, and temporal awareness is reduced; that is, with less attention allotted to the passage of time, temporal experience is decreased. J. B. Priestly's (1968) somewhat impressionistic commentary summarizes this point:

> as soon as we make full use of our faculties, commit ourselves heart and soul to anything, live richly and interestingly instead of merely existing, our inner time spends our ration of clock time as a drunken sailor his pay. What are hours outside seem minutes inside. (pp. 41–42, cited in Hogan, 1978, p. 419)

At present, there is no theory to account for the majority of the findings. Moreover, the role of different factors (e.g., numerosity, complexity, organization, and memory) and attention-processing effort on the sense of time passing may vary with the actual physical time to be estimated. That is, using very brief intervals may induce a different relationship among the temporally sensitive variables than using moderate or relatively long intervals (Poynter & Homa, 1983). In addition, with increases in duration, memory and other, less specifiable cognitive processes are more likely to be engaged (e.g., Ferguson & Martin, 1983; Fortin et al., 1993). Clearly, conclusions about the relation between cognitive variables and time experience must be qualified in terms of the kinds of intervals examined.

Biological versus Cognitive Basis of Time Perception

To review, there appears to be some relationship between bodily activity and a time sense. Similarly, the time perception of complex events is under certain cognitive influences. How can we resolve the discrepancy between the two explanations? It should be pointed out that the temporal experiences and responses assessed by experiments that support a biological clock basis of time perception are generally very different from the experiences employed in experiments supporting time perception based on cognitive processes. The biological clock type of experiment often employs brief intervals and uses response measures such as the rate of tapping. Perhaps the perception of very short intervals invokes a very different psychological process from that employed in the perception of longer intervals. It may be that with very brief intervals attention can focus primarily on the interval itself and thus reflects the effect of physiological rhythms, whereas for longer intervals judgments must rely on indirect cues such as the number and kinds of activities. If this is the case, then both types of explanations may be drawn on: the biological explanation can most usefully be applied to very brief intervals, whereas longer intervals, perceived less directly and with greater reference to external events and nontemporal factors, fall under a cognitive explanation.

AGE AND THE PASSAGE OF TIME

It is clear that both biological and cognitive effects can contribute to the perception of time. Interestingly, *age* is a variable that may involve both biological and cognitive effects on the perception of long intervals of time. Almost everyone senses that as they age, annual events such as holidays and birthdays seem to occur more and more rapidly. Indeed, it is a common and often perplexing and dismal observation that as we grow older time seems to pass more swiftly.

Why does a year (or any large unit of time) seem to pass by faster as we age? One possible explanation is that we automatically perceive the passage of long intervals—such as the time between birthdays—relative to the total amount of time we have already experienced. In other words, one's lifetime serves as a *reference level* for the perception of a given time span. Thus, the duration between annual events (e.g., birthdays) is perceived relative to one's age. For example, the passage of a year to a 4-year-old represents 25% of the child's lifetime; this is a substantial amount and is experienced as a relatively long time. In contrast, the passage of a year to a 60-year-old person represents a very small fraction of the person's life (1/60th, or less than 2%); accordingly, in comparison to the temporal experience of the child, it seems to pass quickly.

TIME PERCEPTION AND THE SIZE OF THE SPATIAL ENVIRONMENT

A. J. DeLong (1981) proposed an **experiential space–time relativity** where space and time are related to each other, each being a psychological manifestation of the same phenomenon. According to this notion, modifying the size of the components that one interacts with should affect our perception of time. Bobko et al. (1986) tested this notion by having groups of subjects interact with two-dimensional visual environments of different sizes and then estimate how

long it took. Display size was varied by using three sizes of television screens, with diagonals of 0.13, 0.28, and 0.58 m. Different groups of subjects viewed each screen and engaged in a modified video game that was constant for all screens and fixed in duration at 55 sec. The video game itself was constant, but the *size* of the images comprising the game varied directly with video screen size.

Subjects' verbal estimates of the 55-sec duration were found to depend on display size. This is shown in Figure 19.3, where time estimations are plotted against screen size. Note that the estimated time plotted on the *y*-axis is a derived score in which each estimation was converted to a ratio of the verbally estimated duration of the interval to its physical duration (i.e., 55 sec). Accordingly, ratios of 1.00 reveal perfect judgment, and ratios above 1.00 reflect an overestimation of the interval (i.e., a lengthening of perceived time or "time passes slowly"). The 55-sec interval was overestimated for each screen size, and the magnitude of the overestimation *increased* as display size *decreased*. Thus, the constant 55-sec duration was experienced as *longest*—2.3 (i.e., 126.5/55)—when viewing the *smallest* visual environment, the 0.13-m video screen. In other words, clock or physical time is experienced as longer when the observed envi-

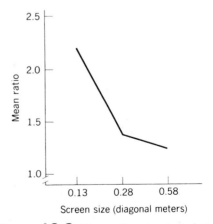

□ *figure* **19.3** Mean ratios of verbally estimated time interval to actual interval (55 sec), plotted by viewing screen size. According to this conversion, ratios of 1.00 show perfect estimation, and ratios above 1.00 represent an overestimation of the interval ("time passes slowly"). (Based on Bobko et al., 1986.)

ronment is *compressed:* the smaller the size of the visual environment, the greater the apparent duration.

Mitchell and Davis (1987) similarly found an inverse relation between the size of model environments (consisting of model railways, living rooms, and abstract nonrepresentational interiors) and apparent duration: smaller environmental size was related to a compression of subjective time relative to physical time. Overall, it appears that environmental size affects perceived duration. Although we have no convincing explanation for this relationship, perhaps, as Mitchell and Davis suggest, subjective time compression is related to differences in the *density* of the information to be processed in environments of different sizes. Clearly, experienced time and space vary together in a consistent fashion. Two further manifestations of this interdependence are given next: tau and kappa effects.

TIME AND DISTANCE: THE TAU AND KAPPA EFFECTS

Tau Effect

A close relationship between experienced time and certain activities exists: each can influence the other. For example, in certain conditions the manipulation of time can affect the perception of distance and variation in distance can influence the perception of time. The effect of time on the perception of distance is called the **tau effect.** An example of the tau effect attributed to Helson and King (1931) is shown in Figure 19.4. Three equidistant points (A, B, C) on the forearm of a subject are stimulated in succession (i.e., forming a tactual equilateral triangle). However, if the interval of time between stimulation of the first point (*A*) and the second point (*B*) is greater than that between the first (*A*) and third (*C*) points, the subject will perceive the *distance* between the first and sec-

ond points as greater than that between the first and third points. In other words, if an observer is judging two equal distances, the distance defined by the longer interval of *time* will appear to be longer. In short, the greater the time interval between successive stimulations, the greater the perceived distance. A similar tau effect has been demonstrated in vision (Abbe, 1937) and in audition (Christensen & Huang, 1979).

Kappa Effect

The converse effect, in which time perception is influenced by the manipulation of distance, has also been identified and termed the **kappa effect** (Cohen et al., 1953, 1955; Huang & Jones, 1982; Jones & Huang, 1982). Consider two equal temporal intervals defined by the onset of two successive stimuli (e.g., three lights arranged in a row, as in Figure 19.5). If the distance between the first and second stimuli is greater than that between the second and third, the first interval will be perceived as longer. A kappa effect also has been shown with audition (Cohen et al., 1954) and with touch (Suto, 1955).

SUMMARY

In this final chapter, we examined the perception of time, or protensity. Two main explanations were reviewed. The biological approach to time perception is linked to the cyclical nature of many bodily processes, such as temperature variation, and general metabolic activities. Its basic assumption is that an internal biological clock controls the speed of metabolic processes and time experience.

The second explanation contends that time perception depends on the kind and degree of cognitive processing and the attentional focus of the individual. According to a major version of this notion (Ornstein's

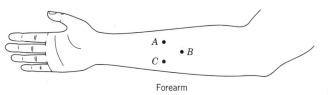

Forearm

□ *figure* **19.4** The tau effect.

A B C

□ *figure* **19.5** The kappa effect.

theory), perceived duration depends on the contents of mental storage. Thus, the amount of information picked up and stored in memory determines the perception of the time interval. Several stimulus factors that seem to affect information storage, and hence time perception, were examined: the number and complexity of events occurring within the interval, empty versus filled intervals, stimulus organization and memory.

An alternative cognitive approach to Ornstein's theory was also outlined. This theory holds that attention is divided between two processors: an information processor and a temporal processor. According to this notion, the less attention paid to information processing and the more attention directed to the passage of time (e.g., "endlessly" waiting in line), the greater the temporal experience. By contrast, when attention is focused on an absorbing task (e.g., solving problems, taking a test), temporal experience shortens.

We briefly discussed the familiar experience that time appears to pass more quickly as we age. We speculated that the passage of long intervals of time (such as between birthdays and holidays) is perceived relative to the total time already experienced: one's lifetime serves as a reference level for the perception of a given period of time.

Next, the effect of the size of the spatial environment on time perception—experiential space–time relativity—was briefly described. It was noted that the smaller the visual environment, the greater is the apparent duration. An experiment analyzing this by employing visual displays of different sizes was outlined.

In the final section, we considered the relation of time perception to the spatial variable of distance. The tau effect refers to the effect of duration on perceived distance; the kappa effect refers to the effect of physical distance on perceived duration.

KEY TERMS

Biological Clock

Circadian Rhythms

Cognitive–Attentional Theory

Cognitive Timer

Experiential Space–Time Relativity

Hoagland's Hypothesis

Information Processor

Kappa Effect

Ornstein's Information-Storage Size Theory

Protensity

Tau Effect

STUDY QUESTIONS

1. Distinguish between physical time and protensity. What sensory structures and physical processes may mediate the subjective experience of time? Examine the possibility that the experience of time is derived immediately from perception.

2. Identify periodic or cyclic variations in bodily processes, including circadian rhythms, that could serve as a biological clock.

3. Outline Hoagland's biological clock theory of time perception and summarize the evidence in its support. How does variation in body temperature affect time perception?

4. Summarize the effects of stimulant and depressant drugs on the experience of time.

5. Outline Ornstein's information-storage theory of time perception and indicate how it incorporates the effects of biological variations. Identify and examine the information-processing demands that influence time perception. Describe the effect of the number of events, stimulus complexity, and the role of memory.

6. How does the cognitive–attentional theory compare to Ornstein's storage model? Describe how the allocation of attention affects time experience. What is the cognitive timer?

7. Based on the cognitive–attentional theory, explain the experiences summarized in the statements "A watched pot never boils" and "Time flies when you're having fun."

8. Explain why time seems to pass by faster as we get older.

9. Discuss the effect that the apparent size of the spatial environment has on time perception. What is experiential space–time relativity?

10. Describe the tau and kappa effects.

GLOSSARY

ABSOLUTE (PERFECT) PITCH The rare ability to identify and reproduce isolated musical notes without any musical reference or standard.

ABSOLUTE THRESHOLD (LIMEN) The least amount of physical intensity of a stimulus required for its detection.

ACCOMMODATION The variable refractive capacity of the lens that brings an image into sharp focus on the retinal surface.

ACHROMATOPSIA A rare condition of total color blindness due to cortical pathology.

ACOUSTIC REFLEX The combined reflexive action of two sets of muscles attached to the ossicles of the middle ear when the auditory system is exposed to intense sounds. The acoustic reflex reduces the efficiency of the middle ear in transmitting intense sounds and thus protects the delicate inner ear structures from damaging sound pressures.

ACTION POTENTIAL (SPIKE POTENTIAL) Brief (1/1000th of a sec) electrical change in a neuron that fires the neuron.

ACUITY The ability to detect, resolve, and perceive fine details of a visual display.

ACUPUNCTURE An ancient Chinese medicinal practice of therapy for the general treatment of disease and control of pain. Acupuncture involves inserting needles into the body at precise loci.

ADAPTATION (1) Relative loss in sensitivity or increase in threshold due to prolonged or repeated stimulation. (2) The process of adjustment to the change in the conditions of lighting, that is, dark or light adaptation. In general, adaptation refers to a reversible change in the state of an organism due to the effects of environmental events.

ADAPTATION-PRODUCED POTENTIATION The effect of imparting a particular taste to water because of adaptation to the taste of certain chemical substances.

ADDITIVE COLOR MIXTURE Mixtures in which the addition of the excitations produced by different wavelengths produce a specific chromatic sensation.

AERIAL PERSPECTIVE (CLEARNESS) A depth or distance cue in which objects whose retinal images are sharp or distinct appear closer than those whose images are blurry or otherwise indistinct.

AFFERENT CODE Neural firing pattern or code for groups of receptor cells or nerve fibers linked to a specific sensation.

AFFERENT SIGNALS Neural excitations toward the brain—sensory input.

AFTEREFFECTS Perceptual effects due to viewing a stimulus of a particular color, shape, intensity, or orientation.

AGEUSIA Absence of taste.

AIR-RIGHTING REFLEX The tendency of some mammals to right themselves during a fall and land upright.

ALBEDO A surface property that refers to the proportion of incident light that is reflected. Also known as *reflectance*.

ALL-OR-NONE PRINCIPLE The phenomenon that a neuron *always* fires when the neural threshold is reached, causing an action potential, and *never* fires when the neural threshold is not reached and no action potential results.

AMBIENT SYSTEM A presumed neural pathway involved in visually locating objects in space. It is presumed to be mediated by the retinotectal visual system.

AMBLYOPIA A loss of visual acuity that is not directly linked to any ocular abnormality and that cannot be corrected optically.

AMPLITUDE A general measure of stimulus magnitude.

ANAGLYPH A form of stereo figure created by printing two different patterns on top of each other in different inks to produce a composite picture. When viewed through the proper filters that enable each eye to sort out a single pattern, a stereo depth effect is perceived.

ANALYTICAL INTROSPECTION A highly disciplined technique of self-observation and mental analysis used by the nineteenth-century structuralists to uncover the fundamental units of sensation.

ANECHOIC CHAMBER A specially constructed acoustic environment that lacks sound-reflecting objects and hence is free of echoes.

ANGLE-OF-REGARD HYPOTHESIS Explanation of the moon illusion that proposes that the size of the moon is affected by the angle of the eyes relative to the position of the head.

ANISEIKONIA An optical anomaly in which the image in one eye is larger than that in the other, resulting in a significant disparity between the images in each eye.

ANOMALOSCOPE A special kind of color mixer that measures the proportions of two colors necessary to match a third color.

ANOMALOUS TRICHROMATISM Defect in color vision in which a proportion of the three primary colors different from normal are needed to match the colors of the spectrum.

ANORTHOSCOPIC PERCEPTION The perception of form resulting from viewing a figure in successive sections through a narrow slit. The term *anorthoscopic* (''abnormally viewed'') was originally used by Zöllner and Helmholtz, in the nineteenth century, to refer to the presentation of stimuli in successive sections.

ANOSMIA Insensitivity to odors.

APHASIA A general class of speech defects.

APPARENT DISTANCE HYPOTHESIS (SIZE-DISTANCE INVARIANCE HYPOTHESIS) The linear relationship between apparent size and apparent distance: the farther away an object appears, the larger it appears.

APPARENT MOVEMENT The perception of movement from a stationary stimulus.

APPARENT OVERLAP The tendency to perceive a form or surface as having distinct contours—called *subjective contours*—overlapping a figure. The subjective contours are illusory; there is no actual physical overlap.

ARISTOTLE'S ILLUSION An illusory tactual experience attributed to Aristotle in which a single stimulus, if applied in a specific manner to two crossed adjacent fingers, produces the experience of two separate sensations. See Figure 16.10.

ASPARTAME A low-calorie sweetener produced by the combination of two amino acids, aspartic acid and phenylalanine. Aspartame is equivalent in calories to sucrose (table sugar), but it is about 200 times sweeter.

ASTIGMATISM Optic defect in which the corneal surface is not spherical.

AUDIOGRAM A graph that shows hearing loss, in decibels, for pure tones as a function of frequency.

AUDIOMETER A device for assessing hearing loss.

AUDITORY ADAPTATION The reduced sensitivity to a specific auditory stimulus due to continued stimulation by the stimulus.

AUDITORY CORTEX The part of the cortex concerned with processing auditory signals.

AUDITORY FATIGUE Elevation of the auditory threshold after the termination of a masking tone. Also called *sound-induced hearing loss* and *auditory adaptation.*

AUDITORY SCENE ANALYSIS The tendency to analyze the complex acoustic environment, which is composed of many distinct sound events, into its constituent sources.

AUDITORY STREAMS   Groups of sounds that share some feature or characteristic and appear to come from a common source.

AUTOKINETIC MOVEMENT   The apparent motion of a stationary point of light in a dark environment.

AUTOSTEREOGRAM   A special stereogram that contains complete information for both eyes on a single printed image. When properly fused, a three-dimensional display is seen (see Figure 9.26).

AXON   The part of the cell or neuron that carries information from the cell body to other neurons.

BACKWARD MASKING   Impairment to the perception of a target stimulus by the immediate presentation of a second stimulus that masks the target.

BASILAR MEMBRANE   A membrane on which lies the organ of Corti.

BEATS   The perception of a single throbbing tone of a single pitch, periodically varying in loudness. Beats can result from the simultaneous occurrence of two tones that are of similar intensity but slightly different in frequency.

BÉKÉSY'S TRACKING PROCEDURE   A procedure used for generating an audiogram that reveals tonal gaps, narrow ranges of frequencies which are inaudible to the individual.

BENHAM'S TOP   A circular design, which when rotated at a rate between 5 to 10 cycles per second, produces subjective colors. See Chapter 5.

BEST (CHARACTERISTIC) FREQUENCY   The frequency or frequency range of an auditory nerve fiber at which the intensity necessary to reach absolute threshold is at a minimum.

BEST STIMULUS   The class of stimuli, specified with reference to one of the primary taste qualities, that is most effective in eliciting neural activity from a given taste fiber.

BEZOLD–BRÜCKE EFFECT   The sensory effect in which the perception of long-wavelength light apparently shifts toward yellow and short-wavelength light shifts toward blue, with an increase in intensity.

BINOCULAR CUES   Cues to the perception of depth and distance that require the use of both eyes.

BINOCULAR DISPARITY (BINOCULAR PARALLAX)   The difference in the two retinal images that provides a strong impression of depth and three-dimensionality of space. Also termed *retinal disparity*.

BINOCULAR OVERLAP   Region of the visual field that is seen by both eyes.

BINOCULAR RIVALRY   The phenomenon that occurs when each eye is presented with different stimuli. At one moment the stimuli from one eye may be dominant, with a suppression of the stimuli from the other eye.

BIOLOGICAL CLOCK   A hypothesized internal clock in the brain that controls the speed of metabolism and the rhythm of subjective time.

BIOLOGICAL MOTION   The perception of the pattern of movement produced by locomoting humans. These forms of motion have been labeled *biological motion* by G. Johansson.

BIPOLAR CELLS   Cells in the intermediate retinal layer that transmit impulses from the receptors to the ganglion cells.

BLIND SPOT   The region of the visual field that is reflected on the optic nerve fibers (optic disk) exiting from the eyeball. No photoreceptors lie at this region; thus, the viewer cannot perceive the corresponding part of the visual field.

BLINDSIGHT   The presumed ability of some blind individuals to localize and orient to objects that they are not consciously aware of seeing.

BLOBS   Distinctively patterned dark regions distributed over the visual or striate cortex that are selectively activated only by color and possess concentric double-opponent receptive fields.

BLOCH'S LAW   Within certain limits, the threshold response to a visual stimulus is a product of stimulus intensity (I) and exposure time (T). That is, $T \times I = $ a constant threshold value. Also known as the *Bunsen–Roscoe law*.

BLOCK PORTRAIT   An image that has been computer processed (or "block averaged") into a pattern of small blocks; each block is uniform in luminance throughout its area and is assigned the same dark-light value as the average value of the original portion of the picture.

BONE CONDUCTION Process by which sound is conducted to the cochlea of the inner ear through the cranial bones rather than by the usual conduction structures.

BOTTOM-UP PROCESSES (DATA-DRIVEN) An approach to perceptual processing that begins with the analysis of simple, basic sensory features, such as luminance differences and spatial frequencies, which are then integrated to form identifiable patterns and shapes.

BRAILLE SYSTEM A tactual reading system composed of dots embossed on a surface that produces patterns of differential stimulation when contacted by the skin, usually the fingertip.

BRIGHTNESS One of the basic psychological dimensions of light. It varies primarily with physical intensity.

BROCA'S AREA A small region in the lower part of the frontal lobe that mediates speech expression or production. It is usually found in the left frontal lobe.

CAPSAICIN An active ingredient in the chili pepper that appears to intensely irritate receptors innervated by the trigeminal nerve mediating the common chemical sense. This irritating quality accounts for the extreme burning sensation that follows the ingestion of even very small amounts of chili pepper.

CAROUSEL EXPERIMENT Classic experiment by Held and Hein (1963) in which kittens are allowed either active experience (coordinated visual and motor experience) or passive (visual *or* motor) experience. The findings are that effective perceptual-motor development requires active experience. See Chapter 11.

CATARACT An opacity of the lens of the eye resulting in impaired vision.

CATCH TRIALS Trials in a signal detection task in which no signal is present.

CATEGORICAL PERCEPTION A phenomenon in which the ability to discriminate among members of the *same* category is inferior to the ability to discriminate between members of *different* categories. As an example applied to speech perception, it is more difficult to discriminate between different forms of the consonant /p/ than it is to discriminate between the two consonants /p/ and /b/.

CENTER-SURROUND RECEPTIVE FIELD A receptive field of a ganglion cell that has a concentric organization. In one type of cell, stimulation of the central area will produce an excitatory response, whereas stimulation of the surround will produce an inhibitory response. In another type of center-surround receptive field, the effects are reversed: stimulation of the center will produce an inhibitory response, whereas stimulation of the surround will produce an excitatory response.

CENTRAL NERVOUS SYSTEM The part of the nervous system that consists of the brain and spinal cord.

CEREBRAL CORTEX A thin (2 mm), very convoluted exterior covering of the cerebral hemispheres. The cerebral cortex is responsible for sensory and motor functions as well as higher mental processes in the human.

CEREBRAL DOMINANCE The relative dominance of one side of the brain over the other for certain perceptual processes. Also referred to as *brain asymmetry.*

CHEMONOCICEPTOR Presumed receptor of the trigeminal nerve and the common chemical sense for the reception of chemical irritants.

CHEMORECEPTORS Specialized sensory receptors for the pick up of chemicals. Taste, smell, and the common chemical sense are mediated by chemoreceptors.

CHLOROLABE A photosensitive pigment for groups of cones selectively responsive to medium wavelengths of light.

CHOROID Layer at the back of the eyeball that provides nutrients for the retina and absorbs light. In some mammals it forms a process called the tapetum which reflects back some light.

CHROMATIC ABERRATION Distortion of chromatic retinal images by the lens due to greater refraction of short wavelengths than of long ones.

CHROMESTHESIA A form of synesthesia in which sounds produce vivid color sensations in addition to aural sensations.

CILIARY MUSCLE Muscle that changes the shape or curvature of the lens of the eye and promotes accommodation.

CIRCADIAN RHYTHMS Activity patterns that occur regularly on a daily (i.e., 24-hour) basis.

CLOSURE A Gestalt principle of perceptual organization; it is a tendency to "fill in" gaps in the structure of a figure or form so that it appears complete or closed.

COCHLEA Spiral-shaped portion of the inner ear containing the receptive elements (transducers) that convert sound to neural activity.

COCHLEAR DUCT Middle canal of the cochlea of the inner ear. It contains the organ of Corti. Also called the *scala media.*

COGNITIVE–ATTENTIONAL THEORY A model of time perception that holds that the focus of attention directly affects temporal experience. Attention is divided between two processors: a nontemporal information processor and a cognitive timer that processes temporal information.

COGNITIVE COMPONENTS Components of a cognitive nature such as past experience, attention, and perceptual constancy that contribute to certain illusions.

COGNITIVE INVENTION A notion proposed by I. Rock to explain the resultant lightness effect that promotes subjective contours and shapes.

COGNITIVE TIMER A presumed mode of attention involved in time perception that processes and encodes temporal information and heightens temporal awareness.

COLOR ADAPTATION Adaptation or adjustment of the visual system to the dominant wavelengths that illuminate a scene. Color adaptation plays a role in explaining color constancy.

COLOR CIRCLE A circular arrangement used to specify the relation among hues and saturations. Hues are arranged around the perimeter of the circle, and saturation extends from the perimeter to the center of the circle.

COLOR CONSTANCY The tendency for the color of an object or surface to appear constant in spite of variations in the wavelengths of light illuminating it.

COLOR MIXTURE CURVES A set of curves derived from the mixture of various amounts of light from the wavelengths of three primaries, enabling the matching of all colors.

COLOR SPINDLE A three-dimensional model used to show the relation among hue, brightness, and saturation. Hues are located around the perimeter, saturation from the center to the perimeter, and brightness is arranged from top to bottom. Also called the *color solid.*

COMMON CHEMICAL SENSE (TRIGEMINAL CHEMORECEPTION) A sensory system whose effective stimuli are typically chemical irritants. The sensory surface for the common chemical sense is the mucosa of the nose, mouth, eyes, respiratory tract, anus and genital apertures, which is innervated by the trigeminal nerve.

COMMON FATE A Gestalt grouping principle in which elements that move in the same direction are grouped together.

COMPARATOR A hypothetical center in the nervous system in which efferent signals from the brain to the eye muscles are compared with the flow of images on the retina, thereby canceling apparent movement due to the stimulation of the image–retina system.

COMPLEMENTARY AFTERIMAGE After prolonged fixation of a color stimulus, the complementary color will appear if fixation is shifted to an achromatic surface.

COMPLEMENTARY COLORS The hues of two wavelengths that, when mixed in the correct proportions, yield achromatic gray or white. Complementary colors lie opposite each other on the color cirlce.

COMPLEX CELLS Cortical cells whose receptive fields are optimally sensitive to stimuli that are at a particular orientation and move in a particular direction. However, the receptive fields of complex cells may fire to stimuli that fall within a relatively large region of the visual field.

COMPLEXITY The acoustic dimension of sound produced by vibrating bodies that do not vibrate at a single frequency. The psychological dimension of the resultant complex waveform is termed *timbre.*

COMPOUND EYE An image-forming eye (of arthropods) consisting of a mosaic of tubular units (ommatidia) that are clustered tightly together and arranged so that the outer surface forms a hemisphere.

COMPUTATIONAL APPROACH An approach to perceptual processing, derived from the application of computer simulation and artificial intelligence, that holds that perception involves solving an information processing problem presented to the visual system. Perception is thus considered to be the end product of a mathematically oriented analysis performed on the retinal image.

CONDITIONED TASTE AVERSION The behavioral effect of pairing a specific taste with an extremely unpleasant stimulus, such as a poison, that produces symptoms of illness. As the result of a conditioned taste aversion, substances with the specific taste are subsequently avoided or rejected.

CONDUCTION HEARING LOSS Deficiency in hearing due to a defect in the conduction mechanism of the auditory system. Hearing loss is distributed about equally over all frequencies. Also known as *transmission hearing loss.*

CONES Photoreceptors of the retina that function in color vision and acuity. Such receptors are most dense in the fovea and relatively absent in the periphery of the retina. There are approximately 6 to 8 million cones in the retina.

CONNECTIONIST MODEL An approach to perceptual processing based on the idea that the sensory system has a large but finite set of functional neural units; the pattern or network of activity across a number of such units represents specific features.

CONSONANCE In audition, those combinations of tones that appear to blend well and sound pleasant together.

CONSTRUCTIVIST APPROACH A psychological approach in which perception is believed to be the outcome of an integrative, constructive process based on cognitive strategies, past experience, biases, expectations, and so on.

CONTEXT The influence of the background or surroundings on perception.

CONTINGENT AFTEREFFECTS The class of aftereffects that results from continued stimulation and selective adaptation or fatigue of combinations of specific stimulus features. Accordingly, the resultant aftereffect is linked to and contingent on the presence of one of the adapted stimulus features. The McCollough effect is the classic example of contingent aftereffects.

CONTRAST ILLUSIONS The set of visual illusions in which the surrounding or contextual stimuli exert opposing effects on the apparent size of an embedded stimulus. See Chapter 10.

CONTRAST SENSITIVITY FUNCTION A figure that represents the visual system's sensitivity for the range of perceived spatial frequencies. Specifically, the figure plots the relation between spatial frequency and threshold levels of contrast.

CONVERGENCE The tendency of the eyes to turn toward each other in a coordinated action to fixate on targets located nearby.

CORNEA The transparent outer surface of the sclerotic coat lying in front of the iris and the lens.

COROLLARY DISCHARGE SIGNALS (OUTFLOW SIGNALS) A presumed set of corollary signals sent to a hypothetical region of the central nervous system that matches the efferent motor command signals produced during self-initiated motor movements.

CORRECT REJECTION A negative response given by an observer in a signal detection task when *no* signal is present.

CORRESPONDING RETINAL POINTS Stimulation of identical areas in the left and right fovea by the same target. The resulting perception is of a single, fused target.

CORTICAL MAGNIFICATION Exaggerated allocation of cortical representation of the area of the fovea relative to the peripheral retina. Functionally, this means that a relatively large area of the cortex is devoted to the small foveal area of the retina that is responsible for perceiving acuity.

CRITERION The stimulus magnitude at and above which an observer will report a stimulus present in a signal detection experiment.

CRITICAL FLICKER FREQUENCY (CFF) The minimum frequency of intermittent light stimulation necessary for flicker to change to fusion. Also called *critical fusion frequency.*

CRITICAL PERIOD A specific developmental period in which the deprivation of visual experience has an extremely harmful effect on the establishment of normal neural organization.

CROSS-ADAPTATION The effect in which adaptation to one taste substance (or odorant) affects the sensitivity or threshold to another taste (or odorant) substance.

CROSS-FIBER PATTERNING The notion that each taste fiber has it own activity profile or pattern of firing; accordingly, taste quality is due to the *pattern* developed across a number of fibers.

CYANOLABE A photosensitive pigment for groups of cones selectively responsive to short wavelengths of light.

CYCLOPEAN PERCEPTION A unique form of stereo viewing devised by Bela Julesz based on the idea that the image on each eye is combined and synthesized in a central visual area of the brain to produce the perception of depth.

d' A term derived in signal detection tasks that serves as a measure of the observer's sensitivity to signal strength that is independent of response bias.

DARK ADAPTATION Increase in sensitivity of the eye during the change from high to low levels of illumination.

DECIBEL (dB) One-tenth of a bel. One bel is the common logarithm of the ratio between two intensities or energies. The bel is often expressed as the logarithm of the ratio of the square of two pressures:

$$\log_{10} \frac{P_1^2}{P_2^2}$$

The decibel is commonly used to specify the amplitude or intensity of a sound wave.

DECORRELATED FEEDBACK Sensory feedback from the environment that is inconsistent with the activity performed. Decorrelated feedback does not enable adaptation.

DENDRITES The part of the cell or neuron that receives neural information from other cells and transmits it to the cell body.

DENSITY A tonal quality that refers to the compactness or tightness of a sound. Generally, greater density occurs with higher-frequency tones.

DETECTION ACUITY Detection of the presence of a target stimulus in the visual field.

DEUTERANOMALY A form of anomalous trichromatism in which the person requires more green than normal in a mixture of red and green to match a yellow in an anomaloscope.

DEUTERANOPIA Color weakness characterized by the inability to distinguish between reds and greens and a relative insensitivity to the medium wavelengths that appear green to normal viewers.

DIABETIC RETINOPATHY A disease of the diabetic elderly in which blood vessels and capillaries in the retina rupture and hemorrhage. Retinal images are blurred and distorted, and close visual tasks become very difficult to perform.

DICHOTIC LISTENING The condition in which each ear hears a different sound or message at the same time.

DICHROMATISM Color-vision defect in which the person matches all wavelengths of the spectrum with two rather than three colors.

DIFFERENCE THRESHOLD The amount of change in stimulus magnitude for a given level of stimulation in order for a change to be detected. Also known as the *difference limen* or *just noticeable difference* (JND).

DIRECT APPROACH Approach to perception proposed by J. J. Gibson which argues that environmental stimuli contain sufficient information for perception, without the contribution of mediation, learning, or cognitive processes.

DIRECT PERCEPTION The notion of J. J. Gibson that the information for perception is fully contained within the patterned input from the environment. It is *direct* in that the spatial layout of the environment is picked up directly, without processing and mediation by cognition.

DISTANCE PARADOX The phenomenon that the horizon moon often appears both larger and closer than the zenith moon (also called the *further-larger-nearer phenomenon*). It poses a problem for explaining the moon illusion on the basis of the apparent distance hypothesis.

DISTORTED ROOM ILLUSION One of the Transactionalists illusions in which objects within an apparently normal (but physically very distorted) room appear distorted. See Chapter 10.

DOCTRINE OF SPECIFIC NERVE ENERGIES A doctrine attributed to Johannes Müller (1826) that holds that a sensory receptor produces only one kind of sensory experience or sensation. The sensory experience depends on the neural connection of a receptor to the brain, not on the form of physical energy that stimulates the receptor. Thus, it is not the stimulus, but rather the nerve stimulated, that determines sensory experience.

DOPPLER SHIFT A change in the frequency and pitch of a moving sound source relative to a stationary listener.

DOUBLE-OPPONENT RECEPTIVE FIELDS Receptive fields for "blob" neurons of the visual (striate) cortex. Double-opponent receptive fields have an antagonistic center-surround organization, with each component possessing a dual effect. The center increases its activity to one color and decreases it to the complementary color; the surround has the exact opposite double-response pattern.

DUPLEX PERCEPTION The unique experience of hearing both speech and nonspeech from the same set of acoustic signals.

DYNAMIC ACUITY An acuity task involving the detection and location of moving targets.

DYSGEUSIA A distortion in taste experience; most common forms of dysgeusia are persistent metallic, burning, and sour tastes that are inappropriate to substances in the mouth.

DYSOSMIA (PAROSMIA) A distortion of odor quality, such as when an unpleasant odor is experienced in the presence of a normally pleasant odor.

EARDRUM A thin, fibrous membrane stretched across the inner end of the external auditory canal that seals off the cavity of the middle ear. The eardrum vibrates in direct response to the pressure waves of the sound reaching the ear.

ECHO DELAY-TUNED NEURONS Neurons in the bat's auditory brain that are tuned to process the time interval between the emission of a tonal pulse by the bat and the return of its echo after the pulse strikes an object.

ECHOLOCATION The use of self-produced echoes to gain location information.

EFFERENT SIGNALS Self-initiated neural excitations that carry messages from the brain to receptors. Self-initiated neural signals that produce eye movements are examples of efferent signals.

ELEVATION (HEIGHT IN THE VISUAL FIELD) A depth or distance cue in which objects appearing higher in the visual field are perceived as being farther away from the viewer than those lower in the visual field.

EMMERT'S LAW The apparent size of an afterimage is directly related to the apparent distance of the surface on which it is perceived.

EMPIRICISM The view that perceptual organization is based primarily on past experience.

ENDORPHIN An endogenous, opiate-like neurotransmitter substance that specifically blocks neural signals in the pain pathways.

ENKEPHALIN An endogenous analgesia. An opiate-like substance secreted by the body (especially the brain and intestines) that serves to suppress pain.

ENVELOPE OF THE TRAVELING WAVE The shape described by the set of locations displaced by a traveling waveform along the basilar membrane. The shape of the envelope is determined by the frequency of the waveform; high frequencies trace out different envelopes than low frequencies.

ENVIRONMENTAL ORIENTATION The orientation of a shape with respect to gravity and to the visual frame of reference of the viewer.

ENVIRONMENTAL SURGERY Restricted visual experience during a critical period that affects the development of cortical units.

EPISODIC ODORS Odors associated with real-life experiences.

EQUAL-LOUDNESS CONTOURS Laboratory-derived contours or curves. Any sound whose frequency and intensity lie on a given equal-loudness curve appears as loud as any other sound on the curve, although their frequencies and intensities may differ. The family of such curves indicates that loudness is secondarily affected by frequency. Also called *isophonic contours* or *Fletcher-Munson* curves.

EUSTACHIAN TUBE Tube that connects the middle ear chamber with the back of the mouth. The tube permits pressure from the outside to be equalized with air pressure in the middle ear. This is accomplished when the mouth is opened.

EXALTOLIDE A musk-like synthetic odorant. For the human, the threshold for Exaltolide varies with gender.

EXPERIENTIAL SPACE–TIME RELATIVITY The notion that the apparent size of the environment with which one interacts affects the apparent duration of events that appear to occur in the environment.

EXTERNAL AUDITORY CANAL A cylindrical canal that creates the pathway for soundwaves to the eardrum.

EYE–HEAD MOVEMENT SYSTEM The system of movement perception in which the eyes track a moving stimulus.

FACILITATIVE INTERACTION The summation of effects that occurs with sequential presentation of stimuli.

FALSE ALARM Reporting the stimulus as present on a trial of a psychophysical or signal detection experiment when it is not actually present. Also called *false positive.*

FAMILIAR SIZE A possible memory cue for depth and distance based on knowledge of the sizes of objects.

FECHNER'S LAW General law proposed by Gustav Fechner (1860) stating that the magnitude of a sensation is a logarithmic function of the stimulus.

FIGURAL AFTEREFFECT Distortion effect after prolonged exposure to a given stimulus pattern or form that occurs when a new stimulus form falls on the same or a nearby retinal region.

FIGURE–GROUND The tendency to perceive part of a stimulus configuration as a figure set apart from the background.

FILLED-UNFILLED SPACE ILLUSION An illusion in which a filled extent appears longer than an unfilled extent of equal length.

FLAVOR A combination of sensory effects that affect the overall palatability of a sapid substance, including its taste, smell, texture, temperature, color, irritability, and sound (when chewed).

FOCAL SYSTEM A neural system for the visual identification and recognition of objects in space, mediated by the geniculostriate visual system.

FOCUSED ATTENTION STAGE The second stage in a two-stage process of perceptual processing that requires the conscious attention of the observer of the stimuli to perceptually group basic elements revealed in the initial preattentive stage.

FORMANT The concentration of acoustic energy that appears in spectrograms.

FORWARD MASKING Impairment to the perception of a target stimulus due to a preceding masking stimulus.

FOURIER ANALYSIS The breakdown of a complex waveform into its component simple sine waves based on the mathematical theorem devised by the nineteenth-century French scientist Jean Baptiste Fourier.

FOURIER SYNTHESIS The physical construction of a complex waveform from a series of simple sine waves.

FOVEA The central region of the retina. It is a small indentation about 0.3 mm across, subtending a visual angle of $1°$ to $2°$. The fovea contains primarily cone photoreceptors.

FRAMING EFFECTS (PONZO ILLUSION) The contribution of the enclosing border or frame surrounding the components of the Ponzo illusion in inducing illusory size effects.

FREE NERVE ENDINGS Unspecialized sensory neural receptors widely distributed throughout the body.

FREQUENCY Characterization of sound waves by the number of cycles or pressure changes completed in a second.

FREQUENCY CUTOFF A procedure in the study of speech perception in which bands of frequencies are selectively removed from a speech sequence.

FREQUENCY-MATCHING THEORY (PERIODICITY OR TELEPHONE THEORY) Theory that the basilar membrane vibrates as a whole to the frequency of the sound wave, thereby reproducing the vibrations of the sound. Pitch is thus determined by the frequency of impulses traveling up the auditory nerve.

FREQUENCY TUNING CURVES Curves for a given auditory nerve fiber that plot the frequency at which absolute threshold is at a minimum.

FUNDAMENTAL FREQUENCY The lowest tone of the series of tones produced by a sound-emitting instrument. Also called the *first harmonic*.

GANGLION CELLS Intermediate layer of neurons of the retina that forms the optic nerve.

GANZFELD A completely textureless and homogeneous field of uniform brightness.

GEONS Basic three-dimensional geometric forms that can be combined and arranged to create the shape of almost any object. Geons are easily distinguished from each other from any angle or viewpoint and are highly resistant to various sorts of visual distortion (see Figure 6.16).

GESTALT GROUPING PRINCIPLES A proposed set of fundamental organizing tendencies to perceive the visual field on the basis of such factors as the similarity, arrangement, and relative location of elements.

GESTALT PSYCHOLOGY A theoretical view of the organized nature of perception developed by a group of German psychologists, especially Wertheimer, Köhler, and Koffka. The German word *Gestalt* means *form* or *configuration*.

GLAUCOMA An age-related disorder due to abnormal intraocular pressure producing retinal damage and atrophy of the optic nerve. Glaucoma causes marked reduction in visual acuity and in the size of the visual field.

GLOBAL STEREOPSIS The matching process of similar elements projected to each eye that yields stereoscopic perception from random-dot stereograms.

GLOMERULUS A relay connection in the olfactory bulb where nerve fibers connect with the brain by olfactory tracts.

GOOD CONFIGURATION The collective tendency, according to Gestalt principles, of a certain pattern of stimuli to have the qualities of good continuation, closure, and symmetry.

GOOD CONTINUATION Gestalt tendency for stimulus elements to be perceptually grouped in such a way as to perceive the continuation of a line or curve in the direction that has been established.

HABITUATION A technique used to assess color perception in infants. An infant will look less at (or habituate to) a stimulus that is repeatedly presented. Habituation may also occur to sustained movement.

HAPTIC SYSTEM From the Greek "to lay hold of." A sensory-perceptual channel that refers to the combined input from the skin and joints.

HARMONICS The set of frequencies that are multiples of and occur simultaneously with the fundamental frequency of a complex waveform.

HERMANN GRID A pattern composed of apparently intersecting white stripes on a black background (see Figure 6.5). Faint gray illusory spots appear at the intersection of corners created by the pattern; the illusory spots are considered to be due to the activity of cells at the retinal ganglion level that have antagonistic center-surround receptive fields.

HERTZ (Hz) The number of cycles completed within 1 sec. Named for the nineteenth-century German physicist Heinrich Hertz.

HIT Correctly detecting the presence of a signal in a trial of a signal detection experiment.

HOAGLAND'S HYPOTHESIS A theory proposing the existence of a biological clock in the brain that regulates the body's rate of metabolism and affects perception of the passage of time.

HOLWAY–BORING EXPERIMENT (1941) A classic experiment that revealed the critical role played by the perception of distance cues in enabling size constancy.

HOMUNCULUS A topographic representation of the relative amount of brain devoted to various parts of the body.

HORIZONTAL-VERTICAL ILLUSION An illusion of length produced by a figure such as an inverted T in which the vertical line appears substantially longer than the horizontal line.

HOROPTER The locus of all points in space whose images fall on corresponding retinal points in each eye and produce single images.

HUE   The chromatic sensation produced mainly by the wavelength of a light.

HYPERACUITY   The acuity for details whose size is less than 10″ of arc, which is smaller than the diameter of an individual photoreceptor.

HYPERCOLUMN   A cluster or module of adjacent columns of the visual cortex that includes all possible orientations, as well as left and right ocular dominance columns.

HYPERCOMPLEX CELLS   Cortical cells whose receptive fields are optimally responsive to moving and specifically oriented stimuli that are of a particular length.

HYPERGEUSIA   Increased sensitivity to taste.

HYPEROPIA (OR HYPERMETROPIA)   Refractive error of the lens of the eye in which the image formed of a nearby target falls on a focal plane behind the retina. Also known as *farsightedness*.

HYPEROSMIA   Increased sensitivity to all or a limited number of odorants.

HYPOGEUSIA   Diminished taste function.

HYPOSMIA   Decreased sensitivity to all or a limited number of odorants.

ILLUMINANCE   The amount of light falling on a surface.

IMAGE–RETINA MOVEMENT SYSTEM   The system of movement perception in which a succession of neighboring retinal locations are stimulated.

IMPEDANCE MISMATCH   The difference in the resistance of sound pressure transmitted from the middle ear to the inner ear, due to the change from the airborne vibrations of the middle ear cavity to the fluid-filled inner chambers of the cochlea.

IMPOSSIBLE FIGURES   Displays containing inconsistent and contradictory sets of depth cues that cannot individually be suppressed. The graphic renderings of E. C. Escher are examples of such displays.

INCUS   One of the chain of three small bones or ossicles of the middle ear. Also known as the *anvil*.

INDUCED MOVEMENT   Apparent movement of a stationary stimulus induced by movement of a nearby moving stimulus.

INFORMATION PROCESSOR   A presumed mode of attention that concerns the nontemporal information processing demands of a task and shortens temporal awareness.

INNER HAIR CELLS   Specialized hair cells that lie on the organ of Corti and are the transducers for sound. Inner hair cells may register the frequency of sounds.

INTENSITY   A general term that refers to the magnitude of the physical energy stimulating a sense organ.

INTERAURAL INTENSITY DIFFERENCE   The intensity difference produced when the sound reaching one ear is of a different intensity than the sound reaching the other ear. This can serve as a cue to sound localization.

INTERAURAL TIME DIFFERENCE   The time difference produced when a sound reaches one ear before the other. This can serve as a cue to sound localization.

INTERPOSITION   A depth or distance cue in which the appearance of one object partially conceals or overlaps another.

INTERSTIMULUS INTERVAL (ISI)   The duration between presentation of two stimuli.

INVARIANTS   A presumed characteristic of the pattern of environmental energy for objects and events that is picked up by the observer and that remains constant as other dimensions of the energy vary. For example, the *rate of change* of the size of texture elements in the light reflected from a surface is invariant for different surfaces and for different distances.

IRIS   Circular diaphragm-like structure forming the colored portion of the eye that controls the size of the pupil opening.

JUST NOTICEABLE DIFFERENCE (JND)   The least change in the magnitude of a stimulus that is detectable.

KAPPA EFFECT   The effect in which time perception is influenced by the distance separating two stimuli.

KINESTHESIS   The perception of body-part position and movement in space of the limbs and other mobile parts of the jointed skeleton.

KINETIC DEPTH EFFECT Moving two-dimensional patterns perceived in three dimensions.

KOFFKA RINGS A contrast effect related to figure–ground segregation showing that perceptual organization affects lightness contrast. See Figure 7.7.

KOHLER EXPERIMENT (1962, 1964) A follow-up to the classic study by Stratton (1896), in which subjects continually wore optical devices that produced a left–right reversal of the visual field.

L CONES Cone pigments sensitive to long wavelengths of light.

LABELED LINE The label of a taste fiber based on the taste quality of the class of stimuli that elicits the greatest impulse discharge from that fiber.

LABYRINTH Bony cavities of the inner ears of mammals.

LATERAL GENICULATE NUCLEUS (LGN) Relay center for vision located in the thalamus. Neural fibers from the LGN project to the visual area in the occipital lobe of the cortex.

LATERAL INHIBITION The phenomenon in which adjacent or neighboring neural units in the eye mutually inhibit each other.

LAW OF PRÄGNANZ General Gestalt principle referring to the tendency to perceive the simplest and most stable figure of all possible perceptual alternatives.

LEMNISCAL PATHWAY A nerve pathway from the skin to the brain comprised of nerve fibers that are relatively large and fast conducting. The fibers transmit precise positional information concerning touch and movement, and their cortical (somatosensory) neurons possess receptive fields that are small and densely packed.

LENS Structure of the eye that aids in focusing light rays on the retina.

LIGHT ADAPTATION Decrease in sensitivity of the retina due to exposure to light.

LIGHTNESS CONSTANCY Constancy of the lightness of an object or surface despite changes in its illumination.

LIGHTNESS CONTRAST An effect in which the intensity of large background regions can modify the lightness of smaller enclosed areas.

LIMBIC SYSTEM Part of the forebrain that serves as a center for emotional experience and memory.

LIMULUS Horseshoe crab, whose eye has been studied as a model for analyzing lateral inhibition.

LINEAR PERSPECTIVE A geometric technique that involves systematically decreasing the size of more distant elements and the space separating them. Linear perspective is a monocular spatial cue.

LINE-BUSY HYPOTHESIS An explanation of masking based on the activity of the masker and the masked test tone on the basilar membrane. The notion assumes that the masker tone excites the same group of fibers as the test tone, preventing the fibers from responding to the test tone.

LINGUISTIC BOUNDARY The intermediate point in a changing speech sound where the perception of the sound changes from one phoneme to another.

LINGUISTIC FEATURE DETECTORS Assumed detectors for speech perception that presumably are specialized to respond to specific, distinctive characteristics and features of the speech signal.

LOBE A distinct area of the cortex, bordered by major fissures and associated with a specific function.

LOCALIZATION (VERNIER) ACUITY The acuity task of detecting whether two lines, laid end to end, are continuous or whether one line is offset relative to the other.

LOCAL STEREOPSIS The matching of corresponding retinal projections of simple, unambiguous elements projected to the left and right eye to yield stereopsis.

LOOMING The spatial and temporal information that signals an imminent collision with an environmental object.

LOUDNESS The attribute of an auditory sensation in which tones are ordered from soft to loud. Loudness is primarily determined by the amplitude of a sound wave.

LUMINANCE The amount of light reflected from an illuminated surface.

M CONES Cone pigments sensitive to medium wavelengths of light.

MACH BANDS Illusory perception of bands of brightness at borders where there are abrupt changes in luminance.

MACULA LUTEA The yellowish retinal area that includes the fovea and adjacent regions.

MACULAR DEGENERATION A retinal disease of the elderly that produces deterioration of the macula region of the retina (which includes the fovea). The result is a serious loss of central vision and a significant reduction in the ability to perform close visual tasks.

MAGNETIC SENSE An orientation mechanism used by honeybees in which navigation is aided by magnetic field information. Evidence of its use by other species is inconclusive.

MAGNITUDE ESTIMATION A psychophysical method employed in scaling sensory magnitudes for Stevens' power law application.

MAGNOCELLULAR DIVISION Division of the LGN consisting of cells that respond quickly and have large receptive fields. Magnocellular cells are neurally linked to Y cells from the ganglia of the retina. These cells are considered to be insensitive to color, but they are intimately involved with depth, movement, and low-contrast stimuli.

MALLEUS The first in the chain of three small bones, or ossicles, attached to the eardrum. Also known as the *hammer.*

MASKING Raising of the threshold for a stimulus due to the presence of a second stimulus.

MCCLINTOCK EFFECT The phenomenon that the menstrual cycles of women who remain in close physical proximity to each other fall into synchrony.

MCGURK EFFECT The phenomenon that auditory and visual information on speech interact with each other and affect the perception of what is heard: seeing the speaker as he or she speaks influences what the listener hears.

MECHANORECEPTORS Receptors whose excitation depends on mechanical stimulation.

MEISSNER'S CORPUSCLE Sensory receptor in touch-sensitive, hairless skin regions, presumed to be a pressure receptor.

MEL A dimension of pitch. By definition, the pitch of a 1000-Hz tone at 40 dB is assigned a value of 1000 mels.

MEMORY COLOR The notion that familiarity with a chromatic stimulus influences its apparent color.

MÉNIÈRE'S DISEASE A disorder due to abnormal pressure of the vestibular organ that produces a wide range of symptoms similar to those of motion sickness.

MERIDIONAL AMBLYOPIA A form of ambylopia in which there is a permanent, uncorrectable reduced acuity for the contours of a specific orientation.

METAMERS Different lights whose mixture produces an apparent match with a third light.

MINIATURE EYE MOVEMENTS A pattern of extremely small, tremor-like eye movements that occurs during fixation.

MISS A negative response made by an observer in a signal detection task when the signal is actually present.

MIXED-MODE EYE MOVEMENTS A functional category of eye movements that involves several distinct eye movements. For example, tracking an object in depth requires the execution of saccadic, pursuit, and vergence eye movements.

MODULUS A standard stimulus of moderate intensity used in Stevens' magnitude estimation for comparison with a series of stimuli.

MONAURAL CUES Stimulation of one ear.

MONOCHROMATISM A color defect in which monochromats match all wavelengths of the spectrum against any other single wavelength or white light.

MONOCULAR CUES Spatial cues requiring only one eye.

MONOCULAR DEPRIVATION An experimental procedure that restricts light experience to one eye.

MONOSODIUM GLUTAMATE (MSG) A chemical that enhances the palatability of food. It is a taste modifier and may also be a primary taste quality ("umami").

MOON ILLUSION The illusory perception that the moon at the horizon appears significantly larger than when it is at the zenith.

MOTION PARALLAX The relative apparent motion of objects in the visual field as the viewer moves the head. Motion parallax is a monocular spatial cue.

MOTION PATHS The predicted path or trajectory that a moving object will follow when set in motion.

MOTION PERSPECTIVE A dynamic cue to depth and distance provided by the continuous change in the perspective or position from which objects are viewed, that is, by the optic flow pattern that is created by movement toward or parallel to surfaces.

MOTION SICKNESS An extremely debilitating effect of abnormal vestibular stimulation, generally produced by passive movement. It is characterized by dizziness, pallor, vertigo, hyperventilation, and nausea, often accompanied by vomiting.

MOTOR NERVES (EFFERENT NERVES) Nerves that send signals from the brain and the spinal cord to muscles.

MOTOR THEORY A theory that the perception of spoken language is a result of knowledge of the articulatory gestures involved in the production of speech. That is, the sounds of speech are perceived by reference to the ways they are generated.

MOVEMENT AFTEREFFECT (MAE) The immediate perceptual effect after viewing a constantly moving display.

MÜLLER-LYER ILLUSION An illusion of length in which two lines of the same length appear to differ in length because of the influence of the ends of each line. See Chapter 10.

MULTISTABLE FIGURES (AMBIGUOUS OR REVERSIBLE FIGURES) Illusory figures that provide ambiguous and equivocal depth information.

MYELIN Protective covering of axons that serves as an insulating sheath. This sheath helps to transmit nerve impulses.

MYOPIA Refractive error of the lens of the eye in which the image of a distant target is brought to a focus in front of the retina. Also known as *nearsightedness.*

NALOXONE A potent opiate-antagonist chemical often used to study the analgesic effect of endorphins.

NANOMETER (NM) A billionth of a meter.

NATIVISM The notion that perceptual organization is inherent in the biological structure of the organism; therefore, experience and learning play a comparatively small role.

NEAR POINT The closest distance to a viewer at which a target can be seen clearly.

NEAR-WORK (USE-ABUSE) THEORY The theory that there is a causal relationship between excessive near vision and myopia.

NERVE A bundle of fibers consisting of axons and dendrites in the nervous system.

NEURON The basic cellular unit of the nervous system that serves to conduct nerve impulses.

NEUROPHYSIOLOGICAL APPROACH An approach proposing that sensory and perceptual phenomena can be explained primarily on the basis of known neural and physiological mechanisms that serve the sensory systems.

NEUROTRANSMITTERS Chemicals released at synapses that either excite or inhibit transmission between neurons.

NIGHT BLINDNESS (NYCTALOPIA) Pathological insensitivity to dim light.

NOCICEPTOR A receptor whose effective stimulation produces injury to the body and whose sensations are unpleasant.

NOISE Extraneous background stimuli in a signal detection task.

NOISE CANCELLATION A technical means of canceling repetitive noise (created by a complex sound wave) by generating an identical sound wave that is 180° out of phase.

NONCORRESPONDING RETINAL POINTS Stimulation of slightly different areas in the left and right retinas by the same target. The resulting perception is a double image.

NUCLEI Regions of the nervous system where groups of neurons converge and make synaptic connections with each other. Nuclei function as relay stations to process, integrate, and transform sensory information.

NULL (HUE) CANCELLATION METHOD A method used to measure the spectral distribution of the chromatic response. The amount of a color response is determined by the amount of energy of a wavelength of the complementary color necessary to cancel or neutralize the color sensation.

OBLIQUE EFFECT The reduction in acuity for oblique or diagonal grating patterns compared to either horizontal or vertical patterns.

OCCIPITAL LOBE Lobe at the back of the brain containing the primary projection area for vision.

OCTAVE The interval between any two tones, one of which is exactly twice the frequency of the other.

OCTAVE EQUIVALENCE The perceptual similarity of tones that are exactly an octave apart.

OHM'S ACOUSTICAL LAW The auditory system performs a crude form of Fourier analysis on a complex sound wave, separating it into its separate components. Functionally, this means that, within limits, we hear the individual frequency components of a complex sound.

OLFACTION The sense of smell.

OLFACTORY BULB A mass of neural tissue located under the temporal lobe into which the olfactory nerve fibers enter. Nerve tracts lead from the olfactory bulb into the brain.

OLFACTORY CILIA Hair-like projections of the olfactory receptor cells that may provide the receptor sites for odorant molecules and are involved in the initial transduction stage of the olfactory process.

OLFACTORY EPITHELIUM (MUCOSA) Odor-sensitive tissue region located on both sides of the nasal cavity.

OMMATIDIUM Element of a compound eye.

OPPONENT-PROCESSES THEORY A theory of color perception stating that there are three classes of neural receptors, each composed of a pair of opponent color processes: white–black, red–green, and blue–yellow.

OPTIC CHIASMA (OR CHIASM) The part of the visual system at which the optic nerve fibers from the nasal part of the retina cross over to the contralateral hemisphere.

OPTIC DISK Region of the retina where the optic nerve fibers leave the eye. There are no photorecep-

tors in this area and thus no visual response when light strikes this region. The corresponding visual field is termed the *blind spot.*

OPTIC FLOW PATTERN The pattern of apparent changes in the optic array of a surface, relative to a fixation point, occurring from an observer's movement parallel to or directly approaching the surface. The spatial information in optic flow patterns is termed *motion perspective.*

OPTICAL-RETINAL COMPONENTS Effects contributing to visual illusions due to structural and neural properties of the visual system.

ORGAN OF CORTI Cochlear structure containing the auditory receptors. It lies between the basilar and tectorial membranes.

ORIENTATION COLUMNS The vertical arrangement of cells of the visual cortex that show the same receptive field or orientation preference.

ORNSTEIN'S INFORMATION-STORAGE SIZE THEORY A theory proposed by Robert Ornstein that the duration of time is constructed from the amount of memory storage; that is, the amount of information registered in the individual's consciousness and stored in memory determines the duration experience of a particular interval of time.

OSSICLES Three small bones of the middle ear that contribute to the conduction of sound to the inner ear: the malleus, incus, and stapes.

OTOCYST Sensory organ in vertebrates that serves as a gravity detector.

OTOLITHS Calcium carbonate particles in vertebrates that lie within the otocyst cavity. They are generally free-moving and react to inertial forces; accordingly, they register gravity and linear movement.

OUTER HAIR CELLS Specialized hair cells that lie on the organ of Corti and are the transducers for sound. Outer hair cells register the presence of weak auditory signals and may be loudness detectors.

OVAL WINDOW A membrane over the inner ear cavity that is connected to the footplate of the stapes; the motion of the stapes causes it to vibrate which, in turn, causes mechanical activity in the inner ear.

PACINIAN CORPUSCLES Bulb-like mechanoreceptors attached to nerve endings in various parts of the body, especially in the mobile regions of the jointed skeleton and deep within the skin surface, and innervated by rapidly acting nerve fibers.

PANUM'S FUSION AREA (PFA) A narrow region around the curved spatial plane of the horopter whose spatial points produce fused images.

PAPILLAE Clusters of taste buds seen as elevations on the tongue. Four have been distinguished on the basis of shape and location: fungiform, foliate, circumvallate, and filiform.

PARADOXICAL COLD A cold sensation produced when a warm stimulus is applied to a cold spot on the skin.

PARIETAL LOBE Part of the brain containing the primary projection area for the skin senses (the somatosensory cortex).

PARVOCELLULAR DIVISION Division of the lateral geniculate nucleus composed of small cells that receives signals from the X cells of the ganglia of the retina. Parvocellular cells have small receptive fields, are considered sensitive to high-contrast stimuli, and are integral to both color and fine detail vision.

PERCEPTION Perception is the process of organizing and interpreting sensations into meaningful experiences. Perception is the result of psychological processes in which meaning, context, judgment, past experience, and memory are invoked.

PERCEPTUAL CONSTANCY Perceptual tendency for physical properties of objects to appear unchanged in spite of changes in their illumination, distance, and viewing position. Four forms are identified in text: color (Chapter 5), and lightness, size, and shape (Chapter 10).

PERCEPTUAL-MOTOR COORDINATION The smooth integration of perceptual signals and motor or muscle activity.

PERCEPTUAL SET Readiness to make a particular perceptual response or class of responses to particular organizations of stimuli. A perceptual set may be established by the prior conditions of exposure.

PERMANENT THRESHOLD SHIFT (PTS) The permanent effect on hearing due to chronic or extended exposure to intense noise.

PERSONAL GUIDANCE SYSTEM A computer-driven, portable navigational system designed to assist the blind, mobile person to maneuver about in a natural environment.

PERSPECTIVE-CONSTANCY THEORY The theory that stimulus features indicative of distance invoke a size constancy mechanism and provoke a compensatory size correction; this perceptually enlarges apparently distant stimuli and promotes the correction that normally occurs for a diminishing retinal image size when distance is increased.

PHANTOGEUSIA A taste abnormality in which the individual perceives specific tastes, either neutral, pleasant, or unpleasant, in the absence of any oral chemical stimulus.

PHANTOM LIMB PAIN The sensation of pain from an amputated limb. It is proposed that the pain arises in the stump tissue that possesses an abnormal amount of small-diameter, slow-conducting nerve fibers relative to large-diameter fibers.

PHANTOSMIA The perception of an odor, either pleasant, neutral, or unpleasant, without the inhalation of any actual odorant.

PHASE The arrival of a sound wave specified with respect to the phase of its cycle. Two sound waves that are at different phases within a cycle when they arrive at the two ears—for example, compressions occurring at different times relative to each other—change the quality of the sound and may serve as a cue for sound localization.

PHASE-LOCKED (TIME-LOCKED) The neural phenomenon that the firing pattern of auditory nerve fibers is synchronized with the frequency of the stimulating sound wave. Thus, the neural activity to a sound wave is time-locked to its frequency.

PHEROMONES Chemical substances that serve as communicants or signals secreted to the external environment and exchanged among members of the same species.

PHON A unit of loudness. It is a measure of the loudness level of a tone specified as the number of decibels of a standard 1000-Hz tone of equal loudness.

PHONEME Smallest speech sound unit of a language that distinguishes one utterance from another.

PHONEMIC RESTORATION EFFECT The perceptual restoration of "filling in" of an omitted but contextually meaningful speech sound (phoneme).

PHONETIC BOUNDARY A point at which a categorical change in a sound is heard when systematically and incrementally varying certain acoustic variables (i.e., the VOT).

PHOTOCHROMATIC INTERVAL The vertical distance between the photopic and scotopic threshold curves that specifies the "colorless" interval of radiant energy for a given wavelength; that is, the interval between seeing only a light and seeing a color or hue.

PHOTON The quantum unit of light energy.

PHOTOPIC Vision accomplished with cones.

PHYSIOLOGICAL ZERO The temperature at which a sensation of neither warmth nor cold occurs.

PICTORIAL CUES The set of static monocular cues for depth. Pictorial cues produce the impression of three-dimensional space on a two-dimensional surface.

PICTORIAL PERCEPTION The impression of depth on a two-dimensional surface, such as a photograph or picture, promoted by the use of pictorial depth cues.

PINNA The earflap part of the outer ear of mammals, which is useful for sound localization. It is also called the *auricle.*

PITCH The psychological attribute of a tone that is described as high or low. Pitch is primarily mediated by the frequency of the tone.

PLACE THEORY A theory maintaining that different auditory nerve fibers linked to specific regions of the basilar membrane are activated by different frequencies.

POGGENDORFF ILLUSION An illusion of misalignment. See Chapter 10.

POINT LOCALIZATION The ability to localize pressure sensations on the region of the skin where the stimulation is applied.

POSTURAL SWAY The sway of an individual who is initially stationary but is surrounded by an environment comprised of walls and ceilings that swing back and forth. In this situation, the individual begins to sway in synchrony with the swinging environment.

POWER LAW Psychophysical statement that sensory magnitude grows in proportion to the physical intensity of the stimulus raised to a power.

PREATTENTIVE STAGE The first stage in a two-stage process of perceptual processing that automatically extracts sensory information and enables the perception of very simple, obvious features.

PRECEDENCE EFFECT The perception of the sound reaching the ears from the farther of two identical sound sources will be suppressed with regard to its localization.

PREFERENTIAL LOOKING METHOD A technique used to assess the characteristics of a stimulus to which an infant will preferentially attend.

PRESBYACUSIS A pathological condition of the auditory system in which there is a progressive loss of sensitivity to high-frequency sounds with increasing age (also called *presbyacusia*).

PRESBYOPIA A refractive error of the lens of the eye in which, with increasing age, the elasticity of the lens progressively diminishes so that it becomes more difficult for the ciliary muscle to change the lens' curvature to accommodate for near objects.

PRIMAL SKETCH According to the computational approach, the primal sketch is the first step in processing basic features of physical structures, such as intensity differences.

PRIMARY COLORS The colors of lights that appear unique, not easily reducible to component colors. With certain restrictions, three primary colors can be combined in various proportions to match all spectral colors. Although red, green, and blue are the usual primaries, many different sets of three primaries are possible as long as no primary can be matched by a mixture of the remaining two or is complementary to another primary (i.e., can cancel out the effect of one of the other two primaries).

PRIMARY CORTICAL PROJECTION AREAS (PRIMARY RECEIVING AREAS) Regions of the brain specific to each sensory system. The primary projection areas lie in the lobes of the brain: frontal (taste), temporal (hearing), parietal (skin), occipital (vision), and the olfactory bulb, located just beneath the temporal lobe (smell).

PRIMER PHEROMONES Pheromones that produce a long-lasting receptive state or physiological change in a receptive organism, usually hormonal, such as that affecting the estrus cycle in the female.

PROTANOPIA A form of color defect (dichromatism) in which the protanope matches the spectrum with combinations of two rather than the three colors required by individuals with normal color vision. The protanope is especially insensitive to long wavelengths of light.

PROTENSITY The subjective experience of time as distinguished from clock or physical time.

PROTOANOMALY A form of anomalous trichromatism in which the person requires more red than normal in a mixture of red and green to match a yellow in an anomaloscope.

PROXIMITY (NEARNESS) A Gestalt principle of perception that individual elements making up a configuration will be perceptually organized into wholes according to their degree of physical closeness.

PSYCHOPHYSICAL METHODS A set of methods used to determine thresholds. The traditional set of psychophysical methods were devised by G. T. Fechner in 1860.

PSYCHOPHYSICS The study of the relation between variation in specified characteristics of the physical stimulation and the attributes and magnitude of subjective experience.

PTC (PHENYLTHIOCARBAMIDE) A chemical substance (or its synthetic equivalent, known as *PROP*) that is either intensely bitter to some individuals or barely detectable or tasteless to all others. The ability to taste PTC appears to have a genetic basis.

PULFRICH PENDULUM EFFECT A perceptual distortion of physical movement produced when each of the two eyes is stimulated by different intensities of light.

PUPIL The opening formed by the iris of the eye through which light enters.

PUPILLOMETRY The analysis of the behavioral and physiological basis of changes in pupil size.

PURKINJE SHIFT The shift in relative brightness of lights from the two ends of the spectrum as illumination decreases owing to the shift from photopic (cone) to scotopic (rod) vision.

PURSUIT MOVEMENTS Involuntary eye movements executed in tracking moving targets.

RANDOM-DOT-STEREOGRAM A computergenerated pair of nearly identical random dot patterns devised by Bela Julsez. The two patterns have identical random dot textures except for a central area that is displaced laterally in opposite directions in both patterns, creating disparity. When the slightly disparate patterns are stereoscopically fused, a three-dimensional display appears (see Fig. 9.24).

RAPIDLY ADAPTING (RA) FIBERS Fibers that innervate and link the skin receptors to the neurons of the brain. RA fibers react only at the onset and offset of pressure stimulation and are unresponsive to sustained skin pressure.

RECEIVER OPERATING CHARACTERISTIC (ROC) CURVE A curve that shows the relationship between the proportion of hits and false alarms in a signal detection experiment.

RECEPTIVE FIELD Precise region of the sensory system (such as the skin or retina) that, when appropriately stimulated, alters the firing rate of specific neurons lying within or en route to the brain.

RECOGNITION ACUITY The task of recognizing target stimuli, such as naming the letters of an eye chart (Snellen letters).

RECOGNITION BY COMPONENTS A theory proposing that object recognition begins with the processing of a set of primitive features called *geons*. Geons, in turn, are basic three-dimensional geometric forms that can be combined and arranged to create the shape of almost any object.

RED-EYE Apparent as red light seen in photographs taken with a flash. Red-eye is the effect of the light of the flash reflected back from the choroid of the retina. It is produced in dim light, where the pupil is maximally dilated.

REFERRED PAIN Condition in which pain originating from internal organs appears to occur from another region of the body, usually the surface of the skin.

REFRACTORY PERIOD The brief period of neural inactivity immediately following an action potential before the neuron can fire again. It is a recovery period for the neuron that lasts for 1 msec.

REISSNER'S MEMBRANE A membrane that divides the vestibular canal from the cochlear duct.

RELATIVE SIZE A depth or distance cue that occurs when two or more similar or identical shapes of different sizes are simultaneously viewed; the larger stimulus generally appears closer to the viewer than the smaller one.

RELEASER PHEROMONES Pheromones that produce an immediate and direct effect on an animal, such as the powerful mating behavior shown by the male dog to the female when she is in estrus ("in heat").

RESOLUTION ACUITY The acuity task of perceiving a separation between discrete elements of a pattern.

RESONANCE The natural vibration frequency of an object. An external driving force matching the resonant frequency will set the object into sympathetic vibration.

RESPONSE BIAS Nonsensory factors, such as expectation and motivation, that may affect the observer's decision as to whether a signal is present or not in a signal detection test.

RESTING POTENTIAL The inactive state of a neuron.

RESTORED SIGHT The clinical studies of the perception of individuals who have been blind from birth or early childhood and have their vision corrected in adulthood.

RETINA A photosensitive layer at the back of the eyeball consisting of interconnected nerve cells and photoreceptors that are responsive to light energy.

RETINAL EXPANSION A source of dynamic movement information that results from expansion of the retinal image when moving toward a stationary surface.

RETINOTOPIC MAP A map-like representation of the retina found in the lateral geniculate nucleus and other regions of the brain.

RHODOPSIN A light-absorbing pigment found in rods. Rhodopsin is sometimes called *visual purple*.

RICCO'S LAW A law stating that a constant threshold response can be maintained by the reciprocal interaction of retinal area (A) and stimulus intensity (I). That is, $A \times I$ = a constant threshold value.

RODS Photoreceptors of the retina found mainly in the periphery of the retina.

ROUGHNESS ENHANCEMENT A method of enhancing the perception of textural information of certain surfaces by rubbing a thin sheet of paper across a surface with the fingertip.

ROUND WINDOW A membrane-covered opening of the tympanic canal.

S CONES Cones sensitive to short wavelengths of light.

SACCADE A rapid, abrupt jump made by the eye as it moves from one fixation to another.

SACCADIC OMISSION Masking of the blurred image formed during saccadic eye movement.

SACCULE Fluid-filled sac that, along with the utricle, acts as an otocyst, registering the extent and direction of linear displacement and bodily position with respect to gravity.

SAPID Capable of being tasted.

SATURATION The apparent concentration of the hue of a spectral light. The corresponding physical dimension is chromatic purity. In general, the narrower the band of wavelengths comprising a light, the greater is its purity and saturation. Accordingly, white light, composed of radiant energy distributed among all wavelengths, lacks purity and appears desaturated.

SCENE PERCEPTION The perception of a scene containing objects that possess rational and coherent spatial and contextual relationships to each other and to the overall background.

SCLERA Outer coat of the eye continuous with the cornea. The sclerotic coat is seen as the "white" of the eye.

SCOTOPIC Vision accomplished with rods.

SELECTIVE ADAPTATION PROCEDURE A procedure that selectively fatigues or adapts a specific linguistic or visual feature by a controlled form of overexposure.

SELF-VECTION An illusion of in which observers experience motion when, in fact, they are stationary and the visual field is moving.

SEMANTIC PRIMING An experimental condition in which one stimulus, usually a word, facilitates or "primes" the perception of another word.

SEMICIRCULAR CANALS Fluid-filled enclosures that lie above the inner ear at approximately right angles to each other and register rotary motion. The three semicircular canals and the utricle and saccule comprise the vestibular organs that register gross bodily orientation.

SENILE MIOSIS An age-related reduction in pupil opening.

SENSATION The initial process of detecting and encoding environmental energy. Sensations also refer to immediate, basic, and direct experiences of stimulus attributes such as "hard," "warm," "loud," "blue," and the like. Sensations are caused by stimulation of a sensory organ.

SENSITIVITY Susceptibility to the perception of stimuli. In vision, sensitivity refers to perception in conditions of low illumination.

SENSORINEURAL HEARING LOSS Hearing loss due to deficiencies in or damage to the neural elements of the cochlea, including the auditory nerve and the organ of Corti.

SENSORY CONFLICT THEORY A theory proposed to explain motion sickness. It holds that periods of unusual passive motion cause disruption of the usual close correspondence between the visual system and the vestibular system concerning spatial orientation. The effect of this disruption of the sensory input to the two sensory systems causes motion sickness.

SENSORY NERVES (AFFERENT NERVES) Nerves that carry sensory information to the brain.

SHADING AND LIGHTING A depth or distance cue in which the pattern of lighting and shading affects the apparent location of objects and surfaces relative to the viewer.

SHAPE AFTEREFFECTS After exposure to curved contours, subsequent exposure to straight lines makes them appear curved in the opposite direction.

SHAPE CONSTANCY The tendency to perceive an object as relatively invariant in shape, regardless of the orientation from which it is viewed or the shape of its image on the retina.

SIMILARITY A Gestalt principle in which elements with similar physical attributes tend to be grouped together.

SIMPLE CELLS Cortical neurons whose receptive field optimally react to linear stimuli at a particular orientation.

SIMULTANEOUS CONTRAST The tendency for the color of one region to affect the perception of the color of the adjacent region. The adjacent region appears tinged with the complementary of the original region. Both hue and brightness are affected.

SIZE CONSTANCY The tendency to perceive the size of objects as relatively constant in spite of changes in viewing distance and changes in the size of the objects' retinal images.

SLOWLY ADAPTING (SA) FIBERS Fibers that innervate and link skin receptors to the neurons of the brain. SA fibers show a steady pattern of discharge to sustained pressure on the skin.

SOMATOSENSORY CORTEX Part of the brain in the parietal lobe for processing the skin or cutaneous sense.

SONAR A technique using sound for navigation in water (*SO*und *N*avigation *A*nd *R*anging).

SONE A unit of loudness. One sone is defined as equivalent in loudness to a pure tone of 1000 Hz at 40 dB.

SOUND- (NOISE-) INDUCED HEARING LOSS A form of hearing loss attributed to exposure to intense sounds. The hearing loss effects may be temporary or permanent. Also called *noise-induced hearing loss.*

SOUND WAVE A graphic description of pressure variations passing by a given point as a function of time.

SPECIFIC ANOSMIAS Olfactory disorders in which individuals are unable to smell one or a limited class of odors.

SPECTOGRAM A graphic reproduction of the frequency spectrum, intensity, and duration of a pattern of acoustic signals.

SPECTRAL PURITY   A physical dimension of light that corresponds to the psychological dimension of saturation. The more wavelengths comprising a light source the less its spectral purity and saturation.

SPECTRAL SENSITIVITY CURVES   The set of curves that specify the effect of the wavelength of light on sensitivity. There is a separate curve for the light adapted (cone-mediated) and dark adapted (rod-mediated) eye.

SPECTRAL THRESHOLD CURVES   The set of curves that plots photopic and scotopic threshold levels of radiant energy by wavelength. Threshold vision is affected by wavelength: maximal sensitivity for photopic vision is at 550 nm and for scotopic vision at 500 nm.

SPEECH BLANKING   In the study of speech, a procedure involving the selective periodic removal of sections of speech flow.

SPEECH MODE   A presumed unique form of specialized processing imposed on acoustic input recognized as speech.

SPHERICAL ABERRATION   Distortion of the retinal image focused by a spherical lens. This is due to the fact that the light rays passing through the periphery of the lens are brought to a shorter focal plane than those passing through the center.

SPINAL GATE CONTROL THEORY   Theory of pain that focuses on afferent nerve impulse transmission from the skin to the spinal cord.

STABILIZED IMAGE   A laboratory effect produced by having a target image continuously fall on the same foveal region.

STAPES   The last in the chain of three small bones, or ossicles, that link the middle to the inner ear. The footplate of the stapes connects to the oval window of the inner ear. Also known as the *stirrup.*

STATOCYSTS   Specialized sensory organs that serve as gravity detectors. Also known as *otocysts* in vertebrates.

STATOLITHS   Anatomical structures that lie within the statocyst cavity. They are generally free-moving and react to inertial forces; accordingly, they register gravity and linear movement. They are also known as *otoliths* in vertebrates.

STEREOBLINDNESS   Total or partial inability to localize depth in the visual scene by means of stereoscopic or binocular disparity cues alone. It is assumed that such individuals lack the necessary binocular disparity detectors.

STEREOCHEMICAL THEORY   A theory of olfaction that attempts to establish direct links between the chemical composition of substances and perceived odors. It assumes that the geometric properties (size and shape) of molecules of odorants "fit" into similar size and shape receptor sites. Also known as the *steric* or *lock-and-key theory.*

STEREOGNOSIS (TACTUAL)   The perception of three-dimensional shape information by palpation and manipulation of the hands.

STEREOGRAM   Specially prepared pairs of pictures, each representing the view of a single object seen by a separate eye. When viewed in a stereoscope, an impression of depth with stereopsis results.

STEREOPHONIC LISTENING   A mild form of dichotic stimulation that produces an experience of aural space.

STEREOPSIS   A perceptual experience of depth occurring as a by-product of the disparity of the images projected on each eye.

STEREOSCOPE   An optical instrument used to produce the fusion of two images, each from a slightly different view, so as to produce an impression of depth.

STIMULUS DEPRIVATION AMBLYOPIA   A form of amblyopia in which the acuity of one eye is permanently reduced due to restricted or significantly reduced use of one eye at an early critical period.

STRABISMUS   Inability to coordinate the movement of the two eyes.

STRATTON EXPERIMENT (1896)   A classic experiment in which George Stratton wore a special optical device that caused the visual field to be continually seen as reversed and upside down.

STREAM SEGREGATION   Perceptual analysis and segregation of a complex auditory signal into its separate auditory streams.

STRIATE CORTEX   Primary visual cortex, also referred to as *Brodmann's area 17 or area V-1.*

STROBOSCOPIC (β) MOVEMENT The phenomenon of apparent movement between two successive presentations of separate light sources. Also referred to as *beta* movement or *phi* movement.

STROOP EFFECT The disruption and delay in naming the colors of words printed in colors when the letters spell incongruous or nonmatching color words.

STRUCTURALISM An early school of psychology, attributed to E. B. Titchener, that focused on the discovery of the basic elements and structure of perception.

SUBJECTIVE COLORS The chromatic sensations produced from black-and-white stimulation.

SUBJECTIVE CONTOUR The perception of a contour across a blank portion of the visual field.

SUBLIMINAL PERCEPTION A controversial form of perception in which stimuli are not detected or consciously perceived but nevertheless exert some measurable influence on certain response outcomes.

SUBTRACTIVE COLOR MIXTURE The apparent result of mixing two chromatic substances, such as pigments, paints, or dyes, in which there is a mutual absorption or subtraction of wavelengths, canceling the reflectance of all wavelengths but those that the two substances jointly reflect.

SUCCESSIVE COLOR CONTRAST A condition in which a chromatic stimulus is fixated, producing an afterimage in the complementary color of the initial stimulus.

SUPERIOR COLLICULUS Region at the top of the midbrain involved in coordinating certain eye movements with visual and postural reflexes.

SYMMETRY Gestalt tendency for the perceptual grouping of stimulus elements to form symmetrical patterns rather than asymmetrical ones.

SYNAPSE The junction at the end of a terminal button that lies between the axon of one neuron and the dendrite of another.

SYNESTHESIA An experience in which stimulation of one sensory modality evokes an experience in a different sensory domain. Chromesthesia, or color hearing, is an example.

SYNTHETIC THERMAL SENSATIONS Thermal sensations induced by thermally neutral chemicals applied directly to the skin, such as menthol, alcohol (both of which produce a cooling sensation), and methyl salicylate (which produces a sensation of warmth).

TACTUAL STEREOGNOSIS The perception of three-dimensional shape information by palpation and manipulation of the hands.

TACTUAL–VISUAL SUBSTITUTION SYSTEM A system in which a video image of an object or display is converted into a cutaneous pattern of stimulation.

TADOMA METHOD A method used by the deaf-blind to receive some information from vocalized speech. The hand, placed in contact with specific regions of a speaker's lips, face, and neck, enables the pickup of spatiotemporal patterns of stimulation closely linked to the speaker's articulation.

TAPETUM A retinal layer (of the choroid) of some nocturnal animals that reflects back some of the light entering the eye. It accounts for the "eye shine" emanating from some animals at night.

TASTE BUD The basic receptor structure for taste, located in microscopically small pits and grooves of the mouth, soft palate, throat, pharynx, inside of the cheeks, and along the dorsal surface of the tongue.

TAU EFFECT The relationship between distance and perceived duration. The greater the time between the presentation of two stimuli, the greater the experienced distance.

TECTORIAL MEMBRANE Membrane extending along the top of the organ of Corti.

TEMPORAL LOBE Lobe of the brain that contains a primary projection area for hearing.

TEMPORARY THRESHOLD SHIFT (TTS) A measure of the temporary hearing loss or a change in threshold sensitivity due to exposure to intense sound stimulation.

TERMINAL BUTTON Structure at the end of an axon where it connects with the dendrite of another axon.

TEXTONS Distinguishable features of the elements comprising a texture, such as shapes, lengths, and angular orientations. Detection of textons facilitates the preattentive stage of perceptual processing.

TEXTURE GRADIENT The gradual refinement of the size, shape, and spacing of the form of a microstructure, generally seen as a texture, that is characteristic of most surfaces. Elements of the texture appear denser as distance is increased.

THALAMUS A bundle or nucleus of neurons in the forebrain that processes incoming signals from most of the senses and sends messages to specific projection regions of the brain.

THERMAL CONDUCTIVITY The rate at which an object or surface draws heat from or conducts heat to the region of the skin in contact with the object or surface.

3-D MODEL REPRESENTATION According to the computational approach, an advanced stage of perceptual processing in which the observer attains a general model of the visual world. At this stage of information processing, the observer recognizes a particular object.

TIMBRE An attribute of auditory sensation corresponding to the physical complexity of a tone.

TINNITUS Auditory pathological condition manifested by a high-pitched ringing in the ears. It is a prominent symptom of many ear disturbances.

TONAL GAP Narrow range of frequencies that is inaudible. Audiometric techniques, such as Békésy's tracking procedure, may uncover the inaudible frequency range.

TONE CHROMA The position of a musical scale note within a given octave. See Figure 14.6.

TONE HEIGHT A dimension assigned to musical notes that represents overall pitch. See Figure 14.6.

TONOTOPIC ORGANIZATION The spatial arrangement of neural elements of the auditory pathway so as to represent similar frequencies in adjacent neural areas.

TOP-DOWN PROCESSES (CONCEPTUALLY DRIVEN) An approach to perceptual processing that holds that global, abstract levels of analysis, involving past experience, meaning, and interpretation, affect the operation of lower, more sensory processes.

TRANSACTIONALISM An empiricist theory stating that the perceptual world is largely constructed from experience. A class of demonstrations (Ames demonstrations) has been devised to illustrate the importance of learning and experience in perception.

TRANSDUCTION The conversion or translation of environmental, physical energy to neural activity.

TRAPEZOIDAL WINDOW One of the Ames demonstrations used to show the importance of experience for perception. The window is a trapezoidal shape that projects a retinal image of a rectangular window at a slant from the viewer's gaze line.

TRAVELING WAVE A waveform whose point of maximal displacement moves within an envelope. Proposed to occur within the cochlea of the inner ear.

TRICHROMATIC RECEPTOR THEORY (YOUNG–HELMHOLTZ THEORY) The color theory that maintains that there are three sets of receptors (cones) that respond differently to different wavelengths. The theory is based on the fact that the light of three different wavelengths, when mixed appropriately, is sufficient to produce almost all the perceptible colors.

TRIGEMINAL NERVE The fifth cranial nerve, which provides innervation to much of the mucous membrane of the head, including the nasal, oral, and corneal regions. The trigeminal nerve is the major neural structure mediating the common chemical sense.

TRITANOPIA A rare form of dichromatism characterized by a deficiency in seeing blue and yellow.

TUNED FIBERS A class of auditory nerve fibers that are maximally sensitive to a very narrow range of sound frequencies. Each such tuned fiber has a characteristic or *best* frequency to which it is most sensitive.

2 1/2-D SKETCH The second stage in the computational approach to perceptual processing, in which the primal sketch is analyzed to yield information on the orientation and depth relationships of structures in the visual environment relative to the observer.

TWO-POINT THRESHOLD The minimal separation in distance of two simultaneous stimuli that gives rise to two distinct impressions of touch.

TYMPANIC CANAL The lower canal of the inner ear.

UMAMI A possible basic taste employed in Japanese psychophysics. *Umami* translates loosely as "delicious taste" and is elicited by monosodium glutamate (MSG).

UTRICLE A membranous, fluid-filled sac that, along with the saccule, registers linear acceleration and gravity.

VERGENCE MOVEMENTS Eye movements that move the eyes in opposite directions in the horizontal plane so that both eyes focus on the same target.

VESTIBULAR CANAL Upper canal of the inner ear of the cochlea.

VESTIBULAR NYSTAGMUS Series of reflexive, tremorlike eye movements of an oscillatory nature.

VESTIBULAR ORGANS The set of organs adjacent to the inner ear that mediate posture, balance, and the general sense of orientation. In mammals the vestibular organs are the saccule, utricle, and semicircular canals.

VESTIBULO-OCULAR EYE MOVEMENTS A pattern of reflexive eye movements initiated when the head or body moves to stabilize the position of the eyes relative to the environment.

VISUAL ANGLE The angle formed by a target on the retina. Visual angle is given in degrees, minutes, and seconds of arc, and specifies the retinal area subtended by a target as a joint function of the target's size and its distance from the viewer's eye.

VISUAL CAPTURE The dominance of vision over touch input. Thus, an object feels as if it has the size or shape based on how it looks.

VISUAL CLIFF An apparatus used to assess depth perception. It consists of a glass surface extending over an apparent void (deep side) and an apparent near surface (shallow side).

VISUAL MASKING The reduction in the perception of a target stimulus when a second stimulus is present close in time to the target stimulus.

VISUAL PERSISTENCE The visual effect that the sensation persists briefly after the offset of the physical stimulus.

VOICE-ONSET TIME (VOT) The short latency between air release and vocal cord vibration when producing certain speech sounds. Thus, the VOT for sounds such as /b/ is very brief relative to the VOT for sounds such as /p/.

VOLLEY PRINCIPLE An assumption about neural transmission of the auditory stimulus that every nerve fiber does not fire at the same moment. Instead, the total neural activity is distributed over a series of auditory nerve fibers so that squads or volleys of fibers fire at different times. Accordingly, the overall neural pattern of firing corresponds to the frequency of the stimulus.

VOLUME A tonal quality that refers to the size and expansiveness of a tone. Various combinations of frequency and intensity produce different volumes.

VOMERONASAL SYSTEM A chemical communication system specialized for evaluating large, relatively nonvolatile molecules that typically require direct physical contact (such as licking) for their reception.

W CELLS Ganglion cells with slow conduction speeds and a variable range of receptive fields. They contrast with the specific receptive fields of X and Y retinal ganglion cells.

WATERFALL ILLUSION An example of movement aftereffects in which fixation of a waterfall for a short period will subsequently cause a stationary scene to apparently move upward.

WAVELENGTH A physical dimension of light and sound. The wavelength of a sound denotes the distance from crest to crest of a soundwave and corresponds to the psychological dimension of pitch. The wavelength of light corresponds to the hue or color of the light.

WEBER'S FRACTION OR RATIO Psychophysical principle that holds that the greater the magnitude of a stimulus (I), the greater the change required for a difference to be detected (ΔI). It is formulated as $\Delta I/I = k$, where k is a constant fraction that differs for different modalities.

WERNIKE'S AREA A region in the left temporal lobe that mediates speech comprehension.

WHYTT'S REFLEX A reflexive constriction of the pupil of the eye in response to bright light.

WOLFF EFFECT An example of figure-ground perception demonstrating that figures show greater contrast effects than grounds. See Figure 7.6.

X CELLS Ganglion cells linked to the fovea that have a slow conduction speed; react in a steady, sustained fashion; have a small center-surround receptive field; and respond to precise, fine details and the color of stationary stimuli.

Y CELLS Ganglion cells linked to the periphery of the retina that have a fast conduction speed, respond abruptly with transient reactions, have large center-surround receptive fields, and respond mainly to stimulus movement.

ZEIGARNIK EFFECT The phenomenon that completed tasks are recalled less well than unfinished tasks.

REFERENCES

Abbe, M. The temporal effect upon the perception of space. *Japanese Journal of Experimental Psychology,* 1937, *4,* 83–93.

Abramov, I., Gordon, J., Henderson, A., Hainline, L., Dobson, V., & LaBrossiere, E. The retina of the newborn human infant. *Science,* 1982, *217,* 265–267.

Ackerman, D. *A natural history of the senses.* New York: Random House, 1990.

Adam, N. Rosner, B. S., Hosick, E. C., & Clark, D. L. Effect of anesthetic drugs on time production and alpha rhythm. *Perception & Psychophysics,* 1971, *10,* 133–136.

Adams, C. L., & Molfese, D. L. Electrophysiological correlates of categorical speech perception for voicing contrasts in dogs. *Developmental Neuropsychology,* 1987, *3,* 175–189.

Adams, J. A., Maurer, D., & Davis, M. Newborn's discrimination of chromatic from achromatic stimuli. *Journal of Experimental Child Psychology,* 1985, *41,* 267–281.

Addams, R. An account of a peculiar optical phenomenon seen after having looked at a moving body. *Philosophy Magazine,* 1834, *5,* 373.

Adler, K., & Pelke, C. Human homing orientation: Critique and alternative hypotheses. In D. S. Jones, B. J. MacFadden, & J. L. Kirschvink (Eds.), *Biomagnetism.* New York: Plenum, 1985.

Ahern, S. K., & Beatty, J. Physiological signs of information processing vary with intelligence. *Science,* 1979, *205,* 1289–1292.

Akil, H., Richardson, D. E., Hughes, J., & Barchas, J. D. Enkephalin-like material elevated in ventricular cerebrospinal fluid of pain patients after analgetic focal stimulation. *Science,* 1978, *201,* 463–465.

Alajouanine, T. Aphasia and artistic realization. *Brain,* 1948, *71,* 229–241.

Albright, T. D. Form-cue invariant motion processing in primate visual cortex. *Science,* 1992, *255,* 1141–1143.

Allport, G. W., & Pettigrew, T. F. Cultural influences on the perception of movement. The trapezoid illusion among Zulus. *Journal of Abnormal and Social Psychology,* 1957, *55,* 104–120.

Alper, J. Antinoise creates the sounds of silence. *Science* 1991, *252,* 508–509.

Alpern, M., Lawrence, M., & Wolsk, D. *Sensory processes.* Belmont, Calif.: Wordsworth, Brooks/Cole, 1967.

Altman, J. *Organic foundations of animal behavior.* New York: Holt, Rinehart and Winston, 1966.

Amato, I. Feeling at your fingertips. *Science* 1992, *258,* 1436.

Ames, A. Binocular vision as affected by relations between uniocular stimulus-patterns in commonplace environments. *American Journal of Psychology,* 1946, *59,* 333–357.

Amoore, J. E. Psychophysics of odor. *Cold Spring Harbor Symposia in Quantitative Biology,* 1965, *30,* 623–637.

Amoore, J. E. Specific anosmias. In T. V. Getchell, R. L. Doty, L. M. Bartoshuk, & J. B. Snow, Jr. (Eds.), *Smell and taste in health and disease.* New York: Raven Press, 1991.

Amoore, J. E., Pelosi, P., & Forrester, L. J. Specific anosmias to 5 α-androst-16-en-3-one and ω-pentadecalactone: The urinous and musky primary odors. *Chemical Senses and Flavor,* 1977, *2,* 401–425.

Angier, N. Bizarre baby raises hopes for an endangered primate. *The New York Times,* May 19, 1992, pp. C1, C10.

Angle, J., & Wissman, D. The epidemiology of myopia. *American Journal of Epidemiology,* 1980, *111,* 220–228.

Annis, R. C., & Frost, B. Human visual ecology and orientation anisotropies in acuity. *Science,* 1973, *182,* 729–731.

Anstis, S. M. A chart demonstrating variations in acuity with retinal position. *Vision Research,* 1974, *14,* 589–592.

Anstis, S. M., & Atkinson, J. Distortions in moving figures viewed through a stationary slit. *American Journal of Psychology,* 1967, *80,* 572–586.

Anstis, S., & Reinhardt-Rutland, A. Interaction between motion aftereffects and induced movement. *Vision Research,* 1976, *16,* 1391–1394.

Appelle, S. Perception and discrimination as a function of stimulus orientation. *Psychological Bulletin,* 1972, *78,* 266–278.

Arlin, M. The effects of physical work, mental work, and quantity on children's time perception. *Perception & Psychophysics,* 1989, *45,* 209–214.

Aronson, E., & Rosenbloom, S. Space perception in early infancy: Perception within a common auditory-visual space. *Science,* 1971, *172,* 1161-1163.

Arvidson, K., & Friberg, U. Human taste: Response and taste bud number in fungiform papillae. *Science,* 1980, *209,* 806-807.

Aslin, R. N., & Salapatek, P. Saccadic localization of visual targets by the very young human infant. *Perception & Psychophysics,* 1975, *17,* 293-302.

Attneave, F. Multistability in perception. *Scientific American,* 1971, *225,* 63-71.

Badcock, D. R., & Westheimer, G. Spatial localisation and hyperacuity: The centre/surround localisation function has two substrates. *Vision Research,* 1985, *25,* 1259-1276.

Baddeley, A. D. Time-estimation at reduced body temperature. *American Journal of Psychology,* 1966, *79,* 475-479.

Bahill, A. T., & LaRitz, T. D. Why can't batters keep their eyes on the ball? *American Scientist,* 1984, *72,* 249-253.

Baird, J. C. The moon illusion: II. A reference theory. *Journal of Experimental Psychology: General,* 1982, *III,* 304-315.

Bakan, P. Attention research in 1896 (note). *Science,* 1967, *143,* 171.

Baker, H. D. The instantaneous threshold and early dark adaptation. *Journal of the Optical Society of America,* 1953, *43,* 798-803.

Baker, H. D., & Rushton, W. A. H. The red-sensitive pigment in normal cones. *Journal of Physiology,* 1965, *176,* 56-72.

Baker, R. R. Goal orientation by blindfolded humans after long-distance displacement: Possible involvement of a magnetic sense. *Science,* 1980, *210,* 555-557.

Baker, R. R., Mather, J. G., & Kennaugh, J. H. Magnetic bones in human sinuses. *Nature,* 1983, *301,* 78-80.

Baker, R. R., & Parker, G. A. The evolution of bird coloration. *Philosophical Transactions of the Royal Society of London,* 1979, *B287,* 63-120.

Ball, W., & Tronick, E. Infant responses to impending collision: Optical and real. *Science,* 1971, *171,* 818-820.

Balota, D. A. Automatic semantic activation and episodic memory encoding. *Journal of Verbal Learning & Verbal Behavior,* 1983, *22,* 88-104.

Balota, D. A., & Rayner, K. Parafoveal visual information and semantic contextual constraints. *Journal of Experimental Psychology: Human Perception and Performance,* 1983, *9,* 726-738.

Banks, M. S. Infant refraction and accommodations. In S. Sokol (Ed.). Electrophysiological and psychophysics: Their use in ophthalmic diagnosis. *International Ophthalmology Clinics,* 1980, *20,* 205-232.

Banks, M. S., Aslin, R. N., & Letson, R. D. Sensitivity period for the development of human binocular vision. *Science,* 1975, *190,* 675-677.

Banks, M. S., & Bennett, P. J. Optical and photoreceptor immaturities limit the spatial and chromatic vision of hu-man neonates. *Journal of the Optical Society of America,* 1988, *5,* 2059-2079.

Banks, M. S., & Salapatek, P. Infant visual perception. In P. H. Mussen (Ed.), *Handbook of child psychology.* Volume II. New York: John Wiley, 1983.

Banton, T. & Levi, D. M. The perceived strength of illusory contours. *Perception & Psychophysics,* 1992, *52,* 676-684.

Barclay, C. D., Cutting, J. E., & Kozlowski, L. T. Temporal and spatial factors in gait perception that influence gender recognition. *Perception & Psychophysics,* 1978, *23,* 145-152.

Barlow, H. B., Blakemore, C., & Pettigrew, J. O. The neural mechanism of binocular depth discrimination. *Journal of Physiology,* 1967, *193,* 327-342.

Baringa, M. Giving personal magnetism a whole new meaning. *Science,* 1992, *256,* 967.

Barlow, J. D. Pupillary size as an index of preference in political candidates. *Perceptual and Motor Skills,* 1969, *28,* 587-590.

Bartley, S. H. The psychophysiology of vision. In S. S. Stevens (Ed.), *Handbook of experimental psychology.* New York: John Wiley, 1951.

Barrow, H. G., & Tenenbaum, J. M. Computational approaches to vision. In K. R. Boff, L. Kaufman, & J. P. Thomas (Eds.), *Handbook of perception and human performance, Vol. II. Cognitive processes and performance.* New York: Wiley, 1986.

Bartoshuk, L. M. Water taste in man. *Perception & Psychophysics,* 1968, *3,* 69-72.

Bartoshuk, L. M. Bitter taste of saccharin related to the genetic ability to taste the bitter substance 6-*n*-propylthiouracil. *Science,* 1979, *205,* 934-935.

Bartoshuk, L. M. Taste. In R. C. Atkinson, R. J. Herrnstein, G. Lindzey, & R. D. Luce (Eds.), *Stevens' handbook of experimental psychology* (2nd ed.). New York: John Wiley, 1988.

Bartoshuk, L. M., Lee, C-H., & Scarpellino, R. Sweet taste of water induced by artichoke (*Cynara scolymus*). *Science,* 1972, *178,* 988-990.

Bashford, J. A., Riener, K. R., & Warren, R. M. Increasing the intelligibility of speech through multiple phonemic restorations. *Perception & Psychophysics,* 1992, *51,* 211-217.

Batteau, D. W. The role of pinna in human localization. *Proceedings of the Royal Society of London,* 1967, *168* (1011), Series B, 158-180.

Batteau, D. W. Listening with the naked ear. In S. J. Freedman (Ed.), *The neuropsychology of spatially oriented behavior.* Homewood, Ill.: Dorsey, 1968.

Bauer, J. A. Development of visual cliff discrimination by infant hooded rats. *Journal of Comparative and Physiological Psychology,* 1973, *84,* 380-385.

Bauer, J. A., & Held, R. Comparison of visually-guided reaching in normal and deprived infant monkeys. *Journal of

Experimental Psychology: Animal Behavior Processes, 1975, *1,* 298–308.

Bauer, J. A., Jr., Owens, D. A., Thomas, J., & Held, R. Monkeys show an oblique effect. *Perception,* 1979, *8,* 247–253.

Baxter, D. W., & Olszewski, J. Congenital universal insensitivity to pain. *Brain,* 1960, *83,* 381–393.

Beagley, W. K. Interaction of Müller-Lyer with filled-unfilled space illusion: An explanation of Müller-Lyer asymmetry. *Perception & Psychophysics,* 1985, *37,* 45–49.

Beatty, J., & Wagoner, B. L. Pupillometric signs of brain activation vary with level of cognitive processing. *Science,* 1978, *199,* 1216–1218.

Beauchamp, G. K. The human preference for excess salt. *American Scientist,* 1987, *75,* 27–33.

Beauchamp, G. K., Bertino, M., Burke, D., & Engelman, K. Experimental sodium depletion and salt taste in normal volunteers. *American Journal of Clinical Nutrition,* 1990, *51,* 881–889.

Beauchamp, G. K., Cowart, B. J., & Moran, M. Developmental changes in salt acceptability in human infants. *Developmental Psychology,* 1986, *19,* 17–25.

Beauchamp, G. K., Cowart, B., & Schmidt, H. J. Development of chemosensory sensitivity and preference. In T. V. Getchell, R. L. Doty, L. M. Bartoshuk, & J. B. Snow (Eds.), *Smell and taste in health and disease.* New York: Raven Press, 1991.

Beauchamp, G. K., & Moran, M. Dietary experience and sweet taste preference in human infants. *Appetite,* 1982, *3,* 139–152.

Beck, J. Effect of orientation and of shape similarity on perceptual grouping. *Perception & Psychophysics,* 1966, *1,* 300–302.

Beck, J. Textural segmentation. In J. Beck (Ed.), *Organization and representation in perception.* Hillsdale, N.J.: Lawrence Erlbaum, 1982.

Becklen, R., & Wallach, H. How does speed change affect induced motion? *Perception & Psychophysics,* 1985, *37,* 231–236.

Bedford, F. L. Constraints on learning new mappings between perceptual dimensions. *Journal of Experimental Psychology: Human Perception and Performance,* 1989, *15,* 232–248.

Beebe-Center, J. G., & Waddell, D. A general psychological scale of taste. *Journal of Psychology,* 1948, *26,* 517–524.

Beidler, L. M. Dynamics of taste cells. In Y. Zotterman (Ed.), *Olfaction and taste,* Volume I. New York: Macmillan, 1963.

Békésy, G. von. On the resonance curve and the decay period at various points on the cochlear partition. *Journal of the Acoustical Society of America,* 1949, *21,* 245–249.

Békésy, G. von. Description of some mechanical properties of the organ of Corti. *Journal of Acoustical Society of America,* 1953, *25,* 770–785.

Békésy, G. von. Human skin perception of traveling waves similar to those on the cochlea. *Journal of the Acoustical Society of America,* 1955, *27,* 830–841.

Békésy, G. von. The ear. *Scientific American,* 1957, *197,* 66–78.

Békésy, G. von. Frequency in the cochleas of various animals. In E. G. Wever (Trans. Ed.), *Experiments in hearing.* New York: McGraw-Hill, 1960, 500–534.

Békésy, G. von. Hearing theories and complex sounds. *Journal of the Acoustical Society of America,* 1963, *35,* 588–601.

Békésy, G. von. *Sensory inhibition.* Princeton, N.J.: Princeton University Press, 1967.

Békésy, G. von. Localization of visceral pain and other sensations before and after anesthesia. *Perception & Psychophysics,* 1971, *9,* 1–4.

Békésy, G. von, & Rosenblith, W. A. The mechanical properties of the ear. In S. S. Stevens (Ed.), *Handbook of experimental psychology.* New York: John Wiley, 1951.

Bell, C. R. Time estimation and increases in body temperature. *Journal of Experimental Psychology,* 1965, *70,* 232–234.

Bell, C. R., & Provins, K. A. Relation between physiological responses to environmental heat and time judgments. *Journal of Experimental Psychology,* 1963, *66,* 572–579.

Bell, F. R. The variation in taste thresholds of ruminants associated with sodium depletion. In Y. Zotterman (Ed.), *Olfaction and taste.* New York: Macmillan, 1963.

Benedetti, F. Processing of tactile spatial information with crossed fingers. *Journal of Experimental Psychology: Human Perception and Performance,* 1985, *11,* 517–525.

Benedetti, F. Tactile diplopia (diplesthesia) on the human fingers. *Perception,* 1986, *15,* 83–91. (*a*)

Benedetti, F. Spatial organization of the diplesthetic and non-diplesthetic areas of the fingers. *Perception,* 1986, *15,* 285–301. (*b*)

Benedetti, F. Exploration of a rod with crossed fingers. *Perception & Psychophysics,* 1988, *44,* 281–284.

Benedetti, F. Perceptual learning following a long-lasting tactile reversal. *Perception & Psychophysics,* 1991, *17,* 267–277.

Benson, C., & Yonas, A. Development of sensitivity to static pictorial depth information. *Perception & Psychophysics,* 1973, *13,* 361–366.

Berbaum, K., Bever, T., & Chung, C. S. Light source position in the perception of object shape. *Perception,* 1983, *12,* 411–416.

Berbaum, K., Bever, T., & Chung, C. S. Extending the perception of shape from known to unknown shading. *Perception,* 1984, *13,* 479–488.

Berbaum, K., Tharp, D., & Mroczek, K. Depth perception of surfaces in pictures: Looking for conventions of depiction in Pandora's box. *Perception,* 1983, *12,* 5–20.

Bergeijk, W. A., van Pierce, J. R., & David, E. E., Jr. *Waves and the ear.* Garden City, N.Y.: Anchor Books/Doubleday, 1960.

Bernstein, I. L. Flavor aversion. In T. V. Getchell, R. L. Doty, L. M. Bartoshuk, & J. B. Snow, Jr. (Eds.), *Smell and taste in health and disease.* New York: Raven Press, 1991.

Bernstein, I. H., Bissonnette, V., Vyas, A., & Barclay, P. Semantic priming. Subliminal perception of context? *Perception & Psychophysics,* 1989, *45,* 153-161.

Bernstein, I. L. Learned taste aversion in children receiving chemotherapy. *Science,* 1978, *200,* 1302-1303.

Bernstein, I. L., & Webster, M. M. Learned taste aversions in humans. *Physiology and Behavior,* 1980, *25,* 363-366.

Berry, K. E., Sink, J. D., Patton, S., & Ziegler, J. H. Characterization of the swine sex odor (SSO) components in boar fat volatiles. *Journal of Food Science,* 1971, *36,* 1086-1090.

Bertenthal, B. I., & Campos, J. J. A systems approach to the organizing effects of self-produced locomotion during infancy. In C. Rovee-Collier & L. P. Lipsett (Eds.), *Advances in infancy research,* Volume 6. Norwood, N.J.: Ablex, 1989.

Besson, J., & Chaouch, A. Peripheral and spinal mechanisms of nociception. *Physiological Review,* 1987, *67,* 67-186.

Best, C. T., Morrongiello, B., & Robson, R. Perceptual equivalence of acoustic cues in speech and nonspeech perception. *Perception & Psychophysics,* 1981, *29,* 191-211.

Bever, T. G., & Chiarello, R. J. Cerebral dominance in musicians and nonmusicians. *Science,* 1974, *185,* 537-539.

Beverley, K. I., & Regan, D. Separable after-effects of changing-size and motion-in-depth: Different neural mechanisms. *Vision Research,* 1979, *19,* 727-732.

Biederman, I. On the semantics of a glance at a scene. In M. Kubovy & J. R. Pomerantz (Eds.), *Perceptual organization.* Hillsdale, N.J.: Lawrence Erlbaum, 1981.

Biederman, I. Recognition-by-components: A theory of human image understanding. *Psychological Review,* 1987, *94,* 115-147. (*a*)

Biederman, I. Matching image edges to object memory. *Proceedings of the First International Conference on Computer Vision* (pp. 384-392). New York: IEE Computer Society, London, 1987. (*b*)

Biederman, I. Higher-level vision. In D. N. Osherson, S. M. Kosslyn, & J. M. Hollerbach (Eds.), *Visual cognition and action* (Vol. 2). Cambridge, Mass.: MIT Press, 1990.

Biederman, I., Mezzanotte, R. J., & Rabinowitz, J. C. Scene perception: Detecting and judging objects undergoing relational violations. *Cognitive Psychology,* 1982, *14,* 143-177.

Bienenstock, E., & Doursat, R. Issues of representation in neural networks. In A. Gorea (Ed.), *Representations of vision.* Cambridge, Mass.: Cambridge University Press, 1991.

Birnholz, J. C. The development of human fetal eye movement patterns. *Science,* 1981, *213,* 679-681.

Birnholz, J. C., & Benacerraf, B. R. The development of human fetal hearing. *Science,* 1983, *222,* 516-518.

Bishop, G. H. Relation of pain sensory threshold to form of mechanical stimulator. *Journal of Neurophysiology,* 1949, *12,* 51-57.

Blake, R. Cats perceive biological motion. *Psychological Science,* 1993, *4,* 54-57.

Blake, R., & Cormack, R. H. Psychophysical evidence for a monocular visual cortex in stereoblind humans. *Science,* 1979, *200,* 1497-1499.

Blakemore, C., & Cooper, G. F. Development of the brain depends on the visual environment. *Nature,* 1970, *228,* 477-478.

Blakemore, C., & Sutton, P. Size adaptation: A new aftereffect. *Science,* 1969, *166,* 245-247.

Block, R. A. Models of psychological time. In R. A. Block (Ed.), *Cognitive models of psychological time.* Hillsdale, N.J.: Lawrence Erlbaum, 1990.

Block, R. A., George, E. J., & Reed, M. A. A watched pot sometimes boils: A study of duration experience. *Acta Psychologica,* 1980, *46,* 81-94.

Bloomer, C. M. *Principles of visual perception.* New York: Van Nostrand Reinhold, 1976.

Bobko, D. J., Bobko, P., & Davis, M. A. Effect of visual display scale on duration estimates. *Human Factors,* 1986, *28,* 153-158.

Bolanowski, S. J., Gescheider, G. A., Verillo, R. T., & Checkosky, C. M. Four channels mediate the mechanical aspects of touch. *Journal of the Acoustical Society of America,* 1988, *84,* 1680-1694.

Boltz, M. The estimation and attentional perspective. *Perception & Psychophysics,* 1991, *49,* 422-433.

Bonnet, C. Thresholds of motion perception. In A. Wertheim, W. Wagenaar, & H. W. Leibowitz (Eds.), *Tutorials in motion perception.* New York: Plenum, 1982.

Boring, E. G. A new ambiguous figure. *American Journal of Psychology,* 1930, *42,* 444-445.

Boring, E. G. *Sensation and perception in the history of experimental psychology.* New York: Appleton-Century-Crofts, 1942.

Boring, E. G. The moon illusion. *American Journal of Physics,* 1943, *11,* 55-60.

Boring, E. G. *A history of experimental psychology* (2nd ed.). New York: Appleton-Century-Crofts, 1950.

Boring, E. G. Size constancy in a picture. *American Journal of Psychology,* 1964, *77,* 494-498.

Boring, E. G., Langfeld, H. S., & Weld, H. P. *Foundations of psychology.* New York: John Wiley, 1948.

Bornstein, M. H., Kessen, W., & Weiskopf, S. The categories of hue in infancy. *Science,* 1976, *191,* 201-202.

Bossom, J., & Hamilton, C. R. Interocular transfer of prism-altered coordinations in split-brain monkeys. *Journal of Comparative and Physiological Psychology,* 1963, *56,* 769-774.

Botstein, D. The molecular biology of color vision. *Science,* 1986, *232,* 142-143.

Bough, E. W. Stereoscopic vision in the macaque monkey: A behavioural demonstration. *Nature,* 1970, *225,* 42-44.

Bowditch, H. P., & Hall, G. S. Optical illusions of motion. *Journal of Physiology,* 1882, *3,* 297-307.

Bower, T. G. R. *Development in infancy.* San Francisco: W. H. Freeman, 1974.

Bower, T. G. R., Broughton, J. M., & Moore, M. K. Infant responses to approaching objects: An indicator of response to distal variables. *Perception & Psychophysics,* 1971, *9,* 193-196.

Braddick, O. J., Wattam-Bell, J., & Atkinson, J. Orientation-specific cortical responses develop in early infancy. *Nature,* 1986, *320,* 617-619.

Bradley, A., Switkes, E., & DeValois, K. Orientation and spatial frequency selectivity of adaptation to color and luminance gratings. *Vision Research,* 1988, *28,* 841-856.

Bradley, D. R., & Dumais, S. T. Ambiguous cognitive contours. *Nature,* 1975, *257,* 582-584.

Bradley, D. R., Dumais, S. T., & Petry, H. M. Reply to Cavonius. *Nature,* 1976, *261,* 77-78.

Bradley, D. R., & Petry, H. M. Organizational determinants of subjective contour: The subjective necker cube. *American Journal of Psychology,* 1977, *90,* 253-262.

Bradshaw, J. L., & Nettleton, N. C. *Human cerebral asymmetry.* Englewood Cliffs, N.J.: Prentice Hall, 1983.

Brauner, J. D., & Lit, A. The Pulfrich effect, simple reaction time, and intensity discrimination. *American Journal of Psychology,* 1976, *89,* 105-114.

Braunstein, M. L. *Depth perception through motion.* New York: Academic Press, 1976.

Bravo, M., Blake, R., & Morrison, S. Cats see subjective contours. *Vision Research,* 1988, *28,* 861-865.

Bregman, A. S. Asking the ''what for'' question in auditory perception. In M. Kubovy & J. R. Pomerantz (Eds.), *Perceptual organization.* Hillsdale, N.J.: Lawrence Erlbaum, 1981.

Bregman, A. S. *Auditory scene analysis: The perceptual organization of sound.* Cambridge, Mass.: MIT Press, 1990.

Breitwisch, R., & Whitesides, G. H. Directionality of singing and non-singing behavior of mated and unmated northern mockingbirds. *Animal Behaviour,* 1987, *35,* 331-339.

Bridgeman, B. Visual receptive fields sensitive to absolute and relative motion during tracking. *Science,* 1972, *178,* 1106-1108.

Bridgeman, B. *The biology of behavior and mind.* New York: John Wiley, 1988.

Bridgeman, B., & Delgardo, D. Sensory effects of eye press are due to efference. *Perception & Psychophysics,* 1984, *36,* 482-484.

Brown, J. F. The thresholds for visual movement. *Psychologische Forschung,* 1931, *14,* 249-268. Reproduced in I. M. Spigel (Ed.), *Readings in the study of visually perceived movement.* New York: Harper & Row, 1965.

Brown, J. L. The structure of the visual system. In C. H. Graham (Ed.), *Vision and visual perception.* New York: John Wiley, 1965.

Brown, J. L., Shively, F. D., LaMotte, R. H., & Sechzer, J. A. Color discrimination in the cat. *Journal of Comparative and Physiological Psychology,* 1973, *84,* 534-544.

Brown, J. M., & Koch, C. Influences of closure, occlusion, and size on the perception of fragmented pictures. *Perception & Psychophysics,* 1993, *53,* 436-442.

Brown, J. M., & Weisstein, N. A phantom context effect: Visual phantoms enhance target visibility. *Perception & Psychophysics,* 1988, *43,* 53-56.

Brown, P. K., & Wald, G. Visual pigments in single rods and cones in the human retina. *Science,* 1964, *144,* 45-52.

Brown, R. J., & Thurmond, J. B. Preattentive and cognitive effects on perceptual completion at the blind spot. *Perception & Psychophysics,* 1993, *53,* 200-209.

Brown, S. W. Time perception and attention: The effects of prospective versus retrospective paradigms and task demands on perceived duration. *Perception & Psychophysics,* 1985, *38,* 115-124.

Bruce, C., Desimone, R., & Gross, C. G. Visual properties of neurons in a polysensory area of the superior temporal sulcus of the macaque. *Journal of Neurophysiology,* 1981, *46,* 369-384.

Bruce, V., & Green, P. *Visual perception physiology, psychology and ecology.* Hillsdale, N.J.: Lawrence Erlbaum, 1985.

Buck, L. B. The olfactory multigene family. *Current Opinion in Neurobiology,* 1992, *2,* 282-288.

Buck, L. B., & Axel, R. A novel multigene family may encode odorant receptors: A molecular basis for odorant recognition. *Cell,* 1991, *65,* 175-187.

Buffardi, L. Factors affecting the filled-duration illusion in the auditory, tactual, and visual modalities. *Perception & Psychophysics,* 1971, *10,* 292-294.

Burnham, R. W., Hanes, R. M., & Bartleson, C. J. *Color: A guide to basic facts and concepts.* New York: John Wiley, 1963.

Burr, D. C., & Ross, J. Contrast sensitivity at high velocities. *Vision Research,* 1982, *22,* 479-484.

Buss, A. H. *Psychology: Man in perspective.* New York: John Wiley, 1973.

Butler, R. A. An analysis of the monaural displacement of sound in space. *Perception & Psychophysics,* 1987, *41,* 159-164.

Butler, R. A., & Humanski, R. A. Localization of sound in the vertical plane with and without high-frequency spectral cues. *Perception & Psychophysics,* 1992, *51,* 182-186.

Butterworth, G., & Hicks, L. Visual proprioception and postural stability in infancy: A developmental study. *Perception,* 1977, *6,* 255-262.

Cagan, R. H. Chemostimulatory protein: A new type of taste stimulus. *Science,* 1973, *181,* 32-35.

Cahoon, D., & Edmonds, E. M. The watched pot still won't boil: Expectancy as a variable in estimating the passage of time. *Bulletin of the Psychonomic Society,* 1980, *16,* 115-116.

Cain, W. S. A history of research on smell. In E. C. Carterette & M. P. Friedman (Eds.), *Handbook of perception, Volume VI, A: Tasting and smelling.* New York: Academic Press, 1978.

Cain, W. S. To know with the nose: Keys to odor identification. *Science,* 1979, *203,* 467-470.

Campbell, F. W., & Wurtz, R. H. Saccadic omission: Why we do not see a grey-out during a saccadic eye movement. *Vision Research*, 1978, *18*, 1297–1303.

Campos, J. J., Hiatt, S., Ramsay, D., Henderson, C., & Svejda, M. The emergence of fear on the visual cliff. In M. Lewis & L. A. Rosenbaum, (Eds.), *The development of affect*. New York: Plenum, 1978.

Cann, A., & Ross, D. A. Olfactory stimuli as context cues in human memory. *American Journal of Psychology*, 1989, *102*, 91–102.

Carlson, N. R. *Physiology of behavior* (4th ed.). Boston: Allyn and Bacon, 1991.

Carmon, A., & Nachshon, I. Ear asymmetry in perception of emotional non-verbal stimuli. *Acta Psychologica*, 1973, *37*, 351–357.

Caron, A. J., Caron, R. F., & Carlson, V. R. Infant perception of the invariant shape of objects varying in slant. *Child Development*, 1979, *50*, 716–721.

Carpenter, J. A. Species difference in taste preferences. *Journal of Comparative and Physiological Psychology*, 1956, *49*, 139–144.

Carr, T. H. Perceiving visual language. In K. R. Boff, L. Kaufman, & J. P. Thomas (Eds.), *Handbook of perception and human performance. Volume II: Cognitive processes and performance*. New York: John Wiley, 1986.

Carr, W. J., & McGuigan, D. I. The stimulus basis and modification of visual cliff performance in the rat. *Animal Behaviour*, 1965, *13*, 25–29.

Cazals, Y., Aran, J-M., Erre, J-P., & Guilhaume, A. Acoustic responses after total destruction of the cochlear receptor: Brainstem and auditory cortex. *Science*, 1980, *210*, 83–85.

Chapanis, A. How we see: A summary of basic principles. In *Human factors in undersea warfare*. Washington, D.C.: National Research Council, 1949.

Chapanis, A., & Mankin, D. A. The vertical-horizontal illusion in a visually-rich environment. *Perception & Psychophysics*, 1967, *2*, 249–255.

Cheesman, J., & Merikle, P. M. Priming with and without awareness. *Perception & Psychophysics*, 1984, *36*, 387–395.

Cholewiak, R. W., & Sherrick, C. E. A computer-controlled matrix system for presentation to the skin of complex spatiotemporal patterns. *Behavioral Research Methods and Instrumentation*, 1981, *13*, 667–673.

Christensen, J. P., & Huang, Y. L. The auditory tau effect and memory for pitch. *Perception & Psychophysics*, 1979, *26*, 489–494.

Christman, R. J. *Sensory experience* (2nd ed.). New York: Harper & Row, 1979.

Cicerone, C. M., & Nerger, J. L. The relative numbers of long-wavelength-sensitive to middle-wavelength-sensitive cones in the human fovea centralis. *Vision Research*, 1989, *29*, 115–128.

Clavadetscher, J. E., Brown, A. M., Ankrum, C., & Teller, D. Y. Spectral sensitivity and chromatic discriminations in 3- and 7-week-old human infants. *Journal of the Optical Society of America A*, 1988, *5*, 2093–2105.

Clocksin, W. F. Perception of surface slant and edge labels from optical flow: A computational approach. *Perception 1980*, *9*, 253–271.

Cohen, J. Psychological time. *Scientific American*, 1964, *211*, 116–124.

Cohen, J., Hansel, C. E. M., & Sylvester, J. D. A new phenomenon in time judgment. *Nature*, 1953, *172*, 901–903.

Cohen, J., Hansel, C. E. M., & Sylvester, J. D. Interdependence of temporal and auditory judgments. *Nature*, 1954, *174*, 642.

Cohen, J., Hansel, C. E. M., & Sylvester, J. D. Interdependence in judgments of space, time and movement. *Acta Psychologica*, 1955, *11*, 360–372.

Cohen, L. A. Analysis of position sense in human shoulder. *Journal of Neurophysiology*, 1958, *21*, 550–562.

Cohen, L. D., Kipnes, D., Kunkle, E. G., & Kubzansky, P. E. Observations of a person with congenital insensitivity to pain. *Journal of Abnormal and Social Psychology*, 1955, *51*, 333–338.

Cohen, W. Spatial and textural characteristics of the Ganzfeld. *American Journal of Psychology*, 1957, *70*, 403–410.

Cohen, W. Color-perception in the chromatic Ganzfeld. *American Journal of Psychology*, 1958, *71*, 390–394.

Cohn, R. Differential cerebral processing of noise and verbal stimuli. *Science*, 1971, *172*, 599–601.

Collings, V. B. Human taste response as a function of locus of stimulation on the tongue and soft palate. *Perception & Psychophysics*, 1974, *16*, 169–174.

Collins, C. C. Tactile vision synthesis. In T. D. Sterling, E. A. Bering, S. V. Pollack, & H. G. Vaughan (Eds.), *Visual prosthesis*. New York: Academic Press, 1971.

Conrad, D. G., Elsmore, T. F., & Sodetz, F. J. Δ^9-Tetrahydrocannabinol: Dose-related effects on timing behavior in chimpanzee. *Science*, 1972, *175*, 547–550.

Cook, M., & Birch, R. Infant perception of the shapes of tilted plane forms. *Infant Behavior and Development*, 1984, *7*, 389–402.

Corbin, A. *The foul and the fragrant*. Cambridge, Mass.: Harvard University Press, 1986.

Coren, S. Subjective contours and apparent depth. *Psychological Review*, 1972, *79*, 359–367.

Coren, S. *The intelligence of dogs: Canine consciousness and capabilities*. New York: Free Press, 1994.

Coren, S., & Aks, D. J. Moon illusion in pictures: A multimechanism approach. *Journal of Experimental Psychology; Human Perception and Performance*, 1990, *16*, 365–380.

Coren, S., & Girgus, J. S. *Seeing is deceiving: The psychology of visual illusion*. Hillsdale, N.J.: Lawrence Erlbaum, 1978. (*a*)

Coren, S., & Girgus, J. S. Visual illusions. In R. Held, H. W. Leibowitz, & H.-L. Teuber (Eds.), *Handbook of sensory physiology, Vol. III: Perception*. New York: Springer-Verlag, 1978. (*b*)

Coren, S., & Girgus, J. S. Principles of perceptual organization: The Gestalt illusions. *Journal of Experimental Psychology: Human Perception and Performance,* 1980, *6,* 404-412.

Coren, S., & Porac, C. The creation and reversal of the Müller-Lyer illusion through attentional manipulation. *Perception,* 1983, *122,* 49-54.

Coren, S., Porac, C., & Theodor, L. H. The effects of perceptual set on the shape and apparent depth of subjective contours. *Perception & Psychophysics,* 1986, *39,* 327-333.

Coren, S., Porac, C., & Ward, L. M. *Sensation and perception* (2nd ed.). New York: Academic Press, 1984.

Corina, D. P., Vaid, J., & Bellugi, U. The linguistic basis of left hemisphere specialization. *Science,* 1992, *255,* 1258-1260.

Cormack, L. K., Stevenson, S. B., & Schor, C. M. (1993). Disparity-tuned channels of the human visual system. *Visual Neuroscience, 10,* 585-596.

Cornfield, R., Frosdick, J. P., & Campbell, F. W. Grey-out elimination: The roles of spatial waveform frequency and phase. *Vision Research,* 1978, *18,* 1305-1311.

Cornsweet, T. N. The staircase-method in psychophysics. *American Journal of Psychology,* 1962, *75,* 485-491.

Cornsweet, T. N. Information processing in human visual systems. *Stanford Research Institute Journal,* 1969, Feature issue 5 (Jan.).

Cornsweet, T. N. *Visual perception.* New York: Academic Press, 1970.

Costanzo, R. M., & Gardner, E. P. A quantitative analysis of responses of direction-sensitive neurons in somatosensory cortex of awake monkeys. *Journal of Neurophysiology,* 1980, *43,* 1319-1341.

Costanzo, R. M., & Graziadei, P. P. C. Development and plasticity of the olfactory system. In T. E. Finger & W. L. Silver (Eds.), *Neurobiology of taste and smell.* New York: John Wiley, 1987.

Costanzo, R. M., & Zasler, N. B. Head trauma. In T. V. Getchell, R. L. Doty, L. M. Bartoshuk, & J. B. Snow (Eds.), *Smell and taste in health and disease.* New York: Raven Press, 1991.

Cotzin, M., & Dallenbach, K. M. "Facial vision:" The role of pitch and loudness in the perception of obstacles by the blind. *American Journal of Psychology,* 1950, *63,* 483-515.

Cowey, A., & Stoerig, P. The neurobiology of blindsight. *Trends in Neuroscience,* 1991, *14,* 140-145.

Crassini, B., Brown, B., & Bowman, K. Age-related changes in contrast sensitivity in central and peripheral retina. *Perception,* 1988, *17,* 315-332.

Crawford, M. L., Smith, E. L., Harwerth, R. S., & von Noorden, G. K. Stereoblind monkeys have few binocular neurons. *Investigative Ophthalmology and Visual Science,* 1984, *25,* 779-781.

Cremieux, J., Orban, G. A., & Duysens, J. Responses of cat visual cortical cells to continuously and stroboscopically illuminated moving light slits compared. *Vision Research,* 1984, *24,* 449-457.

Crescitelli, F., & Pollack, J. D. Color vision in the antelope ground squirrel. *Science,* 1965, *150,* 1336-1338.

Crook, C. K. Taste perception in the newborn infant. *Infant Behavior and Development,* 1978, *1,* 52-69.

Crouch, J. E., & McClintic, J. R. *Human anatomy and physiology.* New York: John Wiley, 1971.

Crovitz, H. F., & Schiffman, H. Visual perception and xerography. *Science,* 1968, *160,* 1251-1252.

Curry, F. K. A comparison of left-handed and right-handed subjects on verbal and nonverbal dichotic listening tasks. *Cortex,* 1967, *3,* 343-352.

Curtin, B. J. Myopia: A review of its etiology pathogenesis and treatment. *Survey of Ophthalmology,* 1970, *15,* 1-17.

Cutietta, R. A., & Haggerty, K. J. A comparative study of color association with music at various age levels. *Journal of Research in Music Education,* 1987, *35,* 78-91.

Cutler, W. B., Preti, G., Krieger, A., Huggins, G. R., Garcia, C. R., & Lawley, H. J. Human axillary secretions influence women's menstrual cycles: The role of donor extract from men. *Hormones and Behavior,* 1986, *20,* 463-473.

Cutting, J. E. Generation of synthetic male and female walkers through manipulation of a biomechanical invariant. *Perception,* 1978, *7,* 393-405.

Cutting, J. E., & Kozlowski, L. T. Recognizing friends by their walk: Gait perception without familiarity cues. *Bulletin of the Psychonomic Society,* 1977, *9,* 353-356.

Cutting, J. E., & Proffitt, D. R. Gait perception as an example of how we may perceive events. In R. Walk & H. Pick (Eds.), *Intersensory perception and sensory integration.* New York: Plenum Press, 1981.

Cutting, J. E., Proffitt, D. R., & Kozlowski, L. T. A biomechanical invariant for gait perception. *Journal of Experimental Psychology: Human Perception and Performance,* 1978, *4,* 357-372.

Czeisler, C. A., Shanahan, T. L., Klerman, E. B., Martens, H., Brotman, D. J., & Desimone, R. Face-selective cells in the temporal cortex of monkeys. *Journal of Cognitive Neuroscience,* 1991, *3,* 1-8.

Czeisler, C. A., Shanahan, T. L., Klerman, E. B., Martens, H., Brotman, D. J., Emens, J. S., Klein, T., & Rizzo, J. F. Suppression of melatonin secretion in some blind patients by exposure to bright light. *The New England Journal of Medicine,* 1995, *332,* 6-11.

Dallenbach, K. M. The temperature spots and end-organs. *American Journal of Psychology,* 1927, *39,* 402-427.

Dallenbach, K. M. A puzzle-picture with a new principle of concealment. *American Journal of Psychology,* 1951, *64,* 431-433.

Dalrymple-Alford, E. C. Associative facilitation and interference in the Stroop color-word task. *Perception & Psychophysics,* 1972, *11,* 274-276.

Dallenbach, K. M. Pain: History and present status. *American Journal of Psychology,* 1939, *52,* 331-347.

Dallos, P. The active cochlea. *Journal of Neuroscience,* 1992, *12,* 4575-4585.

Darian-Smith, I., Sugitan, M., Heywood, J., Darita, K., & Goodwin, A. Touching textured surfaces: Cells in somatosensory cortex respond both to finger movement and to surface features. *Science,* 1982, *218,* 906-909.

Darwin, C. *The descent of man and selection in relation to sex.* 1871, New York: Modern Library Edition, 1948.

Daunton, N., & Thomsen, D. Visual modulation of otolith-dependent units in cat vestibular nuclei. *Experimental Brain Research,* 1979, *37,* 173-176.

Davis, H. *Hearing and deafness: a guide for laymen.* New York: Murray Hill, 1947.

Davis, H., & Silverman, S. R. *Hearing and deafness* (4th ed.). New York: Holt, Rinehart and Winston, 1978.

Davis, J. M., Schiffman, H. R., & Greist-Bousquet, S. Semantic context and figure–ground organization. *Psychological Research,* 1990, *52,* 306-309.

Davis, J. M., & Rovee-Collier, C. Alleviated forgetting of a learned contingency in 8-week-old infants. *Developmental Psychology,* 1983, *19,* 353-365.

Daw, N. W. Goldfish retina: Organization for simultaneous color contrast. *Science,* 1967, *158,* 942-944.

Day, R. H. Visual spatial illusions: A general explanation. *Science,* 1972, *175,* 1335-1340.

Day, R. H. Induced rotation with concentric patterns. *Perception & Psychophysics,* 1981, *29,* 493-499.

Day, R. H., & McKenzie, B. E. Infant perception of the invariant size of approaching and receding objects. *Developmental Psychology,* 1981, *54,* 172-177.

Dear, S. P., Simmons, J. A., & Fritz, J. A possible neuronal basis for representation of acoustic scenes in auditory cortex of the big brown rat. *Nature,* 1993, *364,* 620-623.

DeCasper, A. J., & Fifer, W. P. Of human bonding: Newborns prefer their mother's voices. *Science,* 1980, *208,* 1174-1176.

DeCasper, A. J., & Spence, M. J. Prenatal maternal speech influences newborn's perception of speech sounds. *Infant Behavior and Development,* 1986, *9,* 133-150.

Deems, R. O., Friedman, M. I., Friedman, L. S., & Maddrey, W. C. Clinical manifestations of olfactory and gustatory disorders associated with hepatic and renal disease. In T. V. Getchell, R. L. Doty, L. M. Bartoshuk, & J. B. Snow, Jr. (Eds.), *Smell and taste in health and disease.* New York: Raven Press, 1991.

Deliege, I. Grouping conditions in listening to music: An approach to Lerdahl & Jackendoff's grouping preference rules. *Music Perception,* 1987, *4,* 325-359.

Delk, J. L., & Fillenbaum, S. Difference in perceived color as a function of characteristic color. *American Journal of Psychology,* 1965, *78,* 290-293.

DeLong, A. J. Phenomenological space-time: Toward an experimental relativity. *Science,* 1981, *213,* 681-683.

DeLucia, P., & Hochberg, J. Geometrical illusions in solid objects under ordinary viewing conditions. *Perception & Psychophysics,* 1991, *50,* 447-554.

Dember, W. N., Jenkins, J. J., & Teyler, T. J. *General psychology* (2nd ed.). Hillsdale, N.J.: Lawrence Erlbaum, 1984.

Denes, P. B., & Pinson, E. N. *The speech chain: The physics and biology of spoken language.* Garden City, N.Y.: Anchor Books/ Doubleday, 1973.

Denton, D. A. *The hunger for salt.* New York: Springer-Verlag, 1982.

Denton, D. The most-craved crystal. *The Sciences,* 1986, *26,* 29-34.

Desimone, R., Albright, T. D., Gross, C. G., & Bruce, C. Stimulus-selective properties of inferior temporal neurons in the macaque. *Journal of Neuroscience,* 1984, *4,* 2051-2062.

Desor, J. A., & Beauchamp, G. K. The human capacity to transmit olfactory information. *Perception & Psychophysics,* 1974, *16,* 551-556.

Desor, J. A., Maller, O., & Turner, R. E. Taste acceptance of sugars by human infants. *Journal of Comparative and Physiological Psychology,* 1973, *84,* 496-501.

Dethier, V. G. The taste of salt. *American Scientist,* 1977, *65,* 744-751.

Deutsch, D. The psychology of music. In E. C. Carterette & M. P. Friedman (Eds.), *Handbook of perception.* Volume X: *Perceptual ecology.* New York: Academic Press, 1978.

Deutsch, D. Grouping mechanisms in music. In D. Deutsch (Ed.), *The psychology of music.* New York: Academic Press, 1982.

Deutsch, D. Auditory pattern recognition. In K. R. Boff, L. Kaufman, & J. P. Thomas (Eds.), *Handbook of perception and human performance. Volume II: Cognitive processes and performance.* New York: John Wiley, 1986.

DeValois, R. L. Analysis of coding of color vision in the primate visual system. *Cold Spring Harbor Symposia,* 1965, XXX. (*a*)

DeValois, R. L. Behavioral and electrophysiological studies of primate vision. In W. D. Neff (Ed.), *Contributions to sensory physiology,* Volume 1. New York: Academic Press, 1965. (*b*)

DeValois, R. L. Abramov, I., & Jacobs, G. H. Analysis of response patterns of LGN cells. *Journal of the Optical Society of America,* 1966, *56,* 966-977.

DeValois, R. L., & Jacobs, G. H. Neural mechanisms of color vision. In J. M. Brookhart & V. B. Mountcastle (Eds.), *Handbook of physiology. The nervous system III.* Bethesda, MD: American Physiological Society, 1984.

Dichgans, J., & Brandt, T. Visual-vestibular interaction: Effects on self-motion perception and postural control. In R. Held, H. W. Leibowitz, & H.-L. Teuber (Eds.), *Handbook of sensory physiology, Volume VIII: Perception.* New York: Springer-Verlag, 1978.

Dixon, F. *Subliminal perception: The nature of a controversy,* New York: McGraw-Hill, 1971.

Dobson, V., & Teller, D. Y. Visual acuity in human infants: A review and comparison of behavioral and electrophysical studies. *Vision Research, 1978, 18,* 1469-1483.

Dodd, B. The role of vision in the perception of speech. *Perception,* 1977, *6,* 31-40.

Dodd, J., & Castellucci, V. F. Smell and taste: The chemical senses. In E. R. Kandel, J. H. Schwartz, & T. M. Jessell (Eds.), *Principles of neural science* (3rd ed.). New York: Elsevier, 1991.

Doty, R. L. Olfactory system. In T. V. Getchell, R. L. Doty, L. M. Bartoshuk, & J. B. Snow, Jr. (Eds), *Smell and taste in health and disease.* New York: Raven Press, 1991.

Doty, R. L., Bartoshuk, L. M., & Snow, J. B., Jr. Causes of olfactory and gustatory disorders. In T. V. Getchell, R. L. Doty, L. M. Bartoshuk, & J. B. Snow, Jr. (Eds.), *Smell and taste in health and disease.* New York: Raven Press, 1991.

Doty, R. L., Brugger, W. E., Jurs, P. C., Orndorff, M. A., Snyder, P. J., & Lowry, L. D. Intranasal trigeminal stimulation from odorous volatiles: Psychometric responses from anosmic and normal humans. *Physiology and Behavior,* 1978, *20,* 175-187.

Doty, R. L., Green, P. A., Ram, C., & Yankell, S. L. Communication of gender from human breath odors: Relationship to perceived intensity and pleasantness. *Hormones and Behavior,* 1982, *16,* 13-22.

Doty, R. L., Shaman, P., Applebaum, S. L., Gilberson, R., Sikorski, L., & Rosenberg, L. Smell identification ability: Changes with age. *Science,* 1984, *226,* 1441-1442.

Doty, R. L., Snyder, P. J., Huggins, G. R., & Lowry, L. D. Endocrine, cardiovascular, and psychological correlates of olfactory sensitivity changes during the human menstrual cycle. *Journal of Comparative and Physiological Psychology,* 1981, *95,* 45-60.

Dowling, J. E. Night blindness. *Scientific American,* 1966, *215,* 78-84.

Dowling, J. E., & Wald, G. The biological function of vitamin A acid. *Proceedings of the National Society of Sciences,* 1960, *46,* 587-616.

Dowling, W. J. The perception of interleaved melodies. *Cognitive Psychology,* 1973, *5,* 322-337.

Dowling, W. J. Scale and contour: Two components of a theory of memory for melodies. *Psychological Review,* 1978, *85,* 341-354.

Dowling, W. J., & Harwood, D. L. *Music cognition.* Orlando, Fla.: Academic Press, 1986.

Dravnieks, A. Odor quality: Semantically generated multidimensional profiles are stable. *Science,* 1982, *218,* 799-801.

Duke-Elder, S. *System of ophthalmology. Volume I: The eye in evolution.* St. Louis: C. V. Mosby, 1958.

Dumais, S. T., & Bradley, D. R. The effects of illumination level and retinal size on the apparent strength of subjective contours. *Perception & Psychophysics,* 1976, *19,* 339-345.

Dumbacher, J. P., Beehler, B. M., Spande, T. F., Garraffo, H. M., & Daly, J. W. Homobatrachotoxin in the genus *Pitohui:* Chemical defense in birds. *Science,* 1992, *258,* 799-801.

Duncan, J. Two techniques for investigating perception without awareness. *Perception & Psychophysics,* 1985, *38,* 296-298.

Duncker, K. Uber induzierte Bewegung. *Psychologisch Forschung,* 1929, *12,* 180-259. [Translated as "Induced motion," in W. D. Ellis (Ed.), *A source book of Gestalt psychology.* London: Paul, Trench & Trubner, 1938.]

Duncker, K. The influence of past experience upon perceptual properties. *American Journal of Psychology,* 1939, *52,* 255-265.

Dunkeld, J., & Bower, T. G. R. Infant response to impending optical collision. *Perception,* 1980, *9,* 549-554.

Dzendolet, E., & Meiselman, H. L. Gustatory quality changes as a function of solution concentration. *Perception & Psychophysics,* 1967, *2,* 29-33.

Edminster, J. A., & Vickers, Z. M. Instrumental acoustic measures of crispness in foods. *Journal of Texture Studies,* 1985, *16,* 153-167.

Eggers, H. M., & Blakemore, C. Physiological basis of anisometropic amblyopia. *Science,* 1978, *201,* 264-266.

Ehrenstein, W. Concerning variations on L. Hermann's brightness observations. *Zeitschrift fur Psychologie,* 1941, *150,* 83-91.

Eich, J. E. The cue dependent nature of state-dependent retrieval. *Memory and Cognition,* 1980, *8,* 157-173.

Eimas, P. D., & Corbit, J. D. Selective adaptation of linguistic feature detectors. *Cognitive Psychology,* 1973, *4,* 99-109.

Eimas, P. D., Siqueland, E. R., Jusczyk, P., & Vigorito, J. Speech perception in infants, *Science,* 1971, *171,* 303-306.

Emerson, P. L., & Pesta, B. J. A generalized visual latency explanation of the Pulfrich phenomenon. *Perception & Psychophysics,* 1992, *51,* 319-327.

Engel, E. Binocular fusion of dissimilar figures. *Journal of Psychology,* 1958, *46,* 53-57.

Engen, T. Remembering odors and their names. *American Scientist,* 1987, *75,* 497-503.

Engen, T. *Odor sensation and memory.* New York, Praeger, 1991.

Engen, T., Gilmore, M. M., & Mair, R. G. Odor memory. In T. V. Getchell, R. L. Doty, L. M. Bartoshuk, & J. B. Snow, Jr. (Eds.), *Smell and taste in health and disease.* New York: Raven Press, 1991.

Engen, T., & Ross, B. M. Long-term memory of odors with and without verbal descriptions. *Journal of Experimental Psychology,* 1973, *100,* 221-227.

Enns, J. T., & Girgus, J. S. Perceptual grouping and spatial distortion: A developmental study. *Developmental Psychology,* 1985, *21,* 241-246.

Enns, J. T., & Prinzmetal, W. The role of redundancy in the object-line effect. *Perception & Psychophysics,* 1984, *35,* 22-32.

Enright, J. T. Stereopsis, visual latency, and three-dimensional moving pictures. *American Scientist,* 1970, *58,* 536–545.

Epelboim, J., Booth, J. R., & Steinman, R. M. Reading unspaced text: Implications for theories of reading eye movements. *Vision Research,* 1994, *34,* 1735–1766.

Epstein, W. The influence of assumed size on apparent distance. *American Journal of Psychology,* 1963, *76,* 257–265.

Epstein, W. *Varieties of perceptual learning.* New York: McGraw-Hill, 1967.

Erdelyi, M. A new look at the new look: Perceptual defense and vigilance. *Psychological Review,* 1974, *81,* 1–25.

Erickson, R. P. Sensory neural patterns and gustation. In Y. Zotterman (Ed.), *Olfaction and taste.* New York: Macmillan, 1963.

Erickson, R. P. Definitions: A matter of taste. In D. W. Pfaff (Ed.), *Taste, olfaction, and the central nervous system.* New York: Rockefeller University Press, 1984.

Eriksen, C. W., & Collins, J. F. Some temporal characteristics of visual pattern recognition. *Journal of Experimental Psychology,* 1967, *74,* 476–484.

Escher, M. C. *The graphic work of M. C. Escher.* New York: Ballantine, 1971.

Evans, D. W., & Ginsburg, A. P. Predicting age-related differences in discriminating road signs using contrast sensitivity. *Journal of the Optical Society of America,* 1982, *72,* 1785–1786.

Ewert, P. H. A study of the effect of inverted retinal stimulations upon spatially coordinated behavior. *Genetic Psychology Monographs,* 1930, *7,* 177–363.

Fagan, J. F. Infant's recognition of invariant features of faces. *Child Development,* 1976, *47,* 627–638.

Fanselow, M. S. Naloxone attenuates rat's preference for signaled shock. *Physiological Psychology,* 1979, *7,* 70–74.

Fanselow, M. S. Odors released by stressed rats produce opioid analgesia in unstressed rats. *Behavioral Neuroscience,* 1985, *99,* 589–592.

Fantz, R. L. The origin of form perception. *Scientific American,* 1961, *204,* 66–72.

Fantz, R. L. Pattern vision in newborn infants. *Science,* 1963, *140,* 296–297.

Fantz, R. L. Ontogeny of perception. In A. M. Schrier, H. F. Harlow, & F. Stollnitz (Eds.), *Behavior of nonhuman primate,* Volume II. New York: Academic Press, 1965.

Fantz, R. L. Visual perception from birth as shown by pattern selectivity. *Annals of the New York Academy of Sciences,* 1965, *118,* 793–814.

Fantz, R. L. Pattern discrimination and selective attention. In A. H. Kidd & J. L. Rivoire (Eds.), *Perceptual development in children.* New York: International Universities Press, 1966.

Fantz, R. L., & Miranda, S. B. Newborn infant attention to form of contour. *Child Development,* 1975, *46,* 224–228.

Favreau, O. E., Emerson, V. F., & Corballis, M. C. Motion perception: A color contingent aftereffect. *Science,* 1972, *176,* 78–79.

Fay, R. R. Auditory frequency discrimination in the goldfish (*Carrassius auratus*). *Journal of Comparative and Physiological Psychology,* 1970, *73,* 175–180.

Fendrich, R., Wessinger, C. M., & Gazzaniga, M. S. Residual vision in a scotoma: Implications for blindsight. *Science,* 1992, *258,* 1489–1491.

Ferguson, R. P., & Martin, P. Long-term temporal estimation in humans. *Perception & Psychophysics,* 1983, *33,* 585–592.

Ferster, D. A comparison of binocular depth mechanisms in areas 17 and 18 of the cat visual cortex. *Journal of Physiology,* 1981, *311,* 623–655.

Festinger, L., Allyn, M. R., & White, C. W. The perception of color with achromatic stimulation. *Vision Research,* 1971, *11,* 591–612.

Fillenbaum, S., Schiffman, H. R., & Butcher, J. Perception of off-size versions of a familiar object under conditions of rich information. *Journal of Experimental Psychology,* 1965, *69,* 298–303.

Fineman, M. B. *The inquisitive eye.* New York: Oxford University Press, 1981.

Fisher, G. H. Towards a new explanation for the geometrical illusions: II. Apparent depth or contour proximity. *British Journal of Psychology,* 1973, *64,* 607–621.

Fisher, R. The biological fabric of time. In Interdisciplinary perspectives of time. *Annals of the New York Academy of Sciences,* 1967, *138,* 451–465.

Fitzpatrick, V., Pasnak, R., & Tyler, Z. E. The effect of familiar size at familiar distance. *Perception,* 1982, *11,* 85–91.

Flaherty, C. F. Incentive contrast: A review of behavioral changes following shifts in reward. *Animal Learning & Behavior,* 1982, *19,* 409–440.

Flaherty, C. F., & Grigson, P. S. From contrast to reinforcement: Role of response contingency in anticipatory contrast. *Journal of Experimental Psychology: Animal Behavior Processes,* 1988, *14,* 165–176.

Fletcher, H. *Speech and hearing* (rev. ed.). New York: D. Van Nostrand Co., 1952.

Fletcher, H., & Munson, W. A. Loudness, its definition, measurement, and calculation. *Journal of the Acoustical Society of America,* 1933, *5,* 82–108.

Fogarty, C., & Stern, J. A. Eye movements and blinks: Their relationship to higher cognitive processes. *International Journal of Psychophysiology,* 1989, *8,* 35–42.

Foley, J. P. An experimental investigation of the effect of prolonged inversion of the visual field in the rhesus monkey (*Macaca mulatta*). *Journal of Genetic Psychology,* 1940, *56,* 21–51.

Fortin, C., Rousseau, R., Bourque, P., & Kirouac, E. Time estimation and concurrent nontemporal processing: Specific interference from short-term memory demands. *Perception & Psychophysics,* 1993, *53,* 536–548.

Foster, P. M., & Govier, E. Discrimination without awareness? *Quarterly Journal of Experimental Psychology,* 1978, *30,* 289–295.

Foulke, E., & Berlá, E. P. Visual impairment and the development of perceptual ability. In R. D. Walk & H. L. Pick, Jr. (Eds.), *Perception and experience.* New York: Plenum, 1978.

Fowler, C. A., Wolford, G., Slade, R., & Tassinary, L. Lexical access with and without awareness. *Journal of Experimental Psychology: General,* 1981, *110,* 341-362.

Fox, R., Aslin, R. N., Shea, S. L., & Dumais, S. T. Stereopsis in human infants. *Science,* 1980, *207,* 323-324.

Fox, R., & Blake, R. R. *Stereopsis in the cat.* Paper presented at the tenth meeting of the Psychonomic Society, San Antonio, Tex., November 1970.

Fox, R., Lehmkuhle, S. W., & Bush, R. C. Stereopsis in the falcon. *Science,* 1977, *197,* 79-81.

Fox, R., Lehmkuhle, S. W., & Westendorf, D. H. Falcon visual acuity. *Science,* 1976, *192,* 263-265.

Fox, R., & McDaniel, C. The perception of biological motion by human infants. *Science,* 1982, *218,* 486-487.

Fraisse, P. *The psychology of time.* New York: Harper & Row, 1963.

Fraisse, P. Perception and the estimation of time. *Annual Review of Psychology,* 1984, *35,* 1-36.

Frank, M. An analysis of hamster afferent taste nerve response function. *Journal of General Physiology,* 1973, *61,* 588-618.

Frank, M. The distinctiveness of responses to sweet in the *Chorda tympani* nerve. In J. W. Weiffenbach (Ed.), *Taste and development.* Bethesda, Md.: U.S. Department of Health, Education, and Welfare, Public Health Service, 1977. DHEW Publication No. (NIH) 77-1068.

Frankenhauser, M. *Estimation of time.* Stockholm: Almqvist & Wiksell, 1959.

Freedman, D. H. In the realm of the chemical. *Discover,* June 1993, 69-76.

Freedman, S. J., & Fisher, H. G. The role of the pinna in auditory localization. In S. J. Freedman (Ed.), *The neuropsychology of spatially oriented behavior.* Homewood, Ill.: Dorsey, 1968.

Freeman, R. D., & Bonds, A. B. Cortical plasticity in monocularly deprived immobilized kittens depends on eye movement. *Science,* 1979, *206,* 1093-1095.

Freeman, R., Mallach, R., & Hartley, S. Responsivity of normal kitten striate cortex deteriorates after brief binocular deprivation. *Journal of Neurophysiology,* 1981, *45,* 1074-1082.

Freeman, R. D., Mitchell, D. E., & Millodot, M. A neural effect of partial visual deprivation in humans. *Science,* 1972, *175,* 1384-1386.

Freeman, R. D., & Thibos, L. N. Electrophysiological evidence that abnormal early visual experience can modify the human brain. *Science,* 1973, *180,* 876-878.

French, N. R., & Steinberg, J. C. Factors governing the intelligibility of speech-sounds. *Journal of the Acoustical Society of America,* 1947, *19,* 90-119.

Friederici, A. D., & Wessels, J. M. I. Phonotactic knowledge of word boundaries and its use in infant speech perception. *Perception & Psychophysics,* 1993, *54,* 287-295.

Frisby, J. P. *Seeing.* New York: Oxford University Press, 1980.

Frisby, J. P., & Clatworthy, J. L. Illusory contours: Curious cases of simultaneous brightness contrast? *Perception,* 1975, *4,* 349-357.

Frome, F. S., Piantanida, T. P., & Kelly, D. H. Psychophysical evidence for more than two kinds of cone in dichromatic color blindness. *Science,* 1982, *215,* 417-419.

Frost, B. J., & Nakayama, K. Single visual neurons code opposing motion independent of direction. *Science,* 1983, *220,* 744-745.

Fujita, K., Blough, D. S., & Blough, P. M. Pigeons see the Ponzo illusion. *Animal Learning & Behavior,* 1991, *19,* 283-293.

Fujita, K., Blough, D. S., & Blough, P. M. Effects of the inclination of context lines on perception of the Ponzo illusion by pigeons. *Animal Learning & Behavior,* 1993, *21,* 29-34.

Galambos, R., & Davis, H. The response of single auditory-nerve fibers to acoustic stimulation. *Journal of Neurophysiology,* 1943, *6,* 39-57.

Galanter, E. Contemporary psychophysics. In R. Brown, E. Galanter, E. H. Hess, & G. Mandler (Eds.), *New directions in psychology.* New York: Holt, Rinehart and Winston, 1962.

Galanter, E. *Textbook of elementary psychology.* San Francisco: Holden-Day, 1966.

Galluscio, E. *Biological psychology.* New York: Macmillan, 1990.

Gambert, S. R., Garthwaite, T. L., Pontzer, C. H., & Hagen, T. C. Fasting associated with decrease in hypothalamic β-endorphin. *Science,* 1980, *210,* 1271-1272.

Gandelman, R. *The psychobiology of behavioral development.* New York: Oxford, 1992.

Gandelman, R., Zarrow, M. X., Denenberg, V. H., & Myers, M. Olfactory bulb removal eliminates maternal behavior in the mouse. *Science,* 1971, *171,* 210-211.

Garcia, J., Hankins, W. G., & Rusiniak, K. W. Behavioral regulation of the milieu interne in man and rat. *Science,* 1974, *185,* 824-831.

Gardner, E. *Fundmentals of neurology.* Philadelphia: W. B. Saunders, 1947.

Gardner, E. P., & Palmer, C. I. Stimulation of motion on the skin: III. Mechanisms used by rapidly adapting cutaneous mechanoreceptors on the primate hand for spatiotemporal resolution and two-point discrimination. *Journal of Neurophysiology,* 1990, *63,* 841-859.

Gardner, M. B., & Gardner, R. S. Problem of localization in the median plane: Effect of pinnae cavity occlusion. *Journal of the Acoustical Society of America,* 1973, *53,* 400-408.

Garrett, M. F. Production of speech: Observations from normal and pathological language use. In A. W. Willis (Ed.),

Normality and pathology in cognitive functions. New York: Academic Press, 1982.

Geiger, G., & Poggio, T. The Müller-Lyer figure and the fly. *Science,* 1975, *190,* 479–480.

Geldard, F. A. *The human senses* (2nd ed.). New York: John Wiley, 1972.

Gesteland, R. C. Neurophysiology and psychology of smell. In E. C. Carterette & M. P. Friedman (Eds.), *Handbook of perception. Volume VI, A: Tasting and smelling.* New York: Academic Press, 1978.

Gesteland, R. C., Lettvin, J. Y., & Pitts, W. H. Chemical transmission in the nose of the frog. *Journal of Physiology,* 1965, *181,* 525–559.

Gesteland, R. C., Lettvin, J. Y., Pitts, W. H., & Rojas, A. Odor specificities of the frog's olfactory receptors. In Y. Zotterman (Ed.), *Olfaction and taste.* New York: Pergamon, 1963.

Getchell, T. V., Doty, R. L., Bartoshuk, L. M., & Snow, J. B., Jr. *Smell and taste in health and disease.* New York: Raven Press, 1991.

Getchell, T. V., & Getchell, M. L. Peripheral mechanisms of olfaction: Biochemistry and neurophysiology. In T. E. Finger & W. L. Silver (Eds.), *Neurobiology of taste and smell.* New York: John Wiley, 1987.

Giampapa, V. C. Personal communication, 1989.

Gibbons, B. The intimate sense of smell. *National Geographic,* 1986, *170,* 324–361.

Gibson, E. J. The development of perception as an adaptive process. *American Scientist,* 1970, *58,* 98–107.

Gibson, J. J. Adaptation, after-effect, and contrast in the perception of curved lines. *Journal of Experimental Psychology,* 1993, *16,* 1–31.

Gibson, J. J. *The perception of the visual world.* New York: Houghton Mifflin, 1950.

Gibson, J. J. Observations on active touch. *Psychological Review,* 1962, *69,* 477–491.

Gibson, J. J. *The senses considered as perceptual systems.* New York: Houghton Mifflin, 1966.

Gibson, J. J. What gives rise to the perception of motion? *Psychological Review,* 1968, *75,* 335–346.

Gibson, J. J. *The ecological approach to visual perception.* Boston: Houghton Mifflin, 1979.

Gibson, J. J. & Bridgeman, B. The visual perception of surface texture in photographs. *Psychological Research,* 1987, *49,* 1–5.

Gibson, J. J., & Radner, M. Adaptation, aftereffect and contrast in the perception of tilted lines. I. Quantitative studies. *Journal of Experimental Psychology,* 1937, *20,* 453–467.

Gibson, J. J., & Waddell, D. Homogeneous retinal stimulation and visual perception. *American Journal of Psychology,* 1952, *65,* 263–270.

Gilbert, A. N., & Wysocki, C. J. The smell survey results. *National Geographic,* 1987, *172,* 514–525.

Gilchrist, A. L. Perceived lightness depends on perceived spatial arrangement. *Science,* 1977, *195,* 185–187.

Gilden, D. L., MacDonald, K. E., & Lasaga, M. I. Masking with minimal contours: Selective inhibition with low spatial frequencies. *Perception & Psychophysics,* 1988, *44,* 127–132.

Gillam, B. A depth processing theory of the Poggendorff illusion. *Perception & Psychophysics,* 1971, *10,* 211–216.

Gillam, B. Geometrical illusions. *Scientific American,* 1980, *242,* 102–111.

Gilliland, A. R., Hofeld, J., & Eckstrand, G. Studies in time perception. *Psychological Bulletin,* 1946, *43,* 162–176.

Ginsburg, A. P. Spatial filtering and vision: Implications for normal and abnormal vision. In L. Proenza, J. Enoch, & A. Jampolski (Eds.), *Clinical applications of psychophysics.* New York: Cambridge University Press, 1981.

Ginsburg, A. P. Spatial filtering and visual form perception. In K. R. Boff, L. Kaufman, & J. P. Thomas (Eds.), *Handbook of perception and human performance. Volume II: Cognitive processes and performance.* New York: John Wiley, 1986.

Ginsburg, A. P., Cannon, M. W., Evans, D. W., Owsley, C., & Mulvaney, P. Large sample norms for contrast sensitivity. *American Journal of Optometry and Physiological Optics,* 1984, *61,* 80–84.

Gintzler, A. R. Endorphin-mediated increases in pain threshold during pregnancy. *Science,* 1980, *210,* 193–195.

Glaser, E. M., & Haven, M. Bandpass noise stimulation of the simulated basilar membrane. *Journal of the Acoustical Society of America,* 1972, *52,* 1131–1136.

Glass, B. Foreword to M. P. Kare, & O. Haller (Eds.). *The chemical senses and nutrition.* Baltimore, Md.: Johns Hopkins University Press, 1967.

Godden, D. R., & Baddeley, A. D. Context-dependent memory in two natural environments: On land and underwater. *British Journal of Psychology,* 1975, *66,* 325–331.

Gogel, W. C., & DaSilva, J. A. Familiar size and the theory of off-sized perceptions. *Perception & Psychophysics,* 1987, *41,* 318–328.

Gogel, W. C., & Koslow, M. The adjacency principle and induced movement. *Perception & Psychophysics,* 1972, *11,* 309–314.

Goldfoot, D. A., Essock-Vitale, S. M., Asa, C. S., Thornton, J. E., & Lechner, A. I. Anosmia in male rhesus monkeys does not alter copulatory activity with cycling females. *Science,* 1978, *199,* 1095–1096.

Goldsmith, T. H. Hummingbirds see near ultraviolet light. *Science,* 1980, *207,* 786–788.

Goldstein, A., & Hilgard, E. R. Failure of opiate antagonist naloxone to modify hypnotic analgesia. *Proceedings of the National Academy of Sciences,* 1975, *72,* 2041–2043.

Goldstone, S., Boardman, W. K., & Lhamon, W. T. Effect of quinal barbitone, dextroamphetamine, and placebo on apparent time. *British Journal of Psychology,* 1958, *49,* 324–328.

Golledge, R. G., Loomis, J. M., & Klatzky, R. L. *Auditory maps as alternative to tactual maps.* Paper presented at the 4th International Symposium on Maps and Graphics for the Visually Impaired, São Paulo, Brazil, February 20-26, 1994.

Golledge, R. G., Loomis, J. M., Klatzky, R. L., Flury, A., & Yang, X. L. Designing a personal guidance system to aid navigation without sight: Progress on the GIS component. *International Journal of Geographical Information Systems,* 1991, *5,* 373-395.

Gomez, L. M., & Robertson, L. C. The filled-duration-illusion: The function of temporal and nontemporal set. *Perception & Psychophysics,* 1979, *25,* 432-438.

Gonzalez-Cruzzi, F. *The five senses.* San Diego: Harcourt Brace Jovanovich, 1989.

Good, P. A sculpture is created with the blind in mind. *The New York Times,* October 23, 1988, p. 20 (New Jersey supplement).

Good, P. R., Geary, N., & Engen, T. The effect of estrogen on odor detection. *Chemical Senses and Flavor,* 1976, *2,* 45-50.

Goodwin, M., Gooding, K. M., & Regnier, F. Sex pheromones in the dog. *Science,* 1979, *203,* 559-561.

Goolkasian, P. Cyclic changes in pain perception: An ROC analysis. *Perception & Psychophysics,* 1980, *27,* 499-504.

Gordon, I. E. *Theories of visual perception.* Great Britain: John Wiley & Sons, Ltd., 1989.

Gordon, I. E., & Cooper C. Improving one's touch. *Nature,* 1975, *256,* 203-204.

Gorey, E. *Gorey games.* San Francisco: Troubador Press, 1979.

Gould, J. L., & Able, K. P. Human homing: An elusive phenomenon. *Science,* 1981, *212,* 1061-1063.

Gould, J. L., Kirschvink, J. L., & Deffeyes, K. S. Bees have magnetic remanence. *Science,* 1978, *201,* 1226-1228.

Gouras, P. Color vision. In E. R. Kandel, J. H. Schwartz, & T. M. Jessell (Eds.), *Principles of neural science* (3rd ed.). New York: Elsevier, 1991.

Graham, C. A., & McGrew, W. C. Menstrual synchrony in female undergraduates living on a coeducational campus. *Psychoneuroendocrinology,* 1980, *5,* 245-252.

Graham, C. H., & Hsia, Y. Luminosity curves for normal and dichromatic subjects including a case of unilateral color blindness. *Science,* 1954, *120,* 780.

Graham, C. H., & Hsia, Y. Color defect and color theory. *Science,* 1958, *127,* 675-682.

Graham, N. Spatial-frequency channels in human vision: Detecting edges without edge detectors. In C. S. Harris (Ed.), *Visual coding and adaptability.* Hillsdale, N.J.: Lawrence Erlbaum, 1980.

Granrud, C. E. Binocular vision and spatial perception in 4- and 5-month-old infants. *Journal of Experimental Psychology: Human Perception and Performance,* 1986, *12,* 36-49.

Granrud, C. E., & Yonas, A. Infants' perceptions of pictorially specified interposition. *Journal of Experimental Child Psychology,* 1984, *37,* 500-511.

Granrud, C. E., Yonas, A., & Opland, E. A. Infants' sensitivity to the depth cue of shading. *Perception & Psychophysics,* 1985, *37,* 415-419.

Grau, J. W. Influence of naloxone on shock-induced freezing and analgesia. *Behavioral Neuroscience,* 1984, *98,* 278-292.

Graybiel, A., & Lackner, J. R. Treatment of severe motion sickness with antimotion sickness drug injections. *Aviation, Space, and Environmental Medicine,* 1987, *58,* 773-776.

Green, B. G. Localization of thermal sensation: An illusion and synthetic heat. *Perception & Psychophysics,* 1977, *22,* 331-337.

Green, B. G. Tactile roughness and the "paper effect." *Bulletin of the Psychonomic Society,* 1981, *18,* 155-158.

Green, D. M. *An introduction to hearing.* Hillsdale, N.J.: Lawrence Erlbaum, 1976.

Green, D. M., & Swets, J. A. *Signal detection theory and psychophysics.* New York: John Wiley, 1966.

Green, K. P., Kuhl, P. K., Meltzoff, A. N., & Stevens, E. B. Integrating speech information across talkers, gender, and sensory modality: Female faces and male voices in the McGurk effect. *Perception & Psychophysics,* 1991, *50,* 524-536.

Greene, E. The corner Poggendorff, *Perception,* 1988, *17,* 65-70.

Greene, E. Angular induction is modulated by the orientation of the test segment but not its length. *Perception & Psychophysics,* 1993, *54,* 640-648.

Greene, E., & Fiser, J. Classical illusion effects with nonclassic stimuli: Angular induction from decomposing lines into point arrays. *Perception & Psychophysics,* 1994, *56,* 575-589.

Greene, E., & Verloop, M. Anomalous and luminance contours produce similar angular induction effects. *Perception,* 1994, *23,* 147-156.

Greene, S. L., Plastoe, E., & Braine, L. G. Judging the location of features of naturalistic and geometric shapes. *Perception & Psychophysics,* 1985, *37,* 148-154.

Gregory, R. L. Distortion of visual space as inappropriate constancy scaling. *Nature,* 1963, *199,* 678-680.

Gregory, R. L. *Eye and brain.* New York: World University Library, 1966.

Gregory, R. L. Visual illusions. *Scientific American,* 1968, *219,* 66-76.

Gregory, R. L. *Eye and brain* (2nd ed.). New York: World University Library, 1973.

Gregory, R. L. *Concepts and mechanisms of perception.* New York: Scribners, 1974.

Gregory, R. L. *Eye and brain: The psychology of seeing* (3rd ed.). New York: World University Library, 1977.

Gregory, R. L., & Wallace, J. G. Recovery from early blindness: A case study. *Experimental Psychology Society Monographs* (No. 2). Cambridge: Heffner, 1963.

Greist-Bousquet, S., & Schiffman, H. R. The many illusions of the Müller-Lyer: Comparisons of the wings-in and wings-out illusion and manipulations of standard and dot forms. *Perception*, 1981, *10*, 147-154. (*a*)

Greist-Bousquet, S., & Schiffman, H. R. The rule of structural components in the Müller-Lyer illusion. *Perception & Psychophysics*, 1981, *30*, 505-511. (*b*)

Greist-Bousquet, S., & Schiffman, H. R. Poggendorff and Müller-Lyer illusions: common effects. *Perception*, 1985, *14*, 427-447.

Greist-Bousquet, S., & Schiffman, H. R. The basis of the Poggendorff effect: An additional clue for Day and Kasperczyk. *Perception & Psychophysics*, 1986, *39*, 447-448.

Griffin, D. R. *Listening in the dark*. New Haven, Conn.: Yale University Press, 1958.

Griffin, D. R. *Echoes of bats and men*. Garden City, N.Y.: Anchor Books/Doubleday, 1959.

Griffin, D. R. Foreward to papers on magnetic sensitivity in birds. *Animal Learning & Behavior*, 1987, *15*, 108-109.

Grondin, S. Duration discrimination of empty and filled intervals marked by auditory and visual signals. *Perception & Psychophysics*, 1993, *54*, 383-394.

Grondin, S., & Rousseau, R. Judging the relative duration of multimodal short empty time intervals. *Perception & Psychophysics*, 1991, *49*, 245-256.

Gross, C. G., Rocha-Miranda, C. E., & Bender, D. B. Visual properties of neurons in inferotemporal cortex of the macaque. *Journal of Neurophysiology*, 1972, *35*, 96-111.

Grossberg, S., & Mingolla, E. The role of illusory contours in visual segmentation. In S. Petry & G. E. Meyer (Eds.), *The perception of illusory contours*. New York: Springer-Verlag, 1987.

Grünau, V. M. W., Wiggins, S., & Reed, M. The local character of perspective organization. *Perception & Psychophysics*, 1984, *35*, 319-324.

Grzegorczyk, P. B., Jones, S. W., & Mistretta, C. M. Age-related differences in salt taste acuity. *Journal of Gerontology*, 1979, *34*, 834-840.

Guilford, J. P. *Psychometric methods*. New York: McGraw-Hill, 1954.

Guirao, M., & Stevens, S. S. The measurement of auditory density. *Journal of the Acoustical Society of America*, 1964, *36*, 1176-1182.

Gulick, W. L. *Hearing: Physiology and psychophysics*. New York: Oxford University Press, 1971.

Gulick, W. L., Gescheider, G. A., & Frisina, R. D. *Hearing: Physiological acoustics, neural coding, and psychoacoustics*. New York: Oxford University Press, 1989.

Gulick, W. L., & Lawson, R. B. *Human stereopsis: A psychophysical analysis*. New York: Oxford University Press, 1976.

Gurnsey, R., Humphrey, G. K., & Kapitan, P. Parallel discrimination of subjective contours. *Perception & Psychophysics*, 1992, *52*, 263-276.

Gustavson, C. F., & Garcia, J. Aversive conditioning: Pulling a gag on the wily coyote. *Psychology Today*, 1974, *8*, 68-72.

Gwei-Djen, L., & Needham, J. A scientific basis for acupuncture. *The Sciences*, 1979, *19*, 6-10.

Gwiazda, J., Bauer, J., & Held, R. From visual acuity to hyperacuity: A 10-year update. *Canadian Journal of Psychology*, 1989, *43*, 109-120.

Gwiazda, J., Bauer, J., Thorn, F., & Held, R. Meridional amblyopia *does* result from astigmatism in early childhood. *Clinical Vision Sciences*, 1986, *1*, 145-152.

Gwiazda, J., Brill, S., & Held, R. New methods for testing infant vision. *The Sightsaving Review*, 1979, *49*, 61-69.

Gwiazda, J., Brill, S., Mohindra, I., & Held, R. Infant visual acuity and its meridional variation. *Vision Research*, 1978, *18*, 1557-1564.

Gwiazda, J., Thorn, F., & Bauer, J. Myopic children show insufficient accommodative response to blur. *Investigative Ophthalmology & Visual Science*, 1993, *34*, 690-694.

Haber, R. N., & Hershenson, M. Effects of repeated brief exposure on the growth of a percept. *Journal of Experimental Psychology*, 1965, *69*, 40-46.

Haber, R. N., & Nathanson, L. S. Post-retinal storage? Some further observations of Parks' camel as seen through the eye of a needle. *Perception & Psychophysics*, 1968, *3*, 349-355.

Hafter, E. R., Dye, R. H. Jr., Wenzel, E. M., Knecht, K. The combination of interaural time and intensity in the lateralization of high-frequency complex signals. *Journal of the Acoustical Society of America*, 1990, *87*, 1702-1708.

Haith, M. M. Visual competence in early infancy. In R. Held, H. W. Leibowitz, & H.-L. Teuber (Eds.), *Handbook of sensory physiology, Volume VIII: Perception*. New York: Springer-Verlag, 1978.

Haith, M. M. *Rules that babies look by*. Hillsdale, N.J.: Lawrence Erlbaum, 1980.

Haith, M. M., Bergman, T., & Moore, M. J. Eye contact and face scanning in early infancy. *Science*, 1977, *198*, 853-855.

Hall, J. L. Two-tone distortion products in a nonlinear model of the basilar membrane. *Journal of the Acoustical Society of America*, 1974, *56*, 1818-1828.

Hallett, P. Eye movements. In K. R. Boff, L. Kaufman, & J. P. Thomas (Eds.), *Handbook of perception and human performance. Volume I: Sensory process and perception*. New York: John Wiley, 1986.

Hanson, D. R., & Fearn, R. W. Hearing acuity in young people exposed to pop music and other noise. *Lancet*, Aug. 2, 1975, no. 7927, Vol. II, 203-205.

Hardy, J. D., Stolwijk, J. A. J., & Hoffman, D. Pain following step increase in skin temperature. Chapter 21. In D. R. Kenshalo (Ed.), *The skin senses*. Springfield, Ill.: Charles C. Thomas, 1968.

Hardy, J. D., Wolff, H. G., & Goodell, H. *Pain sensations and reactions*. Baltimore, Md.: Williams & Wilkins, 1952.

Harmon, L. D. The recognition of faces. *Scientific American*, 1973, *229*, 70-82.

Harmon, L. D., & Julesz, B. Masking in visual recognition: Effects of two-dimensional filtered noise. *Science*, 1973, *180*, 1194-1197.

Harris, C. S. Perceptual adaptations to inverted, reversed and displaced vision. *Psychological Review*, 1965, *72*, 419-444.

Harris, C. S. Insight or out of sight? Two examples of perceptual plasticity in the human adult. In C. S. Harris (Ed.), *Visual coding and adaptability*. Hillsdale, N.J.: Lawrence Erlbaum, 1980.

Harris, J. D. *Pitch discrimination*. USN Bureau of Medicine and Surgery Research Report, Project NM 033 041.22.04, No. 205, June 20, 1952.

Harwerth, R. S., Smith III, E. L., Duncan, G. C., Crawford, M. L. J., & von Noorden, G. K. Multiple sensitive periods in the development of the primate visual system. *Science*, 1986, *232*, 235-238.

Hatfield, G., & Epstein, W. The status of minimum principle in the theoretical analysis of visual perception. *Psychological Bulletin*, 1985, *97*, 155-186.

Hay, J. C. Reafference learning in the presence of exafference. *Perception & Psychophysics*, 1981, *30*, 277-282.

Hayes, W. N., & Saiff, E. I. Visual alarm reactions in turtles. *Animal Behavior*, 1967, *15*, 102-106.

Haynes, H., White, B. L., & Held, R. Visual accommodation in human infants. *Science*, 1965, *148*, 528-530.

Hebb, D. O. *The organization of behavior*. New York: John Wiley, 1949.

Hecht, S., & Shlaer, S. An adaptometer for measuring human dark adaptation. *Journal of the Optical Society of America*, 1938, *28*, 269-275.

Hecht, S., Shlaer, S., & Pirenne, M. H. Energy at the threshold of vision. *Science*, 1941, *93*, 585.

Hecht S., Shlaer, S., & Pirenne, M. H. Energy, quanta, and vision. *Journal of General Physiology*, 1942, *25*, 819-840.

Heffner, R., & Heffner, H. Hearing in the elephant (*Elephas maximus*). *Science*, 1980, *208*, 518-520.

Heffner, R. S., & Heffner, H. E. Hearing in larger mammals: Horses (*equus caballus*) and cattle (*Bos taurus*). *Behavioral Neuroscience*, 1983, *97*, 299-309. (*a*)

Heffner, R. S., & Heffner, H. E. Hearing in large and small dogs: Absolute thresholds and size of the tympanic membrane. *Behavioral Neuroscience*, 1983, *97*, 310-318. (*b*)

Heffner, R. S., & Heffner, H. E. Visual factors in sound localization in mammals. *Journal of Comparative Neurology*, 1992, *317*, 219-232.

Hein, A. The development of visually guided behavior. In C. S. Harris (Ed.), *Visual coding and adaptability*. Hillsdale, N.J.: Lawrence Erlbaum, 1980.

Held, R., & Bauer, J. A. Visually guided reaching in infant monkeys after restricted rearing. *Science*, 1967, *155*, 718-720.

Held, R., & Bossom, J. Neonatal deprivation and adult rearrangement: Complementary techniques for analyzing plastic sensory-motor coordinations. *Journal of Comparative and Physiological Psychology*, 1961, *54*, 33-37.

Held, R., & Freedman, S. J. Plasticity in human sensorimotor control. *Science*, 1963, *142*, 455-462.

Held, R., & Gottlieb, N. Techniques for studying adaptation to disarranged hand-eye coordination. *Perceptual and Motor Skills*, 1958, *8*, 83-86.

Held, R., & Hein, A. Adaptation of disarranged hand-eye coordination contingent upon reafferent stimulation. *Perceptual and Motor Skills*, 1958, *8*, 87-90.

Held, R., & Hein, A. Movement-produced stimulation in the development of visually guided behavior. *Journal of Comparative and Physiological Psychology*, 1963, *56*, 872-876.

Held, R., & Schlank, M. Adaptation to disarranged eye-hand coordination in the distance dimension. *American Journal of Psychology*, 1959, *72*, 603-605.

Heller, M. A. Tactile retention: Reading with the skin. *Perception & Psychophysics*, 1980, *27*, 125-130.

Heller, M. A. Haptic dominance in form perception with blurred vision. *Perception*, 1983, *12*, 607-613.

Heller, M. A. Tactile memory in sighted and blind observers: The influence of orientation and rate of presentation. *Perception*, 1989, *18*, 121-133.

Heller, M. A. Haptic perception in blind people. In M. A. Heller & W. Schiff (Eds.), *The psychology of touch*. Hillsdale, N.J.: Lawrence Erlbaum, 1991.

Helson, H. *Adaptation-level theory*. New York: Harper & Row, 1964.

Helson, H., & King, S. M. The *tau*-effect. An example of psychological relativity. *Journal of Experimental Psychology*, 1931, *14*, 202-218.

Henkin, R. I. Metallic taste. *Journal of the American Medical Association*, 1993, *270*, 1369-1370.

Henning, G. J., Brouwer, J. N., Van Der Wel, H., & Francke, A. Miraculin, the sweet-inducing principle from miracle fruit. In C. Pfaffmann (Ed.), *Olfaction and taste*. New York: Rockefeller University Press, 1969.

Hepler, N. Color: A motion-contingent aftereffect. *Science*, 1968, *162*, 376-377.

Hering, E. *Outlines of a theory of the light sense*. Cambridge, Mass.: Harvard University Press, 1964. (Translated from the original 1920 publication by L. M. Hurvich & D. Jameson.)

Herman, B. H., & Panksepp, J. Ascending endorphin inhibition of distress vocalization. *Science*, 1981, *211*, 1060-1062.

Hershberger, W. Attached-shadow orientation perceived as depth by chickens reared in an environment illuminated from below. *Journal of Comparative and Physiological Psychology*, 1970, *73*, 407-411.

Hershenson, M. (Ed.). *The moon illusion*. Hillsdale, N.J.: Lawrence Erlbaum, 1989.

Hess, E. H. Attitude and pupil size. *Scientific American*, 1965, *212*, 46-54.

Hess, E. H. *The tell-tale eye*. New York: Van Nostrand 1975.

Hess, E. H. The role of pupil size in communication. *Scientific American*, 1975, *233*, 110-119.

Hess, E. H., & Polt, J. M. Pupil size as related to interest value of visual stimuli. *Science*, 1960, *132*, 349-350.

Hess, E. H., & Polt, J. M. Pupil size in relation to mental activity during simple problem-solving. *Science*, 1964, *140*, 1190-1192.

Hess, E. H., & Polt, J. M. Changes in pupil size as a measure of taste difference. *Perceptual and Motor Skills*, 1966, *23*, 451-455.

Hill, D. L. Development and plasticity of the gustatory system. In T. E. Finger & W. L. Silver (Eds.), *Neurobiology of taste and smell*. New York: John Wiley, 1987.

Hirsh, H. V. B., & Spinelli, D. N. Visual experience modifies distribution of horizontally and vertically oriented receptive fields in cats. *Science*, 1970, *168*, 869-871.

Hoagland, H. The physiological control of judgments of duration: Evidence for a chemical clock. *Journal of General Psychology*, 1933, *9*, 267-287.

Hoagland, H. *Pacemakers in relation to aspects of behavior*. New York: Macmillan, 1935.

Hochberg, J. E. *Perception*. Englewood Cliffs, N.J.: Prentice Hall, 1964.

Hochberg, J. Perceptual organization. In M. Kubovy & J. R. Pomerantz (Eds.), *Perceptual organization*. Hillsdale, N.J.: Lawrence Erlbaum, 1981.

Hochberg, J. Representation of motion and space in video and cinematic displays. In K. R. Boff, L. Kaufman, & J. P. Thomas (Eds.), *Handbook of perception and human performance. Volume I: Sensory processes and perception*. New York: John Wiley, 1986.

Hochberg, J. Visual perception. In R. C. Atkinson, R. J. Hernnstein, G. Lindzey, & R. D. Luce (Eds.), *Stevens' handbook of experimental psychology* (2nd ed.), Volume 1. New York: John Wiley, 1988.

Hochberg, J. E., & McAlister, E. A quantitative approach to figural goodness. *Journal of Experimental Psychology*, 1953, *46*, 361-364.

Hochberg, J. E., Triebel, W., & Seaman, G. Color adaptation under conditions of homogeneous visual stimulation (Ganzfeld). *Journal of Experimental Psychology*, 1951, *41*, 153-159.

Hogan, H. W. A theoretical reconciliation of competing views of time perception. *American Journal of Psychology*, 1978, *91*, 417-428.

Hohmann, A., & Creutzfeldt, O. D. Squint and the development of binocularity in the humans. *Nature*, 1975, *254*, 613-614.

Hölldobler, B., & Wilson, E. O. *The ants*. Cambridge, Mass.: Harvard University Press, 1990.

Hollins, M., Faldowski, R., Rao, S., & Young, F. Perceptual dimensions of tactile surface texture: A multidimensional scaling analysis. *Perception & Psychophysics*, 1993, *54*, 697-705.

Hollins, M., & Kelley, E. K. Spatial updating in blind and sighted people. *Perception & Psychophysics*, 1988, *43*, 380-388.

Holubář, J. *The sense of time: an electrophysiological study of its mechanism in man*. Cambridge, Mass.: M.I.T. Press, 1969.

Holway, A. H., & Boring, E. G. The moon illusion and the angle of regard. *American Journal of Psychology*, 1940, *53*, 109-116.

Holway, A. H., & Boring, E. G. Determinants of apparent visual size with distance variant. *American Journal of Psychology*, 1941, *54*, 21-37.

Hothersall, D. *History of psychology*. New York: Random House, 1984.

Houpt, K. A., & Houpt, T. R. The neonatal pig: A biological model for the development of taste preferences and controls of ingestive behavior. In J. M. Weiffenbach (Ed.), *The genesis of sweet preference*. Bethesda, Md.: U.S. Department of Health, Education, and Welfare, Public Health Service, National Institutes of Health, 1977. DHEW Publication No. (NIH) 77-1068.

Howard, I. P. *Human visual orientation*. New York: John Wiley, 1982.

Howard, I. P. The perception of posture, self motion, and the visual vertical. In K. R. Boff, L. Kaufman, & J. P. Thomas (Eds.), *Handbook of perception and human performance. Volume I: Sensory processes and perception*. New York: John Wiley, 1986.

Howard, I. P., & Templeton, W. B. *Human spatial orientation*. New York: John Wiley, 1966.

Howe, E. S., & Brandau, C. J. The temporal course of visual pattern encoding: Effects of pattern goodness. *Quarterly Journal of Experimental Psychology*, 1983, *35*, 607-633.

Howe, E. S., & Jung, K. Immediate memory span for two-dimensional spatial arrays: Effects of pattern symmetry and goodness. *Acta Psychologica*, 1986, *61*, 37-51.

Hsia, Y., & Graham, C. H. Color blindness. In C. H. Graham (Ed.), *Vision and visual perception*. New York: John Wiley, 1965.

Huang, Y. L., & Jones, B. On the interdependence of temporal and spatial judgments. *Perception & Psychophysics*, 1982, *32*, 7-14.

Hubel, D. H., The visual cortex of normal and deprived monkeys. *American Scientist*, 1979, *67*, 532-543.

Hubel, D. H. Evolution of ideas on the primary visual cortex, 1955-1978: A biased historical account. *Bioscience Reports*, 1982, *2*, 435-469.

Hubel, D. H. *Eye, brain, and vision*. New York: Scientific American Library, 1988.

Hubel, D. H., & Livingstone, M. S. The 11th J. A. F. Stevenson Memorial Lecture: Blobs and color vision. *Canadian Journal of Physiology and Pharmacology*, 1983, *61*, 1433-1441.

Hubel, D. H., & Livingstone, M. S. Segregation of form, color, and stereopsis in primate area 18. *Journal of Neuroscience,* 1987, *7,* 3378-3415.

Hubel, D. H., & Wiesel, T. N. Receptive fields of single neurons in the cat's striate cortex. *Journal of Physiology,* 1959, *148,* 574-591.

Hubel, D. H., & Wiesel, T. N. Receptive fields, binocular interaction and functional architecture in the cat's visual cortex. *Journal of Physiology,* 1962, *160,* 106-154.

Hubel, D. H., & Wiesel, T. N. Receptive fields of cells in striate cortex of very young, visually inexperienced kittens. *Journal of Neurophysiology,* 1963, *26,* 994-1002.

Hubel, D. H., & Wiesel, T. N. Receptive fields and functional architecture of monkey striate cortex. *Journal of Physiology,* 1968, *195,* 215-243.

Hubel, D. H., & Wiesel, T. N. Stereoscopic vision in macaque monkey. *Nature,* 1970, *225,* 41-42.

Hubel, D. H., & Wiesel, T. N. Sequence regularity and geometry of orientation columns in the monkey striate cortex. *Journal of Comparative Neurology,* 1974, *158,* 267-294.

Hubel, D. H., & Wiesel, T. N. Functional architecture of macaque monkey visual cortex. *Proceedings of the Royal Society of London,* 1977, *198,* Series B, 1-59.

Hubel, D. H., & Wiesel, T. N. Brain mechanisms of vision. *Scientific American,* 1979, *241,* 150-162.

Huffman, K., Vernoy, M., & Vernoy, J. *Essentials of psychology in action.* New York: John Wiley, 1995.

Huggins, A. W. Distortion of the temporal pattern of speech: Interruption and alternation. *Journal of Acoustical Society of America,* 1964, *36,* 1055-1064.

Humphrey, N. K. Vision in a monkey without striate cortex: A case study. *Perception,* 1974, *3,* 105-114.

Hunt, D. M., Dulai, K. S., Bowmaker, J. K., & Mollon, J. D. The chemistry of John Dalton's color blindness. *Science,* 1995, *267,* 984-988.

Hurvich, L. M., & Jameson, D. A quantitative theoretical account of color vision. *Transactions of the New York Academy of Sciences,* 1955, *18,* 33-38.

Hurvich, L. M., & Jameson, D. An opponent-process theory of color vision. *Psychological Review,* 1957, *64,* 384-404.

Hurvich, L. M., & Jameson, D. Opponent processes as a model of neural organization. *American Psychologist,* 1974, *29,* 88-102.

Ingle, D. J. The goldfish as a retinex animal. *Science,* 1985, *227,* 651-654.

Jacobs, G. H., Neitz, J., and Deegan, J. F. Retinal receptors in rodents maximally sensitive to ultraviolet light. *Nature,* 1991, *353,* 655-656.

Jacobs, G. H., & Pulliam, K. A. Vision in the prairie dog. *Journal of Comparative and Physiological Psychology,* 1973, *84,* 240-245.

Jacobs, H. L. Observations on the ontogeny of saccharine preference in the neonate rat. *Psychonomic Science,* 1964, *1,* 105-106.

Jacobs, H. L. Taste and the role of experience in the regulation of food intake. In M. R. Kare & O. Maller (Eds.), *The chemical senses and nutrition.* Baltimore, MD.: Johns Hopkins Press, 1967.

Jacobsen, A., & Gilchrist, A. The ratio principle holds over a million-to-one range of illumination. *Perception & Psychophysics,* 1988, *43,* 1-6.

James, W. *The principles of psychology.* New York: Henry Holt, 1890.

Janisse, M. P. *Pupillometry.* Washington, D.C.: Hemisphere, 1977.

Janson, H. W. *History of art.* Englewood Cliffs, N.J.: Prentice Hall, 1962.

Jastrow, R., & Thompson, M. H. *Astronomy: Fundamentals and frontiers* (2nd ed.). New York: John Wiley, 1974.

Jensen, A. R., & Rohwer, W. D. The Stroop colourword test: A review. *Acta Psychologica,* 1966, *25,* 36-93.

Jerome, N. W. Taste experience and the development of a dietary preference for sweet in humans: Ethnic and cultural variations in early taste experience. In J. W. Weiffenbach (Ed.), *Taste and development.* Bethesda, Md.: U.S. Department of Health, Education, and Welfare, Public Health Service, National Institutes of Health, 1977. DHEW Publication No. (NIH) 77-1068.

Jewesbury, E. C. O. Insensitivity to pain. *Brain,* 1951, *74,* 336-353.

Johansson, G. Visual perception of biological motion and a model for its analysis. *Perception & Psychophysics,* 1973, *14,* 201-211.

Johansson, G. Visual motion perception. *Scientific American,* 1975, *232,* 76-88.

Johansson, G., von Hofsten, C., & Jansson, G. Event perception. *Annual Review of Psychology,* 1980, *31,* 27-64.

Johansson, R. S., & Vallbo, A. B. Tactile sensibility in the human hand: Relative and absolute densities of four types of mechanoreceptive units in glabrous skin. *Journal of Physiology,* 1979, *286,* 283-300.

Johnson, O., & Kozma, A. Effects of concurrent verbal and musical tasks on a unimanual skill. *Cortex,* 1977, *13,* 11-16.

Johnsson, L. G., & Hawkins, J. E. Sensory and neural degeneration with aging, as seen in microdissections of the human inner ear. *Annals of Otology, Rhinology and Laryngology,* 1972, *81,* 179-193.

Johnston, J. C., & McClelland, J. L. Visual factors in word perception. *Perception & Psychophysics,* 1973, *14,* 365-370.

Johnston, J. C., & McClelland, J. L. Perception of letters in words: Seek not and ye shall find. *Science,* 1974, *184,* 1192-1194.

Johnston, J. C., & McClelland, J. L. Experimental tests of a hierarchical model of word identification. *Journal of Verbal Learning and Verbal Behavior,* 1980, *19,* 503-524.

Jones, B., & Gwynn, M. Functional measurement scale of painful electric shocks. *Perception & Psychophysics,* 1984, *35,* 193-200.

Jones, B., & Huang, Y. L. Space-time dependencies in psychophysical judgment of extent and duration: Algebraic models of the tau and kappa effects. *Psychological Bulletin,* 1982, *91,* 128-142.

Jones, L. A., Hunter, I. W., & Irwin, R. J. Differential thresholds for limb movement measured using adaptive techniques. *Perception & Psychophysics,* 1992, *52,* 529-535.

Jones, M. R. Dynamic pattern structure in music: Recent theory and research. *Perception & Psychophysics,* 1987, *41,* 621-634.

Jordan, K., & Randall, J. The effects of framing ratio and oblique length on Ponzo illusion magnitude. *Perception & Psychophysics,* 1987, *41,* 435-439.

Jory, M. K., & Day, R. H. The relationship between brightness contrast and illusory contours. *Perception,* 1979, *8,* 3-9.

Julesz, B. Binocular depth perception without familiarity cues. *Science,* 1964, *145,* 356-362.

Julesz, B. Texture and visual perception. *Scientific American,* 1965, *212,* 38-48.

Julesz, B. *Foundations of cyclopean perception.* Chicago: University of Chicago Press, 1971.

Julesz, B. Global stereopsis: Cooperative phenomena in stereoscopic depth perception. In R. Held. H. W. Leibowitz, & H.-L. Teuber (Eds.) *Handbook of sensory physiology.* Volume VIII: *Perception.* Berlin: Springer-Verlag, 1978.

Julesz, B. Texton gradients: The texton theory revisited. *Biological Cybernetics,* 1986, *54,* 245-251.

Julesz, B., & Bergen, J. R. Textons, the fundamental elements in preattentive vision and perception of textures. *The Bell System Technical Journal,* 1983, *62,* (6), 1619-1645.

Jung, R., & Spi'lman, L. Receptive-field estimation and perceptual integration in human vision. In F. A. Young & D. B. Lindsley (Eds.), *Early experience and visual information processing in perceptual and reading disorders.* Washington, D.C.: National Academy of Sciences, 1970.

Jusczyk, P. Speech perception. In K. R. Boff, L. Kaufman, & J. P. Thomas (Eds.), *Handbook of perception and human performance. Volume II: Cognitive processes and performance.* New York: John Wiley, 1986.

Kagan, J. The determinants of attention in the infant. *American Scientist,* 1970, *58,* 298-306.

Kaiser, M. K., Proffitt, D. R., & Anderson, K. Judgments of natural and anomalous trajectories in the presence and absence of motion. *Journal of Experimental Psychology: Learning, Memory, and Cognition,* 1985, *11,* 795-803.

Kaiser, M. K., Proffitt, D. R., & McCloskey, M. The development of beliefs about falling objects. *Perception & Psychophysics,* 1985, *38,* 533-539.

Kallman, H. J., Corballis, M. C. Ear asymmetry in reaction time to musical sounds. *Perception & Psychophysics,* 1975, *17,* 368-370.

Kandel, E. R. Visual system III: Physiology of the central visua! pathways. In E. R. Kandel & J. H. Schwartz (Eds.), *Principles of neural science.* New York: Elsevier, 1981.

Kandel, E. R. Processing of form and movement in the visual system. In E. R. Kandel & J. H. Schwartz (Eds.), *Principles of neural science* (2nd ed.). New York: Elsevier, 1985.

Kandel, E. R., Schwartz, J. H., & Jessell, T. M. *Essentials of neural science and behavior.* Norwalk, Conn.: Appleton & Lange, 1995.

Kanizsa, G. *Organization in vision: Essays on Gestalt psychology.* New York: Praeger, 1979.

Kare, M. R., & Ficken, M. S. Comparative studies on the sense of taste. In Y. Zotterman (Ed.), *Olfaction and taste.* New York: Macmillan, 1963.

Katsuki, Y. Neural mechanism of auditory sensation in cats. In W. A. Rosenblith (Ed.), *Sensory communication.* Cambridge, Mass.: M.I.T. Press, 1961.

Katsuki, Y., Watanabe, T., & Suga, N. Interactions of auditory neurons in response to two sound stimuli in cat. *Journal of Neurophysiology,* 1959, *22,* 603-623.

Katz, D. *The world of touch.* (L. E. Krueger, Transl.) Hillsdale, N.J.: Lawrence Erlbaum, 1989. (Original work published 1925.)

Katz, J., & Melzack, R. Pain "memories" in phantom limbs: Review and clinical observation. *Pain,* 1990, *43,* 319-336.

Kauer, J. S. Coding in the olfactory system. In T. E. Finger & W. L. Silver (Eds.), *Neurobiology of taste and smell.* New York: John Wiley, 1987.

Kaufman, L. *Perception: The world transformed.* New York: Oxford University Press, 1979.

Kaufman, L., & Rock, I. The moon illusion, I. *Science,* 1962, *136,* 953-961 (*a*).

Kaufman, L., & Rock, I. The moon illusion. *Scientific American,* 1962, *207,* 120-132 (*b*).

Kaufman, L., & Rock, I. The moon illusion thirty years later. In M. Hershenson (Ed.), *The moon illusion.* Hillsdale, N.J.: Lawrence Erlbaum, 1989.

Keele, S. W. Motor control. In K. R. Boff, L. Kaufman, & J. P. Thomas (Eds.), *Handbook of perception and human performance. Volume II: Cognitive processes and performance.* New York: John Wiley, 1986.

Keim, H. A. *How to care for your back.* Englewood Cliffs, N.J.: Prentice-Hall, 1981.

Kellar, L. A., & Bever, T. G. Hemispheric asymmetries in the perception of musical intervals as a function of musical experience and family handedness background. *Brain and Language,* 1980, *10,* 24-38.

Kellogg, W. N. Sonar system of the blind. *Science,* 1962, *137,* 399-404.

Kelly, D. D. Somatic sensory system IV: Central representations of pain and analgesia. Chapter 18. In E. R. Kandel & J. H. Schwartz (Eds.), *Principles of neural science.* New York: Elsevier, 1984.

Kendrick, K. M., & Baldwin, B. A. Cells in temporal cortex of conscious sheep can respond preferentially to the sight of faces. *Science,* 1987, *236,* 448-450.

Kennedy, J. M. What can we learn about pictures from the blind? *American Scientist,* 1983, *71,* 19-26.

Kennedy, J. M. The tangible world of the blind. *Encyclopaedia Britannica Medical and Health Annual.* Chicago, 1984.

Kennedy, J. M. Line endings and subjective contours. *Spatial Vision,* 1988, *3,* 151-158.

Kennedy, J. M. *Drawing and the blind: Pictures to touch.* New Haven, Conn.: Yale University Press, 1993.

Kennedy, J. M., & Campbell, J. Convergence principle in blind people's pointing. *International Journal of Rehabilitation Research,* 1985, *8,* 189-210.

Kennedy, J. M., & Domander, R. Pictorial foreground-background reversal reduces tactual recognition by blind subjects. *Journal of Visual Impairment and Blindness,* 1984, *78,* 215-216.

Kennedy, J. M., Gabias, P., & Nicholls, A. Tactile pictures. In M. A. Heller & W. Schiff (Eds.), *The psychology of touch.* Hillsdale, N.J.: Lawrence Erlbaum, 1991.

Kenshalo, D. R. The cutaneous senses. In J. R. Kling & L. A. Riggs (Eds.), *Experimental psychology* (3rd ed.). New York: Holt, Rinehart and Winston, 1971.

Kenshalo, D. R. Biophysics and psychophysics of feeling. In E. L. Carterette & M. P. Friedman (Eds.), *Handbook of perception,* Volume VI, B. New York: Academic Press, 1978.

Kenshalo, D. R., & Gallegos, E. S. Multiple temperature-sensitive spots innervated by single nerve fibers. *Science,* 1967, *158,* 1064-1065.

Kenshalo, D. R., & Nafe, D. R. A quantitative theory of feeling: 1960. *Psychological Review,* 1962, *69,* 17-33.

Kenshalo, D. R., & Scott, H. A. Temporal course of thermal adaptation. *Science,* 1966, *151,* 1095-1096.

Kessen, W. Sucking and looking: Two organized congenital patterns of behavior in the human newborn. In H. W. Stevenson, E. H. Hess, & H. L. Rheingold (Eds.), *Early behavior: Comparative and developmental approaches.* New York: John Wiley, 1967.

Khanna, S. M., & Leonard, D. G. B. Basilar membrane tuning in the cat cochlea. *Science,* 1982, *215,* 305-306.

Kiang, N. Y. S. Peripheral neural processing of auditory information. In I. Darian-Smith (Ed.), *Handbook of physiology.* Bethesda, Md.: American Physiological Society, 1984.

Kilpatrick, F. P. *Explorations in transactional psychology.* New York: New York University Press, 1961.

Kimble, G. A, Garmezy, N., & Zigler, E. *Principles of general psychology* (5th ed.). New York: John Wiley, 1980.

Kimbrell, G. M., & Furchgott, E. The effect of aging on olfactory threshold. *Journal of Gerontology,* 1968, *18,* 364-365.

Kimura, D. Cerebral dominance and the perception of verbal stimuli. *Canadian Journal of Psychology,* 1961, *15,* 166-171.

Kimura, D. Left-right differences in the perception of melodies. *Quarterly Journal of Experimental Psychology,* 1964, *16,* 355-358.

Kimura, D. Functional asymmetry of the brain in dichotic listening. *Cortex,* 1967, *3,* 163-178.

Kimura, D., & Folb, S. Neural processing of backwards-speech sounds. *Science,* 1968, *161,* 395-396.

Kinsler, L. E., & Frey, A. R. *Fundamentals of acoustics* (2nd ed.). New York: John Wiley, 1962.

Kirk-Smith, M. D., Van Toller, C., & Dodd, G. H. Unconscious odour conditioning in human subjects. *Journal of Biological Psychology,* 1983, *17,* 221-231.

Kirschvink, J. L., Jones, D. S., & MacFadden, F. J. (Eds.), *Magnetite biomineralization and magnetoreception in organisms, a new biomagnetism.* New York: Plenum Press, 1985.

Klatzky, R. L., Lederman, S. J., & Metzger, V. A. Identifying objects by touch: An "expert system." *Perception & Psychophysics,* 1985, *37,* 299-302.

Kleber, R. J., Lhamon, W. T., & Goldstone, S. Hyperthermia, hyperthyroidism, and time judgment. *Journal of Comparative and Physiological Psychology,* 1963, *56,* 362-365.

Kleffner, D. A., & Ramachandran, V. S. On the perception of shape from shading. *Perception & Psychophysics,* 1992, *52,* 18-36.

Klein, G. S. Semantic power of words measured through the interference with color naming. *American Journal of Psychology,* 1964, *77,* 576-588.

Kline, D. W., & Schieber, F. Visual aging: A transient/sustained shift? *Perception & Psychophysics,* 1981, *29,* 181-182.

Kluender, K. R., Diehl, R. L., & Killeen, P. R. Japanese quail can learn phonetic categories. *Science,* 1987, *237,* 1195-1197.

Knouse, K. Citation in *Rutgers Magazine,* 1988, *67* (Sept.-Oct.), 8.

Knox, C., & Kimura, D. Cerebral processing of nonverbal sounds in boys and girls. *Neuropsychologia,* 1970, *8,* 227-237.

Knudsen, E. I., & Brainard, M. S. Visual instruction of the neural map of auditory space in the developing optic tectum. *Science,* 1991, *253,* 85-87.

Knudsen, E. I., & Konishi, M. A neural map of auditory space in the owl. *Science,* 1978, *200,* 795-797.

Koffka, K. *Principles of Gestalt psychology.* New York: Harcourt Brace, 1935.

Kohler, I. Experiments with goggles. *Scientific American,* 1962, *206,* 62-86.

Kohler, I. The formation and transformation of the perceptual world. *Psychological Issues,* 1964, *3* (Whole No. 4).

Köhler, W., & Wallach, H. Figural aftereffects: an investigation of visual processes. *Proceedings of the American Philosophical Society,* 1944, *88,* 269-357.

Kowal, K. H. Apparent duration and numerosity as a function of melodic familiarity. *Perception & Psychophysics,* 1987, *42,* 122-131.

Kowler, E., & Anton, S. Reading twisted text: Implications for the role of saccades. *Vision Research,* 1987, *27,* 45-60.

Kowler, E., & Martins, A. J. Eye movements of preschool children. *Science, 1982, 215,* 997-999.

Krech, D., & Crutchfield, R. S. *Elements of psychology.* New York: Alfred A. Knopf, 1958.

Kristofferson, A. B. Attention and psychophysical time. *Acta Psychologica,* 1967, *27,* 93-100.

Krueger, L. E. David Katz's der Aufbau der Tastwelt (the world of touch): A synopsis. *Perception & Psychophysics,* 1970, *7,* 337-341.

Krueger, L. E. Tactual perception in historical perspective: David Katz's world of touch. In W. Schiff & E. Foulke (Eds.), *Tactual perception: A sourcebook.* New York: Cambridge University Press, 1982. (*a*)

Krueger, L. E. A word-superiority effect with print and Braille characters. *Perception & Psychophysics,* 1982, *31,* 345-352. (*b*)

Krueger, L. E., & Ward, M. E. Letter search by Braille readers: Implications for instruction. *Journal of Visual Impairment and Blindness,* 1983, *77,* 166-169.

Krumhansl, C. L., & Kessler, E. J. Tracing the dynamic changes in perceived tonal organization in a spatial representation of musical keys. *Psychological Review,* 1982, *89,* 334-368.

Kubovy, M. Overview. In K. R. Boff, L. Kaufman, & J. P. Thomas (Eds.), *Handbook of perception and human performance. Volume II: Cognitive processes and performance.* New York: John Wiley, 1986.

Kuffler, S. W. Discharge patterns and functional organization of mammalian retina. *Journal of Neurophysiology,* 1953, *16,* 37-68.

Kuhl, P. A., & Miller, J. D. Speech perception by the chinchilla: Voiced-voiceless distinctions in alveolar plosive consonants. *Science,* 1975, *190,* 69-72.

Kuhl, P. A., & Padden, D. M. Enhanced discriminability at the phonetic boundaries for the place feature in macaques. *Journal of the Acoustical Society of America,* 1983, *73,* 1003-1010.

Kuhl, P. K. Perception of auditory equivalent classes for speech by infants. *Infant Behavior and Development,* 1983, *6,* 263-285.

Lackner, J. R. Adaptation to visual and proprioceptive rearrangement: Origin of the differential effectiveness of active and passive movement. *Perception & Psychophysics,* 1977, *21,* 55-59.

Lackner, J. R., & Graybiel, A. Head movements in nonterrestrial force environments elicit motion sickness: Implications for the etiology of space motion sickness. *Aviation, Space, and Environmental Medicine,* 1986, *57,* 443-448.

Laing, D. G. Natural sniffing gives optimum odour perception for humans. *Perception,* 1983, *12,* 99-118.

Lambert, L., & Lederman, S. J. An evaluation of the legibility and meaningfulness of potential map symbols. *Journal of Visual Impairment and Blindness,* 1989, *83,* 397-403.

Lancet. Noise-induced hearing loss (Editorial Summary). *Lancet,* Aug. 2, 1975, no. 7927, Vol. II, 215-216.

Langfeld, H. S. Note on a case of chromaesthesia. *Psychological Bulletin,* 1914, *11,* 113-114.

Langlois, J. H., Ritter, J. M., Roggman, L. A., & Vaughn, L. S. Facial diversity and infant preferences for attractive faces. *Developmental Psychology,* 1991, *27,* 79-84.

Lanze, M., Macguire, W., & Weisstein, N. Emergent features: A new factor in the object-superiority effect? *Perception & Psychophysics,* 1985, *38,* 438-442.

Lautenbacher, S., & Strian, F. Sex differences in pain and thermal sensitivity: The role of body size. *Perception & Psychophysics,* 1991, *50,* 179-183.

Lawless, H. T. Recognition of common odors, pictures, and simple shapes. *Perception & Psychophysics,* 1978, *24,* 493-495.

Lawless, H. T. Sensory interactions in mixtures. *Journal of Sensory Studies,* 1986, *1,* 259-274.

Lawless, H. T. Gustatory psychophysics. In T. E. Finger & W. L. Silver (Eds.), *Neurobiology of taste and smell.* New York: John Wiley, 1987.

Lawless, H., & Engen, T. Associations to odors: Interference, mnemonics, and verbal labels. *Journal of Experimental Psychology: Human Learning and Memory,* 1977, *3,* 52-59.

Lawless, H. T., Rozin, P., & Shenker, J. Effects of oral capsaicin on gustatory, olfactory and irritant sensation on flavor identification in humans who regularly or rarely consume chili pepper. *Chemical Senses,* 1985, *10,* 579-589.

Lawless, H. T., & Stevens, D. A. Responses by humans to oral chemical irritants as a function of locus of stimulation. *Perception & Psychophysics,* 1988, *43,* 72-78.

Lawson, R. B., Packard, S., Lawrence, D., & Whitmore, C. L. Stereopsis from reversible and irreversible patterns. *Perception & Psychophysics,* 1977, *21,* 65-68.

Lederman, S. J. "Improving one's touch" . . . and more. *Perception & Psychophysics,* 1978, *24,* 154-160.

Lee, D. N., & Aronson, E. Visual proprioceptive control of standing in human infants. *Perception & Psychophysics,* 1974, *15,* 529-532.

Leehey, S. C., Moskowitz-Cook, A., Brill, S., & Held, R. Orientational anisotropy in infant vision. *Science,* 1975, *190,* 900-902.

Le Grand, Y. *Form and space vision.* Bloomington: Indiana University Press, 1967.

Le Grand, Y. *Light, colour and vision.* London: Chapman and Hall, 1968.

Le Grand, Y. History of research on seeing. In E. C. Carterette & M. P. Friedman (Eds.), *Handbook of perception. Volume V: Seeing.* New York: Academic Press, 1975.

Leibowitz, H. W., Brislin, R., Perlmutter, L., & Hennessy, R. Ponzo perspective illusion as a manifestation of space perception. *Science,* 1969, *166,* 1174-1176.

Leibowitz, H. W., & Owens, D. A. Nighttime driving accidents and selective accidents and selective visual degradation. *Science,* 1977, *189,* 646-648.

Leibowitz, H. W., & Pick, H. A. Cross-cultural and educational aspects of the Ponzo perspective illusion. *Perception & Psychophysics,* 1972, *12,* 430-432.

Leibowitz, H. W., Post, R. B., Brandt, T., & Dichgans, J. Implications of recent developments in dynamic spatial orientation and visual resolution for vehicle guidance. In A. Wertheim, W. Wagenaar, & H. W. Leibowitz (Eds.), *Tutorials in motion perception.* New York: Plenum Press, 1982.

Leinbach, M. D., & Fagot, B. I. Categorical habituation to male and female faces: Gender schematic processing in infancy. *Infant Behavior and Development,* 1993, *16,* 317-332.

Lele, P. P., & Weddell, G. The relationship between neurohistology and corneal sensibility. *Brain,* 1956, *79,* 119-154.

Lenneberg, E. H. Understanding language without ability to speak: A case report. *Journal of Abnormal and Social Psychology,* 1962, *65,* 419-425.

Lenneberg, E H. *Biological foundations of language.* New York: Wiley, 1967.

Lenz, R. A., Gracely, R. H., Hope, E. J., Baker, F. H., Rowland, L. H., Dougherty, P. M., & Richardson, R. T. The sensation of angina can be evoked by stimulation of the human thalamus. *Pain,* 1994, *59,* 119-125.

Lettvin, J. Y., Maturana, H. R., McCulloch, W. S., & Pitts, W. H. What the frog's eye tells the frog's brain. *Proceedings of the Institute of Radio Engineers,* 1959, *47,* 1940-1951.

Leukel, F. *Introduction to physiological psychology.* St. Louis: C. V. Mosby, 1972.

LeVay, S., Wiesel, T. N., & Hubel, D. H. The development of ocular dominance columns in normal and visually deprived monkeys. *Journal of Comparative Neurology,* 1980, *191,* 1-51.

Levenson, T. Accounting for taste. *The Sciences,* 1995, *35,* 13-15.

Leventhal, A. G., & Hirsch, H. V. B. Cortical effect of early selective exposure to diagonal lines. *Science,* 1975, *190,* 902-904.

Levy, C. M., Fischler, I. S., & Griggs, R. A. *Laboratory in cognition and perception.* Iowa City, Iowa: Conduit, 1979.

Lewin, R. Mockingbird song aimed at mates, not rivals. *Science,* 1987, *236,* 1521-1522.

Lewis, J. W., Cannon, J. T., & Liebeskind, J. C. Opioid and nonopiod mechanisms of stress analgesia. *Science,* 1980, *208,* 623-625.

Lewis, M. E., Mishkin, M., Bragin, E., Brown, R. M., Pert, C. B., & Pert, A. Opiate receptor gradients in monkey cerebral cortex: Correspondence with sensory processing hierarchies. *Science,* 1981, *211,* 1166-1169.

Lewkowicz, D. J. Infants' responsiveness to the auditory and visual attributes of a sounding/moving stimulus. *Perception & Psychophysics,* 1992, *52,* 519-528.

Lewy, A. J., Wehr, T. A., Goodwin, F. K., Newsome, D. A., & Markey, S. P. Light suppresses melatonin secretion in humans. *Science,* 1980, *210,* 1267-1269.

Liberman, A. M., Cooper, F. S., Harris, K. S., MacNeilage, P. F., & Studdert-Kennedy, M. Some observations on a model for speech perception. In W. Wathen-Dunn (Ed.), *Models for the perception of speech and visual form.* Cambridge, Mass.: M.I.T. Press, 1967. (*a*)

Liberman, A. M., Cooper, F. S., Shankweiler, D. P., & Studdert-Kennedy, M. Perception of the speech code. *Psychological Review,* 1967, *74,* 431-461. (*b*).

Liberman, A. M., & Studdert-Kennedy, M. Phonetic perception. In R. Held, H. W. Leibowitz, & H.-L. Teuber (Eds.), *Handbook of sensory physiology. Volume VIII: Perception.* Berlin: Springer-Verlag, 1978.

Licklider, J. C. R., & Miller, G. A. The perception of speech. In S. S. Stevens (Ed.), *Handbook of experimental psychology.* New York: John Wiley, 1951.

Lieberman, P. *Information, perception, and language.* Research Monograph No. 38. Cambridge, Mass.: M.I.T. Press, 1968.

Lieberman, P., & Crelin, E. S. On the speech of Neanderthal man. *Linguistic Inquiry,* 1971, *2,* 203-222.

Lieberman, P., Crelin, E. S., & Klatt, D. H. Phonetic ability and related anatomy of the newborn and adult human, Neanderthal man, and the chimpanzee. *American Anthropologist,* 1972, *74,* 287-307.

Lindsay, P. H., & Norman, D. A. *Human information processing: An introduction to psychology* (2nd ed.). New York: Academic Press, 1977.

Linn, C. E., Jr., Campbell, M. G., & Roelofs, W. L. Pheromone components and active spaces: What do moths smell and where do they smell it? *Science,* 1987, *237,* 650-652.

Lishman J. R., & Lee, D. N. The autonomy of visual kinaesthesis. *Perception,* 1973, *2,* 287-294.

Livingston, W. K. The vicious circle in causalgia. *Annals of the New York Academy of Sciences,* 1948, *50,* 247-258.

Livingstone, M. S. Art, illusion and the visual system. *Scientific American,* 1987, *258,* 78-85.

Livingstone, M. S., & Hubel, D. H. Anatomy and physiology of a color system in the primate visual cortex. *The Journal of Neuroscience,* 1984, *4,* 309-356.

Livingstone, M. S., & Hubel, D. Segregation of form, color, movement, and depth: Anatomy, physiology, and movement. *Science,* 1988, *240,* 740-749.

Livingstone, M. S., & Hubel, D. H. Psychophysical evidence for separate channels for the perception of form, color, movement, and depth. *Journal of Neuroscience,* 1987, *7,* 3416-3468.

Livingstone, M. S., Rosen, G. D., Drislane, F. W., & Galaburda, A. M. Physiological and anatomical evidence for a magnocellular detect in developmental dyslexia. *Proceedings of the National Academy of Sciences,* 1991, *188,* 7943-7947.

Llewellyn-Thomas, E. Search behavior. *Radiological Clinics of North America,* 1969, *7,* 403-417.

Llewellyn-Thomas, E. Can eye movements save the earth? In D. F. Fisher, R. A. Monty, & J. W. Senders (Eds.), *Eye movements: Cognition and visual perception*. Hillsdale, N.J.: Lawrence Erlbaum, 1981.

Lockhart, J. M. Ambient temperature and time estimation. *Journal of Experimental Psychology*, 1967, *73*, 286–291.

Logethetis, N. K., & Schall, J. D. Neuronal correlates of subjective visual perception. *Science*, 1989, *245*, 761–763.

Logue, A. W. *The psychology of eating and drinking* (2nd ed.). New York: W. H. Freeman, 1991.

Lohmann, K. J., & Lohmann, C. M. F. Acquisition of magnetic directional preference in hatchling loggerhead sea turtles. *Journal of Experimental Biology*, 1994, *190*, 1–8.

London, I. D. A Russian report on the postoperative newly seeing. *American Journal of Psychology*, 1960, *73*, 478–482.

Long, G., & Beaton, R. J. The contribution of visual persistence to the perceived duration of brief targets. *Perception & Psychophysics*, 1980, *28*, 422–430.

Long, G., Toppino, T. C., & Kostenbauder, J. E. As the cube turns: Evidence for two processes in the perception of a dynamic reversible figure. *Perception & Psychophysics*, 1983, *34*, 29–38.

Long, G., & Wurst, S. A. Complexity effects on reaction-time measures of visual persistence: Evidence for peripheral and central contributions. *American Journal of Psychology*, 1984, *97*, 537–561.

Long, G. M., Toppino, T. C., & Mondin, G. W. Prime time: Fatigue and set effects in the perception of reversible figures. *Perception & Psychophysics*, 1992, *52*, 609–616.

Loomis, J. M., Golledge, R. G., Klatzky, R. L., Speigle, J. M., & Tietz, J. Personal guidance system for the visually impaired. *Proceedings of the First Annual International ACM/SIGCAPH Conference on Assistive Technologies*. Marina del Rey, Calif., October 31–November 1, 1994.

Loomis, J. M., Klatzky, R. L., Golledge, R. G., Cicinelli, J. G., Pellegrino, J. W., & Fry, P. A. Nonvisual navigation by blind and sighted: Assessment of path integration ability. *Journal of Experimental Psychology: General*, 1993, *122*, 73–91.

Loomis, J. M., & Lederman, S. J. Tactual perception. In K. R. Boff, L. Kaufman, & J. P. Thomas (Eds.), *Handbook of perception and human performance. Volume II: Cognitive processes and performance*. New York: John Wiley, 1986.

Loop, M. S., & Bruce, L. L. Cat color vision: The effect of stimulus size. *Science*, 1978, *199*, 1221–1222.

Lore, R., & Sawatski, D. Performance of binocular and monocular infant rats on the visual cliff. *Journal of Comparative and Physiological Psychology*, 1969, *67*, 177–181.

Lucas, A., & Fisher, G. H. Illusions in concrete situations: II Experimental studies of the Poggendorff illusion. *Ergonomics*, 1969, *12*, 395–402.

Lucca, A., Dellantonio, A., & Riggio, L. Some observations of the Poggendorff and Müller-Lyer illusions. *Perception & Psychophysics*, 1986, *39*, 374–380.

Luckiesh, M. *Visual illusions*. New York: Dover Publications, 1922. (Reprinted 1965.)

Lyman, B. J., & McDaniel, M. A. Memory for odors and odor names: Modalities of elaboration and imagery. *Journal of Experimental Psychology: Learning, Memory, and Cognition*, 1990, *16*, 656–664.

Lynes, J. A. Brunelleschi's perspective reconsidered. *Perception*, 1980, *9*, 87–99.

Lynn, B. Capsaicin: Actions on nociceptive C-fibres and therapeutic potential. *Pain*, 1990, *41*, 61–69.

Mack, A. Perceptual aspects of motion in the frontal plane. In K. R. Boff, L. Kaufman, & J. P. Thomas (Eds.), *Handbook of perception and human performance. Volume I: Sensory processes and perception*. New York: John Wiley, 1986.

Mack, A., Fendrich, R., Chambers, D., & Heuer, F. Perceived position and saccadic eye movements. *Vision Research*, 1985, *25*, 501–505.

MacKain, K. Studdert-Kennedy, M., Spieker, S., & Stern, D. Infant intermodal speech perception is a left-hemisphere function. *Science*, 1983, *219*, 1347–1349.

MacKay, D. M. Ways of looking at perception. In W. Wathen-Dunn (Ed.), *Models for the perception of speech and visual form*. Cambridge, Mass.: M.I.T. Press, 1967.

MacNichol, E. F. Three-pigment color vision. *Scientific American*, 1964, *211*, 48–56. (*a*)

MacNichol, E. F. Retinal mechanisms of color vision. *Vision Research*, 1964, *4*, 119–133. (*b*)

MacLeod, D. I. A., Chen, B., & Crognale, M. Spatial organization of sensitivity regulation in rod vision. *Vision Research*, 1989, *29*, 965–978.

Madden, R. C., & Phillips, J. B. An attempt to demonstrate magnetic compass orientation in two species of mammals. *Animal Learning & Behavior*, 1987, *15*, 130–134.

Mair, R. G., Bouffard, J. A., Engen, T., & Morton, T. H. Olfactory sensitivity during the menstrual cycle. *Sensory Processes*, 1978, *2*, 90–98.

Maier, S. F., Drugan, R. C., & Grau, J. W. Controllability, coping behavior, and stress-induced analgesia in the rat. *Pain*, 1982, *12*, 47–56.

Maller, O. Specific appetite. In M. R. Kare & O. Maller (Eds.), *The chemical senses and nutrition*. Baltimore, Md.: Johns Hopkins Press, 1967.

Malott, R. W., Malott, M. K., & Pokrzywinski, J. The effects of outward-pointing arrowheads on the Mueller-Lyer illusion in pigeons. *Psychonomic Science*, 1967, *9*, 55–56.

Malott, R. W., & Malott, M. K. Perception and stimulus generalization. In W. C. Stebbins (Ed.), *Animal psychophysics*. New York: Appleton-Century-Crofts, 1970.

Mandenoff, A., Fumeron, F., Apfelbaum, M., & Margules, D. L. Endogenous opiates and energy balance. *Science*, 1982, *215*, 1536–1538.

Manley, G. A. Some aspects on the evolution of hearing in vertebrates. *Nature*, 1971, *230*, 506–509.

Mann, T. *The magic mountain*. New York: Knopf, 1927.

Marcel, A. J. Conscious and unconscious perception: Experiments on visual masking and word recognition. *Cognitive Psychology,* 1983, *15,* 197-237.

Marks, L. E., Synesthesia. *Psychology Today,* 1975, *9,* 48-52.

Marks, L. E. *The unity of the senses.* New York: Academic Press, 1978.

Marks, L. E., & Stevens, J. C. Perceived cold and skin temperature as functions of stimulation level and duration. *American Journal of Psychology,* 1972, *85,* 407-419.

Marks, W. B., Dobelle, W. H., & MacNichol, E. F. Visual pigments of single primate cones. *Science,* 1964, *143,* 1181-1183.

Marler, P. R., & Hamilton, W. J. *Mechanisms of animal behavior.* New York: John Wiley, 1966.

Marr, D. *Vision.* New York: W. H. Freeman, 1982.

Marx, J. L. Brain peptides: Is substance P a transmitter of pain signals? *Science,* 1979, *205,* 886-889.

Masin, S. C., & Vidotto, G. A magnitude estimation study of the inverted-T illusion. *Perception & Psychophysics,* 1983, *33,* 582-584.

Masini, R., Sciaky, R., & Pascarella, A. The orientation of a parallel-line texture between the verticals can modify the strength of the Poggendorff illusion. *Perception & Psychophysics,* 1992, *52,* 235-242.

Mason, J. R., & Silver, W. L. Trigeminally mediated odor aversion in starlings. *Brain Research,* 1983, *269,* 196-199.

Masterton, B., & Diamond, I. T. Hearing: Central neural mechanisms. In E. C. Carterette & M. P. Friedman (Eds.), *Handbook of perception. Volume III: Biology of perceptual systems.* New York: Academic Press, 1973.

Masterton, B., Heffner, H., & Ravizza, R. The evolution of human hearing. *Journal of the Acoustical Society of America,* 1968, *45,* 966-985.

Matin, L. Visual localization and eye movements. In K. R. Boff, L. Kaufman, & J. P. Thomas (Eds.), *Handbook of perception and human performance. Volume I: Sensory processes and perception.* New York: John Wiley, 1986.

Matin, L., Picouh, E., Stevens, J. K., Edwards, M. W., Jr., Young, D., & MacArthur, R. Oculoparalytic illusion: Visual field dependent spatial mislocalization by humans with experimentally paralyzed extraocular muscles. *Science,* 1982, *216,* 198-201.

Matthews, L. H., & Knight, M. *The senses of animals.* London: Museum Press, 1963.

Mattingly, I. G. Speech cues and sign stimuli. *American Scientist,* 1972, *60,* 327-337.

Maurer, D., & Lewis, T. L. Peripheral discrimination by three-month-old infants. *Child Development,* 1979, *50,* 276-279.

Maurer, D., & Salapatek, P. Developmental changes in the scanning of faces by young infants. *Child Development,* 1976, *47,* 523-527.

Mayer, M. Development of anisotropy in late childhood. *Vision Research,* 1977, *17,* 703-710.

Mayer, M. *Sensory perception laboratory manual.* New York: John Wiley, 1982.

Mayer, M. J., Kim, C. B. Y., Svingos, A., & Glucs, A. Foveal flicker sensitivity in healthy aging eyes. I. Compensating for pupil variation. *Journal of the Optical Society of America A,* 1988, *5,* 2201-2209.

Mazur, R. H. Aspartame—a sweet surprise. *Journal of Toxicology and Environmental Health,* 1977, *2,* 243-249.

McBurney, D. H. Effects of adaptation on human taste function. In C. Pfaffman (Ed.), *Olfaction and taste.* New York: Rockefeller University Press, 1969.

McBurney, D. H. Psychological dimensions and perceptual analyses of taste. In E. C. Carterette & M. P. Friedman (Eds.), *Handbook of perception. Volume VI, A: Tasting and smelling.* New York: Academic Press, 1978.

McBurney, D. H., Collings, V. B., & Glanz, L. M. Temperature dependence of human taste responses. *Physiology and Behavior,* 1973, *11,* 89-94.

McBurney, D. H., Levine, J. M., & Cavanaugh, P. H. Psychophysical and social ratings of human body odor. *Personality and Social Psychology Bulletin,* 1977, *3,* 135-138.

McBurney, D. H., & Pfaffmann, C. Gustatory adaptation to saliva and sodium chloride. *Journal of Experimental Psychology,* 1963, *65,* 523-529.

McBurney, D. H., & Shick, T. R. Taste and water taste of twenty-six compounds for man. *Perception & Psychophysics,* 1971, *10,* 249-252.

McBurney, D. H., Smith, D. V., & Shick, T. R. Gustatory cross-adaptation: Sourness and bitterness. *Perception & Psychophysics,* 1972, *11,* 228-232.

McCleod, R. W., & Ross, H. E. Optic-flow and cognitive factors in time-to-collision estimates. *Perception,* 1983, *12,* 417-423.

McClintic, J. R. *Physiology of the human body* (2nd ed.). New York: John Wiley, 1978.

McClintock, M. K. Menstrual synchrony and suppression. *Nature,* 1971, *229,* 244-245.

McClintock, M. K. Estrous synchrony: Modulation of ovarian cycle length by female pheromones. *Physiology & Behavior,* 1984, *32,* 701-705.

McCloskey, M. Intuitive physics. *Scientific American,* 1983, *248,* 122-130. (*a*)

McCloskey, M. Naïve theories of motion. In D. Gentner & A. L. Stevens (Eds.), *Mental models.* Hillsdale, N.J.: Lawrence Erlbaum, 1983. (*b*)

McCloskey, M., Caramazza, A., & Green, B. Curvilinear motion in the absence of external forces: Naïve beliefs about the motions of objects. *Science,* 1980, *210,* 1139-1141.

McCloskey, M., Washburn, A., & Felch, L. Intuitive physics: The straight-down belief and its origin. *Journal of Experimental Psychology: Learning, Memory, and Cognition,* 1983, *9,* 636-649.

McCollough, C. Color adaptation of edge-detectors in the human visual system. *Science,* 1965, *149,* 1115-1116.

McConkie, G. W., Kerr, P. W., Reddix, M. D., Zola, D., & Jacobs, A. M. Eye movement control during reading: II. Frequency of refixating a word. *Perception & Psychophysics,* 1989, *46,* 245-253.

McCready, D. Moon illusion redescribed. *Perception & Psychophysics,* 1986, *39,* 64-72.

McFadden, D., & Plattsmier, H. S. Aspirin can potentiate the temporary hearing loss induced by intense sounds. *Hearing Research,* 1983, *9,* 295-316.

McGivern, R. F., & Berntson, G. G. Mediation of diurnal fluctuations in pain sensitivity in the rat by food intake patterns: Reversal by naloxone. *Science,* 1980, *210,* 210-211.

McGurk, H., & MacDonald, J. Hearing lips and seeing voices. *Nature,* 1976, *264,* 746-748.

McKee, S. P., & Westheimer, G. Improvement in vernier acuity with practice. *Perception & Psychophysics,* 1978, *24,* 258-262.

McKenzie, B. E., Tootell, H. E., & Day, R. H. Development of visual size constancy during the first year of human infancy. *Developmental Psychology,* 1980, *16,* 163-174.

Meltzoff, A. N. Imitation of televised models by infants. *Child Development,* 1988, *59,* 1221-1229.

Melzack, R. Phantom limbs. *Psychology Today,* 1970, *4,* 63-68.

Melzack, R. *The puzzle of pain.* New York: Basic Books, 1973.

Melzack, R. Phantom limbs. *Scientific American,* April 1992, 120-126.

Melzack, R., & Wall, P. D. Pain mechanisms: A new theory. *Science,* 1965, *150,* 971-979.

Merbes, S. L., & Nathans, J. Absorption spectra of human cone pigments. *Nature,* 1992, *356,* 433-435.

Merigan W. H., & Eskin, T. A. Spatio-temporal vision of macaques with severe loss of Pb retinal ganglion cells. *Vision Research,* 1986, *26,* 1751-1761.

Mermelstein, R., Banks, W., & Prinzmetal, W. Figural goodness effects in perception and memory. *Perception & Psychophysics,* 1979, *26,* 472-480.

Mescavage, A. A., Heimer, W. I., Tatz, S. J., & Runyon, R. P. *Time estimation as a function of rate of stimulus change.* Paper presented at the annual meeting of the Eastern Psychological Association, New York, April, 1971.

Messing, R. B., & Campbell, B. A. Summation of pain produced in different anatomical regions. *Perception & Psychophysics,* 1971, *10,* 225-228.

Metalis, S. A., & Hess, E. H. Pupillary response/semantic differential scale relationships. *Journal of Research in Personality,* 1982, *16,* 201-216.

Michael, C. R. Retinal processing of visual images. *Scientific American,* 1969, *220,* 104-114.

Michael, C. R. Color vision mechanisms in monkey striate cortex: Dual-opponent cells with concentric receptive fields. *Journal of Neurophysiology,* 1978, *41,* 572-588. (*a*)

Michael, C. R. Color vision mechanisms in monkey striate cortex: Simple cells with dual opponent-color receptive fields. *Journal of Neurophysiology,* 1978, *41,* 1233-1249. (*b*)

Michael, R. P., Bonsall, R. W., & Warner, P. Human vaginal secretions: Volatile fatty acid content. *Science,* 1974, *186,* 1217-1219.

Michael, R. P., & Keverne, E. B. Pheromones in the communication of sexual status in primates. *Nature,* 1968, *218,* 746-749.

Michels, K. M., & Schumacher, A. W. Color vision in tree squirrels. *Psychonomic Science,* 1968, *10,* 7-8.

Michon, J. Tapping regularity as a measure of perceptual motor load. *Ergonomics,* 1966, *9,* 401-412.

Miczek, K. A., Thompson, M. L., & Shuster, L. Opioid-like analgesia in defeated mice. *Science,* 1982, *215,* 1520-1522.

Middlebrooks, J. C., Clock, A. E., Xu, L., & Green, D. M. A panoramic code for sound location by cortical neurons. *Science,* 1994, *264,* 842-844.

Milewski, A. E. Infant's discrimination of internal and external pattern elements. *Journal of Experimental Child Psychology,* 1976, *22,* 229-246.

Miller, G. A. The masking of speech. *Psychological Bulletin,* 1947, *44,* 105-129.

Miller, J. D., Weir, C. C., Pastore, R., Kelley, W. J., & Dooling, R. J. Discrimination and labelling of noise-burst sequences with varying noise-lead times: An example of categorical perception. *Journal of the Acoustical Society of America,* 1976, *60,* 410-417.

Milne, L. J., & Milne, M. *The senses of animals and men.* New York: Atheneum, 1967.

Mishkin, M., Ungerleider, L. G., & Macko, K. A. Object vision and spatial vision: Two cortical pathways. *Trends in Neuroscience,* 1983, *6,* 414-417.

Mistretta, C. M. Developmental neurobiology of the taste system. In T. V. Getchell, R. L. Doty, L. M. Bartoshuk, & J. B. Snow, Jr. (Eds.), *Smell and taste in health and disease.* New York: Raven Press, 1991.

Mitchell, C. T., & Davis, R. The perception of time in scale model environments. *Perception,* 1987, *16,* 5-16.

Mitchell, D. E. Effect of early visual experience on the development of certain perceptual abilities in animals and man. In R. D. Walk & H. L. Pick (Eds.), *Perception and experience.* New York: Plenum, 1978.

Mitchell, D. E. The influence of early visual experience on visual perception. In C. S. Harris (Ed.), *Visual coding and adaptability.* Hillsdale, N.J.: Lawrence Erlbaum, 1980.

Mitchell, D. E., Reardon, J., & Muir, D. W. Interocular transfer of the motion aftereffect in normal and stereoblind observers. *Experimental Brain Research,* 1975, *22,* 163-173.

Mitchell, D. E., & Ware, C. Interocular transfer of a visual aftereffect in normal and stereoblind humans. *Journal of Physiology,* 1974, *263,* 707-721.

Miyazaki, K. Musical pitch identification by absolute pitch possessors. *Perception & Psychophysics,* 1988, *44,* 501-512.

Mo, S. S. Judgment of temporal duration as a function of numerosity. *Psychonomic Science*, 1971, *24*, 71-72.

Monahan, C. B., Kendall, R. A., & Carterette, E. C. The effect of melodic and temporal contour on recognition memory for pitch change. *Perception & Psychophysics*, 1987, *41*, 576-600.

Moncrieff, R. W. *The chemical senses.* London: Leonard Hill, 1951.

Moncrieff, R. W. *Odour preferences.* New York: John Wiley, 1966.

Money, K. E., & Cheung, B. S. Another function of the inner ear: Facilitation of the emetic response to poisons. *Aviation, Space, and Environmental Medicine*, 1983, *54*, 208-211.

Montagna, W. The skin. *Scientific American*, 1965, *212*, 56-66.

Montgomery, J. C., & MacDonald, J. A. Sensory tuning of lateral line receptors in antarctic fish to the movements of planktonic prey. *Science, 1987, 235*, 195-196.

Moore, B. C. J. *Introduction to the psychology of hearing* (3rd ed.). New York: Academic Press, 1989.

Moore, B. C. J. Hearing. In A. M. Colman (Ed.), *Companion encyclopedia of psychology*. London: Routledge, 1994.

Morse, P. A., & Snowden, C. T. An investigation of categorical speech discrimination by rhesus monkeys. *Perception & Psychophysics*, 1975, *17*, 9-16.

Mosel, J. N., & Kantrowitz, G. The effect of monosodium glutamate on acuity to the primary tastes. *American Journal of Psychology*, 1952, *65*, 573-579.

Movshon, J. A., & Newsome, W. T. Neural foundations of visual motion perception. *Current Directions in Psychological Science*, 1992, *1*, 35-39.

Mozell, M. M. Olfactory discrimination: Electrophysiological spatiotemporal basis. *Science, 1964, 143*, 1336-1337.

Mozell, M. M. The spatiotemporal analysis of odorants at the level of the olfactory receptor sheet. *Journal of General Physiology*, 1966, *50*, 25-41.

Mozell, M. M. Olfaction. In J. W. Kling & L. A. Riggs (Eds.), *Experimental psychology* (3rd ed.). New York: Holt, Rinehart and Winston, 1971.

Mueller, C. G. *Sensory psychology.* Englewood Cliffs, N.J.: Prentice Hall, 1965.

Mueller, C. G., & Rudolph, M. *Light and vision.* New York: Time, Inc., 1966.

Muir, D. W., & Mitchell, D. E. Visual resolution and experience: Acuity deficits in cats following early selective visual deprivation. *Science, 1973, 180*, 420-422.

Mulligan, R. M., & Schiffman, H. R. Temporal experiences as a function of organization in memory. *Bulletin of the Psychonomic Society*, 1979, *14*, 417-420.

Murphy, C. Olfactory psychophysics. In T. E. Finger & W. L. Silver (Eds.), *Neurobiology of taste and smell.* New York: John Wiley, 1987.

Murphy, C., & Gilmore, M. M. Quality-specific effects of aging on the human taste system. *Perception & Psychophysics*, 1989, *45*, 121-128.

Murphy, M. R., & Schneider, G. E. Olfactory bulb removal eliminates mating behavior in the male golden hamster. *Science, 1969, 167*, 302-303.

Nachman, M. Taste preferences for sodium salts by adrenalectomized rats. *Journal of Comparative and Physiological Psychology*, 1962, *55*, 1124-1129.

Nafe, J. P. The pressure, pain, and temperature senses. In C. A. Murchison (Ed.), *A handbook of general experimental psychology*, (Chap. 20). Worcester, Mass.: Clark University Press, 1934.

Nathans, J., Piantanida, T. P., Eddy, R. L., Shows, T. B., & Hogness, D. S. Molecular genetics of inherited variation in human color vision. *Science, 1986, 232*, 203-210.

Nathans, J., Thomas, D., & Hogness, D. S. Molecular genetics of human color vision: The genes encoding blue, green, and red pigments. *Science, 1986, 232*, 193-202.

Nanez, J., Sr. Perception of impending collision in 3- to 6-week-old infants. *Infant Behavior and Development*, 1988, *11*, 447-463.

Nazir, T., Heller, D., & Sussman, C. Letter visibility and word recognition: The optical viewing position in printed words. *Perception & Psychophysics*, 1992, *52*, 315-328.

Neale, J. H., Barker, J. L., Uhl, G. R., & Snyder, S. H. Enkephalin-containing neurons visualized in spinal cord cell cultures. *Science, 1978, 201*, 467-469.

Neill, W. T. Decision processes in selective attention: Response priming in the Stroop color-word task. *Perception & Psychophysics*, 1978, *23*, 80-84.

Neisser, U. The processes of vision. *Scientific American*, 1968, *219*, 204-214.

Nemire, K., & Cohen, M. M. Visual and somesthetic influences on postural orientation in the median plane. *Perception & Psychophysics*, 1993, *53*, 106-116.

Nerger, J. L., & Cicerone, C. M. The ratio of L cones to M cones in the human parafoveal retina. *Vision Research*, 1992, *32*, 879-888.

Newton, I. *Optiks, or a treatise of the reflections, refractions, inflections & colours of light* (1704) (4th ed.). New York: Dover, 1952.

Nicolaus, L. K., Cassel, J. F., Carlson, R. B., & Gustavson, C. R. Taste-aversion conditioning of crows to control predation on eggs. *Science, 1983, 220*, 212-214.

Norcia, A. M., & Tyler, C. W. Spatial frequency sweep VEP: Visual acuity during the first year of life. *Vision Research*, 1985, *25*, 1399-1408.

Novick, A. Echolocation in bats: Some aspects of pulse design. *American Scientist*, 1971, *59*, 198-209.

Nowlis, G. H., Frank, M. E., & Pfaffmann, C. Specificity of acquired aversions to taste qualities in hamsters and rats. *Journal of Comparative and Physiological Psychology*, 1980, *94*, 932-942.

Nygaard, L. C., Sommers, M. S., & Pisoni, D. B. Speech perception as talker-contingent process. *Psychological Science*, 1994, *5*, 42-46.

Nyström, M., & Hansson, S. B. Interaction between early experience and depth avoidance in young eider ducks (*Somateria* molissima L.). *Behavior,* 1974, *48,* 303–314.

Ogle, K. N. The optical space sense. In H. Davson (Ed.), *The eye.* New York: Academic Press, 1962.

Ohzawa, I., DeAngelis, G. C., & Freeman, R. D. Stereoscopic depth discrimination in the visual cortex: Neurons ideally suited as disparity detectors. *Science,* 1990, *249,* 1037–1041.

Oldfield, S. R., & Parker, S. P. A. Acuity of sound localisation: A topography of auditory space. III. Monaural hearing conditions. *Perception,* 1986, *15,* 67–81.

Olson, C. R., & Freeman, R. D. Progressive changes in kitten striate cortex during monocular vision. *Journal of Neurophysiology,* 1975, *38,* 26–32.

Olzak, L. A., & Thomas, J. P. Seeing spatial patterns. In K. R. Boff, L. Kaufman, & J. P. Thomas (Eds.), *Handbook of perception and human performance. Volume I: Sensory processes and perception.* New York: John Wiley, 1986.

O'Mahoney, M., Kingsley, L., Harji, A., & Davies, M. What sensation signals the salt taste threshold? *Chemical Senses and Flavor,* 1976, *2,* 177–188.

O'Mahoney, M., & Wingate, P. The effect of interstimulus procedures on salt taste intensity functions. *Perception & Psychophysics,* 1974, *16,* 494–502.

Orchard, L. N., & Stern, J. A. Blinks as an index of cognitive activity during reading. *Integrative Physiological and Behavioral Science,* 1991, *26,* 108–116.

Ornstein, R. E. *On the experience of time.* Baltimore, Md.: Penguin Books, 1969.

Osgood, C. E. *Method and theory in experimental psychology.* New York: Oxford University Press, 1953.

Oster, G. Auditory beats in the brain. *Scientific American,* 1973, *229,* 94–102.

Owens, D. A., & Wolf-Kelly, K. Near work, visual fatigue, and variations of oculomotor tonus. *Investigative Ophthalmology and Visual Science,* 1987, *28,* 743–749.

Owsley, C., Sekuler, R., & Siemsen, D. Contrast sensitivity throughout adulthood. *Vision Research,* 1983, *23,* 689–699.

Oyama, T. Figure-ground dominance as a function of sector angle, brightness, hue, and orientation. *Journal of Experimental Psychology,* 1960, *60,* 299–305.

Palmer, S. E. The effects of contextual scenes on the identification of objects. *Memory and Cognition,* 1975, *3,* 519–526.

Palmer, E. E., & Hemenway, K. Orientation and symmetry: Effects of multiple, rotational, and near symmetries. *Journal of Experimental Psychology: Human Perception and Performance,* 1978, *4,* 691–702.

Palmeri, T. J., Goldinger, S. D., & Pisoni, D. B. Episodic encoding or voice attributes and recognition memory for spoken words. *Journal of Experimental Psychology: Learning, Memory, and Cognition,* 1993, *19,* 309–328.

Palmerino, C. C., Rusiniak, K. W., & Garcia, J. Flavor-illness aversions: The peculiar roles of odor and taste in memory for poison. *Science,* 1980, *208,* 753–755.

Papanicolaou, A. C., Schmidt, A. C., Moore, B. D., & Eisenberg, H. M. Cerebral activation patterns in an arithmetic and a visuospatial processing task. *International Journal of Neuroscience,* 1983, *20,* 283–288.

Parker, D. E. The vestibular apparatus. *Scientific American,* 1980, *243,* 118–135.

Parks, T. E. Post-retinal visual storage. *American Journal of Psychology,* 1965, *78,* 145–147.

Parks, T. E. Illusory figures: A (mostly) atheoretical review. *Psychological Bulletin,* 1984, *95,* 282–300.

Pasternak, G. W., Childers, S. R., & Snyder, S. H. Opiate analgesia: Evidence for mediation by a subpopulation of opiate receptors. *Science,* 1980, *208,* 514–516.

Pastore, N. *Selective history of theories of visual perception.* New York: Oxford University Press, 1971.

Patterson, J., & Deffenbacher, K. Haptic perception of the Müller-Lyer illusion by the blind. *Perceptual and Motor Skills,* 1972, *35,* 819–824.

Patterson, R. L. S. Identification of 3α-hydroxy-5α-androst-16-ene as the musk odour component of boar submaxillary salivary gland and its relationship to the sex odour taint in pork meat. *Journal of the Science of Food Agriculture,* 1968, *19,* 434–438.

Pearlman, A. L., Birch, J., & Meadows, J. C. Cerebral color blindness: An acquired defect in hue discrimination. *Annals of Neurology,* 1979, *5,* 253–261.

Penfield, W., & Rasmussen, I. *The cerebral cortex of man.* New York: Macmillan, 1950.

Petrig, B., Julesz, B., Kropfl, W., Baumgartner, G., & Ankliker, M. Development of stereopsis and cortical binocularity in human infants: Electrophysiological evidence. *Science,* 1981, *213,* 1402–1405.

Petry, S., & Meyer, G. E. *The perception of illusory contours.* New York: Springer-Verlag, 1987.

Pettigrew, J. D., & Freeman, R. D. Visual experience without lines: Effect on developing cortical neurons. *Science,* 1973, *182,* 599–601.

Pfaff, D. Effects of temperature and time of day on time judgments. *Journal of Experimental Psychology,* 1968, *76,* 419–422.

Pfaffmann, C. The sense of taste. In J. Field, H. W. Magoun, & V. E. Hall (Eds.), *Handbook of physiology, Volume I.* Washington, D.C.: American Physiological Society, 1959.

Pfaffmann, C. Taste stimulation and preference behavior. In Y. Zotterman (Ed.), *Olfaction and taste.* New York: Macmillan, 1963.

Pfaffmann, C. Taste, its sensory and motivating properties. *American Scientist,* 1964, *52,* 187–206.

Pfaffmann, C. Specificity of the sweet receptors of the squirrel monkeys. In *Chemical senses and flavor.* Dordrecht-Holland: D. Reidel Co., 1974.

Pfaffmann, C. The vertebrate phylogeny, neural code, and integrative processes of taste. In E. C. Carterette & M. P. Friedman (Eds.), *Handbook of perception, Volume VI, A: Tasting and smelling.* New York: Academic Press, 1978.

Pfaffmann, C., Frank, M., Bartoshuk, L. M., & Snell, T. C. Coding gustatory information in the squirrel monkey chorda tympani. In J. M. Sprague & A. N. Epstein (Eds.), *Progress in psychobiology and physiological psychology, Volume 6.* New York: Academic Press, 1976.

Pickles, J. O. *An introduction to the physiology of hearing* (2nd ed.). New York, Academic Press, 1988.

Piggins, D. J., Kingham, J. R., & Holmes, S. M. Colour, colour saturation, and pattern induced by intermittent illumination: An initial study. *British Journal of Physiological Optics,* 1972, *27,* 120–125.

Pinker, S. *The language instinct.* New York: Morrow, 1994.

Poggio, G. F. Stereoscopic processing in monkey visual cortex: A review. In T. V. Papathomas, C. Chubb, A. Gorea, & E. Kowler (Eds.), *Early vision and beyond.* Cambridge, MA.: MIT Press, 1995.

Poggio, T., Fahle, M., & Edelman, S. Fast perceptual learning in visual hyperacuity. *Science,* 1992, *256,* 1018–1021.

Poggio, G. F., & Fisher, B. Binocular interaction and depth sensitivity in the striate and prestriate cortex of behaving rhesus monkey. *Journal of Neurophysiology,* 1977, *40,* 1392–1405.

Poggio, G. F., & Poggio, T. The analysis of stereopsis. *Annual Review of Neuroscience,* 1984, *7,* 379–412.

Pollack, I., & Pickett, J. M. The intelligibility of excerpts from conversational speech. *Language & Speech,* 1964, *6,* 165–171.

Pollack, R. H. A theoretical note on the aging of the visual system. *Perception & Psychophysics,* 1978, *23,* 94–95.

Pollack, R. H., & Jaeger, T. B. The effect of lightness contrast on the colored Müller-Lyer illusion. *Perception & Psychophysics,* 1991, *50,* 225–229.

Polyak, S. *The vertebrate visual system.* Chicago: University of Chicago Press, 1957.

Pons, T. P., Garraghty, P. E., Friedman, D. P., & Mishkin, M. Physiological evidence of serial processing in somatosensory cortex. *Science,* 1987, *237,* 417–420.

Post, R. B., & Leibowitz, H. W. A revised analysis of the role of efference in motion perception. *Perception,* 1985, *14,* 631–643.

Postman, L., & Egan, J. P. *Experimental psychology.* New York: Harper & Row, 1949.

Poulton, E. C. Geometric illusions in reading graphs. *Perception & Psychophysics,* 1985, *37,* 543–548.

Povel, D. J., & Essens, P. Perception of temporal patterns. *Music Perception,* 1985, *2,* 411–440.

Power, R. P. The dominance of touch by vision: Sometimes incomplete. *Perception,* 1980, *9,* 457–466.

Poynter, W. D., & Homa, D. Duration judgment and the experience of time. *Perception & Psychophysics,* 1983, *33,* 548–560.

Prah, J. D., & Benignus, V. A. Trigeminal, sensitivity to contact chemical-stimulation—A new method and some results. *Perception & Psychophysics,* 1984, *35,* 65–68.

Pressey, A. W., & Moro, T. L. An explanation of Cooper and Runyan's results on the Müller-Lyer illusion. *Perceptual and Motor Skills,* 1971, *32,* 564–566.

Pressey, A. W., & Pressey, C. A. Attentive fields are related to focal and contextual features: A study of Müller-Lyer distortions. *Perception and Psychophysics,* 1992, *51,* 423–436.

Preti, G., Cutler, W. B., Garcia, C. R., Huggins, G. R., & Lawley, H. J. Human axillary secretions influence women's menstrual cycles: The role of donor extract of females. *Hormones and Behavior,* 1986, *20,* 474–482.

Priestly, J. B. *Man and time.* New York: Dell, 1968.

Prinzmetal, R., & Gettleman, L. Vertical–horizontal illusion: One eye is better than two. *Perception & Psychophysics,* 1993, *53,* 81–88.

Pritchard, R. M., Heron, W., & Hebb, D. O. Visual perception approached by the method of stabilized images. *Canadian Journal of Psychology,* 1960, *14,* 67–77.

Prosen, C. A., Moody, D. B., Stebbins, W. C., & Hawkins, J. E., Jr. Auditory intensity discrimination after selective loss of cochlear outer hair cells. *Science,* 1981, *212,* 1286–1288.

Pugh, E. N., Jr. Vision: Physics and retinal physiology. In R. C. Atkinson, R. J. Herrnstein, G. Lindzey, & R. D. Luce (Eds.), *Stevens' handbook of experimental psychology* (Vol. 1) (2nd ed.). New York: John Wiley, 1988.

Pugliese, L. Auto-random-dot stereograms. *Optics and Photonics News,* 1991, *59,* 62.

Purcell, D. G., & Stewart, A. L. The face-detection effect: Configuration enhances detection. *Perception & Psychophysics,* 1988, *43,* 355–366.

Purghé, F., & Coren, S. Subjective contours 1900–1990: Research trends and bibliography. *Perception & Psychophysics,* 1992, *51,* 291–304.

Purghé, F. Illusory contours from pictorially three-dimensional inducing elements: Counterevidence for Parks and Rock's example. *Perception,* 1993, *22,* 809–818.

Quadagno, D. M., Shubeita, H. E., Deck, J., & Francoeur, D. Influence of male social contacts, exercise and all female living conditions on the menstrual cycle. *Psychoneuroendochronology,* 1981, *6,* 239–244.

Rabin, M. D. Experience facilitates olfactory quality discrimination. *Perception & Psychophysics,* 1988, *44,* 532–540.

Radinsky, L. Cerebral clues. *Natural History,* 1976, *55,* 54–59.

Rakerd, B. Vowels in consonantal context are perceived more linguistically than are isolated vowels: Evidence from an individual differences scaling study. *Perception & Psychophysics,* 1984, *35,* 123–136.

Ramachandran, V. S. Blind spots. *Scientific American,* 1992, *266,* 86–91.

Ramachandran, V. S. Behavioral and magnetoencephalographic correlates of plasticity in the adult human brain. *Proceedings of the National Academy of Sciences*, 1993, *90,* 10,413-10,420.

Rammsayer, T. H., & Lima, S. D. Duration discrimination of filled and empty auditory intervals: Cognitive and perceptual factors. *Perception & Psychophysics*, 1991, *50,* 565-574.

Ratliff, F. Contour and contrast. *Scientific American*, 1972, *226,* 90-101.

Ratliff, F., & Hartline, H. K. The responses of *Limulus* optic nerve fibers to patterns of illumination on the retinal mosaic. *Journal of General Physiology*, 1959, *42,* 1241-1255.

Raviola, E., & Wiesel, T. N. An animal model of myopia. *New England Journal of Medicine*, 1985, *312,* 1609-1615.

Raymond, J. E. The interaction of target size and background pattern on perceived velocity during visual tracking. *Perception & Psychophysics*, 1988, *43,* 425-430.

Reason, J. T., & Brand, J. J. *Motion sickness.* New York: Academic Press, 1975.

Reed, C. M., Doherty, M. J., Braida, L. D., & Durlach, N. I. Analytic study of the Tadoma method: Further experiments with inexperienced observers. *Journal of Speech and Hearing Research*, 1982, *25,* 216-223.

Regan, D., & Beverley, K. I. Visually guided locomotion: Psychophysical evidence for a neural mechanism sensitive to flow patterns. *Science*, 1979, *205,* 311-313.

Regan, D., & Beverley, K. I. How do we avoid confounding the direction we are looking and the direction we are moving. *Science*, 1982, *215,* 194-196.

Regan, D., Beverley, K. I., & Cynader, M. The visual perception of motion in depth. *Scientific American*, 1979, *241,* 136-151.

Regan, D. M., Kaufman, L., & Lincoln, J. Motion in depth and visual acceleration. In K. R. Boff, L. Kaufman, & J. P. Thomas (Eds.), *Handbook of perception and human performance. Volume I: Sensory processes and perception.* New York: John Wiley, 1986.

Remez, R. E., Rubin, P. E., Pisoni, D. B. & Carrell, T. D. Speech perception without traditional speech cues. *Science*, 1981, *212,* 947-950.

Restle, F. Moon illusion explained on the basis of relative size. *Science*, 1970, *167,* 1092-1096.

Reymond, L. Spatial visual acuity of the eagle *Aquila audax:* A behavioral, optical and anatomical investigation. *Vision Research*, 1985, *25,* 1477-1491.

Rice, C. E. Human echo perception. *Science*, 1967, *155,* 656-664.

Richards, W. Stereopsis and stereoblindness. *Experimental Brain Research*, 1970, *10,* 380-388.

Richards, W. Anomalus stereoscopic depth perception. *Journal of the Optical Society of America*, 1971, *61,* 410-414.

Richards, W., & Regan, D. A stereo field map with implications for disparity processing. *Investigative Ophthalmology*, 1973, *12,* 904-909.

Richter, C. P. Salt taste thresholds of normal and adrenalectomized rats. *Endocrinology*, 1939, *24,* 367-371.

Richter, C. P. Total self-regulatory functions in animals and human beings. *Harvey Lectures*, 1942, *38,* 63-103.

Riggs, L. A. Visual acuity. In C. H. Graham (Ed.), *Vision and visual perception.* New York: John Wiley, 1965.

Riggs, L. A. The ''looks'' of Helmholtz. *Perception & Psychophysics*, 1967, *2,* 1-13.

Riggs, L. A., Volkmann, F. C., & Moore, R. K. Suppression of the blackout due to blinks. *Vision Research*, 1981, *21,* 1075-1079.

Rock, I. *Orientation and form.* New York: Academic Press, 1973.

Rock, I. The perception of disoriented figures. *Scientific American*, 1974, *230,* 78-85.

Rock, I. *An introduction to perception.* New York: Macmillan, 1975.

Rock, I. *The logic of perception.* Cambridge, Mass.: Bradford Books/M.I.T. Press, 1983.

Rock, I. *Perception.* New York: Scientific American Library, W.H. Freeman, 1984.

Rock, I. The description and analysis of object and event perception. In K. R. Boff, L. Kaufman, & J. P. Thomas (Eds.), *Handbook of perception and human performance. Volume II: Cognitive processes and performance.* New York: John Wiley, 1986.

Rock, I., & Harris, C. S. Vision and touch. *Scientific American*, 1967, *216,* 96-104.

Rock, I., & Kauffman, L. The moon illusion, II. *Science*, 1962, *136,* 1023-1031.

Rock, I., & Palmer, S. The legacy of Gestalt psychology. *Scientific American*, 1990, *263,* 84-90.

Rock, I., & Victor, J. Vision and touch: An experimentally created conflict between the senses. *Science*, 1964, *143,* 594-596.

Rodgers, W., & Rozin, P. Novel food preferences in thiamine-deficient rats. *Journal of Comparative and Physiological Psychology*, 1966, *61,* 1-4.

Roederer, J. G. *Introduction to the physics and psychophysics of music.* New York: Springer-Verlag, 1973.

Rogel, M. A critical evaluation of the possibility of higher primate reproductive and sexual pheromones. *Psychological Bulletin.* 1978, *85,* 810-830.

Rogers, W. L., & Bregman, A. S. An experimental evaluation of three theories of auditory stream segregation. *Perception & Psychophysics*, 1993, *53,* 179-189.

Rollman, G. B., & Harris, G. The detectability, discriminability, and perceived magnitude of painful electrical shock. *Perception & Psychophysics*, 1987, *42,* 257-268.

Root, A. In Metropolitan Diary (R. Alexander, Ed.), *The New York Times*, November 30, 1994, p. C2.

Rose, J. E., Brugge, J. F., Anderson, D. J., & Hind, J. E. Phase-locked response to low-frequency tones in single auditory nerve fibers of the squirrel monkey. *Journal of Neurophysiology*, 1967, *30,* 769-793.

Rose, L., Yinon, U., & Belkin, M. Myopia induced in cats deprived of distance vision during development. *Vision Research,* 1974, *14,* 1029-1032.

Rosen, R. C., Schiffman, H. R., & Cohen, A. S. Behavior modification and the treatment of myopia. *Behavior Modification,* 1984, *8,* 131-154.

Rosen, R. C., Schiffman, H. R., & Myers, H. Behavioral treatment of myopia: Refractive error and acuity changes in relation to axial length and intraocular pressure. *American Journal of Optometry and Physiological Optics,* 1984, *61,* 100-105.

Rosenblatt, F. *Principles of neurodynamics: Perceptrons and the theory of brain mechanism.* Washington, D.C.: Spartan Books, 1962.

Rosenblum, L. A., & Cross, H. A. Performance of neonatal monkeys in the visual-cliff situation. *American Journal of Psychology,* 1963, *76,* 318-320.

Rosenblum, L. D., & Fowler, C. A. Audiovisual investigation of the loudness-effort effect for speech and nonspeech events. *Journal of Experimental Psychology: Human Perception and Performance,* 1991, *17,* 976-985.

Rosenzweig, M. R. Representations of the two ears at the auditory cortex. *American Journal of Psychology,* 1951, *67,* 147-158.

Rosenzweig, M. R. Cortical correlates of auditory localization and of related perceptual phenomena. *Journal of Comparative and Physiological Psychology,* 1954, *47,* 269-276.

Rosenzweig, M. R. Auditory localization. *Scientific American,* 1961, *205,* 132-142.

Rosenzweig, M. R., & Leiman, A. L. *Physiological psychology.* Lexington, Mass.: D. C. Heath, 1982.

Rossi, P. J. Adaptation and negative aftereffect to lateral optical displacement in newly hatched chicks. *Science,* 1968, *160,* 430-432.

Rossi, P. J. Primacy of the negative aftereffect over positive adaptation in prism adaptation with newly hatched chicks. *Developmental Psychobiology,* 1969, *2,* 43-53.

Rothblat, L. A., & Schwartz, M. L. Altered early environment: Effects on the brain and visual behavior. In R. D. Walk & H. L. Pick (Eds.), *Perception and experience.* New York: Plenum, 1978.

Rovee-Collier, C. The capacity for long-term memory in infancy. *Current Directions in Psychological Science,* 1993, *2,* 130-135.

Rovee-Collier, C., & Hayne, H. Reactivation of infant memory: Implications for cognitive development. *Advances in Child Development and Behavior,* 1987, *20,* 185-238.

Rowell, T. E. Agonistic noises of the rhesus monkeys (*Macaca mulatta*). *Symposium of the Zoological Society of London,* 1962, *8,* 91-96.

Rozin, P., Gruss, L., & Berk, G. Reversal of innate aversions: Attempts to induce a preference for chili peppers in rats. *Journal of Comparative and Physiological Psychology,* 1979, *93,* 1001-1014.

Rubin, D. S., Groth, E., & Goldsmith, D. J. Olfactory cuing of autobiographical memory. *American Journal of Psychology,* 1984, *97,* 493-507.

Rubin, E. Figure and ground. In D. C. Beardslee & M. Wertheimer (Eds.), *Readings in perception.* New York: D. Van Nostrand, 1958. Based on an abridged translation by Michael Wertheimer of pp. 35-101 of Rubin, E., *Visuell wahrgenommene Figuren* (translated by Peter Collett into German from the Danish *Synsoplevede Figurer,* Copenhagen: Gyldendalske, 1915). Copenhagen: Gyldendalske, 1921.

Rubin, M. L., & Walls, G. L. *Fundamentals of visual science.* Springfield, Ill.: Charles C. Thomas, 1969.

Ruch, T. C., Patton, H. B., Woodbury, J. W., & Tawe, A. L. (Eds.), *Neurophysiology* (2nd Ed.). Philadelphia: W. B. Saunders, 1965.

Ruckmick, C. A. A new classification of tonal qualities. *Psychological Review,* 1929, *36,* 172-180.

Rumelhart, D. E., & McClelland, J. L. *Parallel distributed processing: Explorations in the microstructure of cognition. 1. Foundations.* Cambridge, Mass.: M.I.T. Press, 1986.

Runeson, S., & Frykholm, G. Kinematic specifications of dynamics as an informational basis for person-and-action perception: Expectation, gender recognition, and deceptive intention. *Journal of Experimental Psychology: General,* 1983, *112,* 585-615.

Runyon, R. P., & Cooper, M. R. Enhancement of Sander illusion in minimal form. *Perception & Psychophysics,* 1979, *8,* 110-111.

Rushton, W. A. H. Visual pigments in man. *Scientific American,* 1962, *207,* 120-132.

Russell, M. J. Human olfactory communication. *Nature,* 1976, *260,* 520-522.

Russell, M. J., Switz, G. M., & Thompson, K. Olfactory influence on the human menstrual cycle. *Pharmacology, Biochemistry and Behavior,* 1980, *13,* 737-738.

Rymer, W. Z., & D'Almeida, A. Joint position sense: The effects of muscle contraction. *Brain,* 1980, *103,* 1-22.

Sacks, O. A neurologist's notebook. *The New Yorker,* May 10, 1993, pp. 59-73.

Sacks, O. *An anthropologist on Mars.* New York: Knopf, 1995.

Sacks, O., & Wasserman, R. The case of the colorblind painter. *New York Review of Books,* Nov. 19, 1987, 25-34.

Sadza, K. J., & de Weert, C. M. M. Influence of color and luminance on the Müller-Lyer illusion. *Perception & Psychophysics,* 1984, *35,* 214-220.

Safire, W. On language. *The New York Times Magazine,* May 27, 1979, pp. 9-10.

Salapatek, P. *The visual investigation of geometric pattern by one- and two-month-old infants.* Paper read at the annual meeting of the American Association for the Advancement of Science, Boston, December, 1969.

Salapatek, P. Pattern perception in early infancy. In L. B. Cohen & P. Salapatek (Eds.), *Infant perception: From sensation to cognition, Volume I.* New York: Academic Press, 1975.

Salapatek, P., & Kessen, W. Visual scanning of triangles by the human newborn. *Journal of Experimental Child Psychology,* 1966, *3,* 113–122.

Salapatek, P., & Kessen, W. Prolonged investigation of a plane geometric triangle by the human newborn. *Journal of Experimental Child Psychology,* 1973, *15,* 22–29.

Saldaña, H. M., & Rosenblum, L. D. Visual influences on auditory pluck and bow judgments. *Perception & Psychophysics,* 1993, *54,* 406–416.

Salzman, C. D., & Newsome, W. T. Neural mechanisms for forming a perceptual decision. *Science,* 1994, *264,* 231–237.

Samuel, A. G. Red herring detectors and speech perception: In defense of selective adaptation. *Cognitive Psychology,* 1986, *18,* 452–499.

Samuel, A. G. Insights from a failure of selective adaptation: Syllable-initial and syllable-final consonants are different. *Perception & Psychophysics,* 1989, *45,* 485–493.

Samuels, C. A., Butterworth, G., Roberts, T., Graupner, L., & Hole, G. Facial aesthetics: Babies prefer attractiveness to symmetry. *Perception,* 1994, *23,* 823–831.

Sawusch, J. R., & Jusczyk, P. W. Adaptation and contrast in the perception of voicing. *Journal of Experimental Psychology: Human Perception and Performance,* 1981, *7,* 408–421.

Scariano, A. Where time comes from. *The New York Times* (Book Review, Section 7; letter to the editor), July 21, 1991, p. 4.

Schab, F. R. Odors and the remembrance of things past. *Journal of Experimental Psychology: Learning, Memory, and Cognition,* 1990, *16,* 648–655.

Schab, F. R. Odor memory: Taking stock. *Psychological Bulletin,* 1991, *109,* 242–251.

Schapf, J. L., Kraft, T. W., & Baylor, D. A. Spectral sensitivity of human cone photoreceptors. *Nature,* 1987, *325,* 439–441.

Schaeffel, F., Glasser, A., & Howland, H. C. Accommodation, refractive error and eye growth in chickens. *Vision Research,* 1988, *28,* 639–657.

Scharf, B. *Experimental sensory psychology.* Glenview, Ill.: Scott, Foresman, 1975.

Scharf, B., & Buus, S. Audition I: Stimulus, physiology, thresholds. In K. R. Boff, L. Kaufman, & J. P. Thomas (Eds.), *Handbook of perception and human performance. Volume I: Sensory processes and perception.* New York: John Wiley, 1986.

Scharf, B., & Houtsma, A. J. M. Audition II: Loudness, pitch, localization, aural distortion, pathology. In K. R. Boff, L. Kaufman, & J. P. Thomas (Eds.), *Handbook of perception and human performance. Volume I: Sensory processes and perception.* New York: John Wiley, 1986.

Schendel, J. D., & Shaw, P. A test of the generality of the word-context effect. *Perception & Psychophysics,* 1976, *19,* 383–393.

Schiff, W. The perception of impending collision: A study of visually directed avoidant behavior. *Psychological Monographs,* 1965, *79* (Whole No. 604).

Schiff, W. *Perception: An applied approach.* Boston: Houghton Mifflin, 1980.

Schiff, W., Caviness, J. A., & Gibson, J. J. Persistent fear responses in rhesus monkeys to the optical stimulus of "looming." *Science,* 1962, *136,* 982–983.

Schiffman, H. R. Size-estimation of familiar objects under informative and reduced conditions of viewing. *American Journal of Psychology,* 1967, *80,* 229–235.

Schiffman, H. R. Depth perception of the Syrian hamster as a function of age and photic conditions of rearing. *Journal of Comparative and Physiological Psychology,* 1971, *76,* 491–495.

Schiffman, H. R. Some components of sensation and perception for the reading process. *Reading Research Quarterly,* 1972, *VII,* 588–612.

Schiffman, H. R., & Bobko, D. J. Effects of stimulus complexity on the perception of brief temporal intervals. *Journal of Experimental Psychology,* 1974, *103,* 156–159.

Schiffman, H. R., & Bobko, D. J. The role of number and familiarity of stimuli in the perception of brief temporal intervals. *American Journal of Psychology,* 1977, *90,* 85–93.

Schiffman, H. R., & Thompson, J. G. The role of apparent depth and context in the perception of the Ponzo illusion. *Perception,* 1978, *7,* 47–50.

Schiffman, N. Sound localization difficulties of a monaural listener: Personal communication, 1994.

Schiffman, N., & Greist-Bousquet, S. The effect of task interruption and closure on perceived duration. *Bulletin of the Psychonomic Society,* 1992, *30,* 9–11.

Schiffman, S. S. *The range of gustatory quality: Psychophysical and neural approaches.* First Congress of the European Chemoreception Research Organization. Université de Paris. Sud, Campus d'Orsay. July 1974. (*a*)

Schiffman, S. S. Physiochemical correlates of olfactory quality. *Science,* 1974, *185,* 112–117. (*b*)

Schiffman, S. S. Personal communication, 1975.

Schiffman, S. S. Taste and smell in disease. *New England Journal of Medicine,* 1983, *308,* 1275–1279, 1337–1343.

Schiffman, S. S. The use of flavor to enhance efficacy of reducing diets. *Hospital Practice,* 1986, *21,* 44H–44R.

Schiffman, S. S. Recent developments in taste enhancement. *Flavor Trends & Technologies,* 1987, *41,* 72–73, 124.

Schiffman, S. S. Personal communication, 1988.

Schiffman, S. S., & Gatlin, C. A. Clinical physiology of taste and smell. *Annual Review of Nutrition,* 1993, *13,* 405–436.

Schiffman, S. S., Hornack, K., & Reilly, D. Increased taste thresholds of amino acids with age. *American Journal of Clinical Nutrition,* 1979, *32,* 1622–1627.

Schiffman, S. S., Moss, J., & Erickson, R. P. Thresholds of food odors in the elderly. *Experimental Aging Research,* 1976, *2,* 389-398.

Schiller, P. H. The ON and OFF channels of the visual system. *Trends in Neuroscience,* 1992, *15,* 86-92.

Schiller, P. H., & Wiener, M. Binocular and stereoscopic viewing of geometric illusions. *Perceptual and Motor Skills,* 1962, *15,* 739-747.

Schlaug, G., Lutz, J., Huang, Y., & Steinmetz, H. In vivo evidence of structural brain asymmetry in musicians. *Science,* 1995, *267,* 699-701.

Schlosberg, H. Stereoscopic depth from single pictures. *American Journal of Psychology,* 1941, *54,* 601-605.

Schluroff, M. Pupil responses to grammatical complexity of sentences. *Brain and Language,* 1982, *17,* 133-145.

Schnapf, J. L., & Baylor, D. A. How photoreceptor cells respond to light. *Scientific American,* 1987, *256,* 40-47.

Schnapf, J. L., Kraft, T. W., & Baylor, D. A. Spectral sensitivity of human cone photoreceptors. *Nature,* 1987, *325,* 439-441.

Schneider, G. E. Two visual systems. *Science,* 1969, *163,* 895-902.

Schouten, J. F. Subjective stroboscopy and a model of visual movement detectors. In W. Wathen-Dunn (Ed.), *Models for the perception of speech and visual form.* Cambridge, Mass.: M.I.T. Press, 1967.

Scott, T. R., & Plata-Salaman, C. R. Coding of taste quality. In T. V. Getchell, R. L. Doty, L. M. Bartoshuk, & J. B. Snow, Jr. (Eds.), *Smell and taste in health and disease.* New York: Raven Press, 1991.

Scott, T. R., & Chang, F.-C. T. The state of gustatory neural coding. *Chemical Senses,* 1984, *8,* 297-314.

Sedgwick, H. A. Space perception. In K. R. Boff, L. Kaufman, & J. P. Thomas (Eds.), *Handbook of perception and human performance. Volume I: Sensory processes and perception.* New York: John Wiley, 1986.

Sekuler, R., & Blake, R. Sensory underload. *Psychology Today,* 1987, *21,* 48-53.

Sekuler, R., Hutman, L. P., & Owsley, C. J. Human aging and spatial vision. *Science,* 1980, *209,* 1255-1256.

Seyforth, R. M., Cheney, D. L., & Marler, P. Monkey responses to three different alarm calls: Evidence of predator classification and semantic communication. *Science,* 1980, *210,* 801-803.

Sharp, W. L. The floating-finger illusion. *Psychological Review,* 1928, *35,* 171-173.

Shepard, R. N. Recognition memory for words, sentences, and pictures. *Journal of Verbal Learning and Verbal Behavior,* 1967, *6,* 156-163.

Shepard, R. N. Psychophysical complementarity. In M. Kubovy & J. R. Pomeranz (Eds.), *Perceptual organization.* Hillsdale, N.J.: Lawrence Erlbaum, 1981.

Shepard, R. N., & Zare, S. L. Path-guided apparent motion. *Science,* 1983, *220,* 632-634.

Sherif, M. *The psychology of social norms.* New York: Harper & Row, 1936.

Sherrick, C. E., & Cholewiak, R. W. Cutaneous sensitivity. In K. R. Boff, L. Kaufman, & J. P. Thomas (Eds.), *Handbook of perception and human performance. Volume I: Sensory processes and perception.* New York: John Wiley, 1986.

Shimizu, Y. Tactile display terminal for the visually handicapped. *Displays,* 1986, *7,* 116-120.

Shimizu, Y., Saida, S., & Shimura, H. Tactile pattern recognition by graphic display: Importance of 3-D information for haptic perception of familiar objects. *Perception & Psychophysics,* 1993, *53,* 43-48.

Shinkman, P. G. Visual depth discrimination in day-old chicks. *Journal of Comparative and Physiological Psychology,* 1963, *56,* 410-414.

Shlaer, R. Shift in binocular disparity causes compensatory change in the cortical structure of kittens. *Science,* 1971, *173,* 638-641.

Shlaer, R. An eagle's eye: Quality of the retinal image. *Science,* 1972, *176,* 920-922.

Shors, T. J., Wright, K., & Greene, E. Control of interocular suppression as a function of differential image blur. *Vision Research,* 1992, *32,* 1169-1175.

Sidtis, J. J., & Bryden, M. P. Asymmetrical perception of language and music: Evidence for independent processing strategies. *Neuropsychologia,* 1978, *16,* 627-632.

Silver, W. L. The common chemical sense. In T. E. Finger & W. L. Silver (Eds.), *Neurobiology of taste and smell.* New York: John Wiley, 1987.

Silver, W. L., & Finger, T. E. The trigeminal system. In T. V. Getchell, R. L. Doty, L. M. Bartoshuk, & J. B. Snow, Jr. (Eds.), *Smell and taste in health and disease.* New York: Raven Press, 1991.

Silver, W. L., & Maruniak, J. A. Trigeminal chemoreception in the nasal and oral cavities. *Chemical Senses,* 1981, *6,* 295-305.

Silverstein, R. M. Pheromones: Background and potential for use in insect pest control. *Science,* 1981, *213,* 1326-1332.

Simmons, F. B., Epley, J. M., Lummis, R. C., Guttman, N., Frishkopf, L. S., Harmon, L. D., & Zwicker, E. Auditory nerve: Electrical stimulation in man. *Science,* 1965, *148,* 104-106.

Simmons, J. A. The sonar receiver of the bat. *Annals of the New York Academy of Sciences,* 1971, *188,* 161-174.

Simmons, J. A., Fenton, M. B., & O'Farrell, J. Echolocation and pursuit of prey by bats. *Science,* 1979, *203,* 16-21.

Simon, H. A. An information-processing explanation of some perceptual phenomena. *British Journal of Psychology,* 1967, *58,* 1-12.

Singer, G., & Day, R. H. Spatial adaptation and aftereffect with optically transformed vision: Effects of active and passive responding and the relationship between test and exposure responses. *Journal of Experimental Psychology,* 1966, *71,* 725-731.

Sivian, L. J., & White, S. D. On minimum audible sound fields. *Journal of the Acoustical Society of America*, 1933, *4*, 288-321.

Slattery, III, W. H., & Middlebrooks, J. C. Monaural sound localization: Acute versus chronic unilateral impairment. *Hearing Research*, 1994, *75*, 38-46.

Sloboda, J. A. *The musical mind: The cognitive psychology of music.* (Oxford Psychology Series No. 5). Oxford: Oxford University Press, 1985.

Smith, D. V. Brainstem processing of gustatory information. In D. W. Pfaff (Ed.), *Taste, olfaction, and the central nervous system.* New York: Rockefeller University Press, 1984.

Smith, D. V., & McBurney, D. H. Gustatory crossadaptation: Does a single mechanism code the salty taste? *Journal of Experimental Psychology*, 1969, *80*, 101-105.

Smith, J. *Senses and sensibilities.* New York: John Wiley, 1989.

Smith, J. D. Conflicting aesthetic ideals in a musical culture. *Music Perception*, 1987, *4*, 373-391.

Smith, K. U., Thompson, G. F., & Koster, H. Sweat in schizophrenic patients: Identification of the odorous substance. *Science*, 1969, *166*, 398-399.

Snow, J. B., Jr., Doty, R. L., & Bartoshuk, L. M. Clinical evaluation of olfactory and gustatory disorders. In T. V. Getchell, R. L. Doty, L. M. Bartoshuk, & J. B. Snow, Jr. (Eds.), *Smell and taste in health and disease.* New York: Raven Press, 1991.

Snyder, F. W., & Pronko, N. H. *Vision with spatial inversion.* Wichita, Kan.: University of Wichita Press, 1952.

Snyder, S. H. The brain's own opiates. *Chemical & Engineering News*, 1977, *55*, 26-35.

Sokol, S., Moskowitz, A., & Hansen, V. Electrophysiological evidence for the oblique effect in human infants. *Investigative Ophthalmology & Visual Science*, 1987, *28*, 731-735.

Solomon, A. Defiantly deaf. *The New York Times Magazine*, August 28, 1994, p. 44.

Spear, P. D., Penrod, S. D., & Baker, T. B. *Psychology: Perspectives on behavior.* New York: John Wiley, 1988.

Sperling, G. The information available in brief visual presentations. *Psychological Monographs*, 1960, *74* (No. 11).

Sperry, R. W. Mechanisms of neural maturation. In S. S. Stevens (Ed.), *Handbook of experimental psychology.* New York: John Wiley, 1951.

Spigel, I. M. *Visually perceived movement.* New York: Harper & Row, 1965.

Spivey-Knowlton, M. J., & Bridgeman, B. Spatial context affects the Poggendorff illusion. *Perception & Psychophysics*, 1993, *53*, 467-474.

Spreen, O., Spellacy, F. J., & Reid, J. R. The effect of interstimulus interval and intensity on ear asymmetry for nonverbal stimuli in dichotic listening. *Neuropsychologia*, 1970, *8*, 245-250.

Springer, S. P., & Deutsch, G. *Left brain, right brain* (rev. ed.). New York: W. H. Freeman, 1985.

Springer, S. P., & Deutsch, G. *Left brain, right brain* (4th ed.). New York: W. H. Freeman, 1993.

Srinivasan, M. V. Distance perception in insects. *Current Directions in Psychological Science*, 1992, *1*, 22-26.

Steinberg, A. Changes in time perception induced by an anaesthetic drug. *British Journal of Psychology*, 1955, *46*, 273-279.

Steinman, R. M. Eye movement. *Vision Research*, 1986, *26*, 1389-1400.

Steinman, R. M., Haddad, G. M., Skavenski, A. A., & Wyman, D. Miniature eye movements. *Science*, 1973, *181*, 810-819.

Stern, J. A., & Strock, B. D. Oculomotor activity and user-system interaction in the workplace. In A. Gale & B. Christie (Eds.), *Psychophysiology and the electronic workplace.* New York: John Wiley, 1987.

Sternbach, R. A., & Tursky, B. Ethnic differences among housewives in psychophysical and skin potential responses to electric shock. *Psychophysiology*, 1965, *1*, 24-246.

Stevens, J. C. Perceived roughness as a function of body locus. *Perception & Psychophysics*, 1990, *47*, 298-304.

Stevens, J. K., Emerson, R. S., Gerstein, G. L., Kallos, T., Neufeld, G. R., Nichols, C. W., & Rosenquist, A. C. Paralysis of the awake human: Visual perceptions. *Vision Research*, 1976, *16*, 93-98.

Stevens, S. S. The relation of pitch to intensity. *Journal of the Acoustical Society of America*, 1935, *6*, 150-154.

Stevens, S. S. (Ed.), *Handbook of experimental psychology.* New York: John Wiley, 1951.

Stevens, S. S. The direct estimate of sensory magnitudes-loudness. *American Journal of Psychology*, 1956, *69*, 1-25.

Stevens, S. S. To honor Fechner and repeal his law. *Science*, 1961, *133*, 80-86. (*a*)

Stevens, S. S. Psychophysics of sensory function. In W. A. Rosenblith (Ed.), *Sensory Communication.* Cambridge, Mass.: M.I.T. Press, 1961. (*b*)

Stevens, S. S. Neural events and the psychophysical law. *Science*, 1970, *170*, 1043-1050.

Stevens, S. S. *Psychophysics, and social scaling.* Morristown, N.J.: General Learning Press, 1972.

Stevens, S. S. *Psychophysics: Introduction to its perceptual, neural and social prospects.* New York: John Wiley, 1975.

Stevens, S. S., & Davis, H. *Hearing.* New York: John Wiley, 1938.

Stevens, S. S., & Volkman, J. The relation of pitch to frequency. *American Journal of Psychology*, 1940, *53*, 329-356.

Stevens, S. S., & Warshofsky, F. *Sound and hearing.* New York: Life Science Library, 1965.

Stork, D. G., & Rocca, C. Software for generating auto-random-dot stereograms. *Behavior Research Methods, Instruments and Computers*, 1989, *21*, 525-534.

Strange, W., & Jenkins, J. J. Role of linguistic experience in the perception of speech. In R. D. Walk & H. L. Pick, Jr. (Eds.), *Perception and experience.* New York: Plenum, 1978.

Stratton, G. M. Some preliminary experiments on vision without inversion of the retinal image. *Psychological Review,* 1896, *3,* 611-617.

Stratton, G. M. Upright vision and the retinal image. *Psychological Review,* 1897, *4,* 182-187. (*a*)

Stratton, G. M. Vision without inversion of the retinal image. *Psychological Review,* 1897, *4,* 341-360. (*b*)

Stroop, J. R. Studies of interference in serial verbal reactions. *Journal of Experimental Psychology,* 1935, *18,* 643-662.

Stroop, J. R. Factors affecting speed in serial verbal reactions. *Psychological Monographs: General & Applied,* 1938, *50,* 38-48.

Stryker, M. P., Sherk, H., Leventhal, H. G., & Hirsch, H. B. Physiological consequences for the cat's visual cortex of effectively restricting early visual experience with oriented contours. *Journal of Neurophysiology,* 1978, *41,* 896-909.

Stypulkowski, P. H. Mechanisms of salicylate ototoxicity. *Hearing Research,* 1990, *46,* 113-146.

Supra, M., Cotzin, M. E., & Dallenbach, K. M. "Facial vision": The perception of obstacles by the blind. *American Journal of Psychology,* 1944, *57,* 133-183.

Süskind, P. *Perfume* (J. E. Woods, Trans.). New York: Alfred A. Knopf, 1986.

Suto, Y. The effect of space on time estimation (*S* effect) in tactual space. II: The role of vision in the *S* effect upon the skin. *Japanese Journal of Psychology,* 1955, *26,* 94-99.

Suzuki, K. (1991). Moon illusion simulated in complete darkness: Planetarium experiment reexamined. *Perception & Psychophysics,* 1991, *49,* 349-354.

Svaetichin, G. Spectral response curves of single cones. *Acta Physiologica Scandinavica,* 1956, *1,* 93-101.

Taub, E. Prism compensation as a learning phenomenon: A phylogenetic perspective. In S. J. Freedman (Ed.), *The neuropsychology of spatially oriented behavior.* Homewood, Ill.: Dorsey, 1968.

Taylor, D. W., & Boring, E. G. The moon illusion as a function of binocular regard. *American Journal of Psychology,* 1942, *55,* 189-201.

Taylor, H. R., West, S. K., Rosenthal, F. S., Muñoz, B., Newland, H. S., Abbey, H., & Emmett, E. A. Effect of ultraviolet radiation on cataract formation. *New England Journal of Medicine,* 1988, *319,* 1429-1440.

Taylor, W., Pearson, J., Mair, A., & Burns, W. Study of noise and hearing in jute weaving. *Journal of the Acoustical Society of America,* 1965, *38,* 113-120.

Teghtsoonian, R. On the exponents in Stevens' law and the constant in Ekman's law. *Psychological Review,* 1971, *78,* 71-80.

Teghtsoonian, R., & Teghtsoonian, M. Two varieties of perceived length. *Perception & Psychophysics,* 1970, *8,* 389-392.

Terhardt, E. The two-component theory of musical consonance. In E. F. Evans & J. P. Wilson (Eds.), *Psychophysics and physiology of hearing.* New York: Academic Press, 1977.

Terman, i. W., Shavit, Y., Lewis, J. W., Cannon, J. T., & Liebeskind, J. C. Intrinsic mechanisms of pain inhibition: Activation by stress. *Science,* 1984, *226,* 1270-1277.

Teuber, M. L. Sources of ambiguity in the parts of Maurits C. Escher. *Scientific American,* 1974, *231,* 90-104.

Theberge, J. B. Wolf music. *Natural History,* 1971, *80,* 37-42.

Thomas, E. A. C., & Brown, I. Time perception and the filled duration illusion. *Perception & Psychophysics,* 1974, *16,* 449-458.

Thomas, E. A. C., & Weaver, W. B. Cognitive processing and time perception. *Perception & Psychophysics,* 1975, *17,* 363-367.

Thomas, J. Mohindra, I., & Held, R. Stabismic amblyopia in infants. *American Journal of Optometry & Physiological Optics,* 1979, *56,* 197-201.

Thompson, P. Margaret Thatcher—a new illusion. *Perception,* 1980, *9,* 482-484.

Thompson, R. F. *The brain: An introduction to neuroscience.* New York: W. H. Freeman, 1985.

Thompson, R. F. *The brain: A neuroscience primer* (2nd ed.). New York: W. H. Freeman, 1993.

Thor, D. H. Diurnal variability in time estimation. *Perceptual and Motor Skills,* 1962, *15,* 451-454.

Thouless, R. H. Phenomenal regression to the real object. *British Journal of Psychology,* 1931, *21,* 338-359.

Tolansky, S. *Optical illusions.* Oxford: Pergamon, 1964.

Toppino, T. S., & Long, G. Selective adaptation with reversible figures: Don't change that channel. *Perception & Psychophysics,* 1987, *42,* 37-48.

Townshend, B., Cotter, N., van Compernolle, D., & White, R. L. Pitch perception of cochlear implant subjects. *Journal of the Acoustical Society of America,* 1987, *82,* 106-115.

Trefil, J. Which way does time fly? *The New York Times* (Book Review, Section 7), June 23, 1991, p. 6.

Treisman, A. Properties, parts, and objects. In K. R. Boff, L. Kaufman, & J. P. Thomas (Eds.), *Handbook of perception and human performance, Vol. II, Cognitive processes and performance.* New York: Wiley, 1986.

Treisman, M. Temporal discrimination and the indifference interval: Implications for a model of the "internal clock." *Psychological Monographs,* 1963, 77 (Whole No. 576).

Treisman, M. Motion sickness: An evolutionary hypothesis. *Science,* 1977, *197,* 493-495.

Trevarthen, C. B. Two mechanisms of vision in primates. *Pschologische Forschung,* 1968, *31,* 229-337.

Tumosa, N., Tieman, S. B., & Hirsch, H. B. Unequal alternating monocular deprivation causes asymmetric visual fields in cats. *Science,* 1980, *208,* 421-423.

Tyler, C. W., & Clarke, M. B. The autostereogram. In J. O. Merritt & S. S. Fisher (Eds.), Stereoscopic displays and applications. *Proceedings of SPIE—The International Society for Optical Engineering,* 1990, *1256,* 182-197.

Ullman, S. Tacit assumptions in the computational study of vision. In A. Gorea (Ed.), *Representations of vision.* Cambridge, Mass.: Cambridge University Press.

Ullman, S. Against direct perception. *The Behavioural and Brain Sciences,* 1980, *3,* 373-415.

Underwood, G. Attention and perception of duration during encoding and retrieval. *Perception,* 1975, *4,* 291-296.

Uttal, W. R. *The psychobiology of sensory coding.* New York: Harper & Row, 1973.

Valenta, J. G., & Rigby, M. K. Discrimination of the odor of stressed rats. *Science,* 1968, *161,* 599-601.

Van Toller, C., Kirk-Smith, M. D., Wood, N., Lombard, J., & Dodd, G. H. Skin conductance and subjective assessments associated with the odour of 5-ᵃandrostan-3-one. *Journal of Biological Psychology,* 1983, *16,* 85-107.

Varner, D., Cook, J. E., Schneck, M. E., McDonald, M., & Teller, D. Tritan discriminations by 1- and 2-month-old human infants. *Vision Research,* 1985, *6,* 821-831.

Veraart, C., & Wanet-Defalque, M.-C. Representation of locomotor space by the blind. *Perception & Psychophysics,* 1987, *42,* 132-139.

Verrillo, R. T. Cutaneous sensations. In B. Scharf (Ed.), *Experimental sensory psychology.* Glenview, Ill: Scott, Foresman, 1975.

Vickers, Z. M. Sensory, acoustical, and force-deformation measurements of potato chip crispness. *Journal of Food Science,* 1987, *52,* 138-140.

Vierling, J. S., & Rock, J. Variations of olfactory sensitivity to Exaltolide during the menstrual cycle. *Journal of Applied Physiology,* 1967, *22,* 311-315.

Vokey, J. R., & Read, J. D. Subliminal messages: Between the devil and the media. *American Psychologist,* 1985, *40,* 1231-1239.

von der Heydt, R., Adorjani, C., Hanny, P., & Baumgartner, G. Disparity sensitivity and receptive field incongruity of units in the cat striate cortex. *Experimental Brain Research,* 1978, *31,* 523-545.

von der Heydt, R., & Peterhans, E. Mechanisms of contour perception in monkey visual cortex: I. Lines of pattern discontinuity. *Journal of Neuroscience,* 1989, *9,* 1731-1748. (*a*)

von der Heydt, R., & Peterhans, E. Mechanisms of contour perception in monkey visual cortex: II. Contours bridging gaps. *Journal of Neuroscience,* 1989, *9,* 1749-1763. (*b*)

von der Heydt, R., Peterhans, E., & Baumgartner, G. Illusory contours and cortical neuron responses, *Science,* 1984, *224,* 1260-1262.

von Senden, M. *Space and sight: The perception of space and shape in congenitally blind patients before and after operation.* London: Methuen, 1960.

Wade, N. J. A note on the discovery of subjective colours. *Vision Research,* 1977, *17,* 671-672.

Wade, N. Op art and visual perception. *Perception,* 1978, *7,* 47-50.

Wagner, H. G., MacNichol, E. F., & Wolbarsht, M. L. The response properties of single ganglion cells in the goldfish retina. *Journal of General Physiology,* 1960, *43,* 45-62.

Walcott, C., Gould, J. L., & Kirschvink, J. L. Pigeons have magnets. *Science,* 1979, *205,* 1027-1028.

Wald, G. Human vision and the spectrum. *Science,* 1945, *101,* 653-658.

Wald, G. Eye and camera. *Scientific American,* 1950, *183,* 32-41.

Wald, G. Life and light. *Scientific American,* 1959, *201,* 92-108.

Walk, R. D. The study of visual depth and distance perception in animals. In D. S. Lehrman, R. A. Hinde, & E. Shaw (Eds.), *Advances in the study of behavior.* New York: Academic Press, 1965.

Walk, R. D. Depth perception and experience. In R. D. Walk & H. L. Pick (Eds.), *Perception and experience.* New York: Plenum, 1978.

Walk, R. D., & Gibson, E. J. A comparative and analytical study of visual depth perception. *Psychological Monographs,* 1961, *75,* 15 (Whole No. 519).

Walk, R. D., Trychin, S., & Karmel, B. Z. Depth perception in the dark-reared rat as a function of time in the dark. *Psychonomic Science,* 1965, *3,* 9-10.

Walker, J. The amateur scientist (visual illusions that can be achieved by putting a dark filter over one eye). *Scientific American,* 1978, *238,* 142-153.

Walker-Andrews, A. S. Intermodal perception of expressive behaviors: Relation of eye and voice. *Developmental Psychology,* 1986, *22,* 373-377.

Walker-Andrews, A. S. Infant's perception of the affordances of expressive behaviors. In C. Rovee-Collier & L. P. Lipsett (Eds.), *Advances in infancy research, Volume 6.* Norwood, N.J.: Ablex, 1989.

Walker-Andrews, A. S. Taxonomy for intermodal relations. In D. L. Lewkowicz & R. Lickliter (Eds.), *The development of intersensory perception.* Hillsdale, N.J.: Lawrence Earlbaum, 1994.

Walker-Andrews, A. S., Bahrick, L. E., Raglioni, S. S., & Diaz, I. Infants' bimodal perception of gender. *Ecological Psychology,* 1991, *3,* 55-75.

Walker-Andrews, A. S., & Lennon, E. M. Auditory-visual perception of changing distance by human infants. *Child Development,* 1985, *56,* 544-548.

Walker-Andrews, A. S., & Lennon, E. M. Infants' discrimination of vocal expressions: Contributions of auditory and visual information. *Infant Behavior and Development,* 1991, *14,* 131-142.

Wall, D. P., & Sweet, W. H. Temporary abolition of pain in man. *Science,* 1967, *155,* 108-109.

Wallace, P. Individual discrimination of humans by odor. *Physiology and Behavior,* 1977, *19,* 577-579.

Wallach, H. Brightness constancy and the nature of achromatic colors. *Journal of Experimental Psychology,* 1948, *38,* 310-324.

Wallach, H. The perception of neutral colors. *Scientific American,* 1963, *208,* 107-116.

Wallach, H., Newman, E. B., & Rosenzweig, M. R. The precedence effect in sound localization. *American Journal of Psychology,* 1949, *62,* 315-336.

Wallach, H., & O'Connell, D. N. The kinetic depth effect. *Journal of Experimental Psychology,* 1953, *45,* 205-217.

Wallach, H., O'Leary, A., & McMahon, M. L. Three stimuli for visual motion perception compared. *Perception & Psychophysics,* 1982, *32,* 1-6.

Wallach, H., & Slaughter, V. The role of memory in perceiving subjective contours. *Perception & Psychophysics,* 1988, *43,* 101-106.

Wallman, J., Gottlieb, M. D., Rajaram, V., & Fugate-Wentzek, L. A. Local retinal regions control local eye growth and myopia. *Science,* 1987, *237,* 73-77.

Walls, G. L. *The vertebrate eye and its adaptive radiation.* New York: Hafner, 1963.

Wang, Q., Schoenlein, R. W., Peteanu, L. A., Mathies, R. A., & Shank, C. V. Vibrationally coherent photochemistry in the femtosecond primary event of vision. *Science,* 1994, *266,* 422-425.

Warden, C. J., & Baar, J. The Müller-Lyer illusion in the ring dove, *Turtur risorius. Journal of Comparative Psychology,* 1929, *9,* 275-292.

Warkentin, J., & Carmichael, L. A study of the development of the air-righting reflex in cats and rabbits. *Journal of Genetic Psychology,* 1939, *55,* 67-80.

Warren, R. E., & Lasher, M. D. Interference in a typeface variant of the Stroop test. *Perception & Psychophysics,* 1974, *15,* 128-130.

Warren, R. M. Perceptual restoration of missing speech sounds. *Science,* 1970, *167,* 392-393.

Warren, R. M., & Warren, R. P. A critique of S. S. Stevens' "New Psychophysics." *Perceptual and Motor Skills,* 1963, *16,* 797-810.

Warren, R. M., & Warren, R. P. Auditory illusions and confusions. *Scientific American,* 1970, *223,* 30-36.

Warren, W. H., & Hannon, D. J. Direction of self-motion is perceived from optical flow. *Nature,* 1988, *336,* 162-163.

Warren, W. H., & Hannon, D. J. Eye movements and optical flow. *Journal of the Optical Society of America A,* 1990, *7,* 160-169.

Warren, W. H., Morris, M. W., & Kalish, M. L. Perception of translational heading from optical flow. *Journal of Experimental Psychology: Human Perception and Performance,* 1988, *14,* 646-660.

Warrington, E. K. Neuropsychological studies of object recognition. *Philosophical Transactions of the Royal Society of London,* 1982, *B298,* 15-33.

Wasacz, J. Natural and synthetic narcotic drugs. *American Scientist,* 1981, *69,* 318-324.

Watson, M., Greist-Bousquet, S., & Schiffman, H. R. Illusion decrement in wings-in and wings-out Müller-Lyer figures. *Bulleti of the Psychonomic Society,* 1991, *29,* 139-142.

Watt, D. G. Responses of cats to sudden falls: An otolith-originating reflex assisting landing. *Journal of Neurophysiology,* 1976, *39,* 257-265.

Wead, G., & Lellis, G. *Film: Form and function.* Boston: Houghton Mifflin, 1981.

Wegel, R. L., & Lane, C. E. The auditory masking of one pure tone by another and its probable relations to the dynamics of the inner ear. *Physiological Review,* 1924, *23,* 266-285.

Wei, E. T., & Seid, D. A. AG-3-5: A chemical producing sensations of cold. *Journal of Pharmacy and Pharmacology,* 1983, *35,* 110-111.

Weiffenbach, J. M. Chemical senses in aging. In T. V. Getchell, R. L. Doty, L. M. Bartoshuk, & J. B. Snow, Jr. (Eds.), *Smell and taste in health and disease.* New York: Raven Press, 1991.

Weil, A. T., Zinberg, N. E., & Nelson, J. M. Clinical and psychological effects of marijuana in man. *Science,* 1968, *162,* 1234-1242.

Weinstein, S. Intensive and extensive aspects of tactile sensitivity as a function of body part, sex, and laterality. In D. R. Kenshalo (Ed.), *The skin senses.* Springfield, Ill.: Charles C. Thomas, 1968.

Weintraub, M. I. Vestibulopathy induced by high impact aerobics. A new syndrome: Discussion of 30 cases. *Journal of Sports Medicine and Physical Fitness,* 1994, *34,* 56-63.

Weiskrantz, L. Hindsight and blindsight. *Neurosciences Research Program Bulletin,* 1977, *15,* 344-348.

Weiskrantz, L. Unconscious vision: The strange phenomenon of blindsight. *Sciences,* 1992, *32,* 23-28.

Weiskrantz, L., Elliott, J., & Darlington, D. Preliminary observations on tickling oneself. *Nature,* 1971, *230,* 598-599.

Weiss, B. A. Auditory sensitivity in the goldfish. *Journal of Auditory Research,* 1966, *6,* 321-335.

Weiss, B. A. Lateral-line sensitivity in the goldfish (*Carassius auratus*). *Journal of Auditory Research,* 1969, *9,* 71-75.

Weiss, B. A., & Brandspiegel, L. Excessive sound levels generated at sports events. *Sound and Vibration,* July 6-8, 1990.

Weiss, B. A., Hewett, T. T., & Mentzer, J. R. Evidence that line illusions originate in the central nervous system. *Perceptual and Motor Skills,* 1979, *48,* 1165-1166.

Weiss, B. A., & Martini, J. L. Lateral-line sensitivity in the blind cavefish (*Anoptichthys jordani*). *Journal of Comparative and Physiological Psychology,* 1970, *71,* 34-37.

Weiss, B. A., Strother, W. F., & Hartig, G. M. Auditory sensitivity in the bullhead catfish (*Ictalurus nebulosis*). *Proceedings of the National Academy of Science,* 1969, *64,* 552-556.

Weiss, D. J. The impossible dream of Fechner and Stevens. *Perception,* 1981, *10,* 431-434.

Weisstein, N., & Harris, C. S. Masking and the unmasking of distributed representations in the visual system. In C. S.

Harris (Ed.), *Visual coding and adaptability*. Hillsdale, N.J.: Lawrence Erlbaum, 1980.

Welch, R. B. *Perceptual modification: Adapting to altered sensory environments*. New York: Academic Press, 1978.

Welch, R. B. Adaptation of space perception. In K. R. Boff, L. Kaufman, & J. P. Thomas (Eds.), *Handbook of perception and human performance. Volume I: Sensory processes and perception*. New York: John Wiley, 1986.

Welch, R. B., Bridgeman, B., Anand, S., & Browman, K. E. Alternating prism exposure causes dual adaptation and generalization to a novel displacement. *Perception & Psychophysics*, 1993, *54*, 195-204.

Welker, W. I., & Campos, G. B. Physiological significance of sulci in somatic sensory cerebral cortex in mammals of the family *procyonidae. Journal of Comparative Neurology*, 1963, *120*, 19-36.

Wendt, G. R. Vestibular functions. In S. S. Stevens (Ed.), *Handbook of experimental psychology*. New York: John Wiley, 1951.

Wenger, M. A., Jones, F. N., & Jones, M. H. *Physiological psychology*. New York: Holt, Rinehart and Winston, 1956.

Wenzel, B. M. Chemoreception. In E. C. Carterette & M. P. Friedman (Eds.), *Handbook of perception. Volume III: Biology of perceptual systems*. New York: Academic Press, 1973.

Wertheimer, Max. Principles of perceptual organization. In D. C. Beardslee & M. Wertheimer (Eds.), *Readings in perception*. New York: D. Van Nostrand, 1958. An abridged translation by Michael Wertheimer of Untersuchungen zur Lehre von der Gestalt, II. *Psychologische Forschung*, 1923, *4*, 301-350.

Wertheimer, M. Hebb and Senden on the role of learning in perception. *American Journal of Psychology*, 1951, *64*, 133-137.

Wertheimer, M. Constant errors in the measurement of kinesthetic figural aftereffects. *American Journal of Psychology*, 1954, *67*, 543-546.

Wertheimer, M. Psychomotor coordination of auditory and visual space at birth. *Science*, 1961, *134*, 1692.

Westheimer, G. The eye as an optical instrument. In K. R. Boff, L. Kaufman, & J. P. Thomas (Eds.), *Handbook of perception and human performance*. Volume I: *Sensory processes and perception*. New York: John Wiley, 1986.

Westheimer, G. Diffraction theory and visual hyperacuity. *American Journal of Optometry*, 1976, *53*, 362-364.

Westheimer, G. Simultaneous orientation contrast for lines in the human fovea. *Vision Research*, 1990, *30*, 1913-1921.

Wever, E. G. *Theory of hearing*. New York: John Wiley, 1949.

Wever, E. G., & Bray, C. W. Present possibilities for auditory theory. *Psychological Review*, 1930, *37*, 365-380.

Wever, E. G., & Bray, C. W. The perception of low tones and the resonance-volley theory. *Journal of Psychology*, 1937, *3*, 101-114.

Whalen, D. H., & Liberman, A. M. Speech perception takes precedence over nonspeech perception. *Science*, 1987, *237*, 169-171.

White, B. L. Child development research: An edifice without a foundation. *Merrill-Palmer Quarterly of Behavior and Development*, 1969, *15*, 47-78.

White, B. L., Castle, P., & Held, R. Observations on the development of visually-directed reaching. *Child Development*, 1964, *35*, 349-364.

White, B. W., Saunders, F. A., Scadden, L., Bach-y-Rita, P., & Collins, C. C. Seeing with the skin. *Perception & Psychophysics*, 1970, *7*, 23-27.

White, C. W., & Montgomery, D. A. Memory colors in afterimages: A bicentennial demonstration. *Perception & Psychophysics*, 1976, *19*, 371-374.

Wiesel, R. N., & Raviola, E. The mystery of myopia. *The Sciences*, 1986, *26*, 46-52.

Wiesel, T. N., & Hubel, D. H. Single-cell responses in striate cortex of kittens deprived of vision in one eye. *Journal of Neurophysiology*, 1963, *26*, 1003-1017.

Willer, J. C., Dehen, H., & Cambier, J. Stress-induced analgesia in humans: Endogenous opioids and naloxone-reversible depression of pain reflexes. *Science*, 1981, *212*, 689-691.

Wilson, H. C. A critical review of menstrual synchrony research. *Psychoneuroendocrinology*, 1992, *17*, 565-591.

Wilson, H. R. Responses of spatial mechanisms can explain hyperacuity. *Vision Research*, 1986, *26*, 453-469.

Wilson, H. R. Development of spatiotemporal mechanisms in infant vision. *Vision Research*, 1988, *28*, 611-628.

Wilsoncroft, W. E., & Griffiths, R. S. Time perception and body temperature: A review. *Psychological Documents*, 1985, *15*, 1-12.

Winckelgren, I. How the brain "sees" borders where there are none. *Science* 1992, *256*, 1520-1521.

Witelson, S. F. The brain connection: The corpus callosum is larger in left-handers. *Science*, 1985, *229*, 665-668.

Witkin, H. A. The perception of the upright. *Scientific American*, 1959, *200*, 50-70.

Wolf, G. Innate mechanisms for regulation of sodium intake. In C. Pfaffmann (Ed.), *Olfaction and taste*. New York: Rockefeller University Press, 1969.

Wolff, W. Induzierte helligkeitsveranderung. *Psychologische Forschung*, 1935, *20*, 159-194.

Wong, E., & Weisstein, N. A new perceptual context-superiority effect: Line segments are more visible against a figure than against a ground. *Science*, 1982, *218*, 587-589.

Wong, R., & Jones, W. Saline intake in hamsters. *Behavioral Biology*, 1978, *24*, 474-480.

Wood, H. Psychophysics of active kinesthesis. *Journal of Experimental Psychology*, 1969, *79*, 480-485.

Woodhouse, J. M., & Taylor, S. Further studies of the café wall and hollow squares illusions. *Perception*, 1987, *16*, 467-471.

Woodrow, H. Time perception. In S. S. Stevens (Ed.), *Handbook of experimental psychology*. New York: John Wiley, 1951.

Woodworth, R. S. *Experimental psychology*. New York: Henry Holt, 1938.

Woodworth, R. S. *Psychology (4th ed.).* New York: Henry Holt, 1940.

Woodworth, R. S., & Schlosberg, H. *Experimental psychology.* New York: Henry Holt, 1954.

Worshel, P., & Dallenbach, K. M. "Facial vision": Perception of obstacles by the deaf-blind. *American Journal of Psychology,* 1947, *60,* 502-553.

Worshel, P., & Dallenbach, K. M. The vestibular sensitivity of deaf-blind subjects. *American Journal of Psychology,* 1948, *61,* 94-98.

Wright, W. D. A re-determination of trichromatic coefficients of the spectral colours. *Transactions of the Optical Society of London,* 1928-1929, *30,* 141-164.

Wright, W. D. *The rays are not coloured. Nature,* 1963, *198,* 1239-1244.

Wright, W. D. *The rays are not coloured.* New York: American Elsevier, 1967.

Wyatt, H. J. Singly and doubly contingent aftereffects involving color, orientation and spatial frequency. *Vision Research,* 1974, *14,* 1185-1193.

Wyburn, G. M., Pickford, R. W., & Hirst, R. J. *Human senses and perception.* Toronto: University of Toronto Press, 1964.

Wysocki, C. J., & Meredith, M. The vomeronasal system. In T. E. Finger & W. L. Silver (Eds.), *Neurobiology of taste and smell.* New York: John Wiley, 1987.

Wysocki, C. J., Pierce, J. D., & Gilbert, A. N. Geographic, cross-cultural, and individual variation in human olfaction. In T. V. Getchell, R. L. Doty, L. M. Bartoshuk, & J. B. Snow (Eds.), *Smell and taste in health and disease.* New York: Raven Press, 1991.

Yaksh, T. L. Opiate receptors for behavioral analgesia resemble those related to depression of spinal nociceptive neurons. *Science,* 1978, *199,* 1231-1233.

Yarbus, A. L. *Eye movement and vision.* New York: Plenum Press, 1967.

Yang, G., & Masland, R. H. Direct visualization of the dendritic and receptive fields of directionally selective retinal ganglion cells. *Science,* 1992, *258,* 1949-1952.

Yeager, J. Absolute time estimates as a function of complexity and interruptions of melodies. *Psychonomic Science,* 1969, *15,* 177-178.

Yellott, J. I. Binocular depth inversion. *Scientific American,* 1981, *245,* 148-159.

Yin, T. C. T., Kuwada, S., & Sujaku, Y. Interaural time sensitivity of high-frequency neurons in the inferior colliculus. *Journal of the Acoustical Society of America,* 1984, *76,* 1401-1410.

Yonas, A., Granrud, C. E., Arteberry, M. E., & Hanson, B. L. Infants' distance from linear perspective and texture gradients. *Infant Behavior and Development,* 1986, *9,* 247-256.

Yonas, A., Kuskowski, M., & Sternfels, S. The roles of frame of reference in the development of responsiveness to

shading information. *Child Development,* 1979, *50,* 495-500.

Yost, W. A., & Nielsen, D. W. *Fundamentals of hearing.* New York: Holt, Rinehart and Winston, 1977.

Young, F. A. Development of optical characteristics for seeing. In F. A. Young & D. B. Lindsley (Eds.), *Early experience and visual information processing in perceptual and reading disorders.* Washington, D.C.: National Academy of Sciences, 1970.

Young, M. P., & Yamane, S. Sparse population coding of faces in the inferotemporal cortex. *Science,* 1992, *256,* 1327-1331.

Young, R. A. Some observations on temporal coding of color vision: Psychophysical results. *Vision Research,* 1977, *17,* 957-965.

Yuodelis, C., & Hendrickson, A. A qualitative and quantitative analysis of the human fovea during development. *Vision Research,* 1986, *26,* 847-855.

Zadnik, K., Satariano, W. A., Mutti, D. O., Sholtz, R. I., & Adams, A. J. The effect of parental history of myopia on children's eye size. *Journal of the American Medical Association,* 1994, *271,* 1323-1327.

Zahorik, D. M., & Maier, S. F. Appetitive conditioning with recovery from thiamine deficiency as the unconditional stimulus. *Psychonomic Science,* 1969, *17,* 309-310.

Zakay, D. Relative and absolute duration judgments under prospective and retrospective paradigms. *Perception & Psychophysics,* 1993, *54,* 656-664.

Zakay, D., & Fallach, E. Immediate and remote time estimation—A comparison. *Acta Psychologica,* 1984, *57,* 69-81.

Zakay, D., Nitzan, D., & Glicksohn, J. The influence of task difficulty and external tempo on subjective time estimation. *Perception & Psychophysics,* 1983, *34,* 451-456.

Zatorre, R. J., Evans, A. C., Meyer, E., & Gjedde, A. Lateralization of phonetic and pitch discrimination in speech processing. *Science,* 1992, *256,* 846-849.

Zelazo, P. R., Zelazo, N. A., & Kolb, S. "Walking" in the newborn. *Science,* 1972, *176,* 314-315.

Zelman, S. Correlation of smoking history with hearing loss. *Journal of the American Medical Association,* 1973, *223,* 920.

Zhou, H., & May, J. G. Effects of spatial filtering and lack of effects of visual imagery on pattern-contingent color aftereffects. *Perception & Psychophysics,* 1993, *53,* 145-149.

Zihl, J., von Cramon, D., & Mai, N. Selective disturbance of movement vision after bilateral brain damage. *Brain,* 1983, *106,* 313-340.

Zimbardo, P. G., Anderson, S. M., & Kabat, L. G. Induced hearing deficit generates experimental paranoia. *Science,* 1981, *212,* 1529-1531.

Zingale, C. M., & Kowler, E. Planning sequences of saccades. *Vision Research,* 1987, *27,* 1327-1341.

Zola, D. Redundancy and word perception during reading. *Perception & Psychophysics,* 1984, *36,* 280.

Zöllner, F. On a new way of pseudoscopy and its relation to the movement phenomena described by Plateau and Oppel. *Annalen der Physik und Chemie,* 1860, 110 (whole series 86), 500-522.

Zotterman, Y. Studies in the neural mechanism of taste. In W. A. Rosenblith (Ed.), *Sensory communication.* Cambridge, Mass.: M.I.T. Press, 1961.

Zurek, P. M., & Sachs, R. M. Combination tones at frequencies greater than the primary tones. *Science,* 1979, *205,* 600-602.

Zusne, L. *Visual perception of form.* New York: Academic Press, 1970.

Zwicker, E., & Scharf, B. Model of loudness summation. *Psychological Review,* 1965, *72,* 3-26.

Zwislocki, J. J. Sound analysis in the ear: A history of discoveries. *American Scientist,* 1981, *69,* 184-192.

AUTHOR INDEX

SUBJECT INDEX